1953 E1

1 50
6

THE JOY OF COOKING

THE

JOY

OF COOKING

Irma S. Rombauer
Marion Rombauer Becker

Illustrated by Ginnie Hofmann
THE BOBBS-MERRILL COMPANY, INC.
Publishers: Indianapolis • New York

Foreword

ALL previous editions of "The Joy of Cooking" have been dedicated to my friend Mary Whyte Hartrich, and so is this one. It is she who from the beginning volunteered to help me with my undertaking and who compiled the admirable index for each edition so well that my readers say, "You can really find what you are looking for!" In addition she has been an excellent balance wheel for my flights of fancy, advising frequently against too much exuberance and adding a great deal that is valuable to my books.

The first "Joy," a modest volume, was published privately in 1931. It was written at the request of my children, who, on leaving home, asked for a record of "what mother used to cook." In 1936 The Bobbs-Merrill Company brought out an enlarged and revised edition of my timidly launched maiden effort and this was followed by a second enlarged and revised edition in 1943. A new edition is now before you.

My roots are Victorian but I have been modernized by life and my children. My book reflects my life and, as you may see by its timely contents, I have not stood still. So I am bringing you not only much that is old and memorable but also much that is new. Many simply prepared dishes, low in cost, have been included to meet the change in our domestic home front. Every effort has been made to encourage the cook in her daily grind by lifting everyday food out of the commonplace.

The ever-widening scope of this new edition has called for assistance from others. Needless to say, it has continued to come in full measure from Mary Hartrich and from my earliest critic and adviser, my daughter, Marion Rombauer Becker. Also my friend Jane Torno worked with me for a while, capably and well. Marion has been a wonderful co-worker, stimulating and tireless, assuming a large part of our joint responsibility and contributing immeasurably to the enrichment of this book. It was Marion who induced her friend Ginnie Hofmann to do the delightful drawings that enliven these pages. It was Marion whose interest and enthusiasm made of our long and often tedious co-operation a happy experience. Together we have cooked and tested and tasted. We have consulted, argued and agreed, and our families have stood by nobly, actually thriving under an overpowering onslaught of experimentation. Does one laud guinea pigs? If so they should come in for their share of attention.

The book is now yours. Our best effort has gone into it and we submit it with pleasure for your consideration.

I. S. R.

Introduction

"MOTHER," said Marion, "the book needs an introduction." "Why?" said I. "Will cooks ever read it?" She replied: "Perhaps they will read it if you tell them a story, for if they do not, how will they know that an ingredient in parenthesis means 'optional' and 'chocolate' means the bitter kind unless otherwise stated?"

So here is the story. Pete, a farmer's old handy man, suffered an accident that cost him a leg. In due time he was able to get about again much as before. One day he drove the farmer's flivver into a ditch, and as the icy waters rose and the flivver tilted he had only a few inches of head space left in which to breathe. After calling out feebly from time to time, he was rescued two hours later by a passer-by who asked Pete whether he had not been terrified by his precarious position. "Gosh, yes," said Pete. "I was scared green my wooden leg would warp!"

How good is your sense of values? What is your first thought when you prepare a meal? Is it of a decorated cake or a fancy salad? It should be of the nutritional value of the food you plan to serve, not only for the one meal but in relation to the whole day's intake. Gastronomy and nutrition are not synonymous—so don't confound them. Your thought should be of the correct preparation, cooking and timing of the food. It should be an attempt at variety in ingredients, textures and flavors.

If you have little time, choose a menu that may be quickly prepared. Prepare such dishes in advance as are not harmed by early preparation. For all details consult the cookbook and the index. Know at what degree of heat you are going to cook the food and how long it is going to take.

Start with the dish that takes the longest time to cook and follow it up with the others requiring a shorter time. Set the table in one of the intervals.

Serve hot food hot from hot dishes. Serve cold food chilled from chilled dishes. Keep calm even if your hair striggles and you drip unattractively. Brush up before serving. Your appearance and the appearance of the food are important, but eating in a quiet atmosphere is even more important to the family's morale and digestion.

A meal represents effort and money. It is worthy of a dignified hour.

Your first efforts at cooking may result in confusion, but soon you will acquire a skilled routine that will give you confidence and pleasure. You don't believe it? Will it encourage you to know that I was once as ignorant, helpless and awkward a bride as was ever foisted on an impecunious young lawyer? Together we placed many a burnt offering on the altar of matrimony, and I have lived to serve a meal attractively and well and even to write a cookbook that has proved helpful to others.

I. S. R.

Table of Contents

TABLE OF CONTENTS

THE JOY OF COOKING

Cocktails

The chief virtue of cocktails is their informal quality. They loosen tongues and unbutton the reserves of the socially diffident. Serve them by all means, preferably in the living room, and the sooner the better. They may be alcoholic or nonalcoholic. For the benefit of a minority serve the latter with the former.

To give this book the impression of sobriety and stability it deserves, the alcoholic cocktails have been relegated to the chapter on Beverages. There they may blush unseen by those who disapprove of them and they may be readily found in the company of many other good drinks by those who do not.

TOMATO JUICE COCKTAIL
4 Servings
Simmer for ½ hour:
  12 medium-sized raw tomatoes or
    3½ cups tomatoes: No. 2½ can
  ½ cup water
  1 slice onion
  2 ribs celery with leaves
  ½ bay leaf
  3 sprigs parsley
Strain these ingredients. Season with:
  1 teaspoon salt
  ¼ teaspoon paprika
  ¼ teaspoon sugar
Serve the cocktail thoroughly chilled.

CANNED TOMATO JUICE COCKTAIL
4 Servings
Combine in a jar and shake well:
  2½ cups tomato juice
  ½ teaspoon grated onion
  1 teaspoon grated celery
  ½ teaspoon horseradish
  1½ tablespoons lemon juice
  A dash of Worcestershire or
    Tabasco sauce
  ⅛ teaspoon paprika
  ¾ teaspoon salt
  ¼ teaspoon sugar
This cocktail is good served hot or chilled. Curry powder, a few cloves, a stick of cinnamon, tarragon, parsley or some other herb may be steeped in the cocktail and strained out before it is served.

TOMATO CUCUMBER COCKTAIL
4 Servings
Combine in a jar, shake well and chill:
  2 cups tomato juice
  2 tablespoons salad oil
  1 tablespoon vinegar
  ½ teaspoon salt

  ⅛ teaspoon paprika
  (¼ teaspoon basil, page 833)
Peel, seed, grate and add:
  1 cucumber
Just before serving add:
  ½ cup cracked ice
Shake the cocktail well.

CHILLED TOMATO CREAM COCKTAIL OR SOUP
6 Servings
Combine in a cocktail shaker:
  2 cups chilled tomato juice
  1 cup chilled cream
  1 teaspoon grated onion or garlic
    and celery powder to taste
  4 or more ribs grated raw celery
  Salt
  A few drops Tabasco sauce
  A few grains cayenne
Add:
  ¼ cup chopped ice
Shake the soup well. Serve it with:
  Heated salted crackers

Tropical Consommé, page 71; Madrilène and Tomato Juice, page 72.

SAUERKRAUT COCKTAIL
Chill, then combine equal parts of:
  Sauerkraut juice
  Tomato juice
with a little:
  (Prepared horseradish)
Or combine:
  1 teaspoon lemon juice
  ⅛ teaspoon paprika
  2 cups sauerkraut juice

CLAM JUICE COCKTAIL
6 Servings
Combine:
  3 tablespoons lemon juice
  2 tablespoons tomato catsup

1

3 cups clam juice
A drop Tabasco sauce
Salt if needed
(½ teaspoon grated onion)
(1 tablespoon grated celery)

Chill these ingredients. Strain them before serving. This is a good combination but there are many others. Horseradish may be added, so may Worcestershire sauce. The cocktail may be part clam juice and part tomato juice, etc.

Alcoholic Cocktails. See Alcoholic Beverages, page 819.

FRESH PINEAPPLE COCKTAIL I
About 1½ Cupfuls of Juice
A very refreshing drink.
Peel a:
Pineapple

Cut it into cubes. Extract the juice by putting the pineapple through a food grinder or blender. There will be very little pulp.
Strain the juice and serve it with:
Cracked ice
Garnish the cocktail with:
Sprigs of mint

PINEAPPLE AND TOMATO JUICE COCKTAIL
4 Servings
Shake vigorously in a cocktail shaker:
1 cup pineapple juice
1 cup tomato juice
¼ teaspoon salt
¼ cup crushed ice

ORANGE AND TOMATO JUICE COCKTAIL
4 Servings
This is a well-blended, palatable concoction.
Shake vigorously in a cocktail shaker:
1½ cups tomato juice
1 cup orange juice
1 teaspoon sugar
1 tablespoon lemon or lime juice
½ teaspoon salt
¼ cup crushed ice

ORANGE AND LIME JUICE COCKTAIL
4 Servings
Shake vigorously in a cocktail shaker:
2 cups orange juice
1 tablespoon lime juice or 2 tablespoons lemon juice

A pinch of salt
¼ cup cracked ice

FRUIT JUICE COCKTAILS
Good combinations are equal parts of:
Orange juice and pineapple juice
or:
Loganberry juice and pineapple juice
or:
White grape juice and orange juice

PINEAPPLE AND GRAPEFRUIT JUICE COCKTAIL
6 Servings
Boil for 3 minutes:
½ cup sugar
½ cup water
Chill the sirup. Add to it:
1¾ cups grapefruit juice
1 cup pineapple juice
¼ cup lemon juice

GRAPEFRUIT JUICE COCKTAIL
This may be plain fresh or canned grapefruit juice or it may be combined with orange, lemon and other fruit juices, fresh or canned, in any desired proportion or combination.
Minted grapefruit juice is good. Add chopped mint or 1 or 2 drops of oil of peppermint.

CITRUS FRUIT JUICE COCKTAIL
4 Servings
Shake vigorously in a cocktail shaker:
¾ cup grapefruit juice
¼ cup lemon juice
½ cup orange juice
⅓ to ½ cup sugar
1 cup cracked ice
Pour the cocktail into glasses and serve it garnished with:
Sprigs of mint
One cupful chilled carbonated water may be substituted for the cracked ice. In that case chill the fruit juices and serve the cocktail with a very little cracked ice.

GRAPEFRUIT AND CRANBERRY JUICE COCKTAIL
Chill, then combine equal parts of:
Canned or fresh grapefruit juice
Canned cranberry juice

CRANBERRY JUICE COCKTAIL

4 Servings
Cook until very soft:
  1 pint cranberries
  2 cups water
Strain them through a cheesecloth. Add to the juice and boil it for 3 minutes:
  ¼ to ⅓ cup sugar
  (3 cloves)
Cool it. Add:
  ¼ cup orange juice
  1 tablespoon lemon juice
Serve it thoroughly chilled.

MILK EGGNOG

2 Servings
Combine in a cocktail shaker:
  2 cups chilled milk
  2 eggs
  2 tablespoons confectioners' sugar or honey
  ½ teaspoon vanilla or grated orange or lemon rind
  ¼ cup cracked ice
Shake the eggnog well. Sprinkle the top with:
  Freshly grated nutmeg
Of course, it will do no harm to add to this a jigger or two of whisky, cognac or rum.

ORANGE MILK EGGNOG

Add to the preceding rule:
  ¼ cup orange juice

APRICOT OR PRUNE EGGNOG

2 Servings
Combine in a cocktail shaker:
  ¾ cup chilled apricot or prune juice
  1 teaspoon lemon juice
  A pinch of salt
  1 egg
  2 tablespoons cracked ice
Shake the cocktail well. Or, combine for a fruit shake:
  ⅔ cup chilled apricot or prune juice
  1⅓ cups cold milk

PINEAPPLE OR ORANGE EGGNOG

4 Servings
Combine in a cocktail shaker:
  2 cups chilled pineapple or orange juice
  1 tablespoon confectioners' sugar or honey
  1½ tablespoons lemon juice
  1 egg or 2 egg yolks
  A pinch of salt
  ¼ cup cracked ice
Shake the cocktail well.

Eggnog, page 825.

Many of the fruit juice, vegetable and egg drinks may be enriched in texture and in food value if they are prepared in a blender. For further suggestions, see page 896.

TO FROST GLASSES FOR A FRUIT COCKTAIL

Dip the rims of the glasses in:
  Lemon juice
Dip them in:
  Confectioners' sugar
Place them in the refrigerator to frost for about 20 minutes. Fill the glasses with chilled fruit. For example:
  Pitted cherries
  Diced pineapple
  Skinned grapefruit sections
  Skinned orange sections
Pour over them:
  Chilled fruit juice lightly sweetened
Garnish the top with:
  Mint leaves
dusted with:
  Confectioners' sugar

FRUIT COCKTAIL

Chill and prepare for serving:
  Fresh fruit
Five minutes before serving sprinkle it lightly with:
  Confectioners' sugar
Immediately before serving flavor it with:
  Lime juice, lemon juice or sherry
Or partly cover it with:
  Chilled ginger ale
Seedless grapes, watermelon, green and yellow cantaloupes, cut into balls with a French potato cutter, Queen Anne cherries or dates, stoned and stuffed with filberts, and fresh pineapple make good cocktails. Garnish the cocktail with Candied Mint Leaves, page 490.

FRESH PEARS IN LIQUEUR

4 Servings
A cocktail or a dessert. Combine:
  1 cup chilled orange juice
  1 tablespoon confectioners' sugar

Before serving add to the orange juice:

2 tablespoons curaçao

Pare and quarter and core:

4 pears

Cover them with the juice. Chill until ready to serve.

STRAWBERRY COCKTAIL

Place in cocktail glasses:

Sliced strawberries

Boil for 10 minutes equal parts of:

Orange juice
Strawberry juice

with:

¼ as much sugar, or as much as is palatable

Chill the sirup. Season it well with:

Sherry

Add:

Shaved ice

Fill the glasses. Serve the cocktails at once.

Or place on:

Lettuce leaves

Hulled or unhulled:

Strawberries

Immediately before serving moisten them with:

French dressing to which a little confectioners' sugar may be added

Or, cover:

Chilled strawberries

with:

Chilled pineapple juice

Add, if needed:

Confectioners' sugar

Or, sprinkle strawberries lightly with:

Lemon juice
Confectioners' sugar

Decorate the fruit with:

Mint leaves

PINEAPPLE TIDBITS

Method I. 8 Servings

This is alluring in appearance.

Trim ⅔ from the leafy top of:

1 chilled ripe pineapple

If one of the inner leaves of the crown pulls out easily and if the eyes are protruding the pineapple is fully ripe.
Cut the fruit into 8 lengthwise wedges. Cut off the core and place each part so that it will resemble a boat as shown opposite. Pare the skin in 1 piece, leaving it in place, and cut the pulp into 5 or 6 downward slices, retaining the boat shape. Serve each boat on an individual plate with a small mound of:

Confectioners' sugar

Add:

5 or 6 large unhulled strawberries

Method II.

A Texas girl taught me to prepare a pineapple this way: Loosen each section of a chilled pineapple by cutting it down to the core with a sharp knife.

When all sections have been loosened, serve the pineapple, a toothpick stuck into each eye. Let the guests serve themselves.

Method III.

In Mexico I was served a crosswise slice of pineapple that had been cut into pie-shaped wedges on an individual plate. A wedge is lifted with the fingers and dipped in sugar. Every bit is eaten except the peel. A few unhulled strawberries may be placed on the plate.

FRESH PINEAPPLE COCKTAIL II

6 Servings

Peel, core and dice:

1 fresh pineapple

Chill it. Boil for 1 minute:

1 cup sugar
⅓ cup water

Chill this sirup. Add:

½ cup chilled orange juice
3 tablespoons lime juice

Place the pineapple in glasses and pour the sirup mixture over it.

PINEAPPLE AND ORANGE MINT COCKTAIL

Prepare:

1 cup fresh diced pineapple or
1 cup canned diced pineapple

Peel, divide and skin the sections of:

3 oranges

Crush and combine with the fruit:
¼ lb. after-dinner mints
Chill the cocktail for 1 hour or more and serve it with a sprinkling of:
Confectioners' sugar

CANTALOUPE BASKETS

Choose ripe cantaloupes. A vine-ripened cantaloupe will have a deep scar at the stem end and an all-over netted surface. To store ripe melons, cover them closely to keep them from

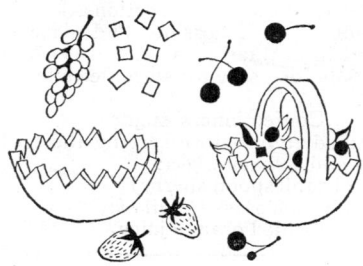

absorbing flavors from other foods in the refrigerator. Chill, then cut into basket shape as shown above:
Small cantaloupes
Remove the seeds. Cut out the pulp. Dice it. Combine it with an equal amount of chilled:
Hulled strawberries
Seeded cherries or
Diced pineapple
Sweeten the fruit slightly. It may be moistened with chilled:
French dressing
Place it in the baskets and serve at once.

MELON MINT COCKTAILS

Boil for 5 minutes:
½ cup sugar
½ cup water
Pour this sirup over:
3 tablespoons chopped mint leaves
Cool the sirup. Strain it. Add to it:
Juice of 1 lemon
Juice of 1 orange
Chill it. Prepare and chill:
Cantaloupe balls
Watermelon balls
Immediately before serving the cocktail place the balls in cocktail glasses and pour the sirup over them. Garnish them with:
Sprigs of mint

HONEYDEW M[...]
CANTALOUPE

Cut into sections:
1 chilled melon
Remove the seeds [...] the sections on:
Lettuce leave[...]
with:
French dressing or with lime or lemon juice

BANANA AND ORANGE COCKTAIL

Cut into thin slices chilled:
Ripe bananas
Place them in cocktail glasses. Cover them with chilled:
Orange juice
You may decorate the tops with:
Orange sections
lightly sprinkled with:
Confectioners' sugar
Garnish with:
Crushed mint or a sprig of mint or a cherry or strawberry

AVOCADO COCKTAIL
Method I.
Chill:
Small avocados
Cut them in halves. Fill the hollows with highly-seasoned, chilled:
Tomato Juice Cocktail, page 1, or chili sauce seasoned with horseradish, marinated seedless grapes or finely chopped dill pickles

Method II.
Or fill them with French dressing. You may add to each half:
1 teaspoon grenadine

Method III.
Chill:
Avocados
Peel them. Slice them. Marinate them for about 5 minutes in chilled, highly seasoned:
French dressing
Tabasco sauce, chili sauce, catsup, etc., may be added.
Sprinkle them with:
Chopped parsley or chopped mint

More Avocado Recipes will be found in the Index.

COCKTAILS

CADO FILLED WITH ANGE SECTIONS
Servings
Cut into halves and remove the seed from:

2 chilled avocados

Peel, then cut into sections without membrane or seeds:

2 chilled oranges

Fill the avocado shells with the sections. Pour over each:

1½ tablespoons chilled French dressing

Garnish each shell with:

A sprig of mint parsley or cress

Serve at once.

CELERY ROOT COCKTAIL
Cook by the rule on page 464:

Celery root

Chill it. Toss it in:

Mayonnaise

to which add:

Catsup and lemon juice

Or in:

Pink Sauce for Shrimp, page 8

Or, best of all, in:

French dressing

to which add:

Minced onion or chives

Serve it on endive or water cress.

Chilled Eggplant Purée or Eggplant Caviar, page 289.
See Salads, page 451—artichokes, Vinaigrette, stuffed with shrimp, crab, etc. Other salads and aspics make good first-course dishes.

GRAPEFRUIT COCKTAIL
Chill:

Grapefruit

Cut them in halves. Loosen the pulp from the peel with a sharp knife. Remove the seeds and cut out the tough fibrous center with a pair of scissors or a patent cutter. Five minutes before serving sprinkle the grapefruit with:

Confectioners' sugar

Add to each half immediately before serving:

1 tablespoon sherry

BROILED GRAPEFRUIT
Delicious as a cocktail or a dessert. Fine for a winter breakfast. Prepare by the preceding rule:

Grapefruit

Sprinkle each half with:

1 tablespoon or more sugar

Place the fruit on a broiler under a moderate flame. When the grapefruit is hot pour over each half:

1 tablespoon sherry

Serve the fruit at once.
When grapefruit is very ripe it is inadvisable to loosen the pulp from the peel as that makes the fruit too juicy.

GRAPEFRUIT IN COCKTAIL GLASSES
4 Servings
Chill:

2 large grapefruit

Peel them, skin the sections, keeping them whole if possible, and place the fruit in cocktail glasses. Fifteen minutes before serving sprinkle it lightly with:

Confectioners' sugar

Immediately before serving the cocktail add to each glass:

(1 tablespoon sherry)

Or fill each glass ¼ full of:

Chilled orange juice

OYSTERS IN GRAPEFRUIT
4 Servings
Prepare as for Grapefruit Cocktail, on this page, omitting the sugar:

2 large chilled grapefruit

Place in the center of each half, immediately before serving the cocktail:

3 small oysters

Season them with:

Lemon juice and salt
Horseradish
1 tablespoon sherry or a drop of Tabasco sauce

If cooking sherry is used omit the salt.

SHRIMP IN GRAPEFRUIT
4 Servings
Prepare as for Grapefruit Cocktail, on this page, omitting the sugar:

2 large chilled grapefruit

Marinate in French dressing for 30 minutes:

12 or 16 shrimp

Immediately before serving season each grapefruit half with:

Salt and paprika

and place 3 or 4 shrimp in each center. Garnish the cocktail with:

Sprigs of parsley

GRAPEFRUIT AND STRAWBERRY COCKTAIL IN GRAPEFRUIT CUPS
4 Servings
Remove the skins in halves from:

3 small grapefruit

Place the skins in cold water to keep them firm. Skin the grapefruit sections. Hull:

2 cups strawberries

Combine them with the grapefruit sections. Sprinkle the fruit well with:

Sugar

Chill the fruit. Wipe the grapefruit shells. Line them with:

Mint leaves

Fill them with the chilled fruit. Garnish the tops with a few:

Unhulled strawberries

LOBSTER OR SHRIMP AND GRAPEFRUIT COCKTAIL

Arrange on:

Lettuce leaves or in glasses

Sections of:

Skinned grapefruit

and:

Pieces of lobster meat

Garnish with:

Mayonnaise and chopped chives

OYSTER COCKTAIL

4 Servings

Measure:

½ cup sherry

Season it with:

Salt and cayenne

Pour these ingredients, immediately before serving, over:

24 small chilled oysters

If cooking sherry is used omit the salt.

OYSTER OR CLAM COCKTAIL

4 Servings

Combine, stir, then chill:

¼ cup tomato catsup
¼ cup lemon juice
1 teaspoon Worcestershire sauce
1 teaspoon salt
A few grains cayenne
2 teaspoons grated horseradish
2 tablespoons vinegar

Immediately before serving pour these ingredients over:

28 small chilled oysters or clams

placed in 4 cocktail glasses.

FRESH CRAB COCKTAIL

Place in a bowl:

Chilled fresh crab meat

Pour over it an equal amount of:

Chilled Russian Dressing, page 496

Toss the salad well before serving it in individual dishes or from a bowl lined with:

Lettuce

Garnish it with:

Chopped parsley
Sliced pimiento olives

CRAB MEAT COCKTAIL

4 Small Servings

Combine:

2 tablespoons mayonnaise
2 tablespoons catsup
1 tablespoon horseradish
¼ chopped green pepper
1 chopped pimiento or 3 tablespoons chopped celery or pepper

Add the contents of:

1 can flaked crab meat: 6½ oz.

SHRIMP OR OTHER SEA FOOD COCKTAIL

Cooked shrimp may be used alone, as may cooked lobster or crab meat, raw oysters or littleneck clams, or several of these sea foods may be combined. Shell and de-vein:

Cooked shrimp

Pick over the other sea food for bits of shell. Discard them. You may line cocktail glasses with:

A small lettuce leaf or a sprig of water cress

Add the shrimp—about ⅓ cupful per person. To serve, imbed the glasses in crushed ice. In any event, whether you have suitable glasses or not, chill the shrimp well. Pour cocktail sauce over them, about 2 tablespoonfuls to each portion.

COCKTAIL SAUCE FOR SEA FOOD

Method I.

10 Servings: About 1¼ Cupfuls

Combine:

1 cup catsup
2 tablespoons cider or wine vinegar or lemon juice
4 to 6 drops Tabasco sauce
1 tablespoon horseradish
1 tablespoon minced chives or grated onion
¼ cup finely chopped celery
1 teaspoon Worcestershire sauce
½ teaspoon salt
(1 tablespoon minced parsley)

Method II.

Fine for dipping shrimp served at cocktail parties.

Measure:
 1 cup mayonnaise
Beat in slowly:
 1 cup heavy cream
 5 tablespoons chili sauce
 ½ teaspoon grated onion
 1 tablespoon grated green pepper
 1 tablespoon Worcestershire
  sauce
 1½ tablespoons lemon juice
Season the sauce with:
 Salt and paprika
Chill it.

Method III. 4 Servings
Stir in a small skillet over low heat until melted and caramelized:
 2 tablespoons sugar
Add:
 2 tablespoons butter
 2 tablespoons finely chopped
  onion
 2 tablespoons cocktail catsup
 6 tablespoons mayonnaise
Chill the sauce. Serve it over chilled clams, oysters, crab or lobster meat in individual glasses.

QUICK SAUCE FOR SHELLFISH COCKTAIL
Combine equal parts of:
 Tomato catsup and cream
You may add to the sauce:
 Chopped celery, cucumber,
  onion, parsley, etc.

FRESH HERB SAUCE FOR RAW OYSTERS
Combine, stir, then chill:
 2 tablespoons chopped parsley
 2 tablespoons minced green
  onions or shallots
 1 tablespoon chopped chervil
 1 tablespoon chopped chives
 3 tablespoons oil
 3 tablespoons vinegar

 ½ teaspoon salt
 ½ teaspoon Worcestershire sauce
 2 drops Tabasco sauce

DRIED HERB SAUCE FOR RAW OYSTERS
Combine, stir, then chill:
 2 tablespoons fresh chopped
  parsley
 2 tablespoons minced onion
 1 teaspoon in all dried chervil,
  basil and tarragon
 3 tablespoons oil
 3 tablespoons vinegar
 ½ teaspoon salt
 ½ teaspoon Worcestershire sauce
 2 drops Tabasco sauce

For other cocktail sauces see Herb Mayonnaise, etc., in Salad Dressings, page 490.
Tomato Cream for Shrimp, page 39.
New Orleans Shrimp Sauce, page 39.

PINK SAUCE FOR SHRIMP
Combine, stir, then chill:
 1 cup mayonnaise
 ½ cup catsup
  A few drops Tabasco sauce
 1½ tablespoons lemon juice
  Salt to taste

TO SERVE WITH COCKTAILS
 Cheese crackers
 Pretzel sticks
 Cheese popcorn
 Hot potato chips
 Salted nut meats
 Canapés
 Olives
 Tiny broiled sausages
 Cocktail almonds, etc.

The following chapter on Canapés and Sandwiches is full of good suggestions.

Canapés and Sandwiches for Cocktails and Teas

Innumerable hostesses—not to mention quick-lunch stands—keep green the memory of Lord Sandwich, whose mania for gambling gave the world the well-known concoction that bears his name.

Suggestions for Making and Keeping Canapés and Sandwiches Fresh. Canapés are small attractive mouthfuls and they may be cut in endless shapes. Sandwiches range in size and complexity until they rival a Dagwood.

One loaf of sandwich bread makes about 24 sandwiches. Day-old bread is best unless the sandwiches are to be rolled. Use fresh bread for rolled sandwiches and secure them with a toothpick or a clove. Cut very fresh bread with a heated sharp knife or chill the bread, closely covered, in the refrigerator for several hours before cutting. To remove crusts quickly use scissors, or if the whole loaf is to be used, remove crusts before slicing. A pound of butter will spread 3 medium-sized loaves. Cream the butter for ease in spreading. If the sandwiches are to be toasted, do so on both sides immediately before serving them. Serve them very hot.

Sandwiches may be made in advance and stored in waxed paper, plastic bags, in a cloth wrung out in cold water, or they may be deep frozen, see page 872. If this method is used, choose ingredients carefully as certain sandwich fillings do not freeze well.

Assembly Line Sandwiches

It is often quicker to make tea sandwiches in quantity by working with a whole loaf rather than with the usual individual slice. Cut the crusts from an unsliced loaf, then cut it in 6 or 7 horizontal slices. These long layers may be spread with

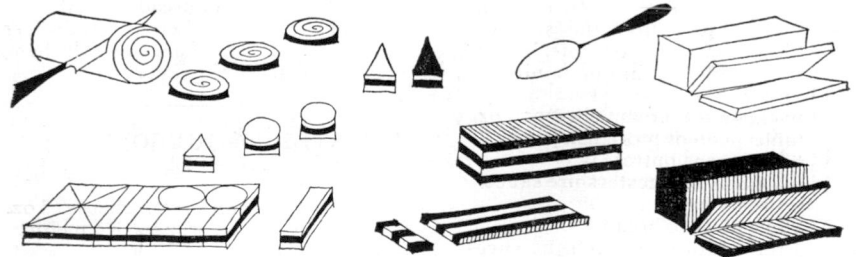

fillings and rolled to make pinwheels. A filling may be placed between 2 of them and the sandwiches cut in oblongs, squares, triangles or fancy shapes. By using both white and dark breads in this manner particolored sandwiches may be achieved. All these methods are shown above.

In making any sandwiches in quantity, time is saved if adequate space is available to allow mass production techniques. Place bread slices in rows. Put dabs of butter or mayonnaise on one row, well-seasoned filling on the next. Then do the final spreading to the edges of the bread. For closed sandwiches do all the assembling, stacking and packing at once. For open sandwiches, after the base is spread, do all the garnishing of one type, then of another, see next page.

9

Quick Canapé Spreads

A large number of canapé and sandwich spreads may be purchased ready for use. Chopped raw onions, herbs, including chives or parsley, chopped celery, olives, etc., may be added to these. They may be seasoned with some favorite condiment if you wish to give them an original touch, but on the whole they are acceptable as they are.

Spread these on potato chips, tortillas or any of the good crackers to be had in all shops, or on toasted rye, white or graham bread cut into attractive shapes. The bread may be buttered.

If you prefer some concoction of your own, have fish paste on hand, anchovy, sardelle, etc., cheese, caviar, antipasto, braunschweiger sausage, etc.

For further suggestions for sandwich fillings and combinations, see page 21.

Hot Canapés and Sandwiches

TOASTED CREAM CHEESE AND FISH PASTE CANAPÉS

My father, a physician, once took to task a scandalously obese patient. "But, doctor," said the patient plaintively, "one must offer the stomach something from time to time." This is a favorite offering in our family.
Combine:
    1 package soft cream cheese: 3 oz.
    ½ tablespoon or more fish paste
    1½ tablespoons butter
    ½ teaspoon Worcestershire sauce
Cut the crusts from:
    Thin slices of bread
Spread the mixture between the slices and cut them into shapes or roll them. Toast and serve them very hot.

TOASTED CREAM CHEESE CANAPÉS

Combine and beat until smooth:
    1 package soft cream cheese: 3 oz.
    1 tablespoon cream
    ⅛ teaspoon salt
Add:
    ½ teaspoon onion juice or 1 teaspoon finely chopped onion,
    chives or other herb
    (1 tablespoon finely chopped celery)
Cut into rounds:
    Thin slices of bread
Spread the mixture between the slices and cut them into shapes or roll them. Toast and serve them very hot.

TOASTED ROQUEFORT CHEESE CANAPÉS

Combine:
    1 package soft cream cheese: 3 oz.
    3 tablespoons or more Roquefort cheese
    ¼ cup chopped walnut or pecan meats
    Seasoning
Cut the crusts from:
    Thin slices of bread
Spread the cheese mixture between the slices and cut them into shapes or roll them. Toast and serve them very hot.

See Cold Canapés and Sandwiches, page 17, for other cream cheese spreads that may be used for toasted sandwiches.

TOASTED MUSHROOM CANAPÉS

Cut the crusts from:
Thin slices of bread
Spread between the slices:
Minced Creamed Mushrooms, page 292
Toast the sandwiches on both sides. Serve them very hot.

TOASTED BRAUNSCHWEIGER SAUSAGE CANAPÉS

Braunschweiger is a refined version of the rather heavy smoked liver sausage. Combine and stir to a smooth paste:
Braunschweiger sausage
Canned tomato soup
(A few drops of cream or Worcestershire sauce)
Cut the crusts from:
Thin slices of bread
Spread them with the sausage mixture. Roll the bread or make double-deck canapés. Toast and serve them very hot. For an emergency spread use canned condensed liver soup with catsup, chili sauce or French dressing.

TOASTED CHEESE ROLLS

This filling is quickly made. It is very good, but the following Cheese Spread is better. Combine and stir to a smooth paste or blend (see page 942):
2 cups soft sharp cheese, grated if necessary
½ teaspoon salt
A few grains cayenne
1 teaspoon prepared mustard
3 tablespoons cream
Cut the crusts from:
Thin slices of white bread
Spread and roll the slices. Serve the rolls very hot.

CHEESE SPREAD FOR TOASTED SANDWICHES OR CHEESE DREAMS

The following delicious sandwich spread will keep for a week or more. Scald in a double boiler:
½ cup milk
Add:
1 beaten egg
¼ teaspoon dry mustard
½ teaspoon salt
¾ lb. diced American cheese
Cook these ingredients over hot water for 15 minutes. Stir them constantly. Cool the mixture and keep it in a closed jar in the refrigerator. When ready to use it spread it between:
Rounds of bread

Place on each side of the canapés or sandwiches a generous dab of:
Butter
Toast them in a moderate oven 350° or under a broiler until they are crisp. For other cheese spreads see page 22. These may be used for hot or cold canapés or sandwiches.

TOASTED CHEESE LOGS OR ROLLS

Trim the crusts from:
Thin slices of bread
Place on each slice not quite covering it:
A thin slice of cheese
Or, place on each slice of bread:
An oblong block of cheese
Spread the cheese lightly with:
Anchovy paste, prepared mustard or horseradish
Gather up 2 opposite corners and fasten them with a toothpick or roll the bread. Seal the ends, using:
Butter
Brush the outside of the logs with:
Melted butter
Broil them under a low flame to toast them lightly and to melt the cheese, or toast them in a moderate oven 350° until light brown. Serve them piping hot on toothpicks.

CHEESE BREAD CUBES

Cut into cubes of any size:
Fresh bread
Beat:
1 egg
1½ tablespoons melted butter
Roll the cubes in the egg mixture, then in:
Finely grated American cheese
Salt and cayenne or paprika
Or, omit the egg and spread rye bread cubes with a paste made of:
Butter
Grated Parmesan cheese
Caraway or celery seed
Salt and a few grains cayenne
(Mustard)
Toast the cubes on a greased sheet in a moderate oven 375° until the cheese is melted. Serve them hot as appetizers. Good with soup or salads.

PUFFED BREAD SQUARES

These may be prepared in advance. Keep at room temperature until soft, then blend well:
½ lb. Cheddar cheese
¼ lb. butter: 1 stick

Season palatably with:
  Mustard
  Curry powder
  Caraway or celery seed
  Salt and pepper or paprika
Cut bread into 1½ inch blocks. Cover them with the cheese spread. Keep them chilled until ready for use. Pop them into a moderately hot oven 375°-400°. They should brown lightly and puff.

CHEESE BALLS
About 24
Cream the contents of:
  1 jar sharp spreading cheese: 5 oz.
  3 tablespoons butter
Sift, then add:
  ¾ cup all-purpose flour
  ½ teaspoon salt
  ¼ teaspoon paprika
When well blended pinch off pieces of dough and form them into ¾ inch balls. They should be chilled for 2 hours but they may be baked at once. Bake the balls in a moderately hot oven 400° for about 10 minutes. Serve them hot or cold.

CHEESE PUFF CANAPÉS
Beat until very stiff:
  2 egg whites
  ¼ teaspoon salt
Fold in:
  1 cup grated American cheese
  1 teaspoon Worcestershire sauce
  ½ teaspoon paprika
  ½ teaspoon dry mustard
Toast on one side:
  Small rounds of bread or crackers
Spread the untoasted side with the cheese mixture. Place the canapés under a moderate broiler flame for about 6 minutes, until the cheese is well puffed and brown.

PUFFED CREAM CHEESE CANAPÉS
Soften:
  1 package cream cheese: 3 oz.
with:
  2 tablespoons mayonnaise
Add:
  1 tablespoon minced onion, chives or other green herb
  (2 tablespoons chopped nut meats)
Spread this ¼ inch thick on salted crackers. Brown them quickly under a broiler.

ONION AND CHEESE CANAPÉS
Method I.
Cut into small rounds:
  Bread or toast
Place on each round:
  A very thin slice of onion
Cover each round with:
  1½ teaspoons mayonnaise seasoned with curry or chutney
Sprinkle the tops with:
  Grated Parmesan cheese
Place the canapés under a broiler until the tops begin to color. Serve them piping hot.

Method II.
Or, spread the onions with:
  Grated cheese
Mixed to a paste with:
  Worcestershire sauce
  Dry mustard and salt
  Paprika or cayenne
Broil as directed above.

BRAN BISCUITS WITH CHEESE
This combination is very popular.
Bake small:
  Bran Biscuits, page 508
When they are cold split them. Prepare:
  Cheese Spread, pages 11, 22
Spread the insides of the biscuits with the cheese. Place on the top of each biscuit:
  A dab of butter
Reheat them in a hot oven 425°. Serve them very hot.

MAYONNAISE PUFFS
Whip until very stiff:
  2 egg whites
  ⅛ teaspoon salt
Fold in:
  1 cup thick mayonnaise
Spread the mixture on crackers. Broil them for 1 minute under a moderate flame.

DEVILED CRACKERS
A quick and easy canapé made with ingredients one is apt to have on hand.
Work into a paste:
  2 teaspoons dry mustard or 1 teaspoon curry powder
  Worcestershire sauce
Beat until soft:
  3 tablespoons butter
Beat the paste into it. Season it with:
  ½ teaspoon paprika or ⅛ teaspoon red pepper
Spread the mixture on thin crackers. Heat the crackers in a moderate oven 350° until they are light brown.

FINGER ROLL CANAPÉS
Cut into lengthwise halves:
  Small soft finger rolls
Hollow them slightly. Fill the hollows with:
  Cheese Spread, pages 11, 22
or with any of the fillings given for toasted sandwiches or hot canapés, such as Lobster, Crab, etc. Reheat them in a hot oven 425°.

PUFF SHELLS I
See Cream Puffs, page 653. Bake:
  1 inch puff shells
Split them on one side. Fill them with:
  Deviled ham, cream cheese and catsup
  Cheese Spread, pages 11, 22
  Creamed Mushrooms, page 292, oysters, fish, etc.
  Braunschweiger sausage thinned with tomato soup and Worcestershire sauce
Reheat them in a hot oven 425°.

PASTRY SNAILS
If the approval of guests is to be taken as a criterion of excellence this is the prize-winning canapé, reminiscent of the guest who hesitated to help himself, saying: "Well, I shouldn't, I've had two already." Which remark was capped by his hostess' brisk and crushing reply: "You've had six, but who's counting?"
Roll into very thin oblongs any:
  Pie Crust, page 564
Spread the oblongs with:
  Filling (see below)
Roll them like a jelly roll. Chill the rolls; cut them in ½ inch slices and bake them on a greased pan in a hot oven 425°.

FILLINGS FOR PASTRY SNAILS
I.
Two parts of soft cream and 1 part anchovy paste or Roquefort.
II.
Grated American cheese seasoned with cayenne, curry or mustard.
III.
Soft cream cheese seasoned with catsup, salt and paprika.
IV.
Roquefort cheese, cream cheese and sherry.
V.
Deviled ham thinned with a very little cream, seasoned with mustard.

VI.
Deviled ham sprinkled with grated American cheese, seasoned with a dash of mustard, salt and paprika.
VII.
Braunschweiger sausage thinned with tomato soup, seasoned with Worcestershire sauce.
VIII.
Mock Paté de Fois Gras, page 23.

See Turnovers Filled with Meat, page 159, and Meat Shortcakes, page 159, for good hot canapés that may be prepared in advance and reheated later.

TOMATO, CHEESE AND BACON CANAPÉS
Cut:
  6 rounds of bread
Toast them on one side. Place on the untoasted sides:
  6 thick slices tomato
Sprinkle them with:
  Salt and pepper
  Minced onion and green pepper
  (Brown sugar)
Dot them with:
  Butter
Place on each slice:
  1 tablespoon grated cheese or a slice of bacon
Place the canapés on the bottom shelf of the broiling oven. Serve them when the tomatoes are soft, the cheese is melted and the bacon is crisp.

See Vegetable Shortcake or Pizza Napolitana, page 169.

TOMATO, BACON AND CHEESE TARTS
Follow the rule for:
  Biscuit Dough, page 505, or
  Pie Dough, page 561
Roll or pat it until it is about ⅛ inch thick. Cut it into 3 inch squares. Place in the center of each square:
  A thin slice of cheese 1½ x 2 inches
Top this with:
  ½ slice tomato
Season the tomato with:
  A grating of pepper
  A little salt
  (A sprinkling of brown sugar)
Sprinkle the top with:
  Cooked diced bacon
Moisten the corners of the dough lightly with water. Fold up the sides of the dough and pinch the corners to make a tart shape. Bake the tarts in a hot oven 425° for 10 to 15 minutes.

BACON AND CHEESE CANAPÉS

Toast on one side:
    Rounds of bread
Spread the untoasted side thickly with:
    2 cups grated cheese
    2 slices minced sautéed bacon
    ¼ teaspoon dry mustard
    A few grains cayenne
    1 tablespoon Worcestershire
        sauce
Toast the canapés under a broiler until the cheese is melted.

CHUTNEY AND CHEESE CANAPÉS

Cover:
    Round crackers or toast
with:
    Chutney
    A thin slice of American cheese
Broil the crackers to melt the cheese.

TOASTED NUT CANAPÉS

Cream until soft enough to stir:
    ½ cup butter
Stir in:
    1 cup ground pecans
    2 tablespoons Worcestershire
        sauce
Toast on one side:
    Slices of bread
Spread the untoasted side with the mixture. Toast the canapés until they are hot.

TOASTED TRISCUIT, ETC.

Spread:
    Triscuit
with:
    Melted butter or partially beaten
        egg white
Sprinkle it with:
    Caraway or celery seed
Or, add:
    Melted butter
to:
    Shredded wheat or rice squares
You may add:
    Grated onion
Heat in a hot oven 400°.

TOASTED POTATO CHIPS

Sprinkle:
    Potato chips
with:
    Grated Parmesan cheese
Toast them in a hot oven 400°.

SALTINE AND BACON CANAPÉS

Surround:
    Long salted soda crackers

with:
    Strips of very thin bacon
Take care that the strips do not overlap. Secure them with toothpicks. Place them on a rack set in a pan. Broil the bacon until it is crisp or bake the crackers in a moderate oven 325°. Turn the crackers. Drain them on absorbent paper. Serve at once.

BROILED SARDINE CANAPÉS

Drain:
    Large sardines
Blend well:
    2 tablespoons butter
    1 teaspoon dry mustard
    A few drops Worcestershire
        sauce
Spread the sardines with this mixture. Dip them in:
    Cracker crumbs
Broil them quickly. Serve them on:
    Strips of toast
with:
    Parsley and slices of lemon

TOASTED SARDINE CANAPÉS

Method I.
Drain well:
    Large sardines
Cut into slices the size of the sardines:
    Bread
Toast it. Dip it in the sardine oil. Spread each slice with:
    Anchovy paste
Sprinkle it with:
    Lemon juice
    Chopped parsley
Place the sardines on the toast. Heat them in a hot oven 400°.

Method II.
Mash with a fork:
    12 skinless, boneless sardines
Add:
    ½ teaspoon Worcestershire sauce
    ½ teaspoon tomato catsup
    1 tablespoon finely cut celery or
        onion
    1 tablespoon chopped stuffed
        olives
Moisten these ingredients until they are a good consistency to spread with:
    Mayonnaise or French dressing
Season them with:
    Salt and pepper
Cut the crusts from:
    Thin slices of white bread
Spread the sardine mixture on the bread. Roll the slices and secure them with toothpicks. Toast the canapés and serve them very hot.

LOBSTER CANAPÉS

In the absence of the lobster, page the crab or tuna fish. Combine:

½ lb. cooked lobster meat
½ lb. Sautéed Mushrooms, page 292
1 cup rich Cream Sauce II, page 428
1 tablespoon finely chopped green pepper
1 tablespoon chopped pimiento
Salt and pepper
¼ teaspoon curry powder or 1 teaspoon Worcestershire sauce or 2 tablespoons sherry

Heap the mixture on rounds of:
Toast, which may be spread with anchovy paste

Sprinkle the tops with:
Grated Parmesan or Swiss cheese
Bread crumbs

Dot them with:
Butter

Heat the canapés under a broiler.

CRAB MEAT CANAPÉS

Follow the above rule for:
Lobster Canapés

Substitute for the lobster:
6½ oz. crab meat

Use only:
¾ cup Cream Sauce II, page 428

TUNA FISH OR CRAB MEAT CANAPÉS

Follow the recipe above or drain the contents of:
1 can tuna fish or crab meat

Mash it with a fork. Add to it sufficient:
Mayonnaise or French dressing

to make a creamy paste. Spread it on:
Rounds or triangles of toast

Sprinkle the canapés well with:
(Grated cheese)

Heat them under a broiler until they are brown. Serve them hot.

CREAMED OYSTER CANAPÉS

Follow the rule for:
Creamed Oysters, page 111

Place the pan containing the oysters over hot water. Toast and butter lightly:
Small rounds of bread

Place an oyster on each round. Sprinkle it with:
Chopped parsley

Serve the canapés at once.

OYSTER AND BACON CANAPÉS

Toast lightly and butter:
Small rounds of bread

Place on each round:
A large drained oyster

Cover each oyster with:
A thin piece of bacon

Place the canapés in a pan and broil them under moderate heat until the bacon is done or bake them in a hot oven 400° for about 3 minutes. Serve them on toothpicks.

Rolled Asparagus Canapés, Toasted, page 19.

TOASTED ROLLS WITH CRAB MEAT AND CHEESE

4 Servings

Fine with beer or cider. Cut into halves:
4 rolls

Cover the 4 lower halves with:
Lettuce leaves

Combine:
¾ cup canned crab meat
¼ cup mayonnaise

Spread this on the lettuce. Spread the remaining halves with:
Butter
Slices of cheese
(Mustard)

Toast the cheese under a broiler until it is soft. Place the tops on the lower halves. Serve the rolls at once.

HOT SLICED CHICKEN, ROQUEFORT CHEESE AND BACON SANDWICHES

Prepare:
Buttered toast

Cover the toast with:
Sliced chicken

Sprinkle it with:
Crumbled Roquefort cheese

Cover it with:
Strips of notched bacon

Broil the sandwiches or bake them in a moderate oven 375° for about 10 minutes, until the bacon is crisp. Sliced tomatoes may be placed on the toast.

CHEESE SANDWICHES WITH BACON

4 Servings

Toast on one side:
4 slices of bread

Place on the untoasted sides:
Slices of cheese

Spread the cheese with:
Mustard or chili sauce

Cover each sandwich with:
    2 slices notched bacon
Arrange between the bacon slices:
    A slice of tomato
    (Sliced stuffed olives)
Bake the sandwiches in a moderate
oven 350° for 10 minutes, or until the
bacon is crisp. These sandwiches may
be placed under a broiler until the
bacon is cooked.

ROLLS WITH BACON AND CHEESE
4 Servings
Cut into halves:
    4 long hard buns
Place between the slices:
    4 thick oblongs yellow cheese
It may be spread with:
    Mustard
Wind around the buns:
    4 strips bacon
Secure them with toothpicks. Bake
the buns on a rack in a quick oven
400°, or place them under a broiler
until the bacon is crisp.

TUNA FISH SANDWICHES WITH CHEESE
4 Servings
Skin, then cut into thick slices:
    Tomatoes
Place them on:
    8 rounds of buttered toast
Season them with:
    Salt and pepper
    A pinch of brown sugar
Drain, then flake the contents of:
    1 can tuna fish: 7 oz.
Combine it lightly with:
    Mayonnaise
Spread the tuna on the tomatoes.
Sprinkle them with:
    Grated cheese
Broil them under a flame until the
cheese is melted. Serve them garnished
with:
    Parsley
You may substitute sardine fillets and
lemon juice for the tuna and mayon-
naise.

CORNED BEEF SANDWICHES
6 Servings
Cut into tiny slivers:
    ¼ cup sharp American cheese
Cream the cheese well with:
    2 tablespoons mayonnaise
Shred finely and add:
    4 oz. canned corned beef or dried
    beef

Chop until fine and add:
    ¼ cup sour-sweet pickles
    1 tablespoon grated onion
    (2 tablespoons minced celery or
    parsley)
Season the spread with:
    Salt, if needed, and paprika
    Curry powder, mustard or
    Worcestershire sauce
Spread it between:
    Slices of bread
The sandwiches may be toasted or
they may be served with sliced toma-
toes and lettuce between the layers.

QUICK CORNED BEEF CANAPÉS
Combine:
    ½ cup minced corned beef
    1½ tablespoons sherry
    ½ teaspoon Worcestershire sauce
Spread this on crackers or toast. Broil
them under a quick flame.

PEANUT BUTTER AND TOMATO SANDWICH
Toast on one side:
    A slice of bread
Spread the untoasted side with:
    Peanut butter.
mixed with:
    Chopped cooked bacon
    Bacon drippings
You may top this with:
    A thick slice of tomato
Season the tomato with:
    ¼ teaspoon brown sugar
    Salt and paprika
Put the sandwich under a broiler for a
minute or two.

LILY SANDWICHES
Combine and work to a paste:
    2 packages cream cheese: 6 oz.
    1 or more tablespoons cream
    ¼ teaspoon salt
    (¼ teaspoon paprika)
Cut very thinly:
    20 slices of bread
Remove the crusts. Spread the slices
with the cheese. Roll the bread into
cornucopia shape by bringing 2 straight
edges together and letting them overlap. Hold the edges together with
additional cheese. Press them gently
or use a toothpick to hold them firmly.
You may substitute for the bread
Swedish wafers steamed in a double
boiler until pliable. Roll and chill before spreading or filling. Insert into
each lily formed:

A thin strip of carrot

You may, in addition, cut into leaf shape:

Green pepper

Attach these with cheese to the sides of the lily. Chill the sandwiches.

DEVILED EGGS ON TOAST WITH SHRIMP AND MAYONNAISE BROILED

4 Servings

Hard-cook by the rule on page 79:
4 eggs

Chill them. Chop them. Add:
2 tablespoons cream
1 teaspoon lemon juice

A few drops Tabasco or Worcestershire sauce
Salt
1 teaspoon dried tarragon or
2 tablespoons chopped chives

Toast:
4 slices of bread

Spread them with the egg mixture. Cover each slice with:
Cooked shrimp

Cover the shrimp with well-seasoned:
Mayonnaise

Broil the sandwiches until the tops are light brown.

Hot and Cold Sandwiches with Hot Sauce or Cold Dressing, page 131.

Cold Canapés and Sandwiches

POTATO CHIPS AND CHEESE

Work to a smooth paste:
Roquefort cheese or soft cream cheese

Season it with:
Worcestershire sauce
Paprika

Spread it on:
Crisp potato chips

PRETZEL AND CHEESE CANAPÉS

Work with a fork until smooth:
1 package soft cream cheese: 3 oz.

Season it well with:
Paprika

Place the cheese in the hollows of:
Small crisp pretzels

Press the pretzels into:
Rolled pretzel crumbs

Chopped pickles may be added to the cheese mixture. Make these canapés shortly before they are served. Chill them.

CHEESE CRACKERS AND FISH PASTE CANAPÉS

An emergency canapé. In the center of:
Crisp round crackers

place:
A small dab of butter
A small dab of fish paste

RIBBON SANDWICHES

Cut the crust from:
White bread
Dark bread

Spread the slices with:
Butter or Cream Cheese Mixture, page 22

Place about 5 slices of bread alternately in stacks. Cut them into bars, squares or triangles (page 9).

CHRISTMAS CANAPÉS

These have a charming, crisp, holiday effect. Cut into 2 inch rounds:
White bread slices

Work until smooth:
1 package soft cream cheese: 3 oz.
1 tablespoon or more cream
A pinch of salt

Spread the rounds with the cheese. Cut into tiny rounds about ⅛ inch:
Maraschino cherries or pimiento or use tiny red decorettes

Chop until fine:
Parsley

Make a narrow ring of the parsley around each piece of bread. Dot it at intervals to look like a holly wreath with the red rounds.

It is hard to cut the cherries or pimiento. I asked my hostess how she had done it and that inventive person told me she had used the point of an empty pencil—the kind into which lead is slipped. When in haste she uses decorettes, but places both the rounds and the decorettes on the sandwiches shortly before serving them to keep the color from running. Bits of cranberry may be used.

CREAM CHEESE, BACON AND CHIVE CANAPÉS

Cook slowly until crisp:
2 slices bacon

When cold chop the slices. Mash with a fork:
1 package soft cream cheese: 3 oz.

If very stiff add:
    1 or 2 tablespoons cream
When mashed to a smooth paste add:
    ¼ teaspoon Worcestershire sauce
and the bacon. Heap on crackers.
Serve them dusted with:
    Finely minced chives or parsley

CHEESE AND CELERY CANAPÉS

Remove the crust from:
    A small loaf of white bread
Cut it into ¼ inch lengthwise slices.
Spread the slices with a thick layer of
paste made with:
    ¼ lb. Roquefort cheese
    ½ cup finely cut celery
    Mayonnaise
    A few drops Worcestershire
      sauce
Roll the slices like a jelly roll. Chill
the rolls. Cut them into ¼ inch slices.

ANCHOVY AND WALNUT CANAPÉS

Combine:
    10 minced anchovies
    6 tablespoons chopped walnut
      meats
    1 tablespoon chopped parsley
    ½ minced clove garlic or 1
      tablespoon chopped olives
    1 tablespoon anchovy oil
    1 teaspoon lemon juice
Heap these ingredients on:
    Toast
The toast may be spread with anchovy
oil.

EGG AND ANCHOVY CANAPÉS

Cut:
    Small rounds of bread
Spread them with:
    Butter
Toast them lightly. Place on each
round a slice of:
    Hard-cooked egg
Place in each center:
    A rolled anchovy
The edges of the canapé may be piped
with:
    Mayonnaise

TOMATO AND SHRIMP CANAPÉS

Prepare:
    Rounds of toast
Cover them with:
    Thick slices of tomato
Place in each center:
    2 or 3 marinated shrimp
Cover the shrimp with:
    A dab of mayonnaise

TOMATO CANAPÉS WITH CAVIAR AND SHRIMP

Cut:
    Thin slices of tomato
Combine:
    Caviar
    Chopped hard-cooked egg yolks
    A few drops lemon juice
Spread this mixture on the tomato
slices. Garnish them with:
    Chopped hard-cooked egg
      whites
Serve them on:
    Lettuce leaves or rounds of
      buttered toast
Garnish the centers with:
    (Marinated shrimp)

CAVIAR AND CUCUMBER CANAPÉS

Dip:
    Slices of cucumber
in:
    French dressing
Drain them. Prepare:
    Small rounds of buttered toast
Peel, then slice crosswise:
    Mild onions
Separate the slices into rings. Place
a ring on each round of toast so that
it will form a wall. Place a slice of
cucumber in each ring. Cover the
cucumber with:
    Small mounds of caviar seasoned
      with lemon and onion juice or
      chives
Garnish the canapés with:
    Capers
    Riced hard-cooked eggs

CAVIAR CANAPÉS

Sauté in butter:
    Rounds of thin toast
Combine and spread on the toast equal
parts of:
    Caviar
    Finely chopped onion
Season them with:
    Lemon juice
Garnish the edges of the canapés with:
    Riced hard-cooked egg yolks
They may be topped with:
    Shrimp or smoked salmon

MUSHROOM CANAPÉS

Sauté by the rule on page 292:
    Mushrooms
Mince the mushrooms. Prepare by the
rule on page 428:
    Cream Sauce II—½ as much
      sauce as mushrooms

Season it with:
Salt and paprika
Freshly grated nutmeg
Combine the sauce and the mushrooms. When cold add a little:
Whipped cream
Heap these ingredients on:
Small rounds of bread or toast
Garnish the canapés with:
Paprika and parsley

Toasted Mushroom Canapés, page 11;
Sandwiches with Sauce, page 131.

WATER CRESS CANAPÉS
This canapé is very refreshing. Chop until fine or chop coarsely:
Water cress
Mix it with:
Soft butter
Grated onion or chives
A dash of salt
Spread it on:
Thin crustless slices white bread
Serve the canapés rolled, open or double-deck, page 9.
Or, spread the slices with:
Cream cheese softened with
cream
A thin layer caviar
Place on each slice:
A sprig of water cress
Roll the sandwiches, letting the green leaves protrude, page 9. Serve them around the edge of a platter, letting the water cress form a wreath. Fill the center with shrimp, curled celery, radishes or olives.

WATER CRESS AND BRAUN-SCHWEIGER SANDWICHES
Combine and mix to a paste:
¼ lb. braunschweiger
1 or more tablespoons cream
Add:
¼ cup or more chopped water
cress
Serve on rye bread or toast.

PICKLE CANAPÉS
A very decorative canapé. Remove the crust from:
A small loaf fresh white bread
Cut it into ¼ inch lengthwise slices.
Combine and work until smooth:
Roquefort or soft cream cheese
thinned with cream
Color the mixture pink with:
Paprika
Spread it on the bread. Roll each slice around:

A jumbo pickle
Wrap the rolls in waxed paper. Chill them and when ready to serve cut them into ¼ inch slices.

ROLLED ASPARAGUS CANAPÉS OR SANDWICHES
Cut the crust from:
Thin slices of bread
Spread the slices thinly with:
Butter and mayonnaise
Sprinkle them lightly with:
Chopped chives
Place on each slice a well-drained:
Asparagus tip
Roll the canapés. Wrap the rolls in waxed paper until ready to serve.
If preferred, the drained asparagus tips may be marinated in French dressing for ½ hour.
These sandwiches may be toasted.

MOCK CHICKEN SANDWICHES
Put in a strainer the contents of:
1 can tuna fish
Pour over it:
2 cups boiling water
Drain the fish well, flake it and combine it with:
Well-seasoned mayonnaise
Spread the mixture between:
Thin slices of bread
Place between the slices:
Lettuce leaves or water cress

TUNA FISH, SALMON OR CRAB MEAT SANDWICH FILLING
Combine lightly with a fork:
½ cup flaked tuna fish
1 chopped hard-cooked egg
½ cup chopped celery
2 tablespoons chopped pimiento
2 tablespoons chopped sweet
pickles
¼ teaspoon salt
¼ teaspoon paprika
⅓ cup mayonnaise
Spread this filling between:
Thin slices of bread

CRAB MEAT OR LOBSTER CANAPÉS
Prepare by the rule on page 15 the mixture for:
Crab Meat Canapés
When cold add a little:
(Whipped cream)
Heap these ingredients on:
Small rounds of bread or toast

CLAM CANAPÉS
Drain the contents of:
> 1 can minced clams: 7 oz.

Combine them with:
> 1 package soft cream cheese: 3 oz.
> 1 tablespoon Worcestershire
>   sauce
> A pinch of dry mustard
> Salt as needed
> 1 tablespoon more or less onion
>   juice

Heap these ingredients on small rounds of bread or toast.

SMOKED SALMON CANAPÉS
Place on round waffle wafers or crackers:
> Squares of smoked salmon

Top them with a slice of:
> Stuffed olive

Brush the canapés with:
> Meat Glaze, page 441

that is about to set. Chill them until set. Place on:
> Lettuce

and serve 2 to a person.

SMOKED SALMON AND PRETZEL CANAPÉS
Cut into very thin slices:
> Smoked salmon

Spread the slices with:
> Prepared mustard

Fasten them about one end of:
> Small pretzels

The mustard will hold the salmon in place.

SHRIMP AND CELERY SANDWICHES
Clean:
> Canned shrimp

Cut them in two lengthwise. Place them flat on slices of:
> Buttered bread

Spread them with:
> Mayonnaise

Sprinkle over them:
> Minced celery and ripe olives

Cover them with a lettuce leaf and a second slice of buttered bread, or place the lettuce under the shrimp and serve the sandwich open.

The shrimp may be marinated in French dressing and you may add slices of mild onions.

LOBSTER SANDWICHES
Flake:
> 6 oz. or more canned lobster or
>   other sea food

Sprinkle over it:
> 1 teaspoon lemon juice

Add:
> ½ cup minced celery
> 1 tablespoon minced onion or
>   chives
> ½ cup mayonnaise

Mayonnaise, if too thick, is fine thinned with sour cream.

Season the sandwich spread as desired with:
> Worcestershire sauce, curry or
>   freshly grated nutmeg

You may add:
> Capers, chopped olives, pickles
>   or parsley, etc.

Spread these ingredients on:
> Buttered rye bread

You may add:
> Crisp lettuce leaves

OPEN-FACED FISH SALAD AND TOMATO SANDWICHES
Prepare:
> Slices of buttered bread

Cover them with:
> Slices of tomato

Top the tomatoes with mounds of:
> Crab Meat Salad, page 468, or
>   other sea food

Garnish with:
> Chopped parsley, olives or
>   chives
> Chopped sautéed bacon

CHICKEN OR FISH SALAD SANDWICHES
The above rule may be followed and any left-over fish or meat may be used to make good sandwiches. If you have only a little and wish to stretch it, add chopped hard-cooked eggs, canned asparagus, drained and cut into pieces, left-over cooked vegetables, etc.

CHICKEN AND CREAM CHEESE SANDWICHES
Spread:
> Slices of whole-wheat bread

with:
> Cream cheese softened with
>   cream

Add:
> Slices of cooked chicken
> Chopped green olives
> Salt

SALAMI SANDWICHES
Grind or chop fine and combine:
> ½ lb. salami
> 1 pimiento

1 green pepper
½ small onion
⅓ cup chopped ripe or green olives
Add to moisten:
    Mayonnaise
Season as needed with:
    Salt and pepper
Spread the filling between slices of rye
or whole-wheat bread.

CLUB SANDWICH
Individual Service
Prepare:
    3 large square slices of toast
Cover Slice 1 with:
    A lettuce leaf
    3 crisp slices hot bacon
    Slices of tomato
    1 tablespoon mayonnaise
    (Drained slices pineapple)
Place Slice 2 on Slice 1 and cover it
with:
    Slices of cold cooked chicken
    1 tablespoon mayonnaise
Place Slice 3 on Slice 2 and cut the
sandwich on the bias.

PECAN SANDWICHES
Trim the crusts from:
    Thin slices of bread
Place between the slices:
    Nasturtium or lettuce leaves
    Finely chopped pecans
    moistened with mayonnaise

HARD ROLLS, STUFFED
AND SLICED
Hollow from one end:
    Long hard rolls

Fill the hollows with:
    A sardine or other sandwich
    spread
Chill the rolls. Cut them into slices
They may be garnished with:
    Capers, parsley, olives, etc.
A good filling may be made with:
    3 chopped hard-cooked eggs
    6 chopped anchovies
    Mayonnaise

FINGER ROLL SANDWICHES
Very good picnic sandwiches. Cut into
lengthwise halves:
    Soft finger rolls
Hollow them slightly. Fill the hollows
with any palatable sandwich spread.
These are easy to handle and will keep
well for a long time. They are delicious filled with:
    Chicken Salad, page 470
    Crab Meat Salad, page 468
    Braunschweiger Sausage
    Canapé Filling, page 11
    Chopped celery and mayonnaise
    Chopped olives and cream
    cheese, etc.

PUFF SHELLS II
Bake:
    1 inch Puff Shells, page 13
Split them on one side. Fill them with:
    Chicken, lobster, crab or fish
    salad, caviar, soft cream cheese
    and Roquefort, or any desired
    sandwich spread
For a decorative canapé cut a thin slice
from the top of the puffs. Fill the puffs
with:
    Soft cream cheese
    A dab of bright jelly

Sandwich Spreads

The following spreads or fillings may be used on:

| White bread | Rye bread, etc. | Buns |
| Graham bread | Small rolls | Crackers |

For teas it is usual to cut the bread into very thin slices and to trim the edges.
The bread may be toasted.

For suppers and picnics it is frequently advisable to have heftier sandwiches.
Sandwiches may be served open or covered.

In addition to the spread the following may be used for flavor or for garnishes:

Lettuce	Parsley	Pimientos
Water cress	Pickles	Nut meats
Nasturtium leaves	Olives	Herbs, etc.

A number of commercial spreads may be purchased. To these you may add
condiments or flavorings to please your palate.

BUTTER SPREADS

There are many ways of preparing good, quick sandwich spreads with a butter basis. Beat butter until soft. Add other ingredients gradually. Chill the butter mixture until it is a good consistency to spread, or cut it into small blocks and serve them with salad.

Beat until soft:
    4 tablespoons butter
Add to the butter slowly one or more of the following:
    ½ teaspoon lemon juice
    ½ teaspoon Worcestershire sauce or ½ teaspoon dry mustard
    ½ teaspoon grated onion or minced garlic
Good additions to the butter mixture are a choice of:
    2 tablespoons chopped parsley
    2 tablespoons chopped chives
    1 tablespoon chopped mixed herbs
    2 tablespoons chopped water cress
    ¼ cup soft or grated cheese
    2 tablespoons fish paste
    2 tablespoons horseradish
    1 tablespoon olive paste
    2 tablespoons catsup or chili sauce
    1 tablespoon chutney
    ¼ teaspoon curry powder
Add if needed:
    Salt and pepper

HONEY BUTTER

Combine by the above rule for butter spreads:
    Equal parts of butter and honey

Lemon Butter, Mint Butter, page 431.

SEA FOOD BUTTER

Put through a sieve or blender or chop:
    1 cup cooked shrimp, lobster, etc.
    ¼ lb. butter
    1 teaspoon or more lemon juice
    A fresh grating of pepper

DRIED HERBS IN WINE FOR BUTTER SPREADS

Combine:
    2 tablespoons crushed dried herbs: basil, tarragon, chervil, orégano, etc.
    ½ cup dry white wine or lemon juice
Permit the herbs to soak for 2 hours or more. Follow the above rule for Butter Spreads, using a little of this mixture. Keep the rest to use combined with melted butter as a dressing for vegetables.

ROQUEFORT AND CREAM CHEESE SPREAD OR SAUCE

This delicious spread keeps well and improves with age—better when 1 week old than when newly made.
Combine to a paste:
    ½ lb. Roquefort cheese
    2 packages soft cream cheese: 6 oz., or use an 8 oz. package
    2 tablespoons butter
    1 small grated onion
    1 tablespoon Worcestershire sauce
    2 tablespoons sherry
    Salt as needed
Keep the spread in a closely covered jar in the refrigerator.
To Make A Sauce: Shortly before using it add, until the right consistency is reached:
    Cream

CREAM CHEESE AND HORSERADISH SPREAD

Work to a smooth paste:
    1 package cream cheese: 3 oz.
    1 teaspoon or more cream
    1 tablespoon or more horseradish
    Salt and paprika
You may add:
    1 tablespoon chopped parsley or chives

CREAM CHEESE AND GARLIC SPREAD

Rub a bowl with:
    Garlic
Place in it and work to a paste:
    1 or more packages soft cream cheese: 3 oz. packages
Season it with:
    Worcestershire sauce

See Toasted Cream Cheese Canapés, page 10.

GINGER CHEESE SPREAD

Moisten:
    Cream cheese
with:
    Rich milk
Add:
    Chopped ginger
    Chopped almonds

ORANGE CHEESE SPREAD
Combine:
  1 package soft cream cheese: 3 oz.
  Rind of 1 orange or 2 table-
  spoons orange marmalade
  ¼ teaspoon salt
  ⅛ teaspoon paprika
Spread:
  Thin slices of bread
with:
  Mayonnaise or butter
Cover them with the cheese and:
  Toasted chopped pecan meats

FRESH HERB AND COTTAGE CHEESE SPREAD
Combine:
  1 lb. dry cottage cheese: 1 pint
  2 tablespoons cream
  1 tablespoon salad oil
  1 teaspoon chopped basil
  1 teaspoon chopped tarragon
  1 teaspoon chopped parsley
  1 teaspoon salt
  (1 teaspoon dill seed)
Place in a covered jar in the refrigerator for 24 hours.

CHEESE AND FISH SPREAD
Cut into pieces and melt in the top of a
double boiler:
  1 package processed Old English
  cheese
Add:
  1 can tuna fish or crab meat: 7 oz.
  ½ cup mayonnaise
  ½ teaspoon Worcestershire sauce
Chill. Use as a cold spread or on
rounds of hot toasted bread.

CRAB MEAT SPREAD
Flake the contents of:
  1 can crab meat: 6½ oz.
Stir in:
  2 tablespoons mayonnaise
  1 or 2 tablespoons tomato paste
  or catsup
  Seasoning as needed
You may add:
  Chopped celery or olives
Good on anything, especially good on
hot potato chips. Encourage your
guests to spread their own. Put the
mix in a bowl, surround it with crackers, etc.

ANCHOVY SPREAD
Combine:
  10 or 12 chopped anchovies
  ¼ cup chopped nut meats

  1 tablespoon minced parsley or
  chives
  ½ minced clove garlic
  1 tablespoon olive oil
Spread this on:
  Toast or crackers

TUNA FISH SPREAD
Combine:
  Tuna fish
  Chopped sour or sweet pickles
  or olives
  Chopped cooked bacon
  Chopped celery or carrots
  Mayonnaise
  Lemon juice

SARDINE SPREAD
Follow the rule for Toasted Sardine
Canapés II, page 14.

LOBSTER SPREAD
Combine:
  Chopped cooked lobster meat
  Chopped hard-cooked eggs
  Chopped cucumbers
  Well-seasoned mayonnaise

MOCK PÂTÉ DE FOIE GRAS SPREAD
Remove the skin from:
  ½ lb. liver sausage
Mash it with a fork. Beat into it:
  1 tablespoon mayonnaise
  1½ tablespoons lemon juice
  ½ teaspoon salt
  ⅛ teaspoon white pepper

*Toasted Braunschweiger Sausage Can-
apés, page 11.*

ALMOND OR BACON AND EGG SANDWICH SPREAD
Combine:
  ¼ cup finely chopped blanched
  almonds or cooked chopped
  bacon
  4 finely chopped hard-cooked eggs
  Salt
  ¼ teaspoon Worcestershire sauce
Add until the mixture is a good consistency to spread:
  Butter
  Mayonnaise or French dressing

HAM OR TONGUE SANDWICH SPREAD
Method I.
Grind:

½ lb. cooked ham or tongue
1 large sour pickle
4 hard-cooked eggs
Season them with:
    Salt and pepper
    Prepared mustard
Moisten the filling until it is a good
consistency to spread with:
    Vinegar

Method II.
Combine:
    Ground cooked ham or tongue
    Chopped onion or chives
    Chopped celery
Moisten them with:
    Cream or salad dressing
If cream is used, season with:
    Paprika and salt if needed
Spread the filling between:
    Thin slices of bread

DEVILED HAM SPREAD
Method I.
Combine:
    2¼ oz. deviled ham
    1 tablespoon finely chopped
        celery
    1 finely chopped hard-cooked egg
Moisten:
    ¼ teaspoon curry powder
with:
    ½ teaspoon olive oil
Add these ingredients to the ham mixture with enough:
    Mayonnaise
to make them a good consistency to
spread. Season the spread with:
    Salt if needed and paprika

Method II.
Combine:
    Equal parts of deviled ham and
        cream cheese
Season them with:
    Catsup

VEGETABLE SPREAD
Chop, then combine:
    1 cup celery
    1 cup drained cucumbers
    ¼ cup Bermuda onion
    ¼ cup green pepper
    6 stuffed olives
Add to make a spread:
    Cooked salad dressing or
    mayonnaise

CHICKEN OR HAM SALAD
SPREAD
Chop until fine:
    1 cup cooked chicken

Add:
    2 tablespoons finely chopped
        celery
    ¼ cup chopped blanched almonds
        or other nut meats
    (¼ cup chopped pineapple)
Combine these ingredients with sufficient:
    Highly-seasoned mayonnaise
to make a paste that will spread easily.

CHICKEN, HAM AND OLIVE
SPREAD
Combine:
    1 cup finely chopped cooked
        chicken
    1 cup finely chopped boiled ham
    ½ cup finely chopped green olives
    Well-seasoned mayonnaise

PECAN OLIVE SPREAD
Combine:
    4 chopped hard-cooked eggs
    1 cup chopped pecan meats
    2 dozen chopped stuffed olives
    Well-seasoned mayonnaise

RIPE OLIVE SANDWICH
SPREAD
Combine:
    ½ cup chopped ripe olives
    ½ chopped green pepper
    1 package cream cheese: 3 oz.
Season the spread with:
    Onion or garlic
    French dressing
Garnish open sandwiches with:
    Sliced ripe olives

STUFFED OLIVE SANDWICH
SPREAD
Combine:
    1 package cream cheese: 3 oz.
    A few drops of cream
    ¼ cup chopped stuffed olives
    ½ cup finely chopped celery
    ½ teaspoon salt
    ¼ teaspoon paprika
Garnish open sandwiches with:
    Sliced stuffed olives
Chopped nut meats and commercial
olive spread may be substituted for
the stuffed olives.

ALMOND SANDWICH SPREAD
Combine:
    1 package cream cheese: 3 oz.
    A few drops of cream
    ½ cup shredded salted almonds
    Paprika
Garnish open sandwiches with:
    Salted almonds

HAWAIIAN SANDWICH FILLING

Grind:
> Cooked ham

Combine it with equal parts of:
> Cream cheese
> Drained crushed pineapple

HARD-COOKED EGG AND HERB SPREAD

Combine and mix to a paste with a fork:
> 2 hard-cooked eggs
> 4 slices crumbled cooked bacon
> 1 tablespoon mayonnaise
> 1 tablespoon herb or wine vinegar
> 1 teaspoon dried or 1 tablespoon fresh herb

HARD-COOKED EGG AND SOUR CREAM SPREAD

Combine and mix to a paste with a fork:
> 2 hard-cooked eggs
> 1 tablespoon or more thick sour cream
> ¼ teaspoon salt
> ⅛ teaspoon paprika
> 1 tablespoon chopped chives
> (1 teaspoon lemon juice)

HARD-COOKED EGG AND ANCHOVY SPREAD

Shell, then chop:
> Hard-cooked eggs

Combine them with:
> Minced anchovies
> Minced celery

Moisten these ingredients with:
> Mayonnaise

AVOCADO SPREAD OR GUACAMOLE

This makes a pretty canapé or a fine dish in which to dip potato chips. Mexicans sometimes add chopped tomato to it, but I prefer it this way. Pare:
> 1 or 2 ripe avocados

Mash the pulp with a fork. Add:
> Onion juice and lemon juice
> Salt

Heap this on small crackers or toast. Garnish with:
> Paprika and parsley

A good holiday touch is a bit of pimiento or a slice of stuffed olive. Or, omit the juices and add chopped pickled onions, or minced sautéed bacon.

GOOSE OR CHICKEN LIVER PASTE OR PÂTÉ DE FOIE GRAS

Pâté de foie gras should of course be goose liver but you will find the more readily obtained chicken liver a fine substitute. Drop into boiling seasoned water and simmer until barely done:
> 1 lb. chicken livers

Drain them. Cook until hard, shell, chop and add:
> 2 eggs

Chop coarsely, then sauté:
> 2 medium-sized onions

in:
> 2 tablespoons butter

Chop or blend these ingredients until they are a fine paste. Season the paste with:
> Salt and pepper
> (1 teaspoon dried herbs or 1 tablespoon fresh herbs)

CHICKEN LIVER, GIZZARD AND HARD-COOKED EGG PASTE

Melt:
> 2 tablespoons butter

Sauté in it until tender:
> 6 chopped chicken livers

Simmer until tender, see Chicken Stock for Gravy, page 394:
> 4 chicken gizzards

Prepare by the rule on page 79:
> 2 hard-cooked eggs

Chop these ingredients until they are very fine. Add:
> 1 tablespoon cream
> A few grains curry powder
> Salt and pepper as needed

Mold the paste. Chill it.

Open Sandwiches

BAR LE DUC SANDWICHES

Spread:
> Rounds or squares of bread

with:
> Soft cream cheese

Place in the center of each sandwich a small mound of:
> Currant Preserves or Bar le Duc, page 805

PINEAPPLE OR ORANGE SANDWICHES
Spread:
> Rounds of white bread

with:
> Soft cream cheese

Cover them with:
> Thin rounds of pineapple or a slice of orange

Garnish with:
> Maraschino cherries

TOMATO OR CUCUMBER SANDWICHES
These sandwiches are very attractive for a spring tea party.
Cut:
> Small rounds of bread

Spread them lightly with:
> Butter

Place on each round, covering it completely:
> Small round of sliced tomato or a large round of pared sliced cucumber or both

Decorate each sandwich with a generous:
> Dab of mayonnaise

For daintiness but not for food value slice tomatoes, then drain them for 2 hours to keep the sandwiches from being soggy.

ITALIAN CANAPÉ OR SALAD
Place on a plate:
> Crisp lettuce or slices of buttered toast

Cover with:
> A thick slice skinned tomato
> A slice of salami

Heap on this to form a cone:
> Well-seasoned slaw

Cross the top of the cone with:
> 2 anchovies

Chill these ingredients, other than the toast of course, in advance.

The 3 following sandwiches are highly decorative.

CREAM CHEESE OR MAYONNAISE AND PIMIENTO SANDWICHES
Cut:
> Small rounds of white bread

Spread them with:
> Soft cream cheese

or spread them lightly with:
> Butter

Spread them heavily with:
> Thick mayonnaise

Cut into narrow 2 inch strips:
> A pimiento

Cross 2 pimiento strips on each sandwich and decorate the center with:
> A slice of stuffed olive

CREAM CHEESE AND PICKLE SANDWICHES
Cut:
> Small rounds of white bread

Spread them with:
> Soft cream cheese

Add to the cheese before spreading, if desired:
> A little anchovy paste

Place across each sandwich a very narrow:
> Strip of green pepper or a sprig of parsley

This represents a stem. Place at the top of the strip:
> Slice of stuffed olive

This represents a flower. Cut into lengthwise slices:
> Small sour-sweet pickles

Place the pickle slices opposite each other on the green pepper stem. These represent leaves.

SHRIMP AND MAYONNAISE SANDWICHES
Cut:
> Small rounds of white bread

Spread them lightly with:
> Butter

Spread them heavily with:
> Thick mayonnaise

Cut thin strips of:
> Green pepper

Place a strip on each sandwich. This represents a stem. Cut leaf shapes of:
> Green pepper

Put 1 or 2 along each stem. Top the stem with a:
> Shrimp

This represents a flower. If shrimp are not available make several stems of green pepper and place on one end of each a slice of pimiento olive.

MARINATED HERRING AND ONIONS ON TOAST
Drain:
> Marinated herring

Place them on:
> Squares or rounds of toast

Cover them with:
> Thin slices Bermuda onion

Sprinkle them with:
> Chopped parsley or water cress

Attractive Ways to Serve Canapés and Hors d'Oeuvres

Place hors d'oeuvres—shrimp and bacon, rolled chipped beef, codfish balls, mushrooms, olives, etc.—on toothpicks:

1. Cut a pineapple in half lengthwise. Place it flat side down and end to end on a long platter. Let the leaves protrude over either side. Place on each leaf a maraschino cherry. This has a very decorative effect. Stud the pineapple halves with hors d'oeuvres on toothpicks.

2. Cut the top from a small red cabbage. Hollow the cabbage. Fill it with mayonnaise or cheese sauce. Surround it with potato chips, cooked shrimp on toothpicks, Stuffed Pickled Beets and Stuffed Brussels Sprouts, page 38.
3. Cut a grapefruit in half, place it flat side down on a plate or platter. Stud the grapefruit with hors d'oeuvres on toothpicks. Place canapés around it.
4. Use a central dipping bowl for sauce. Surround it with dippable tidbits.

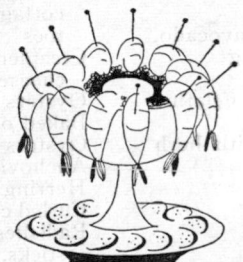

5. Cut a cantaloupe in half. Remove the seeds. Place it flat side down on a platter and stud it with hors d'oeuvres on toothpicks, or place it on a plate round side down and fill the center with cheese balls, olives, etc. You may also stud the sides with hors d'oeuvres on toothpicks and place canapés around it.
6. Cut a large colorful apple in half. Place it flat side down on a plate. Stud it with hors d'oeuvres on toothpicks. Surround it with canapés.

Hors d'Oeuvres

Canapés and hors d'oeuvres are appetizers—consequently any palatable tidbit is suitable for this preliminary step to a repast.

Serve what appeals to your imagination but remember that, unlike the overture to an opera, it is unwise to forecast in this course any of the joys that are to follow during the meal. For instance: Should you serve, either in the drawing room or at table, caviar in pickled beets or eggs and anchovies on tomatoes, forget the very existence of the beet and tomato when planning the vegetables for dinner. This is not a superfluous caution, for one encounters many unnecessarily repetitious meals.

If the hors d'oeuvres are served in the drawing room choose something that can be handled easily. Toothpicks—obnoxious word implying the original purpose, happily diverted, of this article of commerce—are a help, practically and decoratively.

Serve hot food as hot as possible; serve cold food well chilled.

There are recipes given in other chapters of this book that are suitable as hors d'oeuvres. It is difficult to place certain dishes under any one heading as they obligingly play a double or triple role.

An index isn't literature, but a careful perusal of it will sometimes produce a poem. The following foods are suggested as appropriate for hors d'oeuvres:

Aspic salad
Tongue in aspic
Fish salads
Small fresh fruit salads—avocado, grape, etc., with nut dressing
Small vegetable salads
Beets pickled or molded in gelatine salad
Flaked lobster, crab, etc., with herb sauce
Stuffed Brussels sprouts
Deviled eggs de luxe
Masked eggs
Soufflés

Timbales
Small or cherry tomatoes filled with cottage cheese or other filled tomatoes
Creamed oysters with crab meat and cheese
Oysters and sweetbreads on skewers
Baked oysters on toast
Oysters in spinach
Anchovies on marinated lettuce
Herring salad
Curled celery
Radishes, olives, green onions, carrot sticks, etc.

STUFFED PECANS OR WALNUTS

Work to a smooth paste:
  Roquefort cheese
Moisten it with:
  A few drops lemon juice or cream
Spread this mixture on:
  Large pecan halves
Press 2 halves together.

SALTED ALMONDS, ETC.

Place in a skillet:
  1 lb. blanched almonds
  2 tablespoons butter or salad oil
Cook the almonds over slow heat, or place them on a broiler under slow heat, leaving the oven door open, or place them in a moderate oven 350° for about ½ hour. Shake the skillet from time to time. Cook the almonds until they are a light brown. While hot, sprinkle them generously with:
  Salt
Drain them on brown paper. Change the paper after the first 3 minutes to remove the excessive grease.

COCKTAIL ALMONDS

Follow the above rule for:
  Salted almonds
While hot, substitute for the salt a generous sprinkling of:
  Celery salt, garlic salt or some concoction of similar salts, or cayenne pepper or paprika

SALTED BRAZIL NUTS

Shell, then place in a saucepan:
> Brazil nuts

Cover them with:
> Cold water

Bring to a boil, then simmer them for 4 minutes. Drain, dry, then cut them into the thinnest possible lengthwise slices. Place the slices in a shallow baking pan. Add for each pound of nuts:
> 2 tablespoons melted butter

Sprinkle the nuts with:
> Salt

Toast them in a moderate oven 350° for ½ hour, or until brown. Stir them occasionally.

Toasted without salt these slivers make a fine garnish for coffee cake.

TOASTED PUMPKIN OR SQUASH SEEDS

Separate the fiber from:
> Unwashed pumpkin or squash seeds

Add to 2 cupfuls of seeds:
> 1½ tablespoons melted butter or oil
> 1¼ teaspoons salt

Spread them in a shallow pan. Bake them in a very slow oven 250° until crisp and brown. Stir them from time to time.

CELERY CURLS

Separate, then wash:
> A stalk of celery

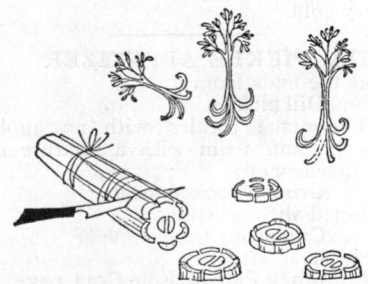

Trim leaves, cut several long gashes into each rib. Soak in ice water until curled.

CELERY RINGS

Separate:
> A stalk of celery

Wash and dry each rib carefully. Cut the heart in half. Cut the ribs into 6 inch lengths. Make your favorite cream cheese spread or use one of the many suggestions in this chapter, or use equal parts of cream cheese and butter, about 3 ounces of each. Season it with salt and pepper. You may add 2 tablespoonfuls of tomato paste or catsup. Stuff the ribs with the paste. Begin with the heart, sticking the halves together, and re-form the ribs around it in much their original shape. Wrap in waxed paper. Chill. Slice thinly as shown in first column.

FILLED CELERY

Combine:
> 1 tablespoon butter
> 1 tablespoon Roquefort cheese
> 1 package soft cream cheese:
> 3 oz.
> Salt
> (1 teaspoon caraway, dill or celery seed)

Place this mixture in:
> Dwarf celery ribs

Sprinkle them with:
> Paprika

Or, fill celery with:
> Avocado Spread, page 25

Chill the celery. Celery ribs may be filled with crab or other fish combined with cream cheese and mayonnaise.

GARLIC OLIVES

Drain the liquid from:
> Green or ripe olives

Add:
> 12 peeled cloves garlic

Cover the olives and garlic with:
> Salad oil

Permit them to stand for 24 hours or more under refrigeration. Drain them. Use the oil for salad dressing. You may dust the olives with:
> Chopped parsley

TIDBITS IN BLANKETS

Surround:
> Cooked shrimp
> Oysters
> Stuffed olives
> Pickled onions
> Watermelon pickle
> Sautéed chicken livers
> Skinned grapefruit sections
> Dates stuffed with pineapple, etc.

with:
> Thin strips of bacon

Secure them with toothpicks. Broil them under moderate heat until the bacon is crisp.

SARDINE AND BACON ROLLS

Drain and mash:
  Sardines
Season them with:
  Mayonnaise
  Mustard
  Onion juice
Spread this mixture on:
  Slices of bacon
Roll the bacon and secure it with toothpicks. Broil the rolls.

PEANUT BUTTER AND BACON ROLLS

Broil until crisp:
  12 slices bacon
Combine:
  6 tablespoons peanut butter
  ½ teaspoon Worcestershire sauce
  Chili sauce to make a stiff paste
Spread the bacon with the paste. Roll it while it is hot. Secure it with toothpicks and serve it at once.

ANTIPASTO

Italian hors d'oeuvres arranged attractively on a platter or on individual plates.
Suggestions:
  Tomato slices cut lengthwise
  Marinated artichoke hearts or centers
  Anchovies
  Smoked Salmon Rolls, page 30
  Marinated Mushrooms, page 460
  Curled celery
  Pickled Beets and Caviar, page 37
  Sardines
  Slices of salami
  Hard-cooked eggs
  Masked Eggs, page 37
  Garlic Olives, page 29
  Cucumber and Green Pepper Sticks, page 35

GLAZED SHRIMP

6 to 8 Servings
Clean and remove the dark vein (page 245) from:
  1½ lbs. boiled shrimp
Soak:
  2 teaspoons gelatine
in:

2 tablespoons cold water
Dissolve it over hot water. Cool it. Add to it:
  ½ cup sharp French dressing
Be careful of salt. Catsup is a good addition to the dressing. Chill the mixture until it begins to set. Spear the shrimp on toothpicks. Dip them into the dressing. When partly set, dip them again. Chill well. Serve cold.

SMOKED SALMON ROLLS

Cut into very thin slices:
  Smoked salmon
Spread them with:
  Cream cheese seasoned with horseradish, chopped chives or parsley
Roll the strips. Secure them with toothpicks. See Smoked Salmon Canapés, page 20.

HERRING, ANCHOVY OR SMOKED SALMON PICKLES

Cut into ½ inch strips:
  Pickled herring or smoked salmon, or use anchovies
Roll the strips around tiny:
  Sour-sweet or other gherkins
Secure the rolls with toothpicks. Serve them as hors d'oeuvres.
A very good first-course dish is an individual plate of shredded lettuce and the pickled onions that usually come with herring moistened with some of the liquor from the jar. Top the salad with 3 herring rolls, or use sliced onions and herring in sour cream. Serve very cold.

DILL PICKLE APPETIZER

Cut the ends from:
  Dill pickles
Hollow the pickles with an apple corer. Stuff them with a mixture of well-seasoned:
  Ground cooked meat
thinned with a little:
  Cream
or with:
  Mock Paté de Foie Gras, page 23
Chill the pickles. Cut them in crosswise slices ⅓ inch thick.

GHERKINS STUFFED WITH NUT MEATS

Split halfway down:
  Pickled gherkins
Insert in the opening:
  Salted nut meats

TIDBITS ON TOOTHPICKS

Alternate on toothpicks:

Small onions with pieces of cocktail sausages or bur gherkins with sausages

Squares of cheese with pickle slices, stuffed olives or small onions

Slices of raw carrot and blocks of tongue or ham

Shrimp lightly flavored with mustard and pieces of celery

Squares of cheese and slices of green onion topped with a ripe olive

Balls of cream cheese sprinkled with paprika or chopped olives, chilled, and pieces of herring or anchovy

Pieces of ham or bacon and watermelon pickle

Pieces of kippered salmon or herring and onions

In short, use your imagination and your left-overs.

ARTICHOKE LEAVES AND SHRIMP

Cook:

Artichokes, page 264

Chill them. Separate the larger leaves. Place on each leaf:

A cooked shrimp

Top it with:

A dab of tart mayonnaise

ARTICHOKES STUFFED WITH SHRIMP OR CRAB MEAT

Cook:

Artichokes, page 264

Chill and cut them in two. Remove the inedible choke (page 264). Marinate:

Shrimp or crab meat

with:

French dressing or lemon juice

Fill the artichokes with the shrimp and serve them with:

Mayonnaise

MARINATED MUSHROOMS

Sauté by the rule on page 292:

Small mushrooms

When they are lightly browned cover them with well-seasoned:

French dressing

Add to the dressing:

(1 sliced clove garlic)

Soak the mushrooms for 12 hours or more.

CHEESE BALLS

Work to a paste:

½ cup Roquefort cheese or part Roquefort and part cream cheese

1 tablespoon butter

½ teaspoon Worcestershire sauce

½ teaspoon paprika

A few grains cayenne

Shape the paste into 1 inch balls. Roll them in:

¼ cup ground nut meats

Chill them.

MARINATED ONIONS

Skin, then slice:

Bermuda onions

Soak them for 30 minutes in:

Brine—⅔ cup water to 1 tablespoon salt

Drain them. Soak them for 30 minutes in:

Vinegar

Drain, then chill them. They are then ready to be served side by side with celery, radishes, olives, etc.

MARINATED CELERIAC

Cook by the rule on page 464:

Celery root or celeriac

When cold cut it into oblongs. Marinate them for several hours in:

Well-seasoned French dressing

SALAMI CORNUCOPIAS

Remove the skin from:

Slices of salami or other sausage

Roll the slices into cornucopias, secure them with toothpicks. Place in each center:

A sour-sweet gherkin, a stuffed olive or a small ball of cream cheese mixed with chopped chives

MARINATED OYSTERS IN PASTRY

Drain well:

24 to 30 small oysters

Permit them to marinate for 3 hours in:

½ cup well-seasoned French dressing

to which you may add:

½ clove garlic

Drain them well. Dry them on absorbent paper. Roll until very thin:

Pie dough

Cut it into 2½ inch rounds. Place an

oyster on each round. Fold the dough over the oyster and press the edges together with a fork. Cut a vent in each patty. Bake them in a hot oven 450° for about 15 minutes. Serve them hot.

LINK SAUSAGES, OLIVES OR SHRIMP IN PASTRY
Very popular items.
Follow the above rule. Substitute for the oysters:
> Marinated shrimp or link sausages or sausage meat seasoned with mustard or stuffed olives

SAUSAGE AND POTATO BALLS
Roll into 1 inch balls:
> Sausage meat

You may season this with:
> (Savory, parsley, etc.)

Coat the balls with:
> Mashed potatoes

Roll them in:
> 1 egg diluted with 1 tablespoon water

then in:
> Sifted seasoned bread crumbs

Roll them again in the egg and in crumbs. Let them dry for about 1 hour. Fry them until brown in deep fat (page 541). Serve them on toothpicks.

TINY BROILED SAUSAGES
Broil:
> Very small sausages

Serve them hot on toothpicks with:
> Mustard Cream, page 440

CODFISH BALLS ON TOOTHPICKS
Fry very small:
> Codfish Balls, page 129

Serve them hot on toothpicks with:
> Tartar Sauce, page 439

HAM AND EGG BALLS
Prepare:
> 3 hard-cooked eggs

Shell them. Separate the yolks from the whites. Mash the yolks with a fork. When they are smooth add:
> ½ teaspoon chopped chives
> Mayonnaise to make a smooth paste

Season the paste with:
> Salt and paprika

Put through a grinder the whites of the eggs and:
> ¼ lb. lean cooked ham

Combine the 2 mixtures. Add to form a paste:
> Mayonnaise

Shape it into 1 inch balls.
Roll them in:
> Crushed cornflakes

Serve them on toothpicks.

HAM AND CHEESE APPETIZERS
Cut into blocks:
> Sliced boiled ham
> Sliced Swiss or American cheese

Alternate the blocks on toothpicks.

BOLOGNA TRIANGLES
Blend:
> 1 package cream cheese: 3 oz.
> 2 tablespoons cream
> 1 tablespoon fresh grated horse-radish

Spread with the mixture:
> ½ lb. thinly sliced bologna

Stack 6 slices. Wrap them in waxed paper. Chill. Cut into 6 or more pie-shaped wedges.

TONGUE AND CREAM CHEESE APPETIZERS
These are decorative and unusually good.
Cut:
> Smoked boiled tongue into ⅓ inch slices

Work until smooth:
> Cream cheese softened with cream

A sandwich is made of 3 slices of tongue and 2 layers of cream cheese ⅓ inch thick. The edges of the sandwich are neatly trimmed and it is cut into 4 or 5 slices. The block effect is very pleasing.

TONGUE, CHIPPED BEEF OR BOLOGNA ROLLS
Work until smooth:
> Soft cream cheese
> A few drops of cream

Season the cheese with:
> Worcestershire sauce
> Grated onion or garlic
> Paprika or freshly ground pepper

Spread this mixture on very thin slices of:
> Smoked boiled tongue or chipped beef

Roll the canapés. Smooth, thick cottage cheese may be substituted for the cream cheese, or the meat may be spread with Sour Cream and Horseradish Sauce, page 439.

BRAUNSCHWEIGER PIE
Skin, then mash:
    1½ lbs. braunschweiger sausage
Beat in:
    ½ cup catsup
    1 teaspoon Worcestershire
        sauce
Press these ingredients into a small pie pan. Chill, then unmold them. Cover the top and sides with a thin coating of:
    Cream cheese
This may be thinned with:
    Cream
Chill the pie. Serve it in cut wedges.

BACON-WRAPPED PRUNES STUFFED WITH NUT MEATS
Place in a colander and wash:
    Prunes
Drop them into:
    Boiling water
Boil them for 2 minutes. Drain them. Remove the pits. Place the prunes in a small jar. Pour over them to cover:
    White wine, red wine or sherry
Close the jar tightly. Soak the prunes for about 48 hours. Drain them and reserve the liquor for sauces, gravies, etc. Place in each cavity:
    A walnut or other nut meat
Surround each prune with:
    A narrow strip of bacon
Secure it with a toothpick. Broil the prunes under a moderate flame or bake them on a cake rack placed over a pan in a moderate oven 375° until the bacon is done. Turn them. Serve them very hot.

PINEAPPLE FINGERS AND BACON
Wrap:
    Pineapple fingers or wedges
with:
    Narrow slices of bacon
Secure them with toothpicks. Broil them or bake them, placed on a rack over a pan in a moderate oven 375° until the bacon is done. Turn them while cooking. Serve them hot.

MEAT BALLS AS APPETIZERS
Cook by any rule in the meat chapter:
    Tiny meat balls, hamburgers
    or nutburgers

Season them well. Serve them very hot on toothpicks or between small biscuits.

BROILED STUFFED MUSHROOMS
4 Small Servings
Prepare for cooking (page 291):
    12 large mushroom caps
Chop the stems. Simmer them for 2 minutes in:
    1 tablespoon butter
Add to them:
    1½ cups dry bread crumbs
    ¼ cup chopped blanched almonds
        or other nut meats
    1½ tablespoons chopped chives or
        other herb
Bind these ingredients with:
    2 tablespoons cream, stock or
        part stock and part sherry
Season with:
    Salt and paprika
Brush the caps with:
    Butter
Place them cap side down on a greased broiler rack. Broil the mushrooms for 2½ minutes under a moderate flame. Reverse them. Place dressing in each cap. Dot the tops with:
    Butter
Broil them 2½ minutes longer.
Serve them sizzling hot.

MUSHROOMS STUFFED WITH SHAD ROE
4 Servings
Prepare:
    12 large mushroom caps
Place them cap side up in a greased oven-proof plate. Stuff each cap with:
    Shad roe
topped with:
    A dab of butter
    A little grated onion
Combine and pour in the bottom of the plate:
    ⅔ cup cream
    2 tablespoons sherry
Bake the mushrooms in a moderately hot oven 400° for about 15 minutes. Serve very hot from the plate.

MUSHROOMS STUFFED WITH SHRIMP
4 Servings
Remove the stems from:
    8 large mushrooms
Wipe caps and stems with a cloth. Chop the stems. Shell, then chop:
    ½ lb. cooked shrimp

Canned shrimp will call for 2 minutes' soaking in cold water before being cut up.

Prepare the sauce. Melt:

3 tablespoons olive oil or butter

Stir in:

4 tablespoons flour

Stir in:

2 cups shrimp, chicken or clam stock

Add the mushroom stems. Lower the heat. Stir and simmer the sauce for 2 minutes. Add the shrimp and:

2 teaspoons chopped chives, parsley or other herb

Stir gently until well blended. Taste and add, if needed:

Salt and pepper

⅛ teaspoon curry powder or 1 tablespoon sherry

Place the filling uncovered over hot water. Brush the caps with:

Butter

Place them cap side down on a greased broiler rack. Broil them gently for 2½ minutes. Turn them cap side up. Add to each cap:

½ teaspoon butter

Broil them 2½ minutes longer.

While the caps are cooking prepare:

8 rounds of buttered toast

Fill the caps, rounding the tops well. Place them on the toast. Place the remaining sauce in the center of a platter. Surround it with the caps on toast. Garnish the dish with:

Parsley

If you want to make this a main dish, add curls of:

Broiled bacon

BRAISED CELERY AND SHRIMP

Allow to each portion:

1 stalk dwarf celery

Wash the stalks. Drop them in a small quantity of:

Boiling highly seasoned Stock, pages 43, 44

Boil them until they are tender. Drain them. Chill them. Serve them on:

Shredded, lightly marinated lettuce

Surround each stalk with:

6 or 8 cooked chilled shrimp

Top the stalks with a tablespoonful of:

Mayonnaise

MUSHROOMS STUFFED WITH ONIONS

4 Servings

Clean, then stem:

12 large mushrooms

Dip the caps in:

Oil or melted butter

Mince the stems. Add:

1½ tablespoons minced onion

Stir and sauté these for 3 minutes in:

3 tablespoons butter

Add:

¾ cup cooked puréed spinach

A fresh grating of nutmeg

Salt

Fill the caps. Sprinkle them with:

Grated cheese

Bake them in a moderate oven 375° for about 15 minutes. Serve them on:

Rounds of toast

ANCHOVY MUSHROOMS

4 to 6 Servings

Prepare for cooking:

1 lb. mushrooms

Marinate them for 2 hours in:

3 tablespoons olive oil

⅓ teaspoon salt

¼ teaspoon paprika

Drain the mushrooms. Melt in a skillet:

3 tablespoons butter

Sauté the mushrooms in this for 5 minutes. Stir them frequently. Remove them from the pan. Add to the juice in the pan:

2 teaspoons grated onion

2 tablespoons chopped parsley

1 teaspoon anchovy paste

3 tablespoons thick cream

Cook these ingredients gently for about 3 minutes. Add:

⅓ cup or more creamed spinach

Pour the sauce over the mushrooms. They are good served on:

Toast with scrambled eggs, omelet or sliced cooked ham

HOT MUSHROOMS AND CLAMS OR OYSTERS

Prepare for cooking by the rule on page 291:

Large mushroom caps

Dip them in:

Melted butter

Place on each one:

A clam or oyster

Cover each clam with:

1 teaspoon horseradish

1 teaspoon or more mayonnaise

A drop or 2 Tabasco or Worcestershire sauce

Place the mushrooms in a pan. Broil them under moderate heat until the tops begin to color. Serve them hot.

SHRIMP PUFFS
24 Puffs
Clean, then cut in half:
    12 shrimp
Whip until stiff:
    1 egg white
Fold in:
    ¼ cup grated cheese
    ⅛ teaspoon salt
    ⅛ teaspoon paprika
    A few grains red pepper
    ½ cup mayonnaise dressing
Heap these ingredients lightly onto crackers or rounds of toast. Garnish each one with ½ shrimp. Broil the puffs under moderate heat until light brown. Serve hot.

HERRING IN SOUR CREAM
Drain a jar of:
    Herring in wine
Cut the pieces into squares. Marinate them in:
    Thick sour cream
    Chopped chives or parsley
    A few drops lemon juice
These may be served on:
    Melba or rye toast
or they may be placed in a bowl and served with toast or hard crackers.

HERRING OR SARDINE HORS D'OEUVRES
Individual Serving
Place on a plate:
    Lettuce leaves
Build up into a cone:
    Finely shredded onion
    Finely shredded cole slaw
    topped with pieces of herring or sardine
Pour over the cone:
    Thick sour cream
Have all ingredients very cold.

RAW VEGETABLE PLATTER WITH DRESSING
Place in the center of a platter a bowl of:
    Herb Mayonnaise, page 495, or
    Sour Cream and Horseradish, page 439, or chives
Surround it with:
    Lettuce
    Cauliflower flowerets
    Carrot, Cucumber and Green Pepper Sticks on this page
    Radishes
    Celery
    Peeled broccoli stems, etc.
Encourage your guests to do their own dipping.

CUCUMBER AND GREEN PEPPER STICKS
Cut into strips:
    Seeded cucumbers and green peppers
Place them in ice water in the refrigerator for ½ hour. Drain them well.
Cut a slice from:
    A clove of garlic
Rub the cut side over a piece of waxed paper. Roll the sticks in the paper, wrap the roll in a cloth and place it in the refrigerator to chill the sticks.
You may serve them with:
    Sour Cream Dressing, page 496

TOMATO SLICES FILLED WITH AVOCADO
Peel, then mash:
    Avocado
Season it with:
    Grated onion and lemon juice
    Salt and paprika
Spread the mixture between thin slices of:
    Tomato
Decorate the slices with a dab of:
    Mayonnaise
Serve them on:
    Lettuce

CELERY ROOT AND TOMATOES WITH FISH SALAD
Cook by the rule on page 464:
    Celery root
Cut it into ¼ inch slices. Marinate them for ½ hour or more in:
    French dressing
Cut into ¼ inch slices:
    Tomatoes
Alternate the celery, the tomatoes and:
    Crab, Shrimp or Tuna Fish Salad, page 468
Serve the stacks on:
    Lettuce

Celery Root Cocktail, page 6.

TOMATOES AND COTTAGE CHEESE
Use small firm tomatoes. Prepare:
    Tomato Cases, page 458
Fill them with:
    Seasoned cottage cheese
Combine the cheese, if desired, with:
    Blanched shredded almonds or pecan meats
    Chopped celery, parsley or chives

Garnish the tomatoes with:
  Ripe or stuffed olives or chopped chives
  A sprig of parsley
Serve the tomatoes with:
  Mayonnaise

TOMATOES FILLED WITH CRAB MEAT OR FISH SALAD

Use small firm tomatoes. Prepare:
  Tomato Cases, page 458
Fill them with:
  Crab meat salad
Or see rule on page 468 for Fish Salad. Substitute crab meat for fish. Garnish the tops with:
  Sprigs of parsley

Tomato and Cheese Canapés, page 13; Green Pepper Slices, page 466; Cucumber Slices, page 459; Rolled Lettuce Leaves and Cottage Cheese, page 466.

CHICKEN SALAD OR FISH SALAD IN ASPIC

Prepare:
  Aspic Jelly, page 475, or Quick Tomato Aspic, page 477
When it is nearly set pour individual molds ⅓ full. Place in each mold:
  A small ball of rather dry Chicken Salad or Fish Salad, page 468
Fill the molds with aspic jelly. Chill the aspic. When firm unmold it on:
  Lettuce leaves
Serve it with:
  Mayonnaise

GRILLED TOMATOES AND MAYONNAISE

Combine until a thick paste is formed:
  Dry bread crumbs
  Mayonnaise
Season it with:
  Worcestershire sauce
  Salt
  A few grains cayenne
Spread it thickly on:
  Tomatoes cut in halves
Place the tomatoes in a buttered pan and broil them for 10 minutes in a quick oven 425°.

TOMATO, EGG AND CAVIAR

Prepare:
  Rounds of toast
Cover them with thick slices of:
  Skinned tomatoes

Prepare:
  Hard-cooked eggs
Shell them, cut them in two, remove the yolks and put them through a ricer. Combine them with:
  Caviar, onion juice, lemon juice and seasonings
Fill the egg whites with this mixture. Place them on the tomato. Garnish the canapés with the riced egg yolks.

TOMATO ASPIC WITH CHEESE CENTERS

8 Servings
Prepare:
  Tomato Aspic, page 476
When it is about to set pour individual molds ⅓ full. Combine and roll into balls:
  1 package soft cream cheese: 3 oz.
  1 tablespoon anchovy paste
  2 drops Worcestershire sauce
Drop a ball into each mold and cover it with aspic. Chill the aspic until it is firm. Unmold it on lettuce leaves. Serve it with:
  Mayonnaise

TOMATOES, ANCHOVIES AND CHEESE

5 Servings
Skin:
  3 large flat tomatoes
Cut them crosswise into slices 1 inch or more thick. There should be 5 slices. Place on the slices:
  10 anchovies
Crush with a fork:
  3 oz. Roquefort cheese
Combine it with:
  6 tablespoons Tartar Sauce, page 439
Cover the tomato slices with a thick layer of this mixture. Serve them on:
  Water cress or lettuce leaves

POACHED EGGS IN ASPIC

Cook in rings by the rule on page 80:
  6 poached eggs
Let them cool in the rings. Pour over them as it is about to set:
  Aspic Jelly, page 475
The amount depends upon the size of your rings—about 1¼ cupfuls. Chill until firm. Unmold the eggs on:
  Rounds of ham
Serve them on:
  Shredded lettuce or water cress
with:
  Mayonnaise

HARD-COOKED EGGS ON TOMATOES WITH SAUCE
4 Servings
Prepare:
    4 hard-cooked eggs
Skin, then cut in halves crosswise:
    4 large tomatoes
Cover each half with:
    A very thin slice cheese
    1 egg cut crosswise
Place crosswise on each egg:
    2 anchovies
Cover them with a sauce made with:
    3 tablespoons olive oil
    ½ minced clove garlic
    ½ cup tomato catsup
    ⅛ teaspoon curry powder
    1 tablespoon chopped parsley

See Index for other Egg Dishes suitable as hors d'oeuvres.

DEVILED EGGS DE LUXE
Prepare:
    Hard-cooked eggs
Shell the eggs, cut them in halves, remove the yolks, crush them with a fork and combine them with:
    Grated onion or chives
    Caviar
    Lemon juice and cream
Fill the egg whites with the paste and garnish the eggs with:
    Capers or sliced olives

DEVILED EGGS IN ASPIC
Prepare:
    Tomato Aspic, page 477, or some other well-seasoned aspic
Prepare:
    Deviled Eggs, page 89
Place ½ an egg, sunny side up, in:
    ½ cup aspic that is about to set
Chill the aspic and when it is firm invert it on:
    Lettuce leaves
Serve it with:
    Mayonnaise

EGGS STUFFED WITH SHRIMP OR CRAB MEAT
Marinate for 30 minutes:
    Shrimp or crab meat
in:
    French dressing or lemon juice
Shell and cut in half:
    Hard-cooked eggs
Remove the yolks and put them through a ricer. Moisten the shrimp with:
    Mayonnaise
    A dash Worcestershire sauce

Fill the egg whites with the shrimp and garnish them with the riced egg yolks.

MAYONNAISE EGGS
8 Servings
Cook and mince:
    4 slices bacon
Shell and rice:
    6 hard-cooked eggs
Combine the eggs and bacon and add:
    4 tablespoons mayonnaise
    ½ teaspoon grated onion
    1 teaspoon prepared mustard
    1 tablespoon chopped parsley
    2 tablespoons chopped green peppers
    1 teaspoon salt
    ½ teaspoon white pepper
Form this mixture into balls or egg shapes and roll them first in:
    Mayonnaise
then in:
    Grated cheese
Chill them and serve on:
    Shredded lettuce

MASKED EGGS
Allow 1 Egg or ½ Egg to a Person
Chill and shell:
    Hard-Cooked Eggs, page 79
Cut them into halves lengthwise. Place them cut side down on:
    Water cress or shredded lettuce
Pour over them:
    Mayonnaise thinned with a little lemon juice or cream
Sprinkle them with:
    Capers, chopped anchovies, bits of ham or cooked bacon
The eggs may be surrounded with the following beets.

PICKLED BEETS AND CAVIAR
Prepare by the rule for Pickled Beets, page 461, leaving them whole:
    Small shapely beets or canned beets
Hollow them slightly. Fill the hollows with:
    Caviar
sprinkled with a very little:
    Lemon juice
Garnish them with:
    A sprig of parsley

PICKLED BEETS STUFFED WITH EGGS AND HERBS
Prepare, leaving them whole:
    Pickled Beets, page 461
Hollow them if small. If large, cut

them in thick slices. Combine:

Chopped hard-cooked eggs
Mayonnaise
Herbs, preferably chives and
tarragon

Fill the beets or top the slices with the dressing.

STUFFED BRUSSELS SPROUTS
Drain well:

Cooked or canned Brussels
sprouts

Cut a small hollow in each one, preferably from the top. Drop into each hollow:

½ teaspoon French dressing

Chill them. Fill them with any good:

Sandwich spread

Liver sausage and tomato soup, cream cheese and chives or anchovy or nut meats, etc., may be used.

You may add the chopped center portion of the sprouts. Garnish with:

A sprig of parsley, savory,
basil, etc.

Serve several as a salad or serve them as hors d'oeuvres.

CHILLED SPINACH DISH
4 Servings
Chop, then chill thoroughly:

1 lb. cooked spinach

Combine and work to a smooth paste:

Juice of 2 lemons
¼ lb. Roquefort cheese

Add and beat to the consistency of whipped cream:

¼ cup sour cream

Add this mixture to the spinach. Serve it very cold.

CABBAGE AND SHRIMP DISH
A decorative platter for a buffet or first course.
Shred:

White cabbage

Dress it with equal parts of:

Mayonnaise
Chili sauce

Arrange it in a mound. Cover the top with:

Marinated shrimp

Surround the mound with:

Deviled eggs topped with caviar
Large sardines

ANCHOVY CHEESE OR
KLEINER LIPTAUER
Work until smooth:

2 packages cream cheese: 6 oz.

Work in:

3 tablespoons soft butter
2 minced anchovies
1½ tablespoons grated onion or 1
minced shallot
1½ teaspoons capers
½ teaspoon caraway seed
¾ teaspoon paprika
2 drops Worcestershire sauce
Salt as needed

Shape the mixture into small patties. Chill them thoroughly.

VICKSBURG CHEESE
Blend with a fork until smooth:

⅓ Roquefort cheese
⅓ Cheddar cheese
⅓ soft cream cheese

Sprinkle a large piece of waxed paper thickly with:

Paprika

Roll the cheese mixture into sausage shape on the paper until it has a generous coating of paprika. Place in refrigerator to chill. Cut in slices to serve.

FILLED EDAM CHEESE
Fine for a buffet meal. Hollow:

An Edam or Gouda cheese

Crumble the removed part. Combine it with:

2 teaspoons or more Worcester-
shire sauce
1 tablespoon prepared mustard
A few grains cayenne
1 or 2 tablespoons fresh or dried
minced herbs

Refill the cheese shell. Serve it surrounded by toasted crackers.

FRIED OYSTERS OR SCALLOPS
AND DUNKING SAUCE
Prepare by the rule on page 251:

Fried Oysters

Have ready a bowlful of:

Sour cream
Tomato Cream Sauce or other
dipping sauce, page 39

Place it on a platter. Surround it with the hot oysters placed on toothpicks. Let the guests dip them in the sauce.

NEW ORLEANS SHRIMP
4 to 6 Servings
Cook by the rule on page 245:

2 lbs. fresh shrimp

Permit them to cool in the water in which they were cooked. Shell and clean them. Serve them well chilled on lettuce. Prepare the following:

New Orleans Shrimp Sauce

Rub a bowl with:

Garlic

Add:

½ cup finely chopped celery
1 stalk finely chopped green onion
1 tablespoon chopped chives
6 tablespoons olive oil
3 tablespoons lemon juice
¼ teaspoon red pepper sauce
5 tablespoons horseradish
2 tablespoons prepared mustard
¼ teaspoon paprika
¾ teaspoon salt
½ teaspoon white pepper

You may marinate the shrimp in this sauce for 12 hours, or the time may be much shorter. A clove of garlic may be added for 2 hours to the shrimp while marinating.

Reserve the water in which the shrimp were cooked. It makes excellent soup. Heat it and add a little cream or use it as a basis for Cream Soup, page 56.

Louisiana Evangeline sauce is recommended for the red pepper sauce, but Tabasco, catsup or chili sauce may be substituted. The donor of this recipe suggests a combination of the 3. A good combination is ¼ teaspoonful Tabasco sauce and 2 tablespoonfuls each of chili sauce and catsup.

SOUR CREAM AND HORSE-RADISH FOR DIPPING SHRIMP, ETC.

Combine:

1 cup sour cream
1 or more tablespoons horse-radish
½ teaspoon salt
¼ teaspoon paprika

SOUR CREAM AND HERBS FOR DIPPING SHRIMP, ETC.

Combine:

2 cups thick sour cream
2 tablespoons chopped parsley
2 tablespoons chopped chives
1 teaspoon dried herbs

⅛ teaspoon curry powder
½ teaspoon salt
¼ teaspoon paprika

TOMATO CREAM SAUCE FOR SHRIMP

Clean:

Cooked or canned shrimp

Whip until stiff:

1 cup heavy cream

Fold into it:

½ cup condensed tomato soup
½ teaspoon salt
¼ teaspoon paprika
⅛ teaspoon ground cloves
½ teaspoon grated onion
¼ teaspoon dried basil, page 833

Place the cream in a bowl surrounded by shrimp, or use it over shrimp in cocktail glasses.

Horseradish Cream Sauce and other combinations with mayonnaise, page 497; Cocktail Sauce for Sea Food, page 7; Herb Sauce for Oysters, Pink Sauce for Shrimp, page 8.

CHEESE FOR DIPPING POTATO CHIPS

Beat until smooth:

2 packages cream cheese: 6 oz.
1½ tablespoons mayonnaise
1 tablespoon cream
¼ teaspoon salt
1 teaspoon grated onion, minced garlic or chives
1 teaspoon Worcestershire sauce

Fill a large hollowed apple with this mixture. Surround it with:

Toasted potato chips

Cheese Spread or Sauce, page 191, Cream Cheese and Roquefort Spread, page 22, thinned with cream, Boiled Sour Cream Dressing, page 498, are all fine for cocktail parties. Place a small bowlful in the center of a platter, surround it with shrimp, potato chips or crackers and let your guests do their own spreading or dunking.

Soups

Soup was once a matter of long cooking, and in the days when soup bones were lagniappe pounds of meat and bone were used to concoct a strong wonderful essence for daily family consumption. That method is now among the luxuries. As you will see later on in this chapter good soup can be economical when concocted from scraps that would otherwise be discarded, and long cooking has been replaced by pressure cookery and the use of the blender, which streamlines the job most acceptably and brings it into the range of even the most casual cook.

Soups are given many enticing names, but they fall into one or the other of the following general classifications:

White Stock, made with white meats and light-colored vegetables.

Brown Stock, made with dark meats and vegetables.

Bouillon, made with beef, part of which is browned in marrow, and vegetables.

Consommé, made with beef, veal, chicken and vegetables.

Broth or Extracts like clam, mushroom, chicken, etc. Vegetable or meat stock may be added to the latter. These soups are served clear.

Vegetable Soup, made with meat stock or fish stock, the water in which fish has been cooked or stock made with fish bones, heads and trimmings, and vegetable stock, the water in which vegetables have been cooked. To these, vegetables, diced or puréed, and cereals are added.

Cream Soup like purée or bisque, made with cooked strained vegetables, or cooked strained fish or chicken, to which a thin sauce usually made with butter, flour or eggs, and milk, cream or stock is added. A food mill is good for this purpose, but an electric blender is ideal.

Cereal Soup, made with stock or cream soup and cereal.

Chowders, thick soups made with fish, meat, salt pork, vegetables, milk and crackers.

The French Government once conferred a decoration upon the cook who prepares Campbell's soup. It is regrettable that this distinction could not be made to include all the soup manufacturers who have brought to us this good and often nutritious product.

It is advisable to keep several cans of soup on the emergency shelf. They may be used in many good combinations, see page 66. A can of bouillon and clear chicken soup should be kept for quick aspics and for use in place of stock. Beef, chicken and vegetable cubes are in general use for stock and gravies. Be sure to have them on hand. No substitute, however, can compare with good homemade soup.

Good soup stock may be kept on hand by utilizing scraps. Keep bits of bone, cooked meat, chicken carcasses and feet, fish and meat trimmings, vegetable parings, the outer leaves of lettuce, unshapely tomatoes, celery tops, pea pods, snapbean ends, the lower ends of asparagus, parsley, etc., for the soup pot. Keep the liquid from cooked and canned vegetables for the same purpose. If your scraps are insufficient add a soup bone or an oxtail and a soup bunch.

The proportions of this type, appropriately named "Icebox soup," vary greatly. See Soup Stock II, page 44, and Scrap Soup, page 44.

When using fresh meat the meat from aged animals is best. You may salt it for one hour before cooking it in soup and you may then soak the meat for a ½ hour in the water in which it is to be cooked. Soaking or salting the meat draws the juices from it. You may omit this step and merely add salt to the cooking water.

The meat may be cut into 1 inch cubes. Salt and soak two thirds of it as directed. Sauté the remaining one third in hot marrow or other fat until it is dark brown before adding it to the soup pot. This will give both flavor and color to the soup. Have the bones for soup cut up, or saw them up or crush them yourself as much as possible. They may be browned like the meat.

If you wish to extract extra calcium from the bones add 2 tablespoonfuls of vinegar to 1 quart of water.

If a strong meat broth is desired, allow 2 cupfuls of water to every pound of meat, fat and bone. When so much meat is used only a few vegetables are needed to give flavor to the stock.

Use lamb and mutton sparingly except for Scotch lamb and barley soup. They are frequently strong in flavor. Pork is too sweet to make good soup.

Use but little seasoning until the soup is to be served, as it is difficult to gauge the amount needed.

Vegetables with few exceptions should be added for the last ½ hour of cooking only, because they are apt to absorb the delicate flavor of the meat. They too add more flavor and calories to the soup if they are gently sautéed until partly tender in a small quantity of fat before being put in the soup kettle. For superb vegetable soup quickly made see Electric Blender, page 895.

Soup Made from Fresh Meat requires at least 4 hours' simmering, covered, in which time the original amount will be reduced by one fifth to one fourth.

Soup Made from Cooked Meat and left-overs requires less cooking than soup made from fresh ingredients. One to 2 hours' simmering in a covered kettle is sufficient to extract the juices from cooked food, in which time the liquid will be reduced by about one sixth of the original amount.

How to Cook and Store Soups. Simmer soups in a closely covered kettle. Cool soups rapidly, uncovered. Store all soup or stock in a tightly covered jar in the refrigerator. Soup and stock will keep for several days stored in this way. You may then bring it to a boil, cool and refrigerate it as directed for several days longer. Soup is best one day old when its flavor is intensified. As its seasoning is higher then, it is wise to season all soups lightly in the beginning and to add seasoning if needed before the soup is served. Grease forms a cake that is easily removed from cold soup. See To Remove Grease from Soup, page 42. See Pressure Cooker Soups, page 878.

VEGETABLES FOR SOUP

Tomatoes, fresh or canned, lettuce, onions, parsnips, cress and leeks make good soup. Use turnips, broccoli stems, green pea pods and carrots sparingly. The first 2 are too strong in flavor, the latter too sweet. For increased flavor you may sauté vegetables lightly in a very little butter before adding them to the pot. Frozen vegetables may be used. These cook more rapidly than fresh vegetables. Use vegetable parings freely. Outer lettuce leaves, green bean and asparagus ends, etc., may all be added, but since the vegetables all cook so much more rapidly than the meat it is wise to add them the last ½ hour or less of cooking. If you wish to serve vegetables in the soup, strain the meat from the soup before the vegetables are added. Chill and remove the fat from the soup. Add the scrubbed and diced vegetables and simmer them covered until they are tender. If you want to use the vegetables as a thickening, put the cooked vegetable through a food mill or the raw vegetables through a blender and reheat them in the soup. Cereals may also be added with the vegetables. See suggestions below.

DRIED CELERY AND PARSLEY FOR SOUP

Place on a rack in an oven, so slow it is barely warm, and dry until brittle:

Celery leaves or parsley

When dry, put them in a closed container and set them aside for future use.

CEREALS AND THICKENING FOR SOUP

Add raw cereals to soup with the vegetables for the last hour of cooking. Allow to the original amount of water approximately:

1 teaspoon barley to 1 cup water
1 teaspoon green kern to 1 cup water
1 teaspoon rice to 1 cup water
1 teaspoon oatmeal to 1 cup water
2 tablespoons wheat germ flour to

1 cup water
2 tablespoons peanut flour to 1 cup water
2 tablespoons soya flour to 1 cup water
½ teaspoon quick-cooking tapioca to 1 cup water

Stir it into the boiling soup and simmer it for 5 minutes before serving. This will be a very light thickening. Add cooked cereal in any desired amount to soup shortly before serving it. Leave it whole or use the blender. Add noodles, etc., to soup for the last 20 minutes of cooking. Add alphabets and vermicelli for the last 7 minutes. Stir them into the rapidly boiling soup.
If you wish to thicken cooked soup with flour, allow:

1½ teaspoons flour

to:

1 cup soup

Make a paste of the flour with about:
Twice as much cold stock, milk or water.

Stir the boiling soup, pour the paste slowly into it, then simmer and stir it for 3 or 4 minutes. Or, as in cream sauce you may make a Roux, page 425, of:

1½ teaspoons flour
1½ teaspoons butter

Pour the soup onto this gradually, stirring constantly until it is smooth and boiling. Or add:

Flour and butter

to cooled soup in the blender and then reheat the soup. Stir and boil it. Additional thickenings are eggs, cream and cream sauce. Add beaten eggs to hot, not boiling soup. Stir the soup over low heat until the eggs thicken slightly. You may beat:

1 egg or 2 egg yolks

with:

2 tablespoons cream or sherry

Stir this slowly into:

2 cups soup

Soups cooked with starchy vegetables such as dried beans, peas, etc., will separate and must be bound. To do this:
Melt:

1 tablespoon butter

Stir in until blended:

1 tablespoon flour

Add a small amount of:
Cold water, stock or milk

Stir this mixture into about:

3 cups strained boiling soup

See Cream Soups, page 56, Chicken Broth with Egg, page 47, and Duchess

Soup, page 58, for examples of soups thickened with flour and with eggs.

SEASONINGS FOR SOUPS

Salt, peppercorns, freshly ground pepper, paprika, cayenne, celery seed, celery salt, bay leaf, garlic, thyme, mace and allspice are in general use for seasoning soups. Also an onion stuck with 2 or 3 cloves. You may place herbs and whole spices in a large aluminum tea ball for easy removal after seasoning soup.
Season soup lightly in the beginning. Add more seasoning, if required, immediately before serving it. See Garnishes for Soup, page 72.

COLORING FOR SOUP

Caramelized sugar and commercial soup coloring are in general use for coloring soups and sauces.
Prepare:
Caramel Sirup, page 754
The sugar is burnt until it loses practically all sweetness. It will keep indefinitely. Or buy:
Commercial soup coloring
Use it sparingly in delicately flavored food. Homemade caramel sirup is preferable.

TO REMOVE GREASE FROM SOUP

I.
Place a lettuce leaf in the hot soup. When it has absorbed the grease remove it.

II.
Float a paper towel on the surface of the soup and when it has absorbed as much grease as it will hold discard the towel. Or roll a paper towel and use

one end to skim over the soup surface to remove the fat. When the end becomes coated with grease cut off the used part with a scissors and repeat the process.

III.
Put an ice cube in a cloth and agitate it just under the surface of the soup letting it collect the rising fat.

IV.
Chill the soup. It is then a simple matter to remove grease from cold soup.

TO TRY TO REMOVE SALT FROM SOUP
When soup is too salty add to it a raw potato sliced; permit the soup to boil. Remove the potato.

WINE IN SOUPS
The addition of wine to soup frequently enhances its flavor. Wines that blend well with bland soups, chicken or veal, are dry sherry or Madeira, ¼ cupful wine to 1 quart soup. A strongly flavored soup like beef or oxtail is improved by the addition of some dry red table wine, ½ cupful wine to 1 quart soup.

A dry white table wine adds zest to a fish, crab or lobster bisque or chowder. Use ⅛ to ¼ cupful wine to 1 quart soup.

Wines should be added to the hot soup shortly before it is served. Do not boil the soup after adding the wine.

STOCK AND STOCK SUBSTITUTES
Whether used for soups, gravies or sauces, stock of all kinds is an invaluable ingredient. See rules for stock and clear soups in this chapter and note the suggestions below, all of which can be used interchangeably:

Stock for Sauces, page 425. Use beef, chicken or vegetable cubes. Add 1 cube to 1 cupful boiling water or homemade stock, or use diluted beef extract, canned bouillon, consommé, chicken or mushroom broth, etc. See Pressure Cooker Soups, page 878, and Blender Soups, page 895.

SOUP STOCK I. Made with Raw Meat
9 Cupfuls Soup After 4 Hours' Cooking.
This is a good basic rule. More meat may be used and a veal bone added or substituted for the beef. Place in a soup kettle:

>3 lbs. brisket, shinbone or other
>soup meat and bone

You may reserve ⅓ of the meat, cut it into 1 inch cubes and brown them in meat fat or butter. The bones may be cracked and browned in the fat. This will give the soup color and flavor. Add them to the soup water. Sprinkle the meat with:

>1 tablespoon salt

Permit it to stand for 1 hour. Add:

>3 quarts cold water

After 30 minutes bring the water to the boiling point. If a clear soup is desired remove the scum. This is not recommended as the scum contains the main nutritive values of the soup. Simmer the soup covered for 3½ hours. Add and simmer covered for ½ hour longer:

>2 cups or more chopped vegetables: onions, carrots, celery stalks with leaves, etc. See Pressure Cooker Soups, page 878, or Blender Soups, page 895
>¾ cup tomatoes
>½ green pepper with 4 or 5 seeds

It improves the flavor of some soups if the vegetables, at least the onion, are simmered briefly in butter or drippings before being added to the soup pot. Leek tops, green onion tops, celery root, etc., may be used. An onion may be stuck with 2 or 3 cloves. Strain the soup. Chill it, remove the fat and reheat the soup. Add more seasoning if required. Serve the soup with:

>2 tablespoons chopped parsley

See Vegetables Strained as a Thickening for Soups, page 41, Garnishes for Soups, page 72. Also, Pressure Cooker Soups, page 878.

CHICKEN OR VEAL SOUP STOCK
This is known as white or light stock. Follow the rule for Soup Stock I. Substitute chicken or veal for the beef. Omit the tomatoes.

BOUILLON
Follow the rule for Soup Stock I. Use lean beef, a beef shinbone and vegetables.

CONSOMMÉ
Follow the rule for Soup Stock I. Use lean beef, a veal bone, a chicken and vegetables.

See Soup Meat, page 45.

SOUP STOCK II. Made with Cooked Meat
About 3½ Cupfuls
Cut the meat from the bone. To:
> 2 cups meat, bones and fat

add:
> 4 or 5 cups water
> ¼ teaspoon salt

Soak the meat and bone in the water for 1 hour. Bring it to the boiling point and simmer it covered for 1½ hours. Add and simmer covered for ½ hour longer:
> 1 cup chopped vegetables: carrots, turnips, celery, parsley, etc.
> 1 small onion
> 1 cup tomatoes
> ½ teaspoon sugar
> ¼ teaspoon salt
> ¼ teaspoon paprika
> ¼ teaspoon celery salt

Strain the soup, chill it. For quick chilling place it in a tall narrow container set in cold water. Remove the fat and reheat the soup. Add more seasoning if required. Serve the soup with:
> Chopped parsley

See paragraph about vegetables in rule for Soup Stock I, page 43, and Vegetables for Soup, page 41. Also, Pressure Cooker Soups, page 878.

"SCRAP" STOCK OR SOUP
My passion is "scrap soup." I cannot resist the appeal of a few celery tops, outer lettuce leaves, sprigs of parsley, a lone carrot flanked by a sprouting onion or bits of meat, fish or left-over bone. Waste is threatened so I hasten to use these oddments languishing in the refrigerator. Allow:
> 2½ cups water

to:
> 1 cup "oddments"

Place every bit of food suitable for soup, and, if you wish, a tablespoonful or two of raw or left-over cereal in a saucepan. Seasoning as needed will be added later, as some of the food is already salted. Simmer the soup from 1 to 2 hours, the longer period when cooked meat or bone is used. Or pressure cook it, page 878, using only 1½ cupfuls of water for 12 minutes. Strain the soup. Serve it or cool and store it. Sometimes the bones, if any, are removed and the vegetables and soup are put through a blender, food mill or strainer. So in a short time a few negligible fragments have become that invaluable substance for the discrim-

inating cook, a few cupfuls of palatable stock.

This may be seasoned and used as it is. A bouillon cube may be added if it seems advisable. If the vegetables have been strained from the soup and no cereal has been added it makes a good clear soup to which you may add a few Dumplings, see page 72, farina, liver sausage, etc. This stock may make its reappearance in gravy, sauce, soufflés or timbales. It may be used to flavor rice or noodles. It will keep for several days. It may then be brought to the boiling point, cooled and replaced in a tightly covered jar to keep for several days longer. The stock may be used in Cream Soups, page 56, and if called upon to serve a number of people the stock may be stretched by the addition of canned soup. See the section on Canned Soups, page 66.

TO CLARIFY SOUP STOCK
Remove the fat from:
> Cold stock

Measure the stock. Allow to every quart of stock:
> 1 egg white
> 1 eggshell

Beat the egg slightly and add to it:
> 2 teaspoons cold water

Add it to the stock with the eggshell broken into small pieces. Stir it over a low flame until it boils. Boil it for 2 minutes. Place it in a warm place 20 minutes. Strain it in a fine strainer placed over a larger fine strainer lined with a double thickness of cheese cloth.

BEEF JUICE OR BEEF TEA FOR INVALIDS AND CHILDREN
About ½ to ¾ Cupful
Cut in small dice:
> 1 lb. lean round steak

Place the meat in a quart mason jar and add:
> 1 cup cold water
> A pinch of salt

Cover the jar lightly. Place the jar in a pan of cold water, as much water as possible without upsetting the jar. Bring the water slowly to a boil. Boil it gently for 1 hour. Remove the jar. Place it on a cake-cooling rack to cool as rapidly as possible. Strain the juice. Store it in a covered container in a cold part of the refrigerator until ready to heat and serve.

SOUP MEAT
Brisket or other soup meat may be taken from the soup before the vegetables are added. Serve it with:
Horseradish Sauce, page 429
Mustard Sauce, page 428
Tomato Sauce, page 433, or
Onion Sauce, page 432

Hash, page 154; Meat Pie Roll, page 158; Left-Over Meat Deviled, page 157.

VEGETABLE STOCK
Prepare vegetables for cooking and follow Vegetables for Soup, page 41. Add to the pot about twice as much cold water as vegetables. Cook them covered until tender. Drain the vegetables. For ways to utilize the cooked vegetables see Vegetables for Soup, page 41.

MUSHROOM STOCK
Place in a saucepan:
Mushroom skins and ends
Add:
Onion
Celery ribs and leaves
Carrots
Parsley
Cover these ingredients with:
Cold water
Simmer them for 30 minutes. Strain the stock. Season it when ready to use it with:
Salt and pepper and sherry

POT AU FEU OR FRENCH BOILED DINNER
This is the French equivalent of a New England boiled dinner. The liquid is similar to our soup stock. Its flavor varies depending on the ingredients the French housewife finds available at her market or in her garden. Hence it may be delicately or coarsely flavored. If you like a stout soup, add cabbage, parsnips and turnips. A meaty beef shank makes an excellent stock and the meat is still juicy after cooking. Have it cut into 4 inch lengths so that marrow lovers may have a treat. If you like fat meat, add a piece of brisket or short ribs. The vegetables are left whole or are cut into halves and require about 1 hour's cooking. Traditionally, the broth is served first. The meat and vegetables are placed on a platter and served with Dijon mustard and coarse salt. A horseradish, onion or other piquant sauce may be served with it. Any meat left over from the stew may be used to advantage in Meat Salad, page 470, or in Hash, page 155, or as a stuffing for vegetable cases, page 198. Use about 3 cupfuls of water for each pound of meat and bone. Follow the process described in Soup Stock I. After the soup has simmered for 3 hours, add, if you can get them:
6 leeks
Use only the white and light green parts. Add:
2 or more onions
3 or more ribs celery cut into 2 or 3 inch lengths
3 carrots, cut up, and turnips and parsnips, if you like them
4 whole black peppercorns
A bay leaf and pinch of thyme
You may add:
Diced potatoes
They have a wonderful flavor although the stock is clearer without them. If the soup is to serve as a main dish add more vegetables. Simmer the soup ½ hour longer.

MY FAVORITE SOUP
About 15 Cupfuls
Place in a soup kettle:
1 gallon water
1 2-lb. beef bone
1 2-lb. veal bone
2 lbs. brisket of beef
1 large onion
Contents of 1 No. 2 can tomatoes
2 teaspoons salt
Cover the pot closely. Simmer the soup for about 3½ hours. Cut up and add:
1 whole stalk celery with leaves
1 bunch parsley
3 or 4 carrots
½ lb. snap beans
Simmer the soup ½ hour longer. Remove the meat. Put the soup through a purée strainer. Chill it. Remove the fat. Reheat the soup. Add:
1¼ cups fine noodles, broken
Simmer the noodles for about 10 minutes or until tender.

OXTAIL SOUP
About 7 Cupfuls
Brown:
A disjointed oxtail: about 2 lbs.
½ cup sliced onions
in:
2 tablespoons butter or fat
Add and simmer covered for 4½ hours:

8 cups water
1½ teaspoons salt
4 peppercorns

Add and simmer covered ½ hour longer:

¼ cup shredded parsley
½ cup diced carrots
1 cup diced celery
½ bay leaf
4 tablespoons barley
½ cup tomato pulp
1 teaspoon dried herbs: thyme, marjoram, basil, etc.

Strain, chill, skim and reheat the stock. The meat and vegetables may be diced or blended and added to the soup later.

Brown in a skillet:

1 tablespoon flour

Add and stir until blended:

2 tablespoons butter

Add the stock slowly and additional seasoning, if needed. Shortly before serving you may add ¼ cupful dry sherry, Madeira or ½ cupful red wine. Serve the soup with:

Fritter Garnish, page 74, or Slices of lemon

See Pressure Cooker Soups, page 878; Blender Soups, page 895.

PEPPER POT
About 5 Cupfuls

Cut into small pieces and sauté in a heavy saucepan until clear:

4 slices of bacon

Add and simmer for 5 minutes:

⅓ cup minced onion
½ cup minced celery
2 seeded minced green peppers

Wash and cut into fine shreds:

¾ lb. honeycomb tripe

Put it into the saucepan with:

8 cups Soup Stock, preferably White Stock, page 43
1 bay leaf
½ teaspoon freshly ground pepper

Bring these ingredients to the boiling point. Add:

1 cup raw peeled and diced potatoes

Simmer the soup covered for 1 hour, or until the tripe is tender. Melt:

2 tablespoons butter

Stir in until blended:

2 tablespoons flour

Add a little of the soup. Bring these ingredients to the boiling point, then add them to the rest of the soup. Season it with:

Salt and paprika

Shortly before serving it add:

½ cup warm cream

TOMATO BOUILLON
About 3 Cupfuls

Bring to the boiling point and simmer for 5 minutes:

3 cups strained tomato juice
½ small bay leaf
¼ cup celery cut up with leaves
2 tablespoons chopped fennel
2 whole cloves
½ teaspoon dried or 1 tablespoon fresh herb, orégano, basil, etc.
(1 small, skinned, chopped and sautéed onion)

Strain these ingredients. Add:

1 tablespoon butter
½ teaspoon salt
A few grains of pepper
A few grains of celery salt

Serve the bouillon hot or cold in cups topped with a spoonful of:

Whipped cream or sour cream

CHICKEN BROTH
About 9 or 10 Cupfuls

You will find canned clear chicken broth a good substitute for this rule. Cover a:

4 or 5 lb. fowl

with:

12 cups cold water

Simmer it covered for 2½ hours or until almost tender. Add:

5 ribs celery with leaves
½ bay leaf
¼ cup chopped onion
½ cup chopped carrots
6 sprigs parsley
1 teaspoon salt

Simmer the chicken for ½ hour longer or until it is very tender. Add:

Salt, if needed

Permit it to cool in the broth. Remove the grease as the broth cools. Strain the broth. Chill it. It will solidify and make a good aspic or jellied soup. Use it in this way or reheat the broth. Add:

(½ cup of cream)

Do not boil it after adding the cream. You may serve the broth with:

**Chopped parsley
Chopped water cress**

See Chicken Broth with Egg, page 47.

CHICKEN BROTH FROM CHICKEN FEET

If there are only 2 feet, add them to other soup. Poultry dealers are still in

a mood to give away chicken feet.
Cover with boiling water:

Chicken feet

Boil them for 3 minutes. Drain them.
Strip the skin from them. Place the
chicken feet in a saucepan with:

Vegetables for Soup, page 41
⅛ teaspoon salt

Avoid tomatoes and turnips. Cover
these ingredients with cold water.
Simmer them covered for 1 hour.
Strain the broth. Season it with:

Salt and paprika

CHICKEN BROTH OR SOUP FROM BACKS, NECKS, ETC.

Many markets now sell cut-up chickens. This is a boon to the cook who
wishes to make chicken stock without
buying a whole bird. Excellent soup
can be made with backs, wings and
necks. The meat may be minced and
used to great advantage in Soufflés,
page 217, Croquettes, page 195, or
other recipes calling for minced chick-
en. Follow the above rule for Chicken
Broth from Chicken Feet, placing
backs, wings, necks, etc., in a pan
and covering them with cold water. If
they are large, simmer them for 2
hours, add the vegetables for the last
½ hour, or pressure cook, see page 878.

CHICKEN BROTH OR BOUILLON WITH EGG

Individual Serving

A good dish for an invalid. Beat well:

1 egg

Pour over it, beating constantly:

1 cup hot chicken broth

Season it if needed with:

Salt and paprika

Add:

(1 tablespoon chopped parsley)

Serve it at once, or keep it hot over
hot water.

LEFT-OVER CHICKEN SOUP

About 3 Cupfuls

Break into small pieces:

1 chicken carcass

Add and simmer covered for 1½ hours:

4 cups water
¼ teaspoon salt

Add and simmer covered ½ hour
longer the following or similar vegetables:

1 cup chopped celery with leaves
1 large sliced onion
½ cup chopped carrots
¼ cup chopped turnips
Lettuce leaves

Left-over gravy
Parsley
¼ teaspoon salt
¼ teaspoon paprika
¼ teaspoon celery salt
(2 tablespoons rice)

Chill, strain and reheat the soup. Season as required. If a clear soup is desired, omit the gravy and the rice. You
may serve in the soup cubes of dressing sautéed in a little butter.

WATER CRESS SOUP

To:

5 cups hot Chicken Stock, page
43, or Cream of Chicken Soup,
page 59

Add:

1 bunch of water cress chopped or
blended

Heat well and serve.

TURKEY SOUP

About 7 Cupfuls

The following is a good swan song for
a turkey dinner. Cut into small pieces:

1 turkey carcass

Add and simmer covered for 1½
hours:

8 cups water

Add and simmer covered for ½ hour
longer:

¼ cup chopped carrots
1 cup celery with leaves
½ cup chopped turnips
½ cup chopped onions
¼ cup parsley
3 tablespoons barley or rice
½ teaspoon salt
¼ teaspoon paprika
(1 cup tomatoes)
(½ bay leaf)

Strain, chill, skim and reheat the soup.
Add more seasoning if required.
Vary this soup according to your fancy
or your materials on hand. It is sure
to be good. You may strain it and add
tomato juice. You may jazz it up with
2 or more tablespoonfuls sherry. Add
left-over gravy if it is not too rich. If
the carcass is small it may be necessary to add 1 or 2 beef or chicken cubes
or a teaspoonful of beef extract to the
soup to help it along. Make this addition shortly before serving the soup.
You may serve in the soup cubes of
dressing sautéed in a little butter.

DRIED LEGUME SOUPS. Lentils, Beans, Peas

These soups may be flavored with a
ham bone, a ham skin or with the

water in which a ham or tongue, fresh, smoked or corned, has been cooked. But if this water is very salty, better dilute it. Also add flavor with bacon or scraps of ham or fresh pork fat. Try them out, see page 946, then brown an onion in the fat. Reserve the cracklings to garnish the soup, or cook them in it. These soups may be served unstrained, although they are usually more digestible if strained. Stir them well before serving. The legumes may be crushed with a potato masher. If cooked with salt pork, serve a thin slice in each plate. These soups are good as a main dish served with Sausage Balls, page 73. To make them quickly, see below.

FRENCH CANADIAN PEA SOUP
6 to 7 Cupfuls
A not too hefty first-course pea soup. It is traditional to make this with yellow peas. Soak (page 268):

> ½ lb. split yellow peas

Rinse and drain them. Bring them to a boil with:

> 6 cups cold water
> ⅛ lb. diced salt pork

Skin and add:

> ¼ cup finely diced carrots
> ½ cup diced onions
> ½ cup diced white turnips
> A small piece of bay leaf
> (A small minced clove garlic)

Simmer the soup covered for 2 or 3 hours, or until the peas have completely disintegrated. Season it with:

> Salt and pepper
> (½ teaspoon dried savory)

Serve the soup unstrained.

SPLIT PEA SOUP
This makes an old-time family quantity, 2 quarts or more, in the good old way. However, this is a good way to utilize a turkey carcass, a bit of salt pork, a ham bone or the water in which a ham was cooked. If you are too impatient to use the following recipe try the Quick Method Pea Soup opposite. Soak (see page 268):

> 2 cups split peas

Drain the peas, reserving the liquid. Add enough water to the reserved liquid to make 12 cupfuls. Add to the peas and simmer covered for 3½ hours:

> A turkey carcass, a ham bone or
> a 2 inch cube salt pork

Add and simmer covered for ½ hour longer:

> ½ cup chopped onions
> 1 cup chopped celery with leaves
> ½ cup chopped carrots

You may add:

> 1 clove garlic
> 1 bay leaf
> 1 teaspoon sugar
> A dash of cayenne or a pod of red pepper
> ¼ teaspoon thyme

Put the soup through a sieve. Serve it clear or with the puréed vegetables. Chill it. Remove the grease. Melt:

> 2 tablespoons butter or soup fat

Add and stir until blended:

> 2 tablespoons flour

Add a little of the soup mixture slowly. Cook and stir it until it boils, then add to the rest of the soup. Season the soup with:

> Salt, if required, and paprika

Serve it with:

> Croutons, page 73, or toasted cheese crackers or a thin slice of salt pork if this has been used in the soup

MONGOLE SOUP
This is the preceding:

> Split Pea Soup

with:

> 3 cups strained tomatoes

added with the other vegetables.

SPLIT PEA AND FISH SOUP
This may be made at low cost, as many fishmongers give away fish heads, tails, fins and scraps. Use the rule for Split Pea Soup to make either a thick or a thin soup. Substitute fish scraps for the turkey carcass or ham bone. You will find this soup worth a trial.

QUICK METHOD PEA SOUP
About 10 Cupfuls
Boil for ½ hour:

> 2 cups split peas

in:

> 6 cups water

or put these ingredients through a blender. Simmer them until tender, about 1½ hours. When cooked in this way or blended the peas need no further puréeing. Add:

> 3 cups well-seasoned stock

Serve with a garnish of crisp bacon or a tablespoonful of sour cream and chopped parsley.

LENTIL SOUP
About 9 or 10 Cupfuls
Follow the rule on page 48 for Split
Pea Soup. Substitute for the peas:
>2 cups lentils

Add just before serving:
>(1 tablespoon of the traditional
>vinegar or lemon juice)
>(1 cup strained tomatoes)

Serve the soup with:
>Croutons, page 73

BLACK BEAN SOUP
About 9 or 10 Cupfuls
Follow the rule for Split Pea Soup.
Substitute for peas:
>2 cups black beans

Add:
>3 tablespoons butter

in place of the 2 tablespoonfuls given
in Split Pea Soup, as this soup is drier.
Serve the soup with:
>Thin slices of lemon
>Thin slices of hard-cooked eggs
>(1 tablespoon sherry for each
>portion)

Canned Black Bean Soup, page 71.

Italian Bean Soup, page 53.

SCOTCH BROTH
About 8 Cupfuls
Soak for 12 hours:
>½ cup pearl barley

in:
>2 cups water

You may use other barley. Soak it for
1 hour. Add this to:
>3 lbs. mutton or lamb with bones
>10 cups water

Simmer the soup covered for 2 hours
or until the meat is tender. Add for the
last ½ hour of cooking:
>2 cups Vegetables for Soup,
>page 41

These vegetables may be sautéed for
5 minutes in:
>3 tablespoons butter

Remove the meat from the soup. Dice
it, add it to the soup, which may be
thickened like cream sauce. Melt:
>2 tablespoons butter

Stir in:
>2 tablespoons flour

When well blended stir in 1 cupful of
the soup. When it boils add it to the
rest of the soup. Season it with:
>Salt and pepper
>Chopped parsley
>(Curry powder)

GREEN KERN SOUP
About 9 Cupfuls
If you are English, corn means wheat,
if Scotch it means oats, but if you come
from "down under" or are American
you **know** corn grows on a cob. Kern
sounds as though it too might be corn
but it isn't. It's dried green wheat and
it makes a favorite European soup.
Soak for ½ hour:
>½ cup green kern

in:
>4 cups water

Tie in a bunch with a string and add:
>3 sprigs parsley
>2 ribs celery cut up with leaves

Cook the kern gently until the water is
absorbed. Watch it. Remove the
bunch. Add:
>2 quarts soup stock

Cook the soup in a double boiler until
the kern is very tender, about 2 hours.
Stir and blend over heat:
>1 tablespoon butter
>1 tablespoon flour

Stir this slowly into the soup. Permit
it to boil. If you wish you may add:
>½ cup or more warm cream
>Seasoning

BARLEY SOUP
About 9 Cupfuls
Wash then drain:
>½ cup barley

Add it to:
>4 cups soup stock

Follow the above rule for:
>Green Kern Soup

without precooking the barley but
adding the parsley and celery to the
soup stock. You may thicken the soup
as directed, and may also add the
cream. If you prefer, you may purée
or blend the barley before making
these additions.

DRIED NAVY BEAN SOUP
5 to 6 Cupfuls
Soak (page 268):
>½ cup dried navy, kidney or Lima
>beans

Add:
>A small piece of ham, a ham
>bone or ⅛ lb. salt pork
>4 cups boiling water
>½ bay leaf
>3 or 4 peppercorns

Cook the soup slowly until the beans
are soft, for about 2½ hours. For the
last 30 minutes you may add:

1 diced carrot
3 ribs celery with leaves
½ sliced onion

Remove and mince the meat. Put the soup through a food mill, blender or sieve. Thin the soup, if required, with boiling water or with milk. Correct the seasoning. Serve the soup with the meat and:

> Croutons, page 73
> Chopped chives or parsley

CLAM BROTH OR SOUP
About 4 Cupfuls

Wash and scrub well with a brush, then place in a kettle:

> 2 quarts clams in shells

Add:

> 1¾ cups water
> 3 ribs celery cut up with leaves
> A pinch of cayenne

Cover the kettle closely. If you wish you may add more water, about 4 cupfuls in all, and minced vegetables that are suitable for soup. See Court Bouillon, page 238. Steam the clams until the shells open, page 252. Strain the liquor through wet double cheese cloth. It may be heated and diluted with warm cream or rich milk. Add:

> 1 teaspoon butter
> Salt if required

Clam broth may be frozen until mushy and served in small glasses or on the shells with wedges of lemon. The clams may be used in various ways. See Index.

CLAM AND CHICKEN BROTH

Combine equal parts of:

> Clam broth
> Chicken stock

If the clam broth is very salty you may have to use more chicken stock or water. You may use both clam and chicken stock canned, or one fresh and the other canned. Season lightly with:

> Pepper

When boiling remove from fire and place in hot cups. Add to each cupful:

> 1 tablespoon heavy cream or top it
>   with 1 tablespoon whipped cream

Have the cream at room temperature. Sprinkle the top for color with:

> Paprika or chopped chives or
>   parsley

Canned Chicken and Clam Broth, page 69.

MUSHROOM BROTH
I. About 6 Cupfuls

Prepare:

> ¾ lb. diced mushrooms
> 2 ribs diced celery
> ½ skinned and diced carrot
> ¼ skinned and diced onion

Cover these vegetables with:

> 3 cups water

Simmer covered for 45 minutes. Strain the broth. Add to make 6 cupfuls of liquid:

> Chicken Stock, page 43

Add, if needed:

> Salt and paprika

Serve very hot. Add to each cupful:

> 1 tablespoon dry sherry

If you wish to serve the vegetables in the broth use boiling water.

II.

Or, blend or chop until fine:

> ¾ lb. mushrooms

Add them to:

> 6 cups Chicken Stock, page 43, or
>   consommé

Simmer covered for about 15 minutes, only 5 if you use the blender. Strain if you like. Serve it as directed above.

VEGETABLE BROTH
About 2½ Cupfuls

This is quickly made and is very good. Chop or blend:

> 3 cups or more Vegetables for
>   Soup, page 41

The vegetables may be sautéed gently for 5 minutes in 3 tablespoonfuls of butter. Add:

> 4 cups boiling water or part water
>   and tomatoes or tomato juice

Simmer the soup covered for 1 hour. See General Directions for Pressure Cooker Soups, page 878. Season, and add if desired:

> 1 bouillon cube

Serve the soup strained or unstrained, hot or chilled.

QUICK VEGETABLE CHOWDER
About 3½ Cupfuls

This is a full and delightful meal—prepared in about 40 minutes or 15 minutes in a pressure cooker. The vegetables may be varied in kind and quantity, but keep about the same proportions of vegetables and water. The soup is very delicately flavored as it is. Pull off the outer leaves of a head of lettuce. Prepare:

> 1 cup shredded lettuce

Pull apart a stalk of celery. Reserve

the heart to be eaten raw. Chop the best of the large ribs. There should be about:

1½ cups shredded celery

Peel, skin and chop:

1 medium-sized onion

Skin and chop:

1 medium-sized carrot

Melt in a saucepan:

4 tablespoons butter

Add the prepared vegetables and simmer them in the butter for about 8 minutes. Add to them:

2 cups boiling water
(½ cup skinned or canned tomatoes)

When the vegetables are boiling stir in:

⅓ cup noodles or 2 tablespoons rice

Simmer these ingredients covered for 30 minutes. Season them lightly with:

Salt and pepper

MEATLESS VEGETABLE SOUP
About 3 Cupfuls

An acceptable, moderately thick vegetable soup. Vary the vegetables if you like, keeping about the same proportions of liquid and solids. Melt:

3 tablespoons butter

Add and cook slowly for 10 minutes:

¼ cup diced carrots
¼ cup diced celery
¼ cup sliced onions

Add and cook for 2 minutes longer:

½ cup peeled diced potatoes

Add and simmer covered for 1 hour:

3 cups water

Melt:

2 tablespoons butter

Add, cook and stir until smooth:

½ tablespoon flour
½ cup tomatoes

Add these ingredients to the soup and simmer it covered for ¼ hour longer. You may add for the last 5 minutes:

1 cup chopped spinach

And if you wish, add:

1 bouillon cube or meat jelly or
½ teaspoon or more beef extract

Beat the soup with a wire whisk or a fork to break up the vegetables or blend the vegetables before cooking and simmer only 5 minutes in all. Add:

½ teaspoon sugar
¾ teaspoon salt
¼ teaspoon paprika
3 tablespoons chopped parsley

LEFT-OVER VEGETABLE SOUP WITH CHEESE CROUTONS
About 5 Cupfuls

Sauté in butter until light brown:

1½ cups diced bread, see Croutons, page 73

Keep them hot. Place in a stew pan:

4 cups Soup Stock, page 44
1 tablespoon butter

Add any cooked vegetables you have on hand, keeping the same proportion of vegetables to stock as follows:

⅓ cup cooked diced carrots
⅓ cup cooked sliced onions
⅓ cup cooked snap beans or celery
1 teaspoon Caramel Sirup, page 754, or a few drops soup coloring

Add if required:

Salt and paprika

Bring these ingredients to the boiling point. Place them in a large flat ovenproof dish or individual oven-proof bowls. Place the croutons in the soup. Sprinkle it with:

½ cup grated cheese

Put the soup under a broiler until the cheese is melted.

Potato Soup, page 57.

SPINACH SOUP
About 6½ Cupfuls

Pick over, wash, drain thoroughly, then chop fine or blend:

2 lbs. tender young spinach

Or you may use 4 cupfuls cooked or two 14 ounce packages of frozen spinach defrosted. Melt in a saucepan:

4 tablespoons butter

Add and sauté until golden brown:

¼ cup minced onion

Add the spinach. Stir to coat it well with the butter. Cover, and cook gently till the spinach is just tender. If you haven't a blender, put the spinach through a food mill or sieve. Return it to the pan and add:

4 cups chicken stock
A bay leaf or a grating of nutmeg
Salt if required
Paprika or freshly ground pepper

Bring the soup slowly to a boil and serve. You may add, just before serving the soup:

½ cup hot cream

CABBAGE SOUP
About 6 Cupfuls

This superb cabbage soup, quick and inexpensive, is from Herman Smith's book "Kitchens Near and Far." You will find this and his incomparable "Stina" most rewarding. Sauté gently in a saucepan until tender and yellow:

1 large minced onion
1½ tablespoons butter
Grate or shred and add:
    1 small head green cabbage: about
        ¾ lb.
Bring to a boil:
    4 cups Beef Stock, page 43
Add the stock to the vegetables. Season as needed with:
    Salt and pepper
Simmer the soup for 10 minutes. If you wish, add this delicious topping:
    ½ cup sour cream
    1 tablespoon minced parsley
    (½ teaspoon caraway seeds)
Place a spoonful of the sour-cream mixture on each plate of soup.

ONION SOUP
About 5½ Cupfuls
Prepare:
    1 cup chopped or thinly sliced
        onions
Stir and sauté them slowly until golden brown in:
    1½ tablespoons butter
Stir in and cook for 1 minute:
    1½ teaspoons flour
Add and simmer for 15 minutes or, if you are a traditionalist, for 1 hour or more:
    5 cups Stock, page 44
Season the soup as needed with:
    ½ teaspoon Worcestershire sauce
    Salt and pepper or paprika
Pour it into a flat oven-proof dish or into individual oven-proof bowls. Arrange on top of the soup:
    Split toasted rolls or pieces of
        toast
Sprinkle the toast well with:
    Grated Parmesan or other
        cheese
Place the dish under a broiler. Broil the cheese slowly until it is melted and brown. Serve the soup at once.

Cream of Onion Soup, page 59.
Consommé into Cream Soup, page 69.

PANADES
About 8 Cupfuls
These bread-thickened vegetable soups are practical, filling and fattening; they are a good way of utilizing left-over bread. Leeks, celery and sorrel are in general use. Water cress, spinach, lettuce, etc., may be substituted. Use:
    2 cups finely chopped celery, leeks
        or onions
Cook the vegetables slowly until soft but not brown in:
    2 tablespoons butter
Cover them with a lid.
If a leafy vegetable is used, add it to the butter, cover it and cook it slowly until wilted and reduced to about ¼. Add:
    4 cups hot water
    1 teaspoon salt
    6 cups diced bread
Stir well and permit the mixture to boil. Simmer it for ½ hour. Beat it well until smooth with a wire whisk or blend it. Combine:
    2 cups rich milk
    2 small or 1 large egg
Stir this slowly into the hot soup. Heat it but do not permit the soup to boil. You may serve it with:
    Chopped parsley
    Freshly grated nutmeg

GREEN PEA SOUP
About 6 Cupfuls
The Potage St. Germain of good French restaurants. Do not attempt this soup with canned peas but if using canned peas try the good Quick Canned Pea Soup, page 72. Hull:
    3 lbs. green peas
There should be about 3 cupfuls of hulled peas. Shred:
    1 head of lettuce
    1 peeled onion
    ½ cup or more celery with leaves
    2 sprigs parsley
Melt in a saucepan:
    2 tablespoons butter
Sauté the vegetables gently in the butter until tender. Add:
    2½ cups chicken stock
    2 cups of the hulled peas
    (⅓ bay leaf)
Simmer these ingredients covered until the peas are very soft. Put the soup through a food mill, a potato ricer or an electric blender, if you are lucky enough to own one. Simmer until tender:
    1 cup of the hulled peas
in:
    1½ cups chicken stock
Add them to the strained soup with:
    Seasoning as needed
You may color the soup with a drop or two of:
    Green coloring
You may serve the soup with:
    Butter Dumplings, page 74, or
    Sponge Dumplings, page 74
    (2 teaspoons chopped mint)

MEATLESS OKRA CHOWDER
About 6 Cupfuls
Cut the stems from:
 1 quart okra
Slice the okra. Prepare:
 2 cups diced celery
Seed and dice:
 1 green pepper
Skin and chop:
 1 small onion
Sauté the vegetables for 5 minutes in:
 ¼ cup butter or bacon drippings
Skin, chop and add:
 2 large ripe tomatoes or 1 cup
  canned tomatoes
 1 teaspoon brown sugar
 ¼ teaspoon paprika
 4 cups boiling water
Stew the vegetables gently until they are tender, for about 1 hour. Add if required:
 Salt and paprika
Cooked chicken, meat, fish or crisp bacon may be diced and added to the chowder. Serve it with:
 Boiled Rice, page 103

CORN CHOWDER
About 6 Cupfuls
Sauté slowly until lightly browned:
 ½ cup chopped salt pork
Add and sauté until golden brown:
 3 tablespoons chopped onion
 ½ cup chopped celery
 3 tablespoons chopped green
  pepper
Add and simmer:
 1 cup raw peeled diced potatoes
 2 cups water
 ½ teaspoon salt
 ¼ teaspoon paprika
 ½ bay leaf
When the potatoes are tender, combine until blended and bring to the boiling point and add to the above:
 3 tablespoons flour
 ½ cup milk
Add:
 1½ cups hot milk
 2 cups whole kernel corn
Heat but do not boil the soup. Serve it sprinkled with:
 Chopped parsley

VEGETABLE BISQUE
About 2½ Cupfuls
This utilizes the water in which vegetables have been cooked. Melt:
 2 tablespoons butter
Add and stir until blended:

 1⅓ tablespoons flour
Add and stir until smooth:
 1½ cups vegetable water
 ½ cup cream or Stock, page 44
Season the bisque with:
 Salt and paprika
 Celery salt
You may add:
 ½ cup cooked diced or strained
  vegetables
 2 tablespoons chopped parsley

CLEAR SOUP WITH VEGETABLES
Add diced vegetables that have been parboiled and drained to boiling soup stock or to the liquor in which the vegetables were cooked, plus a bouillon cube. Simmer them covered until they are tender. If you blend the vegetables add to soup without parboiling. Use approximately ½ cupful vegetables to 1 cupful Stock, page 44.

MEATLESS ITALIAN BEAN SOUP
About 6 Cupfuls
Soak (see page 268):
 1 cup navy beans or garbanzos
Drain them. Add to them:
 5 cups cold water
Simmer the beans until they are tender. Add boiling water, if needed, and:
 ¼ teaspoon salt
Chop until very fine:
 1 clove garlic
 1 tablespoon onion
 2 tablespoons parsley
 ¾ cup or more celery
Heat in a saucepan:
 ¼ cup oil or butter
Sauté the vegetables in the oil until they are golden brown. Add:
 ¼ teaspoon salt
 ⅓ teaspoon pepper
 1 cup fresh or canned tomato
  pulp
 1 cup coarsely chopped cabbage
Bring these ingredients to the boiling point. Combine them with the cooked beans. Add:
 1 cup Boiled Macaroni, page 91
Simmer the soup ¼ hour longer. Add if needed:
 Salt and paprika
Serve the soup in bowls. Sprinkle the tops with:
 ¼ cup or more grated Parmesan
  cheese

BORSCH
About 6 Cupfuls
There are probably as many versions of Borsch as there are Russians. Peel and chop until very fine:

> ½ cup carrots
> 1 cup onions
> 1 cup beets

Use 2 cupfuls if the tomatoes are omitted. Barely cover these ingredients with boiling water. Boil them gently, covered, for 20 minutes. Add to the vegetables and boil for 15 minutes:

> 1 tablespoon butter
> 2 cups beef or other stock
> 1 cup very finely shredded cabbage
> 1 cup tomato pulp or stewed and strained tomatoes

If the tomatoes are omitted, substitute 1 tablespoonful lemon juice. Place the soup in bowls. Add to each bowl of soup:

> 1 tablespoon room temperature thick sour cream
> (Grated cucumber)

Blender Borsch, page 896.

CHICKEN GUMBO
About 12 Cupfuls
Cut into pieces and dredge with flour:

> 1 stewing chicken

Brown it in:

> ¼ cup bacon grease

Pour over it:

> 4 cups boiling water

Simmer the soup covered until the meat falls from the bones. Drain the stock and chop the meat. Place in the soup kettle and simmer covered until the vegetables are tender:

> 2 cups skinned tomatoes
> ½ cup green corn
> 1 cup sliced okra
> ½ teaspoon salt
> ¼ cup diced onion
> ¼ cup rice
> 8 cups water

Combine these ingredients with the chicken meat and stock. Three-fourths cupful cooked rice may be substituted for the uncooked rice and added at this time. Canned corn may be substituted for the green corn and added at this time. Season the soup with:

> Salt and paprika
> (1 teaspoon filé powder moistened with a little water)

Do not boil the soup after adding the filé powder.

CREOLE SHRIMP GUMBO
If this is the main dish of a meal count it as 10 servings, if not you may stretch it to 14.
Sauté lightly in a skillet:

> 1 slice raw ham: ½ lb.

Cut it into pieces. Cut into ¾ inch slices:

> 2 lbs. okra

Sauté it slowly in the ham drippings for 10 minutes. If you use canned okra, omit the sautéing. Add and sauté for the last 2 minutes:

> 1½ cups chopped onion

Add:

> 2 ribs chopped celery with leaves
> ½ chopped green pepper, seeds and membrane removed
> 2 minced cloves garlic
> 1 sprig fresh thyme or ⅓ teaspoon dried thyme
> 1 bay leaf
> 1½ cups skinned fresh tomatoes or the contents of a No. 1 can tomatoes
> 6 cups water

If a thick gumbo is desired use less water. Shell and remove veins from:

> 2 lbs. fresh shrimp

Permit the soup to boil then reduce heat and add the ham, shrimp and:

> 2 tablespoons chopped parsley

Simmer the soup for ½ hour. Serve it with:

> Boiled or Steamed Rice, page 103

SHRIMP, CRAB AND OYSTER GUMBO
About 8 Cupfuls
Melt over a low flame:

> 1 tablespoon butter

Stir in until blended:

> 2 tablespoons flour

Stir in until golden brown:

> ¼ chopped onion

Stir in:

> 1½ cups strained tomatoes
> 4 cups Stock, page 44
> 1 quart thinly sliced okra

Break into small pieces and add:

> ½ lb. raw shelled cleaned shrimp
> ½ lb. raw crab meat

Simmer these ingredients until the okra is tender. Add:

> 16 oysters
> Salt and pepper

Serve the gumbo as soon as the oysters are plump, sprinkled with:

> Chopped parsley

CRAB GUMBO AND RICE
About 7 Cupfuls
Sauté, then mince:
 2 slices of bacon
Add to the bacon and the drippings:
 1 tablespoon butter
One-fourth pound fresh sausage may be substituted for the bacon. Sauté it. Remove it from the pan. Add the drippings to the other ingredients and proceed as directed. Add the sausage to the gumbo with the crab meat.
Sauté in the fat until light brown:
 2 cups finely sliced okra
 ¼ cup chopped onion
Add:
 2 cups canned tomatoes
 ½ teaspoon minced garlic
 ½ lemon, sliced
 1 bay leaf
Bring these ingredients to the boiling point. Add:
 4 cups boiling water or Stock, page 44
 ½ teaspoon salt
 ¼ teaspoon paprika
Simmer these ingredients for 45 minutes. Combine:
 1 tablespoon flour
 2 tablespoons water
Stir this paste into the simmering gumbo. Add:
 ½ lb. fresh or canned crab meat
 Salt and paprika if needed
Serve the gumbo at once with:
 Steamed Rice I, page 103

BEEF GUMBO
About 10 Cupfuls
Melt in a skillet:
 2 tablespoons butter
Add and sauté until dark brown:
 A soup bone with meat: 3 lbs.
Add:
 12 cups water: 3 quarts
Pressure cook (page 878) or simmer these ingredients covered for 2 hours. Add and simmer covered until the meat falls from the bone:
 ¼ cup chopped celery
 ¼ cup shredded parsley
 ¼ cup chopped onion
 ½ teaspoon salt
 ¼ teaspoon paprika
Strain, cool and skim the stock. Melt:
 2 tablespoons butter
Add and sauté for 3 minutes:
 ½ cup chopped onion
 ½ cup fresh or canned sliced okra
 1 cup chopped celery with leaves

Add:
 2½ cups tomatoes: No. 2 can
 2 tablespoons quick-cooking tapioca
 1 tablespoon sugar
 The soup stock
Simmer the soup covered for 1 hour longer. If desired add for the last 15 minutes:
 ½ lb. fresh shrimp or crab meat
Add additional seasoning if required.

TURTLE SOUP
About 8 Cupfuls
Place in a saucepan and bring to the boiling point:
 1 lb. green turtle meat cut into pieces
 6 cups water
 1 bay leaf
 1 sprig fresh thyme or ⅓ teaspoon dried thyme
 2 cloves
 ¼ teaspoon ground allspice
 Juice and thinly sliced peel of ½ lemon
 A few grains cayenne
 ¼ teaspoon freshly ground black pepper
 ½ teaspoon salt
Heat:
 2 tablespoons bacon drippings or oil
Sauté in this for 2 minutes:
 2 medium-sized chopped onions
Stir in:
 1 tablespoon flour
Add:
 1½ cups fresh skinned tomatoes or the contents of a No. 1 can tomatoes
Permit these ingredients to cook for 10 minutes. Combine them with the turtle mixture and:
 1 tablespoon chopped parsley
 2 cloves minced garlic
Simmer the soup until the turtle meat is tender. You may add a few drops of brown coloring.
Add to each serving:
 1 tablespoon sherry
Garnish the soup with:
 2 chopped hard-cooked eggs
 Lemon slices

Turtle or Terrapin Stew, page 257.

Cream Soups

The trouble with cream soups is that they are frequently served with whipped cream as the first course of a heavy meal. The wonderful thing about cream soups is that they are nearly a meal by themselves. Balanced by a green salad or fruit, they make a perfect luncheon for a non-reducing partaker.

Place on top of a serving of cream soup 1 teaspoonful or more room-temperature whipped cream or sour cream. Garnish it with a dash of paprika.

BASIC CREAM SOUP RECIPE
4 Cupfuls
You may use left-over vegetables for this purpose. Melt:
    2 tablespoons butter
Sauté in this for five minutes:
    1 tablespoon minced onion
Blend in:
    1½ tablespoons flour
    ¼ teaspoon salt
    ⅛ teaspoon paprika
Stir in slowly and heat to the boiling point:
    1 cup rich milk
    1 cup stock or vegetable water
Add and heat to the boiling point:
    ¾ to 1 cup cooked minced or sieved vegetables
Season the soup as desired.

CREAM OF TOMATO SOUP
About 5½ Cupfuls
Simmer covered for 15 minutes:
    2 cups canned or fresh cut-up tomatoes
    ½ cup chopped celery
    ¼ cup chopped onion
    2 teaspoons white or brown sugar
Melt in a double boiler:
    4 tablespoons butter
Add:
    4 tablespoons flour
Scald and add:
    4 cups milk or milk and cream
Strain into this the tomato and vegetable stock. Season it with:
    1 teaspoon salt
    ⅛ teaspoon paprika
Place the soup over hot water for 15 minutes before serving it. Serve it with:
    Croutons
    Chopped parsley

Potato Soup with Tomatoes, page 58.

CREAM OF CORN SOUP
About 5 Cupfuls
Put through a food mill or coarse sieve:

    2½ cups cream-style canned corn or
    2½ cups corn cut from the ear,
      simmered until tender in 1 cup milk.
Melt:
    3 tablespoons butter
Simmer in it until soft:
    ½ medium-sized sliced onion
Stir in:
    3 tablespoons flour
    1½ teaspoons salt
    A few grains freshly ground pepper
    (A grating of nutmeg)
Stir in the corn and:
    3 cups milk or 2½ cups milk and
    ½ cup cream
Serve the soup sprinkled with:
    3 tablespoons chopped parsley or chives

CREAM OF ASPARAGUS SOUP
About 6 Cupfuls
Wash and remove the tips from:
    2 bunches of fresh green asparagus
Simmer the tips covered until they are tender in a small amount of:
    Milk or water
Cut the stalks into pieces and place them in a saucepan. Add:
    6 cups Stock, page 44
    ¼ cup chopped onion
    ½ cup chopped celery
Simmer these ingredients covered for ½ hour. Rub them through a sieve. Melt:
    3 tablespoons butter
Stir in until blended:
    3 tablespoons flour
Stir in slowly:
    ½ cup cream
Add the asparagus stock. Heat the soup in a double boiler. When it is hot add the asparagus tips. Season the soup immediately before serving it with:
    Salt and paprika
    White pepper
Garnish it, if you wish, with a diced hard-cooked egg.

CREAM OF CAULIFLOWER SOUP

About 6 Cupfuls
Cut into flowerets, then cook by the rule on page 280:

    1 large cauliflower

Drain it, reserving the water.
Reserve about ⅓ of the flowerets. Put the remainder through a food mill, blender or sieve. Melt:

    4 tablespoons butter

Sauté in it until tender:

    2 tablespoons chopped onion
    3 minced celery ribs

Stir in:

    4 tablespoons flour

Stir in slowly and bring to the boiling point:

    4 cups Chicken or Veal Stock, page 43

Add the strained cauliflower and:

    2 cups scalded rich milk or cream

Add the flowerets and:

    A grating of nutmeg
    Salt and paprika

The soup may be garnished with grated cheese.

CREAM OF GREEN PEA AND CHICKEN SOUP

About 4 Cupfuls
Pour:

    ½ cup boiling water

over:

    1½ cups green peas
    A slice of onion

Cook them until they are very tender. Put them through a fine strainer, food mill or blender. Melt:

    1 tablespoon butter

Stir in:

    1 tablespoon flour

Stir in the pea purée and:

    1 cup strong chicken broth or consommé

Permit the soup to boil. Add:

    2½ cups rich milk or thin cream

Reheat the soup but do not let it boil. Add as needed:

    Salt and paprika

Serve the soup hot or chilled, sprinkled with:

    Chopped basil, chives or parsley

Blender Cream Soups, page 896.

CREAM OF SPINACH SOUP

About 5 Cupfuls
Pick over and wash:

    2 lbs. spinach or two 14 oz. packages frozen spinach

Place it while moist or frozen in a covered saucepan. Cook it for 6 minutes. Drain it. Put it through a strainer or blender.
Melt in a saucepan:

    2 tablespoons butter

Add and sauté for 3 minutes:

    1 tablespoon grated onion, or 1 slice of onion which can be removed easily

Stir in and cook until blended:

    2 tablespoons flour

Stir in gradually:

    4 cups milk, Chicken or other Stock, pages 43, 44, alone or in combination

Season the soup with:

    ¾ teaspoon or more salt
    ¼ teaspoon paprika
    (A grating of nutmeg)

Add the spinach. Heat the soup well.
Serve it sprinkled with:

    (Grated cheese)

CREAM OF CELERY SOUP

About 4 Cupfuls
Melt:

    1 tablespoon butter

Add and sauté for 2 minutes:

    1 cup or more chopped celery with leaves
    (⅓ cup sliced onion)

Add and simmer for 10 minutes:

    2 cups Stock, page 44

Strain the soup. Add and bring to the boiling point:

    1½ cups milk

Dissolve:

    1½ tablespoons cornstarch

in:

    ½ cup milk

Stir these ingredients gradually into the hot soup. Bring it to the boiling point. Stir and cook it for 1 minute. You may add a grating of nutmeg.
Serve it with:

    (2 tablespoons chopped parsley)

POTATO SOUP

About 3 Cupfuls
As old-fashioned as the song: "I Love To Hear My Grandfather Eat Soup."
Peel and slice:

    2 medium-sized potatoes

Skin and chop:

    2 medium-sized onions
    4 ribs celery

You may sauté these ingredients in 1½ tablespoonfuls of butter. Add:

    Boiling water to cover them
    ½ teaspoon salt
    (½ bay leaf)

Boil the vegetables until the potatoes are tender. Put them through a ricer or blender. Beat into them:

2 tablespoons butter

Thin the soup to the desired consistency with:

Rich milk or Chicken Stock, page 43, or both

Add if required:

Salt and paprika
A dash Worcestershire sauce

Serve the soup with:

Chopped parsley, chives or water cress
Sliced frankfurters or 1 cup chopped cooked shrimp

POTATO SOUP WITH TOMATOES
About 6½ Cupfuls
A more sophisticated version of the above recipe for Potato Soup.
Prepare:

2 cups sliced onions

Cook them very gently in:

¼ cup butter

Stir them, cover them, then simmer them for about ½ hour. Add and simmer covered for 20 minutes:

5 cups sliced tomatoes or 3 cups canned tomatoes
2 teaspoons sugar
1 teaspoon salt
⅛ teaspoon paprika
A pinch of chervil

Add:

2 cups sliced potatoes
6 cups boiling water

Simmer the soup covered until the potatoes are very tender. Put it through a fine strainer or blender. Reheat it and add seasoning if required. Scald and stir in:

1 cup cream

Serve the soup at once.

FRENCH LEEK AND POTATO SOUP
Follow the rule on page 64 for Vichyssoise. Substitute water for stock and milk for cream.

COCK-A-LEEKIE
5 to 6 Cupfuls
Old recipes for this leek, chicken and cream soup start with a fowl or cock to be simmered in strong stock, and wind up with the addition of prunes. The following version is delicious, if not traditional. Remove the dark green part of the tops and roots from:

6 leeks

Wash them carefully—they may be sandy. Cut them in half lengthwise. Cut them crosswise in ⅛ inch slices. There should be about 4 cupfuls. Place them in a pan with:

3 cups boiling water
1½ teaspoons salt

Simmer them from 5 to 7 minutes or until they are tender but not mushy. Add and heat to a boil:

2 tablespoons chicken fat or butter
1½ cups well-seasoned strong chicken broth

Scald and stir in:

½ cup cream
Salt as needed

Serve the soup at once.

DUCHESS SOUP
About 4 Cupfuls
A rich cream soup with egg yolks, lightly flavored with cheese. Melt:

1 tablespoon butter

Sauté in it for about 8 minutes over low heat:

¼ cup finely chopped onion

Do not permit the onion to brown. Stir in until blended:

1 tablespoon flour

Stir in slowly:

3 cups milk

Cook these ingredients until the onion is soft. Put them through a strainer. Shortly before serving the soup combine and beat:

2 tablespoons grated cheese
2 egg yolks
¾ cup cream

Add these ingredients to the hot soup. Stir and heat it for 2 minutes, but do not permit it to boil. Season it with:

¾ teaspoon salt
¼ teaspoon paprika
A few grains of cayenne
(A few grains of celery salt)

CHEESE SOUP
About 3 Cupfuls
Sauté for 3 minutes:

2 tablespoons chopped onion

in:

1 tablespoon butter

Stir in until blended:

1 tablespoon flour

Stir in slowly:

¾ cup Stock, page 44

When the sauce is smooth and boiling add:

2 cups milk

Heat the soup, but do not let it boil.
Add and stir until melted:
    ¾ cup grated American cheese
Season the soup with:
    Salt and paprika

CREAM OF CHICKEN SOUP
About 4½ Cupfuls
Simmer:
    3 cups Chicken Stock, page 43
    ½ cup finely chopped celery
When the celery is tender, add and
cook for 5 minutes:
    ½ cup cooked rice
Add:
    ½ cup hot cream
    1 tablespoon chopped parsley
    Salt and paprika
Do not boil the soup after adding the
cream. Or in place of the rice melt:
    2 tablespoons butter
    2 tablespoons flour
Stir in the soup slowly. When it is
boiling, season it and add the hot
cream and parsley as directed.

CHICKEN BISQUE
About 5 Cupfuls
Melt:
    2 tablespoons butter
Add, cook and stir until blended:
    2 tablespoons flour
Add, cook and stir until boiling:
    3 cups Chicken Stock, page 43
    1 cup ground cooked chicken
Scald and add:
    1 cup rich milk
Season the bisque with:
    Salt, if required, and paprika
Serve it with:
    Chopped parsley
    (Whipped cream)

CREAM OF ALMOND SOUP
About 4 Cupfuls
Melt:
    1 tablespoon butter
Stir in until blended:
    1 tablespoon flour
Stir in slowly, then stir and cook for
2 minutes:
    2 cups Chicken or Veal Stock,
        page 43
    ¾ cup ground blanched almonds
Add but do not boil:
    2 cups hot cream
    Salt and paprika
    Grated lemon rind

CREAM OF MUSHROOM SOUP
About 4½ Cupfuls
Prepare for cooking:

    ½ lb. mushrooms with stems
The flavor of the mushrooms and other
vegetables is improved when they are
sautéed lightly in 2 tablespoonfuls of
butter before simmering. Add and
simmer covered for 20 minutes:
    2 cups water or Stock, preferably
        chicken, pages 43, 47
    ½ cup chopped tender celery
    ¼ cup sliced onion
    ⅛ cup shredded parsley
    (⅛ cup diced carrots)
If carrots are used, tie them in a bag.
Discard them before grinding the vegetables as they are apt to make the
soup too sweet. Drain the vegetables,
reserving the stock. Blend them or put
them through a food chopper, using
the finest knife. Melt:
    2 tablespoons butter
Add and stir until smooth:
    2 tablespoons flour
Combine the vegetable stock with:
    2 cups top milk or cream
Pour these liquids slowly onto the
butter mixture, cook and stir them
until the soup boils. Add the ground
vegetables. Season the soup with:
    1¼ teaspoons salt
    ⅛ teaspoon paprika
    (⅛ teaspoon nutmeg)
    (2 tablespoons sherry)
Serve it topped with:
    (Whipped cream)
Garnish it with:
    Paprika
    Sprigs of parsley or chopped
        chives

CREAM OF ONION SOUP
About 4 Cupfuls
Melt:
    3 tablespoons butter
Add and sauté till a golden brown:
    1½ cups thinly sliced onions
Stir in:
    1 tablespoon flour
    ½ teaspoon salt
Add:
    4 cups milk or milk and Stock,
        page 44
Simmer the soup covered until the
onions are very tender. Season it with:
    Salt and paprika
    Freshly grated nutmeg or
    (Worcestershire sauce)
Place in each cup:
    1 tablespoon grated cheese
    1 teaspoon chopped parsley
Pour the hot soup over them.

*Onion Soup, page 52; Canned Consom-
mé into Cream Soup, page 69.*

SALMON BISQUE
About 8 Cupfuls
Place in a saucepan the contents of a:
    1 lb. can of pink salmon, oil
      included
Add:
    1 cup canned tomatoes, or 2 large
      skinned tomatoes
    1/3 cup chopped onion
    2 tablespoons chopped parsley or
      celery leaves
    2 cups water
Simmer these ingredients for 20 minutes. Melt:
    4 tablespoons butter
Stir in until blended:
    4 tablespoons flour
Stir in slowly:
    3 cups milk
Add:
    1½ teaspoons salt
    ½ teaspoon paprika
When the sauce is smooth and boiling,
stir in the salmon mixture slowly. Do
not permit the bisque to boil. Serve it
at once. Serve the soup with a green
salad and waffles.

Quick Crab or Lobster Bisque, page 67.

LOBSTER BISQUE
About 6 Cupfuls
Remove the meat from:
    2 medium-sized boiled lobsters
Dice the body meat, mince the tail and
claw meat. Crush the shells. Add to
them the tough end of the claws and:
    2½ cups water or Chicken Stock,
      page 47
    1 sliced onion
    4 ribs celery with leaves
    2 whole cloves
    1 bay leaf
    6 peppercorns
Simmer these ingredients for ½ hour.
If you have used water, add:
    2 chicken bouillon or vegetable
      cubes
Strain the stock. Melt:
    4 tablespoons butter
Stir in:
    4 tablespoons flour
Add gradually:
    3 cups milk
Season with:
    1 teaspoon salt
    ¼ teaspoon nutmeg
If there is coral roe force it through
a fine sieve, combine it with the butter
in a mortar or bowl, add the flour and
when well blended pour the milk
(heated) slowly upon it stirring until
the mixture is smooth.

When the sauce is smooth and boiling,
add the lobster and the stock. Simmer
the bisque covered for 5 minutes. Turn
off the heat. Stir in:
    1 cup scalded cream
Serve at once with:
    Minced parsley
    Paprika

SHRIMP BISQUE
About 5 Cupfuls
Remove shells and intestines from:
    1½ lbs. Boiled Shrimp, page 245
Put the shrimp through a meat grinder
or blender. Cook covered in the top of
a double boiler for 5 minutes:
    6 tablespoons butter
    2 tablespoons grated onion
Add the ground shrimp and:
    3 cups warm milk
Cook for 2 minutes. Stir in slowly,
heat but do not boil:
    1 cup cream
Add:
    Salt, if needed, paprika or
      freshly ground pepper
    A grating of nutmeg
    3 tablespoons sherry
    2 tablespoons parsley or chives
Serve at once.

MUSHROOM AND CLAM BISQUE
About 4 Cupfuls
Chop until fine:
    ½ lb. mushrooms
Sauté them by the rule on page 292 in:
    2 tablespoons butter
Stir in:
    2 tablespoons flour
Stir in slowly:
    2½ cups clam broth
Simmer these ingredients for 5 minutes. Remove them from the fire. Heat
but do not boil:
    ¾ cup cream
Add the cream to the other ingredients. Season the broth with:
    Paprika and salt if needed
Serve it with:
    Chopped parsley or chives

BOUILLABAISSE
About 8 Cupfuls
A fish and soup dish. The fish and the
soup are served separately but eaten
at the same time. Toast is placed in
individual bowls, fish is added and the
soup ladled over it. The toast may be
omitted and crackers served with the
bouillabaisse. Ingredients for this dish

vary greatly but the basic rule is the same. It calls for vegetables of the onion family sautéed in oil or butter; to these are added tomatoes, stock, seasonings, one or more kinds of fish and one or more kinds of shellfish. This is a case of the more the merrier. Except in the case of oysters it is usual to precook the shellfish. After a brief simmering, wine and chopped parsley complete the dish.
Remove the meat from:
>½ lb. Boiled Shrimp, page 245
>1 small Boiled Lobster, page 247

You may add to the fish:
>½ lb. sliced raw mushrooms

Cut into 2 or 3 inch pieces:
>2 or 3 lbs. fish fillets

Sauté until soft:
>¾ cup sliced onions
>2 sliced leeks
>1 minced clove garlic

in:
>½ cup olive oil

Add:
>¾ cup cooked strained tomatoes
>4 cups Fish Stock, page 230
>1 bay leaf
>4 peppercorns
>A pinch of saffron
>2 cloves
>A small slice of lemon rind
>1 teaspoon salt

Simmer these ingredients covered for ½ hour. Add the fish and mushrooms. Simmer them for 10 minutes. Add the shellfish and:
>(2 dozen oysters)

Simmer them for 5 minutes. Add:
>½ cup or more dry white wine
>Salt as needed

Have ready two hot dishes. Strain the soup into one, place the fish in the other. Sprinkle the fish with:
>2 tablespoons chopped parsley

LOBSTER STEW
About 5 Cupfuls
Sauté for 3 or 4 minutes:
>1 cup diced fresh lobster meat

in:
>3 tablespoons butter

Add slowly:
>4 cups scalded milk with a slice of onion

Season the stew with:
>1 teaspoon salt
>⅛ teaspoon paprika

A Maine correspondent writes that this stew is much improved by the addition, at this time, of ½ to 1 cupful clam broth. If you add the broth, omit

the salt until you find you need it. Add:
>2 tablespoons chopped parsley or
>1 teaspoon dried basil or tarragon

CLAM CHOWDER
About 8 Cupfuls
Prepare:
>1 quart shucked clams

Wash them in:
>3 cups water

Drain the clams, reserving the water. Strain the liquid. If using hard-shelled clams, cut the hard part from the soft part. Chop finely:
>The hard part of the clams
>A 2 inch cube of salt pork or 3 slices of bacon
>1 large onion

Sauté the pork very slowly. Remove and reserve the scraps. Add the minced onions and hard part of the clams to the grease. Stir and cook them slowly for about 5 minutes. Sift over them and stir until blended:
>3 tablespoons flour

Heat and stir in the reserved liquid. Peel, prepare and add:
>2 cups raw potatoes cut into ½ inch dice

Cover the pan and simmer the chowder until the potatoes are done but still firm. Add the pork scraps, the soft part of the clams and:
>3 tablespoons butter

Simmer the chowder for 3 minutes. Heat to the boiling point:
>4 cups milk

Place the chowder in a hot tureen. Pour the milk over it. Season it with:
>Salt and freshly ground pepper

Serve it at once with:
>Pilot biscuit or crackers

Eight of these crackers may be soaked in milk to moisten and added to the chowder.
You may substitute for the fresh clams the contents of:
>1 No. 2 can minced clams

Strain the juice. Add water to make 3 cupfuls of liquid. Use this liquid in place of the water measurement given above.

MANHATTAN CLAM CHOWDER
Most New Englanders consider this an illegitimate child. Follow the above recipe for:
>Clam Chowder

Omit the milk. Add to the chowder with the potatoes:
>3 cups cooked or canned tomatoes

FISH CHOWDER
About 5 Cupfuls
Bone:
    1 lb. haddock or other fish
Place it in a saucepan. Add:
    1 cup cold water
Simmer it for 10 minutes. Remove the fish and skin it. Replace the fish in the water. Try out very slowly:
    ¼ cup diced salt pork
Place it in a saucepan. Add to it and cook covered for 10 minutes:
    2 cups peeled, thinly sliced
        potatoes
    3 tablespoons chopped onion
    ½ cup water
Add the fish and the fish stock and simmer the chowder for 5 minutes. Add and bring to the boiling point:
    3 cups milk
Add just before serving:
    1 tablespoon butter
    Salt and paprika
This may be made in advance and reheated over hot water or a low flame, provided you do not permit the chowder to boil.

QUICK MANHATTAN FISH CHOWDER
About 5 Cupfuls
Heat:
    2 tablespoons salad oil
Sauté in it for 3 minutes:
    1 raw potato, pared and cut into
        ½ inch cubes
    2 tablespoons minced onion
    1 cup diced celery
Add:
    1⅓ cups tomatoes
    2½ cups stock or water
    ½ teaspoon sugar
    ½ teaspoon salt
    ½ teaspoon paprika
    (¼ teaspoon curry powder)
Simmer these ingredients for 15 minutes. Add:
    1 cup cooked or canned flaked
        fish: tuna, fish flakes, etc.
Heat the soup and serve it with:
    Grated Parmesan cheese

CRAWFISH BISQUE
About 4 Cupfuls
Wash and scrub with a brush under running water:
    3 dozen crawfish
Soak them for 30 minutes in salted water, 1 tablespoonful salt to 4 cupfuls of water. Rinse them thoroughly. Place them in a saucepan with:
    6 cups boiling water

    A few grains of cayenne
    ½ teaspoon salt
Bring them to a boil then simmer them for 15 minutes. Drain them, reserving the stock. To clean them, see page 246. Pick the meat from the heads and tails of the crawfish. Set aside 18 of the heads to be stuffed as a garnish for the bisque. Return all remaining shells to the stock. Bring it to a boil. Add:
    4 ribs chopped celery
    2 tablespoons chopped parsley
    ½ diced carrot
    ⅛ teaspoon thyme or a sprig of
        fresh thyme
Simmer these ingredients for 30 minutes. Strain the stock. Meanwhile prepare the stuffing for the heads. Mince the crawfish meat. Sauté until lightly browned:
    2 tablespoons minced onion
in:
    2 tablespoons butter
Add and simmer for 3 minutes:
    2 tablespoons finely minced celery
    1 tablespoon finely minced parsley
Remove from the fire and add ½ the crawfish meat and:
    ½ cup bread crumbs
Beat and add:
    1 egg
    Salt as required and paprika
Stir lightly with a fork. Stuff the heads with this mixture. Place them on a greased shallow pan. Dot each head with butter. For 10 minutes before serving the soup, bake the heads in a hot 425° oven. Melt:
    2 tablespoons butter
Sauté in it until delicately browned:
    1 minced onion
Add and stir until lightly browned:
    2 tablespoons flour
Add the fish stock slowly while stirring and boiling until smooth. Add the remaining crawfish meat and:
    Salt and paprika
Simmer the bisque for 5 minutes, stirring it often. To serve, place the heated heads in hot soup plates, then pour the bisque over them.

OYSTER STEWS
Here are 3 good recipes for oyster soup, which are like the little bear, the big bear and the great big bear in nutritive value and effort.
The first calls for milk and is unthickened; the second for milk and flour; and the third for milk, cream, flour and egg yolks.
To clean oysters, see page 250.

OYSTER STEW WITH VARIATIONS
About 4 Cupfuls
This is foolproof, as the use of a double boiler prevents overcooking of the oysters. Combine in the top of a double boiler:

    2 to 4 tablespoons butter
    1 pint oysters with liquor
    1½ cups milk
    ½ cup cream
    ½ teaspoon salt
    ⅛ teaspoon pepper or paprika

Place the pan over, not in, boiling water. When the butter is melted, the milk hot and the oysters float, add:

    2 tablespoons chopped parsley

and serve the soup.
As variations add to the stew:

    ½ teaspoon or more grated onion
    or leek, or a sliver of garlic

Or, add to the stew for the last ½ minute:

    ½ cup dry white wine

OYSTER STEW
About 6 Cupfuls
Heat well in a double boiler:

    2 tablespoons butter
    1 pint oysters with liquor

Combine and scald in a saucepan:

    3½ cups milk
    2 tablespoons butter
    1 teaspoon salt
    ⅛ teaspoon pepper

Stir and blend well in a cup:

    ½ cup milk
    1½ tablespoons flour

Add these ingredients to the scalded milk, stir and boil it until it thickens and pour it over the hot oysters. Place the stew over, not in, hot water for 15 minutes before serving it.

OYSTER BISQUE
About 5 Cupfuls
Heat well but do not boil:

    1 pint oysters

Drain them, reserving the liquor, and put them through a meat grinder or chop them until they are fine. Melt in a saucepan:

    2 tablespoons butter

You may sauté lightly in this:

    1 tablespoon grated onion

Add, cook and stir until smooth:

    1½ tablespoons flour

Add and stir:

    The oyster liquor
    2½ cups milk
    ½ cup cream
    1 teaspoon salt
    ½ teaspoon paprika or a few grains
    of cayenne
    (⅛ teaspoon nutmeg)

When these ingredients are smooth and boiling add the ground oysters. Remove the bisque from the fire. Combine and beat:

    2 egg yolks
    2 tablespoons water

Add them slowly to the hot bisque. Reduce the heat, stir and cook the bisque very slowly for 1 minute, or place it over, not in, hot water until ready to serve. Sprinkle it with:

    3 tablespoons chopped parsley

If there is little oyster liquor it may be necessary to thin the bisque with hot milk.

Oyster Celery, page 116.

Chilled Soups

There is nothing more refreshing and satisfying than a chilled soup on a hot day. Except for the jellied soups, the cold soups that follow have heft and lots of vitamins and calories. You don't need to add many other dishes. Let's say:

1. Vichyssoise, French Bread or Toasted Bread Loaf, page 76, a fruit salad or fruit dessert, strong hot coffee.
2. Cold Borsch, hot biscuits—unusual Russian- U. S. harmony there—a cheese soufflé, green peas, coffee, possibly a fruit cookie, or
3. A quickie for effort—Madrilène with Sour Cream and Herbs, a toasted ham and cress sandwich, fresh pineapple sliced, laced with rum or something similar, and so on and on.

Cold soups can be prepared quickly in the blender, page 896, and chilled rapidly in the deep freeze or refrigerator. If chilled in a tall jug or cookie jar they may be served directly from it for informal occasions.

At the end of the Canned Soup section, page 71, you will find: Tropical Consommé, Madrilène with Cheese, Madrilène and Tomato Juice, Madrilène with Sour Cream and Herbs. See Hot Weather Menus, page 915.

VICHYSSOISE OR FRENCH POTATO SOUP
About 6 Cupfuls

Yes, the last S **is** pronounced. Most Americans shun it in a "genteel" way as though it were virtuous to ignore it. In fact, they correct me diffidently, still liking me, in spite of my apparent crudeness of speech. Who started this nonsense? Be sure to serve the soup reduced to a velvety smoothness. If you like, do as the Joneses do in regard to the last S, that unfortunately may pass unnoticed, but ostracism should come in the wake of the tiniest ignoble lump left to mar the dish. This soup is served hot or very cold.
Mince the white part of:

3 medium-sized leeks or 8 green onions
1 medium-sized onion

If leeks and green onions are not available use two onions.
Stir and sauté them for 3 minutes in:

2 tablespoons butter

Peel, slice very fine and add:

4 medium-sized potatoes

Add:

4 cups chicken consommé

Simmer the vegetables covered for 15 minutes or until tender. Put them through a very fine sieve, food mill or blender. Add:

1 or 2 cups cream
Salt and pepper
Chopped water cress or chives

See Blender Vichyssoise, page 896.

SPANISH SOUP OR GAZPACHO
About 6 Cupfuls

Another good summer soup—chilled vegetable soup with fresh herbs.
Peel and seed:

2 large ripe tomatoes

Seed and remove membrane from:

1 large sweet pepper

Peel:

1 clove garlic

Wash:

½ cup or more fresh mixed herbs: chives, parsley, basil, chervil, tarragon, etc.

Place all ingredients in a chopping bowl. Chop them. Stir in gradually:

½ cup olive oil
3 tablespoons lemon or lime juice
3 cups chilled water or light stock

Add:

1 peeled thinly sliced mild onion

1 cup peeled, seeded diced or grated cucumber
1½ teaspoons salt or more if needed
½ teaspoon paprika

Place the soup in individual bowls. Sprinkle the tops with:

½ cup dry bread crumbs

Chill the soup for 4 hours or more.

CHILLED CREAM OF CUCUMBER HERB SOUP
6 Cupfuls

Pare, then slice:

2 medium-sized cucumbers

Add to them:

1 cup water
2 slices onion
¼ teaspoon salt
⅛ teaspoon white pepper

Cook the cucumbers covered until very soft. Put them through a fine strainer or an electric blender. Stir until smooth:

4 tablespoons flour
½ cup chicken stock

Stir in:

1½ cups chicken stock

Add the cucumber purée and:

½ bay leaf or 2 cloves

Stir the soup over heat, boil it for 2 minutes. Chill it in a covered jar. Add to it:

¾ cup chilled cream
Seasoning if required
1 tablespoon finely chopped dill, chives or other herb

Serve the soup very cold.

COLD CUCUMBER SOUP
5 Cupfuls

Peel, seed and dice:

2 small cucumbers

Add:

4 cups chicken stock

Cook these ingredients until the cucumber is soft. Cool them slightly. Put them through a food mill or blender with:

1 cup sour cream

Season with:

Grated lemon rind
Salt and pepper as needed

Chill thoroughly. Serve sprinkled with chives.

CHILLED CREAM OF TOMATO SOUP
Follow the rule on page 56 for:

Cream of Tomato Soup

Chill it thoroughly. You may garnish it with:

Chopped chives
Whipped cream and paprika

CHILLED CREAM OF AVOCADO SOUP
6 Servings
Combine and stir until smooth:
4 tablespoons flour
4 tablespoons chicken stock
Stir this into:
4 cups chicken stock
Stir the mixture until it boils.
Peel, remove seed and purée:
2 medium-sized avocados
Add them to the stock. Chill the soup.
When ready to serve stir in:
½ cup chilled cream
⅛ teaspoon white pepper
Serve in cups sprinkled with:
1 teaspoon dill or orégano seed, chopped chives or other herb

CHILLED SPINACH SOUP
About 4 Cupfuls
See Blender Cream Soups, page 896.
Pick over and wash:
1 lb. spinach or one 14 oz. package frozen spinach defrosted
Place it while moist in a covered saucepan. Cook it until it is just tender—about 6 minutes. Drain it. Put it through a strainer, blender or food mill. Add:
3 cups spinach water and stock
Bring the spinach to the boiling point.
Remove it from the fire and add:
1½ tablespoons lemon juice
Chill it thoroughly. Chill and combine:
½ cup sour cream
1 small diced cucumber
1 tablespoon minced scallions or onion
Stir the spinach mixture into the sour-cream mixture. Season the soup with:
Salt and freshly ground pepper.
Serve the soup very cold.

JELLIED SOUPS
Stock made from a veal knuckle bone and a beef bone which jells readily by itself is the best base for jellied soups. To jell other stock use gelatine, see rule for Soup Stock I and II, pages 43 and 44. Allow about 2 tablespoonfuls of gelatine to 4 cupfuls of liquid. Flavor the soup with lemon, vinegar or cooking sherry. Season it well and serve it very cold. See Aspic Salad, page 475.

QUICK JELLIED CONSOMMÉ OR SOUP
I.
A flavored gelatine preparation for jellied soup may be purchased ready to be dissolved and chilled.

II.
Canned jellied consommé of different kinds may be purchased and need only be placed in a refrigerator for about 4 hours to be set sufficiently for use. Full instructions are given on the label of the can. It is wise to keep some of this in the refrigerator ready at all times. This jelly is fine for soup but not quite firm enough for an aspic.

III.
Soak ½ tablespoonful gelatine in ½ cupful Stock, page 44. Dissolve it in 1½ cupfuls hot stock. Flavor it with Worcestershire sauce, lemon juice or sherry. Season it well. Chill it and you have enough jellied soup for 4 small servings. Serve it very cold in cups with wedges of lemon and sprigs of parsley.
Remember that left-over liquid in which vegetables have been cooked, or liquor from canned vegetables, plus a bouillon cube or two, will make a palatable basis for consommé or aspic.
To chill a soup quickly place the dish containing it in a bowl of ice water or cracked ice or in the freezer for a few minutes.

JELLIED TOMATO BOUILLON
8 Cupfuls
Soak for 5 minutes:
2 tablespoons gelatine
in:
½ cup cold water
Heat to the boiling point:
2 cups strained tomato juice
½ teaspoon grated onion
2 cups clear Stock, page 44
A piece of lemon rind
Salt and pepper
Dissolve the gelatine in the hot stock. Cool it. Flavor it with:
Lemon juice, sherry or Worcestershire sauce
Strain the stock and pour it into a wet mold. Chill it. The bouillon may be beaten slightly before it is served. The top may be garnished with:
Lemon slices, chopped chives, mint, nasturtium leaves, parsley or water cress, chopped olives, hard-cooked eggs riced, catsup, relish or horseradish

JELLIED CONSOMMÉ OR CHICKEN CONSOMMÉ
Follow the rule on page 65 for Jellied Tomato Bouillon. Use 4 cupfuls in all of beef or chicken broth in place of the tomato juice and stock.

See *Madrilène with Cheese, page 71.*

Canned and Quick Soup Suggestions

Canned soups are a boon to any housekeeper. If there are women who fail to keep them on hand they are working to their own disadvantage. It would be a mistake, and false economy, to eliminate homemade soup from our menus and to choose only the modern, easier way of preparing soups, gravies and creamed dishes, but it would be equally unfortunate to deny the usefulness of the canned product. As a timesaver canned soups stand supreme. They may be combined in many interesting ways.

Pressure Cooker and Blender Soups, see pages 878, 895, homemade stock and vegetable waters in which vegetables have been cooked, may be added to them. This includes the liquor from canned vegetables and from canned sea food—the latter must be used sparingly because it is apt to be salty. Waste nothing that can possibly be used. Store all juices suitable for soups and gravies including the water in which sweetbreads, fish, etc., have been cooked, and stock—see Soup Stock II, page 44—in tightly closed glass containers in the refrigerator ready for use. See also Stock Substitutes, page 43, and Stock for Sauces, page 425. For unusual seasonings and additions to soups see pages 41 and 42.

Remember, please, that some soups do not call for dilution. They are ready to be heated and served as they are. Be sure to watch this. These diluted soups may be used, without the addition of milk, water or other liquid, in all the combinations suggested in this chapter for condensed soups.

When combining a thick condensed soup with a thinner liquid good results are obtained by stirring the second slowly into the first. Do this over low heat. The quickest and easiest way to combine the two is to use a blender or a wire stirrer, usually called a spiral egg beater, see page 424. This little implement is ideal for sauces and other food inclined to lump and be troublesome. Canned soups are good bases for quick sauces and gravies, see page 441.

In the following chapter you will find many good rules in which canned soups are combined—space alone prevents the listing of more—but you are urged to try out combinations of your own.

In a recent flood disaster a social worker was interrogating an applicant for assistance. In answer to the question, "How many children have you?" the woman replied proudly, "Well, ma'am, it was thissaway. I had two by my first husband and three by my second husband and one all by myself."

Canned Scotch Purée, page 68, is *my* baby. See what you can produce.

Canned Mongole Soup by an unknown author, a wonderful combination, swept the country some years ago. New and tempting combinations will vary your menus especially if you dilute the canned product with stock of your own making, thereby avoiding the otherwise inevitably familiar and easily detected "boughten" quality.

The word "can" may be confusing as cans of ready-to-serve soup contain varying amounts. The usual can of condensed soup contains 10½ ounces, though smaller cans of some soups are available. It is advisable to read the label on a can of soup with which you are unfamiliar. See the Soup Chapter, page 40, for other quick vegetable and fish soups.

CANNED TOMATO SOUP
About 3 Cupfuls
Heat and stir but do not boil the contents of:
 1 can condensed tomato soup:
  10½ oz.

Add:
  An equal amount of milk or ½ fresh and ½ evaporated milk
  ½ teaspoon salt
Heat cups or bowls. You may place in each one:

A very thin slice of cheese

Pour the soup into the cups. Serve it at once. To reheat or to keep the soup hot use a double boiler.

You may use ¼ to 1 teaspoonful curry powder or ¾ teaspoonful anchovy paste, ½ teaspoonful dried herbs or 2 tablespoonfuls minced chives.

Chilled Tomato Cream Soup, page 64.

CANNED TOMATO CELERY SOUP
About 5 Cupfuls

Stir and heat the contents of:
> 1 can condensed tomato soup: 10½ oz.
> 1 can condensed celery soup: 10½ oz.
> 2⅓ cups rich milk or stock or a mixture of both

Heat the soup but do not permit it to boil. Add:
> 1 tablespoon chopped parsley or chives

Serve it with:
> Hot cheese crackers

CANNED TOMATO BEAN SOUP
About 5 Cupfuls

Mince, then sauté lightly:
> 1 slice bacon

Add and cook until light brown:
> ½ cup sliced onions
> ¼ cup sliced celery

Add the contents of:
> 1 can condensed tomato soup: 10½ oz.
> 1 can condensed bean soup: 10½ oz.

and:
> 2⅓ cups water

Heat the soup. Serve it with:
> Croutons

CANNED TOMATO CONSOMMÉ
About 3 Cupfuls

Combine the contents of:
> 1 can condensed consommé: 10½ oz.

And:
> 1¾ cups tomato juice

Heat these ingredients. Serve the consommé in cups topped with:
> 1 teaspoon whipped cream

Garnish the cream with:
> Paprika
> A sprig of parsley

CANNED MONGOLE SOUP
About 5 Cupfuls

I should like to sing a paean of praise about this and the following soups made with a basis of pea and tomato. If there is anything better in the hurry-up culinary art I don't know what it is. Rich? Yes, but you may plan to serve simple food afterward. This is worth adding a fraction of a pound to your avoirdupois. Only don't fall in love with it and serve it too often.

Combine and stir the contents of:
> 1 can condensed tomato soup: 10½ oz.
> 1 can condensed pea soup: 10½ oz.

Add:
> 1 cup Stock, page 44
> 1 cup cream

Heat these ingredients well. Flavor them if needed with:
> Salt and paprika

Add to each portion:
> (1 tablespoon sherry)

Serve the soup sprinkled with:
> (¼ cup grated cheese)

QUICK CRAB OR LOBSTER BISQUE
About 4 Cupfuls

So good that it must be tried. I defy you to eat it without making a noise! Soak for 5 minutes:
> 1 cup more or less flaked canned crab or lobster

in:
> 3 tablespoons sherry or 1 teaspoon Worcestershire sauce

Combine and heat to the boiling point the contents of:
> 1 can condensed tomato soup: 10½ oz.
> 1 can condensed pea soup: 10½ oz.

Stir in slowly:
> 1¼ cups rich hot milk or part cream and bouillon

Add the crab. Heat the soup but do not permit it to boil.

Crab Meat with Piquant Sauce, page 124.

LOBSTER SUPRÉME
About 5 Cupfuls

Combine the contents of:
> 1 can condensed asparagus soup: 10½ oz.
> 1 can condensed mushroom soup: 10½ oz.

Add:
>2 cups light cream

Pick over and add:
>6 to 8 ozs. canned lobster meat

Heat this soup but do not permit it to boil. Add:
>3 tablespoons sherry

CANNED SOUP WITH NOODLES
About 6 Cupfuls

Combine and bring to the boiling point the contents of:
>1 can condensed consommé: 10½ oz.
>1 can condensed clear chicken soup: 10½ oz.
>1 can condensed pea soup: 10½ oz.

Add:
>1⅓ cups water or stock

Add:
>4 ozs. fine noodles
>1 tablespoon Worcestershire sauce
>1 tablespoon chili sauce

Simmer the soup covered until the noodles are done, for about 15 minutes.

CANNED GREEN TURTLE SOUP

This is usually ready to serve. If condensed, dilute the soup as directed.
Add to each serving:
>2 teaspoons sherry
>A thin slice of lemon
>Chopped parsley

ST. GERMAIN SOUP. Canned Pea Soup and Chicken Stock
About 4 Cupfuls

French has been called the language of the alimentary canal. This soup speaks wonderful French. Mince, then sauté slowly until light brown:
>(⅓ cup diced salt pork or ham)

Combine it with the contents of:
>1 can condensed clear chicken soup: 10½ oz.
>1 can condensed green pea soup: 10½ oz.

Add:
>1 cup water

Heat the soup to the boiling point. Serve it with:
>1 tablespoon chopped mint
>Croutons

CHEF'S PRIDE
8 Cupfuls

As this calls for a variety of soups it makes a large quantity. You may, of course, reduce the amounts. It needs no sales talk. It sells itself.
Combine and stir the contents of:
>1 can condensed mock turtle soup: 10½ oz.
>1 can condensed pea soup: 10½ oz.
>1 can condensed consommé: 10½ oz.

Add:
>2⅓ cups water or milk

Heat the soup. Season it if advisable. Serve it hot. Add to each portion:
>(1 tablespoon sherry)

Top each portion with:
>A dab of whipped or sour cream

Garnish the cream with:
>A small sprig of parsley

CANNED SCOTCH PURÉE.
Scotch Broth with Consommé
About 3 Cupfuls

An excellent result with little effort. Run through a food mill, blender or colander the contents of:
>1 can condensed Scotch Broth or Vegetable Soup: 10½ oz.

Add the contents of:
>1 can condensed consommé or strong stock: 10½ oz.
>⅔ cup water or rich milk
>1½ tablespoons catsup

Heat and serve.

CANNED CORN AND MUSHROOM SOUP
About 3 Cupfuls

A good main luncheon dish. Sauté until tender:
>½ cup sliced onion

in:
>2 tablespoons butter

Add them to the contents of:
>1 No. 1 can cream style corn
>1 can condensed mushroom soup: 10½ oz.
>⅔ cup milk or water

You may add:
>Drained, chopped sautéed bacon
>¼ teaspoon curry powder
>2 tablespoons chopped chives

QUICK TOMATO CORN CHOWDER
3 Cupfuls

Combine and heat but do not boil the contents of:
>1 can condensed tomato soup: 10½ oz.

An equal amount of milk
½ cup cream-style corn
¼ teaspoon curry powder
1 teaspoon sugar
¼ teaspoon salt

CANNED OXTAIL, CHICKEN AND CURRY SOUP
About 4 Cupfuls
Combine and heat in a double boiler the contents of:
1 can condensed oxtail soup: 10½ oz.
1 can condensed chicken soup: 10½ oz.
½ teaspoon curry powder
1 teaspoon Worcestershire sauce
1 cup cream
Strain the soup. Add when serving:
2 tablespoons sherry

ONION SOUP WITH CANNED CONSOMMÉ
Follow the rule for:
Onion Soup, page 52
Used canned consommé or bouillon.

CANNED SOUP WITH FARINA BALLS
About 3 Cupfuls
Heat about:
3 cups clear soup
This may be consommé or a combination of Vegetable Stock, page 45, and some other broth or meat cube concoction. Prepare by the rule on page 72:
Farina Balls
Make only ½ the amount given. Drop the batter into the simmering soup and cook it as directed.

CANNED CONSOMMÉ WITH SHERRY
A clear soup is supposed to be better than a clear conscience. Add to each portion of consommé, hot or cold:
1 tablespoon sherry
A good garnish is diced avocado.

CANNED CHICKEN AND CLAM BROTH
Heat equal parts of:
Chicken broth
Clam broth
To this you may add:
Dash of cream
Serve it with:
Chopped parsley or grated cheese
Do not permit soup to boil again.

CREAM OF CLAM SOUP
About 3 Cupfuls
Heat but do not boil:
1 cup clam juice or minced clams
Heat but do not boil:
1 cup cream
1 cup milk
Combine the liquids and add:
1 teaspoon butter
Seasoning
Garnish each cup of soup with:
1 tablespoon whipped cream
Paprika
A sprig parsley

CANNED CELERY, CONSOMMÉ AND CHEESE SOUP
About 4 Cupfuls
Combine and stir over slow heat the contents of:
1 can condensed celery soup: 10½ oz.
1 can condensed consommé: 10½ oz.
1¼ cups water or milk
½ cup grated cheddar or pimiento cheese
You may add:
1 tablespoon chopped onion
¼ teaspoon Worcestershire sauce
Stir the soup over low heat until the cheese is melted. Do not permit the soup to boil. Serve it with:
Chopped parsley

CANNED MULLIGATAWNEY SOUP
About 4 Cupfuls
Heat and stir but do not boil the contents of:
1 can condensed mulligatawny soup: 10½ oz.
Add:
An equal amount of Stock, page 44
No seasoning is required. These ingredients may be strained or put through a food mill or blender. To reheat or to keep the soup hot use a double boiler.

CANNED CONSOMMÉ CHANGED INTO CREAM SOUP
About 3 Cupfuls
Quickly made, delicious, delicately onion flavored. Place in a pan the contents of:
2 cans condensed consommé: 21 oz.
Add:
1 small grated or chopped apple
1 small grated or chopped onion

Cook these ingredients until the apple and onion are very tender. Put them through a strainer. Add:
  1 cup cream
Season the soup as desired with:
  Salt and paprika
  Curry powder
Reheat it but do not permit it to boil. An addition like the above of grated apple and onion to a canned soup does much to enliven it and give it a distinctive flavor.

QUICK CREAM OF CAULIFLOWER SOUP
About 3½ Cupfuls
Make this when you have a cupful, more or less, of left-over cauliflower on hand. Heat:
  2 tablespoons butter
Cook in the butter for 4 minutes:
  ¼ cup sliced onion
  2 small ribs minced celery with leaves
Strain the butter. Add to it:
  1½ cups chicken broth
  1 cup cooked or canned cauliflower, riced or mashed
Heat the soup to the boiling point. Heat, then add:
  1 cup rich milk
  Salt if needed
  ¼ teaspoon paprika
Do not permit the soup to boil after adding the milk. Serve it with:
  1 tablespoon chopped parsley
  A light grating of nutmeg

Canned Borsch, see Blender Borsch, page 896.

CANNED OXTAIL SOUP WITH WINE
About 2½ Cupfuls
Pare thinly (in several strips):
  The rind of 1 lemon
Add to it:
  1 cup water
and the contents of:
  1 can condensed oxtail soup: 10½ oz.
  Salt, if needed
  ¼ teaspoon paprika
  1 teaspoon grated onion
Simmer these ingredients for 5 minutes. Remove the lemon rind. Reduce the heat. Stir in:
  ½ cup claret or ¼ cup very dry sherry
  1 tablespoon minced parsley
Serve the soup at once with:
  Toasted crackers

QUICK OYSTER AND TOMATO SOUP
About 4 Servings
Combine the contents of:
  1 can condensed tomato soup: 10½ oz.
with:
  3 cups rich milk
  1½ teaspoons grated onion
  1 teaspoon salt
  (½ teaspoon curry powder or dried herb)
  (¼ cup minced celery)
Heat the soup. Add:
  1 pint oysters
Simmer the soup until the oysters are plump. Do not let it boil.

CANNED VEGETABLE AND MOCK TURTLE SOUP
About 4 Cupfuls
Combine and stir the contents of:
  1 can condensed mock turtle soup: 10½ oz.
  1 can condensed vegetable soup: 10½ oz.
Add:
  1¼ cups water or Stock, page 44
Heat these ingredients. Add:
  ¼ cup hot cream
  (1 tablespoon chopped parsley)
Do not permit the soup to boil.

CANNED MUSHROOM AND CLAM SOUP
About 5 Cupfuls
Heat in a double boiler the contents of:
  2 cans condensed mushroom soup: 21 oz.
Heat separately:
  2½ cups diluted clam broth
Stir it gradually into the mushroom soup.

CANNED MUSHROOM SOUP WITH BOUILLON
About 4 Cupfuls
Combine, stir and heat the contents of:
  1 can condensed mushroom soup: 10½ oz.
  1 cup condensed bouillon or consommé
  1¼ cups water or milk

CANNED CHICKEN AND MUSHROOM SOUP
Follow the above rule. Substitute Chicken Bouillon for Bouillon.

CANNED BEAN AND FRESH VEGETABLE SOUP
About 4 Cupfuls

Combine and stir the contents of:
> 1 can condensed bean or pea soup: 10½ oz.
> An equal amount of water

Add to it about:
> 1½ cups grated fresh vegetables: carrots, onions, green peppers, finely shredded cabbage, etc.

Simmer the soup until the vegetables are tender, for about 4 minutes.
Then you may add:
> 1 tablespoon chopped parsley

This makes a delicious thick vegetable soup.

FAITH'S QUICK BAKED BEAN SOUP
About 4 Cupfuls

Combine the contents of:
> 1 can baked beans: 11 oz.
> 1 can consommé: 10½ oz.

with:
> 1 cup tomatoes or tomato juice

Heat the soup. You may put it through a strainer or blender.

CANNED BLACK BEAN SOUP
Add to each portion of black bean soup when about to serve:
> A thin slice of lemon
> A slice or two of hard-cooked egg

The soup may be thinned with part water and part red wine.
Or, combine equal parts of:
> Condensed black bean soup
> Condensed Madrilène or bouillon
> 1 cup water

You may add:
> Diced garlic sausage
> 2 tablespoons chopped parsley

Season with sherry or dry red wine and freshly ground pepper.

QUICK CREAM OF CHICKEN SOUP
Easy to make and very good.
Heat in a double boiler:
> Chicken bouillon
> Cream—about ¼ the amount of the bouillon

Add if you wish:
> A dash of nutmeg
> Chopped parsley

Add if you want to be luxurious:
> Ground blanched almonds—use about 2 tablespoons to 1 cup soup.

QUICK CHICKEN CURRY SOUP
About 2 Cupfuls

Melt:
> 1 tablespoon butter

Stir in until blended:
> ¾ tablespoon flour

Stir in slowly:
> 1½ cups canned chicken broth

When the soup is boiling season it with:
> Paprika
> ¼ teaspoon or more curry powder

Reduce the heat. Beat:
> 1 egg yolk
> 3 tablespoons rich milk or cream

When the soup is no longer boiling, stir these ingredients into it. Stir it over low heat until the egg has thickened slightly without boiling.

Vichyssoise, page 64.
This may be made with canned chicken soup. Fine in a blender.

TROPICAL CONSOMMÉ
About 3 Cupfuls

Combine and heat the contents of:
> 1 can condensed consommé: 10½ oz.
> 1 can condensed Madrilène: 10½ oz.

Add and heat:
> The juice of 1 large orange

Or, these ingredients may be combined and chilled.

MADRILÈNE WITH CHEESE
2 Servings

Chill for 12 hours:
> 1 can condensed Madrilène: 10½ oz.

Remove the soup from the can into a chilled bowl. Beat into it with a fork:
> 3 tablespoons crumbled Blue cheese

Place the soup in cups. Garnish the tops with:
> 3 tablespoons sour cream

Sprinkle them with:
> Chopped parsley, chives or some other herb

MADRILÈNE WITH SOUR CREAM AND HERBS
4 Servings

Chill thoroughly the contents of:
> 2 cans condensed consommé Madrilène: 21 oz.

A few drops of red coloring may be added. Whip the jelly with a fork. Place it in a bowl or in individual dishes. Pour over it about:

¾ cup thick sour cream whipped
2 tablespoons or more chopped
chives, parsley, basil, etc.
Top each serving with:
(1 tablespoon red caviar)

MADRILÈNE AND TOMATO JUICE
About 2½ Cupfuls
A superlative summer soup. Combine
the contents of:
1 can condensed Madrilène: 10½ oz.
with:
An equal amount of tomato juice
Add:
1 teaspoon grated onion
1 teaspoon grated celery
Serve this well chilled.

Chilled Tomato Cream Soup, page 64.

QUICK TOMATO SOUP
About 4 Cupfuls
Simmer covered for 15 minutes, or
steam for 2 minutes in a pressure cooker, then strain:
2½ cups tomatoes: No. 2 can
¼ cup sliced onion
½ cup chopped celery with leaves
Melt:
2 tablespoons butter

Add and stir until blended:
2 tablespoons flour
Add, cook and stir until smooth and
boiling:
2 cups Stock, page 44, or canned bouillon
½ teaspoon sugar
⅛ teaspoon paprika
Salt
The strained tomato stock
Add just before serving:
3 tablespoons chopped parsley

QUICK CANNED PEA SOUP
About 6 Cupfuls
Put through a ricer the contents of:
1 No. 2 can peas
Add:
The liquor from the can
2 cups Stock, page 44, or canned bouillon
2 tablespoons lemon juice
1 tablespoon butter
Salt and paprika
Heat and serve the soup.

QUICK SPINACH SOUP
Use:
Left-Over Creamed Spinach, page 313
Thin it with:
Stock, page 44, or spinach
water and milk
Season it palatably.

Garnishes for Soups

The shift from a chiffonade of cress to farina dumplings, using the same clear
soup base, can set the temper of a meal. Scan the garnishes to decide what it
shall be.

CUSTARD
Scald:
½ cup milk or stock
Beat and add:
1 egg
⅛ teaspoon salt
⅛ teaspoon paprika
(⅛ teaspoon nutmeg)
Bake the custard in a bowl or a large
cup in hot water placed in a slow oven
325° until it is set. (See rule for Cup
Custard, page 710.) Drop it from a
spoon into simmering soup just before
serving it. The custard may be cut
into shapes.

FARINA BALLS
6 Servings
Farina balls are heavier than soup cus-

tard, so it is advisable to serve them
with a light meal. They are fine for
invalids and children. Heat to the
boiling point:
2 cups milk
Add, stir and cook until thick:
½ cup farina
1 tablespoon butter
½ teaspoon salt
⅛ teaspoon paprika
(⅛ teaspoon nutmeg)
Remove the batter from the fire and
beat in one at a time:
2 eggs
Drop the batter, a generous teaspoonful at a time, into simmering soup
stock. Cook it for 2 minutes and serve
the soup.

See Gnocchi with Flour, page 102.

HOMEMADE NOODLES
Beat slightly:
  1 egg
  ⅓ teaspoon salt
Add about:
  ⅔ cup all-purpose flour
  ⅛ teaspoon salt
to make a rather stiff dough. Knead it and permit it to stand covered for ½ hour. Roll it until it is very thin and let it dry until it is no longer sticky but not dry or brittle. Before it becomes brittle, fold it over several times and cut it into narrow strips. Toss the noodles lightly with the fingers and spread them until they are dry, when they may be used at once or kept in a closed jar for future use. Drop the noodles into simmering stock or water and cook them for 5 minutes.

SOUP NOCKERLN
Beat until creamy:
  ¼ cup soft butter
  1 egg
Stir in:
  1 cup all-purpose flour
  ⅛ teaspoon salt
Add gradually until a firm batter is formed about:
  6 tablespoons milk
Cut out the batter with a teaspoon to form small balls. Drop them into boiling water or soup to simmer for 10 minutes.

RICE MOLD
In a Swiss home we were frequently served Boiled Rice, page 103, seasoned lightly with freshly grated nutmeg, then pressed into a greased mold placed in hot water. The warm rice was turned onto a dish garnished with parsley and passed at table to be spooned into hot soup. We loved this dish.

CROUTONS
Dice bread and sauté it in butter until it is an even brown, or butter slices of bread, cut them into dice and brown them in a moderate oven.

FORCEMEAT. Chicken, Veal, Clam, Oyster, Fish
Combine:
  ¾ cup raw or cooked ground meat
  1 egg white
    Salt and pepper
  2 tablespoons grated onion
  (A pinch of herb)

Add enough:
  Cream
to make the mixture the right consistency to roll into small balls. Drop them into simmering soup and cook them until they are done, about 5 or 6 minutes.

MEAT BALLS FOR SOUP, SPAGHETTI OR STEW
4 Servings
These added to vegetable soup make a superb main dish. Remove the crust, then soak in water or milk:
  1 slice white bread
Prepare:
  ½ lb. finely ground or scraped beef
Melt:
  2 tablespoons butter
Sauté in it for 3 minutes:
  ¼ cup minced onion
Press the water from the bread. Add to the onion mixture, the bread, meat and:
  1 beaten egg
Season with:
  ½ teaspoon salt
  ⅛ teaspoon pepper
  ¼ teaspoon freshly ground nutmeg
  ½ teaspoon dried thyme, basil, etc., or 1 tablespoon chopped parsley or chives
Mix the ingredients lightly with a fork. Shape them without pressure into 1 inch balls. Drop them into boiling soup or stock. Simmer them until done for about 10 minutes.

Liver Dumplings, page 384.

LIVER SAUSAGE DUMPLINGS
About Twenty 1 Inch Balls
Combine and work with a fork:
  ¼ lb. Braunschweiger sausage
  ½ egg or 1 egg white or yolk
  ½ cup cracker crumbs, or more if the egg is large
  1 tablespoon chopped parsley or chives
  (1 tablespoon catsup)
Shape the mixture into 1 inch balls. Cook them gently for about 2 minutes in soup stock.

SAUSAGE BALLS FOR SOUP
4 Servings
Good in pea, bean or lentil soup. Combine:
  ½ lb. raw sausage meat
  1 egg white
  2 teaspoons chopped parsley

¼ teaspoon basil
½ teaspoon rosemary
1 thin slice white bread, toasted
and rolled fine
Roll this mixture into 1 inch balls.
Drop them into boiling stock. Simmer
the soup until the balls are done, for
about 30 minutes.

CHEESE BALLS FOR SOUP
Combine:
2 beaten egg yolks
2 tablespoons grated cheese:
preferably Parmesan
2 tablespoons dry bread crumbs
⅛ teaspoon paprika
½ teaspoon dried herbs, fresh
chives or parsley
Beat until stiff, then fold in:
2 egg whites
⅛ teaspoon salt
Drop the batter from a spoon into
simmering soup. Simmer the soup
only 1 or 2 minutes longer.

CRACKER BALLS
Pour:
½ cup boiling soup or milk
over:
½ cup cracker crumbs
Add:
1 egg slightly beaten
1 tablespoon chopped parsley
Salt and paprika
Cool the mixture. Drop it from a teaspoon into simmering soup. Simmer
the soup for 5 minutes longer.

MARROW BALLS
Combine and beat until creamy:
¼ cup fresh marrow
2 tablespoons butter
Add:
3 eggs
¼ teaspoon salt
⅛ teaspoon paprika
2 tablespoons chopped parsley
Cracker crumbs
Use just enough cracker crumbs to
make the mixture the right consistency
to shape into balls. Cook the balls in
simmering soup for 15 minutes.

SPONGE DUMPLINGS
4 Servings
Wonderful in fresh green pea soup, or
any other soup. Beat with an egg or
cake beater until blended:
½ cup milk
½ cup flour
1 egg white

Melt over low heat until hot:
3 tablespoons butter
Beat in the milk mixture and continue
to cook and beat until the batter no
longer sticks to the sides of the pan.
Remove it from the fire. Beat in, 1 at a
time, until well blended:
2 egg yolks
Beat until stiff:
2 egg whites
⅛ teaspoon salt
Fold or beat them into the batter.
Drop it from a teaspoon into about 5
cupfuls of simmering soup. Cover the
pot. Cook the dumplings for about 8
minutes.

EGG DROPS
Crush with a fork:
2 hard-cooked egg yolks
Add to them and blend well:
1 tablespoon soft butter
1 raw egg yolk
A few grains of cayenne
A light grating of nutmeg
⅛ teaspoon salt
Form these ingredients into ½ inch
balls. Roll them in:
Flour
Cook the drops in simmering consom-
mé for 1 minute.

FRITTER GARNISH
Beat until light:
1 egg
Add:
¼ teaspoon salt
⅛ teaspoon paprika
½ cup flour
2 tablespoons milk
Heat fat to a temperature of 360°, page
542. Put the batter through a colander
into the fat and fry it until it is brown.
Drain it on paper. Serve it in hot soup.

SPATZEN
Prepare:
Spatzen, page 423
Drop the batter as directed into sim-
mering soup instead of water.

BUTTER DUMPLINGS OR
BUTTERKLOESSE
Beat until soft:
2 tablespoons butter
Beat and add:
2 eggs
Stir in:
6 tablespoons flour
¼ teaspoon salt
Drop the batter from a spoon into sim-

mering soup. Simmer the dumplings for 5 minutes. Or simmer them in the soup for 5 minutes, using a pressure cooker with the vent open.

ALMOND BALLS
Beat:
 1 egg yolk
 ½ cup ground blanched almonds
 ⅛ teaspoon salt
 ⅛ teaspoon grated lemon rind
Fold in:
 1 stiffly beaten egg white
Drop the batter from a teaspoon into hot fat, page 542. Drain the dumplings well on absorbent paper. Add them to clear soup immediately before serving.

ITALIAN SOUP GARNISH
4 Servings
Beat until well combined:
 1 egg
 1½ teaspoons grated Parmesan cheese
 1 tablespoon grated dry bread crumbs
Have ready:
 3 cups boiling consommé or other clear soup
Stir the egg mixture rapidly into the soup. This should result in a ragged fluff effect. Serve at once.

WHIPPED CREAM GARNISH
Whip:
 ½ cup cream
Fold in:
 2 tablespoons horseradish
 ⅛ teaspoon paprika
Place a spoonful on top of an individual serving of soup. Or, omit the horseradish and paprika. Place a spoonful of whipped cream on top of each serving and garnish with:
 Paprika
 A sprig of parsley

PUFFED CEREALS FOR SOUP
Sauté:
 Puffed cereals
in:
 Butter
Or, sprinkle them with:
 Grated cheese
and dot them generously with:
 Butter
Toast them in a slow oven 325°.

RAW VEGETABLES IN SOUP
Mince:
 Celery and parsley

Scrape:
 Carrots
Grate them. Add them to hot soup.

RAW POTATOES IN SOUP
A good thickening for those whose diet does not include flour. Peel:
 A potato
Grate it into clear soup. Simmer the soup for a few minutes until the potato is tender. You may add the raw vegetables given in preceding rule.

ADDITIONAL GARNISHES
For Clear Soup:
 Thin slices of lemon or orange
 Thin slices of avocado
 Minced parsley, chives, water cress, mint or other herbs
In Europe a ring of boiled rice flavored with nutmeg is passed with clear soup.
Cooked in the Soup:
 Fine noodles, marrow or other dumplings as given in this chapter
 Grated apple and onion
 Grated or diced vegetables
For Cream Soup:
 Salted whipped cream
 Blanched, shredded toasted almonds
 Popcorn, or cheese popcorn
 Minced parsley, herbs and spices
For Thick Soups:
 Sliced lemon or orange
 Sliced sausages
 Sliced hard-cooked eggs
 Croutons
 Bits of cooked meat: ham, tongue, chicken, etc.
 Grated cheese
 Sour cream at room temperature

BREADS TO SERVE WITH SOUP
Melba Toast, page 539.
White or rye bread cut into shapes and toasted.
Crackers, plain or spread with butter and fish paste.
Pastry Snails, page 13, spread with deviled ham and cheese, mustard and paprika.
Round crackers sprinkled with grated cheese, mustard, paprika and salt, placed in the oven until the cheese is melted.
Soda crackers spread lightly with butter placed in the oven until they are light brown.
Cheese Bread Cubes, page 11.
Cheese Straws, page 517.
Cream Cheese Pastry, page 565.

Rye Krisp.
Corn Dodgers or Zephyrs, page 516.
Toasted Buttered Loaf, below, or
French bread cut in thick slices. See
French Bread to be served with soup
or salad on this page.
Thinly sliced rolls, Toasted Croutons,
page 422.

TOASTED BUTTERED BREAD LOAF OR GARLIC BREAD

Cut into very thin slices:
**A medium-sized loaf of bread or
French bread**
Do not slice it all the way through;
leave the bottom crust undisturbed.
Spread the bread with:
½ cup melted butter
The butter may be flavored with garlic.

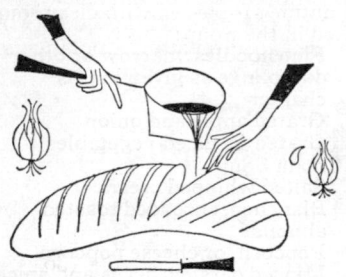

Or crush 2 cloves of garlic with a little
salt until smooth. Spread a little on
each slice. Follow up with melted butter as shown above. Separate the slices
slightly so that the butter will be evenly distributed. Cover the loaf with a
paper bag. Place it in a moderate oven
350° until the bread is light brown, for
about 20 minutes. Remove it from the
bag, place it on a platter and permit
the guests to serve themselves.

FRENCH BREAD TOASTED

Cut very thin slices of:
French bread
Brush them lightly with
Fat from bouillon
Toast them in a moderate oven 375°.
Add them to hot soup.

CHEESE CROUTONS

Prepare by the rule on page 73:
About 3 cups croutons

When sautéed or browned in the oven
drop them while hot in a bag containing:
**1 teaspoon salt
1 teaspoon paprika
Ground Parmesan cheese
Very finely minced chives or
other herb**
Close the bag. Shake it until the croutons are evenly coated. Add them to
hot soup.

PULLED BREAD

Remove the crust from:
A small loaf of bread
Pull the bread apart into irregular
pieces with 2 forks. Place it in a
slow oven 300° until it is dry and light
brown.

TOASTED BREAD STICKS

Follow the rule on page 11 for Bread
Cubes with Cheese. Substitute for the
cubes bread cut into oblong blocks.

SOUFFLÉ CRACKERS

Soak in ice water for 8 minutes:
Soda crackers
Drain them. Dot them with:
Butter
Bake them in a hot oven 450° until
they are puffed and brown.

CORN-MEAL CRACKLES

About 20
Combine and stir well:
**1 cup yellow corn meal
½ cup sifted all-purpose flour
¼ teaspoon salt
¼ teaspoon soda
⅛ teaspoon paprika
2 tablespoons bacon fat, oil or
other shortening
⅓ cup milk**
Knead the dough for 10 minutes. Roll
it into 1 inch balls, flatten them well by
rolling them or slapping them between
the palms of your hands, Mexican tor-
tilla fashion. They should be paper
thin. Bake them on an ungreased
sheet in a moderate oven 350° for
about 15 minutes. While hot brush
them with:
1 tablespoon butter
Sprinkle them with:
Salt
Cool them on a rack.

Luncheon and Supper Dishes

I must confess to an especial fondness for this chapter. Any experimental cook can produce a good meal when her financial means and her sources of supply are unlimited, but it is an art to make delicious dishes with meager means.

A meal should be nutritious, balanced and flavorful. If, as in so many cases, it must at the same time be economical, additional thought and care should go into its preparation.

In this chapter I have tried to call attention to endless good, simple dishes. Many of them may be made with ingredients one is apt to have on hand. The main idea is that no matter what is served—a can of tuna, frankfurters or an omelet—that the dish have the distinction that careful preparation can give it. To quote Mrs. Nussbaum: "To mine husband Pierre I am offering an ultimato." Cooking is a daily job, it may be a daily chore, why not make it a daily adventure?

Luncheon Dishes Served in Pastry, Bread Shells, etc.

Creamed dishes, eggs and left-overs may be attractively served in various ways:
1. In patty shells.
2. On rounds of buttered and toasted bread or on French Toast, page 136.
3. On rusks lightly buttered and heated.
4. In bread cases prepared in the following way: Cut rounds from slices of bread 1¼ inches thick with a large biscuit cutter. Press a small biscuit cutter into these rounds, but not through them. Hollow the centers, leaving a shell and a bottom at least ¼ inch thick. Spread the insides lightly with melted butter and place the shells in a slow oven 300° until toasted.
5. In Melba toast baskets made by pressing thin, crustless slices of fresh white bread lightly buttered on both sides into muffin tins, letting the corners protrude slightly. Toast in a slow oven 300° until crisp.
6. In small rolls that have been hollowed, buttered lightly on the inside and toasted in a slow oven 300°.
7. In a loaf of bread that has been hollowed, buttered lightly and toasted in a slow oven 300°.
8. In a Rice Loaf, page 105.
9. In one large or in individual Pie Shells, page 561, or in Turnovers, page 577.
10. In one large or in individual Noodle Rings, page 98.
11. In one large or in individual Rice Rings, page 105.
12. In a Pastry Roll, page 158.
13. In or between Biscuits or Shortcakes, page 505.
14. In a Mashed Potato Ring, page 302.
15. In a Bread Dressing Ring, page 157.
16. On or in rolled Pancakes, page 117.
17. On or between waffles.
18. In Noodle Baskets or Potato Baskets, pages 98, 302.
19. As a stuffing for tomatoes, peppers, potatoes, cucumbers, apples, acorn squash, etc., as suggested in the recipes in the following chapter.
20. On Cereal Cakes, Grits, Rice or Eggplant, pages 100 and 287.

Before deciding upon your luncheon menu read the Chapter on Hors d'Oeuvres.

Additions that Lend Distinction to Food

Many people cultivate mental allergies toward things they do not know well. Perhaps they have at some time had a dish so generously doused with some spice that they have disliked it ever after. Use your spices and herbs sparingly until you are sure of your ground, but give them a chance. They add a variety and subtlety to food that you should not overlook.

Try: Freshly ground pepper
　　　Cloves stuck into lemon slices for tea
　　　A bit of freshly ground nutmeg on eggplant, squash or rice
　　　Cinnamon with apples
　　　Ginger and lemon with pears
　　　Curry with eggs or meat
　　　Mustard with cheese
　　　Paprika with almost anything
　　　Bay leaf in bouillon or fish stock
　　　Chili in meat or rice dishes
　　　Celery, caraway, fennel, cumin and dill seeds
　　　Fresh and dried herbs
　　　The new vegetable powders (not salts), parsley, celery, onion, garlic, etc., are worth your attention. They may be used in emergencies as a substitute for fresh herbs and vegetable flavoring.
　　　Add a few drops of anise to sponge cake batter and later toast the cake for tea—delicious!

Charles Rector has called garlic the vanilla of vegetables. Use it to rub the inside of a salad bowl or a skillet. If you like a lot of it and don't mind the consequences, mince it and add it to food, preferably to hot butter, or add a whole skinned clove of garlic and fish it out before the food is served. Of course, the humble—well, not so very humble—onion is a good understudy; so is the leek.

As to the Herbs, see page 832 for further suggestions. They are numerous and just now tremendously in vogue. The fashionable woman seems suddenly to be cultivating an herb garden, as less fashionable gardeners have been doing for centuries with far less fuss. Parsley of course reigns supreme, but chives and delicate celery leaves are not to be despised. Tarragon is the perfect herb for salads, although this may be disputed by lovers of fennel or basil. A bit of thyme, either fresh or dried, is a fine thing added to a sauce, soup or gravy. So is chervil and so on down the line. It is a very long one.

Combined herbs—the French call them a bouquet—add a wonderful something to stews, sauces and soups, and combined herbs are marvelous in the salad bowl. Add one or more of your favorite dried herbs to your pantry shelf, also a choice of celery, fennel, caraway and other seeds, Worcestershire, A, A-1 or Tabasco sauce, catsup, poultry seasoning, horseradish, the various new mustard combinations, French dressing, etc., and you are ready for any emergency.

Remember to let the original flavor of the food predominate. When necessary to add character to what is already there do it with a light hand.

Beware of becoming like H. H. Munro's cook who had a way of serving up chicken like beefsteak that bordered on the supernatural.

Eggs and Egg Dishes

Treat eggs gently. They like this consideration and will respond by being tender.

Those who have a "good ear for cooking" find many ways of making eggs palatable. Those who have not may be grateful for the numerous suggestions given in this chapter.

The first thing to impress upon the novice is that eggs cook with a very low degree of heat.

"It was so hot that you could fry an egg upon the sidewalk" is to be taken literally. It can be done under favorable conditions. Eggs solidify so readily that it is well to remember when cooking egg dishes to place them over a low flame, or in a double boiler, to avoid the disaster of a curdled dish. Should a custard or sauce misbehave and curdle, owing to an excess of heat, remove it at once from the fire, dump it into a cold dish and beat it vigorously with a wire whisk. By this treatment it may sometimes be induced to behave.

Salt is supposed to toughen eggs. If preferred, add it to egg dishes when they are cooked.

To prepare powdered eggs add 2 tablespoonfuls of water to 1 tablespoonful of powdered egg. Beat until well blended and entirely smooth. Use this mixture immediately after preparing.

To test eggs for freshness put them one at a time in cold water. If they sink, they are fresh. If they float, they are stale.

When our scarcity of domestic service was first making itself felt, I was approached by a woman of seventy who asked for help in realizing the ambition of her lifetime—to know how to separate an egg. She died happy.

José Ferrer breaks an egg and then, with his admirable dexterity, rolls the contents from palm to palm until the white is separated from the yolk. A less complicated method follows.

To Separate an Egg: Have 2 bowls ready. Holding an egg in one hand, tap the center of the side of the egg lightly, yet sharply, either with the edge of a knife blade or on the edge of one of the bowls, to make an even crosswise break. Then take the egg in both hands with the break on the upper side. Hold the egg over a bowl and tip the egg so that the wider end is down. Hold the edges of the break with the thumbs. Widen the break by pulling the edges apart until the egg shell is broken into halves. As you do this some of the egg white will flow into the bowl; the yolk and the rest of the egg white will remain in the lower half of the shell. Now pour the remaining egg back and forth from one half shell to the other, letting some more of the white flow into the bowl each time until you have only the yolk left. Place the yolk in the other bowl. Be sure that the egg whites in the bowl are entirely free from the yolks. If there are bits of yolk in the bowl, fish them out with a clean piece of shell or a spoon. If you are not careful about this, the egg whites will not whip properly.

To Divide an Egg: Beat the egg, measure it in a measuring cup and divide.

SOFT AND HARD-COOKED OR "BOILED" EGGS

Place in a saucepan:
    Eggs
Cover them with:
    Cold water
Put the pan over medium heat and bring water to the boiling point. Reduce the heat to below the boiling point and let the water simmer. Now watch your time.

Soft-Cooked Eggs:

Remove them from the water 2 to 3 minutes after you reduce the heat.

Medium-Soft Cooked Eggs:

Allow 4 minutes after you reduce the heat.

Hard-Cooked Eggs:

Allow 20 minutes after you reduce the heat.

Place hard-cooked eggs in cold water at once to prevent the yolks from discoloring.

Or, place eggs in boiling water, reduce the heat and keep the water under the boiling point. Allow 6 minutes for delicately coddled eggs; 8 minutes for firmly coddled eggs, and 30 to 35 minutes for hard-cooked eggs. If you have difficulty in regulating the heat, put the eggs in the top of a double boiler, pour boiling water over them and place the pan over boiling water. Keep the eggs hot but do not permit the water in the lower container to boil. The eggs will be hard-cooked in 35 minutes. Plunge hard-cooked eggs, when done, into cold water as directed on preceding page.

Crack the shell and rock the egg between the palms of the hands to remove the shell readily. Should the shell crack while boiling, seal the crack heavily with salt. If you want to slice the eggs smoothly, dip a knife in water before using.

SAUTÉED OR "FRIED" EGGS
4 Servings
Melt in a skillet over a slow fire:
    1 to 2 tablespoons butter
Break into saucer one at a time and slip from the saucer into the skillet:
    4 eggs
Cook them over a very low fire until they are done. While cooking slash across the whites several times with a knife to permit the heat to penetrate the lower crust. When the eggs are firm serve them seasoned with:
    Salt and paprika

EGGS IN BLACK BUTTER OR AU BEURRE NOIR
Follow the preceding rule for:
    Sautéed Eggs
Remove the eggs to a hot platter. You may sprinkle them with:
    A few capers
    Chopped chives
    Grated onion
Add to the butter in the skillet and cook until brown:
    1 tablespoon butter
Add and heat:
    1 tablespoon lemon juice or vinegar
Pour this over the eggs and serve them at once. Garnish them with:
    Chopped parsley

POACHED EGGS
Fill a skillet ⅔ full of water. Allow ½ teaspoonful salt to 4 cupfuls of water. A teaspoonful of vinegar added to the water will keep the whites from spreading. Bring the water to the boiling point, then reduce the heat and keep it under the boiling point. Break an egg into a saucer and slip it gently from the saucer into the water. Repeat this process. As the eggs cook dip some water from the sides with a spoon and pour it over them to cook the tops. When a film forms over the yolks and

the whites are firm, remove them from the water with a buttered skimmer and place them on rounds of buttered toast. Or, after adding the eggs to the hot water, remove the skillet at once from the heat and permit the eggs to stand for 5 minutes in the hot water. Eggs may be poached in a small amount of milk or stock. When they are cooked, you may pour the milk or stock over the toast.

SAUTÉED OR POACHED EGGS PLUS
And it is the plus that gives them the punch. A good luncheon dish.
Try these eggs on a small mound of:
    Boiled rice, noodles or rounds of toast
Pour over them:
    Well-seasoned left-over gravy
    Mushroom, tomato or onion sauce or condensed canned Cream Soups, page 441
    Cream sauce seasoned with mustard or curry, herbs, onion, celery, green peppers, capers, anchovies, etc.

POACHED EGGS IN TOMATO SOUP OR SAUCE
Method I. 4 Servings
The following recipe makes a good, attractive, well-balanced meal—prepared in a few minutes. Combine in an 8 inch skillet and heat to the boiling point over a slow fire the contents of:
    1 can condensed tomato soup:
        10½ oz.
    ½ as much water
    (¼ teaspoon sugar)
Reduce the heat and keep the liquid below the boiling point. Add to the soup:
    4 eggs
To cook and serve the eggs see the rule for Poached Eggs opposite.
Sprinkle them with:
    Chopped parsley

Method II.
Sauté for 10 minutes:
    1 minced clove garlic
in:
    2 tablespoons salad oil
Add:
    1 cup hot water
    3 tablespoons chili sauce
    ¾ teaspoon Worcestershire sauce
    ¼ teaspoon salt
    ¼ teaspoon paprika

Bring the sauce to the boiling point. Reduce the heat. Slip into the simmering sauce:

4 eggs

To cook and serve follow the rule for Poached Eggs, page 80.

Method III. 6 Servings

Or, poach:

6 eggs

Drain them well, place them on an oven-proof plate, pour over them the following sauce, top them with ½ cupful bread crumbs, sprinkle them well with grated Parmesan cheese and bake them in a hot oven 400° until it is melted.

Simmer for 15 minutes:

2½ cups tomatoes
¼ cup minced onion
1 teaspoon sugar
½ teaspoon salt
Freshly grated pepper
2 tablespoons butter
(½ teaspoon dried herb)

POACHED EGGS ON TOMATOES WITH HOLLANDAISE SAUCE OR EGGS BLACKSTONE

6 Servings

Sauté, then mince:

3 slices bacon

Reserve the drippings. Cut:

6 slices tomato ½ inch thick

Season them with:

Salt and pepper

Dip the slices in flour. Sauté them in the bacon grease. Sprinkle them with the minced bacon. Cover each slice with:

A Poached Egg, page 80

Pour over the eggs:

Hollandaise Sauce, page 429

EGGS POACHED IN CREAM

Individual Serving

Follow the rule on page 80 for:

Poached Eggs

Substitute cream for the water. Allow to 2 eggs:

2 tablespoons cream

Add:

⅛ teaspoon salt
A sprinkling of paprika

Use a small skillet so that the bottom is well covered with cream. Move the skillet while the eggs are cooking with a circular motion to keep the eggs from sticking. Serve them on:

Hot buttered toast or on split, buttered, toasted buns

Pour the remaining cream over them.

SEMI-POACHED EGGS

4 Servings

Heat in an 8 inch skillet:

1 teaspoon bacon fat or butter

Break and place in the skillet:

4 eggs

Add at once:

1 tablespoon boiling water

Cover the skillet and cook the eggs for about 1 minute.

Poached Eggs in Aspic, page 36; Poached Eggs, Crab Meat and Cheese on Toast, page 124.

LUNCHEON EGGS OR EGGS BENEDICT

6 Servings

Cut and toast:

6 rounds of bread or halves of toasted English muffins

Cover them with:

Thin slices of cold or hot ham
Broiled Tomatoes II, page 319
Poached Eggs, page 80

Serve them hot with:

Hollandaise Sauce, page 429
or Easy Hollandaise Sauce, page 430

SCRAMBLED EGGS

2 Servings

Melt in a skillet or a well-greased double boiler over a slow fire:

1 tablespoon butter

You may add and cook for 1 minute:

(1 or 2 teaspoons grated onion)

Beat and pour into the skillet:

3 eggs
⅛ teaspoon salt
⅛ teaspoon paprika
(3 tablespoons cream or top milk)

When the eggs begin to thicken break them into shreds with a fork. When they are thick serve them on:

Hot toast lightly buttered or spread with fish paste or deviled ham or liver sausage

Scrambled eggs may be stirred with a wooden spoon, "for creaminess," says Jane, and she likes to add to them chopped chives and bits of ham fat that have been tried out in a slow oven or skillet.

SCRAMBLED EGGS WITH BACON

2 Servings
Sauté in a skillet over low heat until nearly done:
    4 slices minced bacon
Pour off all but a very little grease.
Beat and add to the bacon:
    4 eggs
    4 tablespoons milk
    ⅛ teaspoon paprika
Cook the eggs until they begin to thicken. Break them into shreds with a fork. When they are thick serve them on:
    Hot toast

SCRAMBLED EGGS WITH CREAMED FOOD, VEGE-TABLES, HASH, ETC.

Scrambled eggs combine well with:
    Creamed tuna, shrimp, crab, oysters, etc.
    Creamed or sautéed mushrooms
    Creamed spinach, asparagus, green beans, etc.
    Chicken livers, bacon, hash, ham, sausage, etc.

SCRAMBLED EGGS AND CRAB MEAT

4 Servings
Melt over low heat:
    3 tablespoons butter
Stir in until well heated:
    ¼ teaspoon curry powder
    ½ cup crab meat
    ⅛ teaspoon paprika
Beat until light:
    6 eggs
    ¼ cup cream
Add the eggs to the crab mixture. Stir these ingredients gently until the eggs are scrambled.

SCRAMBLED EGGS WITH CHICKEN BROTH AND CHEESE

4 Servings
Melt in a double boiler:
    ¼ lb. Swiss cheese
    1 tablespoon butter
Add:
    1 cup hot chicken broth
    1 tablespoon grated onion
    1 tablespoon chopped parsley
    A grating of nutmeg
    ¼ teaspoon salt
    ⅛ teaspoon paprika

Beat well and add:
    4 eggs
Cook and stir these ingredients over boiling water until they are firm. Serve them on:
    Rounds of hot toast

SCRAMBLED EGGS WITH ONIONS

2 or 3 Servings
Combine:
    ½ cup chopped onions
    ½ cup milk
    (2 tablespoons chopped green pepper)
Cook these ingredients in a covered saucepan over low heat for 5 minutes. Cool them. Beat in:
    4 eggs
Season them with:
    ¼ teaspoon salt
    ⅛ teaspoon paprika
Melt in a small skillet:
    1½ tablespoons butter
Add the egg mixture. Cook it over low heat. As it thickens break it into shreds with a fork. Serve it at once on:
    Hot buttered toast or rusks

SCRAMBLED EGGS WITH TOMATO SOUP

4 Servings
Melt in a small skillet over a slow fire:
    1½ tablespoons butter
Add and cook for 3 minutes:
    1 tablespoon chopped onion
    (1 tablespoon chopped green pepper)
Combine, beat, then add to the skillet:
    4 eggs
    ¾ cup tomato soup
    ⅛ teaspoon salt
    ⅛ teaspoon paprika
Cook and stir these ingredients until they are thick and creamy. Serve them at once on:
    Hot lightly buttered toast

SCRAMBLED EGGS WITH TOMATOES

4 Servings
Melt in a small skillet over a slow fire:
    1 tablespoon butter
Add and cook covered for 5 minutes:
    1 teaspoon grated onion
    1 cup strained tomatoes
    ¼ teaspoon salt
    ⅛ teaspoon pepper
    ½ teaspoon or more brown sugar

Cool these ingredients slightly and add:

4 beaten eggs

Cook them over a low fire. Break them into large curds as they cook. Serve them on:

Hot toast, lightly buttered or spread with deviled ham

SCRAMBLED EGGS WITH PINEAPPLE
2 Servings

It may be possible to induce children who do not like eggs to eat this tempting combination. Drain the contents of:

1 can crushed pineapple: 9 oz.

Beat until well blended:

4 eggs
4 tablespoons pineapple juice
⅛ teaspoon salt

Melt in a small skillet:

1 tablespoon butter

Pour in the egg mixture. Follow the rule on page 81 for scrambling eggs. Serve the eggs on:

Toast

with the remaining pineapple juice and pineapple which should be heated.

SCRAMBLED EGGS WITH ANCHOVIES AND CRAB CANAPÉS

Prepare by the rule on page 81:

Scrambled Eggs

Serve them on individual plates. Decorate the eggs with:

Whole anchovies

Place on each plate 2:

Crab Meat or Lobster Canapés, page 15

Garnish the plates with:

Parsley

The eggs may be placed in the center of a platter, garnished with anchovies, parsley and toast points and surrounded by Creamed Fish or Sea Food, page 122.

SMOKED SALMON ON TOAST WITH EGGS

A good winter breakfast or luncheon dish. Prepare:

Buttered toast

Dip into boiling water:

Very thin slices smoked salmon

Dry them. Place them on the toast. Cover them with:

Poached or sautéed eggs

EGGS SCRAMBLED WITH CREAM CHEESE
4 Servings

Sauté (page 375) until brown:

12 small sausages

Drain them on absorbent paper. Keep them hot. Melt in a double boiler over simmering water:

1 package cream cheese: 3 oz.
1 tablespoon butter

Scald and stir in:

1 cup rich milk

Add:

½ teaspoon salt
¼ teaspoon paprika

Break into the sauce:

6 eggs

Before the egg whites are firm stir the eggs gently with a fork. Add:

1½ tablespoons sherry

Serve the eggs when they have thickened, surrounded by the sausages and garnished with:

Chopped chives or parsley

CHINESE EGGS OR EGGS FOO YUNG
4 Servings

Sauté for 1 minute:

¾ lb. sliced mushrooms

in:

2 tablespoons butter

Add:

1 cup sliced onions
1 cup diced celery

Stir and sauté these ingredients for about 5 minutes. Cool them. Beat until light:

4 eggs

Season them with:

¼ teaspoon salt
⅛ teaspoon pepper

Add the sautéed vegetables and:

¾ cup well-drained bean sprouts
½ cup cooked shredded pork or chicken

Melt in a skillet over low heat:

2 tablespoons butter or oil

Drop the egg mixture into the butter from a large spoon. Turn the cakes as soon as they are firm on the bottom. Cook the other side and serve them at once with:

Soy sauce or 2 cups brown or cream sauce seasoned with 2 tablespoons soy sauce

---

SHIRRED EGGS
Method I.

Beat until very stiff:

2 egg whites

Heap them in a greased oven-proof dish. Make 2 cavities an equal distance apart, not too near the edge. Slip into the cavities:

2 unbroken egg yolks

Place the dish in a moderate oven 350° for 10 minutes or until the eggs are set. Season the eggs with:

Salt and paprika

Sprinkle them with:

(Chopped chives)

Method II.

Break into a well-buttered oven-proof dish:

Eggs

Bake them on the lower shelf of a moderate oven 375° for about 10 minutes.

EGGS BAKED IN TOMATO OR OTHER SAUCE
4 Servings

Prepare:

1 cup Tomato Sauce, page 433

Butter 4 baking cups. Place in each cup 2 tablespoonfuls of sauce. Add a layer of:

Cracker crumbs

Break into each cup:

1 egg

Cover it with 2 tablespoonfuls of tomato sauce and a second layer of cracker crumbs. Sprinkle the tops with:

Grated cheese

Bake the eggs in a moderate oven 350° for about 12 minutes, until they are firm. The eggs may be baked in 1 small 6 inch baking dish.

One cupful cream sauce flavored with 1 teaspoonful prepared mustard, creamed mushrooms or canned soup—celery, mushroom, asparagus, etc.—diluted with milk or water to the consistency of cream sauce, may be substituted for the tomato sauce. Eggs are good baked in 1 cupful or more of Creamed Onions, page 294.

BAKED EGGS WITH OR WITHOUT CHEESE
4 Servings

Grease a baking dish or 4 individual oven-proof dishes with:

1 tablespoon butter

The baking will be hastened if the dish is thin. Spread the dish with:

Bread crumbs

Break into the dish:

4 eggs

Season them with:

Salt, paprika or white pepper
A few grains cayenne or freshly grated nutmeg

Cover the top with:

(½ cup grated cheese)

Pour over it:

½ cup cream

Bake the eggs in a moderate oven 350° until they are firm. Serve them on:

(Buttered toast)

BAKED EGGS WITH CHEESE
4 Servings

Cover the bottom of a well-buttered baking dish with:

¾ lb. finely chopped American cheese

Combine and pour over the cheese:

½ teaspoon to 1 teaspoon dry mustard
¾ teaspoon salt
A few grains cayenne
¾ cup cream or evaporated milk
(2 teaspoons Worcestershire sauce)

Break over these ingredients:

6 eggs

Keep the yolks whole. Combine and pour over the eggs:

½ cup cream or evaporated milk
⅛ teaspoon salt
⅛ teaspoon paprika

Bake the eggs in a moderate oven 350° until they are firm.

EGGS BAKED IN CHEESE RICE
4 Servings

Prepare (page 103):

1½ cups cooked rice

Add to it:

2 tablespoons melted butter
¼ cup thin cream
A few grains of cayenne
A few grains of nutmeg or curry powder

Line 4 ramekins with the rice. Sprinkle them with:

¼ cup grated cheese

Place in the centers of the ramekins:

4 eggs

Pour over them:

½ cup thin cream

Cover the tops with:

Bread crumbs

Season them with:

Salt and paprika

Dot them with:

2 tablespoons butter

Sprinkle over them:

¼ cup cheese

Place the ramekins in a shallow pan half filled with hot water. Bake the eggs in a moderate oven 375° until they are firm.

EGGS BAKED IN BACON RINGS

Sauté or broil lightly:
    Strips of bacon
Grease the bottom of muffin pans. Line them with the bacon. You may place in each pan:
    1 tablespoon chili sauce
Drop into each pan:
    1 egg
Sprinkle the eggs with :
    Salt and paprika
Bake them in a moderate oven 325° for about 15 minutes or until the eggs are set. Turn them out onto:
    Rounds of toast or slices of
        drained pineapple
Garnish them with:
    Parsley

FLUFFY OMELET
4 Servings

Prepare to make and serve an omelet with dispatch. To quote Archie of Duffy's Tavern, "Leave us not shilly-dally."
Combine and beat with a fork:
    ¼ cup milk
    4 egg yolks
    1 teaspoon baking powder
Combine and beat until stiff, but not dry:
    4 egg whites
    ½ teaspoon salt
Melt in a skillet over a slow fire:
    1 tablespoon butter
Fold the yolk mixture lightly into the egg whites. Pour the batter into the skillet. Cover the skillet with a lid. As the omelet cooks slash through it several times with a knife to permit the heat to penetrate the lower crust. When the omelet is done, after about 12 minutes, it may be placed uncovered on the center grate of a slow oven 275° until the top is set, or it may be folded over and served at once. Make an incision with a knife on either side of the omelet where you want it to fold. Tip the pan and push the omelet gently with a spatula or a broad knife until it folds over. Serve the omelet sprinkled with:
    (Chopped parsley)
Creamed dishes—celery, sweetbreads, spinach, mushrooms, oysters or minced clams, etc.—are good served with om-elet. A good everyday combination is omelet with Boiled Macaroni, page 94, and Tomato Sauce, page 433.

SWEET OMELET

Follow the preceding rule for Fluffy Omelet. Add to the yolk mixture:
    1 tablespoon sugar
Before folding the omelet spread it with:
    Jam or jelly
Sprinkle the top with:
    Confectioners' sugar
Fruit juice may be substituted for the milk and the omelet may be spread with cooked or raw sweetened fruit instead of jelly.
See page 730 for other Sweet Omelets.

OMELET
4 Servings

This is for the benefit of those who say, "But I like a firm omelet."
Beat with a fork until blended:
    4 eggs
Beat in:
    4 tablespoons milk or cream
    ½ teaspoon salt
    ⅛ teaspoon paprika
Melt in a skillet:
    1½ tablespoons butter
When this is fairly hot add the egg mixture. Cook it over low heat. Lift the edges with a pancake turner and tilt the skillet to permit the uncooked custard to run to the bottom, or stick it with a fork in the soft spots to permit the heat to penetrate the bottom crust. When it is all an even consistency, fold the omelet over and serve it.
The Japanese make a good omelet by this rule, substituting stock for milk or cream.

FRENCH OMELET
3 Servings

This dish seems to be highly controversial. Although I have eaten endless French omelets and have watched French cooks make them, both method and ingredients have varied slightly. The following is a crosscut, a good example of an omelet as frequently served in France. You will note that it consists of eggs only, not even salt. Season it later if you like. It is disastrous to make an omelet on a modern stove with more than six eggs. If you wish a larger amount, make 2 omelets.

Beat with a fork until blended:

6 eggs

Melt in a 12 inch skillet over moderate heat:

3 tablespoons butter

Try out a drop or 2 of the omelet at this point. This is to test the heat. Wait until the drops make a slight hissing sound before adding all the eggs. As soon as the eggs are poured into the skillet, tip it to spread them to all sides. If they seem to be cooking rapidly, lower the heat or raise the skillet and hold it well above the burner. Push back the omelet from the sides with a fork to permit the liquid part to run to the bottom of the skillet. Cook it until it is fairly firm—until it is of a jellied consistency throughout. When the heat is right this is a matter of a very short time. Fold over the omelet and serve it at once with the usual accompaniments suggested elsewhere in this chapter. Or sprinkle it with sugar. In France a hot poker is used to sear the sugar by making about 3 slight bias depressions across the top. This adds a delicious caramel flavor. For your first attempt it is advisable to make an individual serving. Use an 8 inch skillet, 2 eggs and 1½ tablespoonfuls butter. You will soon become an expert in making this quick, simple and probably best of omelets.

OMELET WITH BACON OR SALT PORK

2 Servings

Cut into small pieces:

3 slices bacon or ¼ cup salt pork or ham fat

Place them in a 9 inch skillet over a very slow fire. Try out the bacon; that is, cook it until all the fat is melted. Beat with a fork until blended:

4 eggs

Pour them over the bacon and drippings. To cook the dish follow the rule for Fluffy Omelet, page 85. Good served with:

Chopped chives or parsley

SPINACH OMELET

2 Servings

Combine by beating with a fork:

½ cup Creamed Spinach, page 313, or Creamed Broccoli, page 274

4 eggs

Heat in a skillet:

1 tablespoon olive oil

Add the egg mixture. To cook it follow the rule for Fluffy Omelet, page 85.

German Pancake, page 553; Austrian Pancake, page 553.

These pancakes are closely related to the omelet and the soufflé.

CHEESE OMELET

Method I. 4 Servings

Prepare by the rule on page 85:

Fluffy Omelet

Do not fold it over. Sprinkle it with:

½ cup grated cheese
2 tablespoons chopped parsley
(2 tablespoons chopped green pepper)

Bake it in a slow oven 275°, as directed, until the cheese is melted. Serve it garnished with:

Parsley

Method II.

Or, when it is nearly done sprinkle the top with:

6 tablespoons grated cheese
⅛ teaspoon salt
A few grains cayenne

Finish cooking the omelet and fold it over. It is not necessary to bake it.

ANCHOVY OMELET

4 Servings

Rub a small bowl with:

A clove garlic

Follow the rule on page 85 for:

Fluffy Omelet

Place the milk, yolks and baking powder in the bowl. Stir in these ingredients:

1 teaspoon chopped parsley
¾ teaspoon anchovy paste

LOBSTER OR CRAB-MEAT OMELET

4 Servings

Sauté until light brown:

1 tablespoon minced onion

in:

2 tablespoons butter

Stir in and simmer for 3 minutes:

1 tablespoon or more chopped celery
¾ cup diced lobster meat

Prepare in another skillet:

Fluffy Omelet, page 85

Before folding it spread it with the

lobster mixture. You may add at the last moment:

1 tablespoon sherry

Fold it over. Garnish it with:

Parsley

OMELET WITH HERBS
4 Servings

Prepare by a rule on page 85:

Omelet

Before folding it over sprinkle it with:

Dried Herbs, page 833, or fresh minced herbs

OMELET AND SAUSAGES
4 Servings

Broil:

6 breakfast sausages

Drain them on absorbent paper. Keep them hot. Prepare:

Fluffy Omelet, page 85

Place the sausages on the omelet and fold it over. Garnish it with:

Parsley

You may serve it with:

(Tomato Sauce, page 433)

OMELET AND FISH ROE

Prepare:

Fish Roe, page 243

Prepare:

Fluffy Omelet, page 85

Surround the omelet with the roe. Serve it garnished with:

Lemon slices, water cress or parsley

OMELET WITH CREOLE OR OTHER SAUCE

Prepare:

Creole Sauce, page 434

Prepare:

Omelet, page 85

Pour the sauce around it. Try left-over gravy, with bits of meat or cooked fish, vegetables, cheese sauce, canned soups, etc., in place of the sauce.

BREAKFAST DISH
Individual Serving

Place in a colander and let cold water run over:

A shredded wheat biscuit

Have it good and soppy. Drain it. Place it on a greased pan. Place over it:

1 tablespoon butter

Bake it in a slow oven 300° for 15 minutes. Cover it with:

A poached egg

You may glorify it further by adding:

Hollandaise Sauce, page 429

Bacon slices

STEAMED EGGS ON TOAST
6 Servings

Carefully prepared this makes a delicious dish.

Grease individual molds with:

Butter

Place in each one:

1 teaspoon chopped celery, chives or parsley

Break into each one:

1 or 2 eggs

Season them with:

Salt and paprika

Cover the molds with pieces of waxed paper held in place by rubber bands. Place the molds in a pan of hot water on top of the stove and cook the eggs gently until they are firm. Turn them out on:

Rounds of hot buttered toast

Serve them with well-seasoned:

Cream Sauce I, page 428, or Tomato Sauce, page 433

Custard for Timbales, page 212.

EGGS AND CHEESE IN BREAD CASES
4 Servings

Prepare by rule 4 or 6 under Luncheon and Supper Dishes, page 77:

4 Bread Shells or hard rolls

Spread them with:

1 tablespoon melted butter

Sprinkle them with:

¼ cup grated cheese

Break into a bowl:

2 eggs

Add and beat well:

6 tablespoons cream

¼ teaspoon salt

A few grains dry mustard

A few grains cayenne

Fill the cases with this mixture. Sprinkle the tops with:

¼ cup grated cheese

Bake the cases in a moderate oven 350° until the cheese is brown. Or, drop a whole egg in each bread case and cover it with 1 tablespoonful of cream. Bake as directed until the eggs are firm. Season them. Serve them with:

Chopped parsley or chives

Good with a hot sauce, mushroom, tomato, etc. You may use a canned soup.

CREAMED EGGS AND ASPARAGUS
6 Servings

The following recipe always meets with favor. It is a fine Sunday-night dish with a green salad. If you wish to "stretch" the dish, serve it on slices of buttered toast.

Prepare by the rule on page 79:

5 hard-cooked eggs

When cold, peel them and cut them in very thin slices. Drain, then cut in 2 the contents of:

1 can asparagus tips: 16 oz.

Melt in a saucepan over low heat:

4 tablespoons butter

Stir in:

4 tablespoons flour

Add slowly:

2 cups cream, or rich milk and asparagus water

Season the sauce with:

Salt and paprika
(Freshly grated nutmeg)

Stir the sauce until it boils. Fold in the asparagus tips and remove the pan from the fire. Place a layer of sliced eggs in a buttered baking dish, add a layer of asparagus and repeat this process until the dish is filled. Cover the top with:

½ cup bread crumbs

Dot it with:

2 tablespoons butter

Heat but do not cook the dish in a moderate oven 350°, or under a broiler. To reheat place it over hot water. If preferred, this dish may be served without being breaded and baked.

EGGS IN ONION SAUCE
4 Servings

Skin, then dice:

2 medium-sized onions

Cook them for 3 minutes in boiling water. Drain them well. Stir and cook the onions slowly, but do not let them brown, for about 5 minutes in:

4 tablespoons butter

Stir in:

3 tablespoons flour
¾ teaspoon salt
⅛ teaspoon pepper

Stir in:

2 cups rich milk

Cook the onions in a double boiler, with occasional stirring, for 45 minutes. Add:

6 sliced or halved hard-cooked eggs

If desired, the onions may be strained from the sauce before the eggs are added. Or, place these ingredients in an oven-proof dish. Sprinkle the top with:

½ cup bread or cracker crumbs
¼ cup grated Parmesan cheese

Place the dish under a broiler or place it in a 400° oven to brown the top lightly.

CREAMED EGGS WITH CHEESE
4 Servings

Slice into a baking dish:

4 hard-cooked eggs

Combine:

1½ cups cream sauce
4 tablespoons chili sauce

Pour this mixture over the eggs. Top it with:

¼ cup dry bread crumbs
¼ cup grated cheese
¼ teaspoon paprika
¼ teaspoon salt

Place the dish under the broiler or in a hot oven until the cheese is melted.

CURRIED EGGS
Method I. 3 Servings

An occasional curry dish is a treat. Cook by the rule on page 79:

4 hard-cooked eggs

Shell and slice them. Melt:

1½ tablespoons butter

You may brown in it:

1 teaspoon chopped onion

Stir in until blended:

1½ tablespoons flour

Stir in slowly:

1 cup hot milk

Season the sauce with:

¼ teaspoon salt
⅛ teaspoon paprika
½ teaspoon or more curry powder

When the sauce is smooth and boiling fold in the eggs. You may add:

¼ cup seedless raisins

Soak the raisins in the milk for 30 minutes. Strain the milk before adding it to the butter and flour. If raisins are added, omit the onions.

Method II. 4 Servings

Cook by the rule on page 79:

6 hard-cooked eggs

Shell and slice them. Peel and dice:

1 small onion
1 apple

You may pound and add:

(¼ cup blanched almonds)

Sauté these ingredients for 5 minutes in:
> 2 tablespoons butter

Add and simmer for 8 minutes:
> 1¾ cups rich milk, chicken stock or a combination of both

Add, if needed:
> Salt and paprika

Dissolve:
> 1½ teaspoons cornstarch
> ½ to 1½ teaspoons curry powder

in:
> ¼ cup milk or chicken stock

Add this mixture to the other ingredients. Stir and cook them for 2 minutes. Add the eggs. Heat them well. Serve them on:
> Hot buttered toast

garnished with:
> Parsley

Curried Eggs and Mushrooms, page 177; Mushrooms à la King, page 176.

EGGS IN SPINACH WITH CHEESE OR EGGS FLORENTINE

Half fill a buttered baking dish or individual molds with:
> Creamed Spinach, page 313

Sprinkle it with:
> Grated Parmesan or other cheese

Press hollows in the spinach with a large spoon. Break into each hollow:
> 1 egg

Season it with:
> Salt and paprika

Sprinkle the top with:
> Grated cheese

Cover the entire dish with:
> Cream Sauce I, page 428, or Béchamel Sauce, page 429

Place the dish in a pan of hot water in a moderate oven 325° for about 12 minutes, until the eggs are firm.

EGGS IN A NEST
4 Servings
The following is a good sequel to a ham dinner. Prepare:
> 2 cups Mashed Potatoes, page 302

or soften:
> 2 cups cold mashed potatoes

with:
> 5 tablespoons hot milk

Add:
> ½ cup chopped ham or sautéed minced bacon

> 3 tablespoons chopped parsley
> Salt and paprika
> (Celery seed)

Place this mixture in a baking dish and press 4 large hollows in it with a spoon. Break into the hollows:
> 4 eggs

The top may be sprinkled with:
> Bread crumbs

and dotted with:
> Butter

Bake the dish in a moderate oven 325° until the eggs are firm but not hard, for about 12 minutes. If well seasoned, no sauce is needed with this dish. It may be served with Tomato Sauce, page 433.

DEVILED EGGS
Prepare:
> Hard-Cooked Eggs, page 79

Shell the eggs, cut them in halves, remove the yolks. Crush the yolks with a fork and work them into a smooth paste with:
> Mayonnaise, French dressing, cream or butter

Season the paste with:
> Salt, paprika, celery seed
> (A little dry mustard)

Fill the egg whites with the paste and garnish the eggs with:
> Chopped parsley or chives
> Sliced olives, anchovies, capers, etc.
> Paprika

Cream and vinegar or cream and lemon juice may be substituted for the mayonnaise or French dressing. So may anchovy paste, liver sausage, deviled ham, grated Roquefort cheese, etc. Good seasonings are Worcestershire sauce, catsup or chili sauce, Tabasco sauce, etc.

Deviled Eggs de Luxe, page 37.

DEVILED EGGS IN TOMATO OR OTHER SAUCE
4 Servings
Prepare by the above rule:
> 4 Deviled Eggs

Place the halves in a greased dish. Pour over them:
> 1 cup Tomato Sauce, page 433, or Mornay Sauce, page 431, or Béchamel Sauce, page 429, or Mushroom Sauce, page 436, or canned soup sauce

The top may be covered with:
Bread crumbs
dotted with:
Butter
and sprinkled with:
Grated cheese
Bake the dish in a hot oven 425° until
the top is brown.

---

*Hard-Cooked Eggs on Tomatoes with
Sauce, page 37.*

DEVILED EGG AND CRAB CASEROLE
4 Servings

I'm tired of writing definite rules so
this is going to be a beautifully indef-
inite one. If an imagination is not
exercised, doesn't it become atrophied?
I've never given mine a chance to relax
so I don't know. If you have an inventive urge, this is a good practice
dish.
Drain well the contents of:
1 can crab meat: 6½ oz.
Of course this may be shrimp, tuna,
etc. Place it in a 7 or 8 inch greased
baking dish. Prepare by the rule on
page 89:
4 to 6 Deviled Eggs
Devil them any way you like without
giving them any particularly dominant
flavor. Place them over the crab. Now
invent a sauce. Flavor it to suit your
taste. Use a choice of mustard, curry,
celery seed, herbs, onion, etc. There
should be about:
1 cup of sauce
based on 2 tablespoonfuls of butter and
2 tablespoonfuls of flour. Let the 1
cupful of liquid be part fish liquor, if
any, evaporated milk or cream and
stock, either meat or vegetable. Flavor
the sauce well but delicately and if the
fish is salty go easy on the salt. You
may add to the sauce:
**2 or more tablespoons grated
Cheddar cheese**
Heat the dish well in a hot oven 425°.
Serve it with hot bread, a salad, hot
coffee and a fruit dessert if you wish to
win friends and influence people.

HARD-COOKED EGG AND VEGETABLE CASSEROLE
5 Servings
A fine main dish.

Prepare by the rule on page 428:
1 cup Cream Sauce I
Melt:
2 tablespoons fat
Add:
**2 tablespoons chopped onion
2 tablespoons chopped peppers**
Cook them until tender. Add:
**1¼ cups canned or stewed tomatoes
or canned tomato soup
1 minced clove garlic
¼ teaspoon chili or curry powder**
Stir and cook these ingredients until
they are thick. Add them to the cream
sauce. You may add:
**2 teaspoons minced herb, chopped
parsley, thyme, basil, etc.**
Dill or celery seeds are wonderful.
Add if you wish, I do:
½ teaspoon brown sugar
Prepare by the rule on page 79:
5 Hard-Cooked Eggs
Slice them. Grease a baking dish. Place
alternate layers of eggs and sauce in
the dish. Top it with:
**½ cup crushed cornflakes, cracker
or dry bread crumbs**
Dot them with:
Butter
Cover them with:
½ cup grated cheese
Bake the dish in a moderate oven 350°
for about 15 minutes. This is a fine
utility dish. Add scraps of meat, fish,
cooked vegetables, etc.

EGGS AND HERRING IN CREAM SOUP
2 Servings
Grease a baking dish. Break into pieces
the contents of:
**1 can herring snacks or kippered
herring: 6 oz.**
Place them in the dish. Combine, then
pour over them:
**⅔ cup canned cream soup: celery,
asparagus, mushroom, etc.
2 tablespoons onion juice
(1 tablespoon chopped parsley
or ½ teaspoon dried herb)**
Place over the soup:
4 eggs
Put each one in a saucer and then slide
it off. Season them with:
**¼ teaspoon salt
A grating of fresh pepper**
Bake in a moderate oven 325° from 15
to 20 minutes, until the eggs are set.
This may be served au gratin.

Starchy Foods

Spaghetti, Macaroni, Noodles, Etc.

These are inexpensive dishes, good fillers, easily prepared and an ideal accompaniment to any number of foods. They may be cooked in advance and reheated. It is best to moisten them with butter, cream, milk, bouillon or tomato juice, etc., when reheating them on top of a stove or in an oven.

You may combine the starch dishes with other ingredients, cooked meat, sea food, vegetables, herbs, etc. They take a good deal of doctoring to make them interesting. You may place them in a greased oven-proof dish and bake them in a moderately hot to hot oven 375° to 425° until the top is brown. Of course, you may serve them with sauce—tomato, creole, cheese, mushroom, etc. Here are some brief rules for cooking these foods.

Rules for Boiling Spaghetti, Macaroni, Creamettes and Noodles

	Amount	Uncooked	Yield when cooked
Spaghetti Macaroni broken	½ lb.	Approximately 2 cupfuls	4 cupfuls
Creamettes	½ lb.	2 cupfuls	4 cupfuls
Noodles broken	½ lb.	2 cupfuls	2½ cupfuls

The key to good "pasta" or starch foods listed above is to immerse them so gradually into a quantity of rapidly boiling water as not to disturb the boiling point. One-half pound of pasta calls for about 2 quarts of water seasoned with 2 teaspoonfuls of salt. The boiling point is maintained throughout the cooking until the pasta is done.

You ask what is "until done"? This is a matter of individual taste. Authorities are agreed that overcooking is to be avoided, especially if the spaghetti, etc., is to be reheated in sauce or otherwise. An Italian may think 8 to 10 minutes to a point he calls "al dente," so the pasta still resists the teeth, is ideal. My preference is 10 to 15 minutes, according to the thickness of the pasta used.

When done drain the pasta in a strainer. Noodles may be rinsed after cooking. Pour 4 cupfuls of boiling or cold water over them. Reheat them over hot water.

All cooked pasta is good drained, then well doused with melted butter to which chopped rosemary or basil may be added. Serve the dish with grated Parmesan cheese passed at table or with one of the following combinations of cheese:

⅓ part Swiss to ⅔ part American cheese or
½ part Parmesan to ½ part American cheese or
⅓ part Swiss to ⅔ part Cheddar cheese

In the following recipes spaghetti, noodles, macaroni and creamettes may be used interchangeably if the amounts and the time for cooking are properly gauged by the above rules.

SPAGHETTI, ETC.

The basis of this dish is usually an Italian noodle, cooked, to which a tomato sauce is added. Into the tomato sauce you may put garlic or onion, green pepper or other vegetables and ground beef sautéed in olive oil or fat, but you need not confine yourself by any means to beef or to the vegetables given above. Cooked chicken, chicken livers, liver, pork, bacon, sausage meat or sliced sausage, mushrooms, clams, oysters, anchovies, stuffed or green olives, stock, Worcestershire sauce, etc., may be added to the dish, which seems best when largely inspirational. Some recipes call for red wine, cinnamon, cloves and other spices. Herbs give it zest, and cheese, preferably Parmesan, completes it.

SPAGHETTI WITH BEEF
About 2½ Quarts
Cook by the rule on page 91:
    6 oz. spaghetti: 1½ cups
Mince and cook over a very slow fire:
    3 slices bacon
Stir in:
    ¼ cup chopped onion
    2 tablespoons olive oil
    ½ lb. ground round steak
When the meat is nearly done, add:
    2½ cups tomatoes: No. 2 can
    ½ cup chopped green peppers
    1 No. 1 can chopped mushrooms
    or ½ lb. to 1 lb. fresh sliced
    Sautéed Mushrooms, page 292
    Mushroom liquor
    Salt, cayenne or paprika
    ½ lb. grated cheese: 2 cups
Stir in the cooked drained spaghetti. If it is too dry add:
    ½ cup stock or canned bouillon
Steam it in a double boiler or in a mold for 1 hour.

BAKED SPAGHETTI
Follow the preceding rule for:
    Spaghetti with Beef
Reserve the cheese. Place the spaghetti in a baking dish, sprinkle the cheese over it and bake for 15 to 20 minutes in a moderate oven 375°.

ITALIAN SPAGHETTI
About 4 Quarts
Grind:
    1 lb. round steak
    ¼ lb. chicken or calf liver
Chop:
    3 large onions
    3 or 4 carrots
    1 clove garlic
    5 ribs celery
Melt in a large saucepan:
    ½ cup shortening or oil
Sauté the vegetables in it. Stir in the meat. Cook it until it is done. Add the contents of:
    1 No. 3 can tomatoes: 4 cups
Stir in:
    2 tablespoons chili powder
    1 cup canned, dried or sautéed
    mushrooms
    2½ teaspoons salt
Simmer these ingredients until they are thick, for about 1 hour. Add:
    ⅓ cup chopped parsley
    2 teaspoons dried basil
Boil by the rule on page 91:
    2 lbs. spaghetti
Drain it. Place alternate layers of the spaghetti and meat mixture in a dish. Sprinkle the top with:
    Chopped parsley
Serve the spaghetti with:
    Grated Roman cheese

ITALIAN SPAGHETTI WITH SAUCE
About 6 Servings
In Italy spaghetti is served in one dish, the sauce in another and grated cheese in a third. The sauce may be poured over the spaghetti, which is tossed until the two are well blended. Cook by the rule on page 91:
    1 lb. unbroken spaghetti
When well drained pour over it:
    ¼ cup melted butter
Prepare one of the following sauces. Put the spaghetti in a bowl. Pour the sauce over it and toss until well coated.

MEAT SAUCE FOR SPAGHETTI
8 to 10 Servings
Heat:
    ¾ cup olive oil
Slice, add and remove when brown:
    2 cloves garlic
Add and brown lightly:
    ¼ cup chopped onion
Add:
    1 lb. ground round steak
    ½ lb. ground lean pork
    1 can Italian tomatoes: 15 oz.
    1 can Italian tomato paste: 6 oz.
    ½ cup water
    1½ teaspoons salt
    ¼ teaspoon paprika

Simmer the sauce covered for 2 hours.
You may add for the last 15 minutes:
    ½ cup chopped celery
    ½ cup sliced mushrooms
Season it with:
    2 teaspoons dried basil
Serve it as directed above with:
    Grated Parmesan cheese

ANCHOVY SAUCE FOR SPAGHETTI
About 2 Cupfuls
Sauté until light brown:
    ½ cup chopped onion
in:
    2 tablespoons butter
    2 tablespoons olive oil
Add and simmer covered for 15 minutes:
    1½ cups chopped tomatoes
    6 finely minced anchovies
    1 tablespoon chopped parsley
    ½ teaspoon dried basil or thyme
Add:
    2 tablespoons water
    3 tablespoons grated Parmesan cheese
    Salt if needed
    Freshly ground pepper

TUNA FISH SAUCE FOR SPAGHETTI, ETC.
4 Servings
Drain, reserving the oil, the contents of:
    1 can tuna fish: 7 oz.
Heat the oil in a 12 inch skillet. There should be about ¼ cupful. Add salad oil if needed. Add:
    ⅔ cup chopped onions
    1 chopped clove garlic
Simmer these ingredients for about 10 minutes. Stir in the tuna. Cook it until it begins to color. Add:
    1 cup Italian tomato sauce
Simmer the sauce uncovered until it begins to thicken, about 18 minutes. Add:
    2 tablespoons chopped parsley or
    1 teaspoon dried basil
    A grating of pepper
    Salt as needed
    (½ teaspoon brown sugar)
Serve the sauce poured over rice, spaghetti or noodles.

SPAGHETTI CHEESE SAUCE WITH MUSHROOMS AND ANCHOVIES
4 Servings
Melt:

    3 tablespoons butter
Sauté in the butter by the rule on page 292:
    ½ lb. fresh, thinly sliced mushrooms
Cut into small pieces and add:
    8 fillets of anchovy or
    3 cooked chicken livers or
    ½ cup cooked clams
Add and stir over low heat until melted:
    1 cup grated cheese
Add:
    Salt as needed
    ⅛ teaspoon curry powder
    A few grains red pepper
    1 tablespoon chopped parsley
    1 tablespoon chopped chives or other herb
Stir the cheese into the other ingredients. Serve them over cooked spaghetti, noodles, etc.

SPAGHETTI SAUCE WITH LIVER, ONIONS AND TOMATOES
4 Servings
Melt:
    2 tablespoons butter or drippings
Sauté in it until light brown:
    ½ cup chopped onions
Add and sauté very lightly:
    1 cup cubed liver
Add and simmer for 15 minutes:
    ½ cup tomato sauce
Season with:
    1 teaspoon salt
    ⅛ teaspoon pepper
    (¼ teaspoon basil or thyme)
Serve the sauce over noodles, spaghetti, etc., garnished with:
    Parsley

Blender Spaghetti Sauce, page 898. See Italian Macaroni, Spaghetti or Noodles, page 94.

ITALIAN SPAGHETTI WITH SEA FOOD
About 1½ Quarts
Cook by the rule on page 91, then drain well:
    ½ lb. spaghetti
Combine and blend well:
    1 cup meat stock
    1 cup tomato purée
    1 clove minced garlic
    Salt and paprika
    1 teaspoon Worcestershire sauce
    1 cup shredded anchovies, cooked ham and tongue or

1 cup cooked sea food
Stir in the spaghetti. Steam it covered in a double boiler for ½ hour. Add:
   2 tablespoons butter
Serve the spaghetti with:
   Grated Parmesan cheese

SPAGHETTI WITH SEA FOOD
About 2½ Quarts
Cook by the rule on page 91.
   ½ lb. spaghetti: 2 cups
Heat the contents of:
   1 can condensed tomato soup: 10½ oz.
Melt in a saucepan over slow heat:
   4 tablespoons butter
Stir in and cook for 1 minute:
   ¼ cup or more chopped onion
   ¾ cup chopped green pepper
Stir in until blended:
   4 tablespoons flour
Stir in slowly:
   2 cups Stock, page 44, or milk
When the sauce is thick, add very slowly, stirring constantly the hot tomato soup and:
   ½ lb. diced cheese
When the cheese is melted, add:
   ½ lb. cooked or canned diced lobster, crab, shrimp or tuna
and the boiled, drained and rinsed spaghetti. Add seasoning. This dish may be prepared in advance. To reheat place it over boiling water.

QUICK SPAGHETTI WITH SOUP AND BACON
4 Servings
Sauté until nearly crisp:
   8 slices bacon or 1 cup chopped tongue, ham or potted meat
Cut them into large pieces. Combine the contents of:
   1 can condensed mock turtle or pepper pot soup: 10½ oz.
   1 No. 2 can spaghetti
If preferred, cook and substitute 1¼ cupfuls spaghetti or use 2½ cupfuls cooked spaghetti. Add:
   ¼ cup hot water
Place alternate layers of this mixture and the bacon in a greased oven-proof dish. Cover the top with:
   Buttered crumbs
Bake the dish in a moderate oven 375° for about 20 minutes until it is thoroughly heated. If you wish, omit the soup and season the spaghetti with:
   1 teaspoon prepared mustard
   1 teaspoon grated onion

QUICK SPAGHETTI WITH TUNA FISH, SALMON OR BEEF
4 Servings
Drain the contents of:
   1 can tuna fish or salmon: 8 oz.
Or use:
   ½ lb. ground beef
Sauté in the oil:
   ⅓ cup chopped onion
For the beef use:
   4 tablespoons drippings
Add to the onion the contents of:
   1 can condensed tomato soup: 10½ oz.
   1 No. 2 can spaghetti
Fold in the flaked fish. Season with:
   ½ teaspoon sugar
   A few grains cayenne
   Salt and paprika
Cook it until it is thoroughly heated. You may rub a bowl with:
   (A cut clove garlic)
Add the spaghetti. Garnish it with:
   2 tablespoons chopped parsley
This dish may be served in an oven-proof baking dish au gratin. Use a hot oven 400° or a broiler to melt cheese.

Salmon Spaghetti Loaf, page 120; Jambolaya, page 107. The second is a fine rice dish in a spaghetti sauce.

BOILED MACARONI WITH CHEESE
3 Servings
Cook by the rule on page 91.
   4 oz. macaroni: 1 cup
Drain it. Return it to the saucepan. Stir and reheat it over a slow fire with:
   ½ cup cream or rich milk
Place it in a dish and sprinkle it with:
   ½ cup or more grated cheese
Serve it with:
   Tomato Sauce, page 433

ITALIAN MACARONI, SPAGHETTI OR NOODLES
4 to 6 Servings
Cook by the rule on page 91:
   ½ lb. unbroken macaroni or spaghetti
Drain it. Keep it hot. Heat a salad bowl. Rub it with a cut:
   Clove garlic
Place in it:
   ¼ teaspoon salt
   ¼ teaspoon paprika
   4 tablespoons hot oil or melted butter
   1 cup grated cheese

Bring the macaroni to the table. Toss it in the prepared dressing like a salad. Serve it at once.

If you wish to cook macaroni unbroken, place the ends in boiling water until they soften, then bend them, thrust them farther in until the whole is limber and can be gradually submerged.

BAKED MACARONI
4 Servings
Cook by the rule on page 91:
> 4 oz. macaroni: 1 cup

Drain it. Place layers of macaroni in a buttered baking dish. Sprinkle the layers with:
> ⅞ cup grated cheese

Beat until blended:
> 1 or 2 eggs
> ⅔ cup milk
> ¼ teaspoon salt
> ⅛ teaspoon paprika
> A few grains cayenne

Pour this mixture over the macaroni. Sprinkle the top with:
> ¼ cup bread crumbs
> ⅛ cup cheese
> Paprika

Bake the macaroni in a quick oven 400° until it is well browned.
One cupful well-seasoned Cream Sauce I, page 428, may be substituted for the egg and milk mixture.

BAKED MACARONI WITH TOMATOES
Follow the above rule, substitute for the milk:
> ½ cup tomato juice
> ¼ cup cream

Add:
> ½ teaspoon sugar
> (1 tablespoon chopped parsley or 1 teaspoon dried basil or thyme)

MACARONI BAKED WITH SOUR CREAM
4 Servings
Boil by the rule on page 91:
> 1½ cups macaroni

Drain it well. Toss it in:
> 3 tablespoons melted butter

Place it in a greased oven-proof dish. Make a hollow in the center into which pour:
> 1 cup sour cream

You may sprinkle this with:
> ½ cup grated cheese

Bake the macaroni in a quick oven 400° until the top is brown.

MACARONI WITH TOMATOES, CHICKEN LIVERS, MUSHROOMS AND CHEESE
About 2 Quarts
Cook (page 91):
> ½ lb. macaroni

Drain it. Place it in a deep casserole. Sauté (page 292):
> ½ lb. mushrooms

Sauté or boil until tender:
> ½ cup chicken livers or calf liver

Chop the mushrooms and the liver. Boil until fairly thick:
> 4 cups tomatoes: No. 3 can

Strain them. Season them with:
> ¾ tablespoon salt
> 1 teaspoon brown sugar
> A few grains cayenne
> (1 teaspoon dried basil)

Sauté:
> 1 minced onion
> (½ minced clove garlic)

in:
> 2 tablespoons butter

Combine these with the other ingredients and pour them over the macaroni. Mix them well with 2 forks. Sprinkle the top with:
> Grated cheese

Bake or broil the macaroni in a hot oven 400° until the cheese is melted.

MACARONI AND SHRIMP DISH
4 Servings
Boil by the rule on page 91:
> 1½ cups macaroni

Drain it. Sauté:
> 1 tablespoon minced onion

in:
> 3 tablespoons butter

Stir in until blended:
> 1½ tablespoons flour

Stir in until smooth:
> 1½ cups milk
> ¾ cup grated cheese

1 teaspoon Worcestershire sauce
½ teaspoon lemon juice
1 teaspoon salt
¼ teaspoon paprika
    A few grains cayenne
Have ready:
    1½ to 2 cups cleaned shrimp
Place layers of macaroni and shrimp in
a baking dish. Pour the sauce over it.
Cover the top with:
    Bread crumbs
    Grated cheese
Bake the dish in a moderate oven for
about 45 minutes.

MACARONI AND CHICKEN CASSEROLE OR CHICKEN TETRAZZINI
8 to 10 Servings
Cook by the rule on page 402:
    A boiled chicken
Cut the meat from the bones in shreds.
There should be 2 to 3 cupfuls.
Cook by the rule on page 91:
    ½ lb. macaroni
Add to this:
    ½ lb. Sautéed Mushrooms, page
    292
Make a sauce of:
    3 tablespoons butter or chicken fat
    2 tablespoons flour
    2 cups chicken broth
    Seasoning
Remove from fire. Stir in:
    1 cup heavy cream, heated
    2 tablespoons sherry
Add ½ the sauce to the chicken and ½
to the macaroni and mushrooms. Place
the macaroni in a greased baking dish.
Make a hole in the center. Place the
chicken in it. Sprinkle the top with:
    Grated Parmesan cheese
Bake the dish in a moderate oven 375°
until it is lightly browned. You may
add to the chicken:
    ½ cup blanched and shredded
    almonds
A fan writes that she prefers using ¼
pound macaroni and 1 pound mushrooms. A bit more extravagant but
very good.

CANNED MACARONI IN CREAM SAUCE WITH CHEESE
This is a fine base to serve with other
ingredients. Heat the macaroni, make
a mound of it, surround it with a buttered vegetable and serve it with a
meat or fish dish in place of potatoes.
It is delicious au gratin with cheese.

CREAMETTE OR MACARONI LOAF
5 Servings
This delectable dish is very attractive
in appearance. It makes a fine ring
dish.
Boil:
    5 cups water
    1½ teaspoons salt
Add:
    ¾ cup creamettes, macaroni or
    spaghetti
Boil them for 10 minutes. Drain them
in a colander. Place them in a bowl.
Scald:
    ½ cup milk or cream
Beat into it:
    2 or 3 eggs
Melt and add:
    3 tablespoons butter
Pour this over the creamettes. Add:
    ½ cup soft bread crumbs, without
    crusts
    ½ cup grated cheese
    1½ sliced pimientos
    ¼ cup chopped green peppers or
    2 tablespoons chopped parsley
    1 tablespoon grated onion
    ¼ teaspoon salt
    ⅛ teaspoon paprika
    A few grains cayenne
Place these ingredients in a buttered
baking dish. Bake them for 1 hour in a
moderate oven 350°. If baked in a ring,
set the baking dish in a pan of hot
water. Serve with:
    Mushroom Sauce, page 436, or
    Tomato Sauce, page 433
It makes a somewhat lighter dish if
you add only the egg yolks to the
scalded milk. The whites, beaten until
stiff, are then folded into the other
ingredients at the last moment.

MUSTACCIOLI
5 Servings
Melt:
    1 tablespoon butter
Stir and brown in it:
    ¾ to 1 lb. ground round steak
    1 large chopped onion
    1 clove garlic cut into halves
Cover these ingredients with boiling
water. Add:
    ¾ teaspoon salt
    ⅛ teaspoon pepper
Simmer them covered until they are al-
most dry. Fish out the garlic. Add:
    2 cups canned tomatoes
Continue to simmer, stirring frequent-
ly. Cook until the sauce is thick, from

1 to 3 hours. Add mushrooms when the sauce is partly done. Wash well in warm water, then drain:

 ½ lb. dry mushrooms

When the sauce is almost done add:

 ¼ cup olive oil

Cook until tender by the rule on page 91:

 ½ lb. elbow macaroni: about 2 cups

Serve the mustaccioli on a hot platter. First a layer of macaroni, then a layer of sauce, then a layer of macaroni and again a layer of sauce. Sprinkle each meat sauce layer generously with:

 Grated Parmesan cheese
 Freshly grated black pepper

Homemade Noodles, page 73.

SPINACH OR VEGETABLE NOODLES
About 14 Ounces

Cooked vegetables, drained, then finely puréed, may be used to make noodle dough in the following manner. Combine:

 ¼ cup puréed spinach or other drained vegetable
 1 beaten egg
 ¼ teaspoon salt

Stir in gradually, then knead until smooth:

 2 cups flour

Place the dough in a covered dish for 30 minutes. Follow the rule for Homemade Noodles, page 73.

BOILED NOODLES
5 Servings

Drop:

 2 cups noodles

into:

 Boiling salted water—½ teaspoon salt to the quart—or chicken stock, consommé, etc.

Boil them for 20 minutes. If noodles are cooked in chicken stock, consommé, etc., drain but do not rinse these in a colander. If cooked in water, you may rinse them by pouring 4 cupfuls boiling water over them. Drain them well. Moisten them generously with:

 Melted butter or cream (Chicken Stock, page 43)

Serve them with:

 (Grated cheese)

Or sauté:

 ¼ cup bread crumbs

in:

 3 tablespoons butter

and pour them over the noodles. Or see Noodle Topping for Vegetables, page 326. This may be substituted for the bread crumb dressing above. A variation of this is to stir until brown:

 ½ cup blanched chopped almonds

in:

 1 tablespoon butter

Add and melt:

 3 tablespoons butter

Add:

 3 tablespoons poppy seeds

Stir these ingredients into the noodles. Boiled noodles may be arranged in a ring on a platter and the center filled with a creamed meat or vegetable. This is a good simple way of serving hash.

CORN-MEAL NOODLES
About 16 Ounces

Scald:

 1 cup water-ground corn meal

in:

 1½ cups boiling water

Beat in:

 1 tablespoon butter
 1 beaten egg

Sift:

 ½ cup all-purpose flour
 1½ teaspoons any baking powder
 ½ teaspoon salt

To roll, cut and dry follow the rule for Homemade Noodles, page 73.

NOODLES IN CHICKEN BROTH WITH CHEESE

Cook the noodles as directed on page 91. Serve them by the rule given for Italian Macaroni, Spaghetti or Noodles on page 94.

FRIED NOODLES

To be served in the place of a starchy vegetable or as a garnish on vegetables or other dishes, notably Chinese mixtures. Boil in water for 5 minutes:

 Thin noodles

Place them in a colander and rinse them with cold water. Drain them thoroughly. Fry them, a small amount at a time, in deep fat 385°-395° (page 542) until they are a delicate brown. Drain them on absorbent paper. Sprinkle them lightly with:

 Salt

Keep them hot or reheat them in a moderate oven 400°.

NOODLE BASKETS

For these you need a tea strainer about 3 inches in diameter and a second strainer about 3/8 inch smaller that fits into it but leaves space for the swelling of the noodles. Prepare by the rule on page 73:

Noodle Dough

Before the dough is dry fold it over and cut it into 1/4 inch strips. Dip the strainers in hot fat to keep the noodles from sticking. Line the larger strainer with 2 layers of noodles, giving them a crisscross effect. Snip off the ragged edges. Place the smaller strainer over the noodle basket. Fry the noodle basket in deep fat (page 542) heated to 390° until lightly browned. Remove it carefully from the strainers and fry the next one. You may fill the fried baskets at once with creamed food, etc., or you may cool them and reheat them later by dipping them briefly in hot fat without the strainers. Drain them on absorbent paper.

Potato Baskets, page 302.

BAKED NOODLE RING

4 Servings
Cook (page 91):
  1 1/2 cups noodles
Rinse and drain them. Beat:
  2 egg yolks
  1/2 cup milk
  3/4 tablespoon melted butter
  1/4 teaspoon salt
  1/8 teaspoon paprika
  (1/8 teaspoon nutmeg)
Combine this mixture with the noodles. Beat until stiff:
  2 egg whites
Fold them lightly into the noodles. Butter a 7 inch ring mold or individual ring molds. Fill them with the noodle mixture and bake them set in a pan of hot water in a moderate oven 350° until done, about 45 minutes for a large mold or 30 minutes for the small ones. Invert the contents of the molds on hot plates and fill the centers with:
  Creamed spinach, peas, mush-
  rooms, hash, stewed tomatoes,
  etc.

NOODLE RING WITH CHEESE

A great favorite.
Follow the preceding rule for Baked Noodle Ring. Use in all:
  3/4 cup milk

Add to the noodle mixture before folding in the egg whites:
  1 1/2 teaspoons Worcestershire sauce
  1/2 tablespoon catsup
  3/4 cup grated cheese

NOODLE RING WITH WHIPPED CREAM

10 Servings
A famous Eastern house makes a specialty of this dish and sells the recipe to those who are willing to pay the price. Use a 9 inch ring. For 5 servings take half the recipe and use a 7 inch ring. Cook (page 91):
  2 cups fine noodles
Rinse and drain them. Beat and pour over the noodles:
  4 egg yolks
  1/4 teaspoon paprika
  1/2 cup melted butter
Whip until stiff:
  4 egg whites
  1/4 teaspoon salt
Beat:
  1 cup heavy cream, sweet or sour
Fold the egg whites and the cream lightly into the noodle mixture. Fill a well-greased ring. Place it in a pan of hot water. Bake it in a moderate oven 350° until it is firm, for about 1 hour or more. Invert the ring and fill it with:
  Green peas or creamed food,
  sweetbreads, fish, etc.

HAM NOODLES

8 Servings
This rule is capable of a wide interpretation and its proportions may be varied. Cook (page 91):
  1 1/2 cups noodles
Grease a baking dish. Place in it layers of noodles sprinkled with:
  3/4 cup ground ham
  (1/2 cup grated cheese)
  (1/2 cup shredded green pepper and
  celery)
Combine:
  1 1/2 cups milk
  1 or 2 eggs
  1/4 teaspoon paprika
  1/4 to 1/2 teaspoon salt, omit if the
  ham is very salty
Pour this over the noodles. The top may be covered with·
  Bread crumbs
Bake the dish for 1 hour in a moderate oven 350°.

LEFT-OVER NOODLE DISH

Follow the above rule. Substitute for the ham:

> Diced cooked roast, chicken,
> crab, shrimp, chipped beef,
> mushrooms and other vegetables

Part gravy may be substituted for milk.

NOODLES, STEWED PRUNES AND CROUTONS

This is a traditional Good Friday dish in a number of European countries. It is a reminder of how good simple food may be in a tempting combination. Prepare:

> Boiled Noodles, page 97
> Stewed Prunes, page 450
> Croutons, page 73

Serve the noodles hot with the croutons poured over them. Serve the prunes from a separate bowl.

RAVIOLI

An Italian filled pastry made much like a Filled Cookie, page 670, but this process may be mass produced as described below:
Sift onto a board:

> 1½ cups flour
> ⅛ teaspoon salt

Drop into the center:

> 1 whole egg
> 2 egg yolks

Moisten these ingredients lightly with warm water and knead into a stiff, smooth dough. Cover it with a cloth and permit it to stand for 10 minutes. Roll the dough until it is very thin. Cut it into 2 sheets. On one sheet put a teaspoonful of ravioli filling in little mounds 2 inches apart. Cover them with the second sheet which may be brushed lightly with water. Press the top sheet gently around the ravioli mounds. Press the edges. Cut the dough into squares with a mound in each center. Use a pie jagger or a cookie cutter. Dry the ravioli for about 2 hours. Drop them into boiling, salted

water or into chicken broth. Simmer them for 10 minutes. Remove them from the liquid with a skimmer onto a hot platter. Sprinkle them with:

> Grated Parmesan cheese

Serve with sauce or roast gravy.

RAVIOLI FILLING

This is usually a spinach and meat mixture very finely chopped or put through a purée strainer. Grated cheese and light seasoning may be added. Sometimes the filling is thickened slightly with bread crumbs or egg. There may be much leeway in the composition of the filling and you may use any combination of meat and vegetables you like.
Combine:

> ¼ cup cooked puréed spinach
> ¼ cup chopped cooked meat
> 1 egg
> 2 tablespoons cracker crumbs
> 2 tablespoons grated cheese
> Stock, cream or gravy to form
> a stiff paste
> Seasoning
> (½ clove minced garlic)

Or:

> ½ cup cooked drained spinach
> ½ cup cooked minced chicken
> 2 tablespoons grated cheese
> Salt and pepper
> ½ teaspoon dried basil or ⅛ teaspoon nutmeg
> (½ clove minced garlic)

RAVIOLI SAUCE

Melt:

> 2 tablespoons butter

Stir in:

> 2 tablespoons flour

Combine and stir in:

> 4 tablespoons Italian tomato
> paste
> 1¼ cups water

Stir and cook the sauce until it bubbles. The Anchovy Sauce for Spaghetti, page 93, is fine for this.

Cereals

On the train trip from Palermo to Siracusa a stranger leaned toward us to say in the most casual tone that this was the field where Pluto grabbed off Persephone and rushed her to his dark abode. This brought to mind the lamentations of her mother Ceres and a speculation as to how much greater those lamentations would have been had she known what modern processing was to do to the grains that bear her name.

Store all dry cereals in a cool place tightly covered and watch whole grains especially for rancidity or insect infestation.

Scientists tell us that cereals are edible as soon as the starch granules swell to their fullest capacity in hot liquid. This state they speak of glibly as gelatinization, although it remains something of a chemical mystery. To cooks this phenomenon is evident in the thickening of cereals and sauces. While the learned gentlemen insist that the starch and protein in cereals are adequately cooked in a short period of time, many cooks claim that the results are not so nutty and sweet as when the older, slow-heat methods are used.

Whether you back the cook or the scientist, on one point they agree. Cereals must be added slowly to very rapidly boiling water and stirred in so that each individual grain is surrounded and quickly penetrated by the hot liquid. The boiling point of the water, 212°, must be maintained throughout the period of adding the cereal.

With cereals that tend to gumminess this slow addition to the boiling water allows the outer starch layers to stabilize and keeps the grains separated after swelling. Coarsely ground cereals may be added dry. Granular fine cereals may be moistened with part of the measured cold water to form a loose mush and may be poured slowly as described above into the rapidly boiling water. Processed cereals should be cooked according to the directions on the label.

RULE FOR COOKING CEREALS

Cereals increase in bulk depending on the amount of water they absorb. You may count on 4 to 6 servings for each cupful of uncooked cereal. If you cook cereal in advance of use—a convenient but nutritionally wasteful procedure—cover it while still hot from the first cooking so no crust forms on top. To avoid ·lumps on reheating over hot water allow the cereal to heat through before stirring. Cook granular cereals like:

Corn meal, farina, cream of wheat and hominy

for 2 to 3 minutes over direct heat and then from 5 to 15 minutes over hot water. See directions above. Allow:

4 to 6 cups water
1 teaspoon salt

to:

1 cup cereal

Cook coarse grains like:

Brown rice, whole or cracked wheat, samp and whole buck-wheat

or flaky cereals like:

Rolled oats

for 3 to 5 minutes over direct heat and then 20 to 30 minutes over hot water. See directions above. Allow:

2 to 4 cups water
1 teaspoon salt

to:

1 cup cereal

If you want to cook any of these cereals longer, start out as directed above and if necessary add more milk or water during the cooking period. During the last few minutes of cooking you may add:

3 tablespoons dry skim-milk solids
2 teaspoons yeast powder

for:

Each cup dry cereal

These ingredients make no noticeable change in taste and are a great addition in food value. You may add at this time:

Dates, figs, raisins and cooked dried fruits

GRITS OR CORN-MEAL MUSH
4 Servings

Combine and stir:

1 cup water-ground corn meal or grits
1 cup cold water
1 teaspoon salt

Place in the top of a double boiler:

4 cups boiling water

Stir in the corn-meal mixture gradually. Cook and stir the mush over a quick flame from 2 to 3 minutes. Steam it, covered, over boiling water for 15 minutes or more. Stir it frequently.

Grits Ring, page 157; Boiled Rice, page 103.

CHEESE, MEAT OR VEGETABLES IN CEREALS

Grated cheese may be stirred into cooked, hot cereals. So may cooked chopped meat, ham and vegetables.

SAUTÉED CEREAL CAKES

Roll cooked cereal into small balls, then flatten them. Or, pack a cooked, lukewarm cereal firmly into a small loaf pan or a tin can rinsed in cold water. Cover the mush. Chill it well, cut it into slices. Spread the balls or slices with melted butter or drippings. They may be dipped in seasoned egg diluted with 1 tablespoonful of water and then in crumbs, flour or corn meal. Sauté them until well browned in butter or bacon drippings. Do this slowly if you like them crisp, allowing about 15 minutes. Corn-meal mush may be bought ready for use. Serve the cakes with sirup and sausages.

SCRAPPLE

These are of various kinds. The basis is corn-meal mush and finely chopped or ground meat spiced with herbs and well seasoned. Follow the rule for corn-meal mush and the above rule for corn-meal mush sautéed. Fresh meat may be cooked with the corn-meal mush or cooked meat may be added later. Proportions vary—a good one is 1 to 2 cupfuls of meat to 1 cupful of corn meal.

Pork Scrapple, page 147.

SAUTÉED CANNED HOMINY CAKE

4 Servings
Place in a skillet the contents of:
    1 No. 2½ can hominy: 3½ cups
Cover and simmer the hominy for ½ hour. Mash it and beat in:
    1 teaspoon grated onion
    ¼ cup butter
    Seasoning
Spread the hominy in a well-greased skillet. Sauté the cake until it is crisp on the bottom, turn it and crisp the other side.

For other Hominy Dishes see Index.

CANNED HOMINY CAKES

5 Servings
These cakes are a variation on potatoes. Drain the contents of:
    1 No. 2 can hominy
Combine it with:
    2 tablespoons flour
    1 egg
    Salt and pepper
Form these ingredients into flat cakes. Sauté them until they are brown in:
    Butter or drippings

Serve them hot plain or with:
    Honey or sirup

CANNED HOMINY WITH CHILI CON CARNE OR CHEESE SAUCE

6 Large Servings
Drain the contents of:
    1 No. 2 can hominy
Add it to the contents of:
    1 No. 2 can chili con carne
and you may add:
    Minced onion and celery
Place these ingredients in a greased baking dish. Sprinkle the top with:
    Bread crumbs and grated cheese
Or, combine and place in a baking dish:
    2 cups drained hominy
    1 cup Cheese Sauce, page 430
    ½ cup minced green pepper
Cover the top with:
    Strips of bacon
Bake the dish in a hot oven 400° for about 20 minutes.

SCALLOPED CANNED HOMINY WITH TOMATO SAUCE

4 Servings
Combine:
    ½ cup water
    10½ oz. condensed tomato soup or 2 cups cream sauce
Add:
    ½ teaspoon salt
    ½ teaspoon sugar
    ⅛ teaspoon paprika or pepper
Drain, then add the contents of:
    1 No. 2 can hominy
Heat these ingredients. Combine:
    1 cup soft bread crumbs
    1 cup grated cheese
    ⅛ teaspoon paprika
    ¼ teaspoon salt
Place ½ the hominy mixture in a greased baking dish, cover it with ½ the bread mixture. Dot the top with:
    1 tablespoon butter
Repeat the process. Bake the dish in a moderate oven 375° until the top is brown—about 12 minutes.

HOMINY CREOLE

4 Servings
Combine and sauté until brown:
    1 cup pork sausage
    3 cups drained canned hominy
    ½ teaspoon savory
    (2 tablespoons chopped onion)

Add and heat:
  1 cup canned tomato soup
  ¾ teaspoon salt
Serve these ingredients topped with:
  ½ cup buttered crumbs

POLENTA OR CORN-MEAL MUSH WITH CHEESE
About 5½ Cupfuls
This Italian dish resembles American corn-meal mush. It is one of the principal articles of food among the poorer classes of Italians, who frequently buy it fried from street vendors. It lends itself to endless variations. Cheese is sometimes cooked with polenta—sometimes it is served sprinkled over it. Tomato sauce, meat gravy or a combination of both is another favorite accompaniment. Polenta is served as mush or fried mush in the place of a potato dish at dinner or as a main dish with a salad for a lighter meal.
Prepare:
  Corn-Meal Mush, page 100
Add to it for the last 15 minutes of cooking:
  ⅛ teaspoon paprika
  A few grains red pepper
  (½ cup grated cheese)
Or serve it sprinkled generously with:
  Grated cheese, preferably
  Parmesan
  A few grains red pepper

FRIED POLENTA
Follow the rule for Sautéed Cereal Cakes, page 100.

GNOCCHI WITH FLOUR
4 Servings
An Italian dish which is either served as a separate course or in place of potatoes. It is delicate and delicious.
Scald:
  1 cup milk
Melt in a skillet:
  2 tablespoons butter
Stir and blend in until smooth:
  2 tablespoons flour
  2 tablespoons cornstarch
  ¼ teaspoon salt
Stir in the scalded milk. Reduce the heat to a low flame and add:
  1 egg yolk
  (½ cup grated cheese)
Beat the batter until the egg has thickened and the cheese has melted. Pour it onto a shallow greased platter or

pan. When it is cool, cut it into strips 2 inches long. Place the strips in a pan and pour over them:
  Melted butter
Sprinkle them with:
  (Grated cheese)
Bake them in a moderate oven 375° until the cheese is melted. The cheese may be omitted in the batter and later without detracting from the quality of the dish. In that case use an additional tablespoonful of flour.
The above is the recipe given me in Italy, but I prefer poaching the batter, after it has been cut into strips, in gently boiling water or stock for 1 or 2 minutes, draining the strips and serving them with melted butter. Cut into small shapes, this batter is good served in soup. As it is cooked it need only be well heated.

GNOCCHI WITH POTATOES
6 Servings
Boil, then put through a ricer:
  2 medium-sized potatoes
Heat to the boiling point:
  ½ cup milk
  5 tablespoons butter
Stir in until the dough forms a ball:
  1 cup flour
Remove from fire. Beat in:
  2 eggs
  1 teaspoon salt
  ¼ teaspoon paprika
  (3 tablespoons grated cheese)
and the potatoes. Sprinkle the dough with flour. Roll it into sticks ½ inch thick. Cut it into 1 inch lengths. Drop the gnocchi into simmering salted water. Simmer uncovered for 10 minutes. Drain. Place them on a greased pan in a hot oven 400° for about 3 minutes. The baking is optional.
Serve the gnocchi dressed with melted butter and grated cheese.
It makes a satisfying casserole dish. See next rule.
Remember that the good Farina Balls on page 72 may be served with gravy.

GNOCCHI CASSEROLE
4 Servings
Scald:
  2 cups milk
Stir in, all at once:
  ¾ cup farina
Stir the mush over low heat until thick. Remove from heat and beat in until smooth:

1 tablespoon butter
1 egg yolk
¼ teaspoon salt

Spread the mush evenly in an 8 x 8 inch pan lined with waxed paper. Chill it for about 3 hours. Cut it into 1½ inch squares. Place the squares in a well-greased oven-proof dish, letting them overlap slightly. Dot them with:

2 tablespoons butter

Pour over them slowly:

1 cup any good tomato sauce

or try:

Hunters' Sauce, page 434, or
Anchovy Sauce for Spaghetti,
page 93

You may sprinkle the top with:

6 tablespoons grated Parmesan
cheese

Bake the dish in a hot oven 425° until well heated, for about 12 minutes.

RICE

Let's try to keep this sad tale with its moral in reverse from little children. The same amount and kind of rice rations were issued to some nuns and monks in the Philippines. The nuns, being tidy, washed theirs. The monks, being hasty, didn't go to all that bother. Some of the nuns developed beriberi while all the monks remained hale and hearty.

This story coincides with scientific experiments which show that whether rice is short or long-grained, brown or white, tremendous losses in nutrients result from the old method of washing rice before and after cooking. Brown or undermilled rice is richer in taste and a far better buy nutritionally than processed or polished rice. Combined with eggs or sauce it cannot be distinguished at sight from its weaker, handsomer sisters.

To keep rice white when cooked in hard water, add 1 teaspoonful lemon juice or 1 tablespoonful vinegar to the cooking water.

One cupful uncooked rice equals about 3½ cupfuls rice when cooked.

BOILED RICE

Bring to a rolling boil:

1¾ cups water

Add:

¾ teaspoon salt

Stir slowly into the water so as not to disturb the boiling point:

1 cup rice

Cover and cook over slow heat. White rice will take from 20 to 30 minutes, brown from 40 to 50. If the rice becomes too dry add ¼ cupful or more boiling water. When the grains have swelled to capacity, uncover the pot. This is for about the last 5 minutes of cooking. Continue to cook the rice over very slow heat, shaking the pot from time to time until the grains have separated. You may stir the cooked rice with a fork to make it fluffy. If the rice is to be combined later with a cream sauce, cook it uncovered in part milk and water, adding more milk as needed. If it is to be a casserole dish, cook it in stock, adding salt as needed to the cooked rice.

STEAMED RICE
Method I. 6 to 8 Servings

Place in the top of a double boiler over direct heat:

3 cups boiling water
1 teaspoon salt

Stir slowly into the boiling water:

1 cup rice

Cook it for 5 minutes. Place it over boiling water and cook it covered until it is tender, for about 45 minutes. Stir it frequently. Add:

2 tablespoons butter

Uncover it and cook it until it is dry.

Method II.

This is frequently served in place of a starchy vegetable or as a main dish with tomato or some other sauce.

Prepare (see above):

Steamed Rice I

Add to the rice when it is placed over boiling water:

(3 tablespoons or more chopped
celery)

Serve it with:

(1 tablespoon chopped parsley)

RICE IN BROTH

Prepare by the preceding rule:

Steamed Rice I

Substitute for water:

Broth or part broth

Add the salt when the rice is cooked if needed.

Milk Rice, page 716.

JAPANESE RICE
8 Servings

Place in a deep kettle:

1 cup rice

Cover it with:
1½ inches of water

Soak it for 1 hour. Cover the kettle, bring the rice to the boiling point, then let it simmer until the surface water is gone and bubbles come up from the bottom. This takes about ½ hour. Reduce the heat and continue to cook the rice covered for about 20 minutes longer or until it is done. Turn off the heat and let the rice stand for about 20 minutes. It is then ready to be served. You will find it dry and flaky.

GREEN RICE
4 Servings

An outstanding rice dish. This amount will fill a 7 inch ring mold. Doubled, it will fill a 9 inch mold and an individual baking dish.

Beat:
1 egg

Add and mix well:
1 cup milk
½ cup finely chopped parsley
1 finely chopped clove garlic
1 small minced onion
2 cups cooked rice
½ cup sharp grated cheese
Salt to taste

Place these ingredients in a baking dish in which has been poured:
2 tablespoons olive oil

Bake it for 30 or 40 minutes in a moderate oven 325°.

The cheese may be omitted. Substitute 1 teaspoonful celery seed and ½ teaspoonful curry powder. Made with 3 cupfuls of rice this makes a marvelous stuffing for a veal breast.

CHEESE RICE
Method I. 6 to 8 Servings

The following is a good dish to serve with a cold supper.

Boil (page 103):
1 cup rice

When the water is nearly absorbed add:
½ cup or more grated cheese
¼ teaspoon paprika
A few grains cayenne

Stir the rice over low heat until the cheese is melted.

Method II.
Or, boil:
1 cup rice

Add the contents of:
1 can condensed tomato or
   mushroom soup: 10½ oz.
¾ cup grated cheese

Cover the top with:
Buttered bread crumbs

Place the rice in a hot oven 400° until the crumbs are brown.

Method III.
Boil:
½ cup rice

Grease a baking dish and place in it layers of rice sprinkled with:
½ cup or more grated cheese
(¾ cup Sautéed Mushrooms, page 292)

Combine and beat:
1 cup milk
1 egg
½ teaspoon salt
⅛ teaspoon paprika
A few grains cayenne

Pour this over the rice. Cover the top with:
¼ cup bread crumbs

Dot it with:
2 tablespoons butter

Bake the rice in a moderate oven 350° until it is lightly browned.

ITALIAN RICE OR RISOTTO
4 Servings

This unusual way of preparing rice gives the dish a distinctive and piquant quality. Melt:
2 tablespoons butter

Measure:
½ cup rice

Sauté it in the butter for 1 minute. Heat to the boiling point:
2 cups Stock, page 44
(Minced garlic)

Pour it over the rice. Add:
¼ cup grated cheese
A few grains cayenne
⅛ teaspoon paprika
(1/16 teaspoon saffron or ½ teaspoon fennel seed)

Steam the rice in a double boiler for 1 hour. Stir it several times during the steaming. If required add:
Salt

While it is not traditional there is no reason why a slice of onion should not be browned in the butter, or why leftover meat chopped, or sautéed mushrooms should not be added to the dish toward the last of steaming.

BAKED RICE
4 Servings

Combine and stir well in a greased 1½ quart oven-proof baking dish:

1 cup rice
2 tablespoons butter
2 cups boiling water or stock
1 teaspoon salt or less if stock is
used
(2 tablespoons minced onion)
The onion may be sautéed in the butter. Cover the dish. Bake it in a moderate oven 350° for ¾ hour or more until tender.

CHEESE RICE RING
4 Servings
Boil (page 103):
½ cup rice
Add:
1 beaten egg
2 tablespoons olive oil or melted
butter
¼ cup milk
⅓ cup grated cheese
¼ tablespoon grated onion
1 teaspoon Worcestershire sauce
¼ teaspoon salt
3 tablespoons chopped parsley
Grease a 7 inch ring mold. Fill it with the rice mixture. Bake it set in a pan of hot water in a moderate oven 350° for about 45 minutes.

RICE RING WITH CREAMED CHICKEN, ETC.
6 Servings
Boil (page 103):
1 cup rice
Season it with:
½ teaspoon grated nutmeg
Place it in a well-greased 7 inch ring mold. Melt and pour over it:
¼ cup butter
You may add:
¾ cup blanched, coarsely chopped
almonds
Set the mold in a pan of hot water. Bake the rice in a moderate oven 350° for 20 minutes. Loosen the edges, invert the contents of the mold onto a platter. Fill the center with:
Creamed Chicken, page 143
Creamed Mushrooms, page 292,
or with a creamed or buttered
vegetable

MUSHROOM RICE RING
6 Servings
A superlative dish.
Boil (page 103):
1 cup rice
Grind, chop fine or blend:
½ to 1 lb. mushrooms
Sauté them for 2 or 3 minutes in:

2 tablespoons butter
Add:
¼ cup hot stock or water
Combine the mushrooms and rice. Season them as needed with:
Salt and paprika
Place the rice in a greased 7 inch ring mold set in 1 inch of hot water. Bake it in a moderate oven 350° for about ½ hour. Invert the rice onto a platter. Fill the center with a buttered vegetable, creamed fish, etc.

BROWN RICE
6 Servings
Bring to a boil in a saucepan:
2½ cups water
Stir in slowly so as not to disturb the boiling point:
1 cup brown rice
1 teaspoon salt
Shake the pan to level the rice. Cover and cook it over very low heat for about 45 minutes, until the rice is tender and has absorbed all the water.

RICE WITH CHICKEN BROTH AND EGGS
Boil in the top of a double boiler:
3 cups chicken stock
Stir in slowly:
1 cup rice
1 teaspoon salt
Cook the rice closely covered over hot water until it is tender—for about 1 hour. Stir it frequently. Beat:
3 eggs
¼ cup melted butter
¼ teaspoon freshly grated nutmeg
Stir this mixture into the rice. Serve it with:
Chopped parsley

RICE LOAF
10 Servings
Boil (page 103):
⅔ cup rice
Line a buttered mold with it. Reserve ½ cupful for the top. Cook:
1 cup Cream Sauce II, page 428
Stir in and thicken over low heat:
1 egg yolk
Add:
1 cup diced canned salmon, cooked
fish or meat
½ cup bread crumbs
1 tablespoon chopped parsley
1 tablespoon chopped onion
½ cup chopped celery
1 teaspoon lemon juice or 1 teaspoon Worcestershire sauce
Salt, paprika, nutmeg

Fill the mold and place the reserved rice over the top. Cover this with a piece of buttered paper. Set the mold in a pan of hot water and bake or steam it until it is set, for about 30 minutes. Invert the loaf onto a platter. Garnish it with:

Sprigs parsley

Serve it with:

Tomato Sauce, page 433, or
Mushroom Sauce, page 436, etc.

PILAF
6 Servings

A rice dish combined with shrimp or chicken livers, etc. It can be used in many variations.

Boil (page 103):

⅔ cup rice

Brown:

3 tablespoons chopped onion

in:

1 tablespoon butter

Add it to the rice. Boil until thick:

2½ cups tomatoes
½ bay leaf
3 ribs of celery with leaves
⅓ teaspoon salt
¼ teaspoon paprika
½ teaspoon brown sugar

Strain these ingredients. Add and stir over a low fire until melted:

(¼ cup grated cheese)

Add:

1 cup cooked shrimp, lobster meat, crab meat or sautéed or boiled chicken livers

Combine these ingredients with the rice. Season them with:

Salt, if needed, and paprika

You may omit melting the cheese, and reserve it. The rice may be placed in a greased baking dish, the top sprinkled with the cheese and bread crumbs and the dish browned under a broiler or in a moderate oven 375°.

RICE WITH MUSHROOMS AND ALMOND SAUCE
4 Servings

Boil (page 103):

⅔ cup rice

Sauté (page 292):

¼ lb. mushrooms

Prepare:

1 cup Brown Sauce, page 435

Add the mushrooms and:

¼ cup blanched, toasted almonds

Serve the sauce over the rice.

TOMATO RICE WITH CHEESE AND MUSHROOMS
4 Servings

Boil (page 103):

½ cup rice

Sauté (page 292):

½ cup or more mushrooms

Combine the rice and the mushrooms. Add:

1 cup skinned and chopped tomatoes, or canned tomatoes
½ teaspoon brown sugar
½ teaspoon salt
⅛ teaspoon paprika
2 tablespoons chopped onion
2 tablespoons chopped green pepper
(¼ to ½ cup diced cheese)

Place the ingredients in a buttered baking dish. Cover them with:

¼ cup dry bread crumbs

Dot them with:

1 tablespoon butter

Bake the rice in a moderate oven 350° for about 40 minutes.

RICE "TAFEL" OR TABLE
8 Servings

A Javanese dish served with many variations but adaptable to our own favorite foods. As this is a very filling dish—nearly a meal in itself—it is ideal for suppers or luncheons, followed by salad or fruit. It may be made as elaborate or as simple as you wish. I shall give it in its original form with suggestions as to its modification.

If you object to coconut, if you do not like the flavor of curry, do not discard this dish. Instead carry out the idea of the rice tafel by substituting creamed chicken, ragout fin, or some dish you do like, followed by vegetables and condiments served in some attractive way.

Grate:

A fresh coconut or use about 2 cups canned coconut

Scald:

4 cups milk

Add the coconut. Permit these ingredients to stand for 2 hours in a cool place. Melt:

1 tablespoon butter

Sauté in it until light brown:

½ cup finely chopped onion

Add:

2 inches of chopped gingerroot
1 chopped clove garlic
1½ tablespoons curry powder
1 cup coconut milk or Chicken Stock, page 43

Add the milk and grated coconut.
Combine 3 tablespoonfuls of the liquid
with:
>1 tablespoon flour
>1 tablespoon cornstarch

Heat the remaining liquid and stir the
starch paste into it. Cook and stir the
sauce until it boils and thickens. Season it as desired with:
>Salt and paprika

Strain the sauce. Combine ½ this sauce
with about:
>3 cups cooked, diced chicken,
>shrimp, fish, veal, sweetbreads,
>mushrooms, etc., either alone
>or in combination

Boil (page 103):
>2 cups rice

Have it rather dry and flaky.
The ceremony of serving this dish is
part of its charm. In Java one refers to
it by the separate dishes, as a "One boy
curry" or a "Twenty-two boy curry,"
each boy representing one dish. Pass
the rice first. Spread it generously
over your plate forming a base or
table. Pass the food in the sauce next.
Follow this with:
>Fried Noodles, page 97
>Shoestring Onions, page 297
>Sieved hard-cooked eggs
>Grated peanuts
>Grated coconut if there is none
>in the sauce
>Relish
>Chutney or preserved ginger, etc.

and the remaining sauce.
To simplify matters the last 4 or 5
dishes may be served from one large
condiment dish. Servings from these
various dishes are placed upon the rice
tafel. Cut through the layers and proceed to feast with your fork.

JAMBOLAYA

8 Servings
A rice and vegetable dish of unusual
quality—ideal for a picnic supper.
Steam (page 103):
>⅔ cup rice

Sauté lightly in butter:
>¾ to 1 lb. mushrooms

Seed and chop:
>2 medium-sized green peppers

Skin and chop:
>1 medium-sized onion

String and chop:
>1 stalk of celery

Chop:
>2 canned pimientos
>1¼ cups canned tomatoes

Season these ingredients with:
>¾ teaspoon salt
>A few grains cayenne
>½ teaspoon paprika

Add:
>¼ lb. melted butter

These proportions may be varied.
Combine the rice and the other ingredients. Place them in a greased baking
dish. Cover the dish. Bake them in a
slow oven 300° for about 1 hour.
The sautéed mushroom caps and the
pimientos may be used to garnish the
top of the dish. They are highly decorative with a bunch of parsley in the
center.

JAMBOLAYA WITH MEAT OR FISH

8 Servings
Sauté lightly in a saucepan:
>2 slices diced bacon

Add and sauté until it begins to color:
>¼ cup chopped onion

Stir in until slightly browned:
>1 tablespoon flour

Add:
>1 cup tomato pulp
>⅓ cup water
>¼ teaspoon paprika
>¼ teaspoon salt

Bring these ingredients to the boiling
point. Stir in:
>3 cups cooked rice
>2 cups coarsely diced cooked ham,
>chicken, sausage, tongue or
>shrimp, etc., alone or in combi-
>nation

Season these ingredients with:
>¼ teaspoon thyme
>Salt if needed
>(Worcestershire sauce)

Stir the jambolaya over very low heat
for 10 minutes, or cook it over boiling
water for ½ hour. Serve it sprinkled
with:
>Chopped parsley

CHICKEN JAMBOLAYA

10 Servings
Cut into pieces:
>A young chicken
>½ lb. raw ham

Sauté these ingredients for 5 minutes
in:
>¼ cup hot lard or butter

Remove the meat from the pan. Sauté
in the lard for 3 minutes:
>⅓ cup minced onion
>½ cup skinned, minced tomato

Stir in:
>1 diced green pepper
>½ cup diced celery
>1 cup uncooked rice

When the rice is well coated with lard, stir in the sautéed chicken and ham. Cover these ingredients well with:
>Boiling water

Add:
>1 bay leaf
>¼ teaspoon thyme
>¼ cup chopped parsley
>1 teaspoon salt
>¼ teaspoon pepper

Simmer these ingredients until the chicken is tender and the rice is done. Season if needed with additional:
>Salt and pepper

Dry out the jambolaya by placing it for 5 minutes or more in a moderate oven 350°.

SPANISH RICE
4 Servings
Sauté until brown:
>3 slices minced bacon

Remove the bacon. Stir and cook in the drippings until brown:
>½ cup rice

Add and cook until brown:
>½ cup thinly sliced onions

Add the bacon and:
>1¼ cups canned tomatoes
>½ teaspoon salt
>1 teaspoon paprika
>1 seeded and minced green pepper
>(1 clove garlic)

Steam the rice in a double boiler for 1 hour. Stir it frequently. Add water or additional tomato if the rice becomes too dry. It may be served with:
>Cheese Sauce, page 430

CURRIED RICE
4 Servings
An unusual and delicious rice dish. Its popularity is undoubtedly due to the restraint with which the spice is used.
Pour:
>2 cups hot water

over:
>½ cup rice

Place the rice where it will remain hot, but will not cook, for 45 minutes. Add:
>½ cup tomatoes
>¾ teaspoon salt
>¼ cup finely sliced onion
>¼ cup sliced green peppers
>2 tablespoons melted butter
>¾ teaspoon curry powder

Place these ingredients in a baking dish in a moderate oven 350° for 1½

hours or until done. Stir them from time to time. At first there will be a great preponderance of liquid, but gradually the rice will absorb it. Remove the dish from the oven while the rice is still moist.

RICE RAMEKINS WITH FISH
Combine:
>Cooked rice
>An equal amount of crab meat, shrimp or cooked fish

Measure these ingredients and add ½ as much:
>Cream Sauce I, page 428

Season the sauce with:
>Salt and paprika
>Worcestershire sauce or sherry
>Prepared mustard

Fill buttered ramekins or a baking dish. Cover the tops with:
>Bread crumbs

Dot them with:
>Butter

or sprinkle them with:
>Grated cheese

Heat the rice in a quick oven 400° until the crumbs are brown.

KEDGEREE OF LOBSTER OR OTHER FISH
6 Servings
Combine:
>2 cups cooked rice
>1 lb. boiled fresh or canned lobster meat
>4 minced hard-cooked eggs
>4 tablespoons butter
>¼ cup cream
>Salt and paprika

Heat these ingredients in a double boiler.

BACON AND RICE CUSTARD
4 Servings
Cook until partly done:
>8 slices bacon

Use 4 muffin tins. Line each one with 2 slices of bacon. Fill them with the following mixture. Combine:
>2 cups cooked rice
>1 beaten egg
>2 tablespoons cream
>1 tablespoon melted butter
>1 tablespoon grated onion
>1 tablespoon chopped parsley
>⅛ teaspoon salt
>⅛ teaspoon paprika

Bake the custard in a moderate oven 325° until firm, for about ½ hour. Serve with:
>Tomato or other sauce

RICE AND HAM RING
6 Servings
Combine:
    2 cups cooked rice
    1 cup diced cooked ham
Combine and beat:
    1 egg
    ⅔ cup condensed mushroom soup
    ½ cup milk
    ¼ teaspoon salt
    (½ teaspoon dried basil)
Grease a 9 inch ring mold. Place in it layers of rice and ham. Pour the liquid ingredients over them. Sprinkle the top with:
    1 cup crushed potato chips or
        bread crumbs
Bake the ring in 1 inch of hot water in a moderate oven 375° for about ½ hour. Invert it onto a platter. Fill the center with:
    A cooked vegetable, carrots and
    peas, snap beans, etc.

ROMBAUER RICE DISH
6 Servings
Freely varied each time it is made but in such demand that I shall try to write a general rule for it.
Boil by the rule on page 103:
    ½ cup rice
Prepare by the rule on page 357:
    Veal stew: 1½ lbs. meat
Pare, slice and add for the last 20 minutes of cooking:
    ½ parsnip
    2 carrots
    2 onions
    6 sliced ribs celery
    3 sprigs parsley
Drain the stew. To make the gravy see the rule on page 426. There should be about 3 cupfuls of stock. If there is not enough, add chicken bouillon, a bouillon or vegetable cube and water, rice water or sweet or sour cream to make up the difference. If there is not enough fat, add butter. The better the gravy, the better the dish. Combine the rice, meat, vegetables and gravy and reheat them. Garnish the dish with:
    Parsley
You may add a dash of curry powder and some herbs, thyme, basil, etc., page 833. You may use left-over meat, gravy and vegetables. You may serve the stew in a baking dish au gratin or in individual bakers.
A de luxe dish is this recipe made with rice, chicken, sauce (with cream and chicken gravy), blanched slivered al-

monds. An everyday dish is this recipe made with corned beef and some canned soup to substitute for gravy.

TOMATOES WITH PEPPERS AND SOUR CREAM OVER RICE
4 Servings
Remove the blossom ends from:
    4 large firm tomatoes
They may be skinned. Cut them into quarters. Cut into strips:
    1 large green pepper, seeds and
    fibrous portions removed
Place the vegetables in a saucepan with:
    1½ tablespoons butter
    1 teaspoon brown sugar
    ¾ teaspoon salt
    ⅛ teaspoon pepper
Cook them rapidly for about 5 minutes. Fold in just before serving:
    1½ tablespoons sour cream
This dish is fine over lightly buttered:
    Rice or noodles

BAKED PINEAPPLE AND RICE
6 Servings
This good dish may be served with baked ham or fried chicken, or as a dessert with cream.
Cook by the rule on page 103:
    1 cup rice
Drain, then cut into pieces the contents of:
    1 No. 2½ can pineapple
Place in a buttered baking dish ⅓ the rice. Cover with ½ the pineapple. Repeat the layer of rice and pineapple. Place the last ⅓ the rice on top. Dot each layer with:
    1½ tablespoons butter
    ¼ cup brown sugar
Use in all 5½ tablespoonfuls butter and ¾ cupful sugar. Pour over all:
    ¾ cup pineapple juice
Bake the rice covered in a moderate oven 350° for 1 hour. Uncover it and bake it for 1¼ hours longer.

WILD RICE
Wild rice is a seed from a grass growing wild in the northern United States and remains a luxury because of the difficulty of harvesting it.
One cupful of wild rice equals 3 cupfuls of cooked wild rice.

Method I.
Wash well in several waters, pouring off the foreign particles from the top:
    1 cup wild rice

Drain it. Stir it slowly into:
4 cups boiling water
1 teaspoon salt
Cook it without stirring until tender, for about 40 minutes.

Method II.
Or, use only:
3 cups water
Boil the rice for 5 minutes, skim it if necessary, then steam it in a double boiler until tender, for about 1 hour. Stir it frequently.
You may add to the cooked rice:
Sautéed onions and mushrooms

Method III.
Or, cook wild rice until nearly tender by the rule for Steamed Rice, page 103. Use:
½ teaspoon salt
Drain the rice. Add the contents of:
1 can chicken or beef broth:
10½ oz.
Cook the rice until it is tender. Add to it when done:
½ cup sherry

Rice Timbales, page 215.

CREAMED BROWNED WILD RICE WITH MUSHROOMS
4 Servings
Cook by the preceding rule:
1¼ cups wild rice
Scald, combine and stir into it:

½ cup heavy cream
¼ teaspoon paprika
¼ teaspoon freshly grated nutmeg
Salt as needed
Cook and stir the rice over low heat until the cream is absorbed. Melt in a skillet:
2 tablespoons butter
Press the rice down into the skillet. Cook it over low heat until it is browned. Fold it like an omelet. Before folding you may cover it with:
1 cup Creamed Mushrooms, page 292
Or you may serve the rice with creamed mushrooms.

WILD RICE RING
4 Servings
Cook by the second rule opposite:
1 cup wild rice
You may add:
1 sliced clove garlic
Steam the rice as directed. Add:
¼ cup butter
½ teaspoon poultry seasoning or freshly grated nutmeg
(1 cup sautéed onions and mushrooms)
(¼ cup sherry)
Place it in a well-greased 7 inch ring mold. Set the mold in a pan of hot water and bake the rice in a moderate oven 350° for 20 minutes. Loosen the edges with a knife, invert the contents onto a platter and fill the center with:
Creamed Mushrooms, page 292, Sautéed Chicken Livers, page 139, Sautéed Onions, page 296, etc.

Sea Food Dishes

There are various ways of preparing bulk oysters for cooking. The favorite method seems to be to place the oysters with their liquor in a saucepan, to pick them over and discard bits of shell, etc., and to stew them until their edges curl. The oysters must be closely watched, as a degree too much cooking makes them tough. I prefer either of the two following methods:

Drain the oysters, reserving the liquor, place them in a single layer in a large colander over boiling water, cover them and steam them until they are plump; or place the drained oysters in the bottom of a large saucepan, cover them and put the pan in boiling water until the oysters are plump.

In the case of creamed oysters, or other dishes where drained oysters are to be put directly into boiling cream sauce, it is not necessary to cook them beforehand.

The oyster liquor may be used in making cream sauce or in other oyster sauce or soup dishes.

CREAMED OYSTERS
Method I. 4 Servings
Drain:
  1 pint oysters
Reserve the liquor. Melt in a saucepan:
  2 tablespoons butter
Add and stir until blended:
  2 tablespoons flour
Stir in slowly:
  1 cup oyster liquor or oyster
  liquor and cream, milk, chicken
  or beef stock
Add:
  ½ teaspoon salt
  ⅛ teaspoon paprika
When the sauce is smooth and boiling
add the drained oysters. Heat them to
the boiling point but do not allow the
sauce to boil. When the oysters are
thoroughly heated, season them with:
  1 teaspoon lemon juice or
  ½ teaspoon Worcestershire sauce
  or 1 teaspoon sherry
Serve them at once in:
  Bread Cases, page 77, patty
  shells or on hot buttered toast
Sprinkle them generously with:
  Chopped parsley
These oysters may be served au gratin
by placing them in a greased baking
dish or in individual molds, covering
the top with bread crumbs dotted with
butter or sprinkled with cheese. Brown
the crumbs under a broiler.

Method II.
This oyster dish is richer by the addition of egg yolks than Creamed
Oysters I. Follow the preceding rule
for:
  Creamed Oysters I
When the oysters are well heated, reduce the heat. Pour part of the sauce
slowly, beating it constantly, over:
  2 egg yolks
Return the mixture to the pot and permit the yolks to thicken slightly by
cooking the sauce 1 minute longer. Stir
constantly. Add the desired flavoring
and the parsley as given in the preceding rule and serve the oysters on:
  Hot toast or rusks

Method III.
This recipe differs from the 2 preceding ones by calling for chopped
oysters. It lends itself well to filling
small patties or cases.
Heat in their liquor until the edges
begin to curl:
  1 pint oysters

Drain them well, reserving the liquid,
and chop them coarsely. Melt:
  2 tablespoons butter
Add and stir until blended:
  2 tablespoons flour
Stir in slowly:
  2 tablespoons cream and the
  oyster liquor—there should be
  ¾ cup in all; add top milk if
  there is not enough liquor
Season with:
  ½ teaspoon salt
  ¼ teaspoon paprika
When the sauce is smooth and boiling,
add the oysters. Heat them to the boiling point, but do not permit the sauce
to boil. Reduce the heat. Beat part of
the sauce into:
  2 egg yolks
Return it to the pan. Permit the eggs
to thicken slightly by cooking the
sauce 1 minute longer. Stir constantly.
Season the sauce with:
  1 teaspoon lemon juice or ½ teaspoon Worcestershire sauce or
  1 teaspoon sherry
Add:
  2 tablespoons chopped parsley
Fill individual molds or:
  Bread Cases, page 77
Cover the tops with:
  Bread crumbs
Dot them with:
  Butter
or sprinkle them with:
  Grated cheese
Place them under a broiler until the
tops are brown. To keep hot or to reheat, place the oysters in a pan over
hot water.

OYSTERS SAUTÉED WITH CRAB MEAT
4 Servings
Chop:
  ½ cup crab meat
Combine it with:
  ½ cup soft bread crumbs
Season the mixture with:
  Salt and pepper
Drain:
  1 pint oysters
Roll them in the crumbs and crab
meat. Prepare the following batter.
Sift:
  ½ cup flour
  ¼ teaspoon salt
  1 teaspoon any baking powder
Combine and add:
  ¼ cup milk
  1 beaten egg
Beat these ingredients until they are

blended. Dip the oysters in the batter. Sauté them until they are well browned in:

Butter

SCALLOPED OYSTERS
4 Servings
Drain:
1 pint oysters
Combine:
6 tablespoons cream and the oyster liquor
Combine:
½ cup dry bread crumbs
1 cup cracker crumbs
Pour over them:
½ cup melted butter
Plan to use 2 layers of oysters, no more, and 3 layers of crumbs. Grease a baking dish and cover it with a layer of crumbs, then proceed to build up the 4 other alternate layers of oysters and crumbs. Season each layer of oysters with:

Salt and pepper

and pour ½ of the combined oyster liquor and cream over it.
The oysters may be sprinkled with:
½ cup chopped celery or
½ cup chopped green peppers
The top layer of crumbs should be dry. Dot it with:
(Butter or grated cheese)
Bake the oysters for 20 minutes in a hot oven 400°.

SCALLOPED OYSTERS WITH TOMATO JUICE
6 or 8 Servings
Melt:
4 tablespoons butter
Sauté in the butter until tender:
2 tablespoons chopped celery
1 tablespoon chopped onion
2 tablespoons chopped green pepper
Stir in until blended:
¼ cup flour
Add:
¼ teaspoon salt
A few grains pepper
Stir in slowly and cook and stir until thick:
1 cup milk
Remove these ingredients from the heat. Stir in slowly:
1 cup tomato juice
¼ teaspoon sugar
Butter a casserole well. Have ready:
2½ cups coarsely rolled cracker crumbs

Line the casserole with some of the crumbs. Drain:
1 pint oysters: 2 cups
Place ½ of them in the casserole. Cover them with 1 cupful of the crumbs. Add ½ the tomato sauce. Add the rest of the oysters, 1 cupful of the crumbs and the rest of the tomato sauce. Sprinkle the last of the crumbs on top and dot them with:
2 tablespoons butter
or sprinkle them with:
⅛ cup grated cheese
Bake the oysters in a moderate oven 375° for about 40 minutes.

OYSTERS SCALLOPED IN CANNED SOUP
6 Servings
Drain, reserving the liquor:
1 pint small oysters: 2 cups
Combine:
1 cup dry bread crumbs
3 tablespoons melted butter
¼ teaspoon salt
1 teaspoon minced parsley
Heat to the boiling point:
10½ oz. condensed celery, mushroom or asparagus soup
The oyster liquor or 4 table-spoons water
Add the oysters. Cook them until the edges begin to curl. Place ½ the buttered crumbs in a hot casserole, add the oysters and soup. Top with the remaining crumbs. Place the dish under a broiler until the top is brown.

SCALLOP OF OYSTERS AND CANNED FISH FLAKES
4 Servings
Drain:
1 to 1½ cups oysters
Heat them until their edges begin to curl in:
2 tablespoons butter
Drain them. You may add the juice to the soup. Combine the contents of:
1 can fish flakes: 7½ oz.
and:
1 cup condensed celery, asparagus or mushroom soup
The soup should have the consistency of cream sauce. Season it with:
¼ teaspoon curry powder
Place in a 7 inch greased oven-proof baking dish 3 alternate layers of creamed flakes and oysters. Begin and end with the fish; place the oysters between. The top may be sprinkled with:

Bread crumbs
Grated cheese
Bake the dish in a hot oven 400° until
it is well heated—for about 10 minutes.

BROILED OYSTERS
Drain:
    Oysters
Place them in a buttered pan and pour
over them a mixture of:
    Melted butter
    Worcestershire sauce
    Salt, pepper and paprika
Place the pan under a broiler until the
oysters are plump. Serve them at once
with:
    Lemon slices and parsley
on:
    Hot buttered toast

BROILED BREADED OYSTERS
5 Servings
Drain:
    1 pint oysters
Dry them between towels. Place in a
small cup:
    1/4 cup melted butter
Insert a fork in the tough muscle of
the oysters and dip them in the butter,
then in:
    Seasoned bread or cracker
    crumbs
Place the oysters on a buttered metal
sheet and broil them, turning them frequently until they are brown. Serve
them on:
    Buttered toast
with:
    Slices of lemon
    Sprigs of parsley
or with:
    Lemon Butter, page 431

BUTTERED OYSTERS
2 Servings
This is recommended as an excellent
dish, quickly prepared. With grapefruit halves, rusks and a beverage it is
an ideal emergency luncheon. Drain:
    1 pint oysters
Place them in a covered strainer over
boiling water and steam them until
they are thoroughly heated. Place in a
heated serving bowl:
    2 tablespoons butter
Pour the oysters into it. Season them
with:
    Salt and pepper
Serve them at once.

PANNED OYSTERS
4 Servings
Combine:
    1 cup flour
    1 teaspoon salt
    1/8 teaspoon pepper
Combine, then beat:
    1 egg
    1 tablespoon salad oil
Drain:
    24 oysters
Roll them in the flour, in the egg mix-
ture and then in:
    Bread crumbs
Bake the oysters in a greased shallow
pan in a moderate oven 375° until they
are brown—for about 15 minutes.
Serve them with:
    Tartar Sauce, page 439

OYSTERS BAKED IN THE HALF SHELL
This original recipe is the contribution
of a Maryland man. He objects to the
fact that I, a landlubber, should have
recipes for "denuded" oysters only and
suggests that this rule be given a trial.
The trial has taken place and the ver-
dict is "superlative." I shall give the
rule as much as possible in his own
words, but I must begin instead of end
with his final warning: "Do not overlook, unless you are extraordinarily
nimble, that the sauce should be
started well before the oysters go into
the oven." Have the fish merchant
open, on the deep side:
    Oysters
Take them home and with the juice
slightly warmed in a double boiler
make a sauce, adding to it:
    Lemon and onion juice
    Celery seed or salt
    Tarragon vinegar
    Mustard—heavy on this
    Pepper
    Tabasco
    Not too much butter
Meanwhile, the oysters may start
cooking—a 325° oven is about right—
each in its own half shell with a little of
its own juice to prevent its drying out,
propped carefully on the open grid so
as to be level. The heat must come
from below. Do not broil. The fire
must be mild. When the color of the
oysters begins to darken remove from
the fire and serve with the rest of the
sauce drenching them.

OYSTERS ROCKEFELLER

Allow 6 oysters on the half shell per person. If unshucked oysters are not available, buy oyster shells and use bulk oysters. The oysters are seasoned with various ingredients and baked in a hot oven 450° to 500° for about 10 minutes, or until plump. Then they are browned under a broiler. Add to the oysters:

> Butter creamed with onion juice and chopped parsley—reserve some of this
> Salt
> A few grains cayenne
> Cooked, minced bacon
> Puréed spinach
> Bread crumbs and the remaining butter

OYSTERS IN SPINACH

A simpler version of the rule above. Half fill a shell with:

> Creamed Spinach, page 313

Place on spinach:

> 1 large oyster

Cover with:

> 1 teaspoon chopped parsley
> A few drops lemon juice and Worcestershire sauce
> A square inch of bacon

Or combine and cover the oyster with:

> 1 teaspoon well-seasoned cream sauce
> 1 tablespoon crab meat
> 1 teaspoon grated Parmesan cheese

It is a New Orleans idea to sprinkle the oysters with absinthe. Bake and brown as directed above.

PLANKED OYSTERS

Grease a plank or a flat oven-proof dish. Heat the plank or dish. Place in the center:

> Oysters

Season them with:

> Salt and pepper
> Onion or lemon juice

Cover them with:

> Thin strips of bacon

Surround them with thick slices of:

> Raw tomatoes

Sprinkle the tomatoes lightly with:

> Flour, salt and pepper
> (Brown sugar)

Dot them with:

> Butter

Bake the tomatoes and oysters in a moderate oven 350° for 20 minutes. Have ready:

> Hot Mashed Potatoes, page 302

Force them through a pastry tube to form a border. Serve the dish at once.

BAKED OYSTERS AND BACON

4 Servings

Rub a heavy skillet with:

> A clove garlic

Melt in the skillet:

> 4 tablespoons butter

Stir and brown in the butter:

> 1 cup bread crumbs

Season them with:

> ¼ teaspoon salt
> ⅛ teaspoon paprika

Place on an oven-proof pie plate, or in shallow ramekins:

> 1 pint drained oysters

Cover them closely with the crumbs and:

> Strips of bacon cut into 1 inch pieces

Place the plate in a hot oven 425° until the bacon is crisp.

If oysters on the half shell are used, sprinkle the tops with seasoning and crumbs and cover each oyster with a square of bacon.

OYSTERS BAKED WITH CHEESE IN CATSUP SAUCE

4 Servings

Drain:

> 1 pint oysters

Prepare a sauce with:

> ½ cup catsup
> 1 teaspoon Worcestershire sauce
> ½ teaspoon salt
> 1 tablespoon soft butter
> ¼ teaspoon paprika

Pour it into a flat oven-proof plate. Place the oysters on the plate. Dot them with:

> Butter

Sprinkle them with:

> Grated cheese

Bake them in a moderate oven 375° only until they are well heated and the cheese is melted.

OYSTERS BAKED IN MUSHROOM SAUCE

3 Servings

Chop:

> 4 young onions or prepare ¼ cup minced onions

Stir and sauté the onions until they are light brown in:

> 2 tablespoons butter

Drain:

> 1½ cups oysters

Moisten them with:

> 3 tablespoons sherry

Cook them slowly in the butter until they are plump. Sprinkle them with:

> 3 tablespoons chopped parsley
> ¼ teaspoon salt
> ⅛ teaspoon paprika

Combine and boil:

> ¾ cup Cream Sauce I, page 428
> ½ cup chopped Sautéed Mushrooms, page 292

Add the oysters. Place these ingredients in a greased baking dish. Sprinkle the top with:

> Bread crumbs

Dot it with:

> Butter

Bake the dish in a moderate oven 375° until it is well heated. Brown the top under a broiler.

BAKED OYSTERS ON TOAST

Butter and place on a shallow pan:

> Small rounds of toast

Place on each one:

> (A thin slice of boiled ham)
> A large oyster

Sprinkle the oysters with:

> Salt and pepper

Bake them in a moderate oven 375° until they are plump. Cover each oyster with:

> ½ teaspoon lemon butter

Lemon Butter
Season:

> 3 tablespoons butter

with:

> ¼ teaspoon salt
> A few grains cayenne

Add slowly:

> 1 tablespoon lemon juice

Chill the butter before using it.

OYSTERS WITH WINE SAUCE AND CHEESE
4 Servings
Melt:

> 3 tablespoons butter

Stir in until blended:

> 1 tablespoon flour

Stir in slowly:

> ½ cup cream
> 1½ teaspoons anchovy paste or anchovy sauce
> A few grains cayenne
> ¼ teaspoon grated lemon rind
> 2 tablespoons sherry

Bring the sauce to the boiling point, then pour it into a buttered 9 inch oven-proof plate.
Place in the sauce:

> 1 pint drained oysters

Sprinkle them with:

> ½ cup bread crumbs
> ⅓ teaspoon salt
> ¼ teaspoon paprika
> ½ cup grated Parmesan cheese

Bake the oysters in a quick oven 400° until they are plump, for about 5 minutes.

CREAMED OYSTERS WITH CRAB MEAT AND CHEESE
4 Servings
Melt in the top of a double boiler over low heat:

> 2 tablespoons butter

Add and stir until blended:

> 1 teaspoon flour

Add and stir until melted:

> 3 tablespoons grated cheese

Stir in slowly:

> ½ cup cream
> ⅓ cup tomato catsup

Add:

> ⅓ teaspoon salt
> ¼ teaspoon paprika
> 1 teaspoon Worcestershire sauce

When the sauce has reached the boiling point, place it over boiling water.
Cook in their liquor until plump:

> 1 cup oysters: ½ pint

Drain them well. Add them to the hot sauce with:

> ¾ cup crab meat

When these ingredients are hot serve them at once on:

> Hot crackers or toast

CREAMED CANNED SHRIMP AND BAKED OYSTERS
3 Servings
Do not take this dish too literally. Change the proportions and substitute crab, tuna, etc., to suit yourself. It's a grand basic dish with which to work.
Clean, then sauté lightly:

> 1 cup shrimp

in:

> 2 tablespoons butter

Add to the butter:

> 1 tablespoon chopped chives or onion

Prepare and add:

> ½ cup cream sauce or ½ cup condensed mushroom soup

Season it with:

> (½ teaspoon Worcestershire sauce or 1 tablespoon sherry)

Pour these ingredients into a greased 8 inch oven-proof dish. Cover the top with:

> ½ pint drained oysters

The juice may be used in the sauce. Season them lightly with:
Salt and pepper
Lemon juice
Sprinkle them with:
Grated cheese
Bake them in a moderate oven 375° for about 8 minutes, or heat them under a broiler.

Oyster Rarebit, page 188; Oyster and Mushroom Ragout, page 175; Oysters on Mushrooms, page 176; Oysters and Mushrooms on Skewers, page 194; Oysters on Skewers, page 194.

OYSTER LOAF
8 Servings
Prepare:
A loaf of bread
by cutting off the top and taking out the center, leaving a shell ¾ inch thick. Spread the outside of the shell lightly with:
Melted butter
Using a pastry brush, spread the inside with:
1 egg white
This will keep the loaf from becoming soggy. Bake the shell in a moderate oven 350° until it is well toasted. Prepare:
Creamed Oysters I, II or III, page 111, doubling the quantities given
Fill the shell. Sprinkle the top with:
Chopped parsley
Serve the loaf at once.

OYSTER PIE
4 Servings
Prepare:
Pie Dough, page 564
Use ½ the amount given. Strain:
2 cups oysters: 1 pint
Add to the liquor to make 1½ cupfuls in all:
Milk
Add to it:
2 tablespoons butter
3 tablespoons finely chopped celery
1 tablespoon finely chopped parsley
Bring it to the boiling point. Shell, then mash with a fork:
1 hard-cooked egg
Add to it:
2 tablespoons finely crushed dry bread crumbs

Make a paste of these ingredients with a little of the liquor. Add them to the rest of the liquor. Stir and cook the sauce for 2 minutes. Season it with:
½ teaspoon salt
⅛ teaspoon paprika
(½ teaspoon Worcestershire sauce or curry powder)
Dry the oysters between towels. Place them in the bottom of a greased baking dish. Pour the boiling sauce over them. Roll out the pie crust. Prick it as directed. Cover the oysters with the crust. Press down the edges with a fork. Brush the top with:
Milk
Bake the pie in a moderate oven 375° for about ½ hour. Serve it hot.

Beefsteak and Oysters, page 347.

OYSTER CELERY
4 Servings
In regard to this rule I feel like the author of a well-known opera guide who classified von Flotow's "Martha" as a French opera. He stated that of course he knew it was German but he thought it ought to be French. Of course, I know that this is a soup but I prefer to classify it as a luncheon dish, for if I placed it among the soups it might be lost to fame and it deserves attention.
Drain:
2 cups oysters: 1 pint
Reserve the liquor. Melt in a saucepan:
1½ tablespoons butter
Add and sauté for 1 minute:
½ cup finely chopped celery
½ cup finely chopped green peppers
¼ cup finely chopped onion
Add and stir until blended:
1½ tablespoons flour
Stir in slowly:
1½ cups hot top milk and oyster liquor
When the sauce is smooth and boiling add the drained oysters. When the oysters are plump, reduce the heat and add:
1 beaten egg
Cook the oysters for 1 minute longer to permit the egg to thicken. Stir them gently. Serve them at once.

For other Oyster Dishes, see page 250.

See Scallops on Skewers, page 194, and other Scallop Dishes, page 254.

CREAMED SCALLOPS OR OYSTERS AND MUSHROOMS
6 Servings
Simmer until tender, for about 5 minutes, in boiling water:
    2 cups scallops: 1 pint
Drain them well. Sauté for 5 minutes:
    ½ lb. mushrooms
in:
    2 tablespoons butter
Melt in a saucepan:
    2 tablespoons butter
Stir in until blended:
    2 tablespoons flour
Stir in slowly:
    ½ cup milk or chicken broth
    ½ cup cream
When the sauce is smooth and boiling stir in the scallops and the mushrooms. Reduce the heat to a low flame. Add:
    1 beaten egg
Cook and stir these ingredients until the egg thickens, for about 2 minutes. Season them with:
    Salt and pepper
When oysters are substituted cook them in their own juice until the edges begin to curl. Drain them well. Substitute the juice for part of the milk.

PANCAKES FILLED WITH CREAMED SEA FOOD
4 Servings
Cook:
    French Pancakes, page 551
Cook:
    1½ cups Cream Sauce I, page 428
Season it until it is pink with:
    (Paprika)
Moisten with part of the sauce:
    1 cup crab meat, shrimp or lobster cooked or canned or cooked meat or vegetables
Season the crab with:
    Sherry, Worcestershire sauce or curry powder
Add:
    (2 tablespoons chopped parsley)
Spread the pancakes with the mixture. Roll them. Cover them with the remaining sauce. Sprinkle them with:
    Grated cheese
Brown them lightly under broiler.

FISH HASH
3 Servings
Flake:
    1 cup cooked fish
Melt:
    2 tablespoons butter
Heat in the butter:
    1 cup cooked diced potatoes

Add:
    1 chopped hard-cooked egg
    2 tablespoons finely chopped green peppers
Combine:
    ½ cup milk
    1 teaspoon prepared mustard or 1 teaspoon Worcestershire sauce
    ¼ teaspoon salt
    ⅛ teaspoon paprika
Add these ingredients to the potato and egg mixture. Add the fish. Melt in a skillet:
    1 tablespoon butter
Add the hash, cover the pan and cook the hash until it is browned on the bottom. Fold it over and serve it very hot.

BAKED RICE AND FISH BALLS
Twelve 2 Inch Balls
Flake:
    2 cups cooked fish
Add to it:
    2 cups Boiled Rice, page 103
    2 beaten eggs
    Salt and pepper
    1 tablespoon lemon juice or 2 teaspoons Worcestershire sauce
    (2 tablespoons chopped parsley)
Form these ingredients into 2 inch balls. Roll them in:
    Cream
    Crushed cornflakes
Place them in a well-greased pan. Bake them in a moderate oven 350° for about 20 minutes. Serve them with:
    Easy Hollandaise Sauce, page 430, or Tomato Sauce, page 433

The 4 following recipes are all variations on the same theme—a starch, fish of some kind and a sauce. Please do not feel bound to follow them too closely. The first—Rice, Tuna Fish and Cheese Sauce—may become Rice, Tuna Fish and Celery, or some other soup sauce, to which cheese may be added or not. The second—Tuna, Noodle and Mushroom Soup Casserole—may resolve itself, thanks to expediency, into Shrimp, Noodle and Tomato Soup Casserole, and so on. These dishes and many other combinations are good, but there are too many to detail. Try your own hand.

RICE, TUNA FISH AND CHEESE SAUCE
6 Servings
Boil (page 103):
    ⅔ cup rice

There should be about 2 cupfuls of cooked rice. Drain the contents of:
  1 can tuna fish: 7 oz.
Break the tuna into pieces with a fork. Melt in a saucepan:
  2 tablespoons butter
Stir in until blended:
  4 tablespoons flour
Stir in slowly:
  2 cups milk
Add:
  ½ teaspoon salt—more if the rice is unsalted
  ½ teaspoon paprika
  A few grains red pepper
Reduce the heat to low. Stir in until melted:
  2 cups grated American cheese
Place in a baking dish alternate layers of rice, fish and sauce. The top may be covered with:
  Bread crumbs
dotted with:
  Butter
Place the dish in a hot oven 400° or under a broiler until the crumbs are brown.
The proportions of rice and fish in this excellent dish may be varied. Use about ½ as much cream sauce as you do of the other main ingredients combined. If preferred, bake the ingredients in a ring, invert it and serve it with the center filled with Sautéed Mushrooms, page 292.

TUNA, NOODLE AND MUSH-ROOM SOUP CASSEROLE
4 Large Servings
An excellent emergency dish. Cook until tender:
  2 cups noodles
Drain them in a colander. Pour 3 cupfuls of cold water over them. Drain them again. Drain the contents of:
  1 can tuna fish: 7 oz.
Separate it with a fork into large flakes. Be careful not to mince it as that isn't nearly so good. Grease an oven-proof dish. Arrange a layer of noodles, then sprinkle it with fish and so on. Have noodles on top. Pour over this mixture the contents of:
  1 can condensed mushroom soup: 10½ oz.
Season the soup with:
  Worcestershire sauce, curry, sherry, etc.
Cover the top with:
  Buttered cornflakes or cracker crumbs

Bake the dish in a hot oven 450° until the top is brown.

POTATO SCALLOP WITH SEA FOOD
4 Large Servings
Slice the contents of:
  1 No. 2 can potatoes: about 2 cups boiled potatoes
Drain, reserving the oil, then flake:
  7 oz. tuna fish or about the same amount of salmon, shrimp or clams
Add:
  1 tablespoon diced onion
  1 tablespoon chopped parsley
Fill a greased oven-proof dish with alternate layers of these ingredients, and the contents of:
  1 can condensed celery or mushroom soup: 10½ oz.
diluted with:
  6 tablespoons water or milk
Season the layers lightly with:
  Salt, pepper and paprika
Pour over the dish the oil from the can. Bake it in a hot oven 425° for about 25 minutes.

SALMON AND CELERY SOUP DISH
3 Servings
Drain the contents of:
  1 can salmon: 16 oz.
Remove skin and bones, break the fish into large flakes. Place it in a greased baking dish. Combine and heat:
  10½ oz. celery or other soup
  ½ cup rich milk or cream
  ¼ teaspoon paprika
  1 tablespoon chopped parsley or chives
Pour this mixture over the salmon. Cover the top with:
  1½ crushed shredded wheat biscuits
Dot with:
  1 tablespoon butter
Sprinkle with:
  Grated cheese
Place the dish under a broiler until the fish is hot and the top is brown.

TUNA FISH CASSEROLE
4 Large Servings
A good satisfying "quickie." Heat:
  1 cup condensed mushroom soup
  1 cup milk
Add:
  3 chopped hard-cooked eggs
  ¼ cup chopped ripe olives
  1 can grated tuna: 7 oz.

Pour these ingredients into a baking dish. Cover the top with Biscuits, page 505. Bake in a hot oven 425° until the biscuits are brown, about 12 minutes.

TUNA AND POTATO CHIP LOAF
4 Servings

Pat lightly until broken:
> 3 oz. potato chips

Flake and add:
> 1 can tuna fish: 7 oz.

Combine these ingredients lightly with:
> 1 can mushroom soup: 10½ oz.

Add if desired:
> Chopped pimiento, stuffed olives or chopped parsley

Bake the loaf in a greased pan in a moderate oven 350° for about ½ hour.

TUNA FISH BALLS
About 4 Servings

Combine and mix well:
> 7 oz. grated or flaked tuna fish
> 1 cup mashed potatoes
> 4 or 6 chopped olives
> 6 or 8 capers
> ½ minced clove garlic or 1 teaspoon grated onion
> 1 tablespoon minced parsley
> Salt and paprika
> 1 teaspoon brandy or sherry
> (1 teaspoon dried basil)

Shape the mixture into 1 inch balls. Sauté them for 2 or 3 minutes in:
> ½ cup hot olive oil or butter

Drain the balls, roll them in:
> ¾ cup ground nut meats

TUNA FISH PATTIES WITH TOMATOES AND CHEESE

Cooked hot hamburger or other patties may be substituted. Shape into patties and place on a lightly greased oven-proof dish:
> Grated tuna fish

Top each one with:
> A thin slice of tomato
> A thin slice of cheese

Use seasoning if you wish:
> Salt and pepper
> Mustard, Worcestershire sauce, curry or herbs, etc.

Place the patties under a broiler until the cheese is melted.

INDIVIDUAL TUNA FISH PIES
6 Servings

Any other fish or sea food may be substituted. Bake 6 individual Pie Shells, page 561.

Combine:
> 7 oz. flaked tuna fish
> 1 or 1½ cups thick Cream Sauce II, page 428, or condensed cream soup slightly diluted with milk

Heat this mixture. Season it with a choice of:
> ½ teaspoon dried Herbs, page 832
> ¼ teaspoon curry powder
> ½ teaspoon Worcestershire sauce
> 1 tablespoon sherry

Place the hot tuna mixture in the hot pie shells. Serve them garnished with:
> Parsley

The pies may be topped with a:
> Poached egg

sprinkled with:
> Parmesan cheese, chives or parsley

SALMON POT PIE
8 Servings

A meal in one dish. The salmon mixture may be prepared in advance, so may the dough, and combined shortly before baking. A fine thing for the hurry-up housekeeper. Canned vegetables—peas and asparagus, etc.—and, of course, other fish—crab, shrimp, tuna, etc.—may be substituted.

Drain the contents, reserving the oil, of:
> 1 can salmon: 16 oz.

Prepare by the rule on page 505:
> Biscuit dough

Prepare:
> 1 cup cooked celery
> 1 cup cooked peas

Drain the vegetables, reserving the liquid. Melt:
> 4 tablespoons butter

Sauté in it for 2 minutes:
> 1½ tablespoons minced onion

Stir in until smooth:
> 6 tablespoons flour

Stir in until boiling:
> ¾ cup salmon oil and vegetable water
> 1½ cups milk

Add:
> 1 teaspoon salt
> ⅛ teaspoon paprika
> 1 tablespoon lemon juice or 1 teaspoon Worcestershire sauce
> 1 teaspoon or more chopped parsley or other herb

Break the salmon into large pieces. Fold the vegetables and the salmon into the cream sauce. Add, if needed, more salt and flavoring. Place the mixture in a large casserole. Roll the biscuit dough to the thickness of about ¼ inch. Cut it into rounds. Top the salmon mixture with biscuits. Bake in a hot oven 425° until it is done, for about 12 minutes.

SALMON AND TOMATO SCALLOP
4 Large Servings
Drain the contents of:
    1 can salmon: 16 oz.
Combine them with:
    3 cups soft bread crumbs
    2 tablespoons butter or salmon oil
    ¼ cup chopped onion
    ½ teaspoon salt
    1 teaspoon sugar
    ¼ teaspoon paprika or pepper
    2½ cups tomatoes
    (1 beaten egg)
    (1 teaspoon Worcestershire sauce
    or lemon juice)
Place these ingredients in a greased baking dish. The top may be sprinkled with:
    Grated cheese
Bake the dish in a moderate oven 375° until the top is brown.

SALMON IN PARSLEY SAUCE WITH RICE OR NOODLE RING
6 Servings
Drain, reserving the liquid:
    1 can salmon: 16 oz.
Remove skin and bones. Break the fish into large flakes. Combine:
    1½ teaspoons dry mustard
    1½ teaspoons salt
    ⅛ teaspoon pepper
    ½ teaspoon paprika
    3 tablespoons flour
Combine and beat into the dry ingredients:
    1 cup milk
    ¾ cup salmon liquid and water
Place in double boiler over hot, not boiling, water and beat with a wire whisk:
    1 egg
    2 tablespoons lemon juice
Add the milk mixture and stir and cook until the sauce has thickened. Add the salmon and:
    2 tablespoons butter
    ½ cup finely minced parsley
    1 teaspoon Worcestershire sauce
Heat well and serve in:
    Rice Ring, page 105, or
    Noodle Ring, page 98

SALMON CASSEROLE
4 Servings
Skin, bone and flake:
    2 cups cooked or canned salmon
    or other fish
Add:
    Salt—lightly
    Freshly ground pepper
    Freshly ground nutmeg
Place the fish in a greased baking dish.
Pour over it:
    Béchamel Sauce, page 429, or
    Cream Sauce, page 428, or
    Canned Soup Sauce, page 441,
    etc.
Cover the top with:
    Bread crumbs
Dot them with:
    Butter
You may add a border of:
    Mashed potatoes
Bake the dish in a hot oven 425° until the top is lightly browned.

SALMON PUFFS
6 Servings
Remove skin and bones, drain, then flake the contents of:
    1 can salmon: 16 oz.
Add and stir lightly to blend:
    ½ cup fresh bread crumbs
    2 tablespoons grated onion
    1 tablespoon lemon juice
    1 tablespoon melted butter
    ¼ teaspoon salt
    ¼ teaspoon pepper
Beat:
    1 egg
Add and beat:
    ½ cup milk
Combine with the salmon mixture. Place in 6 well-greased baking cups set in hot water. Bake in a moderate oven 350° for 45 minutes. Unmold onto a hot platter. Serve with:
    Egg Sauce II, page 428

SALMON SPAGHETTI LOAF
6 Servings
Heat and stir:
    1 cup milk
    2 cups fresh bread crumbs
Remove from fire, beat in:
    2 beaten egg yolks
Add:
    1 cup cooked spaghetti broken in
    pieces
    ¼ cup cream
    2 cups salmon
    4 tablespoons melted butter
    1 teaspoon salt
    ¼ teaspoon paprika

Cool these ingredients. Beat until stiff, then fold in:
>   2 egg whites

Bake the loaf in a buttered oven-proof dish set in a pan of hot water in a moderate oven 350° for about 50 minutes.

Sauce for Salmon Loaf
Melt in a double boiler:
>   ¼ cup butter

Stir in:
>   2 tablespoons flour

Add gradually:
>   ¾ cup milk

Season with:
>   1 teaspoon salt
>   ⅛ teaspoon pepper

Permit the sauce to thicken. Remove it from the heat. Stir in:
>   ¼ cup lemon juice
>   1 teaspoon grated lemon rind
>   2 egg yolks

Reheat and stir but do not boil the sauce.

SALMON LOAF WITH CHEESE SAUCE
5 Servings
Prepare:
>   1 cup Cream Sauce I, page 428

Stir in over low heat until melted:
>   ¼ lb. grated cheese

Season the sauce with:
>   ¼ teaspoon salt
>   ⅛ teaspoon paprika
>   A few grains cayenne

Prepare:
>   1½ cups Mashed Potatoes, page 302

Grease a baking dish and spread the mashed potatoes in it. Cover them with ½ the sauce. Drain, skin, then flake the contents of:
>   1 can salmon: 16 oz.

Place it over the sauce. Cover it with the remaining sauce. Bake the dish in a moderate oven 350° for 30 minutes. Serve it with:
>   Tomato Sauce, page 433

The cheese may be omitted in the cream sauce and a well-seasoned Cream Sauce I with Herbs, page 428, may be used.

QUICK FISH LOAF
4 Servings
Drain, then flake:
>   1 lb. cooked or canned fish: 2 cups

Combine and beat:
>   1 egg
>   ¼ cup undiluted evaporated milk
>   or rich cream

>   ¾ cup soft bread crumbs
>   ½ teaspoon salt
>   ¼ teaspoon paprika
>   2 teaspoons lemon juice or
>   1 teaspoon Worcestershire sauce
>   1 tablespoon melted butter
>   3 tablespoons minced parsley
>   2 tablespoons chopped celery,
>   onion or green pepper

Add the fish. Place these ingredients in a greased baking dish. Bake them in a hot oven 400° for 30 minutes. This loaf may be served hot with:
>   Cream, Tomato or Cheese
>   Sauce, pages 428, 431, 433

or cold with:
>   Mayonnaise

STEAMED FISH PUDDING OR TIMBALE
6 Servings
This is a delicious way of preparing left-over fish. For 3 people reduce the amount by ½ and boil the pudding in a large baking powder can.
If it is not practical to steam the fish, place it in a greased double boiler and cook it for 1 hour. Combine:
>   2 cups flaked or ground fish or
>   1 lb. drained canned salmon
>   ¼ cup melted butter or 4 table-
>   spoons cream
>   ¾ cup bread crumbs
>   3 egg yolks
>   2 teaspoons lemon juice or 1
>   teaspoon Worcestershire sauce
>   Salt and pepper

Beat until stiff and fold in:
>   3 egg whites

Place these ingredients in a mold and steam them for 1 hour (page 731). Serve the pudding with:
>   Cream Sauce I, page 428

seasoned with:
>   Worcestershire sauce

or with:
>   Mustard Sauce, page 428, or
>   Tomato Sauce, page 433, or
>   Shrimp Sauce for Fish, page
>   258, or Oyster Sauce for Fish,
>   page 259

Crab Meat with Piquant Sauce, page 124; Halibut Soufflé, page 221; Fish Soufflé, page 220; Fish Timbales II, page 215.

BAKED FISH RING OR MOUSSE
6 Servings
This is a soufflé to which whipped cream is added, so it becomes some-

what of a luxury dish—a fish mousse. Grind, put through a ricer or blend:
    1 lb. uncooked fish: 2 cups
Cooked fish may be substituted, but uncooked fish makes a better mousse. Heat over a low fire:
    1½ tablespoons butter
Stir in until blended:
    1 tablespoon flour
Stir in:
    ¼ cup milk
Beat and stir in:
    2 egg yolks
Season these ingredients with:
    ½ teaspoon salt
    ⅛ teaspoon paprika
Stir the yolks for 1 or 2 minutes. Permit them to thicken slightly. Add the ground fish. Cool the mixture. Whip until stiff:
    2 egg whites
    ⅛ teaspoon salt
Whip until stiff:
    1 cup heavy cream
Fold these ingredients lightly into the fish mixture. Garnish a greased 9 inch ring mold with:
    Strips of pimiento
    (Strips of green pepper)
Pour the fish mixture into the mold. Set the mold in a pan of hot water. Bake it in a moderate oven 350° for about ½ hour. Serve it with:
    Hollandaise Sauce, page 429,
    Hot Shrimp Sauce, page 258,
    Horseradish Sauce, page 439,
    Oyster Sauce, page 259, or
    Cucumber Sauce, page 437

CREAMED FISH OR SEA FOOD
4 Servings
Prepare:
    1 cup Cream Sauce I, page 428
Salmon and other fat fish call for only 1 tablespoonful of butter in the Cream Sauce. The liquid used in the sauce may be cream, milk, evaporated milk, tomato juice, Stock, page 43, or a combination of these or other liquids. When it is boiling add:
    1 cup flaked fish, shrimp, crab, etc.
Stir it gently with a fork until the food is hot. Season it as desired with:
    Salt and pepper
    Worcestershire sauce, lemon juice, curry powder or mustard, etc.
    2 tablespoons chopped parsley, celery or green pepper, or ½ teaspoon dried Herb, page 833
    1 teaspoon grated onion
Serve it on:

Hot toast, rusks, waffles, pancakes, etc.
It may be served au gratin. Place the creamed fish in a baking dish or in individual dishes. Cover the top with:
    4 tablespoons bread crumbs
Dot them with:
    2 tablespoons butter
or sprinkle them with:
    ½ cup grated cheese
Brown the crumbs under a broiler or bake the dish set in a pan of hot water in a moderate oven 375° until the crumbs are brown.

FISH OR SEA FOOD IN SOUP
3 Servings
The most quickly made main dish I know is a combination of canned fish and condensed cream soup doctored as suggested above. A winner in the race for time is:
    1 can tuna: 7 oz.
Use the fish can to measure:
    An equal amount of condensed cream soup
Add:
    2 tablespoons of milk
Season, heat and serve.

CREAMED SEA FOOD ON TOAST
12 Servings
Cook:
    2 hard-cooked eggs
Shell and dice them. Sauté (page 292):
    ½ lb. mushrooms
Cut into slices:
    8 stuffed olives
Flake:
    ½ lb. fresh crab meat
Prepare:
    1 lb. Boiled Shrimp, page 245
Cook:
    2 cups rich Cream Sauce I, page 428
Add the sea food, olives, mushrooms and eggs to the boiling cream sauce. Season these ingredients with:
    Salt and pepper
    2 tablespoons sherry
Serve them at once on:
    Toast, buttered or spread with anchovy paste
or in a:
    Rice Ring, page 105

CREAMED SEA FOOD AU GRATIN
10 Servings
Do not overlook this delectable luncheon dish.

Combine 3 or 4 kinds of raw fish or shellfish. For example:
    ½ lb. lobster meat
    1 cup drained oysters cut into pieces
    1 cup minced fillet of haddock
Prepare:
    Sautéed Mushrooms, page 292
Use about the same amount of mushrooms as you have fish, about 3 cupfuls. Prepare:
    4 cups Cream Sauce I, page 428
Use ½ cupful butter, ½ cupful flour, 4 cupfuls rich milk or cream, and seasoning.
When the sauce is smooth and boiling fold in the fish. Add the mushrooms. Fill ramekins or shells with the mixture. Cover the tops with:
    Bread crumbs
Dot them with:
    Butter
or sprinkle them with:
    Cheese
Bake the fish in a moderate oven 350° for about 25 minutes. Before serving it pour over each portion:
    1 or 2 teaspoons sherry
Reheat the fish for 1 minute under a broiler.

SEA FOOD POULETTE
4 to 6 Servings
Prepare:
    12 cooked, shelled shrimp
    1 cup raw cut-up and drained oysters
    1 cup scallops
    1 cup raw cut-up lobster meat
Melt:
    2 tablespoons butter
Chop and add:
    6 mushroom caps
    2 shallots
You may substitute for the shallots green onions, dried onions or leeks, using only the white part—about 2 tablespoonfuls. Stir these ingredients about. Cook the for 2 minutes. Add:
    ½ cup cream
    ½ cup dry white wine
This dish should have low, even heat. Simmer these ingredients for 10 minutes. Season them with:
    Salt and white pepper
Beat:
    1 egg yolk
    Juice of 1 lemon
    2 tablespoons dry white wine
Remove the sea food from the fire. Fold in gently the egg mixture and:
    1 tablespoon chopped parsley
    1 tablespoon chopped chives

Place the sea food uncovered over hot water until ready to serve it on:
    Toast triangles

CRAB MEAT À LA KING
8 Servings
Combine:
    8 oz. canned crab meat: 1 cup
    3 peeled diced hard-cooked eggs
    1 chopped pimiento
Sauté (page 292) and add:
    ½ cup chopped mushrooms
Cook until tender in boiling water, drain and add:
    ¼ cup chopped green peppers
Melt:
    3 tablespoons butter
Stir in until blended:
    3 tablespoons flour
Stir in gradually:
    2 cups milk
Add:
    ½ teaspoon salt
    ¼ teaspoon paprika
When the sauce is smooth and boiling add the other ingredients. Add:
    Salt if needed
Season it when hot, as desired, with:
    1 teaspoon Worcestershire sauce
    or 1 tablespoon lemon juice or
    2 tablespoons sherry
Serve the crab over:
    French Toast, page 136, toast, rusks, or in a patty shell or au gratin in ramekins

----

CRAB MEAT NEWBURG
6 Servings
Heat but do not boil:
    1 cup cream
Melt in a saucepan:
    3 tablespoons butter
Stir in:
    2 cups crab meat
    ¾ teaspoon salt
    ⅓ teaspoon paprika
    ⅓ teaspoon nutmeg
Push the meat to one side, tip the saucepan and stir into the butter:
    1 tablespoon cornstarch
Cook until the butter bubbles, right the saucepan and add the hot cream. Stir until the sauce is boiling, then reduce the heat. Beat and add:
    2 egg yolks
Cook and stir gently for 2 minutes, until the yolks thicken slightly, but do not permit the sauce to boil. Add:
    1 teaspoon Worcestershire sauce
    or 2 tablespoons sherry
Serve the crab meat at once on:
    Buttered toast

MOCK CRAB NEWBURG
3 Servings
Pick over the contents of:
>   1 can crab meat: 6 oz.

Heat the contents of:
>   1 can condensed mushroom soup:
>   10½ oz.
>   4 tablespoons milk

Stir in the crab meat, heat it to the boiling point, remove it from the fire and add:
>   2 tablespoons sherry

CRAB MEAT OR LOBSTER WITH PIQUANT SAUCE
4 Servings
The overworked word "intriguing" applies to this delightful dish. For a perfect luncheon or supper serve it with rice and a salad.

Combine and heat in a double boiler:
>   ¾ cup canned tomato soup
>   ¾ cup canned pea soup
>   ¾ cup cream

Heat in a double boiler:
>   1 cup canned crab meat

Pour a little of the sauce over it. Serve it garnished with:
>   Parsley
>   Steamed or Boiled Rice, page 103

and the remaining sauce. All the sauce may be added to the crab. In that case the dish becomes a thick soup.

Crab Bisque, page 67; Rice Ramekins with Crab or Shrimp, page 108.

CRAB MEAT AND MUSHROOMS IN A PATTY SHELL
6 Servings
Sauté in a skillet:
>   ½ lb. mushrooms

in:
>   1 tablespoon butter

Remove the mushrooms. Melt in the skillet:
>   3 tablespoons butter

Stir in until blended:
>   3 tablespoons flour

Stir in slowly:
>   1 cup Chicken Stock, page 43
>   ½ cup cream

When the sauce is boiling add:
>   1½ cups crab meat

and the mushrooms. When these ingredients are well heated stir in:
>   ½ cup grated Parmesan cheese
>   ½ teaspoon salt
>   ⅛ teaspoon pepper
>   ⅛ teaspoon paprika

Remove the crab from the fire and add:
>   3 tablespoons sherry

Serve it in one large hot:
>   Puff Paste Shell, page 566, in
>   patty shells or on hot toast
>   spread with anchovy paste

CRAB MEAT, POACHED EGGS AND CHEESE ON TOAST
6 Servings
Drain, then pick over the contents of:
>   1 can crab meat: 6 oz.

Melt:
>   1½ tablespoons butter

Add:
>   1½ tablespoons flour

When these ingredients are bubbling stir in slowly:
>   ¾ cup rich milk or use ½ cream
>   and ½ chicken stock

Add and heat the crab meat. Season it as needed with:
>   Salt and pepper

Remove it from the fire. Add:
>   (1 or more tablespoons sherry or
>   ½ teaspoon curry powder)

Place this where it will keep hot. Prepare:
>   6 large rounds of buttered toast

Place on each slice:
>   A poached egg

Heap the crab meat on the eggs. Sprinkle it with:
>   Grated cheese

They are now ready to be served but they may be run under a broiler to permit cheese to melt. Top them with:
>   A sprig of parsley or a bit of
>   pimiento

Deviled Egg and Crab Casserole, page 90.

DEVILED LOBSTER
10 Servings
Prepare:
>   3 hard-cooked eggs

Shell them. Separate the yolks from the whites. While hot crush the yolks with a fork, or rice them. Blend them with:
>   1½ tablespoons butter

Blend:
>   2 tablespoons flour
>   1½ tablespoons butter

Combine the yolk and the flour mixture. Stir in slowly:
>   2½ cups milk

Cook and stir these ingredients over a low flame until they thicken and boil. Add the chopped egg whites and:

2 tablespoons chopped parsley
1 teaspoon minced onion
2 cups boiled diced or canned
    lobster meat
1¼ teaspoons salt
¼ teaspoon paprika
(2 tablespoons sherry or 2 tea-
    spoons Worcestershire sauce)
Pour these ingredients into a greased
casserole. Cover the top with:
    ⅓ cup bread crumbs
Dot it with:
    2 tablespoons butter
Bake the dish in a hot oven 450° for
about 10 minutes.

LOBSTER AND MUSHROOM CASSEROLE

6 Servings
Slice:
    1 lb. mushrooms
Sauté them for 2 minutes in:
    4 tablespoons butter
Add:
    3 tablespoons flour
    1 teaspoon salt
    ⅛ teaspoon paprika
Cook and stir the mushrooms over a
slow fire for 1 minute. Stir in slowly:
    1½ cups milk
    ½ cup Bouillon, Chicken or
        Vegetable Stock, pages 43, 45
Cook and stir these ingredients for 3
minutes. Add:
    2 cups boiled diced or canned
        lobster meat
Beat well and add:
    ½ cup cream
    2 egg yolks
Stir and cook these ingredients over a
low flame until they are well heated.
Pour them into a buttered casserole.
Cover the top with:
    ⅓ cup bread crumbs
Dot it with:
    1½ tablespoons butter
Bake the dish in a hot oven 450° for 10
minutes.

Lobster and Lobster Dishes, page 246.

LOBSTER NEWBURG

6 Servings
Melt in a double boiler:
    4 tablespoons butter
Add, stir and cook for 3 minutes:
    2 cups boiled diced lobster meat
Add and cook for 1 minute longer:
    ½ teaspoon paprika
    ⅓ teaspoon nutmeg
Beat and add:

3 egg yolks
1 cup cream
Cook and stir these ingredients until
they thicken. Do not permit them to
boil. Add:
    ¼ cup sherry
Add if required:
    Salt
Serve the lobster at once on:
    Hot buttered toast

LOBSTER NEWBURG BARBARINI

The following good recipe is a contri-
bution of an English woman living in
Massachusetts. I shall give it in her
own words.
"To serve 2 rather greedy people.
Double the quantity for 5 very average
servings.
Cut into pieces about the size of an
almond:
    The meat of a medium-sized
        boiled lobster or 1 package
        frozen lobster
Set it to simmer in a small double
boiler with:
    1 cup cream
If there is any coral roe in the lobster,
be sure to sieve it into the cream.
Simmer the lobster for ½ hour.
Meanwhile, melt in a saucepan:
    4 tablespoons butter
Stir in:
    2 teaspoons flour
Stir in:
    Hot milk
sufficient to make a smooth thick
sauce. Cook it for 3 minutes. Transfer
lobster and sauce to a large double
boiler. Season it with:
    White pepper
    Paprika and salt
The paprika is to give color and should
be used lavishly. Let the whole Newburg simmer happily along for about
15 minutes, then add:
    2 tablespoons sherry
Simmer for another 15 minutes. Five
minutes before sending to the table add
another dab of butter. Stir it well.
Then add about 1 tablespoonful of cold
water. Do not inquire as to the why of
the cold water. It may be lunacy on
my part, but I firmly believe that it
gives a special smoothnes. Just before
serving add a little extra sherry to
taste.
I serve this Newburg often in a glass
baking dish with a lid of Half-Puff
Pastry, page 565, which has been
cooked just before. We always have

cucumbers in a sharp dressing too—
they give great piquancy.
If using domestic sherry, of course,
cut down a little on the salt. I always
mess with my sauces and add as I go
by rule of palate."

LOBSTER RING
5 Servings
Melt:
　2 tablespoons butter
Stir in until blended:
　3 tablespoons flour
Stir in gradually:
　2 cups chicken bouillon or 1 cup
　　bouillon and 1 cup rich milk or
　　cream
Add:
　1 tablespoon minced parsley
　½ cup grated bread crumbs—not
　　very fresh
　4 beaten egg yolks
　2 cups boiled diced lobster meat
　Salt and pepper
Whip until stiff:
　4 egg whites
　⅛ teaspoon salt
Fold them lightly into the other ingredients. Bake the lobster mixture in a
well-oiled 9 inch ring mold in a moderate oven 325° until it is firm, about 20
minutes. Unmold it and serve it with:
　Mushroom Sauce, page 436

Lobster Croquettes, page 196.

CREAMED SHRIMP AND CELERY, EGGPLANT OR CUCUMBER AU GRATIN
4 Servings
Cook:
　1 cup chopped celery, boiled egg-
　　plant or well-drained cucumber
Drain it well. Prepare:
　¾ cup Cream Sauce I, page 428
When the sauce is boiling add the
celery and:
　½ cup or more boiled shrimp
Season with:
　Salt if needed
　⅛ teaspoon paprika
　(½ teaspoon Worcestershire sauce)
Place these ingredients in greased
ramekins. Sprinkle the tops with:
　Bread crumbs or cornflakes
Dot them with:
　Butter
Brown them under a moderate flame.

Pilaf, page 106. A rice dish with
shrimp, oysters, etc.

SHRIMP WITH CHEESE AND ONION SAUCE
4 Servings
Cook by the rule on page 245:
　1 lb. shrimp
Shell and clean them. Melt:
　4 tablespoons butter
Add:
　½ cup minced onion
Simmer the onion for 3 minutes. Stir
in:
　½ cup grated cheese
　½ teaspoon dry mustard
　½ teaspoon salt
　½ minced clove garlic
Cook and stir these ingredients over
very low heat until the cheese has
melted. Add the shrimp and:
　6 tablespoons sherry
Butter individual baking dishes. Place
the shrimp in them. Brown them lightly under a low flame. Shortly before
they are done sprinkle the tops with:
　Grated coconut
Serve them very hot when the coconut
is light brown.

MASKED CAULIFLOWER WITH SAUCE AND SEA FOOD
4 Servings
A one-dish meal. Quick—good.
Drain:
　Cooked or canned cauliflower
Put it in a colander over steam to heat
it. Prepare about:
　1½ cups sauce, page 428—Celery
　　Soup Sauce with Cheese, Cream
　　Sauce, Tomato or fresh Mush-
　　room, etc.
Add to the hot sauce:
　1 cup cleaned shrimp
Heat them. Place the cauliflower in a
hot dish. Pour the sauce over it.
You may vary this in many ways,
changing your sauce, sea food and
seasoning. It may be served au gratin.
Curry, mustard or a bouquet of herbs
may be added to give the canned food
an "uncanny" flavor.
It is bound to be good and is a dish
with unlimited possibilities.

SHRIMP WITH ONIONS AND CHEESE
4 Servings
Cook by the rule on page 294:
　12 small skinned onions
Drain them well. Cook by the rule on
page 245:
　1 lb. boiled or canned shrimp
Shell them. Remove the vein. Combine, then scald:

3 cups milk
2 ribs celery with leaves
½ sliced clove garlic
½ bay leaf
1 whole clove
Salt as needed
¼ teaspoon white pepper
Strain the liquid. Melt in a double boiler:
4 tablespoons butter: ¼ cup
Stir in:
4 tablespoons flour
Stir in the milk mixture. Cook the sauce over hot water for about 5 minutes, stirring frequently. Stir in:
2 beaten egg yolks
Continue to cook and stir the sauce until the egg yolks begin to thicken, for about 3 minutes. You may add at this time:
2 tablespoons dry white wine or sherry
Fold in the onions and the shrimp. Place them in a baking dish. Sprinkle the top with:
½ cup grated cheese
Place the dish under a broiler until the top is brown. Serve it very hot.

SHRIMP WIGGLE
6 Servings
Melt:
4 tablespoons butter
Stir in and blend:
2 tablespoons flour
Add gradually:
1¼ cups milk
When the sauce is boiling add:
1 cup shrimp
1 cup drained peas
Paprika and celery salt
Lower the heat and stir in:
(1 egg yolk)
Permit the yolk to thicken slightly, then add:
Salt if required
(1 teaspoon lemon juice or 1 tablespoon sherry)
Serve the wiggle at once on rounds of:
Hot buttered toast
Or the wiggle may be placed in a greased baking dish and covered with buttered crumbs or cornflakes. Brown the top under a broiler.

Stuffed Eggs on Rosettes with Savory Sauce, page 174; Boiled Shrimp, page 245; Fried Shrimp, page 245.

SHRIMP IN CURRY SAUCE
6 Servings
Prepare:

1 lb. Boiled Shrimp, page 245
Melt in a skillet:
2 tablespoons butter
Add the shrimp. Stir and cook them over high heat for 2 minutes. Add:
2 cups boiling Cream Sauce I, page 428
Combine and stir in:
½ to 1 tablespoon curry powder
2 tablespoons water
A few grains cayenne
Stir constantly. Reduce the heat. Simmer the shrimp for 5 minutes. Beat:
2 egg yolks
2 tablespoons cream
Stir these ingredients slowly into the shrimp. Permit the sauce to thicken for 1 minute. Stir in:
1 tablespoon butter
Salt as needed
Serve the shrimp in a:
Rice Ring, page 105
Surround the ring with:
Whole Baked Tomatoes, page 318
Garnish the dish with:
Parsley
Canned shrimp may be substituted for the boiled shrimp. Omit seasoning the canned shrimp with salt unless necessary.

SHRIMP IN CREOLE SAUCE
4 Servings
Prepare:
1 lb. Boiled Shrimp, page 245
Melt in a skillet:
2 tablespoons butter
Add the shrimp. Stir and cook them over a hot fire for 2 minutes. Add:
2 cups Creole Sauce, page 434
¼ cup dry white wine
Simmer the shrimp covered for 5 minutes. Add if needed:
Salt and pepper
A few grains cayenne
Serve the shrimp with:
Steamed Rice, page 103
Canned shrimp may be substituted for the boiled shrimp. Omit seasoning the canned shrimp with salt unless necessary.

SHRIMP NEWBURG
4 Servings
Prepare (page 245):
1 lb. cooked shrimp
Melt:
2 tablespoons butter
Stir in until blended:
1¾ tablespoons flour

Stir in slowly:
>   1 cup cream

When the sauce is thick stir in:
>   3 tablespoons tomato catsup
>   ¾ tablespoon Worcestershire sauce
>   (½ teaspoon dry mustard)

Add the shrimp. Stir them about until they are well heated. Season with:
>   Salt and pepper
>   A few grains cayenne

Immediately before serving add:
>   2 tablespoons sherry

Serve the shrimp in a:
>   Grits Ring, page 157

or over:
>   Rice

Or, serve the dish au gratin (page 942).

SOUTHERN CREAMED SHRIMP
4 Servings

Cook by the rule on page 245, then shell and clean:
>   2 lbs. shrimp

Melt:
>   4 tablespoons butter

Sauté in it very lightly:
>   3 chopped ribs celery
>   ½ chopped green pepper, seeds and fibrous portions removed
>   1 teaspoon grated onion

Stir in:
>   4 tablespoons flour

Stir in gradually:
>   2 cups rich milk

When the sauce is boiling add the shrimp. Season with:
>   ¾ teaspoon salt
>   ⅛ teaspoon curry
>   A few grains cayenne
>   1 tablespoon walnut sauce
>   2 teaspoons Worcestershire sauce

Place the shrimp in individual baking dishes or a casserole. Cover the tops with:
>   Bread crumbs

Dot them with:
>   Butter

Sprinkle the tops with:
>   Grated Parmesan cheese

Heat the shrimp in a hot oven 425° until the crumbs are lightly browned.

CANNED FISH ROE IN RAMEKINS
3 Servings

To the contents of:
>   1 can fish roe: 7¾ oz.

Add:
>   1½ teaspoons bread crumbs
>   1½ teaspoons butter
>   1 beaten egg
>   Salt if needed
>   ¼ teaspoon paprika
>   2 teaspoons chopped parsley
>   ½ cup milk

Fill four greased ramekins. Place them in a pan of hot water in a moderate oven 325° until firm—about 20 minutes. Serve the roe with:
>   Slices of lemon

SARDINES AND CANNED SPINACH
4 to 6 Servings

Prepare:
>   1 cup Cream Sauce, page 428, or 1 cup slightly diluted mushroom, celery or tomato soup

Drain the contents of:
>   1 No. 2 can spinach

Chop the spinach or put it through a ricer. Add the sauce and:
>   A fresh grating of nutmeg or a little grated onion
>   (A few drops green coloring)

Heat the spinach well. Drain lightly the contents of:
>   1 can sardines: 10 oz.

Broil the sardines. Heap the spinach on a dish. Place the sardines around it. Garnish it with:
>   Lemon slices
>   Hot potato chips or triangles of toast

EMERGENCY FISH CAKES

Excellent cakes may be made quickly by combining fish or sea food with condensed cream soup. See Fish or Sea Food in Soup, page 112. Keep your mixture rather stiff. Treat it as you would any other fish ball or cake.

SALMON CAKES
6 Servings

Flake the contents of:
>   1 can salmon: 16 oz.

Stir in:
>   ½ cup cracker crumbs
>   2 beaten eggs
>   ½ teaspoon salt
>   ⅛ teaspoon paprika

Form these ingredients into cakes. Sauté them until brown in:
>   Butter

Serve the cakes with:
>   Mushroom Sauce, page 436
>   Celery Soup Sauce, page 441, etc.

SALMON POTATO CAKES
6 Servings
Prepare by the rule on page 309:
     Potato cakes
Use the egg and 2 cupfuls mashed potatoes. Add in small flakes:
     1 cup or more salmon
Season with:
     Chopped parsley, onion juice
     or celery seed
Shape the mixture into cakes. Dip them in:
     Crushed cornflakes or bread
     crumbs
Sauté them slowly in:
     Butter, oil or drippings
See the note under Tuna Fish with Canned Soup Sauce, page 441.

CRABBURGERS
6 to 8 Servings
Combine:
     1 lb. cooked crab meat
     ¼ teaspoon salt
     ⅛ teaspoon pepper
     1 tablespoon Worcestershire
     sauce
     A few drops of Tabasco sauce
     1 small grated onion
     5 beaten egg yolks
     2 tablespoons chopped parsley
Whip until stiff, then fold in:
     5 egg whites
Melt in a skillet:
     ¼ cup oil or butter
Drop the batter from a spoon into the hot fat. When done place the cakes on sandwich buns. Spread them with:
     Mayonnaise seasoned with
     garlic

CANNED CODFISH CAKES, BAKED BEANS AND BACON
Codfish cakes and baked beans may be purchased in cans. Heat them as directed on the can label. One tablespoonful horseradish may be added to a 10 oz. can of codfish. Heat:
     Baked Beans, page 268
Sauté:
     Bacon
Arrange the codfish cakes, the beans and the bacon on a hot platter. Garnish it with:
     Parsley
     Lemon wedges
     Pickles
Serve this dish with:
     Boston brown bread, packaged
     or canned

CODFISH BALLS
Method I. 6 Servings
Soak in cold water for 3 hours:
     1 cup shredded codfish
Drain it. Place it in boiling water. Peel, add and cook until tender:
     6 medium-sized potatoes
Drain these ingredients well, separate them with a fork, permit the steam to evaporate and shake them over heat to dry. Add and mix lightly with a fork:
     1 tablespoon butter
     ⅛ teaspoon pepper
     1 beaten egg
Shape the mixture into balls, or drop it from a spoon. Fry the codfish balls in deep fat (page 542) or sauté them in butter.

Method II.
Soak in cold water for 3 hours, place in boiling water, then simmer for 20 minutes:
     1 cup codfish
Drain it and put it through a chopper or ricer. Rice or mash:
     6 medium-sized boiled potatoes
Combine the fish and potatoes. Beat in one at a time:
     2 eggs
Beat in until fluffy:
     2 tablespoons cream
Season as needed with:
     Salt and pepper
     (1 teaspoon grated onion)
Shape the mixture into balls, or drop it from a spoon. Fry the balls in deep fat (page 541) or sauté them in butter. They may be baked in a greased pan in a moderate oven 375° for about 35 minutes. Dot the tops with butter.

SCALLOPED CODFISH
8 Servings
Soak for 12 hours in water to cover:
     1 lb. dried codfish
Drain it well. There should be about 2 cupfuls of fish when it is picked over and shredded. Combine:
     1 tablespoon flour
     2 cups milk
     1 well-beaten egg
Cook and stir these ingredients over boiling water until they are thick. Season them with:
     A few grains salt
     ¼ teaspoon paprika
Prepare:
     1½ cups bread crumbs
     1½ cups finely chopped celery
These proportions may be varied. Grease a baking dish. Place in it ½ the fish and a layer of ½ the crumbs.

Cover with ½ the sauce and repeat the process. Put a layer of crumbs on the top. Dot it with:
Butter
or sprinkle it with:
Grated cheese
Cover the dish closely and place it in a moderate oven 375° for 15 minutes. Uncover it and bake it until the crumbs are crisp.

CODFISH CREAMED AND BAKED
6 Servings
Soak in cold water for 3 hours, changing the water twice, the contents of:
1 box salt codfish
Drain the fish, cover it with cold water and bring it slowly to the boiling point. Drain it, cover it with cold water, heat and simmer it until tender. Drain the fish well and break it into shreds. Prepare, then beat into the fish:
1½ cups Cream Sauce I, page 428
Heat:
3 tablespoons salad oil
Skin, slice and sauté in it on both sides:
2 large tomatoes
seasoned with:
2 teaspoons grated onion or 1 minced clove garlic
1 teaspoon sugar
Add the tomatoes to the codfish. Beat in:
½ cup cream
Freshly grated pepper
Salt if needed
(1 teaspoon dried basil or other herb)
Place the mixture in a greased ovenproof dish in a moderate oven 400° for about 15 minutes.

CLAM HASH
5 Servings
Steam (page 252), then put through a food chopper:
20 large clams
Combine and add:
½ cup fresh or canned clam broth or chicken stock
3 lightly beaten eggs
1 cup cooked cubed potatoes
1 tablespoon finely minced parsley
1 tablespoon finely minced chives or 2 teaspoons grated onion
1 tablespoon chopped green pepper
¼ teaspoon or more salt
⅛ teaspoon pepper
2 tablespoons sherry

Permit this to stand for ½ hour. Melt in a skillet:
3 tablespoons butter
Stir the clam mixture into this until hot. Spread it evenly in the pan. Cook it over low heat until the bottom is brown, then fold over the hash and place it on a hot plate. Garnish it with:
Lemon wedges and water cress

CLAM GRIDDLE CAKES
4 to 6 Servings
Beat well:
1 cup sour cream
1 egg
Add:
¾ cup minced cooked or canned clams
Sift before measuring:
1½ cups flour
Resift with:
½ teaspoon salt
½ teaspoon soda
Combine the liquid and the sifted ingredients with a few swift strokes. Bake the cakes on a griddle. See rule for Griddle Cakes, page 547.

CRAB, CLAM OR OYSTER CAKES
Six 3 Inch Cakes
You may combine these or use them separately.
Melt:
2 tablespoons butter
Add, stir and simmer for 3 minutes:
2 tablespoons minced onion
½ cup soft bread crumbs
Combine and add:
2 beaten eggs
½ cup cream
2 cups minced clams or flaked crab meat
½ teaspoon dry mustard or 1 tablespoon lemon juice
2 tablespoons chopped parsley
½ teaspoon salt
½ teaspoon paprika
Chill this mixture for 2 hours. Shape into cakes. Dust them lightly with:
Flour or bread crumbs
Fry in deep fat (page 542) or melt in a skillet over a quick fire:
1 tablespoon butter
Brown the cakes on both sides, lower the heat and cook the cakes slowly for about 6 minutes longer.

MARINATED HERRING
Soak for 3 hours in water to cover:
24 milter herring
Change the water twice. Cut off the

heads and tails. Split the herring. Remove the milt. Reserve it. Remove the bones. Discard them. Cut the fillets into pieces about 3 inches long. Place in a crock in alternate layers the herring, ½ the milt and:

2 very thinly sliced lemons
2 skinned and thinly sliced onions
⅓ cup mixed pickle spices
1 tablespoon sugar

Cover these ingredients with:

Malt vinegar or other vinegar

to which the remaining milt is added after being crushed with a fork or put through a sieve. Dilute the vinegar with a little water if it is very strong. Cover the crock and put it in a cool place. The herring are ready to be served after 2 weeks.

MARINATED HERRING WITH SOUR CREAM

Prepare by the preceding rule:

6 milter herring

Follow the rule but use only 1 lemon, 1 onion, 2½ tablespoonfuls mixed spices and ¼ cupful vinegar. Add:

1 cup sour cream

Keep in a cool place. Serve it after 48 hours.

HERRING IN WINE WITH SOUR CREAM

6 Servings

Drain the contents of:

A 2 lb. jar of herring in wine

Reserve the liquor. Add to it:

1 cup thick sour cream
1 tablespoon grated onion
2 tablespoons chopped chives
1 tablespoon chopped basil

Pour this mixture over the herring. Serve them chilled on:

Lettuce

See Index for other Herring Dishes.

Hot and Cold Sandwiches with Hot Sauce or Cold Dressing

A main dish for luncheon or supper. These sandwiches lend themselves to endless variations. Canned biscuits make good sandwiches.

Many fine suggestions for sandwiches will be found in the chapter on Canapés, page 9.

HAM, TOMATO AND EGG SANDWICH WITH CREAM HORSERADISH DRESSING

Slice and butter:

Rye bread

Place on it:

Slices boiled ham
Lettuce leaves
Sliced tomatoes

Garnish the sandwiches with:

Slices hard-cooked egg
Sprigs parsley

Serve them with:

Sour Cream and Horseradish Sauce, page 439, or Horseradish Sauce, page 439, or Russian Dressing, page 496

TOMATO AND BACON SANDWICH WITH CHEESE SAUCE

Trim the crusts from:

Slices light or dark bread

Place on each slice:

Crisp Sautéed Bacon, page 375
Lettuce leaves
Sliced tomatoes
Sliced olives or pickles

Serve the sandwiches with the following Cheese Sauce:

Cheese Sauce II

6 Servings

Rub the top of a double boiler with:

Garlic

Beat in it:

1 egg
1 cup milk

Add:

¾ teaspoon salt
¾ teaspoon dry mustard
¼ teaspoon paprika
A few grains red pepper

Cook and stir these ingredients over boiling water. When they are hot add and stir in until melted:

¾ lb. grated or ground yellow cheese: 3 cups

Serve the sauce hot.

LAMB OR CHICKEN SANDWICH WITH CAVIAR DRESSING

Trim the crusts from:

Large slices rye bread

Spread them with:

Butter

Place on each piece:

Slices cold lamb or chicken
Lettuce leaves

Slices tomato
Slices hard-cooked egg
Serve the sandwich with:

Russian Dressing II
Combine and beat well:
1 cup mayonnaise
2 tablespoons drained chili sauce
1 teaspoon barbecue sauce
A few drops onion juice
2 to 4 oz. caviar

CHEESE SANDWICH WITH MUSHROOM SAUCE

Trim the crusts from:
Slices light or dark bread
Spread them with:
Butter
Place on each piece:
Slices of cheese
Lettuce leaves
Slices tomato or cucumber
Slices hard-cooked egg
Sliced olives or pickles
Serve the sandwiches with:
Mushroom Sauce, page 436

EGG AND CHEESE SANDWICH WITH TOMATO SAUCE

4 Servings
Rub:
4 slices French bread
with:
(Garlic)
Dip them quickly in:
Milk seasoned with a pinch of
salt
Brown them in:
Olive oil
Place them on a hot oven-proof plate.
Cover them with:
4 chopped hard-cooked eggs
1 cup or more grated cheese
6 or more chopped olives
Dots of butter
The slices may be placed in a hot oven
450° or under a broiler until the cheese
is melted. Serve them with:
Tomato Sauce, page 433

TOASTED DEVILED HAM AND CHEESE SANDWICHES

Cover:
Thin slices of toast
with a paste made of:
Deviled ham, French mustard or
horseradish
Cover the ham with thin slices of:
American cheese
Broil the sandwiches until the cheese
is soft.

HOT EMERGENCY SANDWICHES

Bake:
Canned biscuits
Split them. Spread them with:
Deviled ham
Serve them piping hot with:
Condensed cream soup—aspara-
gus, celery, tomato, etc.—
slightly diluted with milk

MEAL-IN-ONE SANDWICH

4 Servings But Better Call It 2
On your toes when you make this. It's
easy if you have all your ingredients
ready before you poach the eggs.
Prepare:
4 large slices of toast
8 slices sautéed bacon
4 skinned and sliced large
tomatoes
½ cup French dressing
1 cup Cream Sauce I, page 428
1 cup grated cheese
Place the toast on a baking sheet,
cover it with the bacon, tomatoes and
dressing. Poach:
4 eggs
Place an egg on each piece of garnished toast, cover it with ¼ of the
cream sauce and ¼ of the grated
cheese. Place the toast under the
broiler until the cheese melts. Serve
the sandwiches piping hot.

Toasted Sardine Canapés, page 14.

HOT ROAST BEEF SANDWICH WITH OLIVE SAUCE

4 Servings
Slice:
Cold roast beef
Prepare by the rule on page 435:
1 cup Brown Sauce
Add to it:
1 tablespoon finely minced sour
pickle or ½ cup chopped olives
Cut:
6 thin slices of light or dark bread
Beat until soft:
2 tablespoons butter
¼ teaspoon prepared mustard or
1 teaspoon horseradish
Spread the bread with this mixture.
Dip the beef slices in the hot sauce.
Place them between the slices of bread.
Serve the sandwiches on a hot platter
covered with remaining sauce.

HOT CHICKEN SANDWICHES
Cut into slices:
>Cold cooked chicken

Dip the slices in:
>Mayonnaise

Prepare:
>Biscuits, page 505

While hot open and spread them with:
>Butter

Place the chicken slices in the biscuits.
Serve them hot with:
>Chicken gravy or Cheese Sauce,
>page 430

BROILED HAMBURGER SANDWICHES
4 Servings
Combine:
>1 lb. ground beef
>1 teaspoon salt
>¼ teaspoon paprika

Add:
>(¼ cup chopped lightly sautéed
>onions)

Toast on one side:
>8 slices bread

Spread the untoasted sides with the
meat mixture. Dot the tops lightly
with:
>Butter

Broil the sandwiches under 325° heat
for about 8 minutes. Serve them with
or without:
>Brown Sauce, page 435, or
>Creole Sauce, page 434, etc.

HOT BISCUITS BAKED WITH FILLINGS
About Eighteen 2½ Inch Biscuits
Combine:
>1 cup cooked, shredded meat—
>chicken, fish, ham, veal, roast,
>etc.
>½ cup thick gravy, cream sauce or
>condensed soup
>1 tablespoon grated onion
>1 chopped hard-cooked egg
>2 tablespoons chopped pickles or
>olives
>Seasoning

Make by the rule on page 505:
>Baking powder biscuit dough

Roll it to the thickness of ¼ inch. Cut
it into rounds. Place on one round:
>1 spoonful meat mixture

Moisten the edges and cover it with
another round. Seal the edges with a
fork. Prick the tops. Place the biscuits
on a baking sheet and bake them until
brown in a very hot oven 450°. You
may serve these with:
>Mushroom Sauce, page 436

MINCED CHICKEN SANDWICHES
About Eight 2½-Inch Biscuits
Combine:
>½ cup cooked minced chicken
>1 chopped hard-cooked egg
>6 chopped stuffed olives
>¼ cup mayonnaise
>(2 tablespoons chopped parsley)

Prepare:
>Biscuits, page 505

While hot open and spread them with:
>Butter

and the minced chicken mixture. Serve
them hot with:
>Chicken gravy or Mushroom
>Sauce, page 436

BAKED BEAN SANDWICHES
2 Servings
Mash, then heat:
>1 cup baked beans

Add:
>1 teaspoon lemon juice or 2 tea-
>spoons catsup, chili sauce or
>prepared mustard
>1 tablespoon melted butter
>¼ cup minced onion or celery
>Seasoning

Spread this on slices of:
>Boston brown or rye bread

Sprinkle it with:
>Chopped parsley

Strips of sautéed or raw bacon may be
placed on the sandwich. If raw, notch
them. Broil them under a moderate
flame until they are crisp.

DRIED BEEF AND SCRAMBLED EGG SANDWICHES WITH TOMATO CHEESE SAUCE
4 Servings
Prepare by the rule on page 434:
>Tomato Cheese Sauce

Prepare:
>12 slices thin toast

Scramble:
>4 eggs

Place the eggs between 2 slices of
toast. Place between the second and
third slices:
>Dried beef

Pour the sauce over the sandwiches.

PEANUT BUTTER AND BACON SANDWICH
4 Servings
Virtue, however admirable, is frequently dull. Peanut butter needs
enlivening. Try this mixture on the
unconverted. Combine:

¾ cup peanut butter
    4 tablespoons mayonnaise
    ¼ teaspoon salt
    2 tablespoons pickle relish or
        chili sauce
    4 tablespoons cooked minced
        bacon
Toast on one side:
    4 slices bread
Spread the untoasted side with the
mixture. Broil the sandwiches until
the tops are brown. Slice them diagonally.

CORNED BEEF OR DRIED BEEF AND CHEESE SANDWICHES

6 Servings
Cut into tiny slivers:
    ¼ cup sharp American cheese
Cream the cheese well with:
    2 tablespoons mayonnaise
Shred finely and add:
    4 oz. canned corned beef or dried
        beef
Chop until fine and add:
    ¼ cup sour-sweet pickles
    1 tablespoon grated onion
    (2 tablespoons minced celery or
        parsley)
Season the spread as needed with:
    Salt and pepper
    Curry powder, mustard or
    Worcestershire sauce
Spread it between:
    Slices of bread
The sandwiches may be toasted or
they may be served with sliced toma-
toes and lettuce between the layers.

CORNED BEEF AND TOMATO SANDWICHES

Prepare:
    Slices of buttered toast
Cover them with:
    Sliced corned beef
seasoned with:
    Mustard or horseradish
    Tomatoes seasoned with French
    dressing
Sprinkle the tops with:
    Grated cheese
Broil the sandwiches until the cheese
is melted.

CHEESE SANDWICHES WITH BACON

4 Servings
Toast on one side:
    4 slices bread
Place on the untoasted sides:
    Slices cheese

Spread the cheese with:
    Mustard or chili sauce
Cover each sandwich with:
    2 slices bacon
Arrange between the bacon slices:
    (Sliced stuffed olives or slices of
        tomato)
Bake the sandwiches in a moderate
oven 350° for 10 minutes or until the
bacon is crisp, or broil them.

Cheese Spreads, pages 22 and 191.
Place one of these spreads between
slices of bread. Toast them.

ROLLS WITH BACON AND CHEESE

4 Servings
Cut into halves:
    4 long hard buns
Place between the slices:
    4 thick oblongs of yellow cheese
It may be spread with:
    Mustard
Wind around the buns:
    4 strips of bacon
Secure them with toothpicks. Bake
the buns on a rack in a quick oven 400°
or place them under a broiler until the
bacon is crisp.

ROLLS STUFFED WITH HAM MIXTURE

4 Servings
Cut the tops from:
    4 large hard rolls
Hollow the centers. Combine and mix
well:
    2 tablespoons chopped onion
    2 tablespoons catsup
    2 tablespoons chopped green
        pepper
    2 tablespoons chopped pickles
    ½ lb. chopped sharp cheese
    3 oz. deviled ham or ½ cup finely
        cut cooked ham
    4 tablespoons cream, melted
        butter or oil
Fill the rolls with this mixture. Wrap
them in waxed paper. Bake them in a
moderate oven 400° for 10 minutes.
These rolls may be served with:
    Tomato Sauce, page 433, etc.

FISH SANDWICH WITH CHEESE ON FRENCH TOAST

4 Servings
Flake with a fork:
    1 cup tuna, salmon, etc.
Add and toss gently:

½ cup minced celery
¼ cup mayonnaise
2 tablespoons lemon juice
¼ teaspoon salt
⅛ teaspoon paprika
Prepare:
8 slices lightly buttered bread
Spread 4 slices with the fish mixture.
Top each slice with:
A thin slice cheese
and a slice of bread.
Beat well:
2 eggs
1 cup milk
⅛ teaspoon salt
Dip the sandwiches on both sides in
this mixture. Sauté them in a skillet
until golden brown in:
Butter

TOASTED ROLLS WITH CRAB MEAT AND CHEESE
4 Servings
Fine with beer or cider.
Cut into halves:
4 rolls
Cover the 4 lower halves with:
Lettuce leaves
Combine:
¾ cup canned crab meat
¼ cup mayonnaise
Spread this on the lettuce. Spread the
remaining halves with:
Butter

Slices of cheese
(Mustard)
Toast the cheese under a broiler until
it is soft. Combine the halves.

SHRIMP SANDWICHES WITH CHEESE SAUCE
3 Servings
Clean:
1½ cups shrimp
Melt:
2 tablespoons butter
Add:
1 tablespoon grated onion
(1 sliced pimiento)
and the shrimp. Stir over low heat for
1 minute. Prepare:
6 slices toast
Heap the shrimp on the toast. Serve
with:
Cheese Sauce, page 431

TUNA FISH PASTE ON TOAST WITH CHEESE SAUCE
Spread:
Toast
with a paste made of:
Tuna fish
Cream
Lemon juice
Grated onion or chopped chives
Broil the sandwiches. Serve them
with:
Cheese Sauce, page 431

Sandwich Suggestions for Individual Servings

2 slices toast, sliced chicken, 2 strips sautéed bacon and grated cheese au gratin, Mushroom Sauce, page 436.

2 slices toast, creamed chicken, Parmesan cheese au gratin, grilled tomatoes and bacon.

2 slices buttered toast, baked ham, creamed chicken and mushrooms.

Ham, chicken and lettuce between toast. American cheese on top, broiled until cheese is soft.

2 slices toast, braunschweiger, sliced tomatoes, lettuce, tart mayonnaise.

2 slices toast, sliced tongue, sliced tomatoes, mayonnaise, sautéed bacon.

2 slices buttered toast, creamed mushrooms, sliced tomatoes and grated cheese on top, broiled until cheese is melted.

2 slices toast, sliced ham, creamed mushrooms.

Hot buttered biscuits filled with ham, mushroom sauce.

2 slices toast, lettuce, French dressing, sliced tomato and avocado, 2 slices crisp sautéed bacon.

2 slices buttered toast, asparagus tips, 2 slices crisp bacon, Welsh Rarebit.

2 slices buttered toast, lettuce, sliced chicken, sliced tomato, crumbled Roquefort cheese, 2 slices crisp bacon.

Miscellaneous Luncheon Dishes

SANDWICH LOAF

This is a meal by itself—an excellent luncheon dish with coffee and a dessert. Cut the crusts from:

    A loaf of white or whole-wheat bread

Cut the loaf into 3 or 4 lengthwise slices. Butter the inner sides of the slices and spread them with a layer of:

    Chicken or shrimp salad

a layer of:

    Drained crushed pineapple and cream cheese

a layer of:

    Drained sliced tomatoes, lettuce or water cress

or with any good combination of salad or sandwich ingredients. Be sure to cut the bread thin enough or spread the fillings thick enough (see below) to keep the bread from dominating.

Wrap the loaf firmly in a moist towel, chill it well, unwrap it and place it on a platter. Cover it with softened cream cheese, smooth cottage cheese or with 1 cupful mayonnaise to which ½ teaspoonful gelatine soaked in 1 tablespoonful water and dissolved over heat has been added and which is ready to set. An individual slice cut from the finished loaf is shown above. If it fits with your fillings, add 2 tablespoonfuls anchovy paste to the cream or cottage cheese.

Garnish the loaf with:

    Hard-cooked eggs
    Stuffed olives
    Red caviar
    Parsley, water cress, pimiento

To serve cut it into slices.

Or if you want festive individual servings, cut the bread into rounds or squares, fill the layers as described above, cover them with the cream cheese which has been put on in decorative patterns and then serve topped with a lighted birthday candle.

TOAST ROLLS WITH HAM AND ASPARAGUS

4 Servings

Drain the contents of:

    1 can asparagus tips: 16 oz.

Remove the crusts from:

    8 thin slices bread

Brush them lightly on both sides with:

    Melted butter

Place on each slice:

    A slice boiled ham
    Several asparagus tips

Roll the bread around the tips or bring 2 corners together. Fasten the bread with toothpicks. Bake these rolls on a baking sheet in a 400° oven until they are lightly browned. Use the asparagus water and cream to make:

    Cream Sauce, page 428, or
    Mushroom Sauce, page 436

Serve the rolls piping hot with the sauce. A fine luncheon or supper dish with a molded grapefruit salad and coffee.

LUNCHETTES

Prepare:

    Rounds of toast

While hot spread them lightly with:

    Butter

Place on each round:

    A thick slice of tomato

Cover the tomatoes with:

    Chopped onion and green pepper

Season them with:

    Salt and pepper

Place on each round:

    A slice of American cheese
    A slice of bacon

Crisp the bacon under a broiler.

FRENCH TOAST

Cut:

    4 or 6 slices of stale bread ½ inch thick

Combine:

    1 slightly beaten egg
    1 cup milk
    ¼ teaspoon salt
    2 tablespoons sugar

Dip the bread in the egg mixture. Soak it well. Cook it on a well-greased griddle or skillet. Brown one side, turn the slices and brown the other. Serve the slices hot with:

Jelly or hot apple sauce sprinkled with cinnamon

HAM AND PINEAPPLE FRENCH TOAST SANDWICH

Combine equal parts:

Ground ham
Crushed pineapple

Season these ingredients with:

French mustard

Spread this filling between slices of:

Buttered bread

See the above rule for French Toast. Spread the outsides of the sandwiches with the egg mixture and sauté them as directed.

FRENCH TOAST AND CHEESE
4 Servings

Prepare (see page 136), omitting the sugar:

French Toast

Toast the bread on a buttered oven-proof plate in a moderate oven 350° for about 5 minutes. Stir over very low heat until smooth:

½ lb. grated or minced cheese
½ teaspoon salt
A few grains cayenne
¼ cup milk
3 tablespoons butter

Spread the toast with the cheese mixture. Return it to the oven to brown lightly.

HAWAIIAN TOAST WITH BACON
4 Servings

Cut:

4 to 6 slices stale bread ½ inch thick

Beat until light:

2 eggs

Beat in:

1 cup pineapple juice
½ teaspoon salt

Dip the bread in the egg mixture. Soak it well. Sauté in a skillet:

8 slices bacon

Remove them to a hot platter. Keep them hot. Fry the bread in the bacon drippings, brown one side and then the other. Remove the bread to the hot platter. Sauté in the bacon drippings:

4 slices drained pineapple cut into halves

Garnish the platter with the bacon and the pineapple. Serve the toast at once.

TOASTED SANDWICHES

These are offered as a luncheon suggestion. Many of the sandwich fillings given in the preceding rules and in the chapter on Canapés and Sandwiches, page 10, may be spread between slices of bread and the bread may be toasted. The sandwiches may be served with a hot sauce or a cold dressing.

SAUTÉED SANDWICHES

Melt in a small skillet large enough to accommodate one sandwich:

1½ teaspoons butter

Sauté a sandwich slowly on one side until browned. Add to the skillet:

1½ teaspoons butter

Brown the second side. Especially good with a thin slice of cheese, mustard, salt and paprika between the bread slices, or with deviled ham, meat mixtures, jam or jelly.

WAFFLE OR TOASTED SANDWICHES

These and the following sandwiches are good for the maidless hostess who has no toaster.

Cut into thin slices:

White or dark bread

Spread it lightly with:

Soft butter

Cut off the crusts and spread between the slices:

Cheese Spread or other sandwich fillings, pages 191, 23

Cut the sandwiches to fit the sections of a waffle iron. Wrap them in a moist cloth until ready to toast. Heat a waffle iron, arrange the sandwiches upon the iron, lower the top and toast them until they are crisp.

BAKED SWEETBREAD PATTIES WITH TOMATOES AND ONIONS
4 Servings

A complete course, therefore an ideal plate-luncheon dish.

Simmer until tender:

1 pair sweetbreads

Skin them. Divide them into 4 parts. If they are very uneven, flatten them by placing a weight on them. Boil:

2 cups water

Add:

(⅛ bay leaf)

Cut and drop into the water:

4 slices Bermuda onion ¾ inch thick

Cook the slices until they are nearly tender. Drain them. Have ready:
    8 slices bacon
Cross the strips for each patty, forming 4 plus signs. Place the pieces of sweetbreads on the bacon, cover them with the onion slices. Then cover the onion slices with:
    4 slices tomato ¾ inch thick
Season the tomatoes with:
    Salt and pepper
    Brown sugar
Bring the ends of the bacon over the top of the patties and fasten them with toothpicks. Arrange the patties in a skillet and sauté them until slightly browned on the bottom, then place the skillet on the top grate of a moderate oven 375° and bake the patties until they are well heated and the bacon is crisp. Serve them on:
    Hot rusks or rounds of toast

WILD RICE AND SWEETBREADS
4 Servings
Cook by the rule on page 109:
    ¾ cup wild rice or use white or brown rice
Simmer by the rule on page 376:
    1 pair sweetbreads
Skin them. Break them into large pieces. Cream by the rule on page 292:
    ½ to 1 lb. mushrooms
Season them as you wish. You may add (it's very good):
    2 tablespoons acid white wine or sherry
Place the rice in a mound in the center of a platter and pour the mushrooms over it. Melt in a skillet:
    2 tablespoons butter
Turn the sweetbread pieces quickly in the butter until heated. Place them on top of the mound. Garnish the dish with:
    Parsley or chopped chives

BAKED SWEETBREADS IN HAM
4 Servings
Simmer by the rule on page 376:
    A large pair sweetbreads
Drain them. Reserve the broth. Chill them in cold water and drain them. Remove the membrane. Break the sweetbreads into 4 parts. Dip them into:
    1 cup Cream Sauce II, page 428, made with part sweetbread or chicken stock and part cream

The sauce should be rich, heavy and hot.
Chill them until the sauce is firm. Roll the sweetbreads in:
    Sifted bread crumbs
Surround them with very thin:
    Slices ham
Wrap them in oiled paper. Broil them under a moderate flame. Serve them with:
    Spinach Ring, page 223, or
    Vegetable Soufflé, page 218

SWEETBREADS AND MUSHROOMS IN CHICKEN SAUCE
6 Servings
Cook, then remove the membrane from:
    2 pairs sweetbreads
Sprinkle them lightly with:
    Salt and pepper
Melt in a skillet:
    1 tablespoon butter
Add the sweetbreads. Sauté them until they begin to brown. Turn them once. Place them on a hot platter. Keep them hot. Place in the skillet and sauté for 3 minutes:
    1 cup sliced mushrooms
    (1 sliced shallot or 1 teaspoon grated onion)
Drain the vegetables and add them to:
    1 cup hot Poulette Sauce, page 432
Pour the sauce over the sweetbreads. Garnish them with:
    Parsley

CREAMED CHICKEN GIBLETS
Dice, put in boiling water or stock, then simmer until tender:
    Chicken giblets
You may add for the last 15 minutes of cooking:
    Chopped green pepper
    Chopped celery
Drain these ingredients, reserving the stock. Make:
    Gravy, page 426
using:
    2 tablespoons butter
    2 tablespoons flour to 1 cup stock
Season the gravy palatably, then reheat in it the giblets and vegetables. See the bottom of the following rule for suggestions for serving this dish.

CHICKEN LIVERS BOILED AND CREAMED
Drop chicken livers in:
    Boiling Vegetable Stock, page 45, or Chicken Stock, page 43, or bouillon

Simmer them until they are tender, for about 10 minutes. Add to them:

> Cream Sauce I, page 428, made with part cream and part stock

Use about ½ as much sauce as there are livers. Or, add to them:

> Brown Sauce, page 435

Serve them with:

> Rice, page 103, or Scrambled Eggs, page 81, or Omelet, page 85

or place them in:

> Filled Pancakes, page 117, or on toast, etc.

CHICKEN LIVERS SAUTÉED WITH ONIONS
4 Servings

Cut in two:

> 12 chicken livers

Roll them in:

> Seasoned flour

Melt in a saucepan:

> 2 tablespoons butter

Sauté in the butter until brown:

> 2 tablespoons chopped onion

Add the chicken livers. Stir and sauté them until they are brown, for about 3 minutes. Stir in until lightly browned:

> 1 teaspoon flour

Stir in slowly:

> ½ cup Chicken or other stock, page 43, or ½ stock and ½ dry red wine

Add:

> ½ teaspoon Worcestershire sauce
> Salt and pepper if needed

Cook these ingredients for 2 minutes. To serve them see the preceding rule for Chicken Livers Boiled.

CHICKEN LIVERS IN CREAM AND SHERRY WITH OR WITHOUT APPLES
4 Servings

Follow the above rule for:

> Chicken livers sautéed with onions

Substitute for the stock:

> ½ cup cream

When smooth and boiling add:

> ¼ cup sherry
> Salt and pepper if needed

Cook until tender:

> 2 pared and sliced large apples

in:

> ½ cup water
> ¼ cup brown sugar
> ⅛ teaspoon salt

Combine them with the chicken livers. Serve with:

> Lemon wedges and parsley

Chicken Livers in Blankets, page 29.

CHICKEN LIVERS, GREEN PEAS AND CARROTS IN INDIVIDUAL CASSEROLES
4 Servings

Cook:

> 2 cups fresh peas: 2 lbs.

Boil:

> ¾ cup chopped carrots

Drain the vegetables. Reserve the liquids. Combine the vegetables and place them in 4 individual casseroles. Melt:

> 3 tablespoons butter

Sauté in the butter until seared only:

> ½ lb. chicken livers

Arrange the chicken livers on top of the vegetables in the casseroles. Stir into the butter in the pan:

> 1½ tablespoons flour

Stir in slowly:

> ⅓ cup Chicken Stock, page 43, or vegetable liquor
> ⅓ cup cream
> Salt and pepper as needed

Pour it over the ingredients in the casseroles. Place the casseroles covered in a moderate oven 350° for 10 minutes. Serve this dish with:

> Corn-Meal Soufflé, page 219, or Hashed Brown Potatoes, page 306, etc.

CHICKEN LIVERS IN BATTER
Wipe with a cloth:

> Chicken livers

Season them lightly with:

> Salt and pepper

Dip them into:

> Batter (see Chicken in Batter, page 399)

Fry them in deep fat (page 542) heated to 375° until well browned. Good with omelet on toast with Brown Sauce, page 435, or other sauce, or as a garnish for a meat or vegetable platter.

BAKED POTATO CUPS AND CHICKEN HASH
4 Servings

Bake (page 301):

> 4 small or 2 large potatoes

Cut the large potatoes into halves. Scoop out the pulp. If small, cut a slice from the flat side and scoop out the pulp from the top. Fill the shells with:

> Chicken or other Hash, page 145

Use the pulp for:

> Mashed Potatoes, page 302

Pipe an edge of mashed potato around the edge of the hash with a pastry bag or a spoon. You may place on each ½:
  A Poached Egg, page 80
Cover it with:
  Mornay Sauce, page 431, or thick cream
Brown the tops under a broiler or in a quick oven 400°. Garnish with:
  Parsley

CALF BRAINS ON TOAST
4 Servings
Cook by the rule on page 378:
  1 set calf brains
Drain, then chop them. Add:
  ½ teaspoon grated lemon rind or 1 teaspoon lemon juice
  Salt and pepper
  Chopped parsley
  1 teaspoon grated onion
  1 whole egg
  3½ tablespoons cracker crumbs, or enough to keep the mixture from being soggy
Toast on one side:
  4 slices bread
Spread the untoasted side with the brain mixture. Dot the top with butter. Broil the slices under a broiler until well heated.

BROILED CALF BRAINS ON TOMATOES
4 Servings
Cook by the rule on page 378:
  2 sets calf brains
Spread them with:
  Butter
Place them on the greased rack of a broiling pan. Broil them for 5 minutes on one side. Cut and place on a greased oven-proof plate:
  8 thick slices tomato
Season them with:
  Salt and pepper
  Brown sugar
Cover one side with:
  Buttered crumbs
Place the brains on the tomatoes, the cooked side down. Broil them for 5 minutes longer. Serve them at once.

Creamed Calf Brains, cream like Sweetbreads, page 376. These make a good filling for Tomato Cases, page 198.
Calf Brains with Wine Sauce, page 378.

CALF BRAIN FRITTERS
3 Servings
Cook by the rule on page 378:
  1 set calf brains

Dry them between towels. Pull them into small pieces. Sift:
  1 cup all-purpose flour
  1 teaspoon any baking powder
  ¼ teaspoon salt
Beat until light:
  2 egg yolks
Beat in the sifted ingredients until blended. Beat in:
  1 tablespoon melted butter
  1 teaspoon grated lemon rind
  A grating nutmeg
  ½ cup milk
  (1 tablespoon wine or brandy)
Beat until stiff:
  2 egg whites
Fold them into the batter. Add the brains. Heat in a skillet:
  Bacon drippings or other shortening
Drop the batter into it by spoonfuls. Sauté the fritters until done, or fry them in hot fat 360° (page 542).

For other Calf Brain Dishes, see page 378.

VEAL KIDNEY, MUSHROOM AND ONION CASSEROLE
4 Servings
Dice:
  4 veal kidneys
Dust them lightly with:
  Paprika
Boil:
  1 cup Stock, page 43
Drop the kidneys slowly into the stock. Simmer them for 3 minutes. Drain them. Reserve the stock. Remove the kidneys to a heated oven-proof dish. Heat in a skillet:
  1 tablespoon butter
Sauté in the butter:
  ¼ to ½ lb. sliced mushrooms
  2 tablespoons minced onion or ¼ clove garlic
  1 tablespoon minced parsley
Stir and cook these ingredients for about 2 minutes. Stir in:
  3 tablespoons flour
Stir in the boiling soup stock. Bring these ingredients to the boiling point. Add:
  ¼ cup sherry, white wine or ½ cup orange juice
  (Seasoning if needed)
Pour these ingredients into the casserole. Cover it closely. Bake it in a moderate oven 350° for about 20 minutes. Toast:
  4 thick slices bread

Sprinkle them with:
    Grated cheese
Place them on top of the kidneys.
Broil them until the cheese is melted.

SAUTÉED KIDNEYS WITH CELERY AND MUSHROOMS
4 Servings
You may use this rule as a basis and omit 1 or more of the ingredients and still have a good stew. But if you follow it closely, you may bring about the illusion of being in France.
Prepare (page 379):
    8 lamb kidneys
Quarter them. Sprinkle them with:
    Lemon juice
Heat:
    3 tablespoons butter or drippings
Sauté lightly in this:
    1 cup chopped celery
    ¼ cup chopped onion
Add the kidneys. Simmer them covered for 5 minutes. Stir in:
    1 tablespoon flour
    1 cup hot Stock, page 43
When these ingredients are blended add:
    ½ lb. chopped mushrooms
Season the kidneys lightly with:
    Paprika
    Worcestershire sauce
Simmer them covered for 15 minutes.
Add:
    Salt if needed
    2 tablespoons sherry
    1 tablespoon chopped parsley

BROILED BEEF KIDNEYS, TOMATOES AND ONIONS
Prepare for cooking by the rule on page 379:
    A beef kidney
Slice it. Simmer it in boiling water to cover until nearly tender.
Simmer in milk or water until nearly tender:
    Sliced onions
Drain these ingredients. Dry them between towels. Grease an oven-proof platter. Arrange the kidneys and onions upon it with:
    Thick slices tomato
Season the vegetables with:
    Salt and pepper
Dot them and the meat with:
    Butter
Broil them under a low flame until the tomatoes are done.

For other Kidney Dishes, see page 379.

JELLIED PIGS' FEET
6 Servings
Wash, leave whole or split in halves:
    6 pigs' feet
You may wrap them in cheesecloth to retain their shape. Cover them with water, bring to the boiling point and simmer them covered for 3 hours. Add boiling water if needed. Season the pigs' feet with:
    1 large sliced onion
    1 cut clove garlic
    1 sliced lemon
    2 bay leaves
    3 or 4 whole black peppers
    6 or 8 whole cloves
Simmer them 1 hour longer. Strain the stock through a sieve. Remove the skin and the bones from the pigs' feet. Place the meat in the stock. Season it with:
    White vinegar or dry wine
    Salt if needed
Chop and add:
    1 pimiento, decorative but optional
Pour the pigs' feet into a mold and chill them until the stock is firm.

BROILED PIGS' FEET
Cook by the preceding rule:
    Pigs' feet
Cut them in two lengthwise. Roll them in:
    Melted butter
then in:
    Corn meal or cracker crumbs
Place the pigs' feet on a greased broiler and broil them, turning them once, for about 15 minutes, or bake them in a moderate oven 375° from 15 to 20 minutes. Serve them with:
    Pickled Beets, page 461, or
    Lemon wedges

CHICKEN POT PIE
6 Servings
The following is a fine way of dressing up a plain chicken stew in an imposing manner.
Cook (page 402):
    1 stewing chicken
Make about 3 cupfuls of gravy as the crust is apt to soak up quite a bit of it. Place the chicken in a baking dish, add the boiling hot gravy and pour Sour Milk Corn Bread Batter, page 515, or the following batter over it at once.
Sift:
    2 cups all-purpose flour
    1½ teaspoons salt
    2 teaspoons any baking powder
Combine:

⅞ cup milk
2 tablespoons melted butter
2 well-beaten eggs

Add these ingredients quickly to the sifted flour mixture. Stir the batter as little as possible. Bake the pie in a moderate oven 375° until it is light brown.

Some cooks prefer a biscuit pie crust top that is cut to fit the casserole, baked separately and adjusted while hot over the cooked chicken.

INDIVIDUAL CHICKEN PIES

These are of two kinds.
Prepare:
Stewed Chicken, page 402
Cut the chicken into pieces and add them to the gravy. Or, prepare:
Creamed Chicken, page 143
Prepare:
Pie Dough, page 561

Method I.
Cut the dough into small rounds. Fit them over the reverse side of muffin tins or small pie pans. Puncture them. Bake the pies in a hot oven 500° for about 12 minutes. Fill the hot or reheated shells with the hot chicken mixture. Serve them garnished with parsley.

Method II.
Line individual pie pans with Pie Dough. Brush the inner surface with white of egg. Fill them with cooked chicken, creamed or in gravy. Cover them with a thin top of pie dough brushed on the inside with white of egg. Press down the edges and puncture the top crusts. Bake the pies in a hot oven 450° for about ½ hour.
You may substitute other meat for the chicken. A delicious addition to the meat is drained asparagus, cooked or canned, cut in pieces and added to the boiling sauce or gravy. You may use the asparagus water and cream for the liquid of the sauce.

MEAT PIES

An agreeable disposition of refrigerator accumulations. Please read the above rules for:
Individual Chicken Pies
One large pie may be made in the same manner. For a filling use stews or leftover meat creamed or in gravy. Make the gravy interesting by seasoning it well. See Gravy, page 426. Cooked vegetables may be added to the meat.

Steak and Kidney Pie, page 160;
Veal and Pork Pie, page 160.

CHICKEN PATTIES
10 Servings

The French make many attractive dishes by grinding uncooked meat or fish, shaping it with other ingredients and poaching, broiling or sautéing the patties.
Cut the breast meat from:
A 4½ lb. chicken
Remove the meat from the legs and wings. Pick over the carcass for bits of meat. Put the meat through a grinder, using a coarse knife, or blend it. Save the juices if any. Combine the ground meat, the juices and:
¾ cup heavy sweet cream
1½ cups soft bread crumbs
1 teaspoon salt
1 teaspoon dried basil or 1 tablespoon chopped parsley
A grating lemon rind
¼ teaspoon paprika
Shape the mixture into 10 patties. Dip them in:
1 egg diluted with
1 tablespoon water
then in:
Seasoned bread crumbs
Place them in a shallow greased pan. Broil them under a moderate flame for about 10 minutes to a side, or until lightly browned.
The patties may be left unbreaded and poached in a small amount of milk or stock, enough to cover the bottom of the skillet, until done. This means very low heat.
Use the carcass for Soup, page 47, or for Gravy, page 426.

CHICKEN OR BEEF CHOP SUEY
8 Servings

Now an international dish. Recently advertised in New York as "Chop Suey Spanish Style." Read Mrs. Buwei Yang Chao's delightful "How To Cook and Eat in Chinese" for real Chinese dishes.
Melt:
1½ tablespoons butter
Sauté in the butter for 3 minutes:
½ cup shredded pepper
½ cup shredded onion
Add and cook for 3 minutes:
1 cup shredded cooked chicken, pork or veal
If raw meat is used, cook it until tender. Add:

1 cup shredded celery with leaves
1 cup canned bean sprouts
¼ cup chicken broth or canned
    chicken bouillon
Make a paste of:
    ¼ cup chicken broth and
    2 tablespoons flour
Add the paste to the other ingredients.
Stir and cook them until they boil.
Stir in:
    ½ cup blanched, shredded toasted
        almonds
    2 tablespoons soy sauce
Add:
    (½ cup Sautéed Mushrooms, page
        292)
Serve hot with rather dry:
    Steamed Rice, page 103

Quick Beef Chop Suey, page 168.

CHICKEN CREOLE
8 Servings
This is a case of stew your chicken
first (page 402). Melt:
    3 tablespoons chicken fat
Sauté in the fat:
    2 tablespoons chopped onion
    2 tablespoons chopped green
        pepper
Stir in:
    3 tablespoons flour
    ¼ teaspoon salt
    ¼ teaspoon paprika
Add:
    ½ cup tomato purée or strained
        tomatoes
    1 cup chicken broth
Stir and cook these ingredients until
they boil. Add:
    1 teaspoon lemon juice
    ½ teaspoon horseradish
    2 cups cooked diced chicken meat
    ½ cup sliced Sautéed Mushrooms,
        page 292
    ½ cup chopped pimiento
    Salt as needed
Serve the chicken in a:
    Rice Ring, page 105, or
    Noodle Ring, page 98

CHICKEN À LA KING
4 Servings
Cut into dice:
    1 cup cooked chicken
    ½ cup Sautéed Mushrooms, page
        292
    ¼ cup canned pimiento
Melt:
    3 tablespoons chicken fat or
        other shortening

Stir in and blend:
    3 tablespoons flour
Add slowly:
    1½ cups Chicken Stock, page 47, or
        cream
When the sauce is smooth and boiling,
add the chicken, mushrooms and pi-
miento. Reduce the heat and add:
    1 egg yolk
Stir and permit it to thicken slightly.
Add:
    Seasoning if required
    (¼ cup blanched slivered almonds)
    (1 tablespoon sherry)
Serve the chicken at once. To reheat
place the chicken in a saucepan over
boiling water.

CREAMED CHICKEN OR VEAL
4 Servings
There is no reason why this dish
should not be delicious, whether it is
made in a luxurious way or with left-
over food. Proportions, seasonings,
etc., are unimportant, provided that
good combinations are chosen. Feel
free to follow any creative urge. Prepare:
    1 cup Cream Sauce I, page 248
Use cream and chicken stock or vegetable water, with part gravy and part
milk, etc. Add:
    2 tablespoons chopped parsley
    2 cups minced chicken or veal
Part of this may be cooked or canned
vegetables. Season these ingredients
with:
    1 teaspoon lemon juice or ½
        teaspoon Worcestershire sauce
        or 2 teaspoons sherry
    (3 tablespoons chopped pickles
        or olives)
Add:
    Salt and pepper
    Celery salt if required
Grease a baking dish and put the
creamed mixture in it. Sprinkle the
top with:
    ½ cup bread crumbs
Dot it with:
    2 tablespoons butter
or sprinkle it with:
    Grated cheese
    (½ cup blanched shredded almonds)
Place the dish under a moderate flame
until the crumbs are brown. The
creamed ingredients may be served
unbreaded on:
    Hot toast or hot waffles or in a
    Noodle or Rice Ring, pages
    98, 105

See Filled Pancakes, page 162.

CREAMED CHICKEN AND MUSHROOMS

Follow the preceding rule. Use part cooked chicken and part Sautéed Mushrooms, page 292.

CHICKEN TAMALE PIE
6 Servings

Good in individual dishes. Cook by the rule for Corn-Meal Mush on page 100:

½ cup water-ground corn meal

There should be about 3 cupfuls of mush. Cut into strips:

3 cups cooked chicken

Line a baking dish with the mush. Place the chicken over it. Combine:

1 can tomato sauce: 8 oz.
1 can whole-kernel corn: 1 lb., 4 oz.
2 tablespoons sugar
2 tablespoons salad or olive oil
10 sliced ripe or stuffed olives
2 teaspoons salt
A few grains cayenne
¼ teaspoon pepper
(1 teaspoon dried basil or tarragon)

Pour these ingredients over the chicken. Sprinkle the top with:

1 cup grated Parmesan cheese

Bake the tamale in a moderate oven 350° for about 45 minutes.

LEFT-OVER CHICKEN OR TURKEY IN SPAGHETTI WITH MUSHROOMS AND ALMONDS
4 Servings

Cream by the rule on page 143:

1 cup cooked minced chicken or turkey

Add to it:

½ cup or more Sautéed Mushrooms, page 292
2 cups cooked spaghetti
¼ cup chopped green peppers
½ cup blanched slivered almonds

Place these ingredients in a greased baking dish or in individual dishes. Cover the top with:

Bread crumbs
Grated Parmesan cheese

Bake in a moderate oven 375° until the top is brown.

CREAMED CHICKEN AND HAM
4 Servings

Creamed dishes combine well with hot waffles or shortcakes. Melt:

1½ tablespoons butter

Add and stir until blended:

1½ tablespoons flour

Stir in slowly:

¾ cup Chicken Stock, page 47
¼ cup cream

When the sauce is smooth and boiling add:

½ cup diced cooked chicken
½ cup diced cooked ham
¼ cup chopped celery
1 tablespoon chopped parsley

Pour a little of the sauce over:

1 beaten egg

Reduce the heat to a low flame. Return the sauce to the pan. Stir the sauce and permit it to thicken slightly. Season the dish, if needed, with:

Salt and pepper

Before serving it stir in:

(1 tablespoon sherry)

TURKEY OR CHICKEN CASSEROLE WITH VEGETABLES
4 Servings

Prepare by the rule for Left-Over Soup, page 47:

Turkey stock

Prepare by cutting into cubes:

2 cups cooked turkey or chicken

Melt:

3 tablespoons butter

Stir in and sauté gently until lightly browned:

½ cup diced celery
⅓ cup thinly sliced onions
⅓ cup thinly sliced green pepper, seeds and fibrous portions removed

Sprinkle over the top, stir in and cook slowly for 5 minutes:

2 tablespoons flour

Stir in gradually:

1½ cups turkey or chicken stock or chicken bouillon cubes dissolved in ½ cup boiling water

Remove the pot from the fire. Stir in:

2 lightly beaten egg yolks
Seasoning as required

and the turkey meat. Stir over low heat just long enough to let the sauce thicken slightly. You may add:

2 tablespoons sherry

Place the mixture in one large or in individual casseroles. Sprinkle the top with:

Minced chives or parsley, nut meats or grated cheese

Serve at once. Good with rice or spoon bread or on toast.

CHICKEN OR TURKEY HASH
4 Servings

The usual way to make hash is to cut the meat from a chicken or turkey carcass, combine it with left-over gravy, reheat it briefly and season it acceptably. There should be about ½ as much gravy as other ingredients. You may add, in addition to the meat, cooked mushrooms, celery or potatoes, chopped olives, green peppers, parsley or some other herb, or anything else that seems suitable. The proportions may be varied. This is a matter of taste and expedience. In the absence of gravy, sweet or sour cream or a sauce—cream, tomato, creole, etc.— may be substituted, or you may add a sauce or cream to the gravy to obtain the desired amount. When using cream reheat the hash in a double boiler as boiling thins it. Sherry, Madeira or dry wine may be added. For seasonings read the chapter on Gravy, page 426.

Hash may be served in a pastry shell, in a rice ring, over noodles, etc. See Index. It is good au gratin. Use a mild cheese.

Combine and heat:

> 1½ cups diced meat
> ½ cup cooked drained celery or boiled potato cubes
> 1 cup left-over gravy or sauce
> 1 tablespoon chopped parsley or chives
> Seasoning as required

Serve the hash as suggested or in a:

> Grits Ring, page 157, or
> Bread Dressing Ring, page 157

TURKEY OR CHICKEN LOAF
4 to 6 Servings

Cook and stir for 1 minute:

> 1½ tablespoons grated onion

in:

> 1 tablespoon butter

Add it to:

> 2 cups diced cooked turkey or chicken
> ¾ teaspoon salt
> 1 cup cracker crumbs
> ¾ cup gravy or thickened Chicken Stock, page 47
> ¾ cup milk
> 2 beaten eggs
> (½ cup finely chopped celery)
> (¾ teaspoon chili powder)

Place these ingredients in a well-greased loaf pan set in a pan of hot water. Bake the loaf in a moderate oven 350° for about 50 minutes. Serve it with:

> Left-over gravy with chopped olives
> Mushroom Sauce, page 436, or
> cream sauce with lots of chopped parsley or chives

CHICKEN LOAF
10 Servings

This good chicken dish is similar to a soufflé but calls for fewer eggs. See Timbales, page 214; Chicken Soufflé, page 221.

Prepare:

> 1 cup rich Cream Sauce I, page 428

Cool it slightly and add:

> 2 egg yolks

Combine the sauce with:

> 2 cups cooked ground chicken
> ½ cup dry bread crumbs
> ½ teaspoon salt
> ½ teaspoon pepper
> 1 tablespoon chopped parsley

Whip until stiff and fold in:

> 2 egg whites

Pour these ingredients into a mold lined with waxed paper. Cover it with waxed paper. Set it in a pan of hot water and bake the mousse in a moderate oven 325° for 1 hour. Serve it with:

> Mushroom Sauce, page 436

JELLIED CHICKEN OR CHICKEN ASPIC
8 Servings

Prepare for cooking:

> A 4 to 5 lb. chicken

Place in a kettle and boil:

> 6 cups water
> 3 ribs celery with leaves
> 1 carrot
> 1 small onion
> 4 or 5 sprigs parsley
> 1 bay leaf
> ½ teaspoon salt
> 6 peppercorns

Drop the chicken into the boiling water, reduce the heat and permit it to simmer covered until it is tender. Remove it from the pot. Boil the stock until there are 3 cupfuls. Clarify the stock by adding:

> 1 slightly beaten egg white

Bring the stock to the boiling point. Remove it to a warm place. After 10 minutes, skim and strain it. Soak:

> 2 tablespoons gelatine

in:

> ¼ cup cold water

Dissolve it in a little boiling stock and add it to the remaining stock. Add:

Seasoning if needed

Chill it until it is nearly set. Cut the chicken from the bones. Cut into pieces:

**1 cup canned mushrooms or
½ lb. Sautéed Mushrooms, page
292, or chopped celery
2 hard-cooked eggs
12 stuffed olives
(½ to 1 cup blanched almonds)**

Rinse a mold in cold water. Fill it to the depth of ½ inch with the chicken jelly. Place the sliced eggs and olives in the jelly in some attractive arrangement. Combine the remaining jelly, the chicken and the mushrooms and fill the mold. Chill the jelly until it is firm. Unmold it and serve it with or without:

Mayonnaise

PRESSED CHICKEN
8 Servings

Pressed chicken is an old-fashioned dish for which many persons have a nostalgic hankering. It was customary to place a weight upon it to spread the meat evenly. This is unnecessary if the chicken is added to stock about to solidify. The preceding Jellied Chicken is an aspic. Pressed chicken, also an aspic, has very little jellied stock and is, therefore, a more solid dish that slices well and may be used as a sandwich filling.

Cut into pieces:

A 4 lb. stewing chicken

Place it in a saucepan and half cover it with:

Boiling water

Add:

**1 small sliced onion
1 small sliced carrot
4 or 5 ribs celery with leaves
1 teaspoon salt
¼ teaspoon paprika or white
pepper**

Cover the chicken closely. Simmer it until it is very tender. Drain the chicken, reserving the stock. Measure the stock. If there is more than 1 cupful, reduce it by boiling it until you have about that amount. Cut the chicken from the bones into very small pieces. Sprinkle it lightly with:

Salt, paprika or white pepper

You may add:

½ cup blanched shredded almonds

Oil a mold or small individual molds.

If you wish, you may garnish the mold with:

**Sliced pimiento olives
Sliced hard-cooked eggs
Tender minced celery**

In hot weather it is wise to soak:

1 teaspoon gelatine

in:

¼ cup of the cold stock

Dissolve it in the remaining boiling stock. Chill this mixture. When it is about to set stir in the chicken and spoon it carefully into the mold. Chill the aspic. Serve it on:

Lettuce garnished with parsley

JELLIED CHICKEN MOUSSE
Method I. 10 Servings

This recipe is given because it is neither so rich nor so expensive as Chicken Mousse II, and I like it just as well.

Use the rule for Ham Mousse on page 149. Use chicken stock. Substitute cooked ground chicken for the ham, or use part chicken and part ham.

Method II. 8 Servings

This is good served with a green or a fruit salad.

Soak:

1½ tablespoons gelatine

in:

¼ cup Stock, page 47

Dissolve it in:

½ cup hot stock

Beat:

3 egg yolks

Add:

1½ cups milk

Cook these ingredients in a double boiler until they are smooth and fairly thick. Stir in the dissolved gelatine. When the mixture is cool add:

**2 cups cooked minced or ground
chicken**

Season it with:

Salt, pepper and paprika

Chill the jelly and when it is about to set fold in:

1 cup heavy cream, whipped

Place the mousse in a wet mold and chill it until it is firm. Unmold it.

GLORIFIED CHICKEN MOUSSE
STEAMED
6 Servings

Well worth the trouble.

Stew until very tender, by the rule on page 402:

A 3½ lb. chicken

Remove meat from bones. Grind it until it is very fine. Put it 3 times through the meat grinder or blend it. Add for the third grinding:

> 1 cup cut-up mushrooms

Make a Cream Sauce, page 428, of:

> 3 tablespoons butter
> 3 tablespoons flour
> 1 cup cream
> ¼ teaspoon salt
> ⅛ teaspoon paprika

Pour it over the chicken. Beat in one at a time:

> 3 eggs

Beat until the mixture is very light. Taste it and add, if you wish:

> Seasoning
> ½ teaspoon dry tarragon or basil

Have ready a greased mold. Fill the mold about ⅔ full. Cover it tightly with a lid. Steam the mousse for 2 hours. See Steamed Puddings, page 731. Serve the mousse with:

> Mushroom Sauce, page 436

Chicken Soufflé, page 221.

SWEET POTATOES, BACON AND PINEAPPLE SLICES

4 Servings

This is a very good and easily prepared luncheon dish.
Cook by the rule on page 309:

> 4 small round or 2 large "fat" sweet potatoes

You may use canned sweet potatoes or Mashed Sweet Potatoes, page 310, shaped into cones.
Peel them and trim them so that they will nearly cover a slice of pineapple. Surround the 4 sweet potatoes with:

> 4 slices bacon

Use toothpicks to secure them. Do not permit the bacon to overlap too heavily. Place in a greased pan:

> 4 slices pineapple

Cover each slice thickly with:

> Brown sugar

Press down the sugar and place a potato on each slice. Bake these ingredients in a moderate oven 375° until the bacon is crisp. Baste the potatoes with:

> Hot pineapple juice

PORK SCRAPPLE

About 6 Servings

Place in a pan:

> 2 lbs. pork neck bones, or other bony piece

Add:

> 1½ quarts boiling water
> 1 sliced onion
> 6 peppercorns
> (1 bay leaf)

Simmer the pork until the meat falls from the bones. Strain it, reserving the liquor. There should be about 4 cupfuls. Add water if necessary to make this amount. Prepare, using this liquid in place of boiling water:

> Corn-Meal Mush, page 100

Remove all meat from the pork bones and chop or grind it fine. Add it to the cooked mush. Season it with:

> Salt if required
> 1 teaspoon or more grated onion
> ½ teaspoon dried thyme or sage
> Nutmeg and a little cayenne

Pour the scrapple into a bread pan that has been rinsed with cold water. Permit it to stand until cold and firm. Slice it. Sauté it slowly in:

> Melted butter or drippings

GROUND HAM ON PINEAPPLE SLICES

4 Servings

Combine:

> 1 cup cooked ground ham
> 1 teaspoon prepared mustard
> 2 tablespoons mayonnaise

Spread this mixture on:

> 4 slices drained pineapple

Bake the slices in a greased pan in a hot oven 400° for 10 minutes.

HAM CAKES AND EGGS

4 Servings

Combine:

> 1 cup cooked ground ham
> 1 egg
> 1 tablespoon water
> ⅛ teaspoon paprika or pepper

Press these ingredients into 4 greased muffin tins. Leave a large hollow in each one. Drop into the hollows:

> 4 eggs

Bake the cakes in a slow oven 325° until the eggs are firm. Turn out the cakes on:

> Rounds of toast

Garnish them with:

> Parsley

HAM CAKES WITH PINEAPPLE AND SWEET POTATOES

6 Servings

Cook by the rule on page 309:

> 3 large sweet potatoes

Combine:

2 cups cooked chopped or ground
    ham
½ cup dry bread crumbs
2 eggs
⅛ teaspoon salt
1 teaspoon prepared mustard

Shape these ingredients into 6 flat
cakes. Melt in a skillet:

5 tablespoons bacon drippings

Brown lightly in the skillet:

6 slices drained pineapple

Remove them and brown the ham
cakes. Place the pine-
apple slices in a baking dish and cover
each slice with a ham cake. Peel the
sweet potatoes. Cut them lengthwise
into halves. Combine and sprinkle over
them:

¼ teaspoon cloves
¼ cup brown sugar

Cook them slowly in the skillet until
they are well caramelized. Place them
in the baking dish. Baste them with:

Pineapple juice

Bake the dish in a moderate oven 375°
for 10 minutes.

HAM AND POTATO CAKES
4 Servings
Combine:

1 cup mashed potatoes
1 cup ground cooked ham
1 tablespoon chopped parsley
½ teaspoon grated onion
⅛ teaspoon pepper
Salt if needed

Shape this mixture into flat cakes.
Dip them lightly in:

Flour

Sauté them in:

Bacon drippings or other fat

BAKED HAM WITH APPLES
4 Servings
Rub:

1 slice smoked ham 1 inch thick

with:

½ teaspoon dry mustard
½ teaspoon pepper
2 tablespoons brown sugar

Place it in a baking pan. Core:

Apples

Cut them in ½ inch slices. Cover the
ham thickly with the apples. Sprinkle
them with:

½ cup sugar

Pour enough water in the pan to cover
the bottom. Cover the pan closely.
Bake the ham in a moderate oven 350°

for 1 hour. Then remove the lid and
permit the top to brown.

---

*For other Baked Ham Dishes see
Index.*

CREAMED HAM
6 Servings
To:

1 lb. ground cooked ham: 2 cups

add:

1 cup boiling Cream Sauce I,
    page 428

Stir in:

¼ cup chopped pickles
(1 teaspoon Worcestershire sauce)

Serve the ham over:

Hot toast or hot corn-bread
muffins or crusty corn bread
cut into squares and split

Garnish it with:

Chopped parsley

HAM LOAF WITH COOKED HAM
6 Servings
Combine:

2 cups cooked ground ham
1½ cups bread or cracker crumbs or
    crushed cornflakes
2 eggs
2 tablespoons grated onion
⅛ teaspoon pepper
1 cup milk
2 tablespoons chili sauce, 2 table-
    spoons chopped parsley or
celery or ½ teaspoon dried herb

Bake these ingredients in a greased
loaf pan in a moderate oven 350° for
about 45 minutes. Serve the loaf with:

Tomato, Horseradish, Mustard,
Mushroom or some other sauce,
pages 433 to 435

Ham Loaf with Smoked Ham, page
374, has some good suggestions for
adding pineapple, etc., to the pan.

Ham Loaf with Raw Ham, page 374.

HAM ROLLS WITH RICE AND RAISIN OR ASPARAGUS FILLING
4 Servings
Make these when you have left-over
rice. Trim:

8 thin slices baked or boiled ham

Spread them lightly with:

Mustard

Place on each slice part of the following filling. Combine:

1½ cups cooked rice
⅓ cup chopped raisins
1 beaten egg
¼ teaspoon paprika
½ teaspoon Worcestershire sauce
(¼ cup chopped celery)
(2 pinches herbs)

Roll the slices and secure them with toothpicks. Brush them with:

Milk

Broil the rolls or bake them in a hot oven 400° until they are thoroughly heated. Serve them with:

Cumberland Sauce, page 438

Another good filling for ham rolls is the following. Place on each slice of ham:

4 asparagus tips

Roll, brush and heat the ham as directed. Serve the rolls with:

1½ cups Cheese Sauce, page 430

CREAMED DEVILED HAM
2 Servings

An emergency dish. Prepare:

1 cup Cream Sauce I, page 428

Stir into this the contents of:

1 can deviled ham: 2¼ oz.

One-fourth teaspoonful dry mustard may be added to the seasoning of the cream sauce. Add:

¼ cup sliced stuffed olives or chopped pickles

Serve the ham on:

Hot toast, rusks or hot Waffles, page 556

One hard-cooked egg, finely chopped, may be substituted for the olives, or it may be added to the other ingredients.

JELLIED HAM MOUSSE
10 Servings

Soak:

1 tablespoon gelatine

in:

¼ cup cold water

Dissolve it in:

1½ cups boiling Stock, page 43

Chill the jelly. When it is nearly set combine it with:

2 cups cooked ground or chopped ham
¼ cup chopped celery
1 tablespoon grated onion
½ cup mayonnaise
¼ cup sour or sour-sweet chopped pickles

Add, if required:

Worcestershire sauce
Seasoning

Moisten a mold with cold water. If desired decorate the sides and bottom with:

Stuffed olives and sliced hard-cooked eggs

Add the other ingredients. Chill the mousse until it is firm.

Baked Fish Ring or Fish Mousse, page 121; Lobster Ring, page 126.

HAM À LA KING
6 Servings

Prepare:

2 cups Cream Sauce I, page 428

When the sauce is boiling add:

2 cups cooked diced ham
2 diced hard-cooked eggs
1 cup Sautéed Mushrooms, page 292, or canned mushrooms with sliced stuffed olives
1 tablespoon chopped green pepper
1 tablespoon chopped pimiento

Serve the ham very hot on:

Rounds of toast, on rusks or in bread cases

SAUTÉED APPLES AND BACON
4 Servings

A fine breakfast or luncheon dish. Pare tart winter:

Apples

Cut them into cubes. There should be about 4 cupfuls. Sauté in a heavy skillet by the rule on page 375:

8 slices bacon

Remove the bacon when crisp. Keep it hot. Leave about 2 tablespoonfuls of grease in the skillet. Add the apples. Sprinkle them with:

2 tablespoons white or brown sugar

Cover them and cook them slowly until they are tender. Remove the cover. Turn the apples carefully. Let them brown lightly. Place them on a hot platter. Surround them with the bacon. Serve them garnished with:

Parsley

Bacon Dredged in Corn Meal, page 375. This is a pleasant variation.

SAUSAGE MEAT AND PINEAPPLE OR APPLE SLICES
4 Servings

Drain:

6 slices canned pineapple or 2 apples cut in ½ inch slices

Rub the slices with:
**Prepared horseradish or
mustard**
Place them in a flat greased baking
dish. Combine:
**1 lb. sausage meat
2 tablespoons flour**
Form these ingredients into 6 flat
cakes slightly smaller than the pineapple slices. Place them on the slices.
Bake them in a moderate oven 350° for
about ½ hour. Baste them with a little:
Pineapple juice
Serve them garnished with:
Parsley or chopped chives

SAUSAGE MEAT WITH APPLES
2 Servings
Shape into 4 flat cakes:
½ lb. sausage meat
Combine and roll the cakes in:
**1 tablespoon flour
¼ teaspoon sugar**
Core and cut into ½ inch slices:
2 firm tart apples
Boil for 5 minutes:
**½ cup sugar
½ cup water**
Add:
1 teaspoon butter
Drop the apple rings into the sirup.
Cook them slowly until they are nearly
tender, about 5 minutes. Drain them.
Broil the meat cakes under a moderate
flame for about 8 minutes. Arrange
the apple slices on a hot platter. Place
the sausage cakes on them. Serve them
garnished with:
Parsley

QUICK SWEET POTATOES
WITH SAUSAGE PATTIES
A complete course in about ½ hour.
Grease a pie pan, fill it with:
Canned mashed sweet potatoes
You may soften them with:
Cream or butter
Sprinkle the top lightly with:
Brown sugar
Cover it with pan-browned:
Sausage patties
Pour the drippings over them. Bake
the pie in a moderate oven 350° for
about 20 minutes. Serve with canned
applesauce.

SAUSAGE MEAT RING
6 Servings
Grease lightly a 7 inch ring mold.
Press into the bottom of the mold:

3 tablespoons cornflakes
Combine well:
**1 lb. sausage meat
1 tablespoon minced onion
¾ cup fine bread crumbs
2 tablespoons chopped parsley
1 beaten egg**
Place these ingredients in the mold.
Bake the ring in a moderate oven 350°
for ½ hour. Drain the fat from it after
15 minutes' baking. Invert the ring
onto a hot platter and fill the center
with:
8 Scrambled Eggs, page 81
Garnish the top with:
Chopped parsley or paprika

SAUSAGE MEAT, APPLES AND
SWEET POTATOES
4 Servings
Boil (page 309):
4 large sweet potatoes
Peel them and cut them into thin
slices. Grease a baking dish. Cover the
bottom with ½ the sweet potatoes.
Shape into 4 flat cakes:
1 lb. sausage meat
Brown them lightly in a greased pan
to which you may add:
1 tablespoon minced bacon
Peel and cut into thick slices:
4 large apples
Place the meat cakes on the sweet potatoes and cover them with apple
slices. Sprinkle them lightly with:
Salt and brown sugar
Place the remaining sweet potatoes
over the apples. Brush the potatoes
with:
Milk
and sprinkle them with:
Brown sugar
Bake the dish in a moderate oven 350°
for about ¾ hour.

*Apples Filled with Sausage Meat, page
208.*

PANCAKES AND SAUSAGES
Cook:
French Pancakes, page 551
Cook:
Sausages, page 375
Roll the sausages in the pancakes.
Serve them very hot with:
Applesauce, page 447
Or if this seems too rich a combina-
tion, serve the sausages with omelet
and applesauce.

SAUSAGE IN PASTRY OR BISCUIT DOUGH
Spread:
> Small sausages or balls of
> sausage meat

with:
> Mustard or horseradish

Prepare:
> Pie Crust, page 561, or
> Biscuit Dough, page 505

Roll it to the thickness of ⅛ inch. Cut it into oblongs. Roll the dough around the sausages. Moisten the ends with a little water and pinch them so that the sausages are entirely enclosed. Bake the sausages in a hot oven 425° for about 20 minutes.

SAUSAGES AND MUSHROOMS
Fine for a late breakfast. Prepare:
> Mashed Potatoes, page 302

Heap them in a mound on a hot platter. Keep them hot. Cook:
> Sausages, page 375

Place them around the potatoes. Sauté in the drippings:
> Mushrooms, page 292

Garnish the platter with them and:
> Sprigs parsley

Pour the drippings over the potatoes.

PIGS IN POTATOES
3 Servings
Combine and beat well:
> 1 teaspoon minced onion
> 1 teaspoon minced parsley
> 2 cups Mashed Potatoes, page 302,
> or left-over potatoes
> 1 egg yolk

Cook:
> 6 small link sausages or cook and
> cut in halves 3 large sausages

Coat them with the potato mixture. Roll the croquettes in:
> Finely crushed bread crumbs

then in:
> 1 egg diluted with 1 tablespoon
> water or milk

then again in the crumbs. Heat to 375° deep fat, hot enough to brown an inch cube of bread in 40 seconds. Fry the croquettes until they are a golden brown.

SAUSAGE STUFFED WITH SAUTÉED ONIONS
4 Servings
Heat in a skillet:
> 2 tablespoons oil or fat

Add:
> 1½ cups slivered onions

Cook and stir these over low heat for about 15 minutes until light brown. Cut a lengthwise slit in:
> 8 wiener sausages or frankfurters

Fill them with the onions. Fasten them with toothpicks. Broil them slowly on both sides. You may place them in:
> Lightly toasted buns

SAUSAGE WITH ONIONS AND SAUCE
4 Servings
Steam or boil:
> 12 Vienna sausages: wieners

Chop until fine:
> 2 cups onions

Add:
> (A chopped clove garlic)

Cover the onions well with boiling water. Boil them for 10 minutes. Drain them. Add to them:
> ¼ cup hot bacon drippings

Keep the onions hot. Prepare the following sauce:
> 2 cups Brown Sauce, page 435
> ¼ cup catsup
> 6 tablespoons chili sauce
> A generous seasoning cayenne
> Salt
> (3 chopped pimientos)

Simmer the sauce for 5 minutes. Split the sausages. Cover them with the onions. Pour the sauce over them.

VIENNA SAUSAGE WITH SAUCE
Boil:
> Wieners

Serve them with:
> Sauce: Mustard, Creole, Onion,
> etc., pages 440, 434, 432

Good with mashed potatoes. Superb with boiled noodles.

SAUSAGE IN CREOLE SAUCE WITH RICE
Prepare:
> Creole Sauce, page 434, or
> Quick Tomato Sauce, page 433

Use no salt. Season it well with:
> Paprika

Boil by the rule on page 375:
> Vienna sausages

Drain them. Heat them in the sauce. Serve them with:
> Steamed or Boiled Rice, page
> 103

FRANKFURTERS ON TOAST
4 Servings

Cut the edges from:
   8 slices bread
Spread the slices with:
   Mustard
   (Grated onion)
Place on the slices on the bias:
   8 frankfurters
Pick up 2 opposite corners of the bread and pin them together with a toothpick. Bake the rolls in a moderate oven 400° until well toasted. Serve piping hot.

___

FRANKFURTERS AND SOUR CREAM
4 Servings

Cut into thin slices:
   6 frankfurters
Brown them lightly in:
   1½ tablespoons fat
   3 tablespoons grated onion
   1½ tablespoons paprika
   ¼ teaspoon salt
   ⅛ teaspoon pepper
Cook these ingredients slowly until the onion is tender. Add:
   1¼ cups sour cream
Stir the mixture lightly. Heat it but do not let it boil. Serve it on:
   Mashed potatoes, noodles, etc.

___

FRANKFURTERS COOKED IN TOMATO SAUCE
3 Servings

Place in a shallow pan:
   6 frankfurter sausages
Season the contents of:
   1 No. 1 can tomatoes or 1 cup Barbecue Sauce, page 436
with:
   Salt if needed
   1 teaspoon brown sugar
   ¼ teaspoon dry mustard
You may add:
   Chopped green peppers
   Grated onions or chives
Pour these ingredients over the sausages. Bake them in a hot oven 400° until they burst and the sauce thickens.

___

SAUSAGES IN TOASTED SHREDDED WHEAT BISCUITS
4 Servings

Split:
   4 shredded wheat biscuits
Toast them on both sides. Sauté:
   12 small sausages

Place 3 sausages between 2 biscuit slices. Spread the tops with:
   Butter
Heat the biscuits in a hot oven 400°. Serve them with:
   Maple sirup

___

Squash Pudding with Bacon and Sausages, page 181; Veal Slices and Pork Sausages on Skewers, page 195.

___

FRANKFURTERS FILLED WITH MASHED POTATOES
Gash lengthwise:
   Frankfurters
Fill the gashes with:
   Mashed potatoes
   Sautéed onions
Sprinkle the sausages with:
   Grated cheese
Or omit the cheese, wrap the frankfurters spiral fashion with strips of bacon. Secure them with toothpicks. Bake them in a hot oven 400° until the cheese is melted and the sausages are light brown.

___

FRANKFURTERS AND PICKLE RELISH
Gash lengthwise:
   Frankfurters
Broil them until they are nearly done. Fill them with:
   Pickle relish or chili sauce
Complete the broiling.

___

FRANKFURTERS AND APPLES WITH CHEESE
4 Servings

Place in a baking dish:
   8 frankfurters
Spread them lightly with:
   Mustard
Cover them with:
   3 peeled, very thinly sliced tart apples
Sprinkle them with:
   ¼ cup white or brown sugar
Bake them in a moderate oven 350° for about 20 minutes. Sprinkle the top with:
   ½ cup grated cheese
Bake or broil the dish until the cheese is melted.

___

FRANKFURTERS FILLED WITH SAUERKRAUT
Spread:
   Frankfurters

with:

Mustard

Gash them lengthwise. Fill the gashes with:

Canned drained sauerkraut

Surround the sausages with:

Bacon

Secure it with toothpicks. Broil the sausages or bake them in a 400° oven until the bacon is crisp and the sausages are well cooked.

Pickles may be substituted for the sauerkraut filling.

CORN-BREAD SAUSAGE
4 Servings

Cook by the rule on page 373 until partially done:

8 frankfurters or wieners

Place them in an 8 x 8 inch baking pan. Pour over them:

Sour Milk Corn Bread Batter, page 515

Bake in a hot oven 425° until the corn bread is done, about 20 minutes.

MASHED POTATO AND SAUSAGE CASSEROLE

Place in boiling water and simmer for 10 minutes:

Link sausages, frankfurters or wieners

Drain them well. Place in a greased oven-proof dish:

Mashed Potatoes, page 302

Place the sausages on top of the potatoes. Bake the dish in a moderate oven 375° for ½ hour. You may serve it with:

Milk gravy (see Salt Pork, page 375)

Use the sausage fat and add chopped chives or parsley.

SAUSAGE IN MACARONI

Prepare by the rule on page 96:

Creamette Loaf

Skin:

6 frankfurters

Place them in a greased casserole between 2 layers of the creamette mixture. Bake as directed. Serve with:

Tomato Sauce, page 433

LENTIL AND SAUSAGE CASSEROLE
4 Servings

Prepare by the rule on page 272:

1 cup lentils

Place them in a greased oven-proof

dish. Place in boiling water and simmer for 10 minutes:

1 lb. small link or other sausages

Drain them. Place them on top of the lentils. Bake the dish uncovered in a moderate oven 400° until the sausages are brown.

SAUSAGE MEAT ON POTATO OR CEREAL CAKES

Prepare:

Sausage Meat, page 375
Potato or Cereal Cakes, pages 100 and 309

Serve the sausage on the cakes with:

Baked apples and parsley

MIXED GRILL

Here is a fine grill—a complete course. Heat your broiler. Cut into slices:

Tomatoes

Brush them with:

Melted butter

Season them with:

Salt and pepper
Brown sugar

Prepare for cooking:

Mushrooms

Brush them with:

Melted butter or heavy cream

Season them lightly with:

Salt
(Lemon juice)

Grease the broiler. Place on it the tomato slices, mushrooms and:

Slices bacon
Sausages

Broil these ingredients until they are done. Meanwhile sauté or poach:

Eggs

Serve the eggs on a hot platter surrounded by the grilled food. Garnish the platter with:

Parsley, olives, radishes, etc.

PORK TENDERLOIN WITH MUSHROOMS AND OLIVES
4 Servings

Cut into 1 inch crosswise slices:

1 lb. or more pork tenderloin

Roll them in:

Seasoned flour

Heat:

2 tablespoons butter

Add and sauté for 2 minutes:

A slice onion

Brown the rounds quickly in the butter. Bring to the boiling point:

1 cup thin cream

Pour this mixture over the chops. You may add at this time:

½ lb. sliced mushrooms
Cover the skillet closely. Simmer the rounds until they are done, about 20 minutes. Add:

6 sliced stuffed olives
2 tablespoons lemon juice

Serve the pork garnished with:

2 tablespoons chopped parsley

The amount of mushrooms and olives is unimportant. You may dispense with them. A few capers or chopped pickles may be added just before serving.

See Index for other Pork Tenderloin Dishes.

VEAL AND PORK GOULASH WITH SAUERKRAUT
4 Servings
Sauté until light brown:

6 tablespoons chopped onions

in:

2 tablespoons butter

Cut into 1 inch cubes and add to the onions:

½ lb. veal
½ lb. lean pork

Heat and add:

1 lb. sauerkraut

Simmer these ingredients covered for 1 hour. Heat and add:

1 cup sour cream
1 teaspoon caraway seed

Simmer the goulash ½ hour longer.

Hash in Creamed Cabbage, page 172.

COLD ROAST BEEF AND TOMATO SAUCE
Prepare:

Creole Sauce, page 434

Arrange slices of beef on a hot platter. Pour the boiling sauce over them. Sprinkle the top with:

Chopped parsley or chopped chives

BEEF REHEATED IN CUMBERLAND SAUCE
4 Servings
Cut into ½ inch cubes:

2 cups cooked roast beef

Melt over slow heat:

1 tablespoon butter
3 tablespoons currant jelly

Add, heat, but do not boil:

¼ cup sherry or Madeira
A dash red pepper
¼ teaspoon or more salt

Stir in the beef last. Heat it without boiling it. Serve it at once on:

Hot toast

BEEF AND HAM HASH WITH POTATOES AND MUSHROOMS
Based on Sam Ward's Hash.
Cut into cubes equal parts of:

Cold roast beef and cooked or smoked ham
Raw pared potatoes

Reserve the beef. Place in a saucepan the ham and potatoes. Cover them with:

Brown Sauce, page 435

Cover these ingredients and simmer them for 45 minutes. Add:

½ lb. or more sliced mushrooms

Simmer them covered for 15 minutes longer. Add the beef. Reheat the hash but do not permit it to boil. Season it with:

Garlic salt
A pinch dried herb: basil, thyme, savory, etc.
Sherry
Salt if needed

Serve it on:

Hot toast

garnished with:

Chopped parsley

This dish may be made without the ham.

HASH WITH CELERY
4 Servings
There is no set rule about making hash. In fact it makes an immense appeal to the imagination. Cooks lacking that nerve-racking quality will find the following recipe helpful. Prepare:

½ cup chopped celery
¼ cup chopped green pepper
¼ cup chopped onion

Drop them into:

¾ cup boiling water

seasoned with:

⅛ teaspoon salt

When the vegetables are tender, drain them. Reserve the liquor, as it may be needed for the gravy. If there is enough roast gravy available, use it. If there is not enough, thicken the vegetable water with:

1 tablespoon flour

and add it to the roast gravy, or make gravy in the following way. Melt:

1½ tablespoons butter

Add and stir until blended:

1½ tablespoons flour

Stir in slowly:
  ¾ cup vegetable water
Add:
  1 tablespoon catsup or
  2 tablespoons tomato pulp
Heat the gravy to the boiling point.
Add and stir until dissolved:
  1 beef cube
If a beef cube is not available, use canned bouillon instead of vegetable water.
Add the drained vegetables and:
  1 cup cooked diced meat
  Salt and pepper as required
Remove the hash from the fire as soon as the meat is heated. Do not let the gravy boil after adding the meat. Unnecessary boiling does not improve the flavor of beef and sometimes causes it to become tough. To keep the hash hot place the saucepan in hot water.
Serve the hash on:
  Hot waffles, hot toast or in a hot pie shell or pancake (see Filled Pancake, page 117)

HASH WITH POTATOES

6 Servings
This is an excellent combination. If it is not feasible to use all the ingredients given, it will still be good. Prepare:
  ½ cup cooked diced potatoes
  ⅓ cup cooked diced onions
  ⅓ cup seeded sliced green peppers
  3 tablespoons diced pimientos
  2 cups cold cooked meat cut into ⅓ inch cubes
Combine:
  1 cup left-over gravy
  ⅓ cup tomato purée
  1 tablespoon butter
  Salt and pepper as required
  1 teaspoon Worcestershire sauce
Heat the sauce and add the meat and vegetables. If there is no available gravy, make it with 2 tablespoonfuls butter, 2 tablespoonfuls flour and 1 cupful of vegetable stock or water in which 1 beef cube has been dissolved. Pour the hash into 1 large baking dish or into 6 individual baking dishes.
Sprinkle the top with:
  Bread crumbs
  Grated cheese
Dot it lightly with:
  Butter
Or cover it with green pepper rings and seasoned slices of tomatoes dotted with butter. Brown the dish in a moderate oven 350°.

SAUTÉED OR BROWNED HASH

4 Servings
Combine and grind:
  1½ cups cooked meat
  ½ cup raw cubed potatoes with or without skins
  1 medium-sized onion
Season with:
  Salt, pepper, celery seed or ½ teaspoon dried herbs
Turn these ingredients into a hot well-greased skillet. Cook the hash over a medium flame until a crust forms on the bottom, turn it and brown the other side. Stir it from time to time to let the hash brown throughout. Shortly before it is done, pat it down firmly to form an unbroken cake. This requires about ½ hour cooking in all.
Serve the hash with:
  Catsup or Tomato Sauce, page 433

QUICK HASH

4 Servings
Heat over a very low flame:
  1 can condensed mushroom soup: 10½ oz.
Stir in gradually:
  ¼ cup milk
Add:
  1 cup cubed cooked ham or meat: frankfurters, hamburgers, etc.
  2 sliced hard-cooked eggs
Season the hash with:
  A pinch dried herb
  Salt and pepper
  (Chopped parsley)
Serve it over:
  Hot corn bread or toast

CANNED STEW POT PIE

4 Servings
Place in the bottom of an oven-proof dish the contents of:
  1 No. 2 can stew: beef, lamb, etc.
Cover it with:
  Pie Dough or Biscuit Dough, pages 561, 505, or slices of bread buttered on both sides
Bake it in a hot oven 400° until it is light brown, about 20 minutes for pie or biscuit dough.

MASHED POTATO PIE

A very good way of using a small quantity of cold mashed potatoes and bits of meat or vegetable scraps.
Line individual molds with a wall ¼ inch thick of:
  Left-over mashed potatoes

If the potatoes are very hard, soften them with:

    1 or 2 tablespoons hot milk

Brush the inner walls with:

    1 egg white

Moisten:

    Chopped cooked meat and
    vegetables

with a small amount of:

    Gravy, Tomato Sauce, page 433,
    Cream Sauce, page 428, or cream

Fill the molds and cover them with a layer of mashed potatoes. Brush the tops with:

    Soft butter

Place the molds in a pan of hot water in a quick oven 400° for 15 minutes, or until the potatoes are brown.

COTTAGE PIE WITH HASH AND SAUERKRAUT

4 Servings

Prepare:

    2 cups mashed potatoes

Combine:

    1 cup cooked diced meat, roast
    beef, canned meat, sausage, etc.
    1½ cups chopped drained canned
    sauerkraut
    1 cup gravy or Stock, page 43
    ¼ teaspoon pepper
    Salt if needed
    (¾ teaspoon celery seed or caraway
    seed)

If stock is used, thicken it with 2 tablespoonfuls butter and 2 tablespoonfuls flour. Place these ingredients in a greased baking dish. Cover them lightly with the potatoes. Dot the top with:

    1½ tablespoons butter

Bake the dish in a moderate oven 375° until the top is brown.

SHEPHERD'S PIE

Method I.

Prepare:

    Hash, page 155

Spread it in a baking dish. Cover it with fresh hot:

    Mashed Potatoes, page 302

Spread the top with:

    Melted butter

Bake the dish in a quick oven 400° until the potatoes are brown.

Method II. 6 Servings

More luxurious than No. I.

Prepare by the rule on page 302:

    2 cups well-seasoned mashed
    potatoes

Beat in until very light:

    2 egg yolks

Whip until stiff:

    2 egg whites
    ⅛ teaspoon salt

Fold them lightly into the potatoes. Spread the bottom of a greased baking dish with ½ the potatoes. Combine and place over them:

    2 cups finely chopped veal or
    other meat
    2 tablespoons chopped parsley
    ½ cup finely chopped celery
    ½ cup gravy or tomato pulp or ⅓
    cup cream
    Salt and pepper

Cover the meat with the remaining potatoes. Dot the top with:

    Butter

or sprinkle it with:

    Grated cheese

Bake the pie in a hot oven 400° until the top is brown. Serve it with:

    (Gravy or Creole Sauce, page
    434)

Do not use the tomato flavor in both meat and sauce—it is too monotonous.

CORN-MEAL MUSH MEAT PIE OR TAMALE PIE

4 Servings

The idea of using a lining of corn-meal mush is excellent. Any cooked meat in sauce may be used for the filling, or raw hamburger browned in fat and cooked in sauce may be substituted. The pie becomes a tamale when the filling is highly seasoned. See Chicken Tamale Pie on page 144 for further suggestions for filling. Do not hesitate to try out new combinations. Freda de Knight has assembled the traditional recipes of the colored people in her interesting book "A Date with a Dish." She adds to her tamale pie mixture cumin seed and other flavorful ingredients. In one rule she boils the corn meal with the meat mixture and then bakes it in a casserole. In another she too uses the corn-meal lining.

Grind or chop:

    1 cup cold roast meat

Moisten it with:

    1 cup meat gravy, brown sauce or
    cream sauce

Add:

    1½ cups tomato purée or stewed
    tomatoes
    ½ small minced clove garlic
    1½ teaspoons chili powder

Boil:
4 cups water or stock
Stir in:
1 cup water-ground corn meal
1½ teaspoons salt
Cook and stir these ingredients over low heat until the mush is thick. You may beat into the slightly cooled mush:
1 egg
Make a thin lining of ¾ of the mush in a buttered baking dish. Pour in the meat. Dot the top with the remaining mush rolled into 1 inch balls. Bake the dish in a moderate oven 350° for about 45 minutes.

CORNED BEEF HASH IN CORN-MEAL MUSH

Follow the preceding rule for:
Corn-Meal Mush Meat Pie
Fill the pie with:
2 cups corned beef hash or
Creamed Chipped Beef, page 161
to which you may add:
¼ cup chopped onion
sautéed in:
2 tablespoons butter and
½ teaspoon thyme

BREAD DRESSING IN A RING FILLED WITH HASH, ETC.

Grease a ring mold. Fill it with:
Bread Dressing, page 416, or
Apple and Bread Dressing,
page 418, etc.
Bake it in a hot oven 400° until it is brown. Invert it onto a hot plate. Fill the center with:
Hash, page 154, or stewed
creamed fresh or left-over
vegetables
Good served with:
Left-over gravy or other sauce

LEFT-OVER DRESSING DISH

4 Servings
Place in a greased baking dish:
2 cups left-over dressing
Cover the top with:
1 lb. seasoned hamburger
Dot it with:
Butter
Sprinkle it with:
Soy sauce
Bake the dish in a hot oven 425° until the hamburger is cooked, about ½ hour. Left-over dressing may be placed

in greased custard cups and reheated in a 425° oven. Serve these with:
Mushroom sauce

GRITS RING WITH HASH OR STEW

10 Servings
Cook until thick in a double boiler, or stir over low heat:
1 cup grits
2½ cups milk
2½ cups water
1¼ teaspoons salt
3 tablespoons butter
Stir these ingredients frequently. Cool them slightly. Stir in:
¼ cup chopped parsley
3 egg yolks
¼ teaspoon paprika
Whip until stiff and fold in:
3 egg whites
⅛ teaspoon salt
Butter a 9 inch ring mold. Fill the mold with the grits mixture. Set it in a pan of hot water in a slow oven 325° for 1¼ hours. Invert the contents of the mold onto a platter. Fill the center with:
Hash or creamed food

LEFT-OVER MEAT LOAF

4 Servings
Rather a light loaf but not quite a soufflé. Prepare:
1 cup Cream Sauce I, page 428
Cool it slightly. Beat in:
1 whole egg
Add to it and mix well:
1 cup chopped cooked meat or
meat and vegetables
½ cup fresh bread crumbs
2 teaspoons chopped parsley
½ teaspoon onion juice or
1 tablespoon minced onion
¼ teaspoon salt
Place these ingredients in a greased baking dish. Bake them in a moderate oven 350° for 15 minutes. This loaf may be served with:
Tomato Sauce, page 433
Mustard Sauce, page 436, etc.
If this recipe is doubled, beat the yolks into the cream sauce. Whip the whites separately and fold them in when all the other ingredients are combined.

LEFT-OVER MEAT DEVILED

Spread:
Cooked sliced meat
with:
Prepared mustard or catsup

Roll the slices in:
    Buttered bread crumbs
Broil them under a good flame until browned. Serve the meat with:
    Piquant Sauce, page 436,
    Green Onion Sauce, page 436

MEAT LOAF IN PASTRY OR BISCUIT DOUGH

Prepare by any rule on page 354:
    Beef Loaf
Bake the loaf until it is nearly done. Or improvise a beef loaf of cooked ground meat. Prepare:
    Pie Crust, page 564, or
    Biscuit Dough, page 505
Roll it until it is very thin and wrap it around the beef loaf, covering the loaf completely. Moisten the edges of the dough to hold them down. Bake the loaf in a quick oven 450° until the dough is done, about 15 minutes. Serve it with:
    Left-over gravy, Olive Sauce, page 435, or Tomato Sauce, page 433

MEAT PIE ROLL OR PIN WHEELS

4 Servings
This is a palatable, quickly made, everyday dish, an attractive way to serve a small quantity of left-over meat.
Make by the rule on pages 505, 561 or with Biscuit Mix:
    Biscuit Dough or Pie Dough: use 2 cups of flour
If you use biscuit dough, make it a little drier than for ordinary biscuits, otherwise it will be difficult to handle. Roll it until it is very thin. Cut it into an oblong. Use a pastry brush and brush it lightly with:
    1 egg white or soft butter
This will keep the crust from being soggy. Spread the dough with the meat filling, being careful not to get it close to the edges. Leave about 1 inch at the sides uncovered. Begin to roll it loosely. Moisten the end with water and plaster it down. Moisten the sides and pinch them together. Bake the roll in a hot oven 450° until it is done, about 20 minutes.
Or, cut the roll into ¾ inch slices. Place the slices in a lightly greased pan. Dot the tops with:
    Butter
This roll may be prepared in advance and placed in the refrigerator until ready for use. Bake the slices in a hot oven 450° until the dough is done. Serve them very hot with:
    Brown Sauce, page 435, or
    Tomato Sauce, page 433

Fillings

I.
Raw sausage meat may be used. It need not be moistened or seasoned.

II.
Grind or mince:
    Cooked meat
Moisten it with:
    Thick gravy, Cream Sauce, page 428, canned condensed soup, Brown Sauce, page 435, or a little cream
Season it lightly with:
    Chopped parsley
    Grated carrot
    Salt and pepper
    Mustard or Worcestershire sauce
    Chopped pickles

III.
Crumble:
    8 oz. corned beef
Combine it with:
    1½ cups Cream Sauce III, page 428
Season the filling with:
    2 teaspoons A-1 or Worcestershire sauce
    Salt if needed
    ⅛ teaspoon paprika
    A pinch thyme, marjoram and sage
    ½ teaspoon curry powder
    1 tablespoon capers or chopped pickles
Any good chopped meat filling may be evolved from this basis. Ham loaf or veal loaf may be substituted for the corned beef, but beware of adding seasoning without tasting the mixture. Chopped cooked meat will do and sea food is highly recommended.

POTATO AND ONION PIE ROLL

Sauté until brown:
    1 cup finely minced onions
in:
    ¼ cup butter
Add these ingredients to:
    2 cups hot Mashed Potatoes, page 302
Follow the rule for making the above Meat Pie Roll, substituting this filling for the meat.

TURNOVERS OR ROLLS FILLED WITH MEAT, ETC.
6 Servings

This recipe and the following one make excellent hot canapés. For canapés cut the dough into small attractive shapes. For hot luncheon sandwiches make them a more generous size. If prepared in advance, keep them chilled until ready to bake. Please have the patience to read to the end of this recipe. The fillings are recommended with gusto.

Prepare, using about 2 cupfuls of flour:

Biscuit or Pie Dough, pages 505, 561

Pat or roll it until it is thin. This is a matter of taste—about ¼ inch for biscuit dough, ⅛ inch for pie dough. Cut it into 3 x 3 inch squares or into rounds. Place a filling on the squares, as much as they will hold properly. Moisten the edges of the dough, fold it over into a triangle and pinch it down with a fork. Place the triangles or crescents in a pan. Brush them lightly with:

(Soft butter)

Bake them in a quick oven 450° until the dough is done, about 20 minutes. This may be served with:

Brown Sauce, page 435

Fillings
I.
Lightly moisten:

Ground or minced cooked meat

with:

Gravy or cream, Worcestershire or chili sauce

Season it well with:

Salt and pepper

II.
Moisten braunschweiger sausage with chili sauce or tomato soup.

III.
Use:

1½ cups ground ham
½ cup Cream Sauce II, page 428, thick cream or evaporated milk
2 tablespoons chopped pickles
1 tablespoon chopped onion
1½ tablespoons catsup
Salt and pepper if needed

IV.
Use Filling for:

Meat Pie Roll, page 158

V.
Sauté gently until yellow:

2 cups chopped onions

in:

3 tablespoons olive or anchovy oil

Add:

¼ cup or more chopped ripe olives
6 or 8 chopped anchovies

VI.
Use Filling for:

Potato and Onion Pie Roll, page 158

Rissoles or Turnovers, page 577.

MEAT SHORTCAKES
10 Cakes

Follow the rule on page 506 for:

Fluffy Biscuit Dough

If a richer dough is desired, use an additional tablespoonful of butter. Combine:

4 tablespoons cream
¾ cup deviled ham

Ground cooked ham or other meat may be substituted. In that case ¼ teaspoonful prepared mustard, 2 teaspoonfuls minced onion or other seasoning may be added.

Roll out the dough on a lightly floured board to the thickness of ¼ to ⅓ inch. Spread ½ of it with the ham mixture. Fold over the other ½ so that the ham is between the layers of dough. Cut the dough with a biscuit cutter. Bake the cakes in a hot oven 450°.

QUICK CANNED VEGETABLE AND MEAT DISH OR PIE
6 to 8 Servings

This is notable for goodness, economy and the rapidity with which it may be made. When making it you may ad lib to your heart's content.

Drain, then cut into cubes the contents of:

1 can roast beef: 16 oz.

Reserve the juices. Drain, reserve the juices of:

1½ to 2 cups cooked or canned mixed vegetables

Add to the juices to make 2 cupfuls of liquid:

Vegetable Stock, page 45, tomato juice, consommé, cream, etc.

Melt:

4 tablespoons butter

Stir in:

4 tablespoons flour

Add the liquid gradually. When the sauce is smooth and boiling, add the vegetables and meat. Season with:

> Salt and pepper
> Onion juice, horseradish,
> mustard or curry, etc.

Serve it as it is, or place it in a baking dish and cover it with:

> Pie Crust, page 561, or
> Biscuit Dough, page 505

Bake it in a hot oven 450° until the top is done. If you prefer, it may be served au gratin, or you may place over it slices of bread buttered on both sides. Bake or broil the dish until the bread is toasted.

LEFT-OVER HAM OR OTHER MEAT IN WAFFLES OR PANCAKES

Add:

> ¾ to 1 cup minced ham

to:

> Waffle Batter, page 556

Bake the waffles. Serve them with:

> Condensed Mushroom Soup
> Sauce, page 441

Or prepare Condensed Mushroom Soup Sauce, cream the ham in part of it. Make pancakes or griddle cakes. Spread the creamed ham on them. Roll them. Serve with the remaining sauce.

BAKED SQUASH AND HAM

Combine:

> 1½ cups cubed smoked or boiled
> ham

with:

> 2 cups peeled diced Hubbard
> squash

Dot it well with:

> Butter

Season it with:

> ½ teaspoon pepper
> 1 teaspoon sugar
> ½ teaspoon grated nutmeg

Cover the dish closely. Bake it in a hot oven 400° for 1 hour. Cooked or uncooked meat may be used. Add salt.

QUICK SPAGHETTI MEAT PIE

4 Servings

Sauté lightly:

> 2 cups cooked cubed meat
> 2 teaspoons grated onion

in:

> 2 tablespoons butter

Add:

> ¼ cup cream

Season it with:

> Salt and pepper
> (½ teaspoon basil)

Place in a greased dish the contents of:

> 1 can spaghetti: 24 oz.

Make a depression in the center. Place the meat in it. Sprinkle the top with:

> Buttered bread crumbs
> Grated cheese

Bake the dish in a moderate oven 375° for 25 minutes.

STEAK AND KIDNEY PIE

6 Servings

Cut into 1½ inch cubes:

> 1½ lbs. chuck or round beef

Prepare (page 379), then slice:

> ¾ lb. veal or lamb kidneys

Melt:

> 3 tablespoons butter or beef fat

Brown in this:

> 1⅓ cups chopped onion

Add meat. Stir it until all sides are well coated and lightly browned. Add:

> 3 cups boiling Stock, page 43
> ½ bay leaf

One-fourth cupful of the liquid may be dry red wine. Cover the dish, simmer the stew for about 2 hours, or until tender. Thicken the stock with:

> Flour (see Gravy, page 426)

Season it with:

> Salt and pepper
> Worcestershire sauce

Place the stew in a baking dish. Cover it while hot with:

> Pie Crust, page 561, or
> Chicken Pot Pie Batter, page
> 141

Bake it in a hot oven 450° for about 20 minutes.

This is the traditional way of cooking this English dish. I like to add the kidneys for the last 30 minutes of cooking only and to add at the same time 2 carrots and 1 stalk of diced celery.

VEAL AND PORK PIE

4 Servings

Cut into 1 inch pieces:

> ½ lb. veal
> ½ lb. lean pork

Stir and brown the meat lightly in:

> 2 tablespoons hot drippings or
> butter

Add and simmer covered for 15 minutes:

> 3 cups boiling water
> 1 teaspoon salt
> ½ teaspoon paprika
> ½ bay leaf
> 2 whole cloves

Remove spices. Add:
> ¼ cup diced carrots
> ¾ cup diced celery
> 1 cup diced potatoes
> 12 small onions

Bring the stew to the boiling point, reduce the heat and simmer it covered until the meat is tender, about 30 minutes longer. Thicken the stock with:
> Flour (see Gravy, page 426)

Add as required:
> Seasoning

Place the stew in a baking dish. Top it while hot with:
> Pie Crust, page 561, or
> Chicken Pot Pie Batter, page 141

Bake it in a hot oven 450° for about 20 minutes.

EGGS IN CANNED CORNED BEEF HASH
4 Servings
Divide into 4 parts the contents of:
> 1 can corned beef hash: 16 oz.

Press each portion into a buttered oven-proof ramekin. Make a depression in each one. Place in each depression:
> 1 egg

Sprinkle the tops with:
> Grated American cheese
> Paprika

Bake the corned beef in a moderate oven 375° until the eggs are set. Garnish them with:
> Chopped parsley

CANNED CORNED BEEF HASH PATTIES
4 Servings
Sauté:
> 3 tablespoons chopped onion

in:
> 2 tablespoons butter

Add:
> 2 tablespoons horseradish
> ½ teaspoon thyme
> 16 oz. canned corned beef hash

Form patties of this mixture. Sauté them on both sides in:
> Hot butter or drippings

Sauté in the same pan:
> Slices firm tomato

Season them with:
> Brown sugar
> Salt and pepper

Arrange the tomatoes and patties on a platter garnished with:
> Parsley

Or serve the patties with:
> 1½ cups Cream Sauce, page 428

to which you may add:
> 2 chopped hard-cooked eggs
> 2 tablespoons chopped pickles

BAKED CORNED BEEF
Remove whole from the can:
> Corned beef

Stud it with:
> Whole cloves

Make a paste by stirring a little water into:
> ¼ cup brown sugar
> 1 teaspoon chili powder

Add to it:
> 2 tablespoons chopped pickles

Spread the beef with the paste. Bake it in a moderate oven 350° for about 10 minutes.

Corned Beef Hash and Potatoes, page 352.

CHIPPED OR DRIED BEEF RECIPES
Chipped beef that is not soaked in boiling water for 10 minutes has a better flavor and more character than beef that is soaked, but you must then be very careful to omit salt in your sauce and filling or you may have too much. If you have soaked it, dry the beef between paper towels.

CREAMED CHIPPED BEEF
Method I. 4 Large Servings
Let's make something good out of this.
Pull apart:
> 8 oz. chipped beef

Melt:
> 3 tablespoons butter

Sauté in it until light brown:
> 3 tablespoons minced onion
> 3 tablespoons minced green pepper

Sprinkle these with:
> 3 tablespoons flour

Add slowly, stirring constantly:
> 2 cups milk

Add the beef. Simmer these ingredients until they thicken. Remove from fire and season with:
> 1 tablespoon chopped parsley or chives
> ¼ teaspoon paprika
> 2 tablespoons sherry
> (2 tablespoons capers or chopped pickles)

Method II.
Or you may omit the vegetables and sherry. Add:

4 sliced hard-cooked eggs
⅓ cup raisins
½ teaspoon or more curry powder
Serve the beef on:
Hot buttered toast or Cereal
Cakes, page 100

CHIPPED BEEF IN CHEESE SAUCE

2 Servings
Prepare:
1 cup Cheese Sauce, page 430
Add to it:
4 oz. or more shredded chipped
beef
Heat it. Serve it over:
Hot corn-bread squares
This and the above combination may
be served in pancakes. See Sea Food
in Pancakes, page 117.

CHIPPED BEEF OR CORNED BEEF IN CANNED SOUP

4 to 5 Servings
A good, economical "quickie."
Combine and heat the contents of:
1 can cream soup—mushroom,
celery, asparagus, etc.: 10½ oz.
6 tablespoons milk or Stock, page
43
⅛ teaspoon freshly ground nutmeg
A grating of black pepper
Add:
8 oz. shredded chipped beef or
diced corned beef
1 cup left-over vegetables
Heat these ingredients. Serve them on:
Toast or hot biscuits
sprinkled with:
Chopped parsley or chives or
grated cheese
Or you may boil until nearly tender:
10 small onions
Drain them and place them in a baking
dish, pour the soup and beef mixture
over them. Cover the top with:
Crushed potato chips
Bake the dish in a hot oven 400° for
about 15 minutes.

CHIPPED BEEF IN CREOLE SAUCE

3 Servings
Prepare:
Quick Creole Sauce, page 435
Melt:
1 tablespoon butter
Sauté in it for 1 minute:
4 oz. shredded chipped beef

Add the sauce. Heat the dish. Serve it
on:
Buttered toast

QUICK DRIED OR CHIPPED BEEF DISH

5 Servings
Cut into cubes:
5 cooked or canned sweet potatoes
Shred:
¼ lb. dried beef
Prepare:
¼ cup grated onion
1½ cups Cream Sauce I, page 428,
or condensed canned soup
Place these ingredients in layers in a
greased casserole. Cover the top with:
Crushed cornflakes
Dot it with:
Butter
or sprinkle it with:
Cheese
Bake in a moderate oven 375° for ½
hour.

PANCAKES FILLED WITH HASH OR VEGETABLES

Follow the rule on page 117 for:
Pancakes Filled with Creamed
Sea Food
Substitute for the sea food:
Hash with gravy, creamed
vegetables, chicken, chipped
beef, etc.

LEFT-OVER MEAT IN BATTER

Follow the rule for:
Calf Brain Fritters, page 140
Substitute for the brains about:
1½ cups chopped cooked meat
Add to the meat, if desired:
2 tablespoons chopped parsley
1 tablespoon lemon juice or
1 teaspoon Worcestershire sauce
Serve the fritters with:
Gravy, Tomato Sauce, page 433,
or Horseradish Sauce, page 439

LEFT-OVER MEAT IN BAKED RICE BALLS

Follow the rule on page 117 for:
Baked Rice and Fish Balls
Substitute for the fish:
2 cups or less chopped cooked
meat

LEFT-OVERS IN BACON

Measure:
Cooked ground meat

Add ⅓ the measure of:
Steamed Rice, page 103
Moisten it lightly with:
Gravy or cream
Season it well with:
Salt and pepper
Minced onion or onion juice
Roll the mixture into small balls, flatten them slightly and wrap around them:
Slices of bacon
Secure the bacon with toothpicks. Place the patties in a greased pan or dish and cook them in a hot oven 450° until the bacon is crisp, about 15 minutes. Serve them with:
Tomato Sauce, page 433

SCALLOPED VEAL AND OYSTERS

Follow the rule on page 112 for:
Scalloped Oysters
Use part:
Cooked chopped veal
and part:
Oysters
Use part:
Milk
and part:
(Gravy)

GERMAN MEAT BALLS OR KOENIGSBERGER KLOPS

6 Servings—About Ten 2 Inch Balls
Introduce this very good dish to your family.
Soak in water to cover:
1 slice of bread 1 inch thick
Put through a meat grinder twice:
1½ lbs meat: ½ lb. beef, ½ lb. veal, ½ lb pork or liver
Beat well and add:
2 eggs
Melt:
1 tablespoon butter
Sauté in it until brown:
¼ cup finely minced onion
Add it to the meat. Wring the water from the bread. Add the bread to the meat and:
3 tablespoons chopped parsley
1¼ teaspoons salt
¼ teaspoon paprika
½ teaspoon grated lemon rind
1 teaspoon lemon juice
1 teaspoon Worcestershire sauce
A few minced sardelles or ¼ herring may be added to the meat balls at this time or they may be added later to the gravy. Combine these ingredients well. Do this lightly with the hands—a bet-

ter method than using a fork or spoon. Shape them lightly into 2 inch balls. Drop them into:
5 cups boiling Vegetable Stock, page 45
Simmer them covered for about 15 minutes. Remove them from the stock. Measure the stock. Make gravy of it (page 426) by using:
2 tablespoons butter for every cup stock
2 tablespoons flour for every cup stock
Season it, if needed, with:
Salt and pepper
Cook and stir it until it is smooth and boiling. Add to it:
2 tablespoons capers or 2 tablespoons chopped pickles or lemon juice or sour cream
2 tablespoons chopped parsley
Reheat the meat balls in the gravy. Serve them with a platter of:
Boiled Noodles, page 91, or Spaetzle, page 423
Cover them generously with:
Buttered Crumbs, page 326

ITALIAN MEAT BALLS

Follow the preceding rule for:
German Meat Balls
Omit the Worcestershire sauce. Add to the meat mixture:
½ chopped clove garlic
3 tablespoons grated Italian cheese
Roll the balls lightly in:
Flour
Place them in a casserole. Half cover them with:
Tomato pulp or canned tomatoes cooked until thick, then strained
Bake them covered in a moderate oven 350° for about 1 hour.

PORK BALLS IN TOMATO SAUCE

4 Servings
Soak in water to cover:
A slice of bread 1½ inches thick
Wring the water from it. Add to the bread:
1 lb. ground pork
⅓ cup chopped onion
1 beaten egg
¾ teaspoon salt
¼ teaspoon paprika
Combine these ingredients lightly with the hands until they are well blended.

Shape them into 2 inch balls. Combine the contents of:

    1 can tomato soup: 10½ oz.
    An equal amount of water

Bring the liquid to the boiling point. Drop the balls into it. Cover the pan and simmer the balls until they are done, about ½ hour.

Meat Balls, page 73.

BEEF TONGUE WITH RAISIN SAUCE

An unusual dish—delicious and inexpensive. As it takes 1 hour to make the sauce it is well to begin to prepare it while the tongue is cooking.

Place in a kettle or pressure cook by the rule for Corned Beef Tongue, page 890:

    A fresh beef tongue

Peel and add:

    2 medium-sized onions
    1 large carrot
    3 or more ribs celery with leaves

Wash and add:

    6 sprigs parsley

Barely cover these ingredients with boiling water. Add:

    8 peppercorns

Simmer the tongue until it is tender, about 3 hours. Drain it. Reserve the liquor. Skin the tongue. Remove the roots. Place the tongue where it will keep hot.

Sauce:

Blanch and split:

    ½ cup almonds: ⅛ lb.

Add and simmer for ½ hour:

    2 cups water

Add and simmer for ½ hour longer:

    ⅔ cup closely packed seedless
        raisins

Drain the sauce. Reserve the liquid. Melt:

    6 tablespoons fat from the tongue
        stock or butter

Stir in until blended:

    3 tablespoons flour

Stir in gradually:

    The raisin and almond liquid
        and tongue stock to make 3 cups
        liquid in all
    ¼ cup crushed ginger snaps
    2 teaspoons Caramel, page 754

Add the almonds, raisins and:

    1 lemon cut into very small cubes

Season the gravy with:

    Salt and pepper

Serve the tongue with:

    Noodles and buttered crumbs
    or with a Noodle Ring, page 98,
    filled with green peas

CALF TONGUES WITH RAISIN SAUCE

Follow the preceding rule.

Substitute for beef tongue:

    Calf tongues

Cooking time: about 2 hours.

SUKIYAKI
10 Servings

This Japanese dish should, I suppose, be labeled "stew," but as it is an unusual dish it had better be known by its unusual name. It is a good thing to serve from a chafing dish. Melt in a saucepan a scant:

    ¼ lb. suet or butter

Cut into very thin slices across the grain and brown in the fat:

    2½ lbs. fillet of beef

Boil and add to it approximately:

    2½ cups Beef Stock, page 43, or
        canned bouillon

Cut into very thin slices and add:

    2 cups bamboo shoots
    20 young green onions
    2 seeded green peppers
    2 stalks celery
    ½ lb. fresh or canned mushrooms

Season the stew with:

    ¼ cup or more soy sauce
    Salt and pepper
    2 tablespoons sugar

Cook these ingredients gently for 15 minutes—no more. Serve them at once with:

    Japanese Rice, page 103

The friend to whom I am indebted for this recipe suggests adding to the stew:

    ⅓ cup tomato juice
    1 teaspoon Worcestershire sauce
    ½ cup blanched almonds

CHOW MEIN WITH FRIED NOODLES
10 Servings

This and the following good dish may be made in advance and reheated.

Cut into cubes:

    ½ lb. lean pork

Melt in a skillet:

    3 tablespoons butter

Add and cook for 2 minutes:

    2 tablespoons minced onion

Brown the meat in the butter. Stir in until blended:

2½ tablespoons flour

Stir in slowly:

2½ cups Chicken Stock, page 43

Add:

3 cups diced cooked chicken
¾ cup diced celery or bean sprouts
¾ cup canned or fresh mushrooms

Simmer these ingredients gently for 15 minutes, or cook them in a double boiler. Add:

2 tablespoons soy sauce
(¾ cup blanched slivered almonds)

and seasoning if needed. Serve the chow mein on a large deep platter. Surround it with:

Fried Noodles, page 97, or canned fried noodles

MEXICAN VEAL STEAK WITH NOODLES
6 Servings

A famous "Madam Malaprop" once announced to her delighted listeners that her son would attend a masquerade in the "Garbage of a monk." Here is an old friend in a new garb—for onion lovers only.

Cut into 8 or 10 portions:

1 lb. thin veal steak

Dredge it with:

¼ cup seasoned flour

Heat:

3 teaspoons shortening

Sauté the meat quickly on both sides until it is brown. Reduce the heat. Cover the meat with:

1½ cups sliced onions
6 tablespoons chili sauce
1¼ cups boiling water

Cover the pan closely. Simmer the steak for ½ hour. Sprinkle it with:

2 oz. grated cheese

Stir the mixture until the cheese is melted. Cook by the rule on page 91:

5 oz. noodles

Drain them. Rinse them with water. Drain them. Melt:

2 tablespoons butter

Stir in:

1 tablespoon flour

Stir in slowly:

½ cup chicken stock or a bouillon cube dissolved in ½ cup boiling water

Reheat the noodles in this sauce. Serve them with:

Buttered crumbs

Serve the meat garnished with:

Parsley

VEAL PATTIES
3 Servings

Combine:

¾ lb. ground veal
2½ tablespoons melted butter or drippings
¼ teaspoon lemon juice
¼ teaspoon salt
¼ teaspoon paprika
⅛ teaspoon nutmeg
A few grains pepper
¼ cup crushed cornflakes

Shape these ingredients with the hands into 6 cakes. Roll them in:

Seasoned bread crumbs or crushed cornflakes

Dip them in:

1 egg diluted with 2 tablespoons water

and again in the crumbs. Heat in a skillet:

3 tablespoons shortening

Sauté the patties on both sides to a rich brown. Drain them on absorbent paper. Serve them with:

Gravy or Sauce, page 426

VEAL AND SPINACH DISH

Herman Smith cooked and served this fine dish when I visited him in his Connecticut home. Its success depends largely upon how well you cook spinach. His, as I remember it, was deliciously creamed and delicately flavored with grated onion and lemon rind. While you are preparing the spinach you may cook enough to make cream of spinach soup for another day. Save the spinach water for this purpose too.

Place in a casserole a 1 inch layer or more of:

Creamed spinach

Place over it:

Slices of roast veal or lamb, etc.

If you have gravy, pour a little of it over the meat or use a little thick cream. Cover the top with:

Bread crumbs

Dot it lightly with:

Dabs of butter

Sprinkle it with:

Grated cheese

Bake the dish in a hot oven 425° until the top is brown. Garnish it with:

Parsley

Herman's dish was handsome without parsley. Possibly he hesitated to disturb the general decorative scheme by gilding this lily, for he served butter wreathed in ivy.

CANNED VEAL MOUSSE
6 to 8 Servings
Mash with a fork the contents of:
>   1 can veal or ham loaf: 16 oz.
Beat in:
>   ¼ cup light cream
Whip until stiff:
>   2 egg whites
>   ⅛ teaspoon salt
Fold them into the meat mixture.
Heap the mousse on an oven-proof
plate. Bake it in a moderate oven 325°
until hot, about 15 minutes. Garnish it
with:
>   Parsley
Serve it with:
>   Lightly seasoned Cream Sauce,
>   page 428
to which add:
>   1 tablespoon capers or
>   2 tablespoons chopped pickles,
>   olives or chopped parsley

CURRIED VEAL AND RICE
4 Servings
This combination of meat, apple and
curry is luscious.
Peel and slice:
>   1 cup onions
Core, peel and slice:
>   2 medium-sized apples
Melt in a saucepan:
>   3 tablespoons butter
Add the onions and apples and sauté
until the onions are tender. Remove
them from the pan. Brown lightly in
the pan about:
>   2 cups sliced or diced cooked veal
Remove it from the pan. Stir into the
pan juices:
>   1 tablespoon curry powder
>   2 teaspoons flour
Stir in slowly:
>   1 cup Stock, page 43
When the sauce is smooth and boiling,
add the onions, apples and meat. Stir
in:
>   1 tablespoon lemon juice
>   Salt as needed
Serve the meat with:
>   Steamed or boiled rice
Caution! Use only ½ teaspoonful
curry to begin with if you are unfamiliar with it.

For other Veal Dishes see Index.

CHOP GRILL WITH
PINEAPPLE AND TOMATO
Heat your broiler. Grease a rack and
place it in a shallow pan or grease a
broiling rack. Place on it:

>   Lamb or pork chops, pork
>   tenderloin slices or pricked
>   sausages
Melt:
>   Butter
Dip in it:
>   Mushroom caps
>   Drained pineapple or apples,
>   cored and cut in thick slices,
>   sprinkled with sugar and
>   cinnamon
>   Tomato slices
Arrange these on the rack. Season the
mushrooms and tomato slices with:
>   Salt and pepper
Add to the tomatoes a sprinkling of:
>   Brown sugar
Stick the pineapple slices with a few:
>   Whole cloves
Place the pan on a rack about 3 inches
under a broiler. When one side of the
chops is done turn them and the other
ingredients and broil the other side,
time dependent on the thickness of the
chops.
Arrange these ingredients on a hot
platter. Pour the drippings over them.
Garnish them with:
>   Parsley

LAMB AND EGGPLANT
CASSEROLE DISH
4 Servings
Pare and chop until fine:
>   1 medium-sized eggplant
Combine it with:
>   2 cups raw ground lamb: 1 lb.
>   ½ cup chopped onion
>   3 tablespoons chopped parsley
>   1 teaspoon salt
>   ¼ teaspoon paprika
>   1 cup canned chopped tomatoes
Butter a casserole. Fill it with the
lamb mixture. Bake it covered in a
moderate oven 350° for about ¾ hour.
Remove the cover and permit the top
to brown.

LAMB TERRAPIN
4 Servings
Cut into dice:
>   2 cups cold cooked lamb
Chop or rice:
>   2 hard-cooked eggs
Combine the lamb, the eggs and:
>   2 tablespoons olive oil
>   1 tablespoon lemon juice
Melt:
>   2 tablespoons butter
Stir in until blended:

3 tablespoons flour
1 teaspoon dry mustard
Stir in slowly:
    2 cups Lamb Stock, see "Scrap"
    Soup, page 44, or milk
Add:
    1 teaspoon Worcestershire sauce
    Salt as needed
Cook and stir the sauce until it is boiling. Add the lamb and egg mixture. Heat the terrapin thoroughly. Serve it on:
    Hot toast

For other Lamb Dishes see Index.

CHICKEN TERRAPIN
6 Servings
Cut into cubes:
    2 cups cooked chicken
Cook, then shell:
    3 hard-cooked eggs
Chop the whites until they are fine. Crush the yolks. Combine them with:
    3 tablespoons cream
Melt in the top of a double boiler over direct heat:
    2 tablespoons butter
Stir in the chicken with a fork. Stir in until blended and bubbling:
    1 tablespoon flour
    ½ teaspoon salt
    A few grains cayenne
    (¾ teaspoon mace)
Stir in gradually:
    1 cup cream
Place the container over boiling water. Stir in the egg whites and the yolk mixture. Serve the terrapin as soon as it is hot.

SPANISH CASSEROLE DISH WITH RICE
6 Servings
This is a one-dish meal.
Cook:
    ⅔ cup Steamed Rice, page 103
Prepare:
    1 cup chopped celery
    ¼ cup chopped green pepper
Melt in a saucepan:
    2 tablespoons butter or other fat
Peel, chop and sauté in the butter until brown:
    1 medium-sized onion
Cut into cubes, add and sear:
    1 lb. round steak
Season it with:
    ¾ teaspoon salt
    ¼ teaspoon paprika
Place in a greased baking dish ⅓ of the

rice and ½ of the meat. Sprinkle over it ½ of the celery and pepper. Repeat this process. Place the last of the rice on top. Pour over these ingredients the contents of:
    1 can condensed tomato soup:
    10½ oz.
    Seasonings
Cover the dish and place it in a moderate oven 350° for ½ hour.

CHILI CON CARNE
8 Servings
This is a mild, very good chili.
Melt:
    2 tablespoons bacon drippings or
    butter
Sauté in the fat:
    ½ cup chopped onion or ½
    chopped clove garlic
Add:
    1 lb. ground beef
Stir and sauté the beef until it is well done. Add:
    1¼ cups canned tomatoes
    2 No. 1½ cans kidney beans
    2 teaspoons to 2 tablespoons chili
    powder
    ¾ teaspoon or more salt
Cover and cook slowly for 1 hour.

HAMBURGER-OLIVE LOAF
4 Servings
A quick meat loaf.
Combine lightly with the hands:
    1½ lbs. ground beef
    ½ cup lightly crushed cornflakes
    1 teaspoon salt
    ¼ teaspoon paprika
    ¼ cup minced onions
Grease a baking dish and spread the beef in it. Cut into pieces:
    10 or more stuffed olives
Sprinkle them over the meat. Cover it with the contents of:
    1 can condensed tomato or
    mushroom soup: 10½ oz.
Bake the loaf in a hot oven 425° for about 30 minutes.

PORCUPINES
6 Servings
Combine:
    1 lb. ground beef
    ½ cup bread crumbs
    1 egg
    ¼ cup chopped onion
    ¾ teaspoon salt
    ¼ teaspoon paprika
    (2 tablespoons chopped green
    peppers)

Roll these ingredients into balls. Press them into flat cakes. Roll them in:
    ¼ cup raw rice
Heat in a heavy pot the contents of:
    1 can condensed tomato soup:
        10½ oz.
    2 cups boiling water
Add:
    6 small skinned onions
    6 ribs celery cut into inch lengths
    1 teaspoon chili powder
Add the meat cakes. Cover the pot. Simmer the meat for 45 minutes. Thicken the sauce with:
    Flour (see Gravy, page 426)
Season it, if needed, with:
    Salt and pepper

DOUGHNUT HAMBURGERS
4 Servings
This recipe comes from a well-known New York quick-lunch stand.
Mix thoroughly:
    2 lbs. ground round steak
    1 egg yolk
    ½ cup matzos or cracker meal
    Juice of 1 lemon
    1 grated Bermuda onion with juice
Form these ingredients into doughnut shapes. Cook them in hot fat 370° (page 542) or sauté them in drippings. Season them after cooking with:
    Salt and pepper
Drain them on absorbent paper.

For other Hamburger Dishes see Index.

HAMBURGER RING
5 Servings
Combine lightly with a fork:
    1 lb. ground beef
    ½ cup rich milk
    1 tablespoon grated onion
    1 teaspoon salt
    ¼ teaspoon paprika
    (½ teaspoon Herbs, page 832)
Bake this mixture in a greased 7 inch ring mold in a moderate oven 350° for about 1 hour. Invert it onto a platter. Use the juices for:
    Gravy, page 426
adding stock, cream or tomato juice to make from 1 to 2 cupfuls. Serve the ring on a platter filled with:
    Butter beans, peas, snap beans, etc.
Surround it with:
    Browned potatoes

Garnish it with:
    Parsley or water cress

NUTBURGERS
6 Servings
You may vary the filling of this good basic recipe. Use chopped celery, pickles, chili sauce with bread crumbs or bread dressing, left-over vegetables, etc.
Sauté lightly:
    6 slices bacon
Season:
    1½ lbs. ground beef
with:
    1 teaspoon salt
Divide it into 12 portions. Shape them into flat cakes. Make a filling with:
    6 tablespoons chopped nut meats
    3 tablespoons chopped parsley
    2 tablespoons grated onion
Spread it on 6 of the cakes. Cover each one with ½ slice of the bacon. Top them with the remaining cakes. Pinch the edges together. Broil the nutburgers under a preheated broiler for about 8 minutes, turning them once, or panbroil them. See Hamburgers, page 352.

QUICK BEEF CHOP SUEY
4 Servings
Melt in a skillet:
    ¼ cup butter
Sauté in it until the meat loses its color:
    1 lb. ground steak
    1 cup minced celery
    1 medium-sized cubed onion
    ½ lb. mushrooms
Add:
    1 teaspoon salt
Place the ingredients in a casserole. Cover them with:
    1 can condensed tomato soup:
        10½ oz.
Bake the suey in a hot oven 400° for about 45 minutes. Serve with:
    Fried Noodles, page 97

Chicken or Beef Chop Suey, page 142.

AVOCADO AND BACON
2 Servings
A breakfast or luncheon dish.
Mash with a fork the pulp of:
    1 avocado
Season it with:
    Lemon juice and salt
    Onion juice

Heap it in small mounds on 2 plates.
Garnish it with:

Strips of sautéed bacon
Paprika and chopped parsley

BANANAS, PINEAPPLE AND BACON

Good as a breakfast dish or served with a meat course.
Cut into lengthwise halves:

Bananas

Place between the halves:

Canned pineapple sticks

Wrap the bananas with:

Slices bacon

Broil them in a pan under a low flame, turning them frequently until the bacon is crisp.

BANANAS IN BLANKETS

Peel and cut into quarters crosswise:

Firm ripe bananas

Dip them in:

Lemon juice

Sprinkle them very lightly with:

Sugar

Roll them in very thin:

Slices bacon or boiled ham

Secure the bacon with toothpicks. Sauté the bananas in a skillet or bake them in a moderate oven 350° until the bacon is crisp. When using ham, grease the skillet lightly.

VEGETABLE SHORTCAKE OR PIZZA NAPOLITANA

12 or 14 Servings

This simple rule may be used as the basis of a one-dish meal, or small portions may be served as hors d'oeuvres. It is capable of many variations, for you may substitute for the bread dough biscuit or pie dough, and the topping may be made from any suitable left-overs or fresh ingredients you happen to have on hand.
Roll out to fit a 12 x 15 inch greased cookie sheet or jelly-roll pan a thin layer of:

Bread dough

This may be rolled right on the greased sheet. Spread on the dough the contents of:

1 can Italian tomato paste: 6 oz.

Combine:

4 tablespoons olive oil
3 tablespoons anchovy paste
1 teaspoon dried orégano

Spread this mixture over the tomato paste. Permit the dough to rise until about doubled in bulk. Bake the pizza

in a hot oven 400° for about 20 minutes, or until the dough is done. Serve it hot or cold.
Italian sausage, finely sliced, is sometimes substituted for the anchovy. Orégano, an herb, may be purchased in most groceries, but basil, marjoram, minced chives or onions may be substituted. Minced left-over meat and vegetables may be moistened with oil and used in place of the anchovy or sausage.
A good combination is:

3 cups lightly packed, chopped cooked meat
4 tablespoons olive oil
3 tablespoons chopped chives or
1 tablespoon minced onion
1 teaspoon orégano

UPSIDE-DOWN LEFT-OVER VEGETABLE PIE

4 Servings

Grease a casserole. Place in it:

3 cups cooked vegetables

Pour over them:

¼ cup cream, Stock, page 43, or a mixture of both

Cover these ingredients with:

Sour Milk Corn Bread Batter, page 515, or Pie Crust, page 561, or Biscuit Dough, page 505

Bake the pie in a hot oven 425° for about 25 minutes. It may be served with Tomato Sauce, page 433, or with left-over gravy.

ONION SHORTCAKE

6 Servings

When it comes to onions don't be a defeatist.
Peel and slice:

10 medium-sized white onions

Sprinkle them with:

½ teaspoon salt

Melt in a saucepan:

3 tablespoons butter

Add the onions. Cover them and simmer until they are tender. Cool them.
Prepare by the rule on page 506:

Fluffy Biscuit Dough: use ½ the amount given

Spread the dough in a deep greased 8 inch pan or in an oven-proof dish.
Cover it with the cooked onions. Add:

¼ teaspoon paprika
2 teaspoons chopped parsley

Prepare by the rule on page 428:

1 cup Cream Sauce I or use
½ cup sour or sweet cream
½ teaspoon salt

A grating nutmeg or black
pepper
Beat into it:
    1 egg
Pour the sauce over the onions. The
top may be sprinkled with:
    ¼ cup grated cheese
Bake the cake in a hot oven 425° for
about 20 minutes, or until the dough is
done.

ONION PIE

Richer and more sophisticated than the
preceding Onion Shortcake. Serve
Onion Shortcake with a meat course.
Have Onion Pie as a main dish with a
green salad.
Line a 9 inch pie pan with:
    Pie Dough, page 561
Chill it. Skin and slice thinly:
    2½ lbs. Bermuda onions: about 10
    medium-sized onions
Melt in a heavy saucepan:
    3 tablespoons butter
Add the onions. Stir and cook them
over low heat until they are clear. Cool
them well. Combine and heat slowly
until blended:
    3 eggs
    1 cup sour cream
    ¼ cup dry sherry
    1 teaspoon salt
    ¼ teaspoon freshly ground pepper
    (1 tablespoon minced fresh herb
    or 1 teaspoon dill or celery seed)
Stir this mixture into the onions.
Brush the bottom of the pie shell with:
    1 slightly beaten egg white
Fill it with the onion mixture. You
may place over the top:
    4 strips bacon cut into squares
Bake the pie in a hot oven 450° for 10
minutes. Reduce the heat to 300° and
bake the pie until the crust is light
brown, about ½ hour.
Serve it piping hot.

CHEESE, NUT AND BREAD LOAF
6 Servings
Combine well:
    2 cups fresh bread crumbs
    1 cup minced walnut or pecan
    meats
    1 cup grated American cheese
    1 cup milk
    ¾ teaspoon salt
    ½ teaspoon paprika
    1 tablespoon finely chopped onion
    1 tablespoon minced parsley
    1 beaten egg

Shape these ingredients in a loaf by
placing them in a bread pan. Invert
the contents of the pan onto a greased
tin. Bake the loaf in a moderate oven
350° for about 25 minutes. Serve it
with:
    Quick Tomato Sauce, page 433,
    Mushroom Sauce, page 436, or
    Onion Sauce, page 432

NUT ROAST
6 Servings
Melt:
    3 tablespoons butter
Sauté in it until soft:
    1 minced onion
    1 seeded chopped green pepper
Add:
    1 cup cooked rice
    ⅓ cup bread crumbs
    1 cup tomatoes
    1 cup chopped or ground walnut
    or other nut meats
    1 beaten egg
    2 tablespoons chopped parsley
    ¾ teaspoon salt
    ¼ teaspoon paprika
Place these ingredients in a greased
baking dish. Bake them in a moderate
oven 375° for 30 minutes. Cover the
top with:
    Mashed potatoes
Dot them generously with:
    Butter
Brown them under a broiler. Serve the
roast with:
    Tomato Sauce, page 433

DRIED BEAN LOAF
4 to 6 Servings
You may use for this and the following
Bean Patties any dried cooked beans:
navy, pea, soy, Lima, etc.
Put through a grinder or mash:
    ½ lb. cooked dried beans
Add and mix well:
    1 teaspoon salt
    ¼ seeded chopped green pepper
    ½ cup tomato pulp
    ½ cup cornflakes
    1 chopped onion
    ¼ teaspoon pepper
    1 teaspoon Worcestershire sauce
    1 teaspoon horseradish sauce
    1 beaten egg
Bake these ingredients in a greased
loaf pan in a moderate oven 350° for
about 1 hour. Serve the loaf with:
    Cheese Sauce, page 430, or
    Tomato Sauce, page 433

DRIED BEAN PATTIES

Grind or mash:
   2 cups cooked dried beans
Add to them:
   1 chopped onion
   1/4 cup chopped parsley
Beat and add:
   2 egg yolks
   2 tablespoons cream or evaporated
      milk
   1/4 teaspoon pepper
   1 teaspoon salt
Shape these ingredients into balls,
flatten them. Dip them in:
   Flour
Chill the patties for 1 hour or more.
Sauté them slowly until brown in:
   Butter, drippings or other fat
Serve them with any:
   Barbecue Sauce, page 346

SCALLOPED CABBAGE

8 Servings
Rather luxurious treatment for this
good bourgeois vegetable.
Chop, then cook (page 275):
   1 medium-sized head cabbage
Drain it well. Prepare:
   1 1/2 cups Cream Sauce I, page 428
Prepare:
   2 tablespoons chopped peppers
   2 tablespoons chopped pimientos
Sauté and mince:
   (6 slices bacon)
Melt:
   2 tablespoons bacon fat or butter
Toss lightly in this:
   1/2 cup bread crumbs
Place layers of drained cabbage in a
greased baking dish. Sprinkle them
with the minced bacon, the peppers
and pimientos and:
   1 cup or less grated cheese
Cover them with the cream sauce. Top
the dish with the sautéed bread
crumbs. Bake the cabbage in a moderate oven 375° for 10 minutes.

*Creamed Cabbage Baked with Nut
Meats and Cheese, page 276.*

CABBAGE WITH SAUSAGE

4 Servings
Prepare by the rule on page 275:
   3 cups boiled cabbage
Drain it well. Combine it with:
   3 whole black peppercorns or 1
      teaspoon caraway seed
Place it in a greased baking dish. Pour
over it:
   1/2 cup Soup Stock, page 43

Place on top of it:
   8 breakfast sausages
Bake it in a hot oven 425° until the
sausages are done.

STUFFED CABBAGE OR GEFUELLTER KRAUTKOPF

6 Servings
Separate the leaves of a large:
   Head of cabbage
Wash them and boil them uncovered
for 5 minutes in a quantity of:
   Boiling water
Drain the cabbage well. Reserve the
liquor. Prepare the following meat
dressing. Soak in water for 2 minutes:
   1 slice of bread 1 inch thick
Press the water from it. Combine the
bread with:
   1/2 lb. ground pork
   1/2 lb. ground beef
   1/2 lb. ground veal
   3 beaten eggs
   3/4 teaspoon salt
   1/4 teaspoon paprika
Or use a filling of:
   1 lb. pork sausages, skins removed
   3 half inch slices of bread
   1 beaten egg
Line a bowl with a large napkin and fill
it with alternate layers of the leaves
and the meat dressing. Cover the top
with 1 or 2 large leaves, gather up the
cloth and tie it with a string. Place the
bag in boiling water to cover well—the
water in which the cabbage was boiled
and as much fresh boiling water as
needed. Boil the cabbage gently for 2
hours if you are old-fashioned, but 45
minutes should be ample time. Drain
it on a colander, untie the bag and
place the cabbage in a hot serving dish.
Serve it with:
Onion Sauce
Brown in a double boiler:
   4 tablespoons butter
Add and stir until brown:
   2 tablespoons flour
Have in readiness:
   2 cups Stock, page 43, or cabbage
      water
Stir 1/2 cupful of this into the butter
mixture. Add:
   1/2 cup or more chopped onion
If required, season with:
   Salt and pepper
Cook the onions covered until they are
very tender. Add the remainder of the
stock gradually. The gravy is best
when it is thick with onions.

CABBAGE WITH TOMATO SAUCE
6 Servings

A practical all-purpose vegetable rule. Good made with Brussels sprouts or left-over cabbage.

Prepare by the rule for Boiled Cabbage, page 275:

    A small firm head cabbage

While the cabbage boils prepare this sauce. Dice and sauté until crisp:

    4 slices bacon

Remove and reserve the bacon. Sauté in the bacon fat until tender:

    1 small minced onion

Add:

    1 cup tomato purée or the contents
    of an 8 oz. can Spanish-style
    tomato sauce
    Salt and pepper
    (2 teaspoons brown sugar)

When the sauce is boiling add the well-drained cabbage and the bits of bacon. Serve very hot garnished with:

    2 tablespoons minced parsley

CABBAGE, TOMATO AND CHEESE DISH
6 Servings

Cook for 5 minutes (page 275):

    3 cups finely shredded cabbage

Drain it well. Cook:

    1½ cups Stewed Tomatoes, page 318
    ¾ teaspoon salt
    ¼ teaspoon paprika
    (2 teaspoons brown sugar)

Butter a baking dish. Place in it alternate layers of tomatoes and cabbage, beginning with tomatoes. Sprinkle the layers with:

    1 cup grated cheese
    1 cup bread crumbs

Dot the top with:

    1 tablespoon butter or 2 strips
    minced bacon

Bake the dish in a moderate oven 325° for about ½ hour, or until the crumbs are brown.

HASH IN CREAMED CABBAGE

Prepare:

    Creamed Cabbage, page 275

Place ½ the cabbage in a greased oven-proof dish. Place on top of it a layer of:

    Hash moistened lightly with
    gravy or cream

Cover it with the remaining cabbage. Sprinkle the top with:

    Bread crumbs or cornflakes

Dot it with:

    Butter

You may sprinkle it with:

    Grated cheese

Bake the cabbage in a hot oven 400° until the top is light brown.

FRESH CABBAGE FILLED WITH CANNED CORNED BEEF HASH
4 Servings

Trim the outer leaves and the stem from:

    A medium-sized head of cabbage

Cook it uncovered until it is barely tender in:

    2 quarts boiling water

Do not overcook cabbage. It is best when still slightly crisp. Drain it well. Scoop out the inside, leaving a 1½ inch shell. Place the shell in a greased oven-proof dish. Keep it hot. Chop the removed part. Add it to the contents of:

    1 can minced corned beef hash:
    16 oz.
    ¼ cup or more sautéed onions
    A pinch of thyme

Moisten it with:

    (Cream, evaporated milk or
    bacon drippings)

Heat these ingredients. Fill the shell. Cover the top with:

    Buttered cornflakes

The cabbage may be heated in a hot oven over 400° for 10 minutes. It may be served with:

    Onion Soup Sauce, page 442

CABBAGE STUFFED WITH HAM AND CHEESE
6 Servings

Trim the loose outer leaves from:

    A firm head cabbage

Cut out enough from the stem end of the cabbage to make a deep well. Prepare a filling by combining:

    2 cups cooked ground or chopped
    ham
    1 cup bread crumbs
    ¾ cup grated American cheese
    ½ teaspoon dry mustard
    Salt
    ½ teaspoon paprika
    A few grains cayenne

Fill the center of the cabbage with the filling. Steam the cabbage in an improvised steamer made of a colander or frying basket, if necessary, until it is tender, from 1 to 2 hours. Place it over boiling water. Cover it with a bowl or lid, or wrap the cabbage in heavy waxed paper and bake it in a moderate oven 375° from 1 to 2 hours.

Serve it with:
Cheese Sauce, page 431, or
Tomato Cheese Sauce, page 434

GROUND BEEF IN CABBAGE LEAVES
4 Servings
Cook for 3 minutes in boiling salted water:
8 large cabbage leaves
Drain them and dry them on a towel. Combine:
1 lb. ground beef or a mixture of beef, veal, pork and liver
3 tablespoons finely chopped onion
2 tablespoons finely chopped parsley
¾ teaspoon salt
½ teaspoon thyme
½ mashed clove garlic
A few grains cayenne
Divide the meat mixture into 8 parts. Put one part on each cabbage leaf. Roll the leaves. Secure them with toothpicks. Place them close together in a buttered baking dish. Dot each roll with:
½ teaspoon butter
Pour into the dish:
½ cup boiling Stock, page 43, water, tomato juice or sour cream and paprika
Bake the rolls in a moderate oven 375° until the cabbage leaves are very tender.

CABBAGE ROLLS STUFFED WITH RICE AND SAUSAGE MEAT
4 Servings
Prepare by the preceding rule:
Cabbage leaves
Prepare the following stuffing. Melt:
1½ tablespoons butter
Sauté in the butter for 2 minutes:
1 seeded chopped green pepper
¼ cup chopped onions
(¼ cup chopped celery)
Add to these ingredients:
1½ cups cooked seasoned rice
1 cup sausage meat: ½ lb.
Fill and roll the cabbage leaves as directed in the preceding rule. Dot them with:
Butter
Place them in a greased baking dish. Bake them in a moderate oven 350° for about 45 minutes. Serve them with:
Tomato Sauce, page 433

CABBAGE ROLLS STUFFED WITH RICE AND CHEESE
6 Servings
A variation of the preceding rule. Omit the vegetables if desired. Substitute for the sausage meat:
¾ cup grated American cheese
Season well with:
Cayenne, paprika and salt

CABBAGE OR LETTUCE AND RICE DISH
6 Servings
This is a good dish to make in the trail of a salad luncheon. You may use the outer leaves of lettuce. Melt:
2 tablespoons bacon drippings
2 tablespoons butter or 3 tablespoons other fat
Stir in, cover and cook gently for 10 minutes:
3 cups finely shredded cabbage or lettuce
½ cup finely chopped onion
1 seeded chopped green pepper
Stir these ingredients frequently. Stir in and cook until well heated:
1 cup cooked rice
2 cups tomato pulp or thick stewed tomatoes
Salt and pepper
This is good served with:
Crisp bacon or cold ham

RED CABBAGE AND CHESTNUTS
6 Servings
In "The House of Exile" I read that the Chinese served red cabbage in green peppers, see Pepper Cases, page 202. This dish is attractive served that way.
Shell and blanch (page 283):
1 cup chestnuts
You may slice the chestnuts. Shred until very fine:
1 small head red cabbage
Place it in a bowl. Cover it with:
Boiling water
Add:
¼ cup white wine or vinegar
Permit it to soak for 15 minutes. Drain it well. Heat in a saucepan:
2½ tablespoons bacon drippings or butter
Add the cabbage. Sprinkle it lightly with:
Salt and pepper
Sauté the cabbage until it browns. Cover it with a lid and simmer it for 10

minutes. In a separate saucepan combine the chestnuts with:

1 cup water
1½ tablespoons sugar
¼ cup white wine or vinegar
⅓ cup seedless raisins
1 peeled thinly sliced apple

Simmer these ingredients covered until the chestnuts are tender. Sprinkle over the cabbage:

1 tablespoon flour

Add it to the chestnut mixture. Cook these ingredients until they are well heated and blended. Season them if needed with:

Salt

and, if vinegar has been used, with:

(1 tablespoon sherry)

Serve them hot.

STUFFED EGGS ON ROSETTES WITH SAVORY SAUCE

8 Servings

This rather elaborate dish is worth the trouble because it is unusual. The rosettes and the sauce may be made the day before they are served.
Prepare:

8 hard-cooked eggs

Cut them crosswise into halves. Remove the yolks. Combine them with equal parts of:

Cooked, finely chopped seasoned spinach, or Creamed Spinach, page 313

Fill the egg whites with the mixture. Prepare:

2 cups Cream Sauce I, page 428

Season it with:

2 tablespoons Worcestershire sauce
2 tablespoons sherry
¾ cup chili sauce
Salt and pepper

When the sauce is smooth and boiling add:

2 cups cooked or canned shrimp or diced cooked sweetbreads

Prepare by the rule on page 546:

16 rosettes

Place a stuffed egg half on each rosette and cover the eggs with sauce. Serve them at once, or make the sauce and the rosettes ahead of time. Reheat the sauce in a double boiler. Reheat the rosettes in a quick oven 400°.

SPINACH, TOMATO AND CHEESE LOAF

8 Servings

Place in a bowl:

2 cups cooked or 1 package frozen, slightly chopped spinach or chard: 14 oz.
2¼ cups canned tomatoes: No. 2 can
¼ cup chili sauce
½ lb. grated cheese
1 cup cracker crumbs
Juice of ½ onion
¼ teaspoon salt
¼ teaspoon freshly ground pepper

Toss these ingredients until they are blended. Place them in a greased loaf pan. Bake the dish in a moderate oven 350° for 1 hour. Serve it garnished with:

Crisp Bacon, page 375

RAGOUT FIN

8 Servings

A very good creamed dish—delicate and far-reaching.
Boil by the rule on page 376:

1 pair sweetbreads

Chill, remove the skin and break them into pieces. Drain and cut in two the contents of:

1 can asparagus tips: 15 oz.

Reserve the liquid. Rub a skillet with:

(A clove of garlic)

Melt in it:

4 tablespoons butter

Sauté in the butter for 3 minutes:

½ lb. mushrooms

Remove them from the skillet. Add to the fat in the skillet:

6 tablespoons butter

Add and stir until blended:

6 tablespoons flour

Stir in slowly:

3 cups liquid: cream, top milk, asparagus water or Stock, page 43

When the sauce is smooth and boiling, add gradually the asparagus tips, the mushrooms and the sweetbreads. Reduce the heat to a low flame and stir in:

2 egg yolks

Season the ragout with:

Salt and paprika
Freshly grated nutmeg

Fold the sauce over the ingredients, taking care not to let it burn at the bottom. Cook it for 1 minute longer to permit the yolks to thicken. Just before serving add:

2 tablespoons sherry or
1 teaspoon Worcestershire sauce

Serve the ragout at once in:

Hot patty shells, on hot buttered toast, in Bread Cases, page 77, in a baked Noodle Ring, page 98, or on hot Waffles, page 556

To reheat the ragout, place it over boiling water.

OYSTER AND MUSHROOM RAGOUT WITH VEAL BALLS
8 Servings

This is a bit troublesome. If you are a cook with the hurry-up approach to meals, don't bother with it. If, however, you care for unusual food, try out this old cherished recipe. It was the specialty of a well-known St. Louis hostess whose reputation as a cook reached a pinnacle.

Prepare by the rule on page 73:
> **Meat Balls**

Use veal instead of beef. Roll the mixture into ¾ inch balls. Cook by the rule on page 376:
> **1 pair sweetbreads**

Drain them, reserving the stock. Skin, then cut into 1 inch dice. Poach the meat balls covered in the simmering stock for 5 minutes. Drain them. Reserve the stock. Sauté:
> **½ lb. mushrooms**

in:
> **4 tablespoons butter**

Sprinkle them with:
> **4 tablespoons flour**

Add gradually:
> **2 cups drained stock**

Season the stock well with:
> **Salt and paprika**
> **1 tablespoon lemon juice**

Add the sweetbreads and veal balls to the boiling sauce. Heat in their liquor until the edges begin to curl:
> **1 pint oysters**

Drain them. Add the juice to the stock. Add the oysters to the boiling sauce. Reduce the heat. Draw off part of the sauce. Beat in:
> **2 egg yolks**

Return the sauce to the pan. Do not let it boil but stir it gently over low heat for about 1 minute. Serve the stew at once in ramekins or over:
> **Buttered toast**

BRUNSWICK STEW
8 Servings

Disjoint for cooking:
> **A 4 lb. chicken**

Sauté it slowly until light brown in:
> **¼ cup butter or drippings**

Remove it from the pan. Brown in the fat:
> **½ cup chopped onions**

Place in a large stewing pan the chicken, onions and:

> **5 peeled quartered tomatoes:**
> about 2 cups
> **1 cup boiling water**
> **6 cloves**
> **A few grains cayenne**

Simmer these ingredients covered until the chicken is nearly tender. Add:
> **3 cups fresh Lima beans**
> **3 cups corn cut from the cob**

Simmer these ingredients covered until the chicken and the vegetables are tender. The meat may be removed from the bones. Season the stew with:
> **Salt**
> **2 teaspoons Worcestershire sauce**

You may stir in:
> **1 cup toasted bread crumbs**

MUSHROOMS UNDER GLASS
4 Servings

In former years the following dish was associated in my mind with extreme luxury. Today it is within the reach of anyone with a few extra cents and a glass bowl that fits closely over a baking dish. Trim the stems from:
> **1 lb. mushrooms**

Beat until creamy:
> **¼ cup butter**

Stir in very slowly:
> **2 teaspoons lemon juice**

Add:
> **1 tablespoon chopped parsley**
> **⅓ teaspoon salt**
> **¼ teaspoon paprika**

Cut with a biscuit cutter and toast:
> **4 rounds bread ½ inch thick**

When cold spread them on both sides with ½ the butter mixture. Spread the rest on the tops of the mushroom caps. Place the toast in the bottom of a small baking dish and heap the mushrooms upon them. Pour over them:
> **½ cup cream**

Cover them closely with a glass bowl. Bake them in a moderate oven 375° for 25 minutes. Add more cream if they become dry. Just before serving add:
> **2 tablespoons sherry**

Serve the mushrooms garnished with:
> **Parsley**

BAKED MUSHROOMS
5 Servings

This is the easiest way I know of preparing mushrooms. It is less troublesome than the preceding recipe and nearly as good.

Remove the stems from:
> **1 lb. large mushrooms**

Place them cap side up in a flat greased

pan or baking dish. Sprinkle them lightly with:
> Salt and paprika
Dot them with:
> 2 tablespoons butter
Pour around them:
> ⅔ cup cream
Bake them in a hot oven 425° for about 10 minutes. Serve them caps up on:
> Rounds of toast
on which you may place:
> Rounds of ham

Anchovy Mushrooms, page 34; Mushrooms Stuffed with Onions, page 34; Broiled Stuffed Mushrooms, page 33; Mushrooms Stuffed with Shrimp, page 34; Lobster and Mushroom Casserole, page 125.

MUSHROOM RING OR MOUSSE
6 Servings
Put through a food chopper:
> 1 lb. mushrooms
Melt:
> 2 tablespoons butter
Stir in:
> 2 tablespoons flour
Brown the flour slightly. Sauté the mushrooms in this mixture for 2 minutes. Cool them. Beat in:
> 4 beaten egg yolks
> ½ teaspoon salt
> ¼ teaspoon paprika
Whip until stiff:
> 1 cup heavy cream
In another bowl whip until stiff:
> 2 egg whites
> ⅛ teaspoon salt
Fold the cream lightly into the mushroom mixture. Fold in the egg whites. Butter a 9 inch ring mold. Pour in the mousse. Cover it with a piece of buttered paper. Place the ring mold in a pan of hot water. Bake it in a slow oven 325° for about 1 hour. Invert the mousse onto a platter. Fill the center with:
> Buttered peas and parsley

Mushroom Soufflé, page 218; Mushroom Soufflé with Sweetbreads or Chicken, page 222.

OYSTERS AND MUSHROOMS AU GRATIN
4 Servings
Sauté (page 292):
> 20 large mushroom caps
in:
> 3 tablespoons butter

Place the mushrooms, caps up, in a greased baking dish. Cover them with:
> 20 large drained oysters
Season them well with:
> Salt and pepper
Cover them with:
> 1 cup boiling Cream Sauce I, page 428
seasoned with:
> Sherry
You may sprinkle the top with:
> Grated cheese
Place the dish in a moderate oven 375° until the top is brown. Or omit the cream sauce and dot each oyster with:
> ¼ teaspoon butter
> A few drops lemon juice
Bake as above until the oysters are plump.

MUSHROOMS IN CHEESE SAUCE
4 Servings
Sauté by the rule on page 292:
> 1 lb. mushrooms
Prepare by the rule on page 431:
> Cheese Sauce II or III
If you choose Cheese Sauce II, you may omit the mustard and substitute ¼ teaspoonful or more curry powder. If you do not like curry or mustard, substitute at the last moment 2 tablespoonfuls sherry. Combine the sauce with the mushrooms. Serve them on:
> Toast

MUSHROOMS À LA KING
6 Servings
This is a delectable concoction. Fine with a rice or noodle ring.
Prepare:
> 1 cup Stewed Celery, page 281
Drain it well. Prepare:
> 3 hard-cooked eggs
Chill, shell and slice them. Melt in a skillet:
> 4 tablespoons butter
Add and sauté for 3 minutes:
> 1 lb. mushrooms
Stir in until blended:
> 4 tablespoons flour
Stir in slowly:
> 2 cups top milk
Much better than the 2 cupfuls of top milk, but a little more troublesome, is the substitution of 1 cupful cream and 1 cupful stock. Make the stock with the mushroom trimmings, the celery water, an onion, a carrot, parsley, etc., or use 1 cupful chicken stock.

Season these ingredients with:
    ½ teaspoon salt
    ¼ teaspoon paprika
When the sauce is smooth and boiling, add the stewed celery, the sliced eggs and:
    ¼ cup sliced stuffed olives
The original recipe calls for, but it is really superfluous:
    ¼ cup grated American cheese
Just before serving season with:
    1 tablespoon cooking sherry or
    ½ teaspoon Worcestershire sauce
Serve the mushrooms in:
    Bread Cases, page 77, on hot Waffles, page 556, etc.

CHICKEN LIVERS À LA KING
Follow the preceding rule for:
    Mushrooms à la King
Substitute for the mushrooms:
    1 cup or more Sautéed Chicken Livers, page 139

CURRIED EGGS AND MUSHROOMS WITH CHEESE
4 Servings
Prepare:
    5 hard-cooked eggs
Chill them in cold water. Peel them and cut them into quarters. Sauté:
    ½ lb. mushrooms
Prepare:
    1 cup Cream Sauce I, page 428
Add to it:
    ¼ cup or more grated cheese
    ½ teaspoon or more curry powder
    1 tablespoon or more chili sauce
When the sauce is boiling add the mushrooms and the eggs. Pour this mixture into a baking dish or into ramekins. Sprinkle the top with:
    Bread crumbs
Dot it with:
    Butter
or sprinkle it with:
    Cheese
Place it under a broiler until the crumbs are brown.

MUSHROOMS AND ONIONS IN WINE SAUCE
4 Servings
Fine for a chafing dish.
Prepare for cooking:
    1 lb. mushrooms
Melt:
    ½ cup butter
Skin, add, stir and sauté for 5 minutes:
    16 tiny white onions

Add the mushrooms. When they are coated with butter add:
    2 tablespoons flour
    4 tablespoons chopped parsley
    ½ bay leaf
    ¼ teaspoon freshly grated nutmeg
    ½ cup bouillon or stock
Cook and stir these ingredients until the onions are tender. Add:
    ¼ cup Madeira or sherry
Serve garnished with:
    Croutons, page 73
    Sprigs of parsley

SAUERKRAUT WITH MUSHROOMS
4 Servings
Wash well in cold water:
    1 lb. sauerkraut
Drain it. Dice and try out—sauté over a very slow fire:
    ¼ cup bacon or ham fat
Combine it with the kraut. Simmer these ingredients covered in a heavy pot for about 1 hour. Watch them closely so that they do not burn. Add to them:
    ⅓ cup sour cream
    ½ lb. Sautéed Mushrooms, page 292
    1 tablespoon sugar
Place these ingredients in a greased baking dish. Cover the top with:
    Bread crumbs
Dot it with:
    Butter
Brown the crumbs under a broiler.

LIMA BEANS
Canned Lima beans, drained or dried Lima beans cooked (page 270) and drained may be substituted in the following recipes.

LIMA BEANS AND MUSHROOMS
6 Servings
Serve this with crisp bacon and grapefruit salad.
Cook:
    2 cups Lima beans
Drain them. Sauté (page 292):
    ½ lb. mushrooms
Drain them, saving the liquor if there is any. Add to the liquor and melt:
    1 tablespoon butter
Stir in:
    2 tablespoons flour
Cook and stir these ingredients until

they are well blended. Stir in slowly:
> ½ cup Chicken Stock, page 47, or
> stock and bean liquor
> ½ cup top milk

Season the sauce with:
> Salt and pepper

Add the beans and mushrooms. Heat them. Add before serving:
> (1 tablespoon sherry)

The dish may be served au gratin. Cover the top with:
> Bread crumbs

Dot it with:
> Butter

Place it under a broiler until the crumbs are brown.

LIMA BEANS WITH CHEESE
4 Servings

This, the preceding, and the following bean dishes are fine for stuffed peppers or onions.
Drain the contents of:
> 1 No. 2 can Lima beans

Stir into them:
> ½ cup chicken stock

Or melt:
> 2 tablespoons butter

Add and sauté for 3 minutes:
> ¼ cup minced onion

Stir into the stock or butter over low heat until melted:
> ½ lb. grated cheese

Add the beans and:
> ½ teaspoon salt
> ¼ teaspoon pepper
> 1 teaspoon dried basil or thyme
> A few grains cayenne
> (1 cup chopped nut meats)

Heat the beans in a moderate oven 350° for ½ hour. Serve them with:
> Tomato Sauce, page 433

MEXICAN LIMA BEAN CASSEROLE
6 Servings

Drain:
> 2 cups cooked Lima beans

Add:
> ¼ lb. salt pork cut in strips
> 1 large minced onion
> 1 tablespoon molasses
> 2 cups cooked tomatoes
> 1 tablespoon brown sugar
> ¼ teaspoon chili powder or pepper
> 1 teaspoon salt

Bake these ingredients in a greased casserole in a moderate oven 375° for 45 minutes.

CANNED BAKED BEANS WITH CHEESE
4 Servings

Stir and melt over hot water:
> ¼ lb. diced American cheese
> 1½ tablespoons butter

Fold in the contents of:
> 1 No. 2 can baked beans with pork

Season with:
> Salt and a few grains red pepper
> 2 teaspoons Worcestershire sauce
> or prepared mustard

Serve on:
> Toast

sprinkled with:
> Chopped parsley, chives or
> other herb

LEFT-OVER BRUSSELS SPROUTS IN CHEESE SAUCE
3 Servings

Prepare:
> 1 cup Cream Sauce I, page 428

When the sauce is boiling, add:
> 1 cup cooked Brussels Sprouts,
> page 274

Stir them carefully to avoid breaking them. When the sprouts are heated, reduce the heat and add:
> ½ cup grated cheese

Stir the sauce gently until the cheese is melted. Serve the sprouts on:
> Hot buttered toast

CAULIFLOWER AND MUSH-ROOMS IN CHEESE SAUCE
6 Servings

Cook (page 280):
> 1 large cauliflower

Drain it well and put it in a greased baking dish. Place it where it will keep hot. Melt in a skillet:
> 2 tablespoons butter

Sauté in it for 2 minutes:
> ½ lb. mushrooms

Cook:
> 1½ cups Cream Sauce I, page 428

Stir into the sauce over a low fire:
> ¾ cup grated cheese

When the cheese is melted, add the sautéed mushrooms and pour the sauce over the cauliflower. Serve it at once.

SCALLOPED CAULIFLOWER AND HAM
6 Servings

Cook (page 280):
> 1 small head cauliflower

Drain it. Separate it into flowerets. Cut into small pieces:
> ½ lb. boiled ham

Place in the top of a double boiler:
> 3 tablespoons quick-cooking
> tapioca
> 2 tablespoons butter
> ½ teaspoon salt
> ⅛ teaspoon pepper
> ⅛ teaspoon paprika
> 2 cups scalded milk

Cook these ingredients over boiling water for 7 minutes, or until the tapioca is clear. Stir them frequently. Place in a greased baking dish alternate layers of the tapioca mixture, the cauliflower and the ham, with the tapioca on top. Sprinkle the top with:
> Bread crumbs

Dot it with:
> Butter

Bake the dish in a moderate oven 350° for 20 minutes, or until brown.

SCALLOPED TOMATOES OR TOMATO PUDDING

This recipe should make enough to serve 6 people, but it is usually only enough for 4 because it is such a wonderful tomato dish. Serve it with meat, fish or omelet.

Place in a saucepan:
> 10 oz. tomato purée

Rinse the can with:
> ¼ cup boiling water

and add it to the purée. Heat these ingredients to the boiling point and add:
> ¼ teaspoon salt
> 6 tablespoons brown sugar
> ½ teaspoon dried basil

Place in a baking dish:
> 1 cup fresh white bread crumbs

Pour over them:
> ¼ cup melted butter

Add the tomato mixture and cover the dish closely. Bake the pudding in a moderate oven 375° for 30 minutes. Do not remove the cover until ready to serve the tomatoes. When fresh tomatoes are plentiful you may follow the rule substituting for the tomato paste about:
> 14 skinned sliced tomatoes

Add:
> 1 teaspoon fresh chives
> 1 teaspoon parsley
> 1 teaspoon basil

If you wish, add:
> A finely chopped onion

Sautéed in:
> Butter

Bake the dish for 3 hours, or until it has cooked down to a pastelike consistency.

TURKISH EGGPLANT
4 Servings

Sauté until nearly done, then cut each slice into 4 pieces:
> 4 slices bacon

Cut into 4 pieces, then remove membrane and fat from:
> 6 lamb kidneys

Cut into about 16 blocks:
> ½ lb. liver

Skin, then cut into quarters:
> (2 or more small onions)

Pare, cut into thick slices, then into about 32 blocks:
> A small eggplant

Arrange these ingredients alternately on 8 skewers. Dip the filled skewers in:
> Fritter batter (see batter for
> Calf Brain Fritters, page 140, or
> use a pancake mix batter)

To do this use a deep pie pan. Place the skewers on a rack to drip and dry briefly. Fry them in deep fat (page 542) until a golden brown.

EGGPLANT AND MINCED CLAM CASSEROLE
4 Servings

This unusual dish has a fine flavor. It may be a main luncheon or dinner dish. Pare:
> 1 medium-sized eggplant

Cut it into dice and cook it (page 180) in boiling water until it is tender. Drain it. You may mash it. Drain, reserving the liquor:
> 1 can minced clams: 7 oz.

Add to the liquor to make 1 cupful:
> Cream

Melt:
> 1 tablespoon butter

Sauté in it:
> 1 tablespoon minced onion

Stir in:
> 1 tablespoon flour

Add the clam liquor and cream gradually, stirring constantly until the sauce boils. Stir in the clams, fold in the eggplant and:
> 1 tablespoon chopped parsley

Place these ingredients in a greased oven-proof dish. The top may be covered with:
> Bread crumbs

dotted with:
> Butter

lightly sprinkled with:
> Paprika

Bake it in a moderate oven 350° for about ½ hour, or until thoroughly heated.

BROILED EGGPLANT AND BAKED TOMATOES

6 Servings

Use:

Tomatoes

cut into six 1 inch slices or 6 small tomatoes. If the whole tomatoes are used, scoop them out.

Chop and combine:

¼ cup onion

¼ cup green pepper or tomato pulp

Place the tomatoes in a greased pan, cover them or fill them with the onions and peppers. Season them with:

2 tablespoons brown sugar

Salt and pepper

Top them with:

6 tablespoons butter

Bake them in a moderate oven 350° for about 30 minutes.

Pare and cut into six ¾ inch slices:

1 eggplant

Spread the slices with:

Soft butter

Sprinkle them lightly with:

Salt

Broil them slowly for 30 minutes. Turn them once. Place the eggplant slices on:

(Rounds of toast)

Cover them with the tomato slices.

EGGPLANT CREOLE

Method I. 4 Servings

This ranks with Vegetable Casserole and Bacon or with Tomatoes Creole. Wonderful combination dishes.

Peel, then cut into dice:

1 medium-sized eggplant

Cook it for 10 minutes in:

Boiling water

Drain it. Place it in a greased baking dish. Melt:

3 tablespoons butter

Add and stir until blended:

3 tablespoons flour

Peel, slice and chop:

3 large tomatoes or 2 cups chopped canned tomatoes

Seed and chop:

1 small green pepper

Peel and chop:

1 small onion

Add the vegetables to the butter mixture with:

1 teaspoon salt

1 tablespoon brown sugar

½ bay leaf

2 cloves

Cook these ingredients for 5 minutes. Pour them over the eggplant. Cover the top with:

Bread crumbs

Dot them lightly with:

Butter or grated cheese

Bake the eggplant in a moderate oven 350° for about 30 minutes.

Method II.

Or, peel, then cut crosswise into ¼ inch slices:

An eggplant

Sauté them very lightly in:

Butter

Or the eggplant slices may be dipped in egg and crumbs, sautéed lightly and built up with tomato purée, cheese and seasoning. Add, if desired:

2 tablespoons grated onion

Sauté in butter in a separate skillet:

4 medium tomatoes cut in halves

Grease a flat oven-proof dish. Cover the bottom with a layer of eggplant and a layer of tomatoes. Season them with:

Salt and pepper

Sprinkle them lightly with:

Grated cheese

(Brown sugar)

Repeat this process until all the vegetables have been used. Bake the dish in a moderate oven 350° for about 1 hour. "Good!"

EGGPLANT WITH SAUSAGES

4 Servings

Slice:

1½ cloves garlic

2 small ripe tomatoes

½ seeded green pepper

2 medium-sized onions

Pare and cut into thick slices:

1 medium-sized eggplant

Place these vegetables in a greased baking dish in alternate layers. Sprinkle them with:

1 teaspoon salt

½ teaspoon pepper

Pour over them:

¼ to ⅓ cup olive oil

Bake the dish in a moderate oven 350° for about 45 minutes, or until the vegetables are tender. Stir in:

(¼ cup sour cream)

You may split:

Wiener or frankfurter sausages

Spread them lightly with:

Mustard or horseradish

Bake them on top of the vegetables.

ARMENIAN EGGPLANT DISH

6 Servings

This is similar to preceding Eggplant Creole, but has the time-saving advantage of being cooked on top of the stove. The old Bostonian who contributed this rule gave it a remarkable name: "And Then the Priest Fainted." She liked it served cold with sour cream. Delectable? Better try it.

Rub a skillet with:

A cut clove garlic

You may leave it in the skillet. Mince, after removing seeds and fibrous portions:

2 green peppers

Skin, if you wish, and dice:

6 ripe tomatoes, or use the contents of 1 can Spanish-style tomato sauce: 16 oz.

Skin and mince:

1 large onion

Pare and cut into 1 inch dice:

2 eggplants

Heat in the skillet:

¼ cup olive oil

Add the eggplant, peppers and onion. Stir and cook them over low heat until they begin to brown. Stir in the tomatoes and:

2 teaspoons salt
¾ teaspoon freshly ground pepper
(1 teaspoon brown sugar)

Cook the vegetables gently until the eggplant is tender. You may bake them au gratin. Either way frankfurters may be heated on top of the vegetables. Served with baked potatoes this is a tempting meal.

MOCK OYSTER CASSEROLE

4 Servings

Prepare:

2 cups cooked Cucumber or Squash, page 285

Drain the vegetables well. Prepare:

1 cup Cream Sauce I, page 428

seasoned with:

1 tablespoon anchovy paste

Place the vegetable in a baking dish. Pour the boiling sauce over it. Cover the top with:

Bread crumbs

Dot it with:

Butter

Sprinkle it, if you like, with:

Grated cheese

Bake the dish in a quick oven 425° until the top is brown or brown it under a broiler.

For other Eggplant Dishes see pages 286-289.

SQUASH CREOLE

6 Servings

Slice thinly, then parboil or steam until partly tender:

Summer or crooked neck squash: about 2½ lbs. ,

If the squash is young, it need not be peeled or seeded.

Follow one of the preceding rules for Eggplant Creole, page 180

ZUCCHINI CREOLE

6 Servings

See the rule on page 180 for:

Eggplant Creole

Substitute for the squash:

6 medium-sized zucchini

Do not boil them. Slice them raw and unpeeled. Place them in the baking dish as directed. Bake them for about 45 minutes.

SQUASH PUDDING WITH BACON OR SAUSAGES

4 Servings

Cook by the rule on page 315 enough:

Summer squash to make 2 cups

Mash it and add:

2 tablespoons butter
1 well-beaten egg
½ cup milk or cream

Season it well with:

Salt and pepper
White or brown sugar
Freshly grated nutmeg

Squash usually calls for a good deal of "doctoring." Place these ingredients in a buttered baking dish. Top the squash with:

Slices bacon or pricked sausages

If preferred, the squash may be closely covered with:

Buttered crumbs or cornflakes with or without grated cheese

Bake it in a quick oven 400° for 15 minutes, or until the bacon is crisp.

For other Squash Dishes see Index.

CREAMED SQUASH

Follow the rule on page 288 for:

Eggplant Sautéed and Creamed

Substitute for the eggplant:

Summer squash

VEGETABLE CASSEROLE WITH BACON
4 Servings

This very good dish served with Spoon Bread, page 423, is a complete and delicious—if somewhat hefty—luncheon.
Cut the tops off:

    2 green peppers

Remove the seeds and veins and slice the peppers. Skin and slice:

    2 large onions
    4 large tomatoes or use about 2
    cups canned drained tomatoes

Grease a baking dish and place in it alternate layers of these vegetables. Season them with:

    1 teaspoon salt
    ½ teaspoon paprika

and sprinkle over the tomatoes:

    2½ teaspoons brown sugar

Cover the dish closely and place it in a hot oven 400° for 30 minutes. Remove the cover and drain the vegetables. Measure the liquid. There should be 1 cupful or more of vegetable stock. Sometimes tomatoes are dry and there is not sufficient stock. Add meat stock or a diluted beef cube or canned bouillon to make at least 1 cupful of liquid in all. To every cupful allow:

    1 tablespoon butter
    2 tablespoons flour

Melt the butter in a saucepan, add the flour and stir it until it is blended. Add the vegetable stock slowly. Cook and stir the sauce until it is smooth and boiling. Taste the sauce to see whether additional seasoning is required. Add the vegetables to the sauce and return them to the baking dish. Cover the top with:

    (Slices of bacon)

Place the dish uncovered in a hot oven 450° until the bacon is crisp, or serve the vegetable dish with:

    Slices of hot Sautéed Bacon,
    page 375

You may substitute ¾ cupful of celery for the green peppers. The proportion of the vegetables may be varied, but in that case use scant seasoning until they are combined and cooked.

TOMATOES CREOLE
4 Servings

This dish is much like the preceding one in ingredients and flavor. It is equally good and is prepared on top of the stove instead of in the oven, which is sometimes an advantage. It makes a delicious quick luncheon dish and a well-rounded one when served with

bacon. Fine for filling peppers or acorn squash.
Melt in a saucepan:

    2 tablespoons butter

Add:

    4 large skinned sliced tomatoes or
    1½ cups canned tomatoes
    1 shredded green pepper
    1 large chopped onion
    2 tablespoons minced celery

Cook the vegetables until they are tender, about 12 minutes. Add:

    ¾ teaspoon salt
    ¼ teaspoon paprika
    2½ teaspoons brown sugar

You may add:

    ¾ teaspoon curry powder

Strain the juice from the vegetables and add to it enough:

    Cream

to make 1½ cupfuls of liquid. Stir in:

    1½ tablespoons flour

Cook and stir the sauce until it is thick and smooth. Combine it with the vegetables and serve them hot on:

    Toast

with:

    Sautéed bacon

CREAMED CANNED TOMATOES
4 Servings

This is similar in flavor to the 2 preceding recipes, but it calls for fewer ingredients and is very quickly made.
Simmer gently for 10 minutes:

    2 cups canned tomatoes
    2 tablespoons minced onion
    ¾ teaspoon salt
    ¼ teaspoon paprika
    2 teaspoons brown sugar
    (½ cup chopped celery)

Combine and boil:

    1 tablespoon flour
    ½ cup cream or milk

If you use the milk, add 2 tablespoonfuls of butter to the tomato mixture. Add the tomato mixture slowly to the cream or milk. Be careful not to reverse the process. Stir constantly to avoid curdling.

TOMATO GRILL WITH CHEESE AND BACON
4 Servings

Prepare:

    4 thick slices toast

They may be buttered. Cut:

    Thick slices tomato

Season them lightly on both sides with:

Salt and pepper
(Brown sugar)
Combine and stir until smooth:
3/4 cup grated cheese
1 teaspoon Worcestershire sauce
1 teaspoon prepared mustard
2 tablespoons soft butter
Place the tomato slices on the toast.
Cover them with the cheese mixture
and:
Strips of bacon
Place the toast on a baking sheet in a
very hot oven 475° until the bacon is
browned and the cheese is melted.

TOMATOES AND OLIVES
3 Servings
If you have any prejudice against tapioca, please dismiss it long enough to
try out this fine dish. Serve it with
ham, scrambled eggs, omelet, etc. Heat
and strain:
1 1/2 cups canned tomatoes
Melt in the top of a double boiler:
1 tablespoon butter
Add and sauté until brown:
1/4 cup minced onion
Add the strained tomato and:
3 tablespoons quick-cooking
tapioca
1/2 teaspoon salt
1/2 teaspoon sugar
1/8 teaspoon paprika
Cook and stir these ingredients in a
double boiler for 7 minutes. Chop
coarsely:
18 stuffed or ripe olives
Grease a baking dish. Fill it with alternate layers of the tomato mixture and
the olives. Sprinkle the layers with:
(1/2 cup grated cheese)
Cover the top with:
Bread crumbs
Dot it with:
1 tablespoon butter
Cook the dish in a moderate oven 350°
for 30 minutes.

TOMATO, CORN AND CHEESE DISH
6 Servings
Seed and chop:
1 green pepper
Skin and chop:
1 small onion
Melt:
2 tablespoons butter
Sauté the vegetables in the butter until
they are brown. Heat in the top of a
double boiler:
1 cup drained canned or fresh
tomatoes

2/3 cup canned corn
Add the sautéed vegetables and:
2 tablespoons quick-cooking
tapioca
1/2 teaspoon salt
1/8 teaspoon pepper
A few grains cayenne
Cook and stir these ingredients over
boiling water for 7 minutes. Stir them
frequently. Stir in until melted:
1 1/3 cups grated cheese
Serve the corn over:
Rusks or rounds of toast

CANNED CORN AND TOMATO PUDDING OR SLUMGULLION
6 to 8 Servings
Combine the contents of:
1 No. 1 can kernel corn
1 No. 1 can tomatoes
1/4 cup chopped onion, celery or
green peppers
3 tablespoons melted butter
Stir in:
1 tablespoon Worcestershire
sauce
3 tablespoons cream
2 beaten eggs
3/4 teaspoon salt
1/2 cup soft bread crumbs
Place these ingredients in a large
greased casserole. Top them with:
Crushed cornflakes or crumbs
(Dabs of butter or grated cheese)
Bake them set in a pan of hot water in
a moderate oven 350° for 25 minutes.

CORN A LA KING
6 Servings
A good filling for peppers.
Place in a double boiler and cook for
20 minutes:
2 1/2 cups corn niblets: 1 No. 2 can
1 shredded green pepper
1 chopped pimiento
You may add:
4 slices sautéed minced bacon
2 tablespoons minced onion that
has been sautéed in the bacon
fat and drained
Combine and beat:
1 egg
1/2 cup milk
1 tablespoon soft butter
3/4 teaspoon salt
1/8 teaspoon paprika
Add these ingredients to the vegetables. Cook and stir them over a low
fire until they are slightly thickened.
Serve them on:
Rounds of hot buttered toast

CANNED CORN AND BACON DISH
4 Servings

Sauté until crisp:

    5 slices bacon

Drain them. Chop them. To the contents of:

    1 No. 1 can whole-kernel corn

add:

    3 tablespoons bacon drippings
    ¼ cup chopped celery or onion

Cook this mixture for 3 minutes. Add:

    ½ cup sour cream or ½ cup cream
    with 1 teaspoon lemon juice
    Salt if needed

Cook it for 3 minutes. Add the bacon.

CORN PUDDING
5 Servings

A good hefty corn dish. For a similar but daintier combination see Corn Soufflé, page 218, and the following Green Corn Pudding.

Drain the contents of:

    1 No. 2 can corn: 2½ cups

Reserve the liquid. Melt:

    2 tablespoons butter

Stir in until blended:

    2 tablespoons flour

Combine and stir in slowly:

    1 cup cream and corn liquid

When the sauce is smooth and boiling stir in the drained corn and:

    1 seeded chopped green pepper
    1 chopped pimiento

When this mixture boils, reduce the heat to a low flame. Beat well:

    2 egg yolks

Pour part of the corn mixture over them. Beat it and return it to the saucepan. Stir and cook it for several minutes to permit the yolks to thicken slightly. Add:

    ¾ teaspoon salt
    ¼ teaspoon paprika

Cool this mixture. You may add:

    ¼ cup crisply cooked, crumbled bacon

or you may cover the bottom of the dish with:

    Minced ham

Place on a platter and whip until stiff:

    2 egg whites
    ⅛ teaspoon salt

Fold them lightly into the corn mixture. Bake the pudding in an ungreased baking dish in a moderate oven 325° for 10 minutes, increase the heat to 350° and bake it until it is firm, about 20 minutes.

GREEN CORN PUDDING
8 Servings

This is a luscious dish but it is a little difficult to give an exact recipe for it because the corn differs with the season. If the corn is watery when scraped, it is sometimes necessary to add a tablespoonful of flour. That is apt to be the case early in the season.

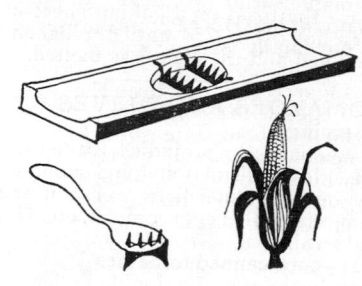

Later it may be necessary to use more cream—up to 1 cupful. When corn is right it looks like thick curdled cream when scraped. There are various scrapers, two of which are shown above.

Scrape:

    18 ears corn

Add:

    1 tablespoon sugar
    ½ cup cream
    Salt and pepper

Place these ingredients in a generously buttered flat baking dish. Dot the top with:

    Butter

Bake the pudding in a moderate oven 325° for about 1 hour.

CORN FRITTERS WITH GREEN CORN

For a short period one of our local newspapers devoted a column to masculine taste in culinary matters. Many men contributed their favorite recipes and the author of the following graciously permitted me to use it when I told him how much it pleased me.

"When I was a child, one of eight, my father frequently promised us a marvelous treat. He, being an amateur horticulturist and arborculturist, would tell us of a fritter tree he was going to plant on the banks of a small lake filled with molasses, maple sirup or honey, to be located in our back yard. When one of us children felt the urge for the most delectable repast, all we had to do was to shake the tree, the fritters would drop into the lake and we could fish them out and eat fritters to our hearts' content.

"Mother was a good cook and a good helpmate, so she developed the fritter that was to grow on and fall from the tree into the lake of molasses or maple sirup or honey, as the case might be. Her recipe as preserved in our family is:

"Grate 12 ears of corn, preferably sugar corn, then beat the yolks of 3 eggs with a very small amount of flour (about a teaspoonful) and a scant teaspoonful of salt; beat the whites thoroughly. Mix the grated corn and yolks, then fold in the beaten whites.

"Fry in butter like pancakes and serve hot. You will want more; so will your guests."

Since writing this, Mr. William N. Matthews tells me that his family has objected strenuously to the addition of the flour, so he asks me to say that the flour "may" be used.

Who could resist the delightful idea of a fritter tree in full fruit? Not I! I'm hungry as I write about it. Wouldn't this be a good thing to read to an invalid to whet his appetite? This makes a great quantity. Please read what is said about corn under Green Corn Pudding, above, then try this unorthodox version. For 4 people use the grated corn of 4 ears, 1½ teaspoonfuls or less of flour, 2 eggs beaten separately and a pinch of salt. Serve the cakes with beef or turkey hash for a meal "out of this world."

CORN FRITTERS WITH GREEN OR CANNED CORN OR CORN OYSTERS

About 16 Fritters
Drain, then mash with a potato masher:

    Green corn or canned cream-
    style corn
There should be 1 cupful. Beat until light and add:

    2 eggs
Add:

    6 tablespoons flour
    ½ teaspoon any baking powder
    ⅛ teaspoon nutmeg

Melt in a small skillet:

    3 tablespoons butter
When it is very hot add the batter by the tablespoonful. Permit the bottom of the cakes to brown, reverse them and brown the other side. Serve them at once with:

    Mushroom Sauce, page 436
    Brown Sauce, page 435, etc.
For best results make the batter immediately before using it, or use a double action baking powder.

CORN AND HAM FRITTERS

6 Servings
Beat until light:

    2 egg yolks
Add and combine with a few swift strokes:

    ½ cup milk
    1⅓ cups sifted flour
    2 teaspoons any baking powder
    ¾ teaspoon salt
    ¼ teaspoon paprika
Fold in:

    2 tablespoons minced parsley or
    onion
    ¼ cup drained cream-style corn
    ¾ cup cooked minced ham
    2 stiffly beaten egg whites
Fry the fritters in deep fat by the rule on page 542.

CREAMED ONIONS AND CHEESE ON TOAST

4 Servings
Here is a homely dish that can be made quite thrilling.
Prepare by the rule on page 294:

    1½ cups Creamed Onions
Prepare:

    4 slices of toast
Sprinkle the slices with:

    Grated cheese
Pour the onions over them. Sprinkle them with:

    Chopped parsley

Scalloped Potatoes and Onions, page 305.

APPLE AND ONION DISH

4 Servings
This, like Vegetable Casserole with Bacon, page 182, is a complete course. It is a complete meal served with a green salad, a beverage and bread. Peel and cut crosswise into ⅛ inch slices:

    6 medium-sized onions
Peel, core and cut in the same way:

    4 medium-sized apples

Sauté, remove from the pan and mince:

    8 slices bacon

Take out 2 tablespoonfuls of the bacon fat. In the remainder toss:

    ½ cup soft bread crumbs

Grease a baking dish. Arrange the onions, apples and bacon in alternate layers. Combine and pour over them:

    ¾ cup hot Stock, page 43, or
    water
    ½ teaspoon salt

Cover the top with the bread crumbs. Cover the dish and bake it in a moderate oven 375° for 30 minutes. Uncover it and cook it 15 minutes longer.

LEFT-OVER VEGETABLES WITH CHEESE

Combine:

    Cooked left-over vegetables

Add to them:

    Raw vegetables: chopped celery,
    shredded green pepper, grated
    or cubed carrots, etc.

The addition of raw vegetables is optional. Moisten the vegetables with:

    Stock, page 43, milk, tomato
    juice or soup

Season them with:

    Salt and pepper

Place them in a shallow greased dish. Sprinkle them with:

    Bread crumbs and grated cheese

Cook them in a moderate oven 375° until they are well heated and the cheese is melted.

LEFT-OVER VEGETABLES WITH HAMBURGER

4 Servings

Combine:

    1 cup cooked sliced potatoes
    ½ cup cooked diced carrots
    ¼ cup cooked or raw celery

    2 tablespoons chopped onion
    ⅛ teaspoon paprika
    ½ lb. ground beef: 1 cup
    1½ tablespoons butter
    1 cup canned tomatoes
    ½ teaspoon salt

Place these ingredients in a greased baking dish. Bake them in a moderate oven 375° for 30 minutes. Other vegetables may be substituted for the carrots, and raw carrots grated may be substituted for the celery.

BACON CORN-MEAL WAFFLES

6 Waffles

This dish is a "find" for the efficiency housekeeper. It requires no scouring of pots or pans. An electric waffle iron may be used. If there is an excess of grease, wipe off the iron with absorbent paper.

Beat slightly:

    2 eggs

Add:

    1¾ cups milk

Sift:

    1 cup cake flour or ⅞ cup all-
    purpose flour
    4 teaspoons tartrate or phosphate
    baking powder or 2½ teaspoons
    combination type (see Baking
    Powder, page 501)
    1 tablespoon sugar
    ½ teaspoon salt

Add:

    1 cup yellow water-ground corn
    meal

Combine these ingredients with the eggs and milk. Add:

    5 tablespoons melted bacon fat
    or other shortening

Cut into halves or quarters:

    6 to 12 slices bacon

Heat a waffle iron. Add the batter. Place a piece of bacon on each section. Cook the waffles until they are crisp.

Cheese Dishes

A question I am called upon to answer frequently is: "Why do my cheese dishes curdle or become stringy?" The answer is: Cheese must be melted over low heat. It must be stirred constantly. It must be removed from the fire at once when it is melted. You may use a double boiler. High heat and overcooking may be responsible for your failures or the cheese may not be sufficiently aged. It should be about six months old for best results.

Brillat-Savarin, the noted French epicure, said that a dinner without cheese is like a one-eyed woman. Housewives, who have many luncheons to plan, like cheese in the middle of the day, but most men prefer it as a midnight snack—the pause that refleshes. Whenever it is served, it is overwhelmingly popular and as a Lenten ingredient it works overtime.

WELSH RAREBIT WITH BEER

6 to 8 Servings
Grate or grind:
   1 lb. yellow cheese
Melt in a double boiler:
   1 tablespoon butter
Stir in:
   1 cup beer
When the beer is warm stir in the cheese. Stir constantly with a fork until the cheese is melted. Beat slightly and add:
   1 whole egg
Season the rarebit with:
   1 teaspoon Worcestershire sauce
   1 teaspoon salt
   ½ teaspoon paprika
   A few grains red pepper
   ¼ teaspoon curry powder
   (¼ teaspoon mustard)
Serve the rarebit at once on:
   Crackers or hot toast

WELSH RAREBIT WITH MILK

4 Servings
Good Welsh rarebit can be bought canned, ready to be heated and served. Melt in a pan over hot water:
   1 tablespoon butter
Stir in and melt:
   1½ cups diced cheese
Add:
   ⅓ teaspoon salt
   ¼ teaspoon dry mustard
   A few grains cayenne
   1 teaspoon Worcestershire sauce
Stir in slowly:
   ½ to ¾ cup cream or top milk
When the mixture is hot remove the pan from the heat. Beat in:
   1 egg yolk
Serve the rarebit at once over:
   Hot toasted crackers or bread

WELSH RAREBIT OVER GRILLED TOMATOES

4 Servings
Cut into ½ inch slices:
   2 large tomatoes
Season them with:
   Salt and pepper
   Brown sugar
Dot them lightly on both sides with:
   Butter
Place them in a pan in a moderate oven 375°. When they are nearly done, broil them on both sides under moderate heat.
Prepare by the preceding rule:
   Welsh Rarebit
Pour it over the tomatoes and serve them at once. Raw tomatoes may be substituted for grilled tomatoes.

QUICK GRILLED TOMATOES AND ONIONS WITH WELSH RAREBIT

6 Servings
Drain the contents of:
   1 No. 1½ can onions
If they are large, cut them into pieces. Fresh onions, peeled and sliced ¼ inch thick, may be substituted. Place them side by side in a skillet. Simmer them covered in a little milk or water for about 10 minutes. Drain them well and proceed. Cut into ¼ inch slices:
   4 large firm tomatoes
Dip the onions and tomatoes in:
   Melted butter
Sprinkle them on both sides with:
   Salt and pepper
   Brown sugar
Dip the slices in:
   Bread crumbs or crushed cornflakes
Broil them on a greased fireproof plate under slow heat. Cook them, turning them once, for about 8 minutes. Prepare as directed on the package or can:
   Welsh Rarebit
or make your own, see this page. Place on a platter:
   Toasted bread
Pour the rarebit over it. Garnish the platter with the grilled tomatoes, the onions and:
   Parsley

TOMATO SOUP, CHEESE AND ONION RAREBIT

4 Servings
Combine and bring to the boiling point the contents of:
   1 can tomato soup: 10½ oz.
   ½ cup water
Add and cook slowly until tender:
   ¾ cup thinly sliced onions
Add and stir until melted:
   ¾ lb. or more thinly sliced cheese
Remove the pan from the fire. Combine, beat and add:
   2 egg yolks
   1 teaspoon Worcestershire sauce
   1 teaspoon dry mustard
   1 teaspoon salt
   ¼ teaspoon paprika
   ⅛ teaspoon white pepper
Stir these ingredients over low heat for 1 or 2 minutes to permit the yolks to thicken slightly. Whip until stiff:
   2 egg whites
   ⅛ teaspoon salt
Fold them into the hot cheese mixture. Serve the rarebit on:
   Hot toast or crackers

TOMATO RAREBIT WITH HARD-COOKED EGGS
4 Servings
Chill, peel and slice:
  4 hard-cooked eggs
Melt in a saucepan:
  2 tablespoons butter
Add and sauté for 2 minutes:
  2 tablespoons grated onion
Add the contents of:
  1 can tomato soup: 10½ oz.
When these ingredients are hot reduce the heat and stir in:
  1½ cups grated cheese
When the cheese is melted pour part of the sauce over:
  1 beaten egg
Return the liquid to the pan. Stir in:
  1 teaspoon Worcestershire sauce
  Salt and paprika
  A few grains cayenne
Stir constantly. Permit the egg to thicken slightly, but do not let the rarebit boil. Prepare:
  4 rounds hot buttered toast or 4 rusks
Cover them with the hard-cooked eggs and pour the rarebit over them. Serve it at once.

RINK TUM DIDDY RAREBIT
4 Servings
Stir and melt over low heat:
  ½ lb. grated cheese: 2 cups
Add, stir and heat:
  1 can condensed tomato soup: 10½ oz.
  3 tablespoons water
  ½ teaspoon salt
  A few grains cayenne
Serve the rarebit on:
  Toast or toasted crackers

OYSTER RAREBIT
4 Servings
Cook in their liquor until plump:
  2 cups oysters: 1 pint
Drain them, keep them hot and reserve the liquor. Cook in a double boiler and stir until smooth:
  2 tablespoons butter
  ¼ lb. diced cheese
  ½ teaspoon salt
  A few grains cayenne
Add and stir until thick:
  The oyster liquor
If there is not enough oyster liquor to make a good sauce, add rich milk until it is the right consistency. Add:
  2 beaten eggs
Add the oysters and:

  Salt
  1 teaspoon Worcestershire sauce
  or 2 teaspoons sherry
Serve it on:
  Toast or rusks
Garnish it with a sprinkling of:
  Paprika
  Sprigs of parsley

FLUFFY TOMATO RAREBIT
8 Servings
This may be kept hot over hot, not boiling, water for an hour or more. Combine in the top of a boiler the contents of:
  1 can condensed tomato soup: 10½ oz.
  1 lb. grated sharp cheese
Cook and stir these ingredients over hot water until the cheese is melted. Combine, beat, then stir in:
  2 egg yolks
  1½ teaspoons Worcestershire sauce
  1 teaspoon dry mustard
Whip until stiff:
  2 egg whites
  ⅛ teaspoon salt
Fold them into the rarebit. Serve it on:
  Hot toast or crackers

WOODCHUCK
4 Servings
Cook until very soft:
  2 cups tomatoes
Beat them with a wire whisk into a purée, or heat:
  1½ cups tomato purée
Stir in over low heat:
  ¼ lb. diced American cheese: 1 cup
Cook and stir these ingredients until the cheese is melted. Add:
  1 beaten egg
Cook and stir the mixture until the egg is slightly thickened. Add:
  Salt and pepper
  Brown sugar
  A few grains cayenne
Serve it at once over:
  Hot toast or hot toasted crackers

CHEESE CUSTARD PIE
4 Servings
In Switzerland we had a vile-tempered cook named Marguerite. Her one idea, after being generally disagreeable, was to earn enough to own a small chalet on some high peak where she could cater to mountain climbers. While she

was certainly not born with a silver spoon in her mouth—although it was large enough to accommodate several—I am convinced she arrived with a cooking spoon in her hand. If she has attained her ideal, many a climber will feel it worth while to scale a perilous peak to reach her kitchen. The following Cheese Custard Pie was always served in solitary state. Its flavor varied with Marguerite's moods and her supply of cheese. It was never twice the same, as she had no written rule, but I have endeavored to make one like hers, for it would be a pity to relegate so good a dish to inaccessible roosts.

Follow the rule on page 561 for making pie crust. Use ½ the ingredients. Roll the dough and line an 8 inch pan or baking dish with it. Bake the crust for 20 minutes in a hot oven 450°. Remove it from the oven, cool it slightly and fill it with the following cheese custard. Scald:

1¾ cups top milk or cream
Reduce the heat and add:

1 cup grated cheese
Stir until the cheese is melted. Add:

½ teaspoon salt
¼ teaspoon paprika
½ teaspoon grated onion
A few grains cayenne

Remove the mixture from the stove and beat in one at a time:

3 eggs
Fill the pie crust and bake it in a slow oven 325° until the custard is firm, about 45 minutes. The size of the pan is not important, but the custard is best when it is about 1½ inches deep.

QUICHE
4 to 6 Servings
Rules similar to the above Cheese Custard Pie are to be found in most foreign cookbooks under the name of Quiche. The dish is attributed to several countries—Belgium, Lorraine, etc. A custard is called for, usually made with:

2 cups scalded cream
4 eggs
1 cup grated Italian or Swiss cheese
½ teaspoon salt
Freshly ground black pepper
A few grains cayenne

Beat with a fork until blended. There are numerous variations of the above. A pie shell made of rich pastry is buttered lightly. Partially cooked bacon is broken or cut up and sprinkled over the bottom. Sometimes the cheese is not added to the custard but sprinkled over the bacon and then covered with the custard. The pie is baked in a hot oven 450° for 12 minutes. The heat is reduced to a slow oven 300° and the pie is baked until the custard is set, about 35 minutes longer. To test use the method given under Cup Custard, page 710. Serve it hot or cold.

PUFFED CHEESE WITH MUSHROOMS ON TOAST
4 Servings
Melt in a saucepan:

1 tablespoon butter
Add and sauté until tender (page 292):

½ cup finely sliced mushrooms
1 teaspoon grated onion
Combine:

2 unbeaten egg yolks
½ lb. grated Swiss cheese: 2 cups
¾ teaspoon salt
¼ teaspoon pepper
A few grains cayenne

Stir in the mushroom and onion mixture. Beat until stiff but not dry:

2 egg whites
Fold them into the mixture. Toast on one side:

6 slices bread
Place them toasted side down on a cookie sheet. Spread the untoasted sides lightly with:

Butter
Heap the cheese mixture on the bread. Bake the slices in a moderate oven 375° until they are firm to the touch and well puffed.

CHEESE TURNOVERS
Sauté until crisp, then mince:

3 slices bacon
Whip until stiff:

1 cup heavy cream
Fold in the bacon and:

1 cup grated cheese
⅛ teaspoon dry mustard
¼ teaspoon salt
A few grains cayenne
⅛ teaspoon curry
1 well-beaten egg

Prepare by the rule on page 561:

Pie Dough
Roll it until it is very thin, cut it into squares or rounds. Place a teaspoonful of filling in the center of each. Moisten the edges lightly with water and fold over the dough. Bake the turnovers in a hot oven 450° for about 20 minutes. Serve them very hot.

CHEESE, BREAD AND EGG DISH
4 Servings
This simple dish goes well with a green salad. Cut ½ inch thick:

 7 slices bread
Spread the slices lightly with:
 Butter
Cut 2 of the slices twice across on the bias, making 8 triangular pieces. Cut the remaining bread into cubes. There should be about 4 cupfuls of diced buttered bread. Place layers of diced bread in a buttered baking dish. Sprinkle the layers with:

 1 cup grated cheese
Combine and beat:
 2 eggs
 1 cup milk
 1 teaspoon salt
 ¼ teaspoon paprika
 A few grains cayenne
 ½ teaspoon dry mustard
Pour these ingredients over the bread and cheese. Place the triangles of bread upright around the edge to form a crown. Bake the dish in a moderate oven 350° for about 25 minutes. Serve it at once.
A fine addition to this dish is ½ pound cooked or canned shrimp.

PUFFED CHEESE CASSEROLE
4 Servings
This is not unlike the preceding rule in ingredients, but different in appearance. Both are grand fillers-in or main dishes. You will be torn between them. Trim the crusts from:

 8 slices bread
Cut them in half on the bias. Place ½ of them in the bottom of a greased 8 inch oven-proof dish, spiral fashion, not letting them overlap. They should resemble a pinwheel. Cut into slices ¼ inch thick:

 6 oz. processed cheese: cheddar, American, Swiss, etc.
Cover the bread layer with the cheese slices, not letting them overlap. Cover the cheese with the rest of the bread, again in spiral fashion. Beat lightly:

 3 eggs
Add and beat well:
 ¼ teaspoon salt
 ⅛ teaspoon paprika
 A few grains cayenne
 2 cups rich milk
You may add:
 1 teaspoon grated onion or
 1 tablespoon parsley or chives or
 ¼ teaspoon mustard

Pour this mixture over the bread. Permit the dish to stand for 1 hour. Bake it in a moderate oven 350° for about 1 hour, or until well browned. Serve it hot.

SCALLOPED BREAD WITH SAUTÉED ONIONS AND CHEESE
6 Servings
An inexpensive luncheon or supper dish. Good balanced by a green vegetable or salad.
Cut the crusts from:

 Stale bread
Cube the bread. There should be 6 cupfuls. Place it in a lightly greased 2 quart oven-proof dish.
Melt:

 4 tablespoons bacon or other fat
Sauté in it gently, stirring constantly:
 ¼ cup chopped onions
Add:
 3 cups milk
 ¼ cup chopped parsley
 Salt as needed
 Freshly ground black pepper
Pour this over the bread. Bake it in a moderate oven 375° for about 15 minutes. Break up the crusts. Combine them with:

 1 tablespoon melted butter
 ¼ cup grated cheese
 (A few grains cayenne)
Spread this over the top of the dish. Bake it until the top is light brown, about 5 minutes.

BAKED ONIONS WITH CHEESE ON TOAST
4 Servings
Peel, slice crosswise and boil or poach in milk until nearly tender:

 6 large white onions
Drain them well. Place in a baking dish:

 4 slices buttered toast
Arrange the onions on the toast. Sprinkle them with:

 ½ cup grated American cheese
Beat well:
 1 egg
 1 cup milk
 ½ teaspoon salt
 ⅛ teaspoon paprika
Pour this mixture over the onions. Dot the top with:

 1 tablespoon butter
Bake the dish in a moderate oven 350° for about 40 minutes. Serve it with:

 Crisp bacon
 Parsley

Or, make a simplified spread of grated cheese, Worcestershire sauce and seasonings. Place the parboiled onions on the toast, spread them with the paste, broil them until the cheese is melted.

CHEESE FONDUE WITH BREAD CRUMBS OR CHEESE MONKEY
5 Servings
Prepare:
> 1½ cups soft bread crumbs
> 1⅓ cups grated cheese or ⅓ lb. melted cheese

If you wish to use melted cheese, cut it into small slivers and dissolve it in the hot milk. Use very low heat and stir it constantly. Heat but do not boil:
> 1 cup milk

Add:
> 2 beaten egg yolks
> ½ teaspoon dry mustard
> (⅛ teaspoon curry)

Add the cheese and the bread. When this is cool, whip until stiff but not dry, then fold in:
> 2 egg whites
> ½ teaspoon salt

Bake the fondue in a buttered 9 inch baking dish set in a pan of hot water in a moderate oven 350° for about ½ hour. It may be cooked in a double boiler. In that case do not trouble to separate the eggs.

CHEESE AND RICE FONDUE
4 Servings
Heat:
> 1 cup cooked rice

in:
> 2 cups milk

Add:
> 4 well-beaten eggs
> 1 cup grated cheese
> ½ teaspoon salt
> A few grains cayenne
> (A few drops Worcestershire or Tabasco sauce)

Stir these ingredients over very low heat until the cheese is melted. Serve the fondue over:
> Hot toast, snap beans, etc.

Spread the toast with:
> (Anchovy paste)

CHEESE FONDUE
Method I. 6 Servings
A fine blend. Serve it as a midnight snack with beer or cocoa.
Cut or break into small pieces:

> ½ lb. American cheese
> ½ lb. pimiento cheese
> ¼ lb. Roquefort cheese

Add:
> 3 tablespoons butter
> 1 teaspoon Worcestershire sauce

Cook and stir these ingredients over hot water. Work them to a smooth paste and whip them until they are fluffy. Add, if the mixture is too stiff to spread, a small amount of:
> Cream or mayonnaise

Serve the fondue at once on:
> Rusks, rye bread or Melba Toast, page 539, etc.

Method II.
This Swiss dish is unusually good. It is appropriate for after-the-theater parties or for suppers. It will serve about 10 people but it usually meets with such favor that it is better to count on only 8 portions if nothing else is being served.
II. Cut into dice:
> 2 lbs. brick cheese

Combine it with:
> ¾ cup butter

Stir these ingredients over low heat until the cheese is melted. Add slowly:
> ¾ cup warm milk

Stir the fondue with a wire whisk until it is smooth. Remove it from the fire and beat in one at a time:
> 2 eggs

Add:
> ½ teaspoon salt

Serve the fondue at once over:
> Hot toast or toasted crackers

Method III. 4 Servings
This is the aristocratic version of an excellent regional dish. The above is the peasants' way of making it.
Cut into small blocks:
> 1 lb. Swiss cheese

Cover it with:
> ¾ cup dry white wine

Permit this to stand for 4 hours. Stir the mixture over very low heat or in a double boiler over, not in, hot water until the cheese melts. Add:
> 2 tablespoons brandy

Serve the fondue very hot over:
> Toasted bread

or serve it with hot:
> French bread

CHEESE SPREAD OR SAUCE
About 1½ Cupfuls
It is a joy to know about this fine mixture, for it is easily made and may be

kept in the refrigerator for days. It makes excellent toasted cheese sandwiches. Use it as a spread or a sauce. For sauce, thin it as you need it with a little milk in a double boiler. Cut into small pieces and stir over very low heat, or in a double boiler, until melted:

    ½ lb. cheese

I find a soft cheese or a processed one preferable for this recipe. Add:

    1 cup evaporated milk
    ¾ teaspoon salt
    ¾ teaspoon dry mustard
    ¼ teaspoon curry powder
    ¼ teaspoon dried herb

Remove from the fire and stir in:

    1 beaten egg

Stir and cook the cheese mixture very slowly until the egg thickens slightly. Remove it from the fire. Pour it into a dish. Cool it slowly, beat it as it cools, to keep a crust from forming, cover and chill it.

TOMATO CHEESE SPREAD
About 1¾ Cupfuls

Place in a saucepan the contents of:

    1 can tomato soup: 10½ oz.

Add:

    1 small skinned grated onion
    1 small seeded grated green
      pepper

Boil and stir these ingredients for 2 minutes. Reduce the heat and stir in until dissolved:

    ½ lb. American cheese cut into
      cubes

Add:

    ¾ teaspoon salt
    A few grains cayenne

Place the mixture in an oiled mold. When it is chilled invert it onto a plate. Serve the cheese with:

    Hot toasted crackers

Cream Cheese Balls on Water Cress, page 489; Roquefort Cheese Balls, page 489.
Remember the good cheese spreads, ideal dunking dishes, on page 39.

COTTAGE CHEESE

Permit milk to sour in a covered jar placed in a warm, not hot, place until the whey separates from the curd. Drain the curd in a bag made of crash toweling until it is firm to the touch. Place it on ice for several hours. Remove it from the bag, put it in a bowl. Work it with a wire whisk until it is smooth and creamy. Beat into it until it is a good consistency:

    Cream

Serve the cheese with:

    Chopped chives

Cottage cheese is good combined with:

    Chopped ripe olives

or served in:

    Tomato Cases, page 458

or served very cold with:

    Stewed cherries, fresh peaches,
    cantaloupe, green grapes, etc.

SOYBEAN CHEESE

Allow Soybean Milk, page 817, to sour. When it is thick cut it in pieces and bring it slowly to a boil in a saucepan. Allow it to drain through a cloth as for cottage cheese, see above. Season with:

    Salt

Add:

    Cinnamon or chives and
    caraway

COOKED CHEESE OR KOCH KAESE

Put in a moderately warm place:

    4 cups rather dry cottage cheese

Stir it daily. It will ferment and in 3 or 4 days the cheese will be waxy throughout and ready to cook. Melt in a double boiler:

    2 tablespoons butter

Add the cheese and:

    ½ teaspoon salt
    (⅛ teaspoon paprika)

Cook and stir these ingredients over low heat. When they are hot add:

    1 cup milk
    2 teaspoons caraway seed

Cook and stir the cheese for about 10 minutes. Pour it into a bowl. Chill it thoroughly. Serve it with:

    Rye bread
    Beer

TO MAKE SOUR CREAM

The mention of sour cream may bring from the uninitiated a disdainful sniff and a vision of a yellowed mass of decomposed solids swimming on a bluish whey. But the seasoned cook responds to the term with delight, for she sees the culinary possibilities of this smooth semiplastic and rolls her tongue in anticipation of its promise. Many uses for sour cream are suggested in this book and if your dairy does not carry it, try making it yourself.
Place in a quart glass jar:

    1 cup 20% pasteurized cream

The cream may be heavier and the heavier the better for the end product.

Add:

5 teaspoons buttermilk

The commercial type which is 1% acid and has carefully controlled bacteria is easier to use than the less acid and less controlled home product. Cover the jar and shake these ingredients vigorously. Stir in:

1 cup 20% pasteurized cream

Cover the jar and allow this mixture to stand at about 80° for 24 hours. The sour cream may then be used at once although storage under refrigeration for another 24 hours makes a finer product.

Food on Skewers

If you have no skewers, invest in a dozen or so, about 5 or 6 inches long and of uniform length. The metal ones are ornamental but the wooden ones are easier to handle. The unadorned pegs the butcher uses will do as well as any if they are thin.

Allow about 2 skewerfuls of food for the average person. Place cooked or uncooked food on the skewers, alternating ingredients to make them look attractive. Brush the food, unless surrounded by bacon, with melted butter or drippings. If the food is to be baked, stick the skewers into a large raw potato.

Bake the food, if cooked, in a hot oven 450° until it is hot; if uncooked, in a moderate oven 350° until it is done. Cooked food on skewers may be heated in a hot, very lightly greased skillet.

If you wish, you may roll filled skewers that are to be baked or sautéed in cracker crumbs or cornflakes. If you do, give them about 10 minutes to dry before cooking them. The crumbs stick better.

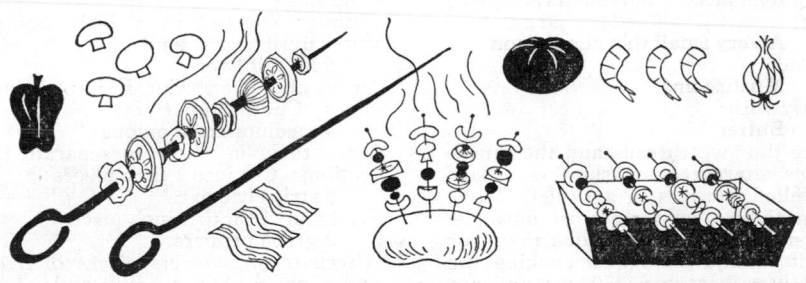

If uncooked food is used, you may broil it 3 inches from the heating unit under moderate heat until done. Leave the oven door partly open. Cooked food is broiled under quick heat. In either case, baste the food several times with melted fat while cooking and turn it frequently to cook evenly. Some cooks like to place the filled skewers over a bread pan for easier handling while broiling or baking.

Suggestions for Food on Skewers

Raw oysters with blocks of bacon and slices of raw onion or firm tomatoes. You may substitute cocktail sausages for the bacon. Or take one strip of bacon to a skewer and wrap it around as you string on the oysters, etc.

Chicken livers or pieces of calf liver or kidney, bacon and celery.

Blocks of cooked meat, bur gherkins and pieces of raw onion or firm tomato.

Diced eggplant or squash, pieces of onion, firm tomatoes and bacon.

Shrimp or lobster, pieces of cucumber or stuffed olives.

Pieces of fresh fish, pickles and celery with or without bacon.

Blocks of cheese, pieces of sausage and pickled onions.

Hamburger balls—ground beef seasoned and shaped, you may add chopped onion—bacon, pieces of unpeeled apple and celery.

Hamburger balls, mushrooms and slices of onion.

Scallops, bacon and onion.

Add to any of the above ½ bay leaf for flavor.

OYSTERS AND SWEETBREADS ON SKEWERS
Surround:
  Large raw oysters
with:
  Strips of bacon
Secure the bacon with toothpicks. Place the oysters on small skewers alternating them with pieces of:
  Boiled Sweetbreads, page 376
Place the filled skewers on a broiler and cook them under moderate heat until the bacon is crisp. Turn them frequently and serve them at once.

SWEETBREADS AND MUSHROOMS ON SKEWERS
Cook:
  Sweetbreads, page 376
Skin them and break them or cut them into 1 inch pieces. Surround each piece with:
  A very small thin slice bacon
Spread:
  Mushrooms
lightly with:
  Butter
Place the sweetbreads and the mushrooms alternately on skewers. Place the filled skewers in a skillet. Move them about over a slow fire until the bacon begins to melt. Cook them for about 3 minutes. Finish cooking the food in a hot oven 450° or under a broiler until the bacon is crisp.

MOCK CHICKEN DRUMSTICKS OR CITY CHICKEN
6 Servings
Cut into 1 x 1½ inch pieces:
  1 lb. veal steak
  1 lb. pork steak
Sprinkle them with:
  Salt and pepper
Arrange the veal and pork cubes alternately on 6 skewers. Press the pieces close together into the shape of a drumstick. Roll the meat in:
  Seasoned flour
Beat:
  1 egg
  2 tablespoons water
Dip the sticks in the diluted egg, then roll them in:

Bread crumbs
Melt in a skillet:
  ¼ cup shortening
Add:
  1 tablespoon grated onion
Brown the meat well. Cover the bottom of the skillet with:
  Boiling Stock, page 43, or water
Put a lid on the skillet and cook the meat over very hot heat until it is tender or, if preferred, the skillet may be covered and placed in a slow oven 325° until the meat is tender. Thicken the gravy with:
  Flour—2 tablespoons flour to 1 cup liquid

LIVER, PEPPER, ONIONS AND OLIVES ON SKEWERS
4 Servings
Simmer covered in a little boiling water until nearly tender:
  ¾ lb. calf liver
Drain the liver. Cut it into 1 inch cubes. Cut into quarters:
  4 medium-sized onions
Place them in water to separate the sections. Cut into 1 inch pieces:
  6 strips bacon
Seed and cut into 1 inch pieces:
  2 green peppers
Alternate on skewers pieces of liver, onion, green pepper, bacon and:
  Stuffed olives
Heat in a skillet over low heat a few bacon scraps or butter. Add the filled skewers. Move them about and cook them for 3 minutes. Place them in a hot oven 450° or under a broiler until the bacon is crisp and the liver is tender.

BROILED LAMB WITH ONIONS ON SKEWERS
4 Servings
Cut into 2 inch squares:
  1 lb. lamb shoulder
Make a dressing of:
  1 tablespoon lemon juice
  2 tablespoons olive oil
  ½ teaspoon salt
  ⅛ teaspoon pepper
Marinate the meat in the dressing for

3 hours. Turn it several times. Place the meat on skewers alternately with:
Slices pineapple
Slices Bermuda onion
Broil it under a flame for about ½ hour. Turn it frequently. Baste it while cooking with mayonnaise or oil.

VEAL SLICES AND PORK SAUSAGES ON SKEWERS
Sauté lightly:
Paper-thin slices veal

Boil or sauté until nearly done:
Tiny pork sausages
Wrap the veal around the sausages. Place three rolls on a skewer alternately with:
½ bay leaf
2 slices onion or 2 small parboiled onions
Roll the skewers in:
Seasoned flour
Cook them as directed under Food on Skewers, page 193.

Croquettes

RULE FOR CROQUETTES
About 12 Croquettes
While croquettes are frequently made with new ingredients—minced cooked chicken, mushrooms, sweetbreads, lobster, oysters, etc.—they are also a good means for utilizing left-over food.
Use about 1 cupful of heavy sauce to 2 cupfuls of ground or minced solids—meat or fish and vegetables. Eggs and bread crumbs may be added.
The following is a good general rule but it need not be followed too closely as a great deal of leeway may be allowed, provided that there is enough thickening to hold the ingredients together.
Prepare:
Cream Sauce III, page 428
When the sauce is smooth and boiling stir in:
2 cups minced solid food: cooked meat and vegetables
1 tablespoon chopped onion
2 tablespoons chopped parsley
When these ingredients are boiling, remove the pan from the heat and beat in:
1 or 2 eggs
Cook and stir them over low heat for 1 minute longer to permit the eggs to thicken slightly. Season the food well with a choice of:
Salt, pepper or paprika
Freshly grated nutmeg or celery salt
2 teaspoons lemon juice
1 teaspoon Worcestershire sauce
½ teaspoon Tabasco sauce
2 teaspoons cooking sherry
½ teaspoon dried herbs
½ teaspoon curry powder
Spread this mixture in a dish. When it is cool shape it as you wish. Roll the croquettes in:
2 cups sifted seasoned bread crumbs

then in:
1 egg diluted with 2 tablespoons water or milk
and again in the bread crumbs. Be careful to cover the entire croquette with the egg mixture to prevent the fat from penetrating. Dry the croquettes for about 2 hours. This will permit the crumbs to adhere to them. Place 4 or 5 croquettes in a frying basket at a time, no more, and fry them in deep fat at 390° (page 542) until they are a delicate brown. Drain them on paper placed in a colander. To reheat, place them in a hot oven 400°. Serve them with:
Onion Sauce, page 432,
Mushroom Sauce, page 436,
Tomato Sauce, page 433, or
Left-over gravy, etc.
In Vienna we were served delicious croquettes. The bread crumbs and egg bath had been omitted. Instead the croquettes were dipped in thin batter, then fried. Use Fritter Batter, page 543.

CHICKEN OR VEAL CROQUETTES
Follow the preceding Rule for Croquettes. The cream sauce may be made with part chicken or veal stock and cream. For the 2 cupfuls of solid food, use chicken or veal, or a combination of both. Substitute part Sautéed Mushrooms, page 292, minced celery or minced nut meats. Serve the croquettes with:
Mushroom Sauce, page 436, or
Poulette Sauce, page 432

SWEETBREAD CROQUETTES
Sweetbreads are delicate and light and it is well to combine them with chicken or mushrooms to give them body. Follow the Rule for Croquettes. Substi-

tute for the solid food part Boiled Sweetbreads, page 376, and part Sautéed Mushrooms, page 292. Boiled brains may be used in croquettes. They are also good combined with mushrooms.

SALMON CROQUETTES

Follow the Rule for Croquettes on page 195. Substitute 2 cupfuls flaked salmon for the solid food, or use:
- 1 lb. drained canned salmon
- 2 cups mashed potatoes
- 1½ teaspoons salt or anchovy paste
- ⅛ teaspoon pepper
- 1 beaten egg
- 1 tablespoon minced parsley
- 1 teaspoon lemon juice or Worcestershire sauce

See the Index for Crab Cakes, Fish Cakes, etc.

LOBSTER CROQUETTES

Follow the Rule for Croquettes on page 195. Substitute 2 cupfuls chopped lobster meat for the solid food.

HAM AND CORN CROQUETTES

4 Servings
Combine and mix well:
- 1¼ cups cream-style corn
- 2 tablespoons chopped green pepper
- 1 cup ground or minced ham
- 1 beaten egg
- ½ cup dry bread crumbs

Chill these ingredients. Shape them into 8 croquettes. Dip them into:
- Dry seasoned bread crumbs

then into:
- 1 egg diluted with 2 tablespoons water

and again in crumbs. Fry them in deep fat (page 542) heated to 390°.
Serve the croquettes with:
- Tomato Sauce, page 433

OYSTER AND CHICKEN CROQUETTES

6 Servings
These whole oysters in chicken croquette mixture are very good.
Heat in their liquor until they are plump:
- 1 pint oysters

Drain them. Reserve the liquor. Dry them. Melt:
- 2 tablespoons butter

Sauté slowly in the butter until yellow:
- (3 tablespoons minced onion)

Stir in until blended:
- ¼ cup flour

Stir in slowly:
- 1 cup oyster liquor and Chicken Stock, page 45

Season the sauce with:
- Salt
- A few grains cayenne
- A few grains nutmeg

Stir in:
- ½ cup cooked minced chicken

Reduce the heat. Whip until stiff:
- ½ cup heavy cream

Fold in:
- 3 egg yolks
- 1 tablespoon minced parsley

Fold these ingredients into the chicken mixture. Cook and stir them over a low flame until they thicken. Spread the mixture on a platter. Cool it. Dip the oysters one at a time in the chicken mixture until they are well coated. Roll them in:
- Sifted bread crumbs

Fry them in deep fat heated to 390° (page 542). Drain them on absorbent paper. Serve them garnished with:
- Lemon slices
- Parsley or water cress

FILLED CROQUETTES

The above rule is a good example of a filled croquette. Use any croquette mixture. Place in the center of each croquette:
- A sautéed mushroom
- A piece cooked chicken liver
- A pimiento olive
- A well-drained seasoned or marinated oyster

Cook them as directed in the Rule for Croquettes, page 195.

RICE CROQUETTES

About 8 Croquettes
Place in a double boiler:
- 2 cups cooked rice

Soften it with:
- 2 or 3 tablespoons hot milk

Add:
- 2 tablespoons butter
- Salt and nutmeg
- 1 or 2 beaten eggs
- (Pepper and 1½ tablespoons chopped parsley)
- 1 or 2 beaten eggs

Cook and stir the rice until the egg thickens. Cool the mixture. For shaping, breading and frying the croquettes follow the rule on page 195.

A little grated lemon rind and dabs of tart jelly may be placed in the center of the croquettes, in which case omit the pepper and parsley. If the croquettes are to be used as dessert, they may be lightly sweetened by adding 3 tablespoonfuls of sugar flavored with 1 teaspoonful of vanilla.

CHEESE AND RICE CROQUETTES
About 10 Croquettes
Combine:
    2 cups Boiled Rice, page 103
    ½ cup grated cheese
    ½ cup Cream Sauce III, page 428
    1 tablespoon chopped parsley
    ½ teaspoon paprika
        A few grains cayenne
        Salt
Shape these ingredients into cones or croquettes. Chill them. Fry them by the rule on page 542.

NUT AND RICE CROQUETTES
About 12 Croquettes
Combine:
    1 cup chopped walnuts
    ½ cup toasted white bread crumbs
    2 cups Boiled Rice, page 103
    1 teaspoon sugar
    ½ teaspoon salt
    1 beaten egg
    1 teaspoon grated lemon rind or
    (1 teaspoon vanilla)
For shaping, breading and frying the croquettes follow the rule on page 542.
Serve them with:
    Tart jelly

Baked Rice and Fish Balls, page 117.

VEGETABLE CROQUETTES
This may be a left-over dish.
Follow the rule on page 195 for:
    Croquettes
For the 2 cupfuls of solid food use:
    2 cups cooked vegetables
Part of these may be mashed potatoes.

MUSHROOM CROQUETTES
About 6 Croquettes
Prepare by the rule on page 428:
    ½ cup Cream Sauce III
Remove it from the fire. Add:
    ½ teaspoon Worcestershire sauce
    ⅛ teaspoon curry powder
    1 slightly beaten egg
    2 tablespoons cracker crumbs
    1 cup chopped mushrooms
    ½ teaspoon salt
    ¼ teaspoon paprika

Shape the mixture. Chill the croquettes. Fry them as directed on page 542.

MACARONI OR SPAGHETTI CROQUETTES
About 10 Croquettes
Combine:
    2 cups cooked macaroni or spaghetti
    ½ cup Cream Sauce III, page 428
    12 sliced stuffed olives
    ½ cup chopped nut meats
    1 tablespoon chopped parsley or chives
    ½ cup Sautéed Mushrooms, page 292, or minced chicken or ham
    Salt and paprika
Shape these ingredients into croquettes. Chill them. Fry them by the Rule for Croquettes on page 542.
Serve them with:
    Horseradish Sauce, page 439

EGG CROQUETTES
6 Servings
Chop until fine:
    7 hard-cooked eggs
Melt and cook until brown:
    1½ tablespoons butter
Stir in:
    2 tablespoons flour
Stir in slowly:
    1 cup cream
When smooth, add the chopped eggs and:
    1 tablespoon finely chopped parsley or other fresh herb
    ½ teaspoon salt
    Pepper or paprika
Permit these ingredients to cool. Shape them into 6 croquettes. Roll them in:
    Dry bread crumbs
Permit them to dry for 1 hour. Fry the croquettes in deep fat by the rule on page 542. Serve them on a platter. Pour over them:
    Creamed Sweetbreads, page 376
Garnish the platter with:
    Crisp bacon
    Parsley

SWISS CHEESE CROQUETTES
Melt:
    4 tablespoons butter
Stir in:
    5 tablespoons flour
Stir in gradually until thickened:
    1 cup milk
    ⅓ cup cream

Stir in over low heat:
 ½ lb. grated Swiss cheese
Cool slightly. Stir in:
 3 beaten egg yolks
 ¾ teaspoon salt
 ⅛ teaspoon paprika
Pour the custard into a well-greased pan about 6 x 9 inches. Chill well. When ready to use immerse pan for a moment in hot water, reverse it and turn the custard onto a flat surface. Cut it into shapes. Roll them in:
 Beaten egg
then in:
 Cracker crumbs or meal
Fry the croquettes in hot fat heated to 390° (page 542) for 1 to 1½ minutes, or until golden brown. Turn out on absorbent paper to drain. Serve with:
 Hot Tomato Sauce, page 433

CHEESE CROQUETTES
About 6 Croquettes
Cook over a low flame:
 ½ cup Cream Sauce III, page 428
Add and stir until melted:
 1½ cups grated cheese
Season the sauce with:
 A few grains cayenne
Cool it. Beat until stiff:
 2 egg whites
Fold them into the mixture. Shape these ingredients lightly into croquettes. Dip them in:
 Sifted bread crumbs
Fry them in deep fat 390° (page 542) until they are light brown. These croquettes are not dipped in egg. A slight depression may be made in the croquettes. When fried, place in the depression:
 A cube tart jelly or a stuffed olive

POTATO CROQUETTES FILLED WITH GREEN PEAS
About 12 Croquettes
Cook:
 2 lbs. Green Peas, page 298, or 2 cups canned peas

Drain them. Peel and boil until tender:
 4 large potatoes
Mash them. There should be about 2 cupfuls. Beat into them:
 1 tablespoon butter
 2 tablespoons cream
 2 egg yolks
Season them with:
 1 teaspoon salt
 10 drops onion juice
 ¼ teaspoon paprika
 ½ teaspoon nutmeg
 1 tablespoon minced parsley
Beat the potatoes until they are smooth. Form them into 2½ inch balls. Scoop out the centers. Place in each one a tablespoonful of peas. Fill the hole with a little of the potato. Re-shape the balls. Dip them in:
 1 egg diluted with 2 tablespoons water
then in:
 Sifted bread crumbs
Fry them in deep fat. Heat the fat to 390°, until a cube of bread dropped into the fat will brown in 2 minutes. Drain the croquettes on absorbent paper. Serve them with:
 Broiled Lamb Chops, page 362, or with roast

POTATO PUFFS
4 Servings
Combine:
 ½ cup sifted flour
 1 teaspoon any baking powder
 ¼ teaspoon salt
Add and mix:
 1 cup mashed potatoes
The potatoes should be soft. If they are not, add a little hot milk or water and beat. Add:
 1 slightly beaten egg
 1 teaspoon minced parsley
Drop by spoonfuls into hot fat (page 542). Fry to a golden brown. Drain on absorbent paper.

Vegetable Fritters, page 324.

Tomato, Pepper and Other Cases for Hot Food

RULE FOR MAKING AND BAKING TOMATO CASES
Cut large hollows in unpeeled tomatoes, salt them and invert them to drain for 15 minutes. Fill them with any desired combination of cooked food. Cover the tops with bread crumbs and dot them with butter or sprinkle them

with cheese. Place the tomato cases in a pan with enough water to keep them from scorching, and bake them in a moderate oven 350° for 10 or 15 minutes, or brown the tops under a broiler. If they are too soft to hold their shape, bake them in well-greased muffin tins. Filled tomatoes are good on toast served with sauce: cheese, mushroom, etc., or gravy. Tomato cases may be stuffed with any of the fillings given for pepper cases and vice versa.

TOMATOES FILLED WITH LEFT-OVER FOOD
Follow the preceding rule for making tomato cases.
Prepare cooked meat or fish, sweetbreads or calf brains, nut meats, raw chopped celery, grated carrots or cooked vegetables. Combine these ingredients with well-seasoned cream sauce, putting the solids into the boiling sauce to prevent it from becoming watery. Use ½ as much sauce as there are solids. Or moisten the food with cream, stock, butter or gravy and add bread crumbs, if thickening is required, to hold the ingredients together.
To fill and bake the tomato cases follow the preceding rule.

TOMATOES FILLED WITH MASHED POTATOES
6 Servings
These are very attractive-looking placed around a baked fish or a roast. Prepare by the rule on page 198:
    6 medium-sized tomato cases
Place the tomatoes in a pan with enough water to keep them from scorching. Bake them for 10 minutes in a moderate oven 350°. Prepare:
    Hot Mashed Potatoes, page 103, using 3 medium-sized potatoes
Add:
    ½ cup broken nut meats
Fill the tomato cases. Garnish the tops with:
    Whole nut meats
    A sprig parsley or sliced stuffed olives
Return the tomatoes to the oven and bake them for 5 minutes, or until they are done.

TOMATOES FILLED WITH BREAD CRUMBS
6 Servings
Prepare by the rule on page 198:
    6 medium-sized tomato cases
Season the cases with:
    3 tablespoons brown sugar
Chop the pulp taken from the tomatoes. Combine it with an equal amount of:
    Soft bread crumbs
Sauté lightly:

    2 tablespoons chopped onion
    2 tablespoons chopped pepper
in:
    2 tablespoons butter
Season the filling with:
    Salt and pepper
Fill the tomato cases. Bake them by the Rule for Tomato Cases, page 198. A good variation of the above is the more sophisticated filling of:
    2 tablespoons chopped onions
browned in:
    2 tablespoons olive oil or drippings
added to:
    1 tablespoon minced parsley
    4 chopped anchovies
    1 cup soft bread crumbs
and the removed tomato pulp. Taste before seasoning as anchovies are salty.

TOMATOES FILLED WITH CORN
4 Servings
Prepare by the rule on page 198:
    4 tomato cases
Sauté, then mince:
    4 slices bacon
Combine:
    1 cup cooked drained corn
    1 chopped pimiento
    ½ chopped green pepper
    2 tablespoons chopped celery
    ½ cup bread crumbs
    2 tablespoons corn liquor or cream
    ½ teaspoon salt
    ¼ teaspoon paprika
    ½ teaspoon sugar if the corn is green
Add the minced bacon. Fill the tomato cases. Sprinkle the tops with:
    ½ cup bread crumbs
Dot them with:
    1 tablespoon butter
or sprinkle them with:
    Grated cheese
Bake them by the Rule for Tomato Cases, page 198.

TOMATOES FILLED WITH CREAMED HAM
Prepare by the rule on page 198:
    Tomato cases
Prepare by the rule on pages 148, 149:
    Creamed Ham or Creamed Deviled Ham
Fill the cases with the ham. Bake them by the Rule for Tomato Cases, page 198.

TOMATOES FILLED WITH SHRIMP
6 Servings
Prepare by the rule on page 198:
    6 tomato cases
Chop the tomato pulp removed from the centers. Melt:
    1 tablespoon butter
Sauté in it for 2 minutes:
    2 tablespoons finely chopped onion
Add the tomato pulp and:
    1 cup chopped cooked or canned shrimp
Stir in:
    1 tablespoon chopped parsley
    3 tablespoons crushed cracker crumbs
    Paprika and salt if needed
Fill the tomatoes with this mixture. Dust the tops with:
    Cracker crumbs
Dot them with:
    Butter
or sprinkle them with:
    Grated cheese
Bake them by the Rule for Tomato Cases, page 198.

TOMATOES FILLED WITH CRAB MEAT IN CHEESE SAUCE
6 Servings
Prepare by the rule on page 198:
    6 tomato cases
Melt over low heat:
    1½ tablespoons butter
Add and cook for 3 minutes:
    3 tablespoons minced green pepper
    3 tablespoons minced onion
Stir in until blended:
    1½ tablespoons flour
Stir in slowly:
    1½ cups milk
When the sauce is thick and boiling add:
    1½ cups crab meat
    ⅓ teaspoon salt
    A few grains red pepper
    2 teaspoons Worcestershire sauce
    1 cup grated American cheese
Cook and stir these ingredients until the cheese is melted. Fill the tomato cases with this mixture. Bake them by the Rule for Tomato Cases, page 198.

TOMATOES FILLED WITH STUFFED OLIVES
6 Servings
Prepare by the rule on page 198:
    6 tomato cases
Place in the center of each tomato:

    1½ teaspoons brown sugar
Chop the removed tomato pulp and add to it:
    ½ cup sliced stuffed olives
    ¾ cup cracker or bread crumbs
    2 tablespoons melted butter
    ¼ teaspoon paprika
    ½ teaspoon salt
Fill the tomato cases. Cover the tops with:
    ½ cup bread crumbs
Dot them with:
    1 tablespoon butter
Bake them by the Rule for Tomato Cases, page 198.

TOMATOES FILLED WITH EGGS
6 Servings
Prepare by the rule on page 198:
    6 tomato cases
Season the centers with:
    Salt and paprika
    Sugar
Place the tomato cases in a baking dish, cover the bottom with enough water to keep them from scorching. Bake them in a moderate oven 350° for 10 minutes. Remove them from the oven and cool them slightly. Break and drop into the hollows:
    6 eggs
Season them with:
    Salt and pepper
Cover the tops with:
    Bread crumbs
Dot them with:
    Butter
or sprinkle them with:
    Grated cheese
Bake the tomato cases in a moderate oven 350° until the eggs are firm but not hard. Serve them on:
    Rounds hot buttered toast
Cover them with the following sauce. Chop the pulp removed from the tomatoes. Melt in a saucepan:
    4 tablespoons butter
Add and stir until blended:
    4 tablespoons flour
Stir in slowly:
    2 cups milk
When the sauce is smooth and boiling add the chopped pulp and:
    2 tablespoons chopped green pepper
    2 tablespoons finely chopped onion
    1 teaspoon Worcestershire sauce
    ¾ teaspoon paprika
    ½ teaspoon sugar
    ⅛ teaspoon celery salt

Add more seasoning, if required, as the sauce should be "peppy."

TOMATOES FILLED WITH ONIONS
6 Servings
Prepare by the rule on page 198:
 6 tomato cases
Melt:
 ¼ cup bacon drippings
Add and sauté until brown:
 ½ cup finely chopped onion
Chop the pulp taken from the tomatoes and combine it with the onions. Add:
 1½ teaspoons brown sugar
 ½ teaspoon salt
 1 tablespoon celery seed
Cook these ingredients for 20 minutes. If the filling is too moist, it may be thickened with bread crumbs. If it is too dry, it may be moistened with cream or milk. Fill the tomato cases. Cover the tops with:
 Bread crumbs
Dot them with:
 Butter
or sprinkle them with:
 Grated cheese
Bake them by the Rule for Tomato Cases, page 198.

TOMATOES FILLED WITH RICE OR WILD RICE
6 Servings
Prepare by the rule on page 198:
 6 tomato cases
Season them lightly with:
 Salt and brown sugar
Cook by the rule on page 109:
 ½ cup rice or wild rice
Rinse it. Fill the tomato cases. Cover the tops with:
 Bread crumbs
Dot them with:
 Butter
Sprinkle them with:
 Cheese
Bake them by the Rule for Tomato Cases, page 198.

TOMATOES FILLED WITH PINEAPPLE
4 Servings
Prepare by the rule on page 198:
 4 medium-sized tomato cases
Sprinkle each hollow with:
 1 teaspoon brown sugar
Place in each hollow:
 1 tablespoon chili sauce
Drain the contents of:
 1 can crushed pineapple: 9 oz.

Fill the tomatoes with the pineapple. Sprinkle the tops with:
 Bread crumbs
 Salt
Dot them generously with:
 Butter
Bake them by the Rule for Tomato Cases, page 198.

TOMATOES FILLED WITH GREEN PEAS
6 Servings
A very decorative dish—a fine garnish for a meat or fish platter.
Prepare by the rule on page 198:
 6 tomato cases
Bake them as directed until they are nearly tender. Boil by the rule on page 298:
 1½ lbs. green peas
Drain them. Moisten the peas with:
 2 tablespoons melted butter or
 ½ cup cream sauce
Fill the tomato cases with the peas. Bake them by the Rule for Tomato Cases, page 198. Garnish them with small:
 Sprigs parsley

TOMATOES FILLED WITH CREAMED MUSHROOMS AND SWEETBREADS
Prepare by the rule on page 198:
 6 tomato cases
Sauté by the rule on page 292:
 ¼ lb. mushrooms
Cook by the rule on page 376:
 ¼ lb. sweetbreads
The mushroom and sweetbread proportions may be varied. Cook by the rule on page 428:
 Cream sauce—½ as much as there are mushrooms and sweetbreads combined
Add the other ingredients to the boiling cream sauce. Thicken them with:
 (¼ cup bread crumbs)
Fill the tomato cases. Cover the tops with:
 Bread crumbs
Dot them with:
 Butter
or sprinkle them with:
 Cheese
Bake them by the Rule for Tomato Cases, page 198.

TOMATOES FILLED WITH CREAMED MUSHROOMS
Substitute for sweetbreads in the preceding rule:
 Mushrooms: ¾ lb. in all

TOMATOES FILLED WITH CHEESE SAUCE OR RAREBIT

Follow one of the rules beginning on page 198 for:

Filled tomato cases

Choose a filling that combines well with cheese—onion, corn, rice, olives, shrimp, etc. Serve the tomatoes on:

Toast

with:

Cheese Sauce, page 430, or Rarebit, page 187

RULE FOR MAKING AND BAKING PEPPER CASES

Gash side or cut stem end from green peppers. Remove seeds and veins.

I.

Rub the outside of raw peppers with butter or drippings. Stuff and place them, without parboiling, in a moderate oven 350°. Bake until tender.

II.

Drop the peppers into rapidly boiling salted water and cook them uncovered until they are nearly tender, about 10 minutes. Drain them well. Fill them with any desired combination of cooked food. Cover the tops with bread crumbs, dot with butter or sprinkle with cheese.

Place the peppers in a pan with enough water to keep them from scorching and bake them in a moderate oven 350° for 10 or 15 minutes.

If they are too soft to hold their shape, bake them in well-greased muffin tins. You may stuff pepper cases with the fillings given for tomato cases and vice versa.

Peppers filled with Creamed Celery, page 281, Mashed Potatoes, page 302, or Creamed Spinach, page 313, etc., are recommended.

PEPPERS FILLED WITH LEFT-OVER FOOD

Follow the preceding Rule for Making and Baking Pepper Cases. For fillings see Tomato Cases, page 199.

To fill and bake the peppers follow the preceding rule.

PEPPERS FILLED WITH CREAMED ASPARAGUS

4 Servings

Cook until tender (page 202):

4 pepper cases

Cut into halves and drain:

1 cup canned asparagus tips

Melt in a saucepan:

1½ tablespoons butter

Stir in until blended:

1½ tablespoons flour

Stir in slowly:

¼ cup asparagus liquor
¼ cup cream

When the sauce is smooth and boiling add the asparagus and:

¼ cup blanched shredded almonds or other nut meats

Season with:

¼ teaspoon salt
⅛ teaspoon paprika
(⅛ teaspoon nutmeg)

Fill the pepper cases. Cover the tops with:

Bread crumbs

Dot them with:

Butter

or sprinkle them with:

Cheese

Brown the tops under a broiler.

PEPPERS FILLED WITH CREAMED OYSTERS

4 Servings

Cook until tender (page 202):

4 pepper cases

Prepare:

½ pint Creamed Oysters, page 111, using ½ the amount

Add:

2 tablespoons chopped parsley

Fill the pepper cases. Cover the tops with:

Bread crumbs

Dot them with:

Butter

or sprinkle them with:

Cheese

Brown the tops under a broiler.

PEPPERS FILLED WITH PEAS

4 Servings

Cook until nearly tender (page 202):

4 pepper cases

Fill them with:

2 cups creamed green peas
2 tablespoons chopped parsley

Do not bake them.

PEPPERS FILLED WITH MACARONI

Cook until nearly tender (page 202):

6 pepper cases

Prepare by the rule on page 91:

½ cup creamettes or macaroni: 1 cup when cooked

Drain them. Add:

¾ cup grated cheese

¾ cup tomato juice and ½ cup
   bread crumbs or ¾ cup condensed tomato soup
¼ teaspoon salt
   A few grains cayenne
⅛ teaspoon paprika
½ teaspoon sugar
   (1 teaspoon Worcestershire sauce)
Fill the pepper cases. Sprinkle the tops
with:
   ½ cup bread crumbs
Dot them with:
   1 tablespoon butter
or sprinkle them with:
   Grated cheese
Bake them by the Rule for Pepper
Cases, page 202.

PEPPERS FILLED WITH RICE
4 Servings
Cook until nearly tender (page 202):
   4 pepper cases
Cook by the rule on page 103:
   ⅓ cup rice or ⅓ cup Wild Rice,
      page 109
Or use:
   1 cup cooked rice
Drain the rice, rinse it and add:
   ½ cup stock, cream or tomato pulp
   Salt and pepper
   A few grains cayenne
   ½ teaspoon curry powder
   ½ cup or more grated cheese
Fill the pepper cases. Cover the tops
with:
   Bread crumbs
Dot them with:
   Butter
or sprinkle them with:
   Cheese
Bake them by the Rule for Pepper
Cases, page 202.

PEPPERS FILLED WITH
CHEESE RICE
Follow the preceding rule for:
   Peppers Filled with Rice
Substitute for the rice mixture:
   Cheese Rice I, page 104
Brown the tops under a broiler.

PEPPERS FILLED WITH
MEAT AND RICE
4 Servings
Cook until nearly tender (page 202):
   4 pepper cases
Melt:
   2 tablespoons drippings or butter
Sauté in it:
   3 tablespoons minced onions
Add, stir and sauté until light colored:
   ½ lb. ground beef

Add:
   1 cup cooked rice
   ½ teaspoon salt
   ⅛ teaspoon paprika
   ¼ teaspoon celery seed, curry
      powder, dried herb or
      Worcestershire sauce
Fill the pepper cases. Bake them by
the Rule for Pepper Cases, page 202.

*Tomatoes Creole, page 182; Lima Beans
with Cheese, page 178; Corn à la King,
page 183.*
These make fine pepper fillings. Serve
the last 2 with tomato sauce.

ZUCCHINI CASES OR
VEGETABLE MARROW
Choose short, round zucchini. Scrub
but do not peel them. This vegetable
cooks very quickly when young. It is
impossible to give exact proportions
for the filling, as zucchini vary in size.
Besides, it is not particularly import-
ant. Cut the stems from:
   Zucchini
Drop the vegetables into:
   Boiling water
Cook them until they are partly done,
2 or 3 minutes. Drain them. Keep the
rounded ends for the cases. To use
center sections, see page 323. Hollow
the ends. Chop the pulp. Melt:
   Butter
Sauté in it:
   Chopped onions
Add the pulp and cook it for 1 minute
longer. Add:
   Bread crumbs, corn-meal mush,
      cooked meat or fish
Moisten these ingredients with:
   Cream, butter, cream sauce,
      stock or gravy
Season them with:
   Salt and pepper
Fill the zucchini cases. Cover the tops
with:
   Bread crumbs
Dot them with:
   Butter
or sprinkle them with:
   Grated cheese
Place them in a pan with a very little
water and bake them in a moderate
oven 375° until they are tender.

RULE FOR MAKING AND
BAKING ONION CASES
Medium-sized onions may be hollowed
and used for this purpose or large
onions may be cut crosswise or lengthwise into halves.

Peel, then steam until nearly tender (page 295):

Large or medium-sized onions

Drain them, cut a slice from the top and hollow them, leaving ¾ inch shell, or cut them into halves and hollow them. Chop the pulp taken from the centers. Combine it with:

Bread crumbs or cooked rice, chopped cooked meat, fish, baked beans, mushrooms and bacon, or with deviled ham or nut meats

Moisten these ingredients with:

Cream sauce, melted butter, stock, cream or gravy

Season them with:

Salt and pepper
Chopped parsley

Fill the onion cases. Cover the tops with:

Bread crumbs

Dot them with:

Butter

Sprinkle them with:

Grated cheese

Place them in a pan with enough water to keep them from scorching and bake them in a moderate oven 375° until they are tender. If they are too soft to hold their shape well, bake them in well-greased muffin tins.

Spanish onions require long cooking. Allow at least 1 hour in all for small ones and longer for large ones. If raw food is used in the filling, shorten the time for boiling and prolong the time for baking the onions.

ONIONS FILLED WITH MUSHROOMS
4 Servings

Good enough for a company main dish. Cook by the preceding rule:

6 medium-sized onion cases

Hollow them. This is easily done with curved scissors. Chop the centers. Sauté:

1½ cups chopped mushrooms

in:

2 tablespoons butter

If mushrooms are not available, substitute canned fish, meat scraps, stuffed olives, etc. Sprinkle over them:

1 tablespoon flour

Stir in:

⅓ cup rich milk

Season the sauce with:

Salt and pepper
Sherry

Fill the onion cases with the mushroom mixture. Melt:

1½ tablespoons butter

Stir in until blended:

1½ tablespoons flour

Stir in slowly:

¾ cup rich milk or part stock and milk

When the sauce is boiling add the chopped onion centers and what is left of the mushrooms, if any. Season the sauce well with:

Salt and pepper
(Worcestershire sauce or sherry)

Pour it into a shallow baking dish. Place the filled onions in the sauce. The tops may be sprinkled with:

Bread crumbs

Dot them with:

Butter

or sprinkle them with:

Cheese

Bake the onions in a hot oven 400° until they are well heated. Garnish them with:

Parsley

They may be served on:

Toast

ONIONS FILLED WITH MASHED POTATOES
4 Servings

Peel:

4 medium-sized Spanish onions

Cut a slice from the top of each onion. Parboil the onions for 10 minutes in a quantity of:

Boiling water

Drain them. Place them for 1 minute in:

Cold water

Drain them well. Scoop out the centers of the onions, leaving a shell ½ inch thick. Reserve the onion pulp. Place the onions in a pan with:

½ cup Soup Stock, page 43

Bake them in a moderate oven 250° for 1 hour, or until they are tender. Prepare by the rule on page 302:

1½ cups Mashed Potatoes: 3 medium-sized potatoes

Fill the onion shells with the mashed potatoes. Chop the onion pulp. Sauté it until tender and brown in:

3 tablespoons butter or bacon fat

Sprinkle the tops of the onions with the sautéed onions. Put them back in the oven until they are thoroughly heated.

BAKED ONIONS AND CHEESE
4 Servings

Cook until nearly tender (page 294):

12 medium-sized onions

Drain them. Cut out the centers. Chop the pulp. Add to it:
> 1 cup grated cheese
> Salt and pepper
> (Chopped parsley)

Fill the cases. Dot them with:
> Butter

Place them in a baking dish in enough stock or water to keep them from scorching. Cover them and bake them in a moderate oven 375° until they are nearly tender. Remove the cover and bake them 5 minutes longer.

For other Onion Dishes see pages 294 to 297.

ONIONS FILLED WITH PEAS
Cook until nearly tender (page 203):
> Onion cases

Fill them with cooked:
> Creamed or buttered green peas

The pulp removed from the centers of the onions may be sautéed in bacon grease or butter and placed on top, either before or after the onions are baked. Sprinkle the tops with:
> Bread crumbs

Dot them with:
> Butter

or sprinkle them with:
> Grated cheese

Follow the same rule for baking them.

ONIONS FILLED WITH SAUERKRAUT
4 Servings
Cook until nearly tender (page 203):
> 6 onion cases

Combine the chopped pulp and:
> 1 cup drained sauerkraut
> ½ cup soft bread crumbs
> ½ cup minced cooked fish or meat
> ¼ teaspoon salt
> ⅛ teaspoon paprika
> (¼ teaspoon caraway.or celery seed)

Heap the mixture into the onion cases. Sprinkle the tops generously with:
> Buttered crumbs

Bake the onions in a pan with a very little water in a hot oven 400° until they are well heated.

RULE FOR EGGPLANT CASES
The following recipes are good examples of how to use an eggplant as a case for food. These cases may be filled with any desired combination of food, to which the cooked eggplant pulp may be added.

EGGPLANT FILLED WITH LEFT-OVER FOOD
4 Servings
Cut the top from:
> A medium-sized eggplant

Cut just under and following the lines of the leafy green cap. This then forms an attractive lid.

Scoop out the pulp, leaving a thin shell. Then, drop the pulp into a small quantity of boiling water and cook it until it is tender. Drain it well and mash it. Combine it with:
> 1 cup chopped cooked meat
> Salt and pepper
> ¼ cup bread crumbs
> (¼ cup chopped nut meats)
> (¼ cup tomato purée)

Fill the shell. Cover the top with:
> Bread crumbs

Dot it with:
> Butter

or sprinkle it with:
> Cheese

Place the eggplant in a hot oven 400° until the filling is well heated.

Eggplant Soufflé and other Eggplant Dishes, pages 286 to 288.

EGGPLANT FILLED WITH RICE AND SHRIMP
Follow the above rule. Substitute for the meat filling:
> 1½ cups cooked rice
> ½ lb. cooked cleaned shrimp
> ¼ minced clove garlic
> 1 teaspoon grated onion
> 2 tablespoons chopped green pepper
> ¼ cup cream
> Salt and pepper

EGGPLANT FILLED WITH MUSHROOMS AND HAM
4 Servings
Cut a slice from:

A medium-sized eggplant

Scoop out the pulp leaving a shell ¼ inch thick. Combine the coarsely chopped pulp with:

1 cup raw sliced mushrooms
½ cup chopped onion

Melt:

4 tablespoons butter

Stir and sauté these ingredients in the butter for 10 minutes. Add:

1 cup minced cooked ham
¼ teaspoon salt
⅛ teaspoon pepper

Fill the eggplant shell. If this is prepared in advance, cover it with waxed paper and keep it in the refrigerator until ready to bake it. Bake the eggplant in a hot oven 400° until it is well heated and browned, about 15 minutes. Garnish it with:

Strips pimiento
Parsley

EGGPLANT SLICES

These make a fine foundation for other food.

Prepare by the rule on page 287:

Steamed and Sautéed Eggplant Slices

or by the rule on page 286:

Baked or Broiled Eggplant Slices

Place them on a hot platter. Cover them with one of the following:

Hot asparagus tips, peas, onions, etc.; buttered or creamed shrimp, tuna, etc.; hash or a combination of left-over meat and vegetables

Garnish the slices with:

Parsley

Try this good combination for an individual serving:

A slice cooked eggplant
A slice raw tomato
A light sprinkling of brown sugar
A light sprinkling salt
A few dots butter

Broil the slices until the tops begin to brown. They may then be covered with:

(A poached egg)

Serve them with:

Cheese Sauce, page 430

CAULIFLOWER FILLED WITH MUSHROOMS OR SHRIMP AND PEAS
6 Servings

This makes a good main dish for a luncheon.

Boil by the rule on page 280:

A large cauliflower

Place it flower side down. Remove the stalk and chop it. Add it to:

1 cup Sautéed Mushrooms, page 292
1 cup cooked peas

These vegetables may be moistened with cream or a little of the sauce. Cooked shrimp may be substituted. Fill the cauliflower. Cover it with:

Buttered crumbs

Sprinkle it with:

Grated cheese

Place it under a broiler or in a hot oven 425° until the cheese is melted. Serve it with:

2 cups rich Cream Sauce, page 428

This may be made with part cream and part water in which the vegetables were cooked. Add to it:

1 tablespoon lemon juice
(½ teaspoon dried tarragon)

ACORN SQUASH CASES

The rule for preparing and baking acorn squash is on page 315. These good and attractively shaped vegetables are ideal for individual service. Choose them of uniform size, either small or medium-sized, to suit your purpose. Bake them filled with sausage or creamed ham or bake or boil them first and fill them afterward with almost any kind of creamed or cooked food suitable for a light meal.

ACORN SQUASH BAKED WITH SAUSAGE, SAUSAGE MEAT OR CREAMED HAM

Prepare uncooked:

Acorn Squash Cases, see above

Omit the butter on the inside and the seasoning. Fill them with:

Little link sausages, sausage meat or Creamed Ham, page 148

Bake them in a moderate oven 375° for about 1 hour. Pour out the fat that collects in the hollows.

ACORN SQUASH FILLED WITH CREAMED FOOD

Prepare cooked:

Acorn Squash Cases, see above

Fill them with:

Creamed oysters, chicken, chipped beef, crab, fish, mushrooms, etc., or with hash or hash and vegetables

Garnish the tops with:

Parsley

Baked Acorn Squash with Spinach or other Vegetables, page 315.

ACORN SQUASH FILLED WITH APPLES

Pare, quarter and core:

Apples

Place them in a covered baking dish in a moderate oven 325°. Cook them until tender. Cut into halves crosswise, remove seeds, bake or boil until nearly tender:

Acorn Squash, page 206

Fill the squash with apples. Place over each top:

1 teaspoon or more chutney or pickle vinegar sweetened with corn sirup

Or, do away with all this bother and substitute canned applesauce. Sprinkle the tops with cinnamon.

SUMMER SQUASH CASES

Method I.

Pare:

Small even summer squash

Allow 1 squash to a person. Remove the seeds. This may be done before or after cooking. It will hollow the squash sufficiently to make an acceptable case. The squash may be steamed or boiled. The former is preferable as squash runs so largely to water. See page 315 for directions for cooking summer squash. Cook them until they are nearly tender. Drain the cases well. Place in each one:

1 tablespoon soft butter

Fill them with a:

Soufflé mixture: Cheese, Spinach, Onion, Chicken, Ham, Fish, etc., pages 217-225

Place them on a buttered pan. Bake them by the Rule for Soufflé, page 217.

Method II.

Cook the squash until they are tender. Keep them hot. Fill them with hot:

Creamed fish, meat, mushrooms, tomatoes, hash, onions, etc.

Garnish them with:

Parsley

These cases may be served au gratin.

TURNIP CUPS

Pare, then boil (page 321):

Medium-sized turnips

Hollow them. Fill them. Place them in a pan with a few tablespoonfuls of water. Bake the cups in a moderate oven 350° until tender and the tops are slightly browned.

FILLED TURNIP CUPS

Prepare by the preceding rule:

8 medium-sized turnip cups

Chop the pulp removed from the centers. Melt:

1 tablespoon butter

Sauté in it for 3 minutes:

1 tablespoon grated onions

Combine the pulp with the onions. Season it with:

Salt and pepper

Thicken it slightly with:

Cracker crumbs or bread crumbs

Fill the turnip cups with this mixture. Place them in a greased baking dish. Combine and pour around them:

½ cup milk
⅛ teaspoon salt

Bake them as directed.

TURNIPS FILLED WITH LEFT-OVER FOOD

Cook and prepare:

Turnip Cups, see this page

Fill them with any good combination of:

Left-over meat, vegetables and turnip pulp

Thicken them slightly with:

Bread crumbs

Moisten them with:

Gravy, Stock, page 43, or cream

Season them well. Fill the turnip cases. Sprinkle the tops with:

Bread crumbs

Dot them with:

Butter

or sprinkle them with:

Cheese

Place the turnips in a baking dish and proceed as directed for Turnip Cups.

TURNIP CUPS FILLED WITH PEAS

Cook and prepare, see this page:

8 medium-sized turnip cups

Combine:

2 cups cooked green peas
2 tablespoons parsley
2 tablespoons butter or ½ cup cream sauce

Fill the cups. Bake them as directed.

RULE FOR CUCUMBER CASES FILLED WITH FOOD

3 Servings

Pare:

3 medium-sized cucumbers

Cut them lengthwise into halves. Remove the seeds and, if the cucumbers are very thick, cut out some of the inner shell, leaving a case about ½ inch thick. Cucumbers may be parboiled in simmering stock for 5 minutes. Chop the pulp if there is any to chop. Melt in a skillet:

2 tablespoons butter

Add and sauté in it for 2 minutes:

2 tablespoons chopped onion

Add the chopped pulp and:

¼ cup bread crumbs
½ cup chopped cooked meat, bacon or fish, creamed deviled ham or nut meats

Moisten these ingredients with:

Melted butter, cream, Stock, page 43, cream sauce or gravy

Season them with:

Salt and pepper

Fill the cucumber cases. Cover the tops with:

Bread crumbs

Dot them with:

Butter

or sprinkle them with:

Grated cheese

Place them in a pan with enough water or stock to keep them from scorching. Bake them in a moderate oven 375° until tender, about ½ hour. Serve them with or without:

Cream Sauce I, page 428, made with sour cream or Tomato Sauce, page 433, or Hollandaise Sauce, page 430

BAKED AVOCADOS FILLED WITH CREAMED FOOD

Cut into halves:

Avocados

Place in each ½:

1 tablespoon Garlic Vinegar, page 494

Permit them to stand for ½ hour. Empty the shells. Fill them with creamed well-seasoned:

Crab, lobster, shrimp, chicken, ham, etc.

Use ¼ as much sauce as crab, etc. Place them on waxed or buttered paper. Cover the tops with:

Grated cheese or buttered crumbs or cornflakes

Bake the pears in a moderate oven 375° for about 15 minutes, until they are well heated and the tops are brown. The recipe for Lobster Sandwiches, page 20, is fine if you are using a lobster filling.

PIMIENTOS FILLED WITH FISH OR MEAT

Highly decorative. Fine for creamed turkey.

Line individual molds with:

Pimientos whole or in strips

Prepare in Cream Sauce II, page 428:

Chopped cooked fish or meat

Use ½ as much cream sauce as fish or meat. Season these ingredients with:

Worcestershire sauce, lemon juice or sherry

Fill the molds and place them in a pan of hot water on top of the stove. Partly cover and steam them gently until they are well heated, about 10 minutes. Serve them hot with:

Chestnut Sauce II, page 433

to which add:

2 tablespoons chopped parsley

Or chill them, unmold them and serve them cold with:

Mayonnaise

BAKED APPLES FILLED WITH SAUSAGE MEAT

6 Servings

A 3 star winter dish. Wash:

6 large tart apples

Cut a slice from the tops. Scoop out the cores and pulp, leaving shells ¾ inch thick. Cut the pulp from the cores. Chop the pulp. Combine it with:

1 cup well-seasoned sausage meat

Sprinkle the shells with:

1 teaspoon salt
(2 tablespoons brown sugar)

Fill them heaping full with the sausage mixture. Bake them in a moderate oven 375° until they are tender. Serve them with:

Potatoes or rice

or place them around a mound of:

Boiled Noodles, page 97

Sausage with Apples, page 150.

APPLES FILLED WITH LINK SAUSAGE

6 Servings

Wash and core:

6 large tart apples

Cut ¼ of the peel from the top of each apple. Fill the apples with:

6 link sausages

Sprinkle the apples with:

Salt and brown sugar

Place them in a pan. Cover the bottom of the pan well with:

Water and a little lemon juice

Bake the apples until they are tender in a moderate oven 375°. Baste them frequently.

POTATOES FILLED WITH LINK SAUSAGES

Wash:
  Small potatoes of uniform size
Grease them with:
  Lard
Cut a hole in each one with an apple corer. Insert in the holes:
  Link sausages or sausage meat
Bake the potatoes until they are done, about 1 hour, in a moderate oven 375°.

POTATO CHEESE PUFFS

6 Puffs

This is a tempting potato dish and a good-looking one.

Beat:
  2 egg yolks
Add and beat until fluffy:
  1⅓ cups hot or cold Mashed
    Potatoes, page 302
  3 tablespoons hot milk
  ⅓ cup grated cheese
Season these ingredients with:
  ¼ teaspoon salt
  ¼ teaspoon paprika
  ¼ teaspoon celery salt
  ½ teaspoon finely grated onion
  1 teaspoon chopped green pepper
    or parsley
Beat until stiff, then fold in:
  2 egg whites
Place the batter in mounds in a greased pan. Brush the tops with:
  1½ tablespoons soft butter
Bake the potatoes in a moderate oven 350° for 20 minutes.

BAKED FILLED POTATOES

Follow one of the rules given for Baked Filled Potatoes or Sweet Potatoes. They may be filled with any kind of cooked food, creamed or buttered. Use left-over fish, meat, vegetables, etc., in any palatable combination. Good additions are Sautéed Mushrooms, page 292, minced bacon, browned onions, chives, celery seed or Herbs, page 832. A grand touch is to add 1 generous tablespoonful deviled ham to a hot split baked potato.

BAKED POTATOES FILLED WITH HASH

6 Servings

Creamed left-over vegetables and/or meat or fish may be substituted. Bake by the rule on page 301:
  6 medium-sized potatoes
Cut a thin slice off the flat side. With a spoon remove as much as you can of the potato without breaking the skin. Do not mash the potato. Add to it and work lightly with a fork until blended:
  1 tablespoon butter
  1 tablespoon cream
  ½ teaspoon salt
  ¼ teaspoon paprika
  1 tablespoon minced onion
  1 tablespoon minced parsley
  1 cup chopped cooked meat
  (¼ cup minced celery)
Moisten these ingredients with:
  Gravy or stock
Season them with:
  2 teaspoons Worcestershire sauce
Combine them with the potato mixture. Fill the skins, heap the tops. Place on each potato:
  ½ teaspoon butter
or sprinkle it with:
  Grated cheese
Brown the potatoes under a broiler or in a hot oven 400°.

BAKED POTATOES FILLED WITH VEGETABLES

8 Servings

Bake (page 301):
  4 Idaho potatoes
Melt:
  2 tablespoons butter
Stir in until blended:
  2 tablespoons flour
Stir in gradually:
  1 cup milk
Add:
  ¼ teaspoon salt
  ½ cup grated cheese
  ½ cup cooked peas
  ½ cup cooked chopped carrots
  ¼ cup diced green peppers
  2 tablespoons diced pimientos
Cut the potatoes lengthwise into halves. Remove the pulp without breaking the skin. Mash the pulp. Add it to the vegetable mixture. Season it with:
  Salt and pepper
Fill the potato shells with the mixture. Cover them with:
  3 cups shredded bread crumbs
browned in:
  4 tablespoons butter
Place the potato shells in a quick oven 400° or under a broiler until the tops are brown. Serve them with:
  Hot or cold meat

BAKED POTATOES AND ROQUEFORT CHEESE

6 Servings

Bake (page 301):
  6 Idaho potatoes

Cut them into halves. Scoop out the pulp, mash and then combine it with:

6 tablespoons butter
3 oz. Roquefort cheese
3 tablespoons hot cream
Salt and pepper

Refill the shells and bake the potatoes in a quick oven 400° until the tops are brown.

BAKED POTATOES FILLED WITH MINCED HAM

Follow the rule on page 302 for:

Potato Boats

Reduce the salt measurement to:

½ teaspoon

Add:

¼ teaspoon paprika
6 tablespoons minced ham or
4 tablespoons deviled ham
3 tablespoons chopped parsley

The use of the grated cheese as a topping is optional.

BAKED SWEET POTATOES FILLED WITH COOKED FOOD

Follow any one of the 4 preceding rules for Baked Filled Idaho Potatoes. Substitute shapely sweet potatoes.

POTATO CUPS OR BOATS

Pare oval:

Potatoes

Hollow out the centers to make cups or boat shapes. Parboil for 10 minutes in:

Boiling water

Drain and dry them. Heat fat to 385°, hot enough to brown a cube of bread in 40 seconds. Fry the potato cups in the fat until they are well browned. Drain them on unglazed paper. Sprinkle them with:

Salt

Fill them with hot:

Creamed meat, fish or vegetables

Suggestions for the Use of Soybeans

This inexpensive and valuable complete protein food may be substituted wholly or in part in recipes calling for ground meat. The beans should be cooked and may then be chopped or ground. As they are apt to be drier than meat they are good moistened with milk, tomato juice or left-over gravy. They require a good bit of seasoning. Vary this. See Seasonings, page 427. See Purée of Dried Lentils, Peas or Beans, page 271. Substitute soybeans and serve them as a vegetable, or use a rather stiff purée as a lining and topping for a meat pie.

Soybeans are good served au gratin. See Dried Bean Loaf and Dried Bean Patties, page 170, Dried Soybeans and Green Soybeans, page 269. Substitute part soybeans in Meal Loaf I or II on page 354 or Left-Over Meat Loaf, page 157.

Soybeans combine well with cheese, tomatoes, onions and other vegetables. They really need an uplift, being rather on the dull side but, like dull people, respond readily to the right contacts.

SOYBEAN LOAF

8 Servings

Sauté until soft:

½ cup chopped onion or celery and green pepper

in:

2 tablespoons butter or drippings

Add and bring to the boiling point:

1 cup tomato purée

Stir in:

1 cup soft bread crumbs
2 beaten eggs
3 cups cooked ground soybeans
2½ teaspoons salt
Chopped parsley or dried Herb, page 833
(½ teaspoon curry powder)

Place in a greased casserole. Bake the loaf in a moderate oven 350° for 30 minutes. You may serve it with:

Gravy or other sauce

You may substitute for the tomato purée 1 cupful of cream sauce and serve the loaf with tomato sauce.

SOYBEAN DINNER IN ONE DISH

4 Servings

Combine:

1 cup cooked corn
1 cup cooked Soybeans, page 269
1 cup lightly drained tomatoes
¾ teaspoon salt
¼ teaspoon paprika
½ teaspoon brown sugar
1 teaspoon grated onion

Place in a greased baking dish. Sprinkle the top with:

Bread crumbs
Cheese or grated peanuts

Bake the dish in a moderate oven 350° for 45 minutes.

SOYBEAN SALAD

Add cooked chopped soybeans to vegetable salads and to French dressing or mayonnaise.

SOYBEAN SOUFFLÉ

4 Servings

Put through a ricer, food mill or blender:

Cooked soybeans

There should be about 2 cupfuls of pulp. Add:

2 teaspoons chopped onion
3 beaten egg yolks
1 teaspoon salt
¼ teaspoon pepper
2 tablespoons chopped parsley or other herb

Whip until stiff, then fold in:

3 egg whites

Bake the soufflé in a slow oven 325° for about 1 hour.

SUGGESTIONS FOR THE USE OF PEANUTS

Add peanuts to cooked food and to salads. Serve them ground over cooked vegetables, macaroni, etc. Use peanut butter freely for sandwiches. Substitute peanuts for other nut meats in Nut Roast, page 170, Nutburgers, page 168, etc. Substitute part chopped peanuts in recipes calling for ground meat, Lima beans, etc.

Make Peanut Brittle, page 794, and Peanut Butter Cookies, page 682. Find other ways of using peanuts or peanut butter to make a generous use of this high protein food.

Entrées

An entrée is meant to be exactly what its name implies—an entrance or an opening wedge to a formal repast. It is also the main dish of an informal meal. I have not devoted a separate chapter to entrées but they are generously scattered through other chapters of this book.

They include: Soufflés, timbales, mousses, various egg dishes, croquettes, sweetbreads, mushrooms, creamed dishes, lobster, oysters, crab, food on skewers—in short, any light dish is appropriate that lacks the heft that is deemed essential for the main course of a formal meal.

Timbales

The timbale is first cousin to the reliable custard and to the flighty soufflé. As it combines the good qualities of both, it is a valuable member of the egg-dish family. It is an attractive and convenient way of serving light food and is therefore admirably suited to luncheon and supper purposes. Usually it is cooked in individual molds, inverted and served with some tempting sauce, but it may be served in a ring or other large mold.

As a disguise for left-over food, the timbale is second only to the soufflé. See page 217. The basis of the latter is cream sauce and egg. In the timbale the cream sauce is omitted and a small amount of cream or stock is substituted. The average timbale has more body than the soufflé. This makes it easier to handle, as it need not be carefully timed for serving and—a very valuable feature—makes it easy to reheat. If you are sure of being able to serve your meal on time, choose the soufflé; if you are uncertain as to when you will be able to serve it, by all means plan for the timbale.

Rule for Timbales

Butter custard molds lightly. Fill them about ⅔ full with timbale mixture. Place them on a rack in a pan of hot water. The water should be as high as the filling in the molds. If a rack is not available, fold several thicknesses of paper and place the molds on it. Bake the timbales for about 20 minutes, or until firm, in a moderate oven 325°. If baked in a large mold, a longer time will be required, about

½ hour. If the molds are covered with waxed paper—use elastic bands to hold the paper in place—the timbale tops will remain soft. Covered in this way the timbales may be steamed on top of the stove. Place the pan over heat, keep the water simmering until the timbales are firm. This takes a little more time than the baking of timbales. A large lid may be placed over them to hasten the process. The timbales are done when a spoon or knife inserted in the mixture and withdrawn remains uncoated. Unmold the timbales onto hot plates. Garnish them with parsley, pimiento, nuts, pickles, olives, etc. Serve them with or without sauce.

CUSTARD FOR TIMBALES
4 Servings
In France the salad is served with the meat course and the vegetable is served in solitary state. It is usually worthy of this exalted position. Sometimes it is accompanied by a mound or ring of delicious custard.
Combine and beat with a wire whisk:

1½ cups warm milk or ½ cup cream and 1 cup chicken stock
4 eggs
¾ teaspoon salt
½ teaspoon paprika
(⅛ teaspoon grated nutmeg or celery salt)
(1 tablespoon chopped parsley)
(A few drops onion or lemon juice)

Place the mixture in a greased ring or mold, or in individual molds, and set it in a pan of hot water. Bake the custard until it is firm. Follow the preceding Rule for Timbales. Invert the contents of the mold onto a hot platter. Serve the timbales with:

Creamed vegetables or Mushroom Sauce, page 292

These ingredients may be poured into the well-greased top of a double boiler, covered, placed over, not in, boiling water and cooked for 15 minutes. Uncover and permit them to cook for 5 or 10 minutes longer. Invert the timbale onto a hot platter. Excellent served with:

Mushroom Sauce, page 436, or other sauce or crisp bacon

You may use this method for any of the timbale rules that follow.

BROCCOLI OR CAULIFLOWER TIMBALES
6 Servings
Follow the preceding rule for:
Custard for Timbales
Add to the custard:

1 to 1½ cups cooked well-drained broccoli or cauliflower chopped or put through a sieve

Add seasoning if required. Bake the

timbales by the rule on page 211. Serve them with:

Hollandaise Sauce, page 429

MUSHROOM TIMBALES
6 Servings
Follow the rule on page 212 for:
Custard for Timbales
Sauté by the rule on page 292:

2 cups chopped mushrooms

Drain them thoroughly. Add them to the timbale mixture. Bake it by the rule on page 211.

For Mushroom Soufflé, Mousse, etc., see Index.

SPINACH TIMBALES
8 Servings
Make a Cream Sauce, page 428, of:

1 tablespoon butter
1 tablespoon flour
1 cup milk

Add to it:

2 cups cooked, finely chopped or strained spinach
3 beaten eggs
½ cup grated cheese
¼ cup chicken stock or other Stock, page 43
Salt and pepper
A few grains cayenne

Place these ingredients in a greased mold or in individual molds. Bake them by the Rule for Timbales on page 211.

CORN TIMBALES
8 Servings
Drain the contents of:

1 No. 2 can corn

There should be about 1½ cupfuls of drained corn. Beat until light:

3 eggs

Add the corn and:

1 teaspoon grated onion
¾ teaspoon salt
⅛ teaspoon paprika

Whip until stiff:

1 cup heavy cream

juice and Worcestershire sauce to taste. Serve the timbales with:

> Left-over gravy or Cream Sauce
> I, page 428, with lots of parsley

CREOLE TIMBALES

A good garnish for a steak or roast platter. Pack greased molds with:

> Pilaf, page 106
> Tomato Rice with Cheese and
> Mushrooms, page 106
> Curried Rice, page 108, or
> Spanish Rice, page 108

Bake them in a pan of hot water in a moderate oven 350° for 10 minutes. Invert them and garnish the timbales with:

> Parsley

Serve them with:

> Onion Sauce, page 432

RICE TIMBALES
6 Servings

Follow the rule for:

> Rice Ring, page 105

Fill buttered timbale molds. Steam them as directed. Serve the timbales with:

> Mushroom Sauce, page 436, or
> Creole Sauce, page 434

Batter Bread, page 423; Steamed Fish Pudding or Timbale, page 121; Halibut Soufflé or Timbale, page 221; Fish Mousse, page 121.

FISH TIMBALES
Method I. 6 Servings

Flake and chop until very fine:

> 2 cups cooked fish

Season it with:

> ¼ teaspoon salt
> ⅛ teaspoon paprika
> ½ teaspoon grated lemon rind
> 1½ teaspoons lemon juice

Whip until stiff:

> ½ cup heavy cream

In a separate bowl whip until stiff:

> 3 egg whites
> ⅛ teaspoon salt

Fold the cream into the fish mixture, then fold in the egg whites. Fill timbale molds ⅔ full. Follow the Rule for Timbales, page 211. Serve them with:

> Shrimp Sauce, page 258, or
> Béchamel Sauce, page 429

Method II. 4 Servings

This is a more economical and somewhat coarser timbale basis.

Melt:

> 3 tablespoons butter

Stir in:

> ¼ cup chopped celery, green
> pepper or onion, or a combina-
> tion of the 3

Stir for 1 minute, then add:

> ⅓ cup soft bread crumbs
> 1 cup milk
> 1¼ cups flaked fish
> (½ cup finely chopped pecans or
> almonds)

Remove the pan from the fire. Stir in:

> 2 beaten eggs
> ¾ teaspoon salt
> ⅛ teaspoon paprika
> 1 teaspoon Worcestershire sauce
> or lemon juice

Pour the mixture into 4 greased individual molds. Place them in a pan of hot water in a moderate oven 350° until the timbales are firm, about ½ hour. Unmold them and serve with:

> Sauce: tartar, cream, cheese or
> tomato

OYSTER TIMBALES
6 Servings

Cook in their juice until the edges begin to curl:

> 1 quart oysters

Strain them. Reserve the liquor. Put the oysters through a food grinder. Reserve the liquor. Stir into the oysters:

> 4 beaten egg yolks

Add:

> 6 tablespoons bread crumbs
> Rind and juice of 1 lemon
> A few drops caramel or com-
> mercial food coloring
> Salt and pepper

Whip until stiff:

> 4 egg whites

Fold them into the oyster mixture. Fill greased timbale molds ⅔ full. Follow the Rule for Timbales on page 211. Serve the timbales with:

Oyster Sauce

Melt:

> 2 tablespoons butter

Stir in until blended:

> 2 tablespoons flour

Stir the oyster liquor in slowly. There should be about 1 cupful of liquor. If there is not enough, add cream or stock. Add the contents of:

> 1 can crab meat: 6½ oz.

Add:

> 1 cup sliced Sautéed Mushrooms,
> page 292

Season the sauce with:

> Salt and pepper
> A few drops Worcestershire
> sauce or 1 tablespoon sherry

SHAD ROE TIMBALES WITH ONION AND CUCUMBER SAUCE

6 Servings

Skin:

3 or 4 pairs canned or fresh shad roe

Break them up with a fork. Add:

1 tablespoon melted butter
½ cup cream
4 egg yolks
Salt, pepper and paprika

Beat until stiff:

4 egg whites

Fold them into the roe mixture. Place it in a greased ring mold. Bake the timbale by the rule on page 211.

Sauce:

Combine:

1 medium-sized chopped onion
1 tablespoon chopped parsley
1 tablespoon capers
1 to 2 tablespoons prepared mustard
4 tablespoons mayonnaise
1 tablespoon lemon juice
2 tablespoons diced cucumber

Thin this sauce to a good consistency with:

Cream

Season it with:

Salt, paprika and pepper

Serve the timbale hot, the sauce cold.

Soufflés

The soufflé is the "misunderstood woman" of the culinary world. This simple and useful everyday dish is held in awe by many people who entertain an exaggerated idea of the difficulties of its composition.

While it should be timed to be served when it is at its peak, it may be held over some 10 or 15 minutes without any more serious injury than a slight shrinkage. Yes, properly made it *will* stay up.

The soufflé is a luxury or an economy dish according to your wishes. It is at all times delicate and tempting, so take your courage in your hands and try it out. The worst that can happen is the sacrifice of a few inexpensive staples, but if you read the following instructions carefully there need be no such sacrifice.

Cream sauce and eggs usually form the basis of the soufflé. To this basis cheese, vegetables, meat, fish, nuts, etc., are added.

Rule for Soufflé

Make a thick cream sauce of 3 tablespoonfuls of butter, 3 tablespoonfuls of flour and 1 cupful of liquid: milk, stock, vegetable water or cream. See Cream Sauce II, page 428.

When it is boiling, stir in about 1 cupful of solids, minced vegetables, cheese, etc. Reduce the heat to a low flame and add three beaten egg yolks. Cook the sauce for 1 or 2 minutes, stirring it constantly, until the yolks thicken slightly, but do not permit it to boil. Season the sauce and remove it from the fire. When it is cool fold in the stiffly beaten whites of eggs and place the mixture in an ungreased baking dish. It will rise higher when the dish is not greased, as it will cling to the dry sides.

The soufflé may be baked with an increasing heat, beginning with a slow oven and increasing the heat slightly every 10 minutes until the oven is moderately hot, 325° to 350°, or by placing the baking dish in a slow oven 325° and baking it until the soufflé is firm, from 25 to 45 minutes, dependent upon the size of the soufflé.

Do not place the dish in hot water unless the recipe calls for it. The water will keep the soufflé soft and in some cases it is preferable to have it crisp and crusty.

However, when making a soufflé in a ring mold, or in any other dish, with the intention of inverting the contents when done, grease the mold well, fill it and set it in a pan of hot water. This will facilitate removing the soufflé from the mold and will give it a uniform consistency.

Soufflés may be prepared in advance, with the exception of the beating of the egg whites, which must be done immediately before the soufflé is put into the oven.

Onions and garlic add greatly to the flavor of the soufflé. If you like them, place finely chopped onions in the butter and sauté them for a minute before making the cream sauce or place a bit of garlic in the butter, sauté it for a minute and remove it before making the cream sauce.

Evaporated milk makes a good soufflé. When using it take ½ milk or stock and ½ evaporated milk.

Carrots, onions and celery may be used raw if they are finely minced or put through a food chopper. Be careful to add these ingredients when the cream sauce is boiling so that their juices will not thin the sauce.

Soufflés may be baked in a double boiler over, not in, hot water. Use a quart

217

size. Grease it well. Pour in the soufflé mixture. Cover it and cook it for about 45 minutes. Turn it out onto a hot plate.

To make a soufflé with a crown—a "high hat soufflé": Just before putting the soufflé into the oven, take a large spoon or a rubber scraper and run a groove abut 1½ inches deep all around the top about 1¼ inches from the edge of the dish.

CHEESE SOUFFLÉ
3 Servings
Prepare:
  1 cup Cream Sauce II, page 428
Reduce the heat and stir in:
  ½ to ¾ cup grated cheese
When the cheese is melted add:
  3 beaten egg yolks
  ¼ teaspoon salt
  ⅛ teaspoon paprika
  A few grains cayenne
Cook and stir these ingredients for 1 minute longer to permit the yolks to thicken. Cool these ingredients. Whip until stiff:
  3 egg whites
Fold them lightly into the cheese mixture. Bake the soufflé in an ungreased 7 inch baking dish in a moderate oven 325° for about 40 minutes, or until firm.

CHEESE AND HAM SOUFFLÉ
Follow the preceding rule for:
  Cheese Soufflé
Go easy on the salt measurement. Add to the cream sauce at the same time the grated cheese is added:
  ½ cup ground cooked ham

CHEESE AND CELERY SOUFFLÉ
Follow the preceding rule for:
  Cheese Soufflé
Add to the cream sauce at the same time the cheese is added:
  1 cup cooked, minced, well-drained celery
Swiss cheese is exceptionally good combined with celery.

TOMATO CHEESE SOUFFLÉ
Follow the preceding rule for:
  Cheese Soufflé
Add to the cream sauce:
  3 tablespoons Italian tomato paste
You may fold into the beaten egg whites:
  2 teaspoons dry sherry

VEGETABLE SOUFFLÉ
4 Servings
Celery, onions and carrots, finely minced or grated, may be used raw. Cooked oyster plant, eggplant, cauli-flower, peas, onions, carrots, celery, canned or fresh asparagus, mushrooms, etc., may be used alone or in any good combination. Small quantities of left-over vegetables may be combined with minced raw carrots, celery and onions.
Prepare:
  1 cup Cream Sauce II, page 428:
  ⅓ cup cream and ⅔ cup vegetable stock
When the sauce is boiling stir in:
  1 cup minced drained vegetables
When the vegetables are hot reduce the heat and add:
  3 beaten egg yolks
Cook and stir for 1 minute longer to permit the yolks to thicken. Season as required with:
  Salt and pepper
  (Nutmeg)
Cool this mixture. Whip until stiff:
  3 egg whites
Fold them lightly into the vegetable mixture. Bake the soufflé in an ungreased 7 inch baking dish in a moderate oven 325° for about 40 minutes, or until firm. If you wish a dish that is a course in itself, serve the soufflé with:
  Mushroom Sauce, page 436

MUSHROOM SOUFFLÉ
Follow the above rule for:
  Vegetable Soufflé
Substitute for the vegetables:
  ½ lb. sautéed mushrooms: ¾ cup
  ¼ cup minced celery
  1 teaspoon grated onion
You may use for the liquid part:
  Chicken stock and cream

Vegetable Timbales, page 213.

CORN SOUFFLÉ
Follow the preceding rule. Use in place of the minced vegetables:
  ¾ cup well-drained corn, canned or cooked (cut from the cob)
Add:
  (1 chopped pimiento)
  (1 chopped green pepper)

Corn Pudding, page 184; Corn Timbales, page 212.

POTATO SOUFFLÉ WITH CHEESE TOPPING
6 Servings

Combine and beat well:

 3 cups hot Mashed Potatoes,
  page 302
 2 egg yolks
 2 tablespoons butter
 ⅓ cup hot cream
 1 teaspoon salt
 ⅛ teaspoon paprika

Shape these ingredients into a mound on an oven-proof dish. Whip until stiff:

 2 egg whites
 ⅛ teaspoon salt

Fold in:

 ⅓ cup dry grated cheese,
  preferably Parmesan

Spread this mixture lightly over the mound. Bake the soufflé in a moderate oven 325° for about 15 minutes.

A good potato soufflé may be made by following the rule for Soufflé on page 217. Use 1 cupful boiled riced potatoes.

SWEET POTATO AND PINEAPPLE OR APPLESAUCE SOUFFLÉ
6 Servings

This is fine with cold or hot ham or other meats.

Prepare by the rule on page 310:

 3 cups mashed sweet potatoes

Add and beat with a fork until the potatoes are fluffy:

 3 tablespoons butter
 ¼ teaspoon salt
 ½ teaspoon grated lemon rind
 2 beaten egg yolks

Drain well and fold in:

 ½ to ¾ cup drained crushed
  pineapple or tart applesauce

Cool these ingredients. Whip until stiff and fold in:

 2 egg whites

Bake the soufflé in a greased 7 inch baking dish in a moderate oven 350° for about 40 minutes.

CORN-MEAL SOUFFLÉ
3 Servings

This is an excellent luncheon dish combined with cold ham and a green salad. It resembles Spoon Bread, page 423.

Heat to the boiling point:

 2 cups milk

Stir in:

 ⅓ cup white or yellow corn meal
 1 tablespoon butter

Reduce the heat and stir in:

 3 tablespoons or more grated
  cheese

Cook these ingredients to the consistency of mush. Season them with:

 1 teaspoon salt
 ¼ teaspoon paprika
  A few grains cayenne

Add:

 3 beaten egg yolks

Cook and stir for 1 minute longer to permit the yolks to thicken. Cool these ingredients. Whip until stiff, then fold in:

 3 egg whites

Bake the soufflé in an ungreased 7 inch baking dish in a moderate oven 350° until it is slightly crusty, about 45 minutes. In Italy bits of ham and sea food are added to the batter which is baked until it is very crisp.

Spoon Bread, page 423; Batter Bread, page 423.

ONION SOUFFLÉ
4 Servings

One of my pet accompaniments to an otherwise slim meal.

Prepare by the rule on page 294:

 1 cup boiled onions

Drain and mince them. Melt:

 2 tablespoons butter

Stir in until blended:

 2 tablespoons flour

Combine and stir in slowly:

 ½ cup milk
 ½ cup evaporated milk or cream

When the sauce is smooth and boiling stir in the minced onion. When the onions are hot reduce the heat and stir in:

 3 beaten egg yolks

Cook and stir for 1 minute longer to permit the yolks to thicken. Season with:

  Salt, paprika and nutmeg
 2 tablespoons chopped parsley
  or ½ teaspoon dried basil

Cool these ingredients. Whip until stiff:

 3 egg whites

Fold them lightly into the onion mixture. Bake the soufflé in an ungreased 7 inch baking dish in a moderate oven 325° until it is firm, about 40 minutes.

Eggplant Soufflé, page 288.

ECONOMY SOUFFLÉ
4 Servings

Cooked left-overs may be utilized to make a very good soufflé.

Prepare:
  1 cup Cream Sauce II, page 428,
    using only 2½ tablespoons flour
When the sauce is smooth and boiling
stir in:
  ¾ cup minced cooked vegetables
    and meat or fish
  ¼ cup mashed potatoes
When these ingredients are hot, stir
in:
  3 beaten egg yolks
Season them as required with:
  Salt and pepper
  Mustard or Worcestershire
  sauce or tomato catsup
  (Nutmeg)
Cool them. Whip until stiff:
  3 egg whites
Fold them lightly into the mixture.
Bake the soufflé in an ungreased 7 inch
baking dish in a moderate oven 325°
until it is firm, about 40 minutes.

JIFFY SOUFFLÉ WITH CANNED SOUP
6 Servings
Use condensed canned soup: cream of
chicken, celery, mushroom, etc., as a
base. Add to this if you wish ¼ cupful
grated cheese, chopped olives, celery,
etc. Place in a bowl the contents of:
  1 can condensed soup: 10½ oz.
Beat in:
  4 egg yolks
Beat until stiff:
  4 egg whites
  ⅛ teaspoon salt
Fold the egg whites into the soup mixture. Place it in an oven-proof dish.
Bake it in a moderate oven 325° for
about 30 minutes.

TUNA FISH OR SALMON AND MASHED POTATO SOUFFLÉ
4 Servings
Drain the contents of:
  1 can tuna fish or salmon: 16 oz.
Break it into pieces with a fork. Melt
in a skillet:
  2 tablespoons butter, or use the
    oil from the can
Add and stir about in it until lightly
browned:
  1 tablespoon finely chopped onion
  2 tablespoons chopped celery
  2 tablespoons chopped parsley
Add:
  1 tablespoon lemon juice
  ¼ teaspoon salt
  A few drops Tabasco Sauce or
  1 teaspoon Worcestershire sauce
Beat these ingredients into:

  2 cups seasoned Mashed
    Potatoes, page 302
If the potatoes are cold, heat them
over hot water. You may add:
  1 teaspoon celery or caraway seed
Beat in the flaked tuna and:
  3 egg yolks
When this mixture is cool, beat until
stiff, then fold in:
  3 egg whites
Pile the soufflé into a greased dish.
Bake it in a moderate oven 350° for
about ½ hour, or until lightly browned.
It may be served with:
  Tomato Sauce, page 433, or
  some other sauce

FISH OR MEAT SOUFFLÉ
4 Servings
Prepare:
  1 cup Cream Sauce II, page 428
When it is smooth and boiling stir in:
  ¾ to 1 cup flaked cooked fish or
    finely chopped meat
  ¼ cup finely chopped raw carrots,
    celery and parsley
When these ingredients are hot reduce
the heat and stir in:
  3 beaten egg yolks
Cook and stir for 1 minute longer to
permit the yolks to thicken. Season
with:
  Salt and paprika
  Nutmeg
  Lemon juice, Worcestershire
  sauce or tomato catsup
  Curry powder (go easy on this!)
Cool these ingredients. Whip until
stiff:
  3 egg whites
Fold them lightly into the mixture.
Bake the soufflé in an ungreased 7 inch
baking dish in a moderate oven 325°
until it is firm, 40 minutes. Serve the
soufflé with:
  (Tomato Sauce, page 433)

HAM SOUFFLÉ
Follow the preceding rule for:
  Fish or Meat Soufflé
Substitute for the fish or meat:
  Cooked chopped or ground ham
This is good flavored with mustard.

CRAB MEAT OR SHRIMP SOUFFLÉ
Follow the rule on this page for:
  Fish or Meat Soufflé
Substitute for the fish or meat the con-
tents of:
  1 can crab meat: 6½ oz., or
    shrimp: 7 oz.

You may add:
    ⅓ cup stuffed sliced olives

OYSTER SOUFFLÉ
4 Servings
This soufflé is very delicate.
Heat in their liquor until they are plump:
    ½ to 1 pint oysters
Drain them. Prepare:
    1 cup Cream Sauce II, page 428:
    part cream and part oyster
    liquor
When it is boiling add the oysters.
Reduce the heat and add:
    3 beaten egg yolks
Cook and stir for 1 minute longer to permit the yolks to thicken. Season with:
    Salt and pepper
    Nutmeg
    (Lemon juice)
Chill these ingredients. Whip until stiff:
    3 egg whites
Fold them lightly into the oyster mixture. Bake the soufflé in an ungreased 7 inch baking dish in a moderate oven 325° until it is firm, about 40 minutes.

HALIBUT SOUFFLÉ WITH ALMOND SAUCE
4 Servings
Combine and cook to a paste:
    1 cup bread crumbs
    ½ cup cream
When it is hot add:
    ½ lb. finely chopped raw halibut
Season with:
    ¼ teaspoon salt
    ⅛ teaspoon paprika
Cool these ingredients. Whip until stiff:
    2 egg whites
Fold them lightly into the fish mixture. Place the soufflé in a 7 inch buttered baking dish; set it in a pan of hot water. Bake it in a moderate oven 325° for 40 minutes. Serve it with:

Almond Sauce
Blanch and slice:
    ⅓ cup almonds
Melt:
    1½ tablespoons butter
Brown the almonds in this. Combine and add:
    2 tablespoons flour
    1 cup cream or top milk
Season with:
    ¼ teaspoon salt
    ⅛ teaspoon pepper

Cook and stir the sauce over low heat until it thickens.

CHICKEN SOUFFLÉ
16 Servings
We use the following soufflé so frequently as a company dish that I am giving it as I first "composed" it. Since, it has gone through endless variations. In a modified form given below it is now our regular follow-up dish to any chicken dinner, provided the partakers thereof have not been too hungry.
Stew by the rule on page 402:
    A 3½ lb. chicken
Mince the chicken meat. There should be about 2¼ cupfuls. Prepare:
    3 cups Cream Sauce II, page 428:
    chicken fat, Chicken Stock, and
    cream or top milk
When the sauce is boiling stir in the minced chicken and:
    1 cup chopped nut meats
    1 cup chopped cooked vegetables
    or raw celery, carrots and onions
When these ingredients are hot, reduce the heat and add:
    9 beaten egg yolks
Cook and stir for 2 minutes longer to permit the yolks to thicken. Season with:
    Salt and pepper
    Nutmeg
Cool this mixture. Whip until stiff:
    9 egg whites
Fold them lightly into the chicken mixture. Bake the soufflé in ungreased baking dishes, or in individual dishes, in a moderate oven 325° until it is firm, about 50 minutes. This soufflé may also be baked in greased dishes placed in a pan of water, if preferred. The size of the dishes is unimportant provided they are filled only about ⅔ full. Serve the soufflé with:
    Cream Sauce I, page 428
Add to the sauce:
    Chopped parsley
    Capers
or with:
    Mushroom Sauce, page 436, or
    Poulette Sauce, page 432, etc.
This recipe has more body than any of the others given. Its proportions may be varied.

FOLLOW-UP CHICKEN SOUFFLÉ
5 Servings
Prepare:
    1 cup Cream Sauce II, page 428:

use chicken fat, Chicken Stock,
page 47, and cream or top milk
When the sauce is boiling add:
1 cup solids: minced chicken, nut
meats, minced and drained
cooked or raw vegetables
Reduce the heat and add:
3 beaten egg yolks
Stir and cook for 1 minute longer to
permit the yolks to thicken. Season
with:
Salt and pepper
Freshly grated nutmeg
Cool these ingredients. Whip until
stiff:
3 egg whites
Fold them lightly into the chicken mixture. Bake the soufflé in an ungreased
baking dish in a moderate oven 325°
until it is firm, about 40 minutes.

MUSHROOM SOUFFLÉ WITH SWEETBREADS OR CHICKEN
8 Servings
Parboil by the rule on page 376:
1 pair sweetbreads or use 1 cup
cooked minced chicken
Remove the skin and membrane and
mince the sweetbreads. Prepare by the
rule on page 428:
1 cup Cream Sauce: 2½ tablespoons butter, 2½ tablespoons
flour, 1 cup liquid—preferably
Chicken Stock, page 47, and
cream
Melt in a pan:
2 tablespoons butter
Add and sauté for 3 minutes:
2 slices onion
Remove the onion. Add to the pan:
1½ cups finely minced mushrooms
and the sweetbreads or chicken. Heat
the cream sauce to the boiling point
and combine it with the mushroom
mixture. Reduce the heat to a low
flame and stir in:
¼ cup dry bread crumbs
1 chopped pimiento
¼ teaspoon salt
2 beaten egg yolks
Cook and stir 1 minute longer to permit the yolks to thicken. Cool these
ingredients. Whip until stiff:
2 egg whites
Fold them lightly into the mushroom
mixture. Place the soufflé in buttered
timbale molds in a pan of hot water
and bake them in a moderate oven
325°, covered with a piece of buttered
paper, for 15 minutes, or until the
soufflé is firm. If a buttered ring mold
or large baking dish is used, bake for

35 minutes. Invert the contents of the
molds onto a platter and surround
them with:

Mushroom Sauce for Soufflé
Melt:
3 tablespoons butter
Add and sauté for 3 minutes:
½ cup thinly sliced mushrooms
Stir in:
2 tablespoons flour
Combine, heat and stir in slowly:
⅓ cup cream
1 cup chicken stock or canned
chicken soup
Season, if required, with:
Salt and paprika
Stir and cook the sauce for 2 minutes.

Mushroom Ring or Mousse, page 176;
Mushroom Timbales, page 212.

RICE AND CHEESE SOUFFLÉ
4 Servings
Combine:
2 cups cooked rice
⅛ to ¼ lb. finely diced or grated
Cheddar cheese
1 tablespoon melted butter
2 beaten egg yolks
1 cup milk
½ teaspoon salt
⅛ teaspoon paprika
A few grains cayenne
(1 tablespoon grated onion)
(1 teaspoon Worcestershire sauce)
(3 tablespoons chopped parsley)
Beat until stiff:
2 egg whites
⅛ teaspoon salt
Fold them into the rice mixture. Bake
the soufflé in a moderate oven 350° for
about 25 minutes.

HOMINY SOUFFLÉ WITH CHEESE
6 Servings
This is a little more delicate than the
Grits Ring on page 157.
Scald in the top of a double boiler over
direct heat:
1 cup milk
1 cup water
Add and stir until thickened:
½ cup hominy grits
Cook these ingredients covered over
hot water for 1 hour. Stir occasionally.
Remove the grits from the fire. Beat
in:
3 egg yolks
2 tablespoons butter

A few grains cayenne
¾ teaspoon salt
(4 tablespoons grated Parmesan
  cheese)
Cool the mixture. Beat until stiff:
3 egg whites
¼ teaspoon salt
Fold the egg whites into the hominy
mixture. Place it in a baking dish.
Bake it in a moderate oven 325° for
about ¾ hour. Good with:
**Creamed Mushrooms, page 292,
or Tomato Sauce, page 433**

Grits Ring, page 157.

SOUFFLÉS IN SQUASH CASES
Prepare by the rule on page 315:
Squash cases
Small squash cases to be served individually or a large one. These should
be steamed or parboiled until they are
nearly tender. Drain them and cool
them. Fill them with any soufflé mixture. Place them in a pan with a very
little water to keep the squash from
scorching. Bake them in a moderate
oven 325° until the soufflé mixture is
firm, about 15 minutes for small squash
and 25 to 30 minutes for large ones.

CANNED LIMA BEAN SOUFFLÉ WITH BACON AND TOMATOES
3 Servings
Sauté until crisp:
8 slices bacon
Keep them hot. Drain, then place in a
double boiler the contents of:
1 No. 2 can Lima beans
Add to them:
3 tablespoons bacon fat
Steam the beans until they are hot.
Mash them with a fork. Beat well:
1 or 2 eggs
¼ cup cream
½ teaspoon salt
¼ teaspoon paprika
⅛ teaspoon marjoram
(⅛ teaspoon thyme)
Stir these ingredients into the beans.
Permit them to heat and to thicken
slightly, a matter of 2 or 3 minutes.
Pile them on a hot platter, cover them
with the bacon. Surround them with:
Tomato slices
The tomato slices may be broiled or
sautéed in the bacon fat.

Ring Mold Soufflés

All the recipes given in the chapter on Soufflés may be used for ring molds, or
for any other mold, with the intention of inverting the contents onto a platter, by
greasing the mold and making the soufflé with the mold set in a dish of hot water.
When the soufflé is firm, run a knife around the edges and invert the mold. Fill the
center of the soufflé with creamed meat, fish or vegetables.

SPINACH RING WITH MUSHROOMS, ETC.
4 Servings
Cook by the rule on page 313:
1½ lbs. spinach: 1 cup when cooked
Drain it, chop it until it is fine, put it
through a purée strainer or blend it.
Melt in a skillet:
3 tablespoons butter
Add and sauté for 1 minute:
1 tablespoon chopped onion
Stir in until blended:
3 tablespoons flour
Combine and stir in slowly:
½ cup milk or Stock, page 43
½ cup cream or evaporated milk
When the sauce is boiling, stir in the
spinach. Reduce the heat and stir in:
3 beaten egg yolks
Cook and stir for 1 minute longer to
permit the yolks to thicken. Season
with:
**Salt and pepper
Nutmeg**
(½ cup grated cheese)
Add just for looks:
A few drops green coloring
Whip until stiff:
3 egg whites
Fold them lightly into the spinach
mixture. Place these ingredients in a
greased 7 inch ring mold set in a pan
of hot water. Bake the soufflé in a
moderate oven 325° until it is firm,
about 30 minutes. Invert it on a
platter and serve it filled with:
**Creamed Mushrooms, page 292,
Chicken à la King, page 143, or
some other creamed dish**

Creamed Eggs and Cheese, page 88.

SPINACH RING WITH NUT MEATS
A fine Lenten dish.
Add to the above rule for spinach soufflé:
    ¾ cup chopped nut meats
Omit the cheese. Fill the center of the ring with:
    Tiny New Potatoes, page 300, with chopped parsley
Serve it with:
    Cheese Sauce, page 431
    Onion Sauce, page 432

BROCCOLI RING
4 Servings
Follow the above rule for:
    Spinach Ring
Substitute for the spinach:
    1 cup cooked minced or puréed Broccoli, page 274

BROCCOLI RING WITH MAYONNAISE
8 Servings
Combine:
    2 cups finely chopped or puréed cooked broccoli
    1 cup Cream Sauce II, page 428
    1 cup mayonnaise
Season with:
    Salt to taste
    ½ teaspoon paprika
    ½ teaspoon onion juice
    (¼ teaspoon dried basil)
Beat in:
    6 egg yolks
Whip until stiff:
    6 egg whites
    ⅛ teaspoon salt
Fold the egg whites into the broccoli mixture. Place these ingredients in a greased 10 inch ring mold set in a pan of hot water. Bake the soufflé in a moderate oven 325° for about ¾ hour. Serve it filled with:
    Creamed shrimp, mushrooms or some other creamed dish

CANNED SPINACH RING SOUFFLÉ
4 Servings
Soak for a few minutes:
    2 cups very loosely packed bread without crusts
in:
    1 cup water
Squeeze the water from it. Break up the bread with a fork. Chop until fine or put through a strainer:

    1½ cups canned or cooked drained spinach
Combine it with the bread and:
    2 egg yolks
Add:
    Seasoning
    A drop or 2 green coloring
Beat until stiff, then fold into the spinach mixture:
    2 egg whites
    A pinch salt
Grease a 7 inch ring mold, fill it with the spinach mixture, set it in a pan of hot water and bake in a moderate oven 325° until it is firm, about 30 minutes. Invert it onto a platter. Fill the center with:
    Chicken à la King, page 143,
    Creamed Mushrooms or Celery, pages 292, 281, creamed fish, etc., or Buttered Carrots, page 278

Mushroom Ring or Mousse, page 176.

CHESTNUT RING MOLD SOUFFLÉ
4 Servings
Combine:
    2 tablespoons flour
    1 teaspoon salt
    ¼ teaspoon paprika
    1 cup riced Boiled Chestnuts, page 283
    ½ teaspoon grated onion
Add gradually:
    ½ cup milk
Stir and cook these ingredients over a slow fire for 5 minutes. Cool them. Whip until stiff, then fold in:
    3 egg whites
Bake the soufflé in a 7 inch ring mold set in a pan of hot water in a moderate oven 325° for about ½ hour. Invert it onto a hot plate. Fill it with:
    Buttered green peas
    Chopped parsley
It may be served with:
    Mushroom Sauce, page 292
to which add:
    2 tablespoons sherry

CELERY ROOT SOUFFLÉ
6 Servings
Cook by the rule on page 282:
    4 medium-sized celery roots
Drain them well. Put them through a grinder, using a coarse knife, or through a ricer. Soak:
    2 slices white bread
in:
    3 tablespoons milk

Stir this into the celery and add:
2 tablespoons melted butter
1 teaspoon grated onion
2 tablespoons cream
4 beaten egg yolks
¾ teaspoon salt
½ teaspoon paprika
A fresh grating nutmeg
Whip until stiff:

4 egg whites
⅛ teaspoon salt
Fold them into the celery mixture. Place the soufflé in a greased ring mold set in a pan of hot water in a moderate oven 350° for about 45 minutes. Invert it onto a hot plate. Fill the center with:
Buttered peas, sautéed mushrooms, etc.

Fish

To many a person a fish is nothing more than a prospective dinner to be found on a shop counter. To the more fortunate a fish opens up an enchanting vista of a quiet pool, a rushing stream or a sparkling ocean, where bent pin, flashing rod or harpoon offer the possibility of bringing in the catch of the season. Above all hovers a prayer—writer unknown to me so forgive the plagiarism—"God grant me grace to catch a fish so big that even I, in speaking of it afterward, need never lie."

To Buy a Fish

Be sure to buy a fish with bright, clear protruding eyes. If the fish is not fresh, the eyes will be dull and sunken. The flesh should feel firm and should leave no impression when pressed with a finger. The gills should be bright, not gray or brown. The scales should have a high sheen. There should be no unpleasant odor. If in doubt about a fish, place it in water. A fresh fish will float.

Allow ⅓ pound per serving of solid fish. Allow ½ pound per serving if fish is bought whole with heads, tails, bones, etc.

To Keep a Fish

Keep fish, wrapped in heavy paper, as short a time as possible in the coldest part of the refrigerator, but not directly on ice. Wrap cleaned fish in waxed paper and place it in a closed container, to avoid contaminating other food, in the coldest part of the refrigerator, but not directly on ice.

If a fish is not freshly caught, you may wash it with acidulated water (water to which a few tablespoonfuls of lemon juice or vinegar have been added) and wipe it until dry with a paper towel or a cloth.

To Clean and Skin a Fish

Place the fish on a large sheet of paper, remove the scales with a fish scaler or a knife. Begin at the tail and work toward the head. If the fish is slippery, hold it with a cloth. If you wish to skin the fish (see below), it need not be scaled. Cut around the back fins and pull them off or grasp the rear part of a fin and give it a

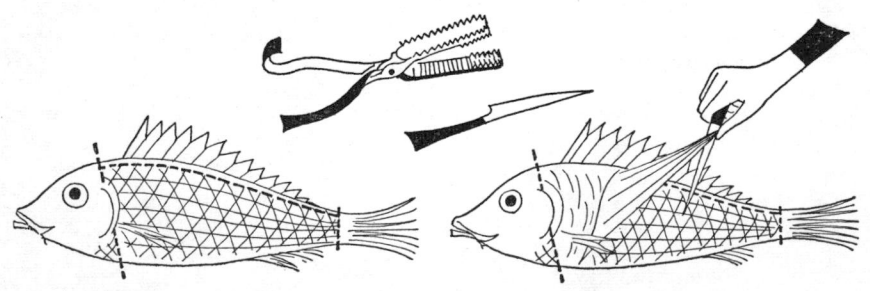

sudden pull toward the fish's head. Both the fin and its bony structure will come away. Or cut off the fins with a scissors allowing a small part to remain visible so the bones may be located easily after the fish is cooked.

If a fish is to be skinned, do it at this time. Place it on a flat surface, run a knife point down the entire length of the backbone as shown on page 226. Loosen the skin near the head of the fish and around the gills, then strip it off toward the tail. Reverse the fish and repeat the process on the other side.

Cut a gash in the abdomen of the fish (a scissors is a help in this operation). Remove the entrails. Remove the congealed blood pocket in the abdominal cavity under the backbone with a few scrapes of a knife tip. You may wish to cook the fish with the head and tail; if not, cut them off at this time. See Fish Stock, page 230. Wash the fish quickly inside and out, but never soak any fish before or after it is cleaned. Dry it thoroughly with a towel.

To Fillet or Bone a Fish

To fillet a small fish: If a fish is scaled (see above) it need be neither skinned, cleaned nor have the fins removed. To prepare the fillet place the fish on its side on a flat surface with the backbone lying toward you, as shown below on the left. With a sharp knife cut the meat off one entire side of the fish in one piece. To do this

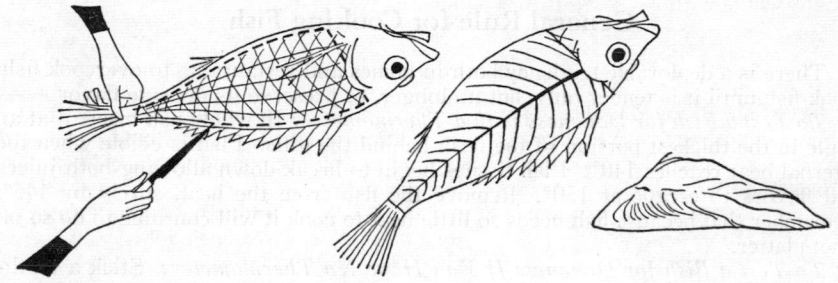

start to cut below the fin near the tail end and continue to work toward the head along the backbone as shown on the drawing on the left above. Cut as close as possible to the backbone, cutting in a sliding motion toward and along the rib bones until the fillet is freed, as shown on the right. Turn the fish over and remove the fillet from the other side. Feel the fish all over with the fingers to find small bones that may have remained in the flesh and remove them with tweezers or a short-bladed knife and the thumb.

To fillet a large fish: Remove the fins. Scale the fish, and clean it, as above. Split it open from the vent to the tail. Cut with a sharp knife, beginning at the tail end as shown on the left below. Separate the flesh from the backbone and loosen it

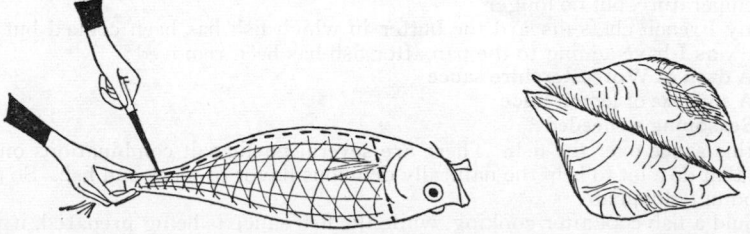

from the rib bones as shown on page 227. Do not cut into the skin on the backbone, because it will hold the fillets together later. Cut the fillet from the other side in the same manner. The double fillet is shown on the right on page 227. Feel the fish all over with the fingers to find small bones that may have remained in the flesh and remove them with tweezers or a short-bladed knife and the thumb.

To Prepare Steaks and Fillets

Fish steaks are slices cut crosswise from a large fish. Fillets are lengthwise pieces taken from fish and freed from bone.

To Remove Fish Odors

To minimize the odor of cooked fish, use wine, vinegar, ginger, spring onions or garlic in the recipe.

To remove the odor of fish from utensils and dish cloths use a solution of baking soda and water, about 1 teaspoonful soda to the quart.

To remove the odor of fish from the hands, rub them with lemon juice, vinegar or salt before washing them.

General Rule for Cooking Fish

There is a deplorable tendency both in homes and restaurants to overcook fish. Cook fish until it is tender only, but no longer, to preserve its delicate flavor.

To Test a Fish for Doneness with a Thermometer: In whole fish insert it at an angle in the thickest portion of the flesh behind the gills. Fish is edible when the internal heat reaches 140°. Fish tissues begin to break down allowing both juices and flavors to escape at 150°. Remove the fish from the heat, surely by 145°. Remember that because fish needs so little heat to cook it will continue to do so on a hot platter.

To Test a Fish for Doneness If You Have No Thermometer: Stick a toothpick in the thickest part of the fish near the backbone and separate the meat from the bone. The fish is done when the flesh is no longer translucent.

Fish is often enhanced by seasonings which are added at the beginning of the cooking process, with the exception of salt which is added last when the fish has been cooked, unless the fish is breaded, floured, covered with batter, or salt is added to the stuffing.

When cooking fish the size and shape of the fish or pieces must be taken into consideration in timing, but the methods themselves for cooking all fish are much the same. A good cook knows through experience how to time her fish but even she will be watchful and hang over the pot, skillet, broiler or oven for best results. For greater detail for each method of cooking see the following pages. These rules apply to fish which has been removed from the refrigerator long enough to reach room temperature, but no longer.

Many French chefs discard the butter in which fish has been cooked but you might try as I have adding to the pan after fish has been removed:

A dash of Worcestershire sauce
A squeeze of lemon juice
Seasoning as needed

Serve this sauce over the fish. There are several garlic salt combinations on the market that do a lot to help the naturally delicious flavor of meat and fish. So does monosodium glutamate.

Should a fish cool after cooking, while the fish sauce is being prepared, it may be reheated briefly in a moderately hot oven 400°.

Frozen Fish

Preferably frozen fish should be thawed before it is cooked but it may be cooked while still frozen. It spoils readily after it is thawed so use it immediately after thawing. If it is cooked frozen, it will require a longer period for cooking than the time given in these recipes, and will tend to be underdone to the center, overdone on the outside. Fish may be defrosted in the refrigerator, at room temperature or in front of an electric fan. For timing, see page 871. Skin frozen fish before cooking it.

To Bake a Fish

Use a moderate oven preheated to 325° to 350° for best results. A fish with the head still on and stuffed will usually require a somewhat longer cooking period than a decapitated unstuffed fish. If using a thermometer insert it in the thick flesh behind the gills. The fish is done when the inner temperature reaches 140°. If not using a thermometer, allow about 20 minutes for 1 inch; 30 minutes for a 2 inch; and 35 minutes for a 3 inch thickness. See "To Test a Fish for Doneness" in the General Rule for Cooking Fish, page 228. When baking fish place a piece of clean muslin or cheesecloth on a rack in the pan; then when fish is baked it can be lifted off the rack and turned over on the serving plate without breaking.

To Steam a Fish

Place fish on an oiled rack above 1½ inches of boiling water or Court Bouillon, page 238. Use a fish steamer if possible so the fish can be lifted out without breaking, page 239. Steam the fish closely covered until tender. See General Rule for Cooking Fish, page 228. Steam a fish 1 inch thick 4 to 6 minutes, a fish 2 inches thick 10 to 15 minutes. If you are using a thermometer, the internal temperature should read 140°.

To Broil a Fish

Whole fish, split fish, boned fish, fish fillets and steaks are good broiled.
There is a great difference of opinion about the heat used in broiling fish. You may preheat a broiler and rack for 10 minutes at 550°. See that the fish is well brushed with a quick browning fat like butter or margarine and is protected by a light dusting of flour. Subject the fish to this high heat for a short period, basting it frequently with additional fat. You may prefer to place the fish, also protected with fat and flour, under a broiler preheated to 375° and keep the fish there for a longer period, also basting it frequently. By this latter method the fish does not brown so readily. You may get a browned effect by covering it liberally with paprika. Fillets are usually placed 2 inches from the source of heat, skin side down, and are not turned during cooking. Whole fish are turned once. Some split fish are placed from 3 to 6 inches from the heat, dependent upon the size and type of fish. Fish are broiled at full heat throughout the cooking period. The length of time depends upon the thickness and texture of the fish. With the 550° oven a fish ½ inch thick takes about 5 minutes; a fish 1 inch thick from 8 to 10 minutes.

To Sauté or Pan Fry a Fish

See pages 236, 241 for Broiling and Sautéing Fish.
Protect fish when cooking it by one of these processes: by spreading it with a coating such as butter, margarine, cream or French dressing (these brown easily), or by using crumbs, flour, paprika, crushed cornflakes or batter, egg white or

whole egg (usually diluted with 1 tablespoonful of water). Unless you are deep fat frying try using 1 tablespoonful of oil instead of water in the usual beaten egg coating and a brown color will result as uniform as that achieved by deep fat frying. Vinegar, lemon juice, dry wine or sherry may be substituted advantageously for the water in the egg coating. Of course, you may bread or flour the fish after it is coated with the egg. See To Flour Food, page 540. To Bread Food, page 540.

To Dredge or Flour a Fish

To Dredge Fish with Flour: See Floured Food, page 540.

To Bread a Fish: Have ready and place on a table in the following order: dressed fish, a bowl of milk or other liquid, a pan of sifted, seasoned bread crumbs and a buttered pan in which to bake the fish. Remember to keep the left hand for

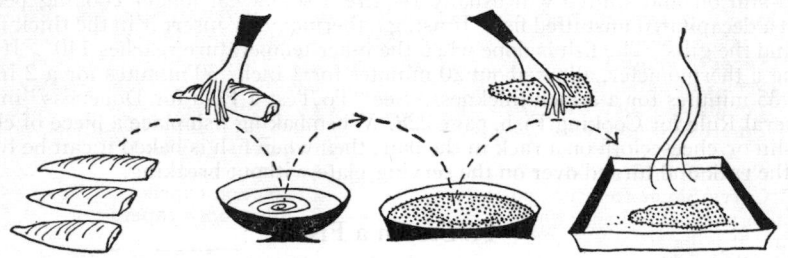

the wet dipping, the right hand for the dry dipping. Dip fish in milk or in egg, see page 540, with the left hand, dip it in crumbs with the right hand, then place it in the pan. Left-handed persons will of course reverse this order. This method is practical and expeditious—only one sticky hand.

To Marinate a Fish

The flavor of a fish is sometimes improved by placing it in a marinade for 1 to 2 hours. Use 1 part vinegar or dry white wine to 2 parts oil. You may add a sliver of garlic. Use what is left of the marinade to baste the fish. Fish may be marinated in vinegar, wine or lemon juice for about ½ hour.

Fish Stock or Fumet

A fumet is a more concentrated stock than Court Bouillon, page 238.

Keep the fish head, tail, fins, skin and bones for stock. Partly cover them with cold water. Add cut-up vegetables suitable for soup: an onion, a half carrot, celery stalks with leaves, etc. Add seasonings at once or later. Simmer the stock for about ½ hour. Strain it. You may add dry white wine to it. Use it for simmering fish. Serve it as soup with a dash of cream added, use as a basis for cream soup, or use it in aspic or sauces. The stock may be kept for several days in a tightly closed container in the refrigerator. It may be combined with meat or vegetable stock.

BAKED FISH
Allow ½ Pound Per Person
This is a decorative and attractive dish.
Scrape, remove the entrails and clean:
    A fish weighing 3 or more lbs.
Stuff it with:
    Dressing

Rub it generously with:
    Soft butter or oil
Dredge it with:
    Flour
Season it with:
    Paprika

Cut 3 or 4 deep gashes in the sides of the fish. Force into the cuts:

Slices of bacon

Do not lard a fat fish. Place the fish in a pan with:

Bacon drippings or 1 or 2
slices bacon

Bake it in a moderate oven 325° for about ¾ hour. Baste it frequently with a mixture of:

Hot water and butter—2 parts
water to 1 part butter

See General Rule for Cooking Fish, page 228.

Season the fish with:

Salt

Serve the fish on a platter garnished with:

Slices of lemon
Sprigs of parsley
Tomatoes Filled with Mashed
Potatoes, page 199

The fish may be served with:

Almond, Shrimp, Mustard or
Curry Sauce for Fish, page 258

The fish may be baked without dressing, but it is better when filled. If the fish is filled, allow at least 10 minutes longer cooking time. This is about the right amount of dressing for a 3 pound fish:

I. Dressing

This is a fine but plain and unsophisticated dressing.

Combine:

1½ cups bread crumbs
2 tablespoons chopped onion
½ cup chopped celery
2 tablespoons chopped parsley
1 or 2 beaten eggs

Season these ingredients well with:

½ teaspoon salt
⅛ teaspoon paprika
½ teaspoon dried tarragon or dill
seed
2 tablespoons capers
(¼ teaspoon nutmeg)

Use enough:

Milk, melted butter or soup
stock

to make a loose dressing. Fill the fish. Sew the sides together with a coarse needle and thread.

II. Dressing

A Southern and more elaborate version of bread dressing is:

Soak for 10 minutes:

1 cup bread crumbs

in:

½ cup sherry

Wring the wine from the bread. Stir and sauté for 3 minutes:

¼ cup finely chopped green pepper
½ cup finely chopped onion

in:

3 tablespoons butter

Add the bread crumbs and:

2 teaspoons chili sauce
½ cup canned or Sautéed Mushrooms, page 292
2 tablespoons chopped parsley

III. Oyster Dressing

For a 4 pound fish.

Melt:

6 tablespoons butter

Sauté in the butter until brown:

¼ cup chopped onion

Add:

1 tablespoon chopped parsley
2 cups bread crumbs
1 cup drained whole or chopped
oysters: ½ pint
¾ teaspoon salt
¼ teaspoon paprika
2 tablespoons capers

BAKED RED SNAPPER WITH SAVORY TOMATO SAUCE

Prepare for cooking:

A 3 lb. red snapper or other large
fish

Dredge it inside and out with:

Seasoned flour

Place it in a baking pan lined with greased paper. Melt:

6 tablespoons butter

Add and simmer for 15 minutes:

½ cup chopped onion
2 cups chopped celery
¼ cup chopped green pepper

Add and simmer until the celery is very tender:

3 cups canned tomatoes
1 tablespoon Worcestershire
sauce
1 tablespoon catsup
1 teaspoon chili powder
½ finely sliced lemon
2 bay leaves
1 minced clove garlic
1 teaspoon salt
A few grains red pepper

Press these ingredients through a potato ricer or food mill. Pour the sauce around the fish. Bake the fish in a moderate oven 325° for about ¾ hour. See General Rule for Cooking Fish, page 228. Baste it frequently with the sauce.

BAKED RED SNAPPER WITH VEGETABLES
Prepare for cooking:
A 6 lb. red snapper
Cut deep gashes in both sides crosswise of the fish about 1½ inches apart. Rub it well inside and out with:
Butter
Place in each gash:
Pepper
A teaspoon of butter
A slice of lemon
Prepare:
½ cup chopped celery
¾ cup chopped green pepper
½ cup chopped parsley
1 minced clove garlic
Stuff the gashes with the chopped ingredients. Place the fish in a pan lined with greased paper. Sprinkle it lightly with:
Cinnamon
If there are vegetables left, sprinkle them over the fish. Melt in a saucepan:
½ cup butter
Stir in and sauté lightly:
1 cup chopped onions
Stir in:
¼ cup flour
Stir in:
1 quart tomatoes or stock
Cook and stir these ingredients until they thicken. Season the sauce very lightly with:
Salt
Pepper
Pour it over the fish. Bake the fish in a moderate oven 325° for about 1 hour. See General Rule for Cooking Fish, page 228. Baste it frequently with the sauce. Serve it with:
Steamed Rice, page 103

BAKED STUFFED FISH WITH CHEESE
6 Servings
Prepare for cooking:
A 3 lb. fish
Prepare this dressing. Melt:
4 tablespoons butter
Add and sauté for 2 minutes:
½ cup minced mushrooms
1 teaspoon chopped onion
¼ cup shredded green pepper
Add:
1½ cups cracker or dry bread crumbs
1 beaten egg
1 teaspoon salt
¼ teaspoon paprika
Fill the fish. Sew the sides together with a coarse needle and thread. Roll the fish in:
½ cup grated cheese
or spread it with softened:
Snappy cheese
Bake it in a pan lined with heavy greased paper in a moderate oven 325° for about 45 minutes. See General Rule for Cooking Fish, page 228. Baste it with a little:
Stock, page 43, or
hot water and butter—2 parts water, 1 part butter
Serve the fish with:
Hollandaise Sauce, page 430

BAKED FISH WITH SOUR CREAM
8 Servings
Split and remove the bones (page 227) from:
A 4 lb. whitefish
Flatten it out. Rub it inside and out with:
Paprika and butter
Place it on an oven-proof dish or shallow baking pan under a flame until it is lightly browned. Cover it with:
2 cups sour cream
Place a lid over it. Bake the fish in a moderate oven 325° for about ¾ hour, or until done. See General Rule for Cooking Fish, page 228. Season it with:
Salt

QUICKLY BAKED FISH
Prepare for cooking:
Small fish, pieces of fish or fish fillets
Combine:
¼ cup rich milk or cream
½ teaspoon salt
⅛ teaspoon paprika or pepper
Dip the pieces in the milk, then in:
Bread crumbs or crushed cornflakes
Permit the fish to dry on a rack for ½ hour. Bake them in a pan lined with greased paper in a moderate oven 325°. See General Rule for Cooking Fish, page 228. Baste them once while cooking with:
Melted butter or bacon drippings

SMALL BAKED FISH WITH ALMOND SAUCE
6 Servings
Prepare for cooking:
6 small fish or 2 lbs. fish fillets

Roll them in:
**¾ cup seasoned crumbs: dry
bread, cracker or crushed
cornflakes**
Place them on a rack to dry for ½
hour. Melt:
4 tablespoons oil, butter or fat
Brown the fish in the oil over a quick
fire. Have the oven heated to 325°.
Bake the fish until done. See General
Rule for Cooking Fish, page 228. Serve
it with:
**Almond Butter Sauce, page 258,
or Wine Butter Sauce, page 258**

FISH BAKED IN PARCHMENT PAPER
Clean:
Small fish
A large fish may be prepared in the
same way but will require more time.
See General Rule for Cooking Fish,
page 228.
Place each fish on a piece of parchment paper or greased brown paper.
Fold it over. Cut it along the lines of
the fish leaving a margin of 1¼ inches.
Remove the paper. Spread it well
with:
Olive oil or butter
Season the fish inside and out with:
Paprika and lemon juice
Replace it in the paper. Fold over the
edges of the paper like a hem. Fasten
it with paper clips so that the paper
will retain the juices. Place the fish in
a greased pan in a moderate oven 350°
for about 20 minutes, or in a 300° oven
for 30 minutes. Unpin the papers.
Slide the fish and the juices onto a
platter. Season them with:
Salt
Garnish them with:
Lemon slices and parsley

FISH BAKED IN A COVERED DISH
4 to 6 Servings
This is a delightful way of preparing
fish with or without sauce. It is simple,
easy and brings about a delicate and
flavorful result. Have at room temperature:
**2 lbs. fish, preferably in 1 chunky
piece**
Combine, then rub the fish on all sides
with:
**2 tablespoons soft butter
¼ teaspoon pepper or paprika
A fresh grating of nutmeg**

Place the fish in an oven-proof dish.
Cover it with a closely fitting lid. Bake
it in a moderate oven 325° until tender.
See General Rule for Cooking Fish,
page 228. The time depends so largely
on the shape of the fish that I hesitate
to estimate it. You may add while
cooking:
**2 tablespoons water or dry white
wine**
Place the fish on a hot platter. Melt
and brown:
3 tablespoons butter
Add:
**2 tablespoons capers or chopped
pickles
1 teaspoon chopped parsley
1 teaspoon chopped chives
¾ teaspoon salt**
Pour this, or any other fish sauce, over
the fish.

BAKED FILLETS OF FISH
Place on a greased oven-proof dish:
Fish fillets
Dot them generously with:
Butter
They may be spread with:
Anchovy paste
or season with:
**Salt
Paprika**
Sprinkle them generously with:
**(Cornflakes)
(Minced onion)
(Grated cheese)**
The cornflakes may be dotted with:
Butter
Bake the fillets in a moderate oven
325° until they are done. See General
Rule for Cooking Fish, page 228.
A cupful of milk may be put in the
dish. Add chopped onion and season-
ing. You may bake the fish until it is
tender, sprinkle it with grated cheese
and place it under a broiler until the
cheese is melted.

BAKED FILLETS OF FISH IN WINE OR VEGETABLE SAUCE
4 Servings
Place in a greased shallow baking pan:
1½ lbs. fillets of sole or other fish
If the fillets are large they may be cut
in half. Sprinkle the fish with:
Paprika
Pour over them:
**1 cup dry white wine or vegetable
stock
(2 tablespoons dry sherry)**
Bake the fish in a moderate oven 325°

until they are just tender. See General Rule for Cooking Fish, page 228. Baste them often with the wine. When tender, remove the fillets carefully to a greased heated oven-proof platter. Reserve the liquid in the pan. Melt:

2 tablespoons butter

Stir in:

1½ tablespoons flour

Add gradually the wine in which the fish was baked. Stir and cook until the sauce is smooth and boiling. Reduce the heat and stir in:

½ cup cream
Salt if needed
Paprika or pepper
(1 teaspoon lemon juice)
(1 cup sautéed mushrooms)

Continue to stir until the sauce is hot, but not boiling. Pour it over the fillets. Place them under the broiler for a few minutes until the sauce is bubbly and lightly browned in spots, or:
Strain the drippings. Place them over, not in, boiling water. Stir in with a wire whisk:

1 egg yolk

Add bit by bit:

2 tablespoons butter

Beat the sauce until it thickens. Season it as needed. Pour it over the fish.

SAUTÉED AND BAKED FILLETS OF FISH
4 Servings

Melt:

4 tablespoons butter

Brown in the butter:

2 small chopped onions

Lightly sauté in the butter:

4 fish fillets

Place them on an oven-proof dish. Add to the skillet:

½ cup dry white wine, stock or cream
½ teaspoon salt

Pour the sauce over the fish. Bake the fish in a moderate oven 350° for about 15 minutes. You may serve it covered with:

Buttered Oysters, page 113

BAKED FILLETS OF HADDOCK IN CREAM SAUCE
4 Servings

Place on an oven-proof dish:

4 haddock or other fish fillets

Prepare:

2 cups Cream Sauce I, page 428, or Cheese Sauce, page 431

Season the sauce well, add:

1 teaspoon Worcestershire sauce or ½ teaspoon dry mustard or 1 teaspoon fennel, dill or celery seed
(2 tablespoons sherry)

Pour it over the fillets. Bake the fish in a moderate oven 325° until it is tender. See General Rule for Cooking Fish, page 228. Remove the fish to a platter. You may sprinkle over it:

1 cup or more fresh boiled or canned shrimp

Place the dish under a broiler until the shrimp are heated. Sprinkle it with:

Chopped chives

QUICK BAKED FILLETS OF FISH
3 Servings

A good hurry-up recipe. Place in an oven-proof dish:

1 lb. fish fillets

Stir and heat until smooth:

5 oz. condensed soup: tomato, celery, mushroom or asparagus
2 tablespoons milk

Add:

A few grains cayenne
½ teaspoon curry powder or 2 tablespoons sherry

Pour the sauce over the fish. Bake it as directed in the preceding rule.

QUICK BAKED FROZEN FISH FILLETS
4 Servings

This exception to the rule that fish is better when thawed before cooking is inserted for the benefit of the hurry-up cook. Cut into quarters:

A 1 lb. block frozen fillets

Combine:

¼ cup all-purpose flour
¾ teaspoon salt
⅛ teaspoon pepper

Roll the pieces in this until well coated. Place them in a greased oven-proof dish. Melt:

3 tablespoons butter or drippings

You may sauté lightly in this:

1 teaspoon grated onion

Add:

½ cup dry white wine or vegetable stock

Pour the sauce over the fish. Cover it closely. Bake it in a hot oven 450° for about 25 minutes. See General Rule for Cooking Fish, page 228.

ROLLED FILLED FILLETS OF FISH BAKED
4 Servings
Cut in two lengthwise:
    4 fillets of fish
Season them with:
    Paprika
Butter muffin tins or custard cups. Line them with the fillets, permitting them to overlap.
Combine and stir with a fork:
    ¼ cup melted butter
    1½ cups soft bread crumbs
    ¼ cup chopped celery
    1 teaspoon grated onion
    1 tablespoon chopped parsley
    ¼ teaspoon dried Herbs, page 832
    ¼ teaspoon salt
Fill the muffin cups with this filling. Or you may place the filling upon the fillets and roll them. In that case secure them with toothpicks and spread with:
    Melted butter or heavy cream
Place them in greased muffin tins or custard cups. Place the tins or cups in a pan of hot water in a moderate oven 375° for about ½ hour. Unmold the fillets on a hot platter. Garnish them with:
    Lemon wedges
    Parsley or water cress
Serve them with:
    Lemon Butter, page 258
    Salt if needed
    (2 teaspoons Worcestershire sauce)

FISH STEAKS OR FILLETS BAKED IN SEA FOOD SAUCE
6 Servings
Place in boiling water or milk and simmer until nearly tender:
    6 fillets or 3 steaks
This will be a quick process if the fillets are thin. Drain them. Place them in a greased baking dish or platter. Keep them where they will remain hot. Melt:
    ¼ cup butter
Stir and sauté in it until done:
    ½ lb. mushrooms
Stir in:
    4 tablespoons flour
Stir in gradually:
    1¾ cups milk
Cook in their liquor until plump:
    ½ pint oysters: 1 cup
Strain them. Add them to the boiling cream sauce. Stir in:
    ¼ lb. cooked shelled shrimp

Remove the sauce from the fire and add the oyster liquor and:
    ½ cup dry white wine
    Seasoning
Pour the sauce over the fillets. Bake them in a moderate oven 350° for about 10 minutes. Serve them garnished. See:
    Garnishes for Fish, page 261

BAKED FISH STEAKS WITH SALT PORK
Place in a shallow pan:
    Thin slices salt pork or bacon
    ½ bay leaf
    2 tablespoons chopped onion
Place over these ingredients a thick:
    Fish steak
Combine and spread the fish with equal parts of:
    Butter and flour
Cover it with:
    Soft bread crumbs
Place over it:
    Several thin slices salt pork or bacon
Bake it in a moderate oven 325° until it is tender. See General Rule for Cooking Fish, page 228. Serve it with:
    Creole Sauce, page 434,
    Mushroom or Horseradish
    Sauce, page 436, 429

BAKED FISH STEAKS WITH CHEESE
Follow the above rule for:
    Baked Fish Steaks with Salt Pork
Omit the pork. Use a well-greased pan. When ½ done sprinkle the steaks well with equal parts of:
    Bread crumbs and grated cheese

BAKED HERRING AND POTATOES
4 Servings
A fine dish reputed to be a favorite among Swedes and Poles. Soak overnight in water to cover:
    2 large salt herring
Drain them. Split them. Remove and discard skin and bones. Cut fillets into 1 inch wide pieces. Pare and slice very thinly:
    6 raw potatoes
    2 medium-sized onions
Butter a baking dish. Place in it alternate layers of potatoes, onions and herring, beginning and ending with potatoes. Cover the top with:
    ¼ cup bread crumbs

dotted with:
    2 tablespoons butter
Bake the dish in a moderate oven 375°
for 45 minutes or more.

___

PLANKED FISH
Allow ½ Pound Fish Per Person
Bone (page 227):
    Fish weighing 2 or more lbs.
Place the fish skin side down on a
greased plank of hickory, oak or ash.
Sprinkle it lightly with:
    Salt
    Paprika
and pour over it:
    ½ cup melted butter
and:
    1 cup rolled cornflakes or dry
    bread crumbs
Bake the fish in a moderate oven 350°.
Allow about 15 minutes to the pound.
See General Rule for Cooking Fish,
page 228. Brown the fish for the last
5 minutes under a broiler. Serve it
garnished with:
    Mashed potatoes
    Beet cups filled with tartar
    sauce
    Parsley, etc.

___

MICHIGAN PANNED FISH
Bone (page 227):
    A fish
Place a piece of heavy greased waxed
paper in a pan and put the fish flat
upon it, skin side down. Season it
with:
    Salt
Dredge it with:
    Flour, cracker crumbs or
    cornflakes
Dot it with:
    Butter
and sprinkle the top with:
    Paprika
Cook the fish on the preheated upper
grate of a hot oven 400° from 20 to 30
minutes. Serve it with:
    Slices of lemon
    Chopped parsley

___

BAKED FINNAN HADDIE
6 Servings
Prepare for cooking:
    2 lbs. finnan haddie
Soak it in warm water for ½ hour,
skin side down. Pour off the water.
Put the fish on a greased oven-proof
pan and cover it with:
    1 cup rich cold milk
Dot it generously with:

Butter
Sprinkle it with:
    ¼ cup chopped onions
    Paprika
Bake it in a moderate oven 350° for
about 40 minutes. See General Rule
for Cooking Fish, page 228. If milk
evaporates, use additional hot milk.
This may be served with:
    Cream Sauce I, page 428

___

BROILED FISH
Bone (page 227):
    A large fish: lake trout, white-
    fish, etc.
Flatten it out or cut it into pieces. Rub
a saucer with:
    Garlic
Place in it and mix:
    1 or 2 tablespoons olive oil
    ¼ teaspoon pepper
Rub the fish inside and out with these
ingredients. Place it in a greased shal-
low pan. Broil it 3 inches from the
heating unit under a moderately hot
broiler until it is brown. Turn it once.
Season it with:
    Salt
Spread it with:
    Maître d'Hôtel Butter, page 431,
    or Lemon Butter Sauce, page
    258, or Soufflé Sauce, page 260
Garnish it with:
    Parsley
    Cucumbers in sour cream with
    herbs

___

BREADED BROILED FILLETS
OF FISH
4 Servings
Cut into pieces suitable for individual
service:
    1½ lbs. fish fillets: haddock, halibut,
    etc.
Roll them in a mixture of:
    ¼ cup oil or melted butter
    Juice of 1 lemon
then in a mixture of:
    ⅓ cup fine dry bread crumbs,
    cornflakes or other crumbs
    3 tablespoons finely chopped
    parsley
    1 teaspoon salt
    ½ teaspoon paprika
Place them on a greased shallow pan
or oven-proof platter in a broiling oven
3 inches below a good flame. Broil
them until they are tender. See General Rule for Cooking Fish, page 228.
Baste them frequently with:
    Oil or melted butter

BROILED SCROD
Split, then remove the bones from:
    A young codfish: scrod
Leave it whole, flatten it out, or cut it in pieces. Follow the above rule for:
    Broiled Fillets of Fish

ROLLED BREADED FILLETS OF FISH
Cut into strips 5 inches by 1:
    Halibut or sole fillets
Sprinkle them with:
    Lemon juice
Brush them with:
    Melted drippings or oil
Dip them in:
    Fine seasoned bread crumbs
Roll the strips. Fasten them with toothpicks. Place them on a sheet in a broiling oven 4 inches below the flame. Baste them frequently with melted drippings or oil. Cook them for 15 minutes. Baste them with:
    Cream
Cook them for about 5 minutes longer. These may be served with:
    Tomato, tartar or other sauce

BROILED MACKEREL WITH ANCHOVY BUTTER
Split and bone (page 228):
    A mackerel
Place it skin down in a greased pan. Sprinkle it with:
    Paprika
Brush it with:
    Melted butter or olive oil
Broil it slowly on one side only until it is tender, for about 20 minutes. Baste it with the drippings as it cooks. Remove it to a hot platter. Spread it with:
    Anchovy Butter, page 258
Garnish it with:
    Parsley and lemon slice
Serve it very hot.

BROILED SALT MACKEREL
Soak by the preceding rule:
    Salt mackerel
Drain, then wipe it dry. Brush the fish with:
    Melted butter
Broil it on a well-greased preheated broiler, skin side down. See To Broil a Fish, page 229. Baste it twice with melted butter as it cooks. Remove it to a hot platter. Pour over it:
    ½ cup Cream Sauce I, page 428
Garnish with:
    Chopped parsley

BOILED SALT MACKEREL
Soak overnight, skin up, well covered with cold water:
    Salt mackerel
Drain it, place it in a shallow pan. Cover it with water and simmer it until tender, for about 12 minutes. Drain it well. Place it on a hot platter. Pour over it:
    Melted butter
to which add:
    Chopped chives or parsley,
    lemon juice or Worcestershire
    sauce

CREAMED FINNAN HADDIE
Barely cover:
    Finnan haddie
with:
    Milk
Soak it for 1 hour. Bring it slowly to the boiling point. Simmer it for 20 minutes. Drain it. Flake it and remove the skin and bones. Place the fish in boiling:
    Cream Sauce I, page 428
Use about ⅔ as much sauce as you have fish. Add for each cupful of flaked fish:
    1 chopped hard-cooked egg
    1 teaspoon chopped green pepper
    1 teaspoon chopped pimiento
Serve the fish on:
    Rounds of toast
Sprinkle it with:
    Lemon juice
    Chopped chives or parsley

BAKED FINNAN HADDIE
If you wish to bake finnan haddie, soak it in equal parts of milk and water. Dry it. Spread it with melted butter. Bake it for about 20 minutes in a moderate oven 350°. Or, spread it with melted butter and broil it under a low flame for about 15 minutes. Serve it with hot Lemon Butter, page 258

"BOILED" FISH
Allow ½ Pound Fish Per Person
My conscience—or is it Marion?—compels me to make this statement: From the nutritional standpoint the boiling of fish is objectionable, for, unless watched carefully and never permitted to go beyond the simmering point, it destroys flavors and nutritional values that are less apt to be lost in the steaming of fish. The latter is a highly recommended method. Sorry, "boiled" fish is one of my favorite dishes.

Scrape, remove the entrails and clean:
A fish weighing 2 or more lbs.
To facilitate handling, the fish may be tied in a cloth, wrapped in parchment paper, or put on an oven-proof dish. Place in a kettle sufficient water to cover the fish. The seasoned water or stock in which fish is boiled is known as court bouillon. This is a very simple rule, the following a more elaborate one. Add:

> 1 tablespoon vinegar or lemon
> juice
> 1 small sliced onion
> ½ cup chopped celery with leaves
> 1 teaspoon salt

When the water boils immerse the fish. Reduce the heat and simmer the fish until it is tender. See General Rule for Cooking Fish, page 228. Do not permit the water to boil as that robs the fish of its delicate flavor. Drain the fish and place it on a platter garnished with:

> Half slices of lemon dipped in
> chopped parsley

or with:

> Wedges of lemon and sprigs of
> parsley

Serve it with:

> Melted butter

or with:

> Cream Sauce I, page 428, and
> capers or Mustard, Shrimp or
> Curry Sauce for Fish, page 258,
> or Onion Sauce I or II, page
> 432, etc.

COURT BOUILLON

A stock in which fish is cooked. Melt:

> 3 tablespoons butter

Stir and sauté in the butter for 5 minutes:

> ¼ cup chopped carrots
> ½ cup chopped celery
> ½ cup chopped onions

Add:

> A few sprigs parsley
> 6 peppercorns
> 3 or 4 cloves
> 1 cup dry white wine or ½ cup
> vinegar
> 2 quarts boiling water
> (A Bouquet Garni, page 832)

The butter may be omitted and the vegetables added directly to the water. Rub a fish with:

> Lemon juice

Immerse it in the boiling court bouillon, reduce the heat at once and simmer the fish until tender. See General Rule for Cooking Fish, page 228.

COLD BOILED SALMON OR OTHER FISH WITH SAUCE

This is fine for a buffet supper—stunning to look at and good to eat. Boil by the rule on page 237:

> A medium-sized salmon or
> other fish

This may be done in Court Bouillon, see the preceding rule. Skin the fish if desired. Place it in a long deep dish. Have ready the following sauce:

> ½ cup finely chopped onions
> ½ cup finely chopped dill pickles
> 6 tablespoons finely chopped
> parsley
> 2 chopped hard-cooked eggs
> 2 tablespoons finely chopped
> chives
> 2 tablespoons capers
> 1 teaspoon sugar
> ¼ cup olive oil
> 6 tablespoons tarragon vinegar
> or lemon juice
> ½ teaspoon freshly ground black
> pepper
> 2 cups hot fish stock

While the fish is warm baste it from time to time with ½ the sauce. Permit it to chill in the sauce. When the fish is cold place it on a platter. Garnish it with:

> Pickled beets
> Marinated cucumbers
> Hard-cooked eggs, etc.
> Water cress or lettuce

Serve it with the remaining sauce. The matter of the sauce is optional. If preferred, omit it and prepare the following aspic.
Season well the stock in which the fish was cooked with:

> Dry white wine, lemon juice or
> vinegar

and, if needed, with:

> Salt if needed and pepper

Strain the stock and measure it. Allow:

> 1 tablespoon gelatine

to:

> 2 cups stock

Soak the gelatine in a little of the stock. Dissolve it over hot water. Add it to the rest of the stock. Chill it. When the gelatine is about to set pour it over the fish or brush it over the fish to glaze it, or permit the gelatine to stiffen in a bowl. Turn it out onto a board and chop it with a knife. Surround the fish with the chopped gelatine. Serve the fish on a garnished platter, see next rule and Fish in Aspic, page 477, with:

> Mayonnaise

COLD SALMON GLAZED

Fine for a buffet supper or luncheon. Very decorative.

Wrap in a piece of cheesecloth or parchment paper:

    A 3 or 4 lb. piece salmon

Follow the rule on pages 237 and 239 for:

    Boiled Fish or Steamed Fish

Simmer it until it is tender. Drain the salmon. Reserve the stock. Let it cool in the cloth. Remove the cloth. Skin the salmon. Use it as it is or glaze it with aspic as directed in the preceding recipe. Arrange it on a bed of:

    Water cress or lettuce

Garnish it with:

    Mayonnaise

Place around it:

    Cucumbers in sour cream with herbs

STEAMED FISH

Allow ½ Pound Fish Per Person

Scrape, remove the entrails, clean and cut into pieces:

    A large fish

A small fish may be steamed whole. Place the fish in a steamer or in a colander over, not in, boiling water. Cover

the colander with a closely fitting lid. Steam the fish until it is tender. See General Rule for Cooking Fish, page 228. Unless the pieces are very thick it will not be necessary to turn them. Serve the fish with:

    Melted butter or some sort of Fish Sauce, page 258

Or make a sauce of the water over which the fish was steamed. Use:

    Butter
    Flour
    The fish stock and cream, see Cream Sauce I, page 428

Season it well with:

    Mustard
    Curry powder

    Worcestershire sauce or lemon juice

Sprinkle the sauce with:

    Salted chopped almonds

Garnish the platter with:

    Grilled Tomatoes and Onions, page 320

POACHED FISH

4 Servings

Fish may be poached in vegetable or meat stock, milk, dry white wine or wine diluted with stock or water. If there is insufficient stock for sauce, add cream or wine.

Combine in a skillet:

    1 cup water
    1 small chopped onion
    2 chopped ribs celery with leaves
    ¼ teaspoon paprika
    A thin slice of lemon

When the water boils add:

    1¾ lbs. fish: small fish, steaks or fillets

Reduce the heat at once and simmer the fish until done. See General Rule for Cooking Fish, page 228. Melt:

    2 tablespoons butter

Stir in:

    2 tablespoons flour

Add about 1 cupful strained fish stock. Permit the sauce to boil. In place of the butter and flour you may add an egg yolk to the stock. Stir the sauce over low heat until slightly thickened but do not let it boil. Season it with:

    Salt
    Lots of chopped parsley

The following are similar rules but suggest other variations.

POACHED FILLETS OF SOLE IN WINE SAUCE WITH MUSHROOMS

3 Servings

Melt:

    2 tablespoons butter

Add and cook lightly:

    A thin slice onion

Add:

    ⅛ teaspoon pepper
    ¾ cup dry white wine

When these ingredients are simmering add:

    1 lb. fillets of sole

Cover the pan and simmer the fish until done. See General Rule for Cooking Fish, page 228. Place the fillets on a greased oven-proof dish. Keep them hot. Strain the stock. Reserve it. Sauté, see page *292*, for 3 minutes:

½ lb. mushrooms
in:
2 tablespoons butter
Or use canned mushrooms, drained and heated in the butter. Beat into the fish stock:
1 egg or 2 egg yolks
Salt
Cook it gently over a low flame or in a double boiler until it thickens slightly. Add the mushrooms to the stock. Add seasoning if needed. Pour the sauce over the fish. You may bake it in a moderate oven 375° until well heated. Serve it garnished with:
Parsley

POACHED HALIBUT STEAK IN CURRY SAUCE
4 Servings
Cut into pieces suitable for individual servings:
1½ lbs. halibut steak or other fish
Place it in a skillet. Cover it with:
Boiling water
Season it with:
4 whole black peppercorns
½ bay leaf
2 teaspoons lemon juice
Simmer it about 10 minutes, or until tender. Remove to a hot platter. Strain the stock. Sauté until brown:
1 tablespoon minced onion
in:
2 tablespoons butter
Stir in until blended:
2 tablespoons flour
Stir in slowly:
1 cup strained fish stock
Cook the sauce until it is smooth and boiling. Add:
½ to 1 teaspoon curry powder
Salt if needed
Stir in until hot but not boiling:
¼ cup cream
Pour the sauce over the fish. Serve it garnished with:
Slices of lemon
Sprigs of parsley
One-half pound sautéed mushrooms may be added to the sauce. You may omit the curry and substitute fresh or dried herb or other flavoring like mustard, catsup, etc.

FISH POACHED IN SOUR CREAM
4 Servings
Prepare for cooking:
1½ lbs. fish
Cut it into small pieces. Sauté until light brown:

¼ cup minced onion
in:
2 tablespoons butter
Stir in and bring to the boiling point:
1½ cups sour cream
½ teaspoon salt
½ teaspoon paprika
Add the fish gradually. Do not disturb the boiling point. Simmer the fish for 5 minutes. Remove it to a hot platter. Pour some of the cream over:
2 beaten egg yolks
Return it to the rest of the cream. Stir and cook the sauce over low heat until the eggs have thickened slightly. Add:
Salt if needed
1½ tablespoons lemon juice or dry white wine
(½ teaspoon dried basil)
Pour the sauce over the fish.

FILLETS OF FISH ON SPINACH WITH SHRIMP AND MUSHROOMS
3 Servings
Cook, then drain:
1 lb. spinach or broccoli
Poach (page 239):
1 lb. fillets of haddock
Cook, then shell (page 245):
½ lb. shrimp
Sauté (page 292):
½ lb. mushrooms
Prepare:
1 cup Cream Sauce, page 428, using the stock in which the fish was poached and cream
Combine:
1 egg yolk
2 tablespoons sherry
Add these ingredients to the cream sauce. Thicken it by stirring it over low heat, but do not permit it to boil. Place the spinach on a buttered oven-proof dish. Place the fillets on it. Pour the sauce over them. Surround them with the mushrooms and shrimp. Place the dish in a moderately hot oven 400° until well heated.

FRENCH FRIED FISH
Method I.
Have fish at room temperature. Clean and prepare for cooking:
Small fish or pieces of fish about 1 inch thick
Dip them in:
Fritter Batter, page 543, sugar omitted, or page 140
Fry them in deep fat heated to 370° (see page 542) for 5 to 8 minutes, or

until a golden brown. The fish will rise to the surface when done. Drain them on absorbent paper. Serve them very hot with:

**Lemon wedges or
Tartar Sauce, page 439**

Method II.

The fish may be dipped in an egg diluted with 1 tablespoonful of water and then in very fine, dry, seasoned bread crumbs or in corn meal, but the most delicious fish ever served to me was in France and it had been dipped in a thin batter and fried as in Method I. The crust crumbled at the touch of my fork.

Method III.

Make a paste of equal parts of flour and water or a little more flour than water. Season it. Dip pieces of fillet of sole into the paste, then in fine bread crumbs. Fry the fish in deep fat heated to 370° for 3 minutes. Drain it on absorbent paper.

Method IV.

See the following rule for Sour Sauce.

FRIED FISH IN SOUR SAUCE
6 Servings
Cut into pieces:
1½ lbs. fish steaks
Marinate them for 30 minutes in:
**6 tablespoons dry white wine or
2 tablespoons lemon juice**
Drain them, dry them and dip each piece separately in:
6 tablespoons thick cream
then in:
½ cup flour
Fry the fish in deep fat 370° (page 542) for about 7 minutes. Serve the fish with the following sauce. Sauté in butter (page 292):
½ lb. mushrooms
Prepare:
1 cup well-seasoned Cream Sauce I, page 428
Use cream and the liquid in which the fish was soaked or dipped. You may add:
1 tablespoon lemon juice or dry white wine
Shortly before serving beat into the sauce one at a time over very low heat:
2 eggs
Keep the sauce hot over hot, not boiling, water. Place the fried fish on a platter. Pour the sauce over it. Garnish it with the sautéed mushrooms and with:
Parsley or chopped chives

SAUTÉED FISH OR "FRIED" FISH
Scrape, remove the entrails and clean (page 226):
A large fish or several small fish
Cut the large fish into pieces and roll them in:
Seasoned flour or corn meal
Or you may dip them in "ready to use" pancake flour. Melt in a skillet to the depth of ⅛ inch:
Bacon drippings and butter
It is inadvisable to use butter when sautéing large fish without the addition of some other fat as it burns more readily than other shortening or drippings. When the fat is hot place the fish in it. To keep the fat from spattering your hands you may cover the pan with an inverted colander. Reduce the heat slightly and cook the fish until it is done, from 3 to 5 minutes. My former cook, Virginia Turner, taught me to complete cooking one side of the fish, to turn it and cook the other until done. This is a very good method.

Fish may be sautéed on both sides until it is seared and then be placed in a moderate oven 375° until it is done, for about 10 minutes.

See Garnishes for Fish, page 261.

BROOK TROUT
4 Servings
Clean and wash:
4 brook trout: 8 inches each
Cut off the fins. Leave the head and tail on. Dip the trout in:
Seasoned flour
Melt:
¼ cup butter
Sauté the trout in this until they are tender and nicely browned. Remove the trout to a hot platter. Add to the drippings in the pan:
3 tablespoons butter
Permit it to brown. Pour it over the fish. Serve them with:
**Lemon wedges
Chopped parsley**

FILLETS SAUTÉED
Sauté:
Fish fillets
in a small amount of:
Hot oil or drippings
This is an unusually quick process requiring only a few minutes. See General Rule for Cooking Fish, page 228. Turn the fish once. While the fish is cooking melt in a small skillet, or cook the fish, remove from pan, keep them

hot and use the same skillet, additional:

Oil or drippings

Sauté in it for 2 minutes:

(Minced mushrooms)

Add:

Chopped parsley
Salt and pepper
A few drops lemon juice

Place the fish on a platter and pour the sauce over it.

FILLETS OF SOLE SAUTÉED

Dip:

Fillets of sole

in:

Milk

Dust them with:

Flour

Sprinkle them lightly with:

Salt
Paprika

Melt in a skillet:

Butter—enough to cover the bottom well

Sauté the fillets in the pan. See General Rule for Cooking Fish, page 228. Turn them once. Place them on a hot platter. Melt in the skillet additional:

Butter

Brown in it lightly:

Blanched shredded almonds

Pour them over the fillets. Garnish them with:

Lemon and parsley

SMELTS
4 Servings

To clean smelts, spread open the outer gills and with the forefinger take hold of the inner gills and pull gently; the parts unfit for food are all attached to these inner gills and come away together, leaving the smelt in perfect shape. Rinse thoroughly and wipe dry.

Clean:

8 to 12 smelts

Leave them whole. Season them with:

Salt
Pepper
Lemon juice

Permit them to stand covered for 15 minutes. Roll the smelts in:

Cream

Dip them in:

Flour or corn meal

Melt:

¼ cup butter

Sauté the smelts gently until they are done, or bake them in a buttered pan in a hot oven 450° for about 5 minutes.

Place them on a hot platter. Add to the butter in the pan:

Juice of 1 lemon
2 tablespoons chopped parsley or chives
2 teaspoons anchovy paste

Or you may place ½ anchovy in each smelt. Pour the sauce over the smelts. Smelts may be dipped in crumbs, egg and crumbs and fried in deep fat at 370° (page 542). Serve them with:

Tartar Sauce, page 439

FILLED FISH

This is either boiled or baked. Scald and clean well:

A fish weighing 2 lbs. or more

Make a gash in the fish, take out the entrails and remove all bones and meat, keeping the skin intact. Mince or grind the meat. Soak in water:

1 cup bread crumbs

Wring the water from the crumbs. Add them to the fish meat with:

½ cup melted butter
2 tablespoons minced parsley
1½ tablespoons grated onions
1 teaspoon salt
¼ teaspoon pepper
Freshly grated nutmeg
(1 egg)

Blend these ingredients lightly with a fork. Stuff the skin with the filling and sew it together, keeping the original shape of the fish. Place the fish in boiling salted water to cover, to which you may add vegetables suitable for soup. Simmer the fish for about 45 minutes. Remove it to a hot platter. You may make a sauce of the strained stock. Thicken it by pouring part of it over 2 egg yolks, blending them well and returning them to the remaining stock. Cook and stir the sauce over very low heat until the eggs thicken slightly. Add:

Seasoning
Lemon juice or sherry

Or, instead of boiling the fish place it in a baking dish, dot it generously with butter and bake it in a moderate oven 375° for about 45 minutes. Baste it frequently with:

Hot butter and water

Serve it with:

Sliced lemon
Chopped parsley

ROE AND MILT

Shad roe is choice, but the roe of other fish—mackerel, flounder, salmon, haddock, etc.—is frequently substituted.

Milt comes from the male fish. The blue vein that runs through salmon milt is removed and discarded. Roe, except the roe of very small shad, and milt are not cooked with the fish. They are sometimes parboiled and the delicate membrane that encloses them is removed and they are then ready to use in various ways. See the preceding and the following rules. Omitting the parboiling, they may be breaded and baked to an internal heat of 150° in a moderate oven 300° for about 30 minutes.

BROILED OR BAKED SHAD WITH CREAMED ROE
Cover:
        Shad roe
with:
        Boiling water
Add to it:
        3 tablespoons dry white wine or lemon juice
Simmer it for 15 minutes. Drain it. Remove the outside membrane. Mash the roe. Melt in a saucepan:
        2 tablespoons butter
You may add and sauté for 5 minutes:
        1 tablespoon grated onion
Add the roe and stir in:
        2 tablespoons flour
        ½ cup cream
When these ingredients begin to boil remove them from the fire. Stir in:
        2 egg yolks
Season the roe well with:
        Dry white wine or lemon juice
Keep it hot. Bone by the rule on page 227:
        A 3 or 4 lb. shad
Place it skin side down on a well-greased broiler rack, a flat pan or a plank. Season the fish with:
        Freshly ground pepper
Brush it with:
        Melted butter
Broil it gently for about 15 minutes, or bake in a moderate oven 350°, allowing about 8 minutes per pound. See General Rule for Cooking Fish, page 242. Remove it from the oven and spread the thin part of the fish with the creamed roe. Cover the fish with:
        Buttered cornflakes or bread crumbs
Return it to the broiler to brown evenly. Season it with:
        Salt
Serve it at once garnished with:
        Lemon slices
        Parsley or water cress
        Pickled beets, cucumbers, etc.

PARBOILED SHAD ROE
Cover with boiling water:
        Shad roe
Add to it:
        1 tablespoon vinegar
Simmer it from 3 to 12 minutes, according to the size of the roe. Drain it. Cool it. Remove the membrane. Add salt if needed.

Canned Fish Roe, page 128.

BROILED ROE
Wipe dry and place on a greased rack:
        Parboiled Shad Roe, see above
Sprinkle it with:
        Pepper
        Lemon juice
Broil it slowly from 5 to 7 minutes. Baste it with:
        Butter
Turn and broil it 5 to 7 minutes more, basting it again. Season it with:
        Salt
Serve the roe split in two on toast garnished with:
        Parsley
        Crisp bacon
        Maître d'Hôtel Butter, page 431

SHAD ROE AND BACON
Sauté or bake (page 375):
        Slices of bacon
Place the bacon on a platter and keep it hot. Sauté in the drippings on both sides for about 10 minutes:
        Parboiled Shad Roe, see above
You may dip the roe in:
        Seasoned flour
Serve the roe surrounded by the bacon, garnished with:
        Lemon slices
        Parsley

SAUTÉED SHAD ROE WITH HERB SAUCE
Heat until light brown:
        2 tablespoons butter
Sauté in this until delicately browned on both sides:
        Parboiled Shad Roe, see above
Season it lightly with:
        Salt and pepper
Remove it to a hot platter. Add to the drippings and heat:
        2 teaspoons lemon juice
        ½ teaspoon chopped chives
        ½ teaspoon chopped parsley
        1 minced shallot
        ½ teaspoon dried tarragon, chervil or basil

Or add to the drippings and brown:
 ¼ cup dry bread crumbs
 1 teaspoon anchovy paste
If you plan doing this, be careful not
to use salt in the first place.
Pour the sauce over the roe. Sautéed
roe is frequently served with Tartar
Sauce, page 439.

FRIED SHAD ROE
Parboil (page 243):
 Shad roe
Cut it into pieces. Sprinkle them with:
 Lemon juice
 Pepper
 Salt
Roll them in:
 Corn meal or cracker crumbs
Dip them in:
 1 egg diluted with 2 tablespoons
 water
and again in corn meal or crumbs.
Fry the roe in deep fat at 390° (page
542).

BAKED SHAD ROE
Parboil (page 243):
 Shad roe
Place it in a buttered pan. Cover it
with:
 Tomato Sauce, page 433
Bake it in a moderate oven 375° for 25
minutes. Baste it every 5 minutes.
Serve it with additional tomato sauce.

CANNED SHAD ROE BROILED
2 Servings
Separate into pieces the contents of:
 1 can shad roe: 7¾ oz., or other
 canned fish roe
Dry them with a paper towel. Brush
them with:
 Melted butter
Sprinkle them with:
 Lemon juice
 Paprika
Place them in a shallow greased pan or
on a greased broiler. Broil the roe
gently for about 10 minutes. Turn it
once. Baste it frequently with:
 Melted butter
Serve it on toast garnished with:
 Slices of lemon
 Chopped parsley

CANNED SHAD ROE CREAMED
2 Servings
Sauté the contents of:
 1 can shad roe: 7¾ oz.
in:

 Butter
Add:
 Salt and paprika
 ¾ cup cream
 ½ teaspoon curry powder
Reheat but do not boil the roe. Serve
it on:
 Toast

TO CLEAN FROG LEGS
Frog legs resemble chicken in texture
and flavor. They are usually bought
skinned and ready to use. Allow 2
large or 6 small frog legs per person.
If the frogs are not prepared, cut off
the hind legs—the only part of the frog
used—close to the body. Wash them
in cold water, begin at the top and
strip off the skin like a glove. Through
an experiment with a twitching frog
leg Galvani discovered the electric
current that bears his name. If you
wish to avoid this seemingly untimely
activity, chill the frog legs well.

FROG LEGS
4 Servings
Clean:
 8 large frog legs
Roll them in:
 Seasoned flour
Melt in a skillet:
 6 tablespoons butter or bacon
 drippings
Rub the skillet with:
 ½ clove garlic
or sauté in the drippings:
 ½ cup chopped onions
Brown the frog legs in the butter.
Reduce the heat and add:
 ¾ cup Boiling Stock, page 43
Cover the skillet closely and cook the
frog legs until they are tender, for
about 10 minutes. Melt:
 6 tablespoons butter
Sauté in the butter:
 1¼ cups seasoned bread crumbs
Add:
 1 teaspoon lemon juice
Roll the frog legs in the bread crumbs
and serve them garnished with:
 Parsley
Or, prepare:
 1½ cups Boiling Cream Sauce,
 page 428
The sauce may be made with the drip-
pings and cream. Flavor it with:
 Sherry
Pour it over the cooked frog legs.
Serve them garnished with:
 Parsley

FROG LEGS FRIED
Clean:
>Frog legs

Season them with:
>Salt and pepper

Dip them in:
>Sifted bread crumbs

then in:
>1 egg diluted with 2 tablespoons
>water

and again in crumbs. Permit them to dry for 1 hour. Fry the frog legs in deep fat 375° (page 542). Drain them. Serve them with:
>Tartar Sauce, page 439

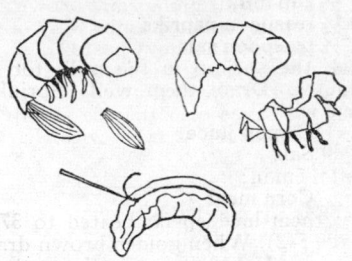

FROG LEGS IN MUSHROOM SAUCE
3 Servings

Clean:
>6 large frog legs

Cut each leg into 3 or 4 pieces. Place them in a saucepan. Cover them with:
>Boiling water

Add:
>2 thin slices lemon
>⅛ teaspoon pepper
>(Celery, parsley, onion or
>vegetables suitable for soup)

Simmer the frog legs covered until they are tender. Drain them well. Melt in a saucepan:
>3 tablespoons butter

Add to it and sauté until light brown:
>1 cup sliced mushrooms

Stir in:
>1½ tablespoons flour

Stir in slowly:
>1½ cups Chicken Stock or stock in
>which the frog legs were cooked

Season the sauce with:
>Salt and paprika

When the sauce is boiling add the frog legs. Reduce the heat to low. Beat well:
>3 egg yolks
>3 tablespoons rich cream

Stir these ingredients into the sauce. Cook them until they thicken. Add:
>1½ teaspoons lemon juice or 2
>teaspoons sherry

Serve the frog legs at once.

SHRIMP
Shrimp are small shellfish which may be boiled or steamed, shelled, deveined and used in many pleasant ways. The shells may be pulled off either before or after cooking. The intestinal vein (harmless but unappetizing), a dark line along the body meat, is removed with a pointed utensil or the blunt end of a toothpick. Allow 1 pound of shrimp in the shell or ½ pound of shelled shrimp for 3 or 4 small servings.

STEAMED SHRIMP
Wash and place fresh or "green" shrimp in the shell in a covered steamer over boiling water. Cook them for 2 minutes. Remove the steamer from the stove, keep it covered and allow the shrimp to remain over hot water 2 minutes longer. Shell, then remove the intestinal vein and use the shrimp in appetizers, see page 39, salads, creamed, etc.

BOILED SHRIMP
Simmer for 15 minutes:
>8 cups water
>¼ cup sliced onion
>1 clove garlic
>1 bay leaf
>2 ribs celery with leaves
>1½ tablespoons salt
>⅛ teaspoon cayenne

Wash, drain and add:
>2 lbs. raw shrimp

Slice and add:
>½ lemon

Simmer the shrimp for 15 minutes. Permit them to cool in the water in which they were cooked. Drain them. Use the water for soup. Usually good as is with a dash of cream added. Chill them. Serve them very cold in their shells (to be shelled at table) with a bowl of:
>Russian Dressing, page 496

or, shell them, remove the intestinal vein and use them as desired.

FRIED SHRIMP
4 Servings

Shell:
>1 lb. raw shrimp

Remove the intestinal vein. Combine:

⅔ cup milk
⅛ teaspoon paprika
¼ teaspoon salt

Soak the shrimp in the milk for 30 minutes. Drain them well. Sprinkle them with:

Lemon juice
Salt

Roll them in:

Corn meal

Fry them in deep fat heated to 375° (page 542). When golden brown drain them on absorbent paper. Serve them hot with:

Lemon juice or mayonnaise seasoned with puréed chutney

SHRIMP FRIED IN BATTER

3 Servings

Shell and clean (page 245):

1 lb. shrimp

You may leave the tails on.

Beat until light:

2 eggs

Beat in until smooth:

½ cup flour
¾ teaspoon salt
¼ teaspoon freshly ground pepper

Stir in:

1 teaspoon butter or olive oil
1 tablespoon brandy or rum or
(1 teaspoon Worcestershire sauce)

Dip a few shrimp at a time in the batter. Fry them in deep fat (page 542) heated to 375° until golden brown. Drain the shrimp on absorbent paper. Serve them with:

Fried Onions, page 297
Lemon wedges or mayonnaise seasoned with catsup and mustard or horseradish

See Index for other Shrimp Dishes.

CRAWFISH

Wash well in several waters:

Crawfish

Drop them one by one into:

Boiling water

You may add to the water minced vegetables suitable for soup.

You may add:

A few grains cayenne
2 teaspoons caraway seed

Boil crawfish 5 minutes. Leave them in the water until cool. Pull out middle tail fin and the intestinal vein with it. Shell the crawfish.

If you have used vegetables, remove the crawfish, continue cooking the stock until the vegetables are tender. This makes good soup.

Crawfish Bisque, page 62.

LOBSTERS

Allow ½ large lobster or 1 small lobster per serving. Buy active lobsters weighing from 1¼ to 2½ pounds. Lobsters weighing 3 pounds and over are apt to be coarse. A 2½ pound lobster will yield about 2 cupfuls of meat. The color of a live lobster is a dark mottled green. Cooked it becomes a bright red.

The female lobster is considered finer than the male by many. (Do you remember Mr. Pontifex's disappointment in "The Way of All Flesh?") Its uppermost finlike appendages near the body are softer than those of the male. The flesh of the male stays firmer when boiled.

To keep live lobsters place them in the refrigerator, but not directly on ice.

When buying a cooked lobster see that its tail is curled. The tail when pulled should roll back into place. This means that the lobster was (properly) alive when cooked.

To Kill a Lobster

Lobsters may be bought with the claws plugged and held together by rubber bands. Kitchen tongs are helpful when handling a lobster. Cut the spinal cord of a live lobster by inserting a sharp pointed knife where the tail and body meet. To split a lobster as shown below see next page.

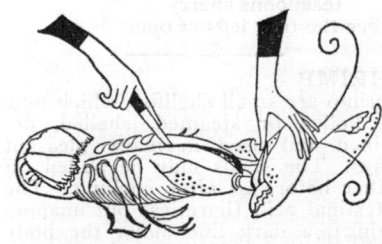

To split a lobster, place it on its back. Cross the claws, hold them firmly and draw a pointed knife through the shell lengthwise from head to tail. To crack the claws sufficiently to permit the meat to be removed use a mallet or a nutcracker.

To Prepare a Lobster for Cooking in the Half Shell

The meat of a lobster is edible all but the stomach or lady—a hard sack near the head—and the intestinal vein that runs through the middle of the underside of the tail meat. Remove and discard these inedible parts. The spongy substance to either side of the body, the lungs, is harmless. They are not removed when a lobster is cooked in the half shell. Neither are the delicious red coral and the greenish liver or tomaly.

To Remove the Meat from a Lobster

Pull off the claws. Place the lobster on its back. Hold it with one hand and with the other, using a sharp scissors or knife, cut a lengthwise gash in the soft undershell. Draw out the tail meat in one piece. Remove and discard the lady or stomach and the intestinal vein. See above. Crack the large claws with a nutcracker or mallet. Draw out the meat. Keep the small claws to use as a garnish. Add the coral and tomaly to the lobster meat or reserve it for use in dressings or sauces for lobster dishes.

BOILED LOBSTER

Allow 1 Small or ½ Large Lobster or About 1¼ Pounds Per Serving
Boil sufficient salted water to cover a lobster generously. Allow:

> 2 tablespoons salt or ⅓ cup rock salt

to:

> 1 quart water

Let the water boil hard and steadily. Add, head first:

> A live lobster

Allow the water to return rapidly to a rolling boil. Count cooking time from this minute, about 20 to 25 minutes according to the size of the lobster. Use kitchen tongs to remove the lobster from the water. Slit the under shell of the lobster from head to tail with a pair of scissors. Clip out the hard sack near the head. Remove the dark intestinal vein. Flatten out the body of the lobster. Chip a small portion from the end of the claws to permit

them to drain. Serve the lobster hot in the shell with:

> Lemon Butter, page 258

in individual dishes into which to dunk the lobster meat. Lobster is delectable with a tossed salad and French bread.

BOILED LOBSTER REMOVED FROM THE SHELL

Cook by the preceding rule:

> Boiled Lobster

Split it in half. Remove the hard sack near the head and the intestinal vein. Take out the body meat. Crack the claws in order to remove the meat from them. Dice the meat. Reheat it in:

> Seasoned melted butter, cream or sauce

Or, serve it cold with:

> Mayonnaise

to which the coral and tomaly may be added. To serve attractively you may replace the lobster meat in the shell.

BAKED STUFFED LOBSTER

2 Servings
Split in half by the preceding rule a freshly:

> Boiled Lobster: about 2½ lbs.

Remove the meat. Chop it. Melt:

> ¾ tablespoon butter

Stir in until blended:

> ¾ tablespoon flour

Stir in slowly:

> ½ cup Chicken or other light Stock, page 45

Season the sauce with:

> 1¼ teaspoons dry mustard
> 1 teaspoon chopped onion
> Salt
> Paprika

Melt in a separate saucepan:

> 2 tablespoons butter

Sauté the lobster meat in the butter until it is heated. Add the boiling sauce. Simmer these ingredients for 2 minutes. Remove them from the fire. Beat, then stir in:

> 1 tablespoon cream
> 2 egg yolks

Add:

> (½ cup chopped Sautéed Mushrooms, page 292)

Fill the lobster shells with the mixture. Cover them with:

> Buttered Crumbs, page 326, or crumbs sprinkled with grated Parmesan cheese

Bake or broil the lobster in a moderate oven 375° until the crumbs are brown.

Season it as it is removed from the oven by pouring over it:

(2 tablespoons sherry)

LOBSTER THERMIDOR
This is similar to the preceding Baked Stuffed Lobster. It is not so highly spiced and calls for cream as well as stock.
Split in halves:

2 freshly Boiled Lobsters, page 247 : 1 to 1½ lbs. each

Remove the meat as directed. Dice the meat. Melt:

2 teaspoons butter

Stir in until blended:

2 teaspoons flour

Add the lobster meat. Stir in slowly:

¼ cup rich cream
1 cup Stock, page 43

Simmer these ingredients for 10 minutes. Stir them frequently. Season them lightly, if required, with:

Salt, paprika and celery salt
A few grains cayenne

Remove the lobster from the pan. Add:

1 tablespoon sherry

Melt:

3 tablespoons butter

Add:

1½ cups shredded white bread

Cook and stir these ingredients until all the butter is absorbed. Wash the lobster shells thoroughly. Fill them with the lobster mixture. Spread the tops with the bread crumbs. Place the lobster in a hot oven 400° for 5 minutes, or brown the crumbs under a broiler. Serve the lobster with:

Wilted Cucumbers, page 459

See Index for other Lobster Dishes.

BROILED OR BAKED LOBSTER
Split and clean by the rule on page 247:

A live lobster

To Broil:
Place the lobster on its back, brush it with:

Olive oil or melted butter

Place it 2 inches from the heat under a moderate broiler flame. Broil it until it is a delicate brown, for about 20 to 25 minutes. Season it with:

Salt and cayenne

Dot it generously with:

Butter

or serve it with:

Lemon Butter Sauce, page 258

To Bake:
Place the lobster in a skillet in a hot oven 450°. Bake it for 15 to 20 minutes. Baste it frequently with:

Olive oil or butter

Season it with:

Salt and cayenne

Serve it with:

Lemon Butter Sauce, page 258

CRABS
Hard-shelled and soft-shelled crabs are one and the same at different stages of their careers. After the crab casts off the old hard shell, the new undeveloped shell is edible—deliciously so. When purchased, crabs should be not only alive but active.

HARD-SHELLED CRABS
Allow 2 Crabs to a Serving
Wash in several waters:

4 live hard-shelled crabs

Use kitchen tongs to drop them, one by one, head first into boiling salted water. For 4 crabs use:

4 cups water
1 tablespoon salt
1 tablespoon lemon juice or vinegar
¼ bay leaf
2 to 6 peppercorns
(1 small sliced onion)

Boil the crabs rapidly the first 5 minutes, then simmer them for 10 to 15 minutes, until they are red. Plunge them into cold water. Drain them. Break off the apron or tail. Take the crab in both hands and, beginning at the tail end, pull the upper and lower shells apart. Discard any substance that sticks to the upper shell. Pull off the waxy substance and the white spongy part between the halves of the body at the side. The edible parts lie in the two remaining compact masses and in the claws. Crack the claws with a nutcracker to remove the meat. Reserve the upper shells if you wish to use them. To clean the shells for stuffing, see below.
Crabs may be served hot or cold. They may be served after being cleaned with the upper shell and the claws. Crab meat is used in cocktails, in creamed dishes and in other ways. See Index for Crab Dishes.
Preparation of Crab Shells
Select large perfect shells. Scrub them well with a brush until they are clean. Place them in a large kettle. Cover them with water to which add 1 tea-

spoonful baking soda. Cover them closely and boil them for 20 minutes. Drain, wash and dry them.

DEVILED CRABS
4 Servings
Flake:
1½ cups fresh or canned crab meat
Melt in a saucepan:
1 tablespoon butter
Add:
1½ tablespoons cracker crumbs
¾ cup milk or cream
Boil these ingredients until they are thick. Remove them from the fire. Beat and add:
2 small eggs
¼ teaspoon salt
1½ teaspoons prepared mustard
A few grains cayenne
Add the crab meat. Pack these ingredients into crab shells or ramekins. Brush the tops with:
Melted butter
Brown them in a quick oven 400° or under a broiler.

For other Crab Dishes see Index.

A "fan" writes from Maryland: I am offering a recipe that you do not give. When I moved into this crab country, I began to boil hard crabs and threw the natives into fainting fits. They were right, so their method follows:

TO STEAM TWO DOZEN HARD-SHELLED CRABS
Allow 6 to 8 Crabs Per Person
Dump the crabs into a large vessel or deep sink and cover them with water just a little hotter than the hand can bear. This anesthetizes them quickly with 2 good results: First, you can handle them safely like soft-shells, and second, they do not appear to suffer when they go on the fire. Otherwise, they struggle woefully in the pot while the steam is rising. Scrub the muck from each crab with a vegetable brush. (So far this is my own discovery, and the natives do not bother, but somehow I like to suck a clean crab better.) If you have a suitable rack, place it in a large pot with close lid and put a little water in the bottom, but not nearly enough to touch the rack. If a rack is lacking, moisten the bottom of the vessel with 2 or 3 tablespoonfuls of water. In any case lay in the crabs and set upon the fire. Sprinkle well with:

1 teaspoon more or less red pepper
2 tablespoons salt
½ cup vinegar
and if desired:
2 tablespoons Old Bay Sea Food seasoning or other favorite
1 tablespoon monosodium glutamate
½ cup beer or what have you
Have no fear that the pot will get dry while steaming. It never does, for the crabs put out a lot of moisture. The problem on the contrary is to keep them from getting sodden. Cover and steam until the aprons begin to rise, about 30 minutes or a little more. Eat hot or cold, preferably over newspapers, and dip each bite in melted butter. Some people use simple French dressing, but not me. If you pull off the apron and open the crab from that point with the fingers, it is easy. Otherwise, a knife is useful to pry off the shell. A mallet or hammer is better than crackers for opening the claws. And don't forget to pry in the points of the top shell for a bite of fat. Some crabs are lean, but some are not. Many crabs, followed by a general hand washing and then green salad, French bread and dessert make a fine dinner for the fanciest guests. The crabs sometimes drop their claws at the touch of hot water, but it is no matter Cook them all and pile the claws on top.

SOFT-SHELLED CRABS
Wash the crabs in several waters. Place live crab face down on a board. Make an incision just back of the eyes. Lift the tapering points on each side of the back shell to remove sandbags and spongy gills. Turn crab on its back and with a pointed knife remove the small pointed apron at the lower part

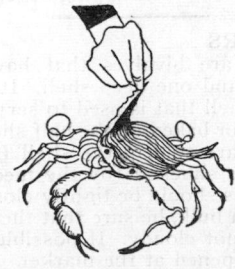

of the shell. These crabs, since the shell is edible, are usually breaded and pan-fried.

SOFT-SHELLED CRABS FRIED

Prepare for cooking (see page 249):
>Soft-shelled crabs

Dip them in:
>Seasoned flour or bread crumbs

then in:
>1 egg diluted with 3 tablespoons water

and then in crumbs.
Fry them from 3 to 5 minutes, or until golden brown in deep fat 375° (page 542). Turn them once while they are frying. Drain on absorbent paper. Sprinkle them well with:
>Salt and pepper

Serve them at once with:
>Tartar Sauce, page 439
>Almond Sauce, page 258, with parsley

SOFT-SHELLED CRABS BROILED

Prepare for cooking (see page 249):
>Soft-shelled crabs

Combine:
>¼ cup butter
>2 tablespoons lemon juice
>A few grains cayenne
>A few grains pepper

Roll the crabs in the butter mixture, then roll them lightly in:
>Flour

Preheat a broiler oven for 10 minutes. Place the crabs on the broiling rack under a hot flame 2 inches from the heat. Broil them for about 10 minutes. Turn them once.

SOFT-SHELLED CRABS SAUTÉED

Follow the above rule for:
>Soft-Shelled Crabs Broiled

Sauté them in butter or other fat over a moderate fire. Place the crabs on a platter. Pour the drippings over them.

OYSTERS

Oysters are bivalves that have one shallow and one deep shell. It is the deeper shell that is used to serve oysters raw or baked on the half shell. Oysters are sold in the shell (by the dozen) or shucked (by the measure). The shells should be tightly closed. If bought in bulk, be sure that the liquor is clear, not cloudy. If possible, have oysters opened at the market. If not, provide yourself with a strainer and

place it over a bowl to catch the oyster juices. Hold a well-scrubbed oyster in the palm of one hand over the strainer. Insert the point of a sharp thin knife blade into the hinged end of the oyster. Push the knife until it cuts through the muscle that holds the shells together. Run it around the shells to separate them. Lift off the shallow shell. The oyster is then ready to be served on the half shell. If you wish to shuck the oyster, loosen it from the shell with a knife. Or, you may treat oysters in the following manner: Place oysters in a moderately hot oven 400° from 5 to 7 minutes, according to size. Drop them into ice water. They may be opened with ease. Examine each oyster with your fingers and remove any bits of shell adhering to it. Drop it into the strainer. A quart of shucked oysters may be rinsed by pouring ½ cupful cold water over them. Add this water to the oyster liquor, then strain it through a fine strainer or cloth. Bulk oysters may be picked over in order to rid them of bits of shell that may adhere. Dry oysters well between towels before breading.

OYSTERS ON THE HALF SHELL

Allow 5 to 6 Oysters Per Serving
Prepare by the preceding rule:
>Oysters

Chill them well. Arrange them in cracked ice on individual plates. You may place in the center a small glass of:
>Cocktail Sauce, page 8

Or you may serve them with:
>Lemon wedges and horseradish

BROILED OYSTERS

Dry well between towels:
>Shucked oysters

Dip them in:
>Melted butter

then in:
>Seasoned cracker crumbs

Place them in a pan. Broil them for about 3 minutes, or until they are lightly browned in a 425° oven. Serve them with:
>Lemon wedges or
>Parsley or Lemon Butter, page 258

Or place them on:
>Toast fingers

Sprinkle them with:
>Grated cheese

Brown them as directed above.

SAUTÉED OR FRIED OYSTERS

Drain:

12 large shucked oysters

Pour 1 cupful cold water over them.
Dry them well between towels. Beat:

1 egg with
2 tablespoons water

Dip the oysters in the egg, inserting a
fork in the tough muscle of the oyster,
then in:

Seasoned bread crumbs

in the egg again and again in the
crumbs. Permit the oysters to stand
for ½ hour. Fry them in deep fat
heated to 375° (page 542) for 4 minutes, or sauté them in butter.

For other Oyster Dishes, see page 111.

CLAMS

Clams are sold in the shell or shucked.
Eight quarts of clams in the shell will
yield about 1 quart of clams shucked.
Allow about 1 quart of unshucked
clams per person for steamed clams;
6 to 8 clams if served in some other
way. If a clam is alive, the shell will
be tightly closed, or if slightly open
will close tightly immediately upon
being touched. Discard all others, including those with broken shells.

Clams are classed as hard-shelled and
soft-shelled. Of the hard-shelled the
large round Quahog is usually cut up
or chopped. The small clams—they are
all the same clam at different ages—
like littlenecks and cherry stones are
eaten raw on the half shell and may be
used without precooking in rules calling for oysters. Recently it has been
found that clams eaten raw are thiev-
ish in that they rob the body of all
available thiamine. There are no such
results when the clams are cooked.

The Atlantic and Pacific both produce
the hard-shelled and the soft-shelled
clam, but the razor clam, considered
unsurpassed in flavor, comes from the
Pacific only.

Soft-shelled clams are edible except
for the black skin or siphon around
the neck. This is usually removed.

Hard-shelled clams have a tough portion that is usually separated from the
soft portion. Their stomachs must be
cleaned. All clams are sandy. Unshucked they are scrubbed and washed
in several waters and the cooked clam
meat is often put under cold running
water to rid it of all sand.

HARD-SHELLED CLAMS

Place clams that have been washed in
several waters in a large dishpan.
Cover them well with cold water.
Sprinkle over the top ¼ cupful corn
meal to about a quart of clams. Leave
them in this bath for at least 3 hours,
preferably for 12. This will whiten
them, rid them of some sand and
cause them to eject the black material
in their stomachs. Wash the clams in
clear water.

To open hard-shelled clams cover
them with water for 5 minutes. They
will open slightly. Lift up a clam
gingerly and insert a strong sharp
knife quickly between the shells. Cut
through the muscle holding the shells
together (save the juices), flatten the
shells and cut away the meat. It requires a strong wrist to shuck an obstinate hard-shelled clam so, if possible, have this done at the market.

If the clams have not been in a corn-
meal bath, open the stomachs with a
pair of sharp scissors and scrape out
the contents.

Or, if you do not mind a slight loss in
flavor, place the clams in boiling water
for 5 minutes or in a moderate oven
until the shells open.

Large hard-shelled clams have a tough
portion which may be separated from
the tender portion, chopped or ground
and used in various dishes, creamed,
scalloped, in fritters, chowders, etc.

SOFT-SHELLED CLAMS
Method I.

Soft-shelled clams are easily opened
with a strong sharp knife. Insert the
blade along the edge of the top shell
and cut the shell off. Reserve the juices.
Slit the skin of the neck or siphon. Cut
the meat from the bottom shell. Pull
off the skin of the neck, see next page.
The skin is too tough to enjoy as
it is. It may be chopped or ground

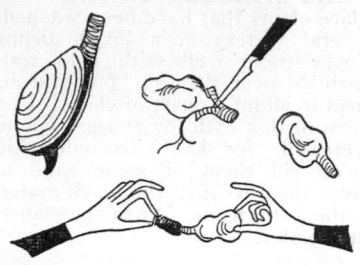

and added to the clam meat, or it may be used in other dishes, in chowders, creamed, scalloped, deviled, etc.

Method II.
Or, if you do not mind a slight loss in flavor, in order to open the clams steam them as directed in the following rule.

CLAM BROTH
Use the clam broth from Steamed Clams, see above, diluted or in its concentrated form, or follow the rule for steamed clams using 4 cupfuls of water and steaming the clams for ½ hour or more. Strain the broth through 2 thicknesses of cheesecloth. The clam meat may be placed in a colander, rinsed well under cold water, chopped and used in chowders, fritters, scalloped and other dishes. You will have about 1 quart of strong broth. It may be diluted with scalded cream or milk but do not boil it after these additions, or it may be combined in equal parts with:
> **Water, chicken broth, consommé or tomato juice**

Each cupful of broth may be topped with a spoonful of:
> **Whipped cream**

CLAM STEW
Follow the rule on page 63 for Oyster Stew. Substitute small raw clams.

STEAMED CLAMS
Allow ¾ to 1 Quart of Clams Per Serving
Scrub thoroughly with a brush and wash in several waters:
> **4 quarts soft-shelled clams**

Place them close together in the bottom of a large kettle or steamer. Place in the bottom:
> **½ cup hot water**

Cover the kettle closely. Steam the clams over moderate heat until they open, but no longer, from 10 to 15 minutes. Overcooking makes clams tough. Lift out the clams. Place them on a platter covered with a folded napkin. Cover them with a folded napkin. Permit the broth to settle briefly and ladle it off the top, or put it through 2 thicknesses of wet cheesecloth. Serve the clams with individual dishes of:
> **Melted butter**

to which you may add:
> **Lemon juice or vinegar**
> **A dash celery salt**

The broth is served in glasses with the clams, or it is used for clam juice cocktail, broth, etc., see below. A clam is picked up from the shell by the neck (usually with the fingers), dipped in broth, then in butter. The clam is edible all but the neck. This is a bathtub dish.

BAKED CLAMS
4 Servings
Scrub with a brush and wash in several waters:
> **36 soft-shelled clams**

Place them flat in a pan. They may be placed in rock salt. Bake them in a hot oven 425° until the shells open. Remove the top shell carefully to avoid spilling the juices. Serve the clams in individual plates with:
> **Butter and celery salt**
> **Pepper and lemon wedges**

CLAMS BROILED ON THE HALF SHELL
Place on an oven-proof dish:
> **Cherry stone clams on the half shell**

Cover each clam with:
> **A dash Worcestershire sauce**
> **A square bacon**

Broil the clams under a hot flame until the bacon is done.

CLAM COCKTAIL
See Oyster Cocktail, page 7. Substitute littleneck or cherry stone clams.

FRIED CLAMS
Shuck (page 251), then wash well in a colander under running water:
> **Soft-shelled clams**

Dry them between towels. Cut away the black skin of the neck or siphon.

see page 251. Follow the rule on page 251 for Fried Oysters. Clams may be fried in batter. See Shrimp Fried in Batter, page 246.

CLAMBAKE CLAMS

A clambake is a rite in coastal regions involving a deep pit, other sea food and sea weed. This is a very simple version.

Put clams on preheated rocks. Cover them with sea weed and a piece of sailcloth. Allow the clams to steam until they open.

DEVILED CLAMS

4 Servings

Chop fine, reserving the liquor:

2 cups shucked clams

Add the liquor and:

1 teaspoon lemon juice

Permit the clams to simmer for 3 minutes. Melt:

3 tablespoons butter

Add and cook until tender:

½ cup finely minced celery
1½ tablespoons minced green pepper
1½ tablespoons minced onion

Add the clams and:

½ cup cracker crumbs
⅛ to ¼ teaspoon prepared mustard
⅛ teaspoon pepper or paprika
Salt if needed

Bake the mixture in large clam shells or in ramekins in a moderate oven 350° for about 12 minutes. You may sprinkle the tops with:

Grated cheese

CLAM FRITTERS

Chop, reserving the juices:

1 pint clams

Prepare by the rule on page 543:

Fritter batter for meats

Measure and substitute the juices for part of the liquid. Fry the fritters in deep fat as directed. Serve the fritters with:

Lemon wedges and water cress

For other clam rules see Index.

OYSTER CRABS

These are tiny boarders found in the oyster shells. They need no preparation as they are eaten whole. They may be shaken in a bag with seasoned flour (see page 540) and fried in deep fat at 390° (page 542) or they may be sautéed in butter, floured or not.

They may be simmered gently until they whiten in water to which onion, celery, parsley and lemon juice may be added. Use this stock in making the cream sauce, about 1 part stock to 1 part cream and about ½ as much sauce as there are crabs.

Season to taste with:

Salt, pepper and mustard

MUSSELS

In France these are called "the oysters of the poor." There are various definitions of poverty.

Mussels are shellfish with a "beard" or ragged fringe. This beard may be removed before the mussels are steamed, or they may be cooked and bearded later at table.

It is customary to serve mussels in several ways: steamed, removed from the shell, bearded and served much like oysters or clams, or served with a sauce poured over the mussels, shell and all. It is permissible—probably because it is necessary—to use the hands in separating the shells. Gourmets suggest that a half shell be used to spoon up the liquor to the last drop. Here are two rules for Moules Marinière—one with an unthickened and one with a thickened sauce.

MUSSELS OR MOULES MARINIÈRE

Method I. 4 to 6 Servings

Wash thoroughly in several waters, then scrub well with a stiff brush:

2 quarts mussels: about 5 dozen

Trim the fringe with kitchen scissors or a sharp knife.

Place the mussels in a large, heavy skillet or saucepan for which you have a tight fitting lid. Add:

1 cup dry white wine
¼ cup chopped celery
¼ cup chopped parsley
6 chopped shallots or
1 sliced clove garlic
¼ cup butter

Cook closely covered over a quick fire until the shells open but no longer. Serve the mussels in bowls, the sauce poured over them.

The sauce may be thickened with:

2 tablespoons or more fresh bread crumbs

Method II.

Cook the mussels as directed in Method I. Omit the butter. When the mussels have opened, drain the liquid and keep the mussels warm. If they have not been bearded, the tufts may be cut off at this time and the mussels removed from the shell. Place the mussel liquor over moderate heat. Cook it until it is reduced by one half. There should be about 2 cupfuls. Strain the liquor. Melt in a skillet:

4 tablespoons butter

Sauté in this for 2 minutes:

(½ lb. sliced mushrooms)

Remove the skillet from the heat. Combine:

1 egg yolk
1 cup cream

Stir this mixture gradually into the sauce. Keep stirring it over low heat until it thickens slightly but do not permit it to boil. Add:

1 tablespoon chopped chives or parsley

Place the mussels in bowls or soup dishes and pour the sauce over them.

BAKED MUSSELS
Place well-cleaned mussels in a pan in a hot oven 450° until the shells open. Remove the upper shell and beard or fringe. Reserve the liquor. Serve the mussels on the lower shell with melted butter and the liquor in small cups or glasses. See Steamed Clams, page 252.

SCALLOPS
Scallops, as bought on the market, are the muscle that holds together the two shells of a mollusk.
There are two types, the small prized cape or bay scallops and the larger sea scallops. They should be creamy rather than dead white in appearance. Scallops are so frequently served fried with tartar sauce that landlubbers are apt to neglect other excellent ways of preparing and using them.
Allow about ⅓ pound of scallops per serving for sautéing or broiling, ¼ pound if used with sauce or any other additions.
Cooked scallops may be used in any recipe for fish salad.

SCALLOPS SAUTÉED OR BAKED
Dip:

Scallops

in:

Seasoned cream or melted butter

You may add:

A dash sherry or Worcestershire sauce

to the cream. Or, you may dip the scallops in 1 beaten egg diluted with 1 tablespoonful water or oil. Roll them in:

(Crushed cornflakes or bread crumbs)

Permit them to dry for about 15 minutes (not necessary but the flakes stick better if dry). They are then ready to be sautéed in a skillet (a very quick process calling for from 5 to 10 minutes' cooking), or they may be put for that same length of time in a moderate oven 375° or they may be broiled. I like them well heated throughout, plus a minute or two in addition, but that's all. Oysters may be prepared by this rule.

BROILED SCALLOPS
Method I. 3 Servings
Wash and drain:

Scallops

Dry them between towels. Dip them in:

Sifted seasoned bread crumbs

then in:

1 egg diluted with 2 tablespoons water or oil

and again in the crumbs. Arrange them on individual oven-proof plates or on a large platter. Pour over them liberally:

Melted butter

Place over each plate of scallops:

A slice bacon

Broil the scallops under a broiler for 5 or 10 minutes, until the bacon is crisp and the scallops are tender. Turn them so they will brown evenly. Serve them on the plates on which they were broiled with:

Tartar Sauce, page 439, or
Tomato Sauce, page 433, or
Lemon wedges

Method II.
Wash, then dry between towels:

1 lb. scallops

Dip them in:

Olive oil

Drain them. Place them in a shallow pan. Season them with:

Pepper

Melt:

4 tablespoons butter or oil

Add, stir and cook for 2 minutes:

1½ tablespoons lemon juice
1¼ tablespoons minced onion, chives or leek

Place the scallops under a broiler preheated to 500° for about 5 minutes. Baste them as they cook with the

sauce. Turn them with a spoon to cook evenly. Season them with:
Salt
Serve them hot.

FRIED SCALLOPS
Wash and pick over:
1 quart scallops: about 2 lbs.
Drain them. Dry them between towels. Season them with:
Salt
Pepper
Celery salt
Dip them in:
1 egg diluted with 2 tablespoons water
and in:
Bread crumbs
Fry them for 2 minutes in deep fat 385°, or sauté in 3 tablespoonfuls butter. Drain them on absorbent paper. Serve them with:
Tartar Sauce, page 439, or Béarnaise Sauce, page 340

SCALLOPS IN WINE
4 Servings
Wash, then drain:
1½ lbs. scallops: 3 cups
Bring to a boil in a saucepan:
1½ cups dry white wine
Add the scallops. Simmer them for 10 minutes. Strain them, reserving the liquor. Cut them into small pieces. Melt:
3 tablespoons butter
Stir in until blended:
3 tablespoons flour
Stir in the scallop liquor. When the sauce is smooth and boiling stir in and heat but do not boil:
¼ cup rich cream
Add:
¼ teaspoon curry powder
Salt to taste
Add the scallops, heat gently and serve. You may place them in ramekins and cover them with a sprinkling of:
Bread crumbs and grated cheese
Brown them lightly under a broiler.

SCALLOPS ON SKEWERS
4 Servings
Drop into boiling salted water and simmer for 2 minutes:
1 lb. scallops
Drain them. Dry them between towels.
Dip them in:
Melted butter

Place them on skewers alternately with:
Pieces of bacon
(Slices of parboiled onions)
Broil them under a moderate flame until the bacon is done. Slip the scallops and the bacon from the skewers onto:
Rounds of toast
Sprinkle them with:
Chopped parsley
Serve them with:
Hollandaise Sauce, page 429, or Tartar Sauce, page 439

Creamed Scallops or Oysters and Mushrooms, page 117.

SCALLOPED SCALLOPS
Follow the rule on page 112 for:
Scalloped Oysters
Substitute scallops for oysters.

ABALONE
1 Pound of Meat Serves 4 People
As it is illegal to ship this shellfish out of the state, these rules are included principally for the benefit of the many Californians who use my "Joy."
Abalone as bought in the market is usually shelled, pounded and ready to be cooked. If it is in the shell, we are told to "pound the shell or head with a wooden mallet to relax the organism, for if the abalone dies in a state of tension it takes a good deal of pounding to tenderize it." (So much for the emotions! Is it too much to assume that they might be tense?)
Remove the edible part, the foot, from the shell. Trim off the dark portions. Pound it whole or cut into ¼ inch strips and pound. (With persistence you may come to rival Carrie Nation.) For steaks slice across the grain, for other dishes slice with the grain. Be careful not to overcook abalone.

I.
It may be dipped in egg and seasoned bread crumbs and sautéed in a hot oiled skillet from 1½ to 2 minutes to the side.

II.
It may be diced and combined with cream sauce—1½ cupfuls abalone to 2 cupfuls sauce and simmered in it for 2 minutes before being served.

III.
It may be made into chowder by simmering 2 abalones until tender in 4

cupfuls water. The stock is reserved, the meat is put through a grinder. Follow any chowder rule, adding potatoes, bacon or salt pork, and the stock.

IV.

It may be broiled 2 inches from a heating unit heated to 400° for about 3 minutes, turned, spread with mayonnaise and broiled about 8 minutes longer, or until tender.

POACHED EEL

6 to 8 Servings

Clean, skin and cut in 1½ inch pieces:
A 3 lb. eel
Melt:
5 tablespoons butter
Add and sauté over moderate heat for 3 minutes:
3 tablespoons chopped onion
Add the pieces of eel and sauté them over high heat, moving them about constantly, for 5 minutes. Add:
1½ cups vegetable stock or dry wine
1 Bouquet Garni, page 832
Cook uncovered over high heat for 10 or 15 minutes, continuing to move the pieces of eel about. Remove the bouquet. Season with:
Salt and pepper
If no wine has been used, lemon juice or wedges make a nice addition.

CANNED FISH

Salmon, crab, shrimp and tuna fish make good aspics, salads, sandwich fillings and creamed dishes.

For "Mock Chicken" (this is surprisingly good), place the contents of a can of tuna fish in a colander and pour 2 cupfuls boiling water over it rapidly.

There are creamed fish recipes to be found in the Chapter on Luncheon and Supper Dishes, and it is fun to concoct new ones. Put cooked or canned fish into boiling cream sauce and serve it at once. Use half as much sauce as there is fish. If you wish to keep creamed fish hot or to reheat it, put it in an uncovered saucepan set in boiling water. This will keep it from being unpleasantly "fishy."

Worcestershire sauce, curry, mustard, lemon, catsup, capers and pickles are good additions to fish dishes.

See Index for Creamed Crab Meat, Tuna, Salmon or Shrimp in Ramekins and other Fish Dishes.

TERRAPIN

Terrapin dishes are shrouded in tradition. The meat of a 6 to 7 inch terrapin should satisfy 2 persons with average appetites. Terrapin is bought alive. It is washed in several waters, scrubbed as well as possible with a long-handled brush and plunged alive into boiling water to cover. After 10 minutes' boiling it is removed from the pot and placed in cold water until cool enough to handle. The black skin of the legs is rubbed off. The head may be pulled out with a pointed utensil and scrubbed with a towel. The terrapin is washed well and is then immersed in boiling salted water to which vegetables suitable for soup may be added for flavor.

It is boiled until tender, from 15 to 45 minutes for a terrapin of moderate size. To test it press the leg with the fingers. It is done when the meat is soft to the touch when pinched. Remove it from the stock. Save the stock. Cool the terrapin. Pull out or cut off the nails. Place the terrapin on its back. Cut away the lower shell. Reserve the juices as much as possible.

Empty the upper shell. The gall bladder, liver and sandbags are found close to the head. Remove the liver. Cut away every bit of the gall bladder carefully; it is attached to the left side of the liver. Discard it. Cut away and discard the green spots, if any, of the liver. Place the liver in cold water.

Take out the eggs, if any, remove the film and drop them in cold water. Cut away and discard the sandbags, the white inside muscles, head, tail, claws, heart, entrails and lights. Here is a moot point. Discard the large intestines. The small intestines are frequently chopped and added to the rest of the meat. Use them or not. Cut up the legs, leaving the bones in, and the rest of the meat into 1 to 2 inch pieces.

Cut up the liver into thin slices. Add it and the eggs to the meat. The terrapin meat is now ready to be simmered.

Barely cover it in its own juices and some of the stock and simmer it for ½ hour. It is seasoned with salt and cayenne and is served, by the traditionalists, with lots of melted butter, added bit by bit, and sherry as a beverage; or it is made into a stew. This stew has degenerated in some sections into a sort of cream sauce affair, but to be right it should be prepared with hard-cooked egg yolks and cream.

TERRAPIN STEW
4 Servings
Hard cook by the rule on page **79**:
>   **5 eggs**

Put the yolks through a ricer. Work them into a paste with:
>   **2 tablespoons butter**

Combine:
>   **2 cups terrapin meat**
>   **1 cup terrapin stock**

Simmer these ingredients for 5 minutes. Stir in the yolk mixture, continue cooking gently and stirring for another 5 minutes. Remove the pan from the fire. Add:
>   **1 cup scalded cream**
>   **½ cup sherry or Madeira**
>   **Salt and cayenne**

Serve the terrapin very hot with:
>   **Corn Sticks, page 515**

TURTLES
Turtles are bought alive. Sometimes they grow to huge size.
Cut off the head of a snapping or soft-shelled turtle. Place the turtle in cold water for ½ hour, or hang it from a nail, neck down, until the blood no longer drips. Follow the preceding rule for Terrapin, cooking the turtle from ½ to 1 hour. Discard the intestines.
Cut the turtle meat into small pieces. Reserve all meat juices for later use. The turtle meat, eggs, thinly sliced liver, juices and stock may be used in stew.
Follow the rule for Terrapin Stew, above, and see Turtle Soup, page 55. If you wish to be highly amused, read the turtle episode in William Alexander Percy's fascinating "Lanterns on the Levee."

SNAILS
4 Servings
Snails are becoming increasingly popular in our country. I realized this one night when I was awakened out of a sound sleep by a long-distance call and an irate voice demanded to know what I knew on the subject. (Being the author of a cookbook is akin to living in an information booth.)
Snails are large and small, but large or small they are a job for the Jobs of the kitchen. Perhaps the French are all descended from him.
First wash about 1 pound of snails (about 25 or 30) in several waters. Next remove the membrane that seals the snail in the shell. Place snails in a pail, pour over them ¼ cupful rock salt diluted in ½ cupful vinegar. Cover the pail. Shake it from time to time. After 2 hours wash the snails in several waters until they are free from impurities.
Boil the snails from 3 to 4 hours in liquid to cover. This may be diluted white wine. Add vegetables suitable for soup and seasonings, shallots or onion, celery, parsley, carrot, bay leaf, cloves, thyme, peppercorns, cloves of garlic, crushed. Or boil the snails in Court Bouillon, page 238. Drain the snails, remove them from the shells with a pointed utensil, cut off the black spot at the end of each one. Dry the snails and dry the shells. Place a dab of Butter Mixture, see below, in each shell. Replace the snails. You may find it advisable to put 2 snails in 1 shell. Pack the shells with Butter Mixture, see below. Place them on a pan or on individual oven-proof dishes. Sprinkle them with fine bread crumbs (optional).
At this point the snails may be chilled and held for later baking.
Bake the snails in a hot oven 425° or under a broiler until they are piping hot.

BUTTER MIXTURE
Cream until soft:
>   **¾ cup butter**

Work into it:
>   **1 teaspoon minced shallots**
>   **2 well-crushed cloves garlic**
>   **1 tablespoon minced celery**
>   **1 tablespoon minced parsley**
>   **½ teaspoon salt**
>   **Freshly ground pepper**

If any of this sauce is left over, remember that it is wonderful on fish, steaks or vegetables.

CANNED SNAILS
These may be purchased in cans with their shells. Boil until reduced by ½:
>   **2 cups dry white wine**
>   **1 teaspoon chopped shallot**

Strain the liquid through a fine sieve. Have ready:
>   **4 dozen small shells**
>   **4 dozen snails**

Add to each shell a scant teaspoonful of the wine. Replace the snails in their shells. Seal them in with the preceding:
>   **Butter Mixture**

Heat the snails thoroughly in a moderately hot oven 400° for about 10 minutes.

Sauces for Fish

LEMON BUTTER SAUCE FOR FISH
Combine:
    4 tablespoons melted butter
    1 tablespoon lemon juice
    A few drops Tabasco
    ¼ teaspoon salt
See Maître d'Hôtel Butter, page 431,
Remoulade Sauce, page 440.

WINE BUTTER SAUCE FOR FISH
Melt:
    4 tablespoons butter
Add:
    ½ cup dry white wine
    Juice of ½ lemon
    2 tablespoons chopped parsley
Heat the sauce well but do not permit
it to boil.

ALMOND SAUCE OR AMANDINE
A Scant ½ Cupful
This sauce is a classic. It glorifies the
most commonplace dish.
Melt:
    4 tablespoons butter
Stir and sauté in it until lightly
browned:
    ¼ cup blanched shredded almonds
    Salt as needed

DEVILED BUTTER
4 Servings
Work until soft:
    4 tablespoons butter
Combine it with:
    ½ teaspoon dry mustard
    2 teaspoons wine vinegar
    2 teaspoons Worcestershire sauce
    ¼ teaspoon salt
    ⅛ teaspoon cayenne
    2 egg yolks
Beat well. Serve this over sea food.

Gravies and Sauces, page 425.
Sauces for Vegetables, page 327.
You will find in these chapters a
number of sauces, cream sauce, Hollandaise, Béarnaise, etc., that may be
served with fish.

ANCHOVY BUTTER FOR FISH, ETC.
Fine spread on hot broiled fish, steak
or canapés. Cream until soft:
    ¼ cup butter

Beat in:
    1 teaspoon anchovy paste
    ⅛ teaspoon onion juice
    ¼ teaspoon lemon juice
    A few grains cayenne

Onion Sauces I and II, page 432.
A reminder for onion fanciers.

MUSTARD SAUCE FOR FISH
About 1 Cupful
Melt:
    3 tablespoons butter
Stir in until blended:
    2 tablespoons flour
Stir in slowly:
    1 cup Fish Stock, page 230
When the sauce is thick add and cook
for 1 minute:
    ½ teaspoon dry mustard
    ¼ teaspoon salt if needed
    ½ teaspoon freshly ground black
    pepper

CURRY SAUCE FOR FISH
About 1⅓ Cupfuls
Melt:
    2 tablespoons butter
Add and cook until slightly brown:
    1 tablespoon chopped onion
Stir in until blended:
    2 tablespoons flour
Stir in slowly:
    1 cup Fish Stock, page 230
Stir and cook the sauce until it is
thick. Add, stir and cook for 1 minute:
    1 teaspoon curry powder
Just before serving stir in slowly and
heat, but do not boil:
    ¼ cup cream or top milk, 2 egg
    yolks or 1 whole egg
Season, if needed, with:
    Paprika

SHRIMP SAUCE FOR FISH
3½ Cupfuls
This is an elaborate sauce. I am giving
it in full. Do not hesitate to deduct
from, add to or alter it.
Prepare:
    2 cups Tomato Sauce, page 433, or
    2 cups Cream Sauce I, page 428
Season the sauce well. Add and heat
to the boiling point:
    1 teaspoon Worcestershire or 2
    teaspoons chili sauce
    2 tablespoons chopped parsley
    ¼ cup chopped olives

½ cup boiled or canned shrimp
½ cup sautéed or canned mushrooms
¼ cup finely chopped celery
Serve the sauce with baked or boiled
fish, or place the fish on a platter and
pour the sauce over it. Heat it under
a broiler.

ANCHOVY SAUCE FOR FISH
1 Cupful
Prepare:
    Cream Sauce I, page 428
Add to it:
    1 teaspoon anchovy paste
Blend it well with the sauce.

OYSTER SAUCE FOR FISH
Prepare:
    1 cup Cream Sauce II, page 428
Season it well with:
    Salt
    (1 teaspoon Worcestershire sauce)
Shortly before serving bring the sauce
to the boiling point and add:
    3 tablespoons chopped parsley
    1 cup finely chopped or ground
    oysters and juice

YELLOW SAUCE FOR FISH OR VEGETABLES
About 1⅓ Cupfuls
Melt:
    2 tablespoons butter
Stir in:
    2 tablespoons flour
Add gradually:
    1 cup fish or vegetable stock
Cook and stir the sauce until it is
smooth and boiling. Reduce the heat
and stir in:
    ⅓ cup light or heavy cream
    Salt, paprika or white pepper
Shortly before serving, place the sauce
over hot water. Beat slightly, then
add:
    2 egg yolks
Stir the sauce until the yolks have
thickened it slightly. Just before serv-
ing stir in:
    1 tablespoon lemon juice or 2
    tablespoons dry white wine
    (2 tablespoons capers)

EGG AND MILK SAUCE FOR FISH
About 1½ Cupfuls
Beat until smooth:
    2 eggs
    ⅓ cup vinegar

Stir and heat to the boiling point:
    1 tablespoon flour
    1 teaspoon butter
    1 cup milk
Remove these ingredients from the
fire. Beat the egg mixture into the
milk mixture with a wire whisk. Place
the sauce over a low fire. Stir it until
it thickens. Beat in:
    1 tablespoon butter
Pour over a cooked fish:
    Melted butter
    Chopped parsley
Serve it with the sauce.

Easy Hollandaise Sauce, page 430.
Remember this sauce when serving
fish, beans, etc.

RITZ FISH SAUCE
M. Louis Diat, whose books on French
cooking are tops, served this luscious
fish sauce when I was the guest of the
management of the New York Ritz.
Into about 2 cupfuls rich cream sauce,
made with stock or fish stock and
cream, put, at the last moment, about
1 cupful seedless green grapes. Pour
the sauce over cooked fillets of fish.
See Baked Fillets of Fish, page 233.
Dribble heavy cream over the top.
Broil the dish briefly to brown the top
partially.

TOMATO CREAM SAUCE FOR FISH
About 1¼ Cupfuls
Prepare:
    1 cup Cream Sauce I, page 428
Skin and slice:
    2 medium or 1 large tomato
Sauté the slices until lightly browned
on both sides in:
    2 tablespoons olive or salad oil
Just before the tomatoes are done add:
    ¼ minced fine clove garlic
Beat the tomato slices into the cream
sauce.

DEVIL'S SAUCE
About 1¾ Cupfuls
For fish or meat.
Place in a small saucepan:
    ⅔ cup tarragon vinegar
    2 sliced cloves garlic
    2½ teaspoons dry mustard
    1 bay leaf
    8 whole peppercorns
    1 teaspoon salt
    ½ teaspoon paprika
    A few grains cayenne

Boil these ingredients until the liquid is reduced to about half. Strain the sauce. Add:
> 1 cup tomato purée

Dissolve:
> 2 bouillon cubes

in:
> ½ cup boiling water

Add:
> 1 teaspoon Worcestershire sauce

Combine this with the sauce. Keep it hot over boiling water. Add:
> 1 tablespoon butter
> 1 teaspoon dried Herbs, page 832

HOT MAYONNAISE SAUCE FOR VEGETABLES OR FISH

About 1 Cupful

Combine in the top of a double boiler:
> ¾ cup mayonnaise
> (⅓ cup milk)

Stir these ingredients over, not in, hot water until smooth and hot, for about 5 minutes. Add:
> ¼ teaspoon salt
> ⅛ teaspoon pepper
> A few grains red pepper
> 1 tablespoon lemon juice

If milk has been omitted, increase lemon juice to 3 tablespoonfuls. Remove from heat. Add:
> 1 tablespoon chopped chives or parsley or
> ⅓ teaspoon dried herb: tarragon, basil, etc.

This sauce may be reheated over hot water.

GREEN SAUCE OR SAUCE VERTE

About 1½ Cupfuls

Fine with cold salmon, glazed, or fish in aspic.

Place in a small bowl and beat:
> 2 egg yolks
> ½ teaspoon salt
> A few grains red pepper
> ¼ teaspoon mustard

Beat in:
> 1 tablespoon cider vinegar
> 1 tablespoon tarragon vinegar

Beat in gradually:
> 1 cup salad oil

When the sauce is thick and smooth beat in:
> 2 tablespoons cream
> 2 tablespoons finely chopped fresh dill
> 2 tablespoons finely chopped water cress

Chill the sauce well.

BROILED TARTAR SAUCE FOR FISH

6 Servings

Combine:
> ½ cup mayonnaise
> A dash cayenne pepper
> 1 tablespoon chopped parsley
> 2 tablespoons chopped pickle

Fold in:
> 1 egg white beaten until stiff but not dry

Spread the sauce over the top of fish fillets or other broiled fish 3 minutes before the end of the broiling time. Broil 3 to 5 minutes, or until the sauce has puffed up and is lightly browned. Serve at once.

SOUFFLÉ SAUCE FOR BROILED FISH

6 Servings

Broil until nearly done (page 236):
> 3 lbs. fish

Transfer them to a hot oven-proof dish. Combine and beat well:
> ½ cup mayonnaise
> ¼ cup pickle relish
> 2 tablespoons chopped parsley
> 1 tablespoon lemon juice
> ¼ teaspoon salt
> A few grains cayenne

Beat until stiff but not dry:
> 2 egg whites

Fold them into the mayonnaise mixture. Spread the sauce evenly on the fish. Broil it until the sauce is puffed and lightly browned.

Good with:
> Broiled Tomatoes, page 319

Dressings for Fish

Oyster dressing
Bread and celery dressing
Mushroom dressing

Onion dressing
Olive or celery dressing
Crab meat dressing

Sauces for Fish

For Boiled or Baked Fish

Mustard sauce for fish
Tomato sauce
Creole sauce
Cream sauce
Curry sauce
Horseradish sauce
Egg sauce
Frozen horseradish

Allemande sauce
Hollandaise sauce
Béarnaise sauce
Figaro sauce
Cheese sauce
Anchovy sauce for fish
Oyster sauce for fish
Yellow sauce for fish

For Sautéed, Fried or Broiled Fish

Lemon butter
Maître d'hôtel butter
Amandine (almond) sauce
Mushroom sauce
Cucumber sauce
Soufflé sauce

Anchovy butter
Fresh horseradish sauce
Tartar sauce
Hot mayonnaise
Hollandaise
Wine butter sauce

For Planked Fish

Melted butter
Parsley butter
Lemon butter

Anchovy butter
Tartar sauce
Maître d'hôtel butter

Garnishes for Fish

Curled celery
Radish roses
Lemons cut in quarters
Lemons slices dipped in chopped parsley
Lemon butter balls
Anchovy butter balls
Shredded almonds browned in butter
Cucumbers and French or sour cream
dressing
Hard-cooked eggs, chopped or riced
Onion rings or chopped onion

Tomatoes, raw or baked
Peeled and shredded carrots
Pickled beets
Cole slaw with green peppers
Pickles
Capers
Hollandaise sauce, tartar sauce or
Figaro sauce in pickled beet cups or
in a thick ring of green pepper
Bacon
Water cress or water cress butter

Green peppers, chopped or sliced

Vegetables

When it comes to cooking vegetables many cooks seem to suffer from arrested development. Delicious meat is usually accompanied by something indescribable that turns out to be a vegetable that has come through a siege. It is drained of all life force and has despairingly surrended to the inevitable.

It is this life force that is of the utmost importance to the consumer, for the loss of vitamin and mineral content through careless cooking robs the vegetable of all flavor and virtually reduces it to a nutritional zero.

High vitamin content depends first on the soil in which the vegetables are grown and next on the handling they receive, factors about which you can do little unless you grow vegetables properly yourself. But once they are in your kitchen you can do much to retain the remaining values and flavors.

Wash all soft-textured vegetables quickly but carefully just before using. Select fresh vegetables if possible, but if they are wilted place them on a rack over ⅛ inch of water in a covered container in the refrigerator. Otherwise store them dry in tightly covered containers or plastic bags. Exceptions to this rule include cauliflower, artichokes, Brussels sprouts and broccoli. Soak these vegetables briefly, immediately before cooking, in several waters for removal of small insects and natural and chemical dusts which would not be released otherwise. The first soaking may be in salted water.

Thick-skinned vegetables should be stored unwashed in a dry, dark, cool place if not used at once. Unless you are planning to use the greens, the tops should be removed at once as the moisture continues to be drawn from the root into the leaf after harvesting. Leave 1 inch of stem on beets and carrots. Work rapidly in paring and slicing so that the vegetable is exposed to the air as short a time as possible before it is covered in cooking. Once pared, do not soak vegetables. Use stainless steel or plastic knives. Where possible scrub the vegetable well and cook it in the skin.

The cooking period for all vegetables should be as short as possible. The exact time is determined by age and size of the vegetable and the cooking method used. Approximate cooking time is given with each recipe in this chapter.

No one method of cooking vegetables can claim superiority over all other types. In any method using water the cooking water should be saved by all means for the valuable vitamins and minerals it contains. Use it for its indispensable flavoring qualities. Added to gravy, sauce or soup, it makes the difference between commonplace and delectable dishes. This stock may be stored for several days in a tightly closed jar in the refrigerator.

For ease, speed and generally favorable results, pressure-pan cooking of vegetables seems advisable (page 882). Follow manufacturers' instructions carefully, especially as to expelling air from the pan before cooking, and timing. Vegetables overcooked by this method, however, have all the drawbacks of other overdone food.

Comparable results are obtained:

1. By steaming in a closed kettle with a perforated tray or colander or by cooking in the top of a double boiler. Flavor is well retained, although for both methods more time must be allowed for the finished product.

2. By cooking vegetables in parchment paper. A sheet of the paper is placed on the table and sprinkled with water like laundry; prepared vegetables are placed on it and salt, pepper, paprika, cream or butter are added. The edges of the paper are gathered up into a bag which is tied tightly, and the corners are turned back to prevent steam or water from entering the bag. It is then placed in a pan of boiling

water and when the vegetable is tender it is taken from the bag ready to serve. Fresh fruit may be stewed by this same process. The paper may be washed and dried for re-use. Other advantages of this method include the cooking of several bags in one pot and the lack of pot scouring.

3. By using heavy, tightly covered saucepans—so-called waterless cookers. The steam from the water naturally within the vegetables, plus a small addition of fluid if the cooking is to be longer than four minutes, keeps the vegetables from scorching if the heat is kept very low after the first few minutes.

It is advisable to cook most vegetables covered. The cabbage and onion tribe act up under too great heat and too long a period of cooking. Their strong disagreeable volatile oils escape and they discolor badly. Therefore, steaming, simmering in milk, or pressure cooking where the time element is short even if the heat is high, are the recommended procedures. They may also be cooked uncovered in a quantity of boiling water. A crust of bread laid on top of them as soon as they are placed in the boiling water helps to trap odors.

Different textures are gained by pan frying and braising.

The crisp but tender effect of mixed greens and roots, where each piece keeps its characteristic flavor, is an achievement of the Chinese. It comes from the use of young, carefully diced and shredded vegetables cooked for a very short time, usually in peanut oil, ⅓ ounce fat to 1 pound of vegetables, over a very hot flame in a specially shaped pan. The vegetables must coat quickly and be sealed in the fat. Constant agitation and split-second timing are needed. If the vegetables are of the thin-leaf type no extra water is needed, but beans and root vegetables need 1 cupful of liquid per pound.

The delicious quality of many French vegetables is the result of gentle sautéing or braising in a small amount of butter. The pot is then covered and the vegetables are cooked until tender in the steam arising from their own juices.

Deep fat frying in batter (page 542) and baking are also variants. While baking keeps the minerals in, the long heat is often destructive of vitamins.

Whatever method you prefer to use, try for ideal conditions: Fresh, young tender produce handled with as little water as possible both in cleaning and cooking. Cook until just tender. Stir as little as possible. Consume the minute it is finished cooking.

If, however, vegetables are mature and not easily tenderized, vary your method. Cook them in a casserole, bake them in an oven, or partially cook them by some other method, and finish the tenderizing by heating them in a sauce. Allow ½ to 1 cupful of sauce to 2 cupfuls of cooked vegetables. Select such recipes also if delay in service is anticipated.

If you cook in hard water as many of us do in the U. S., you are faced with discoloration problems. A few drops of vinegar or lemon juice in the cooking water will help to stabilize the greens. White and red vegetables such as cauliflower, cabbages, onions, turnips and beets will need as much as a teaspoonful of vinegar or lemon juice to 2 cupfuls of water. Simmering vegetables in milk stabilizes color and tenderizes the vegetable more rapidly, although sometimes, due to the acid of the vegetable, the milk curdles slightly and harmlessly.

As salt tends to drain out vitamins, use it during cooking only when absolutely necessary. Leave salting until after the cooking process is completed when most other seasonings may be added as well. Although seasoning is suggested in each recipe, it may be varied to suit individual taste.

Reheating vegetables is frowned on both from a culinary and health standpoint. If you do reheat vegetables, place them with a few teaspoonfuls of water or stock in the top of a covered double boiler or in a covered but unsealed pressure pan, or reheat or bake them in a hot sauce. Allow about half as much sauce as vegetables. Or serve them cold in a salad. Cold food is as nutritious as hot food. Sautéing and hash browning of cooked vegetables involve reheating and are hard on vitamins.

Home or commercially canned vegetables have, of course, already suffered a loss of flavor and vitamins and reheating before serving increases this loss. Be sure to retain the canning water for use in soup or sauce or as the medium in which to reheat the vegetables.

Always clean can tops before opening the cans as they may have been sprayed with poisonous insecticides while in the store. Also avoid metal slivers in opening a can by starting to open it beyond the side seam and stop before you cut through it. Food may be stored safely in opened cans as long as in any other container. However, if the food is acid a disagreeable but harmless taste may result from the acid eating through the tin to the iron in the can.

To cook frozen vegetables, see page 870.

ARTICHOKES
Soak in cold salted water for 30 minutes, or hold by the stem end and dash

up and down quickly in a deep bowl of salted water:
Artichokes
Cut or break off the stems. Pull off the tough bottom row of leaves and cut off ¼ of the tops. For this you may use scissors. To avoid discoloration dip the cut parts in:
Lemon juice
Place the artichokes upright in 1½ inches of boiling water. Add:
1 onion sliced or 1 clove garlic mashed
2 ribs celery with leaves
1½ tablespoons lemon juice
(2 tablespoons salad oil)
Cook them covered for 45 minutes or until tender. Drain them and serve them hot with:
Melted butter, mayonnaise,
Hollandaise Sauce, page 429,
Béchamel Sauce, page 429, or
Vinaigrette Sauce, page 493
Very good results are obtained by dropping artichokes that have been soaked, trimmed and drained into boiling soup and cooking them covered until they are tender. Rather fat, well-seasoned chicken broth is fine for this. Drain the artichokes. Unless completely immersed they will discolor

slightly, but both the soup and the vegetable will gain in flavor. Artichokes may be served chilled. See Index.

CORED ARTICHOKES
Soak and trim by the preceding rule:
Artichokes

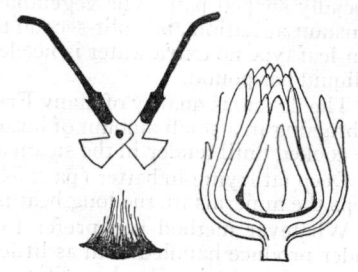

Force the leaves apart slightly and insert a grapefruit corer. Press the handles down to cut out the choke. Remove it. Tie artichokes into shape with string. Boil them, see this page. Drain them well, untie them and serve them either hot or cold, the centers filled with:
Hollandaise Sauce, page 429
Or, serve cold with:
Marinated shrimp and mayonnaise
See To Marinate, page 328.

STUFFED ARTICHOKES BAKED
The following excellent recipe is the contribution of my interested Italian friends and vegetable vendors. Soak and trim (see above):
Artichokes
Drain them well. Make a dressing of:
Bread crumbs
Minced garlic or onion
Chopped celery

Chopped anchovies or anchovy
paste
Grated Parmesan cheese
Chopped parsley
Salt and paprika

Push the dressing down between the leaves. The choke may be removed by the preceding rule, if desired, and the center filled with the dressing. Pour over the artichokes a little:

Olive oil

Place them in a baking dish and cover the bottom of the dish with ¼ inch of:

Boiling water or stock

Bake them covered in a moderate oven until they are done, about 1 hour. Baste them frequently with:

Olive oil or stock

ARTICHOKE HEARTS

Remove all leaves and the chokes from:

Artichokes

Drop the hearts into 1 inch of:

Boiling water

to which you may add:

Lemon juice

Simmer them covered for 20 minutes or until tender. Serve them with:

Brown Butter, page 327
Hollandaise Sauce, page 429

Cooked or canned artichoke hearts, well drained, may be sautéed until hot in:

Butter or drippings

to which you may add:

Garlic, shallots or onions

Season them with:

Salt and paprika
Lemon juice

JERUSALEM ARTICHOKES

A vegetable with agreeable characteristics that needs watching while it is being cooked. Wash and scrape:

1½ lbs. Jerusalem artichokes

Drop them into:

Boiling water

Cook them covered until they are tender only. If permitted to cook beyond this point they will again become tough. Test them with a toothpick after 15 minutes. Drain them. Melt:

2 tablespoons butter

Add:

1 teaspoon mild vinegar or white
wine
2 drops Tabasco sauce
2 teaspoons chopped parsley

Pour these ingredients over the artichokes, or cream them in:

1 cup Cream Sauce I, page 428

Or, you may boil, drain and slice the artichokes, then sauté them in butter. Serve them with lots of chopped parsley.

ASPARAGUS
4-6 Servings

Wash:

2 lbs. asparagus

Cut off or snap off the lower part of the stalks. Keep the trimmings for soup. It is seldom necessary to skin green asparagus. If the asparagus is white, skin the lower ends of the stalks with downward strokes of a knife. Tie the asparagus in bunches. Place them upright in a deep stewpan, or in the bottom part of a double boiler, the lower ends in:

½ cup boiling water

Cook the asparagus closely covered 12

minutes or until tender. An inverted double boiler top may be used. The steam will cook the tips. Drain the asparagus well. Reserve the liquor. Add:

½ teaspoon salt

Melt:

⅓ cup butter

Sauté in it for 1 minute:

1 cup bread crumbs

Pour this mixture over the tips of the asparagus or serve them with:

1 cup Cream Sauce I, page 428,
made with half cream and half
asparagus liquor
Egg Sauce, page 327, or
Hollandaise Sauce, page 429

ASPARAGUS AU GRATIN

Cook by the preceding rule:

Asparagus

Drain it well. Place it in a greased baking dish. Cover it with a little:

Boiling Cream Sauce I, page
428, or melted butter

Sprinkle the top with:

Bread crumbs

Dot it with:
Butter
Brown it under a low flame or in a
moderate oven 375°.
Or, place hot drained asparagus on a
greased hot oven-proof platter. Sprin-
kle it with:
¼ cup grated cheese
Pour over it:
⅓ cup melted butter
Sprinkle it lightly with:
Salt
A few grains of cayenne
Put it under a broiler until the cheese
is browned lightly or, best of all, serve
it with:
Buttered crumbs

___

FRIED ASPARAGUS
Drain well:
Cooked or canned asparagus tips
Dip them in:
1 egg
diluted with:
2 tablespoons water
Roll them in:
Flour, lightly salted
Dip them again in the egg mixture.
Fry them in deep fat (see page 542).
Drain them on absorbent paper. Serve
them very hot.

___

PURÉE OF AVOCADO HEATED
4 Servings
Pare and seed:
2 medium-sized avocados
Mash the pulp. Add:
1 teaspoon lemon juice
¼ teaspoon salt
¼ teaspoon paprika
1 tablespoon chopped chives or
grated onion
1 teaspoon grated lemon rind
Heat the purée in a double boiler.

___

BEANS
Now for a "department of utter confusion" that is all our own. The government bulletins, trade journals, home
economist magazines, etc., are advo-
cating the use of the word "snap
beans" to cover what we once knew as
"string beans." This puts me in mind
of the Japanese official who studied his
English grammar so conscientiously
that a visiting admiral was put to some
embarrassment by being greeted cere-
moniously with: "Sir, Miss or Madam,
as the case may be!" So, henceforth,
green, wax or string beans, as the case
may be, will become mostly "snap"
in these pages.

SNAP OR GREEN BEANS
4 Servings
String and shred lengthwise:
1 lb. snap beans
Drop them into:
1¼ cups boiling water
Cook them, uncovered if you wish to
preserve the color, covered if you wish
to preserve the vitamins, until they are
barely tender, no longer, about 20 minutes. Beans that are cut or slivered
require a shorter cooking time. The
addition of:
A small skinned onion
gives the beans a good flavor. Drain
the beans. Add:
½ teaspoon salt
Return them to the pot and reheat
them in:
2 tablespoons melted butter
or in thin:
Cream Sauce I, page 428
Use ½ as much sauce as there are
beans. Add to the cream sauce as
desired:
(Grated cheese)
Sprinkle the beans with:
Chopped parsley
Hot, well-seasoned stock may be
added to the melted butter, or combined with the cream, in the cream
sauce. Add for a variation to 1 pound
of beans, in place of the butter or
cream sauce:
Almond Sauce, page 258
Minced sautéed bacon and bacon
drippings or olive oil
Brown Onion Butter, page 327
Buttered crumbs
A grating of nutmeg
1 teaspoon celery seed
1 teaspoon dill
Black Butter, page 327

___

Snap Bean Salad II, page 461.

___

SNAP BEANS AND MUSH-
ROOMS IN SOUR CREAM
4 Servings
Sauté:
1 cup mushrooms
in:
2 tablespoons butter
Add:
2 cups cooked snap beans
⅓ cup sour cream
¼ teaspoon salt
Heat and serve with:
2 teaspoons chopped parsley or
basil (see Herbs, page 833)

SNAP BEANS WITH EGG SAUCE
4 Servings
String, tie loosely into small bunches:
> **1 lb. straight young snap beans**
Cook them by the rule on page 266 for Snap Beans. When they are tender, drain and untie the beans. Place them crosswise in a stack on a platter. Have ready the following sauce. Melt:
> **1½ tablespoons butter**
Stir in until blended:
> **1 tablespoon flour**
Stir in slowly:
> **1 cup Stock, page 43, or milk**
When the sauce is smooth and boiling, remove it from the fire and beat in:
> **2 egg yolks**
Reduce the heat and stir and cook the sauce for 1 minute longer to permit the yolks to thicken. Add:
> **¼ teaspoon salt**
> **⅛ teaspoon paprika**
> **1 tablespoon lemon juice**
Pour the sauce in a broad path down the center of the stack. Garnish the beans with:
> **Sautéed mushrooms**
Serve them at once.

SNAP OR GREEN BEAN CASSEROLE DISH
6 Servings
What becomes of the onions and peppers? They frequently disappear, leaving marvelously seasoned beans. An easy dish for the hostess who cooks her own dinner. String:
> **1 lb. snap beans**
Skin and chop:
> **4 medium-sized white onions**
Remove the seeds and membrane from:
> **2 medium-sized green peppers**
Chop the peppers. Butter a baking dish. Place in it alternate layers of the vegetables, beginning and ending with a layer of beans. Sprinkle each layer with:
> **Salt and paprika**
Dot each layer with:
> **Butter**
Cover the dish. Bake the vegetables in a moderate oven 350° for about 1¼ hours, or until the beans are tender. Before serving cover the top with:
> **Buttered Bread Crumbs, page 326**

SNAP BEANS BAKED IN TOMATO SAUCE
6 Servings
A good variation of an old standby. Prepare for cooking:
> **1 lb. tender snap beans**
Place them in a greased dish. Melt:
> **2 tablespoons butter**
> **2 tablespoons flour**
Stir in gradually:
> **2 cups tomato juice or**
> **1 cup Stock, page 43, and**
> **1 cup tomato juice**
> **3 tablespoons prepared horse-radish or**
> **2 teaspoons Worcestershire sauce**
> **¾ teaspoon salt**
> **¼ teaspoon paprika**
Pour this mixture over the beans. Bake the beans covered in a moderate oven 350° for 1 hour and 10 minutes or longer—until tender. Cover the top with:
> **½ cup buttered crumbs or dry crumbs and grated cheese**
Bake them in a hot oven 450° until the crumbs are brown, for about 10 minutes longer.

BAKED SNAP BEANS WITH CHEESE
Prepare for cooking:
> **1½ lbs. snap beans**
Place them in a greased baking dish. Dot them with:
> **1½ tablespoons butter**
Sprinkle them with:
> **1 teaspoon salt**
> **¼ teaspoon paprika**
> **A few grains of cayenne**
> **¾ cup grated cheese**
Pour over them:
> **¾ cup rich milk or part milk and part Stock, page 43**
Cover the dish. Bake the beans in a moderate oven 350° for about 1 hour.

Snap Beans and Cheese, see Snap Beans, page 266.

SNAP OR GREEN BEANS IN MUSHROOM SOUP
4 Servings
Quick if you use canned beans. Wonderful for a buffet supper or that unexpected guest. Cook by the rule on page 266:
> **1 lb. snap beans**
Drain them well. Heat the contents of:
> **1 can condensed mushroom soup: 10½ oz.**
Add:
> **2 tablespoons rich milk**
> **(2 tablespoons sherry or dry white wine)**
Combine this with the hot beans. Place them in a casserole. Sprinkle the top with:

Grated cheese

Place the dish under a broiler until the cheese is melted.

SUCCOTASH WITH SNAP BEANS
5 Servings

Combine and heat:
    2 cups cooked corn cut from the cob
    2 cups finely shredded cooked snap beans
Season the vegetables with:
    Salt and pepper
    Butter

RULE FOR SOAKING AND COOKING DRIED LEGUMES
Dried beans and peas are much more temperamental than they sound. Their cooking time depends on the locality in which they were grown and their age—usually two unknowns for the cook—plus the type of water used in cooking them. Soft water is best but if it is unavailable try boiling the water in which the beans are to cook 20 to 30 minutes before adding the beans. If you have permanently hard water, the odds will still be against you.

Do not use soda as valuable nutrients are lost by its use.

Custom demands soaking to cover, usually overnight, then bringing the beans to a slow boil in the water in which they were soaked and simmering them. If you have forgotten to soak, use a pressure cooker (see pages 876 and 879) or the following alternatives:
Buy treated beans which require no soaking, or drop:
    2 cups dry beans
into:
    1 quart rapidly boiling water
Do this slowly so as not to disturb the boiling point. When the last bean has been added, lower the heat to a simmer and keep it there until the beans are tender.

Navy beans which are usually the toughest take up to 3 hours' simmering. Dried Limas, after soaking for 8 hours, may cook almost as rapidly as the fresh ones—in about ½ hour. Lentils take about 1½ hours.

BAKED BEANS
Method I. 4 Servings
If quick-cooking or precooked beans are used, follow the directions on the package.

Otherwise soak (see this page):
    1½ cups dried beans
Cover them with water. Bring them to a boil, then simmer them slowly for ½ hour or more. Place a few beans in a spoon. Blow on them. If the skins burst, they are sufficiently cooked. Drain them, reserving cooking water, and add:
    ¼ cup chopped onion
    ¼ lb. sliced salt pork
    2 tablespoons or more dark molasses
    2 or 3 tablespoons catsup
    1 tablespoon dry mustard
    1 teaspoon salt
    ½ cup boiling bean water
Place them in a greased baker, decorate them with the salt pork and bake them covered in a very slow oven 250° from 6 to 8 hours. If they become dry, add a little:
    Well-seasoned stock or reserved bean water
Uncover the beans for the last hour of cooking.

Method II. 10 Servings
Pick over, then soak (see this page):
    4 cups beans
Cook them by the rule above. Add:
    ½ cup chopped onion
    ¼ lb. diced salt pork
    ½ to ¾ cup brown sugar or molasses
    ½ cup catsup
    1 teaspoon dry mustard or
    1 teaspoon or more curry
    2 teaspoons salt
    1 cup boiling water
    (1 tablespoon Worcestershire sauce)
Place the beans in a greased baking dish. Decorate the top with:
    ¼ lb. sliced salt pork
Cover the beans with reserved bean water. Bake them as directed above. Uncover the beans for the last hour of cooking. Beans are good served with:
    Marinated Onions, page 31, or sautéed pineapple slices and brown sugar

Pressure Cooked Legumes, page 885.

BLACK BEANS BAKED
4 to 6 Servings
Soak (see this page):
    2 cups black turtle beans
Cook them or see Pressure-Cooked Legumes, page 885, well covered with water in an uncovered pan until they

are tender, but do not permit the shells to burst. Add to the water:

2 teaspoons salt
A cut clove garlic
½ bay leaf

Remove the garlic and bay leaf. Place the beans and water in a bean pot. Add additional water to cover and:

2 skinned sliced onions
1 teaspoon salt
¼ teaspoon pepper
½ teaspoon dried thyme, marjoram, etc.

You may insert in various places:

¼ lb. Canadian bacon, ham fat or diced raw ham

Cook the beans uncovered in a slow oven 250° for about 1½ hours, or until tender. Stir them from time to time. Add more liquid, water or stock, if they become dry. Stir in:

1 tablespoon butter
1 tablespoon lemon juice
½ cup dry red wine

CANNED BAKED BEANS AND BACON OR FRANKFURTERS
6 Servings

To jazz up pepless canned beans add to the contents of:

1 No. 2 can beans

approximately:

4 tablespoons catsup
2 tablespoons molasses
2 tablespoons brown sugar
2 tablespoons bacon drippings
Minced onion, celery and green pepper
Salt if needed
3 drops Tabasco sauce or a few grains of red pepper

Make them moist and palatable. Place the beans in a greased shallow oven-proof dish. Cover the top with:

Bacon, very thin strips of salt pork or skinned sliced frank-furters

Bake the beans in a moderate oven 375° for about 30 minutes. The raw vegetables may first be sautéed in the bacon fat and then added. The bacon may be sautéed and served separately.

BAKED BEANS WITH CHEESE
4 Servings

Stir and melt over hot water:

¾ cup diced American cheese
1½ tablespoons butter

Fold in the contents of:

1 No. 2 can baked beans with bacon

Heat well. Season with:

Salt and a few grains red pepper
2 tablespoons Worcestershire sauce or prepared mustard

Serve on:

Toast

Sprinkle with:

Chopped parsley, chives or other herb

BLACK-EYED PEAS

Cook dried black-eyed peas like dried beans, see Baked Beans I, page 268. Allow ¼ cupful dried peas per serving. Simmer them from 1½ to 2 hours. Cook fresh black-eyed peas like Lima Beans, page 270.

SOYBEANS

Young vegetable type, not field varieties of beans, must be used. The pods should still be green. Immerse them in boiling water. Cover the pot. After 5 minutes drain and cool them. Squeeze the pods to press out the beans. Cook the beans in boiling water until tender, approximately 10 to 15 minutes. Use them as directed in the rules given for Fresh or Canned Lima Beans, etc., page 270.

The cooked beans may also be spread in a greased pan, dotted with butter and roasted in a moderate oven 350° until brown, or they may be browned in deep fat (page 542). Soy milk and cheese can also be made from them. See page 192.

DRIED SOYBEANS

Dried soybeans soaked in 4 times as much water as beans will about double in bulk when cooked. Soak (page 268):

Dried soybeans

If water is bitter, discard it, otherwise boil them in the same water until tender, about 3 hours. Drain if necessary. Tomatoes, bacon, salt pork and onion may be added for the last hour of cooking. Dried soybeans may be substituted for other dried beans, navy, pea, Lima, etc., in the rules given elsewhere in this book.

NAVY OR GREAT NORTHERN BEANS

Soak and cook:

Navy beans

by the rule for Lentils, page 272. Serve them, as in France, with roast lamb.

Bean Loaf, page 170; Bean Patties, page 171.

PURÉE OF DRIED BEANS
A rule for making purées of dried beans, peas, etc., is given under Lentils, page 271.

LIMA OR BUTTER BEANS
Cooked Lima beans of different kinds and in different states—canned, frozen, fresh or dry—may be substituted for one another in most recipes.

If you are hulling fresh Limas, cut a thin strip along inner edge of the pod to which the beans are attached. The beans will pop out easily.

BOILED LIMA BEANS
6 Servings
Cover:
    1 quart fresh shelled Lima beans
with:
    1 inch boiling water
Add:
    1 tablespoon butter
Simmer the beans for 15 minutes. Add:
    1 teaspoon salt
Cook the beans covered over a good flame until tender, for about 20 minutes. Add:
    ¼ cup butter
    1½ tablespoons lemon juice
    1 tablespoon chopped parsley or chives
or add:
    ½ cup cream
Heat them thoroughly in the cream, but do not let them boil. Or dress them with:
    Warm sour cream and freshly ground pepper
A good way of using left-over Lima beans is to combine them with cheese sauce. Add to:
    Lima beans

half as much:
    Cheese Sauce, page 430
Chopped celery, cooked or raw, is good added to Lima beans. So are sautéed onions or creamed mushrooms and crisp bacon, minced.
I know a family whose members feel abused if their beans aren't served, with soup stock thickened with a little flour and butter, in cooked green pepper cases.

LIMA BEAN ONION CASSEROLE
4 Servings
Wash and peel:
    2 cups small onions
Sauté until they are translucent in:
    4 tablespoons butter
Stir in:
    1 tablespoon flour
    1 cup water or stock
Simmer until blended. Add:
    2 cups fresh Lima beans
Continue cooking covered over low heat, shaking occasionally until beans are almost tender. Then add:
    1 tablespoon chopped celery leaves
    1 tablespoon chopped parsley
    ⅛ teaspoon dried thyme
    ½ teaspoon salt
Cover and continue cooking until beans are tender.

CANNED LIMA BEANS WITH PIQUANT SAUCE
4 Servings
In order to provide a canned Lima bean with glamor you must do a fan dance with it. Drain the contents of:
    1 No. 1 can Lima beans
Reserve the liquor. Add to it to make 1½ cupfuls of liquid:
    Cream
Melt:
    3 tablespoons butter or drippings
Sauté in it until light brown:
    ¼ cup chopped onion
    (¼ cup chopped celery)
Stir in until it bubbles:
    2½ tablespoons flour
Stir in the liquid slowly. Reduce the heat and stir in until melted:
    ¼ cup or more minced cheese
Season the sauce with:
    ½ teaspoon salt
    ⅛ teaspoon paprika
    A few grains red pepper
    ¼ teaspoon mustard
    2 teaspoons Worcestershire sauce
    A pinch of three herbs—marjoram, thyme, savory, etc.

Add the beans and heat them. Serve them garnished with:
  Chopped parsley

CANNED LIMA BEAN CASSEROLE
4 Servings
This is a fine main dish. Prepare by the preceding rule:
  Lima beans
Add to them:
  6 sliced frankfurters
Place these ingredients in a baking dish. Cover the top with:
  Bread crumbs
Sprinkle it with:
  (Cheese)
Bake the beans in a moderate oven 375° for about 15 minutes.

For other Lima Bean Dishes, see pages 177, 178.

DRIED RED KIDNEY BEANS
5 Servings
Soak (page 268), then drain:
  1 lb. dried red kidney beans
Place them in a heavy saucepan. Cover them with water. Add:
  6 tablespoons butter
  ⅓ cup chopped onion
  3 whole cloves
  2 teaspoons salt
  ¼ teaspoon freshly ground pepper
  ¼ teaspoon dried thyme
Simmer the beans covered from 1 to 1½ hours. Stir them from time to time. Add and cook for 20 minutes longer:
  1 cup dry red wine or stock
When the beans are tender, serve them hot garnished with:
  Chopped chives or parsley

CANNED KIDNEY BEANS AND TOMATOES
4 Large Servings
Grease a baking dish. Have ready the contents of:
  1 No. 2 can kidney beans
  1 canned tomatoes or diluted
    tomato soup
  ¼ cup chopped onion
  ¼ lb. chopped bacon
If preferred, cut the bacon with a pair of scissors, shown above. Scissors make quick work of celery, green peppers, raisins and ever so many other things. Grand to have around the kitchen.
Cover the bottom of the dish with a layer of beans. Sprinkle it with some of the bacon and onions. Repeat the

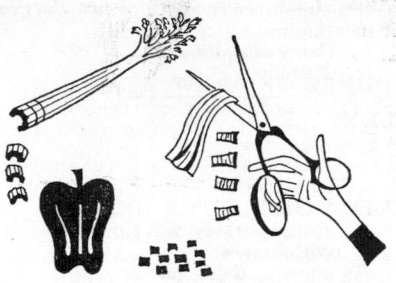

process. Pour the tomatoes over the whole. Cover the top with:
  Bread crumbs or cornflakes
Dot it with:
  Butter
or sprinkle it with:
  Grated cheese
Bake the dish in a moderate oven 350° until the top is browned, for about 30 minutes.

Chile con Carne, page 167; Soybean Dinner, page 210.

QUICK PURÉE OF PEAS
Prepare:
  ¼ cup minced onion, scallions or
    chives
Sauté them until tender in:
  3 tablespoons butter
Heat in a double boiler the contents of:
  2 cans condensed cream of pea
    soup: 21 oz.
Stir in the onions and a few drops of:
  Green coloring
This dish may be served au gratin.

See Lentil and Sausage Casserole, page 153.

PURÉE OF DRIED LENTILS, BEANS OR PEAS
See Pressure Cooked Beans, page 885. Cook by the rule for Dried Beans, page 268:
  Dried lentils, beans or peas
You may add:
  A clove of garlic
After draining the lentils put them through a fine sieve, a purée strainer or blender. Allow to every cupful of purée:
  1 tablespoon butter
  A scant ½ teaspoon salt
  ¼ teaspoon pepper or paprika
You may brown in the butter:
  1 tablespoon flour

Whip the purée over a hot fire. Serve it in a mound garnished with:
> Sautéed onions
> Parsley

LENTILS
4 Servings
Wash, pick over, then soak (page 268):
> 2 cups lentils

Add to them:
> 3 sprigs parsley or a rib celery with leaves
> ¼ cup sliced onions
> ½ bay leaf
> (A piece of fat corned beef, ham skin or bacon rind, tried out pork fat or smoked sausage)
> (2 cloves)
> (A slice of garlic)

Follow the rule for cooking Dried Beans, page 268, using 4 cupfuls of water. Cooking time will be about 1½ hours. Add boiling water, if necessary, during the cooking. Or see Pressure-Cooked Beans, page 885. Remove the onion, parsley and spices. Drain the lentils.

I.
Put them through a ricer, food mill or blender. Beat into them:
> 1 tablespoon butter
> 2 tablespoons cream

Add if needed:
> 1 teaspoon salt or more if the meat has been omitted

You may put them in a greased baking dish in a hot oven 425° until well heated. Serve the lentils with:
> Brown Sauce or Tomato Sauce, pages 435, 433

Use 1 cupful lentil water to make the Brown Sauce.

II.
Lentils may be served whole in:
> Sour Sweet Sauce:

Sauté:
> 3 tablespoons minced bacon
> 3 tablespoons onion

in:
> 2 tablespoons butter

Stir in:
> 1 tablespoon flour

When well blended, add:
> 1 cup lentil or other broth
> 2 tablespoons vinegar or wine
> A fresh grating of nutmeg
> Salt and paprika

Add and heat the drained lentils in the sauce.

Try the lentils in place of some other starchy dish with roast pork.

LENTILS AND PRUNES
4 Servings
Highly caloric but relished by both young and old. Wash:
> 1 cup lentils

Cook them by the rule for Dried Beans, page 268. Cook by the rule on page 450:
> 1 cup dried prunes

Pit the prunes and mash them. Add them to the lentils with:
> ¼ cup sherry
> 1 teaspoon salt
> (Lemon juice and spices)

Cook over low flame until thoroughly heated.

BOILED BEETS
For a quicker approach in cooking beets use a pressure pan or see Young Whole Beets, page 272, Baked Sliced Beets I and II and Beets in a Double Boiler. Cut off the tops of:
> Beets

Leave 1 inch of stem. Wash the beets or pare and dice them. Half cover them with:
> Boiling water

Cook them covered until they are tender. Allow ½ to 1 hour for young beets, 1 to 2 hours for old beets. Add boiling water as needed. When the beets are done, if they are not pared and diced, cool them slightly and skin them. Cut them into quarters, chop them or put them through a ricer. Season them with:
> Salt

Pour over them:
> Melted butter
> Chopped parsley

Or, serve the beets in cream sauce seasoned with mustard, curry powder or horseradish; or you may follow the rule for Cream Sauce, page 428, and use orange juice and water in place of milk. Flavor the sauce with grated orange rind. Sweeten it with:
> (3 tablespoons brown sugar)

BEET GREENS
Beet greens may be prepared like Spinach, page 313. Add a little green coloring, if you like, put the beets in a ring, serve the greens in the center dressed with melted butter.

YOUNG WHOLE BEETS
4 Servings
This recipe using root and leaf is both easy and economical. Scrub well and dice unpared into ¼ inch cubes:

6 or 8 beet roots
Drop them into:
¾ cup hot milk
Stir until you are sure that all surfaces have been coated with the milk. Cook covered over slow heat 8 to 12 minutes depending on age of beets. Cut into ½ inch shreds:
Beet leaves
Add them to the diced beets. Re-cover the pan and continue to simmer 6 to 8 minutes longer. Season with:
Salt and paprika
Freshly ground nutmeg

BOILED BEETS IN SOUR CREAM
4 Servings
Combine in a double boiler:
3 cups cooked sliced beets
½ cup sour cream
1 tablespoon prepared horseradish
1 tablespoon chopped chives
Salt as needed
(1 teaspoon grated onion)
Heat these ingredients.

BAKED BEETS
Beets may be baked like potatoes in their jackets, or pared and wrapped in aluminum foil. Wash:
Beets
Trim the tops, leaving 1 inch of stem. Place them on a pan in a moderate oven 325° and bake them until they are tender, ½ hour for young beets, about 1 hour for old beets. Pull off the skins. Season the beets with:
Salt and paprika
Serve them with:
Melted butter

BAKED SLICED BEETS
Method I. 8 Servings
Beets burn easily and smell to heaven. Thanks to the following rule, you can now serve all the beets you want without giving the household one obnoxious whiff. Pare, then slice or chop fine:
16 medium-sized beets
Grease a 7 inch baking dish. Place the beets in it in layers. Season them with:
¼ cup sugar
¾ teaspoon salt
¼ teaspoon paprika
Dot them with:
3 tablespoons butter
Add:
1 tablespoon lemon juice
⅓ cup water
(Grated or sliced onions)
Cover the dish closely and bake the

beets in a hot oven 400° for 30 minutes, or until they are tender. Stir them twice.

Method II. 6 Servings
Pare and cut into thin slices:
12 medium-sized beets
Place them in a greased baking dish. Combine, stir and pour over them:
2 tablespoons flour
¼ cup sugar
½ teaspoon salt
½ cup orange juice
Dot the beets with:
2 tablespoons butter
Cover the dish closely. Bake the beets in a hot oven 400° for about 30 minutes, or until they are tender.

BEETS COOKED IN A DOUBLE BOILER
Prepare beets for cooking as in the preceding:
Baked Sliced Beets I or II
Place them in a double boiler. Cover the beets and cook them over boiling water for ½ hour, or until they are tender. Stir them frequently.

HARVARD OR SOUR SWEET BEETS
6 Servings
Slice or dice:
3 cups freshly cooked Boiled
Beets, page 272, or canned beets
Stir in a double boiler until smooth:
½ cup sugar
1 tablespoon cornstarch
½ teaspoon salt
2 whole cloves
½ cup mild cider vinegar, or
6 tablespoons strong vinegar and
4 tablespoons cream, or
½ cup dry white wine
Cook and stir these ingredients until they are clear. Add the beets and place them over hot water for 30 minutes. Just before serving heat the beets, but do not boil them, and add:
2 tablespoons butter
Add to the beets for a delicious variation:
1 small ground orange, or
1 tablespoon orange marmalade

Pickled Beets, page 461.

BROCCOLI
Soak for 10 minutes in cold water:
Broccoli
Drain it well. Remove the large leaves and the tough part of the stalks. Cut

deep gashes in the bottom of the stalks. If the broccoli is old, cook it like cabbage, page 275. If it is young, place it in a saucepan in:
    1 inch boiling water
Cook it closely covered until it is barely tender, 10 to 12 minutes. Drain it. Sprinkle it with:
    ½ teaspoon salt
Serve it with:
    Buttered crumbs, melted butter or lemon juice
to which you may add:
    ¼ cup chopped salted almonds
Try serving broccoli au gratin or with:
    Hot Vinaigrette Sauce, page 493
    Chef's Mayonnaise, page 495
    Hollandaise Sauce, page 429
    Easy Hollandaise Sauce, page 430
    Cheese Sauce, page 430
    Onion Sauce I, page 432
    Sour Cream Dressing, page 496

Good ways of using left-over broccoli.
Broccoli Rings, page 224.
Broccoli Timbales, page 212.

CREAMED BROCCOLI WITH BREAD CRUMBS AND CHEESE
6 Servings
Prepare and cook by preceding rule except that you may retain the leaves:
    2 lbs. broccoli
Drain it and chop it until it is very fine. It may be put through a purée strainer. Sauté lightly:
    ½ teaspoon grated onion
in:
    2 tablespoons butter
Stir in until blended:
    2 tablespoons flour
Stir in slowly:
    1 cup milk
    ¼ teaspoon salt
    ⅛ teaspoon paprika
Or use a Canned Soup Sauce, page 441. Add the broccoli. Beat the mixture until it is light. Place it in a baking dish. Sprinkle it with:
    Bread crumbs or crushed cornflakes
    Grated cheese
Bake the broccoli in a hot oven 425° until the cheese is melted, or if the broccoli mixture is hot, melt the cheese under a broiler.

BROCCOLI WITH EGG SAUCE AU GRATIN
Make by the rule on page 429:
    Allemande Sauce
Sauté in the butter:
    1 tablespoon minced onion
Pour the sauce over cooked, drained:
    Broccoli
Sprinkle the top with:
    Chopped parsley or chives
Or, serve it au gratin by sprinkling the top with buttered crumbs or grated cheese and browning it under a broiler.

SAUTÉED OR FRIED BROCCOLI
Prepare by the rule on page 273:
    Broccoli
Drain it before it is tender. Cut it into quarters. Sauté the broccoli in:
    Salad oil
Sprinkle it with:
    Grated cheese
Or, dip the quarters in:
    Batter, page 543
Fry the broccoli in deep fat (page 542) or sauté it in butter.

BRAISED BROCCOLI
6 Servings
Cut the tough stems from:
    2 lbs. or more broccoli
Wash it by the rule on page 237. Drain it. Prepare and place in a baking dish:
    ¼ cup chopped celery or carrots
    ¼ cup chopped onions
Add the broccoli. Cover it well with:
    Chicken Stock, page 47
Cover the dish. Bake the vegetables in a moderate oven 350° until they are tender, for about 1 hour.

BRUSSELS SPROUTS
If wilted, pull the outer leaves from:
    Brussels sprouts
Cut off the stems. Soak the sprouts for 10 minutes in cold water to which a little salt has been added. Drain them. Cut crosswise gashes into the stem ends. Drop them into a quantity of rapidly boiling:
    Water
Reduce heat to simmer and cook uncovered until they are barely tender, about 10 minutes longer. Drain them and serve them with:
    Melted butter—1 tablespoon butter to 1 cup sprouts
You may add to the butter:
    Grated Parmesan cheese and Chopped parsley, or
    1 tablespoon lemon juice
Or sauté in the butter:
    1 tablespoon grated onion, or
    2 tablespoons bread crumbs

Sprouts may be served with:
 Onion Sauce I, page 432
 Use ½ as much sauce as there
 are sprouts
or, best of all, with:
 Lots of Hollandaise Sauce, page
 430, or
 Black Butter, page 327

BRUSSELS SPROUTS AND CHESTNUTS BAKED

6 Servings
Cook by the preceding rule:
 2 cups Brussels sprouts
Cook by the second rule on page 283:
 ½ lb. chestnuts
Butter a baking dish. Fill it with alternate layers of sprouts and chestnuts. Dot the layers with:
 Butter
Season them very lightly with:
 Pepper and salt, if needed
Moisten them lightly with:
 Stock or water
Bake them uncovered in a moderate oven 350° for 30 minutes.

BRUSSELS SPROUTS WITH STOCK AND CHEESE

4 Servings
Prepare and cook by the rule above:
 2 cups Brussels Sprouts
Drain them well. Place them in a buttered baking dish. Pour over them:
 ½ cup chicken stock or bouillon
Sprinkle them with:
 ¼ cup grated cheese
Bake the sprouts in a hot oven 400° until the cheese is melted.

Left-Over Brussels Sprouts in Cheese Sauce, page 178.

BRUSSELS SPROUTS AND CHESTNUTS OR CELERY CREAMED

4 Servings
Cook by the rule above:
 2 cups Brussels Sprouts
Prepare by Method I on page 283:
 1 cup chestnuts
Cover the chestnuts with:
 Boiling water
Cook them until they are tender and the water is absorbed. Heat until brown:
 1 tablespoon butter
Stir in:
 ¼ teaspoon salt
 1 teaspoon sugar

Add the chestnuts, stir and cook them until they are browned. Melt:
 2 tablespoons butter
Stir in until blended:
 2 tablespoons flour
Stir in slowly:
 1 cup Stock, page 43, or the sprouts' liquid and cream
When the sauce is smooth and boiling add the chestnuts and the sprouts. You may substitute for the chestnuts 1 cupful chopped celery sautéed lightly in 2 tablespoonfuls butter.

Brussels Sprouts Cases for hors d'oeuvres, page 38.

BOILED CABBAGE

Method I. 4 Servings
Lemon juice is good added to sauces for the cabbage family. The old way of cooking cabbage is to cut it in sections and boil it for hours. The new way is to shred it finely and barely cook it, allowing only 7 to 8 minutes. Remove the outer leaves from:
 ½ head cabbage
Remove the outer leaves from:
the cabbage. Drop it into a quantity of rapidly boiling:
 Water
Reduce the heat to a simmer. Cook it covered until it is tender but still crisp, 7 or 8 minutes. Drain it. Add:
 ½ teaspoon salt
Place it in a serving dish and pour over it:
 Melted butter—1 tablespoon to 1 cup cabbage
Add to the butter:
 (Bread crumbs, or caraway or poppy seeds or a few drops lemon juice and a teaspoon chopped parsley)

Method II.
All rules have exceptions, so try out this cabbage dish which calls for little water. Cut into wedges:
 A head of cabbage
Trim off part of the core. Drop the wedges into:
 ½ inch boiling water
Cover and cook the cabbage for about 10 minutes. Drain it well. Dress it as above.

CREAMED CABBAGE

6 Servings
Boil by the preceding rule:
 1 medium-sized head cabbage

Drain it well. Prepare:
    1 cup Cream Sauce I, page 428
Add to the sauce:
    ½ teaspoon freshly grated nutmeg
    or 2 teaspoons prepared mustard
    or ½ cup grated cheese
Or you may substitute for the Cream
Sauce:
    1 cup Horseradish Cream Sauce,
    page 429, or
    1 cup creamed canned condensed
    soup
Combine the sauce with the cabbage
and serve it at once.

CREAMED CABBAGE BAKED WITH NUT MEATS AND CHEESE
6 Servings
Cook by the rule on page 275:
    1 medium-sized head cabbage
Drain it well. Place it in layers in a
greased baking dish. Sprinkle the
layers with:
    ¾ cup or more grated cheese
    (½ cup or more chopped nut meats)
Pour over them:
    1 cup boiling Cream Sauce I, page
    428
Cover the top with:
    Bread crumbs or cornflakes
Dot it with:
    Butter
or sprinkle it with:
    Grated cheese
Bake the cabbage in a hot oven 450°
until the crumbs are brown.

CREAMED CABBAGE BAKED WITH EGGS
6 Servings
Boil by the rule on page 275:
    1 medium-sized head cabbage
Drain it well and place it in a greased
baking dish. Combine:
    2 beaten eggs
    1 tablespoon melted butter
    ½ cup cream or milk
    ½ teaspoon salt
    ⅛ teaspoon paprika
Pour these ingredients over the cabbage. Bake it in a slow oven 325° until
it is light brown. Cover the top with:
    Dry bread crumbs
Dot it with:
    Butter
or sprinkle it with:
    Grated cheese
Return it to the oven until the butter
or cheese is melted.

CABBAGE IN MILK
6 Servings
This method makes cabbage more di-
gestible. Cut into very fine shreds:
    3 cups cabbage
Drop it gradually into:
    ¾ cup boiling milk
Boil it for 2 minutes. Stir in:
    ¼ cup cream
    ½ teaspoon salt
    ⅛ teaspoon paprika
Melt:
    1 tablespoon butter
Stir in until blended:
    1 tablespoon flour
Add a little of the liquid from the cab-
bage. Pour this sauce onto the cab-
bage. Cook and stir it over a quick fire
for 3 minutes.

CREOLE CABBAGE
4 Servings
Cook:
    2 lbs. shredded cabbage
Drain it well. Sauté for 5 minutes:
    1 cup chopped onions
in:
    2 tablespoons butter or drippings
Add and simmer for 15 minutes:
    1¾ cups canned tomatoes
    3 tablespoons minced green
    pepper
    3 whole cloves
    ½ bay leaf
    1 tablespoon brown sugar
    ¾ teaspoon salt
Remove the cloves and bay leaf. Add
the drained cabbage. This may be
served au gratin.

AUSTRIAN CABBAGE
4 Servings
Shred:
    1 small head cabbage
Sauté it lightly in:
    Butter or bacon drippings
Add to the hot fat:
    ½ teaspoon salt
    ¼ teaspoon paprika
    Minced garlic or onion
Place the cabbage in a greased baking
dish. Pour over it:
    1 cup sour or sweet cream
Bake it in a moderate oven 375° for
about 20 minutes.

*For Stuffed Cabbage, Scalloped Cab-
bage, Ground Beef in Cabbage Leaves
and other Cabbage Dishes, see Index.*

FRENCH FRIED CABBAGE
Crisp in cold water:
> Finely shredded cabbage

Drain and dry it. Dip it in:
> Milk

then in:
> Flour

Fry a small amount at a time in deep fat heated to 375°, page 542. Drain it on absorbent paper. Season it with salt.

RED CABBAGE
4 Servings

This good old-timer breaks all previously given rules, and should be eaten for auld lang syne rather than nutritional benefit, for it calls for long slow cooking in a covered saucepan. It was once a great favorite and is now enjoying a revival of its former popularity. A cook in St. Louis objects strenuously to following this or any other cook book. Outright rebellion came at the suggestion that apple be added to cabbage. When her employer insisted that the rule be followed, she left the room mumbling darkly: "That ole Mrs. Rombauer! Ought to run **her** out of town, that's what **we** ought to do!"

Pull the outer leaves from:
> A head of red cabbage

Cut it into sections, remove the hard core, shred the cabbage and soak it in cold water. Cut into small pieces, place in a stewpan and sauté over low heat:
> 3 slices bacon

When it is well tried out remove the hard scraps of bacon. Simmer in the fat for 3 minutes:
> (2 tablespoons grated onion)

Or the onion may be sautéed in:
> 3 tablespoons melted butter

Lift the cabbage from the water with the hands, leaving it moist. Place it in the stewpan, cover it and let it simmer for 10 minutes. Core and cut into very thin slices:
> 2 apples

Add them to the cabbage with:
> ¼ teaspoon salt, if bacon is used, **or**
> 1 teaspoon salt if unsalted fat
> is used
> ⅛ cup boiling water

Stir these ingredients. Cover the pan and simmer the cabbage very slowly for 1 hour and 20 minutes. Add boiling water if required. If the water has not been absorbed when the cabbage is done, uncover the pot and cook it until it is absorbed. Dissolve:
> 2 tablespoons flour

in:
> ½ cup diluted vinegar or red wine

Or you may substitute:
> 4 tablespoons brown sugar
> 4 tablespoons undiluted vinegar or
> wine

and omit the flour. Add these ingredients to the cabbage and simmer it 10 minutes longer.

Red Cabbage and Chestnuts, page 173.

RED CABBAGE SIMPLIFIED
4 Servings

The preceding rule is the traditional recipe. The one that follows is the modern version. Prepare:
> 6 cups red cabbage finely
> shredded

Melt:
> 3 tablespoons butter or bacon
> drippings

Sauté lightly in this:
> 2 tablespoons chopped onion

Add:
> 6 tablespoons brown sugar
> 3 tablespoons vinegar or white
> wine
> (1 tablespoon caraway seeds)

Add the cabbage and sauté it covered for 18 minutes over slow heat.

Canned red cabbage may be substituted. Time for cooking—about 5 minutes.

SAUERKRAUT
6 Servings

"Eat all kind nature doth bestow
It will amalgamate below.
If the mind says so, it shall be so.
But, if you once begin to doubt,
The gastric juice will find it out.
Calm courage conquers sauerkraut."

Quoted from Prof. E. P. Cathcart of the University of Glasgow Hastings Lectures. Let's hope so.

Melt in a skillet:
> 2 tablespoons butter or bacon
> drippings

Add and sauté until clear:
> ½ cup sliced onion

Add and sauté for 5 minutes:
> 1 quart sauerkraut

Peel, grate and add:
> 1 medium-sized potato or tart
> apple

Cover the kraut with:
> Boiling Stock, page 43, or water

Cook the kraut uncovered for 30 minutes, cover it and cook or bake it in a moderate oven 325° for 30 minutes longer. The kraut may be seasoned with:

1 or 2 tablespoons brown sugar
1 teaspoon caraway or celery seed

Spareribs or Frankfurters and Sauerkraut, page 369.

CANNED SAUERKRAUT
6 Servings
Canned sauerkraut is excellent. Perhaps you prefer the plain unadulterated variety. If not, try this: Heat until it is brown:

¼ cup butter or drippings

You may sauté in it:

½ cup sliced onions

Add the contents of:

1 No. 3 can kraut

Cover the pot and cook the kraut until it is hot. Add, if you wish:

2 tablespoons brown sugar
1 teaspoon caraway seed or
3 or 4 whole cloves

You may pare, then cut very fine or grate and add:

1 large apple

Some cooks add:

¼ cup vinegar or dry wine

SAUERKRAUT VARIATIONS
Do not feel bound to serve a dish repeatedly in the same way when it is possible to vary its monotony. Sauerkraut is an acceptable food to most persons. Its healthful quality was recognized in 200 B.C. when, history records, it was served to the laborers working on the Great Wall in China. To retain its full flavor serve it raw or barely heated through. Cooking makes kraut milder. See Sauerkraut with Mushrooms, page 177.

I.
Sauté mushrooms and green peppers in butter or fat until nearly done. Add sauerkraut and heat it well. You may add dry wine for flavor.

II.
Combine sauerkraut with thinly sliced apples. Bake it until the apples are tender in a moderate oven 375°.

SAUERKRAUT AND TOMATOES
8 Servings
Lovers of sauerkraut will welcome this old friend in a new guise. Drain well:

1 quart sauerkraut or the contents of a No. 3 can

Put through a strainer the contents of:

1 No. 2½ can tomatoes: 3 cups

Melt:

2 tablespoons bacon or other fat

Add, cook and stir about until lightly browned:

1 small chopped onion

Stir in:

2 tablespoons all-purpose flour

Add the strained tomatoes and:

¼ cup brown sugar

Simmer these ingredients for 15 minutes. Add the drained sauerkraut. Cook it gently for ½ to 1 hour, stirring frequently. Season it with:

Freshly ground pepper

CELERY CABBAGE
Use raw or prepare this vegetable by any of the rules for cabbage. If young, it may require only a few minutes' cooking. Place a stalk of:

Whole or shredded celery cabbage

in:

½ cup boiling water

Cook it until it is barely tender. Drain it thoroughly. Add:

½ teaspoon salt

Serve it with:

Melted butter
Easy Hollandaise Sauce, page 430

BOILED CARROTS BUTTERED, CREAMED OR GLAZED
Carrots are worthy but frequently boring. To be interesting they need stimulating company. For good results combine them with onions, celery, green peppers, olives, mushrooms, etc. Carrots may be boiled, peeled, scraped or unpeeled. They may be cut into slices, into dice, or if small they may be served whole.

Wash and scrape or merely wash:

Carrots

Place them in a small quantity of:

Boiling water

Cook them covered until they are tender, from 20 to 30 minutes. Allow a shorter cooking period for cut up carrots. Permit them to absorb the water in which they are cooked. If necessary, add a small quantity of boiling water. Skin the carrots if they have been cooked in their jackets. Add:

½ teaspoon salt

Celery, onions, etc., may be cooked with peeled carrots or they may be cooked separately and added later. Serve the carrots with:

Chopped parsley
Melted butter, to which you may
add 1 tablespoon grated cheese
or
Cream Sauce I, page 428—⅓
cup sauce to 2 cups carrots—or
Green Onion Sauce, page 327
Or, add to 1 bunch cooked carrots:
3 tablespoons butter
(3 tablespoons sugar)
(½ teaspoon ginger or cinnamon)
Simmer the carrots in this mixture
until well glazed.

BOILED CARROTS IN BUNCHES
Cook by the preceding rule:
Small shapely carrots in their
jackets
Cool them. Skin them. Reheat them
by placing them over steam or by sautéing them for 2 minutes in a little
butter. Serve them in 2 bunches—one
at each end of a meat platter. Place at
the blunt ends to represent carrot
greens:
Bunches of parsley
A little:
Melted seasoned butter
may be poured over the carrots. They
may be seasoned with:
A dash of cloves.

BOILED CARROTS LIGHTLY CREAMED
5 Servings
Prepare:
2 cups sliced Boiled Carrots, page
278
Melt in a saucepan:
2 tablespoons butter
Add the carrots and sprinkle over
them:
1 teaspoon flour
Add:
¼ cup hot Stock, page 43, or
cream
Stir and simmer the carrots until the
sauce bubbles.

CREAMED CARROTS AU GRATIN
6 Servings
Boil (page 278):
2 cups diced carrots
Prepare:
1 cup Cream Sauce I, page 428
Combine these ingredients. Place them
in a greased baking dish. Cover them
with:
Bread crumbs

Dot them with:
Butter
or sprinkle them with:
Cheese
Bake them in a hot oven 400° or place
them under a broiler until the crumbs
are brown.
Sautéed mushrooms combine well with
carrots; so does cooked celery.

MASHED CARROTS OR CARROT RING
4 Servings
Cook (page 278):
2 bunches young carrots in
their jackets
Skin the carrots and put them through
a ricer or mash them with a potato
masher. Beat in:
1 tablespoon butter
Salt and pepper
1 tablespoon chopped parsley or
chives
(A dash of cloves)
Heap the carrots in a mound or in individual mounds. Garnish them with:
Sprigs of parsley
Mashed carrots may be placed in a
small greased ring mold. Heat it in
hot water in a hot oven 400° or on top
of the stove. Invert the mold. Fill the
center of the ring with Green Peas
with Mint Sauce, page 299.

FRENCH CARROTS
4 Servings
Place in a saucepan:
2 cups scraped sliced carrots
½ cup boiling water
2 tablespoons butter
1 tablespoon sugar
¼ teaspoon salt
Cover the pan closely. Cook the carrots
over quick heat until the water evaporates. Permit them to brown in the
butter. Serve them sprinkled with:
Chopped chives or parsley

BAKED CARROTS
4 Servings
Melt:
3 tablespoons butter
Sauté in it for 3 minutes:
¼ cup chopped onion
Add:
2 cups peeled, shredded carrots
Place these ingredients in a baking
dish. Sprinkle them with:
¾ teaspoon salt
1 teaspoon sugar
Pour over them:
½ cup water or stock

Cover the dish. Bake the carrots in a moderate oven 350° until they are tender.

BUTTERED CARROTS COOKED WITHOUT WATER
5 Servings
Peel or scrape:
    2 bunches carrots
Slice them in long thin strips. Place them in a heavy saucepan with:
    2 tablespoons butter
    ½ teaspoon sugar
    ½ teaspoon salt
    1 tablespoon chopped parsley
You may sauté in the butter:
    3 tablespoons chopped onion
Cover the pan closely. Simmer the carrots on top of the stove for about 20 minutes or place them in a moderate oven 350° until they are done. Add:
    1 tablespoon cream
Cook them 2 minutes longer.

CARAMELIZED OR GLAZED CARROTS
Cook in their jackets (page 278):
    Medium-sized or large carrots
Skin them. Cut them into halves or quarters. Dip them in:
    Melted butter
Sprinkle them with:
    Salt, paprika and brown sugar
Place them in a heavy skillet over a low fire until they are well glazed. Baste them from time to time with a little melted butter.

BREADED CARROT BALLS
Cook in their jackets (page 278):
    Small carrots or use very small canned carrots
Skin them. Cut the carrots with a potato-ball cutter. Sprinkle them with:
    Salt
Dip them in:
    Cream
Roll them in:
    Buttered bread crumbs or crushed cornflakes
Place them in a greased baking dish. Cover them and bake them for 20 minutes in a moderate oven 375°. Remove the cover and permit them to brown.

FRIED CARROTS
Scrape:
    Small tender carrots or large quartered carrots
Cook them covered for 10 minutes in a small amount of:
    Boiling water
Drain them. Drop them in:
    Milk
Roll them in:
    Flour, crumbs or crushed cornflakes
Fry them in hot fat or oil 375° (page 542). Drain them on paper.

PARSLEY CARROTS
4 Servings
This is a nice variation of "just plain" carrots. Boil in their jackets (page 278):
    6 large carrots
Scrape and cut them into very thin slices. Melt in a saucepan:
    2 tablespoons butter
Add and sauté for 1 minute:
    1 tablespoon minced onion
Add:
    ¼ teaspoon salt
    ⅛ teaspoon paprika
    ½ teaspoon lemon juice
Add the carrots and cook them quickly until they are well heated, then add:
    2 tablespoons chopped parsley
and serve them at once.

CARROTS AND PEAS
Cook:
    Boiled Carrots, page 278
Combine them in any proportion with:
    Green Peas, page 298, or canned peas
Drain the vegetables well. Season them with:
    Salt and pepper
Pour over them:
    Melted butter—1 tablespoon to 1 cup vegetables
Just before serving them add:
    Chopped parsley
Or heat the peas and carrots in:
    Cream Sauce I, page 428—½ as much cream sauce as there are vegetables
and add:
    Chopped parsley

BOILED CAULIFLOWER
4 Servings
Cut off the tough end of the stem, remove the leaves and soak in cold salted water, head down, for 15 minutes:
    1 medium-sized head cauliflower
Drain it. You may break it into flowerets. Cut deep gashes into the stalk and place it uncovered, head up, in a quantity of:
    Boiling water

To which you may add:
Juice of ½ lemon
Reduce the heat to a simmer and cook covered until the stalk is barely tender. Test for tenderness after 12 minutes. Drain the cauliflower well and place it in a serving dish: Melt:
3 tablespoons butter
Sauté in it:
(2 tablespoons bread crumbs)
Pour the butter over the cauliflower, or omit the butter and the crumbs and pour over it:
1 cup boiling Cream Sauce I, page 428
seasoned with:
¼ teaspoon freshly ground nutmeg
Or use:
Black Butter, page 327, or
Béchamel Sauce, page 429, or
Hollandaise Sauce, page 429
or the following Egg Sauce:

Egg Sauce I
4 Servings
Place in a double boiler over, not in, boiling water:
2 beaten egg yolks
¼ cup cream
⅛ teaspoon salt
⅛ teaspoon freshly ground nutmeg
1 tablespoon lemon juice
Cook and stir these ingredients until they are thick, then add a little at a time:
2 tablespoons butter
Pour the sauce over the cauliflower and serve it at once.

Cauliflowerets are also delicious in Creole Sauce, page 434, or served with Drawn Butter, page 327, and lots of lemon juice and parsley.

STEAMED CAULIFLOWER
Prepare by cooking by the preceding rule:
A medium-sized cauliflower
Have ready a deep saucepan with a closely fitting lid. Place a trivet in the pan. Pour into it to barely cover the bottom:
Boiling water
Place the cauliflower on the trivet. Cover the pan. Steam the cauliflower from 15 to 20 minutes, until it is tender but still firm. Drain and place it in a serving dish. Sprinkle it with:
Salt
Cover it with one of the above sauces.
Or sprinkle over the top:
Buttered crumbs
Chopped nut meats

SAUTÉED CAULIFLOWER
5 Servings
Prepare:
Boiled or steamed cauliflower
Break it into flowerets. Heat:
2 tablespoons butter
2 tablespoons salad oil
Add and cook for 2 minutes:
½ clove garlic or 2 teaspoons grated onion
Remove the garlic. Sauté the flowerets in the fat until they are well coated. Cover and cook for several minutes. Season with:
Salt and paprika
A fresh grating of nutmeg
Or serve the cauliflower with:
Chopped parsley or chives

FRIED CAULIFLOWER
Boil (page 280):
Cauliflower
Drain it well. Separate the flowerets. Beat until light:
2 egg yolks
Add:
½ cup milk
Stir in:
¾ cup flour
¼ teaspoon salt
Beat the batter until it is smooth. Dip each section of cauliflower in the batter. Drop the flowerets into:
Deep hot fat 375°-385° (page 542)
Serve the cauliflower with:
Hollandaise Sauce, page 429, or
Cream Sauce I, page 428, or
Sour Cream Dressing, page 327

Cauliflower Timbales, page 212; Cauliflower and Mushrooms, page 178.

STEWED CELERY IN CREAM SAUCE
4 Servings
Prepare:
2 cups chopped celery
Drop it gradually into:
½ inch boiling water
Cook it covered until it is tender, for about 8 minutes, allowing it to absorb the water. Should there be any liquid, drain the celery and reserve the liquid for the sauce. Drop the celery into:
1 cup boiling Cream Sauce, page 428, or
1 cup boiling cream sauce made with cream and celery liquor
Season the sauce with:
Curry
Celery or dill seed

Freshly grated nutmeg
Herbs, page 833
or season the drained celery with:
Salt and butter

CELERY AU GRATIN
Prepare the preceding:
Stewed Celery in Cream Sauce
Place it in a greased baking dish. Cover
the top with:
Bread crumbs
Dot it with:
Butter
or sprinkle it with:
Grated cheese
Bake it in a hot oven 400° until the
cheese is melted.

CREAMED CELERY AND GREEN PEPPERS
4 to 5 Servings
Follow the rule on page 281 for:
Stewed Celery in Cream Sauce
Follow the rule on page 299 for:
Green Peppers
Drop them into the creamed celery.

BRAISED CELERY
Method I. 3 to 4 Servings
Wash:
3 dwarf celery stalks or 1 large
stalk
Cut off part of the leaves. Place the
stalks in a small quantity of:
Boiling Stock, page 43
Simmer them covered until they are
tender. Large stalks may be used, but
their leaves must be cut off and the
stalks must be quartered. Drain the
celery and place it where it will keep
warm. Reserve the stock. Melt:
2 tablespoons butter
Stir in until blended:
2 tablespoons flour
½ teaspoon salt
Stir in slowly:
1 cup stock or stock and cream
Salt as needed
Place the celery on slices of hot:
Buttered toast
When the sauce is smooth and boiling,
pour it over the celery.
You may vary this by adding to the
finished sauce grated lemon rind and 1
teaspoonful or more lemon juice.

Method II.
Take the outer ribs and the top leaves
from:
4 small stalks celery
Cut the stalks into halves lengthwise.

Melt:
2 tablespoons butter
Sauté in the butter:
1 tablespoon minced onion
Add the celery. Cover the bottom of
the pan with:
Beef stock
Cover the pan with a lid. Simmer the
celery for about 20 minutes, or until
tender. Add:
1 tablespoon butter
Place the pan uncovered in a moderate
oven 350° until most of the liquid has
been absorbed. Baste the celery frequently. Season it if needed with:
Salt and paprika
Serve it hot with the stock or very cold
with:
Mayonnaise or French dressing

Method III.
Simmer dwarf celery until tender in:
Beef stock
Drain it. Marinate it in:
French dressing
for several hours. You may add:
Anchovy paste
to the dressing.

Marinated Celeriac, page 31.
A fine root vegetable, much neglected.
This is good buttered, creamed, au
gratin, made into a pudding, see Squash
Pudding, page 181, or a Soufflé, page
224.

CREAMED CELERY ROOT OR CELERIAC AU GRATIN
4 Servings
Pare, then cube:
1½ lbs. celery root
Half cover it with:
Boiling water
Cook it covered until it is tender, for
about 25 minutes or more. Drain the
celery root. Reserve the water for the
sauce. Prepare:
1½ cups Cream Sauce, page 428
Use:
3 tablespoons butter
2 tablespoons flour
1½ cups cream and celery water
combined
• ½ teaspoon salt
¼ teaspoon paprika
A few grains cayenne
Stir in until melted:
(½ cup grated or cubed cheese)
Fold in the drained celery. Pour the
mixture into an oven-proof dish. Scatter over it:
½ cup dry bread crumbs

Dot the top with:
1 tablespoon butter
Bake the dish in a moderate oven 375°
for about 30 minutes, or until lightly
browned.

CELTUCE
A vegetable recently imported from
China. The large succulent stalk is
edible. Remove the skin down to the
crisp tender part. Celtuce may be
served raw or prepared by any of the
rules given for cabbage.

SWISS CHARD
Follow the rule for Creamed Spinach
on page 313. The middle ribs of the
chard may be cooked separately. Treat
them as you would asparagus, see
Greens, page 290.

CHAYOTE
4 Servings
This vegetable is fairly new in our
markets. Treat it much as you would
zucchini or other squash.
Pare and cut crosswise in ¾ inch
slices:
1 lb. chayote
Boil:
½ cup water
Add the chayote, cover the pan closely
and when the water boils reduce the
heat. Simmer the chayote for about 20
minutes, or until tender. Drain it.
Dress it with:
Salt
Butter
Black Butter, page 327, etc., or
Cream sauce and grated cheese
Chayote may be served chilled with
mayonnaise.

CHESTNUTS—HOW TO
PREPARE THEM
Method I.
Make two crosscut gashes on the flat
side of each chestnut with a sharp
pointed knife. Sometimes the shell
will come off while doing this, but the
inner skin will protect the kernel. Place
the nuts in a pan over a quick fire,
dropping oil or butter over them—1
teaspoonful to 1 pound of nuts. Shake
them until they are coated, then place
them in a moderate oven until the
shells and skins can be removed easily.

Method II.
Or cover chestnuts with boiling water
and boil them from 15 to 25 minutes.
Drain them and remove the shells and
skins. The meats should be sufficiently
tender to be put through a purée
strainer. If not, cover them with boiling water and cook them until tender.
Chestnuts are frequently used as stuffing with fowl and are traditionally
combined with Brussels sprouts and
red cabbage, but their distinctive flavor
is best retained in the following recipes.

POSIE'S CHESTNUTS AND
PRUNES IN WINE
6 Servings
Cook by the above rule until nearly
tender:
1 lb. chestnuts
Drain them. Cook in the water in
which the prunes were soaked, page
450:
½ lb. soaked prunes
2 bay leaves
1 small stick cinnamon
Drain the prunes, pit them. Combine
the chestnuts and prunes. Add:
1 tablespoon butter
½ teaspoon salt
2 tablespoons sugar
1 cup dry white wine
Cook this mixture until the chestnuts
are tender. You may serve this in a
ring or around a mound of coarsely
chopped creamed spinach, page 313.

BOILED CHESTNUTS
4 Servings
Shell and skin (see above):
1 lb. chestnuts
Drop them into:
Boiling water
To which add:
1 tablespoon vinegar
3 ribs celery
1 small peeled onion
Cook them until they are tender. Drain
them well. Mash them with:
1 tablespoon butter
Salt
¼ teaspoon pepper
Add:
2 or more tablespoons hot milk
Beat the chestnuts until they are fluffy.
Keep them hot over hot water. Immediately before serving them stir in:
(1 cup or more finely diced raw
celery)

BAKED CHESTNUTS
4 Servings
Prepare by either rule above:
3 cups chestnuts

Season them with:
   (2 tablespoons or more brown
   sugar)
Grease a baking dish. Place the chestnuts in it. Pour over them:
   1¾ cups chicken stock
Cover them and cook them in a slow
oven 325° for 3 hours. Pour off the
stock. Melt:
   2 tablespoons butter
Stir in until blended:
   1 tablespoon flour
Stir the stock in slowly. When the
sauce is smooth and boiling, pour it
over the chestnuts and serve them.

CORN ON THE COB

Remove the husks and silk from:
   Ears of green corn
Drop them, ear by ear, so as not to
disturb the boiling, into:
   1 inch boiling water or half milk
   and half water
Add:
   (1 tablespoon or more sugar)
Cover the kettle and boil the corn
rapidly until it is tender, from 4 to 10
minutes. Drain and serve it with butter, salt and freshly ground pepper.
See Grilled or Roasted Corn, opposite.
Corn may be steamed in a small quantity of water in a tightly covered kettle.
Young corn will require about 6 minutes' steaming.

COOKED CORN CUT FROM THE COB

Cook the preceding:
   Corn on the Cob
Cut or grate it from the cob. Season it
with:
   Salt and pepper
Moisten it with:
   Butter and cream or butter and
   milk
Reheat the corn.

FRESH CORN CUT FROM THE COB

Cut or grate from the cob:
   Green corn
Cook it covered for several minutes,
until it is tender, in its own juice and a
little:
   Butter
Season it with:
   Salt and pepper
Moisten it with:
   Milk or cream
You may devil it by adding:

   1 tablespoon Worcestershire
   sauce
   Minced garlic
Or, cook the corn in milk in a covered
double boiler for 15 minutes. Season it
with:
   Butter or oil
   Salt and paprika
   Chopped green peppers
   Chopped ripe olives
   (Parsley, onion or chives)

Corn à la King, page 183.

GRILLED OR ROASTED CORN

Cook by the recipe on this page:
   Corn on the Cob
Drain it quickly. Spread the ears generously with:
   Melted butter
Place them on a heated broiler rack
close to the flame. Turn the ears as
they brown and spread them with
more butter. Sprinkle them with:
   Salt
Serve them at once.
Or, after spreading the ears with butter, you may roll them in:
   Grated cheese
Bake in a hot oven 400° for about 10
minutes, or until the cheese is melted.
Corn in husks may be roasted in a
moderate oven 350° until tender, for
about 30 minutes. Remove husks and
silk. Serve the corn with butter. Or,
peel back husks, remove silk, spread
corn with butter. Replace husk and
roast.

*Tomato, Corn and Cheese Dish, page
183; Corn Pudding, page 184.*

SCALLOPED CORN

4 Servings
Combine:
   2 cups uncooked corn cut from the
   ear
   2 beaten eggs
   ½ teaspoon salt
   (¼ cup minced green pepper or
   chopped olives)
Arrange this in 2 layers in a greased
baking dish. Sprinkle the layers with:
   ½ cup cracker crumbs
Dot them with:
   2 tablespoons butter
Pour over them:
   ¾ cup rich milk
Bake the corn in a moderate oven 325°
for about ½ hour.

SUCCOTASH

4 Servings

Combine, then heat in a double boiler:
- 1 cup cooked fresh corn
- 1 cup cooked fresh Lima beans
- 2 tablespoons butter
- ½ teaspoon salt
- ⅛ teaspoon paprika
- Chopped parsley

This is also good made with canned or frozen vegetables.

CORN CREOLE

4 Servings

Melt:
- 3 tablespoons butter

Stir and sauté in it until tender, for about 5 minutes:
- 1½ cups green corn cut from the cob
- ¼ cup chopped onion
- ¼ cup chopped green pepper

Add and heat well:
- ¾ cup canned strained tomatoes
- 1 teaspoon salt
- ¼ teaspoon freshly ground pepper

MULLED CUCUMBERS

4 Servings

The cucumber is banned from many tables as indigestible or even poisonous. Digestion, alas! is an individual matter. Since it is said that good judgment is the result of experience and that experience is the result of bad judgment—why not give the cucumber the benefit of the doubt, at least once, to see whether it has really been maligned? These are most innocuous and very good.

Pare, seed and cut into strips:
- Cucumbers

There should be 2 cupfuls. Drop them into:
- 1½ cups boiling water

Cook them until they are nearly tender. Drain them well. Place in a double boiler:
- ¾ cup Cream Sauce I, page 428

Season the sauce with:
- Salt and pepper
- Freshly grated nutmeg or
- 1 teaspoon chopped fresh herbs
- 1 teaspoon or more lemon juice

When the sauce is boiling add the drained cucumbers. Place the pan over hot water and steam them uncovered for a few minutes before serving them. Cucumbers may be cooked until tender, drained and reheated in a little melted butter or in Tomato Sauce, page 433. They may be served au gratin.

A fine dish is Spinach Ring, page 223, filled with Cucumbers in Sour Cream Dressing, page 328.

SAUTÉED OR FRIED CUCUMBERS

4 Servings

A good garnish for a fish platter. Pare, slice and seed:
- 3 large cucumbers

Dredge them with:
- ½ teaspoon salt
- ⅛ teaspoon paprika

Melt in a small skillet:
- 2 tablespoons oil or bacon fat

Add and sauté until soft:
- Grated onion

Add the cucumbers and sauté them over high heat until they are transparent, for about 5 minutes. Or, cut the cucumbers in strips. Dip them in:
- Seasoned bread crumbs or flour

then in:
- 1 egg diluted with 2 tablespoons water

and again in bread crumbs. Fry them in deep fat 370° (page 542). Serve the cucumbers with:
- 2 tablespoons prepared horseradish
- ¼ cup melted butter

CUCUMBERS IN CREAM

4 Servings

Pare:
- 4 small cucumbers

Place them in a small saucepan. Barely cover them with:
- Stock, page 43

Cover, then cook them gently until they are nearly done. Sauté until crisp:
- 4 slices bacon

Break it into coarse pieces. Add it to the cucumber with:
- 1½ tablespoons finely minced parsley

Simmer the cucumbers 5 minutes longer. Season them with:
- Freshly ground pepper
- Salt, if needed

Combine and beat:
- 1 egg yolk
- 3 tablespoons cream

Remove the cucumbers from the stock into a hot serving dish. Stir the egg mixture into the cooled stock. Stir, heat gently and let this sauce thicken slightly, but do not permit it to boil. Pour it over the cucumbers. Sprinkle the top with:

Fresh dill or celery seed or some
minced herb
Pass at table:
Grated cheese

STEWED CUCUMBERS AND ONIONS

4 Servings

Pare, then cut into quarters lengthwise:
2 large or 3 small cucumbers
Remove the seeds. Cut the cucumbers into strips. Melt in a saucepan:
2 tablespoons butter
Add and sauté gently until soft but not brown:
½ cup sliced onions or 8 very small skinned onions
Stir in:
1 tablespoon flour
½ cup chicken broth or consommé
(¼ cup sherry)
Add the cucumbers. Simmer them until tender. Add stock if needed to keep them from becoming dry. Turn them once or twice to permit them to cook evenly. Season as needed with:
Salt and paprika
Freshly grated nutmeg

CUCUMBER OR SQUASH CASSEROLE WITH CREAM SAUCE

Mock Oyster Casserole

4 Servings

Prepare:
2 cups Boiled Cucumber or Squash, see above
Drain the vegetable well. Prepare:
1 cup Cream Sauce I, page 428
seasoned with:
1 tablespoon anchovy paste
Place the vegetable in a baking dish. Pour the hot sauce over it. Cover the top with:
Bread crumbs
Dot it with:
Butter
Sprinkle it, if you like, with:
Grated cheese
Bake the dish in a quick oven 400° until the top is brown.

CUCUMBER OR SQUASH CASSEROLE WITH TOMATO SAUCE

4 Servings

Pare:
3 large cucumbers
Cut them into ¼ inch slices. They may be seeded and diced. Combine:

½ cup hot chicken or other stock
½ cup hot thick stewed tomatoes
Season with:
Salt, if needed
½ teaspoon grated lemon rind
1 teaspoon lemon juice
Freshly grated pepper
1 teaspoon grated onion
Dried or fresh basil
(1 tablespoon brown sugar)
Place in the bottom of a greased ovenproof dish:
½ cup dry bread crumbs
Add the cucumbers. Pour the sauce over them. Cover it with:
½ cup dry bread crumbs
Dot the top with:
Butter
Bake the dish in a moderate oven 375° for about 35 minutes.

See Index for other Cucumber Dishes.

DASHEENS

Boil without paring:
Dasheens
Follow the rule for Boiled Potatoes, page 300. Skin the dasheens, then put them through a ricer.
Treat them like Mashed Potatoes, page 302.
Dasheens may be baked, but should be parboiled for about 15 minutes. Bake them in a moderate oven 375° until done.

EGGPLANT AND EGGPLANT SHELLS

When cut an eggplant discolors at once. Cut it with a stainless steel knife, work quickly, and dip the pieces as soon as possible into the liquid or fat called for in the recipe. For instance, in the case of Eggplant Slices below. Cut the slices, spread them at once with melted butter or dressing, then pare them. When using eggplant shells cover them as soon as cut with cold water. Shortly before filling them, drain and dry them.

BAKED OR BROILED EGGPLANT

I once heard an artist say: "If only the eggplant were as good as it looks, what a gastronomic treat it would be."
There are several ways of preparing this vegetable that make it taste as wonderful as it looks. The old-fashioned manner of dipping it in batter and frying it in deep fat has given way to newer ones, of which the baked egg-

plant recipe which follows is a good example. Besides being digestible, non-fattening and exceedingly good, it is very quickly prepared.

Pare:

An eggplant

Cut it crosswise into slices ½ inch thick. Spread the slices on both sides with a mixture of:

Soft butter or salad oil

Seasoned with:

Salt and pepper
Grated onion and lemon juice or
French dressing

Place them on a baking sheet and bake them in a quick oven 400° until they are tender, about 12 minutes, turning them once.

Or, broil them until they are tender under a moderate flame. If feasible, finish broiling them under a steak where they can catch the drippings. Serve the eggplant while it is very hot with:

Chopped parsley or tarragon
Lemon Butter, page 431
A sliced lemon or Tomato
Sauce, page 433

EGGPLANT WITH FRENCH DRESSING

This is luscious. Prepare the preceding:

Baked Eggplant

Omit the butter. Marinate the slices for 15 minutes in:

French dressing

You may spread them with:

2 tablespoons anchovy paste

and cover with:

Grated cheese

Bake or broil them as directed. If they tend to become dry, baste with additional French dressing.

EGGPLANT HALVES BAKED

4 to 6 Servings

Wash, dry, then cut into halves lengthwise:

An oval eggplant

Crisscross the top with gashes about ½ inch deep. Sauté the halves cut side down for about 10 minutes in:

3 tablespoons hot olive oil

Set them upright in a shallow ovenproof dish. Make a paste by mashing together until well blended:

8 flat minced anchovy fillets
2 skinned chopped cloves garlic
¼ cup bread crumbs
2 tablespoons strong beef stock
⅛ teaspoon freshly ground pepper

Spread this over the tops of the eggplant. Sprinkle them with:

Dry bread crumbs
Finely minced parsley
A little oil or dabs of butter

Bake the dish in a hot oven 400° for about ½ hour.

STEAMED OR SAUTÉED EGGPLANT SLICES

4 Servings

Pare and cut crosswise into slices 1 inch thick:

A medium-sized eggplant

Place the slices in a colander over boiling water. Cover them closely with a lid. Steam them for 20 minutes. Season them with:

Salt and paprika

Sauté them for 1½ minutes on each side in:

Drippings or butter

or dip them in:

1 egg diluted with 2 tablespoons
water

Dip them in:

Bread crumbs or corn meal

and sauté them as directed until they are light brown.

SAUTÉED OR FRIED EGGPLANT

There is a superstition that an eggplant must have the juice pressed from it. All old recipes read: "Slice, salt and weight an eggplant." I wonder why, when it is so good without all that bother?

If there is time, place eggplant slices that have been dipped in liquid and then in flour or crumbs on a rack to dry for about 15 minutes before cooking. This makes them easier to handle. Peel and cut in ¼ inch slices or into cubes or sticks:

An eggplant

Dip them in:

Milk

Dredge them with:

Seasoned flour

I.

Sauté the slices slowly until tender in a little:

Butter or oil

II.

Or, dip the floured eggplant in:

1 egg diluted with 2 tablespoons
water or in rich milk

then in:

Bread crumbs, corn meal or
flour

Fry the slices in deep fat 370° (page 542). If preferred, the slices may be dipped in batter, page 543. You may place the cooked slices on a hot ovenproof platter. Pour over them:

Tomato Sauce II, page 433

You may sprinkle this with cheese and melt it under a broiler.

EGGPLANT SAUTÉED AND CREAMED

This is a delicate and delicious way of preparing eggplant. Pare:

A medium-sized eggplant

Dice it into ¾ inch pieces. Sauté the pieces slowly in:

4 tablespoons butter

Turn them frequently. Cook them until they are tender, for about 10 minutes. Prepare:

1 cup Cream Sauce I, page 428

You may add to the sauce:

Chopped olives

Pour it over the eggplant. Sprinkle it with:

Chopped parsley, chives or grated cheese

See Index for other Eggplant Dishes.

SCALLOPED EGGPLANT

4 Servings

Pare and cut into dice:

A medium-sized eggplant

Cook it until it is tender in:

½ cup boiling water

Drain it well. Sprinkle it with:

(2 tablespoons chopped parsley)

Chop until very fine:

1 small onion

Melt:

1 tablespoon butter

Sauté the onion in this until it is light brown. Add it to the eggplant. Melt:

3 tablespoons butter

Stir into it until the butter is absorbed:

¾ cup cracker crumbs or ½ cup bread crumbs

Place layers of eggplant and layers of crumbs in a baking dish. Season them if the crackers are unsalted with:

¼ teaspoon salt
⅛ teaspoon paprika

Have the top layer of crumbs. Pour over these ingredients:

½ cup milk

Place on the top:

(Thin slices of cheese or grated cheese)

Bake the eggplant in a moderate oven 375° for ½ hour. Serve it with:

Sautéed Bacon, page 375

Or, for a simpler version, after draining the eggplant mash it and beat it with a fork until it is fluffy. Combine it with the sautéed onion, the butter, seasoning, cracker crumbs and milk. Substitute for the milk if desired:

2 well-beaten eggs

Bake the eggplant as directed.

SCALLOPED EGGPLANT AND OYSTERS

Follow the preceding rule for:

Scalloped eggplant

Heat in their liquor until warm:

1 pint oysters

Place them between the layers of eggplant and crumbs.

EGGPLANT SOUFFLÉ WITH CREAM SAUCE

4 Servings

In the following recipes the pulp is scooped out of the center of the eggplant. It is combined with various ingredients and is replaced in the eggplant shells, in which it is then baked and from which it is served.

Cut into halves:

An eggplant

Scoop out the center, leaving a shell ¼ inch thick. Cook the pulp covered in:

3 cups boiling water

Add to the water:

½ tablespoon vinegar

When the pulp is tender drain it and mash it with a fork. There should be about 1 cupful of pulp. Follow the rule for Vegetable Soufflé, page 218. You may add:

½ cup or less chopped nut meats
Freshly grated nutmeg or onion

Fill the shells and bake them in a moderate oven 325° until the soufflé is set, about 30 minutes. A little water may be placed in the pan to keep the shells from scorching.

EGGPLANT SOUFFLÉ WITH BREAD CRUMBS

Prepare by the preceding rule:

An eggplant

Combine the cooked mashed pulp with:

¾ cup soft bread crumbs
2 beaten egg yolks
1 tablespoon melted butter
½ cup chopped nut meats or grated cheese
Salt and pepper
Grated nutmeg

If the filling seems stiff add:
1 tablespoon or more milk
Beat until stiff:
2 egg whites
Fold them lightly into the other ingredients. Fill the shells. Cover the tops with:
Buttered crumbs or cornflakes
Place them in a pan with a little water and bake them in a moderate oven 325° for 30 minutes.

BAKED EGGPLANT WITH TOMATOES
Cut into halves:
A small eggplant
Scoop out the pulp and chop it. Leave a shell ¼ inch thick. Mince and heat in a skillet:
2 strips bacon
Add to it and sauté until the bacon is cooked:
¼ cup minced onion
¼ cup minced green pepper
Add the eggplant pulp and:
2 cups canned tomatoes
¼ cup diced celery
Simmer these ingredients until the eggplant is tender. Beat them with a fork until they are well blended. Thicken them with:
⅓ cup bread crumbs
Season them with:
Salt and freshly ground pepper
Add to them:
½ cup Sautéed Mushrooms, page 292
Fill the eggplant shells with the mixture. Cover the tops with:
Bread crumbs
Sprinkle them with:
Cheese
or dot them with:
Butter
Place the eggplant in a pan with a very little water in a moderate oven 350° until it is very hot.

Eggplant Filled with Mushrooms and Ham, page 205; Eggplant Fritters, page 325.
Other Eggplant Dishes will be found on page 180.

CHILLED EGGPLANT PURÉE
Eggplant Caviar
4 Servings
Good with cold meat or as an hors d'oeuvre. Wash, then cook in boiling water to cover for about 20 minutes, or until tender:
2 small or 1 large eggplant

Cool it. Cut off the stem end. Pare the eggplant. Chop it until it is well minced. Simmer until the onion is brown:
2 tablespoons olive oil
1 or 2 large skinned, chopped onions
(1 mashed clove garlic)
Add:
4 tablespoons tomato purée and the eggplant
Simmer this with frequent stirring for about ½ hour. Add:
2 tablespoons olive oil
1 teaspoon sugar
Cook the eggplant until it is a thick purée, then add:
2 tablespoons dry wine, lemon juice or vinegar
1½ teaspoons salt
Freshly ground pepper
1 tablespoon chopped basil or other fresh herb
Chill the dish. Serve it with:
Thick sour cream
Rye or French bread

FENNEL OR ANISE
This delicious vegetable may be bought sometimes from Italian hucksters or in neighborhoods frequented by Italians. It is easy to grow.

Method I.
Wash, then peel the bulb and the tender part of:
Fennel stalks
Cut them into slices. Drop them into a small quantity of:
Boiling water
Simmer the fennel covered until it is tender. Serve it seasoned with:
Salt and paprika
Hot olive oil or melted butter, or covered with a hot mustard mayonnaise

Method II.
Fennel may also be braised like Celery, page 282. It makes a very delicate addition to rice dishes.
Cut off the leaves, then cut into quarters lengthwise:
2 stalks fennel
Melt in a large skillet:
6 tablespoons butter
Brown the fennel in this on all sides over a moderate flame. Cover it and let it steam until barely tender. Season it with:
Salt and pepper
Serve it with the pan juices.

GREENS. Turnip, Mustard, Kale, Etc.

To prepare and cook greens follow the rule on page 313 for cooking spinach given under Creamed Spinach. Sometimes it is necessary to add a little water. "Greens" are seldom creamed, although there is no reason why they should not be. The old-fashioned custom is to cook them to death, for an hour or more, with bacon, salt pork or ham hocks and to serve them with vinegar. Try the new way of short cooking. If "side meat" and water are simmered for 2 hours first and then the greens are added and cooked only until tender, an excellent flavor and vitamin retention are both achieved.

A quicker way to flavor the greens is to add, after they are drained and chopped or put through a purée strainer or blender, bacon drippings and crisp sautéed bacon, minced. Lemon juice or vinegar and grated or sautéed onion may be added. Wonderful with sour cream and chives.

WILD GREENS. Dandelion, Poke, Etc.

Edible wild greens are available everywhere seasonally for the picking but great care must be used to avoid poisonous plants. If you are in earnest about pursuing this economical, healthful hobby, consult an authoritative text or better still a local enthusiast.

Although the milder greens may be treated like spinach, see page 313, many of the wildlings are bitter and must be cooked first for a few minutes in boiling water, then drained to remove the bitter and sometimes poisonous elements, and again immersed in fresh boiling water and simmered until tender.

A number, after preliminary boiling, are handled like asparagus, but as each seems to have its peculiarities, such as a delicious shoot but poisonous root and leaf, be sure first that you know what you are gathering for your family.

KOHLRABI
4 Servings
Wash:
    8 large kohlrabi
Cut off the tops and pare the roots. Slice the roots and drop them into a quantity of rapidly:
    Boiling water

Cook them until they are barely tender. Drain them well. Boil the tops separately in the same manner. Drain them well, chop them until they are very fine or purée them and combine them with the roots. Prepare a sauce with the following ingredients.
Melt in a saucepan:
    2 tablespoons butter
Stir in until blended:
    2 tablespoons flour
Stir in and cook slowly:
    1 cup stock or kohlrabi water
    Salt and pepper as needed
    (A grating of nutmeg)
When the sauce is smooth and boiling, add the kohlrabi.

KALE
To cook kale follow the rules for Spinach on page 313, allowing more time for it to become tender, or see Greens above.

LEEKS
Trim the roots and part of the tops, allowing 2 inches of green to remain, from:
    Leeks
Wash them thoroughly. Drop them into:
    1 inch boiling water
Boil them covered until they are tender. Drain them well. Serve them with:
    Melted butter
    Salt and paprika

BRAISED LEEKS
Clean:
    Leeks
Cut off the roots and the green part of the stalks. Use the latter in soup. To braise leeks follow the rule for:
    Braised Celery, page 282

PURÉE OF LEEKS
Cut off the green part of the stalks. Cook the leeks covered until tender in:
    1 inch boiling water
Drain them well. Chop them coarsely. For each cupful of chopped leeks add:
    2 tablespoons butter
    ½ cup fresh bread crumbs
    Salt and pepper
Stir and cook them gently until blended. If they become too thick add:
    A little milk or cream
Serve the purée very hot with:
    Finely chopped parsley

LEEKS AU GRATIN
6 Servings
Clean:
6 or 8 leeks
Cut them into 1 inch lengths using the white part and that which is yellow-green. Use the green tops in the soup pot. Place the leeks in boiling water to cover. Reduce heat and simmer them uncovered until tender. Drain them, reserving the liquid. Season them with:
Salt
Place half the leeks in a shallow buttered baking dish. Prepare:
Boiling Cheese Sauce, page 430
Use the water from the leeks and milk. Pour ½ the sauce over the leeks in the dish. Add the remaining leeks and cover them with the remaining sauce. Dot the top with bits of:
Butter
Bake the dish in a hot oven 475° until light brown.

LETTUCE
Home gardeners in their enthusiasm find themselves with sudden surpluses of lettuce and wish they had rabbits instead of children, failing to realize that nibbling is not the only approach to this vegetable. Try these delectable alternatives: Cook lettuce with soup, use in blender soups, creamed like spinach, page 313, stuffed like cabbage, page 171, or cook and smother it with stewed tomatoes.

BRAISED LETTUCE
This is a very good "quick" hot vegetable. It is frequently served in France with unthickened meat gravy. Remove the outer leaves from:
A head lettuce
Cut the head into quarters and place them in a very small quantity of:
Boiling Stock, page 43
Cook the lettuce covered for about 8 minutes, in which time most of the liquor should be absorbed. Add if required:
Salt and paprika
(1 tablespoon butter)
Lettuce may be braised by the rules for Braised Celery, page 282.

BRAISED LETTUCE OR ENDIVE
4 Servings
Place in a baking dish:
2 slices bacon or 2 tablespoons butter

1 carrot sliced
3 tablespoons chopped onion
2 sprigs parsley
3 heads endive
Cover the dish. Bake it in a moderate oven 375° for 10 minutes. Add:
1 cup hot well-seasoned stock
Bake the dish 10 minutes longer. Drain the stock. Thicken it with:
Flour—2 tablespoons to 1 cup stock
Permit it to boil. Add seasoning as required. Serve the endive on:
(Hot toast)
Pour the boiling sauce over it.

HOW TO PREPARE MUSHROOMS
Mushrooms are now found in the market for the greater part of the year. They give a fine flourish to the everyday menu.
To prepare mushrooms, brush them with a brush or wipe them with a cloth and separate the cups from the stems. If they are washed, dry them thoroughly. When young and fresh they need not be skinned. When old pull off the capskins with the fingers or with a knife and pare the stems with a knife. To cut, slice the mushrooms vertically to retain their shape and cook them rapidly. To mince, break the caps into pieces and slice the stems with a knife or cut them through as shown here. If the stems are tough,

use them for stock and save all the skins and parings for this purpose. See Mushroom Stock, page 45.
If you like mushrooms dark, see Sautéed Mushrooms, page 292.
If you like them pale, simmer:
1 lb. mushrooms
in:
½ cup milk
2 tablespoons butter
in a covered double boiler until tender.

SAUTÉED MUSHROOMS
4 Servings
Prepare for cooking (page 291):
    1 lb. mushrooms
Melt in a skillet:
    2 tablespoons butter
The skillet may be rubbed with a clove of garlic. Add the mushrooms. Sauté them quickly until they are done, 4 or 5 minutes. Shake the skillet or stir the mushrooms. When the mushrooms are well coated, reduce the heat to a moderate flame. You may add:
    Salt as needed
    ½ teaspoon lemon juice or a
    grating of lemon rind
Bacon fat may be substituted for butter. Sautéed mushrooms are surprising things. At first they are so dry you think they will burn, then they relieve your fears suddenly by becoming pleasantly moist.
If you like them black and puffy, add to the sautéed mushrooms and simmer them for 5 minutes longer:
    ¼ cup brandy
If a dramatic touch is wanted, add the brandy to the sautéed mushrooms in a casserole, ignite them and serve them flaming.

SMOTHERED MUSHROOMS
Good served over meat, rice, noodles, etc., or over vegetables. Wonderful added to unthickened pan gravy.
Follow the above rule for:
    Sautéed Mushrooms
After stirring the mushrooms until they become moist, cover the pan closely and simmer them until tender, from 3 to 5 minutes. You may add to the pan:
    Butter
    1 or 2 tablespoons sherry or 1
    teaspoon Madeira
    Seasoning

CREAMED MUSHROOMS
4 Servings
Break into pieces and sauté by the preceding rule:
    1 lb. mushrooms
Sprinkle them with:
    2 tablespoons flour
Stir in gradually:
    1 cup rich milk, cream, sour
    cream, chicken bouillon, mush-
    room or other Stock, page 43
Finely chopped onion may be sautéed with the mushrooms. So may a bit of garlic, but remove this before preparing the sauce. Permit the sauce to come to a boil. Season it with:
    Salt and paprika
    1 tablespoon sherry
    A pinch of herbs
Marjoram is the traditional touch. Chives and parsley are recommended too. Good over baked potato.

MUSHROOMS AU GRATIN
Cook and cream by the preceding rule:
    Mushrooms
Place them in a greased baking dish or in individual dishes. Cover the top with:
    Bread crumbs
Dot it with:
    Butter
or sprinkle it with:
    Cheese
Place the dish under a moderate flame until the crumbs are brown.

FRIED MUSHROOMS
Prepare for cooking (page 291):
    Mushrooms
Dip them into:
    1 egg diluted with
    1 tablespoon water
Then in:
    Seasoned bread crumbs
Allow the crumbs to dry for 1 hour. Fry the mushrooms in deep fat (page 542).

BROILED MUSHROOMS
Method I.
Prepare for cooking (page 291):
    Mushrooms
Brush them lightly with:
    Butter or oil
Place them cap side down on a hot greased broiler and broil them for about 2½ minutes to a side, turning them once. Put in each cap a small lump of:
    Butter or a square of bacon
Season the mushrooms with:
    Salt as needed and paprika
    Chopped parsley and lemon
    juice
Serve them at once on:
    Hot toast
After adding the butter, keep the cap side up to preserve the juices.

Method II.
Marinate for 5 minutes:
    1 lb. mushrooms
in:
    1 tablespoon oil

1 tablespoon lemon juice
1 teaspoon salt
½ teaspoon pepper

Broil them 4 minutes per side. Serve them on:

Toast

with:

Maître d'Hôtel Butter, page 431

BROILED STUFFED MUSHROOMS

Cook (page 292):

Broiled or Sautéed Mushroom Caps

Chop fine:

The stems of 1 lb. mushrooms
1 small skinned onion

Sauté these lightly in:

3 tablespoons butter

Add and heat until warm:

¼ cup bread crumbs
¼ cup chopped pecans
¼ teaspoon dried basil
¼ teaspoon salt
A few grains cayenne
(3 tablespoons grated cheese)

Press this stuffing into the mushroom caps and reheat them under a broiler.

For other rules for Stuffed Mushrooms see Index.

STEAMED MUSHROOMS

Prepare for cooking (page 291):

1 lb. mushrooms

Place them in the top of a double boiler. Dot them with:

2 tablespoons butter

Season with:

¼ teaspoon salt
⅛ teaspoon paprika

Cover closely. Steam for about 20 minutes or until tender.

Mushrooms à la King, page 176; Peas and Mushrooms, page 299; Baked Mushrooms, page 175.

MUSHROOMS AND CHESTNUTS

Boil until tender (page 283):

1 lb. chestnuts

Drain them well. Do not mash them.

Sauté (page 292):

1 lb. mushrooms

The proportions of the chestnuts and mushrooms may be varied.

Stir in until blended:

3 tablespoons flour

Stir in slowly:

1½ cups cream or milk

Season them with:

½ teaspoon salt
⅛ teaspoon paprika

Stir in the chestnuts. Heat these ingredients thoroughly. Serve them garnished with:

Chopped parsley

MUSHROOMS, CHESTNUTS AND CELERY

A variation of the above. Proportions are not particularly important. Follow the preceding rule for:

Mushrooms and Chestnuts

Add and heat:

1 cup chopped celery

Remove the dish from the fire. Add:

2 tablespoons or more sherry

See Index for other Mushroom Dishes.

DRIED MUSHROOMS

Wash well:

Dried mushrooms

Soak them for ½ hour in water to cover. Strain the liquid for use in sauces or soup. Use the mushrooms, which have a strong flavor, as you would fresh ones.

STEWED OKRA

Wash:

Young okra

The stems may be left on or cut off. If the pods are small, leave them whole. If they are large, cut them into 1 inch pieces. Drop the okra into a small amount of:

Boiling water

enough to cover the bottom of the pan by ⅛ inch. Simmer it covered until tender. If whole, it will take about 8 minutes, if cut about 5. Or, the okra may be cooked until half tender, drained and then cooked covered in the butter over low heat until it is tender. Drain it. Season it with:

Salt and pepper

Pour over it:

Melted butter—1 tablespoon to 1 cup okra

Or, serve the boiled whole okra hot or chilled on individual plates with Hollandaise Sauce or mayonnaise. To eat use the fingers, lifting the okra by the stem to dip it in the sauce.

SAUTÉED OKRA

6 Servings

Wash:

1 quart okra: 1 lb.

Dry it well, cut off the stem ends and slice the okra crosswise in thin slices. Melt:

2 tablespoons butter

Add the okra, cover it and cook it gently for 10 minutes. Stir it frequently. Remove the cover and continue cooking the okra until it is tender and a golden brown.

FRIED OKRA
4 Servings
Wash:

1 quart young okra

Cut off the stem ends. Barely cover the okra with:

Boiling water

Boil it covered for 5 minutes. Drain it. Dry it between towels. Sprinkle it with:

Salt and pepper

Roll it until it is well covered in:

Corn meal

Fry it until brown in hot fat, page 542. Drain it on absorbent paper. Serve it hot.

ONIONS
Onions are supposed to be the secret of health. But how can one keep the secret?

Their uses are legion and the results rewarding. Cook them in their jackets

and skin them when tender, or pare them before cooking under running cold water to prevent tears. Then afterward remove the odor of onions from your hands by rubbing them with salt or vinegar.

Use onions, green onion and leek tops in soups. Chives are best chopped and added the last minute, as cooking or standing tend to make their flavor strong. Onion juice or onions grated or minced may be added to salad dressings, hot sauces and stuffings. To mince an onion, pare, cut off a slice, cut exposed surface into ⅛ inch squares as deeply as needed. Slice thinly. If only the juice is wanted, pare and cut off a slice. Then scrape juice from center with edge of spoon. Or ream a cut onion on a lemon squeezer. If not very finely chopped for sauces and stuffings, onions frequently remain raw in taste. Therefore, sauté them over low heat in a little butter until they become translucent and tender but not flabby. Large onions may be held together with toothpicks. Remove the toothpicks when the onions are cooked.

STEAMED ONIONS
This method is recommended in preference to boiling because the onion, like cabbage, releases sulphur compounds under too great heat, causing odors and discoloration.

Place on a rack over hot water:

Dry unpeeled medium-sized onions

Cover the pan and cook them until tender, for 30 minutes or more. Peel, season with:

Melted butter
Salt, paprika or pepper

BUTTERED ONIONS
4 Servings
Steam by the preceding rule:

10 medium-sized onions

Peel them. Dress them with:

¼ cup melted butter
½ teaspoon salt
½ teaspoon cinnamon or cloves
(1 teaspoon sugar)

Or melt:

⅓ cup butter

Add:

1 cup bread crumbs
½ teaspoon salt

Sauté the crumbs for 1 minute and pour them over the onions.

CREAMED ONIONS
4 Servings
If onions were costly, surely they would be considered a great delicacy. The following is a very good vegetable dish, if you like onions. Cook by the above rule:

Steamed Onions

Prepare:

1 cup Cream Sauce, page 428, or 1 cup Cheese Sauce, page 430

You may use ¼ onion water and ¾ cream. When the sauce is smooth and

boiling add the onions. Cook them for
1 minute. Add:
  ¼ cup chopped parsley
  A dash of cloves
  ¼ teaspoon paprika
  (2 tablespoons sherry)
A wonderful addition is ½ cupful or
more of Sautéed Mushrooms, page
292.

ONIONS AU GRATIN
Prepare by the preceding rule:
  Creamed Onions
Place them in a greased baking dish or
in individual dishes. Cover the top
with:
  Bread crumbs
Dot it with:
  Butter
or sprinkle it with:
  Grated cheese
Place the dish on a broiler under a
moderate flame until the top is brown.
If prepared in advance, reheat the
onions over hot water before placing
them in the baking dish.
Minced celery cooked or raw combines
well with this dish.

GLAZED ONIONS
4 Servings
These onions are good with pork
roast. Skin:
  12 small onions
Prick them through the center and
place them in:
  1 inch boiling water
Cook them covered until they are
nearly tender, for about 20 minutes.
Dry them on a cloth. Melt:
  4 tablespoons butter
Add:
  ½ teaspoon salt
  2 tablespoons brown sugar
Cook this sirup for 1 minute. Add the
onions and move them about until they
are well coated. Cook them over low
heat for about 15 minutes, using an asbestos mat toward the end.

ONIONS WITH CREAM AND SHERRY
4 Servings
Very good with turkey, ham or any old
thing. Steam (page 294) until nearly
tender, then peel and slice:
  12 good-sized onions
Place them in a greased baking dish.
Combine and pour over them:
  ½ cup cream or top milk
  2 tablespoons sherry
Add:

Salt and paprika
Dot the top with bits of:
  Butter
Cover the dish and bake it in a mod-
erate oven 350° for ½ hour.

WHOLE BAKED ONIONS
Wash:
  Medium-sized onions
Bake them in a moderate oven 375°
until they are tender, for about 1½
hours. Cut a slice from the root end.
Squeeze the onions to force out the
centers. Discard the outer shells. Pour
over the onions:
  Melted butter
Season them with:
  Salt and paprika
Cover them with:
  (Grated cheese or chopped
  parsley)

SMALL ONIONS BRAISED
Skin:
  Small onions
Pour over them to the depth of ½
inch:
  Boiling Stock, page 43
Cook them covered over a slow fire.
Let them absorb the liquid. When they
are tender season them with:
  Salt and pepper
Add additional stock as required.

SAUTÉED ONIONS WITH STOCK
4 Servings
Prepare:
  2 cups finely sliced onions
Melt in a skillet:
  ¼ cup butter
Stir and sauté the onions in this until
they are soft. Add:
  ¼ teaspoon salt
  ⅛ teaspoon pepper
Sift over them:
  1 tablespoon flour
Stir in:
  ½ cup stock
Seasoned with:
  ½ teaspoon dry mustard or
  1 teaspoon prepared mustard
  1 tablespoon sherry or ¼
  teaspoon curry powder
Stir and cook the onions until the
sauce boils and thickens.

ONIONS AND GREEN PEPPERS
4 Servings
This is a good accompaniment to cold
meat. Skin, then cut into thin slices:
  6 medium-sized onions

Cut coarsely after removing seeds and membranes:

3 green peppers

Or omit the onions and use in all 5 green peppers. Melt in a large skillet:

3 tablespoons butter, ham fat or olive oil

Sauté the onions and peppers in this for about 10 minutes. Add:

2 tablespoons stock or water

Season with:

Salt and pepper

Cover the skillet. Simmer the vegetables until the onions are tender, for about 10 minutes. Serve with:

Tomato Sauce, page 433

BAKED ONIONS
4 Servings

Skin:

12 medium-sized onions

Cut them crosswise into halves. Place them side by side in a buttered baking dish or pan. Season them with:

1 teaspoon salt
⅛ teaspoon paprika
2 teaspoons brown sugar

Dot them with:

3 tablespoons butter

Cook them in a slow oven 325° until they are done, for about 1 hour. Serve them on slices of:

Thin buttered toast

Garnish them with:

Parsley dipped in lemon juice

SPANISH ONIONS ROASTED
Skin:

Spanish onions

Cut them crosswise into 3 slices. Place them side by side in a greased pan. Season them with:

Salt and pepper

Dot them generously with:

Butter

Add to the depth of ¼ inch:

Boiling Stock, page 43

Bake the onions in a moderate oven 325°. Baste them frequently until they have absorbed the stock and are tender and brown. Use additional boiling stock if required.

ONIONS IN TOMATO SAUCE
Follow the excellent rule on page 267 for:

Snap Beans in Tomato Sauce

Substitute:

Small onions or sliced large onions

These may be served in ramekins au gratin.

SCALLOPED ONIONS
4 Servings

Onions build you up physically but run you down socially. When you eat these, you don't care about their disadvantages. Skin and slice:

6 large mild onions

Melt:

4 tablespoons butter or bacon drippings

Sauté the onions in the fat until they are tender. Season them with:

Salt and pepper

Place them in a shallow baking dish. Sprinkle the top well with:

Soft bread crumbs
Grated cheese
Paprika

Bake the onions in a moderate oven 375° until the crumbs are brown.

ONIONS IN RAMEKINS
6 Servings

Cook in an uncovered saucepan:

3 cups skinned, chopped onions:
about 6 medium-sized onions
4 cups boiling water

Reduce the heat and simmer the onions until tender, for about 10 minutes. Drain them. Melt:

1 tablespoon butter

Stir in until blended:

1 tablespoon flour
½ teaspoon salt
⅛ teaspoon pepper

Stir in slowly:

½ cup evaporated milk or cream

Add:

¼ cup soft bread crumbs

Cook and stir these ingredients 2 minutes longer, or until they are thickened. Cool them. Stir in:

1 slightly beaten egg yolk

Add the drained onions and:

2 tablespoons chopped parsley

Cool the onions. Fold in:

1 stiffly beaten egg white

Pour the mixture into 6 greased custard cups or ramekins. Set them in a pan of hot water and bake them in a moderate oven 350° for 1 hour, or until they are firm.

SAUTÉED ONIONS
If you eat onions, don't breathe it to a soul. Skin:

4 medium-sized onions

Cut them into very thin slices or chop them. Melt in a skillet:

2 tablespoons butter or bacon drippings

Add the onions and sauté them until

they are golden brown. Stir them frequently to keep them from burning. Before serving them season with:

> Salt

SMOTHERED ONIONS
4 Servings
Melt:

> 3 tablespoons butter or drippings

Turn in the hot fat:

> 3 cups sliced onions

Cover closely and cook them over a slow fire until tender. Season them while cooking with:

> 1/2 teaspoon Worcestershire sauce
> Salt and pepper

Serve them with scrambled eggs, mashed potatoes, or a meat course.

ONIONS FRENCH FRIED
Skin:

> Onions

Cut them crosswise in 1/4 inch slices. Combine:

> 1/2 cup milk
> 1/2 cup water

Soak the onions in this for 1/2 hour. Drain the onions, spread them on absorbent paper and dredge them with seasoned flour. Fry them until they are light brown in deep fat heated from 350° to 370° (page 542).

SHOESTRING ONIONS
This delicious dish is frequently served by a Filipino chef, who cuts the onions into paper-thin shreds with a cleaver. Skin:

> Onions

Cut them into the thinnest possible shreds. Fry them, a small quantity at a time, in deep fat heated to 370° (page 542). Season them with:

> Salt

Drain them on absorbent paper.

ONION RINGS IN BATTER
6 Servings
Skin:

> 6 large onions

Cut them crosswise into 1/4 inch slices. Separate the slices into rings. Beat:

> 2 egg yolks

Add:

> 1/2 cup milk

Sift, then stir in:

> 3/4 cup cake flour
> 1/2 teaspoon salt

Drop the onion rings into the batter one at a time. Fry them, about 1 cupful at a time, in a kettle of deep fat

heated to 370° (page 542). Drain the onions on absorbent paper. Keep them hot until ready to serve.

YOUNG GREEN ONIONS
Place:

> Young green onions

in a very small quantity of:

> Boiling water

Cook them covered until they are nearly tender. Drain them well. Place them in rows on very thin:

> Slices of toast

Season them with:

> Salt and freshly grated pepper or nutmeg

Pour over them:

> Melted butter

Or, cut the onions into small pieces, cook them and combine them with other cooked vegetables—peas, beans, new potatoes, etc.

YOUNG GREEN ONIONS FRIED
Cut into 1 inch lengths:

> Young green onions

Dip them into:

> 1 egg diluted with 2 tablespoons water

Roll them in:

> Seasoned bread crumbs

Fry them, about 1 cupful at a time, in deep fat. For crumbing and frying, see page 542.

See Index for other Onion Dishes.

OYSTER PLANT
Oyster plant and parsnips, although different in flavor and texture, may be boiled, mashed, seasoned and beaten with cream and an egg, served plain or au gratin, or shaped into cakes and sautéed in butter. Dissolve:

> 1 or 2 tablespoons flour

in:

> 3 cups water

Scrape, slice or leave whole:

> Oyster plant

and drop it at once into the water. This will prevent discoloration. Drain the oyster plant at once and cook it covered in:

> 1 inch boiling water

When it is tender, in about 7 to 15 minutes, drain it. Add:

> 1/2 teaspoon salt

Serve it in:

> Cream Sauce I, page 428—1/2 as much sauce as there is oyster plant
> (Chopped chives or parsley)

or in:
  Melted butter—1 tablespoon
  butter to 1 cup oyster plant
  (½ teaspoon dried herbs)
or in:
  Thin meat gravy

BAKED OYSTER PLANT
4 Servings
Prepare (page 297), drop into boiling
water and cook until nearly tender:
  Oyster plant
Boiled parsnips or oyster plant may be
baked. Drain them, place them in a
baking dish with:
  Salt and paprika
  Brown sugar
  (Dry mustard or nutmeg)
Cover them with:
  Bread crumbs
Dot them generously with:
  Butter
Cover the bottom of the dish with:
  Cream
Bake them in a hot oven 400° until the
top is brown.

SAUTÉED OYSTER PLANT
Drain it. Peel it. Dip it in:
  Milk
Season it with:
  Salt and pepper
Roll it in:
  Flour, bread crumbs or crushed
  cornflakes
Sauté it slowly until brown in:
  Butter
or fry it in:
  Hot fat 395° (page 542)

PARSNIPS
For preparation, treatment to avoid
discoloration and cooking see Oyster
Plant above.

FRENCH PARSNIPS
Follow the rule on page 279 for French
Carrots.

BUTTERED PARSNIPS
4 Servings
Pare, then cut into halves:
  4 medium-sized parsnips
Place them in a greased oven-proof
dish. Brush them with:
  2½ tablespoons butter
Sprinkle them with:
  ½ teaspoon salt
Add to the dish:
  ¾ cup water or stock
Cover the dish and bake it in a moderate oven 375° until the parsnips are

tender, for about 45 minutes. Serve
them with:
  Parsley butter

GREEN PEAS AND LETTUCE
Peas cooked by this rule are delicious.
One pound of peas unhulled is about 1
cupful of peas hulled, about 2 servings.
Wash, then hull:
  Green peas
Place them in the top of a double
boiler. Cover them with large moist:
  Lettuce leaves
Cook them covered until tender over
boiling water. This is sometimes a
slow process, dependent upon the size
of the peas, about ¾ of an hour. Re-
move the lettuce leaves. Add:
  Salt and paprika
  A few grains cayenne
  Butter or cream
Serve the peas sprinkled with:
  Chopped parsley
Or, wash a head of lettuce, remove
the heart. Prepare for cooking:
  Green peas
Season them with:
  Salt and pepper
  Pinch of sugar
Fill the head of lettuce with the peas,
tie up the leaves and place the head in
a small quantity of:
  Boiling water
Steam the peas covered until tender,
about 30 minutes. Serve them with:
  Melted butter or cream
The lettuce leaves may be chopped
and served with the peas.

*French Sautéed or Braised Vegetables,
page 263.*

GREEN PEAS CREAMED
4 Servings
Wash, then hull:
  2 lbs. green peas: 2 cups hulled
Melt in a saucepan:
  1½ tablespoons butter or use 3 slices
  minced, sautéed bacon
Add the peas and:
  1 small onion or 3 young green
  onions
  1 heart of lettuce
  5 or 6 sprigs parsley
  ½ teaspoon salt
  (1 sprig thyme)
Pour over them enough boiling water
to cover the bottom of the pan. Cook
the vegetables over a high flame for 10
minutes, then reduce the heat and simmer them closely covered until the
peas are tender. Remove the lettuce

and the parsley. Combine, heat and pour over the peas:

6 tablespoons cream
3 tablespoons stock from the vegetables

GREEN PEAS AND ONIONS
4 Servings
Cook:

2 lbs. fresh peas

Cook with the peas or cook separately:

1 cup small skinned onions or sliced green onion

Drain the vegetables well. Heat:

2 tablespoons butter or 4 tablespoons thick cream

Pour it over the vegetables. Sprinkle them with:

(Chopped parsley)

GREEN PEAS WITH MINT SAUCE
Cook:

2 cups green peas: 2 lbs.

Drain them and serve them with:

1 cup Cream Sauce I, page 428

Add to the sauce:

3 tablespoons chopped mint leaves

Or, omit the sauce and add the mint to:

2 tablespoons melted butter

GREEN PEAS WITH OR WITHOUT CARROTS
Wash, then hull:

Green peas

Cook them covered in:

⅛ inch boiling water

to keep them from scorching. Add:

½ teaspoon lemon juice

to preserve color. Cooking uncovered will also preserve color but causes some nutritive loss. There is a tradition that one must add to peas:

A pinch of sugar

Two or three pea pods may be cooked with the peas for flavor. When the peas are tender drain them if there is any water left. Season them with:

Chopped sautéed bacon
Salt and paprika

Moisten them with:

Melted butter or hot cream

Peas may be combined in any proportion with:

Boiled Carrots, page 279

PEAS AND MUSHROOMS
6 Servings
The proportions given for peas and mushrooms may be varied. Drain, reserving the liquor:

2 cups: 2 lbs. unshelled fresh boiled peas, or 2 cups canned peas: No. 2 can

Prepare for cooking:

1 lb. mushrooms

Sauté them in:

4 tablespoons butter

The skillet may be rubbed with garlic. Remove the mushrooms. Add to the juice in the skillet:

2 tablespoons flour

Stir and cook it until it bubbles. Combine and stir in slowly:

⅓ cup liquor from the peas
⅓ cup cream

Add if required:

Salt and pepper

When the sauce is smooth and boiling, add the peas and the mushrooms. Simmer them covered for a few minutes. Serve them sprinkled with:

Chopped parsley

Purée of Dried Peas, see Purée of Lentils, page 271.

PODDED PEAS
These small gray-green pods are unusually sweet but seldom available unless you grow them yourself. Extremely young regular peas before they fill out may be substituted. You may cut off the ends and cook them like whole Snap Beans, page 267.

Split Peas, see Dried Beans and Peas.

GREEN PEPPERS IN SAUCE
Stewed green peppers combine well with other vegetables; for example: green peppers with celery or onions. They are good by themselves but may be pepped up with a well-seasoned sauce.

Remove the stem and fibrous portions from:

Green peppers

Cut the peppers into oblongs or strips. Drop them into:

½ inch boiling water

Boil them until they are tender, for about 10 minutes. Drain them well. Serve them in:

Cheese Sauce, or one of the sauces made with canned soups, page 441—equal to about ½ the amount of peppers

Season the cheese sauce with:

Salt
Worcestershire sauce

Pepper Cases Filled with Food, page 202.

Potatoes

For a number of years the mania for girth control has played havoc with the fair name of the potato—bringing "insinuendoes" against it that are almost as damaging as the charges brought against the erstwhile virtue of bread.

Time was when this highly respectable vegetable was held in great repute and it seems to be in for a comeback. Those who have visited Hirschhorn in the sweetly romantic Neckar Valley and who have climbed the hill to the partly ruined castle that dominates the little village, will remember being confronted by a "Potato Monument" dedicated piously "To God and Francis Drake, who brought to Europe for the everlasting benefit of the poor—the Potato." Please don't say that Sir Walter Raleigh or Governor Lane imported the potato, for it really doesn't matter, does it?

BOILED OLD POTATOES
4 Servings
Wash well, remove sprouts and blemishes, then pare:
  6 medium-sized potatoes
When in haste cut them into quarters. Cook them covered from 20 to 40 minutes in:
  4 cups boiling water
When they are done drain them well. Add:
  ½ teaspoon salt

I.
Place a folded towel over the pot for 5 minutes. Shake the pot well. Remove the towel and serve the potatoes at once.

II.
Or place the potatoes in a light saucepan and shake them gently over a good fire for a minute or two. This will dry them and make them mealy. Avoid putting them in a covered dish if you wish to keep the potatoes dry.

BOILED NEW POTATOES
4 Servings
Wash:
  16 new potatoes
Drop them in:
  Boiling water to cover
Cook them covered until they are tender, from 20 to 30 minutes. Remove the skins and serve the potatoes with:
  Chopped parsley, mint or chives
or melt in a skillet:
  2 or more tablespoons butter
Add the potatoes and shake them gently over a low fire until they are well coated. Serve them sprinkled with salt and chopped parsley.
Or serve the potatoes without dressing and pass a bowl of sour cream generously sprinkled with chopped chives.

POTATOES BOILED IN THEIR JACKETS
A favorite dish abroad for informal meals is potatoes (preferably new ones) served in their jackets and peeled at table.
Prepare by the preceding rule:
  Scrubbed and unpared boiled potatoes
Mince and sauté:
  Bacon
Add and sauté at the same time:
  Finely chopped onions
Serve the bacon, the drippings and the onions in a gravy boat with the potatoes or serve them with thick sour cream and chopped parsley or chives.

POTATOES WITH CHEESE COATING
4 Servings
Follow the above rule for Boiled Potatoes, omitting the salt. Combine:
  ½ cup grated cheese
  ¾ teaspoon salt
  ¼ teaspoon paprika
  A few grains cayenne
Roll the potatoes in:
  3 tablespoons melted butter
then in the cheese mixture.
Place them on a buttered sheet in a moderate oven 400° for about 15 minutes, or until the cheese is melted.

POTATOES IN BOUILLON
4 Servings
Pare, then cut into quarters:
  4 large potatoes, or pare 8 small potatoes
Simmer them until nearly tender in:
  1½ cups boiling Stock, page 43
To which you may add:
  3 minced shallots or green onions
Drain. Make a sauce of the stock with:

1 tablespoon butter
1 tablespoon flour
Return the potatoes to the pot. Simmer
them until tender. Season them with:
Salt and pepper
Chopped chives or parsley

STEWED POTATOES
4 Servings
These potatoes are especially good
served with meat which hasn't much
sauce or with cold meat. Try out in a
saucepan:
1 oz. diced salt pork or 1 slice
bacon or
2 tablespoons bacon or chicken fat
Add and sauté until the onions are
lightly browned:
1 medium-sized finely minced
onion
½ bay leaf
Add:
6 medium potatoes pared and cut
in ½ inch dice
Freshly ground white or black
pepper
Pour on to about ¾ the height of the
potatoes:
Boiling water
Cover them and simmer for about 30
minutes, or until tender, but not mushy.
Drain them. Add salt if required. Serve
them garnished with:
Minced parsley

POTATOES COOKED IN SOUR CREAM
4 Servings
Peel, then slice thinly:
4 medium-sized potatoes
1 medium-sized onion
Melt in a skillet:
2 tablespoons fat
Turn the potatoes and onions in the
fat. Sprinkle them with:
Salt
Half cover them with:
Sour cream
Cover the skillet, cook the potatoes
slowly. Turn them several times with
a spatula. When nearly tender uncover
the potatoes and cook them until tender and light brown.

BAKED POTATOES
Wash and scrub even-sized, shapely:
Potatoes
Dry them and grease them lightly
with:
Lard, butter, drippings, etc.
Bake the potatoes in a moderate oven

350° for 1 hour or more. You may bake
potatoes at a higher temperature, 350°
to 450°, allowing about 40 minutes for
the highest temperature. Very large
potatoes require more time. You may
parboil them for 20 minutes. Grease
them and bake them as directed for
about 45 minutes at 350°. When potatoes are ½ done, pull out rack,
quickly puncture skin once with fork,
permitting steam to escape, or cut 2
deep crosswise gashes in each potato.
Return to oven and finish baking.
When done serve them at once with:
Butter or thick sweet or sour
cream
Chopped chives or parsley
To utilize left-over baked potatoes cut
them in 2 while they are still hot.
Scoop out the centers. Combine the
potatoes with:
Milk
Salt and pepper
Grated onion, sautéed or raw,
celery or grated carrots, deviled
ham, crisp bits bacon or ham fat,
etc.
(1 egg)
Beat these ingredients until they are
smooth. Fill the shells. Cover the tops
with:
Bread crumbs
Dot them with:
Butter
or sprinkle them with:
(Cheese)
The potatoes are then ready to be re-
heated for the next day's dinner.

*Baked Potatoes Filled with Ham, Hash,
Vegetables, etc., page 210.*

NEW POTATOES BAKED
New potatoes may be baked like old
potatoes but they require a longer
cooking period as they contain more
moisture than the old potatoes.
Wash and scrub even-sized:
New potatoes
Bake them in moderate oven 400°
about 1½ hours.
Or pare and place in a baking dish:
1 quart new potatoes
Add:
1 can condensed soup: 10½ oz.
1 cup water
Bake the potatoes covered in a 350°
oven for about 1½ hours. Serve them
with:
Chopped parsley or chives

POTATO BOATS
6 Servings
Prepare by the rule on page 301:
6 Baked Potatoes
Cut them in halves. Scoop out the pulp. Add to it:
3 tablespoons butter
3 tablespoons hot milk or cream
1 teaspoon salt
You may sauté:
2 tablespoons grated onion
in the butter.
Beat these ingredients until they are smooth. Whip until stiff:
2 egg whites
Fold them into the potato mixture. Fill the potato shells. Sprinkle them with:
½ cup grated cheese
Paprika
Broil them under a low flame until the cheese is melted. If you plan to serve these with fish add, for piquancy, 1 tablespoonful or more horseradish along with the butter and cream.

For other Baked Potato Dishes, see Index.

BAKED POTATO WAFERS
Potatoes prepared in this way have a distinctive flavor. Select large well-shaped:
Potatoes
Scrub them well. Rub them with:
Butter
Cut them (without peeling them) in rounds ¼ inch thick. Place them in a generously buttered skillet flat side down. Sprinkle them with:
Salt and pepper
Cover them and bake them in a moderate oven 375° for 20 minutes, or until they are tender. Turn the slices as they brown. Serve them garnished with:
Minced parsley

FRENCH POTATO BALLS
Pare:
Potatoes
Place them in cold water for ½ hour. Cut them into balls with a French potato cutter or cut them into cubes. Cook them in:
Boiling water to cover
Drain them. Add:
¾ teaspoon salt to 2 cups potato balls
Serve them with:
Melted butter
Chopped parsley
French potato balls may be prepared by the following rule for Browned Potatoes. Use the potato scraps for potato soup, hashed brown or other potato dishes.

FRANCONIA OR BROWNED POTATOES IN ROAST GRAVY
4 Servings
Parboil (page 300):
8 small old or large new potatoes
When they are nearly tender, drain them. Melt in a pan:
2 tablespoons butter or bacon drippings
Sauté the potatoes in the fat until they are light brown. Shake the pan or turn them frequently. Season with:
Salt and paprika
Bake them in a hot oven 400° until they are crisp and brown. Add more butter if required. Turn the potatoes to brown them evenly.
These potatoes may be placed in the pan in which meat is roasting. If using the new low temperature method, they may not brown sufficiently. In that case place them under a broiler or finish browning them in a skillet on top of the stove.

POTATO BASKETS
Read the rule on page 98 for:
Noodle Baskets
Use a shredder to cut into long ¼ inch strips:
Peeled potatoes
Soak them for 30 minutes in ice water. Drain them well and dry them between towels. Line the larger strainer as directed for noodle baskets. Fit the smaller strainer over it. Fry the potato baskets as directed.

RICED POTATOES
6 Servings
Boil (page 300):
6 medium-sized old potatoes
Put them through a food mill, ricer or strainer. Heap them on a dish and pour over them:
2 tablespoons melted butter

MASHED POTATOES
6 Servings, About 3 Cupfuls
Consult the Index for a large number of mashed potato dishes given elsewhere. Many of the fancier dishes may be prepared in advance and reheated in a moderate oven or under a broiler. Plain mashed potatoes can be kept warm by placing the pan in a larger

pan of hot water. Boil by the rule on page 300:

6 medium-sized old potatoes

You may add to the water a small onion or a cut clove of garlic, a piece of bay leaf and a rib of celery with leaves. Remove these extraneous ingredients. Mash the potatoes with a fork or a potato masher, or put them through a food mill, blender or electric mixer. Add to them:

3 tablespoons butter
1 teaspoon salt
⅓ cup hot milk or cream

Beat them with a fork until they are creamy. Grated or sautéed onions with the drippings, minced crisp bacon, chopped parsley, chives or water cress are all good additions to mashed potatoes. A nice variation is to shape mashed potatoes into small mounds or into 1 large one, make a well in the top of each mound, place a dab of butter in each well and cover it up. Brush the tops with milk. Brown the potatoes lightly on a broiler pan under a moderate flame.

Mashed potatoes may be creamed with:

Canned condensed cream soup diluted with a little milk

MASHED POTATOES BAKED
4 Servings

Richer than mashed potatoes by the addition of 1 egg.

Boil by the rule on page 300:

4 medium-sized potatoes

Two cupfuls cold mashed potatoes may be substituted. In that case use less butter, milk and seasoning.

Beat them with a fork. Beat in:

2 tablespoons butter
1 egg
½ teaspoon salt
⅛ teaspoon pepper
¾ cup hot milk or cream

Place the potatoes in a greased baking dish. Bake them in a moderate oven 380° until they are brown. They may be served au gratin.

POTATO VOLCANO WITH CHEESE
6 Servings

Prepare by the rule on page 302:

Mashed potatoes

There should be 3 cupfuls. Shape them into a mound on a greased oven-proof plate. Make a hollow in the top of the mound as large as a tea cup. Melt:

⅓ cup butter

Reserve 2 tablespoonfuls of this. To the remainder add:

½ cup grated cheese
2 egg yolks
¼ teaspoon salt
⅛ teaspoon paprika

Beat these ingredients well and pour them in the hollow. Spread the sides of the mound lightly with the reserved melted butter. Cover the mound with:

Bread crumbs

Brown the volcano in a moderate oven 375°. These potatoes may be shaped into individual mounds. Try filling the volcano with:

Welsh Rarebit, page 187

This may be canned. Let it overflow. Or, fill it with buttered peas, creamed cauliflower, etc.

Gnocchi with Potatoes, page 102.

CHANTILLY POTATOES
6 Servings

The following recipe is reminiscent of the old colored man who said all he could find that college had done for his children was to put ma on 'lasses and pa on 'taters. Surely this is putting pa on 'taters.

Prepare by the rule on this page:

3 cups Mashed Potatoes or Mashed Potatoes Baked

Whip until stiff:

½ cup cream

Season it with:

Salt and pepper
A few grains cayenne

Combine it with:

½ cup grated cheese

Shape the potatoes into a mound on an oven-proof plate. Cover the mound with the whipped cream mixture. Place the plate in a moderate oven 380° until the cheese is melted and the potatoes are lightly browned.

Potato Soufflé with Cheese Topping, page 219.

POTATO PEARS
6 Servings

Easy to make and very decorative.

Prepare by the rule on page 302:

3 cups Mashed Potatoes

Divide them into 6 parts. Roll them into pear shape. Brush them with:

Yolk of an egg

Dust one cheek of each pear with:

Paprika

Place in the blossom ends:
Cloves
Place in the stem ends:
Bits of parsley or other stems
Place the pears on a greased tin in a moderate oven 375° until they are hot. These potatoes may be prepared in advance and heated shortly before they are served.

FRIED MASHED POTATO BALLS
4 Servings
These are delicious; so are the Potato Apples that follow. The latter are richer by the addition of cheese. Prepare:
    2 cups hot Mashed Potatoes, page 302: 4 medium-sized potatoes
Add to them:
    2 eggs
    1 teaspoon any baking powder
    ¼ teaspoon salt
    ⅛ teaspoon paprika
Beat these ingredients well and drop them by the teaspoonful into hot fat 395° (page 542). Cook the puffs until they are brown and place them to drain on paper in a colander. Serve them while hot, or reheat them in a hot oven 425°. Serve them with:
    Sprigs of parsley

Potato Puffs and Potato Cheese Puffs, pages 198, 209.

FRIED POTATO APPLES
Mashed Potatoes with Eggs and Cheese
6 Servings
Prepare:
    2 cups hot Riced Potatoes, page 302: 4 medium-sized potatoes
Add to them:
    2 tablespoons butter
    ½ cup grated cheese
    ½ teaspoon salt
    A few grains cayenne
    2 tablespoons cream
    2 beaten egg yolks
    ½ teaspoon any baking powder
Whip these ingredients until they are light. Shape them into balls. Roll the balls in:
    Flour
then in:
    1 egg diluted and beaten with 2 tablespoons water
and in:
    Sifted bread crumbs

Fry the balls in deep fat (page 542). Drain them on absorbent paper. Place in the blossom ends:
    Cloves: showing the head
Place in the stem ends:
    Cloves: showing the stem

MASHED POTATO BALLS WITH CORNFLAKES, BAKED OR FRIED
These very good and decorative potato balls may be made long in advance and reheated when ready to serve them. Prepare:
    Mashed Potatoes, page 302
Use the milk sparingly. Roll the potatoes into balls. Dilute:
    1 egg
with:
    2 tablespoons water
Roll the balls in the egg, then in:
    Crushed cornflakes
Or they may be rolled in melted butter and cornflakes if they are to be baked. Place them in a greased pan. Bake the balls in a moderate oven 375° until they are well heated, or fry them in deep fat (page 542).

BAKED MASHED POTATO BALLS
4 Servings
Prepare:
    2 cups well-seasoned Mashed Potatoes, page 302: 4 medium-sized potatoes
Beat in:
    2 egg yolks
    1 tablespoon chopped parsley
Cool these ingredients slightly. Beat until stiff:
    2 egg whites
Fold them lightly into the potato mixture. Shape the mixture into balls. Bake the potatoes in lightly greased muffin tins or drop them on a greased sheet. Bake them in a moderate oven 350° until they are crisp. Turn them to brown evenly.

For other Mashed Potato Dishes see Index.

SCALLOPED POTATOES
Method I. 4 Servings
Grease a baking dish. Place in it in 3 layers:
    3 cups pared, very thinly sliced potatoes
Dredge the layers with flour and dot them with butter. Use in all:

2 tablespoons flour
3 tablespoons butter
Heat:
  1¼ cups milk
Season it with:
  1¼ teaspoons salt
  ¼ teaspoon paprika
Condensed mushroom soup may be substituted for the flour, butter and milk. Pour the sauce over the potatoes. Bake them in a moderate oven 350° for 1½ hours. The potatoes may be turned with a spoon while cooking to insure even baking. They may be covered for the first ½ hour.
Or, pare, then slice thinly into a 7 inch casserole:
  5 medium-sized potatoes
Place in a skillet and sauté slowly until the bacon is crisp:
  2 to 3 slices minced bacon
  1 medium-sized peeled chopped onion
Stir in until bubbling:
  2 tablespoons flour
  ¼ teaspoon salt
  ¼ teaspoon freshly ground black pepper
Stir in:
  1 cup milk, or part milk and water
When boiling, pour the sauce over the potatoes. Bake them in a moderate oven 350° to 375° until tender, for 1 hour or more.

Method II. 8 Servings
Pare and cut into thin slices:
  Raw potatoes
There should be 4 cupfuls. Melt:
  3 tablespoons butter
You may sauté lightly in this:
  2 teaspoons grated onion
Stir in until blended:
  3 tablespoons flour
Cook and stir in slowly:
  1½ cups milk
Season with:
  1½ teaspoons salt
  A few grains cayenne
Cook the sauce until it is smooth and boiling. Reduce the heat and add:
  1 cup grated cheese: ¼ lb.
When the cheese is melted add:
  ¾ cup shredded green pepper and pimiento
Grease a baking dish and fill it with alternate layers of potatoes and cheese sauce. Bake the potatoes in a moderate oven 350° for about 2 hours, or until they are done.
Cover them for the first ½ hour. The potatoes may be turned with a spoon

while cooking to
Parboiling the p
appreciably the

POTATOES
BUTTER
Wash and pare:
  Potatoes
Cut them in slices ⅛ inch thick. F...
them in cold water to cover for 15 minutes. Drain them. Dry them between towels. Butter a shallow baking dish generously. Sprinkle it with:
  Fine dry bread crumbs
Cover the bottom carefully with the potato slices. Dot them generously with:
  Butter
Sprinkle them lightly with:
  Salt and pepper
Repeat this process until the dish is filled. Cover the dish. Bake the potatoes in a moderate oven 375° for about 1 hour, or until they are tender. Turn them out onto a platter. Garnish them with:
  Parsley

SCALLOPED POTATOES AND ONIONS
4 Servings
Pare and cut into very thin slices:
  1½ cups potatoes
  1½ cups onions
Grease a baking dish. Place the vegetables in it in alternate layers. Sprinkle the layers and bake the dish as directed in Scalloped Potatoes I. You may add bits of diced bacon, raw or cooked.

POTATOES AND ONIONS
This is a variation of the preceding Scalloped Potatoes and Onion to be used when an oven is not available. Place in a skillet layers of thinly sliced:
  Raw potatoes and onions
Season them with:
  Salt and pepper
Dot them with:
  Butter or diced raw bacon
Add cold water until it reaches halfway to the top. Cover the skillet closely. Place it on an asbestos mat. Cook the vegetables very slowly until they are thoroughly done.

POTATO, ONION AND ANCHOVY CASSEROLE
4 Servings
Pare:
  5 to 6 medium-sized potatoes

them into very thin slices. Place the potatoes in a greased baking sh. Have ready:

12 anchovies cut in pieces
¼ cup minced chives or onions

Place ½ the anchovies and onions on the potatoes. Sprinkle the layer lightly with:

Salt and pepper

Repeat this. Add until the potatoes are covered:

Cream

Bake the potatoes covered in a moderate oven 350° until tender, for about 1½ hours. Uncover for the last 15 minutes.

SLICED POTATO PIE
6 Servings
Pare and cut into very thin slices:

6 medium-sized potatoes

Soak them in cold water. Place them in the refrigerator for 2 hours. Drain them, then dry them between towels. Heat in a skillet:

2 tablespoons butter or olive oil

When it is hot, add ½ the potatoes. Dot them with:

Butter

Season them with:

Salt and paprika

Add the remaining potatoes and repeat the process. Do not stir them at any time. Cook them over a high flame until the potatoes are brown on the bottom, about 10 minutes. Then cover them and cook them over a low flame until the potatoes are done, ½ to ¾ hour. Dot the top with:

Butter

Brown the potatoes on a broiler under a moderate flame for 15 minutes. Slice them like pie to serve them.

GRATED POTATOES PAN-BROILED
4 Servings
Very good, quick—something like a potato pancake. Wash, grate on a medium grater, skin and all:

3 medium-sized old potatoes

Grated onion may be added.
Spread them in a well-greased skillet to the depth of about ¼ inch. Cook covered over a medium to slow flame until the bottom is brown. Reverse and brown the other side. Season with:

Salt

Serve piping hot.

Potato Pancakes, page 554.

TINY NEW POTATOES SAUTÉED WHOLE
4 Servings
Scrub and scrape well:

24 very small new potatoes

Heat in a heavy saucepan:

2 tablespoons olive oil

Turn the potatoes in the oil, cover them closely and cook them slowly until tender. Shake the pan from time to time. Sprinkle the potatoes with:

Salt
(Chopped chives or parsley)

NEW POTATOES SLICED AND SAUTÉED
Wash well:

New potatoes

Slice them crosswise, without paring them, into thin slices. Soak them in cold water for ½ hour. Dry them. Sprinkle them with:

Salt and paprika

To 3 cupfuls of potatoes allow:

3 tablespoons drippings

Heat the drippings and add the potatoes. Cover them closely. Cook them until they are tender. Remove the lid and permit them to brown. Turn them frequently so that they will brown evenly.

HASHED BROWN POTATOES
4 Servings
Combine with a fork:

3 cups finely diced raw potatoes
1 teaspoon grated onion
1 tablespoon chopped parsley
½ teaspoon salt
¼ teaspoon black pepper
(1 teaspoon lemon juice)

Heat in a 9 inch skillet:

3 tablespoons bacon drippings, oil or other fat

Spread the potato mixture over this. Press it with a broad knife into a cake. Sauté the potatoes slowly, shaking them from time to time to keep them from sticking. When the bottom is brown, cut the potato layer in half and turn each half with 2 spatulas. Pour over them slowly:

¼ cup cream

Brown the second side and serve the potatoes piping hot.

SOUFFLÉ OR PUFFED POTATOES
6 Servings
The story of the discovery of Soufflé Potatoes has become legendary.

Louis XIV, diverted for the moment by his favorite pastime of fighting the Dutch, was inspecting his army at the front. He was to dine at a given point at a given time and a fitting repast had been prepared for him.

His sumptuous traveling coach, that little palace on wheels that was the scene of so many intrigues—of so many tender affairs—swinging along on its great springs was delayed by torrential rains that made the rough roads almost impassable.

The King was due at any moment and would undoubtedly demand food at once to appease his phenomenal appetite. The cook was frantic. His delicious dinner was kept hot over steam, but the potatoes, unfortunately fried ones, were limp and cold.

A tremendous bustle heralded the arrival of the King and in despair the unfortunate cook immersed the potatoes in the hot fat for the **second time**. Behold! there emerged the dish that was to make him rich and famous, the twice fried potato.

Pare, cut with a potato slicer or a knife into even lengthwise slices no more than ⅛ inch thick:

8 medium-sized potatoes

Some experts recommend Idahoes, others Burbanks. Soak them in ice water for 15 minutes. Dry them well with a cloth, preferably linen. See Rule for Deep Fat Frying, page 541. Partly fill 2 frying kettles with a combination of:

Oil and cooking fat

Heat the fat in the first kettle to 275°. Fry a cupful of potato slices at a time in the fat. You may use a frying basket or a sieve. Fry the slices for about 5 minutes. Turn them once to cook evenly. Spread them to drain them on unglazed brown paper or a towel. Repeat this process until all the potato slices have been fried. Cool the slices well. They may be kept in the refrigerator until you are ready to fry them for a second time, or they may be fried as soon as they are cool. Heat the fat in the second kettle to 425°. Plunge the partly fried slices quickly—about 1 cupful at a time, into the hot fat. They should start to puff immediately. Shake them or stir them about. When they are puffed remove at once from the fat and spread them out to drain on unglazed brown paper or on a towel. Sprinkle them lightly with salt. If they are not sufficiently crisp, return them to the hot fat for a few minutes. If you are only partially successful in having the potatoes puff, don't be discouraged—that is usual with this temperamental, unpredictable dish. The duds, the nonco-operative slices are good as French fries so there is no waste. Sometimes after cooling they decide to puff after all, so give them another chance in hot fat.

FRENCH FRIED POTATOES I

Konrad Bercovici tells the following story: Madame Schumann-Heink, the great opera singer, was sitting in front of an enormous steak. Caruso passed her table and seeing the huge portion of meat before the singer, he said: "Stina, you are not going to eat that alone!" "No," Schumann-Heink said, shaking her fine old head. "No, not alone. With potatoes." Two to one, they were French fried potatoes.

Cut into lengthwise strips ¼ inch thick:

Peeled or unpeeled potatoes

Soak them in cold salted water for 1 hour. You may parboil them for 2 minutes before frying. Drain them well, then dry them between towels. Fry them in deep fat heated to 395°, hot enough to brown an inch cube of bread in 20 seconds, until they are a golden brown (page 542). Test a strip by pricking it with a fork to make sure that the potatoes are done in the center. Drain them on paper. Sprinkle them with:

Salt

Serve them very hot.

SHOESTRING POTATOES

Follow the above rule for:

French Fried Potatoes

Cut the potatoes into very thin strips.

FRENCH FRIED POTATOES II

This method involves 2 operations, but is often helpful because the first step may be done several hours before the meal. This is not a soufflé potato. The double process is merely a last minute timesaver. Prepare by the preceding rule:

Potatoes

Those suitable for baking seem best. Fry them, in small lots, in deep fat heated to 350° until they are tender but not brown, for 5 to 7 minutes. Drain them on absorbent paper. Reheat the

fat to 400°. Fry the potatoes again until they are crisp and brown. Drain them on absorbent paper. Sprinkle them with:
>Salt

Serve them very hot.

BAKED "FRENCH FRIED" POTATOES

4 Servings

Pare:
>4 medium-sized potatoes

Cut them lengthwise into strips about ½ inch thick. You may soak them in cold water for 10 minutes. Dry them well between towels. Spread them in a flat oven-proof dish. Pour over them:
>¼ cup melted butter or bacon
>drippings

Stir them about until coated. Bake them in a hot oven 450° for about ½ hour. Turn them several times during this period. Drain them on unglazed brown paper. Sprinkle them with:
>½ teaspoon salt
>¼ teaspoon paprika

Potato Cups, page 210.

CANNED FRENCH FRIED POTATOES

Canned French fried potatoes are easily reheated in a hot oven 450°. Watch them closely lest they burn. Happily they fail to take on that worn and discouraged appearance typical of the lunch-stand variety. Alas! they have an outstanding drawback. A wit has said that a fried potato is "in your mouth a few seconds, in your stomach a few hours and on your hips the rest of your life."

USES FOR COLD BOILED POTATOES

SAUTÉED OR "GERMAN FRIED" POTATOES

4 Servings

Melt in a skillet:
>2 or more tablespoons fat

Add:
>2 cups cold sliced boiled potatoes
>Salt and paprika
>(1 or more teaspoons minced
>onion)

Sauté the potatoes slowly until they are light brown. Turn them frequently.

AU GRATIN POTATOES WITH OR WITHOUT CHEESE

Cut into dice:
>Cold boiled potatoes

Prepare:
>Cream Sauce—½ as much sauce
>as there are potatoes

Combine the potatoes and the sauce. Add:
>(Chopped parsley, minced onion
>or chives)

Heat these ingredients in a double boiler for 30 minutes, or put them in a greased baking dish. Cover them with:
>Bread crumbs

Dot them with:
>Butter

Bake them in a moderate oven 400° until the crumbs are brown.

To prepare the potatoes with cheese, omit the parsley, etc., and substitute grated cheese, or place alternate layers of potatoes and cream sauce in a baking dish and sprinkle the layers with:
>Grated cheese

Season with:
>Paprika or a dash of cayenne

Cover the top with:
>Bread crumbs

Dot it with:
>Butter

Bake the potatoes as directed.

CREAMED POTATO RING

Prepare by the above rule:
>Creamed Potatoes

Pack them into a greased ring mold. Chill them for 6 hours or more. Bake the potatoes as directed. Invert them onto a hot place. Fill the center with:
>A buttered green vegetable, or
>hash

LEFT-OVER POTATOES, O'BRIEN

6 Servings

Boil:
>6 medium-sized potatoes

Chill the potatoes and dice them. Add:
>1 chopped green pepper
>1 chopped onion
>1 tablespoon flour
>Salt and pepper
>A few grains cayenne
>(¾ cup grated cheese)

Place these ingredients in a greased baking dish. Pour over them:
>1 cup rich milk

Cover them with:
>Bread crumbs

Dot them with:
Butter
Bake them in a moderate oven 350°
for 15 minutes.

USES FOR COLD MASHED POTATOES

These make a good soup base.
Cold mashed potatoes, moistened with
hot milk and beaten with a fork until
smooth, may be substituted for fresh
mashed potatoes in any of the recipes
given on pages 303-304. The following
recipe is perhaps the easiest way of
utilizing them:

POTATO CAKES

Shape into little cakes:
Cold mashed potatoes
A beaten egg and a little chopped
parsley, celery or celery seed, grated
onion, or ¼ cupful chopped onions
sautéed in 2 tablespoonfuls butter, or a
grating of nutmeg may be added before shaping the cakes.
Dip them in:
Flour, bread crumbs or crushed
cornflakes
Melt in a skillet:
Butter or other fat
Brown the cakes in this on one side,
reverse them and brown the other side.

Hot Potato Salad, page 464.

BOILED SWEET POTATOES

Sweet potatoes should be treasured
for their high vitamin A content.
To cook sweet potatoes in their jackets, drop them into boiling water to
cover and cook covered until tender,
about 25 minutes. They may also be
pared, dropped into ¼ cupful boiling
water and cooked covered until tender,
about 15 minutes. Salt before serving.
Six medium-sized sweet potatoes will
yield about 2 cupfuls mashed sweet
potatoes.

BAKED SWEET POTATOES

Follow the rule for Baked Potatoes,
page 301. It is well to cut a slice off
one end or to puncture a sweet potato
when half cooked as a safety valve to
prevent its bursting.

FILLED SWEET POTATOES
4 to 6 Servings
Bake by the rule for Baked Potatoes
on page 301.

6 shapely sweet potatoes
Cut them lengthwise into halves and
scrape out the pulp. Add:
2 tablespoons butter
¼ cup hot cream or ¾ cup crushed
pineapple
½ teaspoon salt
(1 tablespoon sherry)
Southern people say "use lots of butter, some brown sugar, nutmeg and
black walnut meats."
Beat these ingredients with a fork
until they are fluffy. Fill the shells
and cover the tops with:
Bread crumbs
Dot them with:
Butter
Bake the potatoes in a moderate oven
375° until they are brown, or reheat
them in a broiler under a moderate
flame.
Marshmallows may be substituted for
the bread crumbs and butter. These
are a matter of taste or lack of taste.

CANDIED SWEET POTATOES
Method I. 4 Servings
Cook covered in boiling water to
cover until nearly tender:
6 sweet potatoes
Pare and cut them lengthwise in ½
inch slices. Place them in a shallow
greased baking dish. Season them
with:
Salt and paprika
Sprinkle them with:
¾ cup brown sugar
½ teaspoon grated lemon rind
1½ tablespoons lemon juice
Dot them with:
2 tablespoons butter
Bake them uncovered in a moderate
oven 375° for 20 minutes.

Method II.

After seasoning the potatoes with salt
and paprika, dot them with:
3 tablespoons butter
Pour over them:
⅓ cup maple sirup
Bake them as directed.

Method III.

Cook for 10 minutes in boiling salted
water:
6 medium-sized sweet potatoes
Pare them, cut them in halves and
place them in a greased baking dish.
Cook for 3 minutes:
¾ cup brown sugar
⅓ cup water

Add:
  2½ tablespoons butter
  (1½ tablespoons lemon juice)
Brush the potatoes with the sirup and
bake them in a moderate oven 375°
until they are done. Baste them several times with the remaining sirup.

FRIED SWEET POTATOES
Method I.
Wash, then parboil for 10 minutes:
  Large sweet potatoes
Pare them and cut them into strips.
Heat deep fat to 375°-385°, hot enough
to brown an inch cube of bread in 40
seconds. Fry the sweet potato strips in
the hot fat until they are a golden
brown. Drain them on absorbent
paper. Sprinkle them with:
  Salt

Method II.
Or pare, then cut into ¼ inch slices:
  Raw sweet potatoes
Fry them in 1 inch of hot fat until
done. Drain them on absorbent paper.
Sprinkle them with:
  Brown sugar
  Salt
  Freshly grated nutmeg

Method III.
Or, cut into dice:
  4 medium-sized boiled sweet
  potatoes
Add to them:
  3 tablespoons melted butter
  Grated rind and juice of 1 small
  orange
  ½ cup brown sugar
  2 tablespoons chopped parsley or
  chives
Shake the sweet potatoes over quick
heat until they are hot.

Method IV.
Or, slice:
  4 medium-sized boiled sweet
  potatoes
Melt:
  3 tablespoons orange marmalade
Sauté the sweet potatoes gently in this
until they are glazed and brown.

FRENCH SWEET POTATOES
Follow the rule on page 279 for
French Carrots.

SAUTÉED SWEET POTATOES
Pare, then slice:
  Left-over boiled or baked sweet
  potatoes

Melt:
  Butter or drippings
Sauté the potatoes slowly until they
are light brown. Sprinkle them with:
  Brown or granulated sugar

MASHED SWEET POTATOES
4 Servings
Boil:
  6 sweet potatoes
Put them through a ricer or mash
them with a potato masher. Add:
  2 tablespoons butter
  ½ teaspoon salt
  A little hot milk, cream, or
  lemon juice or sherry
  (2 teaspoons brown sugar)
Beat them with a fork until they are
very light. Sprinkle them with:
  Grated orange or lemon rind,
  cloves or cinnamon
Chopped dates and nut meats may be
added. Good served with ham.

Substitute sweet potatoes in the rules
given for Mashed Potato Dishes,
page 302. See Index for other Sweet
Potato Dishes.

SWEET POTATO BALLS
Method I.
Prepare by the preceding rule:
  Mashed Sweet Potatoes
You may add:
  Grated orange rind or juice
Form potato balls around:
  Marshmallows or nut meats
Dilute:
  1 egg
with:
  2 tablespoons water
Dip the balls in the egg, then in:
  Crushed cornflakes
Fry them in deep fat 390° (page 542).
Or the balls may be placed in a
greased pan and baked until crisp in
a moderate oven 350°. Turn them to
brown evenly. This method seems to
be quite as satisfactory as the more
troublesome first method.
If desired the balls may be topped
before being baked with a dab of:
  Butter
and a little:
  Brown sugar

Method II.
See any rule for:
  Mashed Potato Balls
Substitute for the mashed potatoes:
  Mashed sweet potatoes

SWEET POTATO PUFFS

Baked in mounds or ramekins. Cold mashed sweet potatoes may be used. Prepared this way they taste a little like pumpkin.
Boil by the rule on page 309:

6 medium-sized sweet potatoes

When they are tender peel and rice them. There should be about 2 cupfuls. Peel, rice and add:

1 large ripe banana

Combine these ingredients and beat them into:

1½ tablespoons butter
1 egg yolk
1½ teaspoons salt
⅓ teaspoon paprika
Hot milk or cream: enough to make the potatoes fluffy
(⅛ teaspoon nutmeg)

Beat until stiff:

1 egg white

Fold it lightly into the potato mixture. Drop the batter by the tablespoonfuls, well apart, on a greased tin. Bake the puffs in a hot oven 500° for 12 minutes.

SPICED SWEET POTATO PUFFS

4 Servings

Boil in their jackets:

3 large sweet potatoes

Drain them, peel, mash and beat them with a fork until they are fluffy. Beat in:

2 tablespoons butter
½ teaspoon salt
A grating of nutmeg
¼ teaspoon cinnamon
⅛ teaspoon allspice

Fold in:

1 cup broken nut meats

Shape the mixture into balls. Roll them in:

Flour

Fry them in deep fat at 390° (page 542) until they are light brown.

Sweet Potato, Bacon and Pineapple Slices, page 147.

CARAMEL SWEET POTATOES OR PUDDING

5 Servings

Prepare by the rule on page 310:

4 cups Mashed Sweet Potatoes

Stir and heat in a heavy skillet:

3 tablespoons butter
½ cup brown sugar

When the sugar is dissolved add:

¼ cup walnut or other nut meats

Spread the potatoes in the skillet. Place the skillet in a moderate oven 350° until the potatoes are firm. Invert them on a platter and serve them with the caramel on top; or when the sugar is dissolved combine all the ingredients, put them in a greased baking dish, top it with:

(Marshmallows)

and bake the dish as directed.

SWEET POTATOES AND APPLES

4 Servings

The following is an exceptionally good dish, especially with roast pork, baked ham or a game course. It has more character than the preceding rule for Caramel Sweet Potatoes. Perhaps I prefer it because it is tart or because I always marvel at any cook who voluntarily dwarfs the possibilities of a sweet potato with marshmallows.
Cook covered until nearly done in boiling water to cover:

6 medium-sized sweet potatoes

Peel them and cut them into ½ inch slices. Cook covered until nearly done in a very little boiling water:

1½ to 2 cups thinly sliced apples

If the apples are not tart, sprinkle them with:

Lemon juice

Grease a baking dish and place in it alternate layers of sweet potatoes and apples. Sprinkle the layers with:

½ cup or more brown sugar
A dash cinnamon or grated
lemon rind

Dot them with:

4 tablespoons butter

Pour over them:

½ cup apple water or water

Bake them in a moderate oven 350° for 1 hour.
To make this dish quickly use canned sweet potatoes, mashed, and canned or fresh applesauce, about ⅔ potato to ⅓ apple, or any proportion you like. Season—you may use cinnamon or lemon juice—then bake until well heated, or make this dish on top of the stove.

APPLES FILLED WITH SWEET POTATOES

8 Servings

Prepare by the rule on page 310:

2 cups Mashed Sweet Potatoes

Remove the peeling from the upper half of:

8 large cooking apples

Remove the core and enough of the pulp to leave a shell ¾ inch thick. Chop the pulp and add it to the mashed sweet potatoes. Add:
    6 tablespoons brown sugar
Roll the apples in:
    Melted butter
then in:
    Sugar
Fill them with the sweet potato mixture. Roll them again in butter and in sugar. Bake them in a greased baking dish in a slow oven 300° for 1½ hours or more. Baste them frequently with the apple juice.

Apple Cups Filled with Sweet Potatoes, page 446.

BAKED SWEET POTATOES AND PINEAPPLE
4 Servings
Drain well:
    4 slices canned pineapple
Boil until nearly tender:
    3 large sweet potatoes
Peel them and cut them into slices. Arrange the sweet potatoes and the pineapple in a small greased baking dish making 3 layers of sweet potatoes and 2 of pineapple. Dot each layer generously with:
    Butter
Melt:
    1½ teaspoons butter
Stir in until blended:
    1½ teaspoons flour
Stir in slowly:
    ¼ cup pineapple juice
When the sauce is smooth and boiling pour it over the ingredients in the baking dish. Bake them in a moderate oven 375° for 20 minutes.
To make this dish quickly use canned sweet potatoes mashed and canned crushed pineapple in a fifty-fifty proportion. Season with butter and salt. Bake until well heated or cook this dish on top of the stove.

Sweet Potato Soufflé, page 219.
Do not overlook this treat.

SWEET POTATOES AND ORANGE JUICE
Cook and mash:
    Sweet potatoes
Allow to every cupful of potatoes:
    1¼ tablespoons butter
    1 tablespoon brown sugar

    ½ teaspoon grated orange or lemon rind
    3 tablespoons orange juice
    ½ teaspoon salt
Combine these ingredients and place them in a baking dish. Sprinkle the top with:
    Brown sugar
    Paprika
Cover the dish closely. Bake the potatoes for 30 minutes in a moderate oven 375°. Remove the cover and bake them until they are brown.

SWEET POTATOES IN ORANGE CUPS
6 Servings
Cut into halves:
    3 oranges
Remove the pulp. Discard the white membrane. Cut the pulp into small pieces. Prepare:
    2½ cups Mashed Sweet Potatoes, page 310
Beat into them:
    ¼ cup cream
    ½ teaspoon salt
    1 tablespoon brown sugar
Add the orange pulp. Fill the orange cups with the potato mixture. Place on each one:
    (1 marshmallow or 2 teaspoons brown sugar)
Bake the cups in a moderate oven 350° for 20 minutes.

BOILED RADISHES
Cut root end and partially clip off leaves of:
    Young radishes
You may pare and slice them. In either case cook them covered until tender in a small quantity of:
    Boiling water
Drain them. Dress them with:
    Salt and pepper
    Melted butter or Cream Sauce I, page 428

RUTABAGA
4 Servings
Pare and dice:
    4 medium rutabaga turnips
Drop them into:
    Boiling water
Cook them until tender, about ½ hour. Drain them well. Add:
    ½ teaspoon salt
Serve them with:
    Melted butter

to which you have added generously:
Lemon juice
Chopped parsley
or mash the turnips and add them in
any proportion to mashed potatoes
with lots of:
Chopped parsley

Baked Turnips or Rutabagas, page 322.

BOILED SPINACH
Pick over and cut the roots and tough
stems from:
½ peck spinach: 2 lbs.
When cooked this is from 1⅓ to 1½
cupfuls. Wash it quickly in several
waters until it is free from sand and
soil. If it is young, tender spinach,
lift it from the water with the hands
and place it moist, but without additional water, in a saucepan, cover it
and cook it for 6 minutes, or until it is
tender. Place old spinach in 1 quart
rapidly boiling water. Reduce heat,
cover and simmer until tender, for
about 20 minutes. Discard the water
if it is strong in flavor. Drain the
spinach well. Add:
½ teaspoon salt
Cut up the spinach with 2 sharp knives
or a triple chopper until it is as fine as
you like it. Sauté:
Diced sweet red pepper or
minced onion
in:
Butter or drippings
Add:
Lemon juice
Salt and pepper
Serve it over the spinach.
The wonderful spinach packaged in
cellophane bags need not be washed.
Sprinkle it well with water and cook it
without adding additional water, as
directed above. Frozen spinach may
be substituted for fresh. Cook it for
about 3 minutes.

CREAMED SPINACH
4 Servings
If this unfortunate vegetable—so often
thrust upon resisting children and
grownups—were given a fair chance
by the following rule it might retire
permanently from the comic papers
and the vaudeville stage. Prepare by
the above rule:
Boiled Spinach
When cooked add:
½ teaspoon salt

Chill the spinach. Chop it until it is as
fine as purée, using a board and a
knife, or a chopping bowl and a knife,
or put it through a coarse strainer or
ricer. You may use a blender or a
food mill. I am devoted to mine and
shall reward it someday with an old
age pension. Melt in a skillet which
may be rubbed lightly with a clove of
garlic:
3 tablespoons butter
Add and cook for 1 minute or, if preferred, until brown:
(1 tablespoon or more very finely
chopped onion)
Stir in until blended:
2½ tablespoons flour
Stir in slowly:
1 cup hot cream, top milk, stock
or diluted evaporated milk
When the sauce is smooth and boiling
add the spinach. Stir and cook it for 3
minutes or until it is thoroughly
blended. If the spinach seems too
thick it may be thinned with additional
cream or milk. Season it well with:
Salt and pepper
(Freshly grated nutmeg)
Serve it garnished with slices of:
1 hard-cooked egg
The French recipes call for 1 teaspoonful powdered sugar and the grated rind
of ½ a lemon. These ingredients and
the onion are optional. The flour is
sometimes browned before it is added
to the butter. Evaporated milk is good
in spinach. Stock, cream or milk may
be used in combination.
Remember that young uncooked spinach makes a good salad; that cooked
buttered spinach and grapefruit salad
are an ideal reducer's luncheon; and
that cooked spinach greens are superb
with Hollandaise Sauce, page 429,
with crisp bacon, minced, or with
sautéed mushrooms.

See Blender Spinach, page 897.

SPINACH WITH WHIPPED CREAM
4 Servings
Cook by the rule for Creamed Spinach
on this page:
2 lbs. spinach
Put it through a purée strainer or
blender. Sprinkle it lightly with:
Salt
A fresh grating of nutmeg
Place the spinach in a baking dish.
Dot it with:
Butter

Whip until stiff:
 ½ cup heavy sweet or sour cream
Fold in:
 2 teaspoons prepared horseradish
 ⅛ teaspoon prepared mustard
 ⅛ teaspoon salt
Heap the cream on the spinach. Place it under a hot broiler until the cream is light brown. Serve it at once.

SPINACH WITH TOMATOES
4 Servings
Cook:
 2 lbs. spinach
Drain it. Chop it or put it through a purée strainer or blender. Add to it:
 6 or 8 oz. Italian tomato paste
 or tomato purée
Sauté:
 1 minced clove garlic or 3
 tablespoons minced onion
in:
 4 tablespoons olive oil
You may fish out the garlic. Add the spinach mixture and:
 Salt and paprika

SHREDDED WILTED SPINACH
4 Servings
This is not only good to look at and to eat but economical too, as the spinach is not cooked long enough for it to mat down. Please give it a trial. Cook it until barely tender. Cut with 2 sharp knives into 1 inch shreds about:
 1 lb. raw spinach: 12 oz. cleaned
Melt in a heavy skillet:
 3 tablespoons butter or drippings
 or try out 2 strips minced bacon
Two tablespoonfuls minced onion may be sautéed in the fat. Add the spinach. Cover it and cook it slowly until tender, a matter of a very few minutes. Season it with:
 Salt
 Lemon juice or tarragon vinegar
You may garnish it with:
 A chopped hard-cooked egg

SICILIAN SPINACH
After cooking spinach by the rule for Boiled Spinach, page 313, squeeze the water from it. Add to a skillet and heat:
 1 tablespoon olive oil
 1 minced clove garlic
Sauté the spinach lightly in the oil. Add:
 2 or more chopped anchovies
 Salt, as needed, and pepper

GROUND SPINACH
Cooked in this way spinach seems to retain all its flavor. Wash:
 2 lbs. spinach
Drain it well. Shortly before you are ready to serve the spinach run it through a food chopper with:
 1 small onion
Reserve the juices. Place it in a saucepan with the juices. Cover it and cook it slowly for 3 minutes. Season it with:
 Butter
 Salt and pepper
Or dispense with the cooking and merely heat the spinach. Season and serve it.

SPINACH IN PANCAKES
Prepare by the rule on page 313:
 Creamed Spinach
Prepare:
 French Pancakes, page 551
 (Chopped Sautéed Mushrooms,
 page 292)
Place the spinach and mushrooms on the pancakes. Roll them like a jelly roll. The tops may be sprinkled with:
 Grated cheese
Place the rolls under a broiler until the cheese is melted.

For Eggs in Spinach, Spinach Ring, Spinach Timbales and other Spinach Dishes see Index.

SPINACH AU GRATIN
Place on an oven-proof dish:
 Canned or cooked drained
 spinach or Creamed Spinach,
 page 313
Spread it in a thin layer. Cover it with:
 Grated cheese
Season it with:
 Salt and pepper
 A few grains cayenne
Pour over it:
 2 or 3 tablespoons cream
Broil it until the cheese is melted. You may dot the dish with:
 Sautéed crumbled bacon

CANNED SPINACH WITH
BACON AND ANCHOVIES
4 Servings
Drain the contents of:
 1 No. 2 can spinach
Mince:
 2 slices bacon
Sauté them very lightly. Add:

¼ cup chopped cucumber, peeled
and seeded, or ¼ cup chopped
celery
4 chopped fillets of anchovy

Turn these ingredients until they are coated with fat, then add the spinach and:

2 to 4 tablespoons butter

Stir the spinach until it is thoroughly heated. Season it with:

Salt and pepper

Vegetable Croquettes, page 197.

ACORN SQUASH OR DES MOINES SQUASH BAKED

On her way to a luncheon a friend stopped to market. Later she telephoned home to give her cook the dinner menu. "And," she added, "cook the acorn squash by some rule in the 'Joy of Cooking.'" "Squash?" said the maid. "Them's eggplant." "No," said her mistress, "acorn squash, and cook them by Mrs. Rombauer's directions." After dinner she complimented the maid on the unusual quality of the squash and asked: "By what rule did you prepare them?" The answer was prompt and triumphant: "By Eggplant Steamed and Sautéed."

Cut into halves and remove the seeds from:

Small acorn squashes

Rub them inside and out with:

Butter

Season each half with about:

⅛ teaspoon salt
A sprinkling of paprika
1 teaspoon sherry
(½ teaspoon brown sugar)

Bake them in a moderate oven 375° for 45 minutes, or until done. The tops of the squash may be covered with buttered paper or squash may be baked cut side down in the pan in:

¼ inch boiling water

Acorn squash may be baked whole in a 375° oven until tender, for about 1¾ hours, or boiled whole or cut into halves until tender. Season the halves and top them with bread crumbs and butter or cheese. Reheat them under a broiler. Squash may be baked or broiled until nearly tender, seasoned, cooled, filled with a soufflé mixture and baked in a moderate oven 325° for about 25 minutes.

I have served the squash filled with Tomatoes Creole, page 182, with great success. See page 206 for further suggestions.

BAKED ACORN SQUASH FILLED WITH SPINACH

Prepare the preceding:

Acorn squash

Prepare:

Creamed Spinach, page 313

It is hard to give the amount of spinach as the squash varies so much in size. Fill the hot squash cups with the spinach. Garnish them with:

Slices of hard-cooked egg or
strips of pimiento

The pimiento is a gay touch for Thanksgiving and Christmas dinners.

BAKED ACORN SQUASH FILLED WITH VEGETABLES

Follow the preceding rule. Substitute for the spinach any creamed or buttered vegetable that combines well with squash.

Acorn Squash Cases Filled with Creamed Food, page 206.

SUMMER SQUASH

To test the freshness of a summer squash press your finger nail against it. If it sinks in easily, the squash is fresh.

WHOLE SUMMER SQUASH

Wash:

Small summer squashes

Pare and seed them if you wish. Steam them covered in a strainer over boiling water until they are tender. Serve them with:

(Melted butter or Tomato Sauce,
page 433)

You may add with fine results:

Chopped tarragon, basil, chives
or freshly grated nutmeg

I have steamed medium-sized whole summer squashes, unpared and unseeded, and have served them without seasoning or butter. There are endless ways of preparing this palatable vegetable. Be sure to become familiar with them by looking up:

Summer Squash Cases, page 207; Soufflés in Squash, page 223; Squash Pudding with Bacon or Sausages, page 181; Squash Creole, page 181.

STUFFED SUMMER SQUASH

Method I. 4 Servings

Wash thoroughly, then cut the stem ends from:

4 summer squashes

Steam them by preceding rule. When tender, drain the squashes, cool them. Scoop out the centers leaving a shell about ½ inch thick. Chop the removed pulp. Add to it:

  ¼ teaspoon paprika
  ½ teaspoon Worcestershire
    sauce
  Minced garlic or onion
  ¼ teaspoon salt
  1 tablespoon butter
  ¼ cup grated cheese
  A few grains cayenne
  ⅛ teaspoon curry powder or dry
    mustard

Refill the shells. Place them in a pan in a very little water. Bake them in a hot oven 400° until hot, for about 10 minutes.

Bread crumbs, chopped ham or other cooked meat, mushrooms and ever so many other ingredients may be used in the stuffing.

Method II.

The preceding rule is for cooked squash stuffed and briefly baked. This one calls for uncooked squash, stuffed and baked for a long time. Either is a fine way for dolling up a good vegetable. Wash:

  4 small summer squash

Cut them down the middle either crosswise or horizontally. Scoop out the pulp leaving a ½ inch shell, unless the seeds are tender. Melt:

  2 tablespoons butter

Sauté in it until tender:

  1 or more tablespoons chopped
    onion

Add the squash pulp and:

  1 chopped hard-cooked egg
  ½ cup grated cheese
  ½ teaspoon salt
  ¼ teaspoon paprika
  A dash of nutmeg or cloves

Stir and cook these ingredients until heated. Remove them from the fire. Add:

  1 beaten egg
  ½ cup dry bread crumbs

You may rub the squash shells with:

  Butter or drippings

Fill them with the stuffing. Place them in an oven-proof dish. Cover the bottom with ⅛ inch water or stock. Sprinkle the tops with:

  Bread crumbs

Dot them with:

  Butter

Bake the squash in a moderate oven 350° until tender, about 1 hour.

BAKED SUMMER SQUASH

4 Servings

If summer squash is young, it need not be pared. Prepare by cutting into strips:

  3 cups summer squash

Place it in a greased baking dish. Dot it with:

  2 tablespoons butter

Sprinkle it with:

  1 teaspoon salt
  ¼ teaspoon paprika

Pour over it:

  ¼ cup rich milk
  (1 teaspoon grated onion)

Cover the dish. Bake the squash in a moderate oven 350° for about ½ hour, or until it is tender.

MASHED SUMMER SQUASH

4 Servings

To be good, this squash must be young and tender. Pare and seed if you wish:

  1½ lbs. summer squash

Cut it into small pieces. Cook it in a small amount of:

  Boiling water

Or—and I find this preferable—cook it covered in a strainer over boiling water until it is tender. Drain it very well. Squash is surprisingly watery. Mash it with a fork. Beat it until it is fluffy. Beat in:

  1 tablespoon cream
  1 tablespoon butter
  ⅛ teaspoon pepper
  (1 teaspoon grated onion or
    chopped fresh herb)

Reheat the squash.

SAUTÉED OR FRIED SUMMER SQUASH

Follow the rule for:

  Cucumbers, page 285

TINY SUMMER SQUASH

Wash:

  Tiny summer squash

Steam them until barely tender by the rule on page 315. Drain them well. Place them in a pan barely covered with water. Place on each squash:

  A square of bacon

Bake them in a moderate oven 375° until the bacon is done.

SUMMER SQUASH OR ZUCCHINI SAUTÉED WITH ONIONS

4 Servings

Wash, seed and pare if old:

  2 summer squash

Dice them. There should be about 2 cupfuls. Melt in a saucepan:

 1/4 cup butter

Add and sauté until light brown:

 1 cup minced onion

Add the squash and:

 1/2 teaspoon salt
 1/4 teaspoon freshly ground pepper

Cover the pan and cook the squash until tender, for about 10 minutes, shaking the pan occasionally to keep the squash from sticking. Serve it sprinkled with:

 Paprika and chopped parsley

YELLOW OR SUMMER SQUASH IN SOUR CREAM
4 Servings

Prepare for cooking by paring, removing seeds and cutting into pieces:

 2 lbs. squash, zucchini or cucumbers

If young, the squash and zucchini need not be pared, but pare the cucumbers, young or old.
Steam the squash (page 315) or cook it covered until tender in a small amount of:

 Boiling water

Drain it well. Melt:

 2 tablespoons butter

Sauté in it:

 1/4 cup chopped onions

Turn the squash gently in the fat until well coated. Combine and heat without boiling:

 1 cup sour cream
 3/4 teaspoon salt
 1/4 teaspoon paprika

Add the vegetables. Heat them without boiling. Serve them garnished with:

 Chopped parsley

CROOKED NECK SQUASH

Treat this vegetable as you would summer squash or zucchini. Wash and cut into 1 inch slices:

 Crooked neck squash

Place it in a buttered baking dish. Sprinkle the squash with:

 (Brown sugar and salt)

Dot it with:

 Butter

Bake it in a moderate oven 350° for about 20 minutes, basting it occasionally. Or boil it until tender. Drain it. Serve it covered with Impromptu Sauce, page 328.

See Squash Creole, page 181. Substitute crooked neck squash.

BAKED HUBBARD SQUASH WITH PINEAPPLE OR ORANGE JUICE
6 Servings

Cut into halves and seed:

 1 medium-sized winter squash

Place it in a colander over boiling water. Cover the colander closely and steam the squash until it is nearly tender. Peel it and cut it into slices 1/4 inch thick. Place the squash in layers in a greased baking dish. Sprinkle each layer with:

 Brown sugar and salt
 1/4 cup crushed pineapple

Dot them with:

 Butter

Or combine and stir:

 1/4 cup sugar
 1/2 cup hot orange juice

Add:

 Grated orange rind
 1/4 teaspoon salt

Brush the squash with this mixture. Dot it generously with:

 Butter

Bake the squash in a moderate oven for about 1 hour.

BAKED HUBBARD SQUASH

Cut into 2 inch pieces and remove the seeds and strings from:

 Hubbard or winter squash

Place the pieces in a dripping pan. Sprinkle them with:

 Salt and pepper
 Brown sugar or molasses
 (Lemon juice)

Dot them generously with:

 Butter

Or place on each piece:

 A square bacon or salt pork

Cook the squash covered for 1/2 hour in a moderate oven 375°. Uncover it and cook it until it is tender, for about 1/2 hour longer. Add butter if necessary. Serve the squash in the shell. Hubbard squash may be baked whole. It may also be steamed or boiled.

MASHED HUBBARD SQUASH
Scrub:

 A 3 to 4 lb. Hubbard squash

Place it on a rack in a moderate oven 375°. Bake it until it can be pierced easily with a toothpick. Cut it in halves, remove the seeds. Peel the squash; mash the pulp. To:

 1 cup squash

add:

 1 tablespoon butter
 1 teaspoon brown sugar

¼ teaspoon salt
⅛ teaspoon ginger
Beat this well with enough:
    Cream
to make it a good consistency. Place it in a serving dish. Sprinkle it with:
    Chopped parsley
    Raisins or nut meats or sautéed onions
Mashed squash is good mixed with:
    Sautéed onions
    Sour cream
    A pinch allspice
Heat it in a double boiler. Try this with quick frozen squash for convenience.

GLAZED SQUASH
6 Servings
Pare, remove seeds and cut into 1 inch cubes:
    Hubbard or other winter squash: about 2 lbs.
enough to make 4 cupfuls cubed squash. Place it in a shallow greased casserole which can be closely covered. Combine:
    1 teaspoon salt
    2 or 3 tablespoons brown sugar
    3 tablespoons lemon juice
    (1 teaspoon grated lemon rind)
Pour this mixture over the squash. Dot it with:
    Butter
Cover the casserole. Bake the squash in a hot oven 400° for about 30 minutes, or until it is tender. Remove the cover and continue to bake the squash until it is glazed, for about 10 minutes.

STUFFED SQUASH BLOSSOMS
Do you wonder why so many of your squash blossoms fall off without maturing? These are male blooms and after they close and drop make decorative as well as edible cases for forcemeat (see page 73). Open each flower and put in only enough of the forcemeat to allow the petals to close again. Place stuffed blossoms side by side in a greased baking dish in a moderate oven until thoroughly heated. Serve them alone or as a garnish for a vegetable platter.

FRESH OR CANNED STEWED TOMATOES
4 Servings
Wash and skin (page 457):
    6 large tomatoes
Cut them into quarters and place them in a stewpan over a slow fire for 20 minutes. You may add:
    1 teaspoon minced onion
    ½ cup chopped celery
    2 or 3 cloves
Stir them occasionally to keep them from scorching. Season them with:
    ¾ teaspoon salt
    ¼ teaspoon paprika
    2 teaspoons white or brown sugar
    ⅛ teaspoon curry powder or ¼ teaspoon basil or 1 teaspoon chopped parsley
    1 tablespoon butter
Tomatoes may be thickened with:
    ½ cup bread crumbs
Or, you may substitute for the fresh tomatoes:
    2½ cups canned tomatoes
Add the celery, onions and cloves and cook them for about 10 minutes. If preferred, omit the stewing and bake the tomato mixture in a hot oven 400°, ½ hour for fresh tomatoes, 20 minutes for canned tomatoes.

Creamed Tomatoes, page 182; Tomatoes Creole, page 182; Tomato Pudding, page 179.

STEWED GREEN TOMATOES
4 Servings
Sauté until light brown:
    2 tablespoons minced onion
in:
    2 tablespoons butter
Add:
    2 cups sliced green tomatoes
Stir and cook the tomatoes slowly until they are tender. Season with:
    ¾ teaspoon salt
    ¼ teaspoon paprika
    ½ teaspoon curry powder
Garnish the tomatoes with:
    1 tablespoon chopped parsley

BAKED TOMATOES
4 Servings
Cut deep narrow holes in:
    6 firm tomatoes
Season them—pushing the seasoning into the hollows—with:
    3 tablespoons brown sugar
    1½ teaspoons salt
    2 tablespoons butter
Fill the remaining space with:
    (4 tablespoons Buttered Bread Crumbs, page 326)
Place the tomatoes in a baking dish or in greased muffin tins. Bake them

in a hot oven 400° for about 15 minutes. You may top each tomato with ½ slice of bacon.

Filled Baked Tomatoes, page 199.

BROILED TOMATOES WITH BREAD CRUMBS
Wash:
>Tomatoes

Cut them crosswise into halves and slice a small piece off the tops and the bottoms. Sprinkle the halves with:
>Salt and pepper
>(Brown sugar)

Dip them in:
>Bread crumbs

then in:
>1 egg diluted with 2 tablespoons water

and again in bread crumbs. Place them on a greased pan in a moderate oven 375° until they are nearly soft, then broil them under a moderate flame, turning them once, until they are brown.

BROILED TOMATOES WITH CHEESE
4 Servings
Wash:
>4 large firm tomatoes

Cut them crosswise into ½ inch slices. Season them well with:
>1 teaspoon salt
>¼ teaspoon pepper
>White or brown sugar
>(Celery salt)

Place them in a greased pan and cover them closely with:
>1 cup bread crumbs

Sprinkle the tops with:
>¼ cup grated cheese
>(2 tablespoons or more grated onion)

Dot them with:
>Butter

Broil them for 10 minutes under a moderate flame, or bake them for 15 minutes in a moderate oven 375°.

BROILED TOMATOES WITH OIL AND MUSTARD
4 Servings
Cut a thin slice from the tops and hollow slightly:
>6 firm medium-sized tomatoes

Combine and blend well:
>6 tablespoons oil
>4 tablespoons brown sugar
>1½ teaspoons salt

>2 tablespoons minced onion
>2 teaspoons prepared mustard
>2 teaspoons vinegar

Place 2 teaspoonfuls of this mixture in each hollow. Sprinkle the tops with:
>3 tablespoons crushed crackers or cornflakes

Place a little of the dressing over the crumbs. Place the tomatoes in a shallow pan. Broil them under a moderate flame for about 10 minutes, or until the tomatoes are tender. Baste them 2 or 3 times during the broiling with some of the dressing.

BROILED TOMATOES WITH BROWN SUGAR SAUCE ON TOAST
Wash:
>Tomatoes

Cut them into halves. Season them with:
>Salt and pepper

Cover them with:
>Brown sugar

Dot them generously with:
>Butter

Place them in a greased pan and broil them under a slow flame or bake them in a moderate oven 350° until tender. Pour off the juice. Add to it:
>Cream—⅓ as much as there is stock

Thicken the gravy with:
>Flour—2 tablespoons to 1 cup stock and cream

Cook and stir it until it boils. Place the tomatoes on rounds of:
>Buttered toast

Pour the gravy over them.

SAUTÉED TOMATOES
4 Servings
This recipe is much like the preceding one but it may be useful when broiling or baking is out of the question. Wash:
>6 firm medium-sized tomatoes

Slice them in ¼ inch slices. Season them with:
>1¼ teaspoons salt
>¼ teaspoon pepper
>(Brown sugar)

Rub a skillet with garlic. Melt in it:
>3 tablespoons butter or bacon drippings

Add the tomato slices. Sauté them on both sides. Remove the tomatoes to a hot platter or place them on:
>Rounds of toast

Blend into the butter in the skillet:
>2½ tablespoons flour

Stir in slowly:
  1 cup rich milk
  1 teaspoon chopped fresh basil
  or chopped parsley
When the sauce is smooth and boiling
pour it over the tomatoes.
For a treat serve them on split toasted
squares of corn bread.
The tomatoes may be dipped in fine
dry bread crumbs, corn meal or flour
before sautéing. If you have not used
garlic, add to the butter:
  1 teaspoon grated onion

SAUTÉED GREEN TOMATOES
Follow the preceding rule for:
  Sautéed Tomatoes
Substitute for ripe tomatoes:
  Green tomatoes
It is wise to cover them at first to let
them cook through. You may dip
them before sautéing in corn meal or
prepared pancake flour.

SAUTÉED CANNED TOMATOES
A good emergency dish. Drain the
contents of:
  1 can tomatoes
Reserve the juice for cocktail or sauce.
Roll the tomatoes in:
  Coarse, well-seasoned bread
  crumbs
Permit them to dry for 25 minutes.
Sauté the tomatoes in:
  Butter
Place them on:
  Buttered toast
Add to the crumbs in the pan:
  Cream
Heat the cream but do not let it boil,
then pour the drippings over the to-
matoes.

CANDIED TOMATOES
4 Servings
Skin:
  12 ripe tomatoes
Place them in a baking pan. Sprinkle
them with:
  A few grains white pepper
  2 cups brown sugar
Dot them with:
  ¼ cup butter
Bake them in a hot oven 400° for ½
hour. Place them on top of the stove
over low heat. Let the juice boil down
to a thick sirup. Bake them again for
½ hour in a hot oven 400°. Season
with:
  Salt

CANDIED CANNED TOMATOES
4 Servings
Melt:
  2 tablespoons butter
Sauté in the butter until brown:
  ¼ cup chopped onion
Add:
  1 quart canned tomatoes
  6 tablespoons brown sugar
Cook these ingredients very slowly
using an asbestos mat until the juice
has been absorbed. Place the tomatoes
in a baking dish. Sprinkle them with:
  ¾ teaspoon salt
  2 tablespoons brown sugar
  1½ cups buttered bread crumbs
Bake them in a moderate oven 375°
until the crumbs are brown.

TOMATOES AND CELERY
Prepare:
  Stewed Tomatoes, page 318
Shortly before serving them add:
  1 cup or more finely chopped
  celery
The celery may be added 10 minutes
earlier, but as most people prefer it
crisp, it is better to cook it only long
enough to heat it. This, however, is
a matter of taste.

*Filled Tomatoes with Cheese Sauce,
page 202.*

BAKED TOMATO SLICES WITH PEPPERS AND ONIONS
These make an attractive garnish for
a meat platter. Wash:
  Tomatoes
Cut them crosswise into halves or, if
large, into thick slices. Season them
with:
  Brown sugar
Place them in a greased pan. Cover
the tops closely with:
  Chopped green peppers
  Chopped onions
Season them with:
  Salt and pepper
Place on each slice:
  ½ tablespoon butter
Bake the tomatoes in a moderate oven
350° for about 30 minutes. Place them
on:
  Rounds of toast

GRILLED TOMATOES AND ONIONS
Skin:
  Onions

Cut them crosswise into ⅓ inch slices.
Drop them into:
>Boiling water

Simmer them for 5 minutes, then drain
them. Wash an equal number of:
>Tomatoes

Cut them crosswise in ½ inch slices.
Season the onions with:
>Pepper

Season the tomatoes with:
>Salt and paprika
>Brown sugar

Dot the onions and the tomatoes generously with:
>Butter

Place them in a pan in a moderate
oven 350°. When they are nearly
tender broil them on both sides under
a good flame. Serve them stacked in
alternate layers.

GRILLED TOMATOES, ONIONS AND EGGPLANT

Prepare the preceding:
>Grilled Tomatoes and Onions

Prepare:
>Sautéed Eggplant, page 287

Serve the 3 vegetables stacked in alternate layers.

TOMATOES AND OKRA

4 Servings
Melt:
>2 tablespoons butter or bacon
>drippings

Add and sauté until brown:
>½ cup finely chopped onion

Add and sauté for 5 minutes:
>1 lb. sliced okra

Add:
>2½ cups fresh, skinned or canned
>tomatoes: No. 2 can
>1¼ teaspoons salt
>½ teaspoon paprika
>¼ teaspoon curry powder
>2 teaspoons brown sugar

You may add:
>½ cup corn cut from the cob or
>drained canned corn niblets

Simmer these ingredients covered until the okra is tender. Green peppers
chopped and garlic may be added.
This dish is good au gratin.

CANNED TOMATOES, OKRA AND CORN

Combine and heat in any proportion
desired:
>Canned tomatoes, okra and corn

Rinse the okra with cold water before

adding it. You may sauté in butter
and add:
>Chopped onion

Season these vegetables with:
>Salt and pepper
>Brown sugar
>Butter

You may thicken them with:
>Bread or cracker crumbs

You may add:
>(Thinly sliced cheese)

Cook and stir the dish over a low
flame until the cheese is melted.

TURNIPS

6 Servings
Wash, cut off top and bottom. Slice
the rest in about 4 pieces, then pare:
>2 lbs. white turnips

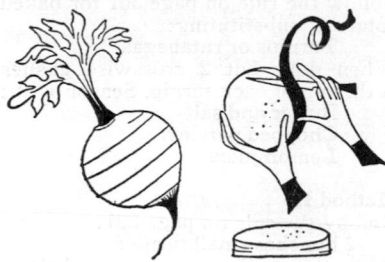

You may prefer to leave the skins on
but the taste is strong and the turnips
are sweeter without it.
Drop them into:
>1 inch boiling water

Cook them covered until they are
tender, from about 9 to 12 minutes.
Season them with:
>¾ teaspoon salt
>1 teaspoon sugar
>¼ teaspoon paprika

and serve them with:
>2 tablespoons melted butter

Or, mash them with a fork, season
them as above, add melted butter and
beat them until they are fluffy. Turnips may be drained and placed in
boiling:
>Cream Sauce I, page 428—½ as
>much sauce as there are turnips

A nice variation is to chop:
>Hot boiled turnips

Add:
>Butter
>Chopped parsley

Season them with:
>Salt and pepper
>Lemon juice or vinegar

TO GLAZE TURNIPS:
Cook as directed above:
>Young turnips

Drain them. Brown them in:
>Hot melted butter

Season them with:
>Paprika and sugar

Dissolve in a little boiling water:
>A beef cube

Pour it over the turnips. Simmer them until they are nearly dry. Serve them at once with:
>Salt if needed
>Chopped parsley

Turnip Cups, page 207.

BAKED TURNIPS OR RUTABAGAS
Method I.
Follow the rule on page 301 for baked potatoes, substituting:
>Turnips or rutabagas

When done cut 2 crosswise gashes in the top of each turnip. Season with:
>Butter and salt
>Chopped parsley
>Lemon juice

Method II.
Boil by the rule on page 321:
>2 bunches small turnips

Drain them. Place them in a shallow baking dish. Spread them with:
>Buttered seasoned bread crumbs

Add:
>½ cup rich milk or sweet or sour cream
>¼ teaspoon paprika
>1 teaspoon grated onion

Bake the turnips in a hot oven 400° until brown. Garnish them with:
>Chopped parsley

MASHED TURNIPS OR SOUFFLÉ TURNIPS
4 Servings
A turnip is not necessarily a depressant. Drain, then mash the contents of:
>1 No. 2 can turnips: about 2½ cups boiled turnips

Melt:
>2 tablespoons butter

Sauté in it until light brown:
>1 tablespoon minced onion

Add the turnips and:
>¾ teaspoon salt
>¾ teaspoon sugar
>¼ teaspoon paprika
>A few grains cayenne

>2 beaten egg yolks or 1 whole egg

Beat the mixture well. Stir and heat the turnips over low heat and serve them piled in a mound garnished with:
>Parsley

If you wish to make the dish a soufflé, use the 2 egg yolks and cool the mixture. Beat until stiff:
>2 egg whites
>⅛ teaspoon salt

Fold them into the turnip mixture. Place the soufflé in a greased baking dish. Bake it in a moderate oven 325° for about 25 minutes.

SCALLOPED TURNIPS
Wash, slice thinly, then pare:
>Turnips

Place them in layers in a baking dish. Dredge them lightly with:
>Flour

Sprinkle them with:
>Salt and freshly ground pepper

Dot them with:
>Butter

Nearly cover them with:
>Milk

Bake the dish in a hot oven 400° until the turnips are tender, for 1 hour or more.

TURNIPS AND ONIONS
Pare and cut into thin slices:
>Turnips
>Onions

Arrange them in layers in a greased baking dish. Sprinkle them lightly with:
>Salt and pepper
>¼ cup stock

Dot them with:
>Butter or grated cheese

Cover the dish closely. Bake the vegetables in a hot oven 400° for about ¾ hour, or until tender.

TURNIPS AND APPLES
4 Servings
Cut into quarters:
>3 large apples

Cook them covered in a little water until they are soft. Put them through a strainer. There should be about 1 cupful of pulp. You may substitute tart applesauce. Cook:
>Turnips

There should be about 3 cupfuls. Mash them if you like. Add:
>Salt and pepper
>2 tablespoons butter

Stir in the apple pulp. Reheat these ingredients and serve them hot.

WATER CRESS
Usually thought of only as salad and sandwich material, water cress not only adds greatly in flavoring soups and vegetables but is good cooked with other greens or by itself. Prepare like Spinach, page 313.

ZUCCHINI
Zucchini are a delectable addition to the vegetable list. Marion's farm neighbor asks: "Want any 'keenies' today?" Scrub, but do not pare:
> Young zucchini

Cut them crosswise in 1 inch slices. Drop them into:
> ½ inch boiling water

Cook them covered until they are tender, sometimes a matter of only a few minutes. Drain them well. Pour over them a little:
> Melted butter or hot olive oil

Zucchini may be dressed with:
> 2 tablespoons melted butter
> ½ teaspoon sugar
> 2 tablespoons lemon juice
> ½ cup sour cream
> 1 tablespoon chopped chives or other herb
> Salt

Zucchini may be boiled by this rule and creamed or they may be served with:
> Tomato Sauce, page 433

SAUTÉED ZUCCHINI
Scrub young:
> Zucchini

Cut them crosswise into thin slices. Heat in a skillet:
> Olive oil or butter

Sauté the zucchini slowly in the oil until they are tender. Turn them frequently. Season them with:
> Salt and pepper
> Sweet basil or marjoram

Garlic or onion may be added to the oil. You may serve the zucchini with:
> Grated cheese or sour cream and chopped parsley or chives or Tomato Sauce, page 433

ZUCCHINI FANS
An attractive way to sauté Zucchini. Allow to each person:
> 1 small zucchini

Parboil them in salted water. Drain and dry them. When cold, slice them lengthwise into ⅓ inch slices to within 1 inch of the stem. Press them gently to spread them like a fan. Sprinkle them with:

> Salt and pepper
> Flour
> Chopped parsley

Sauté them in hot butter or oil until delicately browned on both sides. Place them on a platter. Add lemon juice to the drippings and pour the sauce over them.

Squash or Zucchini Sautéed. See Sautéed Cucumbers, page 285.

FRIED ZUCCHINI
Dip in:
> Batter, page 543

sliced:
> Zucchini

Fry it in oil or in deep fat (page 542). Zucchini is a very good substitute for eggplant in Eggplant Creole, second rule, on page 180.

BAKED YOUNG ZUCCHINI
4 Servings
Scrub well:
> 8 small zucchini

Place them in:
> ½ inch boiling water

Cook them covered for about 5 minutes. Drain them well. Place them in a baking dish. Dot them with:
> Butter

Season them with:
> Paprika
> Grated lemon rind
> Lemon juice
> (Grated onion)

You may place over them:
> Buttered crumbs
> Grated cheese

Bake them in a moderate oven 375° for about ½ hour, or until tender. Good served with:
> Crisp Bacon, page 375

BAKED ZUCCHINI, CROOKED NECK OR SUMMER SQUASH WITH BACON AND CHEESE
4 Servings
Wash well, then cut lengthwise into halves:
> 6 medium-sized zucchini or crooked neck or small summer squash

Scoop out the seeds if you wish. Drop the halves into boiling water to cover. Cook them covered until nearly tender, about 8 minutes for the zucchini, about 10 minutes for the squash. Drain them well. Combine:

¾ cup dry bread crumbs or cracker
crumbs or cornflakes
½ teaspoon salt
¼ teaspoon paprika or freshly
ground black pepper
Roll the halves in this mixture. Place
them on a greased oven-proof dish.
Sprinkle them with:
Finely chopped onion or leeks
Dot each half lightly with:
Butter
Place on each:
A slice bacon
(A sprinkling grated cheese)
Add to the bottom of the dish:
3 tablespoons stock or water
Cook the zucchini in a moderate oven
375° until the bacon is done.

ZUCCHINI CASSEROLE WITH SOUR CREAM
4 Servings
Cut into small pieces:
3 medium-sized zucchini
Simmer them covered until tender, for
about 6-8 minutes, in a small amount
of boiling water. Shake the pan to keep
them from sticking. Drain them well.
Combine:
¼ cup sour or sweet cream
1 tablespoon butter
1 tablespoon grated cheese
½ teaspoon salt
⅛ teaspoon paprika
If sweet cream is used add:
1 tablespoon lemon juice
Stir this mixture over a low flame
until the cheese is melted. Remove it
from the fire. Stir in:
1 beaten egg yolk
1 tablespoon chopped chives
Add the zucchini. Place the mixture
in a baking dish. Cover the top with:
Bread crumbs
Dot the top with:
Butter
Sprinkle it with:
Grated cheese
Brown it in a moderate oven 375° or
under a broiler.

See Index for other Zucchini Dishes.

VEGETABLE PLATTER
An attractive way of serving cooked
vegetables is to place 2 or more varieties on a platter in a decorative manner. For instance, place in the center
of a platter a mound of:
Boiled New Potatoes, page 300,
with drawn butter and chopped
parsley

Place at either end:
Snap Beans and Cheese, page
267, or Snap Beans with Egg
Sauce, page 267
Or place in the center of a platter a
head of:
Cauliflower with Egg Sauce,
page 280
Surround it with a ring of:
Green Peas and chopped parsley
or mint
Surround the peas with a ring of:
Boiled Beets, page 272, or
Harvard Beets, page 273
Or place in the center of a platter:
Browned Potatoes, page 302
Place on one end of the platter:
Baked Onions, page 296
Place at the other end:
Broccoli with Hollandaise
Sauce, page 273
and so on building up, if desired, an
elaborate platter with as many vege-
tables as you wish to serve. Don't
forget:
Tomatoes filled with mashed
potatoes garnished with parsley
flanked by:
Creamed onions garnished with
paprika
and:
Brussels sprouts
Or such delicious looking and tasting
things as:
Red Cabbage in Green Peppers,
page 173
Tomatoes Filled with Pineapple,
page 201
Small whole Boiled Carrots,
page 278
placed on the ends of a platter in
bunches with imitation tops of:
Bunches of parsley
Or:
Turnip cups filled with Green
Peas, page 207, etc.
Rice ring or noodle ring filled
with a creamed vegetable and
surrounded by a buttered vegetable

VEGETABLE FRITTERS
Delicious fritters may be made with
most cooked vegetables—cauliflower,
broccoli, squash, celery, young parsnips, etc. In some instances the vegetables may be raw, as with tomatoes
and whole scrubbed mushrooms which,
if small, may be used attached to their
stems. Dip the vegetables in the following batter. Cook them in deep hot
fat at 365° as directed on page 542.

FRITTER BATTER FOR VEGETABLES
Combine:
>   1 cup sifted all-purpose flour
>   1 teaspoon any baking powder
>   ¼ teaspoon salt

Beat, then stir in with a few swift strokes:
>   ½ cup milk
>   2 eggs

A more delicate texture is achieved if the eggs are separated and whites beaten and folded in the last minute. If a thin batter is desired, use only ⅔ cupful flour.

EGGPLANT FRITTERS
6 Servings
Try these for a treat. Pare and slice:
>   A small-sized eggplant

Cook it until it is tender in:
>   Boiling water to cover

Add:
>   1 teaspoon vinegar

Drain the eggplant. Mash it. Beat in:
>   1 egg
>   ½ teaspoon salt
>   3 tablespoons flour
>   ½ teaspoon any baking powder

Drop the batter from a spoon into hot fat, page 542. Serve the fritters with a meat course.

MUSHROOM FRITTERS
6 Servings
Combine:
>   1 cup sifted all-purpose flour
>   1 teaspoon any baking powder
>   ¾ teaspoon salt
>   ⅛ teaspoon paprika

Combine and beat:
>   2 egg yolks
>   2 tablespoons milk

Add:
>   ¾ cup cooked minced mushrooms
>   1 tablespoon melted butter

Beat until stiff, then fold in:
>   2 egg whites

Drop the batter from a spoon into hot fat (page 542). Cook the fritters for about 3 minutes.

Corn Fritters, page 184.

TOMATO FRITTERS
6 Servings
Chill:
>   6 firm medium-sized tomatoes

Combine:
>   1 cup sifted all-purpose flour
>   2 teaspoons any baking powder

>   ¼ teaspoon salt

Combine and beat:
>   1 egg
>   ½ cup milk
>   1 tablespoon melted butter

Stir the liquid into the dry ingredients with a few swift strokes. You may peel the tomatoes, then cut them into thick slices. Dip them in the batter. Fry them in hot fat (page 542) until browned or sauté them in ½ inch of hot fat.

CARROT, PARSNIP, BUTTER BEAN, ETC., FRITTERS
3 Servings
Beat until light:
>   1 egg

Add and beat well:
>   1 cup mashed or puréed carrots, etc.

Stir in:
>   ¼ teaspoon salt
>   1½ tablespoons melted butter
>   1½ tablespoons flour
>   6 tablespoons milk
>   1 teaspoon Worcestershire sauce or 2½ teaspoons onion juice
>   ½ teaspoon dried Herb, page 833, or 2 tablespoons chopped parsley

Spread these ingredients on a greased platter. When they are cold shape them into balls. You may roll the balls in:
>   1 egg diluted with
>   2 tablespoons water

then in:
>   Sifted bread crumbs

and again in the egg mixture. Fry the balls in deep fat (page 542) heated to 390° or sauté them in butter.

Onion Griddle Cakes, page 548; Corn Oysters, page 185.

SPINACH AND CHEESE BALLS
Measure by packing closely:
>   1 cup cooked, well-drained spinach

Put it through a purée strainer or chop until it is fine. Stir in:
>   2 beaten eggs
>   1½ cups fine dry bread crumbs
>   1 tablespoon grated onion
>   ½ cup grated cheese
>   1 teaspoon salt
>   1 tablespoon lemon juice

Shape this mixture into 1½ inch balls. Fry them in deep fat (page 542) heated to 375° until they are brown and crisp.

Drain them on absorbent paper. Serve them with:

Tomato Sauce, page 433

Spoonfuls of this mixture may be sautéed in hot butter. Good with Hollandaise Sauce, page 429. The balls may be rolled in 1 egg beaten with 2 tablespoonfuls water, in sifted seasoned bread crumbs and again in the egg mixture before being fried or sautéed. Permit the crumbs to dry for 20 minutes before frying.

SAUTÉED VEGETABLES IN EGG AND CRUMBS

While not strictly a fritter, the effect of vegetables cooked in this way is much the same and the method simpler. Follow the rule on page 292 for:

Fried Mushrooms

Substitute:

Parboiled cauliflower, broccoli, okra, celery, etc., raw mushrooms, cucumbers, summer squash or zucchini

Dressings for Vegetables

Drain cooked vegetables. Be careful not to overcook them. I like my vegetables with enough spirit left to fight back, also with their individual flavors intact.

Use a little imagination in dressings. The great favorite is melted butter. To this you may add lemon juice, grated onion, garlic, celery salt, freshly grated nutmeg, grated lemon or orange rind, paprika, salt, chives, parsley or other herbs (page 833), curry powder, mustard, Worcestershire or chili sauce, grated cheese, horseradish, etc.

Cooked vegetables are fine dressed in brown butter—butter that is cooked until it is dark, to which vinegar or lemon juice is then added. Grated onion may be sautéed in butter, or chopped parsley or other herb may be added just before serving.

Next in popularity come buttered crumbs (see below).

Then comes the creamed vegetable. Prepare Cream Sauce I, page 428. You may use milk or part cream and part vegetable stock or meat stock. You may remove the sauce from the heat and beat an egg yolk into it, return it to the heat, stir and cook it gently until it has thickened slightly and pour it over a vegetable. This sauce is good flavored with lemon juice. It is particularly good over asparagus and snap beans. See Allemande and Béchamel Sauce, page 429. If you wish to cream a watery vegetable—cauliflower, cabbage, etc.—drain it well and add it to boiling cream sauce, or pour very hot cream sauce over it. If you do not take this precaution the sauce may become thin.

Cooked vegetables are frequently served with a bread crumb top crust—au gratin. Spread dry bread crumbs over a cooked or creamed vegetable. Dot the top with butter. You may sprinkle it with grated cheese. Place the vegetable in a hot oven 400° or under a broiler until the cheese is melted. You will find a variety of dressings given under the recipes for vegetables. The chapter on Sauces for Meat and Fish also contains a number of suggestions that may be useful to you. Here are several others I hope you will try.

BUTTERED CRUMBS

Sauté:

1 cup bread crumbs

in:

⅓ cup hot butter or bacon drippings

You may add a choice of:

Chopped minced bacon
Minced onions
Chopped parsley
Chopped nut meats
Curry powder
Paprika
Grated cheese

NOODLE TOPPING FOR VEGETABLES

Crush:

¼ cup noodles

Stir them into:

½ cup melted butter

Stir them about over heat until they are brown. Pour the topping over cooked vegetables or noodles.

Croutons, page 422. These are a pleasant addition to the following Drawn or Black Butter.

DRAWN BUTTER FOR VEGETABLES
4 Servings
Combine:
    4 tablespoons melted butter
    4 tablespoons minced parsley,
    chives or mint
    (1 tablespoon lemon juice or 1
    teaspoon Worcestershire sauce)

BROWN OR BLACK BUTTER
4 Servings
Melt:
    4 tablespoons butter
You may add to it:
    (2 teaspoons grated onion,
    chopped chives or ½ teaspoon
    minced garlic)
Cook the butter until it is brown. Add:
    1 tablespoon lemon juice or
    vinegar
    Salt as needed
    (Blanched shredded almonds)

BROWNED ONION BUTTER
4 Servings
Melt:
    4 tablespoons butter
Stir and sauté in it until brown:
    1 tablespoon minced onion
Add:
    Salt and paprika

HERB BUTTER FOR VEGETABLES
4 Servings
Melt:
    4 tablespoons butter
Add:
    1 teaspoon dried or 1 tablespoon
    chopped fresh Herbs, page 833

EGG DRESSING FOR VEGETABLES
4 Servings
Combine, then stir and cook in a double boiler until thickened:
    ¼ teaspoon dry mustard
    ¾ teaspoon salt
    1 teaspoon sugar
    ¼ teaspoon paprika
    1 beaten egg
    ¼ cup mild vinegar or lemon juice
    2 tablespoons olive oil
Add:
    1 tablespoon melted butter
    ¼ teaspoon curry powder
    ½ teaspoon grated onion
Good over cabbage, cauliflower, snap beans, etc.

GREEN ONION SAUCE FOR VEGETABLES
12 Servings
Beat until fluffy:
    ½ cup soft butter
Add gradually:
    2 tablespoons lemon juice
Season with:
    Salt and paprika
    3 tablespoons minced green onions
    1 tablespoon minced parsley
Serve this sauce hot or cold on carrots, peas, beans, cauliflower, etc.

SOUR-SWEET HORSERADISH SAUCE FOR BEETS OR CABBAGE
4 Servings
Combine and stir:
    ¼ cup horseradish
    ¼ cup vinegar
    1 teaspoon salt
    1 tablespoon sugar

DEVILED SAUCE
4 Servings
Combine and stir:
    ⅓ cup vinegar
    ⅓ cup melted butter
    1 tablespoon powdered sugar
    1 teaspoon Worcestershire sauce
    ½ teaspoon salt
    ½ teaspoon paprika
    ½ teaspoon dry mustard

SOUR CREAM HORSERADISH DRESSING
A fine change from the well-liked but often monotonous butter or cream sauce. Combine and stir:
    1 cup sour cream
    ½ teaspoon prepared mustard
    ½ teaspoon horseradish
    ¼ teaspoon salt

SOUR-SWEET CREAM DRESSING
For snap beans, cabbage, etc. Combine and stir over very low heat until the sauce thickens slightly:
    1 beaten egg
    ½ cup sour cream
    2 tablespoons sugar
    ¼ cup vinegar
    ½ teaspoon salt
    ¼ teaspoon paprika
Serve it hot over hot vegetables or cold over chilled vegetables.

Egg Sauce I, page 281.

SWEET SOUR SAUCE

Usually served over snap beans or lentils, dried bean or pea purée. Melt:
  2 tablespoons butter
Stir in:
  2 tablespoons flour
Add gradually:
  1 cup Vegetable or Meat Stock, page 43
Stir until the sauce is boiling. Add:
  2 tablespoons vinegar or lemon juice
  2 tablespoons sugar
  Salt as needed
  ¼ teaspoon paprika

SAUCE FOR CANNED OR BOILED VEGETABLES

Drain the vegetables. Permit the stock or juice to boil until it is reduced by ½. Add to it:
  Melted butter
  Seasonings

MARINATED VEGETABLES

Drain cooked vegetables. Reserve the juices. See Stock for Sauces, page 425. Pour over the vegetables:
  French dressing
Permit them to stand in a cold place for 1 hour or more.

CANNED SOUP SAUCES

Canned condensed soup makes a good emergency sauce. See page 441.

IMPROMPTU VEGETABLE SAUCE

This is my favorite quick mix for squash, zucchini, snap beans, etc.— but I do not use it too frequently. While the vegetable is cooking melt:
  2 tablespoons butter
Sauté in it briefly:
  1 teaspoon or more grated onion
Blend in:
  2 tablespoons flour
Drain the cooked vegetable. Measure the vegetable liquid. Stir it into the sauce. Boil it. Add, to make 1 cupful liquid in all:
  Cream or top milk

Add seasoning:
  Salt and freshly ground pepper
  A pinch curry powder
  1 teaspoon catsup
Do not boil the sauce again. Pour it over the drained vegetable. Of course chopped parsley always helps things along.

HOT SOUR CREAM SAUCE FOR VEGETABLES

1 Cupful

Delicious over broccoli, cabbage, etc. A little more delicate than the following rule. Blend in the top of a double boiler:
  1 tablespoon butter
  1 tablespoon flour
Stir in:
  1 cup sour cream
  ¼ teaspoon salt
Heat these ingredients over a low fire, stirring constantly until thickened. Cover them and place them over, not in, hot water for 5 minutes. If you wish, add:
  1 or 2 tablespoons chopped parsley, chives or peppers

SOUR CREAM HERB SAUCE FOR VEGETABLES

1½ Cupfuls

Melt over low heat:
  2½ tablespoons butter
You may cook briefly in this:
  1 teaspoon grated onion
Add and blend in:
  2½ tablespoons all-purpose flour
Stir in slowly:
  ½ cup milk
Cook and stir the sauce with a wire whisk until it is smooth and boiling. Cool the sauce slightly. Stir in, heat but do not boil:
  1 cup sour cream or 1 cup cream and 1 tablespoon lemon juice
  ½ teaspoon salt
  ⅛ teaspoon paprika
  1 teaspoon or more chopped chives if onion was not used above
  1 teaspoon or more chopped parsley, or 1 teaspoon dried herb
  (A pinch curry powder)

Meat

When a novice approaches a meat counter with a slim purse and an even slimmer knowledge of meat values she may well reach a state of panic. What does one do with all those strange cuts that aren't T-bones? Will a hesitant request reveal her ignorance? Does it take hours and a complicated sauce to serve the brisket the woman next to her had just ordered so authoritatively?

These and other unsolved problems confuse her and check any adventurous impulses she might have toward the unknown. It is hoped that a study of the following meat charts with correspondingly numbered groups of recipes will give her the practical information she lacks until experience has taught her that the meat counter is not a matter of unsolved "who-done-its" but an easily recognized source of supply which she can put to excellent use.

All grades of meat in interstate commerce are government-inspected for sanitary conditions. They are officially labeled for quality by 7 stamps. *Prime* meats are pen-fattened steers and represent a very limited percentage of the total. *Choice* is the affluent buyers' pick. *Good* and *Commercial* are as nutritious as the first 2 but not so tender. *Utility, Cutter* and *Canner* are almost devoid of fat within the tissues. They lend themselves to sausage, potted meats and chili.

While better cuts have the advantage of tenderness, juiciness and fat-marbling, intelligent cooking can give equal nourishment and sometimes better flavors to lower grades at a lower cost.

Meats from muscles that are frequently moved have much connective tissue, little fat, and they increase in flavor with the age of the animal. They are not to be scorned.

Meats from muscles that are least exercised are tender, delicate in flavor, and have the most juice and fat content when the animal is mature but not old. Young meat from these less-used muscles is often lean, so read the sections on veal and spring lamb for their special handling.

Raw meats are tender if they have little connective tissue, tough if they have much. In tough cuts this connective tissue may be broken down by grinding, pounding or slow internal heating, see chart, page 336. If high internal heat is used it forces the connective tissues to break down too rapidly, and the shrinking of protein and loss of juices results. The meat becomes stringy, dry and tough.

Tender cuts are best cooked by dry heat, such as roasting, sautéing, broiling and pan-broiling.

Tough cuts are best approached with moist but slow heat. So-called "boiling," a misleading term as any such violent temperature ruins meat, stewing, fricasseeing, braising or pot-roasting are preferable procedures. The temperature of the liquid should never go over 185°, or the simmering point.

Innards, variety or glandular meats like liver, sweetbreads, brains, kidneys, tripe and the muscle meats like heart and tongue are all extremely valuable nutritively as well as great delicacies when properly presented, so look into their possibilities when ideas on the usual cuts run low. Many families are prejudiced against their use, a frame of mind that can be broken down gradually by serving them in combinations, like liver in wine, creole kidney stew, etc.

Bones are not without their advantages for flavor and especially for calcium, which can be extracted to advantage in recipes calling for vinegar or wine soaking and cooking.

On tougher cuts a marinade, page 340, also helps with tenderizing the meat, and when the cut contains bone is valuable in extracting the calcium.

MATCH CHART AGAINST PAGE NUMBERS—SEE INDEX

LAMB

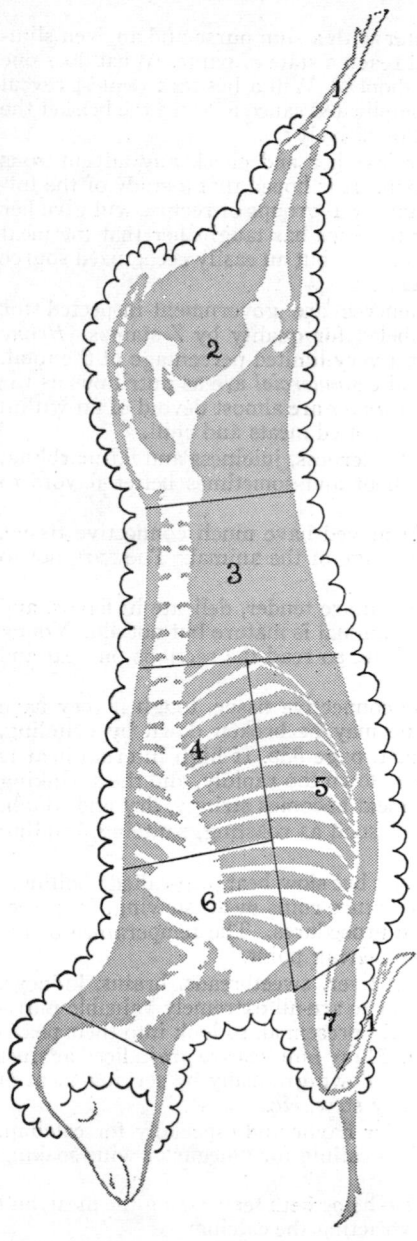

1. Scotch Broth, page 49; Braised Lamb Shanks, page 363; Lamb and Eggplant Casserole, page 166.

2. Leg of Lamb, page 360; Leg of Mutton with Caper Sauce, page 364; Mock Venison, page 362; Lamb Terrapin, page 166.

3. Loin Lamb Chops Broiled, Pan-Broiled and Stuffed, page 362; Creole, page 363.

4. Rib Lamb Chops Broiled, etc. (see 3); Chop Grill, page 166; Crown Roast of Lamb, page 361.

5. Lamb Stew, page 363.

6. Cushion Shoulder of Lamb, Braised Stuffed Shoulder and Braised Roast, page 361; Kabobs, page 364; Broiled Lamb with Onions on Skewers, page 194.

7. Mock Duck II, page 362; Kabobs, page 364; Lamb Terrapin, page 166.

8. Lamb Kidneys in Wine Sauce, page 379; Sautéed Kidneys, page 379; Steak and Kidney Pie, page 160; Turkish Eggplant, page 179; Kidney Patties, page 380.

9. Liver, Pepper, Onions and Olives on Skewers, page 194. See Index for other liver recipes.

10. Sweetbread Croquettes, page 195; Oysters and Sweetbreads, page 194.

11. Tongue and Tongue in Creole Sauce, page 385.

12. Baked Heart and Braised Heart Slices in Sour Sauce, page 381.

13. Boiled Brain Croquettes, page 196.

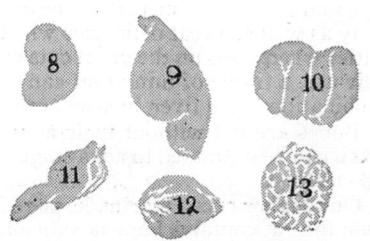

YOU PAY FOR BONES, SO UTILIZE THEIR VALUES

PORK

1. Sausage and Sausage combinations, see Index; Pork Hocks and Sauerkraut, page 369; Stewed Pork Hocks, page 370; Stewed Pigs' Feet, page 369; Jellied and Broiled Pigs' Feet, page 141.

2. Ham and Ham combinations, see Index; Fresh Ham, page 365; Ham Steaks, page 373; Baked Ham with Barbecue Sauce, page 371.

3. Roast Pork, page 365; Pork Tenderloin and Pork Tenderloin Frenched, page 366; Canadian Bacon baked or boiled, page 374; Pork Chops Breaded, page 367; also see Pork Chop recipes under 4 below.

4. Crown Roast of Pork, page 365; Pork Chops and Pineapple, Deviled, Creole and Sour Cream, page 367; Stuffed, page 368.

5. Bacon, page 375; Salt Pork and Milk Gravy, page 375.

6. Baked Spareribs with Dressing, with Sauerkraut, page 368; Barbecued, Boiled, page 369.

7. Stewed Neckbones, page 370; Rolled Shoulder, page 365; Scrapple, page 147; Pork Roast with Sauerkraut, page 366; Pork Birds, page 368; Cottage Roll, page 373.

8. Ham Butt, Shank or Picnic Ham, page 373.

9. Kidneys, page 379; Kidney Patties, page 380.

10. Brains, page 378; Baked Brains, Tomatoes and Egg, page 379.

11. Heart, page 381.

12. Liver Patties, page 384.

13. Tongue, page 385.

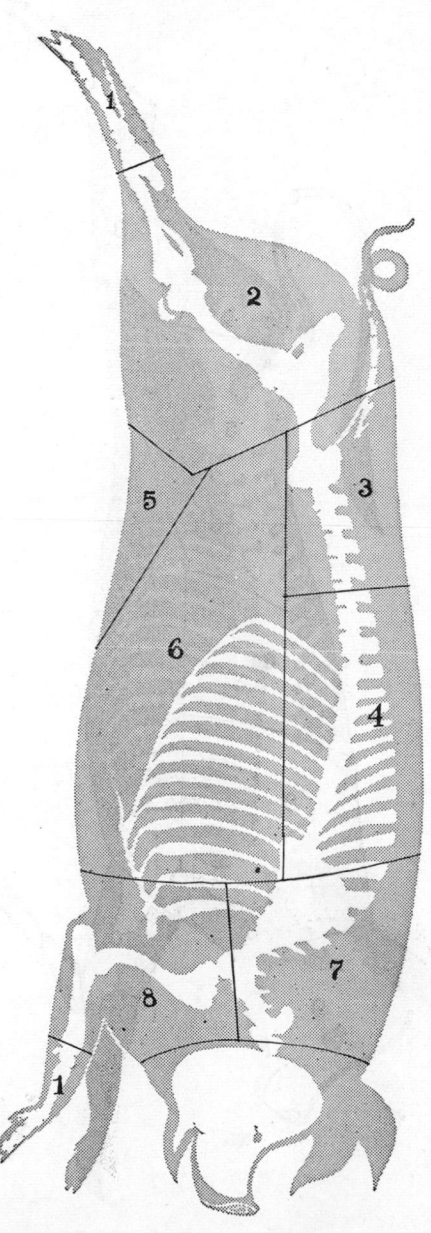

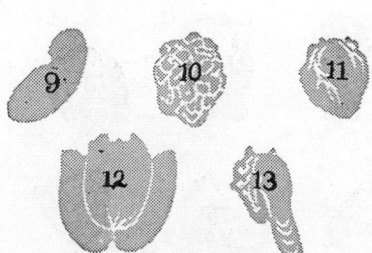

MATCH CHART AGAINST PAGE NUMBERS—SEE INDEX

VEAL

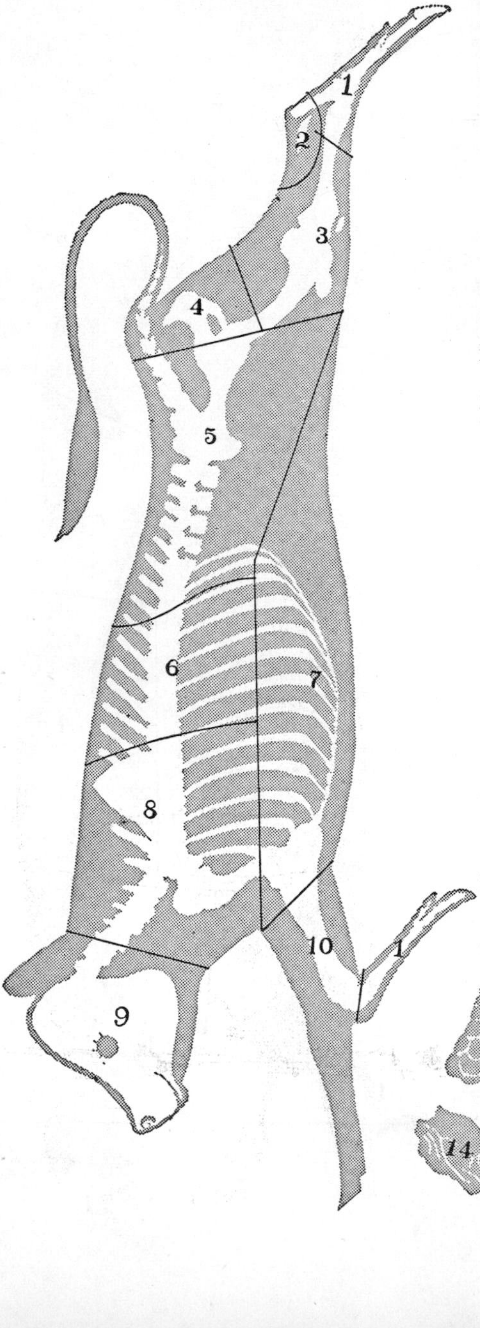

1. Veal Soup Stock, page 43; Stew, page 357; Veal Loaf, page 359; Veal Croquettes, page 195.

2. Veal Baked in Sour Cream, page 357; Veal Stew with Red Wine, page 358; Veal Soufflé, page 360; Veal and Pork Pie, page 160; Curried Veal and Rice, page 166.

3. Veal Cutlet, page 356; Veal Steak or Wiener Schnitzel, page 356; Breaded Veal Slices, page 357; Scallopini, page 357; Veal Birds, page 359; Veal in Batter, page 359.

4. Veal Baked in Sour Cream, page 357; Veal Pot Roast, page 356.

5. Veal Kidney Roast, page 356.

6. Veal Paprika, page 359; Mexican Veal Steak, page 165.

7. Stuffed Veal Breast, page 356.

8. Veal Shoulder Stuffed, page 356; Elaborate Veal Stew, page 358; Veal Slices on Skewers, page 195.

9. Calf's Head, page 386; Head Cheese, page 387.

10. Veal Loaf, page 359; Veal Chop Suey, page 142; Creamed Veal, page 143; Veal Timbales, page 214; City Chicken, page 194.

11. Sautéed Kidney, page 141. Also see Index.

12. Calf Liver Cooked in Wine, Italian Liver and Swiss Liver, page 382; Liver Dumplings, page 384.

13. Brains in Blankets, page 378. Also see Index.

14. Veal Tongue in Creole Sauce, page 385; Calf Tongues Baked, page 386; Calf Tongues in Raisin Sauce, page 164.

15. Ragout Fin, page 174; Tomatoes Filled with Creamed Sweetbreads, page 201; Sweetbread Croquettes, page 195. Also see Index.

16. Braised Heart Slices in Sour Sauce, page 381.

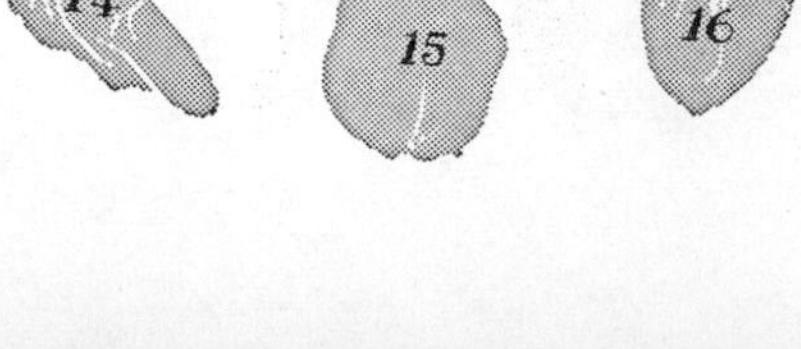

YOU PAY FOR BONES, SO UTILIZE THEIR VALUES

1. Oxtail Soup, page 45; and Oxtail Soup and Stew, page 879; Braised Oxtails, page 386.

2. Pot au Feu, page 45; Stew, page 350; Hamburgers, pages 352-3 and see Index; Meat Loaf, page 354; Meat Loaf in Pastry, page 158; Stuffed Cabbage, page 171; Ground Beef in Cabbage Leaves, page 173; Italian Meat Balls, page 163.

3. Gaston Stew, page 349; Nutburgers, page 168; Hamburgers, pages 352-3 and see Index.

4. Pot Roast, page 343; Round Steak with Onions, pages 347-8; Beef Kabobs, page 348; Scraped Beef, page 353; Beef à la Lindstrom, page 354; Spanish Casserole, page 167.

5. Corned Beef, page 351.

6. Hip Bone Steak, page 345.

7. Steak Broiled and other steaks, pages 345-6.

8. Beef Rolls, page 348; Flank Steak with Dressing, page 348; Mock Duck I, page 349.

9. Anna's Short Ribs, page 344.

10. Roast Beef, page 342; Beef Fillet, page 342; Beef Stroganoff, page 347; Sukiyaki, page 164; Cold and Reheated Roast Beef, page 154.

11. Beef Brisket with Sauerkraut, page 344; Boiled Beef, page 351; Corned Beef, page 351.

12. Pot Roasts, page 343; Spiced Beef, page 343; Beef à la Mode, page 344; Sauerbraten, page 344; Stew, page 350.

BEEF

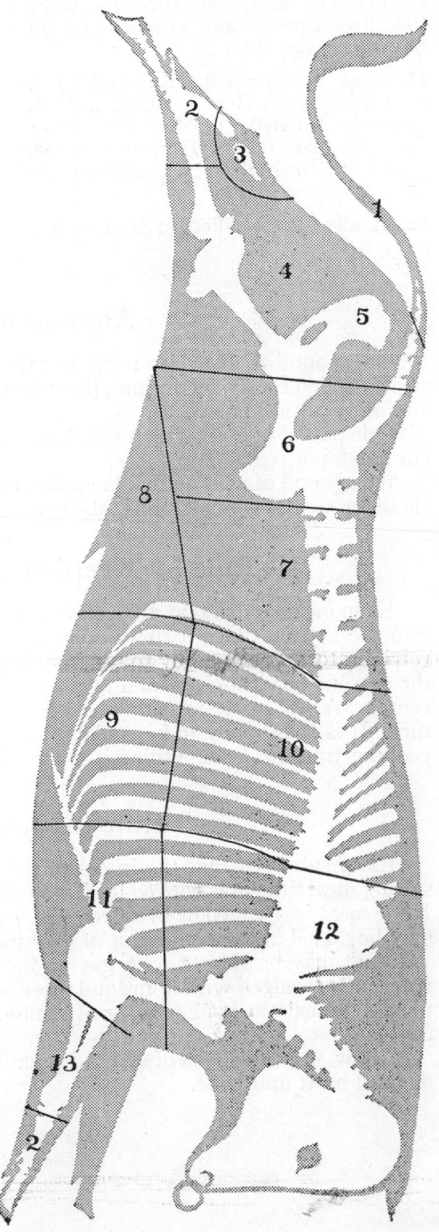

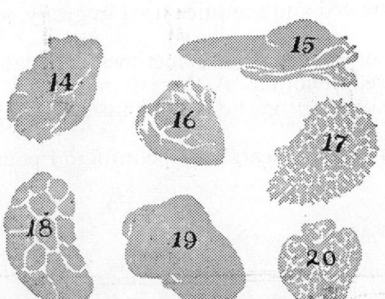

13. Braised Beef with Vegetables, page 345; Gaston Stew, page 349; Meat Loaf, page 354; Hamburger, see Index; Chili Con Carne, page 167; Koenigsberger Klops, page 163.

14. Oysters and Sweetbreads, page 194; Sweetbreads and Mushrooms on Skewers, page 194.

15. Beef Tongue with Raisin Sauce, page 164; Fresh Beef Tongue, Boiled, Corned, Pickled, or Smoked Beef Tongue, page 385; Tongue Creole, page 385; Braised Beef Tongue, page 386.

16. Braised Heart Slices in Sour Sauce, page 381.

17. Pepperpot, page 46; Tripe Stewed and Spanish, page 387; Tripe Fried, Piquant and Broiled, page 388.

18. Broiled Beef Kidney, page 141; Beef Kidneys and Broiled Beef Kidneys, page 380; Kidney Stew and Kidney Creole, page 380.

19. Liver, page 381; Braised Liver with Vegetables, page 383; Beef Liver Creole, page 383; Liver Loaf and Patties, page 384.

20. Boiled Brain Croquettes, page 196; Broiled, Fried, Sautéed or Steamed Brains, page 378.

Amount to Purchase

One pound of boneless meat equals 4 servings. Boned meats include: flank steaks, rolled roasts, tenderloin, liver, heart, kidneys, sausages, brains, sweetbreads, and most canned meats.

One pound of meat with a small amount of bone equals 3 servings: round steak, rib roast, pot roast, ham slices.

One pound of meat with a large amount of bone equals 2 servings: most steaks, shoulder steaks, shoulder cuts, short ribs, neck chops, breast, plate, brisket.

Rule for Keeping and Preparing Meat

Keep meat cold and at an even temperature. Unwrap it as soon as it is brought into the house. Place it in an open dish, loosely covered with wax paper, in the refrigerator. When ready to use, dry it with a cloth. Trim off the hard edges and the surplus fat. Store ground meat flattened in pans so the cold can penetrate the center. When ready to use meat permit it to stand until it is at room temperature. It is then ready to be cooked. Meat for stewing may be tenderized and the cooking time cut by one third if it is soaked overnight in vinegar.

Rule for Seasoning Meat

Early salting brings the juices to the surface of the meat and into the pan. By salting meat after it is cooked its food values and naturally salty juices are retained. If the meat is dredged or breaded or if it is stewed and the juice used in gravy, salt may be added at the beginning of cooking.

Meat may be rubbed with garlic, herbs or spices. It is sometimes marinated, frequently dredged with flour, and often seared in hot fat. A clove of garlic may be tucked in near the bone of a leg of lamb or slivers of garlic may be inserted under the skin.

Allow ¾ teaspoonful of salt to 1 pound of ground meat, 1 teaspoonful to 1 pound of solid meat and bone.

The Modern Way of Roasting Meat by Low Heat

This economical method for roasting meat and fowl is generally followed today. If you doubt the economy, look at the evidence in the accompanying illustration.

As there are a few people who fail to advance with the times or who, being otherwise progressive, hanker nostalgically for the roasts that Mother used to make, a chart for roasting by the old-fashioned method is appended.

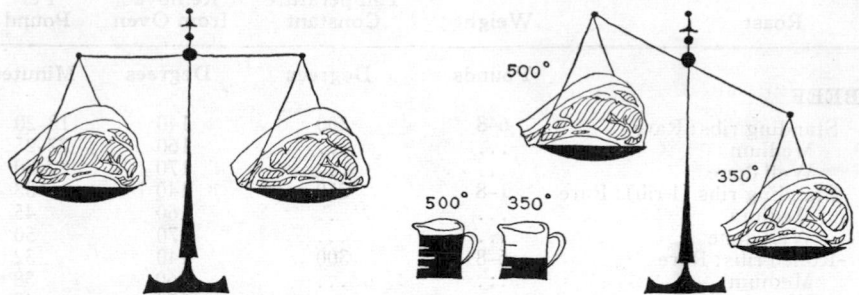

To prepare a roast for cooking by the modern method, take it from the refrigerator at least ½ hour before roasting it.

Place the meat in a pan on a rack, unless the bones form a rack, fat side up, in a preheated oven. See the following chart. Do not increase or decrease the heat at any time. It is not necessary to add liquid. Do not cover or baste the meat. To cook meat uniformly turn boneless and large roasts at least once while cooking. Make gravy with the pan drippings and vegetable stock, page 426.

Time for Roasting Meat by the Modern Method

It is impossible to give an absolutely accurate timetable for roasting meat, as too many factors are involved, such as the lean and the fat, the shape, the size and the quality of the roast. Lean meat cooks more rapidly than fat meat. The degree of aging also affects the time of cooking.

A meat thermometer is essential for absolute accuracy. Insert the bulb of the thermometer in the center of the lean part of the meat before you place it in the oven. Be sure that it does not rest upon either fat or bone. Make a gash in the meat with a pointed knife or a skewer in order to facilitate the insertion of the thermometer. Keep the top as far away from the source of heat as possible.

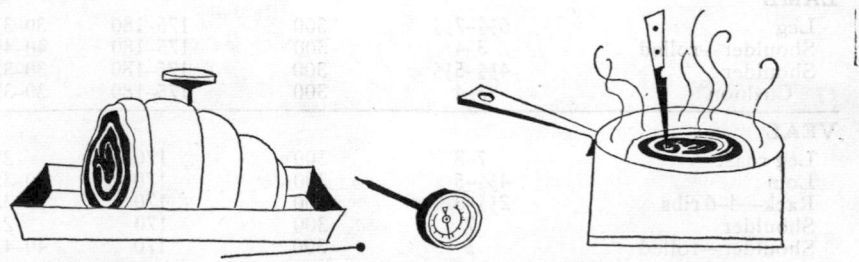

If you have no meat thermometer, a good way to test for doneness is to prick the meat with a skewer. If the juice runs red, it is rare; pink, medium rare; colorless, done and except in the case of pork and fowl, overdone. Cut boiled meat with a sharp knife close to the bone to test for doneness.

Timetable for Roasting Fresh or Defrosted Meats

(Courtesy National Livestock and Meat Board, Chicago, Ill.)

Roast	Weight	Oven Temperature Constant	Interior Temperature when Removed from Oven	Approximate Time Per Pound
	Pounds	Degrees	Degrees	Minutes
BEEF				
Standing ribs: Rare	6–8	300	140	18–20
Medium	...	...	160	22–25
Well done	...	...	170	27–30
Standing ribs (1 rib): Rare	1–8	350	140	33
Medium	...	...	160	45
Well done	...	...	170	50
Rolled ribs: Rare	6–8	300	140	32
Medium	...	...	160	38
Well done	...	...	170	48
Rump (high quality)	5–7	300	150–170	25–30
PORK—Fresh				
Loin: Center	3–4	350	185	35–40
Whole	12–15	350	185	15–20
Ends	3–4	350	185	45–50
Shoulder: Whole	12–14	350	185	30–35
Boned and rolled	4–6	350	185	40–45
Cushion	4–6	350	185	35–40
Pork butt	4–6	350	185	45–50
Fresh ham	10–12	350	185	30–35
PORK—Smoked				
Ham: Whole	10–12	300	170	25
Tendered	10–12	300	160	15
Half	6	300	170	30
Tendered	6	300	160	20
Shank end	3	300	170	40
Butt end	3	300	170	45
Cottage butt	2–4	300	170	35
Picnic	3–10	300	170	35
LAMB				
Leg	6½–7½	300	175–180	30–35
Shoulder—rolled	3–4	300	175–180	40–45
Shoulder	4½–5½	300	175–180	30–35
Cushion	3–4	300	175–180	30–35
VEAL				
Leg roast	7–8	300	170	25
Loin	4½–5	300	170	30–35
Rack—4–6 ribs	2½–3	300	170	30–35
Shoulder	7	300	170	25
Shoulder—rolled	5	300	170	40–45

This table serves as a guide for the Modern Way of Roasting Meat (see above) and the Old-Fashioned Way of Roasting Meat (see below).
For defrosting and cooking frozen meats, see page 870.

The Old-Fashioned Way of Roasting Meat

Prepare the meat as directed in the rule on page 334.

A roast of beef is sometimes seared in a pan on top of the stove until light brown on all sides and then placed in a 350° oven as directed below. Fillet of beef comes under a different rule, page 342.

If the meat has not been previously seared, place it in a pan on a dripping rack in a very hot oven 480° to 500° until it is browned. Reduce the heat to a moderate oven 350°, pour a cup of boiling stock over the roast and cover the pan. Cook the roast until it is done. See Timetable for Roasting Meats. Allow the shorter amount of time for these roasts. Baste the roast frequently. A large dropper-type baster is fine for this or use a spoon.

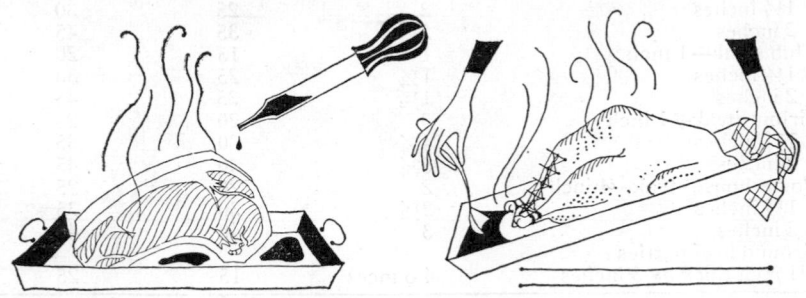

The roast may be uncovered for the last half hour. Turn a boneless roast at least once to permit it to cook uniformly. If stock is not available for basting meat, use vegetable stock or part stock and part dry wine: white wine for veal, red wine for beef and lamb. See the paragraph on Gravy, page 424.

To Broil Meat

Tender meats like beef steak and lamb chops are the best ones for broiling.

Preheat a broiler to 350°, for about 10 minutes. Have the meat at room temperature. Score it about every 2 inches around the edge to keep it from curling. Cut off excess fat, if any.

You may place the meat on a hot greased rack or you may remove the rack while the broiler unit is heating and grease the cold rack. This will keep the meat from sticking. Place the meat on the middle of the broiler rack about 3 inches from the heating unit. If you are broiling only a small amount of meat place it on a rack in a flat pan on the broiler rack. This saves cleaning the broiler rack and pan. Leave the door of the broiling oven slightly open.

Broil the meat until the top side is well browned. Turn and broil until the second side is browned. Only one turning is necessary. Season and serve the meat on a hot platter.

A neat trick is to place pieces of bread in the broiling pan. They take up any drippings and toast at the same time.

Broiling time depends upon the thickness of the meat and the degree of doneness desired. You may use a meat thermometer (see page 335).

Rare steaks are broiled to an internal temperature of 130°; medium to 160°. Lamb chops are broiled to 170°. Ham is cooked well done. The time for broiling bacon is influenced by personal preference as to crispness, but the heat must be low.

Approximate length of time for broiling follows:

Timetable for Broiling Fresh or Defrosted Meats at Moderate Temperature (350°)

(Courtesy National Livestock and Meat Board, Chicago, Ill.)

Cut	Weight	Approximate Total Cooking Time	
		Rare	Medium
	Pounds	Minutes	Minutes
BEEF			
Chuck steak—1 inch	2⅓	24	30
1½ inches	4	40	45
Rib steak—1 inch	1½	15	20
1½ inches	2	25	30
2 inches	2¼	35	45
Club steak—1 inch	1	15	20
1½ inches	1¼	25	30
2 inches	1½	35	45
Sirloin steak—1 inch	3	20	25
1½ inches	4¼	30	35
2 inches	5¾	40	45
Porterhouse steak—1 inch	2	20	25
1½ inches	2½	30	35
2 inches	3	40	45
Ground beef patties			
1 inch thick by 3 inches	4 ounces	15	25
LAMB			
Shoulder chops—1 inch	3 ounces	Lamb chops	12
1½ inches	6 ounces	are not	18
2 inches	10 ounces	served rare	22
Rib chops—1 inch	2 ounces		12
1½ inches	4 ounces		18
2 inches	5 ounces		22
Loin chops—1 inch	3 ounces		12
1½ inches	5 ounces		18
2 inches	6 ounces		22
Ground beef patties			
1 inch by 3 inches	4 ounces		18
PORK			
Ham slice		Ham always	20 (well
½ inch	¾–1	cooked well done	25–30 done)
Ham slice—tendered			
½ inch	¾–1		10–12
1 inch	1½–2		16–20
Bacon			4–5

Broiled and Roasted Meats

This increasingly popular way of preparing thick cuts of beef is a boon to the cook-hostess.

Preheat your oven to 350°. See Broiled Meat Timetable above. Meat is placed on a greased broiling rack 1½ to 3 inches from the source of heat and browned quickly, first on one side and then on the other. It is then spread with butter and placed on an oven-proof dish, frequently surrounded by partially cooked, nearly tender, hot vegetables dressed with butter or sauce. Bake the meat in a slow oven 250° to 300° until done. Use a meat thermometer (see page 335).

To Pan-Broil Meats

This is best done in a heavy skillet. You will find examples of pan-broiling in the following rules: Pan-broiled Steak, page 346; Lamb Chops Pan-broiled, page 362, and Pork Chops, page 367.

To Braise Meats

The less tender cuts of meat are frequently braised. See Marinade for Tenderizing Meat, page 340. Drain and dry the meat. You may dredge it with flour. Brown it quickly in a very little fat—the fat of the meat rendered intensifies the flavor, or you may use hot butter, lard, oil or drippings. Place the meat in a heavy kettle. Add enough boiling water or stock to cover the bottom of the pot, about ¾ cupful. Cover the pot closely. Simmer the meat on top of the stove until it is tender. Add stock as required. The time will depend on the size or cut of the meat.

Or dredge with flour and brown the meat in melted fat. Pour over it 2 to 4 cupfuls of boiling water or stock, cover the pot or casserole closely. Place it in a slow oven 275° to 325°. Baste it every 30 minutes. Turn the meat once at about the middle of the cooking period. This method will require a somewhat longer time than braising meat over direct heat. When done season it.

Vegetables, pared and quartered, may be added to the braised meat, either when the meat is half done or later. Carrots, turnips, parsnips, onions, celery, tomatoes, etc., are good for this dish. Allow double the time for cooking them in the oven, or parboil them. See the section on Pressure Cooked Meats, page 886.

Timetable for Braising Fresh or Defrosted Meats

(Courtesy National Livestock and Meat Board, Chicago, Ill.)

Cut	Average Weight or Thickness	Approximate Total Cooking Time
BEEF		
Pot roast	3–5 lbs.	3–4 hours
Swiss steak	1½–2½ inches	2–3 hours
Fricassee	2 inch cubes	1½ hours
Beef birds	½ inch (x 2 x 4 inches)	1½ hours
Short ribs	Pieces (2 x 2 x 4 inches)	1½ hours
Round steak	¾ inch	45–60 minutes
Stuffed steak	½–¾ inch	1½ hours
PORK		
Chops	¾–1½ inches	45–60 minutes
Spareribs	2–3 lbs.	1½ hours
Tenderloin:		
Whole	¾–1 lb.	45–60 minutes
Fillets	½ inch	30 minutes
Shoulder steak	¾ inch	30–45 minutes
LAMB		
Breast—stuffed	2–3 lbs.	1½–2 hours
Breast—rolled	1½–2 lbs.	1½–2 hours
Neck slices	¾ inch	1 hour
Shanks	½ lb. each	1–1½ hours
VEAL		
Breast—stuffed	3–4 lbs.	1½–2 hours
Breast—rolled	2–3 lbs.	1½–2 hours
Birds	½ inch (x 2 x 4 inches)	45–60 minutes
Chops	½–¾ inch	45–60 minutes
Chops—breaded	½–¾ inch	45–60 minutes
Steaks or cutlets	½–¾ inch	45–60 minutes
Shoulder chops	½–¾ inch	45–60 minutes

To Stew Meat

Stews are meat usually cut into pieces covered with liquid and simmered until tender. The meat may be lightly browned in fat before it is stewed. Examples: Gaston Beef Stew, page 349, Lamb Stew, page 363, "Boiled" Beef, page 351, Veal Stew, page 358, Mutton with Caper Sauce, page 364, etc.

Spices may be added to the stock. Vegetables may be added for the last half hour or so of cooking.

If you wish to stew meat in one piece follow the rule given above and use the following chart as a guide for the approximate length of time to cook it:

BEEF ....40 to 60 minutes to the pound
MUTTON ....20 minutes to the pound
VEAL ....25 minutes to the pound
CHICKEN ....20 minutes or more to the pound

Season the stew. For gravy see the chapter on Gravy, page 424.

To Fricassee Meat

Fricassees are really stews. It is customary to brown the meat before stewing it, or to stew it until tender, brown it in butter or fat and return it to the stock or gravy.

To "Boil" Ham, Corned or Fresh Beef

Individual rules are given in this chapter to cover this subject. These meats are never "boiled," but they are simmered immersed in water or other liquid for long periods. Spices and vegetables are added toward the end of the cooking to give them flavor.

To Barbecue Meat

Barbecued meat—lamb, pork, beef, fowl—is usually cooked in the open very slowly and for a long time over a pit of coals. It is basted with a highly seasoned sauce. To barbecue meat indoors, place it in a hot oven 500° for 20 minutes, reduce the heat to 300° and begin basting it with Barbecue Sauce, page 436. Baste it frequently throughout the cooking period, which may be as much longer as you like than the time given in the Timetable for Roasting Meat, page 336. The sauce is served, unthickened, with the meat.

Marinade for Tenderizing Meat

The less tender cuts of meat may be improved by being placed for several hours in a marinade.

1. Combine:
    1 cup French dressing with garlic
    2 teaspoons mixed dried herbs or
    (2 tablespoons mixed, chopped fresh herbs: parsley, chives, basil, savory, etc.)
2. Combine:
    2 cups acid white wine
    ½ cup cooking oil
    1 teaspoon pepper
    A bouquet garni, page 832
    1 grated onion

3. Combine:
> 1 quart astringent red wine or wine vinegar
> A bay leaf and other herbs

Larding

Lean meat is frequently "larded" to give it additional juiciness and flavor. Lardoons are thin strips of salt pork or bacon. French cooks rub them with garlic and other herbs and dust them with cloves or cinnamon. Lardoons are cut into about 2 inch strips ¼ inch thick.

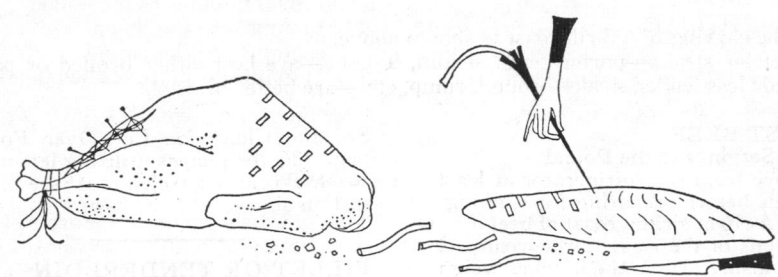

A larding needle is used to draw them through the surface of the meat. Or a gash made with a thin pointed knife or ice pick will permit you to force the lardoons into the meat. Insert them about 1 inch apart. Bacon, salt pork or suet may be placed or tied over a roast to gain a similar effect. When larding a fowl place the lardoons at right angles to the breast bone. Larger strips of salt pork may be forced through meat like chuck and round from surface to surface.

How to Cook Frozen Meat

Complete directions for cooking frozen meat appear on page 870.

Pressure Cooked Meat

Complete directions for pressure cooking meats appear on page 889.

How to Keep Cooked Meat

Cooked meat is stored in a refrigerator in a covered receptacle, well wrapped in waxed paper, in a plastic bag or in whatever will prevent the surface from becoming dry and hard.

Beef

The best cuts of beef for roasting are the rib and loin. The round, cross arm, rump, chuck, ribs and clod may be roasted, but as these cuts are less tender than the rib and loin, it is better to braise or to pot-roast them. See Marinade, page 340. Neck, shoulder, shank, brisket, plate, flank and the heel of the round may be either stewed or braised.

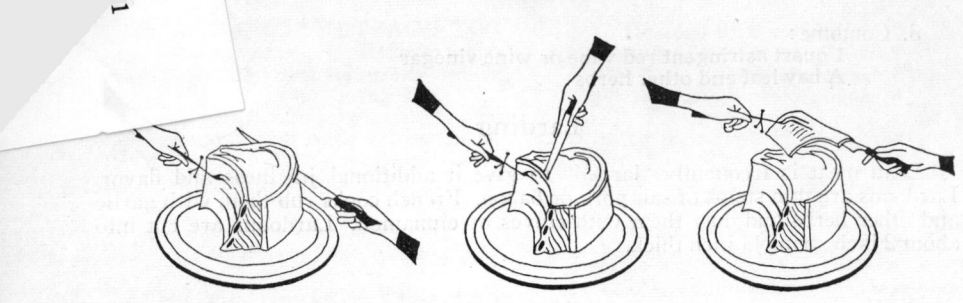

The carving of a 3 rib roast is shown above.

Tender steaks—porterhouse, sirloin, T-bone—are best either broiled or pan-broiled; less tender steaks—round, rump, etc.—are better braised.

ROAST BEEF
3 to 4 Servings to the Pound
Remove from the refrigerator at least ½ hour before preparing for cooking:

A rib or sirloin roast of beef

The ends of the ribs may be removed for braising. Have the butcher weigh the trimmed roast to gauge the roasting time.

Trim off the excess fat and hard edges. The surface may be rubbed with:

A cut clove garlic

and it may be dredged with:

Flour

Place the roast fat side up in a pan in an oven preheated to 300°. If the roast is very lean, tie or skewer over it:

A piece of suet or salt pork

Cook it as directed by the Rules and Timetable for Roasting Meat on page 338 in a slow oven 300° for 18 to 30 minutes to the pound. A rolled roast will require 5 to 10 minutes longer to the pound. Turn it every ½ hour.

You may add parboiled vegetables, onions, carrots, potatoes, etc., for the last ½ hour or so of cooking. If there are insufficient drippings, add a little fat to the pan. Season the roast with:

Salt and freshly ground pepper

If you wish to brown a roast after it is done, place it under a broiler for a few minutes. You may remove a roast from the oven about 20 minutes before serving to allow it to set for easier carving. Comparatively little heat is lost by this process. Use the fat and drippings in the pan for making Gravy, page 426. Serve the roast with:

Creamette or Macaroni Loaf, page 96

Yorkshire Pudding, page 423, or Tomato Pudding, page 179

See the Chart for Left-Over Food, page 926, for recipes utilizing left-over roast. To carve a rolled roast see illustration above.

FILLET OR TENDERLOIN OF BEEF
Allow ⅓ Pound Per Serving
Have the meat at room temperature. Remove the surplus fat and skin from:

A fillet of beef

Lard (page 341) with narrow strips of:

Salt pork or bacon

Fold over the thin ends of the fillet and secure them with string or skewers. If the fillet is not larded, spread it generously with butter or tie strips of bacon over it. A professional cook taught me to stud a fillet of beef with blanched slivered almonds. Dredge it with:

Flour

Roast the fillet in a moderate oven 300° from 20 to 25 minutes to the pound. Do not cover or baste it. A fillet is usually served rare. Season it when it is done.

Or, prepare the fillet as directed and place it on a rack in a roasting pan in a very hot oven 500°. Place a piece of salt pork or bacon in the bottom of the pan. Bake the fillet from 20 to 30 minutes in all. Baste it frequently. Season it when it is done. Prepare:

Gravy, page 426

This is good made with pan drippings and sour cream. You may add to the gravy:

(Minced Sautéed Mushrooms, page 292)

or surround the fillet with:

(Broiled Mushrooms, page 292)

Garnish the platter with dabs of:
    Tart jelly on slices of orange
    Sprigs of parsley
    Mashed Potato Balls, page 304
Fillet is frequently served with:
    Marchand de Vin Sauce, page
    436

POT ROAST
6 Servings
Beef shoulder, chuck, blade bone,
boneless neck and rump make good
pot roasts.
Prepare for cooking:
    3 lbs. chuck, round or other beef
The meat is improved by being larded,
page 341, with:
    Salt pork or bacon
Rub the meat with:
    (Garlic)
Dredge it with:
    Flour
Heat in a heavy pot over a hot fire:
    2 tablespoons fat
Sauté lightly in the fat:
    ¼ cup chopped onion
Remove the onion. Sear the meat on
all sides in the fat until it is dark
brown. Pour over it:
    **2 cups or more boiling stock,
    Vegetable Stock, page 425, or
    1 cup stock and 1 cup canned
    tomatoes**
There should be about ½ inch of liquid
in the pot. Reduce the heat and cover
the pot closely. Do not boil the meat
at any time. Simmer it slowly until it
is done, for 2 or 3 hours. Add stock if
the roast becomes dry. Remove the
roast from the pot. Pot roast may be
baked covered in a slow oven 300° to
325° after the stock has been poured
over it. Season it when it is nearly
done with:
    **Salt and pepper
    (Spices and herbs)**
Strain the stock and thicken it with:
    Flour (see Gravy, page 426)
Some cooks like a sour sweet gravy.
You may get this effect by adding 1
teaspoonful of sugar and 1½ tablespoonfuls lemon juice, acid wine or
vinegar.
Vegetables may be cooked and served
in the stock—about 1½ cupfuls in all
of green pepper, celery, carrots, parsley, potatoes, etc. Peel and slice them
or grind them and add for the last ½
hour or so of cooking. Serve the pot
roast with:
    **Noodles, page 97, or
    Dumplings, page 421**

POT ROAST IN SOUR CREAM
AND WINE
Follow the above rule for:
    Pot Roast
For the liquid, warm:
    **¾ cup dry wine, preferably red
    ¼ cup water**
Pour it around the roast. Heat over
hot water and stir in:
    ¾ cup warm sour cream
Proceed to cook the roast as directed.

POT ROAST WITH CIDER
Combine:
    **2 cups cider
    2 small sliced onions
    ¼ teaspoon ginger
    3 cloves
    ¼ teaspoon cinnamon
    2 tablespoons sugar**
Soak the meat for 12 hours in this
marinade. Keep it in a cold place, turn
it once. Cook the roast by the above
rule for Pot Roast. Use the marinade
in place of other liquid.

POT ROAST WITH
CRANBERRIES
Follow the rule for Pot Roast. Substitute for the liquid:
    2 cups boiling water
Add after 1 hour of cooking:
    2 cups cranberries
and additional boiling water if needed.

SPICED BEEF
8 Servings
Good served hot—fine for a cold meat
platter.
Cover:
    4 or 5 lbs. chuck roast
with:
    **Cider vinegar or dry wine
    2 sliced onions
    ½ bay leaf
    1 teaspoon cinnamon
    1 teaspoon allspice
    1 teaspoon cloves
    1½ teaspoons salt
    1 teaspoon pepper**
Permit the roast to stand in this marinade for 12 hours or more. Drain it.
Reserve the liquor. Place the meat in
a roasting pan. Heat to the boiling
point and pour over it:
    **½ the vinegar
    2 cups water**
Cover it closely and roast it in a slow
oven 275° for 3 hours. Put through a
grinder, then sauté in butter until a
golden brown:

2 onions
4 large carrots
1 medium yellow turnip
1 stalk celery

Add these ingredients to the roast for the last ½ hour of cooking. Add if needed:

Salt

The stock may be thickened with:

Flour (see Gravy, page 426)

BEEF À LA MODE

This is similar to Sauerbraten (see below), but the meat is marinated for only 18 hours. Prepare a marinade of:

1 quart astringent red wine
1 bay leaf per 5 lbs. meat
Herbs and seasoning
(1 crushed clove garlic)

After marinating, follow the rule for Pot Roast, page 343. Substitute the marinade for the stock. Heat but do not boil it.

SAUERBRATEN

10 to 12 Servings

Prepare for cooking:

3 lbs. beef shoulder

Lard it (page 341) with pieces of:

Salt pork or bacon

or choose a cut of meat with fat. Rub it with:

Pepper
(Garlic)

Place it in a crock or bowl. Heat but do not boil:

Equal parts mild vinegar or white wine and water
½ cup sliced onion
2 bay leaves
1 teaspoon peppercorns
¼ cup sugar

Pour this while hot over the beef so that it is more than ½ covered. Place a lid over the crock and put it in the refrigerator. Leave the meat there for a week or 10 days, turning it once a day. Drain it, saving the vinegar, and cook the meat like Pot Roast, page 343. Use the vinegar mixture in place of stock. When the meat is tender remove it from the pot. Thicken the stock with:

Flour (see Gravy, page 426)

Add:

1 cup sweet or sour cream

I like the gravy "straight." Some cooks add raisins, catsup and gingersnaps, but I have never had the courage to do so. Serve the roast with:

Potato Dumplings, page 422

and you will have a treat.

BEEF BRISKET WITH SAUERKRAUT

6 Servings

Tie into a compact shape:

3 lbs. beef brisket

Melt in a deep kettle:

3 tablespoons bacon or other fat

Add, stir about and brown lightly:

(¼ cup chopped onions)

Add the meat and place over it:

2 lbs. sauerkraut

Add:

2 cups boiling water

Simmer the meat covered for about 2½ hours, or until tender. Season with:

Salt and pepper
Dry white wine
(Caraway seed)

Serve the meat with:

Boiled Potatoes, page 300

Pour over them:

Thick sour cream
Chopped parsley or chives

ANNA'S SHORT RIBS OF BEEF

4 Servings

This comparatively inexpensive dish is worth a trial. It is good enough to serve frequently. Choose short ribs that are lean if you do not like fat.

Cut into about 3 inch pieces:

2 lbs. short ribs of beef

Place in a heavy pot with a lid:

5 cups water
1 small sliced onion
1 small sliced carrot
4 or more ribs celery with leaves

Bring these ingredients to the boiling point. Add the short ribs. Simmer them covered until nearly tender, for about 2 hours. Take out the meat. Strain the stock. Make about 3 cupfuls of thin gravy, page 426, using:

4 tablespoons fat
4 tablespoons flour
3 cups stock

Season the gravy mildly with:

Salt and pepper
A few drops brown coloring
(¼ teaspoon curry powder)

Heat in a heavy skillet:

4 tablespoons fat

Slice, add and stir about until light brown:

1 small onion

Brown the meat in the hot fat. Pour over it ½ the gravy. Place it uncovered in a moderate oven at 325° for about 45 minutes and permit it to get brown and crisp. It may be basted occasionally with the drippings. Reheat the

remaining gravy. Season it palatably.
You may add to it:
(2 or more tablespoons sour cream)
Place the meat on a hot platter. Pour
the gravy around it. Serve it piping
hot.

BRAISED BEEF WITH VEGETABLES
4 Servings
Dice and heat in a skillet over a low
fire until the fat is tried out:
4 cubic inches salt pork
Cut into cubes or slices:
2 lbs. beef: inexpensive cut
Brown the meat in the fat. Sear it on
all sides. Place the meat in a casserole.
Rinse the skillet with:
2 cups boiling water
Pour it into the casserole. Cover the
dish closely. Bake the meat in a slow
oven 250°. Baste it every ½ hour.
Turn it after 2 hours. Bake it until it
is tender, for 3½ hours. Add for the
last hour of cooking:
½ cup scraped diced carrots
¼ cup pared diced turnips
¼ cup pared diced onions
¼ cup diced celery
Thicken the drippings with:
Flour (see Gravy, page 426)
Season the dish palatably with:
Salt and pepper

BROILED STEAK
Prepare for cooking (page 334):
A beefsteak 2 inches thick
Have the steak at room temperature.
You may rub the steak with a cut
clove of garlic. You may spread it an
hour before it is cooked with olive oil.
Add, if desired, grated onion and prepared mustard. Or you may spread it
when ¾ cooked with French dressing
or with a paste made of soft butter,
grated onion and prepared mustard.
Preheat the broiler for about 10 minutes at 350°. For method and time of
broiling, see pages 337 and 338.
A very thick steak may be browned on
both sides, then cooked until done
under a lowered flame, or it may be
cooked 4 inches from the flame. When
it is done spread it with:
**Butter or the pan drippings after
removing most of the fat**
Add:
Chopped parsley or chives
If the drippings are meager, you may
add 1 or 2 tablespoonfuls boiling
water. Serve the steak garnished with:

**Smothered Mushrooms, page
292, French Fried Onions, page
297**
Or serve it with:
**Sauce for Steak, page 436
Marchand de Vin Sauce, page
436, or
Green Onion Sauce, page 436**

SAUCE FOR STEAK
This may be prepared while the steak
is being broiled.
Heat:
**2 tablespoons steak drippings or
butter**
Sauté in the fat for 5 minutes:
¼ cup finely chopped onion
Add:
**½ teaspoon mustard
1 teaspoon Worcestershire
sauce
½ teaspoon salt
⅛ teaspoon pepper
½ cup boiling water**
Cover these ingredients and simmer
them for 10 minutes. Shortly before
serving the steak, strain the sauce and
pour it slowly, beating it constantly,
over:
1 beaten egg
Stir and cook the sauce for 1 minute
over low heat. If desired, stir in the
steak drippings. Pour the sauce over
the steak. See Sauces, page 424.

FILLET OF BEEFSTEAKS
Upon request a butcher usually will
cut fillet steaks, shape them and surround them with a strip of bacon secured by a wooden pick. If not, it must
be done at home. The thickness of the
steaks varies from ¾ inch to 1 inch or
more.
Prepare for cooking:
Fillet steaks 1 to 2 inches thick
Spread them with butter. Follow the
rule for Broiled Steak, opposite. When
done spread the steaks with:
**Butter or Hollandaise or
Béarnaise Sauce, page 430**
Serve them on a hot platter garnished
with:
**Lemon and parsley
Broiled Mushrooms, page 292
Mashed Potato Balls, Fried,
page 304**

THIN BEEFSTEAKS WITH CHEESE
Pound:
**Grated Parmesan or Sapsago
cheese**

into:
Thin steaks
Roll them lightly in:
Flour
Season with:
Salt and paprika
Sauté the steaks slowly in:
Hot fat

PAN-BROILED STEAK
Prepare for cooking (page 334):
A beefsteak
Heat a heavy frying pan over a good flame until it is hot. Rub it very lightly with:
A bit of beef fat
Put the steak in the pan and sear it for 1 minute, or until the blood rises on the uncooked surface, turn it and sear the other side.
Reduce the heat to a low flame and continue cooking the steak until it is done, about 10 minutes for a 1½ inch steak. Pour off the fat in the pan. If it is allowed to accumulate, the steak will be sautéed and not broiled. If at all doubtful of the tenderness of the steak, cover it partly with a lid when the flame is reduced. This gives it more of a steamed than a broiled quality but it does help to soften it. Season the steak with:
Salt and freshly ground pepper
The drippings may be thickened with:
Flour (see Gravy, page 426)
or the preceding rule for Sauce may be followed. Serve the steak with:
German Fried Potatoes, page 308

BARBECUED SIRLOIN STEAK
Cream:
6 tablespoons butter
3 tablespoons dry mustard
3 teaspoons salt
3 teaspoons sugar
½ teaspoon pepper
1 teaspoon paprika
Rub this well into:
A whole sirloin steak 2 or 3 inches thick
Sear it on both sides in a heavy pan over a quick fire. Prepare a sauce of:
3 tablespoons Worcestershire sauce
6 tablespoons olive oil
3 tablespoons catsup
1 teaspoon sugar
1 teaspoon salt
Brush part of this over the meat. Broil it ¾ to 1 hour. See Broiled Steak, page 345. The heat may be reduced

for the last ½ hour of cooking. Leave the door of the broiling oven partly open. Turn the steak once. Brush it frequently with the remaining liquid.

PLANKED STEAK
Prepare:
Mashed Potatoes, page 302
to which you may add for color:
1 egg yolk
Brush a large plank with:
Oil
Preheat it. Broil by the rule on page 338 until about ½ done:
A beefsteak
Place it on the hot plank. Brush the steak with:
Melted butter
Season it with:
Salt and pepper
Use a bag and large tube to pipe a border of mashed potatoes around the edge of the plank. Place it in a moderate oven 350° until the steak is done and the potatoes are lightly colored. Don't sacrifice the steak to the potatoes if you have misjudged your time. Remove the plank from the oven and fill in the spaces between the steak and the border with hot cooked vegetables:
Mushrooms, peas, broccoli, grilled tomatoes, etc.
These may be dressed with melted butter or sauce. Garnish with:
Lemon wedges, parsley, etc.

CUBE STEAKS
4 Servings
Prepare for cooking:
4 cube steaks
Heat a heavy skillet. Rub it well with:
A piece of beef fat or a little butter
Put in the cube steaks and cook them 1 minute on one side. Turn them and cook them 1 minute on the other side. Remove them to a hot platter. Pour into the skillet:
1 tablespoon water
Let it boil up. Pour the sauce over the steaks. Season the steaks lightly with:
Salt and pepper

STEAK CREOLE
Prepare for cooking (page 334):
A Porterhouse steak
Sauté in butter sufficient:
Onions
to cover the steak. Prepare the following sauce. Combine:

1½ cups tomato juice
    1 tablespoon Worcestershire
    sauce
    2 tablespoons diced ham
    1 tablespoon butter
Simmer these ingredients for 10 minutes. Combine:
    2½ tablespoons flour
    ¼ cup tomato juice
Stir these ingredients slowly into the simmering stock. Season the sauce with:
    Salt and pepper
Place it over hot water. Add:
    1 tablespoon sherry
Broil the steak, page 338. Place it on a hot platter. Cover it with the sautéed onions. Serve it with the sauce.

BEEFSTEAK AND OYSTERS
Broil until nearly done:
    A beefsteak
Place it in a pan. Cover it with:
    Drained oysters
Season them lightly with:
    Salt and pepper
Dot them with:
    Butter
Bake the steak in a moderate oven 375° until the oysters are plump. Serve it with:
    Lemon Butter, page 431
    Chopped parsley
    Hashed Brown Potatoes, page 306

SWISS STEAK
6 Servings
Trim the edges of:
    A 2 lb. round steak
Rub it with:
    ½ clove garlic
Pound into both sides of the steak with the edge of a heavy plate or a mallet:
    As much flour as the steak will hold
    1 teaspoon salt
    ⅛ teaspoon pepper
Cut the steak into pieces or leave it whole. Heat in a large casserole or skillet:
    ¼ cup bacon or ham drippings
Add and sauté until brown:
    ½ cup chopped onion
Sear the steak in the fat. Add:
    2 cups strained boiling tomatoes
or substitute:
    1 cup boiling water and 1 cup or more chopped carrots, celery and green peppers
Or, these vegetables may be added to

the tomato juice or to 2 cupfuls of condensed soup.
Cover the casserole closely and place it in a slow oven 275° for 2 hours or more. Remove the steak to a hot platter. Strain the drippings. Thicken them with:
    Flour (see Gravy, page 426)
Pour the gravy over the steak. Serve it with:
    Baked Potatoes, page 301

BEEF STROGANOFF
4 Servings
Cut into ½ inch slices:
    1½ lbs. fillet of beef
Pound the beef with a mallet until it is thin. Cut it into strips about 1 inch wide. Melt in a pan:
    1 tablespoon butter
Sauté in the butter for 2 minutes:
    ¾ tablespoon grated onion
Sauté the beef quickly in the butter for about 5 minutes. Turn it so that it will be browned evenly. Remove it. Keep it hot. Add to the pan:
    2 tablespoons butter
Stir and sauté in the butter:
    ¾ lb. sliced mushrooms
Add the beef. Season it with:
    Salt and pepper
    A grating of nutmeg
    (½ teaspoon basil)
Add and heat, but do not boil:
    ½ cup warm sour cream

ROUND STEAK SMOTHERED IN ONIONS
6 Servings
Peel and cut into very thin slices:
    5 medium-sized onions
Trim a:
    2 lb. round steak
Rub it with:
    Seasoned flour
Heat in a heavy skillet over a good flame:
    1 tablespoon bacon drippings
Put the onions in the skillet. Sauté them lightly. Push them to one side. Add the steak to the pan. Permit it to brown on one side, turn it and brown the other. When the steak and onions are brown cover the skillet closely and simmer them over very low heat for 15 minutes. Add:
    1 cup boiling water
Chopped celery and carrots may be added to the water.
Simmer the steak covered for about 1 hour or more, or until it is very tender. After the water has been poured on

the steak, the steak may be covered closely and placed in a slow oven 275° and cooked until it is done, for about 1½ hours. Serve it on a hot platter. Place the onions on top of it. Garnish it with:

    3 tablespoons chopped parsley

Serve the steak with:

    Mashed sweet potatoes flavored with sherry
    Snap beans or zucchini

DICED ROUND STEAK WITH ONIONS AND SOUR CREAM
4 Servings

Melt in a skillet:

    4 tablespoons butter

Sauté in the butter until light brown:

    ½ cup finely minced onions

Cut into ½ inch dice:

    1½ lbs. round steak

Sear it in the hot butter on all sides. Simmer these ingredients covered for 20 minutes. Add:

    ½ cup minced Sautéed Mushrooms, page 292

Combine:

    1 cup sour cream
    2 tablespoons flour

Pour these ingredients into the skillet. Stir and simmer them for 5 minutes. Add:

    ¾ teaspoon salt
    ¼ teaspoon pepper

Serve the meat with:

    Boiled Rice, page 103, or
    Grits Ring Filled with Peas, page 157

Spanish Casserole Dish, page 167.

SAUTÉED ROUND STEAK

Cut into 2 x 4 inch pieces:

    A round steak ⅓ inch thick

Dip the pieces in:

    Flour

Sauté them until brown over a quick fire in:

    Hot butter or drippings

Reduce the heat to a low flame, cover the pan and cook the steak until it is tender.

BEEF ROLLS

Prepare for cooking:

    A round or flank steak ⅓ inch thick

Cut it into 2 x 4 inch pieces. Place on each strip:

    A thick slice carrot
    A piece celery rib

    A small piece salt pork or a slice bacon

For other fillings see Veal Birds, page 359.

Roll the strips and tie them with thread. Brown them in:

    Hot salt pork or bacon drippings

Cover them with ¼ inch of:

    Boiling Vegetable Stock, page 425

Simmer them closely covered for 2 hours. Or, the rolls may be closely covered and baked in a moderate oven 325° for 2 hours. In this case it may be necessary to add more stock during the cooking. Do not let the stock boil at any time. Remove the rolls and cut the threads. Thicken the stock with:

    Flour (see Gravy, page 426)

Try adding a little red wine to the gravy stock—about ½ cupful.

Add as needed:

    Salt and pepper

Pour the gravy over the rolls. Serve them with:

    Mashed Potatoes, page 302
    Noodles, page 97

BEEF KABOBS OR BEEF ON SKEWERS
4 Servings

Use:

    1½ lbs. good grade of round or better

Cut the beef into about 1½ inch cubes. Alternate the cubes on skewers with thin slices of:

    Raw or parboiled onion, chunks of firm, slightly underripe tomatoes, mushrooms, bacon, etc.

Roll the filled skewers in:

    Melted butter

Broil them under a preheated broiler at 375° 3 inches below the heating unit with the oven door partly open. Brush them while broiling with melted butter. Turn them to cook evenly. Cook them until done, according to taste, about 18 minutes for rare, about 25 for well done. Season them. The kabobs may be breaded.

Lamb Kabobs, page 364.

FLANK STEAK WITH DRESSING
4 Servings

Prepare for cooking (page 334):

    A flank steak

Trim the edges. Season it with:

1 teaspoon salt
⅛ teaspoon paprika
(⅛ teaspoon ginger)
Melt:
¼ cup butter or bacon drippings
Add and sauté until brown:
2 tablespoons chopped onion
Add:
1 cup bread crumbs
¼ teaspoon salt
A few grains paprika
2 tablespoons chopped parsley
3 tablespoons chopped celery
1 slightly beaten egg
Spread this dressing over the flank steak, roll it loosely and tie it. Heat in a skillet:
3 tablespoons fat
Sear the steak in the hot fat on all sides. Place the steak in a casserole or closely covered dish. Stir into the fat in the skillet:
2 tablespoons flour
Add:
1 cup water or stock
1 cup tomato juice or dry wine
¼ teaspoon salt
Pour this over the steak. Bake it in a slow oven 250° closely covered for 1½ hours. Add seasoning if required. Serve the steak with a:
Green vegetable

MOCK DUCK I
Follow the preceding rule for:
Flank steak
or prepare for cooking:
2 small rump steaks 1 inch thick
Spread the dressing over ½ of the flank steak and fold over the other ½ or spread it over 1 of the rump steaks and cover it with the second steak. Sew the edges together with a coarse needle and thread. Place the meat in a skillet. Sear it on both sides in:
3 tablespoons hot fat
Add:
2 cups boiling Vegetable Stock, page 425
Cover the skillet closely, reduce the heat and simmer the meat until it is tender, about 2 hours. Remove the thread. Place the meat uncovered in a moderate oven 375°. Baste it frequently. Permit it to brown. Thicken the drippings with:
Flour (see Gravy, page 426)

Mock Duck II, page 362.
This is made with a forequarter of lamb.

GASTON BEEF STEW
6 Servings
This seems best when cooked a day ahead, but it is fine at any time. Perhaps I think that because it is frequently served by a well-known hostess, Mrs. Charles M. Rice, at her country parties. It is a one-dish meal.
Cut into small pieces:
½ lb. salt pork
Cut into pieces suitable for stewing:
2 lbs. beef
Sauté the pork in a large skillet over a slow fire. Brown the meat in the hot drippings over a quick fire. Sprinkle it with:
Seasoned flour
Combine and heat until boiling:
1½ cloves chopped garlic
1 large chopped onion
1 bouillon cube dissolved in 1 cup hot water
8 oz. canned tomato sauce
12 peppercorns
3 whole cloves
¼ cup chopped parsley
½ bay leaf
Place the meat in a heavy saucepan. Pour the above ingredients over it. Simmer it closely covered for about 4 hours. After 3 hours add:
½ cup sherry or acid white wine
Cook separately until nearly tender:
6 medium-sized pared quartered potatoes
6 pared quartered carrots
1 stalk chopped celery
Add these vegetables for the last 15 minutes of cooking.

BEEF STEW WITH WINE OR BOEF BOURGUIGNON
4 to 6 Servings
Try out:
½ lb. thinly sliced salt pork or use
3 tablespoons butter
Peel, add and sauté lightly:
12 small onions
Remove pork and onions from the pan. Cut into 1 inch dice and sauté in the hot fat until light brown:
2 lbs. lean beef
Place it in an oven-proof dish with:
1½ tablespoons flour
1 teaspoon salt
4 peppercorns
½ bay leaf
(½ teaspoon thyme)
Cover the meat with:
Red wine and water—¾ part wine to 1 part water
Cook the beef covered in a slow oven

275° for 1 hour. Place the pork and onions on top and continue to cook it for another hour or until the beef is tender. Or simmer the beef covered on top of the stove for about 1½ hours in all. Correct the seasoning and serve the stew sprinkled with:

Chopped parsley

Sliced shallots, carrots and mushrooms are sometimes sautéed with the onions and added later to the stew. A pinch of marjoram or other herbs may be used to vary the flavor. One-fourth cupful cognac may be added at the last minute and ignited.

BEEF GOULASH
6 Servings

This Hungarian dish is made in many different ways. Beef, veal and other meats are used separately and in combination. Vegetables are sometimes added for the last hour of cooking. Goulash is always highly spiced, some epicures insisting that peppercorns freshly ground are the requisite, others preferring the imported Rosen Paprika or some other spice. Some cooks use water, others prefer stock, sour milk, cream or dry red wine. This is a good general rule:

Cut into 1 inch cubes:
> 2 lbs. beef: round steak, shinbone or 1 lb. beef and 1 lb. lean veal

Melt in a heavy pot:
> 4 tablespoons butter or fat

Sauté in this:
> 1½ cups chopped onion

Brown the meat in the hot fat. Add:
> 1 cup or less boiling Stock, page 43, or tomato juice
> 1 teaspoon salt
> ½ teaspoon paprika

The amount of boiling liquid used is another moot point. Some use just enough to keep the meat from scorching and add more gradually during the cooking. Cover the pot closely and simmer the meat for 1½ hours. If the larger amount of liquid is used, 6 small peeled potatoes may be added for the last ½ hour of cooking, but they do soak up the gravy and the gravy is apt to be the best part of the goulash. Remove the meat from the pot and thicken the stock for:

Gravy, page 426

It may be necessary to add stock or tomato juice. Add if required:
> **Seasoning**

Serve the goulash with:
> **Polenta, page 102, Spaetzle, page 423, or Noodles, page 97**

Veal and Pork Goulash, page 154.

SHINBONE STEW
4 Servings

Buy:
> A 2½ lb. shinbone with meat

Brown it in:
> 3 tablespoons hot butter or drippings

Partly cover it with:
> Boiling water

Season it with:
> Salt and paprika

Simmer the meat closely covered until it is nearly tender, about 2 hours. Add:
> 4 cups peeled diced vegetables

These may be carrots, okra, onions, celery, potatoes, tomatoes, etc. Simmer the stew until the meat and the vegetables are tender. Thicken the stock, if desired, with:
> Flour (see Gravy, page 426)

Season the stew and serve it with:
> Chopped parsley
> Corn Bread, page 515, or Spoon Bread, page 423, or Farina Dumplings, page 421

THRIFT STEWS
Use:
> Flank, chuck, shank, neck, heel of round, or brisket of beef

To Stew, see page 340.

IRISH STEW
4 to 6 Servings

Cut into 1½ inch cubes:
> 1½ lbs. beef or lamb

Dredge it with:
> Seasoned flour

Heat in a pot:
> 3 tablespoons fat

Brown the meat in the hot fat, then remove it from the pot. Add to the fat and brown:
> ¼ cup sliced onions

Add the meat and cover it with:
> Boiling water

Cover the pot closely, reduce the heat and simmer the meat for 1½ hours. Parboil for 5 minutes:
> 1½ cups diced potatoes

Drain them. Add to the stew:
> ¼ cup diced carrots
> ⅓ cup diced turnips

Simmer the stew for 10 minutes. Add the drained potatoes and simmer it for 20 minutes. Dissolve:
> 2 tablespoons flour

in:
> ½ cup cold stew stock

Stir it into the stew and bring the gravy to the boiling point. Serve the stew with:

> Dumplings, page 421
> Biscuits, page 505

"BOILED" BEEF WITH HORSERADISH SAUCE
4 to 6 Servings
Place in a pot:

> 3 lbs. lean first cut brisket

Add to it:

> ½ cup sliced onions
> ½ cup sliced carrots
> ½ cup sliced celery with leaves
> ½ teaspoon salt

Pour over it boiling water to cover. Cover the pot closely and simmer the meat until it is tender, about 3 or 4 hours. Prepare the following:

> **Sauce**

Melt:

> 4 tablespoons butter

Brown lightly in the butter:

> ¼ cup chopped onions

Stir until blended:

> 2 tablespoons flour

Stir in slowly:

> 2 cups pot liquor
> ½ cup freshly grated horseradish
> or prepared horseradish

Season the sauce with:

> Salt
> Vinegar or lemon juice
> (Sugar)

The matter of seasoning is optional. The original recipe calls for 1 cupful pot liquor, 1 cupful horseradish, 1 cupful cider vinegar and ½ cupful sugar. This seems excessive to me. I substitute a cupful of pot liquor for the vinegar, then flavor the sauce as I like. Prepared horseradish contains vinegar, so it is difficult to give exact proportions. Cut the meat into slices. Reheat it in the boiling gravy. Serve the dish garnished with:

> Chopped parsley

Serve the beef with:

> Boiled New Potatoes in their jackets, page 300
> Sauerkraut, page 277
> Dumplings, page 421

New England Boiled Dinner, page 352; Bread Dressing in a Ring filled with Hash, page 157.

TO CORN BEEF
Combine and stir well in a crock:

> 8 cups water
> 1 cup salt
> 3 tablespoons sugar
> 1 bay leaf
> 6 peppercorns
> 1 minced clove garlic
> 2 teaspoons mixed pickle spices

Add:

> 5 or 6 lbs. beef: brisket or rump

Cover it with a plate and place a heavy weight on it. Leave the meat in the brine for 36 hours.

CORNED BEEF
Tie to keep it in shape:

> A 5 lb. piece of corned beef

It is wise to ask your butcher whether or not the beef requires previous soaking in water to keep from being too salty. Soak it if advised to do so. Discard the water.
Place beef in cold water to cover. Add:

> 6 peppercorns
> (½ clove garlic)

Bring it to the boiling point, remove the scum, reduce the heat, cover the pot and simmer the meat for about 5 hours, or until it is tender. You may have to add boiling water to keep the beef covered. Vegetables suitable for soup and cut up potatoes may be added for the last ½ hour of cooking; also a bay leaf and a teaspoon of thyme may be added. Leave the meat in the water in which it was cooked until it is lukewarm. Remove it and press it with a weight, or serve it warm and unpressed with:

> Horseradish Sauce, page 439
> Boiled Potatoes, page 300,
> Corn-Meal Dumplings, page 421, cooked in the corned beef stock, Spinach, page 313

CORNED BEEF AND CABBAGE
Admirers of Jiggs of the funny sheet and his beautifully drawn hands and feet will remember his insatiable desire for this dish.
Prepare by the preceding rule:

> Corned Beef

Peel, quarter and add for the last ½ hour of cooking:

> 3 onions
> 3 carrots

Cut into wedges and add for the last 10 to 15 minutes of cooking:

> A head of cabbage

This is not traditional but modern. Cabbage used to be cooked with the beef for hours.
Serve the beef surrounded by the vegetables and:

Farina or Corn-Meal Dumplings, page 421
These may be cooked in the stock. The vegetables may be dressed with:
Melted butter

CANNED CORNED BEEF AND CABBAGE
Follow the preceding rule. Substitute canned corned beef. Put it into boiling water with the vegetables. Cook it until the vegetables are tender.

NEW ENGLAND BOILED DINNER
10 to 12 Servings
Follow the rule for Corned Beef. After the meat has cooked for 4 hours, remove it from the pot. You may add about:
(2 lbs. salt pork)
for the last 2 hours. Peel, quarter and simmer in the stock for 30 minutes:
3 small parsnips
6 large carrots
3 large yellow turnips
Skin and add:
8 small onions
Peel, quarter and simmer in the stock for 15 minutes longer:
6 medium-sized potatoes
Cut into wedges, add and simmer until tender, for about 10 to 15 minutes:
A head of cabbage
Reheat the meat in the stock. Serve it on a platter surrounded by the vegetables, garnished with:
Parsley
It is customary to cook 10 or 12 beets separately. Skin them and serve them with the rest of the dinner.

CORNED BEEF HASH AND POTATOES
6 Servings
Grind, using coarse blade, or dice:
1½ lbs. cooked or canned corned beef: about 3 cups
Dice:
2 cups boiled potatoes
Melt in a large saucepan:
2 tablespoons butter
Stir in and simmer until tender:
½ cup chopped onion
1 diced green pepper, seeds and fibers removed
2 ribs chopped celery
(1 clove garlic)
(1 cup mushrooms)
Remove the garlic. Add the beef and potatoes and:

1 tablespoon Worcestershire sauce
2 tablespoons minced parsley or chives
Salt and pepper as needed
Cook and stir lightly over medium heat while adding gradually:
⅓ to ⅔ cup Stock, page 43,
or Cream Sauce III, page 428
Stir and cook till well blended and thoroughly heated. Place on a hot platter and serve topped with:
6 Poached Eggs, page 80
Or sauté the hash in a greased skillet until well browned on the bottom. Remove carefully, folding like an omelet, to serve.

Corned Beef Hash in Corn-Meal Mush, page 157.
Other Corned Beef Dishes, page 161.

HAMBURGER PATTIES
5 Servings
Use chuck, flank, shank, neck, heel or round. These patties are good—so good that one need not hesitate to serve them at any time. Grind:
1 lb. beef
Add:
¾ teaspoon salt
¼ teaspoon paprika
(¼ cup chopped onions)
(2 tablespoons thick cream)
Work the meat lightly with the hands. Shape it loosely into 5 cakes about 1 inch thick. You may surround each cake with:
(A strip of bacon)
Secure the bacon with a toothpick. Brush a hot frying pan very lightly with bacon grease. Brown the patties on both sides. Pour off the fat as the patties cook. Reduce the heat and cook them slowly until they are done. Hamburgers may be baked instead of sautéed. Cook them in a greased pan in a moderate oven 375° for about ½ hour. Don't go on a sour cream jag, but you may add it occasionally to the pan drippings to make a distinguished gravy for an everyday dish (in place of Brown Sauce, page 435). Heat but do not boil it. Serve the patties with:
Scalloped Potatoes and Onions, page 305

HAMBURGER VARIATIONS
You may add to the above hamburger mixture a choice of:
Italian Tomato Paste, page 434; catsup or chili sauce

Sautéed Mushrooms, page 292;. chopped pickles, celery or olives, herbs or capers, etc.
Serve cooked hamburgers with:
Onion Soup Sauce, page 442
This may make you an isolationist.
Or add to the pan drippings:
3 tablespoons lemon juice
⅛ teaspoon nutmeg
Or spread the patties with:
Finely chopped olives or chives mixed with butter
Or serve the patties with:
Barbecue Sauce, page 436
Or cook 2 very thin patties with a thin slice of parboiled onion sandwiched between them.

HAMBURGER CASSEROLE
4 Servings
Cook until tender, then drain:
8 medium-sized onions
Combine with the hands:
1 lb. hamburger
1 teaspoon salt
⅛ teaspoon pepper
1 beaten egg
½ cup soft bread crumbs
Divide this into 8 portions. Make a little cup of each portion around each onion. Place them in a greased oven-proof dish. Pour over them the contents of:
1 can tomato or other soup: 10½ oz.
to which you may add:
(½ teaspoon dried basil or 2 tablespoons chopped parsley)
Bake the onion patties in a moderate oven 350° for about ½ hour. Baste them frequently.

HAMBURGER STEAK BALLS OR CAKES
4 Servings
Combine lightly with a fork:
1 lb. ground beef: round steak or shoulder
¼ lb. ground salt pork
3 tablespoons rich milk
1 tablespoon or more chopped onion
1 tablespoon chopped parsley or other herb
¼ teaspoon paprika
If preferred, the onion may be sautéed for 2 minutes in part of the salt pork and then added to the other ingredients.
Vary the seasonings by adding:
1 teaspoon Worcestershire sauce

or 1 or 2 teaspoons prepared mustard or 2 teaspoons drained horseradish
Shape the meat into balls. Handle them lightly so they will not become too solid. Flatten them into cakes.
Surround the cakes with:
(Strips of bacon)
Secure them with toothpicks. Heat in a skillet:
2 tablespoons butter or fat
Add the balls or cakes and brown them. Add:
¾ cup stock or sour cream
Cover the pan and simmer the balls until they are done, about 5 minutes.
Season the balls with:
Celery salt
Salt and pepper
Thicken the drippings with:
Flour (see Gravy, page 426)
Serve the balls with:
Gnocchi, page 102

See Index for Ground Beef in Cabbage Leaves, Stuffed Cabbage, Hamburger with Olives and Tomato Sauce, Hamburger with Mushroom Sauce, Doughnut Hamburgers, Ground Beef and Kidney Beans, Chili con Carne, etc.

Broiled Hamburger Sandwiches, page 133.

SCRAPED BEEF
The following is a good way of preparing meat for a convalescent or a young child.
Scrape with a spoon or a dull knife:
Round steak
Roll the scrapings into a ball, flatten it slightly and pan-broil it in a hot skillet that has been rubbed with a very little:
Butter or suet
Sear the meat on both sides over a good flame, reduce the heat, turn the meat several times, dotting the upper side each time with a very little:
Butter
Season the meat lightly and serve it on:
Toast
Put the part of the steak that will not scrape in the stock pot.

See Index for Left-Over Meat in Biscuit Dough and other ground meat dishes.

BEEF À LA LINDSTROM OR SWEDISH MEAT BALLS
6 Servings or About Eighteen 1½ Inch Balls
There are many rules for this dish, all similar to, and in my opinion none superior to:
German Meat Balls, page 163
Follow this rule. Shape the meat into 1½ inch balls. Brown them in:
1 tablespoon butter or drippings
Simmer them closely covered until done, about 15 minutes, in:
2 cups consommé or other stock
Thicken the stock with:
Flour (see Gravy, page 426)
Season it with:
Sherry
Reheat the balls in the gravy. Serve them with:
Potato Dumplings, page 422

BEEF À LA LINDSTROM II
4 to 5 Servings
Put through a meat chopper 3 times:
1 lb. round steak
Beat and add:
2 egg yolks
1 teaspoon salt
Sauté until light brown:
¼ cup finely minced onions
in:
2 tablespoons butter
Remove from the fire, add:
1 tablespoon capers
½ cup drained, chopped pickled beets
¾ cup chopped cooked potatoes
¼ cup cream
Add the meat. Shape these ingredients into cakes. Sauté them quickly on both sides until done in:
2 tablespoons hot butter

MEAT LOAF
Meat loaf may be shaped and placed on a greased pan or it may be put into a greased ring mold or loaf pan. You may pour about ½ cupful of catsup in the bottom of the mold or pan before you fill it with the meat; or you may pour about 2 tablespoonfuls of chili sauce over the meat loaf when it is half baked. This gives it a good flavor and a light crust. Individual meat loaves may be baked in greased muffin tins and glazed as above. Bake the loaf and baste it as directed in the recipe below. You may cover it with a piece of greased paper for all but the last ¼ hour of baking. If using chili sauce on top or covering the loaf with

paper do not baste it. Remove the paper for the last ¼ hour of the baking period. Invert the mold. Serve the ring hot, filled with green peas or some other vegetable. Or serve it cold filled with potato or some other vegetable salad.

Method I. 4 to 6 Servings
Combine and shape into a loaf:
1 lb. ground beef: ¼ this amount may be pork
1 egg yolk
2 tablespoons chopped parsley
1 tablespoon soft butter
1 tablespoon bread crumbs
1 teaspoon lemon juice
1 teaspoon salt
¼ teaspoon pepper
½ teaspoon onion juice
Place the loaf in a lightly greased pan. Bake it in a moderate oven 350° for 1 hour. Pour over it and baste it every 5 minutes with part of:
¼ cup butter
1 cup boiling water or Vegetable Stock, page 425
Thicken the drippings with:
Flour (see Gravy, page 426)
Serve the loaf with:
Sweet Potato Puffs, page 311

Method II. 8 to 10 Servings
Grind or blend:
3 large peppers
1 large onion
1 cup broken up crackers or cornflakes
Drain, reserving the juice:
3½ cups tomatoes: No. 2½ can
Combine the vegetables and add:
1 lb. ground beef
1 lb. ground pork
1 teaspoon salt
¼ teaspoon pepper
Shape these ingredients into a loaf. Dredge it with:
Flour
Cover it with:
5 or 6 slices bacon
Bake the loaf for 1 hour in a moderate oven 350°. Baste it frequently with the tomato juice. Remove it from the pan. Thicken the drippings with:
Flour (see Gravy, page 426)
If there are insufficient drippings add:
Vegetable Stock, page 425, or sour cream
Serve the loaf with:
Riced Potatoes, page 302

Method III. 8 Servings
Place in a bowl:
2½ lbs. ground round steak

2 to 4 tablespoons horseradish
2 tablespoons catsup
1 teaspoon salt
½ teaspoon pepper
½ cup top milk or light cream

Grind in a food chopper or blend, then add:

6 slices bacon
2 medium-sized onions
1 cup broken up crackers

Mix and knead the mixture with the hands. Mold it into a loaf. Roll the loaf in:

¼ cup cracker crumbs

Place the loaf in a shallow baking pan. Pour into the pan:

½ cup water or stock

Bake the loaf in a moderate oven 350° for 1½ hours. Baste it occasionally, adding more liquid if necessary. Thicken the drippings with:

Flour (see Gravy, page 426)

Method IV. 6 Servings

Grind twice:

½ lb. pork
½ lb. beef
½ lb. veal

Soak for 10 minutes, then add:

½ cup soft bread

in:

¼ cup milk

Or use ½ cupful of stale bread and 6 tablespoonfuls of milk. Add it to the meat.

Chop fine and add:

1 medium-sized bunch celery
10 or 12 sprigs parsley
½ onion or 1 teaspoon onion juice

Season these ingredients with:

⅛ teaspoon pepper
1 teaspoon salt
1 tablespoon catsup
(¼ crushed bay leaf or ½ teaspoon dried herb)

Use your hands to blend and to shape them into a loaf. Place it in a greased skillet, or press the meat gently into a greased pan that has been rubbed with garlic. Place over it:

2 slices bacon

Bake the loaf in a moderate oven 325° for 1½ hours. Remove it to a hot platter. Combine, stir, then place in the pan:

1½ cups cold Stock, page 425
3 tablespoons flour

Cook and stir the sauce until it boils. Remove it from the heat. Add:

Seasoning
(½ cup warm sour cream)

Serve the sauce in a gravy boat. A sprinkling of ½ cupful of chopped nut meats on top of the loaf when it is put in the oven is fine for flavor and crustiness.

Veal

Veal requires longer cooking than beef. It is always served well done, except abroad, where it is served while still a luscious pink color. It may be kept juicy by having a generous coating of fat rubbed into its surface. This also gives it a fine brown color when cooked. Cook veal uncovered at a low even temperature 300°. Do not sear veal roast at any time. It may be dredged with flour. Several strips of salt pork or bacon may be placed on the roast or in the pan, and the roast, if dry, may be basted with drippings. Roast veal 25 to 30 minutes to the pound. A shoulder roast or rolled roast will require a few minutes longer per pound.

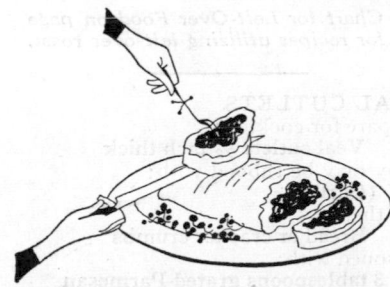

The best cuts for roasting are: Kidney roast or rib, leg, loin, breast, shoulder, shown stuffed above, cushion shoulder and rolled roast.

VEAL ROAST STUFFED BREAST OR SHOULDER

Have a pocket cut in:
> A breast or shoulder of veal

Remove the meat from the refrigerator at least ½ hour before preparing. Fill the pocket with:
> Bread Dressing, page 416, with 2 slices chopped salt pork added, or Oyster Dressing, page 416, or about 3 cups other dressing, or Green Rice, page 104, the cheese omitted

Sew it up with a coarse needle and thread. If it is not fat rub it with:
> Butter

Here are a few added fancy touches: The meat may be rubbed first with garlic, or gashes may be cut in a shoulder roast in which fine slivers of garlic, marjoram and peppercorns, anchovies or anchovy paste may be inserted. Or, rub the roast with oil, pepper, garlic and rosemary and wrap it in waxed paper for several hours before roasting it.
Dredge it with:
> Seasoned flour

Place it in a greased roasting pan in a slow oven 300°. Bake it uncovered until it is done, 25 to 30 minutes to the pound. See rule above or chart on page 336. You may place on the roast several strips of:
> (Bacon)

Thicken the drippings with:
> Flour (see Gravy, page 426)

When the gravy is done you may remove it from the fire and add ¼ cupful sour cream, 1 or 2 tablespoonfuls dry white wine. Heat the gravy but do not let it boil.
To carve a stuffed veal shoulder see illustration on page 355.

See Chart for Left-Over Food on page 926 for recipes utilizing left-over roast.

VEAL CUTLETS

Prepare for cooking:
> Veal cutlets ½ inch thick

They may be rubbed with:
> (Garlic)

Dip them in:
> Bread or cracker crumbs

seasoned with:
> 3 tablespoons grated Parmesan cheese or ½ teaspoon dried herbs: rosemary, savory, chervil, etc.

then in:
> 1 egg diluted with 2 tablespoons water

and again in the crumbs. Heat in a skillet:
> Butter or drippings

Brown the cutlets in the butter over a quick flame, then cook them covered over a very low flame until they are tender, about ½ hour, or in a moderate oven 325° for about 50 minutes.

VEAL ROAST, KIDNEY, LOIN, ETC., OR ROLLED ROAST

Follow the preceding rule for preparing and cooking breast or shoulder. Allow 35 to 40 minutes to the pound for rolled roast, turn it every ½ hour. You may add parboiled vegetables—potatoes, carrots, etc.—for the last ½ hour or so of cooking. If there are insufficient drippings add a little fat to the pan. This roast is good served with:
> Dumplings, page 421
> Spatzen, page 423, and
> Prunes Wrapped in Bacon, page 33

VEAL POT ROAST

Prepare by boning and rolling:
> A rump roast of veal

Follow the rule on page 343 for:
> Pot Roast

Pot Roast in Sour Cream and Wine is good made with veal. You may add to the finished gravy:
> (Capers and herbs: marjoram, thyme, etc.)

VEAL STEAK OR WIENER SCHNITZEL

Trim the edges of:
> A slice of veal from the round
> ½ inch or preferably less thick

Dredge it with:
> Flour

Heat in a skillet:
> ¼ cup butter or drippings

Add until the fat becomes red:
> Paprika

Sauté lightly in the fat:
> ½ cup or more sliced onions

Brown the meat in the hot fat. Remove it from the heat. Add:
> ½ cup sour cream or boiling vegetable stock

Cover the skillet and cook the veal over a very low flame until it is tender, about ½ hour or less. Season it with:
> Salt

Thin the drippings with:

Boiling stock
Sprinkle the Schnitzel with:
  Lemon juice
Serve it garnished with:
  Parsley, capers, sardelles
and if you wish to add a truly European touch:
  A sautéed or poached egg

BREADED VEAL SLICES

The following Veal Slices are so delicate that they may be served as a company dish in preference to some more elaborate meat course.
Trim the edges from:
  2 lbs. veal steak from the round 3/4 inch thick
The meat may be rubbed with:
  (Garlic)
Pound the meat well with the edge of a plate and cut the surface lightly with crisscross gashes. Cut the meat into pieces the size of a large oyster. Dip them in:
  Seasoned bread crumbs
then in:
  1 egg diluted with 2 tablespoons water
and again in the crumbs. Heat in a skillet:
  Butter
Brown the slices in the hot butter over a quick fire. Pour over them:
  1 cup cream and 1/2 cup stock
Cover the skillet with a lid. Reduce the heat to a very, very low flame, or place the covered skillet in a slow oven 325°. Cook the meat for 1 hour. Season it with:
  Salt and paprika
Thicken the drippings with:
  Flour (see Gravy, page 426)
The following variation meets with great favor. Stone and drain:
  Queen Anne cherries
In the place of all cream use 2/3 cream and 1/3 cherry juice. Cook the stoned cherries in the gravy with the meat for the last 5 minutes. Or, cook the meat as directed and add to the stock 5 minutes before the meat is done:
  1 cup seedless grapes or peeled and seeded white grapes
Another variation is to garnish the platter with anchovies and lemon wedges.

SCALLOPINI OR VEAL IN WINE

4 Servings
Cut into very thin slices from the loin or round:

1½ lbs. veal
Pound the meat with a mallet until it is even thinner. Dredge it with:
  Seasoned flour
Grated cheese is sometimes added at this time. Sauté the slices until a golden brown on both sides in:
  4 tablespoons hot butter
Remove them to a hot platter. Dissolve:
  1 bouillon cube
in:
  1/4 cup boiling water
Add this to the pan and stir in:
  3 tablespoons marsala, Madeira or sherry
while scraping the pan well. Pour the sauce over the meat.

CUBED VEAL BAKED IN SOUR CREAM

4 Servings
Cut into cubes:
  1½ lbs. boneless veal
Brown them in:
  1½ tablespoons butter
Remove the meat to an oven-proof baking dish. Add to the butter, stir and sauté lightly:
  1 tablespoon chopped onion
  1/2 lb. sliced mushrooms
Remove it from the heat. Stir in slowly:
  1 tablespoon flour
  3 tablespoons water or stock
  3/4 cup sour cream
  1/2 teaspoon salt
  1/8 teaspoon pepper
Pour sauce over the meat. Cover the dish. Bake the meat in a slow oven 250° for 1 hour.

VEAL STEW

4 Servings
Select:
  1½ lbs. veal with little bone or 2 lbs. neck or shanks
The meat may be cooked in one piece, or cut into 3 inch pieces, or into 1½ inch cubes. Melt in a heavy pot or saucepan over a moderate flame:
  3 tablespoons butter or drippings
Sear the meat in the hot drippings. Reduce the heat to a very low flame. Cover the bottom of the pot to the depth of 1/2 inch with boiling:
  Vegetable Stock, page 425
Cover the pot closely and simmer the meat until it is tender, 45 minutes or more. Remove the meat from the pot. Strain the stock. Thicken it with:
  Flour (see Gravy, page 426)

Return the meat to the pot, heat it
and serve it sprinkled with:
  Chopped parsley
The browning of the meat in fat is
optional. For a pleasant change drop
it directly into boiling vegetable stock
and cook it as directed.
Another approach to veal stew is to
sauté ½ cupful of sliced onions in the
fat and substitute boiling water for
the stock. Celery, carrots, turnips, etc.,
may be peeled and cubed and added to
the stock for the last ½ hour of cooking or the vegetables may be ground
and added. A good proportion is:
  1½ lbs. veal
  1 cup celery and carrots
  1 cup onions: small whole skinned
    onions or sliced onions
  (1 cup potatoes)
If vegetables are added, do not strain
the stock. Thicken it if required with:
  1 or 2 tablespoons quick-cooking
    tapioca or flour combined with
    a little water (see Gravy, page
    426)
Cook the tapioca in the gravy for 5
minutes. Stir it from time to time.
Cook and stir the flour until the gravy
thickens. Serve the stew with:
  Noodles, page 97
  Farina Balls, page 421, or
  Rice Ring, page 105, and
  Fried Apples, page 447
Veal stew is also good with a baked
top crust. Follow the rule for Chicken
Pot Pie crust, page 141, or serve it in
Corn-Meal Mush Pie, page 156, or
Grits Ring, page 157.

VEAL STEW WITH RED WINE
4 Servings
A topnotch dish for a maidless or any
other household. Cut into 12 chunks:
  1½ lbs. boneless veal or beef
Roll each piece in:
  ½ slice bacon: 6 slices in all
Dredge the meat lightly with:
  Flour
Melt in a heavy skillet:
  2 tablespoons bacon or other fat
Add the meat and:
  12 small peeled onions
Stir these ingredients about and permit them to brown on all sides. Remove them from the pan. Pour off all
but 1 tablespoonful of fat. Stir in:
  1 tablespoon flour
Add and stir until smooth:
  1½ cups consommé or stock
  ½ cup dry red wine
Add the beef and onions. Simmer

these ingredients closely covered for
1½ to 2 hours, until the meat is very
tender. Season and serve them with
some baked dish. Try this with one
of my favorites:
  Corn-Meal Soufflé, page 219

ELABORATE VEAL STEW
6 Servings
The traditional Blanquette de Veau is
soaked in water for 1 hour. It is put on
in cold water which is skimmed frequently. It is boiled, not simmered, for
45 minutes. The result is a fine gravy,
but meat that is robbed of nearly all
flavor. I prefer the American version
given below:
Cut into 2 inch squares:
  2½ lbs. veal shoulder
Place in a saucepan and bring slowly
to the boiling point:
  4 cups water
  6 chopped ribs celery with leaves
  4 sprigs parsley
  1 bay leaf
  2 cloves
  ½ teaspoon salt
  ¼ teaspoon white pepper
  ⅛ teaspoon grated nutmeg
  (½ teaspoon thyme)
Drop the meat piece by piece into the
pot. Do not check the boiling of the
stock. Reduce the heat. Simmer these
ingredients covered until the meat is
tender, 45 minutes or more. Add for
the last ½ hour of cooking:
  8 or 10 small peeled onions
Remove the meat and the onions from
the pot. Place them where they will
keep hot. Strain the stock. Skim it.
Melt:
  3 tablespoons fat or butter
Stir in until blended:
  3 tablespoons flour
Stir in slowly:
  2 cups stock
Add, if needed:
  Salt and paprika
Cook and stir the stock until it is
smooth and boiling. Remove it from
the heat. Beat in:
  3 beaten egg yolks
Stir the gravy over a low flame to
permit the yolks to thicken slightly.
Remove it from the fire. Beat in:
  3 tablespoons lemon juice or
    sherry
Arrange the meat and the onions on a
platter around a mound of:
  Boiled Rice, page 103
Pour the gravy over the meat. Place
at each end:

A bunch of parsley
6 or 8 cooked whole carrots
Serve it at once.

VEAL PAPRIKA
Cut into 2 inch squares:
  2 lbs. veal steak 1 inch thick
Sprinkle it with:
  1 teaspoon salt
  ⅛ teaspoon pepper
Peel and cut in two:
  1 clove garlic or use 2 minced
  onions
Sauté it for 3 minutes in:
  2 to 6 tablespoons butter or fat
Add the meat and sauté it until it is
lightly browned. Add:
  1½ cups boiling Vegetable Stock,
  page 425
Cover the saucepan and simmer the
meat for 1 hour, or until it is tender.
Remove the garlic. Add:
  ¾ cup sweet or sour cream
  1 teaspoon paprika
Heat the cream, but do not let the
sauce boil. Serve the stew with:
  Potato Dumplings, page 422

VEAL BIRDS
Trim the edges from:
  Slices of veal from the round ⅓
  inch thick
Pound the meat with the edge of a
plate and cut it into pieces about 2 x 4
inches. Make the following dressing:
Chop the meat trimmings and com-
bine them with an equal amount of
chopped:
  Salt pork
Measure the salt pork and trimmings
and add to them ½ the amount of:
  Bread crumbs
Add:
  Chopped onion or chopped
  raisins or seedless grapes
  Chopped celery
Moisten these ingredients with suffi-
cient:
  Cream or stock
to hold them together. Spread the
meat lightly with the dressing and roll
it. Secure it with skewers or thread.
Roll the birds in:
  Seasoned flour
Sauté them in hot:
  Butter
over a moderate fire until they are
brown. Reduce the heat and add:
  Hot cream, milk, stock or dry
  wine
until the birds are half covered. Cover
the pot closely and cook them until

they are tender, about 20 minutes.
Season them with:
  Salt and pepper
Thicken the drippings with:
  Flour (see Gravy, page 426)
Add to the gravy for a company dish:
  ½ lb. Sautéed Mushrooms, page
  292
Pour it over the meat.
For a simplified way of making veal
birds follow the rule for Beef Rolls,
page 348. In place of the dressing the
meat may be rolled around small sau-
sages or sausage meat.

---

*Goulash, Veal and Pork with Sauer-
kraut, page 154; Mock Chicken Drumsticks or City Chicken, page 194.*

VEAL IN BATTER
Prepare:
  Fritter Batter for Meat, page 543
Pound until very thin a:
  ½ inch slice veal from the round
Cut it into small pieces. Add:
  Chopped parsley
  (Lemon juice)
Follow the rule for cooking Brain
Fritters, page 140. Serve them with:
  Figaro Sauce, page 430

VEAL LOAF
6 to 8 Servings
Grind:
  1½ lbs. veal
Grind it a second time with:
  ¼ lb. salt pork
Remove the seeds and grind:
  1 small green pepper
Peel and chop:
  ¾ cup onion
Melt:
  2 tablespoons butter
Brown the onion in the butter and add
it to the ground ingredients. Add and
combine well:
  2 tablespoons cream or stock
  1 tablespoon lemon juice
  1½ teaspoons salt
  ¾ teaspoon paprika or pepper
  6 tablespoons rolled crackers or
  crushed cornflakes
Place these ingredients in a small
greased loaf pan. Brush the top of the
loaf with:
  White of an egg
Bake it in a slow oven 300° for 2 hours
or more. Baste it with:
  ½ cup stock or ¼ cup pork fat
Thicken the drippings with:
  Flour (see Gravy, page 426)

Cooked ground veal may be prepared by the same rule. It requires a shorter time for baking, about 1 hour.

STEAMED VEAL SOUFFLÉ
8 Servings
The following is an excellent soufflé.
Combine:
　1½ lbs. ground veal
　½ lb. ground pork
　1½ cups finely rolled cracker crumbs
　3 egg yolks
　¾ cup milk
　¼ teaspoon nutmeg
　1 tablespoon melted butter
　1 tablespoon onion juice
　1¼ teaspoons salt

　¼ teaspoon pepper
　¼ cup chopped celery
　⅛ cup chopped parsley
Beat until stiff:
　3 egg whites
Fold them into the other ingredients. Grease a pudding mold, fill it with the mixture, close it tightly and steam the soufflé for 2½ hours. See Rule for Steaming Pudding, page 731. Serve the soufflé with:
　Mushroom Sauce and Capers, page 436, or Allemande Sauce, page 429
or with the more plebeian but always admirable:
　Quick Tomato Sauce, page 433

For other Veal Dishes see Index.

Lamb and Mutton

　Lamb is a tender meat. All cuts may be roasted. The best-known cuts for roasting are a quarter of spring lamb, leg, crown roast or rack, loin, shoulder or chuck, rolled shoulder, cushion shoulder and breast. The leg, shoulder and breast may be stuffed. Other cuts may be braised or stewed. The thriftier cuts are square cut shoulder and cushion shoulder. Mutton is mature lamb. Its flavor is a bit strong, so it is braised or boiled more frequently than roasted in this country. You may substitute mutton for lamb in any of the following recipes. Cook it 5 to 10 minutes longer per pound. The carving of a French leg of lamb is shown below.

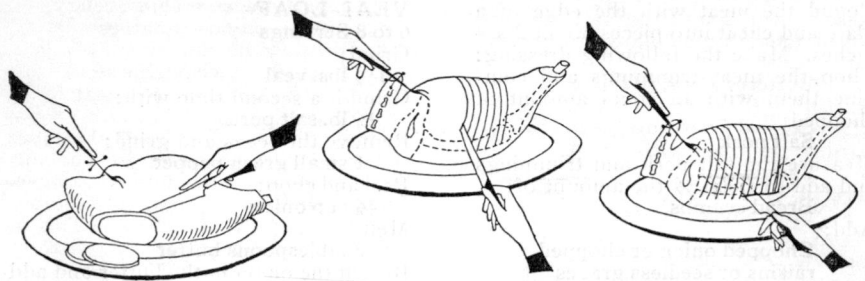

LAMB ROAST
Remove from the refrigerator at least ½ hour before cooking:
　A leg of lamb
You need not remove the fell. It helps retain the shape and flavor. You may rub the meat with:
　(Cut garlic or lemon)
Dredge it with:
　Flour
You may insert under the skin, using a pointed knife:
　(Slivers of garlic or herbs)
Place the lamb fat side up in a pan in a slow oven, preheated to 300°. Roast it as directed by the chart on page 336, 30 to 35 minutes to the pound. The roast will be well done, according to our American custom. Europeans like it slightly rare. Do not cover it or baste it. Season it with:
　Salt and freshly ground pepper
Thicken the drippings with:
　Flour (see Gravy, page 426)
Add to it:
　(Sour cream or milk)
Or serve the roast with unthickened gravy and:
　Mint Sauce, page 431
If the mint sauce is not desired, see:

Currant Jelly Sauce, page 436
You may add 1 or 2 tablespoonfuls
Madeira or sherry to the drippings.
To carve a French lamb roast see illustration on preceding page.

*See the chart for Left-Over Food, page
926, for ways of utilizing left-over lamb.*

CROWN ROAST OF LAMB
Allow 2 Ribs Per Person
Wipe with a cloth:
A crown roast of lamb
Protect the ends of the bones in a slow
oven 300°. Allow 30 to 35 minutes to
the pound. Remove the roast before
the last hour of cooking. Fill the center with:
**Bread Dressing or Dressing for
Crown Roast of Lamb, page 419**
Return it to the oven and complete
the cooking. Season it with:
Salt and freshly ground pepper
Remove the covering from the bones.
Garnish them with a paper frill, a
slice of pickle or a stuffed olive. Thicken the drippings with:
**Flour (see Gravy, page 426)
(See Currant Jelly Sauce, page
436)**
An unfilled crown roast may be cooked
upside down. Omit covering the bones.
When done fill the hollow of the roast
with:
Buttered Peas, page 298
or with:
Cooked Chestnuts, page 283
Garnish the roast with:
Parsley
Serve it with the gravy and:
Mint Sauce, page 431
Parboiled vegetables, potatoes, carrots, etc., may be added to the pan for
the last ½ hour or so of roasting. If
there are insufficient drippings in the
pan, add a little fat.
To carve a crown roast see illustration, page 364.

CUSHION SHOULDER ROAST
OF LAMB
Prepare or have prepared with one
side left open for inserting dressing:
A cushion shoulder of lamb
Rub the meat with:
A cut clove of garlic
Fill the cavity with:
**Bread or other dressing, page
416**
Sew or skewer up the open side. Roast

the meat uncovered in a slow oven
300° until done, about 40 minutes to
the pound. Season it with:
Salt and freshly ground pepper
Another way of preparing this is to
baste the roast every ½ hour with tart
French dressing. Serve the roast with:
Gravy, page 426

BRAISED STUFFED
SHOULDER OF LAMB
WITH VEGETABLES
6 Servings
Bone:
A shoulder of lamb
You may rub it with:
(Garlic)
Or insert slivers of garlic under the
skin. Prepare about:
3 cups Bread Dressing, page 416
Spread the dressing on the meat. Roll
it like a jelly roll. Secure it with
string. The roast may be cooked in a
300° oven, allowing 40 minutes to the
pound. Or place it in a dry pan on a
dripping rack in a hot oven 500° for 15
minutes. Add:
1 cup Vegetable Stock, page 425
Reduce the heat to 350°. Some of the
bones may be placed in the pan. Cover
the meat and cook it for 45 minutes.
Prepare for cooking:
**3 cups diced vegetables: celery,
carrots, onions, potatoes**
Place them in the pan with:
About 1 cup vegetable stock
Cover the pan. Cook the meat for 1
hour longer.
Pour off the liquid. Permit the meat
and vegetables to glaze by cooking
them uncovered for 10 minutes longer.
Prepare the gravy by boiling it rapidly
until it is somewhat reduced. This is
traditional. Pour off the fat. Season
and serve.

BRAISED ROAST OF LAMB
Melt in a heavy kettle:
¼ cup melted drippings or butter
Sear on all sides in the hot fat:
A rolled shoulder of lamb
Remove it from the kettle. Cook
slowly in the fat for 10 minutes:
**½ cup chopped onion
¼ cup chopped carrots
¼ cup chopped turnips
½ cup chopped celery with leaves
(1 sliced clove garlic)**
Return the meat to the kettle. Add:
**½ bay leaf
4 whole peppercorns
1 teaspoon salt**

4 cups boiling water or 2 cups
water and 2 cups tomato pulp or
other **Vegetable Stock, page 425**
Cover the pot closely. Simmer the
meat until it is tender, about 2 hours.
The meat may be baked closely covered until it is tender in a slow oven
325°, allowing about 40 minutes to the
pound. In that case, it may be necessary to add boiling stock or water.
When the meat is done the stock may
be poured off and thickened with:
Flour (see Gravy, page 426)
Serve the roast surrounded by the
vegetables.

Mock Duck I, page 349.
This is made with a beef flank or rump
steak.

MOCK DUCK II
Have a butcher prepare for mock
duck:
A forequarter of lamb
Rub the roast with:
A cut clove garlic
Place pieces of buttered paper on the
parts representing the "head" and the
"tail." Put the roast on a rack in a
roasting pan. Dredge it with:
Flour
Place on top of the meat:
4 thin slices salt pork
Mince and place in the bottom of the
pan:
¼ cup salt pork
Cook the roast in a 300° oven through-
out without basting, allowing 30 min-
utes to the pound.
Or, place the roast in a hot oven 450°
for 15 minutes. Reduce the heat to
300°. Allow 30 minutes to the pound.
Baste several times while cooking.
Season it with:
Salt and freshly ground pepper
Thicken the drippings with:
Flour (see Gravy, page 426)

MOCK VENISON
This is both delicate and delicious.
Wipe with a damp cloth:
A leg of lamb or mutton
Cover it with:
Sour milk
Soak it for 24 hours or more. Drain it.
Lard it (page 341) with:
Salt pork or bacon
Dot it with:
Butter
Dredge it with:
Flour

The roast may be cooked in a 300°
oven, allowing 35 minutes to the
pound.
Or roast it in a very hot oven 480° for
15 minutes. Add:
**½ cup hot Vegetable Stock, page
425**
Reduce the heat to 300° and cover the
roast closely. Baste it frequently.
When it is nearly done remove the
cover and pour over the roast:
1 cup sour cream
Permit the roast to brown uncovered
for 10 minutes. Season it with:
Salt and freshly ground pepper
Thicken the drippings with:
Flour (see Gravy, page 426)
Serve the roast surrounded by:
Browned Potatoes, page 302
Garnish it with:
Parsley

LAMB CHOPS—BROILED
Follow directions for Broiled Steak,
page 345, allowing a shorter time for
cooking according to the thickness of
the chops (see page 338).

LAMB CHOPS—PAN-BROILED
Trim the edges of:
Lamb chops
The outer skin is too strong in flavor.
Sear the chops in a hot dry skillet.
Reduce the heat and cook them slowly
until they are done. Pour off the fat
as it accumulates in the pan. Season
them with:
Salt and freshly ground pepper
Place in the center of a platter a
mound of:
Mashed Potatoes, page 302
Make a slight depression in the top
and pour the hot drippings into it.
Surround the potatoes with the broiled
chops. Garnish them with:
Parsley
Place a sprig of parsley in the center
of the potato mound. Serve the dish
while the chops are very hot.

STUFFED LAMB CHOPS
6 Servings
To prepare and stuff lamb chops follow
the rule for:
Stuffed Pork Chops, page 368
Substitute:
6 lamb chops
The chops may be surrounded by:
Strips of bacon
Use toothpicks to hold them in place.
Or cut lamb chops from the bone.

Place a small ball of sausage meat against each chop. Wrap the tail around it. Secure it with a toothpick. Broil or pan-broil the chops.

BRAISED LAMB SHANKS
4 Servings

Thanks to the high cost of food, interest has been aroused in the less expensive cuts of meat. Cooks with a flair for good eating have always included these dishes in their menus. Short ribs, shanks, flank steak, etc., properly cooked are a treat to be remembered.

Roll:

4 lamb shanks: 3½ to 4 lbs.

in:

Seasoned flour

Rub a roaster with garlic. Melt in it:

2 tablespoons fat

Add:

2 tablespoons cut up onion

Sear the shanks in the hot fat on all sides until a deep brown. Then you may pour off the fat. The meat may be raised in the pan by placing a trivet under it. Add:

1¼ cups boiling water
⅓ teaspoon pepper
1½ teaspoons salt
½ bay leaf

Cover the pan closely. Simmer the meat for about 3 hours, or bake it covered in a slow oven 300° for about 3½ hours, or until tender. Turn it frequently.

You may add for the last ½ hour of cooking:

3 cups diced vegetables
¼ cup boiling water

These may be onions, carrots, celery, peppers, turnips, tomatoes and/or potatoes. The vegetables are a matter of choice and expediency. Add, if you wish:

(½ teaspoon herb)

It is not necessary to thicken the gravy but it may be thickened with:

Flour (see Gravy, page 426)

Correct the seasoning, adding salt, pepper, etc., as needed. If you wish a Creole Sauce, brown lightly:

1 large minced onion

in:

2 tablespoons butter

Add:

2 chopped green peppers with seeds and membranes removed
3 cups tomatoes, partly drained
A pinch of cayenne

½ bay leaf or ½ teaspoon dried herb
Salt and freshly ground pepper

Stir this over low heat until slightly thickened. Add it to the browned shanks in place of the vegetables and water.

CREOLE LAMB CHOPS OR STEAKS
Follow the rule on page 367 for:

Creole Pork Chops

Serve the chops with:

New potatoes creamed, sprinkled with chopped parsley

Lamb Terrapin, page 166.

LAMB STEW
Follow the rule for Veal Stew, page 358. Do not sear the meat unless it is very lean, then sear it in hot fat with chopped onions added. Drop it as directed into boiling:

Vegetable Stock, page 425, or ½ vegetable stock and ½ tomato juice, or vegetable stock and 1 tablespoon tomato paste with a sliver of garlic

Cover it and simmer it until it is tender. Serve the stew, if desired, with a top crust. See Chicken Pot Pie, page 141, or serve it in Corn-Meal Mush Pie, page 156, Grits Ring, page 157, or on Dumplings, page 421.

Capers or chopped pickles may be added to the gravy.

See Irish Stew, page 350. This may be made with lamb. Neck cut in thick crosswise slices makes an excellent stew. The slices look like chops.

CURRY OF LAMB WITH RICE
4 Servings

Remove the gristle and fat from:

A 2 lb. lamb shoulder

Cut the meat into 1 inch cubes. Heat:

3 tablespoons fat

Brown the meat in the hot fat with:

1 tablespoon chopped onion

Add:

1 cup boiling water
⅔ teaspoon curry powder
¼ cup or more chopped celery
2 tablespoons chopped parsley
(1 tablespoon chopped pimiento)

Cover the meat and simmer it until it is done, about ½ hour. Stir it frequently. Season it with:

½ teaspoon salt
¼ teaspoon pepper

Thicken the stock with:
Flour (see Gravy, page 426)
Cook and stir it for 2 minutes. Place
on a platter a mound of:
Hot Boiled or Steamed Rice,
page 103
Arrange the meat and gravy around it.
Garnish the platter with:
Parsley

LEG OF MUTTON WITH CAPER SAUCE

You may leave the fell on:
A leg of mutton
You may place the meat for several
hours in a marinade, page 340, or you
may rub it all over with:
(A cut clove of garlic)
Rub the meat with:
Butter
Melt in a heavy kettle:
¼ cup fat or drippings
Brown the meat in it on all sides. Add:
4 cups boiling water
Cover the pot. Simmer the meat until
it is tender. Allow 30 minutes to the
pound. Add boiling water if necessary.
When the meat has cooked for 1 hour
add:

2 small whole onions
3 peppercorns
3 cloves
A sprig of thyme or ½ teaspoon
dried thyme
½ bay leaf
When the meat is tender remove it
from the pot. Season it with:
Salt
Place it where it will remain hot. Skim
the fat from the stock. Melt:
6 tablespoons butter or use fat
removed from stock
Stir in:
4 tablespoons flour
Stir in slowly:
3 cups strained lamb stock
Cook and stir the sauce until it is thick
and smooth. Add:
¼ cup cream
½ cup drained capers
Seasoning as needed

LAMB KABOBS

Follow the rule for Beef Kabobs on
page 348, substituting lamb for beef.
Good outdoor fare. For other lamb
rules see Index.

Pork

Mrs. Beeton in her vast, wonderful old-timey cookbook adds to her meat chapter some "observations on the common hog." To us, the most welcome observation would be a much reduced price tag attached to the expensive pork on the butcher's counter.

The carving of a crown roast of pork is shown below.

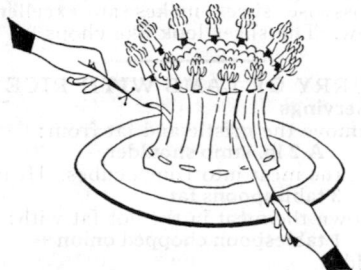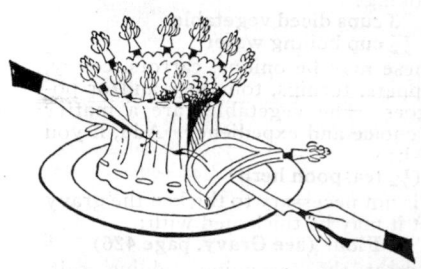

Any part of pork may be roasted. The choice roasts are the rib, loin and shoulder. The lower half of the foreleg or picnic may be boned and rolled or flattened, stuffed and rolled. Allow 5 to 10 minutes longer per pound for a rolled roast.

Fresh hams or legs of pork are good roasted or braised.

The first rule for pork is that it must be thoroughly cooked. Otherwise the trichinae or parasites which exist in most pork may be transmitted to the eater. Avoid "pink pork;" cook the meat until it is white or grayish. Bake it uncovered in a 350° oven 30 to 45 minutes to the pound.

PORK ROAST

The rib end of loin makes a fine juicy roast. Take the roast from the refrigerator at least ½ hour before cooking it. Cut off the edges and surplus fat. It may be rubbed well with:

> (A cut clove of garlic, fresh sage leaves or dried rosemary, tarragon or thyme)

It may be dredged with:

> (Flour)

Place it fat side up in a pan in an oven preheated to 350°. Cook it 30 to 45 minutes to the pound (see chart on page 336). Season it with:

> Salt and pepper

Thicken the drippings with:

> Flour (see Gravy, page 426)

You may roast apples and parboiled onions in the pan for the last hour of cooking or, if you prefer, parboiled sweet potatoes or parsnips. Serve the roast with:

> Applesauce, page 447, seasoned with 2 tablespoons horseradish and a grating of nutmeg
> Sweet Potatoes and Apples, page 311
> Apples with Sauerkraut, page 278
> Apple and Onion Dish, page 185
> Turnips and Apples, page 322, or Purée of Lentils or Peas, page 271

A rib roast may be boned, stuffed, rolled and cooked by the above method. Cooked prunes and apricots are sometimes used for the dressing.

A pork roast is good served with lots of freshly ground pepper and it is superb served with sauerkraut and caraway seeds. The chart for left-overs, page 926, may give you new suggestions for utilizing left-over meat.

ROLLED SHOULDER OF PORK

This is a good cut for roasting. Have the roast boned and rolled. Prepare meat as suggested under Pork Roast. Place it on a rack in a pan. Add the removed bones to the pan. Roast the meat in a 350° oven for 45 minutes to the pound. Turn it every ½ hour. Prepare:

> Gravy, page 426

Serve the roast with:

> Spoon Bread, page 423

FRESH HAM

You may place in a marinade (see Beef à la Mode and Sauerbraten, page 344:

> A fresh ham

After 3 days remove the ham. Wipe it dry. Cook it by the rule for:

> Pork Roast

Baste it every ½ hour with part of the marinade or with a traditional addition: beer. Serve it with:

> Gravy, page 426

CROWN ROAST OF PORK

Prepare like Crown Roast of Lamb, page 361:

> A crown roast of pork

Place it in a moderate oven 350°, allow 30 to 45 minutes to the pound.

If the roast is not to be filled with dressing, omit the covering of the bones and cook the roast upside down. Serve it filled with a cooked vegetable. If the roast is to be filled, remove it 1 hour before it is done. Combine:

> 2½ lbs. pork sausage
> ½ cup bread crumbs
> ¼ cup chopped onions
> ½ cup chopped celery

Moisten these ingredients with a very little:

> Milk

Season with:

> Savory or other herb
> Paprika or pepper

Fill the crown with this dressing or fill it with:

> Apple and Bread Dressing, page 418, or Fruit Dressing, page 419

Return the roast to the oven and complete the cooking. Thicken the drippings with:

> Flour (see Gravy, page 426)

To garnish or to carve it see Crown Roast of Lamb. Serve the roast with:

> Glazed Onions, page 295
> Cinnamon Apples, page 446
> Water cress

ROAST SUCKLING PIG

This recipe for the old-fashioned way of cooking a young pig is given because it is pleasant to preserve traditional rules. However, there is no reason why you should not dress a pig and roast it throughout in a moderate oven 350°, allowing 30 to 45 minutes to the pound. Do not cover or baste it. Dress, by drawing, scraping and cleaning:

> A suckling pig

The dressed pig should weigh about 12 pounds. Fill the pig with:

> Dressing

Onion Dressing, page 419, is traditional, but choose your favorite kind. It takes 2½ quarts of dressing to stuff a pig of this size. Multiply all your ingredients but not the seasonings. Use these sparingly until the dressing is combined, then taste it and add what is lacking. Sew up the pig. Put a block of wood in the pig's mouth to hold it open. Skewer the legs into position, pulling the forelegs forward and the hindlegs backward. Rub the pig with:

Oil or soft butter
(A cut clove of garlic)

Dredge it with:

Flour

Cover the ears with pieces of well-greased paper. Secure them with paper clips. Place the pig in a pan in a hot oven 480° for 15 minutes. Reduce the heat to a moderate oven 350°. Roast the pig until it is tender, allowing 30 minutes to the pound. If you wish the surface of the roast to be soft, baste it every 15 minutes with:

About 2 cups boiling stock

If you wish it to be crusty, baste it every 15 minutes with:

Oil or melted butter

and dredge it with:

Flour

It may be sprinkled lightly toward the end with:

Salt and paprika

Remove the paper from the ears for the last 30 minutes of baking. Place the roast on a platter. Remove the wood from the mouth. Replace it with a small:

Lemon, apple or carrot

Place in the eyes:

Raisins or cranberries

Place around the neck a wreath of:

Small green leaves

or garnish the platter with:

Parsley or water cress

The pig may be surrounded with:

Cinnamon Apples, page 446, Apples filled with Sweet Potatoes, page 446, Apples filled with Mincemeat, page 446, Baked Tomatoes filled with Pineapple, page 201, etc.

Serve the roast with:

Gravy

made with the pan drippings or the liquid in the pan (page 426).

PORK ROAST WITH SAUERKRAUT

Have the butcher remove the bones from:

A pork shoulder

Fill the shoulder with:

Drained sauerkraut

Dredge it with:

Flour

Follow the rule for Cushion Shoulder Roast of Lamb, page 361. If there is no dripping rack available, put ½ cupful of water in the pan to keep the roast from sticking. For time and temperature see Rule for Roasting Meat, page 336.

PORK TENDERLOIN

Split lengthwise:

A pork tenderloin

Flatten it out. Rub it lightly with:

Butter
(Garlic)

Spread it with:

Bread Dressing, page 416, using ¼ the amount given, or with Apple and Sweet Potato Dressing, page 419, using about ⅓ the amount given, or with stewed pitted prunes

Sew it or tie it up. Dredge it with:

Seasoned flour

Place the tenderloin in a moderate oven 350°. Cook it 30 to 45 minutes to the pound. Thicken the drippings with:

Flour (see Gravy, page 426)

You may add to the gravy:

(Sour cream and cooked mushrooms or sweet cream and currant jelly)

Pork tenderloin may be cut into lengthwise strips, spread with dressing—apple is good—rolled and tied up. Roll the rolls in:

Seasoned flour

Sear them in a very little:

Fat

If the garlic has been omitted, a little onion may be added to the fat. Brown the rolls well. Add:

½ cup sour cream

Cover them closely and cook them slowly for 30 minutes.

Pork Tenderloin with Mushrooms, Olives and Cream, page 153.

PORK TENDERLOIN FRENCHED

Cut crosswise into ¾ inch slices:

Pork tenderloin

Flatten the slices slightly. Cover them with:

Paprika

Broil them (page 337) or sauté them like Pork Chops (page 367).

PORK CHOPS

Sear in a hot pan:
    Pork chops
in just enough grease to keep them from sticking. They may be rubbed with garlic or powdered rosemary before searing. Reduce the heat. Season the chops with:
    Salt and pepper
Cook them slowly, covered or uncovered, until they are done. Pour off the excess grease as they cook. Thicken the drippings with:
    Flour (see Gravy, page 426)

BREADED PORK CHOPS

Prepare the chops like Veal Cutlets, page 356. Cook them in a minimum of grease in a hot pan. Reduce the heat. Pour off the excess grease and cook them until they are done. Season them palatably. Thicken the drippings with:
    Flour (see Gravy, page 426)

PORK CHOPS AND APPLES

Trim:
    Pork chops ¾ inch or more thick
Sear the chops in a hot lightly greased skillet. Season them with:
    Salt and paprika
You may sprinkle them with:
    (Chopped onion)
Cut in halves crosswise and core:
    Apples
Place them on the chops, skin side down. Cover the apples with:
    Brown sugar
Cover the bottom of the skillet well with:
    Hot sweet or sour cream
Cover the pan closely. Bake the chops in a moderate oven 350° from 30 to 40 minutes. Season them with:
    Salt and freshly ground pepper
Baste them frequently. When they are done thicken the drippings with:
    Flour (see Gravy, page 426)

PORK CHOPS AND PINEAPPLE

Follow the preceding rule. Sear the chops in:
    1½ tablespoons bacon fat
Place them in a casserole. Brown lightly in the fat:
    6 slices pineapple
Place them on the chops. Pour around them:
    ¾ cup pineapple juice
Proceed as directed.

DEVILED PORK CHOPS
4 Servings

Place in a dish:
    4 pork chops 1 inch thick
Marinate the chops for 1 hour in:
    3 tablespoons chili sauce
    1½ tablespoons lemon juice
    1 tablespoon grated onion
    ¼ teaspoon dry mustard
    2 teaspoons Worcestershire sauce
    ⅛ teaspoon curry
    ½ teaspoon salt
    ¼ teaspoon paprika
Drain the chops, reserving the marinade. Wipe them dry. Brown them in a hot greased skillet. Heat the marinade and:
    ½ cup water
Pour it around the chops. Reduce the heat. Simmer the chops covered until they are nearly tender, uncover them and continue cooking until they are done. Or, bake them covered in a moderate oven 350° until they are tender, about 1 hour.

PORK CHOPS BAKED IN SOUR CREAM
4 Servings

Prepare for cooking:
    4 loin pork chops ½ inch thick
Dredge them with:
    Seasoned flour
Insert in each chop:
    1 clove
Brown them lightly in a little hot pork fat or lard. Place them in a baking dish. Combine, heat and pour over them:
    ½ cup water
    ½ bay leaf
    2 tablespoons vinegar
    1 tablespoon sugar
    ½ cup sour cream
    (¼ teaspoon savory)
Cover the dish. Bake the chops in a moderate oven 350° for about 1 hour.

PORK CHOPS CREOLE
6 Servings

Dredge:
    6 pork chops ½ inch or more thick
with:
    Flour
Brown them in hot fat. Place the chops in a baking dish. Combine, heat and pour around them:
    10½ oz. condensed tomato or other soup
    10½ oz. water
    ½ cup chopped celery

1 seeded chopped green pepper
¾ cup minced onions
¾ teaspoon salt
¼ teaspoon paprika

Cover the dish. Bake the chops in a moderate oven 350° for about 1¼ hours. Remove the cover for the last 15 minutes. Cover the top for this time with:

Crushed cornflakes

STUFFED PORK CHOPS
6 Servings

These are so good that if I were writing a Baedeker I would give them triple stars ★ ★ ★.
Trim:

6 rib pork chops ¾ inch or more thick

Cut the bone from the meat. Trim off the excess fat and cut a large gash or pocket into the side of each chop. Prepare a dressing of:

1 cup bread crumbs
¼ cup chopped celery
¼ cup chopped onions
2 tablespoons chopped parsley
Milk to moisten the dressing
¼ teaspoon salt
⅛ teaspoon paprika

These proportions and ingredients may be varied. Fill the pockets with the dressing. Sew them up with a coarse needle and thread. Sear the chops in a hot skillet and place them in a pan with a little:

Milk or cream

Cover the pan and bake the chops in a moderate oven 350° until they are done, ¾ to 1 hour. Thicken the drippings with:

Flour (see Gravy, page 426)

FRESH SAUSAGE PATTIES
4 Servings

Grind with some of the fat:
1 lb. pork
Add:
1 teaspoon salt
⅛ teaspoon black pepper
⅛ teaspoon sage
1 egg

Mold the meat into cakes. Sauté them until brown.

PORK BIRDS
6 Servings

Pound to the thickness of ¼ inch:
2 lbs. pork steaks cut from the shoulder

Cut them into 6 oblong pieces. Rub them with a mixture of:

½ teaspoon salt
¼ teaspoon pepper
2 teaspoons lemon juice

Combine:
½ cup seeded raisins cut in halves
2 cups dry bread crumbs
¾ cup evaporated milk or cream
1 teaspoon salt

Spread the meat with the dressing. Roll it. Secure the rolls with string or toothpicks. Dredge the rolls in:

2 tablespoons flour

Melt:
2 tablespoons fat

Brown the rolls in the fat. Add:
1 cup boiling water or Stock, page 425

Cover the pan and simmer the rolls for about 20 minutes. Serve them with the liquor in the pan.

Mock Chicken Drumsticks, page 194; Pork Balls in Tomato Sauce, page 163.

BAKED SPARERIBS WITH DRESSING
4 Servings

As there is much bone and little meat to spareribs—I love the self-explanatory name—it is well to allow 1 pound of ribs to a person. Buy:

4 lbs. spareribs in 2 pieces

Spread 1 piece with a dressing made of:

1 cup bread crumbs
1 cup chopped apples
1 tablespoon chopped onion
½ teaspoon salt
⅛ teaspoon paprika
1 tablespoon sugar

Cover the dressing with the other piece of meat. Tie the 2 pieces together. Rub the outside of the meat with:

2 tablespoons flour
⅛ teaspoon salt
A few grains pepper

Place it on a rack in a roasting pan. Bake it in a hot oven 480° for 20 minutes. Reduce the heat and bake it in a moderate oven 325° for 1 hour. Baste the meat every 10 minutes with the fat in the pan.

BAKED SPARERIBS WITH SAUERKRAUT
4 Servings

Place in a mound in the center of a small roasting pan:

1½ quarts sauerkraut

Season:

4 lbs. spareribs
lightly with:
    Salt and pepper
Fold the ribs into halves. Place between the folds:
    Slices of onion
Cover the kraut with the folded spareribs. Bake them in a hot oven 400° until they are nicely browned. Baste them frequently with the kraut juice. Turn the ribs and brown the other side. Add water if necessary. Cover the pan. Reduce the temperature to 350°. Parboil until nearly tender:
    6 medium-sized potatoes
When the meat is nearly done, after about 1¼ hours cooking in all, uncover it, place the peeled whole potatoes around it. Turn them frequently to permit them to brown. Serve the ribs and vegetables when the meat is tender.
Or omit the potatoes. Remove the meat. Place the sauerkraut on top of the stove. Add to it some form of:
    Drop Dumplings, page 421
Cover the pot and cook the dumplings until tender, about 10 minutes.

BARBECUED SPARERIBS
4 Servings
Barbecue Sauce
Sauté until brown:
    ¼ cup chopped onions
in:
    1 tablespoon drippings or other fat
Add and simmer for 20 minutes:
    ½ cup water
    2 tablespoons vinegar
    1 tablespoon Worcestershire sauce
    ¼ cup lemon juice
    2 tablespoons brown sugar
    1 cup chili sauce
    ½ teaspoon salt
    ¼ teaspoon paprika
Cut into pieces for serving:
    2 lbs. spareribs
Place them in a pan. Cover them with waxed paper. Bake the ribs in a very hot oven 500° for 15 minutes. Reduce the heat to 350°.
Remove the paper and pour the barbecue sauce over the meat. Bake the spareribs for 1 hour longer. Baste them frequently with the pan liquor.

BOILED SPARERIBS
Place:
    Spareribs
in:

Boiling water to cover
Add:
    Salt and pepper
    Chopped onion, celery, parsley and carrots
Simmer the meat covered until it is tender, from 1½ to 2 hours. Drain it and serve it on a mound of hot:
    Sauerkraut, page 277
Surrounded by:
    Mashed Potatoes, page 302

BOILED SPARERIBS OR FRANKFURTER SAUSAGES WITH SAUERKRAUT
Sear:
    Spareribs
in a small amount of:
    Pork fat
Season them with:
    Salt and paprika
Place them in a casserole between layers of:
    Raw sauerkraut
    Chopped onions
Cover these ingredients with:
    Boiling water
Cover them closely and bake them in a slow oven 325° for 2 hours. Frankfurter sausages or ham hocks may be substituted for spareribs. If you substitute frankfurters, add them for the last ½ hour of the cooking. Omit salt until the dish is cooked, then season it as needed. Serve the spareribs with:
    Mashed Potatoes, page 302

SAUERKRAUT AND PORK HOCKS
4 Servings
Place in a casserole:
    4 unskinned pork hocks
Cover them with:
    3 cups drained sauerkraut
    ¾ cup sliced onions
    (1 teaspoon caraway or celery seed)
Pour over them:
    1 cup sauerkraut juice or water
Cover the dish closely. Bake it in a moderate oven 350° for about 4 hours.

STEWED PIGS' FEET
Simmer by the rule on page 141 for Jellied Pigs' Feet:
    Pigs' feet
The spices may be omitted. Toward the end of the cooking add:
    Green beans or cabbage or sauerkraut
Cook the vegetables until they are tender.

STEWED PORK HOCKS

Cover with seasoned boiling water:

Pork hocks

Simmer them covered from 1½ to 3 hours. You may add potatoes for the last ½ hour of cooking or greens or cabbage for the last 15 minutes of cooking.

STEWED NECK BONES

Partly cover with seasoned boiling water:

Neck bones

Simmer them covered until tender. Vegetables may be added to the stew for the last ½ hour or so of cooking.

Ham

A definition of eternity: A ham and 2 people.

In former years ham required soaking in cold water to cover for 12 hours or more. Modern methods permit us to dispense with this step, but it is advisable to soak home-cured hams for 6 hours or more.

A "boiled" ham should be simmered, never boiled. Allow 30 minutes per pound for simmering a medium-sized ham; allow slightly more for a small ham and slightly less for a large ham. A thermometer will register 165° when the ham is done.

For a ham that is to be "boiled" and then baked, allow 25 minutes' simmering to the pound for a medium-sized ham, and slightly more for a small ham and slightly less for a large ham. A thermometer will register 150° when the ham is ready to be baked. Be sure to cook all tenderized hams sufficiently. The fact that hams are tenderized does not necessarily mean that the trichinae have been destroyed. A carved and garnished ham are shown below.

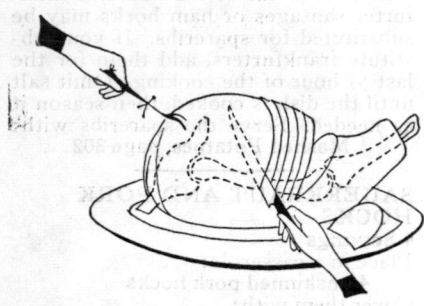

HAM, BOILED AND BAKED

Processed hams need not be boiled. They are sold ready to be baked. Follow the rule on page 371 for Processed Ham, Baked.

Scrub well:

A smoked ham

Place it in a kettle of fresh simmering water that barely covers it. Add:

Vegetables suitable for soup
1 bay leaf
8 peppercorns
(6 allspice)

Simmer the ham. See the preceding rule. Permit it to cool partly in the water in which it was cooked, drain it and strip off the skin. Cover the top of the ham with:

Brown sugar
(A little dry mustard)

Stud it with:

Whole cloves

Bake the ham in a hot oven 425° for 20 minutes. Baste it with a choice of:

1 cup cider, pineapple or orange juice, the juice of pickled peaches, cooked prunes or apricots, wine, ginger ale or molasses

Dredge it with:

Brown sugar

Sprinkle it with:

Grated orange rind

Lower the heat to 350°. Cook it without basting for 30 minutes. For the last 15 minutes put into the pan:

Pineapple slices

Garnish the ham with the pineapple and:

Maraschino cherries
Parsley

Serve it with:

Raisin Cider Sauce, page 437,
Sour Cream and Horseradish
Sauce, page 439, Barbecue
Sauce, page 436, or horseradish
mixed with currant jelly

Consult the Left-Over Chart, page 926, for various ways of utilizing scraps of ham and a ham bone.

"COUNTRY" HAMS. Virginia, Smithfield, etc.

It is a custom in some parts of the United States to "hang" hams for a long period of time. They become old and even moldy before they are used. This means that they must be thoroughly scrubbed with a brush and rinsed before being soaked. Yellow soap may be used when necessary to remove the mold.

After cleaning the ham, soak it overnight in cold water to cover. Rinse it and follow the above rule for Ham, Boiled and Baked. Allow 30 minutes to the pound for boiling an old ham. Bake it as directed above.

BAKED HAM

Scrub well:

A smoked ham

Bake it on a rack uncovered in a slow oven 325°. Allow 25 minutes to the pound for ½ a ham, 30 minutes for a whole ham. It is done when the meat thermometer registers 170°. Take the ham from the oven 1 hour before it is done. Remove the rind, all but a collar around the shank bone. Combine:

1⅓ cups brown sugar
2 teaspoons dry mustard
⅓ cup fine bread crumbs

Moisten these ingredients with:

3 tablespoons cider vinegar, prune
juice, wine or ham drippings

Spread them over the fat side of the ham. Cut diagonal gashes across the fat side of the ham in diamond shape. Stud the fat with:

Cloves

Return the ham to the oven for 45 minutes. Increase the heat to 425°. Bake the ham 15 minutes longer. Place it on a platter. Garnish it with:

Maraschino cherries or
cranberries

Surround it with:

Pineapple slices

heated in the pan for the last 15 minutes, or

Apple Cups Filled with Sweet
Potatoes, page 446

It may be served with:

Wine Sauce, page 437, or some
other sauce for ham (see Sauces,
page 425)

NEW PROCESSED HAMS, BAKED

Hams, processed for tenderness now purchasable everywhere, require no soaking or boiling. Directions for cooking them are usually given on the wrapper. See that the ham is at room temperature, unwrap it and wipe it with a damp cloth. You may replace it in the paper in which it was wrapped. Place the ham, fat side up, in a pan in a 350° oven. A ham that is processed requires 1 to 2 hours. Internal temperature when done is 150° to 160°. Remove the ham from the oven ½ hour before cooking time is over, unwrap it, score it, stud it with cloves, etc., as suggested in the last part of the above rule for:

Ham, Boiled and Baked, or
Baked Ham

Return it to the oven for the last ½ hour of cooking. Baste it frequently for the first 15 minutes of this period.

BAKED HAM WITH BARBECUE SAUCE

Trim and place in a casserole:

A 2 lb. slice smoked ham

Combine:

¼ cup chopped onion
½ chopped clove garlic
¼ cup tomato catsup
2 tablespoons Worcestershire
sauce
¼ cup cider vinegar
1 can tomato soup: 10½ oz.
2 teaspoons butter
1 teaspoon brown sugar
⅛ teaspoon pepper

Pour these ingredients over the ham. Cover the casserole. Bake the ham in a moderate oven 350° until it is tender, for about 1 hour.

HAM BAKED WITH CRANBERRIES

Trim the edges of:

2 slices raw ham 1 or more
inches thick

Combine:

2 cups raw cranberries cut into
   halves
1 cup strained honey or 1 cup
   white or brown sugar
Place a slice of ham in a roasting pan
or casserole. Cover it with ½ the cranberries. Place the second slice of ham
on top of the cranberries. Cover it
with the remaining cranberries. Stud
the edge of the top slice of ham with:
   Whole cloves
Bake the ham in a moderate oven 350°
for about 1½ hours, or until tender.
Baste it frequently with the liquid in
the pan. The cranberries may be put
through a meat grinder. You may add
to the cranberry mixture:
   3 tablespoons freshly ground or
      prepared horseradish

SLICE OF HAM BAKED OR SIMMERED

This is one of the finest everyday
dishes I know, but I find it curiously
neglected by most cookbook writers.
There are 2 methods of preparing a
ham slice—with scarcely a preference
for one or the other method, so that
becomes a matter of convenience.
Ham is prepared, covered with other
ingredients and baked until done, covered or uncovered, in a moderate oven
350°. Or it is seared, covered with
other ingredients and simmered, covered or uncovered, on top of a stove
until done. The ingredients added are
so varied that it is impossible to list
them all, but any one of them seems to
result in a good dish.

HAM BAKED OR SIMMERED IN MILK

4 to 6 Servings
Trim the edges of:
   A small slice smoked ham 1¼
      inches thick
Stud the fat with:
   3 or more cloves
Combine:
   3 tablespoons brown sugar
   2 teaspoons prepared mustard
Or make a paste of brown sugar,
mustard and wine or horseradish, or
of mustard and currant jelly.
Rub these ingredients into both sides
of the ham. Sear it on both sides over
quick heat in:
   A little fat
Pour around it:
   ½ cup hot rich milk or diluted
      evaporated milk
Cook the ham covered in a moderate

oven 350° for 1 hour or longer. Bake
it uncovered for the last 10 minutes.
Baste it frequently. Add hot milk if
needed.
Or prepare by the above rule:
   A slice of ham ½ inch thick
Sear it. Reduce the heat. Simmer the
ham covered on top of the stove for
about 10 minutes. Uncover it for the
last 3 minutes. Test the ham, whether
baked or simmered, for doneness.
There are now so many differently
prepared hams on the market that it is
difficult to give the exact time.

HAM BAKED OR SIMMERED WITH FRUIT

Prepare by one of the preceding rules:
   A slice of smoked ham
Sear it. Add a little fruit juice or water
to the skillet. Cover the ham with a
choice of:
   Thinly sliced apples or oranges
      and brown sugar
   Drained slices canned pineapple,
      apricots, peaches, red plums,
      sour cherries, etc.
   Apricot or prune purée
   Cranberries cut in two and
      sugared, etc.
   Raisins and cider or sherry or
      grapefruit juice
The fruits may be sprinkled with:
   Spice: cinnamon, cloves, curry
or studded with:
   Cloves
Cover the skillet with a lid. Baste sev-
eral times with ham fat or hot fruit
juice. Uncover the ham as directed for
the last few minutes.

SAUTÉED HAM SLICE WITH ONIONS

2 Servings
Melt:
   2 tablespoons butter
Sauté in the hot butter until lightly
browned:
   ½ cup sliced onions
Place on top of the onions:
   A ¾ lb. slice of ham
Sauté it slowly, turning it once, until
tender and browned. If needed, add to
the pan:
   Butter
Make a sauce by melting and blending
over heat:
   ⅓ cup guava or currant jelly
   1 tablespoon prepared mustard
   2 tablespoons butter
   (¼ teaspoon ground cloves)
Place the ham on a hot platter. Sur-

round it with the onions. Pour the sauce over it.

Ham Baked with Apples, page 148.

BAKED HAM, POTATOES AND ONIONS
6 to 8 Servings
Place in a roasting pan:
    A 2 lb. slice of smoked ham
Peel and slice and spread over it:
    6 medium-sized potatoes
Sift over the potatoes:
    ½ cup all-purpose flour
    A little paprika
Peel, slice and add:
    2 large onions
Half cover these ingredients with:
    Milk
Cover the dish. Bake the ham in a moderate oven 350° for about 1½ hours. Uncover it for the last 10 minutes of cooking.

HAM BAKED WITH TOMATOES AND CHEESE
Place in a baking dish:
    A thick slice of smoked ham
Pour over it:
    2 cups canned tomatoes
Cover them with:
    ¼ lb. sliced American cheese
Cover the dish. Bake the ham in a moderate oven 350° until it is tender, about ¾ hour. Uncover it for the last 10 minutes of cooking.

SAUTÉED HAM AND EGGS
Trim the edges of:
    A thin slice of smoked ham
Rub a skillet with ham fat. Heat it. Brown the ham on one side, reverse it and brown it on the other. Remove it to a hot platter. Keep it hot. Reduce the heat. Cook gently in the tried out ham fat:
    Eggs
Or by pushing the ham aside you may cook the eggs in the ham fat when the ham is done without removing the ham from the pan.

BROILED HAM
Method I.
Trim the edges from:
    A slice of smoked ham 2 inches thick
Cover it with:
    Cold water
Simmer it slowly allowing 30 minutes to the pound. Drain it well. Cover one side with:

    Brown sugar
Stick into it:
    Cloves
Broil the ham until the sugar melts.

Method II.
Soak for 1 hour in lukewarm water:
    Slices of smoked ham ⅓ inch thick
Drain them, wipe them and broil them for 3 minutes under a quick flame.

Method III.
Allow ⅓ Pound Per Person
Slash the fat edge in several places of:
    A piece of smoked ham about 1 inch thick
Place the ham on a broiler rack 3 inches below the heating unit, under a moderately hot flame. Broil it for 10 to 12 minutes to a side. A tenderized ham slice will require from 8 to 10 minutes to a side.

HAM STEAK AND CORN FRITTERS
4 Servings
This is as American as a cigar-store Indian.
Melt in a skillet:
    ¾ tablespoon butter
Sauté in this, 2 minutes on each side:
    4 ham steaks: 6 oz. each
Remove them to a hot platter. Stir into the fat in the skillet:
    3 tablespoons flour
Permit this to darken. Stir in:
    1½ cups milk
    1 teaspoon Worcestershire sauce
    Paprika
Pour the sauce over the steak. Serve it surrounded by:
    Corn Fritters, page 184
Garnish it with:
    Thick slices of tomato
    Parsley

HAM BUTT, SHANK OR PICNIC HAM OR CALI
Use these comparatively inexpensive cuts of ham for:
    New England Boiled Dinner, page 352
Cook the ham until it is nearly tender. Add the vegetables and cook until tender.

SMOKED SHOULDER BUTT OR COTTAGE ROLL
This cut may be boned. You may cut slices from this piece for broiling or sautéing, or you may roast or "boil" it.

CANNED HAM LOAF
3 Servings
Place on an oven-proof dish the contents of:
    1 can ham loaf: 12 oz.
Score the top. Stick into it:
    8 or 10 cloves
Bake the loaf in a moderate oven 350°
for 10 minutes. Make a paste of:
    ½ teaspoon cinnamon
    ⅓ cup light brown sugar
    1 teaspoon prepared mustard
    ½ teaspoon vinegar
    1 teaspoon water
Place this over the top of the loaf.
Bake it for 15 minutes longer. Baste
it frequently.

HAM LOAF
The 2 following rules call for much
the same ingredients but suggest different ways of using them. Method I.
calls for less meat and more thickening, like crumbs, flakes, etc., than II,
so it is a little more economical. Ham
loaf may be baked in muffin tins.

HAM LOAF WITH SMOKED HAM
Method I. 4 to 6 Servings
Grind:
    1 lb. raw smoked ham
    ½ lb. lean pork
    (½ onion)
Add, mix with the hands and shape
into a loaf:
    2 well-beaten eggs
    1 cup milk
    1 cup cracker or dry bread crumbs
      or 2 cups crushed cornflakes
    ⅛ teaspoon pepper
    2 tablespoons chopped parsley
Bake the loaf in a moderate oven 350°
for about 2 hours. Baste it frequently
with the following sirup:
    1½ cups brown sugar
    1 tablespoon prepared mustard
    ¼ cup vinegar
    ½ cup water
To make a milder sauce use:
    ½ cup brown sugar
    1 teaspoon mustard
    ½ cup water

Method II. 6 to 8 Servings
Grind until fine:
    1½ lbs. lean pork or veal
    ¾ lb. smoked ham
    (1 small onion)
Add:
    ½ cup cracker crumbs or 1 cup
      crushed cornflakes
    2 beaten eggs

    ½ cup milk
    ½ teaspoon paprika
    ½ teaspoon herbs or Worcestershire sauce
    (½ teaspoon dry mustard)
Shape these ingredients into a loaf.
Place it in a greased bread pan. You
may place in the bottom of the pan a
mixture of:
    ½ cup crushed pineapple, pineapple
      juice or 4 slices canned pineapple
    ½ teaspoon dry mustard
Bake the loaf in a moderate oven 350°
for about 1½ hours. Baste it frequently. After 45 minutes baste the loaf
with about:
    ½ cup chili sauce
    ¼ cup water
    1 cup diluted condensed soup:
      tomato, celery, mushroom, or
      pineapple juice
Baste it several times after that. Good
served with:
    Mashed sweet potatoes

*Ham Loaf with Tomato Soup, Ham Loaf
with Cooked Ham, page 148.*

CANADIAN BACON BAKED
8 Servings
Combine:
    ½ cup brown sugar
    ½ teaspoon dry mustard
    2 tablespoons fine bread crumbs
    1 tablespoon cider vinegar
Spread this over the fat side of:
    A 2 lb. piece of Canadian bacon
Bake the bacon uncovered in a slow
oven 325° for 1 hour. Baste it every
15 minutes with:
    ½ cup pineapple or other rather
      acid fruit juice, sherry or cider,
      etc.

CANADIAN BACON BOILED
This is a very practical thing to have
on hand. It keeps for a long time,
there is no waste and one is ready on
short notice to make a deliciously
flavored sandwich.
Place in boiling water to cover:
    1 lb. or more Canadian bacon
Simmer it until it is tender, for about
1 hour. If you have no freezer, this
keeps well wrapped in waxed paper in
the refrigerator.

CANADIAN BACON SAUTÉED
Place in a heavy skillet:
    Slices of Canadian bacon
Cook them over low heat for about 5

minutes. Turn them frequently. When done the lean part is a red brown and the fat is a light golden brown.

This is good served with Wine Sauce for Ham, page 437, Cumberland or Raisin Cider Sauce, pages 438 and 437.

BACON BAKED OR SAUTÉED
Method I.
When Charles Dickens honored us with his famous American tour he ventured into the wilds around St. Louis. There he stopped at a country inn where the waitress asked him if he would have "the white bread and chicken fixings or the corn bread and common doings?" Upon inquiry, I have found the latter to be bacon.

The following method is a good way to prepare bacon in large quantities. Place on a fine wire broiler or rack in a dripping pan:

Strips of bacon

Bake them in a moderate oven 350° until the bacon is crisp and brown.

Method II.
Or place bacon in a cold skillet and cook it slowly until it is done. Pour off the drippings while cooking the bacon to insure crispness. Turn it frequently. If you wish to remove the excess fat, place the bacon between paper towels. Bacon may be dredged, before it is cooked, in:

Corn meal

SALT PORK AND MILK GRAVY
4 Servings

Dip thin slices of:
1 lb. salt pork
in:
Boiling water
Then in:
Corn meal
Brown it slowly in a skillet. Turn it frequently. Thicken:
2 tablespoons drippings
With:
2 tablespoons flour (see Gravy, page 426)
Pour in slowly:
1 cup milk
Serve the pork with:
Boiled or baked potatoes

BROILED SAUSAGE
4 Servings

Cut apart and place in a skillet:
8 sausages
Add:

½ cup boiling water
Cover the pan. Cook the sausage gently for 8 minutes. Pour off the liquid. Return the sausages to the pan. Cook them over low heat shaking the pan constantly until they are an even brown.

Drain them. Serve them with:
Prepared mustard
For picnics serve them between:
Rolls

Sausage in Pastry or Biscuit Dough, page 151.

BAKED SAUSAGE
Place on a rack over a pan:
Sausages
Cook them in a moderate oven 350° until they are done.

SAUSAGE BAKED WITH APPLES
4 Servings

Arrange in a baking dish:
8 sausages
Core:
6 tart apples
Cut them into ¼ inch slices and place them around the sausages. Sprinkle them with:
¾ cup brown sugar
Bake the dish in a hot oven 400° for 10 minutes, reduce the heat to 350° and continue baking for 15 minutes longer. Baste with the drippings.

BOILED SAUSAGE MEAT
Place in a kettle:
Smoked sausage meat
Cover it with:
Boiling water
Simmer it for 8 or 10 minutes. Drain it and serve it with:
Sauerkraut, page 277

SAUSAGE MEAT
4 Servings

Combine:
1 lb. sausage meat
2 tablespoons flour
(¼ cup drained crushed pineapple)
Shape the meat into cakes ½ inch thick. Sprinkle them with:
Flour
Heat a skillet. No fat is required. Add the cakes and brown them quickly on both sides. Cover them with a lid. Reduce the heat to a low flame. Cook

the sausage until it is done. Serve the cakes with:

Applesauce

See Index for Sausage Meat with Pineapple and other Sausage Dishes.

BARBECUED FRANKFURTERS
4 Servings
Sauté:

¼ cup chopped onion

in:

2 tablespoons salad oil

Add and simmer for 15 minutes:

2 teaspoons sugar
¾ teaspoon dry mustard
¼ teaspoon salt
⅛ teaspoon pepper
¾ teaspoon paprika
6 tablespoons catsup
6 tablespoons water
3 tablespoons vinegar
2 teaspoons Worcestershire sauce
2 drops Tabasco sauce

Split and place in a baking dish:

8 frankfurters

Pour the sauce over them. Bake them in a moderate oven 375° for ½ hour. Baste them several times while cooking.

See Index for other Frankfurter recipes.

Sweetbreads, Brains, Kidneys, Liver, Heart, Tongue, Oxtails, etc.

The following is a hush-hush section, "just between us girls."

Today's skeleton, shamelessly revealed, is apt to be the housekeeper's slenderized pocketbook. Faced with the responsibility of producing meals that are nutritionally sound, acceptable to the family and not noticeably economical, she may well feel "as broke as the ten commandments." Her marketing jaunts find her "just eyeballing around" as far as the luxuries are concerned, and the question foremost in her mind is how to vary her menus without increasing their cost. She knows no substitute for a juicy steak or a glistening roast, for there is none. She has little chance of emulating the French, who pity us for our limited range of gastronomic enjoyment, by using the less expensive variety meats like brains, kidneys, heart, tripe, tongue, etc., for serving these meats frequently means the re-education of family taste. A suggestion on my part that they be tried usually meets with a vociferous and virtuous "Why, my husband wouldn't eat that stuff." Since "that stuff" is relished by countless thousands who have thrived on it, it seems reasonable to give it a trial. Charles Dickens said: "Her hair was false but it deceived no one." So don't try to coat the pill. Serve these delicacies and let the chips fall where they may.

For menu suggestions, see page 917.

SWEETBREADS
Clean under cold running water:

Sweetbreads

Drain them well. Place in a kettle sufficient water to cover the sweetbreads but do not place the sweetbreads in it at this time. Add to the water:

2 tablespoons lemon juice
2 or 3 ribs celery with leaves
or sprigs of parsley
¼ cup chopped onion
A few peppercorns

Bring the water to the boiling point. Drop the sweetbreads into it, lower the heat and simmer them for 20 minutes. Drain them. Reserve the stock. For easier handling you may place them in cold water to harden for 15 minutes. Drain them and remove the skin and membrane. The sweetbreads are now ready to be creamed, broiled, etc.

The liquid in which the sweetbreads were cooked makes an acceptable stock. If you wish, more vegetables may be used in the making of it. The vegetables may be cooked until they are tender after the sweetbreads have been removed. The stock may be flavored with:

A beef cube

It may be used strained or unstrained. It makes a good aspic in which to mold the sweetbreads (see Aspic Salads, page 475) and is useful in making Braised Sweetbreads, page 377, etc.

CREAMED SWEETBREADS
Cook by the preceding rule:

Sweetbreads

Break them into pieces. Drop them into:

Boiling Cream Sauce I, page 428—about 1 cup sauce to 1 pair sweetbreads

The sauce may be made with stock and cream. Just before serving add:

Sherry—1 tablespoon to 1 cup sauce

SAUTÉED SWEETBREADS

Cook by the rule on page 376:

Sweetbreads

Dry them well. Dip them in:

Seasoned, very fine bread crumbs

then in:

1 egg diluted with 2 tablespoons water

and again in crumbs. Sauté them in:

Hot butter

until they are a rich brown. Serve them with:

Cream sauce of sweetbread stock and cream

Season the stock with:

Sherry or lemon juice
Chopped parsley

Serve the sweetbreads with:

New potatoes and green peas

BROILED SWEETBREADS

Cook by the rule on page 376:

Sweetbreads

Dry them well. Break them into large pieces. Roll them in:

Seasoned flour

Surround them with:

Strips of bacon

Secure the bacon with toothpicks. Dot them well with:

Butter

Broil them under a good flame. Baste them frequently with the juices that drip from them and if they are rather dry with additional:

Butter

Add to the drippings a small amount of:

(Sherry or lemon juice)

BRAISED SWEETBREADS

These are outstanding as a main luncheon dish. Cook by the rule on page 376:

Sweetbreads

Break them into large pieces. Surround the pieces with:

Strips of bacon

Secure the bacon with toothpicks. Place the pieces in a baking dish. Bare-

ly cover the bottom of the dish with:

Stock

The stock may be the water in which the sweetbreads were cooked. Finely minced carrots and celery may be added to the boiling stock and cooked in it until tender, and sautéed mushrooms may be added when the vegetables and stock are thickened with flour. This is a luxurious and delicious touch to a very good dish, but not a necessary one.

Cook the sweetbreads covered in a moderate oven 375° for about 10 minutes. Remove the lid. Pour over the sweetbreads additional stock thickened with:

1 or 2 teaspoons flour

Only a small amount of gravy is required.

Cook the sweetbreads uncovered until the bacon is done. Baste them frequently. You may add to the gravy for the last 2 minutes of cooking:

Seasoning
(Sherry or lemon juice)

LARDED SWEETBREADS WITH WINE SAUCE

4 Servings

Prepare and parboil for 15 minutes by the rule on page 376:

2 pairs sweetbreads

Lard them (page 341) with very small pieces of:

Salt pork

Place them in a pan. Pour over them:

2 tablespoons salad oil

Dust them with:

Paprika

Dot them with small dabs of:

Butter

Bake them in a quick oven 400° for about 20 minutes. Serve them with:

Wine sauce

Melt:

2 tablespoons butter

Stir in until blended:

2 tablespoons flour

Stir in slowly:

1½ cups sweetbread or chicken stock

When the sauce is smooth and boiling add:

1 teaspoon Caramel, page 754
¼ cup sherry

Wild Rice and Sweetbreads, page 138; Baked Sweetbread Patties with Tomatoes and Onions, page 137; Baked Sweetbreads in Ham, page 138; Sweet-

breads and Mushrooms in Chicken Sauce, page 138.

BRAINS

Brains are generally in bad repute. They are charged with being too soft, but properly treated they become palatable and there are several good ways of preparing them. They combine well with other food—eggs, salads, soufflés, ragout, etc.—and need only a little pep in flavor—sherry, Worcestershire sauce, etc.—to make them very good. You may use calf, pork, lamb or beef brains. Clean and remove all membrane under running cold water from:

Brains

They need not be precooked, but you may steam them. See below. Drain them and break them into pieces. Brains may be substituted for or combined with sweetbreads. They make a delicious soufflé. In fact, their flavor is, to use an overworked word, intriguing. Add a set of brains cooked by the following rule to 4 eggs before they are scrambled (see Scrambled Eggs, page 81) or serve the brains creamed with Omelet, page 85, sprinkled with chopped parsley.

STEAMED BRAINS

2 Servings

Prepare for cooking by the above rule:

1 pair brains

Put them in a saucepan with:

3 tablespoons water
1 tablespoon vinegar

Cover them closely and simmer them for 15 minutes. Chill them.

FRIED OR SAUTÉED BRAINS

Method I. 4 Servings

Prepare for cooking, see above:

2 sets brains

Cut them in two lengthwise. Dry them between towels. Season them with:

Salt and paprika

Roll them in:

Corn meal or flour

Melt in a skillet rubbed with garlic:

⅓ cup butter or bacon grease

Cook the brains on each side for about 3 minutes. Cover them, reduce the heat and complete the cooking, about 15 minutes in all. Serve them with:

Lemon wedges
Tomato or Worcestershire sauce or Black Butter, pages 433, 327

Thick slices of tomato may be sautéed in the same pan. Add previously sau-

téed bacon to these and you have a fine meal.

Method II.

Or dip them in:

1 egg diluted with
2 tablespoons water

Roll them in:

Sifted seasoned bread crumbs

Sauté them uncovered or fry them in deep fat heated to 370° (page 542). Serve them with:

Pickled beets or relish

or with:

Wine Sauce for Brains

Add to the pan drippings and sauté until light yellow:

1 tablespoon chopped onion

Stir in until smooth:

1½ tablespoons flour

Stir in gradually until the sauce is smooth and boiling:

½ cup chicken or other stock
½ cup dry white wine

Add:

1 tablespoon chopped parsley or chives
Salt as needed

Pour the sauce over the brains.

BROILED BRAINS

Prepare for cooking by the rule on this page:

Brains

Brush them with:

Oil or melted butter

Dust them with:

Paprika

Broil them under moderate heat for about 12 minutes on each side, or until done. Baste them with oil or butter. Serve them piping hot with:

Baked Bacon, page 375
Chopped parsley and lemon wedges

BRAINS IN BLANKETS

4 Servings

Prepare for cooking by the rule on this page:

2 sets brains

Cut them into 6 or 8 pieces. Surround each piece with:

A strip of bacon

Secure with a toothpick. Place them on an oiled tin. Dust them with:

Paprika

Dot them with butter. Bake the rings in a moderate oven 350° for 20 minutes, or until the brains and bacon are done.

BAKED BRAINS
3 Servings
Prepare for cooking by the rule on page 378:

 1 set brains

Chop them coarsely. Combine them with:

 ½ cup bread crumbs
 2 chopped hard-cooked eggs
 6 tablespoons cream
 1 tablespoon catsup or 1 teaspoon
  Worcestershire sauce
 ½ tablespoon lemon juice
 ⅓ teaspoon salt
 ⅛ teaspoon pepper or paprika

Place these ingredients in a greased baking dish or in individual dishes. Sprinkle the top with:

 Bread crumbs

Dot it generously with:

 Butter

Bake the brains for 15 minutes in a hot oven 400°.

Broiled Calf Brains on Tomatoes, page 140; Calf Brain Fritters, page 140.

BAKED BRAINS, TOMATOES AND EGGS
4 Servings
Steam by the rule on page 378:

 2 sets brains

Cut them into 1 inch dice. Place them in 4 small greased casseroles. Peel:

 4 tomatoes

Dice them. Combine them with:

 1½ tablespoons hot olive oil
 1 teaspoon chopped parsley
 1 teaspoon chopped onion or
  chives
 Salt and paprika
 1 teaspoon brown sugar

Pour these ingredients into the casseroles. Break into each dish:

 1 egg

Place the casseroles in a moderate oven 350° for about 5 minutes until the eggs are firm. Melt and brown lightly:

 4 tablespoons butter

Add:

 2 teaspoons lemon juice

Pour this over the eggs. Garnish them with:

 Parsley

Serve them at once.

KIDNEYS
All white membrane should be snipped from beef, lamb and pork kidneys before they are washed. Curved scissors are a great help. Allow 1 veal, 2 or 3 lamb, 1½ to 2 mutton, ½ beef and 1 small pork kidney per person. Cook kidneys as short a time as possible. Long cooking tends to make them tough.

BROILED KIDNEYS
Remove some of the fat from:

 Veal kidneys

Cut them crosswise into slices. Broil them for about 10 minutes. Turn them and baste them with:

 Melted butter

Season them with:

 Lemon juice
 Salt and paprika

BAKED VEAL KIDNEYS
Note for the lone housekeeper: 1 kidney makes a fine little roast for 1 person. Prepare and bake kidneys leaving the fat on. Place in a pan, fat side up:

 Veal kidneys

Bake them uncovered in a slow oven 300° until tender, about 1¼ hours.

SAUTÉED KIDNEYS
3 Servings
Remove some of the fat from:

 3 veal or 9 lamb kidneys

Cut them crosswise into slices. Cut away all the white tissue with curved scissors. Rub a pan with:

 (Garlic)

Melt in it:

 4 tablespoons butter

Sauté in the butter:

 (½ cup sliced onions)

Then sauté the kidneys in the hot fat, a quick process, about 5 minutes. Season with:

 Salt and paprika
 1 tablespoon lemon juice or ¼ cup
  sherry or dry red wine

Sautéed Kidneys with Celery and Mushrooms, page 141; Veal Kidney, Mushroom and Onion Casserole, page 140.

LAMB KIDNEYS IN WINE SAUCE
3 Servings
Cut into thin slices:

 9 lamb kidneys

Cut away all the white tissue with curved scissors. Melt in a saucepan:

 2½ tablespoons butter

Sauté and stir the kidneys quickly in

the hot fat for about 5 minutes. Sprinkle over them and stir in:

    2 tablespoons flour
    ½ teaspoon grated onion

Add slowly, stirring constantly:

    1 cup Stock, page 425, or consommé

When the sauce is smooth and boiling season the kidneys with:

    Salt and paprika

Remove them from the fire. Add:

    2 tablespoons sherry or Madeira

Serve hot on:

    Toast

Sprinkled with:

    Chopped parsley

BEEF KIDNEYS

Remove some of the fat, split the kidneys lengthwise and cut out the white center and tubes with curved scissors. Then place the kidneys in a Marinade (see page 340) for several hours.

BROILED BEEF KIDNEYS
4 Servings

This fine dish makes you feel like an epicure. Prepare by the above rule and cut into ½ inch slices:

    1 beef kidney

If not marinated, dip the slices in:

    French dressing or salad oil

Broil them under moderate heat for 10 to 15 minutes. Baste them with:

    Melted butter
    Lemon juice

Season with:

    Salt and paprika

They are good with Grilled Tomatoes and Onions, page 320.

KIDNEY STEW
4 Servings

This is a contribution—the favorite recipe of a family who likes this dish for Sunday breakfast.

Cut away all the white tissue from:

    2 small beef kidneys

Drop them into boiling, unsalted water to cover. Add:

    1 tablespoon vinegar

Simmer them covered until tender. Remove the kidneys from the stock. Cool them. If you wish, place them in a covered dish in the refrigerator. Reserve the stock. When cold cut the meat into wafer-thin slices. Remove the fat from the stock. Add to the stock:

    1 bay leaf
    A few drops brown coloring

Simmer it gently. There should be about 1 cupful. You may add to flavor it:

    1 beef or vegetable cube

Melt:

    1 to 2 tablespoons butter

Sauté the kidneys lightly in the hot butter. Stir in:

    1½ to 2 tablespoons flour

Pour the strained stock onto this and stir the gravy until it is smooth and boiling. Flavor by adding:

    1 slice lemon or 2 tablespoons sherry
    Salt and paprika as needed

Serve the kidneys on:

    Toast

Garnished with:

    Chopped parsley

CREOLE KIDNEY STEW
4 Servings

Prepare for cooking by the rule on this page, then cut into ½ inch slices:

    2 medium-sized beef kidneys

Sprinkle them with:

    1 tablespoon vinegar
    ¼ cup flour

Sauté slowly until light brown:

    2 slices minced bacon

Add:

    2 tablespoons drippings or butter

Brown the kidney slices in the fat with:

    ½ cup chopped onions
    ½ cup coarsely chopped celery

Simmer covered for 10 minutes, then heat and add to the above:

    1 No. 2 can tomatoes
    1 seeded shredded green pepper
    1 teaspoon salt
    ⅛ teaspoon red pepper
    (⅛ teaspoon curry powder)

Cover the pan, simmer the stew for about 15 minutes. Stir it frequently. Serve it with:

    Rice or noodles or on toast

KIDNEY PATTIES
4 Servings

For these you may use 1 beef, 2 pork or veal or 5 lamb kidneys. Or substitute raw liver or brains. To prepare brains, see page 378. Slice lengthwise, remove all white tissue with curved scissors, then chop until fine:

    Kidneys

Sprinkle them with:

    2 teaspoons vinegar

Rub a skillet with:

    Garlic

Heat in it:

2 tablespoons bacon drippings or
butter
Sauté in this lightly:
1 chopped onion or leek
½ cup minced celery
¼ cup minced green pepper
Remove from fire. Add the chopped
kidneys and:
¼ cup dry bread crumbs
¼ cup milk
1 egg
¼ teaspoon salt
¼ teaspoon freshly ground pepper
4 drops Worcestershire sauce or
¼ teaspoon dried herb
¼ teaspoon caraway or dill seed
Drop these ingredients by the spoonful
into a hot pan that has been brushed
with:
Bacon drippings
Brown them lightly on both sides.
Serve the patties with:
Tomato Sauce or slaw or
something piquant

HEART

This frequently despised and neglected
meat is useful supplemented in any
dish that calls for sliced, diced or
ground meat. To prepare wash well,
remove veins, arteries and blood from
a heart.

BRAISED HEART SLICES IN SOUR SAUCE
6 Servings
Prepare (see above):
1 beef or 2 calf hearts
If beef, cut it across the fiber into ¼
inch slices. Pour into a saucepan or
oven-proof dish to the depth of ¾
inch:
Boiling water
Add:
¼ cup diced carrots
¼ cup chopped celery with leaves
¼ cup sliced onion
½ teaspoon salt
(¼ cup diced green pepper)
Place the heart slices on a rack in the
pan well above the water. Cover the
pan closely. Simmer the meat until
tender, for about 1½ hours, or bake it
in a 250° oven until tender, about 2
hours. Strain the stock. Chill it. Remove the fat and if you like, use it in
the gravy. Use about 2 cupfuls of the
stock.
Melt:
3 tablespoons butter or fat
Stir in:
3 tablespoons flour
Stir in the stock. When it is boiling

add the meat and vegetables. You may
add:
2 tablespoons lemon juice or dry
wine
½ teaspoon dried herb or 2 tablespoons chopped parsley or
olives
Correct the seasoning, that is, add as
needed:
Salt and pepper
Good with Spoon Bread, page 423, rice
or noodles.

BAKED HEART
4 Servings
Prepare (see opposite):
A beef heart or 2 veal hearts
Tie it with a string. Place it on a rack
in an oven-proof dish. Place in the
bottom of the dish:
2 cups stock or diluted tomato
soup
Place over it:
4 slices bacon
Cover the dish closely and bake the
heart in a moderate oven 325° until
tender, sometimes if beef, a matter of
3 to 5 hours, if veal about 2 hours. Remove the heart to a plate and cool it
slightly. Heat in a double boiler, then
fill the heart cavity with:
1½ cups Bread Dressing, page 416,
or other dressing or Green Rice,
page 104
Sprinkle the heart with:
Paprika
Return it briefly to a hot oven 400° or
place it under a broiler to reheat. The
drippings may be thickened with:
Flour (see Gravy, page 426)

LIVER
Except for liver from spring lamb, calf
liver is the most desirable, but beef,
lamb and pork liver may be used.
Remove skin and membrane, keep the
liver whole or slice it. If you wish to
sauté old beef liver, place the slices in
a Marinade, page 340, for 10 minutes
to tenderize it. Dry the liver, then
proceed with any of the recipes given
for calf liver.

SAUTÉED LIVER
4 Servings
Remove the skin and membrane from:
1 lb. calf liver
Cut it into ⅓ inch slices. Dredge them
with:
(Seasoned flour)
Sauté them until done, a matter of 2 or
3 minutes, in:

A very little hot bacon drippings
or melted butter

The pan may be rubbed with a cut
clove of garlic or you may flavor the
liver when cooked with grated lemon
rind and juice.

Remove the liver to a hot platter. You
may rinse the skillet with 3 tablespoonfuls of dry red wine and use this
for sauce.

If you wish to serve onions with sautéed liver, sauté them, keep them hot,
cook liver as directed on one side, turn
it, heap the onions on the cooked side
and continue to cook the liver until
done. If you wish to serve bacon,
sauté it first and keep it hot.

BROILED LIVER
Method I.

Some epicures have a preference for
liver prepared in the following way;
doctors have, too. I lean toward the
sautéed liver above, but must acknowl-
edge the good qualities of this rule,
which calls for liver pure and simple.
Place on a broiling rack about 3 inches
from moderate heat:

Slices of liver ⅓ inch thick

Leave the door of the broiling oven
open. Broil the liver exactly 1 minute
on each side. Season it, if you wish.
It is remarkably good as it is.

Method II.

Or dip the slices in:

2 tablespoons melted butter or oil

Broil them under a broiler, 1½ minutes to a side. Season them lightly
with:

Salt and paprika

Broil previously:

Slices of bacon
Bermuda onions

Serve the liver, bacon and onions on a
hot platter garnished with:

Parsley
A lemon cut into quarters

*Liver, Pepper, Onions and Olives on
Skewers, page 194.*

SWISS LIVER
4 Servings

Remove the skin and membrane from:

¾ lb. calf liver

Cut the liver into 2½ x ½ inch oblongs. Roll the strips, one at a time, in:

Seasoned flour

Place them on a rack to dry. Melt
over moderate heat:

4 tablespoons butter

to which you may add:

(A sliver of garlic or 2 teaspoons
grated onion)

Add the liver. Move it about to keep it
from sticking. Permit it to brown
lightly. Turn it. Add:

1 teaspoon lemon juice
1 or 2 tablespoons dry white wine

Serve the strips hot.

ITALIAN LIVER
4 to 6 Servings

Prepare a mixture of:

3 tablespoons grated Parmesan
cheese
6 tablespoons fine bread crumbs
1 tablespoon chopped parsley
½ teaspoon salt
Freshly ground pepper

Place these ingredients on a plate. In
another plate place:

3 tablespoons vinegar or dry wine

Have ready:

8 slices calf liver

Dip the slices quickly in the vinegar,
bathing both sides, then in the crumb
mixture, covering both sides. Sauté
the liver quickly and briefly in:

4 tablespoons hot oil, butter or
other fat

*Creamed Chicken Livers and other
Chicken Liver Dishes, page 138.*

CALF LIVER COOKED IN
WINE
6 Servings

Slice, then cut into 2 x 2 inch pieces:

A small calf liver

Melt:

3 tablespoons butter

When moderately hot turn the pieces
in it until well coated. Add:

1 teaspoon minced parsley
1 tablespoon chopped chives
1 tablespoon minced celery
2 cloves

Heat and add:

1 cup dry red wine
¾ teaspoon salt
¼ teaspoon paprika

Cover the liver. Simmer it for 3 minutes. Remove the liver. Add to the
stock, cover and simmer for 3 minutes:

1 cup thinly sliced mushrooms

Thicken the stock with:

Flour (see Gravy, page 426)

Place the liver in the sauce. Heat it.
Serve it at once over:

Toast

BRAISED LIVER WITH VEGETABLES
Method I. 6 Servings
Cut into 1 inch slices:
> 1½ lbs. beef liver

Dredge it with:
> Seasoned flour

Brown the liver in:
> ½ cup hot bacon drippings

Combine and heap on the slices:
> 2 diced carrots
> 2 seeded chopped green peppers
> 6 small onions
> 1 cup sliced celery

Add to the pan:
> 1 cup boiling water or stock

Cover it. Simmer the stew for about ¾ hour, or until the liver is tender. Add, if necessary, more boiling water and seasonings.
A calf liver may be substituted. It will be tender in about 20 minutes.

Method II.
Rub:
> Salt pork or bacon

with:
> A cut clove of garlic

Cut it into strips. Use the strips to lard:
> 2 lbs. liver in 1 piece

Follow the above rule, but bake the liver covered in a slow oven 300° for about 2 hours, or until tender. Add the vegetables for the last hour of cooking.

BRAISED LIVER WITH WINE AND VEGETABLES
8 Servings
Rub:
> ¼ lb. salt pork or bacon

with a cut clove of:
> Garlic

Cut it into small strips. Dip them in:
> Freshly ground pepper
> Ground cloves
> Minced parsley or chives

Use the strips to lard:
> 2½ lbs. liver in 1 piece

Place the liver in the following marinade for 1 hour or more:
> ⅓ cup salad oil
> 1½ tablespoons lemon juice
> ¼ teaspoon salt
> ⅛ teaspoon paprika
> ¼ bay leaf

Turn it from time to time. Melt in an oven-proof baking dish:
> 3 tablespoons butter

Add and stir about until lightly cooked:
> 1 small chopped onion or leek

> 1 diced carrot
> 2 or 3 diced ribs celery
> 2 or 3 sprigs minced parsley
> 1 teaspoon dried basil or tarragon, or 1 tablespoon fresh

Place the liver, marinade and all, in an oven-proof dish. Cover it closely. Cook it in a moderate oven 325° until nearly tender, for about 1½ hours. Baste it from time to time. If you wish to serve the liver without further additions, continue cooking it until it is very tender. The addition of the following ingredients is optional, but it completes the dish.
While the liver is cooking place in a heavy skillet:
> 4 slices diced bacon

Cook this over a very slow fire until the bacon is clear. Add and stir about until well glazed:
> 18 small peeled onions
> 6 large or 8 small sliced carrots
> 3 ribs sliced celery

Add:
> 1 cup Stock, page 425, or canned consommé

Cover the skillet and cook the vegetables on top of the stove for 15 minutes over low heat. Add them to the liver in the baking dish, cover and cook them for 15 minutes longer. Drain the contents of the baking dish, reserving the liquor. Place the liver on a hot platter. Add to the liquor:
> ½ cup dry white wine or ¼ cup sherry
> (2 beaten egg yolks)

Cook and stir the sauce over very low heat until it is hot. Do not permit it to boil. Pour the sauce over the liver. Serve it garnished with:
> Chopped parsley

BEEF LIVER CREOLE
Cut into thin slices:
> 1 lb. beef liver

Remove the skin and veins. Dust the slices lightly with:
> Flour

Melt, then brown the liver in:
> 3 tablespoons hot butter or drippings

Add:
> 1¼ cups sliced onions
> 1½ cups heated canned tomatoes
> ½ cup diced celery
> 1 thinly sliced green pepper
> ½ teaspoon salt
> A few grains cayenne

Cover the pan and simmer these ingredients for about 20 minutes. Drain

them. Then thicken the liquid with:
Flour (see Gravy, page 426)
Add the liver and vegetables. Simmer
them 2 minutes longer. Serve with:
Boiled Rice, page 103, or
Noodles, page 97, etc.

LIVER LOAF
6 to 8 Servings
Boil for 5 minutes:
1 cup water
1 medium-sized chopped onion
3 ribs celery with leaves
Prepare for cooking (page 381), slice,
add and simmer for 2 minutes:
1 lb. liver: beef, lamb or pork
Drain, reserving liquid. Put liver and
vegetables through a meat chopper
with:
2 slices bacon or a 1½ inch cube
salt pork
Add and blend well:
1 or 2 beaten eggs
¾ teaspoon salt
⅛ teaspoon pepper
1 cup cracker or dry bread crumbs
½ teaspoon dried marjoram or
thyme
1 cup liquid: liver stock, milk,
tomato juice, etc.
Pour into a greased loaf pan:
(½ cup catsup)
Pack the meat into the pan. Bake it in
a moderate oven 350° for about 40
minutes.
This makes a good everyday liver-
spread.

LIVER LUNCHEON OR
BREAKFAST SPREAD
My unknown friend, the Maryland
man who contributed the delicious
recipe for Oysters Baked in the Half
Shell, page 113, is responsible for the
following equally good and unusual
dish. I am giving it in his own words.
"Marinate calf's liver ½ hour or more,
perhaps overnight, in a mixture of
milk and red wine. The liver is, of
course, already prepared à la Rombauer, page 381.
"Sauté in butter until nearly done, but
when less than halfway done add to
the skillet thinly sliced mushrooms to
about equal the weight of the liver.
Add more butter if necessary. Be sure
that both liver and mushrooms are
cooked to the point of tenderness, but
not beyond. Cut the liver in strips for
the chopper and put it and the mushrooms through a very fine chopper,
alternately, so that they mix.

"Add the milk and wine in which the
liver was soaked to the remaining butter, etc., in the skillet and heat. Economical, what? Thoroughly moisten
the chopped mixture with this, adding
more wine only if necessary for more
moisture. Add salt, pepper, onion salt
and Worcestershire sauce. Also paprika. Also lemon juice. All these
seasonings in moderate quantities. Stir
thoroughly and finish cooking in a
double boiler or chafing dish over boiling water, stirring again from time to
time.
"Serve on toast, French bread, if available, or, for canapés, on crackers. It is
not bad even when cold, but for breakfast or lunch, the hotter the plates,
toast and mixture the better."
Editorial comment. Some cook!

LIVER PATTIES
6 Servings
Combine:
1 lb. ground liver
1 slice chopped bacon
½ cup dry bread crumbs
¼ cup evaporated milk or cream
½ teaspoon salt
⅛ teaspoon pepper
2 teaspoons grated onion
2 tablespoons chopped parsley
Shape these ingredients into 6 cakes.
Wrap around the cakes:
6 slices bacon
Secure the bacon with toothpicks.
Place the cakes in a lightly greased
pan in a hot oven 425°. Cook them
until they are well browned. Turn
them to insure even baking.

Chicken Liver Paste, page 25.

LIVER DUMPLINGS OR
LEBERKLOESSE
6 Servings
Being the child of a South German, I
cannot well compile a cookbook without including a dish that is typical of
that neck of the woods—not exactly a
handsome one, but it has qualities.
Besides, liver is now de rigueur.
Skin and remove the fiber from:
1 lb. calf liver or use chicken livers
Grind or chop it until it is very fine.
Slightly frozen liver is easy to grind.
Soak in water for 3 minutes, then
wring the water from:
2 slices white bread: 1 cup
Beat, then stir into liver and bread:

2 egg yolks
¼ cup soft butter
2 teaspoons chopped onion
2 tablespoons chopped parsley
1½ teaspoons salt
½ teaspoon pepper
2 tablespoons flour
Beat until stiff:
2 egg whites
Fold them into the other ingredients.
Shape this mixture into 1½ inch balls.
Drop them into gently boiling:
Soup Stock, page 43
Cook them for 5 or 6 minutes. Serve
them with the soup. Or, drop them
into boiling water, drain them and
serve them with:
Sautéed Onions, page 296
A good left-over is liver dumplings
sliced and sautéed in onion·butter.

TONGUE
Use beef, calf, lamb or pork tongues.
The best known, beef tongue, may be
purchased fresh, corned, smoked or
boiled. The smaller tongues make
delicious dishes that should not be
neglected.

FRESH BEEF TONGUE BOILED
The only way to make both ends meet
today, says Frank Morgan, is to live
on oxtail soup and beef tongue.
Place in a kettle:
A fresh beef tongue
Peel and add:
2 medium-sized onions
1 large carrot
3 or more ribs celery with leaves
6 sprigs parsley
Barely cover these ingredients with
boiling water. Add:
8 peppercorns
1 teaspoon salt
Simmer the tongue until it is tender,
about 3 hours. Drain it. Reserve the
liquor. Skin the tongue. Remove the
roots. Serve it with:
Mustard Sauce, page 428
Piquant Sauce, page 436
Hot Vinaigrette Sauce, page 493

CORNED OR PICKLED
TONGUE BOILED
My favorite economical dish is a boiled
tongue. It keeps for days and supplies
me at all times with an emergency
meat. I find it preferable to sausage.
Follow the above rule for:
Fresh Beef Tongue Boiled

Substitute:
A corned or pickled beef tongue
If the tongue is very salty, soak it in
cold water to cover for several hours.

SMOKED TONGUE BOILED
Cover with cold water and soak for 12
hours:
A 3 lb. smoked beef tongue
Cover the tongue with fresh water.
Add:
1 sliced or whole onion stuck with
3 cloves
½ cup chopped celery with leaves
3 bay leaves
1 teaspoon peppercorns
Simmer it until it is tender, from 2 to
4 hours. Leave it in the stock until it
is slightly cooled. When cold enough
to handle, skin it and remove all the
dry, hard portions and the roots. It is
then ready to be sliced and served.
The tongue may be served hot with:
Creamed Spinach, page 313
Horseradish Sauce, page 429

Pressure Cooked Tongue, page 890.

TONGUE, BEEF, VEAL OR
LAMB IN CREOLE SAUCE
6 Servings
Cook by the rule for tongue on this
page:
A fresh beef tongue, about 1½
lbs., or 2 veal or 8 lamb tongues
Skin it. Melt:
2½ tablespoons butter
Add and brown lightly:
2 slices onion
1 chopped green pepper, seeds
removed
1 sliced clove garlic
Stir in:
2 teaspoons flour
2½ cups tomatoes
½ bay leaf
1 teaspoon salt
6 or 8 peppercorns
½ teaspoon paprika
1 tablespoon brown sugar
Stir and cook these ingredients for 2
minutes. You may add:
3 tablespoons chopped olives
¼ cup blanched slivered almonds
or 1 cup sliced mushrooms
Place the drained tongue in a casserole. It may be sliced. Pour the sauce
over it. Bake it covered in a moderate
oven 375° for ½ hour. Serve it with:
Chopped parsley

BRAISED BEEF TONGUE

Place in boiling water and simmer for
1 hour:

A fresh beef tongue

Skin it, remove the roots and place it
on a dripping rack in a roasting pan.
Pour over it:

**4 cups of the water in which the
tongue was boiled**

Cover the pan closely and bake the
tongue in a slow oven 275° until it is
tender, about 2 hours. Add for the last
hour of cooking:

**2 cups diced vegetables: carrots,
turnips, onions, celery, etc.**

lightly sautéed in:

3 tablespoons butter

Remove the tongue and place it on a
platter. Strain the vegetables and arrange them around the tongue or serve
the tongue with:

Creamed Spinach, page 313

Thicken the stock with:

Flour (see Gravy, page 426)

*Boiled Beef Tongue with Raisin Sauce,
page 164; Tongue in Aspic, page 481.*

CALF TONGUES

6 Servings

Place in a stewpan:

2 calf tongues

Boil in another stewpan:

**Water to cover the tongues
Several stalks celery with leaves
A sliced onion
1 or 2 carrots
½ bay leaf
6 or 8 peppercorns
1½ teaspoons salt
1 teaspoon lemon juice or vinegar**

Dry wine may be substituted for part
of the water. Pour the mixture over
the tongues. Simmer them covered
until they are tender, about 1 hour; or
bake them covered in a slow oven 275°
for about 2 hours, until tender. Thick-
en the stock with:

Flour (see Gravy, page 426)

Season it, if required, with:

Salt and pepper

Add:

**Prepared horseradish or capers
or chopped pickle**

BAKED CALF TONGUES

Prepare 2 calf tongues by the preceding rule. Place them in a baking dish,
pour the gravy over them and bake
them covered in a moderate oven 350°
for 15 minutes.

For other Tongue Dishes see Index.

BRAISED OXTAILS

5 to 6 Servings

Cut into joints:

2 oxtails

Melt in a skillet:

**4 tablespoons butter or beef
drippings**

Sauté the oxtail sections in the butter
until they are browned. Season them
with:

Salt and paprika

Add:

**2 cups boiling Beef Stock, page
43, or tomato juice
4 peppercorns**

Bring these ingredients to the boiling
point. Place them in a casserole. Cover
it closely. Bake the oxtails in a moderate oven 350° until they are tender,
3 to 5 hours. Add additional stock as
needed. For the last hour of cooking
add:

**8 small peeled onions
½ cup diced celery
¼ cup peeled diced carrots**

When the oxtails are tender strain the
stock from them. Skim off most of
the fat. Thicken the stock with:

Flour (see Gravy, page 426)

Return the meat, the vegetables and
the gravy to the casserole. Serve the
dish with a platter of:

Noodles, page 97

Cover the noodles with:

Buttered Crumbs, page 326

Or, you may prepare oxtails in the
following manner:

Place in a casserole:

2 disjointed oxtails

Add to them the contents of:

**1 No. 2 can tomatoes
2 cups beef stock
1 bay leaf
A split clove of garlic**

Bake them covered as directed, omitting the addition of the vegetables.
Skim all the fat from the stock, which
should be sufficiently thickened. Dry
wine may be added or lemon juice,
also seasonings. Good served with:

Parsley Dumplings, page 421

CALF HEAD

This recipe in an old family cookbook
reads: "Calf's head with tongue and
brain, 25 cents." That notation belongs
to the past, so does the manner in
which the recipe is written, but the
dish remains a great favorite with
gourmets.

Remove the brain from:
A calf head
Boil:
2 quarts water
1 carrot
1 onion
½ sliced lemon
1 bay leaf
4 cloves
1 tablespoon salt
¼ teaspoon pepper
Add the head. The brains and tongue may be simmered separately. Simmer it covered until the meat is tender, about 2 hours. If the tongue is not cooked separately, it will take longer. Add the brains for the last 15 minutes of cooking. Dice them. Cut the meat from the bone and into small pieces. Skin, remove the roots, then slice the tongue. Prepare a sauce with:
4 tablespoons butter
4 tablespoons flour
2 cups liquid in which the meat was cooked
If the tongue is used, treble the amount of water and vegetables but not the seasoning. Add seasoning as required when the head is almost done. Reheat the meat in the sauce. Season it if needed. It is sometimes made rather acid with lemon, vinegar or wine. Serve it with:
Chopped parsley
This dish is sometimes served with the addition at the last moment of:
½ cup scalded cream
Or part of the sauce is drained off. Beat into it:
2 egg yolks
Return the sauce to the pot. Heat but do not boil the sauce after adding the yolks.
If you add cream or egg yolks do not add lemon, vinegar or wine until the last moment.

HEAD CHEESE
A well-liked old-fashioned dish. Quarter:
A calf head
Remove ears, brains, eyes, snout and most of the fat. Soak the quarters in cold water to extract the blood. Wash them. Cover with cold water. Simmer until the meat is ready to fall from the bones. Drain. Separate the meat from the bones. Dice it, cover it well with the stock. Add salt, pepper and herbs. Cook for ½ hour. Pour into a mold, cover with a cloth. Put a weight on

top. Chill. Serve cut into slices. Serve it with:
Vinaigrette Sauce, page 493

TRIPE
Tripe is the inner muscular lining of the stomach of meat animals. Honeycomb, the most delicate tripe, is the lining of the stomach of beef. Any may be used in the following recipes. Simmering in water is a preliminary to all ways of serving tripe. Tripe is partly cooked before it is sold. It may also be bought pickled or canned. Pickled tripe requires a shorter period of simmering, about 2 hours. Fresh tripe whole calls for 4 hours' or more simmering; if it is cut into strips you may allow 2 hours or more.

STEWED TRIPE
3 Servings
Wash several times:
1 lb. honeycomb tripe
Cut it into strips. Tripe that is not cut requires 4 hours or more of cooking in all. Cover the strips with cold water. Bring the water to the boiling point. Add:
¼ teaspoon salt
¼ teaspoon sugar
Cover the pot. Simmer the tripe for 2 hours. Add:
1 sliced clove garlic
⅓ cup chopped onion
1 cup chopped celery and parsley
4 peppercorns
Simmer the tripe until it is tender, about 1 hour longer. Watch it, as it burns easily. Thicken the stock with:
Flour (see Gravy, page 426)
Season the gravy with:
Salt
½ teaspoon prepared mustard
1 teaspoon Worcestershire sauce
Tripe may be served with Cream Sauce, page 428, made with part stock and part cream, Onion Sauce, page 432, etc. You may flavor it with Worcestershire sauce or mustard.

SPANISH TRIPE
Follow the above rule for:
Stewed Tripe
Add to the vegetables:
1 cup more or less tomato purée
A few grains cayenne
1 teaspoon Worcestershire sauce
Add for the last 15 minutes:
½ cup cooked minced ham
½ cup sliced mushrooms

FRIED TRIPE
Cut into squares or strips:
  Stewed Tripe, page 387
Sprinkle it with:
  Salt and paprika
Dip it into:
  Fritter Batter, page 543
Fry it in deep fat (page 542). Serve it with:
  Tartar Sauce, page 439

TRIPE PIQUANT
6 Servings
Cut into strips:
  2 lbs. cooked honeycomb tripe
Melt:
  2 tablespoons butter
Stir and sauté in it until light brown:
  3 tablespoons chopped onion
  1 minced clove garlic
  ¼ cup sliced carrots
Add the tripe and:
  2 tablespoons chopped parsley
  ½ bay leaf
  ¼ teaspoon dried thyme
  2 teaspoons vinegar or lemon juice
Simmer these ingredients for 1 or 2 minutes. Sprinkle them with:

  1 tablespoon flour
Pour over them:
  1 cup boiling water
Season the stew with:
  Salt and paprika
Permit it to simmer covered for 20 minutes.

BROILED TRIPE
4 Servings
Cook in one piece by rule on page 387:
  Stewed Tripe
Drain it. Wrap it in a towel. Twist the towel to wring the remaining water from the tripe. Dip it in:
  Seasoned flour
Dip it in:
  Melted butter or salad oil
and again in the flour. Dip it in:
  Bread crumbs
Broil the tripe on the smooth side for 3 minutes, then on the other for about 2½ minutes. Serve it garnished with:
  Melted butter
  Lemon wedges
  Minced parsley

Poultry and Game

The chicken is a world-citizen to be found everywhere along with Coca Cola, the Singer sewing machine, the *Christian Science Monitor* and Hollywood movies. Ducks, geese and game are also cosmopolites. In fact, we eat many of the same foods the world round, but each nation prepares them in a distinctive manner that marks them as its own.

A provincial will stick to his chicken with dumplings, half-roasted duck and quail on toast, but he should at least have a speaking acquaintance with—an appreciation of the existence of—chicken cacciatore, curry, duck Bigarade, Hasenpfeffer and that Eurasian dish without a country—chop suey. In time he may get to like these foreigners. At least it will widen his horizon and tickle his self-righteousness to tip his hat to them.

Poultry is usually plucked and drawn when purchased. Buy dry picked poultry whenever possible. If it is not plucked, do so at once. It is much easier to pluck and draw a bird that is thoroughly chilled. Pick the feathers from a bird. Remove all pin feathers—use a pair of tweezers or grasp each feather between forefinger and the tip of a knife, then pull.

It is unwise to keep fresh poultry longer than 24 hours before cooking it.

To Draw a Bird

Make an incision through the skin below the breast bone large enough to admit the hand, as shown on the left below. Insert the hand, palm down, into the cavity between the organs and the breast bone, as shown in the center. Feel for the gizzard

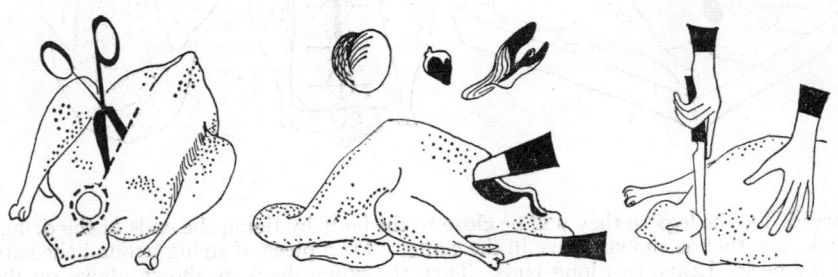

which is firm and roundish and pull it out steadily. It will bring most of the other entrails with it. Remove the kidneys in the hollows near the base of the backbone and the spongy red lungs to either side of the spine between the ribs. Remove surplus cavity fat because it may be too strong in flavor. Cut off the head and draw down the neck skin. Cut off the neck close to the body. Leave a generous flap of skin. Remove the crop and windpipe by making an incision at the base of the neck and drawing them out. Cut out the oil sac at the base of the tail, as shown on the right, making a small oyster-shaped scoop. Hold the bird by the legs and singe the pin feathers over a gas flame or candle. Turn it so that all parts of the skin are exposed to the heat.

Now cut off the feet. Most butchers use a clever gadget that breaks the foot, holds it securely and draws the tendons at the same time that the foot separates from the body. Amateurs have a somewhat harder time. In large birds the tendons are apt to be tough and they are, therefore, removed. Cut through the skin one and one-half inches below the knee joint. Be careful not to cut the tendons. Lay the chicken leg just where the skin is cut at the edge of a table or board. Press the end down sharply to snap the bone at the joint, then pull steadily. The tendons should pull away with the foot and lower leg bone. If they do not come out, remove them by forcing a skewer under each one and pulling out the tendons one by one. Removing tendons sounds complicated and troublesome, but all authorities recommend it.

Do not soak the bird in water at any time. Hold it under running water to clean the insides. Insert the fingers in the cavities to remove the last bits of viscera. Dry the bird well with a cloth. You may season the inside with salt—about ⅓ teaspoonful to the pound. You may rub the outside with a cut lemon.

To Stuff and Truss a Bird

Fill the bird about three-fourths full as the dressing will expand. Stuff it loosely as shown on the left below. Your task will be easier if you place the bird in a large pan. The crop cavity may be stuffed, too. You may also loosen the breast skin with a spoon and fill out the breast between the skin and the flesh with dressing. Close the openings with small skewers and a crisscrossed string as shown in the center drawing. Or use a spiral skewer or sew them with the old-fashioned needle and

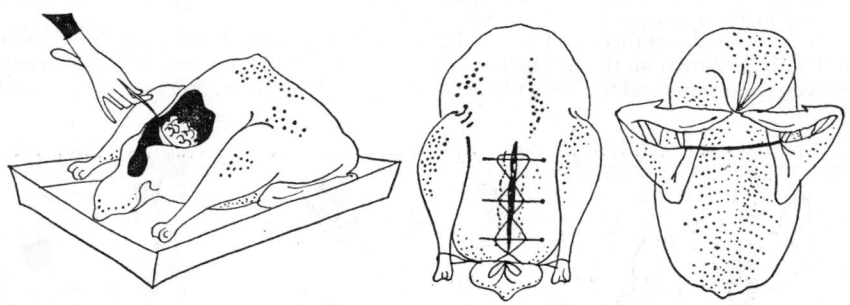

thread. Tie the legs so they will be close to the body by tieing the ends of the drumsticks together as shown above in the center. Tie a piece of string around the skin of the neck. Leave two long ends. Turn the wings back as shown above on the right, and pass the string around them and secure it.

To Cut Up a Bird

Prepare a bird for cooking as described on page 389. Hold the drawn bird up by the wing, letting the weight of the bird tug against the skin at the wing joint, as shown on the next page. Slash through the skin, flesh and joint, severing the wing from the body. Use the same method to sever the second wing and the legs. You will have to cut a longer gash into the skin of the legs and continue the cut until it nearly meets in the back. Press the legs outward and down. If the bird is young the joint will break easily under this pressure. In the case of the older bird you may

have to cut through the joint to sever the leg from the body. Now cut the body
apart in two pieces, separating the breast from the back, cutting along the dotted
line as shown in the center below. In the case of a young chicken it is possible to
make a gash toward the back on either side of the opening made to eviscerate the

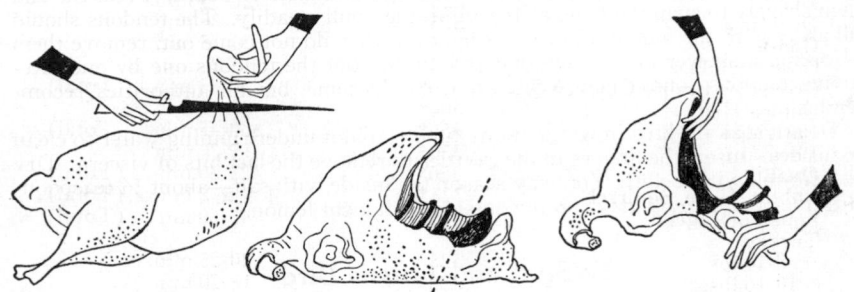

chicken and to pry the body apart until the back cracks, as shown on the right
above. Leave the breast in one piece or cut it into pieces.

    Chicken Wings into Legs. Separate the wings from the body. Cut off the wing
tips. Straighten the 2 remaining joints with the hands (you may have to cut
through the skin), pulling them into a straight line to look like a small double leg.
Silly, but the wings seem to taste better this way.

Giblets

These are the heart, liver and gizzard. Remove the thin veins and blood from
around the heart. Discard them. Cut the green sac, the gall bladder, away from
the liver very carefully. Do not cut too close to the gall bladder. It is better to leave
a small piece of liver tissue clinging to it than to sever the sac which contains a
bitter fluid. Discard the gall bladder. Cut away any part of the liver that is dis-
colored. Sever the intestines from the gizzard. Cut a shallow slit along the curve
of the gizzard. Be careful not to cut into the lining of the inner sac. Push the gizzard with the thumbs to force out the inner sac. Discard it. Wash the giblets.
Cook them by the rule on page 394 or consult the Index for the numerous dishes in
which the liver is used.

Time and Temperature Chart for Roasting
Poultry and Game

The old method of roasting poultry and game has been discarded by moderns.
It called for a hot oven at first, then a reduced heat and much basting. The new
method teaches us that a constant low temperature results in less shrinkage and
juicier and more tender meat.

To figure the time for roasting fowl or game, weigh the fowl before it is drawn
or after it is stuffed. Multiply the weight of the fowl by the minutes per pound
given in the following chart. Use the lower figure for large birds, the higher figure
for small birds. The meat should be at room temperature. If chilled, add 15 to 30
minutes to the total cooking time.

Birds and Game	Oven Temperature	Time per Pound
Capon	325°	22-30 min.
Chicken, roasting	300°	30-45 min.
Duck	325°	20-30 min.
Duckling	325°	15-20 min.
Goose	325°	20-25 min.
Goose, wild	325°	15-20 min.
Grouse or Prairie Chicken	300°	30-45 min. (Total)
Guinea Hen	300°	30-45 min.
Partridge	350°	30-45 min. (Total)
Pheasant	350°	15-20 min.
Quail	350°	25-30 min. (Total)
Rabbit, Hare, Squirrel	325°	1½ to 2 hours (Total)
Squab or Pigeon	325°	45-60 min. (Total)
Turkey		
8-10 lbs.	325°	20-25 min.
10-16 lbs.	325°	18-20 min.
18-25 lbs.	300°	13-15 min.
Turkey, wild	325°	20-25 min.
Wild Duck, rare	325°	10-12 min.
Wild Duck, well done	325°	15-20 min.
Venison, rare	325°	25 min.

Fowl cooked by the above chart will be moist and firm. It will not "fall from the bone" nor should it, as this state frequently lauded by chicken lovers is disastrous to food value and flavor. If you like somewhat overdone fowl, increase your cooking periods slightly.

How to Size Up a Chicken

Chickens fall loosely into the following categories, age determining whether their last mile is to be to the broiler, the skillet, the oven or the pot.

Very Young Chickens: 1 to 2 pounds, juicy, tender and a bit spindly go under the broiler or sometimes in the oven.

Young Chickens: 2 to 3½ pounds, "jeune encore," in the flapper stage, delicately rounded, becoming sightly, go into the skillet.

Full-Blown Chickens: 3½ to 5 pounds, buxom, curvaceous, but not yet lacking in grace go into the oven.

Old Chickens: 4½ pounds and over, tug bottomed, piano legged, obese and awkward; or long, stringy, gaunt and tough go into the pot.

Capons: unsexed male birds, average 6 to 8 pounds in weight and are larger and plumper than chickens of the same age. They are usually roasted (page 395).

Chickens are deceptive, inspect them carefully.

To test them for tenderness try to bend the breast bone. If it is still flexible the chicken is young; if hard and unbending, the chicken is old. Look for a moist skin, soft legs and feet. Press the wing tip backward. It should yield readily. Twist the skin. It should break easily. In addition, pin feathers, bright eyes and a red comb are indicative of youth or partial fulfillment.

Beware of a dry, hard, purplish or scaly skin, long hairs and a stiff breast bone, for that bird is past its prime. Yes, it will be of some good. Use it for a marvelous soup, possibly a stew or a fricassee, or cooked for a long time and ground later for croquettes, soufflés, etc.

The role a chicken is to play on the kitchen stage calls for intelligent casting.

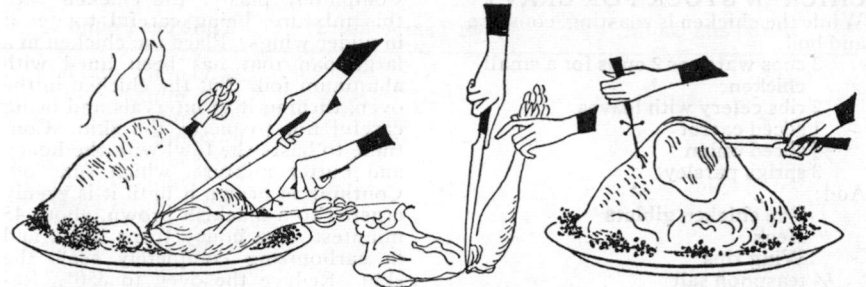

To Carve Poultry

There is a subtle art to graceful carving that is not easily mastered, but a sharp long-bladed carving knife and a two-tined carving fork with a guard are helpful to the amateur.

Place the bird, breast up, on a platter. Place the platter before you so that the legs are to your right, insert the fork into the thigh nearest you and begin to carve the bird by removing the leg that lies away from you. Strike for the joint between the leg and the body, cutting through the meat close to the body. Have an extra platter close at hand. Lift the leg onto it and cut the joint between the thigh and the drumstick. Repeat with the other leg. Begin to arrange the pieces on the extra platter so they will look attractive when the platter is passed. If a large bird is being carved some slices of meat may be cut from the thigh and from the drumstick at this time. Proceed by removing the wings in a similar manner and if the bird is large divide the wings at the major joint. To carve the breast, stick the fork astride the ridge at the peak of the breast bone. Cut thin slices down from the ridge and arrange them one at a time on the extra platter, removing the fork each time to assist in the transfer.

If the bird is very large, such as a turkey, carve only one side unless more is needed at the time.

ROAST CHICKEN
6 Servings

A 4 to 5 pound chicken requires from 30 to 35 minutes' baking per pound. A small chicken requires from 30 to 45 minutes per pound unless wrapped in aluminum foil, page 394. The fowl should be weighed before it is drawn or after it is stuffed. Have the fowl at room temperature for the most satisfactory results. If the fowl is chilled, add 15 to 30 minutes to the cooking time. You may season the inside of the chicken with salt—use about 1/3 teaspoonful to the pound. The outside of a fowl may be rubbed with a cut lemon in preference to wiping it with a moist cloth. Stuff a bird loosely as the filling will grow in bulk:

> A 4 lb. chicken

with:

> Boiled Rice, page 103
> Potato, Oyster or Bread
> Dressing, page 416

Stuff the body cavity and the crop cavity. Sew the edges together with a needle and thread or use a circular skewer or skewers and a piece of string to crisscross them together. Truss the chicken (page 390). It may be rubbed all over with unsalted soft butter or fat and roasted for all but the last 1/2 hour of cooking, breast down; or a buttered chicken may be placed uncovered in a roasting pan. If you like a chicken crusty, you may dredge it now or later with flour. Place over the breast a cloth dipped into melted unsalted fat. Roast the chicken uncovered in a slow oven 300° until tender, basting occasionally with the drippings. To test for doneness, move a leg up and down. It should have some give. The fleshy part of the thigh should feel soft. Remove the cloth for the last 1/2 hour of the roasting period to finish browning. Serve the chicken with:

> Gravy, page 394

CHICKEN STOCK FOR GRAVY

While the chicken is roasting, combine and boil:

> 3 cups water or 2 cups for a small chicken
> 2 ribs celery with leaves
> 1 sliced carrot
> ½ sliced onion
> 3 sprigs parsley

Add:

> The chicken giblets
> Neck
> Wing tips
> ½ teaspoon salt

Simmer these ingredients covered until the liver is tender. Remove the liver. Simmer the remaining ingredients until the gizzard is tender. Remove the meat and strain the stock.

CHICKEN GRAVY
About 2 Cupfuls

Strain the drippings from the roast chicken. Pour off the fat. Heat:

> 4 tablespoons fat

Add and stir until blended:

> 4 tablespoons flour

Stir in slowly:

> 2 cups pan drippings and Chicken Stock, see above

Cook and stir the gravy until it is smooth and boiling. Add:

> The chopped chicken giblets
> ¼ cup or more cream

The cream is optional but very good. Add if required:

> Salt and paprika

If the gravy is very rich it may separate. Add the cream slowly, stir it constantly. This will usually remedy the difficulty.

CHICKEN OTHELLO OR CHINESE CHICKEN
6 Servings

Named by Jin for its color and so no one would be frightened when it got dark brown.

Preheat the oven to 450°. Wipe the interior of:

> A 4½ lb. chicken

with:

> Soy sauce

Stuff it with:

> Any delicate mildly seasoned dressing or the one at the end of this recipe

Beat to a froth:

> ⅓ cup honey
> ¼ cup soft, not melted, unsalted butter

Completely plaster the chicken with this mixture, being careful to get it in under wings. Place the chicken in a large pan that has been lined with aluminum foil. Put the chicken in the oven, turning it at intervals and being careful not to pierce the skin. Continue to baste the fowl with the honey and butter mixture, which runs off. Continue to brown it until it is evenly crusted to a blackish brown, about 45 minutes. The honey turns black and in carbonizing completely seals the skin. Reduce the oven to 350°. Remove aluminum foil from bottom of pan. Cover pan but do not baste for first ½ hour. There will be only a few tablespoonfuls of fat from the skin, but use these for 2 or 3 bastings before the chicken is finished, approximately 1½ hours after covering. If a smaller or larger chicken is used, allow 25 minutes to the pound after browning. Use the drippings for:

> Gravy, this page

A dressing Jin used, her own invention, and was enthusiastic about is:

> 4 ribs Pascal celery, leaves and stem cut up
> ¼ cup chopped parsley
> ⅔ cup dry rice lightly sautéed in chicken fat
> 6 Julienne strips tangerine rind
> (¼ cup lightly sautéed onions)
> (¼ cup lightly sautéed mushrooms)

CHICKEN ROASTED IN PARCHMENT OR WAXED PAPER
4 to 5 Servings

Prepare by the rule for Roast Chicken on page 393, greasing the fowl but omitting the cloth:

> A 3½ to 5 lb. chicken

It may be stuffed. Wrap it in parchment paper. Double the paper over the breast. Fasten it with large pins. Roast the chicken in a moderate oven 325° from 30 to 45 minutes to the pound. Unwrap it for the last ½ hour. Thicken the juices, if any, with:

> Flour (see Gravy, this page)

or make a cream gravy by combining:

> 1 can cream of mushroom soup: 10½ oz.
> 1 cup stock and the pan drippings
> ¼ teaspoon poultry seasoning
> Salt and pepper

CHICKEN IN ALUMINUM FOIL

Follow the rule on page 404 for:

> Turkey in Aluminum Foil

ROAST CAPON
6 to 8 Servings
Prepare for cooking (page 389):
    A 6 lb. capon
Rub the inside well with salt. Stuff it lightly with about 6 cupfuls of:
    Chestnut or Bread Dressing,
        page 416
Rub the fowl well with:
    2 tablespoons unsalted fat
Melt in a roasting pan:
    2 tablespoons unsalted fat
Brown in it:
    1 tablespoon minced onion
    Leaves from a stalk of celery
Place the capon in the pan breast up, cover it with a cloth dipped in fat. Bake it in a slow oven 325° from 22 to 30 minutes to the pound. Baste it frequently with the drippings. A half hour before the capon is tender remove the cloth. Take the bird from the pan. Drain the drippings, replace them in the pan. Place the capon in it. Brush the breast with:
    ½ cup cream
Continue to cook the capon until it is tender. Thicken the drippings with:
    Flour (see Gravy, page 394)
Or see the rule for chicken stock and gravy under the rule for roast chicken.

BAKED YOUNG CHICKENS
Allow ¾ Pound Per Person
Clean and cut into quarters:
    Young chickens
Heat in a skillet:
    Butter
Add the chickens and sauté them until they are brown. Place them in a baking dish. Pour over them:
    ½ cup boiling Chicken Stock, page 47, or milk
Cover the dish and place it in a slow oven 325° for 1 hour or more. Baste the chickens frequently. When they are tender remove them from the dish. Thicken the drippings with:
    Flour (see Gravy, page 394)
Add to the stock, if required:
    Chicken Stock, page 47
    Cream
    Salt and pepper

BROILED SPRING CHICKEN
Allow ¾ Pound Per Person
Clean and cut into halves:
    Spring chickens
Rub them on both sides with:
    Butter
Place them in a pan skin side down. The skin side will brown quicker than the under side. Broil the chickens until they are brown under a good flame, 375°. Turn them frequently. After 15 minutes add, if needed:
    Butter
Place in the bottom of the pan:
    ½ cup chicken stock
Cover the pan and bake the chickens in a slow oven 275°. Baste them every 10 minutes. Bake them for about ½ hour. Very small chickens may be broiled for 20 minutes and require no baking. Strain the drippings. Thicken them, if desired, with:
    Flour (see Gravy, page 394)
or serve the gravy unthickened seasoned with:
    1 tablespoon sherry
Or the chicken may be split, spread with butter, seasoned and baked in a greased pan skin side down in a hot oven 425°. After 15 minutes broil the chicken on both sides for about 5 minutes. Baste it frequently.

BAKED BROILERS
2 Servings
These are as good as fried chicken and very simple to prepare. Split down the back:
    A 1¾ lb. broiler
Rub each half generously with:
    Unsalted butter
Place them in a pan. You may place over them:
    1 tablespoon grated onion
Bake them in a 400° oven for about 30 minutes. Turn them once. Baste them several times. Serve them on toast with the drippings poured over them, to which you may add:
    Salt and pepper
    A pinch of tarragon, etc.

SIMMERED AND BROILED CHICKEN
4 Servings
Split into halves:
    2 broiling chickens
Melt:
    ¾ cup fat
Brown the chicken lightly in the fat. Add:
    6 sprigs parsley
    2 small skinned quartered onions
    ½ lb. cut-up mushrooms
    1 clove garlic cut in two
Cover and simmer the chicken for 15 minutes. Drain the chicken. Roll it in:
    Seasoned bread crumbs
Broil it until it is browned. To serve pour the drippings over it.

BAKED BROILERS WITH PARSLEY DRESSING

Wash well, then dry:

> Parsley

Stuff fryers or young baking chickens with it. Rub them with butter.
To bake them, follow the preceding rule. Serve them hot or chilled.

BAKED WHOLE STUFFED BROILERS

Allow 1 Small Broiler Per Person

Dress for cooking:

> Broilers

Rub the inside with salt. They may be stuffed lightly with:

> Bread Dressing or Oyster
> Dressing, page 416

Allow about ½ cupful for each broiler. Rub them with:

> 2 tablespoons unsalted butter or chicken fat

Truss them. Place them on a rack in a pan. Place in the pan:

> ⅓ cup boiling water
> A slice of onion

Roast them uncovered in a moderate oven 350° for about 25 minutes. Cover them with a piece of greased waxed paper. Turn them to brown evenly. Baste them frequently. Add water as needed. Cook them about 40 to 60 minutes in all. Test them for doneness, page 335. Season the pan drippings. They may be served clear or thickened with a very little:

> Flour (see Gravy, page 394)

Pour the sauce over the chickens.

BAKED HALF BROILERS STUFFED

Allow ½ Chicken Per Person

Clean:

> 1½ lb. chickens

Split them. Rub them inside with:

> Salt

Brush the chickens with:

> Melted butter or salad oil

Fill them with:

> Celery, Bread or other
> Dressing, page 416

Place them skin side down in a pan. Bake them in a moderate oven 350° for 45 minutes. Cover the dressing side with pieces of greased waxed paper or aluminum foil. Turn and baste the chicken with the pan drippings. Increase the heat to 450° and bake them for about 10 minutes longer. Season the chickens before serving with:

> Salt and pepper

BROILERS BAKED IN CREAM

4 Servings

Prepare for cooking:

> 4 broilers

Rub the cavities with:

> Salt

Soak:

> 8 pieces crustless bread

in:

> Milk

Squeeze the moisture from the bread. Season it lightly with:

> Salt and paprika
> Freshly grated nutmeg

Stuff the broilers with this dressing. Place them in a casserole. Add:

> 10 small skinned onions
> 12 skinned new potatoes

Cover these ingredients with:

> 1½ cups seasoned cream

Bake the broilers covered in a moderate oven 325° for about 1 hour, or until tender. You may add cream if needed and for the last ½ hour of cooking:

> 2 cups green peas
> ½ lb. mushrooms
> Seasoning as required

CHICKEN BAKED IN BATTER

Clean and cut up:

> A tender 3½ lb. chicken

Use the back, neck and giblets for Chicken Stock, page 47. You may rub the remaining pieces with a cut lemon. Place in a paper bag:

> ¼ cup all-purpose flour
> 1 teaspoon salt
> ¼ teaspoon freshly grated pepper

Add the chicken and shake the bag vigorously. Melt in a large frying pan:

> ¼ cup butter

Brown the chicken in this on all sides. Remove it from the pan. Drain it on unglazed brown paper. Prepare the following batter. Sift into a bowl:

> 1½ cups all-purpose flour
> 1¼ teaspoons any baking powder
> 1 teaspoon salt

Beat until light:

> 4 eggs

Stir in:

> 1½ cups milk
> 3 tablespoons melted butter

Stir in the flour mixture slowly until blended. Grease a 12 x 7½ x 2 inch baking dish. Pour the batter into it and place the chicken on top of the batter. Bake the dish in a moderate oven 350° for about 1 hour until the batter is light brown. Use the previously prepared Chicken Stock, page 47, to make Gravy, page 394.

CHICKEN WITH WINE AND TARRAGON
4 Servings
Soak for 1 hour:
   ¼ cup fresh or 2 tablespoons dried
      tarragon leaves
in:
   1 cup dry white wine
Disjoint:
   2 broiling chickens
Melt in a heavy skillet:
   ½ cup butter
When very hot add the chicken. Sear
it on all sides until it is light brown.
Mince finely, then add:
   8 shallots or scallions
Lower the heat, cover the skillet closely and simmer the chicken for about
20 minutes, or until tender. Add the
wine. Increase the heat until the sauce
is hot, but do not boil it. Add:
   Seasoning if needed
Serve the chicken on a hot platter.
Garnish it with:
   Chopped parsley

BRAISED CHICKEN IN WINE OR COQ AU VIN
4 Servings
This is best with a youngish chicken,
although an old one may be used and
exposed to longer, slower cooking. Let
us assume that you are going to disjoint:
   A frying or roasting chicken
Use the back and neck for the stock
pot. Melt:
   3 tablespoons butter or olive oil
Add and brown lightly:
   ¼ lb. minced salt pork
   ¾ cup chopped mild onions or 6
      small skinned onions
   1 sliced carrot
   3 minced shallots
   1 peeled clove garlic
Push the vegetables aside. Brown the
chicken in the fat. Add and stir:
   2 tablespoons flour
   2 tablespoons minced parsley
   1 tablespoon fresh chervil or
      marjoram: 1 teaspeon if dried
   ½ bay leaf
   ½ teaspoon thyme
   1 teaspoon salt
   ⅛ teaspoon freshly ground pepper
   (1 tablespoon brandy)
Stir in:
   1½ cups dry wine or sherry
Cook the chicken on high heat until
done, about 20 minutes. Keep it covered for the first 15 minutes. Add for
the last 5 minutes:

   ½ lb. sliced mushrooms
Skim off the excess fat. Correct the
seasoning. Serve the chicken on a hot
platter, the sauce and vegetables
poured over it.

BREASTS OF CHICKEN
Allow 1 Breast for 1 Serving
Remove the breasts from:
   2 or 3 young chickens
Leave the wing bone attached. Dip
them in:
   Cream
Season them with:
   Salt and pepper
Dust them lightly with:
   Flour
Melt in a skillet:
   2 tablespoons butter
Sauté the fillets lightly in the butter
and arrange them in a well-buttered
pan. Dot the fillets with:
   Butter
Cover them with:
   Buttered paper or aluminum foil
Bake them from 10 to 15 minutes in a
hot oven 425°. Baste them frequently
with the fat in the pan. Serve them on
thin slices of:
   Boiled ham or Broiled Ham,
      page 370
Garnish them with:
   Sautéed Mushrooms, page 292
Serve them with the ham and mush-
room drippings thinned with:
   Chicken stock and cream
and thickened with:
   Flour (see Gravy, page 394)
Or with the following sauce.
Melt:
   2 tablespoons butter or pan
      drippings
Stir in until blended:
   2 tablespoons flour
Stir in slowly:
   1 cup chicken stock
   ½ cup cream
Season the sauce with:
   Salt and paprika
Pour part of it over:
   1 slightly beaten egg yolk
Return the sauce to the pan. Stir and
cook it over a slow fire until the egg is
slightly thickened. Season the sauce
with:
   1 tablespoon or more sherry

MARYLAND CHICKEN
4 to 5 Servings
Cut into pieces for serving:
   A young roasting chicken about
      3½ lbs., or 2 broiling chickens

Place in a paper bag:
   ¼ cup flour
   ½ teaspoon salt
   ¼ teaspoon paprika
Add the chicken and shake the bag vigorously. Remove the chicken from the bag. Dip it in:
   1 beaten egg diluted with
   2 tablespoons water
Dip it in:
   Soft bread crumbs
Permit the crumbs to dry for 1 hour. Heat in a heavy skillet:
   1 inch of fat, rendered salt pork, bacon drippings or butter
Add the chicken. Brown it on all sides over high heat, reduce the heat and cook it slowly until tender, from 35 to 45 minutes.
This is usually served with cream gravy. That is, some of the fat thickened with:
   Flour (see Gravy, page 394)
to which milk is added.

SAUTÉED CHICKEN
Allow ¾ Pound Per Person
In ordinary parlance—Fried Chicken. Do not attempt to sauté chicken in this way unless it is young and tender. Clean and cut into halves:
   Young chickens
Dredge them lightly with:
   (Seasoned flour)
A quick and efficient way to flour food is to place it in a paper bag with seasoned flour or pancake flour, close the bag and shake it vigorously. The food will be evenly coated. Some prefer chicken coated with corn meal. A heavy coating is apt to be tough.
Melt in a skillet:
   Butter or bacon drippings
The amount of fat to be used always raises a domestic discussion. My cook, Sarah Brown, likes about ½ inch of fat in the skillet—part butter and part lard. She claims that the lard gives the chicken a better color. I like just enough fat to cover the bottom of the skillet and prefer to have it all butter, but I must admit that Sarah's chicken is mighty good. Lard seems to make a coarse gravy. Use 2 skillets if several chickens are to be fried. When the fat is hot add the chicken. Cook and turn it in the hot fat until it is brown. Reduce the heat, cover the skillet and continue cooking the chicken until it is done, from 20 to 30 minutes, according to the size. Remove the chicken from

the pan and thicken the drippings with:
   Flour (see Gravy, page 394)
Add if required:
   Cream
   Salt and paprika
Serve the chicken garnished with:
   Parsley
If preferred the chicken may be cooked uncovered.

See Chicken Wings into Legs, page 391.

SAUTÉED OR FRIED CHICKEN SOUTHERN STYLE
Allow ¾ Pound Per Person
Clean and cut into small pieces:
   A 2½ lb. baking chicken
Sprinkle it lightly with:
   Seasoned flour
Combine and beat:
   1 egg
   ¼ cup milk
Dip the chicken in the egg mixture and then in:
   Fine bread or cracker crumbs
Melt in a skillet:
   ¼ cup butter, lard or drippings
When it is very hot brown the chicken in it. Pour into the skillet:
   ¼ cup boiling chicken stock or water
Cover it closely and place it in a slow oven 300°. Cook the chicken until it is tender. A 2½ pound chicken calls for about 1 hour's cooking in all, 30 minutes on top of the stove and 30 minutes in the oven. Thicken the drippings, if desired, with:
   Flour (see Gravy, page 394)
Add if required:
   Chicken stock
   Cream
   Salt and paprika

SOUTH CAROLINA "CRUNCHY FRIED" CHICKEN
4 Servings
An American correspondent in the Dominican Republic, about to become a resident of Venezuela, writes nostalgically of her favorite native dish, which she asks me to add to my collection. This dish is easy for the hostess as the gravy may be made in advance. Cook the necks, wing tips, feet and giblets for the Chicken Gravy, page 394. See Chicken Stock, page 47.
Cut up and disjoint:
   A 3 lb. fowl

Dip the pieces in:
> Seasoned flour or pancake flour

Dip them in:
> 1 egg white diluted with
> 2 tablespoons water

then in the flour again. Fry them lightly, a few pieces at a time, in about:
> 1 inch hot fat

Remove them and place them on paper toweling. When all the pieces are lightly browned, but be careful not to overcook them, place them on absorbent paper toweling in a wide flat pan so they do not touch one another. Cook it in a slow oven, about 250°, for 2 hours.

FRENCH FRIED CHICKEN IN BATTER

A 3 Pound Chicken Serves 4 Persons

Clean and cut into pieces:
> Young roasting chickens

You may drop the pieces slowly one by one into:
> Boiling salt water to cover

Do not disturb the boiling point. Add to the water for flavor:
> Vegetables such as onion,
> carrot, parsley, celery

Simmer the chickens until they are tender. Cool them thoroughly. Dry them between towels. Prepare the following batter. Sift:
> 2 cups flour
> 3 teaspoons tartrate or phosphate
> baking powder or 2 teaspoons
> combination type baking powder
> (see Baking Powder, page 501)
> ½ teaspoon salt

Beat:
> 2 eggs
> 1½ cups milk

Stir the liquid into the dry ingredients. Dip each piece of chicken in the batter. Drop it into deep fat heated to 375° (page 542). Fry the chicken until the pieces are a golden brown. Serve it with Gravy, page 394, made with the chicken stock and cream.

SAUTÉED CHICKEN BAKED IN CREAM WITH MUSHROOMS

3 Servings

Clean and cut into pieces:
> A frying chicken: 2 or 2½ lbs.

Dip it in:
> Milk

Dredge it with:
> Seasoned Flour, page 540

Melt in a skillet:
> ½ cup lard or bacon drippings

Add the chicken. Sauté it until it is brown. Drain it on absorbent paper. Slice:
> ½ lb. mushrooms

Sauté them in the skillet for 2 minutes. Place the chicken in a deep baking dish. Place the mushrooms on top of it. Pour over it:
> 2 cups hot cream

Season it with:
> ¼ teaspoon salt
> ¼ teaspoon paprika

Bake the chicken in a moderate oven 325° until it is tender and the cream is a thick sauce, about ½ hour.

SMOTHERED CHICKEN

A 3 Pound Chicken Serves 4 Persons

A good way of preparing middle-aged chickens.

Clean and cut into pieces:
> A chicken

Roll the pieces in:
> Seasoned Flour, page 540

Melt in a pot or skillet:
> ¼ cup fat

Add and sauté for 2 minutes:
> ½ sliced onion

Brown the chicken in the fat.
Heat to the boiling point:
> 1 cup Chicken Stock, page 47
> ½ cup cream

One and one-half cupfuls rich milk may be substituted for the chicken stock and cream. Two slices of sautéed bacon may be added to the milk. Or try canned mushroom soup, diluted, the suggestion of a correspondent.
Pour this over the chicken. Cover the pot and simmer the chicken until it is tender. Remove the chicken from the pot. Strain the stock. Thicken, if desired, with:
> Flour (see Gravy, page 394)

Reheat the chicken in the gravy and serve it.

CASSEROLE CHICKEN

6 to 7 Servings

Prepare for cooking:
> A 4 lb. roasting chicken

Disjoint it. Place the chicken in a paper bag with:
> ¼ cup Seasoned Flour, page 540

Close the bag and shake it vigorously. Brown the chicken in:
> ¼ cup olive or salad oil

Place it in a casserole. Cook in the fat for 10 minutes:
> 1 small sliced onion
> 1 sliced clove garlic
> 3 or 4 stalks chopped celery
> 1 medium-sized carrot

Place the vegetables in the casserole. Pour over them:

1½ cups hot chicken stock

Cover the dish. Bake the chicken in a slow oven 325° for about 1½ hours, or until tender. Sauté for 5 minutes:

1 cup sliced mushrooms

in:

2 tablespoons oil or fat

Add:

12 stuffed sliced olives

Add these ingredients to the chicken 5 minutes before it is done.

HUNTER'S CHICKEN OR CHICKEN CACCIATORE
4 Servings

This and the following dish are flavored with tomatoes.

Cut into individual pieces:

A 3 lb. chicken

Sauté the pieces until golden brown in:

¼ cup olive or salad oil

Add:

½ cup chopped onions
1 can Italian peeled tomatoes:
2 lb. 3 oz.
½ cup dry white wine
1 teaspoon salt
¼ teaspoon pepper
½ bay leaf
⅛ teaspoon thyme
¼ teaspoon marjoram

Cover the chicken. Simmer it for 1 hour. Remove the cover to permit the sauce to reduce somewhat. Cook the chicken until it is tender. Serve it with:

Boiled Spaghetti, page 91

SPANISH CASSEROLE CHICKEN
4 Servings

Cut into pieces:

A 3 lb. frying chicken

Dredge them with:

Seasoned Flour, page 540

Heat in a skillet:

¼ cup olive oil

Brown the chicken in the oil. Place the pieces in a casserole. Sauté in the oil in the skillet:

¼ cup chopped onion
3 tablespoons chopped green pepper
1 minced clove garlic

Add:

½ cup chopped carrots
½ cup chopped celery
1½ cups tomato juice

Pour these ingredients over the chicken in the casserole. Cover it with a lid. Bake the chicken in a moderate oven

325° for about 1 hour, or until it is tender. Add if needed:

Boiling vegetable stock or boiling water

Five minutes before the chicken is done add:

¾ cup Sautéed Mushrooms, page 292
⅓ cup sliced stuffed olives

Thicken the drippings with:

Flour (see Gravy, page 394)

FRENCH CASSEROLE CHICKEN
4 Servings

Whenever I see one of my contemporaries, we are now, alas! all authentic Helen Hokinsons, trying to regain her youthful allure by sophisticated sartorial trappings, I think of a dish I found in a collection of college alumnae recipes called: "Suprême of Old Hen." This French rule makes so fascinating a dish out of a poorish bird that the old girl is still an acceptable morsel.

Prepare for cooking and disjoint:

A 4½ lb. fowl

Sear the pieces in:

4 tablespoons hot butter

Add:

4 tablespoons sherry

Remove the chicken from the pot. Place in the pot:

2 pared, cored, sliced tart apples
6 chopped ribs celery with leaves
1 minced or grated onion
3 sprigs parsley
½ teaspoon salt
¼ teaspoon paprika

Cover and cook these ingredients gently until tender. Stir in:

2½ tablespoons flour
2 cups Stock, page 47

Cook and stir the sauce until it boils. Add the chicken. Cover and simmer it until it is tender, 1 hour or more. Remove the chicken to a hot oven-proof serving dish. Strain the sauce. Warm over hot water:

⅓ cup sweet or sour cream

Add it to the sauce with:

Salt and freshly grated pepper
1 teaspoon dried tarragon or basil

Pour the sauce over the chicken. Sprinkle it generously with:

Grated cheese

Place it under a broiler until the cheese is melted.

CHICKEN PAPRIKA
3 Servings

Cut up as for frying:

A young chicken: about 2⅓ lbs.
Melt in a heavy pot:

    1½ tablespoons butter
    1½ tablespoons lard

Add and simmer until browned:

    1 cup chopped onions

Add:

    ½ teaspoon salt
    2 teaspoons paprika
    2 cups vegetable stock or water

When these ingredients are boiling add
the chicken. Simmer it covered until it
is tender, about 1½ hours. Stir:

    1 teaspoon flour

into:

    1 cup sour cream

Stir it slowly into the pot. Cook the
chicken 5 minutes longer.

THE FRICASSEE

A fricassee is a simmered meat. It is
usually made of chicken, veal or rabbit.
How this meat is to be simmered, in
stock or in water; whether it is to be
turned first in butter or put directly
into boiling liquid; whether it is to be
simmered first and browned afterward; what the additions are to be;
whether or not a thickening of flour is
to be used; whether the stock is to be
thickened at the last with cream and
eggs—these are all matters of tradition, personal taste and convenience.
A typical dish is the following:

FRENCH CHICKEN FRICASSEE

Disjoint and cut up:

    A tender stewing chicken

Place it in a pot and cover it with:

    3 cups boiling water or veal or
        chicken stock

Add to the pot:

    1 medium-sized peeled onion
        stuck with 1 clove
    1 small diced carrot
    ¼ bay leaf
    A bouquet of Herbs, page 831,
        or parsley or chopped chives
    ½ teaspoon salt
    2 or 3 peppercorns
    (The white part of 1 leek)

Cover the chicken, leaving a small vent
hole. Simmer it until it is tender, 1
hour or more. Take out the pieces of
chicken. Keep them hot. Strain the
stock. Chill it. Skim it. Meanwhile,
cook until tender:

    12 small skinned onions
    (¼ lb. mushrooms)

Do this in stock or stock and butter.
Melt:

    3 tablespoons butter

Stir in:

    3 tablespoons flour

Add the chicken stock. Permit this
sauce to cook gently for 10 minutes.
Remove it from the fire. In the words
of French cooks "correct the seasoning." Combine:

    2 egg yolks
    3 tablespoons cream

Place the chicken on a hot platter.
Garnish it with the onions and mushrooms. Stir the cream and egg mixture
into the hot stock. Return it to the
stove. Stir the sauce over low heat
until it is hot, but do not permit it to
boil. Add:

    (½ teaspoon lemon juice)

Pour the sauce over the chicken. Serve
it at once garnished with:

    Parsley or chopped chives

AMERICAN CHICKEN FRICASSEE

A more simple version of the above.
Sometimes the chicken is cooked without browning until tender. It is then
dried, floured and browned in butter.
Disjoint and cut up:

    A tender stewing chicken

Turn the pieces briefly in:

    3 tablespoons hot butter

to which you may add:

    1 medium sliced onion

Cover the chicken with:

    3 cups boiling water

Add:

    ½ teaspoon salt
    ⅛ teaspoon white pepper
    1 carrot
    3 ribs celery with leaves

If you have not added an onion to the
butter, place it in the water.
Simmer the chicken covered, leaving a
small vent hole, until it is tender, 1
hour or more. Remove it from the
stock. Strain the stock. Chill it. Remove the fat on top. Melt:

    4 tablespoons butter or chicken
        fat

Add:

    4 tablespoons flour

Stir in the stock. Correct the seasoning. The stock may be thickened with
egg yolk and cream, using the directions above in French Chicken Fricassee. In this case, use only 3 tablespoonfuls butter and 3 tablespoonfuls
flour. Add:

    (½ teaspoon lemon juice)

Place the chicken in the stock. Serve it
hot garnished with:

    Parsley

This is good with:
  Rice, page 103
  Noodles, page 97
or served with a border of:
  Mashed Potatoes, page 302

STEWED CHICKEN
A 5 Pound Stewing Chicken Serves 5 to 6 People
The following is the best way to prepare a large chicken of doubtful age. Clean and cut into pieces:
  A stewing chicken
Place in a stewing pan and bring to the boiling point:
  3 cups water
  1 sliced carrot
  1 small sliced onion
  2 ribs celery with leaves
Drop the chicken piece by piece into the boiling liquid. Do this slowly so as not to disturb the boiling point. As the liquid will increase in volume, the chicken need only be covered to the depth of ½ inch. Cover the pot closely and simmer the chicken until it is tender, 2 hours or more, but do not boil it at any time. At the end of the first hour of cooking add:
  ⅛ teaspoon paprika or 3 or 4 peppercorns
If you plan to use the chicken in a salad or cut up in other dishes, permit it to cool in the broth. Otherwise, remove the chicken from the pot.
I.
Strain the stock. Thicken it with:
  Flour (see Gravy, page 394)
If a very concentrated gravy is desired, boil the stock before thickening it until it is reduced to 1½ cupfuls. If the gravy threatens to separate, stir into it slowly:
  2 or more tablespoons cream
Return the chicken to the boiling gravy. Serve it as directed in the second method.
II.
A richer gravy is made in the following way. Melt:
  1½ tablespoons chicken fat
Stir in until blended:
  ¾ tablespoon flour
Stir in slowly:
  2 cups chicken stock
Stir and cook these ingredients for 2 minutes.
Beat well:
  2 egg yolks
  2 tablespoons cream
Reduce the heat to low. Stir the yolk mixture gradually into the gravy. Permit the yolks to thicken slightly. Add if needed:
  Salt and paprika
Pour the gravy over the chicken. Garnish it with:
  Parsley
Serve it with:
  Noodles, page 97, Dumplings, page 421, Boiled Rice, page 103, or Baked Macaroni, page 95

Chicken Pot Pie, page 141; Creamed Chicken, page 143.

STEWED CHICKEN AND ONIONS
4 Servings
This recipe calls for a young hen. Follow the preceding rule for:
  Stewed Chicken
Peel:
  24 small white onions
After the chicken has simmered for 1 hour add the seasoning as directed and drop in the onions slowly so as not to disturb the boiling point. Simmer the stew until the chicken and the onions are tender. Remove the chicken to a hot platter. Arrange the onions around it. Keep it hot. Prepare the gravy by the second method above. Add to it:
  1 teaspoon lemon juice
  2 tablespoons chopped parsley
Pour the gravy over the chicken.

CHICKEN WITH RICE
Rice cooked with chicken stock is frequently served with Stewed Chicken, on this page. Melt in a saucepan:
  2 tablespoons butter
Add and stir until golden brown:
  ½ chopped onion
Add and shake until the grains are coated:
  1 cup rice
Add:
  2 cups hot chicken stock
Cover the pot and simmer the rice, or bake it in a moderate oven 375° until the liquid is absorbed. Add:
  2 tablespoons melted butter
Toss the rice with a fork to distribute it.

CHICKEN CURRY
A 5 Pound Chicken Serves 6 to 7 Persons
Cook by the rule for Stewed Chicken, on this page:
  A large chicken
Remove it from the bone in large

pieces. Add to the stock if the chicken is dry:

2 tablespoons butter

Peel, chop until very fine and add:

1 large onion
1 cucumber
1 apple
1 sweet potato

Simmer these ingredients until they are tender. Add:

¼ cup seedless raisins
1 to 2 tablespoons curry powder

Allow to every cupful stock:

1 tablespoon cornstarch

Moisten the cornstarch in a little cold stock. Stir it into the boiling stock. Shortly before serving stir in:

1 cup cream

Heat the sauce but do not let it boil. Pour it over the hot chicken or reheat the chicken in the sauce. Serve it with a border of:

Boiled Rice, page 103
Green Peas, page 298

BARBECUED CHICKEN

Allow ½ Chicken Per Person
6 Servings

Clean, then split down the back:

3 broiling chickens

Brush them with:

Melted butter

Place them on a broiling rack skin side down. Broil them about 5 inches from the heat for 15 minutes, brush with melted butter, turn and broil the other side for the same length of time. Turn the chickens a second time. Allow ¾ to 1 hour in all. Baste them frequently during the last period with:

Barbecue Sauce, page 436

STUFFED CHICKEN LEGS

Allow 1 or 2 Legs Per Person

Prepare for cooking by removing bone and tendons (page 390):

Large chicken legs

Stuff the cavities with:

Olive, Bread or other Dressing, page 419

Close the openings by sewing them or use poultry pins or circular skewers. You may brown the legs lightly in:

Butter or fat

to which you may add:

A slice of onion

Place the stuffed legs in a casserole. Cover the bottom of the dish with:

⅓ inch boiling Chicken Stock, page 394, or Vegetable Stock, page 425

Bake the chickens covered in a moderate oven 350° until they are tender, about 1 hour. Thicken the stock with:

Flour (see Gravy, page 394)

Turkey

A young turkey has black feet, a 3-year-old turkey has pink feet, and an old turkey has gray feet. A good turkey is plump and full breasted. The ideal size is from 10 to 12 pounds. The favorite method of cooking turkey is roasted, but it may be braised or fricasseed, and very young turkeys may be broiled (page 395) like chicken. Turkey cocks are better for cooking than turkey hens.

ROAST TURKEY

Allow ¾ to 1 Pound of Turkey Per Person

Draw (page 389):

A turkey

Remove the windpipe and crop from the neck opening. Cut off the neck close to the body but leave the neck skin on.

Clean the turkey by letting cold water run through it. Dry inside and out with a cloth. Rub it well on the inside with salt. Fill the body cavity loosely—the dressing will increase in bulk—with:

Chestnut, Bread or other Dressing, page 420

Sew up the incision or secure it with skewers. Wrap a string crisscross fashion about them. Fill the neck cav-

ity or crop with one kind of dressing, the body with another. Example: Sausage dressing in the crop, celery dressing in the body; oysters in the crop, bread dressing in the body. Sew up the openings or use skewers to close them. Tie back the flap of neck skin. Truss the bird so that the wings are bent behind the back and the legs are close to the body. Tie the leg bones together. Place the bird breast up in a roasting pan. Brush the breast, legs and wings with:

Unsalted melted fat

Dip a cloth in the fat and place it over the bird, or place a thick layer of body fat on the bird and cover it with a piece of waxed paper or a cloth. Roast the turkey uncovered in a slow oven 300°

until tender. Allow 25 minutes per pound for a bird under 12 pounds, weighed after being dressed, or 20 minutes per pound for a larger bird. Baste the turkey every ½ hour with the pan drippings. Remove the paper or cloth for the last ½ hour of cooking. To prepare the gravy see:

Chicken Stock and Chicken Gravy, page 394

Double or treble the amounts according to the size of the turkey. The turkey liver may be placed in the pan for the last hour of cooking, or you may cook the giblets by the rule for Chicken Giblets, see Chicken Stock, page 394, allowing a somewhat longer time for cooking.

TURKEY ROASTED IN FOIL

Be sure to have the bird at room temperature.

After preparing a turkey for cooking wrap it completely in aluminum foil. Roast it in a moderately hot oven 400° for 20 minutes. Reduce the heat to 350° and roast it from then on 20 minutes to the pound. If the bird is under 10 pounds allow 25 minutes to the pound. About 45 minutes before the cooking time is over you may open the foil and expose the bird for browning. Use pan drippings for frequent bastings during this period.

TURKEY OTHELLO

Follow the rule on page 394 for:
Chicken Othello
Dress:
A 15 lb. turkey
Stuff it as desired. Preheat an oven to 550°. Make a paste as directed of:
1 cup honey
¾ cup butter
Spread it as directed. Place the bird in the hot oven for ½ hour until it is evenly colored. Turn it several times with wooden spoons, being careful not to break the skin. Reduce the heat to 325°, cover the turkey. Cook it 3 to 4 hours—3 for a hen, 4 for an old tom. Baste with the drippings after the first hour of cooking and every 20 minutes afterward. Use the drippings for:
Gravy, page 394

TURKEY FRICASSEE

Wings are usually braised or fricasseed, so are the leg joints. Place in a paper bag:
Seasoned Flour, page 540

Add the turkey parts and shake the bag vigorously. Melt:
Turkey or other fat
You may add:
A slice or two of onion
Brown the turkey parts lightly in the fat. Add:
½ cup vegetable stock or water
Vegetables suitable for soup
Cover the pot closely and simmer the meat until tender, about 1½ hours, or bake the meat in the stock, closely covered, for about 2 hours in a slow oven 250°.

You may follow any rule for casserole chicken or stew, substituting turkey for chicken and allowing a somewhat longer cooking period. See also Stuffed Chicken Legs, page 403.

You may substitute turkey meat in any rule calling for cut-up chicken: creamed, à la king, etc.

A HALF TURKEY OR PARTS OF TURKEY ROASTED
About 6 Servings

Prepare for cooking by the rule on page 390:
A half turkey weighing about 6 lbs.
You may use any desired:
Dressing for Fowl, page 416
Allow 1 cupful dressing for every pound of bird, weighed after being dressed. Place the turkey, skin up, on a rack in a roaster. Brush it with melted butter or drippings. Roast it in a moderate oven 325°. Allow 25 to 30 minutes to the pound. Cook it uncovered, without the addition of water, until ½ done. Remove it from the rack. Place on the rack well-greased heavy brown paper or several thicknesses of waxed paper or aluminum foil. Place the dressing on it in an oval mound. Place the turkey skin side up over the dressing. If using foil, turn up the edges in pan-shape to catch the drippings.

You may baste the turkey every 15 minutes with drippings or butter. Roast it until done. A thermometer placed between the second joint and the body will register 190°. Or see Test for Doneness, page 335. Follow the rule under Roast Turkey, page 403, for preparing the gravy.

A half breast or a leg of turkey may be roasted by this same rule. If the breast is not stuffed, secure the turkey skin to the sides with thread or small skewers to keep it from shrinking. Brown the breast or the leg lightly in melted butter or fat on top of the stove, then bake it as directed. You may add a slice of onion to the fat. The time will be about 2 to 2½ hours for a breast, about 1½ to 2 hours for a leg.

BROILED TURKEY
Prepare for cooking:
> Turkeys weighing from 3 to 4 lbs.

Cut them into 4 pieces. Cook them by the rule on page 395 for:
> Broiled Chickens

Allow about 45 minutes cooking time.

ROAST GOOSE
6 Servings
Prepare for cooking (page 390):
> An 8 lb. goose

This weight is for a bird dressed but not drawn. Rub the inside with:
> Salt

Fill the cavities with:
> Apple, Prune, Chestnut or other Dressing, page 416

Allow 1 cupful dressing to each pound of bird. If very fat, prick through the skin into the fat layer around the legs and wings. Truss the goose. Roast it on a rack in an uncovered pan in a moderate oven 325° allowing 25 minutes to the pound. You may place in the pan a cut clove of garlic or onion and several stalks of celery with leaves. Pour off the fat as it accumulates in the pan. Thicken the drippings with:
> Flour (see Gravy, page 426), or see Chicken Stock and Chicken Gravy, page 394

Season it with:
> Salt
> Pepper
> ½ teaspoon ginger

Goose liver is considered a great delicacy. Remove the gall bladder. Soak the liver in cold salted water for 2 hours. Dry it with a cloth.

I.
Sprinkle it with:
> ⅛ teaspoon paprika
> ½ teaspoon sugar
> ⅛ teaspoon ginger

Sauté it in hot goose fat until it is tender.

II.
Prepare and soak the liver as directed. Place it in an oven-proof dish. Cover it with:
> 1 cup brown sugar
> ¼ teaspoon salt
> 1 cup sherry

Broil it under low heat for ½ hour. Watch it so that it does not burn. Baste it frequently to prevent a crust from forming. Cook sliced apples in a thick sirup until well glazed. Place them around the liver. Continue to baste with apple sirup until the liver is tender.

BRAISED PARTS OF GOOSE OR GAENSEKLEIN
Rub with garlic:
> Goose back, neck, gizzard, wings and heart

Permit these to stand for several hours. Place them in a kettle. Half cover them with boiling water. Simmer them closely covered until nearly tender, about 1½ hours. Add:
> Salt
> Pepper
> Vegetables for Soup, page 41
> (A pinch of ginger)

Cover and simmer the meat until tender, about ½ hour longer. Remove the meat from the pot. Strain the stock. Reserve the vegetables. Remove the grease. Make:
> Gravy, page 394

Pour it over the meat. You may surround it with the vegetables.
Good with:
> Chopped parsley
> Dumplings and applesauce

ROAST DOMESTIC DUCK
5 Servings
Pick, singe and clean (see page 390):
> A 5 lb. duck

Rub it with:
> (Garlic)

Season the inside with:
> Salt

Fill the cavities with:
> Apple dressing, cubed apples and raisins
> Mashed Potato Dressing, page 417

Or you may use coarsely cut celery, sliced onions or drained sauerkraut. Add 3 tablespoonfuls sugar to the kraut. Truss the duck. Roast it in an uncovered pan in a slow oven 325° allowing 20 to 30 minutes per pound. If the duck is very fat, prick the breast to let some of the fat run out. Baste it every 10 minutes with the drippings and:
> 1 cup hot orange juice or stock, see Chicken Stock, page 47

You may thicken the drippings with:

Flour (see Gravy, page 426), or
see Chicken Stock and Chicken
Gravy, page 394
Serve the duck with:
  Fruit on skewers or currant jelly
If it has been basted with stock, serve
it with:
  A grating of orange rind

ROAST DUCK BIGARADE
4 Servings
Prepare for cooking as in preceding
rule:
  A 3½ to 4 lb. duck
Place it unstuffed on a rack in a pan in
a moderate oven 325°. Roast the duck
uncovered, allowing 20 to 30 minutes
to the pound. Skin:
  An orange
Scrape the white pulp from the skin
with a spoon and discard it. Cut the
yellow peel into very thin strips (julienne). Add a cupful of boiling water
and simmer the peel for 15 minutes.
Drain it. Reserve the liquid. Remove
all membrane from the orange sections and discard it. Fifteen minutes

before the duck is done pour the
drippings from the pan. Replace them
by:
  ½ cup boiling consommé
Continue to cook the duck. Add to the
drippings the orange liquid and:
  ½ teaspoon salt
  1 teaspoon sugar
  ½ teaspoon lemon juice
Simmer these ingredients for 10 minutes. Add and stir until dissolved:
  2 tablespoons currant jelly
Add the orange peel and simmer 10
minutes longer. Add the consommé
from the pan and:
  1½ tablespoons Madeira wine
Sprinkle the orange sections with:
  3 teaspoons sugar
Broil them for 3 minutes. Cut the duck
into individual servings. Arrange it on
a hot platter. Garnish it with the
orange sections and dabs of:
  Currant jelly
Pour the sauce over it. Duck sauce is
also flavored with kuemmel, curaçao
or white wine and a more generous
amount of orange juice.

Game and Game Birds

Game is hung in order to tenderize the meat. How long? Few cooks and
hunters agree on this point, but it is inadvisable to hang small birds as they are apt
to become too gamey. If you are a European, you may insist on hanging game until
it begins to decay. This is an extreme but applauded by many. Freshly shot game
birds may be hung, without being drawn, in a dry, cool, airy place for several days
or a week. If you wish to keep birds for a longer period, draw them, unpicked, and
place a piece of charcoal in the cavity. Powdered charcoal is then sifted into the
feathers. When ready to cook them, but no sooner, pick the birds. Examine them
carefully for shot and remove it with a pointed utensil. You may wipe the birds
with damp cloth. Never scald or wash game birds. Small birds, especially wood-
cock, may be cooked without being drawn. This is a matter of preference. Cut off
the heads and feet. Small birds may be skinned when drawn.
    Birds with dark meat—duck, pheasant, grouse or prairie chicken, woodcock,
snipe, pigeon or squab—are usually served rare.
    Birds with white meat—partridge and quail—are served well done.
    Wild birds have very little fat. This must be supplemented in cooking. Butter
or larding (page 341), bacon and salt pork are the usual additions.

WILD DUCK
Allow 1 Pound of Duck Per Person
Two students in their cups approached
a man with a long flowing red beard.
Said they: "We have a little bet which
we are asking you to settle. How do
you sleep? Do you sleep with it (using
an expressive gesture) under the cover
or over the cover?" "Well, well," said
the bearded man with an indulgent
smile, "I'll have to think about that, I
really do not know." This satisfied the

students until they met the man a few
days later. They sallied up to him at
once with a genial: "Have you made
up your mind? What's the answer?"
To which they received a dark scowl
and a vociferous "Damn you two, now
I can't sleep!"
    In our family we cooked wild duck
until well done. My brother, a crack
shot, sent them to us in those days of
thoughtless plenty by the barrelfuls.
It seems strange now that we never

varied our rule. The manner of cooking duck, I lived to discover, is a "mooty" point. Some epicures think 20 minutes in a hot oven the right time, so that when carved the juice of the duck, hardly more than heated through, runs red. Others hold out for meat that is somewhat better done, but still roseate. Then there is the misguided "cook until the meat falls from the bone" school—and recently a correspondent gave me a new angle by urging me to boil wild duck by a rule popular in his family.

You undoubtedly have your own version of what to do with the cherished gift of a wild duck or two. Having reached the man-with-the-red-beard stage, I shall not try to convert you to any specified standard, but offer instead the following rules for your consideration:

TO CLEAN WILD DUCK

Clip the wing tips and remove the coarse guard feathers, leaving the duck covered with down. Melt a cake of paraffin and paint the duck, using a brush and covering the entire surface of the bird with hot wax. Use ⅜ pound of paraffin to 7 quarts of boiling water. Allow the paraffin to harden and then pull it off. It will carry the feathers with it. Duck is sometimes strong flavored. Stuff it with sliced apple, celery, onion or a raw potato. Remove and discard the stuffing before serving the duck as it will have absorbed the strong flavors.

ROAST WILD DUCK

Method I. 4 to 6 Servings

Prepare for cooking (see above):
>   2 wild ducks: 2½ lbs. each

Have ducks at room temperature. Dry them thoroughly inside and out. Rub the insides with:
>   Salt

Fill the cavities loosely with:
>   Skinned onions, drained sauerkraut or peeled, cored and chopped apples with raisins or Apple and Sweet Potato Dressing, page 419

Place the ducks in an uncovered roasting pan. Cover the breasts with:
>   Thin slices salt pork or bacon

or brush them with:
>   Butter

Roast the ducks in a moderate oven 325°: rare duck, 10 to 12 minutes to the pound; well done, 15 to 20 minutes to the pound.

Baste frequently with the fat in the pan. Another school of thought advises roasting duck in a hot oven 500° for a total time of 18 to 20 minutes. Baste every 5 minutes with the fat in the pan to which you may add:
>   Dry red wine

This method seems to be the hunter's ideal. The juices are red and flow freely when the duck is carved. Thicken the drippings with:
>   Flour (see Gravy, page 394)

Add:
>   (Sour cream)

Serve the duck with:
>   Currant jelly or cranberries

or with overlapping:
>   Slices of small oranges, each topped with a dab of bright jelly

Method II.

A good way to cook wild duck and an easy way of serving it is to split it down the back, clean it well and wipe it until it is dry. Rub it with:
>   (Garlic)

Spread it with:
>   Unsalted butter

Season it with:
>   Paprika

Place it in a pan in a hot oven 450°. Baste it frequently with the fat in the pan. Cook it until it has reached the right degree of doneness. Remove it to a hot platter. Season it with salt. You may thicken the drippings with:
>   Flour (see Gravy, page 394)

Serve the duck with:
>   Boiled Oranges or Kumquats, pages 448, 449

An unusual way to cook duck is to fill each duck with:
>   3 medium-sized skinned onions
>   A quartered orange

Follow the rule for cooking Wild Duck. Place in the bottom of the pan:
>   ¼ cup Kiefer berries
>   1 cup grape juice or orange juice

Fried hominy is a well-known accompaniment to duck—so are grilled sweet potatoes or apples stuffed with sweet potatoes.

BRAISED WILD DUCK

Dress (see above):
>   Wild duck, preferably Mallards

Stuff them with:
>   Apple, Celery, Apricot or Bread Dressing, etc., page 416

Place them in a roaster. Add boiling water to the depth of ½ inch. Add:

½ sliced onion
3 stalks celery with leaves
½ teaspoon dry thyme

Cover the roaster. Cook the duck in a slow oven 325° for about 1 hour. Add water as needed. Remove the cover. Cook the duck for ½ hour longer. Thicken the drippings with:

Flour (see Gravy, page 394)

You may add to the gravy:

1 tablespoon orange marmalade

or you may serve the duck sprinkled with:

A grating of orange rind

and garnished with:

Currant jelly

Or serve the duck with:

Orange Salad for Game, page 471

BARBECUED DUCK
4 Servings
Dress (see page 407), then cut the breasts from:

2 large wild ducks

Cook them under the broiler until they are brown. Baste them frequently with the following sauce. Combine and stir over heat:

4 teaspoons lemon juice
1 teaspoon Worcestershire sauce
1 teaspoon tomato catsup
1 tablespoon butter

Sprinkle the duck before serving with:

Salt and paprika

DUCK PILAF
A left-over duck and rice dish. Remove the meat from:

Roast duck

There should be about 2 cupfuls. Break the carcasses apart. Add to them:

4 cups water
1 chopped onion
Some celery leaves

Simmer this stock covered for 1 hour. Strain it. Bring it to the boiling point. Stir into it slowly so as not to disturb the boiling:

⅔ cup rice

Cook the rice until it is tender, for about ½ hour. Strain it. Reserve the liquor. Drain it. Melt:

2 tablespoons butter

Add and sauté covered for 5 minutes:

¾ cup finely chopped celery
1 teaspoon grated onion

Add the duck scraps, the rice and:

1 cup left-over gravy, duck liquor or cream combined

Mix these ingredients well with a fork. Season them, if needed, with:

Salt and paprika

Serve the pilaf hot with:

Stewed plums or apricots

BREAST OF WILD DUCK SAUTÉED
When duck is plentiful cooks frequently cut away the breast and sauté them like chicken in butter. The remaining parts of the ducks are braised or fricasseed like chicken.

GUINEA FOWL
Allow ¾ to 1 Pound for Each Person
The guinea fowl, a domesticated animal, is usually classed as game. It resembles a chicken but is the sweater girl of the fowl world. Its meat is dry and so thin strips of salt pork called lardoons are inserted generously under the breast skin and additional fat is used in cooking the bird. Otherwise it may be prepared, stuffed, trussed and roasted like chicken, page 390, that is, in a slow oven 300° allowing 30 minutes for each pound of bird. Stuff, using any dressing, page 416, suitable for chicken, or place in the cavity 2 small skinned onions, or 1 apple and 2 tablespoonfuls butter. Rub the larded bird well with melted fat, truss it and roast it in a pan on a rack, breast down, for ½ hour. Place several pieces of salt pork on the back. Then turn the bird right side up and roast it until it is done. Be sure to baste it frequently. You may roast a guinea fowl for 15 minutes in a hot oven 500°, then reduce the heat to 350°. Allow 35 to 45 minutes cooking in all for a medium-sized bird. You may use the drippings for:

Gravy, page 394

or you may keep the bird hot and boil the drippings rapidly for about 12 minutes, then pour them over the bird. The usual accompaniment to guinea fowl is:

Cumberland Sauce, page 438

If the following rule for Breasts of Guinea Hen is used, remember that the rest of the fowl makes a grand fricassee, page 401.

BREASTS OF GUINEA HEN
Allow 1 Breast Per Person
Since I have become known as a con-

sultant on culinary matters, endless strangers call up, sometimes for advice but usually for confirmation of what they planned to do in the first place. I am also called on in moments of stress. A frenzied voice came over the telephone one day saying: "I use your cookbook, I do. She's gone out. She's left me with breast of guinea hen. My God! What do I do?"
Lard (page 341) each:

> **Breast of guinea hen**

with:

> **4 lardoons: small, very thin strips salt pork**

Follow the rule for Breasts of Chicken, page 397. After 10 minutes' baking in a hot oven 425°, reduce the heat to a moderate oven 325°. Baste the fillets frequently. Cook them for about 1 hour, or until they are tender. To serve them follow the rule for Breasts of Chicken, page 397.

GROUSE OR PRAIRIE CHICKEN

Allow 1 Pound of Bird Per Person
Prepare for cooking as you would a chicken:

> **Grouse**

You may lard the breast, page 341, with thin strips of:

> **Salt pork**

Do not truss the bird. You may stuff it with:

> **A small apple, a skinned onion or ribs of celery**

If not larded, cover the breast well with thin slices of salt pork or bacon. Roast the bird in a slow oven 300° until done. Grouse is served rare. Allow about 30 to 45 minutes cooking in all. Baste it frequently with:

> **Melted butter or drippings**

Remove the bacon. Brush the bird with:

> **Butter**

Dredge it lightly with:

> **Flour**

Place it in a hot oven 500° until brown. Thicken the drippings with:

> **Flour (see Gravy, page 394)**

PHEASANT IN SOUR CREAM

Prepare for cooking:

> **Pheasants**

Dredge them with:

> **Flour**

Melt in a skillet:

> **Butter or other fat**

Sauté lightly:

> **(1 slice onion)**

Brown the pheasants lightly in the fat. Pour over each pheasant:

> **1 tablespoon sour cream**

Cover the pheasants and cook them in a moderate oven 375° for 1 hour. Baste them every 10 minutes with:

> **Sour cream**

Season them with:

> **Salt and pepper**

Use the drippings for gravy adding more sour cream if needed and Sautéed Mushrooms, page 292. Serve the birds hot with:

> **Wild Rice, page 109**

ROAST PHEASANT

Allow 1 Pound of Bird Per Person
Follow the rule below for:

> **Roast Partridge**

Allow 15 to 20 minutes to the pound.

ROAST PARTRIDGE

These birds may be sautéed, smothered or stewed by any rule for chicken. As they are somewhat drier a little additional fat helps them along. Rub the inside of a drawn and cleaned:

> **Partridge**

with:

> **Salt and butter**

They are frequently larded, page 341, or the breast is covered with:

> **Salt pork**

Truss the bird. Roast it like chicken in a moderate oven 300° for a total cooking period of 30 to 45 minutes in all. Baste it frequently. The bacon or pork but not the larding is removed for the last 15 minutes of cooking. It may be browned separately and served. It is customary to serve the bird with the unthickened pan drippings to which lemon juice, sherry or port may be added.

BRAISED PHEASANT

This rule was sent to me by a gentleman who writes that it is his favorite way of preparing pheasant.
Prepare for cooking:

> **A pheasant**

Pound:

> **A thin slice salt pork**

Separate the skin from the breast flesh of the pheasant and insert the salt pork. Place in the body cavity the pheasant liver and:

> **A small peeled tangerine**

Lace the opening tightly. Truss the pheasant. Melt:

> **4 tablespoons lard**

Roll the pheasant in it turning and basting until it is a golden brown all over. Place it in a casserole. Add and turn in the fat:

12 sliced mushroom caps

Pour these over the pheasant. Melt in a saucepan:

4 tablespoons butter

Stir in, cook but do not permit to brown:

3 shallots or 1 small minced onion
2 teaspoons flour

Stir in gradually:

¼ to ⅓ cup Marsala or Madeira
½ teaspoon salt and freshly ground pepper

Pour this into the casserole.

My correspondent adds a sprig of fresh fennel and 2 crushed juniper berries. As you are not apt to have these on hand and the pheasant may be an unexpected acquisition, you may add:

1 teaspoon fresh herb or ⅓ teaspoon dried herb

Cover the casserole and bake the pheasant in a hot oven 400° for about ½ hour. Serve it from the casserole with:

Fried hominy and currant jelly
A green salad

SMALL GAME BIRDS BROILED
Method I.

Small game birds are delicious prepared in this way.

Pick, then split down the back and draw:

Small game birds

Dust them lightly with:

Flour

Place them breast down on a rack under moderate heat 350°. Broil them, turning them once. Allow for:

Quail . . . . 10 to 15 minutes
Grouse . . . . 15 to 20 minutes
Young partridge . . . . . 20 to 40 minutes
Young pheasants . . . . 20 to 40 minutes
Young duck . . . . 10 to 20 minutes

If the birds have heavy breasts, use low heat and broil them somewhat longer. Baste them frequently with:

Melted butter

Season them with:

Salt and pepper

Serve them on:

Toast

Pour the drippings over them.

Method II.

Pick, draw, although the French do

not draw, then cut off the heads and feet of:

6 small game birds

Rub them with:

2 tablespoons unsalted butter

Surround them with:

6 strips bacon

Truss them with string. Place them on a broiler under low heat. Cook them from 12 to 20 minutes, according to their size. Turn them frequently. The bacon may be removed, if desired, and the birds browned briefly by further broiling. Thicken the drippings with:

Flour (see Gravy, page 394)

Add the juice of:

1 lemon
Stock if there is an insufficient amount of drippings
Salt and pepper as needed

Serve the birds on:

Toast

Pour the gravy over them. Garnish them with:

Parsley

Permit the gravy to soak into the toast.

SMALL GAME BIRDS ROASTED

Prepare by the preceding rule:

6 small birds

Place over each breast:

A thin slice salt pork or bacon

Place in the pan:

1 tablespoon butter

Bake the birds in a hot oven 450° for 5 minutes, reduce the heat to 325° and bake them from 15 to 25 minutes longer according to their size. Baste them frequently with the drippings. Thicken the drippings with:

Flour (see Gravy, page 394)

Serve the birds with:

Panada, page 441

SMALL GAME BIRDS SMOTHERED

Prepare by the preceding rule:

6 birds

Melt in a saucepan:

2 tablespoons butter

Add and sauté for 1 minute:

¼ cup carrots or celery
¼ cup onions

Add the birds and sauté them until they are brown. Add:

½ cup boiling stock or water

Cover the birds with waxed paper. Place them in a moderate oven 350° for 20 minutes. Serve them on:

Toast

Thicken the drippings with:
Flour (see Gravy, page 394)
Add to the gravy:
(2 tablespoons lemon juice or sour
cream)
Serve the birds garnished with:
Parsley

PIGEONS AND SQUABS
Allow ½ to 1 Pigeon Per Person; 1
Squab Per Person
Squabs are young pigeons.

ROAST PIGEONS OR SQUABS
Pick and draw:
Small pigeons or squabs
Rub them inside with:
Salt
They may be stuffed with:
Cooked wild rice, Bread Dressing, etc., pages 109, 416
A thin piece of bacon or salt pork may
be placed across the breasts, or they
may be brushed with melted butter and
dredged with flour. Roast them uncovered in a moderate oven 325° for 45
minutes or more, or until tender. They
may be basted while cooking. Remove
the bacon. Thicken the drippings with:
Flour (see Gravy, page 394)

BROILED PIGEONS OR SQUABS
Pick, then split down the back and re-
move entrails from:
Squabs
Flatten them. Put them on a greased
broiler skin side up. Brush them well
with:
Melted butter
Place them 4 inches from the heat.
Broil them from 15 to 30 minutes.
Turn them once. Season them when
you turn them with:

Salt and paprika
Serve them on:
Buttered toast
Pour the drippings over them. Good
with:
Chopped parsley
Cranberry jelly
Crusty Spoon Bread, page 423

SMOTHERED PIGEONS OR SQUABS—POTTED PIGEONS
6 Servings
Cut into pieces or leave whole:
4 large pigeons or 6 squabs
Dredge them with:
Seasoned flour
Melt:
4 tablespoons butter
Sauté the birds slowly in the butter
until they are seared. Place them in a
casserole. Add to the fat in the pan:
¼ cup chopped onion
1 diced carrot
¼ cup chopped celery
Stir these ingredients for about 3 min-
utes. Add:
1 cup boiling chicken stock or
water
Pour this over the birds. Cover them
closely. Roast them in a moderate
oven 350° until they are tender, about
45 to 60 minutes. You may add for the
last ½ hour:
1 cup sliced mushrooms
Do not permit the birds to become dry.
If they do, add more stock or water
Thicken the drippings with:
Flour (see Gravy, page 394)
You may add:
Sour or sweet cream
Serve the squabs in a border of:
Rice
Sprinkle them with:
Chopped parsley or chives

Rabbit, Hare and Squirrel

The preparation and cooking of these animals is much the same, although they
vary in size. You may substitute them in chicken recipes shown on pages 389
to 403.

If you are choosing rabbits, select them with soft ears and paws and sharp claws,
all signs of youth. If you have hunted your own, you are probably aware of the
precautions needed to avoid tularemia. Never handle rabbit or other wild meat
with your bare hands and be sure that the flesh of these animals is sufficiently
cooked. Draw rabbits at once. You may hang them 3 or 4 days.

To Dress Rabbit, Hare and Squirrel:

Sever the front legs at the joint as shown on the dotted line. Cut through the skin around the hind legs as shown again by a dotted line. Tie the feet together securely. Hang the rabbit on a hook where tied. Pull the skin down off the legs,

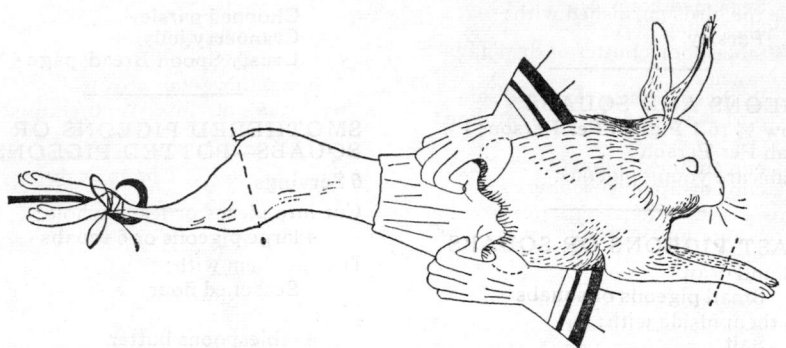

stripping it inside out like a glove and over the body and forelegs. Sever the head and discard it with the skin. Slit the rabbit down the front. Remove the entrails and discard except for the heart and liver. Wash inside and out with acidulated water, that is, water to which 1 or 2 tablespoonfuls of vinegar are added. Rinse and dry carefully.

There are proverbially many ways to skin a squirrel, but some hunters claim the one below is the cleanest and the quickest. It needs a sharp knife.

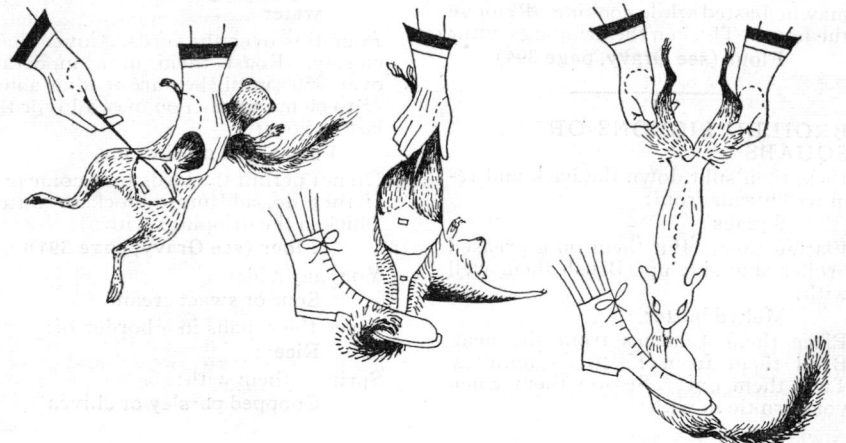

Cut the tail bone through from beneath, but take care not to cut through the skin of the tail. Hold the tail as shown on the left and then cut the skin the width of the back as shown in the dotted lines. Turn the squirrel over on its back and step on the base of the tail. Hold the hind legs in one hand and pull steadily and slowly as shown in the center above until the skin has worked itself over the front legs and head. While holding the squirrel in the same position, pull the remaining skin from the hind legs. Proceed then as for rabbit, above, cutting off the head and the feet and removing the internal organs, plus two small glands found in the small of the back and under each foreleg between the ribs and the shoulders.

STEW OR FRICASSEE OF RABBIT OR HARE

Skin and cut into pieces:
>A rabbit

Dredge it with:
>Seasoned flour

Melt in a skillet:
>4 tablespoons butter or drippings

You may use:
>¼ lb. diced, lightly rendered salt pork—a wonderful substitution

Add:
>¼ cup chopped onions
>(1 cup cut-up mushrooms)

Remove the onions and mushrooms before sautéing the rabbit in the drippings until it is lightly browned. Pour over it:
>1½ cups stock or dry wine

The French use wine and tomatoes or tomato sauce. You may add:
>A piece of lemon rind
>10 peppercorns
>2 sprigs parsley
>2 ribs celery with leaves

Cover the pot closely. Simmer the meat until it is done, for 1 hour or more, but do not boil it at any time. Ten minutes before you remove the rabbit from the pot add the mushrooms and onions. Thicken the drippings with:
>Flour (see Gravy, page 426)

You may add to it:
>Sour cream or milk
>A few drops commercial coloring or Caramel, page 754
>A pinch tarragon or chervil

A friend contributes her favorite rule for rabbit.

Cut up a rabbit, sear it in 2 tablespoonfuls hot butter, season it with salt and pepper. Pour over it a jigger of brandy. Light and burn it. Add and cook gently 2 chopped shallots. Add 1 cupful white wine, 1 cupful stock, a "bouquet," page 832, of parsley, thyme and bay leaf. Simmer the rabbit covered until tender. The drippings may be thickened lightly with flour.

SAUTÉED RABBIT

If rabbit is young, follow the rule for Sautéed Chicken, page 398. Add sour cream to the gravy.

SMOTHERED RABBIT OR HARE WITH ONIONS

Skin and cut into pieces:
>A rabbit

Dredge it with:
>Seasoned flour

Melt in a pot or skillet:
>3 tablespoons drippings or butter

Sauté the rabbit in the drippings until it is browned. Cover it thickly with:
>Sliced onions

Pour over them:
>1 cup thick sour cream

Cover the pot closely and simmer the rabbit for 1 hour, or place the pot in a slow oven 300° and bake the rabbit until it is tender, 1 hour or more.

RABBIT OR HARE À LA MODE OR HASENPFEFFER

Skin and cut into pieces:
>A rabbit

Place the pieces in a crock or jar. Cover them with:
>Vinegar or dry wine and water, in equal parts

Add:
>1 sliced onion
>½ teaspoon salt
>6 peppercorns
>1 bay leaf

Soak the rabbit for 2 days. Then remove the meat, keeping the liquor. Follow the rule on this page for Rabbit Stew. Use the vinegar water in the place of stock and add sour or sweet cream to the gravy, see Gravy, page 426.

ROAST RABBIT OR HARE

A rabbit is usually too small to stuff. A hare may be stuffed with any dressing suitable for fowl.

Skin (page 412):
>A rabbit or hare

You may season it inside with salt, stuff it, close the opening and truss it. Brush it all over with:
>Melted butter, drippings or olive oil

Dredge it with:
>Seasoned flour

Place it on its side in a roasting pan. Roast it uncovered in a moderate oven 325° for 1½ to 2 hours. Baste it every 15 minutes with the drippings in the pan. If it becomes dry, baste with ½ butter and ½ water or stock. Turn the rabbit when ½ cooked. Thicken the drippings with:
>Flour (see Gravy, page 426)

Venison

Hang venison in a cool airy place. Some authorities say "from 4 to 5 days"; others say "for two weeks or more." This is a matter of taste. In Europe game is hung until it is so ripe that a guest is aware of the type of dinner to be served him as soon as he enters the front door.

Venison may be prepared in as many ways as beef and much in the same manner. However, today this meat is an unusual treat and the addition of wine, mushrooms, cream, etc., seems in order to make a super dish of a super meat. There is a consensus that venison must be served rare.

Port, Madeira, sherry or claret is frequently added to the gravy served with venison.

SADDLE OF VENISON
8 Servings
Lard (page 341):
　　A 6 to 7 lb. saddle of venison
Rub it with:
　　A cut clove of garlic
　　Butter
Sprinkle it with:
　　¼ teaspoon pepper or ½ teaspoon paprika
　　A few grains cayenne
Place the roast uncovered in a moderate oven 325°. Allow 25 to 30 minutes to the pound.
Or you may place the roast in a hot oven 450° for ½ hour, then reduce the heat and continue to cook it at 300°, allowing in all 20 minutes to the pound.
Thicken the drippings with:
　　Flour (see Gravy, page 426)
You may add:
　　Consommé or chicken stock
　　Salt as needed
　　Port, Madeira or claret and sour or sweet cream
Garnish the platter with:
　　Orange slices, currant jelly, Orange Sauce for Game, page 437, or Cumberland Sauce, page 438
Serve venison with:
　　Wild Rice, page 109

ROAST LEG OF VENISON
Follow the above rule for Saddle of Venison. Roast a leg skin side down. If the venison is very dry, place several pieces of bacon over the top.

VENISON STEAKS
Have meat at room temperature. See that the steaks are crisp and brown on the outside, rare and juicy within. This means a moderately quick fire. Rub:
　　Venison steaks
with:
　　A cut clove of garlic
　　A generous amount of butter
Broil the steaks under a broiler or over an open fire. Make this a short process unless the steaks are very thick. Turn them once. Season with:
　　Salt and paprika or pepper
You may flavor the drippings with sherry. Pour them over the steaks. Or serve them with:
　　Currant Jelly Sauce, page 436
or with:
　　Maître d'Hôtel Butter, page 431

VENISON LOIN STEAKS OR CUTLETS
Method I.
These may be dipped in:
　　Olive oil
then in:
　　Seasoned bread crumbs
Broil the steaks or sauté them quickly in butter.

Method II.
Or, rub:
　　2 venison steaks
with:
　　A cut clove of garlic
Heat until sizzling:
　　1 tablespoon olive oil
Sauté the steaks quickly in this until both sides are brown. Season the steaks with:
　　Salt and paprika
Remove them to a hot platter. Stir into the pan until blended:
　　¼ cup dry sherry
　　⅓ cup thick cream
　　1½ tablespoons currant jelly
　　2 tablespoons butter
Add additional seasoning if required. Heat but do not boil the sauce. Pour it over the steaks.

VENISON POT ROAST OR STEW

For this use the less tender cuts of meat cut into small pieces or 1 large piece. Place the meat in a marinade, or this step may be omitted and the meat may be prepared like Pot Roast, page 343.

Marinade for Venison:

Cover venison with:

Equal parts of water and dry wine, preferably claret

Add:

6 or 8 black peppercorns
1 bay leaf
10 to 12 whole cloves
1 sliced onion

Permit the meat to remain in the marinade from 2 to 6 days. Turn it from time to time. Dry the meat, dredge it lightly with:

Flour

Follow the rule on page 343 for Pot Roast. Use the marinade for basting. Simmer the meat covered until tender. The time will vary with the age of the animal.

You may skim the fat from the drippings. Add to them:

1 teaspoon grated lemon rind
3 tablespoons lemon juice
⅓ cup port wine
1½ tablespoons butter
Seasoning if needed

Reheat but do not boil the drippings. Place the meat in them and serve.

Garnishes for Meats

Parsley.
Water cress.
Mushrooms, canned or fresh, sautéed.
Truffles.
Sautéed olives or broiled bacon.
Sliced lemons dipped in chopped parsley.
Lemon baskets—lemons cut in basket shape and hollowed, the edges pinked—filled with sauce: Tartar, page 439, Horseradish, page 439, etc., or with cranberry or other jelly.
Oranges sliced, topped with mint, currant, cranberry or other jelly or with Boiled Kumquats, page 449.
Orange halves hollowed and filled with cranberry jelly.
Pimientos shredded or cut into shapes.
Peppers sliced or cut into shapes.
Pepper rings parboiled, filled with sautéed or raw onions.
Carrots, raw or cooked, cut into shapes.
Boiled turnip cups filled with peas.
Boiled beets cut into shapes.
Boiled Beet Cups Filled with Horseradish Sauce, page 439.
Pickled beets.
Baked Tomatoes Filled with Mashed Potatoes, page 199.

Baked Tomatoes Filled with Pineapple, page 201.
Filled Turnip Cups, page 207.
Pineapple slices or pineapple slices sautéed in butter or bacon fat, garnished with maraschino cherries, jelly or cranberry jelly.
Sautéed Bananas, page 448, or peaches.
Baked Apples Filled with Mincemeat, page 446.
Peach halves filled with jam or jelly.
Cinnamon Apples, page 446.
Baked Oranges, page 449.
Boiled Oranges, page 448.
Baked Pears, page 445, or peaches.
Apple Rings, page 447.
Prunes in Wine, page 450.
Prunes on Skewers, page 450.
Cranberry Jelly, page 443.
Apple Cups Filled with Sweet Potatoes, page 446.
Mashed potatoes forced through a tube in a border or as individual roses.
Queen Anne cherries, greengage plums or apricots, heated.
Raw cucumber relish.
Raw tomato relish.
Green Pepper or Pimiento Slices I, II and III for cold meat, page 466.

Dressings for Meat or Fowl

These are an interesting part of the menu, especially on holidays. Vary them according to your means and your imagination. Stuff a bird lightly. The dressing will swell as it cooks. An abundance of liquid will make a dressing soggy. Allow a generous cupful of dressing for every pound of bird. As it is better to have too much rather than too little of it, place the surplus in a greased dish. Bake it in the oven with the bird for the last hour of cooking. It is advisable to wait to stuff birds until shortly before roasting time.

BREAD DRESSING WITH MUSHROOMS, OYSTERS, NUTS, GIBLETS, ETC.

About 4 Cupfuls
Sufficient for a 4 Pound Chicken
Allow about 1 cupful dressing to 1 pound of dressed bird.
There is no set rule for the proportions of ingredients for bread dressing. It should be palatable, light and slightly moist, well flavored but bland. One-day-old bread is preferable. Fresh bread may be toasted for a light dressing. Chopped green peppers, nut meats, sautéed mushrooms and drained or lightly sautéed oysters may be added to it. Stock or oyster liquor may be substituted for milk.
Chop the giblets. Melt:
> ¼ cup butter

Add and sauté for 2 minutes:
> (2 tablespoons or more chopped onion and the chopped giblets)

Combine these ingredients with:
> 4 cups crustless, diced white, graham or whole-wheat bread or bread or corn-bread crumbs
> 4 tablespoons chopped parsley
> ¼ to 1 cup chopped celery
> 1 teaspoon dried tarragon or basil
> ¾ teaspoon salt
> ½ teaspoon paprika
> ⅛ teaspoon nutmeg
> Milk, stock or melted butter to moisten the dressing very lightly
> (2 or 3 eggs)
> (1½ cups nut meats, preferably black walnuts)

In place of the nut meats you may use:
> 6 skinned, sliced and browned pork sausages or
> 1 cup or more sliced mushrooms sautéed with the onion

OYSTER DRESSING

Follow the preceding rule. Omit the giblets and the nut meats. Add:
> ½ to 1 pint drained oysters

Chop them or leave them whole. Drain, then preheat them in the hot butter. Use part milk and part oyster liquor to moisten the dressing.

LEFT-OVER DRESSING

Place left-over dressing in a greased baking dish. Spread it about 1 inch thick. Place over the top:
> Whole or sliced mushrooms

Dot them well with:
> Butter

Sprinkle them with:
> Cream

Bake the dressing in a hot oven 400° for about 15 minutes.

"DRY" DRESSING

This name is given by my cook, Sarah Brown, to a dressing she frequently makes, which is by no means dry when served. Combine:
> Shredded bread: white, graham or whole wheat
> Chopped celery
> Chopped onion

Season the inside of a chicken, quail, turkey, etc., with:
> Salt and paprika

Partly fill it with the dressing. Melt:
> Butter

Pour ½ of it onto the dressing. Fill the cavity lightly with the remaining dressing and pour the remaining butter on it.
Sew up the opening. Proportions seem to be of no importance whatever in this case as the ingredients are never measured and the dressing is always light and good. Chopped pecans, oysters, olives, etc., may be added to it.

RICE DRESSING

Sufficient for Two 3 Pound Chickens or One Large Flank Steak. Double the Recipe for a 12 Pound Turkey
Mince:
> 6 slices bacon

Sauté it lightly for 5 minutes with:
> 3 tablespoons chopped onion

Pour off all but 2 tablespoonfuls of the fat. Combine the contents of the skillet with:
> 4 cups cooked rice
> 1 cup dry bread crumbs
> 1 cup chopped celery
> ¾ teaspoon salt
> ¼ teaspoon pepper
> ⅛ teaspoon sage or nutmeg
> 1 cup rich milk or evaporated milk

SAUSAGE DRESSING FOR TURKEY OR FOWL

Place in a saucepan:
> Turkey giblets
> Turkey neck
> 3 cups boiling water
> 1 small chopped onion
> Some celery ribs and leaves
> (½ bay leaf)

Simmer the giblets until they are very tender. Chop them until fine and add them later to the turkey gravy. Use the stock for the gravy. Crush or grind enough toasted bread to make:

6 cups dry bread crumbs: corn,
  graham, whole wheat or white
Melt:
  6 tablespoons butter
Sauté in it:
  3 tablespoons finely grated onions
Add these to the crumbs with:
  1 teaspoon salt
  3 tablespoons chopped parsley
  ¾ teaspoon pepper or paprika
  ¾ lb. sausage meat
  1½ cups chopped celery
Mix well. Moisten these ingredients
lightly with the:
  Giblet stock
The dressing should be crumbly—not
very moist.

OYSTER RICE DRESSING
Sufficient for a Small Goose or Turkey
Melt:
  ½ cup butter
Sauté lightly in the fat:
  Chopped giblets
  ⅓ cup chopped onions
Add:
  1½ quarts drained oysters
Cook them until their edges just begin
to curl. Add:
  3 cups cooked rice
  ½ cup or more chopped celery
  ¼ cup chopped parsley
  1 small minced clove garlic
  1 teaspoon or more salt
  ½ teaspoon paprika
Shrimp may be substituted for the
oysters. Use less salt if the shrimp are
salty.

WILD RICE DRESSING FOR GAME
Sufficient for a 3½ Pound Chicken
Chop:
  Giblets
Bring to the boiling point:
  4 cups water
  1 teaspoon salt
Drop the giblets into the water and
simmer them for 15 minutes. Remove
them from the water and stir into it:
  1 cup wild rice
Cook it until it is nearly tender.
Melt in a skillet:
  ¼ cup butter
Sauté in it for 3 minutes:
  2 tablespoons chopped onion
  1 tablespoon chopped green
    pepper
  ¼ cup chopped celery
Add the hot drained rice and the
chopped giblets.

GREEN DRESSING FOR FISH OR FOWL
About 1 Cupful
This has a tempting pistachio green
color. Sauté until transparent:
  2 tablespoons chopped onion
in:
  2 tablespoons butter
Cool slightly. Place this in a blender
and blend to a paste with:
  1 egg
  ½ cup tender celery with leaves
  ½ cup parsley
  ¼ cup water cress
  1½ cups crumbled crustless bread
  ½ teaspoon salt
  ⅛ teaspoon dried basil
Blend in with a fork:
  ½ cup crumbled crustless bread

POTATO DRESSING
Method I.
Stuff a fowl lightly with:
  Mashed Potatoes, page 302
You may beat into the potatoes:
  1 or 2 eggs, chopped celery, nut
    meats, sautéed mushrooms,
    onions, etc.

Method II.
Stuff a fowl lightly with the following:
Peel and cut into very thin slices:
  Raw potatoes
Parboil them for 6 minutes. Drain
them. Dry them well. Sprinkle them
with:
  Flour
Season them with:
  Salt and pepper
Dot them with:
  Butter
Moisten them with:
  Stock or milk
Add, if desired:
  Chopped celery

Method III.
Stuff a fowl lightly with the following:
Dice:
  Cold cooked potatoes
Melt:
  Butter or bacon drippings
Sauté in them for 1 minute:
  Chopped onion
Add the potatoes and cook them until
they are lightly browned. Season them
with:
  Salt and pepper
  Sage or other herb
  Chopped parsley
  Chopped celery

RAW POTATO AND CELERY DRESSING FOR POULTRY
Sufficient for a 3½ Pound Chicken
Peel, then grate or put through a food chopper or blend:
> 5 large raw potatoes
> 2 stalks celery
> 1 medium-sized onion

Melt:
> 2 tablespoons butter or poultry drippings

Sauté in the fat until golden brown:
> 1 large diced onion

Add:
> ¼ cup chopped celery leaves or parsley
> ½ cup shortening

Cook these ingredients for 2 minutes. Add them to the potato mixture. Season the dressing with:
> 1 teaspoon salt
> ½ teaspoon paprika

SWEET POTATO DRESSING FOR PORK OR TURKEY
The proportions given below should be increased by ½ for turkey.
Prepare:
> 4 cups Mashed Sweet Potatoes, page 310

While hot stir into them:
> 2 tablespoons butter
> 1½ teaspoons salt (less if the potatoes are salted)
> ¼ teaspoon paprika
> ⅓ cup cream
> 2 cups soft bread crumbs
> 2 whole eggs
> 3 slices sautéed chopped bacon
> ¼ cup finely chopped onion
> ½ cup chopped celery
> 1 tablespoon chopped parsley

SWEET POTATO AND SAUSAGE DRESSING FOR TURKEY
Sufficient for a 10 Pound Turkey
Prepare:
> 4 cups Mashed Sweet Potatoes, page 310

Sauté until light brown:
> ½ lb. sausage meat: 1 cup

Break it up with a fork. Remove it from the pan. Add to the pan and sauté for 3 minutes:
> 3 tablespoons chopped onion
> 1 cup chopped celery

Add the sausage meat, the sweet potatoes and:
> 2 cups dry bread crumbs
> 2 teaspoons salt—less if the potatoes are salted

> ¼ teaspoon paprika
> (3 tablespoons chopped parsley)

Mix these ingredients well.

SAUSAGE AND APPLE DRESSING FOR A FLANK STEAK
Heat and stir in a skillet:
> ½ cup sausage meat

Drain off the surplus fat. Add:
> ½ cup chopped tart apples
> 2 cups cracker crumbs
> ¼ teaspoon minced onion
> ¼ teaspoon salt
> ⅛ teaspoon paprika

Moisten the dressing with:
> ½ cup hot water

APPLE DRESSING FOR DUCK
Peel, quarter and core:
> Cooking apples

Combine them with:
> (Currants or raisins—about 1 cup currants or raisins to 6 cups apples)

You may steam the currants or raisins in 2 tablespoonfuls of water in the top of a double boiler for 15 minutes before combining.

APPLE, ONION AND RAISIN DRESSING
Sufficient for a 12 Pound Turkey
Place in boiling water for 5 minutes:
> 1 cup raisins

Drain them well. Add them to:
> 7 cups soft bread crumbs

Melt:
> ¾ cup butter

Sauté in it for 3 minutes:
> 1 cup chopped onion
> 1 chopped clove garlic
> 1 cup chopped celery

Add these ingredients to the bread crumbs with:
> 3 cups tart diced apples
> ¼ cup finely chopped parsley
> 1½ teaspoons salt
> ¼ teaspoon paprika

APPLE AND BREAD DRESSING
For a small crown roast of pork or for a duck. Melt in a saucepan:
> 2 tablespoons fat

Add and sauté until light brown:
> 1 tablespoon chopped onion

Combine these ingredients with:
> 1 cup soft bread cubes
> 2 cups finely chopped tart apples
> (½ cup chopped celery)

Moisten them with a very little:
> Rich milk

Season them with:
> Salt and paprika

APPLE AND SWEET POTATO DRESSING
Sufficient for a 4 Pound Chicken
Follow the rule on page 311 for Sweet Potatoes and Apples using 2 cupfuls cored apples, 4 cupfuls cooked sweet potatoes. Add:
    ½ cup brown sugar
    ¼ teaspoon salt
Moisten them with:
    About ½ cup apple water—enough to make them a good consistency for dressing
Double this recipe for a goose or turkey.

LIVER DRESSING
Sufficient for a 4 Pound Chicken
Chop:
    ½ lb. calf or baby beef liver
Sauté it lightly in:
    1½ tablespoons butter
to which you may add:
    1 tablespoon grated onion
Combine these ingredients with:
    2 cups soft bread crumbs
    ¾ cup chopped nut meats
    2 beaten eggs
    ½ cup rich milk, or cream and stock
    1 teaspoon salt
    ½ teaspoon paprika
    1½ tablespoons minced chives, parsley or other fresh herbs
    ½ teaspoon lemon juice
    (2 tablespoons sherry)

DRESSING FOR A CROWN ROAST OF LAMB
Heat:
    3 tablespoons salad oil
Brown in it lightly:
    ¼ cup finely chopped onion
Add and cook for 1 minute:
    ⅓ cup chopped carrot
    1 cup chopped celery
    2 tablespoons chopped parsley
    1 cup boiled rice
    2 teaspoons salt
    1 teaspoon pepper
    1 teaspoon paprika
    ¼ teaspoon cloves
Add and mix well:
    1 cup drained crushed pineapple
    ½ cup raisins
    2 cups dry bread crumbs

ONION DRESSING
Sufficient for a 3½ Pound Fowl
Cook for 10 minutes:
    2 cups chopped onions

in:
    4 cups boiling salted water
Drain them. Add:
    3 cups dry bread crumbs
    1 beaten egg
    ½ cup melted butter
    ¾ teaspoon salt
    ⅛ teaspoon paprika
    ½ teaspoon poultry seasoning

CRAB MEAT DRESSING
This recipe won a $500 prize. Flake the contents of:
    1 can crab meat: 6½ oz.
Add:
    2 slightly beaten eggs
Melt:
    2 tablespoons butter
Sauté in it:
    ½ cup chopped onion
    ¾ cup chopped celery
    2 slices minced bacon
    1 cup fresh bread crumbs
Combine these ingredients with the crab meat. Season them with:
    Salt and pepper
An addition of my own, not in the recipe:
    1 teaspoon Worcestershire sauce or 1 tablespoon sherry
This amount will fill a small fowl or 4 green peppers or 6 tomato cases.

OLIVE OR CELERY DRESSING
Sufficient for a 3½ Pound Chicken
Pull apart:
    3 cups stale bread
Moisten it lightly with:
    Chicken Stock, page 47, or canned chicken bouillon
Add:
    1 beaten egg
Melt:
    ¼ cup butter
Add and sauté for 1 minute:
    ¼ cup chopped Spanish onion
Combine this with the bread mixture. Add:
    ¼ cup chopped parsley
    ¾ teaspoon salt
    ⅛ teaspoon pepper
    ½ cup stoned chopped olives or
    ½ cup chopped celery
    (½ chopped pimiento)

APRICOT DRESSING FOR FOWL OR PORK TENDERLOIN
Sufficient for a 4 Pound Chicken
Combine:
    1 cup dried apricots
    1 cup cold water

Bring these ingredients to the boiling point. Simmer them for 5 minutes. Drain them. Cut them into strips. Combine them with:

    4 cups dry bread crumbs
    ¼ cup melted butter
    ½ teaspoon salt
    ⅛ teaspoon pepper
    ½ cup chopped green pepper or celery

Moisten them lightly with:

    Stock or apricot water

PRUNE DRESSING

Follow the preceding rule for:

    Apricot Dressing

Substitute for the apricots:

    1⅓ cups dried prunes

APPLE AND PRUNE DRESSING

Sufficient for a 5 Pound Bird
Combine lightly:

    3 cups diced crustless bread
    ¼ cup melted butter or drippings
    1 cup cubed apples
    ¾ cup chopped cooked prunes
    ½ cup chopped nut meats
    1 teaspoon salt
    ½ teaspoon paprika
    1 tablespoon lemon juice

CHESTNUT DRESSING

Sufficient for a 3½ Pound Chicken.
Double or Treble the Recipe for a Turkey

Shell and skin (page 283):

    3 cups chestnuts

Drop the chestnuts into:

    Boiling water

Cook them until they are soft. Put them through a potato ricer, food mill or blender. Combine them with:

    ½ cup melted butter
    1 teaspoon salt
    ⅛ teaspoon pepper
    ¼ cup cream
    1 cup dry bread or cracker crumbs
    2 tablespoons chopped parsley
    ½ cup chopped celery
    1 tablespoon grated onion
    (¼ cup seedless raisins)

CHESTNUT OYSTER DRESSING

Sufficient for a 12 Pound Turkey
Follow the above rule for:

    Chestnut Dressing

Use part chestnuts and part:

    Oysters

The oysters may be chopped and cooked lightly in melted butter. The oyster liquor may be added to or used in the place of cream. A fine dressing may be made with:

    2 lbs. Chestnuts Boiled and Riced, page 283
    1 pint Creamed Oysters, page 111

Add if desired:

    Bread crumbs
    Chopped parsley
    Chopped celery
    Seasoning

Dumplings, Spoon Bread, Yorkshire Pudding

Rule for Dumplings

Dumplings are apt to be heavy if the lid is lifted frequently before they are done. In order to see how the dumplings are progressing while cooking, cover the pan with a glass pie plate. This will tell you what you want to know without curbing their desire for Lebensraum.

DUMPLINGS

4 Servings
These dumplings are worth a trial and the experiment is apt to be repeated. Measure, then sift 3 times:

    1 cup cake flour
    4 teaspoons tartrate or phosphate baking powder or 2 teaspoons combination type (see Baking Powder, page 501)
    ½ teaspoon salt

Break into a measuring cup:

    1 egg

Add until the cup is half full:

    Milk

Beat well and stir the liquid slowly into the sifted ingredients. Add more milk if necessary but keep the batter as stiff as possible. Thicken:

    2 or 3 cups stock

with:

    Flour—allow 1½ tablespoons flour to 1 cup stock

Heat the stock in a 9 inch saucepan. To drop dumpling batter from a spoon easily, dip the spoon in water first. Then dip the spoon in the batter, fill it and drop the batter into the stock. Continue doing this until the dumplings are barely touching. Then cover

them and simmer for 2 minutes, turn them, cook them 2 minutes longer and serve them at once.
For a newer way to cook the dumplings see page 891.

PARSLEY DUMPLINGS
Follow the above rule. Add to the batter:
    ¼ cup finely chopped parsley

VEGETABLE DUMPLINGS
Follow the above rule. Add to the batter:
    ½ teaspoon grated onion
    3 tablespoons minced green peppers

CHEESE DUMPLINGS
To the above rule for:
    Dumplings
Add:
    2 tablespoons grated cheese
Cook the dumplings in:
    Tomato juice
Thicken this as suggested under the next rule or dilute condensed tomato soup. If in haste, use the following rule for dumplings.

QUICK CHEESE DUMPLINGS IN TOMATO SAUCE
Ten 2 Inch Dumplings
Combine:
    2 cups biscuit mix
    2 tablespoons grated cheese
You will need about ⅔ cupful grated cheese for the entire recipe. Follow the recipe for biscuits as given on the label of the package or prepare and add the cheese to Biscuit Mix, page 506. Pat or roll out the dough to the thickness of ⅛ inch. Cut it into 3 inch rounds. Place in the center of each round:
    1 tablespoon grated cheese
Wet the edges of the rounds with cold water. Gather up the edges to form a ball. Pinch them well. Drop the dumplings into boiling:
    Thin tomato soup or juice, stock or bouillon
Cover them tightly with a lid. Steam them for 15 minutes. Subdue your curiosity and do not lift the lid, no, not even to peek. This takes an 8 or 9 inch pot and a lot of liquid. I use about 5 cupfuls. It may be slightly thickened but it must not be thick. It is best to cook your dumplings and then thicken the stock as for Cream Sauce, page 428,

using 1½ tablespoonfuls butter and the same amount of flour to every cupful of stock. Serve the dumplings at once. They may be sprinkled with:
    Chopped parsley

CORN-MEAL DUMPLINGS
Cooking in the United States is on the up and coming side but it seemed to me that a peak was reached in a small Kentucky town where I was served chicken with dumplings. The latter were like thistledown. "Oh, yes!" said the hotel proprietress wearily when I exclaimed over them. "They are always like that when our cook is drunk."
Far be it from me to limit your sources of inspiration, but I am convinced that the following rules will give you superlative dumplings without dissipation. Sift:
    1 cup corn meal
    ¼ cup all-purpose flour
    1 teaspoon any baking powder
    ½ teaspoon salt
Beat:
    2 eggs
    ½ cup milk
Combine the egg mixture and the dry ingredients. Stir in:
    1 tablespoon melted butter
Have simmering:
    5 or 6 cups corned beef stock, consommé or any clear soup or stock
Drop the batter by the spoonful into the hot stock. Cover the pan closely. Simmer the dumplings for 15 minutes. Remove them at once from the liquor.

FARINA DUMPLINGS
6 Servings
Prepare:
    Farina Balls, page 72
These remain after many tests the queen of dumplings. Though usually served in soup they may be simmered in stock or boiling water, then served with meat gravy. They may be drained, placed in a greased baking dish and covered with a cupful of cream sauce, to which you may add onion juice and parsley, or chopped chives. Sprinkle the top with ¼ cupful grated Parmesan cheese, dot it with butter and bake the dish in an oven 425° for 15 minutes.

For other dumplings see Garnishes for Soups, page 72; Gnocchi Casserole, page 102.

RAISED DUMPLINGS OR DAMPFNUDELN

About 16 Dumplings

It has been fun to dig in old cookbooks for this recipe, if only to realize that the modern method of writing for cooks is an immense improvement over the old. Our grandmothers had to wade through a labyrinth, doubtlessly armed with a ball of string, plus a rabbit's foot, in order to arrive at their goal. This homely old-time favorite is worth resurrecting. Try it in its modern form. A well-known Cincinnati hostess serves this dish as a dessert at formal dinners with much success.

Dissolve:
> ½ cake yeast

in:
> ½ cup lukewarm milk

Work in:
> 1 tablespoon sugar
> 1¼ cups sifted all-purpose flour

Permit this heavy sponge to rise covered with a cloth in a warm place until light, for about 1 hour.

Cream:
> 1 tablespoon butter
> 2 tablespoons sugar
> ½ teaspoon salt

Beat in and stir until light:
> 1 whole egg

Add this to the sponge and work in about:
> ½ cup sifted all-purpose flour

Posie says enough to stiffen as for yeast cake. Cover the bowl with a cloth.

Permit the dough to rise until doubled in bulk. Shape the dough into about 16 biscuits. They may be rolled out and cut. If you have time, permit them to rise again. From here on there is a great divergence in the treatment of the dumplings. The old method was to use a Dutch oven but a covered deep 10 inch oven-proof glass baking dish is preferable as it enables you to watch the cooking process. Place in this a hot liquid and then the dumplings. If they are to be served with a meat course with lots of gravy, use ½ cupful butter and ½ cupful scalded milk. If they are to be a dessert, use 1½ cupfuls sirup, fruit juice, preserves or stewed fruit. Cover the pot closely, place it in a very slow oven 275° and cook the dumplings for about 1½ hours. Do not lift the lid, even to peek. Old recipes add that your sense of smell must be your guide as to when to lift the lid. Do it when the dumplings begin to give off a tempting odor of baked goods, telling you that the liquid has been absorbed. Test the dumplings with a straw. Remove them from the pot and serve them at once.

An outstanding accompaniment if the dumpling is a dessert is stewed blue plums or prunes. Use part of the sirup in the pot. Serve the dumplings with the remaining fruit. The plums or prunes may be stewed with part white wine and part water. In addition it is customary to serve:

> A Custard Sauce, page 710, or
> Posie's Custard, page 713

POTATO DUMPLINGS OR KARTOFFELKLOESSE

These are light and tender, especially good with beef à la mode or other roast gravy. It is traditional to serve them with sauerbraten.

Boil uncovered in their jackets until tender:
> 6 medium-sized potatoes

Chill them thoroughly for 12 hours or more. Peel them and grate or rice them. Add:
> 2 eggs
> 1½ teaspoons salt
> ½ cup flour

Beat the batter with a fork until it is fluffy. Roll it lightly into balls 1 inch in diameter. Many cooks prefer to put the croutons in the balls. Put 1 crouton in the center of each 1 inch ball. If you wish to make large balls, roll several croutons into each ball. Drop them into gently boiling salted water for 10 minutes. Drain them well. Melt:
> ½ cup butter or drippings

Stir in:
> ¼ cup dry bread crumbs

Or prepare:
> ½ cup Croutons, see below

Pour them over the dumplings.

CROUTONS

Cut into ½ inch cubes:
> Bread

Sauté the cubes in:
> Hot butter

You may rub the skillet with garlic or add grated onion to the butter. Stir them gently, or shake the skillet until they are toasted. Serve them over:

> Noodles, page 97
> Spaetzle, page 423
> Potato Dumplings, see above

or serve them in soup.

SPATZEN OR SPAETZLE— GERMAN EGG DUMPLINGS
4 Servings

Spatzen are good at any time but they are particularly good served with roast veal. Beat:

2 eggs

Combine them with:

1½ cups flour
½ cup water
½ teaspoon salt
¼ teaspoon any baking powder

Beat these ingredients well. Drop small bits of the batter from a spoon into simmering salted water, or place it on a plate and cut shreds of the batter with a knife from the side of the plate into the water, or put the batter through a colander.

Spatzen should be very light and delicate.

Try out a sample and if it is too heavy, add water to the batter. Simmer them until they are done. Drain them, place them in a dish and cover them with:

Croutons, see above, or ¼ cup bread crumbs sautéed in ½ cup butter

Spatzen may be cooked and served in soup.

Liver Dumplings, page 384.
Pie Dough, page 564, cut into strips or shapes, simmered in stock, is frequently substituted for a dumpling mixture. Remember the good Vegetable Noodles on page 97.

SPOON BREAD WITH SOUR OR BUTTERMILK
4 Servings

This is fine served with Vegetable Casserole and Bacon, page 182.

Pour:

1½ cups boiling water

over:

1 cup white corn meal

Beat these ingredients well and permit them to cool slightly. Beat in:

1 egg
1 tablespoon butter
1 cup buttermilk
1 teaspoon soda
¾ teaspoon salt

Pour the batter into a hot, greased 7 inch baking dish. Bake it in a moderate oven 350° until it is done, for 30 to 40 minutes. If you wish to keep the top soft, add from time to time while the bread is baking a few tablespoonfuls of milk. Use in all for this purpose:

½ cup milk or thin cream, sour or sweet

This will call for longer baking, about 1 hour in all.

BATTER OR RICE SPOON BREAD
6 Servings

Combine in the order given, then stir until blended:

1 cup boiled rice
¼ cup corn meal
2 cups rich sour milk
½ teaspoon soda
1 teaspoon salt
2 beaten eggs
2 tablespoons melted fat or butter

Place the batter in a greased ovenproof dish. Bake it in a moderate oven 325° for about 1 hour. This dish is good with a meat course or served as a main dish with:

Mushroom Sauce, page 436, or
Tomatoes Creole, page 182, etc.

CRUSTY OR SOFT CENTER SPOON BREAD
4 Servings

Combine, then sift:

½ cup yellow corn meal
¼ cup all-purpose flour
1 tablespoon sugar
¾ teaspoon salt
1 teaspoon any baking powder

Stir in:

1 beaten egg
1 cup milk

Beat the batter until it is well blended. Melt in an 8 x 8 inch baking dish:

2 tablespoons butter

Pour in the batter. Place it in a 375° oven. Pour over the top:

½ cup milk

Bake the bread for 45 minutes or more, until good and crusty.

Corn-Meal Soufflé, page 219. A delightful spoon bread.

YORKSHIRE PUDDING
6 Servings

It was customary to cook this old and delicious dish in the pan with the roast or under the roast, letting the drippings fall upon it. As we now cook roast beef in a slow oven we must revise the cooking of Yorkshire pudding. It is best to cook it separately in the hot oven it requires to puff it up and brown it quickly.

Place the batter in a hot pan containing hot fat or drippings. Cook it as directed and you will have a dish not unlike a popover. Serve it from the dish in which it was cooked, cut into squares. Substitute the pudding for the usual starch served with a main course—potatoes, rice, spaghetti, etc. Sift into a bowl:

7/8 cup flour
1/2 teaspoon salt

Make a well in the center into which pour:

1/2 cup milk

Stir in the milk. Beat until fluffy:

2 eggs

Beat them into the batter. Add:

1/2 cup water

Beat the batter well until large bubbles rise to the surface. You may permit this to stand for 1 hour and then beat it again.

Have ready a hot oven-proof dish, about 10 x 10, or hot muffin tins containing about 1/4 inch hot beef drippings or melted butter. Pour in the batter. It should be about 5/8 inch high. Bake the pudding in a hot oven 400° for about 20 minutes. Reduce the heat to 350° and bake it 10 to 15 minutes longer. Some cooks recommend a 350° oven for 1/2 hour. Serve it at once.

Sauces and Gravies for Meat and Fish

Having once been asked my opinion of a newcomer I gave it unhesitatingly. "She is the kind of person who serves *gray gravy!*"

Sauces are not only the hallmark of the good cook—they are an indication of her aesthetic sense as well. There is nothing about them that is synonymous with the bogey man. On the whole they are simple and in order to excel with them it is necessary to master only 1 or 2 basic principles.

Handy hand-size tools that can be wielded right above the cooking pot involving no extra dishes or surface space often encourage the addition of those extra ingredients which make a great difference in sauce results.

My favorite cooking utensil is shown hanging to the left below. It costs little, it is not an imposing implement, but armed with it you may scoff at lumps and curdles. It is a tremendous timesaver. Vigorously handled it will insure the smoothest of gravies and sauces. I use it in preference to a rotary beater because its action requires only one hand instead of two, and because it will do anything a rotary beater can do and more. It is called a spiral wire whisk or a spiral egg beater. Next to it hangs another beater handy for use in a cup. All these tools encourage sauce experimentation.

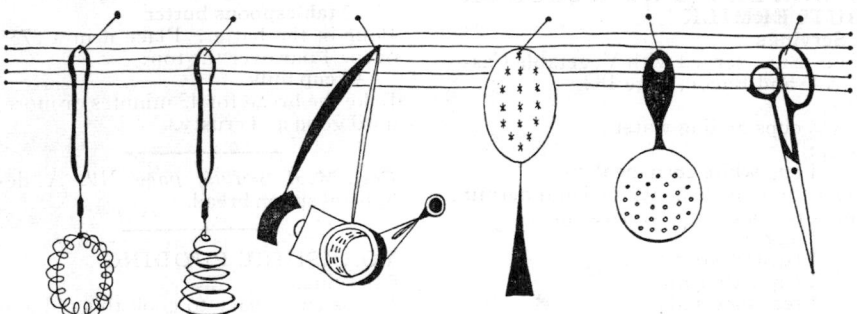

For that little grating of cheese, onion or bread crumbs try a small rotary grater, shown next.

For a sprinkling of lemon rind or nutmeg use a small grating surface.

For straining the seeds from a dash of lemon juice try a wide flat spoon type strainer.

For that snibblet of parsley, basil or chives use your kitchen shears.

Stock for Sauces and Gravies

The word stock usually applies to the liquid gained by simmering meat or fish and vegetables in water. The resulting essence is used in soups, sauces, aspics, etc.

There are many sources for obtaining stock. An enlightened housekeeper will keep a closely covered jar in her refrigerator in which to collect the stock that would otherwise be wasted.

Celery tops and parings, bean parings, peapods, carrot skins, parsley stems, a bit of onion, etc., may be combined, barely covered with water and simmered for about ½ hour. A meat cube may be added to the strained stock, or it may be used as it is as a basis for a sauce or soup.

The juices from mild flavored vegetables such as beans, asparagus, etc., whether freshly cooked or canned, should be saved in this way.

The juice from vegetables that are pronounced in flavor, cabbage, Brussels sprouts, turnips, etc., are too strong for the stock-pot but they may be kept separately and used as a basis for a soup or a sauce that is to accompany a heavily flavored dish.

The maintenance of a stock-pot is a bit of thrift that not only eliminates all waste, but adds materially to the nutritional value of the food served your family. Remember that vegetable juices are rich in vitamins and minerals.

After the little household economies mentioned above, in behalf of better gravies, come commercial aids that are valuable: meat cubes, vegetable cubes, condensed broths, essences, pastes, jellies, etc. My favorites are clear chicken broth, mushroom broth, garlic salt combination and monosodium glutamate. These combine well with cream and other ingredients in sauces adding distinction and flavor to fish and vegetable dishes.

For good gravies keep the following ingredients on hand—all available juices from cooked or canned food, homemade stock and the commercial substitutes listed above. For flavoring various meats distinctively read the Herb Chapter, page 831.

Plain gravies are of 2 kinds:

1. Gravy made with drippings in which meat has been sautéed.

2. Gravy made with the juices of stews and roasts and stock. See rules for making gravy on page 426.

Roux

Flour and butter or fat are blended in varying proportions and heated slowly in a double boiler or over extremely low heat for 10-15 minutes if you are in a hurry or 15 hours if you are a devotee of Escoffier. The darker the roux, the darker and more highly seasoned the sauce in which it is used. The proportion of butter determines the consistency. For typical examples of blond roux see Cream Sauces, page 428. Roux may be made in quantity and stored covered under refrigeration until ready to use. Reheat in a double boiler and proceed with the making of the sauce.

Browned Flour

Many gravies are made with browned flour for color and flavor. Brown flour by stirring it in a dry pan over very low heat. Browned flour has only about ½ the thickening power of other flour.

RULE FOR MAKING GRAVY WITH PAN DRIPPINGS IN WHICH MEAT HAS BEEN SAUTÉED
1 Cupful

Remove the meat from the pan. Place it where it will remain hot. Pour off all but 2 tablespoonfuls of the drippings. Blend into them:

1 or 2 tablespoons flour

Stir the gravy with a wire whisk until the flour has thickened, at least 5 minutes. Cook it slowly and stir it constantly while stirring in:

1 cup Stock, page 43, milk or water and cream

Season the gravy with:

Salt, pepper, fresh or dried minced herbs, grated lemon rind, etc.

See the following Seasonings for Sauces. Color it with:

A few drops Caramel, page 754, or commercial coloring

Strain the gravy, reheat it and serve it.

RULE FOR MAKING GRAVY FOR STEWS

Use soup stock, water in which vegetables were cooked, or prepare the following:

Vegetable Stock

Combine:

**2 cups water
1 sliced onion
Asparagus scrapings or vegetables that are used in soups
2 or 3 chopped celery ribs and leaves
1 sliced carrot
Parsley
Scant seasoning**

If the stock is to be used for pot roast or stew, bring these ingredients to the boiling point and pour them over the seared meat.

RULE FOR MAKING GRAVY FOR ROASTS
About 1 Cupful

Modern meat cookery keeps the juices where they should be, in the roast. You will find very little in the pan. Strain what there is into a tall cup and place it in cold water. The fat will rise quickly. Take what you need of it for your gravy measurement. Skim off the rest and use it later as drippings. The remaining liquid in the cup will be good for your gravy, but if there is not enough you will have to add stock, see preceding rule, a diluted meat cube or canned soup to make up the remainder. Don't use water unless driven to it. Melt over low heat:

3 tablespoons fat

Blend in:

2 tablespoons flour

Stir in slowly:

1 cup Stock, page 43

Cook and stir the gravy over low heat until it is smooth, for at least 5 to 10 minutes. Season it with:

Salt, paprika, pepper, minced herbs, grated lemon rind, etc.

See the following Seasonings for Sauces. Color it with:

A few drops Caramel, page 754, or commercial coloring

When making gravy from fat meats it will sometimes separate. This looks calamitous, but it is easily remedied. Add a little cream very slowly, continue stirring all the time and the gravy will become smooth and thick. Taste the gravy and if it is not good, make it so. Add paprika, celery salt and catsup sparingly. If you add pepper, grind it fresh.

Stock or meat or vegetable cubes give it character. Having made it good, a great deal has been accomplished, but not enough—it must also look good. Brown the flour as directed above or use Caramel, page 754, or commercial coloring. Add enough of this to make the gravy a fine color and it is ready to serve. Never overseason or add unnecessarily to good gravy. Doctor only the indifferent ones and color them to make them attractive. There is no excuse, except inefficiency, for whitish, lumpy, tasteless gravies, but one encounters them, alas! in endless varieties. Therefore these instructions.

FLOUR PASTE FOR THICKENING GRAVIES AND SAUCES

For good results in thickening gravies make a thin paste of flour and cold water or stock. Use about 1 part water and two parts flour. If made with water, the paste may be kept on hand in a covered jar for ready use. Stir as much of the paste as needed into the boiling stock or drippings. Permit the sauce to boil until it thickens.

UNTHICKENED GRAVIES OR SAUCES

These are such a welcome change after the monotonous flour-thickened type. Pan juices and scrapings are precious. Use them to good advantage. Add to the pan in which meat has been cooked after removing it:

1 tablespoon or more hot water

Scrape the pan well. Add to the pan just before removing unfloured sautéed chicken, casserole chicken, steak or chops:

2 teaspoons or more fresh tarragon or ½ teaspoon dried herb

2 tablespoons or more sherry (Butter)

Scrape the pan well.

Small lean roasts, cooked by the slow method, are apt to have very few "drippings." When there are pan drippings from a large roast Jane stirs into them about 1 hour after the roast has been put into the oven:

A sizable chopped onion

2 or 3 ribs cut-up celery with leaves

¼ bay leaf

½ crushed clove garlic

About 20 minutes before the roast is done stir in ½ cupful stock, tomato juice or water. When the roast is done remove both roast and rack. Place the pan over heat. Stir the precious residue well from the bottom, add additional stock, etc., according to the amount and strength of the drippings and seasonings. Strain and serve.

Seasonings and Ingredients for Sauces

Sauces can be made interesting in so many different ways by varying the seasonings and ingredients used. The highly flavored sauces like those with tomato may also be given added nutritional value by using ⅓ cupful powdered milk and 1 teaspoonful debittered brewers' yeast to each cupful of fluid in the sauce. In doubling the ingredients in recipes season cautiously. It is easy to overdo it. The Herb Chapter, page 831, and the following list offer many suggestions.

Fresh or dried parsley, basil, tarragon, thyme, chervil, shallot, savory, etc.
Grated onion
Freshly ground nutmeg
2 or 3 cloves, heads removed
Part of a bay leaf
Freshly ground pepper
Paprika
Curry powder
Celery seed
French celery seed
Caraway seed
Dill seed
Fennel seed
Chili powder
Mustard
Sautéed mushrooms
Capers

Chopped pickles
Chopped lemons
Lemon rind
Lemon juice
Sherry
Madeira
Worcestershire sauce
Tabasco sauce
Horseradish
Catsup
Soy sauce
Pepper sauce
Garlic
Leeks
· Celery salt
Onion salt
Garlic salt combination
Monosodium glutamate

DUXELLES AND MIREPOIX

These mixtures are placed in the pan when meat is being cooked or they are used in preparing gravies and sauces for meat. They may be strained out before the sauce is served.

DUXELLES

Mince equal parts of:

Mushrooms, parsley, shallots

Sauté them for 1 minute in:

Butter

Add minced ham or bacon if desired.

MIREPOIX

Dice:

1 carrot

1 onion

1 celery heart: the inner ribs

Add:

½ bay leaf

½ clove garlic

1 sprig thyme

1 tablespoon minced ham or bacon

The incomparable "Tilda" of the "funny sheet" says: "There's many a live wire around that would be a dead one except for its connections." Apply this to indifferent food enlivened by sauces. Remember, please, that there are sauces other than white, brown and red.

CREAM SAUCE OR WHITE SAUCE I

1 Cupful

This sauce is used for creaming vegetables, fish, etc.

Cream sauce and all its relations are best made in a double boiler. As this is a rather tedious process, requiring 15 minutes' cooking and stirring, most cooks prefer the shorter way. I do, but I feel constrained to draw attention to the fact that it is unconventional.

Melt over low heat:

    2 tablespoons butter

For a delicate flavor even restaurant chefs have found no substitute for butter. Add and blend in over low heat for 5 to 10 minutes:

    1½ to 2 tablespoons flour

Stir in slowly:

    1 cup milk

Cream may be substituted for milk. Or the sauce may be made with part stock and part milk or cream.

Season these ingredients with:

    ¼ teaspoon salt
    ⅛ teaspoon paprika or pepper

Or vary your flavor with:

    Celery salt
    A grating nutmeg
    1 teaspoon lemon juice
    ½ teaspoon Worcestershire sauce
    1 teaspoon sherry
    1 teaspoon onion juice
    2 tablespoons chopped parsley
    2 tablespoons chopped chives

Cook and stir the sauce with a wire whisk until it is smooth and comes to a boil. Combine it with other ingredients just as it boils so that it will not become watery.

For creamed dishes use about ½ as much sauce as there are solids.

CREAM SAUCE II OR HEAVY CREAM SAUCE

1 Cupful

This sauce is used in soufflés. Follow the preceding rule for:

    Cream Sauce I

Use in all:

    3 tablespoons butter
    3 tablespoons flour
    1 cup liquid

CREAM SAUCE III

1 Cupful

This sauce is used in croquettes. Follow the preceding rule for:

    Cream Sauce I

Use in all:

    3 tablespoons butter
    ⅓ cup flour
    1 cup liquid

CURRY SAUCE

Method I. 1 Cupful

Fine for eggs, fish and meat.

Prepare:

    1 cup Cream Sauce I, see this page

Add to it:

    1 teaspoon minced onion
    1 teaspoon or more curry powder
    1 teaspoon lemon juice

Method II. About 2 Cupfuls

Sauté slowly until tender:

    ¼ cup chopped onion
    ¼ cup chopped apple

in:

    4 tablespoons butter

Stir in until smooth:

    2½ tablespoons flour

Stir in slowly, stir and boil until well blended:

    1 cup chicken broth
    1 cup cream
    ½ to 2 teaspoons curry powder

"I have Indian blood in my ancestry." "Indeed, what tribe?" "Oh! It wasn't a tribe. Just a wandering Indian." Use as much or as little curry as you like.

Egg Sauce I, page 281.

EGG SAUCE II

1¼ Cupfuls

This is good made with chicken stock and cream.

Prepare:

    Cream Sauce I

Add to it:

    2 chopped hard-cooked eggs
    1 tablespoon capers or chopped pickles

MUSTARD SAUCE I

1 Cupful

This sauce is good served with corned beef, fish, etc. Add 1 teaspoonful prepared mustard to 1 cupful Cream Sauce I, see above, or make the sauce of the following ingredients. Melt:

    3 tablespoons butter

Stir in until blended:
1½ to 2 tablespoons flour
Add:
1 teaspoon prepared mustard
1 cup stock
Salt if required
Stir the sauce until it boils.

HORSERADISH SAUCE
1 Cupful
Usually used with boiled meat—beef,
corned beef, etc.
Prepare:
Cream Sauce I, page 428
Remove it from the fire, add:
**3 tablespoons prepared horse-
radish**
Or prepare:
Brown Sauce, page 435
Add:
**3 tablespoons prepared horse-
radish**

VELOUTÉ SAUCE
This, and the following Béchamel
Sauce, are good with both meat and
vegetables.
Prepare:
Cream Sauce I, page 428
Substitute for the milk:
Stock, page 43

BÉCHAMEL SAUCE
1 Cupful
Melt:
2 tablespoons butter
Stir in until blended:
1½ to 2 tablespoons flour
Stir in slowly:
½ cup milk
**½ cup well-flavored light meat
or Vegetable Stock, page 425**
Cook and stir the sauce until it is
smooth and boiling. Season it with:
Salt and paprika
The addition of an egg yolk may be
made to this very good sauce. Beat a
little of the sauce into it, combine it
with the rest of the sauce, then stir the
sauce over very low heat until the yolk
thickens slightly. Do not boil the sauce
after adding the yolk.

ALLEMANDE SAUCE
1 Cupful
This is fine with asparagus or beans.
Prepare:
Cream Sauce I, page 428
Substitute for milk:
**Stock, preferably a light stock—
veal or chicken, or vegetable
water**

Just before removing the sauce from
the fire reduce the heat and beat in:
1 egg yolk
Permit the egg to thicken slightly.
Add:
1 teaspoon lemon juice
and serve the sauce.

NEVER FAIL HOLLANDAISE SAUCE
Method I. 1 Cupful
My cook calls this "holiday sauce"—
isn't that a grand name for it? Hollandaise sauce made by this method
may be prepared long in advance. It
may be kept hot for ½ hour or more
over, not in, hot water, or it may be set
aside, chilled and reheated when needed, over, not in, hot water, provided it
is placed in a small crock and is stirred
constantly with a wire whisk until it is
hot.
Place where it will melt slowly and
keep warm:
½ cup butter
The top of the oven is a good place.
Heat in the same way:
**1½ tablespoons lemon juice, sherry
or tarragon vinegar**
Have ready a small saucepan of boiling
water and a tablespoon with which to
measure it when ready.

Find a small thick bowl or crock that
will fit closely on a double boiler base.
The heat will penetrate the crock slowly. Have boiling water in the double
boiler to the depth of about 1 inch. The
bottom of the crock must be well over,
not in, the boiling water. Put the crock
on a table. Place in it:
3 egg yolks
Place the crock on the kettle. Beat the
yolks with a wire whisk until they
begin to thicken. Add 1 tablespoonful
boiling water. Beat again until the
eggs begin to thicken. Repeat this
process until you have added in all 4

tablespoonfuls boiling water. Then beat in the hot lemon juice. Remove the crock from the fire. Beat the sauce well with a wire whisk. Beat constantly while adding the melted butter slowly and:

    ¼ teaspoon salt—less if butter is salted
    ⅛ teaspoon paprika
    A few grains cayenne

Put the crock back on the kettle in which the water must now be hot but not boiling. Cover the crock partially. Beat the sauce again before serving it. Should the sauce separate—a remote contingency when made in this way—beat into it gradually:

    1 tablespoon cream

Method II.

A friend who is a wonder with sauces contributes the following version of the above Hollandaise Sauce. She says it is excellent and made in one fell swoop. "Use your favorite recipe as to quantities. Use the top of a double boiler. Cream all the butter at once. Beat in the egg yolks, lemon juice and seasonings gradually. Mix well. Stir in the boiling water slowly. Place the sauce in a pan over the bottom of a double boiler in which 1 inch of water is simmering. Stir well for 5 minutes until the sauce thickens. Remove from heat and beat for 1 minute."

Method III.

And here is still another version—this one being richer than the other 2 for no water is used. Beat well:

    3 egg yolks

Add very slowly beating constantly:

    ½ cup melted butter

Beat in:

    1 tablespoon lemon juice

Beat the sauce in a small crock over, not in, simmering water until it thickens slightly. Do not permit the water to boil at any time.

SOUR CREAM HOLLANDAISE SAUCE

About 1¼ Cupfuls

This rule became popular during butter rationing. Mix in the top of a double boiler:

    1 cup thick sour cream
    Juice of 1 lemon
    2 egg yolks
    ½ teaspoon salt
    ¼ teaspoon paprika

Stir over, not in, hot water until thick.

SAUCE BÉARNAISE

Follow the preceding rule for:
    Hollandaise Sauce

Add:

    Finely chopped parsley, tarragon, shallot or onion
    ½ teaspoon grated horseradish

FIGARO SAUCE

A variation of the well-known Hollandaise sauce.

Prepare:

    1 cup Hollandaise Sauce, page 429

Beat in very slowly:

    ¼ cup warm tomato pulp

Add:

    2 tablespoons chopped parsley

EASY HOLLANDAISE SAUCE

1¼ Cupfuls

Soften:

    3 tablespoons butter

Add and beat well:

    3 egg yolks

Add:

    1 teaspoon cornstarch
    2 to 3 tablespoons lemon juice

Just before serving the sauce add very, very slowly:

    1 cup boiling water

Place the pan over boiling water, or hold it high over a low flame and stir the sauce until it thickens. Add:

    ½ teaspoon salt
    ⅛ teaspoon paprika

This sauce may be placed over, not in, hot water until ready for use. It may be reheated over very slow heat. Stir it constantly.

CHEESE SAUCE I

About 2 Cupfuls

Melt in a saucepan:

    2 tablespoons butter

Stir in until blended:

    2 tablespoons flour

Stir in slowly:

    1½ cups milk

When the sauce is smooth and boiling reduce the heat and stir in:

    1 cup or less mild grated cheese or diced processed cheese

Season the sauce with:

    ½ teaspoon salt
    ⅛ teaspoon paprika
    A few grains cayenne
    (½ teaspoon dry mustard)

Stir the sauce until the cheese is melted.

Cheese Sauce II, page 191.
This sauce is made without flour. It is heavier in cheese than Cheese Sauce I and more highly seasoned—a paragon among sauces.

CHEESE SAUCE III
About 1½ Cupfuls
Scald:
> 1 cup rich or evaporated milk

Stir in:
> ½ lb. diced processed cheese or grated naturally aged cheese
> 1 teaspoon salt
> ¼ teaspoon paprika
> ¼ teaspoon celery salt, curry powder or mustard
> A few grains cayenne

Cook the sauce over very low heat. Stir it constantly until smooth. This sauce will keep a long time in a refrigerator.

MORNAY SAUCE
About 1¼ Cupfuls
Sometimes served over hash—good with fillets of fish and egg dishes.
Prepare:
> Cream Sauce I, page 428

When very hot reduce the heat and stir in gradually:
> 2 tablespoons butter
> A few grains cayenne
> 2 tablespoons each of 2 kinds grated cheese

Try a combination of Parmesan and Swiss cheeses.

BUTTER SAUCE WITH HERBS
About ½ Cupful
For meat, vegetable or egg dishes. Place in a double boiler, cook and stir until smooth:
> 1 tablespoon flour
> ½ cup butter
> 2 tablespoons milk
> ⅛ teaspoon salt
> 2 tablespoons fresh fennel, parsley, chives, basil or other herb, chopped, or 1 tablespoon of the dried herbs

DRAWN BUTTER SAUCE
About 1½ Cupfuls
Melt:
> 3 tablespoons butter

Stir in:
> 3 tablespoons flour

Stir in slowly and boil for 3 minutes:
> 1½ cups vegetable or fish stock

Stir in, bit by bit:
> 3 tablespoons butter

alternately with:
> 1 teaspoon lemon juice

Season with:
> Salt and paprika or pepper

PARSLEY BUTTER SAUCE
For asparagus, other vegetables and fish. Fine for new potatoes.
Melt:
> ¼ cup butter

Add to it:
> 2 tablespoons chopped parsley or blanched shredded almonds
> Salt and paprika

Lemon juice and Worcestershire sauce may be added when this sauce is used for fish.

MAÎTRE D'HÔTEL BUTTER
Good over broiled steak, etc.
Cream until it is soft:
> ¼ cup butter

Add:
> ½ teaspoon salt
> ⅛ teaspoon pepper
> ½ tablespoon chopped parsley

Add very slowly, stirring the sauce constantly:
> ¾ to 1½ tablespoons lemon juice

LEMON BUTTER FOR MEAT OR VEGETABLES
A nice thing to serve in individual portions. When chilled shape into balls for artichokes, steaks, etc.
Beat until soft:
> ¼ cup butter

Add very slowly:
> 1 tablespoon lemon juice

Add:
> ⅛ teaspoon salt if the butter is unsalted
> (¼ teaspoon curry powder)

MINT BUTTER FOR LAMB, ETC.
Follow the preceding rule for:
> Lemon Butter

Omit the curry and add:
> ¼ cup finely chopped mint leaves

SMITANE SAUCE
About 1¼ Cupfuls
Especially good over cooked meat, fowl, etc.
Melt:
> 1½ tablespoons butter

Sauté in it until clear:
> 2 small chopped onions

Add and cook until the onions are very soft:

    ½ cup dry white wine

Scald, then stir into the onions:

    1 cup sour cream

Simmer these ingredients for 5 minutes. Strain the sauce. Season it with:

    1 teaspoon lemon juice
    Salt and pepper

Sauces for Fish, page 258.
These sauces are good over bland food other than fish.

POULETTE SAUCE
About 2 Cupfuls

This and the following sauce are good with soufflés, sweetbreads, cucumbers, etc. Simmer for 3 minutes:

    1½ cups Chicken or Veal Stock,
        page 43, or canned bouillon
    1 sliced shallot or 2 teaspoons
        chopped onion
    2 tablespoons chopped celery
    1 tablespoon butter
    A dash Tabasco sauce
    A few grains cayenne

Strain, then reheat this stock. Beat well until blended:

    2 egg yolks
    2 teaspoons flour

Add:

    1 tablespoon cold stock

Pour the simmering ingredients on the yolk mixture. Return them to the saucepan. Stir them over low heat until they thicken. Do not permit them to boil. Season them, if needed, with:

    Salt

Add to the sauce:

    2 teaspoons dry white wine, sherry
        or lemon juice
    2 teaspoons chopped parsley

Serve the sauce at once or keep it hot over hot water.

POULETTE SAUCE WITH CREAM
About 1½ Cupfuls

Melt:

    1½ tablespoons butter

Stir in until blended:

    1 tablespoon flour

Stir in slowly:

    1 cup chicken broth or canned
        chicken stock

Reduce the heat to low. Beat together:

    ⅓ cup cream
    1 egg yolk

Stir these ingredients slowly into the

hot sauce. Stir and cook them until the egg yolk has thickened. Do not permit the sauce to boil. Season the sauce if needed with:

    Salt and paprika

Stir in slowly:

    1 teaspoon lemon juice

Serve the sauce at once or keep it hot over hot water.

À la King Sauce, see Chicken à la King, page 143.

ONION SAUCE WITH MILK AND EGGS
About 2 Cupfuls

This is good over cabbage, cauliflower, etc.

Boil until tender:

    1¼ cups chopped onions

Drain them. Strain them through a ricer or sieve. There should be about 1 cupful of pulp. Add the pulp to:

    1½ cups hot top milk

Season the sauce with:

    Salt and paprika

When it is thoroughly heated remove it from the fire and beat in:

    2 beaten egg yolks

Pour the sauce over a vegetable. Top it with:

    Buttered Crumbs, page 326, or
    Croutons, page 422

ONION SAUCE WITH STOCK
About 2 Cupfuls

This sauce, like the preceding one, is fine for vegetables, fish and meat.

Cover with boiling water and cook for 5 minutes:

    2 cups sliced onions

Drain them. Cover them with:

    2 cups boiling water

Boil them until they are soft. Rub them through a sieve. Add to the onions and juice enough water to make 1½ cupfuls and:

    1 bouillon cube

Melt:

    3 tablespoons butter

Stir in until blended:

    3 tablespoons flour

Stir in the onion purée. Season the sauce, if needed, with:

    Salt and paprika

Stir the sauce until it boils.

An Onion Sauce will be found on page 171.
Onion Soup Sauce, page 442.

CHESTNUT SAUCE
Method I.   About 2½ Cupfuls
To be served with game or roast.
Sauté for 5 minutes:
> 2 tablespoons chopped carrot
> 2 tablespoons chopped onion

in:
> 3 tablespoons butter

Stir in until blended:
> 3 tablespoons flour

Add and simmer for 20 minutes:
> 1½ cups stock
> ¼ bay leaf
> 2 tablespoons chopped parsley
> 8 peppercorns

Strain the sauce. Season it with:
> Salt

Add:
> A few drops coloring
> 3 tablespoons Madeira or sherry wine
> 1 tablespoon butter
> 1 cup finely chopped Boiled Chestnuts, page 283

Method II.   About 2 Cupfuls
Prepare:
> Brown Sauce, page 435

Boil (page 283):
> 1 cup chestnuts

Chop the chestnuts. Add them to the sauce.

HOT MAYONNAISE
Method I.   1 Cupful
Place in a double boiler:
> ½ cup Cream Sauce I, page 428

Add to it:
> ½ cup mayonnaise

Stir these ingredients until they are hot. Serve the sauce over:
> Cooked vegetables: cauliflower, cabbage, asparagus, etc.

Method II.
Good over steak.
Heat and stir:
> Mayonnaise

Add:
> Lemon juice and capers

CAPER SAUCE FOR BOILED MEATS, MUTTON, TONGUE, ETC.
Follow the rule for:
> Cream Sauce I, page 428

Use the stock in which the meat was boiled instead of milk, or part stock and part rich milk. Add, just before removing the sauce from the fire:
> 2 tablespoons or more capers

TOMATO SAUCE
About 1½ Cupfuls
Cook for 15 minutes, then strain:
> 2 cups or more canned tomatoes, or fresh stewed tomatoes
> 1 slice onion
> 2 ribs celery with leaves
> (Parsley)
> (1 carrot)
> (½ green pepper)

Melt in a saucepan:
> 3 tablespoons butter

Stir in until blended:
> 3 tablespoons flour

Add the strained stock slowly. Cook and stir the sauce until it is smooth and boiling. Season it with:
> ¼ teaspoon salt
> ⅛ teaspoon pepper
> ¼ teaspoon sugar

TOMATO SAUCE UNTHICKENED
About 4 Cupfuls
Heat over a low fire:
> 3 tablespoons olive oil

Add and stir for about 3 minutes:
> 1 large chopped Bermuda onion
> ½ chopped green pepper, seeds and fibrous portions removed
> 2 ribs celery with leaves
> 1 carrot cut in small pieces
> (1 chopped clove garlic)

Add:
> 4 cups canned tomatoes or 6 large fresh tomatoes
> ½ bay leaf
> 1 teaspoon brown sugar
> 2 sprigs parsley or 1 sprig other fresh herb or 1 teaspoon dried basil or tarragon
> 1 teaspoon salt
> ⅛ teaspoon pepper

Cook the sauce gently until thick, for about 45 minutes. Watch it so that it does not burn. Put it through a fine strainer. Add seasoning if needed. This sauce will keep for several days.

Tomato Cream Sauce for Fish, page 259.

QUICK TOMATO SAUCE
About 2 Cupfuls
Heat the contents of:
> 1 can condensed tomato soup:
> 10½ oz.

Add:
> 2 tablespoons butter

The sauce may be thinned with:
> A little boiling stock or water

QUICK CATSUP SAUCE
About 2½ Cupfuls
Melt:
   4 tablespoons butter
Blend in:
   4 tablespoons flour
Stir in until well blended and boiling:
   1 cup cream
Stir in:
   1½ cups catsup
   1 tablespoon Worcestershire
   sauce
   Salt and paprika
Heat well and serve with rice, mushroom ring, soufflés and what not.

TOMATO PASTE OR VELVET
Wash, pare, then mash:
   6 large ripe tomatoes
Melt:
   2 tablespoons butter
Add the tomatoes and:
   1 teaspoon brown sugar
   ¼ teaspoon paprika
   ¾ teaspoon salt
Cook the tomatoes over low heat, stirring constantly, or in a double boiler, until they are the consistency of thick paste. Put the paste through a strainer. This makes a good sandwich spread or relish. It is a fine addition to sauces.

ITALIAN TOMATO PASTE
This flavorful paste is diluted in a little boiling water and added to sauces and soups. Fine in spaghetti and noodle dishes and as a dressing for cooked vegetables, salads, etc.
Wash and cut into slices:
   1½ pecks ripe tomatoes: 6 quarts
Add:
   3 teaspoons salt
You may add:
   1 large stalk celery cut up with
   some leaves
   ¾ cup chopped onion
   3 tablespoons fresh herbs or
   1 tablespoon dried herbs
   ¾ teaspoon peppercorns
   12 cloves
   1 two inch stick cinnamon
   (1 minced clove garlic)
Simmer these ingredients until the tomatoes are soft. Stir frequently. Put the vegetables through a fine sieve. Simmer the pulp over hot water or simmer it over direct heat with some means of protecting it from the bottom by using an asbestos plate, etc. Stir it frequently as it burns easily. After several hours when the pulp is thick

and reduced by about ½ spread the paste to the depth of ½ inch on moist plates. Cut into the paste to permit the air to penetrate. Place the paste in the sun to dry, or dry it in a slow oven 250°. When the paste is dry enough to roll, roll it into balls. The balls may be dipped in salad oil. Store them in airtight jars or store the paste in a tin box with waxed paper between the layers.

HUNTERS' SAUCE
About 2 Cupfuls
Sauté gently until very tender:
   2 tablespoons minced onion
in:
   2 tablespoons butter
Strain the butter. Stir in and sauté gently for 2 minutes:
   1 cup sliced mushrooms
Stir in the contents of:
   2 cans tomato sauce: 8 oz.
   1 beef cube
   ½ cup dry white wine
Simmer the sauce until thick, for about ¼ hour. Season it with:
   Salt and paprika
You may add:
   2 tablespoons brandy

QUICK TOMATO CHEESE SAUCE
About 1½ Cupfuls
Heat in a double boiler the contents of:
   1 can condensed tomato soup:
   10½ oz.
Add:
   ¼ teaspoon salt
   ¼ teaspoon pepper or paprika
Stir and cook these ingredients until they are hot. Beat in:
   1 cup or more grated American
   cheese
Use a wire whisk. Beat the sauce until the cheese is melted.

CREOLE SAUCE
About 2 Cupfuls
Melt over low heat:
   2 tablespoons butter
Add and cook covered for 2 minutes:
   1 tablespoon chopped onion
   (6 shredded olives)
Add and cook until the sauce is thick:
   1½ cups tomatoes or ½ cup tomatoes and 1 cup brown sauce, see
   below
   ½ chopped green pepper
The thickening process can be hastened by adding:
   1 tablespoon flour

Stir it until it is blended with:
  1 tablespoon water
Add:
  ⅓ teaspoon salt
  A few grains cayenne
  1 teaspoon white or brown sugar
  (1 tablespoon capers)
The amount of onion may be increased
to ¼ cupful. Add to the sauce if you
like it hot:
  ¼ cup chili sauce

QUICK CREOLE SAUCE
To:
  Quick Tomato Sauce, page 433
Add:
  ½ cup finely chopped green peppers, onion, celery, olives and
  pickles

BROWN SAUCE
1 Cupful
Melt in a small saucepan:
  2 tablespoons butter
Add and sauté until light brown:
  ½ slice onion
Remove the onion. Cook and stir the
butter until it is light brown. Stir in
and permit to brown:
  2 tablespoons flour
Stir in slowly:
  1 cup stock—¼ of this may be
  tomato pulp or paste
Stir and cook the sauce until it is
smooth and boiling. Season it with:
  Salt and paprika
  (Sherry, Madeira or Worcestershire sauce)
This sauce is good with left-over meat
dishes.

EMERGENCY BROWN SAUCE OR GRAVY
About 1 Cupful
You may rub your pan with:
  ½ clove garlic
Melt:
  2 tablespoons butter
Let it brown. Stir in until blended:
  2 tablespoons flour
Stir in:
  1 cup canned bouillon or 1 or 2
  bouillon cubes dissolved in 1
  cup boiling water
Permit the gravy to boil. Stir it con-
stantly. Season it as required with:
  Salt and pepper or paprika
  Sherry or Worcestershire sauce
  Lemon juice, catsup or chili
  sauce
  Dried herbs

Or reduce the butter measurement to 1
tablespoonful, use for liquid ⅔ cupful
bouillon and ⅓ cupful rich cream. A
delicious addition to brown sauce is
the following. Pare, then grate:
  1 small apple
  1 small onion
Simmer these for 1 minute in the
gravy. Remove it from the fire. Add:
  2 tablespoons sherry

OLIVE SAUCE
About 1¼ Cupfuls
Remove the pits from:
  12 green, ripe or stuffed olives
Slice the olives. Add them to the pre-
ceding:
  Brown Sauce or Emergency
  Brown Sauce

CURRY SAUCE FOR COLD MEATS
About 1 Cupful
Melt:
  2 tablespoons butter
Sauté in it until light brown:
  1 large minced onion
Stir in:
  8 peppercorns
  ¼ teaspoon freshly grated nutmeg
  1 bay leaf
  1 tablespoon or less curry powder
  2 tablespoons flour
  2 tablespoons vinegar
  1½ cups boiling stock or water
  Salt to taste
Stir the sauce until it bubbles. Strain
and serve it hot or cold.

RAVIGOTE SAUCE FOR MEAT OR FISH
This sauce is served lukewarm.
Chop until very fine:
  2 shallots
Add:
  1 tablespoon wine vinegar
Cook these ingredients rapidly, stirring
constantly for about 3 minutes. Dilute:
  1 tablespoon tomato paste in 1 cup
  meat or Fish Stock, page 230
Add this to the shallots and simmer
the sauce for 10 minutes. Stir:
  1 teaspoon flour
into:
  2 tablespoons stock
Blend it into the sauce and simmer it
for 5 minutes longer. Stir it from time
to time. Add:
  Salt and freshly ground pepper
Cool the sauce to lukewarm. Add:

1 tablespoon chopped parsley
1 teaspoon prepared mustard
1 tablespoon chopped chervil or 1
   teaspoon dried chervil
1 tablespoon chopped capers
½ teaspoon chopped chives
(½ teaspoon chopped tarragon)

MUSHROOM SAUCE I
About 2 Cupfuls
Sauté:
      ¼ lb. mushrooms
in:
      2 tablespoons butter
Remove the mushrooms from the
skillet. Reserve the drippings. Slice
the mushrooms. Make:
      Brown Sauce or Emergency
      Brown Sauce, page 435
Mushroom Stock, page 45, or part
mushroom stock and cream may be
substituted for other stock.
Use the drippings from the mushrooms and add butter if necessary.
When the sauce is smooth and boiling
add the sautéed mushrooms. Heat
them well.

Mushroom Sauce for Soufflé, page 222.

PIQUANT SAUCE
About 1¼ Cupfuls
Combine:
      Brown Sauce, page 435
1 tablespoon lemon juice
1 tablespoon minced onion
1 tablespoon chopped green
   pepper
1 tablespoon capers or chopped
   pickles
A few grains cayenne

CURRANT JELLY SAUCE
1¼ Cupfuls
Good with roast, game or cold meat.
Heat:
      1 cup Brown Sauce, page 435,
      or lamb gravy
Stir in and dissolve in it:
      ¼ cup currant jelly
Add:
      1 tablespoon sherry or 2 teaspoons
      lemon juice
Or, dissolve over low heat equal parts
of:
      Currant jelly
      Prepared mustard
Or, in place of sauce serve:
      Blocks of currant jelly
sprinkled with:
      Chopped mint or
      Grated orange rind

BARBECUE SAUCE
About 1½ Cupfuls
See "To Barbecue Meat" on page 340.
Simmer for 15 minutes, stirring fre-
quently:
      12 to 14 oz. tomato catsup
      ½ cup white distilled vinegar
      1 teaspoon sugar
      A liberal seasoning of red and
         black pepper
      ⅛ teaspoon salt

*Other Barbecue Sauces will be found
under Barbecued Sirloin Steak, page
346; Barbecued Spareribs, page 369.*

SAUCE FOR STEAK I
About ¼ Cupful
Good on broiled meat or fish. Melt:
      3 tablespoons butter
Add:
      3 tablespoons lemon juice
      ½ teaspoon dry mustard
      Salt and pepper or paprika
      (1 tablespoon Worcestershire
      sauce)

Sauce for Steak II, page 345.

GREEN ONION SAUCE FOR STEAK
Chop:
      Young green onions
Sauté them for 5 minutes in:
      Butter
Season them with:
      Salt and paprika
Add to the butter:
      Worcestershire sauce
Bring the sauce to the boiling point
and serve it.

*Maître d'Hôtel Butter, page 431;
Anchovy Butter, page 258.*

MARCHAND DE VIN SAUCE FOR BROILED STEAK OR RED WINE MUSHROOM SAUCE
6 Servings
Sauté:
      ½ lb. finely sliced mushrooms
in:
      2 tablespoons butter
Add and simmer covered for 10 minutes:
      ½ cup hot stock
In another pan sauté:
      ½ cup sliced onions
in:

2 tablespoons butter
Add and cook covered for 20 minutes:
  1 cup hot stock
  ½ cup dry red wine
Stir until blended a little of the onion stock and:
  2 teaspoons flour
Stir it into the onion mixture. Permit the onions to boil again, then remove them from the fire. Add the mushrooms and season with:
  Salt and paprika
Serve the sauce with:
  Broiled Steak, page 345

WINE SAUCE FOR HAM
Method I. About 1 Cupful
Melt:
  1½ tablespoons butter
Add and brown slowly:
  1½ tablespoons flour
Stir in slowly the contents of:
  1 can consommé: 10½ oz.
Add:
  1 bay leaf
  ⅛ teaspoon dried thyme
Simmer these ingredients for 20 minutes. Strain them. Add:
  1 tablespoon sherry or Madeira

Method II.
This calls for many ingredients but you may omit some or substitute others. Combine:
  1 teaspoon dry mustard
  1 tablespoon brown sugar
  ¼ teaspoon powdered ginger
  A few grains cayenne
  ¼ teaspoon salt
  ¼ teaspoon ground cloves
  1½ cups red wine, preferably port
  ½ cup seedless raisins
  ½ cup blanched slivered almonds
Simmer the sauce covered for 8 minutes. Dissolve:
  2 teaspoons cornstarch
in:
  2 tablespoons cold water
Stir this into the sauce. Let it simmer for 2 minutes. Stir in:
  ¼ cup tart jelly
  1 tablespoon grated orange and lemon rind
  ¼ cup orange juice
  2 tablespoons lemon juice

Wine Butter Sauce, page 258.

RAISIN CIDER SAUCE
About 1½ Cupfuls
Good with hot or cold ham or ham sandwiches.

Combine in a saucepan:
  ¼ cup firmly packed brown sugar
  1½ tablespoons cornstarch
  ⅛ teaspoon salt
Stir in:
  1 cup fresh or bottled cider
  ¼ cup raisins cut in halves
  8 whole cloves
  1 two inch stick cinnamon
Cook and stir these ingredients for 10 minutes. Add:
  1 tablespoon butter
Remove the spices. Serve the sauce very hot.

ORANGE SAUCE FOR GAME
About 2 Cupfuls
Melt:
  3 tablespoons butter
Stir in until browned:
  4 tablespoons flour
Stir in slowly:
  1⅓ cups Stock, page 394
Season with:
  Salt and paprika
Keep the sauce hot over hot water. Shortly before serving add:
  1 tablespoon grated orange rind
  ⅔ cup hot orange juice
  2 tablespoons sherry

CUCUMBER SAUCE
Method I. About 1½ Cupfuls
For fish or meat, preferably cold food.
Beat until stiff:
  ¾ cup heavy sweet or sour cream
If the cream is sweet, add slowly:
  2 tablespoons vinegar or lemon juice
Season the sauce with:
  ¼ teaspoon salt
  ⅛ teaspoon paprika
Pare, seed, cut finely and drain well:
  1 large cucumber
Add it to the sauce.

Method II.
For hot or cold fish.
Pare, seed and grate:
  Cucumbers
Season them with:
  Salt and paprika
  Vinegar

MEXICAN SAUCE
About 1 Cupful
Just what you might expect. You will feel hot inside down to your toes. Place in a small saucepan and simmer until fairly thick:

¾ cup canned tomatoes or about 3
    large skinned and quartered
    fresh tomatoes
6 tablespoons chili sauce
2 teaspoons dry mustard
3 tablespoons grated or prepared
    horseradish
½ teaspoon sugar
¾ teaspoon salt
¼ teaspoon pepper
    A few grains cayenne
¾ teaspoon curry powder
6 tablespoons vinegar
1 teaspoon onion juice
1 sliced clove garlic
Strain the sauce. Add:
    1 teaspoon dried or 1 tablespoon
    fresh Herb, page 833
This may be served—in discreet quantities—by itself, but it combines excel-
lently with hot cream sauce or hot or
cold mayonnaise. Use as much of the
Mexican sauce as you find palatable.

CUMBERLAND SAUCE
Method I. About 1 Cupful
Good over ham.
Stir over hot water until soft:
    1 glass currant jelly
Beat in:
    1 egg yolk
    2 tablespoons vinegar
    ¾ teaspoon dry mustard
    2 tablespoons sugar
    Salt and pepper
Stir the sauce until it is thickened, for
about 15 minutes. You may add:
    ¼ cup raisins

Method II. About 1⅓ Cupfuls
Good with cold meat.
Combine and beat well:
    Grated rind of 2 lemons
    Juice of 2 lemons
    Grated rind of 1 orange
    Juice of 1 orange
    1 tablespoon confectioners' sugar
    1 tablespoon grated horseradish
    or prepared horseradish
    ½ cup currant or plum jelly
If the jelly is very stiff, it may have to
be diluted over heat with 1 or 2 table-
spoonfuls hot water.

CURRANT JELLY AND
CHUTNEY SAUCE
About 1¼ Cupfuls
For game or cold meat.
Heat in a double boiler just before
serving:
    1 glass currant jelly: ¾ cup
Stir in:

½ cup Indian chutney
1 teaspoon lemon juice
1 tablespoon brandy
Salt
Or, make a simplified version of:
    ½ cup jelly
    2 tablespoons horseradish
    ½ teaspoon dry mustard

Currant Jelly Sauce, page 436.

PIQUANT SAUCE FOR COLD
MEAT OR FISH
¾ Cupful
Combine and work to a paste:
    1 tablespoon anchovy paste
    2 tablespoons chopped parsley
    2 tablespoons chopped sour-sweet
    pickles
    1 tablespoon prepared mustard
    Yolks of 2 minced hard-cooked
    eggs or 1 whole egg
Stir in slowly:
    3 tablespoons olive oil
    2 tablespoons vinegar

HARD-COOKED EGG DRESS-
ING FOR COLD MEATS
Cook until hard:
    Eggs
Chop them. Measure them. Chop until
you have about an equal amount of a
mixture of:
    Parsley, thyme and chives
Add to make a paste that will spread
easily:
    French dressing
Season with:
    Garlic
    Salt and pepper

RAVIGOTE BUTTER
Chop until fine:
    2 shallots
    1½ teaspoons fresh tarragon
    1½ teaspoons fresh chives
    1½ teaspoons fresh parsley
Pound all these ingredients in a mortar
or bowl. Work in gradually:
    ¼ cup butter
    Salt if needed
You may add:
    A drop or 2 green vegetable
    coloring

RAW VEGETABLE SAUCE
Combine:
    ¾ cup tomato purée or 2 large raw
    skinned tomatoes (the juice
    pressed from them) mashed
    into a purée

1 medium-sized grated or chopped onion
1 chopped green pepper, seeds and membrane removed
¼ cup chopped celery or 1 teaspoon celery and/or dill seeds
2 tablespoons chopped parsley or chives
½ teaspoon salt
¼ teaspoon freshly ground pepper
(2 tablespoons French dressing)

Chill the sauce for ½ hour. Serve it over bland foods, sweetbreads, cold veal, hot or cold fish.

CRANBERRY HORSERADISH SAUCE

Excellent with hot or cold pork or other meat dishes. Place in a bowl and beat well with a fork:
1 cup Whole Cranberry Sauce, page 443
Add and beat to blend well:
1 tablespoon or more horseradish

FRESH HORSERADISH SAUCE
About ½ Cupful

This, and the following sauce, may be served in beet cups as a garnish for a meat platter.
Combine:
¼ cup fresh grated horseradish
2 teaspoons prepared mustard
2 teaspoons vinegar
1 teaspoon salt
½ teaspoon pepper
1 teaspoon sugar
3 or 4 tablespoons cream

Heat but do not boil the sauce.

SOUR CREAM AND HORSERADISH SAUCE

Beat well:
Thick sour cream
Add a generous amount of:
Grated horseradish, fresh or prepared
Vinegar or lemon, if the horseradish is fresh
Salt if needed

MINT SAUCE
About 1 Cupful

The usual accompaniment to roast lamb. Heat:
3 tablespoons water
Dissolve in it:
1½ tablespoons confectioners' sugar
Cool the sirup and add:
⅓ cup finely chopped mint leaves
½ cup strong vinegar

This is best made ½ hour before serving it.

HOT ORANGE AND LEMON MINT SAUCE
About ⅔ Cupful

For lamb or game.
Combine and stir well:
1 teaspoon grated orange rind
¼ cup orange juice
1 teaspoon grated lemon rind
¼ cup lemon juice
¼ cup fresh chopped mint
1 tablespoon confectioners' sugar
⅛ teaspoon salt
⅛ teaspoon paprika
⅛ teaspoon nutmeg

Place these ingredients over hot water for 30 minutes.

BORDELAISE SAUCE
About 2 Cupfuls

For oysters, sweetbreads, etc. Brown:
2 tablespoons butter
Stir in until brown:
2 tablespoons flour
Stir in gradually:
2 cups stock
3 minced cloves garlic
2 tablespoons chopped onion
2 tablespoons chopped ham
1 bay leaf
1 tablespoon Worcestershire sauce
1 tablespoon catsup
½ teaspoon celery salt

Simmer these ingredients for 5 minutes. Strain the sauce. Season it, if needed, with:
Salt and paprika
Add:
2 tablespoons sherry

Believe it or not, the original recipe called for a grain of asafetida! Why bring that up?

TARTAR SAUCE
Method I. About 1¼ Cupfuls

Usually served with fried scallops, oysters, frog legs, etc.
Combine and beat:
1 teaspoon mustard
⅛ teaspoon pepper
1 teaspoon confectioners' sugar
¼ teaspoon salt
Onion juice
2 egg yolks

Add to these ingredients very slowly as in Mayonnaise Dressing, page 495:
½ cup olive oil
3 tablespoons vinegar

When the sauce is thick add:
>1 tablespoon chopped olives
>1 tablespoon capers
>1 tablespoon chopped cucumber
>pickle
>1 tablespoon chopped parsley

If the parsley is omitted, this sauce will keep for weeks in a cold place.

Method II. About 2 Cupfuls
This unusual Tartar sauce has a flour and stock basis.
Stir:
>⅓ cup flour

into:
>1 cup stock or bouillon

Cook and stir these ingredients until they thicken.
Remove the sauce from the fire. Beat in very slowly:
>2 egg yolks
>1 cup salad oil

Continue to beat while adding:
>2 tablespoons vinegar
>2 tablespoons lemon juice
>1 teaspoon dry mustard
>1 cup pickle relish
>Salt if needed

Chill the sauce thoroughly.

Method III. About 1¼ Cupfuls
Combine and beat to blend:
>¾ cup thick sour cream or
>mayonnaise
>2 tablespoons chopped parsley
>2 tablespoons chopped pickle
>1 tablespoon grated onion or
>chopped chives
>¼ cup chopped olives
>1 tablespoon fresh or 1 teaspoon
>dried tarragon

REMOULADE SAUCE
About 1½ Cupfuls
Mash:
>3 hard-cooked egg yolks

Add and beat with a wire whisk:
>2 raw egg yolks
>1 teaspoon dry mustard
>¼ teaspoon salt
>⅛ teaspoon pepper

Add to these ingredients very slowly as in Mayonnaise Dressing, page 495:
>¾ cup olive oil
>3 tablespoons lemon juice or
>vinegar

When the sauce is thick add:
>¼ cup thick sour cream
>1 tablespoon chopped capers
>1 teaspoon chopped anchovies
>1 tablespoon chopped "fine"
>Herbs, page 832

**REMOULADE SAUCE
SIMPLIFIED**
About 1¾ Cupfuls
Chop until very fine:
>6 tablespoons pickles
>1½ tablespoons capers

Press all moisture from them. Mix them well with:
>2 teaspoons prepared mustard or
>½ teaspoon dry mustard
>1 tablespoon chopped parsley,
>chervil, tarragon and chives
>1½ cups mayonnaise

QUICK MUSTARD SAUCE
About ½ Cupful
Stir:
>2 teaspoons prepared mustard

in:
>½ cup thick cream

Season with:
>¼ teaspoon salt
>⅛ teaspoon paprika
>A pinch curry powder

Stir the sauce over low heat. Heat it but do not permit it to boil. Serve it hot.

MUSTARD SAUCE II
About 1 Cupful
Try this over raw or cooked vegetables or sea food.
Combine:
>6 oz. Italian tomato paste
>1 teaspoon dry mustard
>1 tablespoon sugar
>½ teaspoon salt
>1 tablespoon vinegar
>1 tablespoon drained horseradish
>(1 tablespoon chopped onion,
>chives or fresh herbs)

Mustard Sauce I, page 428.
You will find many good sauces for vegetables on page 327.

**MUSTARD SAUCE FOR BOILED
OR COLD MEATS**
This is in the nature of a relish.
Combine:
>2 teaspoons grated onion
>1 tablespoon prepared mustard
>1½ teaspoons sugar
>1 teaspoon oil
>(1 teaspoon vinegar)

MUSTARD CREAM
A highly seasoned sauce for cold meats or broiled sausages.
Blend gradually:

2 tablespoons or more dry
   mustard
with a little:
   Water
until it is the consistency of thick
cream. Fold this paste into:
   ½ cup heavy cream or evaporated
   milk, whipped
Season the sauce, if desired, with:
   Salt and paprika

BREAD SAUCE OR PANADA
About 3 Cupfuls
Usually served with small roasted wild
birds or roast meat.
Skin:
   A small onion
Stud it with:
   3 whole cloves
Place the onion in a saucepan with:
   2 cups milk
Bring the milk to a boil. Pour it over:
   3 cups fine dry bread crumbs
Place it over hot, not boiling, water
and permit the crumbs to absorb the
milk. Remove the onion. Discard it.
Beat the crumbs with a fork. Season
them with:

¾ teaspoon salt
¼ teaspoon paprika
This should be neither thick nor thin.
Add more bread crumbs or milk to suit
your taste. Cut up and beat in:
   2 tablespoons butter
or you may beat in:
   1 tablespoon butter
and cover the top of the sauce when
served with:
   ½ cup coarse stale bread crumbs
browned in:
   2 tablespoons butter

ASPIC GLAZE FOR MEATS
Use this also for salads and canapés.
Soak:
   1 tablespoon gelatine
in:
   ½ cup meat or vegetable stock
Dissolve it over hot water. Add it to:
   1½ cups stock
Season it mildly. Chill it until it thickens somewhat. Brush it over cold
roast, cold fish, canapés, etc.

Fish Glaze, page 238.

Sauces Made with Canned Soups and Other
Quick Sauces

Good quick sauces may be made with canned soup or, if a household is very
small, for reasons of economy with powdered soup. You may purchase canned
gravies of various kinds and sauces galore, but even the most limited emergency
shelf is apt to boast a tin or two of canned soup—so we shall rank that first as a basis
for emergency gravy.

It is a little difficult to write about canned soups in a sweeping way because they
have not the same consistency. Some are thicker than others, also some people like
a thick gravy and others a thin one. The best I can urge upon you is to make a selection of the same soup made by various companies, to determine your preference,
then keep that particular brand on hand for future use.

The thick soups may be thinned to the consistency you like with milk, cream or
stock. The thinner soups may be thickened by melting a tablespoonful or two of butter in a pan, stirring in the same amount of flour and then slowly stirring in the soup
and cooking it until it boils. Or, you may add a thin paste of flour and water or
stock. See note under rule for making Gravy for Roasts, page 426.

As to seasoning, that is an individual matter. Most soups converted into gravies
require little additional seasoning, but if you like your gravy sharp, add it by all
means. You will find suggestions for the usual, and a few unusual, seasonings in
the section on Gravy, page 424.

SAUCES MADE WITH CANNED
SOUPS
Heat the contents of:
   1 can condensed soup—mushroom, celery, asparagus, tomato,
   etc.: 10½ oz.
It may be just the consistency you like
for gravy. If not, thin it with about:

6 tablespoons milk or stock
Or, thicken, like Cream Sauce, page
428:
   Ready-to-serve soup
with about:
   1½ tablespoons butter and the same
   amount of flour
For a highly seasoned sauce add:

Salt, red pepper, chili, Tabasco
or Worcestershire sauce
For a more sophisticated sauce add,
after removing the sauce from the fire:
2 tablespoons sherry
For a fish sauce dilute the sauce with:
¼ cup or more dry white wine or
add 1 tablespoon lemon juice
Do not permit the sauce to boil after
adding the wine. For a variation add:
¼ teaspoon or more curry powder
or dry mustard
1 tablespoon horseradish or a
pinch or 2 dried herb
For a creole sauce add finely chopped
or grated:
Green pepper, onion and celery
You may add:
Chopped pickles, peppers or
capers
and anything that appeals to you that
will give your sauce distinction.
To achieve this follow your feminine
hunch with abandon. After all, one
need not be inhibited about a sauce
that is to be eaten en famille.

Emergency Brown Sauce, page 435;
Quick Tomato Sauce, page 433; Quick
Tomato Cheese Sauce, page 434.

ONION SOUP SAUCE
Good over bland vegetables—green
beans, cauliflower, etc.
Heat:
Ready-to-serve onion soup
You may thicken it with a little:
Flour
If you do, boil the sauce for 5 minutes.
You may add to it:
Grated cheese

MOCK TURTLE SOUP SAUCE
About 1½ Cupfuls
Good over bland food, noodles, etc.
Heat the contents of:

1 can condensed mock turtle soup:
10½ oz.
Add:
6 tablespoons water

Quick Creole Sauce, page 435; Hot
Mayonnaise II, page 433.

CELERY CHEESE SAUCE
1½ Cupfuls
Stir and heat over low heat:
1 cup condensed celery soup
6 tablespoons milk
2 oz. pimiento cheese
A few grains cayenne

QUICK À LA KING SAUCE
About 1½ Cupfuls
To the rescue whenever this type of
sauce is required.
Sauté until tender:
1 minced green pepper
in:
1 tablespoon butter
Add the contents of:
1 can condensed mushroom soup:
10½ oz.
¼ cup milk
Heat the sauce and add:
1 pimiento cut into strips

ASPARAGUS, CHEESE AND
BACON SAUCE
About 2 Cupfuls
Fine on toast or waffles.
Stir and heat over low heat until the
cheese is melted the contents of:
1 can condensed asparagus soup:
10½ oz.
¾ cup milk
1 oz. grated strong cheese
2 pieces sautéed minced bacon

Currant Jelly Sauce, page 436.

Cooked Fruits To Be Served with Meats

Fruit compote makes a pleasant addition to the meat course provided fruit
juices have not been used in basting the meat. If the rules given below are used,
the fruit retains its shape and vitamins well.

If you wish to save on sugar, only about half as much is needed for the same
degree of sweetness, if the sugar is added after the fruit is tender or when it has
cooled.

RULE FOR STEWING UNPARED FRUIT

Boil:

    2 cups water

Prepare and add:

    1 quart unpared fruit

Simmer it until it is nearly tender.
Add:

    ½ to 1 cup sugar

Cook the fruit until it is tender. This
method will keep the skin soft.

RULE FOR STEWING PARED FRUIT

Boil for 3 minutes:

    2 cups water
    ½ to 1 cup sugar
    ⅛ teaspoon salt

Drop into the boiling sirup about:

    1 quart prepared fruit

Cook it gently until it is tender.

CRANBERRY JELLY

Wash and pick over:

    1 lb. cranberries

Place them in a saucepan. Cover them
with:

    2 cups boiling water

As soon as the water begins to boil
again, cover the saucepan with a lid.
Boil the berries for 3 or 4 minutes, or
until the skins burst. Put them through
a strainer or ricer. Stir in:

    2 cups sugar

Place the berries over heat and bring
them to a rolling boil. If you wish to
have a cranberry sauce, remove them
at once. If you wish to mold the cranberry jelly, boil them for about 5 minutes, then pour them into a wet mold.
These cooking periods are right for
firm berries. Very ripe berries require
a few minutes longer.

SPICED CRANBERRY JELLY

Follow the preceding rule. Add to the
water:

    2 inches stick cinnamon
    2 whole cloves
    ¼ teaspoon salt

WHOLE CRANBERRY SAUCE

Place in a saucepan and stir until the
sugar is dissolved:

    2 cups water
    2 cups sugar

Then boil the sirup for 5 minutes. Pick
over, wash and add:

    1 lb. cranberries

Cook the cranberries uncovered very
gently without stirring until they are
thick and clear. Skim, then pour them
into 1 large or several individual molds,
which have been rinsed in cold water.
Chill until firm. Unmold to serve.
After the cranberries are cooked you
may add:

    2 teaspoons grated orange rind

If you prefer a liquid sauce, cook the
cranberries until the skins pop, for
3 to 5 minutes, then chill and serve the
sauce.

BAKED CRANBERRIES

Wash, drain, then place in an oven-
proof dish:

    1 quart cranberries

Sprinkle them with:

    1¼ cups sugar

Make a hole in the center. Pour into it:

    ½ cup water

Bake the berries covered in a slow
oven 300° for about ¾ hour.

ORNAMENTAL CRANBERRIES

"What is this?" I asked a pretty young
waitress, pointing to an item on the
menu. "Oh!" she said, "that's a garnation."

Wash, drain and pick over:

    1 quart cranberries

Prick each berry with a pin. Combine,
heat and stir until the sugar is dissolved:

    2 cups sugar
    ½ cup water

Add the cranberries to the boiling
sirup. Bake them in a slow oven 325°
for 40 minutes. Spread them on
greased waxed paper until nearly dry,
then roll them in:

    Granulated sugar

You may use them on toothpicks to
stud a baked ham or in any other way
as a "garnation."

CRANBERRY APPLESAUCE

Combine and stir:

    2 cups cranberries
    2 cups quartered apples
    ¾ cup water

Cook these ingredients slowly until the
fruit is soft. Put it through a colander.
Add:

    1 cup sugar

Cook and stir the purée until the sugar
is dissolved. It may be sprinkled with:

    Grated orange rind

UNCOOKED CRANBERRY RELISH OR CONSERVE

This relish is to be served like a compote. It will keep, if placed in a cold

place, for 3 or 4 days. Grind:

1 quart cranberries

Remove the seeds, grind and add:

1 orange, skin and all

Stir in:

2 cups sugar

Place these ingredients in covered jars in the refrigerator. Permit them to ripen for 2 days before using them. Serve the relish with meat, fowl or bread.

FRIED PEACHES OR APRICOTS

Cut into halves and remove the stone from unpeeled:

Fresh peaches or apricots

Sauté the fruit soft side down in:

Butter

Baste it frequently with the drippings. Turn the fruit. Sauté it until it is tender. Sprinkle it with:

Sugar

Cook the fruit until the sugar is melted.

STEWED PEACHES

Pare:

12 large peaches

Leave them whole or cut them in halves and remove the stones.

To cook them follow the rule for Stewing Pared Fruit at the beginning of this chapter.

STEWED APPLES

Pare and core:

6 large apples

Follow the rule for Stewing Pared Fruit at the beginning of this chapter. Add to the sirup:

1 stick cinnamon

If the apples are not tart add:

½ to 1 sliced lemon

STEWED PLUMS

Cut into halves and remove the seeds from, or use whole:

4 cups plums

Drop them into:

1½ cups boiling water

When they are nearly tender add:

½ to 1 cup sugar

Cook them a few minutes longer.

STEWED CHERRIES

Remove the stems from cherries. You may pit the cherries. Follow the preceding rule for Stewed Plums. Cherries require only a few minutes' cooking.

STEWED PEARS

Even the uncompromising Kieffer Pears have been known to respond readily to this treatment.

Pare, quarter and core:

6 large pears

Follow the rule for Stewing Pared Fruit at the beginning of this chapter. Add to the sirup:

2 sticks cinnamon

½ sliced lemon

Or omit the spices and add when the pears are cold:

1 to 3 tablespoons rum or crème de menthe

A little red or green coloring

STEAMED RHUBARB

Wash and cut, without peeling, into 1 inch blocks:

1 quart rhubarb

Place it in the upper part of a double boiler over boiling water. Cover it closely. Steam it for 20 or 30 minutes until it is nearly tender. Do not stir it at any time. Dissolve:

½ to ¾ cup sugar

¼ teaspoon soda

in:

½ cup hot water

Pour this over the rhubarb and steam it for 2 minutes longer.

This is a good and a nice-looking dish.

STEWED RHUBARB

Peel and cut into small pieces:

Rhubarb

Place it in an earthen or enameled dish. Sprinkle it generously with:

Sugar

Use about ½ as much sugar as there is fruit. Permit it to stand for 12 hours or more. Put it in a saucepan and cook it without the addition of water. Simmer it gently until it is tender, or bake it covered in a slow oven 325°.

STEWED RHUBARB AND PINEAPPLE

Wash, peel and cut into 1 inch cubes:

Rhubarb

Pare, cut into 1 inch cubes and add an equal amount of:

Fresh pineapple

Sprinkle with:

Sugar

Use about ½ as much sugar as there is fruit. Permit these ingredients to stand for 1 hour. Cook them without stirring over slow heat until the sugar is dissolved. Increase the heat slightly and cook them until the rhubarb is soft but unbroken. Chill the fruit before serving it.

BAKED RHUBARB
Place in a buttered baking dish alternate layers of:
    Sliced rhubarb
    Sugar
Have a layer of sugar on top. Use about ½ as much sugar as there is fruit. Dot the layers with:
    Butter
Sprinkle them with:
    Grated lemon rind or cinnamon
Bake the rhubarb in a slow oven 300° until it is red.

STEWED BLUEBERRIES
Cook in a very little water:
    Blueberries
When they are nearly tender add:
    A few grains salt
    Sugar
Cook them a minute longer.

BAKED PEACHES
Pare, cut in halves and remove the stones from:
    Firm juicy peaches
Place them in a baking dish. Fill each hollow with:
    ½ teaspoon butter
    1 teaspoon sugar
    A sprinkling of lemon juice
    A dusting of cinnamon or
        nutmeg
Place in the bottom of the dish:
    2 tablespoons water
Bake the peaches for 20 minutes in a moderate oven 350°.

BAKED PEARS
Pare, cut in halves and core:
    Pears
Place them in a baking dish. Sprinkle them with:
    Sugar
Dust them with:
    Cinnamon
Add to the bottom of the dish:
    1 tablespoon water for each pear
Cover them closely and cook them until tender in a very slow oven 300°. Varieties differ in baking time, from 1 to 3 hours. The pears may be dotted with:
    Butter
Seckel and other small pears are good baked whole.

PEARS BAKED IN PINEAPPLE JUICE
4 Servings
Peel, then cut into halves:
    4 pears
Core them. Place them on an oven-proof plate. Sprinkle them with:
    ¼ cup sugar
    1 teaspoon grated orange rind
Pour over them:
    ½ cup pineapple juice
    2 tablespoons lemon juice
You may add:
    ½ inch stick cinnamon or 3 cloves
Cover the pears and bake them in a moderate oven 350° for ½ hour, or until tender. Baste them twice while cooking.

BAKED APPLES
6 Servings
Apples are baked in a hot oven, in a moderate oven and in a very slow one with results that seem to be equally satisfactory to cooks and their victims. The addition of grated lemon rind, lemon juice, cinnamon or nutmeg is recommended when apples lack flavor. Wash and core without cutting through the stem end:
    6 apples
Pare the upper ¼ of each apple. Place them in a baking dish.
Fill each center with about:
    1 tablespoon white or brown sugar
        or a diced marshmallow
    ¼ teaspoon butter
    (8 blanched almonds or other nut
        meats)
Pour into the dish:
    1 tablespoon water for each apple
Cook the apples, covered or uncovered, in a hot oven until they are tender. Baste them frequently. Test them with a straw. The time will depend upon the oven and the apple, 45 minutes or more. They may be served with:
    Cream

See Baked Apples, Pressure Cooked, page 892.

GLAZED APPLES
Prepare by the preceding rule:
    Baked Apples
Sprinkle them with:
    Sugar
Broil them under a moderate flame until the sugar is melted.

FILLED APPLE HALVES
Cut into halves and bake by one of the
preceding rules:
> Cored apples

When cold fill the halves with:
> Mint, currant or cranberry jelly

See Baked Apples and Mincemeat on
this page and Apples with Orange
Juice, page 750, and Index for other
Apple Dishes.

CINNAMON APPLES
4 Servings

Pare and core without cutting through
the stem end:
> 4 Rome Beauty apples

Stir and boil in a saucepan until dissolved:
> ½ cup sugar
> 1 cup water
> ¼ cup cinnamon drops

Add the apples slowly one at a time.
Cook them gently until they are tender. Test them with a straw. Remove
them from the sirup. Fill the hollows
with:
> (Blanched almonds or other nut
> meats and raisins)

Boil the sirup until it falls heavily from
a spoon. Pour it over the apples. Chill
them.

GREEN MINT APPLES
4 Servings

Prepare the preceding:
> Cinnamon Apples

Substitute for the cinnamon drops:
> 2 drops peppermint oil
> A very little green vegetable
> coloring

APPLE CUPS FILLED WITH SWEET POTATOES
These are lovely to look at and good to
eat. I like them tart. They may be prepared in advance—another virtue.
Prepare by the preceding rule, omitting the cinnamon drops:
> Large red or yellow apples

When cool enough to handle, hollow
the apples. Reserve the removed pulp.
Prepare by the rule on page 310:
> 1¼ cups Mashed Sweet Potatoes

Mash the apple pulp and add it to the
sweet potatoes with:
> 1 or 2 tablespoons brown sugar

Fill the apples. Decorate the tops with:
> (Nut meats)

Refrain if possible but, if you cannot,
cover the tops with marshmallows. I
am not putting them in the ingredient
column because they are less likely to
be seen here. Place the apples in a
baking dish with a little of the apple
sirup. Reheat them in a moderate oven
375° for 10 minutes. If the apples are
prepared in advance, cover them with
waxed paper. If they have become
chilled, it will take longer to reheat
them. Baste them with apple sirup. If
there is no other decoration, garnish
the tops with:
> Sprigs of parsley

BAKED APPLES AND MINCEMEAT
Wash and core without cutting through
the stem end:
> Apples

Hollow them—leave a shell ⅓ inch
thick. Chop the pulp and combine it
with:
> Mincemeat

Add:
> Brown sugar—allowing 1 table-
> spoon or more for each apple

Fill the apples. Place them in a baking
dish with:
> Water—allowing 1 tablespoon
> for each apple

Sprinkle the apples with:
> Brown sugar

Bake them in a moderate oven 350°
until they are done. Baste them frequently. These apples may be served
as a dessert with or without:
> Hard Sauce, page 753

Flavor the sauce with:
> Brandy or sherry

BAKED PEACHES AND MINCEMEAT
Drain:
> Canned peaches

Fill each half with:
> Mincemeat

Place the peach halves in a shallow pan
with enough peach juice to keep them
from scorching. Bake them in a slow
oven for 25 or 30 minutes. Serve them
with roast fowl or ham.

BROILED PEACHES
This and the above—Baked Peaches
and Mincemeat—make a good garnish
for a meat platter.
Drain:
> Canned peaches

Place them, hollow side up, in a shallow pan. Place in each hollow:
> A dab of butter

Sprinkle each peach lightly with:
Salt and cinnamon
Broil the peaches under moderate heat until they are light brown. You may fill them with:
Cranberry or other jelly

See Index for other Peach Dishes.

APPLESAUCE
Wash and cut into quarters:
Apples
Place them in a saucepan and partly cover them with water. Old apples require more water than new ones. New apples require very little water. Add to tasteless apples:
Sliced lemon
Canned applesauce may be seasoned in the same way.
Stew the apples until they are tender. Put them through a purée strainer or ricer. Return the strained apples to the saucepan. Add enough:
Sugar
to make them palatable. Boil them for 3 minutes. Sprinkle the applesauce, if desired, with:
Cinnamon
Serve it hot or cold. If served hot add:
1 or 2 teaspoons butter
If served cold add:
½ teaspoon vanilla or a few drops almond extract
If applesauce is to be served with pork add:
1 or 2 tablespoons horseradish

SAUTÉED OR "FRIED" APPLES
The following recipe is good only when made with tart, well-flavored apples. Then it is delicious.
Core and slice:
6 large apples
Melt in a skillet over quick heat:
2 tablespoons butter or bacon drippings
When it is hot, fold in the apples. Cover them until they are steaming. Sprinkle the apples with:
½ cup sugar
⅛ teaspoon salt
Cook them covered over a gentle fire until the apples are nearly tender. If the apples are dry, a little hot water may be added. Uncover them and cook them until they are tender. Add additional butter as needed. Serve the apples with a meat course or with:
Bacon
Ripe firm peaches peeled may be sub-

stituted for the apples in this rule. Onion lovers may begin making this dish by placing a layer of onions, about 1 cupful, in the butter. Cook them slowly for 5 minutes. Season with salt and paprika. Add the apples and proceed as directed.

Apple and Onion Dish, page 185.

APPLE RINGS
Wash, core and cut crosswise into slices:
3 large perfect cooking apples
Heat in a skillet:
3 tablespoons bacon fat or butter
Place in it a single layer of apple rings. Sprinkle them lightly with:
Powdered sugar
Add to the skillet:
2 tablespoons water
Cover the skillet and cook the apples until they are tender. Remove the cover and brown the rings on both sides. Serve them hot, the centers filled with:
Bright red jelly
Or dust the rings with:
Cinnamon

APPLES STUFFED WITH SAUERKRAUT
4 Servings
Pare the tops of:
4 large baking apples
Remove the pulp and discard the core, leaving a ½ inch shell. Chop the pulp, add to it:
2 cups drained canned or cooked sauerkraut
⅛ teaspoon pepper
¼ teaspoon caraway seeds
Salt as needed
Fill the shells. Place them in a dish with 4 tablespoonfuls water or dry wine. Bake them in a moderate oven 375° until tender. Baste them frequently.

PICKLED CANNED APRICOTS
Drain the contents of:
A No. 2½ can whole peeled apricots
Add to the juice and simmer for 10 minutes:
⅓ cup vinegar
2 sticks cinnamon
2 or 3 pieces gingerroot
2 whole cloves
Add the apricots and simmer them for 10 minutes. Chill before serving.

BAKED BANANAS

Butter, sugar, lemon juice and salt are called for in most recipes for baked bananas. These additions are good but optional. Peel:

Bananas

Place them in a well-greased baking dish. Bake them in a moderate oven 350° until they are very tender, about 30 minutes. If desired, sprinkle them after baking with:

Lemon juice
Confectioners' sugar
(Salt)

Bananas may be baked in their skins. Bake them in a moderate oven 375° for about 20 minutes.

FRIED BANANAS

4 Servings

Combine:

¾ teaspoon salt
3 tablespoons cream
1 slightly beaten egg

Peel, then cut into 1 inch pieces:

4 firm bananas

Roll them in the egg mixture, then in:

3 tablespoons crushed cornflakes,
dry bread crumbs or corn meal

Permit them to dry for ½ hour. Fry the bananas in deep fat (page 542).

SAUTÉED BANANAS

Peel and cut in half and then into lengthwise slices:

Bananas

They may be sprinkled with:

Lemon juice

Dredge them with:

Seasoned flour

Heat in a skillet:

Butter or bacon drippings

Sauté the bananas in the fat. Serve them very hot sprinkled with:

Confectioners' sugar

SAUTÉED OR BROILED PINEAPPLE

Drain and dry between towels:

Large slices canned pineapple

Cut them into halves. Dip them in:

Flour

Heat in a skillet:

Butter or bacon drippings

Sauté the pineapple in the fat. Serve the slices hot. Use them with:

Parsley

to garnish a meat platter.

To broil the slices, dip them in:

Melted butter
Brown sugar

Melt the sugar under moderate heat.

GLAZED PINEAPPLE

Drain:

Canned pineapple slices or
spears

Dip them in:

Brown sugar

Brown them by cooking them in hot:

Bacon drippings, pan drippings
or butter

or dust them with:

Grated cheese
A few grains red pepper

Broil or bake the pineapple in a moderate oven to melt the cheese.

SPICED PINEAPPLE

Drain the contents of:

1 No. 3 can pineapple

Reserve the juice. Combine it with:

1 cup sugar
1 cup vinegar
2 sticks cinnamon
20 whole cloves

Boil these ingredients for 10 minutes. Add the pineapple slices. Simmer them in the sirup for 10 minutes.

GRILLED PINEAPPLE

4 Servings

Drain:

8 pineapple spears

Wrap around them:

8 slices bacon

Fasten the slices with toothpicks. Broil the bacon under moderate heat.

BOILED OR STEWED ORANGES

6 Servings

Wash and cut into halves or thick slices crosswise:

3 navel oranges

Place them in a saucepan. Pour over them:

Boiling water to cover

Cook them for 1 hour. Drain them well. Discard the water. Cook for 5 minutes:

1 cup sugar
1¼ cups water
3 tablespoons lemon juice

Place the oranges in the sirup. Cook them until they are tender, for about 1 hour. Place them in a jar in the sirup. Keep them in a cold place until ready to use them. The centers may be slightly hollowed and filled with:

Crushed pineapple, chopped nut
meats, maraschino cherries or a
dab tart jelly

Good served with baked ham, spoon bread and a green salad.

BAKED ORANGES
Method I.
Select medium-sized:
   Oranges
Soak them for 12 hours in cold water.
Cut off the tops and take out the cores.
Loosen the peel with a knife to the
depth of 1½ inches. Fill the centers
with:
   Sugar
   1 tablespoon butter
Place the oranges in a baking pan ½
full of water, cover them and bake
them slowly until they are done, for
about 2 hours, in a 325° oven. Remove
the cover and brown them slightly.
They may be topped with:
   Marshmallows
The marshmallows may be roasted.
As I do not belong to the marshmallow
school of cooking, I prefer seasoning
the oranges with:
   Sherry
The juice in the pan may be thickened
with:
   Flour (see Gravy, page 426)
Heat it to the boiling point, stir it
constantly and flavor it with sherry.

Method II.
Wash:
   Thin-skinned oranges of even
   size
Soak them for 12 hours in cold water.
Cut a slice from the top of each orange
and remove the meat. Remove the fiber
and the seeds from the pulp and chop
it. Add an equal measure of:
   Crushed drained pineapple
Sweeten it with:
   Sugar
Fill the shell with the mixture. Put on
each orange:
   1 tablespoon butter
Place them in a baking dish with a
little pineapple juice. Cover them
closely and bake them in a slow oven
325° until the skins are tender, for
about 2 hours. Refill the shells as the
filling cooks down and baste the
oranges frequently with:
   Pineapple juice

ORANGE COMPOTE
4 Servings
Cut the yellow rind off:
   2 California oranges
Cut into thin slices, add to it and boil
for 20 minutes:
   1 cup water
   ¾ cup sugar
   ⅛ teaspoon salt

Skin and remove membrane (page 472)
from the 2 oranges and from:
   3 additional oranges
Place the sections in a serving bowl.
Pour the hot sirup and rind over them.
Chill the compote. You may add to it
before serving:
   1 tablespoon rum or liqueur

CANNED PEARS, PEACHES OR APRICOTS
Drain:
   Canned pears, peaches or
   apricots
Fill them with:
   Mint or other jelly
Use them to garnish a platter or plate.
You may add butter to the fruit and
heat it gently before adding the jelly.
Whole canned apricots seeded are
good stuffed with cream cheese, to
which you may add grated onion or
chopped nut meats.

ORANGE SLICES WITH JELLY OR CRANBERRY JELLY
Wash and cut into ⅓ inch slices:
   2 oranges
Remove the seeds. Cover the slices
with:
   Tart jelly, mint or Cranberry
   Jelly, page 443
Mold the cranberry jelly in a straight
glass. Unmold it, cut it into slices and
cover the orange slices with the jelly.
Try to have it the same size as the
orange slices. Decorative on a platter
or for individual plate service.

BOILED KUMQUATS
Place:
   1 quart kumquats
in water to cover well. Bring them to
the boiling point. Drain them. Repeat
this process twice so that the kumquats
will have been boiled in 3 waters. Boil
them in the last water until they are
tender. Boil for 5 minutes.
   ¾ cup water
   2 cups sugar
Cook the kumquats in this sirup for 5
minutes. The kumquats may be served
whole or they may be cut into halves,
in which case remove the seeds. Chill
the kumquats thoroughly. Use them
as a garnish for a meat plater or in
salads.

Kumquat Salad, page 473.

FROSTED GRAPES

Very decorative on top of a Christmas basket or fruit bowl.
Beat until slightly frothy:
    1 egg white
Spread it on a bunch of grapes. Sprinkle them with:

Granulated sugar

Permit the sugar to dry. Tie a bow of silver or white gauze ribbon around the main stem of the grapes. You may shock the garden club by using sprays of ivy as a garnish. Very pretty, if somewhat irregular.

Dried Fruits

Modern methods of dehydrating have removed the necessity of long soaking of dried fruits. Wash them quickly in several waters or until the water is clear. See Index for dishes calling for diced fruits.

APRICOTS

Wash:
    1 lb. dried apricots
Add:
    4 cups water
Simmer the fruit for 35 minutes. Add:
    1 to 2 cups sugar
Boil the fruit 5 minutes longer.

FIGS

Wash and remove the stems from:
    1 lb. dried figs
Add:
    Cold water to cover well
    1½ tablespoons lemon juice
    A piece of lemon rind
    (A large piece gingerroot)
Stew the figs covered until they are soft. Drain them. Measure the juice. Add:
    ½ as much sugar as there is juice
Simmer the sirup until it is thick. Add:
    1 tablespoon lemon juice
Replace the figs in the sirup. Cook them for 1 minute. Cool them. Add:
    (1 tablespoon sherry)
Chill them and serve them with:
    Cream

PRUNES

Cover with hot water and soak for 2 hours:
    1 lb. dried prunes
Bring them to the boiling point in the water in which they were soaked. Cook them gently for ½ hour. Add:
    ¼ cup or more sugar
Cook them 10 minutes longer. You may add to prunes while cooking:
    ½ sliced lemon
    1 stick cinnamon

PRUNES WITH WINE

4 Servings
Cook by the above rule until almost tender:
    ½ lb. prunes
Add:
    3 tablespoons sugar

Cook them 5 minutes longer. Remove from the heat and add:
    ¼ cup or more sherry or
    ½ to ¾ cup port wine
    6 very thin slices lemon
Place the prunes in a screw-top jar. Chill them thoroughly. Shortly before serving the prunes may be pitted and filled with:
    Halves of walnuts or blanched almonds

PRUNES FOR DRESSINGS

These are best steamed until soft, but boiling water may be poured over prunes and they may be soaked in it for 12 hours. Remove pits.

PRUNES OR APRICOTS ON SKEWERS

Steam until nearly tender in a double boiler or in a covered colander over boiling water:
    Large prunes or apricots
Remove the stones. Stuff the prunes or apricots with prunes or with pieces of:
    Canned drained pineapple
    Unbroken nut meats
Place 2 or more prunes on a skewer. Surround them with:
    Slices of bacon
Place them on a broiler under a moderate flame. Turn them frequently. Cook them until the bacon is crisp.
Or, alternate on skewers:
    Steamed apricots and prunes
Pit the prunes. They may be stuffed as suggested above. Roll the skewers in:
    Melted butter
    Brown sugar
Bake them in a greased pan in a moderate oven 325° to 350° with a roast, duck, etc., for about 15 minutes. Turn them once. Sprinkle them with:
    Brown sugar
Broil the fruit under moderate heat until glazed.

Salads

I remember the final scene of a medieval Maeterlink play. The stage is strewed with those dead or dying. The sweet young heroine whimpers, "I am not happy here." Then the head of the house, or what remains of it, an ancient noble, asks quaveringly, "Will there be a salad for supper?"

Nor can I forget the kindly prelate in Willa Cather's "Death Comes to the Archbishop." Wherever he went, no matter how torrid the climate, how dry the soil, he tended carefully a few leaves and herbs that would provide him with a salad.

I have seen the most pathetic little bunches of wilted greens in rural English towns marked "lettuces"; and a soldier writing to me from abroad said, "I long for salads. I dream of great mountains of lettuce which I climb and climb to slide blissfully down the other side on the Roquefort dressing."

Great piles of green globes, to be decimated by nightfall, are a daily sight in our markets. They supply an entire urban population with country succulence. There is an ever-increasing demand for salads of all kinds, and a greater and greater appreciation of their contribution to our gastronomical enjoyment and our improved health.

Tossed Salads

The general acceptance of ready-made salad dressing has deprived many of us of a function that was once a matter of routine—the making of French dressing at the table. The prerogative of presiding over cruets, seasonings and greens was exercised by either the host or the hostess. If the host officiated it was apt to have a markedly meticulous and conversational quality. Methods of mixing the dressing differed with individual taste, but there was no question of the importance of the moment or of its dignity.

Salad making is always important. Ingredients prepared long in advance suffer a loss of nutritive value. Salads dressed long in advance lose their chief charm by becoming limp. To serve one of the choicest treats of the table take great care to have ingredients fresh, cold, crisp and dry.

Wash the greens several hours in advance and dry them thoroughly by shaking them in a colander, drying them between towels or by whirling them in a wire lettuce basket, a job often relegated to the small fry. Keep the greens well chilled until ready to serve. It is also usual to tear rather than cut the greens if you desire smaller pieces. Dress salads a split second before serving them. Toss them lightly but well.

From the standpoint of nutrition as well as gastronomy you will improve a tossed salad by giving it a preliminary coating of oil. About 1 tablespoonful of salad oil will coat a medium-sized head of lettuce. Toss it until every leaf is completely coated with oil. Then follow up with dressing for further tossing. If the salad is mixed on this principle it will stay crisp, although it is usually eaten too rapidly to prove it. The dressing whether freshly made or freshly taken off the shelf should be ready to be added to the greens. The less time that elapses between the addition of vinegar or salt to the leaves, even in wilted salads, the more vitamins and flavor will be retained.

Place the salad leaves in an ample bowl, preferably wooden, and toss them repeatedly by lifting them gently with a large fork and spoon, again preferably

451

wooden, until they are thinly but completely coated. At this point additional dressing, condiments and trimmings may be added to give that endless variation which is one of the chief charms of salad.

A little garlic is one of the most essential flavorings. A wit has said there is no such thing, but there are 2 ways of giving to salad a delicate touch of this pungent product. Split a clove of garlic and rub the inside of the salad bowl with it, or rub a rather dry crust or toasted piece of bread on all sides with a split clove of garlic. This is called a "chapon." Place the bread in the bowl with the salad ingredients. Add the dressing and toss the salad lightly to distribute the flavor. You may remove the chapon. Serve the salad at once.

It is customary to wipe wooden salad bowls until dry, not to wash them. Garlic as well as other flavoring seasons the bowl as well as the salad.

Gourmets treasure their old well-seasoned salad bowls. A great epicure, the late Charles Rector, made a special provision so that his bowl, his choicest possession, would go to a truly appreciative friend.

A bit of cream, catsup, strong meat stock, horseradish, anchovy or other canned fish oil, potato or cheese may transfigure an otherwise commonplace dish. Chopped chives, parsley or other fresh or dried herbs (see page 833) may make it the success of the meal.

Sliced hard-cooked eggs or radishes, chopped olives, nut meats, pimiento or green pepper, sardelle, anchovy, slivered cheese, ham, grated carrots, cut-up celery, onions pickled, grated or as juice, and many other additions may be made to French dressing, boiled salad dressing or mayonnaise.

It is unwise to add cut-up tomatoes to a tossed salad as their juices thin the dressing. Dress them separately and use them for garnishing the salad bowl. The French cut tomatoes in vertical slices. They bleed less this way. Another nice last-minute addition are small hot Croutons, page 422, placed over a tossed salad just before serving.

CLEANING OF SALAD GREENS

To prepare lettuce, separate the leaves and wash them thoroughly. With Iceberg lettuce this is difficult unless you core the solid part of the stem and hold the head upside down under running

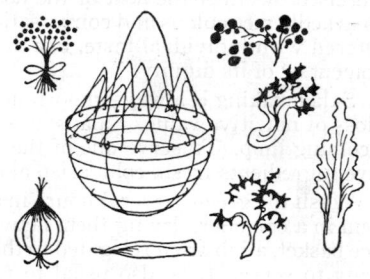

After careful washing, dry the lettuce between towels or in a salad basket.

water. The water pressure pushes the leaves apart without bruising them. Boston and field lettuces must be inspected carefully for grit and sand. Many seasonal lettuces are worth trying when available as their texture and flavors differ markedly.

LETTUCE OR MIXED SALAD WITH SOUR CREAM

4 Servings

Chill:

½ cup sour cream

Add:

¼ teaspoon salt

A fresh grating of pepper

You may add:

1 teaspoon lemon juice

1 teaspoon grated onion or 2
  tablespoons chopped chives
2 tablespoons chopped parsley
Other herbs, fresh or dried, or seeds
like dill, caraway or fennel, may be
added.
Immediately before serving toss this
dressing into a mixed salad or lettuce
leaves.

LETTUCE AND EGGS WITH ANCHOVIES
6 Servings
Rub a bowl with:
  Garlic
Place in it:
  1 head lettuce, separated
Peel, slice and add:
  3 hard-cooked eggs
Drain and chop:
  6 or 8 anchovies
Toss the salad in:
  ⅓ cup French Dressing (page 491)
Have ready:
  2 skinned sliced tomatoes
to add at the last minute as a garnish
for the salad. Serve it at once.

LETTUCE AND HERRING SALAD
4 Servings
Change these ingredients to suit yourself. Add hard-cooked eggs, substitute
pickled beets for the carrots and celery,
etc. Place in a salad bowl:
  1 head lettuce, separated
  ½ cup grated carrots
  ¼ cup chopped celery
  1 chopped pickled herring
Toss the salad in a bowl with:
  ¼ cup French dressing
seasoned with:
  Catsup or chili sauce
Serve it at once. If the herring is not
available, see Beet and Anchovy
Dressing, page 493.

SALAD CAESAR
4 Servings
This California recipe calls for ½ cupful of olive oil, none other, in which a
clove of garlic, peeled and sliced, has
been placed for at least 24 hours.
Prepare:
  1 cup cubed French bread
Toast the cubes. Place them in a bowl.
Pour over them.
  2 tablespoons garlic oil, see above
Cut up (yes, cut up):
  2 heads romaine

Place the romaine in a salad bowl.
Sprinkle over it:
  1½ teaspoons salt
  ¼ teaspoon dry mustard
  A generous grating of black
    pepper
Add:
  3 tablespoons wine vinegar
  6 tablespoons olive oil
Cook gently in simmering water for
1½ minutes:
  1 egg
Drop the contents from the shell onto
the ingredients in the bowl. Add the
croutons and:
  2 tablespoons or more grated
    Parmesan cheese
Toss the salad well. Serve it at once.

WESTERN SALAD
4 to 6 Servings
Similar to the preceding Salad Caesar
with the addition of cheese.
Place in a cup and set aside for several
hours:
  ¼ cup salad oil
  1 halved clove garlic
Remove the garlic. Toast:
  2 cups cubed bread
Place in a large bowl in the order
given:
  6 cups crisp salad greens
  3 tablespoons salad oil
  1½ teaspoons Worcestershire
    sauce
  ½ teaspoon freshly grated pepper
  1½ teaspoons salt
  2 tablespoons grated Parmesan
    cheese
  2 tablespoons crumbled Blue
    cheese
  1 or 2 egg yolks
  ¼ cup lemon juice
Toss and toss the salad. Add the croutons after dipping them quickly in the
garlic oil, see above. Toss the salad
lightly. Serve it at once.

WATER CRESS SALAD
Water cress in France is the invariable
accompaniment to a roast chicken. In
America it is one of our most interesting greens and it is frequently available in the wild. Eating it, however, is
often discouraged by the fact that it
may be growing in polluted water. To
settle any doubts you may have, soak
the cress first in 2 quarts of water to
which 1 tablet of Chlorazene, Hala-
zone or its equivalent has been dissolved. Then rinse the cress in clear

water. Dry and chill it before serving.
The tough ends are cut off before it is
tossed, page 451.

WATER CRESS WITH SOUR CREAM DRESSING
4 Servings
Wash according to preceding recipe,
dry in a cloth and place in a refrigerator for 1 hour or more:
 Water cress
There should be about 4 cupfuls. Immediately before serving cut off the
coarse stems. Place the cress in a
bowl. Pour over it the following dressing:
 1 cup sour cream
 1 tablespoon vinegar or lemon
  juice
 ½ teaspoon salt
 Freshly ground black pepper
 ½ teaspoon celery seed
Serve it at once.

SPINACH SALAD
Method I. 6 Servings
Wash well:
 4 cups young spinach
Dry it. Crisp it in the refrigerator.
Shred the spinach and toss it, page 451,
in:
 ¼ cup French dressing
to which you may add:
 1 teaspoon anchovy paste
Garnish it with:
 Grated hard-cooked egg
 Chopped parsley or chives

Method II. 6 Servings
Wash young spinach until you have
about:
 4 cups spinach leaves
Use the old tougher leaves for cooking. Wash the tender leaves in cold
water until they are free from all grit
and dirt. Drain them well. Dry them
between towels. Cut them into 1 inch
strips. Set them in the refrigerator to
chill. Combine and pour over them:
 2 tablespoons olive oil
 1 tablespoon lemon juice
 ½ teaspoon salt
 ⅛ teaspoon pepper
Toss the leaves. Chop and add:
 1 hard-cooked egg
Place the spinach in a bowl. Garnish
it with:
 Sliced tomatoes
 (Well-drained asparagus)
Serve with:
 Sweet or Sour Cream Dressing
 for Vegetable Salad, page 496
 Chef's Mayonnaise, page 495

WILTED LETTUCE, DANDELIONS, SPINACH OR OTHER GREENS
4 Servings
Sauté:
 4 or 5 slices bacon
Remove from the pan. Cut the bacon
into small pieces. Or use:
 2 tablespoons melted butter,
  drippings or oil
Add to the drippings:
 ¼ cup mild vinegar
 (1 teaspoon chopped fresh Herbs,
  page 833)
Heat this and add the bacon. You
may add at this time:
 (1 teaspoon grated onion)
Pour the dressing while hot over:
 1 head lettuce, separated, or
  other greens
Serve it at once from a warm bowl onto warm plates garnished with:
 Sliced hard-cooked eggs

WILTED LETTUCE WITH CREAM DRESSING
4 Servings
Follow the above rule for:
 Wilted Greens
Use only:
 2 tablespoons vinegar
Add:
 ½ cup thick cream
 ⅛ teaspoon dry mustard

CELERY CABBAGE SALAD
Wash well, then crisp:
 1 stalk celery cabbage
Cut it crosswise into shreds. Serve it
very cold with:
 French dressing
This cabbage combines superbly with:
 Water cress
Use any convenient proportion. You
may garnish the salad with:
 Pickled Beets, page 461

COMBINATION SALAD
Rub a large salad bowl with:
 Garlic
Place in it:
 Lettuce leaves
 Sliced cucumbers
 Pitted shredded ripe olives
 Shredded green pepper
 Diced celery with leaves
 Minced onion and parsley
 Fresh or dried herbs or fennel,
  dill, celery or caraway seeds
Dress the salad with:
 French dressing

Garnish it with:
    Sliced or quartered tomatoes
Serve it at once.

CHEF SALAD
Rub a salad bowl with:
    Garlic
Place in it:
    Lettuce leaves
    Cut-up anchovies
    Chopped pitted ripe olives
    Sliced radishes
    Sliced hard-cooked eggs
    Shredded Swiss cheese
Dress the salad with:
    French Dressing I, page 491
Garnish it with:
    Peeled and quartered tomatoes

SMITH SALAD
Combine:
    Lettuce
    Endive
    Romaine
    Water cress
Cut into narrow strips:
    Salami
    Sautéed bacon
    Anchovies
    Swiss cheese
Dice and add:
    Raw cauliflower
    Cooked string beans
Marinate these ingredients for ½ hour in:
    French dressing
Serve the salad half wilted.

RAW VEGETABLE SALAD
Chop or put through a grinder in any desired amounts:
    Young spinach
    Carrots
    Celery
    Cabbage
    Onions
Moisten these ingredients with:
    French dressing or French
    Dressing with Potato, page 492,
    or thin mayonnaise
Shape them into mounds. Serve the salad with or without additional dressing. Garnish the mounds with:
    Stuffed olives
    Sliced pimiento
    Nut meats

RAW VEGETABLE AND FRUIT SALAD
Follow the above rule. Use, in addition to the vegetables, cut-up apples,

peaches, raisins, pears, nut meats, olives in any combination that appeals to you. Serve as directed above.

COLE SLAW
6 Servings
Remove the outer leaves and the core from:
    A small head of cabbage
Shred or chop the remainder, cutting only as much as is needed for immediate use. Formerly one soaked the chopped cabbage in ice water for 1 hour. If you do, drain it well, dry it between towels and chill it. Immediately before serving it, moisten the cabbage with:
    French dressing, boiled dressing,
    boiled sour cream dressing, equal
    parts of mayonnaise and chili
    sauce, or thick cream, sweet or
    sour, vinegar, salt and sugar
To the last you may add:
    Chopped anchovies
    Dill, caraway or celery seed
    Chopped parsley, chives or other
    herbs
Red cabbage may be used. Very finely shredded red and white cabbage may be combined with good effect. Pared and diced apples, pineapple, etc., may be added.

COLE SLAW IN TOMATO ASPIC RING
Prepare by the above rule:
    Cole slaw
Combine it as directed with:
    Dressing, preferably Sour
    Cream, page 496
    Blanched chopped almonds
Place it in a:
    Tomato Aspic Ring, page 476
Serve it garnished with:
    Parsley

COLE SLAW WITH ROQUEFORT DRESSING
4 Servings
This is based on a Herman Smith rule. I owe him a great deal as a friend and a cook. His splendid books "Stina" and "Kitchens Near and Far," with which all lovers of good eating and reading should be familiar, are inspirational.
Shred finely:
    1½ cups young cabbage
Peel and cut into long, narrow strips:
    2 medium-sized apples: 1 cup
In order to keep them from discoloring sprinkle them with:
    Lemon juice

Prepare the following Roquefort
dressing: Combine:
> ¼ lb. Roquefort or crumbled Blue
> cheese
> 1 tablespoon vinegar
> 2 tablespoons grated American
> cheese
> 1 tablespoon finely minced chives
> or onions
> A pinch of salt
> A generous grinding of black
> pepper

Beat until stiff:
> 1 cup sour cream

Fold in the cheese mixture. Pour the
whole over the cabbage and apple.
Toss the salad lightly until blended.
Serve it at once garnished with:
> Parsley

HOT SLAW WITH APPLE
6 Servings
Place in a stewpan:
> 3 cups shredded cabbage

Add:
> 3 tablespoons vinegar
> 2 tablespoons water
> 1 tablespoon sugar
> 1 teaspoon caraway or celery
> seed
> 1 teaspoon salt
> 2 tablespoons butter

Cook and stir these ingredients over
quick heat until they boil. Reduce the
heat to a low flame. Stir in:
> 1 large peeled grated apple

Heat the slaw for 1 minute longer.

COLE SLAW, APPLES AND NUTS
6 Servings
Prepare:
> 1 cup shredded cabbage
> 1 cup diced apples or pineapple

Combine these ingredients with:
> ½ cup walnut or pecan meats
> ¾ cup mayonnaise or Sour Cream
> Dressing, page 496

TOSSED COLE SLAW
8 Servings
Shortly before serving time cut into
the thinnest shreds possible:
> A small head of cabbage

Remove the core if you like. Place the
cabbage in a deep bowl. You may add:
> (Fresh herbs, chopped parsley,
> chives, etc.)

Beat until stiff:
> ¾ cup whipping cream

Fold in:

> ½ teaspoon celery seed
> ¾ teaspoon salt
> ½ teaspoon sugar
> ¼ teaspoon freshly ground black
> pepper

Fold in until the dressing is palatable:
> About 1½ teaspoons wine or
> cider vinegar

Pour it over the cabbage. Toss it
quickly until it is well coated. Serve it
at once with:
> Tomatoes or in an Aspic Ring,
> page 476

COLE SLAW, CELERY AND OLIVES
8 Servings
Shred:
> 4 cups cabbage

Dice:
> 1½ cups celery

Peel and mince:
> 1 small onion

Seed and chop:
> ½ green pepper

Chill these ingredients. Immediately
before serving moisten them with:
> Mayonnaise

to which add:
> ¼ cup chili sauce
> 10 sliced pimiento olives

GINGHAM SALAD WITH COTTAGE CHEESE
4 Servings
Place in a mixing bowl and toss:
> 1½ cups coarsely chopped young
> spinach leaves
> 2 cups shredded red cabbage
> ⅓ teaspoon salt
> ¼ teaspoon celery seed
> 3 tablespoons chopped olives
> or chives
> 1 cup cottage cheese

Place these ingredients on:
> 4 large lettuce leaves

Serve the salad with:
> French dressing

APPLE AND SAUERKRAUT SALAD
4 Servings
Combine:
> 2 cups drained raw sauerkraut
> 2 thinly sliced apples
> 2 tablespoons lemon juice or dry
> wine
> Freshly grated black pepper
> (1 tablespoon chopped chives or
> onions)

To this you may add celery or other
ingredients.

SAUERKRAUT SALAD

Roll raw drained sauerkraut in lettuce leaves. Use them as a garnish on a hot or cold meat platter. You may sprinkle the kraut with caraway seed or chopped chives.

SAUERKRAUT OR BEAN SPROUT SALAD

Sauerkraut or bean sprouts, drained, may be added to any green salad and tossed along with the other ingredients. Good with sour cream—but then what isn't?

CELERY SALAD

Wash and chill:
> Celery

Cut it into small crosswise pieces. You may add:
> Chopped sweet red or green peppers

Serve it moistened with:
> French dressing, mayonnaise or boiled salad dressing

to which you may add:
> (Sour cream and herbs)

Celeriac or Celery Root Salad, page 464.

RULE FOR SKINNING TOMATOES

A bit of tomato skin was once as much out of place at a dinner table as a bowie knife. The discovery that tomato skins contain highly valued vitamins makes them salonfähig, so whether to serve tomatoes skinned or unskinned rests with the hostess' sense of delicacy or her desire for health. Wash tomatoes. Skin them by one of the following methods:

I.

Rub the surface of very ripe tomatoes with the back of a knife, then pull off the skin with a knife.

II.

Immerse tomatoes in boiling water for 2 minutes. Drain them and skin them.

III.

Turn a tomato on a fork over heat. The skin will crack and it is then easily removed.

TOMATO SALAD

Skin:
> Chilled tomatoes

Cut them from the top into quarters or eighths, but do not cut them all the way through, or slice the tomatoes. Serve them on:
> Lettuce

with:
> French dressing

The centers may be filled with:
> Cream cheese
> Nut meats, etc.
> (Diced cucumbers)
> (Chopped celery)

Substitute for French dressing, if desired:
> Mayonnaise, boiled sour cream dressing, anchovy dressing, etc.

CHILLED CANNED TOMATOES

Chill the contents of a can of:
> Whole tomatoes

or use the firm part of any canned tomatoes. Place them in individual dishes. Sprinkle them with:
> Celery salt and salt
> Lemon juice
> Brown sugar

or anything you like. The main thing is to serve them cold.

FRENCH TOMATO SALAD

Cut into very thin slices vertically:
> 6 medium unpeeled tomatoes

Place them so that they overlap around a cold platter, or across it. Pour over them a dressing of:
> 4 tablespoons oil
> 1 tablespoon vinegar
> 1 teaspoon salt
> Freshly ground black pepper
> ¼ cup minced parsley
> 2 minced shallots or green onions

Use only the white part of the onions. You may substitute grated onion.

TOMATO AND ONION OR CUCUMBER SALAD

Skin and chill:
> Medium-sized tomatoes

Cut 5 or 6 crosswise gashes in the to-

matoes equal distances apart. Place in
each gash a thin slice of:
>Bermuda onion or cucumber

Serve the tomatoes on:
>Lettuce or water cress

with:
>French dressing or sour cream
>dressing, etc.

FRESH TOMATO RELISH
About 2 Cupfuls
This is fine at times when it is incon-
venient to serve a salad.
Combine these ingredients and chill
them for 2 hours before serving them:
>2 cups skinned diced tomatoes
>1 tablespoon lemon juice
>¼ cup chopped onion
>1 teaspoon salt
>(1 teaspoon sugar)

Serve the relish from a bowl.

RULE FOR PREPARING AND FILLING TOMATO CASES FOR SALAD
Skin (page 457):
>Chilled tomatoes

Hollow them. Invert the tomatoes to
drain for 20 minutes. Chill them and
fill the hollows with one of the following fillings, or if you do not wish
to serve large portions, cut the tomatoes in halves or in slices. Place
on each slice a ring of green pepper ½
inch or more thick. Fill the ring with
any one of the fillings suggested:

I. Pineapple and Nut Meats
Combine equal parts of:
>Chopped celery
>Fresh shredded pineapple
>A few walnut meats
>Mayonnaise

II. Eggs and Anchovies
Combine:
>Chopped hard-cooked eggs
>Chopped anchovies or anchovy
>paste
>Onion juice or grated onion
>Chopped parsley or other herb
>Mayonnaise or thick sour cream
>Paprika and salt

III. Eggs and Ham
Combine:
>2 chopped hard-cooked eggs
>1 cup ground or minced ham
>½ cup chopped celery
>12 sliced olives
>Fresh or dried savory

>2 chopped sweet pickles
>Sour cream dressing or
>mayonnaise

IV. Eggs and Olives
Prepare:
>6 tomato cases

Shell, then chop:
>4 hard-cooked eggs

Combine them with:
>½ cup pitted ripe olives or stuffed
>olives
>2 tablespoons anchovy paste or
>4 tablespoons liver sausage

If required add:
>Seasoning

Fill the tomato cases with this mixture. Decorate the tops with:
>Chopped parsley or chives

Serve the tomatoes with:
>Mayonnaise

V. Deviled Eggs
An easily handled picnic salad. Place
in each hollow:
>½ Deviled Egg, page 89

Serve the tomatoes on:
>Lettuce

with:
>Anchovy Dressing, page 492

VI. Aspic
Prepare:
>6 tomato cases

Chill them. Prepare by any rule about:
>1½ cups aspic

This may be an Aspic Salad, page 475,
to which chopped meat or fish and
vegetables, etc., may be added, or it
may be Foundation Recipe I or II
with vegetables or fruit added.
When the aspic is about to set fill the
tomato cases. Chill them until the
aspic is firm. Garnish them with:
>Olives, parsley, etc.

Serve them with:
>Mayonnaise

CUCUMBER SALAD WITH FRENCH DRESSING
Select ripe cucumbers. These should
be green but not flabby and should
show no yellow coloration.
Chill, pare and slice:
>Cucumbers

Combine them with:
>French dressing or sour cream
>dressing

to which add:
>Finely minced parsley

Serve them at once.

If you wish to make them more decorative, leave unpared and score the skin with a fork as shown below.

CUCUMBER SALAD WITH SOUR CREAM
Pare, then slice very thin:
    3 cucumbers
Add:
    1 tablespoon salt
You may allow the cucumbers to stand for ½ hour and then squeeze all the salt from them. Chop very fine:
    1 medium-sized onion
Combine the cucumbers, onion and:
    ½ cup vinegar
Mix well, then add:
    3 tablespoons thick sweet cream
Garnish with:
    Pepper or paprika
You may use this somewhat acid dressing or you may combine the vegetables with thick sour cream generously sprinkled with chopped chives, parsley or some other herb. See Sour Cream Dressing, page 496. Cucumbers are delicious pared and cut into very thin slices, then marinated for 10 minutes in cream, sour cream or yogurt. Season them as desired.

WILTED CUCUMBERS
In Russian plays and books the characters frequently munch cucumbers—yes, skin and all. That seems unnecessarily strenuous for our non-Russian actors, but night after night they live up to their parts heroically.
In old cookbooks you are urged to soak cucumbers in brine or to marinate them, and to soak eggplant too. The only easily digestible cucumber I have found is mulled (see page 285). However, there are stout souls and stout stomachs that take kindly to this dish, frequently served with fish and as an appetizer. It is very good, even if it has lost some of its food value through soaking. Pare, then slice:
    Cucumbers
Soak them in ice water in the refrigerator for ½ hour. Sprinkle them with:
    2 tablespoons salt
    2 tablespoons sugar
Combine and pour over them:
    ½ cup ice water
    ½ cup herb, cider or wine vinegar
Permit them to stand in the refrigerator for 1 hour. Drain them well. You may add:
    (Freshly grated pepper)
Serve them very cold.

RAW CUCUMBER RELISH
About 1 Cupful
Pare and seed:
    1 large cucumber
Chop it until it is fine. Add to it:
    1 tablespoon lemon juice or vinegar
    ½ teaspoon salt
    ⅛ teaspoon paprika
    A few grains cayenne
    1 teaspoon finely minced onion

CUCUMBER SLICES
Pare:
    Cucumbers
Cut off one end and hollow the cucumbers with an apple corer. Fill the centers with one of the cheese mixtures given on page 466 in the rule for Green Pepper Slices. Wrap the cucumbers in waxed paper. Chill them thoroughly. Slice them and serve them on:
    Lettuce
with:
    French dressing or mayonnaise

FILLED CUCUMBERS
Good for a luncheon plate or as hors d'oeuvre. Growers now promise us a burpless cucumber.
Chill:
    Small shapely cucumbers
Pare them. Cut them in halves lengthwise or cut off a slice lengthwise and remove the seeds. The cucumber boats may be wrapped in waxed paper and chilled. Fill them with:
    Chicken Salad, page 470, or Fish Salad, page 468, or crab or shrimp
or anything that is suitable that you can think of, such as celery, nut meats, olives, etc. These ingredients may be moistened with or served with:

(Mayonnaise or Beet and Anchovy Dressing, page 493, or Chutney Dressing, page 493, etc.)
Serve the cucumbers on:
Shredded lettuce or water cress

CARROT SALAD
Raw carrots are served pared and cut in lengthwise strips, or they are grated or ground in a food chopper and combined with shredded celery, green peppers and cabbage or drained sauerkraut. They are served with mayonnaise or French dressing. Ground carrots may be used for gelatine salads, alone, combined with other vegetables or with fruits. See Golden Glow Salad, page 485.

RADISH SALAD
Wash, stem, then cut crosswise:
Red radishes
Combine them with:
French dressing
Serve them at once on lettuce or use them as a garnish for other salads.

CARROT SALAD WITH RAISINS, NUTS AND SOUR CREAM
4 Servings
Scrape well:
4 large carrots
Place them on ice for 1 hour. Grate them coarsely into a bowl. Add and mix lightly:
½ cup seedless raisins
½ cup coarsely chopped pecans or peanuts
¾ teaspoon salt
Freshly ground black pepper
2 teaspoons grated lemon peel
1 tablespoon lemon juice
Place the salad in a bowl. Pour over it:
1 cup or more sour cream
Toss the salad if you wish.

MARINATED MUSHROOMS
The ranchers of the West when hungry frequently resort to a repast of raw mushrooms. Here is a variation. Cut into thin vertical slices:
Large firm mushrooms
Marinate them for 1 hour or more in:
French dressing
Add to the dressing:
Chopped chives or onion juice
Chopped parsley
Serve the mushrooms on:
Lettuce or water cress

MEXICAN AVOCADO SALAD
Method I.
To test an avocado for ripeness, hold it in the palm of your hand and press. If it yields, it is ripe.
Peel and mash the pulp of:
1 large, very ripe avocado
Add:
2 small skinned chopped onions
2 ripe skinned chopped tomatoes, seeds removed
⅛ teaspoon paprika
½ teaspoon salt
Shape these ingredients into 4 mounds on:
Lettuce leaves
Serve the salad with:
French dressing

Method II.
Peel and mash the pulp of:
1 large, very ripe avocado
Add:
6 chopped stuffed olives
1 tablespoon French or 2 tablespoons mayonnaise dressing
Season these ingredients with:
Tabasco sauce
Salt and paprika
This mixture may be used to stuff a cucumber (page 459) or a pepper (page 466) or it may be pressed into small molds. Chill it well before serving it. Serve the salad on:
Lettuce leaves
or as hors d'oeuvre.

Avocado Spread, page 25.

FILLED PIMIENTOS OR CHRISTMAS SALAD
6 Servings
A decorative and delicious salad. Drain the contents of:
1 No. 2 can pimientos: 6 pimientos
Drain the contents of:
1 No. 2 can pineapple
Dice the pineapple. Add to it:
1½ cups diced celery
1⅛ oz. imported pearl onions: a generous tablespoon
Whip until stiff:
¼ cup cream
Combine it with:
1 cup mayonnaise
Fold into these ingredients the pineapple, celery and onions. Stuff the pimientos with the mixture. Chill them. Bed them on a nest of:
Shredded lettuce
Roll into small balls:
2 packages soft cream cheese: 6 oz.

Roll the balls in:
    Chopped parsley
Place them around the pimientos, or
if they are served individually, beside
them.

SNAP BEAN SALAD
This is the most delectable picnic salad
I know except, perhaps, Italian Salad,
page 463.
Cook by the rule on page 266:
    Snap beans
Drain them well. While warm toss
them in:
    French dressing
to which you may add a little:
    Catsup or chili sauce
Chill the beans thoroughly. Add:
    Chopped or grated onion, chives
    or pearl onions
Serve them on:
    Lettuce

HOT SNAP BEAN SALAD
6 Servings
Cook by the rule on page 266:
    1 lb. snap beans
Drain them. Sauté in a skillet:
    4 slices bacon
    ½ cup chopped onions
Remove and mince the bacon. Return
it to the skillet. Add:
    ½ cup mild vinegar
Heat these ingredients and combine
them with the beans. Season them as
desired. Serve them from a warm bowl
onto warm plates.

BEET SALAD OR PICKLED
BEETS
Prepare:
    Boiled Beets, page 272
Skin them. Cut them into crosswise
slices or quarters. While hot pour over
them a dressing of equal parts of:
    Vinegar and water
Season it well with:
    Salt, peppercorns and paprika
    A bay leaf
    A few cloves
    Herbs or seeds: celery, dill or
    fennel
Or, try:
    2 cups cooked or canned sliced
    beets
    1 teaspoon sugar
    1 teaspoon salt
    ½ teaspoon horseradish
    ¼ cup mild vinegar
Chill the beets well before serving
them. You may add to them:
    Sliced mild onions

PICKLED CANNED BEETS
Drain the contents of:
    1 No. 2 can beets
Reserve the juice. Slice the beets.
Place them in a fruit jar. Boil:
    ½ cup sharp vinegar
    ½ cup beet water
Add and heat to boiling:
    2 tablespoons sugar
    2 cloves
    ½ teaspoon salt
    3 peppercorns
    ¼ bay leaf
    (1 sliced green pepper)
    (1 small sliced onion)
Pour these ingredients over the beets.
Cover the jar. Serve the beets very
cold.

BEETS, ONIONS AND HARD-
COOKED EGGS IN SOUR
CREAM DRESSING
4 to 6 Servings
Prepare by the above rule:
    Beet Salad or Pickled Canned
    Beets
Drain them well. Combine about:
    2 cups sliced beets
    ½ cup chopped onion
    1 or 2 sliced hard-cooked eggs
Pour over the ingredients:
    Sour Cream Dressing, page 496

BEET RELISH
About 1 Pint
Combine:
    2 cups finely chopped cooked or
    canned beets
    6 tablespoons horseradish
    4 teaspoons sugar
    4 teaspoons vinegar
Season the mixture well with:
    Cayenne pepper
    Black pepper and salt

ASPARAGUS SALAD
Cook:
    Asparagus, page 265
Drain and chill them. Cover the tips
with:
    Mayonnaise or boiled salad
    dressing
Thin the dressing with a little:
    Sour cream
My country friends serve this salad
made of great white asparagus. To the
dressing they add that most aromatic
and delicious of herbs:
    Chopped tarragon
If that is not available add:
    Chopped parsley or chives
Or serve asparagus salad with:
    Vinaigrette Dressing, page 493

ASPARAGUS TIP SALAD

Drain the contents of a can of:
    Asparagus tips
Place around 4 or 5 tips a ring of:
    Red or green pepper or pimiento
Place the asparagus in the ring on:
    Shredded lettuce
Serve the salad with:
    French dressing or mayonnaise

EGG AND ASPARAGUS SALAD

6 Servings
Chill in a dish:
    2 cups cooked, well-drained
    asparagus cut in pieces
    3 sliced hard-cooked eggs
    6 sliced stuffed olives
Wash, drain and place in refrigerator to crisp:
    1 bunch water cress
    1 small head lettuce
When ready to serve combine:
    ½ cup sour cream
    2 teaspoons grated onion or
    chopped chives
    2 tablespoons lemon juice, caper
    liquor or vinegar
    1 teaspoon salt
    ¼ teaspoon paprika
    1/16 teaspoon curry powder
    (2 tablespoons capers)
Line a serving dish with the larger lettuce leaves. Break the rest into pieces. Add these to the asparagus mixture. Chop and add the water cress. Pour the dressing over these ingredients. Toss them lightly. Place them in the serving dish. Serve the salad at once garnished with:
    Parsley
Note: Heat the asparagus liquid, add a dash of cream and a bit of salt for a fine ½ cupful or so of soup, or use it in place of other liquid with cream in cream sauce.

ZUCCHINI

Zucchini served in the following manner are similar to avocados. Follow the rule on page 323 for boiling:
    Zucchini
Drain and chill them. Serve them on:
    Lettuce with French dressing
or one of its many variations, catsup, nut, tomato soup dressing, etc.

GUMBO OR OKRA SALAD

A fine hot-weather salad. The marinated pods are slightly reminiscent of oysters.
Wash well:
    Okra

You may cut off the stems. Drop the pods into boiling water. Cook them gently until they are tender, about 8 minutes. Drain the okra and rinse the pods with 2 cupfuls of hot water. The rinsing is optional. Drain them again. Place them on a platter and cover them with well-seasoned:
    French dressing or Horseradish
    Dressing, page 492
Chill them. Serve them very cold on:
    Lettuce

COOKED VEGETABLE SALAD PLATTER

Cook separately a variety of:
    Vegetables: cauliflower, carrots,
    snap beans, Lima beans, beets,
    etc.
Marinate these vegetables in separate bowls for several hours with:
    French dressing
Use about ¼ cupful of dressing to 2 cupfuls of vegetables. Drain the vegetables well. Arrange them in some attractive way on a large platter. For example, place the cauliflower or the beets in the center and alternate the other vegetables according to color in mounds about them on:
    Lettuce leaves
Garnish the platter with:
    Curled celery, radishes, sliced or
    riced hard-cooked eggs, or
    deviled eggs
Or, place in the center of a platter chilled:
    Snap Bean Salad I or II,
    page 461
Surround it with overlapping slices of skinned:
    Tomatoes or dwarf tomatoes
    filled with cottage cheese
Garnish the platter with:
    Shredded lettuce or water cress
    Deviled eggs or sardines

COOKED VEGETABLE SALAD PLATTER WITH FISH, CHICKEN OR ASPIC SALAD

This recipe shows a little more imagination than the first one. Follow the preceding rule for:
    Vegetable Salad Platter
Place in the center of the platter:
    Cooked shrimp, flaked cooked
    fish, Chicken or Fish Salad,
    page 468, Chicken Jelly Salad,
    page 482, or Tomato, Meat or
    Fish Aspic, pages 476, 482, 477
Try cooked flaked fish marinated in French dressing, topped with mayon-

naise, garnished with shrimp and stuffed olives. Place the marinated vegetables in mounds around the edge of the platter. Top any one of these with:

> Mayonnaise, Boiled Salad Dressing, page 498, or Boiled Sour Cream Dressing, page 498

ITALIAN SALAD
6 Servings
Prepare and dice:
> 1 cup Boiled Beets, page 272
> 1 cup Boiled Carrots, page 279

These proportions may be varied. Chill the vegetables. Combine them with:
> 1 cup chopped celery
> ½ cup cooked or canned green peas
> (½ cup pared, seeded and diced cucumbers)

Moisten the vegetables with:
> Boiled salad dressing or mayonnaise thinned with sweet or sour cream

Serve the salad in a bowl garnished with:
> Lettuce

COOKED GREEN PEPPERS AS SALAD
This unusual salad was served at a picnic on the West Coast, the contribution of a Near Easterner. The guests picked up the peppers by the stems, held them aloft and guzzled inelegantly but happily. In order to enjoy them fully, we were told, it is necessary to use this technique.
Wash well:
> Long green peppers

Cut gashes into them from the blossom end down to, but not through, the stem end, leaving the peppers whole. Remove the seeds and membranes. Drop the peppers into boiling water. Cook them until they are tender. Drain them well. Marinate them for 12 hours in:
> French dressing

Serve them chilled, dressing and all.

POTATO SALAD WITH MAYONNAISE
Make this salad very moist, as it will absorb a great deal of liquid. It may be made in advance; in fact, it seems to be better the second day.
Boil in their jackets in a covered saucepan until they are tender:
> Old potatoes

Chill them for several hours, peel and slice them. Marinate them well with:

> French dressing
> Soup Stock, page 43, 44, or canned bouillon

Chop or slice and add:
> Hard-cooked eggs, onions, olives, pickles, celery with leaves, cucumbers, capers
> Salt and paprika
> A few grains cayenne
> (2 tablespoons horseradish)

After 1 hour or more add:
> Mayonnaise dressing, boiled salad dressing or sour cream or cream

Shortly before serving you may toss in coarsely chopped water cress or nasturtium leaves.

POTATO SALAD WITH FRENCH DRESSING
4 Servings
Prepare by the preceding rule:
> 2 cups sliced boiled potatoes

Marinate them for several hours in:
> ½ cup French dressing

to which you may add:
> 2 teaspoons mustard, celery or caraway seed
> ⅓ cup chopped onions or
> (2 tablespoons chopped chives)

POTATO SALAD WITH SOUR CREAM DRESSING AND WATER CRESS
6 Servings
Prepare:
> 3 cups cooked sliced or diced potatoes

Pour over them:
> ½ cup well-seasoned French Dressing, page 491, or Stock, page 43

Toss the potatoes with a fork until they are well coated. Permit them to marinate for 3 hours or more. Prepare by the rule on page 492:
> Sour Cream Dressing

Fold it into the potato mixture. Season it palatably with:
> Salt and pepper

Permit the salad to stand for about 1 hour. Serve it cold. Shortly before serving it fold in:
> 1½ cups chopped water cress

Water cress is a good last-minute addition to any potato salad.

POTATO AND HERRING SALAD
6 Servings
Place in a large bowl and toss gently:

2 cups diced boiled potatoes
1¼ cups diced marinated or pickled
herring fillets
¾ cup chopped celery with leaves
1 tablespoon minced parsley
1 tablespoon minced chives
6 tablespoons sour cream
1½ tablespoons lemon juice
¾ teaspoon paprika
Serve the salad chilled in:
Lettuce cups

HOT POTATO SALAD
6 Servings
Cook in their jackets in a covered
saucepan until tender:
6 medium-sized potatoes
Peel and slice them while they are hot.
Heat in a skillet:
4 strips minced bacon or
2 tablespoons bacon drippings
Add and sauté until brown:
¼ cup chopped onion
¼ cup chopped celery
1 chopped dill pickle
Heat to the boiling point:
¼ cup water
½ cup vinegar
½ teaspoon sugar
½ teaspoon salt
⅛ teaspoon paprika
(¼ teaspoon dry mustard)
Pour these ingredients into the skillet.
Combine them with the potatoes and
serve them at once with chopped
parsley or chives.

MASHED POTATO SALAD
4 Servings
Chop or dice:
2 hard-cooked eggs
1 small grated onion
½ cup celery
2 cups cold mashed potatoes
Stir in lightly:
2 tablespoons French dressing
4 tablespoons or more
mayonnaise
Season the salad palatably with:
Salt and paprika
Chopped chives or parsley
Mold it in cups. Chill it. Serve garnished with:
Lettuce

MACARONI OR SPAGHETTI
SALAD OR CALICO SALAD
5 Servings
This is so much better than it sounds.
One of my friends, a born cook, insists
that exact proportions are unimportant.

Break into 1 inch pieces:
1 cup macaroni
Cook it by the rule on page 91. Drain
it. Beat well:
1½ tablespoons lemon juice or 2
tablespoons vinegar
1 tablespoon salad oil
Toss this into the macaroni. There
should be about 2 cupfuls of cooked
macaroni. Chill the salad for several
hours. Toss into it:
1 teaspoon grated onion or 2
tablespoons chopped chives
1 cup diced celery with leaves
1 cup minced parsley
½ cup chopped stuffed olives
¾ teaspoon salt
Freshly ground black pepper
3 tablespoons sour cream
2 tablespoons chopped pimiento
Serve the salad on:
Lettuce
This makes an attractive filling for a
tomato aspic ring.

CELERIAC OR CELERY ROOT
SALAD
8 to 10 Servings
This is fine with cold meat or sausage.
The French pare young celeriac, slice
it, marinate it for 12 hours or more and
serve it uncooked. Pare:
3 or 4 celery roots
Drop them into:
Boiling water
A sliced onion or other soup vegeta-
bles may be added to the water. Cover
them and cook them for about 2 hours
until they are tender, or see Pressure
Cookery, page 876, or quarter the roots
and steam them until they are tender.
Drain the celery and slice it. Heat an
equal amount of:
Vinegar and celery water
Season it with:
Salt and pepper
Moisten the sliced celery with this
mixture. Serve it hot or cold, or slice
the celery, chill it and serve it with:
Mayonnaise, boiled dressing,
French dressing with cream or
Remoulade Sauce, page 440

COOKED BROCCOLI SALAD
Pour:
French Dressing, plain or
elaborate, page 491, or Vinai-
grette Dressing, page 493
over:
Cooked hot drained broccoli
Serve it chilled on:
Lettuce or water cress

It may be garnished with:
Sliced hard-cooked eggs
and sprinkled with:
Chopped parsley or some other
herb
Caviar Beets, page 37, make a good
garnish for this.

RAW BROCCOLI STEM SALAD
Pare:
Broccoli stems
Cut them into strips. Serve them with:
French dressing
on:
Lettuce

CORN SALAD
4 Servings
Drain the contents of:
1 No. 2 can whole kernel corn
Chop and add:
1 pimiento
1 onion
1 green pepper
1 small cucumber
Combine these ingredients with:
½ cup well-seasoned French
dressing
Serve them on:
Lettuce cups
Or use this filling combined with well-
seasoned mayonnaise as a stuffing for
8 hollowed tomatoes.

KIDNEY OR LIMA BEAN SALAD WITH MAYONNAISE
4 to 6 Servings
Men like the heft of this. Place on a
colander the contents of:
1 No. 2 can kidney or Lima beans
Drain them well. Chill them. Combine them with:
3 sliced hard-cooked eggs
½ cup chopped celery
2 tablespoons grated onion or
chopped chives
6 small chopped sour-sweet
pickles
¼ cup mayonnaise thinned with
¼ cup tomato catsup or India
relish
1 teaspoon salt
Add, if needed, additional seasoning.
Serve the salad in:
Lettuce cups
Garnish it with:
Parsley
Lima beans are good combined with
raw chopped onions, carrots, celery
and French dressing.

KIDNEY OR LIMA BEAN SALAD WITH FRENCH DRESSING
5 Servings
Drain the contents of:
1 No. 2 can kidney or Lima beans,
cecci or miniature green
soybeans
Pour over them:
¼ cup French dressing
Toss them until they are well coated.
Serve them on:
Lettuce
Sprinkled with:
Chopped parsley
Chopped chives or grated onion

BEAN SPROUT SALAD
Use fresh or drained canned bean
sprouts. Combine them with salad
dressing, add them to other salads or
use them as a garnish.

HARD-COOKED EGG AND CREAM CHEESE RING
8 Servings
Place in a bowl and work until blended:
2 packages cream cheese: 6 oz.
¼ cup mayonnaise
1½ teaspoons salt
½ teaspoon paprika
2 tablespoons catsup or 1 teaspoon
Worcestershire sauce and 2
tablespoons cream
Add, if you wish:
A pinch of curry powder
Cook until hard then shell and dice:
10 eggs
Add them to the cheese mixture with:
½ cup diced celery
2 tablespoons chopped chives
2 tablespoons chopped parsley
¼ cup chopped green pepper
(¼ cup chopped pimiento)
(1 teaspoon dried basil)
Press these ingredients gently into an
oiled 9 inch ring mold. Chill them for
6 hours or more. Invert the contents
onto a plate garnished with:
Shredded lettuce
The center may be filled with well
drained:
Spiced Beets, page 461, or
Cucumbers in French dressing

MOLDED EGG AND CAVIAR SALAD
A good hors d'oeuvre. Crush with a
fork:
8 hard-cooked eggs
Stir into them:

3 tablespoons soft butter
⅓ teaspoon dry mustard
2 oz. caviar
3 tablespoons lemon juice
1 tablespoon Worcestershire
sauce

Pack these ingredients into a tall, oiled glass. Chill them. Unmold them. Cut them into slices. Serve on slices of:

Tomato

or use them to decorate a salad platter. Cover them with a dab of:

Mayonnaise

and place on top of each one:

A rolled anchovy

CREAM CHEESE AND OLIVE SALAD
6 Servings

Crush with a fork:

2 packages soft cream cheese: 6 oz.

Stir in:

2 tablespoons cream
⅛ teaspoon salt
⅛ teaspoon paprika
12 ripe stuffed or green chopped olives
1 chopped pimiento

Pack the cheese into a small straight oiled glass. Chill it until it is firm. Unmold and cut it into slices. Serve it on:

Water cress or lettuce

with:

Mayonnaise

PEPPER SLICES WITH CREAM CHEESE
8 to 10 Slices

These slices are highly decorative. They make good hors d'oeuvres on toast or crackers.

Method I.
Beat:

2 packages soft cream cheese: 6 oz.

Moisten it slightly with:

Cream or mayonnaise

Add if it does not interfere with the color scheme:

Paprika

Method II.
Or, soak:

1 teaspoon gelatine

in:

2 teaspoons canned pineapple juice

Dissolve it by placing it over hot water. Cool and combine it with:

2 packages soft cream cheese: 6 oz.
½ cup drained crushed canned pineapple
1 chopped pimiento
2 tablespoons chopped nut meats

Wash:

2 medium-sized red or green peppers

Cut a piece from the stem end of the peppers. Remove the seeds and the membranes. Stuff the peppers with the cheese mixture and chill them for 12 hours. Slice them with a sharp, hot knife and replace them on ice. Serve the pepper slices on:

Lettuce

with:

French dressing or mayonnaise

Method III.
If you do not want to go to the trouble of chilling the peppers, cut the rings of pepper about ⅓ inch thick. Add to the cheese:

Grated onion and salt
A little mayonnaise

and fill the rings. Serve them on slices of:

Tomatoes on lettuce

with:

French dressing

These slices are a good addition to Tomato Salad, page 491, or any other suitable salad.

Method IV.
You may use as a filling the following combination for 12 slices:

1 cup cooked ground ham
1 cup finely chopped celery
2 packages cream cheese: 6 oz.
¼ cup chopped parsley
Salt if required

Wash:

4 medium-sized green peppers

Follow the above rule for Green Pepper Slices. See other Green Pepper Slices, page 490.

ROLLED LETTUCE LEAVES AND COTTAGE CHEESE SALAD
Beat until smooth:

Cottage cheese

Add:

(A sprinkling of chives or grated onion)
(Chopped boiled ham)

Seedless raisins, chopped celery, green peppers and nut meats may be added. Spread a thick layer of the cheese on:

Large lettuce leaves

Roll the leaves and secure them with toothpicks. Chill them. Garnish them with:

> Pearl onions, crisp celery, radishes, shredded carrots

Allow 2 or 3 rolls to a person and serve them with:

> Mayonnaise or French dressing

ROLLED TONGUE OR CHIPPED BEEF ROLLS

Prepare:

> Rolled Tongue or Chipped Beef Canapés, page 32

Follow the preceding rule for serving them.

ARTICHOKE HEARTS

Cooked or canned these are delicious in salad. They may be cut up and added to green salads or aspics or they may be used as a basis on which to build up an attractive individual salad plate. Example:
Use a cooked or canned:

> Artichoke heart

that has been marinated for 1 hour in:

> French dressing

Place it on:

> Shredded lettuce

Place on it:

> A ball of cream cheese rolled in chopped chives

A bit of anchovy paste may be added to this. Surround it with:

> Grapefruit sections

Serve the salad with:

> French dressing

ARTICHOKE SALAD

Follow the rule on page 264 for cooking:

> Artichokes

Drain them well. Chill them. Serve them on salad plates on which place an individual dish of:

> Mayonnaise or other dressing

ARTICHOKES STUFFED WITH CRAB MEAT

8 Servings

Cook:

> 8 large artichokes

Add to the water in which they are boiled:

> ¼ cup vinegar

Drain and cool the artichokes. Spread the leaves outward. Pull out the tight conical center of the leaves. Scrape out the choke, the thorny, fuzzy substance, with a teaspoon or a grapefruit knife. Combine the following salad mixture:

> 3 cups crab meat or shrimp, lobster or even the overworked tuna fish, or diced chicken or veal
> 1¾ cups chopped celery
> ¼ cup finely chopped green pepper
> ¾ cup mayonnaise
> (2 tablespoons chopped chives or parsley)

Almost any palatable salad mixture that is not sweet will do. Fill the artichokes. Decorate each one with:

> 1 tablespoon mayonnaise

To eat, remove the leaves one by one and dip them in the mayonnaise. This leaves the remaining salad to be eaten with the artichoke hearts.

AVOCADO AND SHRIMP

Place:

> ½ avocado

on:

> Water cress

Partly fill the center with:

> Chili sauce or catsup

Surround it with:

> Marinated shrimp or other sea food

AVOCADO FILLED WITH LOBSTER OR CRAB MEAT SALAD

Cut into halves:

> Chilled avocados

Season:

> Cooked or canned shredded lobster meat

with:

> Lime juice
> Chili sauce
> Tabasco sauce (go easy here)

Fill the pear cups. Or, combine and fill 4 of them with:

> 1 cup chopped celery
> 2 tablespoons capers
> ½ cup tart mayonnaise

Serve the cups on:

> Endive or water cress

SHRIMP SALAD

4 Servings

If canned shrimp are used soak them in cold water for 2 minutes. Drain them. Moisten:

> 1 cup cooked shrimp

with:

> 1 teaspoon lemon juice

Add:

1 cup diced celery or cucumbers
½ cup mayonnaise
Salt and pepper
Celery salt
Garnish the salad with:
Hard-cooked eggs, sliced olives
and water cress
or serve it on:
Tomato slices

TUNA FISH SALAD
4 Servings
When making this salad, utilize the oil
from the can. Drain the contents of:
1 can tuna fish
Flake it with a fork. Add:
¼ to 1 cup diced celery or
cucumber
Make a French dressing using:
2 tablespoons tuna fish oil
2 tablespoons lemon juice
Or use ¼ cupful mayonnaise. You
may add:
(1 tablespoon chopped chives)
(1 tablespoon chopped parsley)
Serve very cold on:
Lettuce

FISH SALAD
4 Servings
Flake:
2 cups cold cooked or canned fish
Prepare and pour over the fish the following dressing:
¼ cup salad oil or oil from the can
3 tablespoons lemon juice
3 tablespoons chili sauce
2 tablespoons grated onion
⅛ teaspoon white pepper
½ to 1 teaspoon Worcestershire
sauce
½ teaspoon salt
½ teaspoon paprika
1 tablespoon chopped parsley
Chill the fish well for 1 hour. Serve it
on:
Lettuce or water cress
garnished with:
Hard-cooked eggs and olives
You may add to the salad:
1 cup chopped celery
¼ cup chopped green pepper
1 chopped pickle

CRAB MEAT SALAD
4 Servings
Crab meat may be substituted in the
preceding rules for Chicken, Fish or
Shrimp Salad. Or, combine:
1 cup crab meat
1 cup pared shredded apples
½ cup mayonnaise

CRAB LOUIS
4 Servings
This salad is a product of the West
Coast where the magnificent Pacific
crab is frequently served in this way.
Arrange around the inside of a bowl:
Lettuce leaves
Place on the bottom:
¾ cup shredded lettuce leaves
Heap on these:
2 cups crab meat
Prepare the following dressing, then
pour it over the crab. Combine and
beat:
½ cup French dressing
⅓ cup chili sauce
2 tablespoons mayonnaise
½ teaspoon Worcestershire sauce
Salt as needed
Freshly grated black pepper
Sometimes eggs are added to the salad.
Slice:
(2 hard-cooked eggs)
Place them on top of the crab. Sprinkle
over them:
Chopped chives

LOBSTER SALAD
4 Servings
Dice:
1 cup canned or cooked lobster
meat
Add to it:
(Grated onion)
Marinate it with:
¼ cup French dressing
Chill it for 1 hour. Combine it with:
1 cup chopped celery
Place it on:
Lettuce
Cover it or combine it with:
½ cup mayonnaise
to which you may add:
(2 tablespoons sherry)
Garnish it with:
Lobster claws
Olives and radishes
Hard-cooked eggs
Capers and pickles
Or prepare:
Tomato Aspic, page 476
Place it in a ring or in individual
molds. Invert the aspic on:
Lettuce
Fill the ring or surround the molds
with lobster salad.

HERRING SALAD
Method I. About 20 Servings
One of the recollections of my child-
hood is herring salad. Served at Christmastime, its rich color, thanks to the

red of beets, and elaborate garnishing made this dish an imposing sight.
Soak in water for 12 hours:

6 milter herring

Skin them, remove the milt and the bones. Rub the milt through a colander with:

1 cup dry red wine or vinegar

Cut into ¼ inch cubes the herring and:

1½ cups cold cooked veal
2 hard-cooked eggs
1½ cups Pickled Beets, page 461
½ cup onions
½ cup pickles
2 stalks celery
½ cup cold boiled potatoes

Prepare and add:

3 cups diced apples

Blanch, shred and add:

1 cup almonds

Combine the milt mixture with:

1 cup sugar
2 tablespoons horseradish
2 tablespoons chopped parsley

Pour this over the other ingredients. Mix them well. Shape the salad into a mound or place it in a bowl. Garnish it with:

Riced hard-cooked eggs
Pickles and olives
Sardelles and parsley

Method II. 8 Servings
Unusual and delicious. Begin its preparation one day before serving salad.
Cut into ½ inch pieces:

9 large milter herring

You may use herring put up in glass. Add:

2 thinly sliced apples
3 thinly sliced large salt pickles
¾ cup sugar
1 cup broken pecan meats

Shortly before serving whip until it begins to thicken, then fold in:

2 cups heavy cream

Herring or Sardine Hors d'Oeuvres, page 35.

SALAD OF SWEETBREADS, CUCUMBERS, MUSHROOMS

There is nothing set about this good salad.
Combine a choice of:

Boiled Sweetbreads, page 376
Cucumbers
Canned or Raw Mushrooms, page 291
Celery
Hard-cooked eggs
Walnut or pecan meats

Chicken
Peppers
Apples
Olives

Dice the ingredients and marinate them lightly if you wish with:

French dressing

Serve the salad garnished with:

Mayonnaise

Or combine the mayonnaise with the salad. Use about ½ as much mayonnaise as there are other ingredients.

PICKLED LAMB TONGUE SALAD

6 Servings
Drain:

6 pickled lamb tongues

These are usually bought in jars. Cut them into very thin slices. Add:

2 cups minced celery
2 tablespoons grated onion
2 tablespoons green peppers
3 sliced hard-cooked eggs
(2 tablespoons capers)

Combine these ingredients with:

1½ cups Sour Cream Dressing, page 496, or mayonnaise

Add as required:

Vinegar or lemon juice
Seasoning

You may fold into the salad shortly before serving it:

1 cup diced cucumbers

Serve it on:

Lettuce

garnished with:

Parsley

MOCK HAM SALAD

4 Servings
Put through a food chopper, using a medium blade:

1 lb. bologna

Chop, then add:

1 green pepper, seeds and membranes removed
4 small sweet pickles
1 hard-cooked egg

Mix lightly to blend well. Add:

1 tablespoon pickle juice
4 tablespoons mayonnaise

Serve in small mounds on lettuce. Use this mixture also as a sandwich spread.

HAM, COOKED CORNED BEEF, VEAL OR BEEF SALAD

Let this be a matter of inspiration.
Dice:

Cooked ham, corned beef, veal or beef

Hard-cooked eggs
Celery with leaves
(Green peppers or pickles)
Combine these ingredients with:
Tart mayonnaise or French
dressing
Garnish with:
Chopped chives, parsley or other
herbs
Surround the meat with tomatoes, sliced or whole, or use the salad as a stuffing for tomatoes.

Tomatoes Filled with Ham Salad, page 458; Jellied Ham Salad, page 482.

MEAT SALAD
This is a popular salad in Europe.
Dice:
Cooked meat or flaked firm
cooked fish
You may add about ½ as much:
Cooked diced potatoes
and some:
Chopped onion
Chopped celery
Season these ingredients with:
Tart French dressing
Garnish them with:
Parsley:

Quick Aspic Salad, page 480.

CHICKEN SALAD
8 Servings
Dice:
2 cups cooked chicken
1 cup celery
(¼ cup salted almonds)
Chill these ingredients. They may be marinated lightly with:
French dressing
When ready to serve, combine them with:
1 cup oil mayonnaise
Season the salad as required with:
Salt and paprika
Serve it on:
Lettuce
Garnish it with:
Pimiento and olives

VARIATIONS OF CHICKEN SALAD
Follow the preceding rule. Use in any desired proportions:
Chicken and celery
Chicken and bean sprouts
Chicken, cucumber and English
walnut meats

Chicken, Boiled Chestnuts, page 283, and celery. Pimiento may be added.
Chicken and parboiled oysters
Chicken and fruit, such as seedless grapes, fresh chopped pineapple
You may add to the mayonnaise:
(Strained chili sauce)

Chicken Salad Spread, page 24; Chicken Salad in Aspic, page 36.

SEEDLESS GRAPES
Seedless grapes are good served on lettuce leaves with French dressing, in Lemon or Orange Jelly, page 734, served with Yogurt or added to fruit and vegetable salads. See Seedless Grape and Celery Ring, page 484.

MALAGA AND TOKAY GRAPE SALAD
Skin and seed grapes and serve them in Lemon or Orange Jelly, page 734, or as an addition to any fruit salad. Prepared grapes may be tossed lightly in French dressing and served in a mound on lettuce or from a bowl. See Ginger Ale Salad, page 486.

GRAPE AND COTTAGE CHEESE SALAD WITH FRENCH DRESSING
Place in an oiled ring mold, or in individual molds:
Cottage cheese
Chill it and invert it onto:
Lettuce
Dust it with:
Paprika
Serve it filled with:
Seedless grapes
French dressing
Or use chopped ripe olives as an alternate for the grapes. If the cottage cheese is too soft to hold its shape, prepare Molded Cottage Cheese, page 488.

JAPANESE PERSIMMON SALAD
This is an attractive-looking salad.
Chill:
Ripe Japanese persimmons
Serve them whole or cut in halves on:
Lettuce
You may garnish them with:
(Chopped green peppers)
Serve them with:
French dressing

A good way of serving the dressing is to place on each plate ½ a small unpeeled avocado partly filled with French dressing.

If desired, the persimmons may be peeled. Cut gashes in the sides and pull the skin off with the back of a knife. Do not remove the decorative blossom ends.

MELON SALAD
Method I.
Cut into lengthwise slices:
> Ripe chilled melons

Remove the rind and serve the slices whole, or in pieces on:
> Lettuce

Sprinkle the pieces with:
> Lemon or lime juice

Or serve them with:
> French dressing

Method II.
Cut into balls with a potato cutter:
> Melon meat

Serve the balls in cocktail glasses or on:
> Lettuce

Use pink and green melons for a decorative effect. Sprinkle them with:
> Salt or confectioners' sugar

Or serve them with:
> Lime or lemon juice or
> French dressing

MELON AND COTTAGE CHEESE SALAD
Prepare as above:
> Melon Salad I or II

Serve them with:
> Cottage cheese

Or cut melons in halves, remove the seeds and serve the halves filled with cottage cheese sprinkled with:
> Paprika or chopped chives

Or garnish the cheese generously with:
> Seeded green grapes

Serve the salad with:
> (Mayonnaise)

Honeydew melon served this way is an ideal summer luncheon or supper dish.

MELON ROUNDS FILLED WITH RASPBERRIES OR STRAWBERRIES
Cut into 1 to 2 inch crosswise slices:
> Chilled honeydew melon or
> cantaloupe

Allow 1 slice for each person. Remove the seeds. Fill the centers with:
> Chilled sugared raspberries or
> strawberries

Serve them on individual plates with:
> Lime or lemon wedges

Melons are good sprinkled with ginger and served with limes.

HAWAIIAN SALAD
Individual Service
Place on a plate:
> A lettuce leaf
> A slice of pineapple

Pile on it in cone shape:
> Skinned grapefruit and orange
> sections

Place on top of the cone:
> A maraschino cherry

Decorate the sides of the cone with:
> Diamond-shaped pieces green
> pepper

Serve the salad with:
> French dressing

You may add to the dressing:
> (1 tablespoon grated fresh or
> prepared horseradish)

ORANGE AND BERMUDA ONION SALAD
Arrange:
> Lettuce leaves
> Skinned orange sections
> Thin slices Bermuda onion

Serve the salad with:
> French dressing

ORANGE SALAD FOR GAME
4 Servings
Peel and separate the skin from the sections of:
> 4 oranges

Arrange them on:
> Water cress

Combine and pour over them:
> 2 tablespoons brandy
> 2 tablespoons olive oil
> 1 teaspoon sugar
> ¼ teaspoon salt
> A few grains cayenne

Sprinkle the tops with:
> Chopped tarragon

AVOCADO SALAD
Pare and cut into lengthwise slices:
> Avocados

Serve them on:
> Lettuce

with:
> French dressing seasoned with
> ½ teaspoon or more anchovy
> paste or
> Roquefort dressing

alone or combined with pineapple, orange and grapefruit slices or with very thin slices of onion. The pears may also be served in halves, unpeeled, partly filled with French dressing or with chili sauce.

AVOCADO, ORANGE AND GRAPEFRUIT SALAD

Pare:

Avocados

Slice them lengthwise and arrange them with skinned sections of:

Orange and grapefruit

in wheel shape on:

Lettuce

Serve the salad with:

French dressing or Nut Dressing, page 493

Prepare the dressing with lime juice in preference to lemon juice or vinegar. Or, make a rounded salad in this way: Alternate skinned sections of yellow grapefruit and pink grapefruit or orange. Build them up into a half globe and place between the sections a rounded sliver of avocado or green pepper. This is a delightfully tempting salad for looks and taste.

Avocado and Shrimp, page 467.
Mexican Avocado Salad I and II, page 460.

TO PREPARE GRAPEFRUIT OR ORANGE SECTIONS

Remove outer hulls from:

A grapefruit

Pull the fruit apart into halves. Place

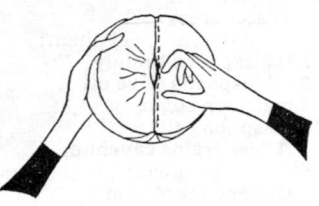

one half in your left hand the flat side up with the fruit sections lying crosswise of the fingers. If the grapefruit is prime you may proceed to work without a knife; if not, a sharply pointed knife is helpful. Split the membrane of the exposed upper section as shown above to the right by tearing it open with the thumb and forefinger. Pull the membrane parallel with the outer edge, first toward one end and then toward

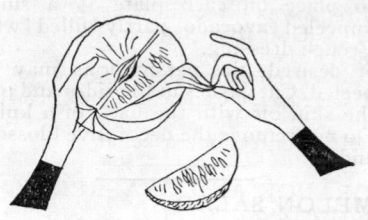

the other. In each case loosen it with a downward movement and continue the downward movement toward the base of the section until the surface of the segment is free from membrane. If this is done with a firm but light touch the segment, still adhering to the other side wall, will lie exposed and ready for easy removal with the fingers or knife. Lift up the segment and free it from the inner and outer membrane. Repeat this with each section, using the portion remaining in the left hand as a base of operations. The segment may break, but this method is worth pursuing even so, for virtually none of the juice is lost. A thin white rib may remain partly embedded in the base of the segment but it need not be entirely removed.

The method given above for grapefruit may be used with some oranges and the method below for oranges may be used for grapefruit although following it results in a considerable loss of juice. Wash and dry:

An orange

Hold the fruit over a bowl to catch all the juices and use a sharp knife to re-

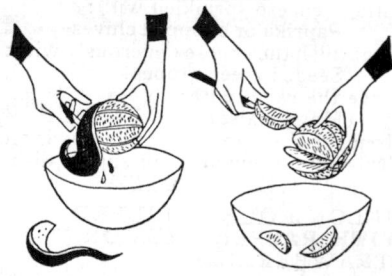

move the rind and the white skin. Pare it around and around like an apple so that the cells are exposed. Loosen the sections by cutting down along the membrane. Lift out the segment in one piece and remove any seeds.

GRAPEFRUIT SALAD
Prepare as directed, page 472:
    Grapefruit segments
Serve them with:
    French dressing
Use grapefruit juice in place of vinegar and add a little:
    Confectioners' sugar

ORANGE AND GRAPEFRUIT SALAD
Prepare as directed, page 472:
    Orange and grapefruit segments
Place them on individual plates on:
    Lettuce
You may place between alternate segments of the fruit:
    Long slivers green pepper
    and pimiento
Serve them with:
    French dressing

CHERRY AND HAZELNUT SALAD
Drain and pit:
    Canned white cherries
Insert in each cherry:
    A hazelnut meat
Serve them very cold with:
    Cottage cheese
    Mayonnaise

BLACK-EYED SUSAN
Skin unbroken whole or half sections of:
    Orange or grapefruit
Arrange them on:
    Lettuce
around a center of:
    Chopped dates and nuts
Serve the salad with:
    French dressing

WALDORF SALAD
6 Servings
Prepare:
    1 cup diced celery
    1 cup diced apples
Combine them with:
    ½ cup walnut or pecan meats
    ¾ cup mayonnaise or boiled
    dressing

PRUNE SALAD
Stew (page 450) or steam in a double boiler:
    Large prunes
Pit and drain them. Fill the centers with:
    Cream cheese combined with
    nut meats and mayonnaise
Serve them on:

    Lettuce
Or, omit the mayonnaise in the filling and serve the prunes with:
    French dressing

KUMQUAT SALAD
Cook:
    Kumquats, page 449
Split them. Remove the seeds. Chill the kumquats thoroughly. Stuff them with:
    Slightly salted cream cheese
Serve them on:
    Water cress or shredded lettuce
with:
    French dressing

APPLE OR PEAR SALAD WITH SHERRY DRESSING
Easy to make. Unusually good. Try this with an omelet, French bread and coffee.
Pare, core and slice:
    Well-flavored apples or pears
Serve them on:
    Lettuce
with:
    Lemon and Sherry Dressing,
    page 494
Garnish the salad with:
    Cream cheese and nut balls or
    Roquefort cheese balls
The apples may be cut into rings and the cheese balls placed in the center. Sprinkle the rings with lemon juice to keep them from discoloring.

FRESH PEACH SALAD
Chill:
    Fresh peaches
Pare them just before serving them, or pare them and place them in a glass jar and screw the lid tight before chilling them. They may be cut into halves or slices. Either way roll them in:
    Lemon juice
Serve them on:
    Cress, etc., with French dressing

FRESH PEACH AND CHEESE SALAD
6 Servings
Cut into 6 parts:
    1 package cream cheese: 3 oz.
Roll the cheese into balls, then in:
    Chopped nut meats
Pare, cut into halves and pit:
    6 peaches
Place a ball of cheese between 2 peach halves. Press the peach into shape. Roll it in lemon juice. If the peaches are not to be served at once, chill them

in closed containers. Serve the peaches on:
> **Water cress**

with:
> **French dressing**

A bit of cress, stem and several leaves may be placed in the stem end of each peach. Decorative, though it may affront a horticulturist.

PEAR SALAD
Method I.
Chill and pare:
> **Fresh pears or drained canned pears**

Follow the preceding rule for Peach Salad. Brush the side of each pear with:
> **Red coloring or paprika**

Place in the blossom ends:
> **A clove**

and in the stem ends:
> **A bit of water cress**

Serve the pears with:
> **French dressing**

Garnish them with:
> **Nut Creams, page 489, or large black cherries seeded and stuffed with cottage cheese**

Or fill the hollows with cream cheese combined with chopped ginger.

Method II.
Prepare as above:
> **Pear Salad**

Serve the pears on:
> **Water cress**

with a choice of:
> **Chutney Dressing, page 493**
> **French dressing with chili sauce, stuffed olives, chopped chives, parsley or other Herb, page 833**

PEAR AND GRAPE SALAD
Pare:
> **Fresh pears**

or drain:
> **Canned pears**

Place half a pear, cut side down, on a plate. Thin:
> **Cream cheese**

with:
> **Cream**

to make a good consistency to spread. Cover each pear half with a coating of cheese. Press into the cheese, close together to look like a bunch of grapes:
> **Stemmed seedless grapes**

Add a leaf of some kind, preferably grape, but an ivy leaf and a bit of stem is a good substitute. Serve with:
> **Mayonnaise or French dressing**

PINEAPPLE AND TOMATO SALAD
Method I. 4 Servings
Skin and slice:
> **4 medium-sized tomatoes**

Drain and cut into eighths:
> **4 slices canned or fresh pineapple**

Arrange the tomatoes and pineapple on:
> **Lettuce**

Serve the salad with:
> **French dressing**

Add to the dressing a little:
> **Pineapple juice**

or serve the salad with:
> **Cream Horseradish Dressing, page 497**

Method II.
Or place on a plate:
> **Lettuce or water cress**

Cover it with:
> **A slice of pineapple**

Cover the pineapple with:
> **A thick slice of skinned tomato**

Place on the tomato:
> **A ring of green pepper**

Place in the pepper ring:
> **Cream Cucumber, page 497, or other dressing**

PINEAPPLE SALAD
Drain:
> **Slices canned pineapple**

Serve them on:
> **Lettuce with French dressing**

Add to the French dressing:
> **A little confectioners' sugar**

or cover the slices with:
> **Riced soft cream cheese**

Top them with:
> **A spoonful currant jelly**

Serve the salad with:
> **French dressing or mayonnaise**

PINEAPPLE AND CUCUMBER SALAD
Peel, core and dice:
> **Fresh pineapple, or use canned pineapple**

Pare, seed and dice:
> **Cucumbers**

The proportions may be varied. Immediately before serving combine these ingredients with:
> **Mayonnaise or French dressing**

Serve them on:
> **Lettuce**

or in:
> **Tomatoes**

Aspic Salads

Chicken, Veal, Fish, Etc.

Any clever person can take a few desolate-looking refrigerator left-overs and glorify them into a tempting aspic salad. For utilizing left-overs an aspic is second only to a soufflé—well-combined scraps resulting in a dish that is sometimes as good as one composed of delicacies. Molds may be filled when dry, but a jellied mixture is more readily removed when a mold has been moistened with water or lightly brushed with oil.

A choice or a combination of the following ingredients may be used:

Cooked diced meat	Diced celery	Cooked beets
Cooked flaked fish	Diced cucumbers	Cooked or raw carrots
Hard-cooked eggs	Cooked celeriac	Skinned grapefruit sections
Seedless grapes	Nut meats	Stuffed ripe or green olives
Shredded cabbage	Cooked sweetbreads	Canned asparagus
Pickles	Sliced green peppers	Halved cranberries

Chopped parsley, chives or other Herbs (page 833)

BASIC RECIPE FOR ASPIC SALAD

5 Servings
Soak:
    ¾ tablespoon gelatine
in:
    ¼ cup cold Stock, page 43
Dissolve it in:
    ¼ cup boiling stock
Add this to:
    ½ cup cold stock
    2 tablespoons vinegar or 1½ tablespoons lemon juice
    Salt and paprika
    Celery salt
    (½ teaspoon sugar)
You may substitute for the stock canned bouillon or a beef cube dissolved in a cupful of boiling water or vegetable stock.
If the aspic is to cover unseasoned food, make the gelatine mixture "peppy." Chill it and when it is about to set combine it with:
    1½ cups solid ingredients
Pour the aspic into a wet mold and chill it until it is firm. Unmold it on lettuce leaves, as shown below, and serve it with or without:

Mayonnaise, Cream Horse-radish Dressing, page 497, etc.
If a jellied mixture persists in sticking to the mold, wring a towel out of hot water and place it briefly over the bottom and sides of the mold to loosen the contents.

JELLIED VEAL STOCK

4 to 6 Servings
Sometimes it is fun to make an aspic without gelatine. Place in a saucepan or pressure cooker:
    A knuckle of veal
    ¼ cup cut-up onion
    ½ carrot
    6 ribs celery with leaves
    1 teaspoon salt
    ¼ teaspoon pepper
Cover the veal with:
    Boiling water
Simmer the meat until it is tender. Strain the liquid. Reserve it. Remove the veal. When cold, cut the meat into small cubes. Remove the fat from the stock. Heat the stock. Add the veal. Correct the seasoning, adding if desired:
    1 teaspoon dried herb: basil, tarragon, etc.
Rinse a mold in cold water or spread it with oil. Pour in the veal mixture. Cover it and place it in a cold place to set. Serve it cold cut in slices.

FOUNDATION RECIPE FOR JELLY I—FOR VEGETABLE SALADS

6 Servings
Soak:

1 tablespoon gelatine

in:

½ cup cold water

Dissolve it in:

1 cup boiling water or Light
Colored Stock, page 43

Add:

2 to 4 tablespoons sugar
½ teaspoon salt if water is used
¼ cup mild vinegar or lemon juice
(1 tablespoon grated onion)

Chill the aspic and when it is about to
set combine it with:

1½ cups cooked or raw diced
vegetables

Place the salad in a wet mold. Chill it
until it is set. Serve it on:

Lettuce

with:

Mayonnaise

FOUNDATION RECIPE FOR JELLY II—FOR FRUIT SALADS
6 Servings

It is well to know that fresh pineapple
cannot be added to a gelatine salad
without ruining it. The pineapple must
be cooked. Canned pineapple complies
with this rule and may be used as it is.

Soak:

1 tablespoon gelatine

in:

½ cup cold water

Dissolve it in:

1 cup boiling water or fruit juice

Add:

4 to 6 tablespoons sugar, less if
sweetened fruit juice is used
⅛ teaspoon salt
¼ cup lemon juice

Chill the aspic and when it is about to
set combine it with:

1½ cups prepared drained fruit

Place it in a wet mold and chill it until
it is firm. Serve it with:

Cream mayonnaise

MINT GELATINE FOR FRUIT SALADS

Pour:

1 cup boiling water

over:

¼ cup crushed mint leaves

Allow them to steep for 5 minutes.
Drain this infusion. Add a few drops
of:

Green coloring

Prepare by the rule on this page:

Foundation Jelly II, substituting
the mint infusion for the boiling
water

TOMATO ASPIC
Method. I. 8 Servings Without the
Addition of Solid Ingredients

Boil for 30 minutes, then strain:

3½ cups tomatoes: contents of a
No. 2½ can

1 teaspoon salt
½ teaspoon paprika
1½ teaspoons sugar
2 tablespoons lemon juice
3 tablespoons chopped onion
1 bay leaf
4 ribs celery with leaves
(1 teaspoon dried basil or tarragon)

Soak:

2 tablespoons gelatine

in:

½ cup cold water

Dissolve it in the strained hot juice.
Add water to make 4 cupfuls of liquid.
Chill the aspic. When it is about to set
add 1 or 2 cupfuls of solid ingredients—a choice or a combination of:

Sliced olives
Chopped celery
Chopped green peppers
Grated or chopped carrots
Chopped meat
Flaked fish
Well-drained oysters, etc.

Chill the aspic until it is firm. Unmold
it and serve it with:

Mayonnaise or boiled dressing

If the aspic is made without the addition of solid ingredients, serve it with:

Cream Horseradish Dressing,
page 497, or Almond and Cucumber Dressing, page 497

See Tomato Aspic Ring below.

Method II. 8 Servings

Soak:

1 tablespoon gelatine

in:

2 tablespoons cold water

Dissolve it in:

2 tablespoons boiling water

Add the contents of:

1 can tomato soup: 10½ oz.

Heat about:

2 cups tomato juice

Dissolve in it:

1 package lemon-flavored gelatine:
3¼ oz.

Combine the 2 mixtures. Add:

⅛ teaspoon salt

Mold and chill the aspic.

TOMATO ASPIC RING
Prepare the preceding:

Tomato Aspic I or II

Make it with or without the addition

of the solid ingredients. Pour it into a wet ring mold or into individual ring molds lined with thin layers of caviar. If you use the caviar lining, wait to fill the molds until the aspic is about to set. Chill it until it is firm. Unmold it on:

> Lettuce

Fill the center with:

> Cole slaw
> Sliced cucumbers
> Shrimp, etc., or
> Diced avocado

Combine these ingredients with:

> Mayonnaise or boiled salad dressing

or fill the ring with:

> Chicken or Fish Salad, page 468, chilled oysters, crab meat, etc., or cottage cheese and chives

Or prepare a highly-seasoned aspic ring with fish or oysters and fill the ring with something bland like:

> Celeriac Salad, page 464, or marinated cucumbers

QUICK TOMATO OR VEGETABLE JUICE ASPIC
8 Servings

Soak:

> 2 tablespoons gelatine

in:

> ½ cup cold tomato juice

Dissolve it in:

> 3½ cups hot tomato juice or tomato and vegetable juice

Tomato juice varies. It is wise to taste the aspic to see whether additional seasoning is required. Lemon juice is good, so is a teaspoonful of chopped or dried herbs, page 833, preferably basil. Add, if desired, 1 or 2 cupfuls of solid ingredients. See Tomato Aspic, page 476. Mold, chill, unmold and serve the aspic as directed.

JIFFY TOMATO ASPIC
6 Small Servings

Bring to the boiling point the contents of:

> 1 can tomato juice: 14 oz.

Dissolve in it:

> 1 package lemon or meat-flavored gelatine

Stir in:

> 1 tablespoon vinegar
> 1 cup minced celery
> 3 tablespoons minced green pepper
> 1 tablespoon grated onion
> ½ teaspoon salt

You may use in all about 2 cupfuls of solid ingredients. These may be cubed cooked meat, cooked or canned fish, cucumbers, etc. Pour the gelatine into oiled molds. Permit it to solidify. Serve it with:

> Mayonnaise

FISH IN ASPIC
8 Servings

This and the preceding rule may be classed with my 3-star recipes. Prepare for cooking (page 228), then cut into 4 or 5 pieces:

> A fish weighing about 2½ lbs.

Bring to the boiling point:

> 5 cups water
> 3 or 4 ribs celery with leaves
> 1 small sliced onion
> 4 or 5 sprigs parsley
> 3 tablespoons lemon juice
> 1 inch lemon rind
> 3 peppercorns
> ½ teaspoon dried herbs: tarragon, basil, etc.
> ½ teaspoon paprika
> 1 teaspoon salt

Drop the fish into the boiling stock. Simmer it until it is tender. Do not permit it to boil at any time. This is a quick process requiring only 5 minutes or so. Test the fish, page 228. Remove it at once from the stock. Strain the stock. There should be about 3½ cupfuls. If there is not, add water, chicken stock, etc. Soak:

> 2 tablespoons gelatine

in:

> ¼ cup cold fish stock

Dissolve it in the hot stock. Add:

> 2 tablespoons or more capers
> 1 tablespoon caper juice

Season the stock well with:

> Salt and paprika
> Lemon juice or dry white wine

Chill it until it begins to thicken. Remove the skin and bone from the fish. Leave it in large flakes or pieces. Place a layer of aspic in a wet mold, cover it with flaked fish and repeat this process until the ingredients are all used. Wind up with aspic on top. Chill the aspic. Serve it very cold with:

> Mayonnaise, page 495, or sour cream

To either of which you may add:

> 1 or 2 tablespoons chopped herbs: chives, tarragon, parsley, etc.
> Diced cucumbers

This makes a fine dish. Decorate the platter with water cress or shredded lettuce, surround it with deviled eggs, radishes and olives. Serve with it:

> **Luncheon Bread, page 534, or Garlic Bread, page 76**

MOLDED LOBSTER RING
6 Servings
Soak:
> 1½ tablespoons gelatine

in:
> ¼ cup cold water

Dissolve it in:
> 2 cups hot chicken or veal broth

Season with:
> Salt and paprika

Chill the aspic until it is about to set. Line an oiled mold with:
> 1 lb. drained asparagus tips

Add part of the aspic and:
> 1 lb. cooked lobster meat

Add the remaining aspic. Chill the salad. Serve it on:
> Lettuce

with:
> Mayonnaise

JELLIED SALMON, CRAB OR TUNA FISH AND CUCUMBER SALAD
6 Servings
Prepare:
> Foundation Recipe for Jelly I, page 476

Dice:
> Celery

Pare, seed and dice:
> Cucumbers or green peppers

Drain and flake:
> Salmon, crab or tuna fish: 1½ cups fish and vegetables in all

When the jelly is nearly set combine it with the solid ingredients. Pour it into a wet mold and chill it until it is firm. Unmold it and serve it on:
> Lettuce

with:
> Mayonnaise or boiled dressing

You may add:
> 2 chopped hard-cooked eggs
> 6 or more sliced stuffed olives

Madrilène Ring with Shad Roe, page 481.

CRAB OR TUNA FISH MOLD
6 Servings
Soak:
> 2 teaspoons gelatine

in:
> ¼ cup cold water

Dissolve it in:
> ¼ cup boiling water

Add it to:
> ¾ cup mayonnaise

Combine it with:
> 1 cup flaked crab meat or flaked tuna fish
> ½ cup chopped celery
> 2 tablespoons chopped parsley
> ½ cup chopped cucumber
> 2 tablespoons chopped stuffed olives
> Salt if required
> ¼ teaspoon paprika
> 1 tablespoon or more lemon juice

Carrots, apples, etc., may be substituted for the cucumber and celery. Place these ingredients in a wet mold. Chill them until they are firm. Unmold them on:
> Cress or shredded lettuce

LOBSTER MOUSSE
6 Servings
Soak:
> 1 tablespoon gelatine

in:
> ¼ cup water

Dissolve it over boiling water. Combine:
> ¾ cup minced celery
> 1½ cups canned or cooked lobster meat
> (⅔ cup minced apple)

Season these ingredients with:
> Salt and paprika

Stir the gelatine into:
> ¾ cup mayonnaise
> 3 tablespoons lemon juice

Whip until stiff, then fold in:
> ⅓ cup heavy cream

Fold this mixture into the other ingredients.
Place the mousse in a wet mold. Chill it thoroughly. Unmold it on a platter garnished with:
> Water cress
> Marinated cucumbers

This is an attractive salad made in a 9 inch ring mold. Serve it filled with the following sauce:
Simmer:
> 1 cup tomatoes

When reduced to ½ cupful chill the tomatoes. Add to them:
> ½ cup olive oil
> ½ teaspoon sugar
> ½ teaspoon salt
> 1 tablespoon chopped parsley
> Freshly grated pepper
> ½ teaspoon Worcestershire or A-1 sauce

Definitely not for reducers, this dish and sauce.

MOLDED FISH MOUSSE WITH WHIPPED CREAM BASIS
6 to 8 Servings
Soak:
> 1 tablespoon gelatine

in:
> ¼ cup water

Dissolve it in:
> ½ cup boiling stock or water

Cool it. Add to it:
> ½ cup mayonnaise
> 1 tablespoon lemon juice
> Salt and paprika
> 1 teaspoon Worcestershire sauce
> ½ tablespoon grated onion

Chill this mixture until it begins to stiffen. Whip until stiff, then fold in:
> ⅓ to ½ cup heavy cream

Chill these ingredients until they are about to set. Prepare:
> 2 to 2¼ cups cooked or canned, finely flaked or ground fish

This may be part finely chopped celery or pickles or 2 tablespoonfuls of capers. Fold this into the gelatine mixture. Place the salad in an oiled mold. Chill it. Serve it with:
> Artichoke bottoms
> Sliced tomatoes, etc.

MOLDED FISH WITH CREAM SAUCE BASIS
6 Servings
Soak:
> ¾ tablespoon gelatine

in:
> 2 tablespoons water

Combine, then stir constantly over boiling water until thickened:
> 2 egg yolks
> 1½ tablespoons soft butter
> ½ tablespoon flour
> 1½ teaspoons salt
> 2 teaspoons sugar
> 1 teaspoon Worcestershire sauce
> or ¾ teaspoon curry
> or 1 teaspoon dry mustard
> 1 teaspoon grated onion
> A few grains red pepper
> ¼ cup vinegar
> ¾ cup milk

Add dissolved gelatine and stir until it is dissolved. Prepare:
> 1½ cups sea food: cooked or canned shrimp, salmon, etc.

Or use part fish and part chopped celery.
When the gelatine is nearly set place part of it in the bottom of an oiled ring mold, add part of the fish, then more gelatine. Repeat this until all ingredients have been used, finishing with

gelatine on top. Chill the salad until it is firm. Serve it on:
> Water cress

Fill the ring with:
> Marinated cucumbers

Surround it with:
> Sliced tomatoes

CLAM JUICE RING
8 Servings
It is difficult to write about this as clam juice varies greatly in strength, but it is too good a dish to neglect. The basic rule is simple.
Dilute with water to make a palatable mixture:
> Clam juice

There should be 3¾ cupfuls of liquid.
Season this with:
> Lemon juice and paprika
> A few drops Worcestershire sauce

Soak:
> 2 tablespoons gelatine

in:
> ½ cup of the liquid

Heat to the boiling point 1 cupful of the liquid. Dissolve the soaked gelatine in it. Return it to the remaining liquid. Place it in an oiled 9 inch ring mold. Chill it until it is firm. Invert the jelly onto a plate. Fill the center with:
> Cottage cheese

Surround it with:
> Tomato slices
> Cucumber slices

Serve the salad with:
> Mayonnaise

GRAPEFRUIT JELLY WITH SHERRY
10 Servings
Soak:
> 2½ tablespoons gelatine

in:
> ½ cup cold water

Stir over heat until the sugar is dissolved:
> ½ cup water
> 1 cup sugar

Dissolve the gelatine in the hot sirup.
Cool it. Add:
> 2 cups and 6 tablespoons fresh grapefruit juice
> 3 tablespoons lemon juice
> ½ cup sherry
> ¼ teaspoon salt

Pour these ingredients into a well-oiled 9 inch ring mold. Chill the jelly until it is firm. Turn it out on a platter. Fill the center with:

Soft cream cheese balls rolled in chopped nuts
Garnish the outer edge of the platter with:
Avocado slices
alternating with skinned:
Graperfruit or orange sections
on:
Water cress or shredded lettuce
Sprinkle it with:
Pomegranate seeds
Serve the salad with:
Mayonnaise and French dressing

GRAPEFRUIT ASPIC
8 Servings
Soak:
1½ tablespoons gelatine
in:
1 cup cold water
Dissolve it in:
1 cup boiling water
Add to it:
3 tablespoons lemon juice
¾ cup sugar
Chill the jelly until it is about to set. Peel:
3 large grapefruit
Separate the inner skin from the sections. Reserve the juice. Add the juice and the fruit to the gelatine mixture. Chop and add:
¾ cup tender celery
(½ cup blanched shredded almonds)
Place the aspic in a wet ring mold or in individual molds. Chill it until it is firm. Unmold it and serve it on:
Lettuce
with:
Mayonnaise or Cream Cucumber Dressing, page 497

ASPIC WITH GRAPEFRUIT, SWEETBREADS AND CELERY
12 to 14 Servings
Sometimes with the luck of a Madame Galvani—only with less far-reaching results—a hostess will hit upon an unusual combination. This is one:
Soak:
2½ tablespoons gelatine
in:
½ cup cold Stock, page 43
Dissolve it in:
3½ cups boiling stock
Add:
Grated lemon rind and as much grapefruit or lemon juice as is palatable
As the aspic is to go over unseasoned food season it highly with:

Salt and paprika
A few grains cayenne
Chill it. When it is about to set place a layer of it in a wet mold. Place over it layers of the following ingredients alternated with other layers of aspic, ending with aspic on top:
Skinned sections of 2 large grapefruit
1 large diced stalk celery
1 pair boiled diced Sweetbreads, page 000
(½ cup nut meats)
You may mold the salad in one large mold or in individual molds. Chill it and unmold it on:
Lettuce
Serve it with:
Mayonnaise

QUICK ASPIC SALAD
8 Servings
This dish—my own palate-child—has saved my life—at least my reputation—on so many occasions that I dedicate it gratefully with all good wishes to any hostess caught in a pinch.
Proportions are unimportant for this refreshing, quickly made salad, and ingredients may be altered freely to suit the cook's taste or materials on hand. Celery, olives, hard-cooked eggs, etc., may be added.
Drain, reserving the juices:
1 No. 2 can grapefruit sections
1 can green or white asparagus: 10½ oz.
1 can crab meat or shrimp: 6½ oz.
Cut the asparagus into pieces. Pick over the crab meat or remove the intestinal vein from the shrimp. Add to the juices to make 2¾ cupfuls of liquid:
Chicken broth, Stock, page 43, canned consommé or dissolved chicken bouillon cubes
Soak:
1½ tablespoons gelatine
in:
½ cup of this liquid
Dissolve it in:
1 cup hot liquid
Combine the gelatine and the remaining liquid. Season well with:
Juice of 1 or more lemons or with ¼ cup dry white wine
Add if needed:
Salt
You may add:
(3 or more tablespoons capers, caper liquor)
Chill the gelatine until it begins to

thicken. Have ready an oiled mold. Pour part of the gelatine into it, sprinkle some grapefruit, crab and asparagus over it, then alternate layers of gelatine and the other ingredients. Wind up with gelatine on top. Chill the aspic until it is very cold. Serve it on:

Lettuce

with:

Herb Mayonnaise, page 495

SWEETBREAD SALAD MOUSSE
4 Servings
Parboil and prepare by the rule on page 376:

¾ lb. sweetbreads

Reserve the stock and break the sweetbreads into small pieces. Soak:

1 tablespoon gelatine

in:

¼ cup cold sweetbread or chicken stock

Dissolve it in:

¼ cup boiling sweetbread or chicken stock

Chill the mixture until it begins to set. Whip until stiff:

½ pint heavy cream

Fold it lightly into the gelatine, then chill it. When the cream begins to set, fold in the sweetbreads and:

Juice of ½ lemon
½ tablespoon chopped onion
½ tablespoon chopped celery
2 tablespoons chopped green pepper
Salt
Paprika or white pepper

Pour the mousse into oiled molds. Chill until well set. Serve the salad inverted on:

Lettuce

with:

Mayonnaise

TONGUE IN ASPIC
8 Servings
A fine looking, palatable dish. Cook by the rule on page 385 or pressure cook, page 890:

A smoked beef tongue

Leave it in the stock until it is cool, then prepare it as directed. A fresh beef tongue may be substituted. Do not soak it. Cover it with boiling water to which the onion, celery, etc., have been added. Make the following aspic. Soak:

1½ tablespoons gelatine

in:

½ cup cold tongue stock

Dissolve it in:

2½ cups boiling tongue stock to which beef cubes may be added
½ cup vinegar or dry white wine or the juice of 2 lemons
1 tablespoon sugar
Salt if required
A few drops Caramel, page 754, or commercial coloring
1 teaspoon Worcestershire sauce

Chill the aspic and when it is about to set add:

½ cup chopped sour-sweet pickles
1 cup chopped celery
½ cup chopped green peppers

Have ready a mold or bread pan that has been moistened with cold water. Place a small amount of aspic in the bottom of the mold. If desired mold into this sliced eggs, carrots, cooked beets, canned mushrooms, etc. Put the tongue into the mold and pour the remaining aspic around and over it. When well chilled, unmold the aspic on a platter. Garnish it with:

Lettuce leaves
Deviled eggs
Parsley
Slices of lemon

Serve it with:

Mayonnaise or see Mayonnaise for Masking, below

MADRILÈNE RING WITH SHAD ROE
A fine summer dish.
Fill a ring mold with:

Canned Madrilène or any meat stock aspic

Chill it. Invert it on:

Shredded lettuce

Place in the center:

Chilled canned shad roe

You may garnish the dish with:

Mayonnaise
Lemon wedges
Parsley

If the Madrilène is a wobbly type, serve it from a small dish surrounded by pieces of roe on lettuce.

MAYONNAISE FOR MASKING COLD FOODS. Aspic, Fish, Meats, Chicken Salad, Etc.
Soak:

1 teaspoon gelatine

in:

2 tablespoons cold water

Dissolve it over hot water Stir it into:

1 cup mayonnaise

Cool it. Spread it as you would frost-

ing, with firm strokes of a spatula.
Garnish the dish with:
    Capers
    Sliced pimiento olives
    Pimiento cut into shapes
    Sliced hard-cooked eggs, etc.
Chill the dish until the mask is set.

JELLIED HAM LOAF
Method I.   6 Servings
Prepare:
    Foundation Recipe I for Vege-
    table Salad, page 476
When the aspic is about to set add:
    1 cup cooked diced ham
    ½ cup diced celery
    ¼ cup chopped green peppers
    2 tablespoons finely chopped
    onions
    2 diced hard-cooked eggs
Pour the aspic into a mold. Chill
until firm. Unmold and serve with:
    (Mayonnaise)

Method II.
Dissolve:
    1 package lemon-flavored
    gelatine: 3¼ oz.
in:
    2 cups boiling water
Cool and add:
    2 tablespoons lemon juice
    ¼ teaspoon salt
    ¼ teaspoon paprika
When the aspic is about to set, add the
solid ingredients and proceed as above.

Ham Mousse, page 149.

CHICKEN JELLY SALAD
6 Servings
Soak:
    1 tablespoon gelatine
in:
    ¾ cup hot chicken stock
Season it with:
    ½ teaspoon grated onion
    Salt and paprika
Cool this mixture until it is about to
thicken. Beat it with a wire whisk
until it is frothy. In a separate bowl
beat until stiff:
    1 cup heavy cream or evaporated
    milk
Fold in the gelatine mixture and:
    1½ cups cooked diced chicken
Pour the jelly into lightly oiled individual molds. Chill it until it is firm.
Unmold it. Serve it on:
    Lettuce

with:
    Mayonnaise or Almond and
    Cucumber Dressing, page 497

*Jellied Chicken, page 145; Chicken
Mousse, page 146.*

CUCUMBER MOUSSE
6 Servings
Soak:
    2 teaspoons gelatine
in:
    3 tablespoons cold water
Dissolve these ingredients over heat.
Add:
    2 teaspoons vinegar or lemon
    juice
    1 teaspoon grated onion
    ¾ teaspoon salt
    ¼ teaspoon paprika
Chill this mixture until it is about to
set. Drain well:
    1 cup pared, seeded, chopped
    cucumbers
Whip until stiff:
    1 cup cream
Beat the gelatine mixture gradually
into the cream. Fold in the cucumbers.
Oil individual molds. Fill them with
the jelly. When they are thoroughly
chilled invert the jelly onto a platter.
Garnish it with:
    Parsley and lettuce leaves
    Chilled sliced tomatoes
Serve the salad with:
    Mayonnaise
Or invert the contents of the molds
onto thick slices of peeled tomato and
garnish them with mayonnaise. Use
somewhere, in the mayonnaise or as a
garnish, because they are a decided
addition:
    Chopped chives

CUCUMBER JELLY AND
CHEESE MOUSSE
8 Servings
The clear green cucumber jelly and
the white cheese mixture make a very
decorative salad.
Pare and slice:
    3 cucumbers
Add and simmer until the cucumbers
are very tender:
    1 slice onion
    1 tablespoon chopped green
    pepper
    1 tablespoon tarragon or other
    vinegar
    2 cups cold water
    (1 tablespoon minced nasturtium
    pods)

Soak:
2 tablespoons gelatine
in:
2 tablespoons cold water
Dissolve it in the cucumber mixture.
Strain these ingredients through a fine
sieve. Add:
A few drops green coloring
½ teaspoon salt
Place the jelly in a wet 9 inch ring
mold. Mash with a fork:
**2 packages soft cream cheese: 6
oz.**
Stir in:
Salt and paprika
A few drops onion juice
Soak:
1 tablespoon gelatine
in:
2 tablespoons cold water
Dissolve it in:
¼ cup boiling water
Cool it. Add it to the cheese. Add:
**3 tablespoons blanched chopped
almonds**
Whip until stiff, then **fold** into the
cheese mixture:
1 cup heavy cream
Heap the cheese on top of the cucumber jelly. Chill the salad until it is
firm. Unmold it. Garnish it with:
Sliced tomatoes
Water cress or lettuce
Serve it with:
Mayonnaise

CUCUMBER JELLY ON TOMATO SLICES
8 Servings
Fine for a meat platter or a ring mold.
Pare and seed:
Cucumbers
Grate them. There should be 4 cupfuls
of pulp and juice. Soak:
2 tablespoons gelatine
in:
½ cup cold water or chicken stock
Dissolve it in:
**¾ cup boiling water or chicken
stock**
Add:
6 tablespoons lemon juice
2 teaspoons grated onion
Add the gelatine mixture to the cucumber pulp with:
1 teaspoon sugar
Salt as needed
¼ teaspoon paprika
A few drops green coloring
Strain the jelly. Place it in small
molds. When it is firm invert it onto:
Thick slices skinned tomatoes

Garnish the slices with:
Water cress
Serve the salad with:
Mayonnaise
Or, place in a 9 inch ring mold. Chill
the jelly. When firm invert it onto a
platter. Fill the center with:
Marinated shrimp
Garnish the edge with alternating:
Tomato slices
Cucumber slices
Serve the ring with:
Herb Mayonnaise, page 495

CELERY ASPIC IN RING MOLDS ON TOMATO SLICES
6 Servings
Prepare:
Foundation Jelly I, page 476
Add to it a very little:
(Green coloring)
When it is about to set add:
1½ cups minced celery
Fill individual ring molds and chill the
jelly until it is firm. Invert the con-
tents of the molds onto:
Thick slices skinned tomatoes
Place in the center of each ring:
3 stuffed olives
Serve the aspic with:
Lettuce or water cress
Mayonnaise

CARDINAL SALAD
8 Servings
Wash well, then boil (page 272):
**8 medium-sized beets, or use
canned beets**
Drain them. Reserve the beet juice.
Peel the beets and dice them. There
should be about 1 cupful. Prepare:
¾ cup diced celery
Dissolve the contents of:
**1 package lemon-flavored gelatine:
3¼ oz.**
in:
1 cup boiling water
Add to it:
¾ cup beet juice
3 tablespoons vinegar
½ teaspoon salt
2 teaspoons grated onion
**1 tablespoon prepared horse-
radish**
Chill these ingredients until they are
about to set. Fold in the beets and the
celery. Place the salad in a wet mold.
Chill it until it is firm. Unmold it on:
Lettuce
Serve it with:
**Mayonnaise or Boiled Salad
Dressing, page 498**

BEET GELATINE SALAD
6 Servings
Prepare:
Foundation Recipe for Jelly I,
page 476
When the jelly is about to set add:
1 cup cooked diced Beets, page 272
½ cup diced celery
The jelly may be colored with a little
red coloring or a little beet juice may
be substituted for part of the water.

QUICK MOLDED VEGETABLE GELATINE SALAD
Method I. 6 Servings
Dissolve the contents of:
1 package lime or lemon-flavored
gelatine: 3¼ oz.
in:
2 cups warm water
Prepare and add when the jelly is
about to set:
1½ cups finely diced vegetables:
equal parts of cucumber, carrot,
celery, unpeeled radish
½ diced green pepper
2 teaspoons grated onion
¾ teaspoon salt
¼ teaspoon paprika
Place the salad in well-oiled individual
ring molds. Chill it thoroughly. Unmold it on:
Lettuce or water cress
Fill the centers with:
Mayonnaise or
Boiled Salad Dressing II, page
498

Method II.
Prepare:
Foundation Recipe for Jelly I,
page 476
When it is about to set add:
1½ cups chopped vegetables:
cabbage, celery, carrots, green
peppers, a few mint leaves, etc.
Chill the salad.

Method III.
Prepare:
Foundation Recipe for Jelly I,
page 476
When it is about to set add:
1½ cups diced avocado, celery and
olives or pimiento
Chill the salad.

SEEDLESS GRAPE AND ASPARAGUS ASPIC
10 Servings
A refreshing summer salad. Drain the
contents of:

1 can asparagus tips: 15 oz.
Reserve the liquor. The tips may be
cut in two or they may be used whole
as a garnish around the edge of the
mold. Soak:
1 tablespoon gelatine
in:
3 tablespoons asparagus liquor
Heat the remaining asparagus liquor
and dissolve the gelatine in it. Add to
it to make 2 cupfuls of liquor in all:
Chicken bouillon or canned
bouillon
Season these ingredients with:
Salt and paprika
Chill them. When they are nearly set
combine them with:
2 cups seedless grapes
1 cup chopped celery
The asparagus tips
Chill the salad until it is firm. Unmold
it and serve it with:
Mayonnaise

SEEDLESS GRAPE AND CELERY RING
8 to 10 Servings
Prepare:
Lemon Jelly or Orange Jelly,
page 734, or Foundation Jelly,
page 476
When it is about to set add to it:
3 cups seedless grapes and diced
celery combined in any proportion
Place the jelly in a wet 9 inch mold and
chill it. Unmold it on:
Lettuce
Fill the center with:
Cream mayonnaise

DUCHESS SALAD
10 Servings
Boil:
1⅔ cups water
Pour it over:
1 package lemon-flavored gelatine: 3¼ oz.
Add:
¼ cup sugar
3 tablespoons lemon juice
3 tablespoons pineapple juice
½ teaspoon salt
Chill the jelly until it is about to set.
Combine it with:
2 cups shredded cabbage
1 cup diced canned pineapple or
fresh cooked pineapple
½ cup chopped celery
2 tablespoons chopped pimiento
The solid ingredients may be combined with Foundation Jelly II, page

476, in place of the gelatine mixture. Pour the salad into a wet mold. Chill it until it is set. Unmold it on:
  Lettuce
Serve it with:
  Mayonnaise or Boiled Salad Dressing, page 498

GOLDEN GLOW SALAD
8 to 10 Servings
Good in flavor and lovely in color. Grate or grind:
  2 cups raw carrots
Drain:
  1 cup crushed canned pineapple
Heat to the boiling point:
  7/8 cup pineapple juice
  7/8 cup water
  1/2 teaspoon salt
Dissolve in the hot liquid:
  1 package lemon-flavored gelatine: 3 1/4 oz.
Chill the jelly and when it is about to set combine it with the carrots and pineapple. Place it in a wet mold. Chill the jelly until it is firm. Unmold it on:
  Lettuce
Serve it with:
  Mayonnaise

MOLDED AVOCADO SALAD
Method I.   4 Servings
Dissolve:
  1 package lemon-flavored gelatine: 3 1/4 oz.
in:
  1 3/4 cups boiling water
Add:
  2 tablespoons lemon juice
  1 tablespoon prepared horse-radish
  1 teaspoon grated onion
Chill these ingredients until they begin to set. Beat the jelly with an egg beater. Fold in:
  2 pared diced avocados
  1/2 cup finely diced celery
Place the salad in an oiled mold or in individual molds. When chilled invert it onto:
  Lettuce leaves
Serve it with:
  Herb Mayonnaise, page 495

Method II.
Or soak:
  1 tablespoon gelatine
in:
  2 tablespoons water
Dissolve it in:
  1 cup boiling water

Add:
  1/4 cup lemon juice
  1 cup mashed avocado
  1/4 teaspoon celery salt
  1 teaspoon salt
  1/2 teaspoon Worcestershire sauce
  A few grains cayenne
  1/4 cup chopped pimiento
To mold and serve the salad follow the above rule.

CELERY ROOT RING SALAD
8 Servings
Cook by the rule on page 282:
  4 celery roots
Put the celery roots through a purée strainer. Add:
  1 can pâté de foie gras: 2 oz., or a very good quality liver sausage
Soak:
  2 tablespoons gelatine
in:
  1/2 cup chicken bouillon
Heat, then dissolve the gelatine in:
  1 1/2 cups chicken bouillon
Add it to the celery mixture. Stir in:
  4 egg yolks
Stir and cook these ingredients over a low flame to permit the yolks to thicken slightly. Season with:
  Salt and paprika
Cool the mixture. Fold in:
  1/2 cup cream, whipped
  4 stiffly beaten egg whites
Place the salad in an oiled 9 inch ring mold. Fill the mold with:
  Marinated Cucumbers, page 458, shrimp, etc.
Surround it with:
  Tomatoes

PINEAPPLE AND CUCUMBER SALAD
5 Servings
Drain the contents of:
  1 can crushed pineapple: 9 oz.
Reserve the juice. Soak:
  1 tablespoon gelatine
in:
  1/4 cup cold water
Dissolve it in:
  1/4 cup boiling water
Add and stir well:
  1/8 teaspoon salt
  1/3 cup sugar
  1/2 cup lemon juice
  2 drops green coloring
Combine this with the pineapple pulp and juice. Pare, seed, grate and add:
  1 small cucumber
Pour these ingredients into a wet mold

or in individual molds. Unmold the salad on lettuce leaves. Serve it with:

Cream Mayonnaise, page 496

MOLDED PINEAPPLE RING

8 Servings

Soak:

2 tablespoons gelatine

in:

½ cup cold water

Strain the contents of:

1 No. 2 can crushed pineapple: 3½ cups

Add to the juice:

½ cup hot water

Bring these ingredients to the boiling point. Stir in the soaked gelatine until it is dissolved. Add:

⅝ cup sugar—½ cup plus 2 tablespoons

Cool the mixture. Add the pineapple and:

The grated rind of 1 orange or lemon

¾ cup orange juice

5 tablespoons lemon juice

Pour these ingredients into a wet 9 inch ring mold. Chill the gelatine. Unmold it on a bed of:

Lettuce or water cress

Fill the center with:

Cottage cheese, soft cream cheese balls rolled in chopped nut meats or chicken salad, etc.

Serve it with or without:

Mayonnaise

PINEAPPLE MINT JELLY SALAD

Drain well:

Canned pineapple

Prepare by the rule on page 476:

Mint jelly

Mold it in the pineapple can. When it is set unmold the jelly and cut it into slices. Place a slice of pineapple on a plate, cover it with a slice of mint jelly. Garnish it with:

Mayonnaise

Candied Mint Leaves, page 490

Nut Creams, page 489

GINGER ALE SALAD

10 Servings

This is about the best molded fruit salad given.

Soak:

2 tablespoons gelatine

in:

4 tablespoons cold water

Dissolve it in:

½ cup boiling fruit juice

Add:

½ cup sugar

⅛ teaspoon salt

1 pint ginger ale

Juice of 1 lemon

Chill these ingredients until the jelly is nearly set. Combine it with:

½ lb. skinned seeded Malaga grapes

1 skinned sliced orange

1 grapefruit in skinned sections

6 slices canned pineapple cut in pieces

¼ lb. Canton ginger

Place the salad in a wet mold. Chill it and unmold it on:

Lettuce

Serve it with:

Cream mayonnaise

STUFFED NECTARINES MOLDED

8 Servings

Soak:

2½ tablespoons gelatine

in:

½ cup water

Drain:

1 No. 2½ can nectarines

Combine and boil:

2 cups of the juice

1½ cups sugar

Dissolve the gelatine in it. Add these ingredients to the remaining juice with:

¾ cup lemon juice

3 tablespoons lime juice

Add until there are 4 cupfuls of liquid in all. Add water or other fruit juice to make up this amount. Chill the gelatine until it is about to set. Soften:

Cream cheese

with a little:

Mayonnaise

Roll it into balls. Roll the balls in:

Chopped nut meats

Place a stuffed nectarine in an oiled individual mold. Pour the gelatine over it. Chill the salad well. Invert it onto:

Water cress

It may be served with:

Mayonnaise

MOLDED PEAR SALAD

6 Servings

Drain the contents of:

1 No. 2½ can Bartlett pears

Soak:

1 tablespoon gelatine

in:

¼ cup cold water

Add to the pear juice enough water to make 1¾ cupfuls of liquid. Heat part of the liquid to the boiling point. Dissolve the soaked gelatine in it. Combine it with the rest of the liquid. Add:

    3 tablespoons lemon juice
    ¼ teaspoon salt

Cool these ingredients. Moisten:

    1 package soft cream cheese or
        pimiento cheese: 3 oz.

with a very little:

    Cream

Use just enough to soften it. Add to the cheese:

    ¼ cup chopped nut meats
    (¼ teaspoon salt)

Form the cheese into balls. Place one in the center of a half pear and cover it with another half pear. If the pears are large, do not cover them. Place the stuffed pears in a ring mold or in cups. Pour the gelatine mixture over them. Add, if desired:

    1 cup or more seedless grapes

Chill the gelatine until it is firm. Unmold it on:

    Crisp lettuce

Serve it with:

    Mayonnaise

This recipe may also be made with:

    1 package lime or lemon gelatine:
        3¼ oz.
    1 cup boiling water
    1 cup pear juice
    1½ tablespoons lemon juice
    ⅛ teaspoon ginger
    ¼ teaspoon salt

Substitute this for the gelatine mixture given in the recipe.

MOLDED CRANBERRY AND ORANGE SALAD
10 to 12 Servings
Soak:

    1 tablespoon gelatine

in:

    ¼ cup water

Wash:

    1 quart cranberries: 4 cups
    2 small oranges

Cut the oranges into quarters. Remove the seeds. Put the oranges and cranberries through a meat grinder. Use a medium knife. Reserve the juices. Dissolve over heat:

    ¾ to 1 cup sugar

in:

    ¼ cup water

Add:

    1 package lemon gelatine: 3¼ oz.

and the soaked gelatine over heat.

Stir until the gelatine is dissolved. Add the ground fruit. Place the salad in a wet mold. It is also fine in a ring mold. Chill it until it is firm. Unmold it on:

    Lettuce

Serve it with:

    Mayonnaise

MOLDED CRANBERRY, CELERY AND NUT SALAD
6 to 8 Servings
Soak:

    1 tablespoon gelatine

in:

    3 tablespoons water

Cook until the skins pop:

    2 cups cranberries: 1 pint

in:

    1 cup boiling water

Use the cranberries strained or unstrained. If the former, strain them at this time. Add and cook for 5 minutes:

    ½ cup sugar
    ¼ teaspoon salt

Add the soaked gelatine. Chill the jelly. When it is about to set fold in:

    ⅔ cup diced celery
    ½ cup chopped nut meats
    (1 cup drained crushed pineapple)

Place it in a wet mold and chill it until it is firm. Serve it with:

    Mayonnaise

MOLDED CRANBERRY AND APPLE SALAD
8 to 10 Servings
Put through a food grinder:

    1 lb. cranberries

Add:

    The grated rind of 1 orange
    ½ cup orange juice
    3½ tablespoons lemon juice
    1½ cups sugar

Let this stand overnight. Soak:

    1 tablespoon gelatine

in:

    3 tablespoons cold water

Dissolve:

    1 package lemon-flavored gelatine: 3¼ oz.

in:

    1 cup boiling water

Add the soaked gelatine. Stir it until dissolved. Combine these ingredients with the cranberry mixture. Pare, then chop and add:

    3 tart apples

Place the salad in a greased mold.

When firm unmold it and serve it on:
> Water cress

with:
> Cream Mayonnaise, page 496

BLACK CHERRY AND ALMOND ASPIC
6 Servings

Prepare:
> Foundation Recipe for Jelly II, page 476

Substitute for part of the boiling water:
> Fruit juice

Cool the gelatine mixture. When it is about to set add:
> 1¼ cups pitted black cherries
> ⅓ cup blanched shredded almonds

These proportions may be varied. Place the aspic in a wet mold. Chill it until it is firm. Unmold it and serve it with:
> Mayonnaise

TWENTY-FOUR-HOUR FRUIT SALAD WITH CREAM
12 to 14 Servings

Cook in a double boiler until thick:
> 2 egg yolks
> ¼ cup sugar
> ¼ cup cream
> Juice of 2 lemons
> ⅛ teaspoon salt

Stir these ingredients constantly. Chill them and add:
> 6 slices diced canned pineapple
> 2 cups pitted Queen Anne cherries
> 1 cup blanched shredded almonds
> ½ lb. marshmallows cut in pieces
> 1 cup heavy cream, whipped
> (½ lb. peeled seeded grapes)

Chill the salad for 24 hours. Serve it on:
> Lettuce

with:
> Mayonnaise

or as a dessert garnished with:
> Whipped cream

FROZEN FRUIT SALAD
10 to 12 Servings

Drain the contents of:
> 1 No. 2 can pineapple

Reserve the juice. Cut the pineapple in pieces. Drain the contents of:
> 1 No. 2½ can white cherries

Pit them. Drain the contents of:
> 1 No. 2½ can apricots

Cut them in pieces. Melt in a double boiler:
> 1 tablespoon butter

Add and stir until blended:
> 1 tablespoon flour

Add:
> The pineapple juice
> 1 tablespoon sugar
> 1 tablespoon lemon juice
> 1 beaten egg

Cook and stir these ingredients until they are smooth. Cool them, then fold in:
> 1 cup heavy cream, whipped

Fold in the fruit. Freeze the salad in a refrigerator, or in a mold packed in ice and salt (see page 766). Unmold it and serve it with:
> Cream Mayonnaise, page 496

MOLDED COTTAGE CHEESE
6 to 8 Servings

Soak:
> 1 tablespoon gelatine

in:
> ¼ cup cold water

Dissolve it by placing it over hot water. Beat until smooth:
> 2 cups cottage cheese
> ¾ teaspoon salt
> ⅛ teaspoon paprika
> ½ cup cream
> ½ cup crumbled Roquefort cheese
> 12 chopped stuffed olives
> ¼ cup chopped nut meats

Add the cooled gelatine. Pour the salad into a wet 7 inch ring mold. Chill it until it is set. Unmold it on:
> Lettuce

Fill the center with:
> Fresh fruit or vegetable salad

French Cheese Cream, page 748.

MOLDED PINEAPPLE CHEESE SALAD
4 Servings

Soak:
> 1½ teaspoons gelatine

in:
> ⅓ cup cold water

Add:
> 2 tablespoons sugar
> ⅛ teaspoon salt
> 2 tablespoons lemon juice

Chill the jelly until it begins to set. Combine it with:
> ⅔ cup cottage cheese

Beat it until it is smooth. Fold in:
> ⅔ cup diced canned pineapple

Place the salad in a wet mold and chill it until it is firm. Unmold it on:
> Lettuce

Garnishes for Salads

To garnish salads use the following:

Tomato slices dipped in finely chopped parsley or chives.
Parsley or water cress in bunches or chopped.
Lettuce leaves, cress, endive, Romaine, etc.
Heads of lettuce cut into slices or wedges.
Lemon slices with pinked edges dipped in chopped parsley.
Shredded olives, or sliced stuffed olives.
Cooked beets cut into shapes or sticks.
Carrots cut into shapes.
Pearl onions.
Pickles.
Capers.
Pomegranate seeds.
Fennel slices.
Cucumbers or Cucumber Slices, page 459.
Green and red peppers shredded. Pepper Slices, page 466.
Mayonnaise or soft cream cheese forced through a tube.
Aspic jellies in small molds, or chopped aspic.
Eggs hard-cooked, sliced, riced or stuffed.
Dwarf tomatoes stuffed with cottage cheese.
Cherry tomatoes.
Fresh herbs, sprigs or chopped.

NUT CREAMS
Roll into ¾ inch balls:
Soft cream cheese
Flatten them slightly between 2:
English walnut or large pecan meats

CHEESE CARROTS
Grate:
Yellow cheese
Moisten it until it is a good consistency to handle with:
Cream or salad dressing
Shape it into small carrots. In the blunt end place:
A sprig of parsley

CREAM CHEESE BALLS ON WATER CRESS
14 to 20 Balls
Work with a fork until smooth:
2 packages soft cream cheese: 6 oz.
Stir in:
¼ lb. Roquefort cheese
1 pony brandy or 2 tablespoons sherry
Add until the cheese is a good consistency to shape:
Cream
Form the cheese into 1 inch balls. They may be rolled in chopped parsley, chives or olives. Chill them. Serve them bedded on:
Water cress
This mixture may also be used as cheese spread.

CREAM CHEESE AND NUT BALLS
12 to 16 Balls
Work with a fork until smooth:
2 packages soft cream cheese: 6 oz.
Stir in until the cheese is a good consistency to shape:
Cream
Add:
¼ cup coarsely chopped nut meats
Shape the cheese into 1 inch balls. They may be rolled in chopped chives.

ROQUEFORT CHEESE BALLS
Mash:
¼ lb. Roquefort cheese
Beat in:
1 teaspoon soft butter
1 teaspoon Worcestershire sauce
1 teaspoon brandy
Roll the cheese into balls. Garnish them with:
Paprika
Sprigs of parsley

CRAB-APPLE GARNISH

Roll into 1 inch balls:
　Coarsely grated yellow cheese
Place in one side of each ball:
　A whole clove
Place in the opposite side:
　The stem of a clove
Sprinkle one cheek of each ball with:
　Paprika

Cucumber Jelly, page 483.

FRIED CHEESE BALLS

Add to firm, dry:
　Cottage cheese or soya cheese
a generous seasoning of:
　Paprika
Shape it into small balls. Roll the balls in:
　Finely crushed salted cracker
　crumbs
Fry the balls in deep fat (page 542).

PEPPER GARNISH

Cut rings of:
　Green or red pepper ⅓ inch
　thick
Place a ring of pepper on an individual salad to cover a slice of pineapple, tomato, etc. Fill it with:
　Mayonnaise or other dressing

Green Pepper Slices, page 466.

EGG APPLES

Prepare:
　Hard-cooked eggs
While they are warm shell them and press them gently between the palms of the hands until they are round. Color them by placing them in beet juice or red coloring. Place in 2 sides of each egg to represent the blossom ends and the stems:
　Cloves
Or shape the eggs, add the cloves and paint the cheeks of the eggs with a dash of red and a dash of green color.

BEET CUPS

Fine for a plate luncheon.
Prepare, leaving them whole:
　Pickled Beets, page 461
or prepare:
　Boiled Beets, page 272
Drain them. Hollow them into cup shape. You may pink the edges with a knife. Fill the beets with:
　Cream Horseradish Dressing,
　page 497, or prepared horse-
　radish
or any dressing that is suitable to the food you are serving.

CANDIED MINT LEAVES

A good garnish for fruit salads or cocktails.
Remove from stem:
　Fresh mint leaves
Coat both sides with:
　White of egg
Combine:
　6 drops oil of peppermint
　½ cup granulated sugar
Dip the leaves in the sugar on both sides. Place them to dry on waxed paper or in a slow oven.

Salad Dressings

Salad ingredients may be simple but they must be good. While a peppy salad dressing has been known to lift an indifferent salad to unexpected heights, a poor dressing is sure to depress a good salad to incredible dreariness of taste and texture.

Ingredients for good dressings should be mutually stimulating without incongruities or an individual striving for supremacy of flavor. They should be keyed to compliment the salad ingredients they are to accompany.

The first consideration is a choice of oil. There is a distinctive unsurpassed flavor in olive oil. Use it by all means if your budget gives you the green light and remember that the best is "first press" or "virgin." Lemon juice is frequently used to flavor dressings but vinegar remains the accepted favorite. Vinegars have varied personalities according to the base on which they are made: wine, cider, malt, etc. The addition of herbs, spices, condiments and seasonings comes later after a choice of vinegar has been made. The rules in this chapter may inspire you to make spiced or herb vinegars in quantity or to add touches to individual servings of salad dressing that will give them character and appeal. Store dressings in a cool place in closed containers.

Bread to Be Served with Salads

The breads and crackers served with soup, page 75, are suitable to serve with salads.

Rule for French Dressing

There are many variations of French dressing, but the basis is usually 3 parts oil to 1 part vinegar, lemon or lime juice, seasoned with salt and pepper or paprika. These proportions and the seasonings may be varied. Some epicures prefer 4 parts oil to 1 part vinegar and they also prefer to make the dressing at table. If made in advance French dressing should be placed in a tightly closed jar. Shake the jar well before using the dressing.

Onion and garlic add flavor to French dressing. A clove of garlic, peeled, may be placed in a quart of vinegar for 6 or 7 days. The clove is then removed and the delicately flavored vinegar is used for dressings. Or the bowl in which a dressing is to be made may be rubbed with garlic. Very finely minced or grated onion or onion juice may be substituted for garlic, or the dressing may be made without either.

Herb, Wine, Garlic and Spiced Vinegar, page 494, are fine for French dressing.

Please read the paragraph on Lettuce, page 451. In addition to the ingredients suggested do not hesitate to add others, such as Worcestershire sauce, chili sauce, chutney, a dash of curry powder, ½ teaspoonful or more of dried or fresh herbs, sour or sweet cream, cottage or Roquefort cheese.

FRENCH DRESSING
About ½ Cupful

Combine in a small bowl:
- ¼ teaspoon salt
- ¼ teaspoon paprika
- 1 tablespoon olive oil
- 1 tablespoon vinegar or lemon juice
- (¼ teaspoon dry mustard)
- (1 teaspoon sugar)

Beat these ingredients well with a wire whisk or a fork until they are smooth. Add:
- 2 tablespoons olive oil

Beat well again. Add:
- 1 tablespoon vinegar or lemon juice
- 3 tablespoons olive oil

Peel and add:
- (1 clove garlic)

Place the dressing in a jar, cover it well. Put it in a cold place ready for use. It will keep indefinitely. Remove the garlic after 6 or 7 days. Shake the dressing well before serving it. French dressing may be made with an electric mixer or blender. Combine all ingredients in the small bowl. Beat them at high speed for about 4 minutes. Good additions to French dressing shortly before serving are given on page 492. Remember to add, occasionally, lots of chopped parsley, chives or other herb, and 1 teaspoonful of celery seed.

LORENZO DRESSING
About ½ Cupful

Prepare:
- ½ cup French dressing

Add:
- 2 tablespoons chili sauce
- 2 tablespoons chopped water cress

CATSUP DRESSING
About ½ Cupful

Prepare:
- ½ cup French dressing

Beat in:
- 1 tablespoon catsup

Add:
- 1 tablespoon finely chopped celery or 1 teaspoon celery seed
- ½ tablespoon grated onion

ROQUEFORT CHEESE DRESSING I
About ⅔ Cupful

Prepare:
- ½ cup French dressing

Beat into it:
- 2 tablespoons or more crumbled Roquefort cheese

SPECIAL ROQUEFORT SALAD DRESSING

2 Servings

A poet's contribution.

Combine and blend well:

1 tablespoon tarragon vinegar
2 tablespoons tomato catsup
4 tablespoons olive oil
1½ square inches crumbled Roquefort cheese
1 teaspoon grated onion or ½ teaspoon minced garlic

HORSERADISH DRESSING

About ½ Cupful

Prepare:

½ cup French dressing

Beat into it:

1 tablespoon or more fresh or prepared horseradish

ANCHOVY DRESSING

About ½ Cupful

Prepare:

½ cup French dressing

Beat into it:

1 tablespoon or more anchovy or other fish paste

CHIFFONADE DRESSING

About 1½ Cupfuls

Prepare:

½ cup French dressing

Add to it:

2 chopped hard-cooked eggs
2 tablespoons chopped pepper
2 tablespoons chopped parsley
2 teaspoons chopped chives
1 teaspoon chopped onion

CRANBERRY DRESSING

About ⅔ Cupful

Prepare:

½ cup French dressing with lemon juice

Beat into it:

2 tablespoons or more Cranberry Jelly, page 443

MINT DRESSING

About ½ Cupful

Heat:

½ cup vinegar
2 tablespoons sugar
¼ teaspoon salt
A few grains red pepper

Pour this over:

2 tablespoons chopped mint

Chill the dressing.

WATER CRESS DRESSING

About 1 Cupful

Put through a sieve:

2 hard-cooked eggs

Rub them to a paste with:

Olive oil

Add:

½ cup chopped water cress
½ cup French dressing
Lemon juice

WATER CRESS DRESSING OR SAUCE AU CRESSON

About 1 Cupful

Wash, then dry between cloths:

1 cup water cress

Rub it through a fine sieve. The French do not mind trouble, but a blender (see page 898) makes puréeing much easier. Combine it with:

¾ cup mayonnaise
2 tablespoons chili sauce

FRENCH DRESSING WITH POTATO

About ¾ Cupful

This is very good, especially over chicory or endive.

Boil until very tender:

1 small potato: ¼ cup

Peel it and crush it with a fork. When it is free from lumps beat into it slowly until smooth:

½ cup French dressing

FRENCH DRESSING WITH CREAM

About ¾ Cupful

Prepare:

½ cup French dressing

Beat into it slowly:

¼ cup cream

FRENCH DRESSING WITH CREAM CHEESE

About ⅞ Cupful

Mash with a fork and beat until smooth:

1 package cream cheese: 3 oz.

Beat in:

1 teaspoon finely minced onion
½ teaspoon dry mustard
1 teaspoon salt
Freshly ground black pepper
2 tablespoons chopped parsley

Beat in gradually:

¼ cup salad oil
1½ tablespoons vinegar

Serve the dressing over a green salad or a vegetable salad.

FRENCH DRESSING WITH TOMATO SOUP
About 3 Cupfuls
Place in a jar with a screw top:
- 1 can tomato soup: 10½ oz.
- 1 cup vinegar: malt, cider, tarragon, or a combination of all 3
- ½ cup oil
- 1 tablespoon Worcestershire sauce
- 2 teaspoons salt
- ½ teaspoon paprika
- ½ teaspoon pepper
- 1 teaspoon dry mustard
- ¼ cup sugar
- 1 teaspoon onion juice
- 1 peeled clove garlic

Chill the dressing. Shake it well before serving it.

ANCHOVY AND BEET DRESSING
About 1 Cupful
Place in a jar with a screw top:
- ½ cup French dressing
- 3 or 4 chopped anchovies
- 2 small chopped cooked beets
- 1 chopped hard-cooked egg

Season the dressing highly. Shake the bottle well. Pour the dressing over a large bowlful of:
- Endive or lettuce

CHUTNEY DRESSING
About 1 Cupful
Combine in a bottle and chill:
- 1 tablespoon chopped hard-cooked egg
- 1 tablespoon chopped chutney
- ¼ teaspoon curry powder
- 1 tablespoon lemon juice
- ½ cup olive oil
- 3 tablespoons vinegar
- ¼ teaspoon salt
- 1 teaspoon sugar
- A few grains black pepper

Shortly before serving the dressing beat it well with a fork.

VINAIGRETTE DRESSING OR SAUCE
About 1 Cupful
Combine:
- 1 teaspoon salt
- ⅛ teaspoon freshly ground black pepper
- A few grains cayenne
- ¼ teaspoon paprika

Add slowly and beat thoroughly:
- 3 tablespoons vinegar
- ½ cup olive oil

Chop until fine and add:
- 1 tablespoon pimiento
- 1 tablespoon cucumber pickle
- ¾ tablespoon green pepper
- ½ tablespoon parsley
- ½ tablespoon chives or onion

This dressing may be served cold or hot. To heat it use a double boiler. Good cold with a green salad or meat aspic. Good hot over hot asparagus, broccoli, Brussels sprouts, etc.

DRESSING WITHOUT OIL
About ¾ Cupful
No, it isn't particularly good but it may be eaten by the bulging with a clear conscience. This recipe takes the place of mineral oil dressings which are not recommended. Soak:
- ½ teaspoon gelatine

in:
- 1 tablespoon cold water

Dissolve it in:
- ¼ cup boiling water

Add:
- 1 tablespoon sugar
- ½ teaspoon salt

Cool this mixture. Add:
- 1 teaspoon grated lemon rind
- ½ cup lemon juice
- ⅛ teaspoon dry mustard
- ¼ teaspoon paprika
- A few grains cayenne
- ⅛ teaspoon pepper
- ¼ teaspoon onion juice
- (⅛ teaspoon curry powder)

Shake the dressing. Chill it. Before serving it beat it well with a wire beater. Add if you wish:
- 2 tablespoons minced parsley
- 1 tablespoon minced chives

FRENCH FRUIT SALAD DRESSING
About ⅔ Cupful
Prepare:
- ½ cup French dressing

Substitute for the vinegar:
- 3 tablespoons grapefruit or lemon juice

NUT DRESSING
About ½ Cupful
Pound to a paste:
- 2 tablespoons pecan nut meats
- 2 tablespoons blanched almonds

Beat in:
- ¼ cup lemon juice
- ¼ cup olive oil
- ¾ teaspoon salt
- ¾ teaspoon paprika

LEMON AND SHERRY DRESSING FOR FRUIT SALAD
About ½ Cupful
Delightful over tart fruit, apples, grapefruit, etc.
Combine:
> 4 tablespoons lemon juice
> ⅛ teaspoon salt

Stir in slowly:
> 4 tablespoons sugar

Stir in:
> 2 tablespoons sherry

AVOCADO DRESSING
About 1 Cupful
Combine and beat well:
> 2 tablespoons rich cream
> 1 tablespoon lemon juice
> ½ teaspoon salt
> 1 teaspoon prepared mustard
> 6 drops Tabasco sauce

Add and beat well:
> ¾ cup sieved avocado pulp

Chill the dressing.

GARLIC VINEGAR
Heat to the boiling point:
> 1 cup vinegar

Cut into halves and add:
> 4 cloves garlic

When the vinegar is cold place it in a closed jar. After 2 weeks strain it. Use it in dressings or sauces.

FRESH HERB VINEGAR
Combine:
> 1 gallon cider or white wine vinegar
> 2 dozen peppercorns
> 1 dozen sliced shallots
> ¾ cup tarragon
> 8 sprigs rosemary
> 8 sprigs thyme
> 4 branches white savory
> 1 sprig chervil
> 1 well-cleaned, unpeeled, then sliced celeriac root
> ½ cup parsley
> 1 sliced parsley root

Bottle these ingredients. Place them in a sunny window for 2 weeks. Strain the vinegar through cheesecloth.

SPICED VINEGAR
An excellent if deceptive mixture. It tastes like a delicious blend of herbs but it is flavored with spices whole or ground. If ground spices are used filter the vinegar before using it. Combine, stir and heat slowly until just under the boiling point:

> ¼ cup whole cloves
> ¼ cup allspice
> 2 tablespoons mace
> 3 tablespoons celery seed
> ¼ cup mustard seed
> 6 tablespoons whole black pepper
> 3 tablespoons turmeric
> 4 tablespoons white gingerroot
> 1½ gallons cider vinegar
> 2 cups sugar

Place these ingredients in jugs or fruit jars. Slice and add:
> 4 or more cloves garlic

Cork the jugs or screw down the jar lids tightly. The vinegar is ready for use in 3 weeks. Combine it with oil for French Dressing, page 491.

TARRAGON VINEGAR
About 2 Cupfuls
Wash, then dry well:
> 2 cups fresh tarragon leaves

Crush them to bruise them slightly. Add them to:
> 2 cups good warmed vinegar
> 2 whole cloves
> 1 skinned halved clove garlic

Place these ingredients in a covered jar. After 24 hours remove the garlic. After 2 weeks strain and bottle the vinegar. This makes a strong infusion that may be diluted later with more vinegar.

IMPROMPTU SPICED VINEGAR
About 1 Quart
This is a quickly made spiced vinegar which meets with general approval. I serve it frequently in salad dressing. As there is something decidedly haphazard about it the usual question as to how it is made is somewhat embarrassing. The first thing to do is to select a well-flavored vinegar, wine, cider, etc.
To:
> 1 quart vinegar

Add:
> 3 or 4 peppercorns
> 2 tablespoons fennel seed
> 2 tablespoons anise seed
> 2 teaspoons cumin seed
> 2 teaspoons celery seed
> 2 teaspoons caraway seed
> 2 teaspoons dill seed
> 2 teaspoons salt
> 1 or 2 sliced cloves garlic
> ½ teaspoon curry powder
> 2 or 3 cloves
> 2 tablespoons sugar

Add any or all of these and in addition anything you find in your spice or herb cabinet you like. Give the vinegar flavor. If it is too strong you may dilute it later with more vinegar. Bring these ingredients slowly to the boiling point. Place the vinegar in a closed jar. After 2 weeks serve it drained, combined with salad oil in any proportion you like—half and half, 3 parts oil to 1 part vinegar, etc. If you like you may add to it when about to serve it:

Chopped parsley
Chopped chives
Dried or fresh herbs of some other kind

Omit the fennel if you do not like it. It tastes something like licorice. And omit the anise if you wish. You will still have a good blend but it will not be as distinctive as when these ingredients are added.

QUICK HERB VINEGAR
About 1 Cupful
Combine:

    1 cup well-flavored vinegar:
        wine, cider, etc.
    1 teaspoon dried crushed herbs:
        basil, tarragon, etc.

You may use this at once with salad oil. You may add ½ clove of garlic and fish it out later. Shortly before you serve it, add:

    2 tablespoons chopped parsley
    1 tablespoon chopped chives

MAYONNAISE DRESSING
About 1¼ Cupfuls
Mayonnaise is a great favorite not only as a dressing but for combining with other foods. Care must be used in storing all mayonnaise combinations under refrigeration as they are subject to bacterial activity which may be very toxic without showing any evidence of spoilage.
Use chilled ingredients. Place in a medium-sized bowl and beat with a wire whisk:

    2 egg yolks

Beat in:

    ¼ to ½ teaspoon dry mustard
    ½ teaspoon salt
    A few grains cayenne
    ½ teaspoon vinegar or lemon
        juice
    (½ teaspoon confectioners' sugar)

Beat in very slowly ½ teaspoonful at a time:

    ½ cup olive oil

Combine in a cup or small pitcher:

    1½ tablespoons vinegar
    2 tablespoons lemon juice

Beat into the dressing ½ teaspoonful at a time:

    ½ cup olive oil

Alternate the oil with a few drops of the lemon and vinegar mixture. If the ingredients are cold and are added slowly during constant beating this will make a good thick dressing. In summer place the bowl in which the dressing is made over cracked ice. Should the dressing separate, place 1 egg yolk in a bowl. Stir it constantly and add the dressing to it very, very slowly at first, and slowly as the mixture thickens. If the dressing is too heavy thin it with:

    Cream or whipped cream

When making mayonnaise with an electric beater, beat the egg yolks at medium speed for 4 minutes. Combine the dry ingredients and add them. Add 1½ tablespoonfuls of cold water. Adjust the oil dripper. Place ½ of the oil in the container. Add the oil drop by drop. When the dressing begins to thicken add the lemon juice. Place the remaining oil in the container. Let it flow more freely. Beat constantly at medium speed. Time required, about 20 minutes.

CHEF'S MAYONNAISE
About 1½ Cupfuls
Rub a bowl with:

    A cut clove garlic

Place in the bowl and work until smooth:

    1 egg
    ½ teaspoon salt
    ¼ teaspoon paprika
    ¼ teaspoon dry mustard
    ½ teaspoon Worcestershire
        sauce
    ¼ cup catsup
    (1 teaspoon sugar)

Beat in gradually and alternately:

    1 cup salad oil
    ¼ cup vinegar

Beat until thick. An electric mixer is fine for this. Beat in, a little at a time:

    ⅓ cup warm water

Chill until ready to use.

HERB MAYONNAISE DRESSING
About 1½ Cupfuls
This may be made with a good grade of commercial mayonnaise. Combine:

1 cup mayonnaise
½ tablespoon lemon juice
¼ teaspoon salt
¼ teaspoon paprika
1 teaspoon minced dried herbs,
page 831, or ¼ cup finely
chopped parsley
1 tablespoon grated onion
1 tablespoon chopped chives
⅛ teaspoon curry powder
½ teaspoon Worcestershire sauce
(1 minced clove garlic)
(1 tablespoon capers)
Fold in:
½ cup cream, whipped, or thick
sour cream
Make this quite salty if it is to go over
fairly bland food, less salty if you use
shrimp, etc. In that case you may not
need any salt.
For shrimp, etc., you may make the
dressing tart by adding more lemon
juice. Also 2 teaspoonfuls of celery
seed are a good addition.

CREAM MAYONNAISE DRESSING
About 2¼ to 2¾ Cupfuls
Prepare:
1 cup mayonnaise
Add to it shortly before serving:
½ to 1 cup heavy cream, whipped

Mayonnaise for Masking, page 481.

RUSSIAN DRESSING I
About 1¾ Cupfuls
Prepare:
1 cup mayonnaise
Drain:
½ cup chili sauce or ¼ cup chili
sauce and
¼ cup India relish or ¼ cup
chopped celery, peppers and
pimiento
Add it to the mayonnaise with:
(1 teaspoon confectioners' sugar)
Or combine:
¾ cup mayonnaise
1½ tablespoons horseradish
3 tablespoons caviar

THOUSAND ISLAND DRESSING
About 2 to 2½ Cupfuls
Prepare:
1 cup mayonnaise dressing
Add to it:
2 tablespoons chili sauce
2 tablespoons minced stuffed
olives

1 tablespoon chopped green
pepper
1 tablespoon minced onion or
chives
¼ to ½ cup heavy cream, whipped
or plain

ROQUEFORT CHEESE DRESSING II
About 1½ Cupfuls
Prepare:
1 cup mayonnaise dressing
Add to it:
¼ cup or more crumbled
Roquefort cheese
(½ teaspoon Worcestershire sauce)

GREEN SALAD DRESSING
About 2 Cupfuls
Combine in a bowl:
1 cup mayonnaise
½ cup heavy sour cream
1 tablespoon lemon juice
2 tablespoons tarragon vinegar,
wine vinegar, or other
2 tablespoons garlic vinegar
2 tablespoons herb vinegar
2 tablespoons anchovy paste
⅓ cup finely chopped parsley
¼ cup finely chopped onion or
chives
Mix these ingredients well. Serve
them over vegetables or fish.

AIOLI SAUCE
Skin, then chop very finely:
4 garlic clove sections
Beat in:
1 egg yolk
⅛ teaspoon salt
Add in a slow stream, beating constantly:
1 cup oil
As the sauce thickens beat in:
½ teaspoon cold water
1 teaspoon lemon juice
In case the sauce fails to thicken beat
an egg yolk and add the sauce to it
very slowly, beating constantly.

SOUR CREAM DRESSING FOR VEGETABLE SALAD
Method I. About 1 Cupful
Beat until smooth:
1 cup thick sour cream
Add to it:
1 teaspoon grated onion or fresh
onion juice
1 teaspoon celery or dill seed
½ teaspoon salt
A fresh grating of black pepper

To this you may add:
2 tablespoons chopped green or
sweet red pepper

Method II. About ¾ Cupful
Beat with a wire whisk or a fork:
½ cup thick sweet or sour cream
Add to it slowly:
1 tablespoon chopped tarragon,
parsley or chives
3 tablespoons vinegar or lemon
juice
¼ teaspoon salt
⅛ teaspoon paprika
Serve the dressing over home-grown
lettuce or cold Boiled Asparagus, page
265.

Boiled Sour Cream Dressing, page 498.

HARD-COOKED EGG DRESSING
A Scant Cupful
Put through a sieve:
The yolks of 4 hard-cooked eggs
Add:
6 tablespoons olive oil
2½ tablespoons wine or herb
vinegar
1 teaspoon herb mustard or 1
teaspoon prepared mustard plus
½ teaspoon dried herb: tarragon, basil, etc.
½ teaspoon salt
Freshly grated pepper

CREAM HORSERADISH MAYONNAISE
About 1½ Cupfuls
Whip:
½ cup cream
Fold in:
3 tablespoons mayonnaise
2 tablespoons grated horseradish
½ to 1 teaspoon dry mustard
1 tablespoon vinegar
¼ teaspoon dried Herbs, page 833
A few grains cayenne

CREAM HORSERADISH DRESSING
About 1¼ Cupfuls
This dressing is good with cold meat.
Beat until stiff:
½ cup heavy cream
Add slowly, beating constantly:
3 tablespoons lemon juice or
vinegar
¼ teaspoon salt
⅛ teaspoon paprika
A few grains cayenne
2 tablespoons grated horseradish

CREAM CHEESE DRESSING FOR FRUIT SALAD
About 1¼ Cupfuls
Mash with a fork and beat until
smooth:
1 package cream cheese: 3 oz.
Beat in slowly:
1 tablespoon lemon juice
2 tablespoons currant jelly
¾ cup cream
Chill the dressing for 1 hour or more
before serving it.

WHIPPED CHEESE DRESSING
2 Cupfuls
Mash with a fork in a small bowl:
1 package soft cream cheese:
3 oz.
Blend in:
3 tablespoons mayonnaise
dressing
Pour into a cold bowl:
½ cup chilled heavy cream
Whip it vigorously with a rotary egg-
beater until it is fluffy. Add:
2 tablespoons lemon juice
Continue whipping until the cream is
stiff. Fold it into the cheese mixture.
Serve the dressing over:
Fruit salad

CREAM CUCUMBER DRESSING
Pare and seed:
A medium-sized cucumber
Grate it or chop it until it is fine. Drain
it well. Whip until stiff:
½ cup heavy cream
Add, beating constantly:
¼ teaspoon salt
⅛ teaspoon paprika
2 tablespoons lemon juice
Fold in the drained cucumber.

ALMOND AND CUCUMBER DRESSING
About 2 Cupfuls
This is good fruit salad dressing. Pre-
pare:
Boiled Salad Dressing II, page
498
Pare and slice:
½ cup cucumbers
Blanch and shred:
¼ cup almonds
Add these ingredients to the dressing.

COOKED SALAD DRESSINGS
Three recipes for boiled salad dressings are given. No. I made with 1 egg
or 2 yolks, is a very economical, acceptable boiled dressing. It may be

thinned with cream, but is good as it is over vegetable and potato salad. No. II is made with milk and 2 whole eggs. Use these dressings over slaw, tomatoes, aspics, etc. No. III is a fruit salad dressing.

BOILED SALAD DRESSING
Method I.   About 1¼ Cupfuls
Dissolve:
    ½ to 1 teaspoon dry mustard
    1 to 2 tablespoons sugar
    ½ teaspoon salt
    2 tablespoons flour
    ¼ teaspoon paprika
in:
    ½ cup cold water
Beat in the top of double boiler:
    1 whole egg or 2 yolks
    ¼ cup vinegar
Add the dissolved ingredients. Cook and stir the dressing over boiling water until it is thick and smooth. Add:
    2 tablespoons butter
Chill the dressing. It may be thinned with:
    Sweet or sour cream

Method II.   About 1½ Cupfuls
Beat in the top of a double boiler:
    2 egg yolks
    2 teaspoons sugar
    1 tablespoon melted butter
    ⅔ cup milk
    ¼ cup vinegar
    2 teaspoons salt

    A few grains cayenne
    1 teaspoon dry mustard
Dissolve:
    2 teaspoons cornstarch
in:
    ⅓ cup milk
Add it to the ingredients in the double boiler. Cook and stir the dressing over boiling water until it is thick. Cool it. You may add chopped parsley, chives or other herbs, celery or dill seeds, etc. Fold it into:
    2 stiffly beaten egg whites

Method III.   About 1¼ Cupfuls
Beat in the top of a double boiler:
    1 teaspoon salt
    ⅓ teaspoon paprika
    ¼ to ½ cup sugar
    2 tablespoons melted butter
    6 tablespoons cream or fruit
        juice
    3 eggs
    (½ teaspoon mustard)
Stir and cook the dressing over boiling water until it is thick. Add slowly:
    6 tablespoons lemon juice
The dressing may be thinned with:
    Fruit juice or cream

BOILED SOUR CREAM DRESSING
Follow the above rule for:
    Boiled Salad Dressing I
When cold, fold into it:
    1 cup sour cream, whipped

Breads

French bread, biscuit, tortillas, pumpernickel, corn pone, scones, rice cakes and so forth—the very names conjure up old cultures that produced breads as characteristic as their makers. Will our characteristics be judged by the pallid commercial bread loaf in general use today? What a heritage for our children! Let's see what we can do about it.

Flour

In our miraculously mechanical but standardized economy the average housewife, oddly enough, finds to hand only two kinds of white flour, both the result of highly milled or "patent" processing. They are "all-purpose" flour and "cake" flour, used as their names imply. All-purpose is a blend of hard and soft wheat flours. The presence of more and tougher gluten in the hard wheat constituent results in a much more elastic and porous product than when cake flour is used. Cake flour is made of soft wheats, and their delicate, less expansive gluten bakes to a crumblier texture. With these differences in mind, you may substitute for 1 cupful of cake flour, ⅞ cupful of all-purpose flour, or you may substitute for 1 cupful of all-purpose flour 1⅛ cupfuls of cake flour.

While the distinction between these two kinds of white flour is very important in the texture of baked goods, there is an even greater importance between the cooking and nutritional qualities of white and whole-grain flours. Whole-grain flours, whether coarsely or finely milled, retain their original vitamins, mineral salts, fats and other still unknown factors. Scientists are aware of about twenty of these substances, even if they have so far failed to isolate them all or to produce them synthetically. Most grains are similar in their structure, carrying in the outer coatings a generous share of their minerals, vitamins and roughage; in the germ lies the greatest concentration of mineral, vitamin and fat; in the endosperm mainly starch and some protein.

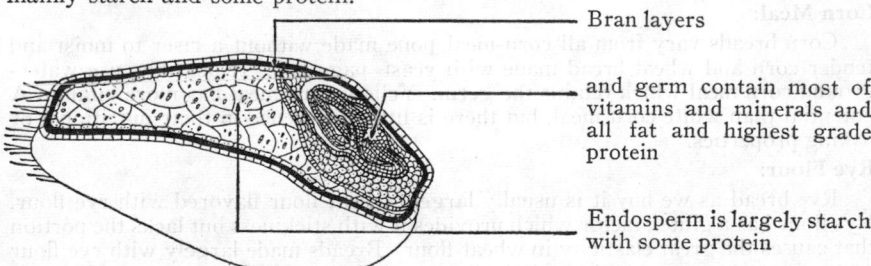

Bran layers

and germ contain most of vitamins and minerals and all fat and highest grade protein

Endosperm is largely starch with some protein

But the outer coating and germ, small as you can see they are compared with the whole kernel in this enlarged drawing of wheat, are of unchallenged importance in content and irreplaceable in flavor.

We have been so accustomed in the last decades to our very much bleached white flours that we are apt to forget that earlier chefs knew only whole-grain or whole-kernel flours. This was not the whole wheat, so called, of our commercial world but the whole grain which includes the germ. Even the finest manchet flour contained the germ. But flours in general use today completely lack it. As Dr. A. J. Carlson, a leading investigator on foods and nutrition says so graphically, "When rats and gray squirrels are given corn in abundance they eat the germ and leave the rest.

People leave the germ and eat the rest." This nutritious and tasty entity, the germ, is removed in modern milling because flours made with it are both harder to mill and to keep. After the removal of the outer coats and germ, our flours are sometimes "enriched" but the term is misleading. As a rule only about three of the known substances in the germ are replaced. Compared to whole-grain flour "enriched" flour is still impoverished.

Most housewives, like wholesalers, prefer white flours because they keep indefinitely and need not be stored in a cool dark place as must the whole-grain flours if the fat in the germ is to be kept fresh. Housewives also hesitate to substitute whole grains even when they are well aware of their values, because they so seldom know their cooking peculiarities and dread failures in using them.

If you do a great deal of baking you probably have your favorite brand of white flour for certain cake and bread recipes, and you can easily imagine the variations that would result from using flours with completely different properties. But the staff of life as now presented to us commercially is frequently such a weak reed that even if faint-hearted you may be encouraged to try for fuller returns by baking your own bread. Try the whole-grain recipes in this chapter or experiment independently on the basis of the following suggestions.

The best flour substitutions are made by weight rather than volume. A rule of thumb formula for substituting coarsely ground whole grains for all-purpose flour is to add 20% more liquid and cut the shortening 10%. But you may also consider whole-grain flours and their peculiarities separately and substitute the following approximate amounts of flour.

Whole-Grain or Graham Flour:

Use 1 cupful of very finely milled whole-grain flour, sometimes called whole-kernel or graham flour, for 1 cupful of all-purpose flour. For coarsely ground whole-grain flour substitute ⅞ cupful to 1 cupful of all-purpose flour. This is stirred lightly rather than sifted before measuring.

Wheat Germ:

You may also use ⅓ cupful of powdered wheat germ and ⅔ cupful of all-purpose flour for 1 cupful of all-purpose flour. Be sure that the wheat germ either powdered or whole is very slightly toasted before combining it with the dough.

Corn Meal:

Corn breads vary from all corn-meal pone made without a riser to moist and tender corn and wheat bread made with yeast, page 530. If possible, use water-ground corn meal which retains the germ. Yellow corn meal has more vitamin A potential than white corn meal, but there is little difference in their nutritional or baking properties.

Rye Flour:

Rye bread as we buy it is usually largely wheat flour flavored with rye flour. Rye flour has a gluten factor which provides it with stickiness but lacks the portion that causes the great elasticity in wheat flour. Breads made largely with rye flour are moist and compact and usually call for a sour dough leavener, page 532.

Soy Flour:

Soy flour has both a high protein and a high fat content. Because of the fat it is not mixed with the dry ingredients but is creamed with the shortening or blended with the liquids. It is usually substituted: 2 tablespoonfuls of soy flour plus ⅞ cupful of all-purpose flour for 1 cupful of all-purpose flour. But it may be used, if you like the flavor, up to 20% of the weight of the flour in the recipe. Soy flour causes heavy browning of the crust so watch temperature.

Cotton Seed and Peanut Flours:

Cotton seed and peanut flours are also substituted: 2 tablespoonfuls of either with ⅞ cupful of all-purpose flour for 1 cupful of all-purpose flour.

Rice and Potato Flours:

Rice and potato flours used straight in recipes heavy in eggs make a very delicate but close dough. Potato flour used in part in bread recipes gives a moist, slow-staling loaf. Substitute ½ cupful of rice flour or potato flour for 1 cupful of all-purpose flour.

Oatmeal:

If you add oats to white flour, use steel-cut rather than rolled oats as they have more nutritional value. Oats or oatmeal may replace up to one third of each cupful of all-purpose flour, but first pour boiling water over the oatmeal and shortening and let it cool to lukewarm before adding the yeast.

Bean Flour:

You may substitute 4 to 5 cupfuls of bean flour for 1 cupful of all-purpose flour.

Improvers:

Various improvers such as fruits and nuts, wheat germ or milk solids are added to doughs. They should never be used in greater quantity than 20% to 30% of the weight of the flour and except for milk solids should always be added last to the dough.

Brewers' yeast, which has no leavening power but adds nutritive value, may be added in the proportion of 1 teaspoonful to 1 cupful of all-purpose flour.

Yeast

Yeast is sold in moist and dry form. Moist yeast, compressed yeast, comes in a small cake. It must be kept under refrigeration. It will keep for about two weeks in a refrigerator, for about 4 months in a freezer. When at its best it is a light grayish tan in color, crumbles readily, breaks with a clean edge and smells pleasantly aromatic. When old it becomes brownish in color.

Dry yeast comes in granular form. It is packaged, labeled and dated. Stored in a cool place it will keep for several months. Its span of usefulness may be lengthened by refrigeration. One cake of compressed yeast may be substituted for one package of dry yeast and vice versa.

For further information on yeast see Yeast Breads, page 526.

Rule for Baking Powder

When confronted with the questions growing out of the use of the various forms of baking powder now on the market the puzzled layman is apt to sigh for the good old days when this article was made at home, rather haphazardly, according to a formula handed down from one generation to the other.

Had I died in 1933 baking powder would have been found written on my heart. Due to the complexity of the problem it became one of life's major issues.

When William Beebe's nerves became overwrought due to the study of the personal relationships of birds, he turned from them to occupy himself with the habits of the less emotional fishes. I had no such outlet. I had to battle with many new things, to discover that calcium phosphate baking powder while not necessarily so labeled has a double action, that both calcium and tartrate baking powders may be used in smaller amounts than usually designated in recipes without other harm to the baked product than a slightly smaller volume, that when eggs are added to a batter the usual measurement of 1 teaspoonful baking powder to a cupful of flour may be reduced, etc. etc.

I do not pretend to have solved the baking-powder problem scientifically, but endless experiments have enabled me to solve it to my own present satisfaction.

Baking powders come under the following general classifications:

Tartrate Baking Powder
Calcium Phosphate Baking Powder
Combination Type or Double Acting Baking Powder (also called S. A. S.)

Look at the label of your baking-powder can. There you will find distinctly marked the type of baking powder you are using.

The recipes in this book will tell you plainly how much of each type of baking powder I find it advisable to use to make a successful bread or cake.

If you wish to determine whether baking powder is still active, mix 1 teaspoonful baking powder with ⅓ cupful hot water. Use the baking powder only if it bubbles enthusiastically.

Sweet and Sour Milk Substitutions and Equivalents

Sour milk is best for baking purposes when it has reached the clabbered stage. The curd is thick and heavy, and the whey has not separated to any great extent. It should be kept in a clean, covered container. If milk is placed in the refrigerator as soon as it reaches the clabbered stage, it will remain in this condition for 3 or 4 days and it may be used as needed.

To Substitute Sour Milk for Sweet Milk: Sour milk may be used in recipes calling for sweet milk if soda is added to the dry ingredients.

Allow ¼ to ½ teaspoonful baking soda—according to the acidity of the milk—to 1 cupful clabbered milk or buttermilk to leaven 2 cupfuls flour.

Baking soda should not be mixed with the sour milk because in this way some of the gas that should go to leaven the product is lost. Baking soda should be sifted with the flour. This is an important factor in the success of baking soda recipes.

One cupful heavy sour cream may be substituted for ⅓ cupful butter and ⅔ cupful milk in any sour milk recipe.

One cupful thin sour cream may be substituted for 3 tablespoonfuls butter and ¾ cupful milk in any sour milk recipe.

To Sour Milk or Cream add 1½ tablespoonfuls of lemon juice or 1⅓ tablespoonfuls of vinegar to each cupful of lukewarm sweet milk, fresh or evaporated. Let stand for a few minutes before using.

Milk is the usual fluid in cake recipes and water is used in true pastries. Many people use dry skim milk as an economical substitute for fresh milk in cooking or as an enricher. If you are interested in either use, read the following:

Powdered milk comes in 2 forms, whole and skim. The skim is without fat and is better for use in yeast doughs than the whole. All powdered milk must be kept in a closely covered light-proof container but need not be refrigerated.

One cupful dry milk solids plus 1 quart of water is the cooking equivalent of 1 quart of liquid milk. Beat the mixture in a blender or mixer or blend it with a rotary beater.

Cooked cereals may be enriched by adding dry milk to the dry ingredients. Add 3 tablespoonfuls to each ½ cupful cereal and the amount of water or milk given in the rule.

To enrich cocoa, custards and puddings, add 3 tablespoonfuls of dry milk for each cupful of liquid.

As dry milk solids scorch easily use low heat or a double boiler in the making of gravies, etc., and low baking temperatures for meats and mixtures to which the dry milk has been added.

In making sauces mix the dry milk with the flour and melted fat away from heat and add the liquid, warm but not hot, gradually to avoid lumps.

One tablespoonful nonfat dry milk solids equals ¼ ounce.

Four cupfuls nonfat dry milk solids equal 1 pound.

If you use evaporated milk, substitute ½ cupful of evaporated milk and ½ cupful of water for 1 cupful of fresh milk.

To make evaporated milk flow easily from a can punch 2 holes, one directly opposite the other, near the rim of the can.

If you use Soya Milk, page 817, substitute 1 cupful for 1 cupful of milk.

In recipes calling for scalded milk rinse a pan in water before adding the milk to prevent sticking. Place the pan over low heat until tiny bubbles form around the edges.

Keep all milk away from direct sun as its riboflavin content deteriorates very fast on exposure to strong light.

To pasteurize raw milk or cream at home, place the milk or cream in glass heat-proof jars on a rack in a deep well or large kettle filled with water. Heat the water surrounding the milk jars to 160° for 20 minutes. Cool rapidly to 50° and refrigerate, or see that the milk itself reaches a temperature not lower than 143° for 30 minutes. Cool to 50° and refrigerate.

Substitutions in Cooking Fats and Oils

Watch your cooking fats and oils as they have different properties and flavors. Unless you interchange them carefully you may have a failure instead of a success.

Butter and hydrogenated fats like oleomargarine, which are increased in bulk by the addition of gas, can be used cupful for cupful.

Cooking oils and lard are substituted ⅞ cupful for 1 cupful of butter.

Chicken fat is measured ⅔ cupful for 1 cupful of butter, but the liquid must be reduced by ¼ cupful for each cupful called for in the recipe.

To grease pans for baking use only unsalted and waterless fats such as unsalted butter, hydrogenated fat or oil.

In any type of fat the amount of fat when melted equals the same amount of solid fat. Melted fat should never be substituted for solid fat unless the recipe calls for it.

To measure fats see page 593.

Sugar Substitutions and Information

Sugar is added to bread dough in small amounts to make the dough rise more quickly and give the crust a golden brown color.

Like fats sugars are not always interchangeable measure for measure, and their properties vary greatly. Also where yeast is used, if the sugar or salt content of a recipe is increased unduly, it may lessen the leavening power.

Granulated white sugar is either cane or beet sugar. Its variants are powdered sugar, which is a more finely granulated product, sometimes used in cakes, sauces and icings, but usually reserved for cold drinks and fruits because it dissolves easily in a cold fluid.

Do not confuse powdered sugar with confectioners' sugar, the finest form marked XXXX, or substitute it when confectioners' sugar is called for in a recipe.

Brown sugar, both light and dark, is a less refined form of cane or beet sugar and contains more moisture. It tends to lump and cake in drying out and should be stored in a closed tin container. If hard, it may be set in a slow oven until it softens.

The following comparative weights may be valuable in gauging substitutions:
One-half pound granulated sugar equals 1 cupful
One-half pound confectioners' sugar equals 1¾ cupfuls
One-half pound brown sugar equals 1⅛ cupfuls firmly packed

To measure brown sugar pack it in a dry measuring cup until in unmolding it holds its shape like a perfect sand tower.

Honey is highly variable as it is often adulterated harmlessly as far as use goes by the addition of a glucose sirup. The general rule for combining it with any flour mixture is: Use honey cupful for cupful with sugar but omit ¼ cupful of the liquid called for in the recipe. If the honey is acid, you may add ¼ to ½ teaspoonful of soda. Honey cakes and breads have very good keeping qualities.

To redeem honey that has crystallized, stand jar in a pan of hot water until honey liquefies.

Molasses and black strap molasses may be used interchangeably with honey, but the soda must be added to the molasses in baking. Black strap has a very distinct flavor so use it only in small quantities.

Sorghum and cane sirup may be used like molasses.

Maple sirup is substituted for sugar by using 1 cupful sirup for ½ cupful of sugar and lessening the liquid in the recipe about ¼ cupful.

Maple sugar because of its cost is frequently confined to flavoring. It dissolves slowly and may be grated or slivered before combining with other ingredients.

Sucaryl sodium and saccharine are two colorless sugar substitutes. Sucaryl retains its sweetness even in boiling solutions and with some cooked foods its sweetening power is increased. An ⅛ grain Sucaryl tablet equals 1 teaspoonful of sugar; ¼ teaspoonful Sucaryl solution equals 2 teaspoonfuls of sugar.

Saccharine can never be used in baking or cooking. It can only be added after the product is cooked. A ¼ grain tablet equals 1 teaspoonful of sugar in sweetening power.

Oven Temperatures

Correct oven temperatures are extremely important and are indicated in each recipe. Set your regulator and preheat your oven to the degree given in the recipe. This will take about 10 to 15 minutes for a gas oven. Electric stoves have an indicator to show when the right degree of heat has been reached. When you have no regulator an oven thermometer is helpful.

	Degrees
Slow oven	250 to 325
Moderate oven	325 to 400
Quick or hot oven	400 to 450
Very hot oven	450 to 550

Oven Temperature Tests

For those who have no thermometer the following tests are suggested:
Sprinkle flour on a pan and place it in a heated oven.
If it turns a *delicate brown* in 5 minutes the oven is *slow*—250° to 325°.
If it turns a *medium golden brown* in 5 minutes the oven is *moderate*—325° to 400°.
If it turns a *deep dark brown* in 5 minutes the oven is *hot*—400° to 450°.
If it turns a *deep dark brown* in 3 minutes the oven is *very hot*—450° to 500°.
A piece of white tissue paper may be used in place of the flour.

General Rules and Terms for Baking

Preheat the Oven to the degree given in the recipe before placing the dough in it.
Ingredients: Have all ingredients at room temperature.
To Beat: Mix with vigorous strokes with a circular over and over motion (page 592).
To Blend: Combine ingredients until they are thoroughly mixed.
To Cream: Combine shortening and sugar with a slotted spoon or with the hand until these ingredients are well blended and fluffy—like whipped cream. Use butter that has been in room temperature long enough to be fairly soft. Take care

that it is not very soft or melted for that will make it oily, unless the recipe calls for melted butter. To measure shortening pack it firmly into the cup or use displacement method illustrated on page 593. Shortening, melted or solid, measures about the same.

To Cut In: Combine butter or shortening with flour by cutting the fat into the flour with a pastry blender or 2 knives until it is reduced to small particles.

To Dredge: Cover the ingredients completely with flour or crumbs.

To Fold In: This usually applies to ingredients into which air has been beaten and in which you wish to retain the air. Fold the lighter into the heavier mixture by a downward and over action enclosing all the air possible until the ingredients are blended. See Cakes, page 592.

To Grease: Spread cake pans or tins with unsalted fat.

To Knead: Press dough with the palms of the hands, then fold the farthest edge to the center. Repeat this action, turning the dough as you knead it (page 527).

To Stir: Mix with a flat circular motion (page 592).

To Whip: This applies to the whites of eggs or to heavy cream. Beat lightly with a circular over and over motion to incorporate air (page 592).

To Work: Combine rather stiff ingredients with a spoon or the hand until they hold together.

To Blanch Almonds: Pour boiling water over shelled almonds. Permit them to stand for 5 minutes. Drain them. Pour cold water over them and slip off the skins. When blanched in advance cover and store in a refrigerator. For ease in shredding or cutting the nuts have them moist and warm.

Eggs: Eggs that have been for some time at room temperature will beat more quickly and lightly than eggs that are very cold. If you are changing the amount of a recipe and you run into a puzzler like dividing 5 eggs—beat up 1 egg, measure it in a measuring cup and divide it.

To Fill: Allow for the rising of bread, cake, soufflés, etc. Fill pans only ⅔ full.

To Measure Brown Sugar: Pack it firmly into the cup (page 593).

To Measure Molasses, Sirup or Honey: Pour it into a greased spoon or cup. If you immerse the spoon or cup, the liquid will cling to the bottom and sides and your measurement will be inaccurate.

To Scald Milk: Put it in a saucepan over slow heat or in a double boiler. It is scalded when small beads appear around the edge.

To Handle Frozen Dough: Doughs may be made in advance and frozen until convenient to bake. Baked breads and rolls may be frozen after baking, page 873.

To Freshen French or Italian Bread: Let cold water run over it a second, then place it in a hot oven 425° or in a covered double boiler over boiling water until it is crisp again.

To Prevent Mold on Bread: Keep it uncovered in a well-ventilated bread box, or keep it well covered in a plastic bag or box in the refrigerator.

Biscuits

The pretzel was the pilgrims' food—the biscuit the pioneers'. A waitress in our early days was a "Biscuit slinger" so perhaps this little round of daily bread served as a handy weapon of defense. Biscuits still call for a quick hand but a light one. Make them thick or thin, crusty or doughy. Serve them piping hot.

To enrich the batter, see suggestions for the use of dried milk solids, etc., page 501.

BISCUITS
About Twenty-Four 1½ Inch Biscuits
Use chilled shortening and liquids.
Sift before measuring:
  2 cups cake flour or 1¾ cups all-
    purpose flour

Resift with:
  1 teaspoon salt
  4 teaspoons tartrate or phosphate
    baking powder or 2½ teaspoons
    combination type (see Baking
    Powder, page 501)

Add:

2 to 6 tablespoons butter

For equivalents of other shortening, see page 503. If oil or melted shortening is substituted, it should be added to the liquid.

Cut the solid shortening into the dry ingredients with a pastry blender, or 2 knives, until the mixture is the consistency of coarse corn meal. Make a well in the center of these ingredients. Pour into it:

⅔ to ¾ cup milk or milk and water

Stir the milk in cautiously until there is no danger of spilling it, then stir it vigorously until the dough is fairly free from the sides of the bowl. The time for stirring should be a scant ½ minute. Turn the dough onto a lightly floured board. A large powder puff dipped in flour makes an even dusting on both board and roller. Knead the dough gently and quickly for a scant ½ minute. Roll it with a lightly floured rolling pin or pat it gently with the palm of the hand until it has the desired thickness—about ¼ inch is right for a plain biscuit, ½ inch or less for a tea biscuit and 1 inch or more for shortcake. Cut the dough with a biscuit cutter. If it sticks, dip the cutter in a very little flour.

Brush the tops of the biscuits with:

(Milk or melted butter)

Use a spatula to place them on a greased baking sheet. Place biscuits 1 inch apart if you like them crusty all over, close together if not. Biscuits may be prepared ahead of time, see Mix below. Cover them with waxed paper and place them in the refrigerator for several hours or until ready to use. Bake them in a quick oven 425° until done, about 12 minutes—a little longer if they have been chilled.

To reheat biscuits, place them in a paper bag, close the bag and place it in a quick oven 425°, or sprinkle a very little water on the biscuits and reheat them in a covered double boiler.

An herb may be added to any biscuit dough. This gives zest to a meat shortcake or chicken pot pie. Add ½ teaspoonful dried rosemary or ¼ cupful finely chopped fresh parsley, chives, etc.

DROP BISCUITS

The kneading and rolling called for in the preceding rule are avoided in this emergency recipe. These biscuits are less shapely but are equally palatable. Add to the preceding rule for Biscuits:

2 tablespoons or more milk

Stir the dough for a scant minute. Drop it by the spoonful on a greased baking sheet. Follow the preceding rule for baking and reheating biscuits. You may stir in lightly 1 cupful blueberries, washed and drained.

BISCUIT STICKS

Prepare by any rule:

Biscuit dough

Cut it into sticks ½ inch high, ½ inch wide, 3 inches long. Brush the sticks with:

Melted butter

Bake them and stack them log cabin fashion.

FLUFFY BISCUITS OR SHORTCAKE DOUGH

About Twenty-Four 1½ Inch Biscuits

Follow the rule for combining and baking biscuits, page 505. Sift before measuring:

2 cups cake flour or 1¾ cups all-purpose flour

Resift with:

4 teaspoons tartrate or phosphate baking powder or 2½ teaspoons combination type (see Baking Powder, page 501)
1¼ teaspoons salt
1 tablespoon sugar

Cut in as directed:

2 tablespoons butter or 4 tablespoons for richer dough

Add:

¾ cup rich milk or cream

Fluffy Biscuits make good shortcake. For other Shortcake Recipes see Index.

MOCK ROLLS

Follow the preceding rule for Fluffy Biscuit Dough. Substitute for 1 tablespoonful sugar:

½ teaspoon sugar

Roll the dough to the thickness of ⅓ inch. Cut it with a biscuit cutter. Brush the biscuits with:

Melted butter

Fold them over like pocketbook rolls. Brush the tops with:

Melted butter

Place the biscuits in a greased pan and permit them to rise in a warm place for 30 minutes. Bake them like biscuits (page 505).

HOMEMADE BISCUIT MIX

Ninety-Six 1½ Inch Biscuits

Sift:

8 cups all-purpose flour

Resift with:

    1 tablespoon salt
    ¼ cup combination-type baking
      powder
    (1 cup skim-milk solids)

Using milk solids is a good way to add flavor and nutritive value to the biscuits without anyone knowing the secret except the cook. Cut into these ingredients, using pastry blender or a fork, until the mixture is like coarse corn meal:

    1 cup shortening

Place the mix in a closely covered container. It will keep for weeks in a cool dark place, for months in a refrigerator. Use it as a basis for biscuit dough, adding milk as needed.

BISCUITS WITH PREPARED BISCUIT FLOUR

Try moistening these "boughten" flours with cream instead of milk. Roll and cut the dough. Dip the biscuits in melted butter and bake them as directed on the label.

SOUR MILK BISCUITS

About Twenty-Four 1½ Inch Biscuits
This recipe makes a very tender dough. Follow the rule for combining and baking:

    Biscuits, page 505

Use the following ingredients, sifting before measuring:

    2 cups cake flour or 1¾ cups all-
      purpose flour
    1 teaspoon salt
    3 teaspoons tartrate or phosphate
      baking powder or 2 teaspoons
      combination type (see Baking
      Powder, page 501)
    1 teaspoon sugar
    ½ teaspoon soda

Cut in:

    4 tablespoons lard or 5 table-
      spoons butter

Add as directed:

    ⅔ to ¾ cup sour milk or buttermilk

WHIPPED CREAM BISCUITS

About Eighteen 2 Inch Biscuits
Sift before measuring:

    2 cups all-purpose flour

Resift with:

    3 teaspoons tartrate or phosphate
      baking powder or 2¼ teaspoons
      combination type (see Baking
      Powder, page 501)
    ¾ teaspoon salt

Whip until stiff:

    1 cup heavy cream

Fold it lightly into the flour mixture

using a fork. Turn the dough onto a floured board. Knead it lightly for 1 minute. Pat the dough to the thickness of ¼ inch. Cut it with a biscuit cutter. Bake the biscuits in a hot oven 425° from 10 to 12 minutes.

ORANGE BISCUITS

For those "as likes them." Prepare:

    Fluffy Biscuits, page 506

Add to the dry ingredients:

    The grated rind of 1 orange
    1 tablespoon sugar

Place the biscuits on a greased sheet or pan. Dip a piece of:

    Cube loaf sugar

quickly into:

    Orange juice

Press it gently into a biscuit. Repeat the process until each biscuit is filled with a cube of sugar. Bake the biscuits in a hot oven 425° for 15 or 20 minutes.

PINEAPPLE BISCUITS

Prepare:

    Fluffy Biscuits, page 506

Use part rich milk and part:

    Canned pineapple juice

Dent the top of each biscuit. Fill the dent with:

    Drained canned crushed pine-
      apple

Sprinkle the biscuits lightly with:

    Confectioners' sugar

Bake the biscuits in a hot oven 425° for 15 or 20 minutes.

BLUEBERRY BISCUITS

Prepare by any rule:

    Biscuit dough

Roll it to the thickness of ¼ inch. Line greased muffin tins halfway up with the dough. Fill the middle with:

    Sugared blueberries

Cover them with a round of dough. Moisten the edges of the shells and the rounds and press them lightly together; or cut the dough into squares, fit them into greased muffin tins, fill them with sugared berries and pinch the corners of the dough together. Bake the biscuits in a quick oven 450° from 12 to 15 minutes.

CHEESE BISCUITS

Follow the rule for:

    Biscuits, page 505

Add to the dry ingredients:

    ¾ cup grated or finely chopped
      cheese

Substitute for ¾ cupful milk:

    ¾ cup milk and water in equal
      parts

BROWN SUGAR ROLL OR PINWHEEL BISCUIT

Prepare by any rule:
    Biscuit dough
Roll it to the thickness of ½ inch.
Spread the surface with:
    4 tablespoons soft butter
    ¾ cup brown sugar
    (Chopped nuts)
    (Chopped raisins)
Roll the dough like a jelly roll, see page
648. Cut it into 1 inch slices. Bake the
slices set well apart in a greased pan in
a quick oven 425° for 15 to 20 minutes.

FILLED BISCUITS OR PINWHEEL BISCUITS

Many of the good fillings for sandwiches, turnovers and pastry snails
may be used to make filled biscuits.
Follow the rule for:
    Biscuits, page 505
Pat or roll it to the thickness of ¼ inch.
Cut the dough into rounds. Spread one
round with a filling like cheese, deviled
ham, etc.; cap it with a second round.
Or, spread the dough with a filling, roll
it loosely and permit it to chill. Cut the
roll into slices. Bake the biscuits or
slices in a hot oven 425° for about 12
minutes.

STREUSSEL BISCUITS

Follow any rule for:
    Biscuit dough
Roll it to the thickness of ¼ inch. Cut
it into rounds. Place the rounds on a
greased sheet. Sprinkle the tops with:
    Streussel, page 624
Bake the biscuits as directed.

GRIDDLE BISCUITS

A good rule for the ovenless housekeeper. Prepare by any rule:
    Biscuit Dough
Bake the biscuits on a hot, lightly
greased griddle 1 inch apart. Brown
them on one side for about 5 minutes,
turn and brown them on the other side.

BISCUIT EASTER BUNNIES

Diverting for children.
Prepare by the rule on page 505:
    Biscuits
You may add:
    2 tablespoons sugar
Pat or roll out the dough to the thick-
ness of ½ inch. Cut it out with 3 sizes
of cutters. I. Large, about 3 inches,
II. ½ as large, and III. ¼ as large.
Assemble your bunnies as shown here.
Use the large biscuit for the body, use

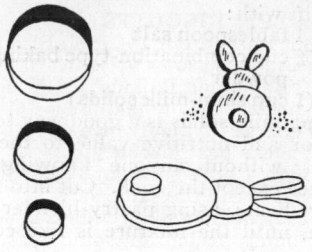

the second biscuit for the head and roll
the third biscuit into a ball for the tail.
Flatten some of the second size biscuits slightly and shape them into ovals
for the ears.
Place the bunnies on a greased sheet.
Bake them in a hot oven 425° for about
15 minutes, or until done.

Birthday Bread Horse, page 538.

WHOLE-WHEAT BISCUITS

Follow the rule for:
    Biscuits, page 505
Substitute for white flour:
    2 cups unsifted whole-wheat flour
Use in all:
    3 tablespoons shortening
When the biscuits are ready to be put
in the oven dot them with:
    A dab of butter

BRAN BISCUITS
About Twenty 1½ Inch Biscuits

Fine to serve for a change. Very good
with a cheese spread.
Sift before measuring:
    1 cup all-purpose flour
Add:
    1 cup bran flakes or whole bran
    ½ teaspoon salt
    4 teaspoons tartrate or phosphate
    baking powder or 2½ teaspoons
    combination type (see Baking
    Powder, page 501)
Cut into these ingredients with a
pastry blender or 2 knives:
    ¼ cup lard
Stir in enough milk to make a soft
dough, about:
    ⅔ cup milk
Pat the dough on a piece of waxed
paper to the thickness of ⅓ inch. Cut
it into rounds. Top the biscuits with:
    A dab of butter
Bake them in a hot oven 425° for
about 15 minutes.

BEATEN BISCUITS
About Forty-Four 1½ Inch Biscuits
The following lines by Howard Weeden ("Bandanna Ballads") sum up in a nutshell the art of making biscuits:

"Of course I'll gladly give de rule
  I meks beat biscuit by,
Dough I ain't sure dat you will mek
  Dat bread the same as I.

"'Case cookin's like religion is—
  Some's 'lected an' some ain't,
An' rules don't no more mek a cook
  Den sermons mek a Saint."

Sift 3 times:

> 1 tablespoon sugar
> 4 cups all-purpose flour
> 1 teaspoon salt

One teaspoonful of any baking powder may be added at this time.
Cut into the flour with a pastry blender or 2 knives:

> 4 tablespoons chilled lard

When ingredients are the consistency of corn meal add to make a stiff dough:

> Equal parts of chilled milk and ice water, approximately 1 cupful

Knead the dough with a biscuit machine, or beat it with a mallet until it is well blistered. Fold it over frequently. This is a long process requiring ½ hour or more. (Miss Weeden's verse goes on to say:

"Two hundred licks is what I gives
  For home-folks, never fewer,
An' if I'm 'specting company in,
  I gives five hundred sure!")

When the dough is smooth and glossy, roll it to the thickness of ½ inch and cut it with a biscuit cutter. Spread the tops with:

> Melted butter

Pierce through the biscuits with a fork. Bake them in a slow oven 325° for about 30 minutes.

SWEET POTATO BISCUITS
Into:

> ¾ cup cooked mashed sweet potatoes

Beat:

> 4 tablespoons melted butter

Stir in:

> ⅔ cup milk

Sift, then measure:

> 1¼ cups all-purpose flour

Resift with:

> 4 teaspoons tartrate or phosphate baking powder or 2½ teaspoons combination type (see Baking Powder, page 501)
> 1 tablespoon sugar
> ½ teaspoon salt

Stir the sifted ingredients into the sweet potato mixture. Turn the dough out on a floured board and toss it lightly until it is smooth on the outside. Roll or pat it to the thickness of ½ inch. Cut it into shapes with a floured biscuit cutter. Bake the biscuits on a greased pan in a hot oven 450° for about 15 minutes.

BAKING POWDER SCONES
About 12 Scones
These are richer than biscuit by the addition of cream and eggs. Fine with a light luncheon. Sift:

> 2 cups cake flour or 1¾ cups all-purpose flour
> 3 teaspoons tartrate or phosphate baking powder or 2¼ teaspoons combination type (see Baking Powder, page 501)
> 1 tablespoon sugar
> ½ teaspoon salt

Cut into these ingredients until the butter is the size of a small pea, using a pastry blender or 2 knives:

> 4 tablespoons butter

Beat in a separate bowl:

> 2 eggs

Reserve 2 tablespoonfuls of this. Add to the remainder and beat:

> ⅓ cup cream

Make a well in the dry ingredients. Pour the liquid into it. Combine the ingredients with a few swift strokes. Handle the dough as little as possible. Place it on a lightly floured board. Pat it until it is ¾ inch thick. Cut it with a knife into diamond shapes or Biscuit Sticks, page 506. Brush them with the reserved egg, sprinkle them with:

> Salt or sugar

Bake them in a hot oven 450° for about 15 minutes.

SALLY LUNN
6 Servings
Combine and cream well:

> ½ cup shortening
> ½ cup sugar

Beat in one at a time:

> 3 eggs

Sift before measuring:

> 2 cups all-purpose flour

Resift with:

> 3 teaspoons tartrate or phosphate baking powder or 2¼ teaspoons combination type (see Baking Powder, page 501)
> ¾ teaspoon salt

Add the sifted ingredients to the batter in about 3 parts alternately with:

> 1 cup milk

Beat the batter lightly until the ingredients are blended only. Bake it in a greased 9 x 12 inch pan in a hot oven 425° for about 30 minutes. Break the bread into squares. Serve it hot.

YEAST SALLY LUNN

Follow the rule for Brioche, page 522, or for Yeast Coffee Cake Dough, page 623. Place the dough in a shallow greased pan. Bake it as directed.

Muffins

Good muffins are straight sided and slightly rounded on top, as shown on the left below. The grain of the muffin is not fine but uniform and the crumb is moist. This shape and texture can be achieved by the proper mixing and baking only, as described in the following rules.

The center drawings show first, the weary muffin peak caused by oven heat that is too slow. The next drawing shows the cracked, wobbly peaked, unsymmetrical form caused by oven heat that is too high.

If the batter has been beaten too long, the grain of the muffin will be coarse and full of tunnels, as shown in the drawing on the right.

The dry ingredients of muffins may be premixed and stored closely covered until ready to use, a breakfast timesaver. Muffins may also be enriched with milk solids and yeast (page 501).

MUFFINS
About Twenty-Four 2 Inch Muffins
Sift before measuring:
> 2 cups cake flour or 1¾ cups all-
> purpose flour

Resift with:
> ¾ teaspoon salt
> ¼ cup sugar
> 3 teaspoons tartrate or phosphate
> baking powder or 2 teaspoons
> combination type (see Baking
> Powder, page 501)

Beat in a separate bowl:
> 2 eggs

Combine and add:
> 2 tablespoons melted butter
> ¾ cup milk

Stir the liquid quickly into the dry ingredients. Do this in only 10 to 15 strokes. Make no attempt to stir or beat out the lumps. Ignore them. Unnecessary handling of the batter results in tough muffins. Pour the batter at once into greased tins, custard cups or paper baking cups. Fill them about ⅔ full. The tops may be sprinkled with 2 tablespoonfuls of poppy seeds or chopped nut meats. Bake the muffins from 15 to 20 minutes in a hot oven 425°. Remove them at once from the tins. To reheat them, place them in a paper bag, close the bag and place it in a hot oven 425° for about 5 minutes.

BLUEBERRY MUFFINS
About Thirty-Six 2 Inch Muffins
Follow the preceding rule for:
> Muffins

Use in all:
> ⅓ cup sugar
> 4 tablespoons melted butter

Fold into the batter:
> 1 cup lightly floured blueberries,
> or 1 cup canned, well-drained
> blueberries, lightly floured
> (1 teaspoon grated orange or
> lemon rind)

NUT OR DATE MUFFINS
Follow the rule on this page for:
> Muffins

Add to the dry ingredients:
> ½ cup chopped nut meats or dates
> or a combination of both

PINEAPPLE MUFFINS
A pleasant variation of a good old standby.
Prepare by the rule on this page:
> Muffin batter

Add to the liquid ingredients:
> ½ cup well-drained crushed
> pineapple

APPLE MUFFINS
Try these for breakfast.
Prepare by the rule on this page:

Muffin batter
Fold into it:
½ cup peeled chopped apples
Pare and core:
Cooking apples
Try to have them about the same diameter as the tops of your muffin cups. Cut them into ½ inch slices. Dip them in a mixture of:
1 part cinnamon
4 parts sugar
Place a slice of apple on the top of each partially filled muffin cup or place these apple rings on plain muffin batter. Bake them as directed on page 510.

BANANA MUFFINS
Prepare by the preceding rule:
Muffin batter
Fold into the liquid ingredients:
½ cup diced mashed bananas

CRUMB MUFFINS
Twelve 2 Inch Muffins
Acceptable muffins that help to utilize stale bread.
Soak for 10 minutes:
1 cup dry bread crumbs
(⅓ cup raisins)
in:
¾ cup milk
Sift before measuring:
½ cup all-purpose flour
Resift:
2 teaspoons tartrate or phosphate baking powder or 1½ teaspoons combination type (see Baking Powder, page 501)
½ teaspoon salt
Melt:
½ tablespoon butter
Beat it with:
1 egg
Add the sifted ingredients to the soaked bread crumbs. Add the egg mixture and stir the batter with a few swift strokes until the ingredients are blended. Partly fill greased muffin tins. Bake the muffins in a hot oven 425° for 20 minutes.

SOUR CREAM MUFFINS
Twenty-Four 2 Inch Muffins
Sift before measuring:
2 cups cake flour or 1¾ cups all-purpose flour
Resift with:
2 teaspoons tartrate or phosphate baking powder or 1 teaspoon combination type (see Baking Powder, page 501)

½ teaspoon salt
2 tablespoons sugar
½ teaspoon soda
Measure:
1 cup sour cream
Beat and add:
1 egg
Stir the liquid into the dry ingredients by the rule for Muffins, page 510. Bake them by the same rule.

SOUR MILK MUFFINS
Follow the preceding rule. Substitute for the sour cream:
1 cup sour milk
Add to the milk:
3 tablespoons melted butter

APRICOT OR PRUNE MUFFINS
Eighteen 2 Inch Muffins
Cream:
¼ cup shortening
½ cup brown sugar
Beat in:
1 egg
Sift before measuring:
2 cups cake flour or 1¾ cups all-purpose flour
Resift with:
1 teaspoon salt
3 teaspoons tartrate or phosphate baking powder or 2 teaspoons combination type (see Baking Powder, page 501)
Add these ingredients to the butter mixture alternately with:
¾ cup milk
Fold in:
¾ cup chopped or riced stewed prunes or apricots
Pour the batter into greased and lightly floured muffin tins. Bake the muffins in a moderate oven 400° for about 25 minutes.

CHEESE MUFFINS
About Thirty-Two 2 Inch Muffins
Permit to stand at room temperature until it is softened:
½ lb. American cheese
Force it through a ricer or rotating grater. Measure before sifting:
2 cups cake flour or 1¾ cups all-purpose flour
Resift with:
4 teaspoons tartrate or phosphate baking powder or 3 teaspoons combination type (see Baking Powder, page 501)
1 tablespoon sugar
½ teaspoon salt
Stir the cheese into the sifted ingredi-

ents until all the particles of cheese have been separated. Combine and beat well:

1 egg
1 cup milk

Add these ingredients to the flour mixture. Beat the batter until blended only. Fold in:

3 tablespoons melted butter

Place the batter in greased muffin tins. Bake the muffins in a moderate oven 350° for about 20 minutes.

BACON MUFFINS

Follow the rule on page 510 for:

Muffins

Add to the batter:

6 to 8 slices cooked crumbled bacon

You may substitute for the butter:

Bacon drippings

RICE MUFFINS

About Thirty 2 Inch Muffins

A good way of utilizing left-over rice. See Batter Bread, page 423.

Beat:

2 egg yolks

Add:

1 cup Boiled Rice, page 103
1¼ cups milk
2 tablespoons melted butter

Sift before measuring:

1½ cups all-purpose flour

Resift with:

1 tablespoon sugar
½ teaspoon salt
3 teaspoons tartrate or phosphate baking powder or 2 teaspoons combination type (see Baking Powder, page 501)

Combine the liquid and the dry ingredients with a few swift strokes. Beat until stiff:

2 egg whites

Fold in the egg whites. Pour the batter into hot, greased pans and bake the muffins in a hot oven 425° for 25 or 30 minutes.

WHOLE-GRAIN MUFFINS

Twenty 2 Inch Muffins

Combine:

⅔ cup all-purpose flour
1⅓ cups whole-grain flour
1½ teaspoons sugar
1 teaspoon salt
3 teaspoons tartrate or phosphate baking powder or 2 teaspoons combination type (see Baking Powder, page 501)
(¼ cup chopped dates or raisins)

Beat in a separate bowl:

(1 egg)

Beat in:

1 cup milk
2 teaspoons melted butter

Stir the liquid into the dry ingredients by the rule for Muffins on page 510. Bake the muffins by the same rule.

GRAHAM MUFFINS

Twenty 2 Inch Muffins

Sift before measuring:

1 cup all-purpose flour

Resift with:

¼ cup sugar
½ teaspoon salt
1 teaspoon soda
1 teaspoon tartrate or phosphate baking powder or ¾ teaspoon combination type (see Baking Powder, page 501)

Add:

1½ cups graham flour

In a separate bowl beat:

2 eggs

The eggs are optional as the muffins remain crisp and good without them. Add and beat in:

3 tablespoons melted butter
1½ cups sour milk

Combine the liquid and the dry ingredients with a few swift strokes. Place the batter in greased muffin tins. Bake the muffins in a hot oven 425° from 15 to 20 minutes.

COOKED OATMEAL MUFFINS

Twenty 2 Inch Muffins

A good muffin and a good way of utilizing left-over oatmeal.

Combine:

1½ cups scalded milk
1 cup cooked oatmeal

Beat well and add:

2 whole eggs

Stir in:

1 tablespoon melted butter

Sift before measuring:

1⅔ cups all-purpose flour

Resift with:

3 teaspoons tartrate or phosphate baking powder or 2 teaspoons combination type (see Baking Powder, page 501)
½ teaspoon salt
2 teaspoons sugar

Combine the sifted ingredients with the milk mixture with a few swift strokes. Place the batter in greased muffin tins. Bake the muffins in a hot oven 425° for about 15 minutes.

FLOURLESS OATMEAL DATE MUFFINS

Twelve 3 Inch Muffins

These are good! Put through a food chopper:

3¾ cups quick oats

There should be 3 cupfuls of oatmeal resembling corn meal in texture. Combine it well with:

1¼ teaspoons salt
4½ teaspoons tartrate or phosphate baking powder or 3¼ teaspoons combination type (see Baking Powder, page 501)
½ cup sugar

Add:

(½ cup chopped nut meats)
(½ cup chopped dates or raisins)

Beat in a separate bowl:

2 eggs

Combine and beat in:

1 cup lukewarm milk
6 tablespoons melted butter

Stir the liquid quickly into the dry ingredients. See Muffins, page 510. Fill greased muffin pans ⅔ full. Bake the muffins in a hot oven 425° for about 25 minutes.

BRAN MUFFINS

Method I.

About Twenty 2 Inch Muffins

A crisp bran muffin good for general use.

Sift before measuring:

2 cups all-purpose flour

Resift with:

2 teaspoons salt
⅓ cup sugar
1 teaspoon any baking powder

1½ teaspoons soda
(1 or 2 teaspoons grated orange rind)

Stir in:

2 cups bran

Combine:

½ cup water
2 cups sour milk
2 tablespoons melted butter
1 beaten egg

Combine the dry and the liquid ingredients with a few swift strokes. Add:

(½ cup raisins)

To bake the batter follow the rule for Muffins, page 510.

Method II.

About Twenty-Two 2 Inch Muffins

These muffins are heavier and sweeter than No. I. Served with cheese they are excellent picnic sandwiches.

Combine and stir well:

2 cups graham flour
1½ cups bran
2 tablespoons sugar
¼ teaspoon salt
1¼ teaspoons soda

Beat:

2 cups sour milk
1 beaten egg
½ cup molasses
2 tablespoons melted butter

Combine the dry and the liquid ingredients with a few swift strokes. Fold in:

1 cup nut meats or nut meats and raisins combined

Bake the muffins in a moderate oven 350° for about 25 minutes.

English Muffins, page 524.

Popovers

Every now and then an excited young woman will rush up to me and say: "I made popovers by your recipe and *they popped!*" Well, that is what they are supposed to do, in fact, these are guaranteed to pop. However, the rise or fall of the popover depends upon having the ingredients at room temperature, mixing the ingredients properly and using the right heat at which to bake them. Evolution has not spared the popover—at one time the batter for this bag of wind was beaten for a long time. Now the authorities suggest that you beat it for about 2 minutes by hand and 1 minute if you are using an electric beater.

As to the insistence that popovers be baked in greased, preheated iron pans, that too, is dated. You may bake them in greased or oiled stone-cold metal pans or in greased or oiled cold custard cups. The cups are filled one third or one half full. You may bake popovers in different degrees of heat too. The old way—hot oven 450° for ½ hour, followed by a moderate oven 350° for 15 minutes, or until done—

has given way to an even oven temperature throughout the baking period—425° or 450° degrees for about 40 minutes, or until done—the time varying slightly with the amount of batter and the size of the cups. My capable friend, Faith, likes to use an oven heat of 500° for 15 minutes and then a slow oven 250° until they are done. This enables her to "hold the popovers over" and to serve them when she is ready rather than when they are ready.

What is "until done"? A popover should be crisp, brown and glossy to the outside and soft but not soggy to the inside. The good old toothpick may be used as a tester. It should come out dry. If you like the centers to be fairly dry, puncture the popover in 4 or 5 places with a toothpick about 5 minutes before the end of the baking period to let out the steam. When done, remove the popovers at once from the pans. To reheat them, place them in a paper bag in a hot oven 425° for 5 minutes.

POPOVERS
8 to 10 Popovers

Spread popover pans with oil. You may heat them for 5 to 8 minutes in a hot oven 500° or not. Heavy oven-proof glass custard cups may be substituted for iron pans. Butter them well but do not heat them. Place them on a cookie sheet. Sift:

1 cup all-purpose flour

Add:

¼ teaspoon salt

Beat in a separate bowl until frothy:

2 large or 3 small eggs

Add:

⅞ cup milk
1 tablespoon melted butter

Stir the liquid slowly into the sifted ingredients. Beat the ingredients until they are well blended, then pour the batter into the oiled pans, filling them only ⅓ full. Bake the popovers in a hot oven 500° for 15 minutes, then reduce the heat and dry them in a slow oven 250° for 15 minutes, or bake them by some other method suggested above. Remove them at once from the pans. Puncture them to let the steam escape.

POPOVERS OR BOUNCING BABIES
6 Servings

These are big, fat popovers, grand to serve for Sunday supper—or at any other time for that matter.
Sift before measuring:

1 cup all-purpose flour

Place in a large bowl:

1 cup milk

Stir in the flour with a wire whisk or an egg beater. Add:

1 tablespoon confectioners' sugar

½ teaspoon salt

Beat in one at a time:

4 whole eggs

Beat the batter well after adding each egg. Have ready 6 oven-proof dishes. These should be about 3½ inches wide and 1½ inches deep. Spread them well with salad oil. Pour the batter into the dishes, about ⅓ cupful to each dish. Bake the popovers for 20 minutes in a hot oven 400°. Then lower the heat to 350° and bake them for 10 minutes longer, or until done. You may stick them with a sharp fork or a skewer to permit the steam to escape 5 minutes before they are done. Serve them piping hot with:

Maple sirup or powdered sugar

The babies are delicious sprinkled at table with lemon juice, so serve:

Wedges of lemon

WHOLE-GRAIN POPOVERS

Follow one of the preceding rules.
Substitute for the flour:

⅔ cup fine whole-grain flour
⅓ cup all-purpose flour

CHEESE POPOVERS

Prepare the batter given in the preceding rule. Add to it:

½ teaspoon salt

Grate into a separate bowl:

¼ lb. cheese: 1 cup when grated

Add:

⅛ teaspoon paprika
A few grains cayenne

Pour 1 scant tablespoonful in each cup; cover it with a teaspoonful of cheese and another teaspoonful of batter. Bake the popovers in a hot oven 475° for about 20 minutes.

Corn Breads

The best of corn bread is made from water-ground corn meal which retains the germ. Use heavy metal utensils. A thin pan permits the bread to overcook on the outside before the inside is done. Grease the pans heavily and heat them well for 5 minutes before adding the batter. To enrich the batter see suggestions for use of dry milk solids and yeast, page 501.

CORN BREAD
Method I.
About 5 Servings of Corn Bread or Sixteen 2 Inch Muffins
This corn bread never fails to elicit a paean of praise.

Heat the oven to 425°. Grease an 8 x 8 inch pan with butter, oil or bacon drippings. Place it in the oven until it is sizzling hot. Sift:

3/4 cup all-purpose flour
3 teaspoons tartrate or phosphate baking powder or 2½ teaspoons combination type (see Baking Powder, page 501)
2 tablespoons sugar
3/4 teaspoon salt

Add:

3/4 cup yellow or white water-ground corn meal

Beat in a separate bowl:

1 egg

Beat into it:

2 to 3 tablespoons melted butter or drippings
3/4 cup milk

Pour the liquid into the dry ingredients. Combine them with a few rapid strokes. Place the batter in the hot pan. You may scatter bits of raw bacon over the top or you may use bits of cooked ham or bacon. Stick these into the batter when it is ½ cooked. You may add to any corn bread batter 1 teaspoonful or more finely chopped chives. Bake the corn bread in a hot oven 425° for about 25 minutes.

Method II. Twelve 2 Inch Muffins
Those who like a very gritty corn bread may prefer this recipe to No. I. Combine:

1 cup water-ground corn meal
2 tablespoons all-purpose flour
1 tablespoon sugar
2 teaspoons tartrate or phosphate baking powder or 1¼ teaspoons combination type (see Baking Powder, page 501)
½ teaspoon salt

Beat in a separate bowl:

1 egg

Add and beat:

1 tablespoon melted lard or butter
½ cup milk

Follow the preceding rule for combining and baking these ingredients.

BUTTERMILK OR SOUR MILK CORN BREAD
6 to 8 Servings or Twenty-Two 2 Inch Muffins
Sift, then measure:

1 cup all-purpose flour

Resift with:

½ teaspoon soda
2 teaspoons tartrate or phosphate baking powder or 1½ teaspoons combination type (see Baking Powder, page 501)
1 tablespoon sugar
1 teaspoon salt

Add:

3/4 cup yellow water-ground corn meal

Combine and beat:

1 cup buttermilk
2 eggs
3 tablespoons melted butter or bacon fat

Stir the liquid into the dry ingredients with a few swift strokes. Pour them into a greased 8 x 10 inch pan. Bake the bread in a hot oven 425° for about ½ hour. If you wish a crisp bread, you may grease the pan well and heat it in a 450° oven until it is very hot before adding the batter.

CORN-BREAD MUFFINS OR STICKS
Heat the oven to 425°. Follow one of the preceding rules for Corn-bread batter. You may add 1 teaspoonful or more chopped chives. Use muffin pans or corn stick pans. Fill the greased and heated pans—preferably heavy metal ones—2/3 full. The pans should be well heated but not sizzling hot. Bake the muffins in a hot oven 425° for about 25 minutes.

BACON CORN-BREAD MUFFINS

Follow one of the preceding rules for Corn-bread batter. Substitute for butter:

> Bacon fat

Sauté, mince and add:

> 4 to 6 slices bacon

CORN-MEAL JELLY MUFFINS

Follow one of the preceding rules for:

> Corn-bread batter

Fill greased and heated muffin pans ⅓ full of batter. Place in each pan:

> 1 teaspoon jelly or thick jam

Cover it with additional batter. Fill the cups ⅔ full. Bake the muffins in a hot oven 425° for about 25 minutes.

CORN DODGERS OR VERY QUICK CORN BREAD

This batter is frequently baked on a griddle. Combine:

> 1 cup water-ground corn meal
> 1 teaspoon salt
> 1½ teaspoons sugar
> 1 tablespoon butter or bacon drippings

The butter measurement may be increased to 2½ tablespoonfuls and 1 egg may be beaten into the batter.
Boil:

> 1 cup water

Pour the water over the dry ingredients. Beat them until they are blended. Drop the batter from a spoon onto a greased sheet or dip the hand in cold water, fill it with batter and reverse the hand, releasing the batter on the sheet. The hand method was learned from Sarah, who, as a child, helped her father make dodgers at the Kentucky Derby. Bake it in a quick oven 400° for about 20 minutes.

CORN-BREAD WAFERS

Follow the above rule for Corn Dodgers. Use in all:

> 1½ cups boiling water

Drop the batter from a teaspoon on a very hot greased sheet and flatten the wafers with a wet spatula. Bake them in a quick oven 400° until crisp.

TOP OF THE STOVE CORN BREAD

Follow the rule for:

> Corn Bread I, page 515

Use:

> 3 tablespoons drippings

Grease well a 10 inch skillet. Pour the batter into it. Cover it closely with a lid. Place it over low heat. Cook it for about ½ hour, or until done. Add ham or bacon as suggested under Corn Bread.

RICE CORN MUFFINS

Twelve 2½ Inch Flourless Muffins
Combine and stir until blended:

> 1⅛ cups cooked rice
> 1 cup yellow water-ground corn meal
> 2 tablespoons sugar
> 2 tablespoons melted butter
> ¾ teaspoon salt
> 2 teaspoons any baking powder
> ⅞ cup milk
> 2 egg yolks

Whip until stiff, then fold in:

> 2 egg whites
> ⅛ teaspoon salt

Bake the batter in well-greased muffin tins in a hot oven 400° for about 20 minutes.

CORN ZEPHYRS

Method I. About Twenty 2 Inch Puffs
This recipe for Zephyrs I calls for whole eggs; Zephyrs II for egg whites only. Pour:

> 2¼ cups boiling water

over:

> 1 cup water-ground corn meal

Add:

> 1 tablespoon sugar
> 1 teaspoon salt
> 2 tablespoons butter

Cook and stir this over low heat until it is a thick mush. Cool it. Beat in:

> 2 beaten egg yolks

Beat until stiff, then fold in:

> 2 egg whites

Drop the batter from a spoon onto a hot buttered pan. Bake the zephyrs in a hot oven 425° for about 20 minutes.

Method II. About Twenty 2 Inch Puffs
Delicate and delicious. Combine:

> 1 cup water-ground corn meal
> 1 tablespoon lard

Scald these ingredients by pouring over them:

> 4 cups boiling water

Add:

> 1 teaspoon salt

Cook the corn meal in a double boiler for 30 minutes. Stir it frequently. Cool it. Whip until stiff:

> 4 egg whites
> ⅛ teaspoon salt

Fold them lightly into the corn-meal mixture. Drop the batter from a spoon onto a greased baking sheet. Bake it in a moderate oven 350° for about ½ hour. Serve the zephyrs piping hot. Fine with a salad course or luncheon dish.

Spoon Bread, page 423; Corn-Meal Soufflé, page 219; Batter Bread, page 423.

CHEESE STRAWS
Method I.
Combine:
> 4 tablespoons soft butter
> 3 tablespoons grated cheese
> 1 egg
> 1 teaspoon sugar
> ½ teaspoon salt
> ⅛ teaspoon paprika
> ⅛ teaspoon nutmeg

Add:

> 2 tablespoons cream
> Enough all-purpose flour to
> make a dough that will roll

Roll the dough. Cut it into strips. Place them on a lightly greased tin. Bake the cheese straws in a quick oven 400° until they are a delicate brown.

Method II.
Roll until very thin:
> Pie Crust, page 561, or
> Hot Water Pie Crust, page 564

Cut it into long strips. Sprinkle the strips with:
> Grated cheese
> Paprika

or add grated cheese to the pie crust. Bake the strips in a very hot oven 450° for about 12 minutes.

Cream Cheese Pastry, page 565.

Rule for Reheating Bread or Buns

Put the bread or buns in a paper bag. Close the bag and and place it in a hot oven 425° for 5 minutes; or put the bread or buns in a hot covered double boiler over boiling water for about the same length of time. If the bread is old, it may be sprinkled lightly with water.

Yeast Rolls and Buns

Please see Breads Made with Yeast, page 526.

You may sprinkle buns or bread when ready for the oven with poppy, caraway, celery or sesame seeds. The latter should be lightly toasted before using.

NEVER FAIL BREAD ROLLS
Eighteen 2 Inch Rolls
These rolls, incredibly light in texture, are not unlike a Brioche (page 522). They require no kneading.
Dissolve:
> 1 cake yeast

in:
> ¼ cup lukewarm water: 80°

Place in a separate bowl:
> ¼ cup lard
> 1¼ teaspoons salt
> 2 tablespoons sugar

Pour over these ingredients and stir until they are dissolved:
> 1 cup boiling water

When they are lukewarm add the dissolved yeast. With a wire whisk beat in:
> 1 egg

Stir in:
> About 2¾ cups sifted all-purpose flour to make a soft dough

Place the dough in a large bowl, cover it with a plate and put it in the refrigerator. The dough will treble in bulk. Chill it from 2 to 12 hours. Pinch off small pieces of dough with buttered hands and place them in greased muffin pans, preferably heavy metal ones, filling the pans about ⅓ full. Cover the tops with:
> Melted butter

Permit the rolls to rise for about 2 hours in a warm place. Bake them in a hot oven 425° for about 20 minutes. Remove them at once from the pans. See above Rule for Reheating Bread or Buns.

FOUR-HOUR BREAD ROLLS
Twenty-Four 2 Inch Rolls
Cream:
> 1 tablespoon lard
> 1 tablespoon butter
> 1½ tablespoons sugar

Add and beat well:
> 1 cup warm milk
> (1 egg or 1 egg white)

Dissolve (page 526):
1 cake yeast
in:
¼ cup lukewarm water
Add these ingredients to the milk mixture. Sift before measuring and add:
1½ cups all-purpose flour
Beat the batter well. Cover it with a cloth and permit the dough to rise in a warm place for 1½ hours. Sift before measuring:
1½ cups all-purpose flour
Add it to the batter with:
1¼ teaspoons salt
Beat the batter well. Place the dough in a bowl, cover it with a cloth and permit it to rise for 1½ hours. Pinch off bits of dough with buttered hands, shape them into small balls and place them in greased muffin tins. The tins should be about ⅓ full. Or place 3 very small balls in greased muffin tins to make Clover Leaf Rolls (page 519). Brush the tops with:
Melted butter
Permit the rolls to rise uncovered in a warm place for 45 minutes. Bake them in a hot oven 425° for about 20 minutes. Remove them at once from the pans.
See preceding Rule for Reheating Bread or Buns.

QUICK PAN ROLLS
Pat bread or roll dough to fit a shallow greased pan. Use a well-greased scissors to cut the dough into squares or oblongs. Brush top with melted butter. Let rise and bake as directed for the rule you are following.

"OVERNIGHT" ROLLS
About 44 Rolls
Combine:
1 crumbled cake yeast
2 teaspoons sugar
Permit these ingredients to stand until they are dissolved and stringy.
Scald (page 945):
1 cup milk
Add and stir until melted:
7 tablespoons lard
Cool these ingredients. Combine and beat well:
7 tablespoons sugar
3 beaten eggs
1 teaspoon salt
Stir in the milk mixture. Stir in the yeast mixture. Stir in:
4½ cups all-purpose flour
Beat the dough until it blisters, about 5 minutes. Place it in a covered bowl

in the refrigerator overnight. Take it out 3½ hours before baking it. Divide

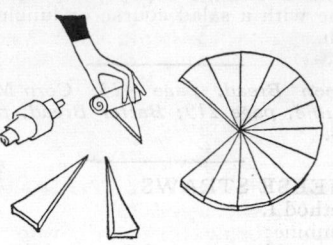

it into 3 parts. Roll each part into a circle about 9 inches in diameter. Cut each circle into 16 wedge-shaped pieces. These pieces may be spread before they are rolled with:
Melted butter
and dusted with:
Sugar and cinnamon
Roll each piece by beginning at the wide end. Stretch the wide end a bit as you start to roll it. Brush the rolls with:
1 beaten egg
Permit the rolls to rise for 3 hours. Bake them for about 12 minutes on a greased sheet in a hot oven 450°. Take care. They burn easily.

PARKER HOUSE ROLLS
About Thirty 2 Inch Rolls
Scald:
1 cup milk
Add and stir until dissolved:
1 tablespoon sugar
2 tablespoons butter
¾ teaspoon salt
When these ingredients are lukewarm, add:
½ cake yeast
dissolved in:
2 tablespoons lukewarm water
Beat in:
(1 egg)
Sift before measuring and add:
2⅝ cups all-purpose flour
Stir in part of the flour, knead in the rest. Use only enough flour to form a dough that can be handled easily. Place the dough in a bowl. Brush the top with:
Melted butter
Cover it and let it rise in a warm place until it doubles in bulk, about 2 hours. Roll the dough and cut it into rounds with a floured biscuit cutter. Dip the handle of a knife in flour and use it to make a deep crease across the middle

of each biscuit. Fold the biscuits over and press the edges together lightly. Place the biscuits in rows in a greased pan. Permit them to rise in a warm place until they are light, about 35 minutes. Bake them in a hot oven 425° for about 20 minutes. Remove them at once from the pans. See Rule for Reheating Bread or Buns, page 517.

THREE-HOUR POTATO ROLLS
Thirty-Two 2 Inch Rolls
Peel and cook until tender in water to cover:

    2 medium-sized potatoes

Rice them. There should be 1 cupful. Dissolve (page 526):

    1 cake yeast

in:

    ½ cup lukewarm water

Scald:

    1 cup milk

Add and beat until melted:

    ¾ cup lard

Add the potatoes and stir in:

    1 cup all-purpose flour
    2 well-beaten eggs
    ½ cup sugar
    2 teaspoons salt

Permit the sponge to rise in a warm place for 2 hours. Sift before measuring and stir in:

    4 cups all-purpose flour

Cover the bowl with a cloth and permit the dough to rise in a warm place for 1 hour. Make it into rolls. Permit them to rise for 15 minutes. Bake them in a hot oven 420° for about 20 minutes. Remove them at once from the pans. See Rule for Reheating Bread or Buns, page 517.

CLOVER LEAF ROLLS
Shape bread dough into small balls and brush them with:

    Soft butter

Grease muffin tins and drop 3 balls in each tin, filling them less than ½ full. Permit the rolls to rise until double in

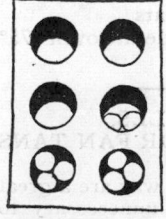
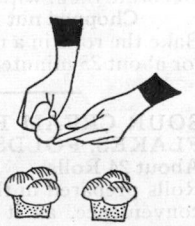

bulk, about 2 hours, and bake them in a hot oven 425° for about 20 minutes. Remove them at once from the pans. You may follow the rule on page 520 for Caramel Buns. Put part of the shortening and brown-sugar mixture in the bottom of heavy muffin tins. Add the 3 small balls of dough and proceed as directed for Caramel Buns. See Rule for Reheating Bread or Buns, page 517.

CLOTHESPIN ROLLS
Roll kneaded bread dough to the thickness of ¼ inch. Cut it into ½ inch strips. Wrap strips of dough in spirals around greased clothespins so that the edges barely touch.

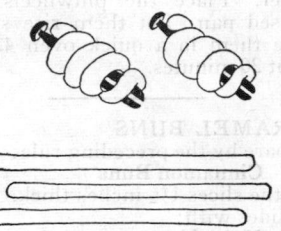

Place them on a baking sheet and permit them to rise until the dough has doubled in bulk. Bake as directed in your roll recipe. When baked, twist clothespins and pull them out.

CINNAMON BUNS OR PINWHEELS
Follow the rule for:

    Parker House Rolls, page 518

Prepare the dough and let it rise until it has doubled in bulk. Roll it to the thickness of ¼ inch. Spread it generously with:

    Melted butter
    Brown sugar and cinnamon
    Raisins

Roll it as for jelly roll, cut it in ¾ inch slices and place them in a greased pan. Let the buns rise slightly and bake them in a quick oven 425° for about 20 minutes.

For Pinwheels
After preparing the dough for the above cinnamon buns and rolling it to the thickness of ¼ inch, cut it into 4 inch squares. Spread them generously with:

    Butter
    Sugar and cinnamon

Place in the center of each square:
6 or more raisins
Cut diagonally into the dough from each corner to within ½ inch of the

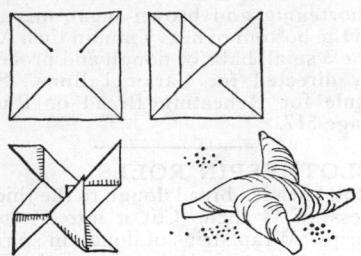

center. Fold the points toward the center. Place the pinwheels on a greased pan. Let them rise slightly. Bake them in a quick oven 425° for about 20 minutes.

CARAMEL BUNS
Prepare by the preceding rule:
Cinnamon Buns
Cut the slices 1½ inches thick. Spread the sides with:
Melted butter
Cream:
6 tablespoons shortening
6 tablespoons brown sugar
Spread this mixture on the bottom and sides of a heavy skillet. Place the slices in the skillet and permit them to rise for 15 minutes. Bake them in a moderate oven 375° for 25 minutes. Watch them, as the sugar burns easily. Serve the buns upside down.

BUTTERMILK POTATO ROLLS—BREAD OR COFFEE CAKE
About 46 Clover Leaf Rolls
This dough is delicious. It may be prepared and baked as directed in this rule or the ingredients may be combined, covered and placed in the refrigerator for 5 or 6 days. To use the chilled dough follow the rule for Refrigerator Rolls, page 524.
This dough makes good coffee cake. Follow the rule on page 624 for putting sugar and fruit on yeast coffee cake dough. Substitute buttermilk potato dough.
Peel and boil:
1 large potato
Rice it. There should be about ¾ cupful. Cut into this while hot:

½ cup lard
Crumble and beat in:
1 cake yeast
Stir in:
2 tablespoons sugar
2 cups buttermilk (not cold)
1 teaspoon salt
Beat until light and add:
2 eggs
Sift before measuring:
7½ cups all-purpose flour
Stir in 6 cupfuls of the flour. Knead in the rest. Place the dough in a bowl and cover it with a cloth. Permit the dough to rise in a warm place for 3 hours. Shape the dough with buttered hands into Clover Leaf Rolls, page 519. Spread the tops with:
1 beaten egg
(Poppy seeds)
Permit the rolls to rise until they have doubled in bulk, about 2 hours. Bake them in a hot oven 425°.

SOUR CREAM ROLLS OR KOLATCHEN
About Thirty-Six 2 Inch Rolls
Beat until creamy:
6 tablespoons butter
Grated rind of 1 lemon
2 tablespoons sugar
Beat in well:
4 beaten eggs
1 cup thick sour cream
Dissolve (page 526):
1 cake yeast
in:
2 tablespoons lukewarm water
Beat this into the egg mixture.
Measure:
3 cups sifted flour
Resift with:
½ teaspoon salt
1 teaspoon soda
Beat these ingredients into the egg mixture. Fill greased muffin tins ½ full. Cover the dough and let it rise in a warm place 85° until doubled in bulk, for about 2 hours. Brush the tops with:
1 slightly beaten egg white
Decorate them with:
Chopped nut meats
Bake the rolls in a moderate oven 375° for about 25 minutes.

SOUR CREAM ROLLS, FLAKES, FOLDS OR FAN TANS
About 24 Rolls
Rolls prepared in this way are a great convenience, as it is unnecessary to

serve them with butter. Fine for a plate lunch or serve-yourself party. Sift before measuring:

4 cups all-purpose flour

Scald:

2 cups thick sour cream

Cool this until lukewarm. Dissolve (page 526):

1 cake yeast

in:

⅓ cup of the lukewarm cream

Add it to the remaining cream with:

¼ teaspoon soda
2 teaspoons salt
¼ cup sugar

Beat this mixture well, then stir the flour in gradually. Place the dough in a greased bowl. Spread the top lightly with:

Melted butter

Cover the dough. Put it in a warm place. Permit it to rise until it has almost tripled in bulk. Knead it lightly for 1 minute. Separate it into 2 parts. Roll one part at a time into a square about ⅛ inch thick. Brush the dough with melted butter. Cut the dough into strips 1½ inches wide. Stack them. There should be from 6 to 8

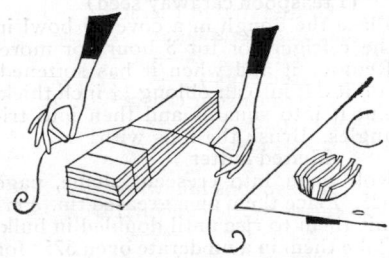

layers of strips stacked. Cut off pieces about 1½ inches wide. Place the cut, stacked strips in buttered muffin tins with the cut edges up. Permit the rolls to rise in a warm place until they have doubled in size. Bake them in a hot oven 425° from 15 to 20 minutes until a good brown.

BUTTERMILK ROLLS

Follow the preceding rule. Substitute for the sour cream:

2 cups buttermilk

After stirring in ½ the flour add:

2 tablespoons melted butter

and the rest of the flour. If you do not wish to make flakes, roll out the dough to the thickness of ½ inch, cut it with a biscuit cutter, place the rolls well apart on a greased sheet, permit them to rise until doubled in bulk and bake them in a hot oven 425° for about 15 minutes.

CHEESE FLAKES, FOLDS OR FAN TANS

Please read the comment under Sour Cream Rolls opposite.

Combine, stir and heat in a double boiler until the cheese is melted:

1½ cups grated cheese
3 tablespoons butter
3 tablespoons milk
¼ teaspoon paprika
½ teaspoon salt

Prepare the dough for:

Sour Cream Rolls, page 520,
Refrigerator Rolls I, page 524,
or other roll dough

Roll the dough into a large very thin square ⅛ inch thick. Spread half of it with the cheese mixture. Fold over the other half. Fold it over once more. You will then have 4 thin layers of dough. Cut it into strips 1½ inches wide, then cut the strips into squares. Place the squares cut side up in greased muffin tins. Permit them to rise in a warm place until they have doubled in bulk. Bake the flakes in a hot oven 400° for 20 to 25 minutes.

CHEESE ROLLS
24 Clover Leaf Rolls or 1 Loaf of Bread

This bread makes delicious sandwiches or toast for breakfast or tea. Sift before measuring:

4 cups all-purpose flour

Dissolve (page 526):

1 cake yeast

in:

¼ cup lukewarm milk

Add:

2 tablespoons sugar

Stir until melted:

1½ cups grated American cheese

in:

1¼ cups lukewarm milk

Beat in 1 cupful of the flour. Permit this sponge to rise in a warm place for 1 hour. Beat in the remaining flour and:

1½ teaspoons salt

Toss the dough onto a lightly floured board. Knead it until it is easily handled, about 2 minutes. Permit it to rise until it has doubled in bulk. Form pieces of the dough into balls ¾ inch in diameter by folding the edges of each ball under until the top is smooth. Place 3 balls in each section of a greased muffin pan. Cover the pan with a cloth. Permit the rolls to rise in a warm place until nearly double in bulk, about 20 minutes. Bake them in a hot oven 425° for about 15 minutes. Remove them from the oven and brush them with:

> **Melted butter**

Remove them at once from the pans. See Rule for Reheating Bread or Buns, page 517.

ROLLED OATS AND MOLASSES ROLLS
Thirty-Eight 2 Inch Rolls
Good, inexpensive and a pleasant change in flavor.
Combine and cook with occasional stirring for 1 hour in a double boiler:

> **1 cup steel-cut or rolled oats**
> **½ tablespoon lard**
> **¾ teaspoon salt**
> **1½ cups boiling water**

Cool these ingredients until they are lukewarm. Add:

> **1 cake yeast dissolved in 1 tablespoon lukewarm water**
> **½ cup molasses**

Sift before measuring and add:

> **4 cups all-purpose flour**

Knead the dough in the bowl until the ingredients are well blended. Cover the dough and permit it to rise in a warm place until it has doubled in bulk, about 2 hours. Pinch pieces off with buttered hands and place them in greased muffin tins. Permit the rolls to rise for about 2 hours. Bake them in a hot oven 425° for about 20 minutes.

WHOLE-GRAIN ROLLS
About Fourteen 2 Inch Rolls
Place in a bowl:

> **2 tablespoons sugar**
> **1½ teaspoons salt**
> **1 crumbled cake yeast, page 526**

Stir in:

> **2 cups lukewarm water**
> **1 well-beaten egg**

Sift before measuring:

> **2 cups all-purpose flour**

Add to it:

> **3 cups finely milled whole-grain flour**

Beat ½ the flour mixture into the yeast mixture. Add:

> **2 tablespoons melted butter**

Beat in the remaining flour mixture. Place the batter in a covered bowl. Put it in a warm place and permit it to rise until it has doubled in bulk. Pinch off pieces of dough and half fill greased muffin tins. Brush the tops with:

> **Melted butter**

Permit the dough to rise again until it has doubled in bulk, about 1 hour. Bake the rolls in a hot oven 425° for about 20 minutes. Brush them once while baking with:

> **Melted butter**

They may be sprinkled before baking with:

> **Coarse salt or chopped nut meats**

RYE ROLLS
About 30 Rolls
Dissolve (page 526):

> **½ cake yeast**

in:

> **1 cup lukewarm water**

Beat until creamy, then beat into the yeast mixture:

> **¼ cup sugar**
> **¼ cup lard**

Beat in, then knead in thoroughly:

> **1½ cups rye flour**
> **2 cups all-purpose flour**
> **1½ teaspoons salt**
> **(1 teaspoon caraway seed)**

Place the dough in a covered bowl in the refrigerator for 3 hours or more. Remove it and when it has softened, roll it out into an oblong ¼ inch thick. Cut it into squares and then into triangles. Brush the tops with:

> **Melted butter**

Roll them into crescent shape, page 625. Place them on a greased tin. Permit them to rise until doubled in bulk. Bake them in a moderate oven 375° for about 25 minutes. Brush them while hot with:

> **A beaten egg yolk**

Sprinkle them with:

> **Coarse salt**

BRIOCHE
This French Recipe Makes 32 Delicious 2 Inch Buns
Scald:

> **1 cup milk**

Add and stir until dissolved:

> **½ to ⅔ cup butter or lard**
> **2 teaspoons salt**
> **¼ to ½ cup sugar**

Cool these ingredients slightly. Dissolve (page 526):

> **2 cakes yeast**

in:

> **¼ cup lukewarm water**

Add:

> 3 or 4 beaten eggs
> (1 teaspoon grated lemon rind)

Add these ingredients to the milk mixture. Sift before measuring, then stir in:

> 4½ cups all-purpose flour

Beat the dough well. Cover it with a cloth and permit it to rise until very light in a warm place for 6 hours. Grease muffin tins, fill them ⅓ full with dough. Brush the tops with:

> Melted butter

Permit the brioche to rise uncovered in a warm place, about 1 hour. Bake the rolls in a hot oven 425° for about 20 minutes. Remove them at once from the pans. See Rule for Reheating Bread or Buns, page 517.

CROISSANTS
About 18 French Crescents
Rich, somewhat troublesome, but unequaled by any other form of roll.
Scald:

> ⅞ cup milk

Stir into it until melted and dissolved:

> 1 tablespoon lard
> 1½ tablespoons sugar
> ¾ teaspoon salt

Cool these ingredients until they are lukewarm. Add:

> 1 cake yeast dissolved in ⅓ cup
> lukewarm water, page 526

Stir in or knead in to make a soft dough about:

> 2½ cups sifted all-purpose flour

Knead the dough on a lightly floured surface until it is smooth and elastic. Place the dough in a bowl. Cover it with a cloth. Permit it to rise until it has doubled in bulk, about 1½ hours. Cover the dough with a lid and place it in the refrigerator until it is thoroughly chilled. Roll out the dough into an oblong ¼ inch thick. Beat until creamy:

> 1 cup butter

Dot the dough with ¼ cupful of the butter. Fold the right end over the center, then fold the left end over the center, so that the dough is in 3 layers. Swing the dough around, bring the right end to the bottom, or as in bridge problems, the East to the South. Roll the dough again to the thickness of ¼ inch. Dot it with ¼ cupful of butter and fold it as before. Do this twice again, so that you have rolled the dough, dotted it with butter and folded it and swung it around 4 times in all. Cover it and chill it for 2 hours or more. Roll it again on a slightly floured surface to the thickness of ¼ inch.

Cut the dough into 3 inch squares. Cut the squares on the bias. Roll the triangular pieces beginning with the wide side and stretching it slightly as you roll. Shape the rolls into crescents, page 625. Place the crescents on a tin. Chill them for ½ hour. Bake them for 10 minutes in a hot oven 350° and bake them until they are done, about 10 minutes longer.

$50,000 NO-KNEAD WATER-RISING TWISTS
2 Dozen Twists
The following rule won the first prize in the Grand National Recipe and Baking Contest recently sponsored by the Pillsbury Mills, Inc., of Minneapolis, Minnesota. Ann Pillsbury has kindly permitted me to publish this rule. It is based on the use of Pillsbury Flour.
Combine:

> ½ cup shortening
> 3 tablespoons sugar
> 1½ teaspoons salt
> 1 teaspoon vanilla
> ½ cup scalded milk

If dry yeast is used, decrease milk to ¼ cupful. Add and mix well:

> 2 cakes crumbled compressed
> yeast or 2 packages dry granu-
> lar yeast dissolved in ¼ cup
> lukewarm water

Blend in:

> 1½ cups sifted all-purpose flour

Beat until smooth. Cover and let rest for 15 minutes. Add:

> 3 eggs

one at a time, beating well after each addition. Blend in:

> 1½ cups sifted all-purpose flour

and mix thoroughly. The dough will be quite soft. Let rise in one of 2 ways: Either set covered dough in warm place, 80° to 90°, about ½ hour; or, tie dough in a tea towel, allowing ample space for dough to rise. Then place in large mixing bowl and fill with water 75° to 80°. Let stand until dough rises to top of water, about 30 to 45 minutes. Remove from water. The dough will be soft and moist.
Combine:

> ¾ cup chopped nut meats
> ½ cup sugar
> 1 teaspoon cinnamon

Divide the dough into small pieces with a tablespoon. Roll each piece in sugar-nut mixture; stretch to about an 8 inch length. Twist into desired shapes. Place on greased baking sheet. Let stand for 5 minutes. Bake in moderate oven 375° for 12 to 15 minutes.

ENGLISH OR RAISED MUFFINS
About Twenty 3 Inch Muffins
Combine in a mixing bowl:
  1 cup hot water
  ½ cup scalded milk
  2 teaspoons sugar
  1 teaspoon salt
When lukewarm, add:
  1 cake yeast dissolved in 2 tablespoons lukewarm water
Sift before measuring:
  4 cups all-purpose flour
Beat 2 cupfuls of this gradually into the milk mixture. Cover the bowl with a damp cloth. Permit the sponge to rise in a warm place 85°, for about 1½ hours, or until it collapses back in the bowl. Beat in:
  3 tablespoons softened shortening
Beat or knead in the remaining flour. Let the dough rise again until doubled

in bulk. Place it on a lightly floured board. Pat or press it until it is about ¾ inch thick. Cut it into rounds about 3 inches in diameter. Let them stand until light. Cook them until they are light brown on a fairly hot, well-buttered griddle. Turn them while cooking. Use a pancake turner. Cool them. Split and toast them.

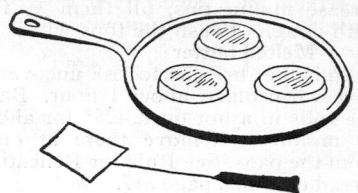

Muffin rings made for this purpose may be used. Put the dough in the rings for the final rising, filling them ½ full. The rings make more shapely muffins. English muffins may be baked in rings on a griddle as described above, or they may be baked, with or without rings, on a greased sheet in a moderate oven 350° for about ½ hour.

Refrigerator Breads

The following recipes make good loaf breads or rolls. None of them requires kneading (page 527) at any time, although some of the recipes suggest it. Keep the dough in the refrigerator, usually 12 hours before using it unless otherwise stated, but it may be kept there for 5 or 6 days.

Place the dough in a large well-greased bowl and then turn the dough bottom side up so as to grease the top automatically. Cover it with waxed paper and a plate, or with a cloth which should be kept moist.

Or you may put the dough in an oiled plastic bag. Close the bag tightly to keep out the air, but allow enough slack for the expansion of the dough. In spite of the fact that yeast has its preferred temperature (page 526) it does rise in the refrigerator.

When the dough has doubled in bulk it may be kneaded, should you care to do so, without taking it out of the bowl or bag. About 2 hours before baking, shape the loaves or rolls (page 528) and allow them to rise. Bake according to instructions below.

REFRIGERATOR ROLLS
Eighteen 2½ Inch Rolls
Sift before measuring:
  3½ cups all-purpose flour
Scald:
  1 cup milk
Stir in until dissolved:
  6 tablespoons shortening or butter
  6 tablespoons sugar
  1½ teaspoons salt
Cool to lukewarm. Place in a measuring cup:
  1 cake yeast

Dissolve (page 526) it in:
  ¼ cup lukewarm water
Beat in:
  1 egg
Add these ingredients to the first mixture. Beat in ½ the flour. Beat the dough for 2 minutes. Add the remaining flour and beat the dough until it blisters. Place it in a greased bowl. Spread the top lightly with grease. Cover it closely. Keep it in a refrigerator for at least 24 hours. When it has doubled in bulk, cut through the dough

to permit the gases to escape. Take out the quantity needed with a spoon or with buttered hands 4 hours before baking it. Place the dough in greased muffin pans, filling the pans ⅓ full. Spread the tops of the rolls with:

Soft butter

Permit them to rise uncovered in a warm place until doubled in bulk. Bake them in a quick oven 425° for about 20 minutes. Remove them at once from the pans. See Rule for Reheating Bread or Buns, page 517.

These and other rolls are good baked in a greased ring mold. Allow space between them. Serve the hot ring of rolls and let the guests pull them apart.

REFRIGERATOR BUTTER HORNS OR ROLLS
Approximately 24 Rolls

Among the bewilderingly numerous rules for Butter Horns this contribution of an amateur chef is an outstanding recipe.

Dissolve (page 526):

2½ cakes yeast

in:

¼ cup lukewarm water

Scald:

1 cup milk

Melt in it:

½ cup butter
½ cup lard

Cool this slightly. Beat in:

3 eggs

Beat in the yeast mixture. Sift before measuring:

4 cups all-purpose flour

Resift with:

½ cup sugar
¾ teaspoon salt

Stir in the sifted ingredients gradually. When blended place the dough in a greased bowl. Cover it closely. Keep the dough in a refrigerator for 12 hours or more. Then roll it out into a thin sheet about ⅛ inch thick. Cut it into squares. Cut the squares across on the bias into 2 triangles. Brush them lightly with:

Melted butter

You may sprinkle them with:

Sugar
Cinnamon

Roll the triangles beginning with the wide side. Shape them into crescent form by curving the rolls slightly. Place them on a greased baking sheet. Let them rise until light, for about 2

hours. Bake them in a hot oven 400° for about 12 minutes.

You may use this dough like coffee cake dough, topping it with fruit, crumbs, etc. See Coffee Cake, page 623.

REFRIGERATOR POTATO ROLLS
Approximately Forty 2 Inch Rolls

This dough makes good coffee cake as well as unusually good rolls.

Peel and boil until tender:

2 medium-sized potatoes

Put them through a ricer. There should be 1 cupful. Dissolve (page 526):

1 cake yeast

in:

½ cup lukewarm water

Place in a separate bowl:

½ cup lard

Scald and pour over it:

1 cup milk

Stir until the lard is melted, then add the dissolved yeast and the riced potatoes. Add:

3 beaten eggs
¾ cup sugar
2 teaspoons salt

Beat these ingredients well. Sift before measuring:

5 cups all-purpose flour

Add 4 cupfuls of the flour and beat the batter well. Stir in the remaining flour, or toss the dough on a board and knead it in. Place the dough in a bowl. Spread the top lightly with shortening. Cover the bowl. Chill the dough for at least 24 hours. It will keep for a week. Take it out of the refrigerator 2 hours before baking it. To shape and bake the dough follow the preceding rule for Refrigerator Rolls.

REFRIGERATOR WHOLE-GRAIN ROLLS
About Twenty 2 Inch Rolls

Dissolve (page 526):

½ cake yeast

in:

1 cup lukewarm water

Beat until creamy:

¼ cup lard
6 tablespoons sugar

Stir in the yeast mixture. Sift before measuring:

1¾ cups all-purpose flour

Add:

1¼ teaspoons salt
1½ cups whole-grain flour

Stir the flour mixture gradually into the yeast mixture. Beat it well. Place the dough in a bowl, spread the top lightly with shortening. Cover the bowl. Chill the dough for at least 24 hours. Take it out 2 hours before baking it. To make out and bake the dough follow the preceding rule for Refrigerator Rolls.

The tops of the rolls may be brushed with:

> Beaten egg yolk

and sprinkled with:

> Chopped nut meats or coarse salt

REFRIGERATOR BRAN ROLLS
Approximately Forty-Eight 2 Inch Rolls

These are crisp, crunchy and light. Choose your own adjective. Mine is delectable.

Combine:

> 1 cup shortening
> ¾ cup sugar
> 1½ teaspoons salt

Pour over these ingredients and stir until the shortening is melted:

> 1 cup boiling water

Add:

> 1 cup bran or bran cereal

In a separate bowl dissolve (page 526):

> 2 cakes yeast

in:

> 1 cup lukewarm water

When the first mixture is lukewarm, add to it:

> 2 well-beaten eggs

and the dissolved yeast. Sift before measuring and add:

> 6 cups all-purpose flour

Beat the batter. Put it in a bowl, spread the top lightly with shortening, cover it and place it in the refrigerator for at least 24 hours. Take out the dough 2 hours before baking it. To make out and bake the rolls, follow the rule for Refrigerator Rolls, page 524.

Breads Made with Yeast

For years I was unfortunate in having what a foreign woman called "a preconceited idea" in connection with all recipes calling for yeast. Someone had given me an exaggerated aspect of the difficulties of handling it and thus deprived me for a long time of the pleasure of making and serving the best of all breads.

The recipes for yeast breads in this section are so simple that no one need hesitate to try them.

The two forms of commercial yeast in general use are described on page 501.

Yeast is alive and has a way of its own, not a very complicated way, but one that must be taken into consideration. It is a plant that, combined with other ingredients, grows when exposed to heat and moisture. It then gives off the gases that supply the leaven needed to make dough rise. If exposed to a high temperature the plant will grow too fast and the bread will be unpleasantly porous. To meet its ideal heat requirements keep yeast dough at from 80° to 85°.

To Use Compressed Yeast: Crumble a cake of yeast into a lukewarm liquid, as directed in the following recipes. Rest it for about 5 minutes. Stir it until it is dissolved.

To Use Dry Granular Yeast: Follow the instructions on the package label.

Since one cake compressed yeast equals one package of dry granular yeast, you may use them interchangeably.

The best bread must be given time to rise slowly, the entire process taking about 4 to 5 hours before baking. If you use 1 cake of yeast to 1½ cupfuls of liquid and if the temperature is right, you can count about 2 hours or more to the first rising, 1 or more to the second and 1 hour in the pans. You may increase the yeast content in any recipe and reduce your rising time considerably. Some successful quick recipes are given, but if you are going to the effort of making bread, you might as well work for the superlative result which comes from the slower process.

The liquids added to yeast, either alone or in combination, are water, which brings out the wheat flavor and makes a crisp crust, milk, which not only adds to the nutritive value but also gives a softer crumb, and potato water, which hastens the action of the yeast and gives a somewhat coarser, moister texture to the bread. Both milk and potato water increase the keeping quality of bread somewhat. The

other ingredients are flour, sugar, salt and shortening. For the extremely important qualities of various flours, see page 500. Sugar is not essential but in the right
quantity hastens the action of the yeast. Too much sugar or salt will inhibit it.
Shortening is optional but the addition of fat gives a tenderer crumb, a browner
crust and a better keeping quality. To increase the food value of bread, milk solids,
debittered brewers' yeast, which has no leavening power, and wheat germ may be
added to the dough. For amounts and when to add them, see pages 501, 502.

Combine the ingredients as directed in the following rules. Mix them at first
with a spoon and later, as more flour is added, by hand. When the dough begins to
leave the sides of the bowl turn it out onto a lightly floured board or pastry cloth.
Now the kneading begins. At first when the dough is turned out on the board it is
slightly sticky, as can be seen on the left in the drawing. Then as the gluten
develops in the flour through continued kneading the dough becomes smooth and
elastic. The first working should be thorough but the pressure exerted on the

dough should not be a heavy or rough one. Fold the dough over toward you.
Then press it with the heel of the hand, as shown above, give it a slight turn, fold it
and press it again. Repeat this process until the dough becomes smooth and elastic
and no longer sticks to the board or cloth. Next, set the dough to rise as directed in
a bowl or on the board. Grease the bowl evenly, put the dough in it and then turn
it over so that the entire surface will be lightly greased. In either case cover the

bread with a damp cloth. This and the covering step after separating the bread
into loaf sizes is shown graphically, not because the text cannot be followed easily,
but to emphasize the importance of these steps. Yeast dough should rise at
a temperature of about 80° until it has doubled in bulk. If the room is cold, you
may place the dough in the bowl on a rack over a pan of warm water. If the dough
rises to more than double its bulk, it will fall back in the bowl. Do not permit this to
happen unless the recipe calls for it as it may result in a coarse dry bread. To make
sure that dough has risen sufficiently, press it well with the finger-tips. When it
has doubled in bulk the imprint of the finger-tips will remain in the dough. Punch
down the dough with a balled hand, work the edges to the center and turn the bottom
to the top. At this point you are ready for the second kneading; a light kneading and

not too long may be done in the bowl. Permit the dough to rise again until it has almost doubled in bulk. This second rising and kneading is omitted if soft flour is used.

When the bread has almost doubled in bulk you are ready to shape the loaves. Pinch the dough into the number of pieces called for in the recipe. Shape them lightly into mounds. Place the pieces on a board, cover them with a cloth and allow them to rest for 10 minutes. This rest enables you to shape the dough easily and without undue handling into loaves. Place the loaf in the pan. You may grease the top lightly. Cover with a damp cloth and let the dough rise until a slight pressure

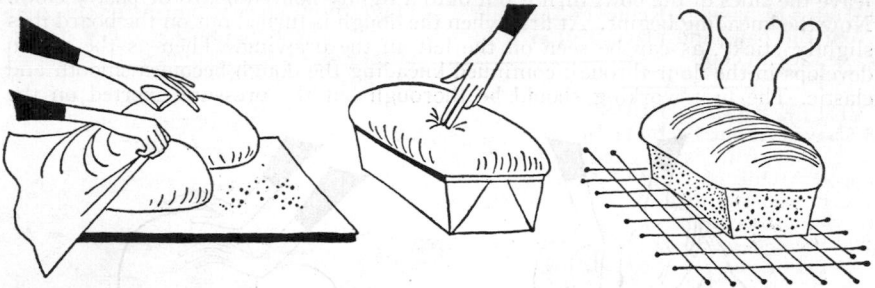

from the finger leaves its imprint. The loaves are now ready to bake. Glass and enamel pans require lower temperature than tin or aluminum ones. If you are shaping the dough for rolls, pinch off portions with greased fingers. If the dough is very light, use a spoon and place the dough in greased muffin tins.

Be sure that the oven has been preheated to the required degree before the bread is put in to bake. The loaf will shrink from the sides of the pan when done. Another test for doneness is to tap the bottom of the pan to release the loaf. Then tap the bottom of the loaf and if a hollow sound emerges the bread is done. Otherwise return the loaf to the pan and bake a few minutes longer. When the bread has finished baking, remove it at once from the pan and place it on a wire rack.

Bread crusts can be made to vary tremendously. Sometimes this is due to the ingredients used (see above). For a very hard crust on bread or rolls place a pan of boiling water in the bottom of the oven during the baking period. For a very brown crust you may bake the bread until it is almost done. Remove it from the pan. Brush it with melted butter or cream. Return it to the oven without the pans. Bake it 15 minutes longer. For a glazed crust you may brush the tops of bread and rolls just before baking with water and beaten egg yolk. Permit the bread to become cold before wrapping each loaf in waxed paper. Store the bread in a bread box or in a refrigerator.

WHITE BREAD
Two 5 by 10 Inch Loaves

Scald:

    1 cup milk

Add:

    1 cup hot water

Pour these ingredients over:

    1 tablespoon lard
    1 tablespoon butter
    2 tablespoons sugar
    2½ teaspoons salt

In a separate bowl dissolve (page 526):

    1 cake yeast

in:

    ¼ cup warm water

When the first mixture is lukewarm, combine it with the dissolved yeast. Sift before measuring:

    6½ cups all-purpose flour

Stir in slowly 3 cupfuls of the flour. Beat the batter for 1 minute, then add the remaining flour. Toss the dough on a floured board. Knead it well, folding the edges of the dough toward the center and pressing it down, repeating this motion until it no longer adheres to the board and is smooth, elastic and full of bubbles. Place the dough in a bowl, cover it with a cloth. Permit it to rise in a warm place until it has doubled in bulk, about 1 hour.

Cut it down by kneading it to its original bulk and let it rise again until doubled in bulk, about 1½ hours. Shape the dough lightly into loaves, place them in greased tins, filling the tins only ½ full. Let the dough rise again until doubled in bulk. Bake the loaves in a hot oven 450° for 10 minutes. Reduce the heat to 350°. Bake the bread until it shrinks from the sides of the pan. It requires about 40 minutes of baking. Remove it at once from the pans and place it on a wire cake rack to cool.

WHITE BREAD PLUS
3 Loaves About 5½ by 11 Inches
The above rule is excellent but if, to quote Archie of Duffy's Tavern, you yearn to be "a little more couth" try this superb version.
Dissolve (page 526):
> 1 cake yeast

in:
> ½ cup lukewarm water

Add:
> 1 tablespoon sugar

Permit this to stand in a warm place for 45 minutes. Beat in:
> 1 beaten egg
> ¼ cup melted lard
> 2 cups lukewarm water
> 1½ teaspoons salt
> ¼ cup sugar

Sift:
> 8 cups all-purpose flour

Stir some of the flour gradually into the other ingredients until a fairly thick batter is formed, then pour the dough onto a floured board and knead in the remaining flour, about 10 minutes. Place the dough in a well-greased bowl and let it stand until double in size. Knead the edges in, turn the dough and let it stand in a warm place until double in size. Cut the dough into 3 portions. Shape them into loaves. Place each loaf in a well-greased loaf pan. Permit the loaves to rise until double in bulk. Place them in a cold oven. Turn the heat to a moderately hot oven 400°. After 15 minutes reduce the heat to moderate 375° and bake the bread 25 minutes longer. Remove the loaves from the oven. Brush them with:
> Melted shortening

Turn them out on a rack to cool.

WHOLE-GRAIN BREAD PLUS
Follow the preceding rule for:
> White Bread Plus

Substitute for the all-purpose flour:
> 4 cups all-purpose flour
> 4 cups whole-grain flour

Reduce the shortening to ¼ cupful. Increase the lukewarm water measurement to 2½ cupfuls. Mix and bake as directed.

QUICK WHITE BREAD
One 5 by 10 Inch Loaf
Time from start to finish for this and the following Quick White-Grain Bread is about 2½ hours. In order to achieve these quick results in the wintertime the ingredients must be warmed. Sift before measuring:
> 3 cups all-purpose flour

Resift with:
> 2 teaspoons sugar
> 1½ teaspoons salt

Dissolve (page 526):
> 1½ cakes yeast

in:
> 2 tablespoons lukewarm water: 105°

Add it to:
> 1 cup lukewarm liquid—½ cup milk, ½ cup water: 105°

Stir the liquid into the sifted ingredients. Stir in:
> 3 tablespoons melted lard and butter combined

Blend these ingredients until the dough is smooth. Knead them on a board into a ball. Cover the dough with a cloth and permit it to stand in a warm place for 15 minutes. Knead the dough for about 10 minutes. Shape it into a loaf. Place it in a greased 5 x 10 inch pan. Permit it to rise in a warm place for 1 hour. Bake it for about 40 minutes in a moderate oven 375°.

QUICK WHOLE-GRAIN BREAD
One 5 by 10 Inch Loaf
Whole-Grain Roll Dough, page 522, may be baked in a loaf.
Sift before measuring:
> 1⅞ cups all-purpose flour

Add to it:
> 1⅞ cups whole-grain flour

Dissolve (page 526):
> 1½ cakes yeast

in:
> 3 tablespoons lukewarm water or milk and water

Add to it:
> 1¼ cups lukewarm water
> 2 tablespoons honey or brown sugar
> 1½ teaspoons salt

Combine the liquid and the sifted ingredients. Add:

3 tablespoons melted shortening

Knead the dough until it is smooth. Shape it into a ball. Cover it with a cloth and permit it to stand in a warm place for 30 minutes. Knead it for 10 minutes (optional). Shape it into a loaf. Place it in a greased 5 x 10 inch pan. Permit it to stand for about 1 hour. Bake it in a moderate oven 385° for about 45 minutes.

RAISIN BREAD

Follow one of the preceding rules for:

Quick White Bread
Quick Whole-Grain Bread

Sprinkle:

1 tablespoon flour

over:

1 cup washed, well-drained seeded raisins

Blend the flour with the raisins. Add them to the dough after the shortening has been kneaded in.

WHOLE-GRAIN BREAD
Two 5 by 10 Inch Loaves

Sift before measuring:

2¼ cups all-purpose flour

Crumble (page 526):

1 cake yeast

into:

¼ cup lukewarm water

Stir in:

1 tablespoon sugar

Permit this to stand until foamy. Combine in a mixing bowl:

2 cups scalded milk
2 tablespoons sugar
1 tablespoon salt

When lukewarm stir in the yeast mixture. Stir in, then beat well:

3¾ cups or less whole-grain flour

Beat in:

2 tablespoons softened shortening

Stir in enough of the all-purpose flour to make a soft dough. Permit this to stand for 10 minutes, then knead it on a lightly floured board for 10 minutes. Work in, kneading constantly, as much of the remaining all-purpose flour as needed to make a soft dough. Knead until the dough is pliable but not sticky. Shape the dough into a ball. Place it in a large bowl greased with shortening. Brush the top of the dough with shortening. Cover it with a damp towel. Let it stand in a warm place 85° free from draughts until it has doubled in bulk. Shape the dough into 2 loaves. Place them in 5 x 10

inch greased bread pans. Brush the tops lightly with soft shortening. Cover the pans with a cloth. Permit the dough to rise until it has nearly doubled in bulk. Bake it in a hot oven 400° for 10 minutes, then in a moderate oven 375° for 40 minutes longer. Three minutes before the bread is done you may brush it with:

Melted shortening

WHOLE-GRAIN BREAD WITH MOLASSES
2 Medium-Sized Loaves

I. Measure:

5½ cups whole-grain flour

II. Combine:

2 cups scalded milk
1½ tablespoons or more bacon, ham or beef fat
1 tablespoon salt
6 tablespoons black strap molasses or honey

III. Dissolve (page 526):

½ cake yeast

in:

¼ cup lukewarm water

Add:

2 tablespoons brown sugar

Combine and stir III and II. Beat, then work into I. If the dough tends to be stiff, you may add a little water. Knead the dough briefly. Place it in a greased bowl in a warm place covered with a damp cloth. Permit it to rise until doubled in bulk. Mold lightly, do not press it, into 2 medium-sized greased bread pans. Cover it as before and permit it to rise in a warm place until doubled in bulk. Bake the bread in a moderate oven 375°, reduce the heat after 20 minutes to 325°. Bake the bread until done, no longer than 1¼ hours in all.

YEAST CORN-MEAL BREAD
One 9½ x 4 Inch Loaf

Sift, then measure:

2¼ cups all-purpose flour

Place in a bowl:

2 tablespoons sugar
2½ teaspoons salt
2 tablespoons shortening

Pour over this and stir well:

1 cup scalding milk

When lukewarm pour off about ¼ cupful of this. Dissolve in it:

1 cake yeast

Stir the yeast into the milk mixture. Stir in until smooth about 1⅔ cupfuls of the sifted flour. Place this sponge in a greased bowl and permit it to stand covered in a warm place, about 82°, until it has almost doubled in bulk, about 1 hour. Stir into it:

½ cup yellow corn meal

Knead into it on a lightly floured board as much of the remaining sifted flour as needed to make a smooth and elastic dough. When the dough is soft place it in a greased mixing bowl, cover it and let it rise in a warm place until it has about doubled in bulk, about 2 hours. Shape the dough into a loaf and place it in a greased 4 x 9½ inch bread pan. Cover it and permit it to rise until double in bulk, about 1 hour. Bake it in a moderate oven 350° for about 45 minutes.

OATMEAL BREAD
Two 5 by 9 Inch Loaves
Combine:

2½ cups lukewarm milk, water or potato water
¼ cup closely packed brown sugar
1 tablespoon salt
2 tablespoons soft shortening

Crumble into this and stir until dissolved (page 526):

1 compressed cake yeast

Stir in:

2 cups steel-cut or regular rolled oats

Measure:

5 to 5½ cups all-purpose flour

If you use quick-cooking oats, measure 5½ to 6 cupfuls of flour. Stir in ½ the flour with a spoon, work in the second ½ by hand. Use only enough flour to make the dough easy to handle. Turn the dough onto a lightly floured board, cover it and permit it to stand for 10 minutes. Knead it until smooth. Shape it into a ball and place it in a greased bowl. Permit the dough to rise in a warm place 85° until double in bulk, about 1 to 2 hours. Punch down the dough. Divide it into halves. Shape each half into a loaf. Place the loaves in 2 lightly greased 5 x 9 x 3 inch bread pans. Cover them with a damp cloth and permit the loaves to rise until double in bulk, about 1 hour. Bake them in a moderately hot oven 400° for 30 to 40 minutes.

STEEL-CUT OATS NUT BREAD
One 4 by 10 Inch Loaf
Good without nuts, too.
Measure into a mixing bowl:

1 cup steel-cut oats
¼ cup dark molasses

1 tablespoon soft shortening
¾ teaspoon salt

Pour over these:

2 cups boiling water

Stir in:

2 cups all-purpose flour

Cool, then add:

1 cake yeast

dissolved in:

¼ cup lukewarm water

Work in:

2 cups all-purpose flour

Knead the dough on a floured board until it is soft and pliable and no longer sticks to the hands. Use a little additional flour if needed. You may work in:

1 cup broken pecan meats

Place the dough in a greased bread pan. Punch it down so that the pan is only ½ full. Cover it with a cloth. Permit the dough to rise in a warm place until it has doubled in bulk. Bake it in a moderate oven 375° for about 40 minutes. Remove it from the pan. Cool it on a rack.

GRAHAM BREAD
Two 3 by 7 Inch Loaves
Dissolve (page 526):

¾ cake yeast

in:

¼ cup lukewarm water

Add:

1¾ cups lukewarm water
¼ cup brown sugar or honey
2 tablespoons melted shortening

Combine:

2 cups graham flour
2 cups sifted all-purpose flour
1 teaspoon salt

Stir the liquid into the sifted ingredients. Cover the bowl with a cloth. Permit the dough to rise in a warm place until it has nearly doubled in bulk. Place it in 2 greased 3 x 7 inch bread pans. Brush the tops with:

Melted shortening

Permit them to rise until they have doubled in bulk. Bake the bread in a moderate oven 350° until it is done, about 40 minutes. Three minutes before the bread is done you may brush the tops with:

Melted shortening

HEALTH BREAD
3 Loaves
A coarse, well-flavored bread. Grand for snacks with cheese; superb with Canadian bacon or smoked salmon and coarsely grated pepper.

Stir until smooth:
> ¾ cup water-ground corn meal
> 1½ cups cold water

Stir this slowly into:
> 1½ cups boiling water

Cook and stir this constantly for about 2 minutes. Add:
> 2 tablespoons salt
> 1 tablespoon sugar
> 2 tablespoons shortening

Permit this to stand until lukewarm. Add:
> 2 cups mashed Boiled Potatoes, page 300

Dissolve:
> 1 cake yeast

in:
> ¼ cup lukewarm water

Add it to the corn-meal mixture with:
> 2 cups all-purpose flour
> 6 cups rye meal

Mix, then knead the dough on a floured board until smooth. Cover it and permit to rise in a warm place until doubled in bulk. Shape it into 3 loaves. Place them in pans heavily lined with greased waxed paper. Let them rise until nearly double in bulk. Bake them in a moderate oven 375° for 1 hour or longer. Place in the bottom of the oven a pan with ¼ inch of boiling water.

MYRNA'S RYE BREAD
2 Loaves

If you live near a corner grocery store, you may not want this rule. If you live in the hinterland—my book travels to distant countries—you may welcome it.

This calls for time and effort as it is necessary, in order to have a true rye bread, to make a sour dough. Once you have made a batter of sour dough you may reserve a cupful of it, place it in a covered stone crock and permit it to ferment. When ready to make fresh bread use ½ cupful of the fermented dough in place of 1 cake of yeast. For the sour dough and bread batter use in all:
> 1 cake yeast

Sour dough

Mix in the order given ½ cake of yeast and:
> ¼ cup water
> ½ cup rye flour

Work this mixture until it will hold together. Cover the sour dough with a damp cloth and keep it in a warm place 85° for 24 hours. Then work into it:

> 1 cup rye flour
> ¾ cup water

Permit the dough to ferment for 4 hours longer. This completes the sour dough.

Batter

Measure into separate bowls:
> 3½ cups rye flour
> 5 cups all-purpose flour

Combine the sour dough with ⅔ of the remaining yeast. Knead in until smooth 1¾ cupfuls of the rye flour. Cover this sponge with a damp cloth and allow the dough to rise until it doubles in bulk. Knead in the remaining rye flour, 1¾ cupfuls of the all-purpose flour, the remaining yeast and:
> 1 cup water

Mix and knead until the dough is smooth. Cover it with a damp cloth and permit the dough to rise until it doubles in bulk. Add to it:
> 1 cup water
> 1 tablespoon salt
> 1 tablespoon caraway seed

Add 1¾ cupfuls of the remaining all-purpose flour. Knead this dough until it is smooth. Permit this to rest for 20 minutes. Then turn it onto a floured board and knead it with the remaining all-purpose flour, adding enough to make a rather firm dough. About 2 cupfuls can be worked in at this point, depending on the flour. Divide the dough and shape it into 2 loaves. Permit them to rise but be careful not to let them double in bulk as rye bread dough that rises too high results in a flat loaf. When the loaves are about half risen bake them in a hot oven 425° for about 1 hour. In order to create steam place a flat pan containing ¼ inch or less of boiling water in the oven before baking the loaves. You may have to replenish the water. Remove the pan after 20 minutes. As soon as the bread is done spread it with melted butter, or if you wish a glazed crust spread it with salted water, 1 teaspoonful salt to ½ cupful water. Cool the loaves on a rack protected from draughts.

GLUTEN BREAD
2 Loaves

Combine and beat:
> 3 cups lukewarm milk or water
> 1 crumbled cake yeast
> 2 cups gluten flour

Permit this sponge to rise in a warm

place until light. Combine, beat and then stir into the sponge:

1 beaten egg
2 tablespoons melted shortening
½ teaspoon salt
(2 tablespoons sugar)

Stir in, then knead in:

Gluten flour: about 4 cupfuls

Use only enough flour to make a dough that will knead well. Knead it until it is smooth and elastic. Shape it into 2 loaves. Bake them in a moderate oven 350° for about 1 hour.

WHITE, WHOLE-GRAIN, GRAHAM OR RYE BREAD STICKS

Pinch off small pieces of:

Bread dough or Refrigerator Roll Dough, page 524, that has risen once

This may be done with buttered hands. Roll the dough into sticks. Brush the sticks with:

Melted butter or 1 beaten egg

Place the sticks on a buttered sheet. Sprinkle them with a choice of:

(Coarse salt)
(Poppy seed)
(Fresh celery seed)
(Chopped nut meats)

Permit them to rise until they have doubled in bulk. Bake them in a hot oven 425° until they are brown and crisp.

SALT-RISING BREAD
Method I.
Three 5 by 10 Inch Loaves

This fine bread is as temperamental as a prima donna. Do not attempt it in damp, cold weather unless the house is heated. Protect the batter from draughts.
Measure:

½ cup coarse white water-ground corn meal

Scald and pour over the corn meal:

1 cup milk

Permit it to stand in a warm place until it ferments, about 24 hours. An old cookbook says: "Keep it warm with a hot water bottle or a hot iron." Heat until lukewarm:

3 cups milk
¾ tablespoon salt
1 tablespoon sugar
5 tablespoons lard

Stir in:

3½ cups sifted all-purpose flour

Stir in the corn mixture. Place the bowl containing these ingredients in a pan of lukewarm water for about 2 hours, until bubbles work up from the bottom. Stir in:

5 cups sifted all-purpose flour

Knead in until smooth:

2½ cups sifted all-purpose flour

Place the dough in 3 greased 5 x 10 inch pans until it has doubled in bulk. Place the loaves in a moderate oven 350° for about 15 minutes. Increase the heat gradually to 425°. Bake the bread for about 1 hour.

Method II.

In some sections of the country a salt-rising bread made with potatoes is anathema. This rule is given because water-ground corn meal is hard to come by and processed corn meal is less apt to make good "Salt-risin'."
Pare, then cut into thin slices:

2½ cups potatoes

Sprinkle over them:

1 tablespoon salt
2 tablespoons corn meal

Add and stir until the salt is dissolved:

4 cups boiling water

Permit the potato mixture to stand covered with a cloth for 18 hours. A good way to regulate the heat in the wintertime is to place the bowl in warm water over the pilot light of a gas stove or in an oven with the pilot light on. Squeeze out the potatoes. Discard them. Drain the liquid into a bowl to which add and stir until very well blended:

1 teaspoon soda
1½ teaspoons salt
5 cups flour

Beat and beat "until the arm rebels." Set the sponge in a warm place to rise until light. Again you may follow the pilot light suggestion given above. The lightness test according to my correspondent: "Bubbles should rise to the surface, the sponge should increase its volume by about ⅓ and smell simply awful." This will take about 1½ hours.
Scald:

1 cup milk
1 teaspoon sugar

When lukewarm add:

1½ tablespoons butter

Add this mixture to the potato sponge with:

6 cups flour

Knead the dough for about 10 minutes before shaping it into 3 loaves. Place them in greased pans. Permit them to rise until light and not quite double in bulk. Bake them in a moderate oven 350° for about 1 hour.

LUNCHEON BREAD

This is a very rich, tender bread—a fine thing to serve hot. Bring the loaf from the oven to the table. Pull it apart with 2 forks.
Beat well:

    3 tablespoons sugar
    3 eggs

Add:

    ½ cup soft butter
    2 cups sifted all-purpose flour
    ½ teaspoon salt

Dissolve:

    2 cakes yeast

in:

    3 tablespoons warm milk

Add these ingredients to the batter. Beat it well for 3 minutes. Place it in a greased bread pan or a 9 inch tube pan. Permit it to rise in a warm place until it has doubled in bulk, about 2½ hours. Bake the bread in a hot oven 450° for about 20 minutes.

CHEESE BREAD

Follow the rule on page 521 for:
    Cheese Rolls

FRENCH BREAD

Mr. Julian Street, who kindly permitted me to use this rule, said, "We believe the following recipe will make as good a French loaf as it is possible to make in the ordinary American household range, gas or electric, with heat coming, not evenly from all sides of the oven, but only from the bottom. To make up for the lack of the characteristic brittle crust we slice the loaf diagonally and lightly toast the slices."
Scald:

    ½ cup milk

Boil:

    1 cup water

Combine and cool to lukewarm. Break:

    1 cake yeast

into:

    ¼ cup lukewarm water

Add it to the above mixture with:

    1½ tablespoons shortening
    1 tablespoon sugar

Measure into a large mixing bowl:

    4 cups all-purpose flour
    2 teaspoons salt
    ½ tablespoon sugar

Make a hole in the center. Pour in the liquid mixture. Stir thoroughly but do not knead. The dough will be soft. Cover with waxed paper or a damp cloth and set in warm place to rise, allowing about 2 hours for rising. Break down the dough. Place on lightly floured board and pat into 2 equal oblongs. Form each into a French loaf by rolling the dough toward you as shown here. Continue rolling, pressing

outward with the hands and tapering the dough toward the ends until a long, thin roll is achieved. Place the

2 loaves on a buttered cookie sheet, cut diagonal slits across top with sharp-pointed scissors to form customary indentations. Set in warm place to rise to somewhat less than double in bulk. Preheat oven to 400°. On bottom of oven place a pie tin filled with ½ inch boiling water. Bake 15 minutes at 400°; 30 minutes at 350°. Five minutes before bread is finished brush loaves with a glazing mixture of:

    1 beaten egg white
    1 tablespoon cold water

Recently I received a letter from a gentleman in Junction City, Kansas, which began: "My wife is too old to cook, and I am too old to do anything else." It seems that he is an enthusiastic baker of French bread but he complained that his loaves turned out to be too flat. I suggested that he try shaping them in the following manner: Make a long oblong of the dough, fold over one edge to the center and then fold the second end over to the center and taper the ends slightly.

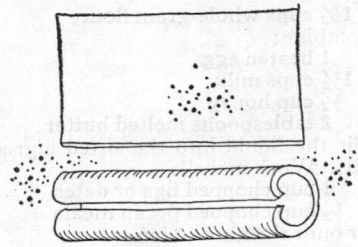

My correspondent made several batches of bread and then wrote me again: "Your plan works fine in shaping the loaves and I am also using ¼ cupful less water. This makes the loaves come up a better shape although it makes the dough harder to mix thoroughly. I think, however, the bread is just as good, and my French son-in-law says it is the best French bread he has eaten outside of France." This communication was followed by a letter from Middleburg, Virginia. "With all respect to Mr. Julian Street, it is possible to make a much better loaf of French bread in the ordinary range than he describes. You may have as thick a crust as you wish if you will bake it at 300° instead of 400° or 350°. Try liquefying ½ cake yeast with 1 tablespoonful of sugar. Add 1 cupful of scalded and cooled milk and 2 cupfuls of water. Omit all fat. Sift in a pint of flour, stir well and let rise until very light and bubbly. Then add a quart of flour, mix it any way you please, knead it and throw it down hard on the board; it doesn't matter what you do so long as you get it smooth. Cover the bowl with a tight heavy lid. Then leave it in not too warm a place overnight. It should be very nearly tripled in bulk. Roll out your loaves the next morning as he says, and let them rise again until the pans feel empty when you pick them up, keeping the tops of the loaves wet with warm milk until they go into the oven. Slow rising and slow baking give the flavor and the crust. They must bake about an hour; it is impossible to be more definite because of the difference in stoves, and the weather.

"The bread should continue to rise after it goes into the oven, but for mercy's sake, leave out that pan of hot water! I have baked bread at 275°. This bread keeps fresh longer than any other and if baked thoroughly it is as good cold as it is when hot.

"The dough should be stiff enough to hold its shape. If in doubt, roll the loaves in flour and wait 10 minutes before wetting them with the warm milk. No one has ever eaten this bread without saying it is the best ever tasted. A French neighbor says: 'Eet is like Franch braid but eet is better than ayny braid I've eaten in France.'

"P.S. Always bake the loaf a little longer than you think necessary."

Baking Powder Breads

These quick breads are delicious when fresh but they have not the keeping qualities of yeast breads and they wither young.

WHITE NUT BREAD
Beat until soft:
    2 tablespoons butter
Add and blend until creamy:
    ⅓ to ½ cup sugar
Sift before measuring:
    2 cups all-purpose flour
Resift with:
    3 teaspoons tartrate or phosphate
      baking powder or 2¼ teaspoons
      combination type (see Baking
      Powder, page 501)
    ⅔ teaspoon salt
Beat until light:
    1 egg
Add and beat:
    1 cup milk

Stir the liquid into the dry ingredients until blended only. Add:
    ¾ cup broken nut meats or part nut
      meats and part chopped dates
Place the dough in a greased 9 x 5 inch bread pan. Bake the bread in a moderate oven 350° for about ½ hour.

ORANGE BREAD
Two 8 by 3½ Inch Loaves
This is an economical, easily made tea bread. If you want a quick treat, break it apart and eat it while hot, with or without lots of good butter. If you wish to use it for sandwiches, you will find it easier to slice on the second day.

Have all ingredients at room temperature. Sift, then measure:

3 cups all-purpose flour

Resift it into a large bowl with:

4 teaspoons tartrate or phosphate baking powder or 3 teaspoons combination type (see Baking Powder, page 501)

Combine and add:

1 tablespoon grated orange rind

½ to ¾ cup sugar

If you wish a cakelike result, use the larger amount of sugar. Combine and beat:

1 egg

¼ cup orange juice

1¼ cups milk

2 tablespoons melted shortening

You may add:

1 cup chopped or broken nut meats

Pour the liquid ingredients into the bowl. Combine all ingredients with a few swift strokes. Stir them lightly until barely blended. Bake the bread in two 8 x 3½ inch loaf pans lined with lightly greased waxed paper in a moderate oven 350° for about 50 minutes, or until done.

WHOLE-GRAIN NUT BREAD WITH BROWN SUGAR

Sift before measuring:

¾ cup all-purpose flour

1½ cups whole-grain flour

Resift with:

2½ teaspoons tartrate or phosphate baking powder or 2 teaspoons combination type (see Baking Powder, page 501)

1 teaspoon soda

¾ teaspoon salt

Pack firmly, then stir in:

½ to ¾ cup brown sugar

Add:

¾ cup broken nut meats or raisins

Stir in quickly:

3 tablespoons melted shortening

1½ cups sour milk or buttermilk

Bake the batter in a greased 4 x 9½ inch bread pan in a moderate oven 350° for about 1¼ hours.

WHOLE-GRAIN FIG OR DATE BREAD

Sift before measuring:

1½ cups all-purpose flour

You may dust the figs or dates with a little of the flour. Resift with:

2 teaspoons any baking powder

¼ cup brown sugar

½ teaspoon salt

¾ teaspoon soda

Add:

1½ cups whole-grain flour

Combine:

1 beaten egg

1½ cups milk

½ cup honey

2 tablespoons melted butter

Stir the liquid into the sifted ingredients. Work in well:

1 cup chopped figs or dates

½ cup chopped pecan meats

Or omit the nuts and use:

1½ cups chopped figs or dates

Place the dough in a greased 6 x 10 inch pan or in two 4 x 7 inch bread pans. Permit it to rise for 20 minutes. Bake it in a slow oven 350° for about 1 hour.

BANANA BREAD

Blend until creamy:

⅓ cup shortening

⅔ cup sugar

¾ teaspoon grated lemon rind

Beat in:

1 beaten egg

Sift before measuring:

1¾ cups all-purpose flour

Resift with:

2 teaspoons tartrate or phosphate baking powder or 1½ teaspoons combination type (see Baking Powder, page 501)

¼ teaspoon soda

Mash 2 or 3 fully ripe bananas to make:

1 cup banana pulp

Add the sifted ingredients in about 3 parts to the sugar mixture alternately with the banana pulp. Beat the batter after each addition until smooth. Place it in a greased bread pan, about 4 x 8 inches. Bake the bread in a moderate oven 350° for about 1 hour, or until done. You may add to the batter 1 cupful raisins, soft dried prunes, or apricots or dates and/or ½ cupful nut meats.

PRUNE OR APRICOT BREAD

This bread may be made with sweetened prune pulp, in which case the sugar given in the recipe is omitted.

Cream:

¼ cup shortening

with:

½ cup sugar

Beat in:

1 egg

Add:
  ¾ cup unsweetened, cooked prune
    or apricot pulp: Stewed Prunes
    or Apricots, page 450, mashed
    or put through a ricer or food
    mill
  ¼ cup prune or apricot juice
Have ready:
  1 cup sour milk
Sift before measuring:
  1½ cups all-purpose flour
Resift with:
  ½ teaspoon salt
  1 teaspoon soda
Add:
  1½ cups whole-grain flour
Add the sifted ingredients alternately
with the milk to the butter mixture.
Stir the batter with a few swift strokes
until blended only. Fold in:
  1 cup broken nut meats
Place the dough in 2 small or in 1 large
greased loaf pan. Bake the bread in a
moderate oven 350° for 1¼ hours.
Permit it to cool in the pan.

BOSTON BROWN BREAD
Two 1 Pound Loaves
Combine:
  1 cup yellow water-ground corn
    meal
  1 cup rye flour
  1 cup graham flour
  ¾ tablespoon soda
  1 teaspoon salt
Combine in a separate bowl:
  2 cups sour milk
  ¾ cup molasses
  1 cup chopped raisins
Add the liquid to the dry ingredients.
Pour the batter into a buttered 2 quart
pudding mold. Fill it ⅔ full. Steam it
for 3½ hours (page 731). This batter
may be steamed in smaller molds or
baking powder cans for 1½ to 2 hours.

BRAN BREAD WITH MOLASSES
Combine:
  2 cups bran
  2 cups whole-grain flour
  2 teaspoons any baking powder
  1 teaspoon salt
  1 teaspoon soda
Combine and beat:
  1 egg
  1¾ cups sour milk
  ½ cup molasses or ¾ cup brown
    sugar
Beat in the dry ingredients. You may
add:

  1 cup raisins, figs or nut meats
You may dust the fruit with a little of
the flour. Place the batter in 2 greased
8 x 4 inch bread pans. Permit it to
stand for 1 hour. Bake the bread in a
moderate oven 375° for 1 hour or
more.

BRAN DATE BREAD DE LUXE
This recipe is worthy of 3 stars. It
makes a wonderful tea sandwich with
butter or cream cheese.
Prepare:
  2 cups chopped dates
Pour over them:
  2 cups boiling water
In a separate bowl beat until light:
  2 eggs
Add slowly, beating constantly:
  ¾ cup brown sugar or ½ cup
    molasses
When these ingredients are creamy
sift in:
  1 cup whole-grain flour
  2 teaspoons any baking powder
  1 teaspoon soda
Add ½ the date mixture and:
  1 cup whole-grain flour
  2 cups bran
  1 teaspoon vanilla
Add the remaining date mixture and:
  1 cup or less chopped nut meats
Place the dough in a lightly greased
9 x 5 inch bread pan. Bake it in a
moderate oven 350° for about 1 hour.

BRAN CORN-MEAL BREAD
Beat until soft:
  ½ cup butter
Add gradually and mix until light and
creamy:
  ½ cup sugar
Beat in one at a time:
  2 eggs
Stir in:
  2 cups bran
Sift before measuring:
  ⅔ cup all-purpose flour
You may dust the fruit with a little of
the flour. Resift with:
  1⅓ teaspoons any baking powder
  ½ teaspoon salt
Add:
  5½ tablespoons water-ground corn
    meal
Beat in the sifted ingredients in about
3 parts alternately with thirds of:
  1 cup milk
Add:
  1 cup raisins, chopped dates or
    nut meats

Spread the batter in a greased 9 x 12 inch bread pan. Bake the bread in a moderate oven 375° for about 20 minutes.

GINGERBREAD
Method I.
Serve this piping hot for a grand dessert. No sauce is needed but you may add a vanilla or lemon sauce, etc.
Cream:
> ½ cup shortening or bacon grease
> 1 cup white or brown sugar

Beat in one at a time:
> 2 eggs

Add:
> 1 teaspoon grated lemon or orange rind

Sift before measuring:
> 2 cups all-purpose flour

Resift with:
> 1 teaspoon nutmeg
> 1 teaspoon soda
> ½ teaspoon salt
> 1½ teaspoons ginger

In a separate bowl combine:
> ½ cup boiling water
> ½ cup molasses

Add the sifted and the liquid ingredients alternately to the butter mixture. Beat the batter after each addition until the ingredients are blended. Bake it in a greased 8 x 11 inch pan in a moderate oven 350° for about 40 minutes.

Method II.
Less cakelike, considerably coarser, a bit more economical than Gingerbread I.
Combine and beat:
> 1 well-beaten egg
> ½ cup sugar
> ½ cup dark molasses

Combine and beat until melted:
> ¼ cup butter: 4 tablespoons
> ½ cup hot water

Add these ingredients to the egg mixture. Beat them until blended. Sift before measuring:
> 2 cups cake flour

Resift with:
> ¼ teaspoon salt
> 1 teaspoon ginger
> 1 teaspoon cinnamon
> 1 teaspoon soda
> (1 tablespoon grated orange rind)

Add the sifted ingredients in about 3 parts to the first mixture. Beat after each addition until blended only. Pour the batter into a lightly greased 8 x 8 inch pan or into 12 greased muffin cups, filling them ⅔ full. Bake the

bread in a 350° oven for about 50 minutes, the muffins in a 400° for 12 or 15 minutes.

TOPPING FOR GINGERBREAD
Combine and work with the hands or 2 knives until crumbly:
> ¼ cup brown sugar
> 1 teaspoon cinnamon
> 2 tablespoons flour
> 2 tablespoons soft butter

Add:
> ½ cup chopped nut meats

Spread this over gingerbread for the last 10 minutes of baking.

Biscuit Easter Bunnies, page 508.

BIRTHDAY BREAD HORSE
As Marion's children have always demanded a piece of their birthday cake for breakfast, she concocted a bread horse to be supplemented later in the day by the candle-lighted birthday cake of richer content. This also makes a good Christmas or Fourth of July breakfast decoration.
You will need a well-rounded loaf of bread—a log-shaped cinnamon roll is fine—an oval bun or roll, about 2½ x 3½ inches, 2 braided rolls about 1 x 3½ inches, 5 peppermint candy sticks 1 x 8 inches, 2 raisins, 2 almonds and a

piece of cherry or a redhot. Use the loaf for the body. Mount it on 4 of the candy sticks. Break off about ⅓ or less of the fifth candy stick. Use it for the neck. Stick it into one end of the loaf at an angle. Put the oval roll on the other end for the head. Use the braided rolls for the mane and tail, the raisins for eyes, the almonds for ears and the piece of cherry for the lips. Bed the horse on ivy or other leaves or grass. Add a ribbon bridle if you care to.

Toast

TOAST MELBA
Cut into the thinnest possible slices:
White or other bread
Remove the crusts. Place the bread in an oven that is barely warm. Permit it to become crisp and slightly browned.

MILK TOAST
Individual Service
Toast lightly on both sides:
A slice of bread ¾ inch thick
Spread it lightly with:
Butter
Sprinkle it with:
(Salt)
Place it in a bowl and pour over it:
1 cup hot milk

FRENCH TOAST
Beat slightly:
2 eggs
Add:
½ teaspoon salt
⅔ cup milk
Flavor with ½ teaspoonful of vanilla or 1 tablespoonful of rum for added zest. Dip in this mixture:
8 slices of bread
The bread may be cut in rounds with a doughnut cutter. Brown the bread on each side on a hot, well-buttered griddle. Serve it hot sprinkled with:
Sugar
Cinnamon
Garnish the cooked rounds with:
Bright red jelly
Or serve with pie cherries, sweetened, slightly thickened and flavored with lemon or applesauce flavored with cinnamon and cloves.

HONEY BUTTER TOAST
Prepare:
Honey Butter, page 22
Spread it on a slice of bread. Cover it with another. Cut the bread into 1 inch strips. Toast the strips under a broiler, first on one side and then on the other. Serve them hot, sprinkled with cinnamon.

FRENCH TOAST JAM SANDWICHES
Prepare the batter in the above rule for:
French Toast
Add:
3 tablespoons sugar
Spread 4 of the bread slices with:

Apricot jam, marmalade or apple butter, etc.
Cover them with the remaining slices. Cut each sandwich into 3 strips. Sauté them as directed.

FRENCH TOMATO TOAST
Beat until light:
2 eggs
½ teaspoon salt
¼ teaspoon paprika
½ cup condensed tomato soup
Dip in this:
6 slices of bread
Sauté the slices in hot:
Butter or drippings
When a good brown serve them with:
Cheese Sauce, page 430
Minced parsley or chives

CINNAMON SPREAD FOR TOAST OR WAFFLES
Cream:
2 tablespoons butter
Blend in:
⅓ cup confectioners' sugar
1 teaspoon cinnamon

CINNAMON TOAST
Method I.
Spread:
Thin slices of bread or rusks
with the preceding:
Cinnamon Spread
Place them in a moderate oven 350° or under a broiler to crisp them.
A Filipino cook I know varies the flavor of cinnamon toast by using part cinnamon and part freshly grated nutmeg with good results.
Method II.
Cut thin slices of:
Bread
Remove the crusts. Spread the bread with a thick layer of:
Butter
Sprinkle it generously with:
Sugar and nutmeg or cinnamon
Allow 1 teaspoonful of spice mixture for every 3 tablespoonfuls of brown or white sugar. Place 1 piece of bread on top of another with the prepared sides to the center. Toast the slices under or over a quick fire. Separate them and serve them at once, cinnamon side up.

ORANGE TOAST
Good with tea. Combine:
Grated rind of 1 orange

¼ cup orange juice
½ cup sugar
Cut:
6 slices of bread
Remove the crusts and toast the bread. Spread it while hot with:
Butter
Cover it with the orange mixture. Put the toast in the oven or under a broiler just long enough to brown the tops lightly.

CINNAMON TOAST STICKS
Cut the crust from:
Bread
Cut the bread into ¾ inch slices. Cut the slices in ¾ inch strips. The strips may be sprinkled with rum. Dip the strips in:

Melted butter or creamed butter
Roll them in:
1 part cinnamon
3 parts sugar
or in:
½ cup confectioners' sugar
½ cup brown sugar
1 tablespoon cinnamon
Toast the strips on 4 sides, or place them in a hot oven 400° for 8 minutes. These are good put together with applesauce.

Orange Marmalade Toasted Sandwiches, page 685; Toasted Buttered Bread Loaf, page 76; Pulled Bread, page 76; Toasted Bread Sticks, page 76.

How to Prepare, Store and Use Bread Crumbs

Dry bread, zwieback and crackers may be put through a food chopper. If the bread is stale, cut it in pieces, place them in a slow oven 250° until crisp before grinding. Use a medium chopping blade, a food mill or an electric blender if they are to be made in quantity. If only a few crumbs are needed, use a small rotary hand grinder. To prevent molding during storage, place the crumbs in a glass jar covered with a cloth secured with a rubber band rather than with a tight lid.

TO PREPARE BREADED AND AU GRATIN FOODS
Prepare (see above):
Cracker crumbs, bread crumbs, or use crumbs from crushed cheese crackers, potato chips, cornflakes, corn chips or bran
The crumbs may be sifted and seasoned.
For Deep Fat Frying:
Combine and beat lightly:
1 egg
2 tablespoons water or oil
The oil browns the food pleasantly. Roll the food to be breaded in the crumbs, dip them in the egg mixture and roll them again in the crumbs. To avoid sticky hands, bread with one hand and dip with the other. If this is done ½ hour before the food is fried, the crumbs will have a better chance to adhere. It is important to cover the entire surface of the food well with the egg mixture. When placed in the hot fat the egg at once forms a coating which the fat cannot penetrate.
For Sautéing:
Prepare food as suggested above, or the egg bath may be omitted and the food may be dipped in oil alone and then breaded; or it may be floured, as shown opposite, or sautéed as it is in butter, oil or drippings.
For Au Gratin Foods:
Spread the surface of the food about to

be baked with crumbs. Dot it with butter and/or sprinkle it with cheese. Bake the dish in a moderately hot oven until the crumbs are brown.

FLOURED FOOD
Place in a large paper or plastic bag:
1 cup flour
1 tablespoon salt
(⅛ teaspoon pepper)
Add food that is to be floured, cut-up uncooked chicken, veal, fish, etc. Shake

the bag vigorously. The food will be evenly floured.

SEASONED FLOUR
Mix:
1 cup all-purpose flour
1 teaspoon salt
¼ teaspoon pepper or ½ teaspoon paprika

Fritters, Doughnuts, Pancakes and Waffles

The everlasting popularity of deep-fat-fried and sautéed foods is balanced by imprecations on their caloric content and their slow digestibility. While their delicious flavor and weight-increasing powers are undeniable, the first can be heightened and the second lessened by proper cooking. If the fat is maintained at the right temperature and if the food is not fried too long there is little danger of excessive fat absorption, for then the moisture in the food itself starts boiling and giving off steam so fast that the outgoing steam does not permit the fat to penetrate the food. The digestibility of fried foods is slow as all fats are slow to leave the stomach, but their value as food need not be scorned if the fats used are not rancid and if they have not been heated to the smoking point. When fats smoke, acrolein, a substance irritating to the lining membranes of the body, is being formed. Acrolein also destroys good flavor and prevents fried foods from keeping well.

With these factors in mind let's find out how to fry foods so that they are both nutritious and delicious. First keep all fats and oils in covered, light-proof containers; oils at cool temperatures and fats refrigerated but not congealed. Never use a fat unless it has a pleasant odor and by all means choose the right fat for the right job.

Hydrogenated fats, chicken fat, corn and peanut oil will withstand any of the temperatures given below. Lard and olive oil smoke before any of these temperatures is reached but both are used. Olive oil has some very definite flavor advantages and is often combined with peanut and corn oil to raise its smoking point and give better results. Bacon fat, suet, drippings and butter all smoke long before they reach the temperatures required for deep-fat frying and are best reserved for sautéing over moderate heat. If you want a luster on foods, such as potato chips, which are to be served cold, use peanut or corn oil brought to room temperature before heating.

Having decided on the food and the type of the fat we are going to use, let us look at our frying equipment and the rules on how to use the fat and how to add the food.

Rule for Deep Fat Frying

Choose a deep heavy saucepan with straight sides. This will answer well for occasional frying. If a great deal of frying is done, a heavy kettle and a wire basket with a handle that fits into it will be found a great convenience. In addition, provide yourself with a long-handled skimmer or a slotted spoon and a long-handled fork.

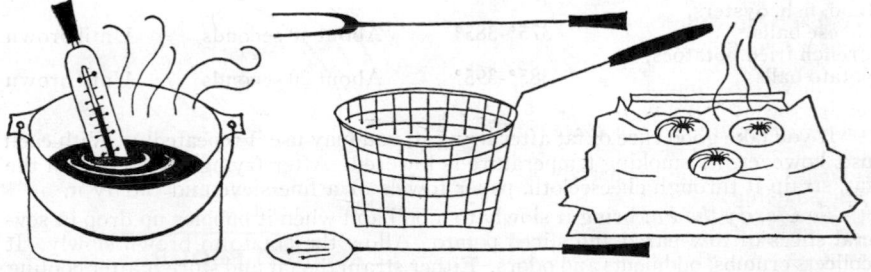

The fat or oil should be deep enough to cover the food generously, at least 4 inches deep. Two or 3 inches must be allowed between the fat and the top of the pan to keep the fat from bubbling over.

Heat the fat or oil slowly to the desired temperature. See the following Chart for Frying Food in Deep Fat.

Fry only a small quantity of food at a time, otherwise you will reduce the temperature of the fat too much. Have the food to be fried at room temperature for the same reason. If it has been chilled, remove it from the refrigerator about an hour before frying. To bread food for frying, see page 540.

To a 3 quart size kettle filled with 1 quart of fat or oil allow about 3 doughnuts, 3 croquettes or 1 cupful of potatoes at a time.

Lower the basket slowly into the fat. The bubbling will soon subside. If a frying basket is not available, place the food on a long-handled spoon and lower it slowly into the fat. When it is cooked on one side, turn it and cook the other. Do not let the food touch while frying. Separate it with a fork or skimmer. As soon as the food is well browned remove it from the fat and drain it on absorbent paper— paper towels, napkins or unglazed paper.

A colander lined with paper toweling is good for this purpose. Keep the fried food warm in a slow oven. Watch the fat temperature constantly and always retest before adding new food to be fried. Skim off all food scraps from the fat to prevent smoke.

Doughnuts, potatoes, fish and other foods all have optimal frying temperatures. Rules for the foods most commonly fried are given in the following chart. It is better to use a thermometer but for lack of one use the following bread test:

To Test the Heat of Fat without a Thermometer

Heat the fat slowly. Drop a 1 inch cube of 1-day-old bread into it. If the bread browns in 40 seconds, the fat is ready for frying cooked food. If the bread browns in 1 minute, the fat is ready for frying uncooked food. The exception to this rule is French Fried Potatoes. Fry these when a cube of bread browns in 20 seconds.

Chart for Frying Food in Deep Fat

	Temperature	Time required to brown a 1 inch cube of day-old bread in hot fat	Cook
Onions, oysters or fish	345°-355°	About 65 seconds	Until brown
Doughnuts, fritters, raw dough mixtures and croquettes with raw food	350°-365°	About 60 seconds	Until brown
Croquettes with cooked food, fish, oysters, cheese balls	375°-385°	About 40 seconds	Until brown
French fried potatoes, potato balls	385°-395°	About 20 seconds	Until brown

If you take good care of fat after using it, you may use it repeatedly. With each use, however, its smoking temperature is lowered. After frying the food, cool the fat, strain it through cheesecloth, paper towels or a fine sieve and clarify it.

To Clarify the Fat bring it slowly to a boil and when it bubbles up drop in several slices of raw pared and sliced potato. Allow the potato to brown slowly. It collects crumbs, oddments and odors. Either strain the fat and store it after cooling or let it cool below 212° and sprinkle the surface of the fat with cold water. When the fat has hardened lift the fat cake out of the pan. The sediment will have sunk to the bottom of the pan and is ready for the discard. Refrigerate the fat in a covered jar.

Fritters

Rule for Frying Fritters

Fritters may be sautéed in butter but are better when prepared in deep fat.
Heat a kettle of fat from 370° to 390°. Dip food in batter, see below. Fry the fritters until they are a delicate brown. Drain them on unglazed paper.

FRITTER BATTER FOR FRUIT

Beat:
> 2 egg yolks
> ⅓ cup water
> ⅓ cup evaporated milk or rich milk

Or ⅔ cupful water may be substituted for the milk and water. Add and beat:
> 1 tablespoon lemon juice, dry wine, brandy or rum
> 1 tablespoon melted butter

Sift before measuring:
> 1 cup all-purpose flour

Resift with:
> ¼ teaspoon salt
> (2 tablespoons sugar)

Combine the liquid and the dry ingredients with a few swift strokes. Add:
> ⅛ teaspoon salt

to:
> 2 egg whites

Whip them until they are stiff. Fold them into the batter.
Serve them with lemon juice and confectioners' sugar, or serve them with Crimson Sauce, page 544.

FRITTER BATTER FOR MEATS

For an alternate recipe to use in a skillet, see page 140. Sift:
> 1½ cups all-purpose flour
> 1 teaspoon any baking powder
> ¼ teaspoon salt
> ¼ teaspoon paprika

Combine, beat and add to the sifted ingredients:
> 1 egg
> 1¼ cups milk

FRITTER BATTER FOR VEGETABLES

Follow the rule on page 325.

APPLE FRITTERS

Peel and core:
> 6 medium-sized apples

Cut them crosswise into ½ inch slices. They may be soaked for 2 hours in:
> Wine or lemon juice and powdered sugar

Drain them. Dip them in:
> Fritter Batter for Fruit

Fry them in deep fat (page 541). Drain them on absorbent paper. Sprinkle them with:
> Cinnamon and sugar

PINEAPPLE FRITTERS

Drain well, then dry between towels:
> 8 slices canned pineapple

These are good sprinkled with:
> Kirsch

This is sometimes unavailable and always, alas! expensive. Its flavor cannot be matched by a substitution. To vary our usual household standby, vanilla, use almond flavoring, sparingly, if you like it, or the 2 flavors combined.
Follow the preceding rule for Apple Fritters.

BANANA FRITTERS

Peel and cut into halves lengthwise:
> 6 bananas

A sprinkling of rum goes well with these. Dip them in:
> Fritter Batter for Fruit

Fry them in deep fat (page 541).

APRICOT FRITTERS

Drain well, then dry between towels:
> Canned or stewed apricots

Dip them in:
> Fritter Batter for Fruit

Fry them in deep fat (page 541).

FRENCH FRITTERS WITH LEMON SAUCE

4 to 6 Servings
These are as light as air.
Combine in a saucepan and boil and stir over a low flame for 5 minutes:
> 6 tablespoons water
> 1 tablespoon butter
> 6 tablespoons all-purpose flour

Remove the pan from the fire. Beat in one at a time:
> 4 eggs

Beat the batter for 3 minutes after each addition. Add:

1 teaspoon vanilla

Drop the batter from a teaspoon into hot fat (page 541). Drain the fritters on absorbent paper. Dust them with:

Confectioners' sugar

Serve them at once with:

Lemon Sauce, page 757

ORANGE FRITTERS

Peel:

4 oranges

Cut them into slices and remove the seeds. Sprinkle the slices with:

Confectioners' sugar

Dip them in:

Fritter Batter for Fruit, page 543

Fry them in deep fat (page 541).

RICE CRULLERS OR FRITTERS

4 to 5 Servings

Boil:

⅔ cup rice or 2 cups cooked rice

Permit the water to absorb. Do not drain the rice. Cool it. Add to it:

3 beaten eggs
½ cup sugar
½ teaspoon vanilla
½ teaspoon nutmeg or grated lemon rind
3 teaspoons tartrate or phosphate baking powder or 2¼ teaspoons combination type (see Baking Powder, page 501)
6 tablespoons all-purpose flour

Heat deep fat to 365°, or hot enough to brown a cube of bread in 1 minute. Drop the batter into the fat from a teaspoon. Fry the fritters until they are golden brown. Drain them on absorbent paper. Sprinkle them with:

Confectioners' sugar

Serve them with:

Tart jelly

CRIMSON SAUCE FOR FRITTERS

About 1 Cupful

Combine and beat well:

½ cup currant jelly
2 tablespoons hot water
2 teaspoons lemon juice
⅛ teaspoon salt

Add:

2 tablespoons chopped raisins
4 chopped maraschino cherries
1 teaspoon maraschino cherry juice

CRULLERS

A Lot—Hard to Gauge the Amount

Sift:

⅔ cup sugar

Beat until light:

4 eggs

Add the sugar gradually. Blend these ingredients until they are creamy. Add:

¾ teaspoon grated lemon rind
⅓ cup melted shortening
⅓ cup milk

Sift before measuring:

3½ cups all-purpose flour

Resift with:

½ teaspoon cream of tartar
½ teaspoon soda
(¼ teaspoon salt)

Stir the sifted ingredients into the egg mixture. Roll the dough to the thickness of ¼ inch. Cut it into strips with a pie jagger. Fry the crullers in deep fat (page 541) 375° until brown, about 3 minutes. Drain them on unglazed brown paper. Sprinkle them when slightly cooled with:

Confectioners' sugar

Vegetable Fritters, page 324; Elderberry Pancakes, page 555.

Doughnuts

Rule for Frying Doughnuts

Doughnuts that are dried for 15 minutes before they are fried absorb little fat. When frying doughnuts have a wide saucepan of boiling water in readiness. Lift each doughnut, as soon as it is fried, rapidly in and out of the boiling water. Be careful to wipe the water from the utensil used in handling the doughnuts before putting it again in the hot fat.

When the water in the saucepan is cold a cake of fat will gather on it. This may be removed and used again.

Place the doughnuts in a moderate oven 375° until they are dry and crisp. Sprinkle them with confectioners' sugar. A good way to coat food with sugar or flour is to place it in a paper bag, add the sugar, close the bag and shake it well. Or ice the doughnuts, when cold, with cake icing.

You may split and toast slightly stale doughnuts.

DOUGHNUTS WITH SWEET MILK
About 36 Doughnuts
Beat:
  2 eggs
Add slowly, beating constantly:
  1 cup sugar
Stir in:
  1 cup milk
  5 tablespoons melted shortening
Sift before measuring:
  4 cups all-purpose flour
Resift with:
  4 teaspoons any baking powder
  ¼ teaspoon cinnamon or 1 teaspoon grated lemon rind
  ½ teaspoon salt
  (¼ teaspoon nutmeg)
Stir the sifted ingredients and the egg mixture until they are blended. The dough may be chilled until it is easy to handle. Roll the dough to the thickness of ¼ inch. Cut it into shapes. Fry the doughnuts in deep fat (page 541) heated to 370° or hot enough to brown a cube of bread in 1 minute. Brown them on one side, turn them and brown them on the other, about 3 minutes in all. See the preceding Rule for Frying Doughnuts.
Doughnuts cut with a small cutter are good for tea. Sprinkle them with:
  Cinnamon and sugar

DOUGHNUTS WITH POTATOES
Peel and cook by the rule on page 300:
  2 medium-sized potatoes
Rice or mash them. There should be 1 cupful. Beat well:
  2 eggs
Add very slowly, beating constantly:
  ⅔ cup sugar
Stir in the potatoes and:
  1 cup milk
  2 tablespoons melted butter
Sift before measuring:
  1 cup all-purpose flour
Resift with:
  3 teaspoons any baking powder
  ⅔ teaspoon salt
  (¼ teaspoon nutmeg or ¼ teaspoon cinnamon)
Stir in the sifted ingredients and the butter mixture until they are blended. Add sufficient sifted:
  All-purpose flour
to form a soft dough. Chill the dough until it is easy to handle. To roll, cut and fry the dough follow the rule for Doughnuts with Sweet Milk.

DOUGHNUTS WITH SOUR MILK OR CREAM
About 36 Doughnuts
Beat well:
  3 eggs
Add slowly, beating constantly:
  1¼ cups sugar
Stir in:
  1½ tablespoons melted butter
  1 cup sour milk
Sour cream may be substituted for the milk. In that case omit the butter.
Sift before measuring:
  4 cups all-purpose flour
Resift with:
  1 teaspoon soda
  2 teaspoons any baking powder
  (¼ teaspoon cinnamon or ½ teaspoon nutmeg)
  (½ teaspoon salt)
Stir the sifted ingredients and the egg mixture until they are blended. The dough may be chilled until it is easy to handle. To roll, cut and dry the doughnuts follow the preceding rule.
Or if you want molasses doughnuts, use the preceding recipe and add:
  ½ cup molasses
  1½ teaspoons ginger

ORANGE DOUGHNUTS
Follow one of the preceding rules for:
  Doughnuts
Deduct:
  4 tablespoons milk
Substitute:
  The grated rind of 1 orange
  4 tablespoons orange juice

CHOCOLATE DOUGHNUTS
Follow any of the preceding rules for:
  Doughnuts
Deduct:
  5 tablespoons flour
Substitute:
  1½ oz. melted chocolate
Add it to the melted shortening. Stir in:
  1½ teaspoons vanilla

PECAN DOUGHNUTS
Add to any of the preceding recipes for doughnuts:
  ½ cup broken nut meats

RAISED DOUGHNUTS
About Twenty-Four 3½ Inch Doughnuts
Follow the rule on page 623 for:
  Coffee Cake Dough
When it is ready to shape pat it to the

thickness of ½ inch. Cut it into rings. Place the rings on a floured board. Permit them to rise until they have doubled in bulk. Follow the Rule for Frying Doughnuts, page 544.

BERLIN DOUGHNUTS
Follow the preceding rule. Cut the dough into 2½ inch rounds instead of rings. Place on one round:
   1 heaping teaspoon jelly or
   preserves
Brush the edges of the round with:
   Egg white
Cap it with another round. Press the edges together. Repeat the process. Follow the preceding rule for letting the doughnuts rise. Fry them as directed in the Rule for Frying Doughnuts, page 544.

FRENCH DOUGHNUTS OR CRULLERS
About 8 Doughnuts
To make this delicious confection follow the recipe on page 653 for:
   Cream Puffs
You may add:
   ½ teaspoon grated orange or lemon
   rind, or 1 teaspoon vanilla
   1 tablespoon sugar
Permit this to cool for 5 minutes. Use a pastry tube to make circles or figure 8 doughnuts on squares of heavily greased paper, or on the end of a well-greased pancake turner. Turn the paper upside-down to drop the doughnuts into hot fat. Fry by the Rule for Frying Doughnuts on page 544. Omit the hot water bath. When cold these doughnuts are sometimes iced with confectioners' sugar diluted with lemon juice.
Or, hot or cold the doughnuts may be iced with Icing under Stollen, page 627.

ROSETTES
About Thirty-Six 2½ Inch Rosettes
Rosettes are shaped with a small iron made for the purpose. They are very good served with creamed food, sweet sauce, stewed fruit, etc.
Beat until blended:
   2 eggs
Add and beat:
   ¼ teaspoon salt
   1 teaspoon sugar
If the rosettes are to be used as patties, omit the sugar. Sift before measuring:
   1 cup all-purpose flour

Stir it into the egg mixture alternately with:
   1 cup milk
To fry rosettes prepare the iron by immersing the head of it in deep fat. Heat the fat to 370°, or hot enough to brown a cube of bread in 1 minute. Dip the hot iron in the batter, but do not let the batter run over the top of the iron, for then it is difficult to get the rosette, when cooked, off the iron. Return the batter-coated iron to the fat, immersing it completely from 20 to 35 seconds. Remove the rosette from the iron with a fork. Reheat the iron in the deep fat and repeat the process. Drain the rosettes on absorbent paper and serve them sprinkled with:
   Confectioners' sugar

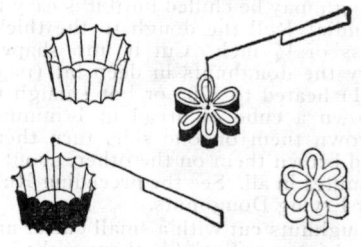

TIMBALE CASES FOR FOOD
Select a timbale iron that is fluted. It is easier to handle than a plain one. Sift:
   ¾ cup all-purpose flour
   ½ teaspoon salt
Combine and beat:
   1 egg
   ½ cup milk
Combine the liquid and the sifted ingredients with a few swift strokes. Add:
   1 teaspoon olive oil or melted
   butter
Let the batter stand for 1 hour to avoid bubbles which disfigure the timbales. To fry timbale cases prepare the iron by immersing its head in deep fat. Heat the fat to 370°, hot enough to brown a cube of bread in 1 minute. Wipe the iron with a cloth wrapped around a fork. Plunge the iron into the batter, within ¾ inch of the top. Remove it. Allow the batter to dry on the iron. Flatten bubbles that may appear with the fingers. Fry the timbale in the hot fat until it is golden brown, about 1 to 1½ minutes. Remove it from the iron and drain it on a paper towel. Repeat the process.

Griddle Cakes

Rule for Baking Griddle Cakes

Prepare griddle cake batter by one of the following rules. Meanwhile heat a heavy griddle. It may be greased with a bit of bacon or a turnip cut in two, but this is usually unnecessary. However, if a griddle has once been greased the process will probably have to be repeated. If this is the case, wipe the griddle with an oiled cloth between "bakings."

Test the griddle by letting a few drops of cold water fall upon it. If the water bounces and sputters a good deal the griddle is ready for the cakes.

Drop the batter by the spoonfuls on the griddle. Pour it from the tip of the spoon to get a round cake. The cakes are ready for their first turning after they have been baked from 2 to 3 minutes. When bubbles appear on their surface and begin to burst, lift the cakes with a spatula to see that the under surface is well browned, then turn them and continue baking them until the other side is browned. If the griddle has been greased, wipe it with an oiled cloth before baking more cakes on it. Watch your fingers!

Griddle or pancake batter may be adjusted to the cook's taste. After making a small test cake, if too thick, thin the batter with a tablespoonful or more of milk; if too thin, with a tablespoonful or more of flour.

Serve the cakes as soon as possible. If they cannot be served at once, keep them on a sheet in a slow oven separated by and covered with a tea towel to keep them from getting soggy. Or you may get much the same result by simply keeping the cakes between the folds of a tea towel.

GRIDDLE CAKES OR BATTER CAKES WITH SWEET MILK

About Fourteen 4 Inch Cakes

Sift before measuring:

1½ cups all-purpose flour

Resift with:

1 teaspoon salt
3 tablespoons sugar
2½ teaspoons tartrate or phosphate baking powder or 1¾ teaspoons combination type (see Baking Powder, page 501)

Beat lightly:

1 or 2 eggs

When using 2 eggs you may separate them. Add the yolks to the milk mixture. Beat the whites until stiff and fold them into the blended batter. Add:

3 tablespoons melted butter
1 cup milk

Make a hole in the center of the dry ingredients. Pour in the liquid ingredients. Stir them with a few swift strokes until they are blended only. Ignore the lumps; they are harmless. This process should take only 20 seconds. The batter may be prepared ahead of time if covered at once and placed in the refrigerator. It may be kept overnight or longer and give excellent results. Follow the preceding rule for baking the cakes.

WHOLE-GRAIN GRIDDLE CAKES

Follow the preceding rule for Griddle Cakes. Use:

¾ cup cake flour
¾ cup whole-grain flour

Add to the liquid ingredients:
 2 tablespoons molasses
Serve the cakes with:
 (Sausages and sirup)

BANANA GRIDDLE CAKES
Follow the rule on page 547 for:
 Griddle Cakes
Slice thinly and add to the liquid ingredients:
 1 large ripe banana

APPLE GRIDDLE CAKES
Follow the rule on page 547 for:
 Griddle Cakes
Peel, slice thinly and add to the liquid ingredients:
 1 tart juicy apple

BLUEBERRY GRIDDLE CAKES
Follow the rule on page 547 for:
 Griddle Cakes
Add to the batter:
 ¾ cup washed thoroughly drained blueberries
Serve the cakes with a mixture of:
 Sugar and cinnamon

PECAN GRIDDLE CAKES
Follow the rule on page 547 for:
 Griddle Cakes
Add to the dry ingredients
 ¾ cup finely chopped pecan meats

ONION GRIDDLE CAKES
This makes a good luncheon dish served with tomato or other sauce and a green salad. Sauté gently until tender but not brown:
 1½ cups finely chopped onion
in:
 2 tablespoons fat
Add them to Griddle Cake Batter with Sweet Milk or Sour Milk, pages 547, 548.

GRIDDLE CAKES WITH SOUR MILK
About Nine 4 Inch Cakes
Sift before measuring:
 1 cup cake flour or ⅞ cup all-purpose flour
Resift with:
 ½ teaspoon soda
 ½ teaspoon salt
Beat lightly:
 1 egg
Add:
 1 tablespoon melted butter
 1 cup sour milk

Combine these ingredients and bake the cakes by the Rule for Baking Griddle Cakes, page 547.

GRAHAM GRIDDLE CAKES
About Sixteen 4 Inch Cakes
Sift before measuring:
 ½ cup all-purpose flour
Resift with:
 2 tablespoons sugar
 ½ teaspoon salt
 ½ teaspoon any baking powder
 ¾ teaspoon soda
Stir in:
 1 cup graham or finely milled whole-wheat flour
Combine and beat:
 1 egg
 2 cups sour milk
 2 tablespoons melted butter or bacon drippings
Stir this into the sifted ingredients. Follow the Rule for Baking Griddle Cakes, page 547.

OATMEAL GRIDDLE CAKES
About Twelve 4 Inch Cakes
Sift before measuring:
 ½ cup all-purpose flour
Resift with:
 1 teaspoon any baking powder
 ½ teaspoon salt
Beat:
 1 egg
Stir in:
 1½ cups cooked oatmeal
 ½ cup evaporated milk
 ¼ cup water
 2 tablespoons melted butter or bacon drippings
Stir this mixture into the sifted ingredients. Follow the Rule for Baking Griddle Cakes, page 547.

BREAD CRUMB GRIDDLE CAKES
About Sixteen 4 Inch Cakes
This practical use of old bread makes a delicious griddle cake. Prepare:
 1 cup dry bread crumbs
Scald:
 1½ cups milk
Add and melt:
 2 tablespoons butter
Pour these ingredients over the crumbs. Beat until light:
 2 eggs
Add them to the crumb mixture. You may separate the eggs. Beat the yolks into the milk mixture. Beat the whites until stiff and fold them into the

blended batter. A good sweet cake may be made by adding 2 tablespoonfuls brown sugar and ¾ teaspoonful cinnamon to the ingredients.
Sift before measuring:
    ½ cup all-purpose flour
    ½ teaspoon salt
    4 teaspoons tartrate or phosphate baking powder or 2 teaspoons combination type (see Baking Powder, page 501)
Add the sifted ingredients to the batter. Stir it until they are blended. Follow the Rule for Baking Griddle Cakes, page 547.

BUCKWHEAT CAKES
About Forty 3 Inch Cakes
This batter is so light that it makes a lot of cakes. It keeps well covered in the refrigerator for several days.
Sift before measuring:
    ½ cup all-purpose flour
Resift with:
    ½ teaspoon any baking powder
    ½ teaspoon salt
    1 teaspoon soda
    2 teaspoons sugar
Two teaspoonfuls molasses may be substituted. Add it to the milk.
Add:
    1½ cups buckwheat flour
Pour into a bowl:
    3¼ cups sour milk or buttermilk
Add:
    2 tablespoons melted shortening
Add the dry ingredients. Beat the batter until it is blended only. Follow the Rule for Baking Griddle Cakes, page 547.

RAISED BUCKWHEAT CAKES
About Eighteen 2½ Inch Cakes
Scald, then cool to lukewarm:
    2 cups milk or water
Add and stir until dissolved:
    ¼ crumbled cake yeast
Add and stir to a smooth batter:
    1¾ cups buckwheat flour
    ½ teaspoon salt
Cover the batter with a cloth and permit it to rise at room temperature for 12 hours. Stir in:
    1 tablespoon molasses
    ½ teaspoon soda dissolved in ¼ cup lukewarm water
    (1 egg or ¼ cup melted shortening)
Follow the Rule for Baking Griddle Cakes, page 547. Serve them with:
    Maple sirup

RHODE ISLAND CORN-MEAL GRIDDLE CAKES
10 or 12 Cakes
Combine and stir:
    1 cup water-ground corn meal
    1 tablespoon flour
    1 teaspoon sugar
    ½ teaspoon salt
Pour over them and stir in:
    1 cup boiling water
Add:
    ½ cup milk
Cook on a griddle generously greased with bacon fat.

CRISP CORN-MEAL CAKES
About Twenty Thin 2 Inch Cakes
Place in a bowl:
    1⅓ cups white corn meal
    1¼ teaspoons salt
    ½ teaspoon soda
    ¼ cup sifted all-purpose flour
Cut into this with a pastry blender:
    ¼ cup butter
Combine and beat:
    2 cups sour milk
    2 eggs
Stir the liquid into the sifted ingredients with a few swift strokes. Make the cakes small for easier turning. The batter settles readily. Beat it between spoonfuls. Follow the Rule for Baking Griddle Cakes, page 547.

LACY CORN-MEAL CAKES
About Twenty-Four Thin 2 Inch Cakes
Place in a bowl:
    1⅓ cups white corn meal
    1¼ teaspoons salt
    ¾ teaspoon soda
    1 tablespoon all-purpose flour
Combine and beat:
    2 cups sour milk
    ¼ cup melted butter
Stir the liquid into the sifted ingredients with a few swift strokes. Make these cakes small for easy turning. The batter settles readily. Beat it between spoonfuls. Follow the Rule for Baking Griddle Cakes, page 547.

RICE CORN-MEAL GRIDDLE CAKES
Twelve 4 Inch Cakes
Sift before measuring:
    ½ cup all-purpose flour
Resift with:
    1 teaspoon salt
    ½ teaspoon soda
    1 tablespoon sugar

Add:

½ cup water-ground corn meal
1 cup cold boiled rice

Combine, beat, then stir into the sifted ingredients with a few swift strokes:

2 cups buttermilk
2 egg yolks
2 tablespoons melted cooled shortening

Beat until stiff:

2 egg whites
⅛ teaspoon salt

Fold them into the batter. Follow the Rule for Baking Griddle Cakes, page 547. This batter may be used for waffles.

LEFT-OVER RICE BATTER CAKES

Stir:

Grated cheese

into:

Cooked rice

Season with:

Salt and paprika

Shape the rice into small flat cakes. You may add 1 beaten egg to every cupful of rice. In that case drop the batter by the spoonful into hot fat. Sauté them slowly in:

Butter

PICNIC BATTER CAKES

This recipe is planned to satisfy the appetites of from 10 to 12 picnickers. Sift before measuring:

3 cups all-purpose flour

Resift with:

¼ cup sugar
2 cups cornmeal
2 teaspoons salt
4 teaspoons tartrate or phosphate baking powder or 3 teaspoons combination type (see Baking Powder, page 501)

Beat:

3 egg yolks
2 tablespoons melted butter
4 cups milk

Follow the rule for Griddle Cakes with Sweet Milk, page 547, for combining the ingredients. Beat until stiff:

3 egg whites

Heap them on top of the batter. Place the batter in glass jars. Keep cool. Beat it with a whisk or fork just before using it. Bake the cakes and wrap them around small:

Broiled sausages or bacon

PANCAKES

Basic Rule for Pancakes
About Eight 3 Inch Cakes

Heat slowly for 15 minutes an ungreased griddle. Prepare a salt bag by tying up about 3 tablespoonfuls of table salt in a 6 inch square of cheesecloth. Sift before measuring:

1¼ cups all-purpose flour

Resift it into a bowl with:

½ teaspoon salt
3 teaspoons tartrate or phosphate baking powder or 2¼ teaspoons combination type (see Baking Powder, page 501)
1 tablespoon sugar

Combine, beat until blended and then add to the flour mixture:

1 beaten egg
1 cup milk
2 tablespoons shortening

Beat the batter until the flour is dampened only. Ignore the lumps. Place a few drops of cold water on the griddle. If they dash about briskly it is ready for use (page 547). Rub it with the salt bag. Clean it this way between bakings, too. You may make a small test cake if you wish. The batter should go zizz, and should begin to bubble at once. If the griddle is ready, begin to bake the pancakes. Pour about ¼ cupful of batter quickly onto the griddle. Repeat until the griddle is covered with cakes. When the edges of the cakes become dry and some of the bubbles break, turn them. The second side will take only about ½ as long to bake as the first side. You may keep the cakes hot in a covered skillet in a slow oven or over slow heat, or in an oven (page 547). You may place on the cakes marmalade, jam, jelly, cottage cheese, puréed fruit, etc. Roll them and sprinkle them with sugar. Or fill them with creamed fish, chicken, vegetables or hash. Roll them, sprinkle them with grated cheese and put them briefly under the broiler to melt it.

ADDITIONS TO PANCAKE BATTER

You may add to the above or to the following pancake batter ½ cupful finely chopped apples or well-drained canned pineapple, chopped pecans or other nut meats, dates, raisins, etc. Or you may add ½ cupful cooked leftover vegetables, minced celery, beans, broccoli or corn, but see that they are well drained.

SOUR MILK PANCAKES
About Fourteen 5 Inch Cakes
Sift before measuring:

    ⅞ cup all-purpose flour or 1 cup
       cake flour

Resift with:

    1 teaspoon sugar
    ½ teaspoon salt
    ¾ teaspoon any baking powder
    ½ teaspoon soda

Beat until light:

    1 egg

Add:

    1 cup sour milk

Combine the sifted and the liquid ingredients with a few swift strokes.
Beat in:

    2 tablespoons melted butter

To bake the pancakes follow the rule for French Pancakes below.

FRENCH PANCAKES
About Fourteen to Sixteen 5 Inch Cakes
Sift:

    ¾ cup all-purpose flour

Resift with:

    ½ teaspoon salt
    1 teaspoon any baking powder
    2 tablespoons powdered sugar

Beat:

    2 eggs

Add and beat:

    ⅔ cup milk
    ⅓ cup water
    ½ teaspoon vanilla or
    (½ teaspoon grated lemon rind)

Make a well in the sifted ingredients. Pour in the liquid ingredients. Combine them with a few swift strokes. Ignore the lumps; they will take care of themselves. Heat a 5 inch skillet. Grease it with a few drops of oil. Add a small quantity of batter. Tip the skillet and let the batter spread over the bottom. Cook the pancake over moderate heat. When it is brown underneath reverse it and brown the other side. Use a few drops of oil for each pancake. Spread the cake with:

    Jelly

Roll it and sprinkle it with:

    Confectioners' sugar

CRÊPES SUZETTE
At the age of 14 the famous Franco-American cook, Henri Charpentier, invented crêpes Suzette—a glorified French pancake. His patron was Albert, Prince of Wales, whose penchant for all that was bright and gay seemed a defense against his incredibly dull upbringing. In "Life à la Henri" (Simon and Schuster, 1934) Henri Charpentier and Boyden Sparkes tell amusingly of Henri's delight in tempting the jaded palate of this gourmet.

One day he was composing a crêpe sauce—a most complicated affair—a blend of orange and lemon peel, sugar, butter, maraschino, curaçao and kirsch. By accident the cordials caught fire and the poor boy thought that both he and his sauce were ruined. The Prince was waiting, how could Henri begin all over again? He tasted the sauce—it was delicious. Quickly he plunged the crêpes into the boiling liquid, added more of the cordials and let the sauce burn again. The dish was a triumph.

Asked by the Prince what he called these fabulous cakes, Henri stammered, "Crêpes Princesse." The Prince, acknowledging the compliment to himself, answered gallantly that there was a lady present. There was, a very small girl—would Henri consent to changing the name to crêpes Suzette? Henri would and did. Later he received from the Prince a jeweled ring, a hat and a cane, but best of all he had put his foot on the first rung of the ladder to his future success.

This is Henri's recipe, condensed and put into what approximates American form. It makes 8 cakes—"enough for 4 people," says Henri.
Combine and stir until the ingredients are the consistency of thin cream:

    3 eggs
    2 tablespoons all-purpose flour
    1 tablespoon water
    1 tablespoon milk
    A pinch of salt

Some cooks then recommend keeping this batter overnight. Place in a small skillet:

    Butter "as one joint of your
      thumb"

When this bubbles pour in enough paste to cover the bottom of the pan with a thin coating—"almost like the white of an egg." Keep the pan moving, for this is a delicate substance. A minute of cooking and the job is ¾ done. Turn the cake. Now again and again and again until the cake is well browned. Now fold the cake twice. It will be triangular in shape "like a lady's handkerchief." The crêpes may be stacked and reheated much later in sauce.

Method I.
Henri's Butter Sauce for Crêpes Suzette
This may be made in advance and kept for months in a cool place.
Cut into very thin strips pieces of:
>   Lemon rind ¾ inch square
>   Orange rind ¾ inch square

"Enough to put a patch on the ball of your thumb." Use only the thin yellow rind. Add:
>   1 teaspoon Vanilla Sugar, page 709

I say (not Henri) you may substitute a few drops of vanilla and 1 teaspoonful of sugar. Permit these ingredients to stand closely covered for 12 hours or more. Melt in a large thin skillet (Henri says a silver skillet):
>   ½ cup sweet butter

When it starts to bubble add:
>   1 pony maraschino
>   1 pony curaçao
>   1 pony kirsch

Put a lighted match to the sauce. As the flame dies down add the lemon and orange mixture. Place the sauce in a cool place until ready for use, if you wish. Make the crêpes. Plunge the cakes in boiling sauce. Turn them. Add:
>   1 pony maraschino
>   1 pony curaçao
>   1 pony kirsch

Put a lighted match to the sauce. Permit it to burn. Serve the cakes at once. The final performance—plunging the folded crêpes into the boiling sauce, adding and burning the liquor—is done in the presence of the one to be fêted.
Having given the original version of this famous dish, I shall follow it by a less complicated and very good, if not authentic, recipe.

Method II.
There are now endless ways of preparing crêpes Suzette. The rule for French Pancakes will answer as well as any for everyday use. Needless to say, but being said for the benefit of those who need an introduction, these cakes are about as good to eat as anything man or superman can make.
Follow the rule for:
>   French Pancakes, page 551

Substitute for the lemon and vanilla:
>   (1 teaspoon cognac or curaçao)

Bake the cakes as directed. Spread them at once with the following sauce. Stir until blended and creamy:

>   ½ cup butter
>   1 cup confectioners' sugar

Add:
>   5 tablespoons orange juice
>   1 tablespoon lemon juice
>   2 teaspoons grated orange rind or orange marmalade

Method III.
Other filling and sauce suggestions include tangerine juice and rind for the orange and marmalade or the crêpes may be spread with any good Hard Sauce, page 753, and served with or without the addition of the brandy and wine. Here is another simple rule.
Heat and stir in a double boiler until smooth:
>   1 teaspoon grated orange rind
>   ½ cup orange juice
>   3 tablespoons butter
>   1½ cups confectioners' sugar

Add:
>   (Rum, sherry or dessert wine)

Roll the cakes and sprinkle them with:
>   Confectioners' sugar

Put the crêpes on a hot platter. Place them in a fairly hot oven 400° to melt the sugar. Have it brought to the table. Cover the bottom of the platter to the depth of ¼ inch:
>   2 parts brandy
>   1 part wine

Put a lighted match to the liquor. Permit it to burn down. Serve the crêpes at once.
Another way to serve the crêpes is to spread them generously with jelly, roll them and cover them with whipped cream dotted with jelly. Place them in a hot oven 400° until the cream and jelly are melted. Raspberry jam flavored with rum makes a good filling. So does bar le duc jelly.

CRÊPES WITH PINEAPPLE
Slice, then pare and remove the eyes from:
>   1 large pineapple

Dice the pulp. Cook and stir until dissolved:
>   ½ cup sugar
>   ½ cup water

Add the pineapple. Let it cook until it has absorbed the sirup. Stir it frequently. Cool it slightly. Or use well-drained canned pineapple with good results—about 1½ cupfuls. Add:
>   2 tablespoons apricot or raspberry jam
>   1 tablespoon rum

Prepare by the rule on page 551:

Thin French Pancakes
and spread them with the pineapple filling. Roll them, then sprinkle them with:

Confectioners' sugar

Place them low under a broiler to let the sugar melt and glaze. Pour over the crêpes:

¼ cup rum

Set it afire at the table. Baste the crêpes while the rum is burning. Serve them on hot plates.

RUSSIAN RAISED PANCAKES OR BLINI

Dissolve in a deep bowl (page 526):

½ cake yeast in 2 cups lukewarm milk

Stir in until well blended:

1½ cups sifted all-purpose flour
2 tablespoons sugar

Set this sponge to rise in a warm place for 1½ hours. Cover the bowl with a cloth. Beat until well blended:

3 egg yolks
6 tablespoons soft butter

Stir in:

1½ cups sifted all-purpose flour
¾ teaspoon salt

Beat these ingredients into the sponge. Permit the sponge to rise again for 1½ hours. Whip until stiff:

3 egg whites

Fold them into the batter. After 10 minutes bake the batter, a very small quantity at a time, in a 5 inch skillet spread with butter. As the cakes bake spread the unbaked side with:

Soft butter

The blini should be paper thin. Serve them with:

Caviar or salmon

AUSTRIAN PANCAKE OR OMELET SOUFFLÉ

4 Small Servings—If You Are Not Very Hungry
Known in Salzburg as a "Nockerl." Few visitors failed to indulge in one or more between the delights of the Annual Musical Festival, and it is safe to suppose that the inhabitants indulge in them the year around. This rich omelet soufflé or pancake is good as a breakfast or supper dish and wonderful as a dessert with rum or fruit sauce. Make it immediately before it is to be served. It has very little body and shrinks quickly.
Melt in a 9 or 10 inch skillet:

1 tablespoon butter

The skillet should be hot when the soufflé mixture is put into it. Beat until very light:

4 egg yolks
2 to 4 tablespoons sugar

Add:

⅛ to ¼ teaspoon vanilla

Whip until stiff:

4 egg whites
A pinch salt

Fold the yolk mixture lightly into the egg whites. Heap the soufflé into the hot skillet by the spoonful. Allow about 5 minutes in all for cooking it. Brown the under side, turn the puffs and brown the other side. The center should remain soft. If you are serving the nockerl without fruit or sauce, sprinkle it with:

Confectioners' sugar

GERMAN PANCAKE

2 Servings
Henriette Davides, the German counterpart of the fabulous English Mrs. Beeton, says that the heat under this pancake must be neither "too weak nor too strong," that it is advisable to put "enough butter in the skillet but not too much" and that the best results are obtained in making no more than a 4 egg pancake at one time. Henriette's recipes make mouth-watering reading. That, as Archie of "Duffy's Tavern" would say, is the "ipso," but the "facto" is that they are almost impossible to follow. Only a strongly intuitive person on speaking terms with his imagination has a chance of success. The following rule is Henriette's but the interpretation is mine.
Combine and stir until smooth:

4 beaten egg yolks
2 tablespoons cornstarch
¼ cup lukewarm milk
¼ cup lukewarm water
¾ teaspoon salt
1 tablespoon sugar
Grated rind of 1 lemon

Beat until stiff:

4 egg whites

Fold them into the yolk mixture. Melt in a heavy skillet about 10 inches in diameter:

2 tablespoons butter

When the skillet is hot pour in the pancake batter. Cook it over low to medium heat, partly covered with a pan, for about 5 minutes. Or the batter may be cooked until it begins to set and then be placed in a moderately hot oven 400° until it is puffed and firm. Cooking time in all is about 7 minutes.

It should puff up well, but it may fall. As Horace Walpole said of a noted beauty: "She is pretty with the bloom of youth but has no features and her beauty cannot last." So serve it at once with:

Confectioners' sugar and cinnamon or lemon juice, covered with jam or jelly and rolled, or with wine, fruit or rum sauce

CORN-MEAL PANCAKES
About Twelve 4 Inch Cakes
Delicate and good. Measure:

1 cup white or yellow corn meal

Place it in a bowl. Add:

1 teaspoon salt
1 to 2 tablespoons sirup or sugar

Stir in slowly:

1 cup boiling water

Cover these ingredients and permit them to stand for 10 minutes. Beat:

1 egg
½ cup milk
2 tablespoons melted butter

Add these ingredients to the corn meal. Sift before measuring:

½ cup all-purpose flour

Resift with:

2 teaspoons any baking powder

Stir the sifted ingredients into the batter with a few swift strokes. To bake the pancakes follow the rule for French Pancakes, page 551. For a special treat have a main dish of these pancakes by making them large, about 5 inches across. When done, place on each one creamed chicken, fish or hash. Fold the cakes over, sprinkle them with grated cheese and place them briefly under the broiler to melt the cheese.

BLINTZES OR COTTAGE CHEESE PANCAKES
4 Servings
Prepare by the rule on page 551:

French Pancake batter

Use a 6 inch skillet. Fry very thin cakes on one side only, until the top is bubbly. Place them on a tea towel, browned side up. Prepare the following filling. Mix well:

1½ cups smooth rather dry cottage cheese: 12 oz.
1 egg yolk
1 teaspoon soft butter
1 teaspoon vanilla or grated lemon rind

Place about 2 tablespoonfuls of filling on the center of each cake. Roll the edges over from 2 sides. At this point the blintzes may be placed in a closely covered dish and chilled for several hours or they may be cooked at once. Melt in a large skillet:

1 tablespoon oil or butter

Place several blintzes in it, lapped side down. Fry them to a golden brown, turning them once. Repeat, adding more oil or butter to the skillet, until all are done. Serve them hot sprinkled with:

Sugar and cinnamon

You may pass:

Sour cream

Blintzes are also made with a filling of finely ground meat moistened with gravy and served with additional gravy.

POTATO PANCAKES
About Twelve 3 Inch Cakes
Pare:

6 large potatoes

Grate them coarsely into a small bowl of water. Drain them quickly. Place them on a towel, wring the towel to extract as much moisture as possible from the potatoes. There should be about 2 cupfuls of potatoes. Place them in a bowl. Beat well, then stir in:

2 eggs

Combine and sift:

1½ tablespoons all-purpose flour
¼ teaspoon baking powder
1¼ teaspoons salt

Add the flour to the potato mixture with:

1 teaspoon grated onion

Sauté by spoonfuls in ¼ inch or more of hot fat. Turn and brown the second side. These are usually served with:

Applesauce

Grated Potatoes, Pan-Broiled, page 306.

TOMATO PANCAKES
About Four 4 Inch Cakes
These sound "queerish" but they have an attractive red brown color, a good flavor and are highly esteemed by cake fanciers. Strain:

2 cups stewed tomatoes or canned tomatoes

Sift and combine with the tomatoes:

1 teaspoon salt
¼ teaspoon pepper
½ teaspoon sugar
1½ cups all-purpose flour
1 teaspoon any baking powder

Melt in a skillet:
2 tablespoons butter

Add the tomato batter by the table-spoonful and sauté the cakes until they are a good brown. Serve them with or without sirup.

APPLE PANCAKES

Prepare by the rule on page 551:
French Pancake batter

Melt in a skillet:
1 tablespoon butter
1 tablespoon lard

When the fat is hot pour in ½ the batter. Sprinkle it generously with:
Pared, cored, thinly sliced apples, peaches, bananas, etc.

Pour the remaining batter over the apples. Turn the cake when it is browned underneath. Brown the other side. Serve the pancake hot with:
Powdered sugar

FRUIT PANCAKES

Follow the preceding rule.

Substitute for the apples:
1 cup or more blueberries, sliced bananas, peach, etc., or ½ cup elderberry blossoms stripped from the stem

Elderberry fritters may be made by leaving the blossoms on the stem. Wash the flowers. When dry dip them in Fritter Batter for Fruit, page 543, or

French Pancake batter, page 551. Fry them in deep fat.

CHOCOLATE PANCAKES

About Fourteen 4 Inch Cakes

Beat until light:
2 egg yolks

Combine and stir:
1 tablespoon soft butter
1 tablespoon sugar
1 teaspoon salt
2 tablespoons cocoa
2 tablespoons milk

Add these ingredients to the yolk mixture. Sift before measuring:
1½ cups all-purpose flour

Resift with:
2 teaspoons tartrate or phosphate baking powder or 1½ teaspoons combination type (see Baking Powder, page 501)

Add the ingredients to the yolk mixture with:
1 cup milk

Or sour milk may be substituted. In that case omit the baking powder and use 1 teaspoonful soda.

Beat until stiff:
2 egg whites

Fold them into the batter. Melt in a skillet:
2 tablespoons butter

Sauté the pancakes in the butter on both sides. While hot sprinkle them with:
Powdered sugar

Waffles

Rule for Making Waffles

Heat a waffle iron. To test the heat of the iron, if there is no indicator, throw a drop of water upon it. If the water boils and forms a small ball, the iron is ready to use. If it sizzles vigorously, it is too hot. Or, put a teaspoonful of water on the iron. Close it. When the steaming stops the iron is ready for use.

Have the batter ready. Place it in a medium-sized pitcher. Fill the iron about two-thirds full as shown on the following page. It takes from 4 to 5 minutes to bake the average waffle—a little longer for a thin batter.

The majority of waffle recipes call for cake flour. If that is not available, substitute all-purpose flour, deducting 2 tablespoonfuls from every cupful given in the recipe.

The majority of recipes call for the separate beating of the egg whites. I am following this rule but I find that good waffles may be made without this additional effort.

Waffles are fine as a main dish with creamed chicken, fish or left-over food, or with bacon as shown cooking in the center on page 556. Or serve them filled with creamed food as shown on the right. They may also be served as a dessert with ice cream, crushed or stewed fruit. sirup, etc.

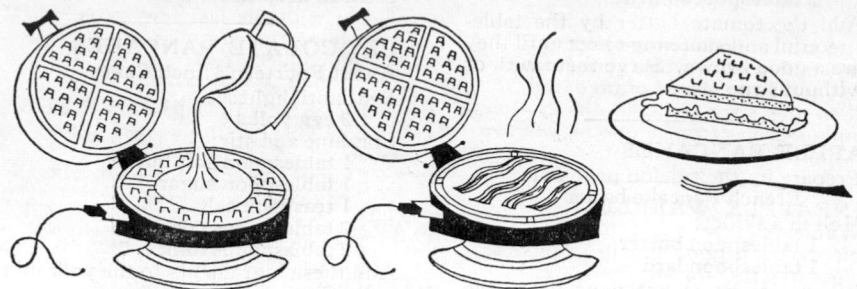

Waffle batter may be stored in the refrigerator for about 3 days if kept in a covered container. If you plan to store the dough use double-action baking powder, page 501. When ready to bake do not stir batter any more than necessary.

See Waffles with Homemade Biscuit Mix, page 557. Use this as a basis for other waffles given in this chapter—raisin, pecan, etc.

To clean a waffle iron, wash off the outside with a cloth wrung out of hot soapy water. Polish it with a dry cloth. Use slightly dampened steel wool to clean excess batter from the grids. Apply a thin film of melted unsalted fat. Close the baker, turn on the current. Heat for about 2 minutes. Wipe off excess fat with paper toweling.

WAFFLES
6 Waffles
Sift before measuring:
   1¾ cups cake flour, see preceding
      rule
Resift with:
   3 teaspoons tartrate or phosphate
      baking powder or 2 teaspoons
      combination type (see Baking
      Powder, page 501)
   ½ teaspoon salt
   1 tablespoon sugar
Beat well:
   3 egg yolks
Add:
   2 to 7 tablespoons melted butter
      or salad oil
   1½ cups milk
Make a hole in the center of the sifted ingredients. Pour in the liquid ingredients. Combine them with a few swift strokes. The batter should have a pebbled look similar to a muffin batter. Beat until stiff but not dry:
   3 egg whites
Fold them into the batter until they are barely blended. Bake the waffles by the preceding rule.
Good served with:
   Honey and melted butter or
   Honey Cream, page 558
   Sweetened strawberries and
   whipped cream or

Waffle Sauce
Cream, then chill:
   3 tablespoons butter
   ½ cup confectioners' sugar
   ¾ teaspoon cinnamon
Waffles are quickly made with an electric mixer. Beat the egg whites at high speed until they stand up in peaks. Combine the remaining ingredients. Beat them at medium speed for 2 minutes. Fold in the egg whites at low speed, for not more than ½ minute.

RAISIN AND NUT WAFFLES
6 Waffles
Follow the preceding rule for:
   Waffles
Add to the sifted ingredients:
   ½ cup chopped seeded raisins
   ½ cup chopped nut meats or
   ¾ cup shredded coconut

PECAN WAFFLES
6 Waffles
Follow the above rule for:
   Waffles
Add to the liquid ingredients:
   1 teaspoon vanilla
Beat in with the last few strokes before adding the egg whites:
   ¾ cup broken pecan meats
Serve the waffles with:

Orange Sirup
Boil slowly for about 8 minutes:
1 cup sugar
6 tablespoons orange juice
1½ tablespoons white corn sirup
½ teaspoon grated orange rind
When the sirup falls in thick, slow running drops from a spoon, remove it from the fire and chill it.

PINEAPPLE WAFFLES
6 Waffles
This makes a good luncheon dessert.
Follow the rule for:
Waffles, page 556
Add to the dry ingredients:
2 tablespoons sugar
(1 teaspoon grated lemon rind)
Beat in with the last few strokes before adding the egg whites:
½ cup drained crushed pineapple
Serve the waffles with the following sauce.

Pineapple Cream Sauce
Cook for 3 minutes:
½ cup pineapple juice
1½ tablespoons sugar
Chill the sirup. Add:
½ cup cream
⅛ teaspoon salt

BANANA WAFFLES
6 Waffles
Prepare by the rule on page 556:
Waffles
Add to the sifted ingredients:
1 tablespoon sugar
1 teaspoon grated lemon rind
Beat in with the last few strokes before adding the egg whites:
1 cup thinly sliced bananas

APRICOT OR PRUNE WAFFLES
Prepare by the rule on page 556:
Waffles
Add to the sifted ingredients:
1 tablespoon sugar
Fold in with the last few strokes before adding the egg whites:
¾ cup stewed, drained, diced apricots or prunes
Bake the waffles. Serve them with:
Apricot or prune juice
Dilute the juice if desired with:
Cream

BLUEBERRY WAFFLES
Prepare by the rule on page 556:
Waffles

Add to the sifted ingredients:
1 tablespoon sugar
Fold in with the last few strokes before adding the egg whites:
1 cup blueberries

WAFFLES WITH HOMEMADE BISCUIT MIX
Measure:
2 cups Homemade Biscuit Mix, page 506
Add:
1 teaspoon sugar
⅛ teaspoon salt
Combine:
1½ cups sweet or sour milk
1 beaten egg
2 tablespoons melted butter or salad oil
Beat the liquid into the dry ingredients until blended only. Proceed as with any waffle batter.

ORANGE WAFFLES
4 Waffles
Sift:
1½ cups cake flour
Resift with:
1 teaspoon any baking powder
1 tablespoon sugar
⅓ teaspoon salt
Add:
1 tablespoon grated orange rind
Beat in a separate bowl until light:
2 egg yolks
Combine and beat in with a few swift strokes:
5 tablespoons melted butter
¼ cup milk
¼ cup orange juice
1 teaspoon lemon juice
Beat until stiff but not dry:
2 egg whites
Fold them lightly into the batter. Bake it by the rule for Waffles, page 556.

RICE WAFFLES
6 Waffles
Stir until smooth (page 103):
½ cup cold cooked rice
Add and beat well:
2 egg yolks
2 tablespoons sugar
1 teaspoon salt
5 tablespoons melted butter
Sift before measuring:
2 cups all-purpose flour
Resift with:
2 teaspoons tartrate or phosphate baking powder or 1½ teaspoons combination type (see Baking Powder, page 501)

Stir these ingredients into the rice mixture with a few swift strokes alternately with:

2 cups milk

You may use sour milk or buttermilk. In that case omit the baking powder. Substitute 1 teaspoonful soda. Deduct ½ teaspoonful salt. Beat until stiff:

2 egg whites

Fold them lightly into the batter. Bake it by the rule for Waffles, page 556.

See Rice Corn-Meal Griddle Cakes, page 549.

BRAN WAFFLES
4 Waffles

Sift before measuring:

1½ cups all-purpose flour

Resift with:

¾ teaspoon salt
1½ tablespoons sugar
4 teaspoons tartrate or phosphate baking powder or 3 teaspoons combination type (see Baking Powder, page 501)

Add:

6 tablespoons bran

Beat in a separate bowl until light:

2 egg yolks

Add:

1½ cups milk
6 tablespoons melted shortening

Combine the liquid and the dry ingredients. Then beat until stiff but not dry:

2 egg whites
¼ teaspoon salt

Fold them into the batter. Bake it by the rule for Waffles, page 556. Serve the waffles with:

Honey Cream

Heat but do not boil:

1 cup honey

Stir in slowly:

½ cup cream

or beat well:

¼ cup honey
2 tablespoons soft butter
2 tablespoons thick cream

CHEESE WAFFLES
6 Waffles

Sift:

2 cups all-purpose flour

Resift with:

2 tablespoons sugar
1 teaspoon salt

4 teaspoons tartrate or phosphate baking powder or 3 teaspoons combination type (see Baking Powder, page 501)

Beat in a separate bowl until light:

3 egg yolks

Add and beat:

2 cups milk
7 tablespoons melted shortening
¾ cup grated cheese

Combine the liquid and the dry ingredients with a few swift strokes. Beat until stiff but not dry:

3 egg whites

Fold them into the batter. Bake it by the rule for Waffles, page 556. Serve them with:

Tart jelly

SOUR MILK WAFFLES
6 Waffles

Sift before measuring:

2 cups all-purpose flour

Resift with:

¼ teaspoon soda
2 teaspoons tartrate or phosphate baking powder or 1⅓ teaspoons combination type (see Baking Powder, page 501)
1 tablespoon sugar
½ teaspoon salt

Beat in a separate bowl until light:

2 egg yolks

Add and beat:

1¾ cups sour milk
6 tablespoons melted butter

Combine the liquid and the dry ingredients with a few swift strokes. Beat until stiff but not dry:

2 egg whites

Fold them into the batter. Bake it by the rule for Waffles, page 556.

SOUR CREAM WAFFLES
About 4 Waffles

These waffles are superlative.

Sift before measuring:

1 cup cake flour

Resift with:

2 teaspoons tartrate or phosphate baking powder or 1⅓ teaspoons combination type (see Baking Powder, page 501)
⅛ teaspoon salt
1 teaspoon sugar
1 teaspoon soda

Beat in a separate bowl until light:

3 egg yolks

Add:

2 cups thick sour cream

Combine the liquid and the dry ingredients with a few swift strokes. Beat until stiff but not dry:

 3 egg whites

Fold them into the batter. Bake it by the rule for Waffles, page 556.

CORN-MEAL WAFFLES
6 Waffles

Combine and stir until smooth:

 1½ cups corn meal
 1½ cups boiling water

Add and stir until melted:

 6 tablespoons shortening

Cool these ingredients thoroughly, cover them and keep them until ready for use. Beat until light:

 3 egg yolks

Add them to the corn meal. Beat in:

 1½ cups sour milk or butter milk

Sift before measuring:

 1 cup all-purpose flour

Resift with:

 ½ teaspoon soda
 1 tablespoon sugar
 ½ teaspoon salt
 3 teaspoons tartrate or phosphate
 baking powder or 2 teaspoons
 combination type (see Baking
 Powder, page 501)

Add the sifted ingredients to the batter. Beat until stiff but not dry:

 3 egg whites

Fold them into the batter. Bake it by the rule for Waffles, page 556.

Bacon and Corn-Meal Waffles, page 186.

HAM WAFFLES
Prepare:

 Waffles, page 556, or Sour
 Milk Waffles, page 558

Just before closing the iron sprinkle the batter with:

 1 cup finely diced uncooked
 smoked ham or ground or
 minced cooked ham

GINGERBREAD WAFFLES
6 Waffles
Sift:

 1½ cups all-purpose flour

Resift with:

 1 teaspoon ginger
 ½ teaspoon salt
 1 teaspoon soda
 1 teaspoon any baking powder
 (¼ teaspoon cinnamon)

Beat in a separate bowl until light:

 3 eggs

Add and beat:

 ¼ cup sugar
 ½ cup molasses
 1 cup sour milk
 ⅓ cup melted shortening

Combine the liquid and the sifted ingredients with a few swift strokes. Bake the batter by the rule for Waffles, page 556. These waffles are a good dessert served with:

 Ice cream or whipped cream

or with:

 Cinnamon and sugar

CHOCOLATE WAFFLES
6 Waffles

This is a delectable waffle with ice cream. Sift before measuring:

 1½ cups cake flour

Resift with:

 2½ teaspoons tartrate or phosphate
 baking powder or 2 teaspoons
 combination type (see Baking
 Powder, page 501)
 ¼ teaspoon salt
 (¼ teaspoon cinnamon)
 (¼ teaspoon nutmeg)

Cream:

 ½ cup butter

with:

 1 cup sugar

Beat in one at a time:

 2 eggs

Add:

 1 teaspoon vanilla

Melt, cool and add:

 2 oz. chocolate

Add the sifted ingredients in about 3 parts alternately with:

 ½ cup milk

Bake the batter by the rule for Waffles, page 556.

CRISP SPONGE CAKE WAFFLES
6 Waffles

This is a good substitute for shortcake. Sift before measuring:

 1 cup cake flour

Resift with:

 1 teaspoon tartrate or phosphate
 baking powder or ¾ teaspoon
 combination type (see Baking
 Powder, page 501)
 ¼ teaspoon salt

Beat in a separate bowl until light:

 3 eggs

Add and beat:

 1 cup sugar

Beat the sifted ingredients into the egg with:

 3 tablespoons melted butter

¼ cup cold water
1 teaspoon vanilla or 2 teaspoons
    orange rind or 1 tablespoon rum

Bake the batter on a hot waffle iron until delicately browned, about 2 minutes.

For shortcakes sprinkle the waffles with:

Powdered sugar

Serve them with:

Berries
Whipped cream or ice cream

FRENCH TOAST WAFFLES

Combine:

1 beaten egg
¼ cup milk
2 tablespoons melted butter
⅛ teaspoon salt

Cut into pieces to fit a waffle iron:

Sliced bread

Coat the bread well in the batter. Toast it on a hot waffle iron.

PEANUT BUTTER WAFFLES
6 Waffles

Cream together:

¼ cup peanut butter
2 tablespoons shortening

Add:

3 tablespoons sugar

Beat and add:

2 eggs

Add:

1½ cups milk

Sift, then measure:

1¾ cups all-purpose flour

Resift with:

3 teaspoons tartrate or phosphate
    baking powder or 2 teaspoons
    combination type (see Baking
    Powder, page 501)
¼ to ½ teaspoon salt depending
    upon the saltiness of peanut
    butter

Add the sifted ingredients to the liquid ingredients. Beat until smooth. Bake by the rule for Waffles, page 556.

Pies

In spite of the old saw, "The American cocktail follows the flag," our pies seem to "beat the cocktail to it." Pie is the most popular of all our foods, especially when allied to the runner-up, ice cream. That combination puts the cocktail in the background, but fortunately not in the doghouse.

Time Chart for Baking Pies

Novices, I find, frequently fail to *preheat* the oven. The oven should be at the temperature given in these recipes when the food to be baked is placed in it.

Double Crust Fruit Pies:	Hot oven 450° for 10 minutes. Moderate oven 350° for an additional 35 minutes, 45 minutes to 1 hour in all.
Mince Pie or any other double crust pie with a previously cooked filling:	Hot oven 450° for 30 minutes.
Open Fruit Pies:	Hot oven 450° for 20 minutes.
Custard, Pumpkin and other open pies:	Hot oven 450° for 15 minutes. Slow oven 325° for an additional 30 minutes.
Deep Fruit Pies:	Hot oven 450° for 10 minutes. 350° for an additional 40 minutes.
Pie Shells without filling:	Hot oven 450° for 15 to 20 minutes.
Dumplings or turnovers with: cooked fillings: raw fruit:	450° for 15 minutes. 350° for 30 minutes.
Meringue Topping:	300° for 15-20 minutes.

Pie Pans

If a pie is to have a deep filling, and to me this is the ideal pie, a deep pie pan will be a great help. I have tried to indicate accurately in each recipe how large a shell is required for each filling, but the matter is, of course, one of individual preference. The kind of pan—heat-resistant glass, enamel, aluminum or tin—is also a matter of preference. But if you use new tins you are not apt to get a well-browned under crust until the shininess has worn off the tin through exposure to heat. Some people prefer to use pans with a screening bottom. Others pierce the bottoms of their pans in 3 or 4 places.

Rule for Making Pie Crust
One Two-Crust or Two Single-Crust 9 Inch Pies

All the materials used should be as cold as possible. The water should be iced. Pie dough should be handled lightly and as little as possible.

Sift, then measure:
  1¾ cups cake flour or
  1½ cups all-purpose flour
Resift with:
  ½ teaspoon salt

1 teaspoon any baking powder
Measure:
  4 tablespoons lard
  2 tablespoons butter
Have in readiness ¼ cup ice water.

561

If you find this measurement scant—it makes excellent pie crust—increase the shortening to ½ cupful in all, or follow the fine rule on page 565 for Rough or Half Puff Paste, treating the ingredients as suggested in this Rule for Pie Crust. Divide the shortening into two parts, about one third in one part and two thirds in the other. Cut the larger part of the shortening into the flour mixture with 2 knives or a pastry blender until it looks like corn meal. Cut in the remaining shortening coarsely until it is the size of a large pea.

Sprinkle 3 tablespoonfuls water over the mixture. Blend it in lightly. If the dough will hold together so that it may be gathered up in a ball, as shown on the left below, stop handling it. If not, use additional water. A good rule for making pastry is: "Keep the moisture out and the air in." Add the last of the water where the ingredients are driest. Some cooks make fine pie crust with a fork, lifting the ingredients to permit the moisture to spread. Others use a spoon deftly, or touch the dough very lightly with the fingertips. If feasible chill it for 12 hours. This tenderizes it. If not, chill it for 10 minutes to make handling easier.

As soon as the dough will hold together, stop handling it. Divide it into two parts, one slightly larger than the other. Keep the smaller part for the top crust. If the room is hot place this part where it will be cold. Roll out the larger part for the bottom crust to the thickness of ⅛ inch, using as little flour as possible on the board and on the roller, or roll the dough between sheets of waxed paper.

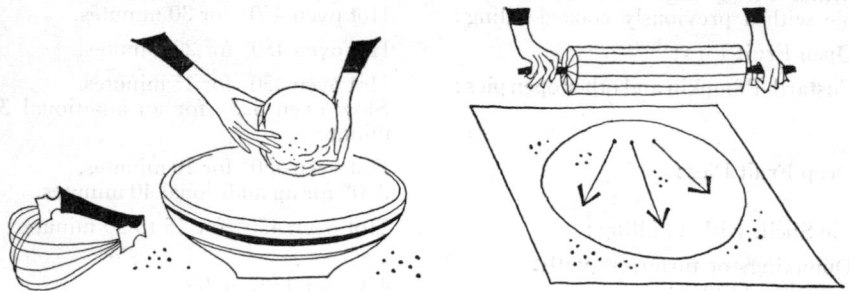

You may purchase a heavy pastry cloth and a cloth covering for a rolling pin that practically eliminate the sticking of the dough. Roll the dough in one direction only, as shown above on the right. Lift the roller, do not push it to and fro. Do not stretch the dough. Cut it 1 inch larger than the pan to allow for shrinkage, as shown below on the left.

To lift the pastry from the board, fold it in half, lay the fold across the center of the pan and unfold it, or roll it around the rolling pin, unroll it onto the pan as shown above on the right. Prick it with a fork in several places. Do not grease the pan. Good pastry makes this unnecessary.

For a one-crust pie make a fluted edge with the dough that laps over or build up a rim with a strip of pastry. Full it on. Use a fork to press it down, or pinch it with the thumb and forefinger, as shown below on the left. This edge is important as it will help to hold the juices in the pie. If the pie is to be filled with a juicy filling, brush the bottom crust lightly with the white of an egg or with melted butter to keep it from being soggy. Fill the pie and moisten the edges with a little water.

If a lattice of pastry is desired, cut long narrow strips of dough with a knife or a pie jagger. The latter makes a pinked edge. Place the strips across the top of the pie and moisten them slightly with water where they meet the edge of the pie or weave a lattice on a piece of waxed paper and invert it onto the top of the pie.

Roll the dough for the top crust, cut it 1 inch larger than the pan and prick it with a fork in several places, or fold it over and gash it with a knife, to allow the steam to escape. Place the top crust on the pie. Full in the surplus dough and press it down around the edges with a fork or tuck it under the lower crust and press it around the edge with a fork, or cut the lower crust ½ inch larger than the upper crust and fold it over like a hem.

The top may be brushed with milk or with 1 egg diluted with 1 tablespoonful of water. This will make it glossy.

If the pie is filled with juicy fruit or custard, wring a strip of cotton 1 inch wide out of cold water and fasten it around the edge or use a piece of parchment tape. This will keep the juices from boiling out. So will 2 pieces of macaroni—about 3 inches long—placed in the pie through a puncture in the upper crust like vents.

To bake the pie consult the preceding Temperature Chart.

If only a shell or a pie crust is desired, bake it on the bottom of a pie pan, that is, invert the pan and fit the dough over the bottom. Prick it with a fork and press it down lightly around the edge. Cut a round for the top crust, prick it and bake it on a baking sheet. When making individual pies, use an inverted muffin tin, or custard cups for deeper pie shells. Cut the rounds of dough 4½ or 5½ inches in diameter and fit them over the cups. You may pinch the dough in about 5 places around the edge to make a fluted cup. Prick the pies before baking them. Bake large or individual pie shells for 12 minutes in a very hot oven 500°.

Pie dough may be made in advance, wrapped in waxed paper and placed in a refrigerator. Chilled dough handles more easily than fresh dough, and it will keep for days.

Hints for Pie Making

1. Too much flour makes pie crust tough.
2. Too much shortening makes it dry and crumbly.
3. Too much liquid makes it heavy and soggy.

For pies frozen either before or after baking, see page 875.

PIE CRUST MADE WITH FLOUR PASTE

A new method joyously acclaimed by many as an improvement over the old. Sift, then measure:

2 cups all-purpose flour

Resift it into a bowl with:

1 teaspoon salt

Measure ⅓ cupful of this mixture and place it in a small bowl or cup. Stir into it to form a smooth paste:

¼ cup water

Cut into the flour mixture in the first bowl until it is the size of small peas:

⅔ cup shortening

To do this use 2 knives or a pastry blender. Stir the flour paste into the dough. Work it with your hand until it is well incorporated and the dough may be gathered into a ball. Treat the dough as you would any pie crust. It may be chilled before it is rolled. Roll it by the preceding Rule for Pie Crust.

HOT WATER PIE CRUST
A 9 Inch 2 Crust Pie

This recipe is an amazingly quick way of making pie crust—almost like magic. The process is so simple that it is absolutely fool-proof. The dough will keep for a week in a cold place. Age improves it.

Place in a bowl:

½ cup lard

Pour over it:

¼ cup boiling water

Beat these ingredients until they are cold and creamy. If there is time, chill them. Sift before measuring:

1½ cups cake flour

Resift with:

½ teaspoon any baking powder
½ teaspoon salt

Combine the liquid and the sifted ingredients and stir them until they form a smooth ball. Cover the dough and chill it until it is firm. Roll it by the Rule for Pie Crust, page 561. Bake it by the Chart for Baking Pie, page 561.

FIVE-MINUTE PIE CRUST
A 9 Inch 2 Crust Pie

Sift into a bowl:

2 cups sifted all-purpose flour
1½ teaspoons salt

Pour over the top, all at once without mixing:

½ cup salad oil
¼ cup cold milk or water

Stir these ingredients lightly until blended. Form them into a ball. Di-

vide it into 2 parts. Flatten them slightly. Roll the dough between sheets of waxed paper to the desired thinness. Patch tears, if any, by sticking them together or by adding a small piece of dough. Remove top paper. Invert the rolled dough, paper and all, onto a pie pan. Remove paper. Proceed as with any pie crust. Prick both bottom and top crust well with a fork. Fill the pie and place the top crust over it. Bake it in a hot oven 425° for about 40 minutes. For a baked pie shell, to be filled later, use ½ the ingredients. Bake it in a hot oven 475° for about 10 minutes.

CHEESE PIE CRUST

Prepare by one of the preceding rules:

Pie Crust

Add to the portion of dough reserved for the upper crust:

⅔ cup grated American cheese

Bake the pie as directed.

Or bake an open apple pie and cover it with very thin slices of:

Cheese

Place the pie in a slow oven 325° or under a low broiler flame until the cheese is melted. Serve the pie hot.

Cheese Pastry, page 565.

CHEESE GLAZE

Grate:

About 1½ cups American cheese

Add:

¼ teaspoon salt

Melt the cheese in a double boiler. Add:

Milk

to make a smooth paste. Spread it over a cooked pie crust. Brown it lightly under a broiler.

NUT PIE CRUST

Prepare by the preceding rules:

Pie Crust or Hot Water Pie Crust

Add to the dough:

½ cup ground black walnuts or other nut meats

SPICED PIE CRUST

Add to the sifted ingredients for pie dough using one of the preceding rules:

2 tablespoons confectioners' sugar
⅛ teaspoon cinnamon
⅛ teaspoon nutmeg

LEMON OR ORANGE PIE CRUST OR TARTELETTE PASTE

This makes fine tart shells. They are especially good with delicately flavored pie fillings: custard, banana cream, etc.

Prepare:

> Pie Crust or Hot Water Pie
> Crust, page 564

Use instead of ¼ cupful water:

> 2 tablespoons water
> 2 tablespoons lemon juice

Add to the sifted ingredients:

> 1 teaspoon grated lemon or orange rind
> ½ tablespoon sugar

If desired add:

> 1 egg yolk for color

Beat the egg yolk for pie crust with the lemon juice. Add just enough ice water to make the dough hold together. If you are making Hot Water Pie Crust, add the egg yolk when the lard, water and lemon juice are cool.

KUCHEN DOUGH

The nearest approach to pie under this heading is the very good German Cherry Cake, page 637. This dough is similar to galette dough. There are many forms of Fruit Kuchen, one being a raised Coffee Cake Dough, pages 626-627; and a more cakelike dough— Dutch Apple, Peach or Plum Cake, page 634. Do not neglect:

> Apple Paradise or Crisp, page 637
> Custard and Fruit Pie, page 581
> Sour Cream Cherry Cake, page 638
> Blueberry Tart, page 570

GALETTE DOUGH
Method I. A 9 Inch Pie or Four 3 Inch Tart Shells

In France one is frequently served rich flat pastry covered with fruit called a galette. It is baked until it is a golden brown.

Sift before measuring:

> 1 cup all-purpose flour

Resift with:

> ½ teaspoon salt
> 1 tablespoon sugar

Work in with a pastry blender:

> 6 tablespoons butter

Beat, then work in with the fingers:

> 1 egg yolk
> 1 tablespoon water
> 1½ tablespoons lemon juice

Chill these ingredients thoroughly. Roll them or pat them until the dough is ⅛ inch thick. Place it in the bottom of a 9 x 12 inch pan. Chill the dough thoroughly. Cover it with about:

> 3 cups sugared fruit

Bake the galette in a hot oven 425° for about 25 minutes.

For a round 8 inch pie pan or ovenproof dish use half the amounts given.

Method II.

There is a good galette or pie base in the rule for Nut Bars, page 666.

CREAM CHEESE PASTRY OR VIENNA TARTS

Delicious for turnovers or with the soup or salad course.

Sift before measuring:

> 1 cup all-purpose flour

Resift with:

> (¼ teaspoon salt)

Cut into these ingredients with a pastry blender or 2 knives:

> ½ cup butter
> 1½ packages soft cream cheese or dry cottage cheese: 4½ oz.

When the ingredients are well blended wrap the dough in waxed paper. Place it on ice for 12 hours. Roll it on a piece of waxed paper to the thickness of ⅛ inch. For the soup or salad course cut the dough into rounds. Bake them on an ungreased tin in a hot oven 450° for about 12 minutes. Serve them hot.

For Turnovers

Cut the dough into squares. Place on each square:

> A dab of jelly, preserves,
> stewed drained fruit, puréed prunes, etc.

Gather up the corners and pinch them together. Bake the turnovers in a hot oven 450° for about 15 minutes. Serve them hot sprinkled with:

> Confectioners' sugar

ROUGH OR HALF PUFF PASTE
A 9 Inch Pie Crust or Top

A simple substitute for the more troublesome Puff Paste of the following rule. Fine as a top crust for a creamed dish.

Sift before measuring:

> 2 cups all-purpose flour

Resift with:

> ½ teaspoon salt

Cut into pieces about 1 inch in size:

> 6 tablespoons unsalted butter
> 6 tablespoons lard

Combine:

½ teaspoon lemon juice
6 tablespoons ice water

Mix the shortening lightly with the flour mixture. Make a well in the center. Add a little of the water. Mix lightly, keeping the shortening intact. Add enough of the rest of the liquid to form a moderately stiff dough. Roll the dough into a long oblong. Fold it equally in 3. Turn it so that you have the folded edges to the right and left. Roll it out again. Repeat this process until the dough has been rolled 4 times. It may be kept in a cool place for 1 hour but should rest for at least ½ hour. Treat it as you would any pie crust but moisten the edge of the pie pan in order to have it stick to the rim. This dough may be used for rolls, vol au vent, hors d'oeuvres, etc.—excellent with sausage meat filling. It is improved by using a glaze made of:

1 egg diluted with
1 tablespoon water

Brush it with this when the dough is half cooked.

PUFF PASTE

Before beginning the adventure with puff paste there is one thing to be explained that will make its composition comparatively easy. The butter used must be washed. The purpose of washing it is to make it elastic. It should be soft through being kneaded, but in no sense soft through being melted—quite the contrary, it must be soft and cold at the same time. In winter turn on the cold water faucet. Manipulate the butter with the hands under the stream of cold water until it is creamy and waxy. At other seasons, do this in a quart of ice water placed in a bowl. The butter may be kneaded with a spoon if preferred. The final kneading of the butter is done on a board or it is patted briskly in the hands until no water flies.

This is the recipe of a professional cook. As it calls for egg yolks it differs from the orthodox rule for puff paste. However, her results are remarkable and her method is simple, so I am giving it in preference to the usual rather complicated recipes. She stresses two points: Keep the hands, the bowl, the board and the rolling pin as cold as possible. A cold windy day is best for making puff paste.

Work with the hands (see the first paragraph):

1 cup butter

Place ¼ cupful of the butter in a cold bowl. Form the remainder into a square and place it where it will keep cold. Add to the butter in the bowl:

2 cups sifted all-purpose flour
¼ teaspoon salt

Work these ingredients with a pastry blender, 2 knives or the finger-tips. Beat and add:

¼ cup ice water
2 egg yolks

The egg yolks may be omitted. In that case use in all 6 tablespoonfuls of water. Work these ingredients well with the hands. If necessary add, to loosen the dough from the bowl:

A pinch of flour

Place the dough where it will be cold but will not freeze, preferably in the open air. If it is not possible to do this, fold the dough in a clean cloth and place it in a dripping pan that has been placed between 2 dripping pans filled with ice. Do not let the dough come in direct contact with the ice. After 15 minutes, roll the dough into a square on a floured board. Roll it one way only, not back and forth. A good way is out from the center.

Put the square of butter in the center of the dough and fold the 4 corners to the center completely covering the butter. Permit the dough to stand on a cloth or piece of waxed paper in a cold place for ½ hour. Turn it once to keep it from becoming dry. Roll out the dough again into a square and fold the corners to the center. Permit it to stand again for ½ hour. Repeat this process. The dough must be chilled and rolled at least 4 times in all.

Chill the dough until you are ready to use it. Wrapped in waxed paper it may be kept in a refrigerator for several days. Roll it, cut it into shapes. Chill it again and bake it. One of the success secrets of puff paste is to have it ice cold when placed in a hot oven. The matter of baking puff paste is a moot point. In all rules the very cold paste is put into a very hot oven—500°. In some it is baked at this temperature throughout. In this case the pastry is covered with waxed paper after 10 minutes' baking. In other rules the heat is reduced 50° every 5 minutes until the temperature is 350° for the final baking.

PATTY SHELLS

Prepare by the preceding rule:

Puff Paste

Roll the paste ¼ inch thick. Cut as many rounds with a 3 inch cutter as you wish to have patties. Cut twice as many additional rounds and cut the centers from them with a smaller cutter, making rings. Place 2 rings on each round. Press them lightly together. Place the shells on 2 layers of heavy brown paper placed on a sheet or in a pan. Chill them. Bake the shells in a hot oven 500° for 5 minutes. Bake them with a decreasing heat, as in the preceding rule, for about 20 to 25 minutes.

Serve the shells hot, filled with:

Creamed food

The patty shells may be reheated in a hot oven 500°.

NAPOLEONS

The blame for the fit of indigestion that is supposed to have lost Napoleon the battle of Waterloo is commemorated in this pastry that bears his name.

Prepare:

Puff Paste, page 566

Roll the paste ¼ inch thick. Cut it into 2 x 4 inch strips. Prick them with a fork. Place them on 2 layers of heavy brown paper on a sheet or in a pan. Chill them. Bake them in a hot oven 500° for 5 minutes. Reduce the heat as in the last paragraph of the rule for puff paste and bake them for about 10 minutes longer. Cool the cakes. Split them lengthwise into halves. Fill them with:

Custard Filling, page 705

Serve them with:

Fluffy Strawberry Sauce, page 758

Crumb Crusts

These crusts are a fine short cut to pie making. They are popular for they are good and easy to make.

GRAHAM CRACKER OR ZWIEBACK CRUST

A 9 Inch Pie

Crush, grind or put in a blender until very fine:

1½ cups graham cracker or zwieback crumbs

This recipe is sufficient for a bottom crust and a generous sprinkling of crumbs on top of a 9 inch pie. One cupful of crumbs will suffice for the bottom of a 7 inch pie and a light sprinkling for the top.

Stir into them:

¼ cup confectioners' sugar
6 tablespoons melted butter
(1 teaspoon cinnamon)

Sugar in crumb crusts is a matter of taste. The amount used is best determined by the type of filling to be used. Reserve ½ cupful of the crumb mixture. Place the remainder in a deep 9 inch pie pan. Pat it firmly with the palm of the hand or with a spoon against the bottom and sides of the pan to form a pie shell. Chill the crust thoroughly. It may be prepared long in advance. It is not necessary to bake it before it is filled. If well chilled it may be baked at the same time as the meringue. If you wish to use the crust at once, bake it without chilling it in a moderate oven 375° for 15 minutes.

After being chilled, or baked, fill the crust with any previously cooked:

Custard filling, cream filling or fresh or dried fruit filling

Cover it with a:

Meringue, page 578

Sprinkle the reserved crumbs over the top. Bake the pie in a slow oven 300° for 15 minutes.

A previously baked crumb crust is good filled with:

Gelatine Chiffon Pie Filling, page 587, or sweetened fresh or stewed fruit

Top it with:

Whipped cream

LUXURY GRAHAM CRACKER OR ZWIEBACK CRUST

Crush or grind until very fine:

1½ cups graham cracker or zwieback crumbs

Stir into them:

6 tablespoons ground unblanched almonds
6 tablespoons sugar
¼ cup top milk or light cream
½ cup melted butter
(⅓ teaspoon cinnamon)

Follow the preceding rule for Graham Cracker or Zwieback Crust. Bake it in a moderate oven 375° for 15 minutes.

BREAD CRUMB CRUST
A good way of utilizing stale bread.
Follow the rule for:
    Graham Cracker Crust, page 567
Substitute for the graham cracker or
zwieback crumbs:
    **1½ cups toasted sifted bread
        crumbs, page 540**
This crust, to be good, must be baked
before it is filled. Place it in a moder-
ate oven 375° for 15 minutes.

CORNFLAKE PIE CRUST
A 7 Inch Crust.
Use ½ again as much if you want a 9
inch shell and crumbs for the top.
Roll or grind:
    4 cups cornflakes
There should be 1 cupful crushed

flakes. Combine it with:
    ⅓ cup melted butter
    ¼ cup sugar
    (¼ teaspoon cinnamon)
Press the crust firmly on the bottom
and sides of the pan. Chill the crust.
To bake it or to fill and bake it follow
the rule for Graham Cracker Crust,
page 567.

GINGER SNAP PIE CRUST
Follow the rule for:
    Graham Cracker Crust, page 567
Substitute:
    Ginger snap crumbs

*Danish or Swedish Apple Pie Topping,
page 569.*

Pies Baked with Fillings

A friend of mine is so fond of apple pie that he says his coat of arms bears an
apple pie rampant. Every attempt has been made to make the following couchant.
    Most fruit fillings like to bubble over. Sprinkle fruit juice spilled in the oven
with salt to prevent smoke and smell.

APPLE PIE
A 9 Inch Double Crust Pie
Line a 9 inch pie pan with:
    Pie Crust, page 564, or
    Cheese Pie Crust, page 564
Peel, core and cut into very thin
pieces:
    6 medium-sized apples
Combine and sift over the apples:
    ½ to ⅔ cup white or brown sugar
    ⅛ teaspoon salt
    **1 tablespoon to 1½ tablespoons
        cornstarch**
    (¼ teaspoon cinnamon)
    (⅛ teaspoon nutmeg)
Only very tart apples require the
larger amount of sugar. Only very
juicy apples require the larger amount
of cornstarch. Stir the apples gently
until they are well coated. Place them
in layers in the pie shell. Dot them
with:
    1½ tablespoons butter
If the apples lack flavor sprinkle them
with:
    1 tablespoon lemon juice
    ½ teaspoon grated lemon rind
    (1 teaspoon vanilla)
If the apples are very dry add:
    2 tablespoons water or cream
Cover the pie with a pricked upper
crust, see Pie Crust, page 561. Bake
the pie in a hot oven 450° for 10 minutes. Reduce the heat to 350°. Bake

the pie until done, from ¾ to 1 hour
in all.
A delicious touch is to sprinkle the top
crust lightly with sugar and cinnamon
as you put it into the oven. Some
cooks brush it first with milk. The pie
may be baked without an upper crust.
Bake it in a hot oven 450° for 20 minutes. Sprinkle over the top:
    1 cup grated cheese
Place the pie under a broiler to melt
the cheese.

*Apple Pie II, page 578; Danish Apple
Pie Topping, page 569.*

SOUR CREAM APPLE PIE
A 9 Inch Single Crust Pie
Follow the preceding rule for:
    Apple Pie
Use the larger amount of sugar.
Brown sugar is preferable to white.
Omit the butter. After filling the pie
with the apples, pour over them:
    1 cup thick sour cream

Cranberry Apple Pie, page 575.

INDIVIDUAL APPLE PIES
8 Pies
Line eight 3 inch muffin cups with:
    Pie Crust, page 564

PIES

569

Fill them with:
    4 cups peeled, thinly sliced
        apples
Combine and pour over the fruit:
    ½ cup sugar
    2 slightly beaten eggs
    2 tablespoons melted butter
    1 tablespoon lemon juice
    1 cup cream or ½ cup evaporated
        milk and ½ cup water
    (½ teaspoon cinnamon)
    (⅛ teaspoon nutmeg)
Bake the pies in a moderate oven 375°
for 40 minutes.

OPEN-FACED APPLE PIE WITH CRUMB TOPPING
A Montana fan writes that she has concocted a sure-fire, he-man pie by baking by my rule an open-faced apple pie without sugar, topped with the crumb mixture given under Apple Paradise, page 637.

DANISH APPLE PIE TOPPING
Topping for a 9 Inch Pie.
Frequently called Swedish—take your choice. This is a crumb topping usually served in place of a top crust on apple or applesauce pie.
Melt:
    6 tablespoons butter
Stir in and brown lightly:
    1 cup fine dry crumbs: zwieback,
        rusk, bread, etc.
    ¾ teaspoon cinnamon
Substitute this mixture for a top crust over any apple or other tart fruit pie.

Apple Paradise, page 637; French Apple Cake, page 635; Grandmother's Apple Cake, page 637.

FRENCH APPLE PIE
The prince of apple pies!
Prepare by the rule on page 565:
    Galette Dough I or II
Spread it to paper thinness in a 9 x 12 inch pan or spread ½ the dough in an 8 inch oven-proof plate. Cover it closely with:
    Peeled, cored quartered apples
Sprinkle them with about:
    ¼ cup sugar
    ¼ teaspoon cinnamon
    ¼ cup melted butter
Bake the pie in a hot oven 450° for about 10 minutes. Reduce the heat and bake it in a moderate oven 350° until the apples are tender and the crust is crisp.

GRATED APPLE PIE
A 9 Inch Pie
Prepare by the rule on page 567:
    Graham Cracker Crust
Grate on a coarse grater:
    6 or 7 tart apples
Add:
    ¾ cup sugar
    Grated rind of 1 lemon
    1½ tablespoons lemon juice
    2 tablespoons sherry
    ¼ teaspoon cinnamon
Cook and stir these ingredients over a low fire until they reach the boiling point. Stir in:
    2 teaspoons arrowroot
Stir and cook the mixture until it looks glazed. Fill the crust with it, cover the top with crumbs and bake it in a moderate oven 350° for about 40 minutes.

PEACH PIE I
Follow the rule on page 568 for:
    Apple Pie or Sour Cream
    Apple Pie
Substitute for the apples:
    5 cups peeled sliced peaches
Use the smaller amount of sugar or less if the peaches are sweet.

Peach Pie II, page 579.

BERRY PIE I. Strawberry, Gooseberry, Currant, Blackberry, Raspberry
A 9 Inch Pie
Line a pie pan with:
    Pie Crust, page 564
Prepare by picking over and hulling:
    4 cups fresh berries
Three cupfuls of fruit will make a 7 inch pie.
Combine:
    ⅔ to 1 cup or more sugar,
        according to the acidity of
        the fruit
    4 tablespoons flour
    2 teaspoons quick-cooking tapioca
    1½ tablespoons lemon juice or
    ½ teaspoon cinnamon
Sprinkle these ingredients over the berries and stir them gently until they are well blended. Pour them into the pie crust. Dot them with:
    1 tablespoon butter
Permit them to stand for 15 minutes. Cover them, if desired, with a top crust or with a Lattice of Pastry, page 563. Bake the pie in a hot oven 450° for 10 minutes. Reduce the heat to

350°. Bake the pie until the crust is golden brown, about 40 minutes in all.

BLUEBERRY PIE
Follow the preceding rule. Use the lemon juice.

BERRY PIES WITH CANNED FRUIT
A 9 Inch Pie
Allow approximately:
>2 cups canned berries
>½ cup juice

Proceed as directed in the rule for Berry Pie I. The minimum amount of sugar is usually sufficient. The flour may be omitted.

Berry Pie II, page 579.
This is a baked pie shell filled with cooked filling.

FRESH CHERRY PIE
A 9 Inch Pie
Follow the rule for Berry Pie I. Use pitted sour cherries. Omit the cinnamon. Add:
>2 drops almond flavoring or 2 tablespoons kirsch

This pie may call for as much as 1⅓ cupfuls of sugar. Fine made with a lattice top.

CANNED CHERRY PIE
A 9 Inch Pie
Combine, stir lightly and permit to stand for 15 minutes:
>2½ cups canned drained pie cherries
>1 cup cherry juice
>1 cup sugar
>⅛ teaspoon salt
>2 drops almond flavoring
>1 tablespoon quick-cooking tapioca
>1 tablespoon melted butter

Follow the rule for baking Berry Pie I, page 569.

RHUBARB PIE
A 9 Inch Pie
Use:
>4 cups young, unpeeled diced rhubarb stalks
>6 tablespoons flour
>1¼ to 2 cups sugar
>1 tablespoon butter
>(1 teaspoon grated orange rind)

Follow the rule for baking Berry Pie I, page 569.

RHUBARB AND STRAWBERRY PIE
This is a very good combination. Follow the above rule for Rhubarb Pie. Use equal amounts or varied amounts of rhubarb and strawberries.

GRAPE PIE
A 9 Inch Pie
Stem:
>4 cups blue grapes

Slip the pulp out of the skins. Reserve the skins. Cook the pulp until the seeds loosen. Press it through a colander to remove the seeds. Combine the pulp, the skins and:
>¾ cup sugar
>1½ tablespoons lemon juice
>1 tablespoon grated orange rind
>1 tablespoon quick-cooking tapioca

Permit these ingredients to stand for 15 minutes. Prepare:
>Pie Crust, page 564, or
>Hot Water Pie Crust, page 564

Line a 9 inch pie pan with the pastry. Fill it with the grape mixture. Place a lattice of pastry over the top. Moisten the edges of the bottom crust. Place a long strip of pastry around the edge of the pie. Crimp it down with a fork. Bake the pie in a hot oven 450° for 10 minutes; lower the heat and bake it in a moderate oven 350° for 20 minutes longer.

German Cherry Cake, page 638.

BLUEBERRY TART
OR KUCHEN WITH CUSTARD
Prepare by the rule on page 565:
>Galette Dough

Place it in a pan and chill it as directed. Bake it in a hot oven 450° for 15 minutes. Cover it with:
>1 quart blueberries
>½ cup sugar
>(3 tablespoons lemon juice)

Bake the tart in a moderate oven 375° for 10 minutes.
Cook and stir over boiling water until thick:
>½ cup cream
>2 or 3 beaten egg yolks
>½ cup sugar
>⅛ teaspoon salt

Cool the custard and pour it over the slightly cooled tart. Cool it well. Make a Meringue, page 578, of:

3 egg whites
6 tablespoons sugar
1 teaspoon vanilla

Heap it on the tart. Bake it in a slow oven 300° for 15 to 20 minutes. The meringue is optional.

DEEP FRUIT PIES
A 7 Inch Pie

Peaches and apples are usually used for deep pies, but other fruits are equally good.
Prepare for cooking:

6 cups apples or peaches or 5
cups berries

Combine:

1 to 1½ cups sugar
1½ teaspoons grated lemon or
orange rind
¼ teaspoon salt
(1 tablespoon lemon juice)
(3 tablespoons flour)

If the fruit is dry, add:

1 or 2 tablespoons water

Stir these ingredients into the fruit until the fruit is coated. Place it in a baking dish or in individual dishes. Dot it with:

1 tablespoon or more butter

Roll to the thickness of ¼ inch:

Pie Crust, page 561

Prick the dough. Cover the fruit and full the dough around the edge of the dish. Bake the pies in a hot oven 450° for 10 minutes and in a moderate oven 350° for 40 minutes longer.

COBBLERS

See Cobblers, page 635, Apple Paradise, page 637, French Apple Cake, page 635, Shortcake, page 633.

CHERRY OR RHUBARB CREAM PIE
A 9 Inch Pie

Line a pie pan with:

Pie Crust, page 564

Prepare by pitting or by peeling and dicing:

2 cups cherries or 2 cups pink
rhubarb

Place the fruit in the pie shell. Combine and beat:

⅔ cup sugar
2 tablespoons flour
2 egg yolks
2 teaspoons lemon juice or
water
⅛ teaspoon salt

Spread these ingredients over the fruit. Bake the pie in a hot oven 400°

for 20 minutes. Reduce the heat and bake it in a moderate oven 350° for 20 minutes.

CUSTARD PIE I
A 9 Inch Pie

The partial baking of this pie shell before filling insures a crisp under crust.
Line a pie pan with any:

Pie Crust, page 564

Build up a fluted rim. Prick the crust and bake it in a hot oven 500° for 10 minutes. Fill it with the following custard by pulling the rack part-way out and pouring the filling into the crust, or remove it from the oven only long enough to fill it.
Beat slightly:

3 eggs or 6 egg yolks

Add and stir well:

½ cup sugar
¼ teaspoon salt
2 cups scalded milk
1 teaspoon vanilla

Pour these ingredients into the partly baked pie shell. Sprinkle the top with:

(¼ teaspoon nutmeg)

Place the pie in a slow oven 325° for about 30 minutes, or until the custard is firm to the touch. Serve the pie plain or with fresh fruit.

CHOCOLATE TOPPED CUSTARD PIE

Follow the preceding rule for:

Custard Pie

Omit the nutmeg. Stir and cook in a double boiler:

1½ oz. chocolate
5 tablespoons sugar
2 beaten eggs
⅛ teaspoon salt

Cook these ingredients until slightly thickened, about 4 minutes. Cool slightly. Add:

1 tablespoon rum or ½ teaspoon
vanilla

Pour the mixture over the baked custard.

Custard Pie II, page 581; Chocolate Topped Gelatine Custard Chiffon Pie, page 589.

APPLE OR PEACH CUSTARD PIE
A 9 Inch Pie

This makes delectable individual pies.
Line a pie pan with any:

Pie Crust, page 564

Core, peel and add:
  2 large apples or peaches
Beat:
  2 egg yolks
  ⅔ cup sugar
  2 cups milk
Pour this custard over the apples.
Cover the pie with a lattice of pastry.
Bake the pie in a hot oven 450° for 15
minutes, then bake it in a slow oven
325° for 30 minutes longer.
Or the lattice may be omitted and the
pie may be baked, cooled and topped
with a Meringue, page 578, made with:
  2 egg whites
  4 tablespoons sugar
  ½ teaspoon vanilla
  3 tablespoons finely chopped
    nut meats
Bake the meringue in a slow oven
300° for 15 or 20 minutes

TRANSPARENT PIE
A 7 Inch Pie
A Southern recipe. Fielding says: "No
man is wise at all hours." Loose or
lose your buttons for this hour.
Line a 7 inch pan with:
  Pie Crust, page 564, or
  Hot Water Pie Crust, page 564
Prick the crust. Bake it in a hot oven
500° for 10 minutes. Beat until very
light:
  4 egg yolks
Beat until soft:
  ½ cup butter
Add very slowly:
  1 cup white or brown sugar
Blend these ingredients until they are
creamy. Beat in the egg yolks and:
  3 tablespoons tart jelly or lemon
    juice and 1½ teaspoons grated
    lemon rind
Fill the pie shell with this mixture.
Bake the pie in a slow oven 325° until
it is firm, about 30 minutes. When the
pie is baked it may be cooled and a
Meringue, page 578, may be placed on
it made with:
  2 egg whites
  ⅛ teaspoon salt
  ¼ cup sugar
  ½ teaspoon vanilla
Bake it in a slow oven 300° for 15 to
20 minutes.

CHESS TARTS
This may be classed with the rubber
plant, the aspidistra and other fading
institutions. It is worthy of a revival.
Line twelve 3 inch muffin tins with:

Hot Water Pie Crust, page 564,
  or Pie Crust, page 564
Prick the pie shells. Bake them in a
hot oven 500° for 10 minutes. Cool
them. Sift:
  1 cup sugar
Beat until soft:
  ½ cup butter
Add the sugar gradually. Blend these
ingredients until they are creamy.
Beat in one at a time:
  2 or 3 eggs
Add:
  1 teaspoon vanilla or 2 table-
    spoons lemon juice
  ¼ cup thick cream
  1 cup chopped walnut meats
  1¼ cups raisins
The raisins may be soaked in boiling
water for 30 minutes. Drain them well.
Fill the pie shells with this mixture.
Bake the pies in a slow oven 325° until the filling is firm. Let them cool in
the pans. Serve them topped with:
  Whipped cream

Jefferson Davis Pie, page 583.

ENGLISH LEMON CHEESE TARTS
So-called, although devoid of cheese.
A rich dish so let us say 4 to 6 servings.
Have ready:
  4 to 6 baked individual Pie Shells,
    page 563
They should be small, about 2½ inches
across, and rather shallow.
Beat well in the top of a double boiler:
  3 eggs
Add:
  2 tablespoons grated lemon rind
  6 tablespoons lemon juice
  ⅛ teaspoon salt
  ¾ cup sugar
  ¾ cup soft butter
Stir these ingredients over, not in, hot
water until they are thick. Chill the
custard. Fill the shells shortly before
serving.

HOW TO COOK PUMPKIN
Wash the pumpkin and cut it in half
crosswise. Remove the seeds and the
strings. Place the pumpkin in a pan
shell side up and bake it in a moderate
oven 325° for 1 hour or more depending on size until it is tender and begins
to fall apart. Scrape the pulp from the
shell and put it through a ricer or
strainer.

PUMPKIN PIE
A 9 Inch Pie
Blend well:
> 6 tablespoons brown sugar
> 2 tablespoons white sugar
> ½ teaspoon salt
> 1 teaspoon cinnamon
> ½ teaspoon ginger
> ⅛ teaspoon cloves
> ½ cup dark corn sirup
> 3 slightly beaten eggs

The egg whites may be beaten separately and folded in last. Add:
> 1½ cups cooked, see page 572, or canned pumpkin
> 1½ cups undiluted evaporated milk or rich cream
> (1 teaspoon vanilla or 2 tablespoons brandy or rum)
> (¾ cup black walnut meats)

Line a 9 inch pan with:
> Pie Crust, page 561

Build up a high fluted edge. Pour the pumpkin mixture into the pie shell. Bake the pie in a hot oven 425° for about 1 hour, or until a silver knife inserted in the filling comes out clean.

Gelatine Pumpkin Chiffon Pie, page 590.

CRUMB PIE
A 7 Inch Pie
Line a pie pan with any:
> Pie Crust, page 564

The shell may be baked in a hot oven 500° for 10 minutes. Sprinkle the bottom with:
> (½ cup raisins)

Combine:
> ¾ cup brown sugar, mild molasses or honey
> ¼ cup hot water
> 1 beaten egg

Pour these ingredients into the pie shell. Combine and work like pastry:
> ¾ cup dry bread, cake or cookie crumbs
> ¼ cup flour
> ½ to 1 teaspoon cinnamon
> ¼ teaspoon nutmeg
> ⅛ teaspoon ginger
> ¼ cup soft butter

Sprinkle this mixture over the filling. If the shell has not been prebaked, bake the pie first in a hot oven 450° until it begins to brown, then reduce the heat to 325° and bake it 20 to 30 minutes longer. If the shell has been prebaked, bake the pie at 325° for 20 to 30 minutes.

SHOO FLY PIE
The above rule is a version of the well-known controversial Pennsylvania Dutch Pie. Follow preceding rule for:
> Crumb Pie

Omit the egg in the filling. Dissolve in the hot water:
> ¼ teaspoon soda

For the crumb mixture, omit the cake crumbs and use in all:
> 1 cup all-purpose flour
> ½ cup brown sugar
> The spices and butter

The shell is not prebaked.

SOUR CREAM PIE I
Sour Cream Pie II, on page 584, is made with a baked pie shell, a cooked filling and meringue. It is possible to make an equally good pie in the following way.
Make:
> A 9 inch pie shell

Bake it in a hot even 500° for 10 minutes. Combine the ingredients given for Sour Cream Pie II, page 584, without separating the eggs. Use:
> 2 eggs

Pour the filling, uncooked, into the partly cooked pie shell. Cook the pie in a slow oven 325° for 30 minutes. This pie is good served hot or cold.

SWEET POTATO PIE
Method I. A 7 Inch Pie
Peel, then cut into ¼ inch slices:
> 4 medium-sized red sweet potatoes

Place them side by side in a stewing pan. Cover them with:
> Boiling water
> ¼ teaspoon salt

Boil them until they are barely tender. Transfer the slices carefully to a greased baking dish. Cover them with the remaining liquor in the pan and:
> ¾ cup white or brown sugar
> ½ teaspoon freshly grated nutmeg
> 1 teaspoon cinnamon
> 1 teaspoon grated orange or tangerine peel
> 2 tablespoons or more whisky, rum or orange juice
> (½ cup pecan meats)

Dot the potatoes generously with:
> Butter

Place over them a lattice of:
> Pie Crust, page 561

Bake the pie in a hot oven 450° for about 20 minutes, or until the lattice is brown.

Method II.
Follow the rule on page 573 for:
Pumpkin Pie
Substitute for the mashed pumpkin:
Mashed sweet potatoes

MAPLE NUT TARTS
8 Small Tarts or an 8 Inch Pie
Line muffin tins with any:
Pie Crust, page 564
Beat lightly:
2 egg yolks
Add:
6 tablespoons sugar
½ cup coarsely chopped nut meats
¾ teaspoon vanilla
¼ teaspoon salt
¼ cup light corn sirup
6 tablespoons maple sirup
Fill the shells. Bake them in a moderate oven 325° for about 45 minutes.

Pecan Pie, page 583.

CARAMEL NUT PIE
A 7 Inch Pie
Line a pie pan with any:
Pie Crust, page 564
Combine and stir:
½ cup dark brown sugar
½ cup maple-flavored corn sirup
½ teaspoon flour
½ teaspoon vinegar
⅛ teaspoon salt
2 whole unbeaten eggs
Place in the bottom of the pie shell:
¼ cup pecan meats
Pour the combined ingredients over them. Bake the pie in a hot oven 450° for 10 minutes, then in a slow oven 300° for 30 minutes.

MOLASSES PIE
A 9 Inch Pie
Combine and beat:
1 cup dark brown sugar
½ cup molasses
1 tablespoon flour
2 tablespoons melted butter
⅛ teaspoon salt
3 eggs
(½ cup black walnut meats)
Follow the preceding rule for Caramel Nut Pie.

RAISIN MOLASSES PIE
A 9 Inch Pie
Line a pie pan with any:
Pie Crust, page 564
Stir well, then cook for 15 minutes in a double boiler, stirring occasionally:

1¼ cups seeded raisins
½ cup sugar
½ cup molasses
½ cup water
⅛ teaspoon salt
Combine, then stir in:
4 tablespoons all-purpose flour
3 tablespoons water
Cook the filling for 15 minutes longer. Stir it from time to time. Cool it slightly. You may flavor it with:
½ teaspoon cinnamon
Fill the pie shell. Bake the pie in a hot oven 450° for 10 minutes, reduce the heat to 350° and bake it ½ hour longer.

CRANBERRY PIE
Method I. A 9 Inch Pie
Combine:
1 cup chopped dates or raisins
⅓ cup chopped nut meats
1½ cups Cranberry Jelly, page 443
Prepare any:
Pie Crust, page 564
Line a pie pan with the crust, fill it with the fruit filling and cover it with a lattice of pastry. Bake it in a hot oven 450° for 20 minutes.

Method II. A 9 Inch Pie
Prepare any:
Pie Crust, page 564
Line a pie pan with the crust. Combine:
3 tablespoons all-purpose flour
½ teaspoon salt
1⅔ cups sugar
Sprinkle the pie shell with 3 tablespoonfuls of this mixture. Cut into thirds:
3 cups cranberries
Combine them with the sugar mixture and:
¾ cup cold water
Place the berries in the pie shell. Dot them with:
3 tablespoons butter
Sprinkle them with:
1 tablespoon grated orange rind
(¼ teaspoon nutmeg)
Cover the berries with a lattice top made by cutting pie crust into ½ inch strips. Bake the pie in a hot oven 475° for 15 minutes. Reduce the heat and bake it at 375° for 35 minutes. This pie keeps well and may be reheated.

CRANBERRY RAISIN PIE
Follow the preceding rule. Substitute for ¾ cupful of the cranberries:
¾ cup raisins

CRANBERRY APPLE PIE
A 9 Inch Pie

Prepare:
    2½ cups chopped cranberries
    1½ cups peeled sliced apples
Combine these ingredients with:
    1½ cups sugar
    3 tablespoons quick-cooking
        tapioca
    3 tablespoons water
Prepare an unbaked Pie Shell, page 561. Fill it with the fruit mixture. Cover it with a lattice top. Bake the pie in a hot oven 425° for ½ hour or more.

MINCEMEAT
About 10 Quarts

Combine:
    4 lbs. lean chopped beef
    2 lbs. chopped beef suet
    1 peck peeled, cored, sliced
        Baldwin apples
    3 lbs. sugar
    2 quarts cider
    4 lbs. seeded raisins
    3 lbs. currants
    1½ lbs. chopped citron
    ½ lb. dried chopped orange peel
    ½ lb. dried chopped lemon peel
        Juice and rind of 1 lemon
    1 tablespoon cinnamon
    1 tablespoon mace
    1 tablespoon cloves
    1 teaspoon pepper
    1 teaspoon salt
    2 whole grated nutmegs
    1 gallon sour cherries with juice
    2 lbs. broken nut meats
Cook these ingredients slowly for 2 hours. Stir them frequently. Seal them in jars.

MOCK MINCEMEAT
Yield About 12 Quarts

Chop:
    1 peck green tomatoes: 11¼ lbs.
Scald them twice by pouring over them each time:
    2 quarts boiling water
Drain them well. Combine them with:
    1 peck, pared, chopped tart apples:
        12½ lbs.
    5 lbs. brown sugar: 13½ cups
    1 lb. seeded raisins: ½ of these
        chopped
    1 lb. currants
    ½ lb. finely chopped suet
    3 tablespoons salt
    2 tablespoons ground cloves
    4 tablespoons cinnamon

    3 tablespoons nutmeg
    2 cups vinegar
If the apples are sweet, instead of tart, do not add the full amount of sugar at first. Taste the mixture to see how much is needed.
Boil these ingredients for 20 minutes. Pack the mincemeat into sterilized jars and seal them.

MINCE PIE
Line a pie pan with:
    Pie Crust, page 564
Fill it with:
    Mincemeat or Mock Mincemeat,
        see preceding rules
Add to the mincemeat:
    (1 or 2 tablespoons brandy)
Cover the pie with an upper crust, see Pie Crust, page 561. Bake it in a hot oven 450° for 30 minutes.

MOCK MINCE PIE
A 9 Inch Pie

Cut into pieces:
    1½ cups seeded raisins
Pare, core and slice:
    4 medium-sized tart apples
Combine the raisins and apples. Add:
    Grated rind of 1 orange
    Juice of 1 orange
    ½ cup cider or other fruit juice
Cover these ingredients and simmer them until the apples are very soft. Stir in until well blended:
    ¾ cup sugar
    ½ teaspoon cinnamon
    ½ teaspoon cloves
    2 or 3 tablespoons finely crushed
        crackers
If the apples are dry, use the smaller amount.
This mixture will keep for several days. Shortly before using it add:
    (1 or 2 tablespoons brandy)
Line a pie pan with any:
    Pie Crust, page 564
Fill it with mock mincemeat. Cover it with an upper crust or with a lattice of pastry. Bake the pie in a hot oven 450° for 30 minutes.

KENTUCKY MINCE PIE
Line a pie pan with any:
    Pie Crust, page 564
Combine:
    2 cups mincemeat
    1½ cups unsweetened applesauce
    ½ cup drained crushed pineapple
Fill the pie with this mixture. Cover it with a lattice top. Bake it in a hot oven 450° for about ½ hour.

APPLE PRUNE PIE

Chop and combine:

    4 cups tart peeled apples
    1 cup cooked pitted prunes

Add:

    Grated rind and juice of 1 small
    orange

Combine and blend:

    ½ teaspoon salt
    ½ teaspoon cinnamon
    ¼ teaspoon cloves
    ⅔ cup sugar
    2 tablespoons flour
    ¼ cup prune juice
    ¼ cup light molasses

Stir this into the first mixture. Place it in 9 inch unbaked Pie Shell, page 561. Combine, then cover the top with:

    2 tablespoons melted butter
    1 tablespoon brown sugar
    ¾ cup chopped nut meats

Bake the pie in a hot oven 450° for 10 minutes. Reduce the heat to a moderate oven 350° and bake it until done, about 50 minutes longer.

FRUIT TARTS

This recipe makes such marvelous tarts to be served with tea.

Prepare:

    Lemon or Orange Pie Crust,
    page 565, or Cream Cheese
    Pastry, page 565

Roll it to the thickness of ⅛ inch and cut it into squares. Drain well:

    Preserved quince, canned pine-
    apple, apricots or peaches

Add:

    1 tablespoon or more brandy or
    rum

Place 1 or 2 slices of fruit on each square. Moisten the edges, gather up the corners and pinch them together. Bake the tarts in a hot oven 450° for 15 minutes.

Turnovers and Dumplings

APPLE DUMPLINGS

4 Dumplings

Prepare:

    Pie Crust, page 564, Cheese Pie
    Crust, page 564, or Biscuit
    Dough, page 505

Chill it. Pare and core:

    4 medium-sized apples

Combine until blended:

    ¾ cup brown sugar
    4 tablespoons soft butter
    ½ teaspoon salt
    ½ teaspoon cinnamon
    (Grated lemon rind)

Fill the core hollows with this mixture and spread the remainder over the fruit. Or you may substitute for the whole apples the following mixture. Combine and permit to stand for about 15 minutes:

    3 cups coarsely chopped apples
    ¾ cup brown or white sugar
    ¾ teaspoon cinnamon

Roll out the dough in a thin sheet, ⅛ inch for pastry, ¼ inch for biscuit dough. Cut it into 4 squares. These squares may be brushed with the white of an egg. This keeps the dough from becoming soggy. Place an apple on each square. Enclose the apple entirely with the dough. Press the edges together; use a little water if necessary to make them stick. Prick the tops of the dumplings in several places. They may be chilled for several hours or they may be baked at once. You may brush the top with milk. Bake the dumplings in a hot oven 425° for 10 minutes, reduce the heat to 350° and bake them for about 45 minutes, until the apples are tender. Test them with a toothpick. Serve them with:

    Brown Sugar Butter Sauce,
    page 755

If you wish to bake the dumplings in sauce, combine and simmer for 5 minutes:

    1 cup water
    ½ cup sugar
    2 tablespoons butter
    ½ teaspoon cinnamon

For enhanced flavor you may simmer the apple cores and peelings in 1½ cupfuls water for 15 minutes. Drain and use the liquid in place of the water. Pour this boiling hot over the dumplings when they begin to color. Dumplings that are not baked in sauce may be served hot or cold with:

    Cream, Hard Sauce with rum,
    page 753, Foamy Sauce, page
    754, or Lemon Sauce, page 757

FRESH OR CANNED PEACH OR APRICOT DUMPLINGS

Follow the preceding rule. If the fruit is small, use a smaller amount of the sugar mixture. Sprinkle canned peaches with:

    Lemon juice or rum

Raised Dumplings or Dampfnudeln,
page 422.

TURNOVERS OR RISSOLES

These triangular or crescent-shaped pastries make attractive canapés and tidbits for tea.
Roll to the thickness of ⅛ inch any:

Pie Crust, page 564, or Biscuit
Dough, page 505

Cut it into 2½ inch rounds or squares. Place in the center of each round 1 teaspoonful or more of the following ingredients:

Applesauce flavored with cinnamon or nutmeg
Preserves or jam
Mincemeat and a block of cheese
Cheese Spread, pages 11, 191
Anchovy paste and soft cream cheese
Well-seasoned oysters
Mushrooms heavily creamed and well seasoned
Chicken or other croquette mixtures highly seasoned
Braunschweiger seasoned with catsup, etc.
Sausage meat

Brush the edges of the rounds lightly with water. Fold the dough over into crescents. The tops of the turnovers may be brushed with:

1 egg yolk diluted with 2 tablespoons cream

Bake them in a hot oven 450° for about 15 minutes.

FRIED PIES

Follow the above rule for:

Turnovers

Fill the rounds with:

Applesauce or other fruit filling

Moisten the edges well. Press them together with a fork. Fry the turnovers in deep fat about 360° to 370° (page 542) until brown.
Or fry them in 1½ inches of hot fat 350° in a heavy skillet. When brown on one side turn to brown on the other. Drain the excess fat from the pies by placing them on absorbent paper. If you wish, you may roll them in cinnamon and sugar before serving.

RULE FOR SPONGE CAKE PIES

These recipes are hard to classify as the fillings may be cooked in unbaked pie shells or in baked pie shells. After trials both ways, the matter seems to be largely one of convenience.
Line a pie pan with any:

Pie Crust, page 564

It may be baked in a very hot oven 500° for 10 minutes, or it may be used without being baked. If it has been baked, fill it with one of the following fillings and bake it in a moderate oven 375° for about 30 minutes, or until the top is brown. If it is unbaked, fill it with one of the following fillings and bake it in a hot oven 450° for 15 minutes. Reduce the heat and finish baking it in a moderate oven 350° for 30 minutes longer, or until it is firm. The following sponge cake pie fillings may be baked by the first method in custard cups. See Orange Sponge Custard, etc., page 714.

FILLING FOR CHOCOLATE SPONGE CAKE PIE
A 9 Inch Pie

Please read the above rule for Sponge Cake Pies.
Sift:

1 cup sugar
2 tablespoons all-purpose flour
¼ teaspoon salt

Combine the sifted ingredients with:

3 well-beaten egg yolks

Melt and stir in:

1½ oz. chocolate

Add:

1 cup top milk or ½ cup evaporated milk and ½ cup water

Beat until stiff:

3 egg whites

Fold them lightly into the chocolate custard.

FILLING FOR ORANGE, LEMON OR PINEAPPLE SPONGE CAKE PIE
A 7 or 9 Inch Pie

Please read the above rule for Sponge Cake Pies. Do not overlook these good fillings. To make them follow the rules on page 714 for:

Orange Sponge Custard
Lemon Sponge Custard
Pineapple Sponge Custard

Sour Cream Pie I, page 573.

SOUR CREAM MERINGUE PIE
Two 7 Inch Pies

Prepare by any rule, page 564:

2 baked Pie Shells

Blend:
  2 cups thick sour cream
  ½ cup sugar
  1 tablespoon all-purpose flour
  ⅛ teaspoon salt
  1½ teaspoons vanilla
Beat until stiff:
  3 egg whites

Fold them lightly into the cream mixture. Sprinkle the top with:
  Cinnamon or grated coconut
Bake the pies in a moderate oven 350°
for 30 minutes.

Cheese Pie or Cake, page 585.

Meringue Pies and Fillings for Baked Pie Shells

RULES FOR MERINGUE
A meringue is beaten constantly until it is spread. Its success depends upon the proper beating of the egg whites, the slow addition of the sugar and the slow oven in which it is baked. Beat the egg whites on a platter or in a large bowl. Use a flat wire whisk.
Method I.
Combine:
  ⅛ teaspoon salt
  2 egg whites
  (2 teaspoons water)
Whip them until they are frothy. Add:
  ¼ teaspoon cream of tartar
Whip them until they are stiff but not dry, until they stand in peaks that lean over slightly when the beater is removed. Beat in ½ teaspoonful at a time:
  4 tablespoons granulated or confectioners' sugar
Beat in:
  ½ teaspoon vanilla

Method II.
Some of the rules call for meringues made with:
  3 egg whites
  1 tablespoon water
In that case use:
  ⅛ teaspoon salt
  ¼ teaspoon cream of tartar
  6 tablespoons sugar
  ¾ teaspoon vanilla
After the ingredients are combined, continue beating the meringue for several minutes, until it holds its shape well. Pile it lightly on a filled pie shell. Be sure that the filling is cool. Spread it lightly with a spatula to the very edges of the pie. Bake it in a slow oven 300° for 15 to 20 minutes. Permit it to cool slowly.

Method III.
A new way to make a meringue reads:
Beat until frothy:
  2 egg whites
  ⅛ teaspoon salt
  ¼ teaspoon cream of tartar

Add gradually, beating constantly:
  4 tablespoons sugar
Whip the meringue until it is stiff and glossy. Heap it on the pie or pudding. Spread it to the edges of the dish. Bake this meringue in a hot oven 400° from 8 to 10 minutes.

RULE FOR MAKING MERINGUE WITH AN ELECTRIC MIXER
Use the ingredients given in the preceding rule. Beat egg whites, cream of tartar and water in the small bowl at high speed for 3 minutes. Add sugar gradually, 1 tablespoonful at a time. Add salt and flavoring. Continue beating at high speed until mixture will stand in peaks, 4 to 5 minutes. Bake it by the preceding rule.

RULE FOR CUSTARD FOR PIES
Cook all egg fillings in a pan over, not in, hot water. Stir them constantly.

Three Minute Icing, page 632.

CRUMB CRUST PIES
Do not neglect these unusually tempting desserts—Custard, Butterscotch, Banana, Coconut, Chocolate and other meringue pies made with crumb crusts. These are best made with a previously baked Crumb Pie Shell, page 567. Sprinkle the reserved crumbs over the meringue before baking it.

APPLE PIE II
A 7 Inch Pie
Prepare by any rule, page 564:
  A baked Pie Shell
Peel, core and slice:
  5 medium-sized apples
Make a sirup of:
  ¼ cup water
  ½ cup white or brown sugar
Very tart apples may require additional sugar. Add:

1 tablespoon butter

Add the apples. Stir them gently, cover them and cook them until they are nearly tender. Stir them from time to time so that they do not burn. If the apples are not tart add:

1 teaspoon or more lemon juice
1 teaspoon grated lemon rind

Pour off a little of the juice, cool, then stir into it:

½ tablespoon cornstarch
(¼ teaspoon cinnamon)
(⅛ teaspoon nutmeg)

Pour this over the apples. Cook and stir them until they boil. Pour the apples into the pie shell. Cover them if you wish with a Meringue, page 578, made with:

2 egg whites

Bake the meringue in a slow oven 300° for 15 to 20 minutes; or cover the top with crumb crust. Brown the top crust under a broiler.
Instead of following these instructions you may vary your fruit pie fillings in the following way:
Cook the fruit with the sugar and water until it is tender. Omit the butter. Add the lemon juice and rind. Cool the fruit slightly. Beat in 2 egg yolks. Stir and cook the fruit over hot water until the yolks thicken. Fill the pie shell and proceed with the meringue.

Apple Pie I, page 568.

PEACH PIE II

Follow the preceding rule for Apple Pie II. If the peaches are very sweet, use less sugar.

Peach Pie I, page 569; Gelatine Raspberry or Loganberry Cream Pie, page 588; Gelatine Fruit Chiffon Pie, page 588; Gelatine Strawberry Chiffon Pie, page 587.

STRAWBERRY AND BANANA PIE

A 9 Inch Pie
Prepare:

A baked Crumb Crust Shell, page 567

Hull:

1 cup strawberries

Prepare:

1 cup sliced bananas

Combine the fruit and sweeten it with:

Sugar

Fill the pie shell. Cover the top with:

Whipped cream or
Three Minute Icing, page 632

BERRY PIE II

A 9 Inch Pie
Try a fine combination—raspberries and currants.
Prepare by any rule, page 564:

A baked Pie Shell

Pick over:

4 cups berries

For a 7 inch pie use 3 cupfuls of berries. Wash them, if necessary, before hulling them. Place them in a saucepan. Crush a few of the berries with a spoon so that the juice will run and they will not scorch. Add to them:

⅔ to 1 cup sugar, according to the acidity of the fruit

Blueberries, for instance, require the smaller amount of sugar and 1 tablespoonful lemon juice.
Cook them over a low fire until they are soft. Stir them from the bottom to prevent them from burning. Pour off a little of the juice. Add to it:

3 tablespoons all-purpose flour
or 1½ tablespoons cornstarch
⅛ teaspoon salt

Return it to the pan. Stir the berries until they boil and thicken. Add:

2 tablespoons butter

Cool the fruit. Pour it into the pie shell shortly before serving the pie. Top the fruit with:

Meringue, page 578

Bake it as directed. Or top the fruit with:

Three Minute Icing, page 632

Glazed Strawberries, page 633.

LEMON MERINGUE PIE

Method I. A 9 Inch Pie
Prepare by any rule, page 564:

A baked Pie Shell

Combine in the top of a double boiler and stir until smooth:

1 cup sugar
5 to 6 tablespoons cornstarch
⅛ teaspoon salt
2 cups water

Cook and stir these ingredients over low heat until the mixture thickens and boils. Place it over boiling water and cook it covered for 10 minutes longer. Pour a little of it over:

3 beaten egg yolks

Beat this, then add it to the mixture in the double boiler. Cook and stir the custard for 3 minutes over boiling water. Remove it from the heat. Beat in:

  3 tablespoons butter
  ⅓ cup lemon juice
  2 teaspoons grated lemon rind

Very coarsely grated rind appeals to many people.

Cool the custard. Pour it into the cold pie shell. Cover it with Meringue, page 578, made with:

  3 egg whites
  ⅛ teaspoon salt

Bake it in a slow oven 300° for 15 or 20 minutes.

Method II. A 9 Inch Pie

This resembles a chiffon pie, as part of the egg white is put into the filling. Prepare by any rule, page 564:

  A baked Pie Shell

Cook and stir in a double boiler until thick and smooth:

  4 egg yolks
  ½ cup sugar
  2 tablespoons flour
  3 tablespoons water

Cool these ingredients. Add:

  Rind and juice of 1 large lemon

Whip until stiff:

  2 egg whites
  ⅛ teaspoon salt

Fold them into the custard. Fill the baked pie shell. Cover the pie with Meringue, page 578, made with:

  2 egg whites

Bake it in a slow oven 300° for 15 to 20 minutes.

Method III. A 7 Inch Pie

A cousin was highly indignant when I failed to put this luxurious recipe in my first cookbook. It has been in the family for many years and he thinks it the only lemon pie worth consideration. Prepare by any rule, page 564:

  A baked Pie Shell

Combine and beat until blended, then cook and stir in a double boiler until melted, over, not in simmering hot water:

  ½ cup butter
  1 cup sugar
  Rind and juice of 2 lemons

Beat well, add and cook until the custard thickens:

  3 eggs
  1 egg yolk

Cool the custard. Pour it into the baked pie shell. Cover it with a Me-

ringue, page 578, made with:

  2 egg whites

Bake the pie in a slow oven 300° for 15 to 20 minutes. This filling is not firm. If you wish a firmer filling use Method I or II.

Lemon Cream Pie, page 582; Lemon Chiffon Pie, page 586; Gelatine Lemon Chiffon Pie or Fairy Tart, page 587; Frozen Lemon Pie, page 715; Orange Cream Pie with Pecans, page 582; Orange Chiffon Pie, page 586.

ORANGE MERINGUE PIE
A 9 Inch Pie

Prepare by any rule, page 564:

  A baked Pie Shell

Combine in the top of a double boiler:

  1 cup sugar
  5 to 6 tablespoons all-purpose
    flour
  ¼ teaspoon salt
  ¾ cup warm water
  ¾ cup orange juice

Cook and stir these ingredients over direct heat until they boil. Place them over boiling water and cook for 10 minutes longer. Pour a little of this mixture over:

  3 beaten egg yolks

Beat this, then add it to the mixture in the double boiler. Cook and stir the custard for 5 minutes over boiling water. Beat in:

  1 tablespoon butter
  2 tablespoons lemon juice
  1 teaspoon grated lemon rind
  1 teaspoon grated orange rind

Cool the custard. Pour it into the cold pie shell. Cover it with a Meringue, page 578, made with:

  3 egg whites

Bake it in a slow oven 300° for 15 to 20 minutes.

PINEAPPLE MERINGUE PIE
A 9 Inch Pie

Prepare by any rule, page 564:

  A baked Pie Shell

Cook and stir over very low heat until thick:

  2 cups crushed pineapple
  1 tablespoon cornstarch
  ¾ cup sugar

Add:

  1 tablespoon butter

Pour part of this mixture over:

  2 lightly beaten egg yolks

Beat it with the yolks and return it to

the saucepan. Stir the mixture and permit the yolks to cook and thicken for 1 minute. Cool the custard. Fill the pie shell. Cover it with a Meringue, page 578, made with:

    2 egg whites

Bake it in a slow oven 300° for 15 to 20 minutes.

Custard Pie I, page 571.
This custard is baked in the pie shell.

CUSTARD PIE II OR CREAM PIE
A 9 Inch Pie
Prepare by any rule, page 564:

    A baked Pie Shell

Beat:

    3 egg yolks

Beat in gradually:

    ⅓ **cup sugar**
    ¼ **teaspoon salt**
    2½ **tablespoons cornstarch**
    1 tablespoon butter

Pour over these ingredients:

    2 cups scalded milk

Cook and stir the custard over boiling water or over very low heat. Stir it constantly until it thickens. Cool it. Add:

    1 teaspoon vanilla or rum
    (¼ teaspoon grated nutmeg)

Pour the custard into the baked pie shell. Cover it with Meringue, page 578, made with:

    2 egg whites

You may top this with:

    ¼ **cup blanched shredded almonds**

Bake it in a slow oven 300° for 15 to 20 minutes.

Chocolate Topped Gelatine Custard Chiffon Pie, page 589.

BANANA CREAM PIE
Follow the preceding rule for:

    Custard Pie Filling II or any one of the Lemon Pie Fillings, pages 579, 580

Peel and cut into very thin slices:

    2 ripe bananas

Place them in the baked pie shell. Pour the filling over them.

COCONUT CREAM PIE
Follow the rule above for:

    Custard Pie II

See Crumb Crusts, page 567.
Add to the hot ingredients:

    ½ **to 1 cup grated coconut**

Fill the pie shell. Or sprinkle the coconut on the bottom of the pie shell and pour the filling over it. Cover the custard with a:

    Meringue, page 578

and bake it as directed. Or omit the coconut in the filling. Top the meringue before baking it with:

    1½ **cups grated coconut**

MACAROON PIE
Prepare:

    Custard Pie II

Use:

    ¼ **cup sugar**

When the custard is cooked add to it:

    6 dry crushed macaroons

Top the custard with a:

    Meringue, page 578

and bake it as directed.

CUSTARD AND FRUIT PIE
This is a tempting filling good in individiual tarts. Prepare by any rule, page 564:

    A baked Pie Shell

Prepare ½ the amount of:

    Custard Pie II Filling, page 581

Place it in the shell. Fill the shell with:

    Fresh sugared fruit or drained stewed fruit

Fresh Stewed Cherries, page 444, or Glazed Strawberries, page 633, or seedless grapes are highly recommended. The fruit may be topped with:

    Whipped cream

German Cherry Cake, page 637.

PINEAPPLE CREAM PIE
Prepare by any rule, page 564:

    A baked Pie Shell

Combine, stir and cook over very low heat until thick:

    ½ **cup sugar**
    ⅛ **teaspoon salt**
    6 tablespoons all-purpose flour
    1 cup drained grated pineapple
    3 beaten egg yolks
    3 tablespoons butter
    1¼ **cups milk**

Add:

    Juice of 1 lemon

Cool the custard. Pour it into the pie shell and cover it with a Meringue, page 578, made with:

    2 egg whites

Bake it in a slow oven 300° for 15 to 20 minutes.

Gelatine Pineapple Chiffon Pie, page 587.

LEMON CREAM PIE
A 9 Inch Pie
Prepare by any rule, page 564:
   A baked Pie Shell
Combine, cook and stir over very low heat until thick:
   ¾ cup sugar
   2 tablespoons cornstarch
   ⅛ teaspoon salt
   1½ cups rich milk
   2 well-beaten egg yolks
Stir in:
   ¼ cup lemon juice
   ¼ teaspoon grated lemon rind
Cool the custard. Fill the pie shell. Cover it with a Meringue, page 578, made with:
   2 egg whites
Bake it in a slow oven 300° for 15 to 20 minutes.

ORANGE CREAM PIE WITH PECANS
A 9 Inch Pie
Prepare by any rule, page 564:
   A baked Pie Shell
Mix thoroughly:
   ½ cup sugar or more if the oranges are very tart
   ¼ cup all-purpose flour
   ⅛ teaspoon salt
Add:
   1 cup scalded milk
Cook and stir these ingredients over very low heat until they are thick. Pour part of this mixture over:
   3 well-beaten egg yolks
Return it to the pan. Add:
   ⅔ cup orange juice
   2 teaspoons grated orange rind
   1 teaspoon butter
Stir and cook the custard over very low heat until the eggs thicken slightly. Add:
   ½ cup pecan meats
Cool the custard and pour it into the baked pie shell. Cover it with a Meringue, page 578, made with:
   3 egg whites
Bake it in a slow oven 300° for 15 to 20 minutes.

CARAMEL PIE
A 9 Inch Pie
Prepare by any rule, page 564:
   A baked Pie Shell
Heat and stir in a skillet until melted:

½ cup sugar
Stir in and boil for 2 minutes:
   ½ cup boiling water
Blend:
   ½ cup sugar
   ¼ cup all-purpose flour
   ⅛ teaspoon salt
Add:
   1½ cups milk
Stir in the caramel sirup. Cook and stir this mixture in a double boiler. When it is hot pour part of it over:
   2 beaten egg yolks
Beat it with the yolks and return it to double boiler. Cook and stir it until it coats a spoon. Add:
   2 tablespoons butter
   1 teaspoon vanilla
   (¼ to ½ cup nut meats)
Cool the filling. Fill the pie shell. Make a Meringue, page 578, with:
   2 egg whites
   ⅛ teaspoon salt
   ¼ cup sugar
   ½ teaspoon vanilla
Pile the meringue on the pie. Bake it in a slow oven 300° for 15 to 20 minutes. Or dispense with the meringue and place around the edge of the pie a ring of whipped cream sprinkled with grated coconut.

BUTTERSCOTCH PIE
A 7 Inch Pie
Prepare by any rule, page 564:
   A baked Pie Shell
Combine in a double boiler:
   ¾ cup firmly packed brown sugar, page 593
   2 tablespoons all-purpose flour
   2 tablespoons butter
   ¼ teaspoon salt
Stir and cook these ingredients until they are blended. Add:
   1 cup scalded milk
Beat until light:
   3 egg yolks
Pour a little of the milk mixture over them. Beat it with the yolks and return it to the double boiler. Stir and cook it until the yolks thicken slightly. Cool the custard and flavor it with:
   ½ teaspoon vanilla
Add:
   (½ cup nut meats or crushed peanut brittle)
Pour the custard into the baked pie shell. Cover it with a Meringue, page 578, made with:
   3 egg whites
Bake it in a slow oven 300° for 15 to 20 minutes.

PECAN PIE
An 8 Inch Pie
Prepare by any rule, page 564:
A baked Pie Shell
Cream:
⅓ cup butter
¾ cup firmly packed brown sugar, page 593
Beat in one at a time:
3 eggs
Stir in:
1 cup light corn sirup
1 cup broken pecans
1 teaspoon vanilla
¼ teaspoon salt
Fill the shell. Bake the pie in a moderate oven 375° for ½ hour.

Caramel Nut Pie, page 574.

JEFFERSON DAVIS PIE
A 9 Inch Pie
Prepare by any rule, page 564:
A baked Pie Shell
Cream:
½ cup butter
2 cups light brown sugar
Beat in:
4 egg yolks
Sift, then add:
2 tablespoons all-purpose flour
1 teaspoon cinnamon
½ teaspoon allspice
1 teaspoon freshly grated nutmeg
Add:
1 cup cream
½ cup chopped dates
½ cup raisins
½ cup broken pecan meats
Fill the shell. Bake the pie in a slow oven 300° until set, about 40 minutes. When cool top it with a:
Meringue, page 578
Bake it as directed.

Chess Tarts, page 572.

CHOCOLATE PIE
A 7 Inch Pie
Prepare by any rule, page 564:
A baked Pie Shell
Scald in a double boiler or over very low heat with constant stirring:
2 cups milk
Cut up and add:
1½ squares (1½ oz.) chocolate or
¼ cup cocoa
If you use the cocoa, use 3 tablespoonfuls of butter in all. Stir until it is dissolved. In a separate bowl dissolve:
2 tablespoons cornstarch
in:
¼ cup milk
Add:
¼ teaspoon salt
1 cup sugar
Add these ingredients to the mixture in the double boiler. Cook and stir them for 15 minutes. Pour a small quantity over:
2 to 4 beaten egg yolks
Beat and add it to the mixture in the double boiler. Stir and cook the custard for 3 minutes. Add:
1 tablespoon butter
Remove the custard from the fire. Beat it until it is very smooth. Add:
1 teaspoon vanilla
(½ cup chopped nut meats)
Cool this. Pour it into the pie shell. Cover it with a Meringue, page 578, made with:
2 egg whites
4 tablespoons sugar
Bake it in a slow oven 300° for 15 to 20 minutes.

Gelatine Chocolate Chiffon Pie, page 590.

FUDGE PIE
This is a crustless pie or cake unexcelled in quality. It is deliciously and devastatingly rich. Do not let that deter you.
Sift:
1 cup sugar
Beat until soft:
½ cup butter
Add the sugar gradually. Blend these ingredients until they are creamy. Beat in:
2 egg yolks
Melt over hot water, cool slightly and beat in:
2 oz. chocolate
Sift before measuring:
½ cup all-purpose flour
Beat the flour into the butter mixture. Add:
1 teaspoon vanilla
Whip until stiff:
2 egg whites
⅛ teaspoon salt
Fold them into the batter. Bake the batter in a greased 8½ inch pie plate in a slow oven 325° for about ½ hour. Serve the pie topped with:
Ice cream

Fudge Cake, page 610.

COFFEE TARTS

Prepare by any rule for pie crusts:
  6 baked tart shells
Prepare:
  2 cups strong coffee
Combine and stir until smooth:
  1 cup cream or evaporated milk
  6 tablespoons sifted all-purpose
    flour
  2/3 cup sugar
  1/4 teaspoon salt
Stir these ingredients into the hot
coffee. Cook and stir the mixture over
low heat until it thickens, about 20
minutes. Pour part of it over:
  2 beaten eggs or 5 egg yolks
Return this to the pan, stir and cook it
for 2 or 3 minutes over low heat to
permit the eggs to thicken slightly.
Add:
  2 tablespoons butter
Cool, then add:
  1 teaspoon vanilla or
  2 teaspoons rum
Fill the tart shells. Chill them. Serve
the tarts topped with:
  Whipped cream
  Crushed Nut Brittle, page 794

LOGANBERRY PIE OR TARTS
A 9 Inch Pie

An excellent winter pie.
Prepare by any rule, page 564:
  A baked Pie Shell or Individual
    Pie Shells
Place in a saucepan the contents of:
  1 No. 2½ can loganberries: 3½
    cups
Dissolve in a cup:
  1½ tablespoons cornstarch
in ½ cupful of the loganberry juice.
Heat the berries to the boiling point.
Add:
  1 tablespoon butter
  ⅛ teaspoon salt
Stir in the dissolved cornstarch. Stir
and cook the berries until they boil
and thicken. Cool the filling. Fill the
pie shells. The pie may be covered
with a:
  Meringue, page 578
Bake the meringue in a slow oven
300° for 15 to 20 minutes.

PRUNE OR APRICOT PIE
A 9 Inch Pie

Prepare by any rule, page 564:
  A baked Pie Shell
Put stewed, unsweetened prunes or
apricots through a ricer. Combine:

  ¾ cup prune or apricot pulp
  ½ teaspoon grated lemon rind
  1 tablespoon lemon juice
  ½ cup sugar
Beat until stiff:
  3 egg whites
  ⅛ teaspoon salt
Beat in very slowly:
  ½ cup sugar
Fold the egg whites into the fruit mixture. Fill the pie shell. Bake the pie in
a slow oven 325° for about 20 minutes,
or until it is set.

BANBURY TARTS
About Six 4 Inch Tarts

Combine:
  1 cup seeded raisins
  1 cup sugar
  2 tablespoons cracker crumbs
  1 well-beaten egg
  Grated rind of 1 lemon
  1½ tablespoons lemon juice
  2 tablespoons butter
Cook and stir these ingredients over
low heat until they begin to thicken.
Remove them from the fire. Cool
them. Partly fill individual baked Pie
Shells, page 563. Top the tarts with:
  Whipped cream
Or use this filling in Turnovers, page
576.

SOUR CREAM PIE II WITH OR WITHOUT RAISINS
A 9 Inch Pie

Prepare by any rule, page 564:
  A baked Pie Shell
Cook and stir in a double boiler until
thick:
  2 egg yolks
  1 whole egg
  ½ cup white or brown sugar
  ¼ teaspoon cloves
  ½ teaspoon cinnamon
  1 cup thick sour cream
  1½ teaspoons lemon juice (optional,
    dependent upon the acidity of
    the cream)
  (½ cup finely chopped seeded
    raisins or dates)
Cool these ingredients. Pour them into
the baked pie shell. If you care to,
cover them with a Meringue, page 578,
made with:
  2 egg whites
Bake the pie in a slow oven 300° for
15 to 20 minutes. This is a good pie
served hot or cold.

Sour Cream Pie I, page 573.

RAISIN PIE I
A 9 Inch Pie
Prepare by any rule, page 564:
  A baked Pie Shell
Cook to the boiling point:
  1 cup seedless white raisins
  1 cup water
Add:
  ½ cup sugar
Cool ½ cupful of this mixture. Stir into it gently:
  2 tablespoons butter
  2 tablespoons all-purpose flour
Return it to the saucepan. Cook and stir these ingredients over low heat until the flour has thickened. Remove the pan from the fire. Beat in:
  2 egg yolks
  1 teaspoon grated lemon rind
  3 tablespoons lemon juice
Cool the filling. Fill the pie shell. Cover it with a Meringue, page 578, made with:
  2 egg whites
Bake it in a slow oven 300° for 15 to 20 minutes.

STRAWBERRY MERINGUE PIE
A 9 Inch Pie
Prepare by any rule, page 564:
  A 9 inch baked Pie Shell
Place in a double boiler and beat:
  1½ cups sugar
  ¼ cup water
  ½ teaspoon cream of tartar
  ⅛ teaspoon salt
  2 unbeaten egg whites
Place the container over rapidly boiling water. Beat steadily with a wire whisk or rotary beater until the meringue will hold a peak, from 6 to 8 minutes. Remove the container from the heat and continue to beat for 3 minutes. Fill the baked pie shell with:
  2 to 3 cups hulled strawberries
or other tart fruit. Cover them with the meringue. Swirl it around on top with a spoon for a professional effect. You may place the pie under a broiler to color the top lightly, for about 2 minutes. Watch it closely. When cool, chill the pie.

CHEESE PIE OR CAKE
Method I. 8 Servings
This cheese pie or cake is luscious. It should be 1½ inches or more in depth. Bake it in a pan with a removable rim or in an oven-proof baking dish 9 inches wide, 2⅜ inches high.
Prepare:

  Zwieback Crust or Crumb
  Crust, page 567
Reserve ½ cupful of the mixture. Line a deep baking dish and press the crust lightly on the bottom and against the sides. Chill it thoroughly. It is best made a day in advance. Fill it with the following:

Cheese Filling
Dissolve:
  1 cup sugar
in:
  ¼ cup cream
If the cheese is dry, double the amount of cream. Add:
  2 lbs. smooth cottage cheese:
    about 2 pints
  4 beaten egg yolks
  3 tablespoons flour
  1 teaspoon vanilla or 2½ tablespoons lemon juice and 1 teaspoon grated lemon rind
Whip until stiff:
  4 egg whites
  ¼ teaspoon salt
Fold them into the cheese mixture. Fill the shell and sprinkle the reserved crumbs over the top. Bake the pie in a moderate oven 350° for about 1 hour. A friend who has been very successful with this recipe asked me to add that she prefers beating the 4 eggs without separating them.

Method II. A Deep 9 Inch Pie
Very delicate, as the filling is made without flour.
Prepare by the rule for Galette Dough II, page 565, Pie Crust, page 564, or Crumb Crust, page 567:
  A baked Pie Shell
Combine and beat:
  3 cups smooth cottage cheese
  3 whole eggs
Add:
  ¾ cup thick cream
  3 tablespoons melted butter
  5 tablespoons sugar
  ½ teaspoon vanilla or
  1 tablespoon lemon juice and
  ½ teaspoon grated lemon rind
  ¼ cup blanched chopped almonds
Bake the pie in a moderate oven 350° until the filling is firm, about 45 minutes. Sprinkle it while hot with:
  4 tablespoons confectioners' sugar
  1 teaspoon cinnamon

Sour Cream Meringue Pie, page 577, Refrigerator Cheese Cakes, page 658.

CHEESE CAKE WITH WHIPPED CREAM
16 Servings
Similar to the preceding cheese cakes or pies but richer.
Combine:

> 2 cups zwieback or graham cracker crumbs
> 1½ teaspoons cinnamon
> ¾ cup melted butter

Reserve 1 cupful of this mixture. Press the remainder with a spoon or the palm of the hand on the bottom and sides of a 12 inch spring form pan. Chill this shell thoroughly, see Crumb Crust, page 567. Or line a spring mold with Galette Dough, page 565. Fill it with the following:

Cheese Filling
Sift:

> 1½ cups sugar

Beat until light:

> 6 eggs

Add the sugar gradually. Beat these ingredients until they are very light. Add:

> ⅛ teaspoon salt
> 2 teaspoons grated lemon rind
> 3 tablespoons lemon juice
> 1 teaspoon vanilla

Fold in:

> 2 cups heavy cream, whipped

Blend well:

> ½ cup all-purpose flour
> 3½ pints smooth cottage cheese:
> 2¼ lbs.

Put these ingredients through a sieve. Fold them into the egg and cream mixture. Fill the pie shell. Sprinkle the reserved crumb mixture over the filling. Bake the pie in a moderate oven 350° for about 1 hour. Turn off the heat and permit the pie to stand in the oven for 1 hour longer or until cooled.

Sour Cream Cherry Cake, page 638.

APPLESAUCE CHEESE PIE
Prepare by any rule, page 567:

> **Crumb Crust**

Reserve ½ cupful of the crumbs. Press the remainder into a deep 9 inch oven-proof dish. Combine and beat the contents of:

> 1 No. 2 can applesauce
> 1 can condensed milk: 15 oz.

with:

> Rind and juice of 1 lemon
> 3 egg yolks

Beat until stiff, then fold in:

> 3 egg whites
> ⅛ teaspoon salt

Cover the top with the reserved crumbs. Bake the pie in a moderate oven 375° for about 50 minutes. Sprinkle the top with:

> Cinnamon

LEMON CHIFFON PIE
A 9 Inch Pie
A delicate and delectable pie usually made with a paper thin crust. Prepare by any rule, page 564:

> **A baked Pie Shell**

Combine in a double boiler:

> 5 tablespoons sugar
> 2 tablespoons water
> 3 egg yolks
> Grated rind of 1 lemon
> 3 tablespoons lemon juice

Cook and stir these ingredients over boiling water until they are thick. Cool them. Add:

> ⅛ teaspoon salt

to:

> 3 egg whites

Whip them until they are stiff but not dry. Fold in:

> 3 tablespoons sugar

Fold this mixture lightly into the custard. Fill the pie shell. Brown the pie in a hot oven 400° for 10 minutes, or place it under a broiler to brown.

ORANGE CHIFFON PIE
A 9 Inch Pie
Use well-flavored orange juice for this pie. Indifferently-flavored orange juice may be improved by the addition of 2 teaspoonfuls of vanilla. Prepare by any rule, page 564:

> **A baked Pie Shell**

Cook and stir in a double boiler until thick:

> 3 tablespoons all-purpose flour
> 3 egg yolks
> 2 tablespoons lemon juice
> ¾ cup orange juice
> ½ teaspoon grated orange rind
> 2 tablespoons water
> ¼ cup sugar

Use more sugar if the orange juice is acid. Cool these ingredients. Whip until stiff:

> ⅛ teaspoon salt
> 3 egg whites

Fold them into the orange custard. Fill the pie shell. Brown the pie in a hot oven 400° for 10 minutes, or place it under a broiler to brown.

Gelatine Chiffon Cream Pies

The following rules are for baked pie shells or crumb crusts filled with gelatine mixtures and cream. They make delicious desserts. As they may be prepared well in advance, if kept in a cold place, they have a practical value that is desirable in many instances.

GELATINE STRAWBERRY CHIFFON PIE
Method I. A 9 Inch Pie

The first method calls for both egg whites and yolks, which makes it like a strawberry custard. Method II, made with egg whites only and with whipped cream, is more like a Bavarian dessert. Prepare by any rule, page 564:

A baked Pie Shell

Soften:

1 tablespoon gelatine

in:

¼ cup water

Beat in the top of a double boiler:

3 egg yolks

Add:

1 tablespoon lemon juice
¼ teaspoon salt
½ cup sugar

Stir and cook these ingredients over hot water until thickened. Remove them from the fire and stir in the gelatine until dissolved. Crush and stir in:

1½ cups strawberries

Chill this mixture. When it begins to thicken whip until stiff:

3 egg whites

Beat in gradually:

2 tablespoons sugar

Fold in the thickened strawberry mixture. Heap it into the pie shell, chill it well. You may garnish the top with:

½ cup heavy cream, whipped
A few whole strawberries

Method II.

Prepare by any rule, page 564:

A baked Pie Shell

Chill it for 3 hours. Hull, then slice or crush:

1½ cups strawberries

Pour over them:

¾ cup sugar

Permit these ingredients to stand for 30 minutes. Soak:

1 tablespoon gelatine

in:

¼ cup cold water

Dissolve it in:

½ cup boiling water or strawberry juice

Add:

1 tablespoon lemon juice

Add the gelatine to the berry mixture. Chill these ingredients until they are about to set. Whip until stiff and fold in:

½ cup heavy cream

Whip until stiff and fold in:

2 egg whites
⅛ teaspoon salt

Fill the pie shell with the strawberry mixture. Chill it. Garnish the pie with:

(Whipped cream)

GELATINE LEMON OR LIME CHIFFON PIE
A Deep 9 Inch Pie

Prepare by any rule, page 564:

A baked Pie Shell

Soak:

1 tablespoon gelatine

in:

¼ cup water

Combine, stir and cook in a double boiler until the consistency of custard:

½ cup sugar
½ cup lemon or lime juice
½ teaspoon salt
4 beaten egg yolks

Stir in the dissolved gelatine and:

1 teaspoon grated lemon or lime rind

Chill these ingredients. Whip until stiff:

4 egg whites

Beat in very slowly:

½ cup sugar

In a separate bowl beat until stiff:

1 cup heavy cream

When the custard begins to thicken, beat it with a wire whisk until it is fluffy. Fold in the egg whites. Fold in the cream. Fill the pie shell. Chill the pie thoroughly before serving it. The cream may be reserved for the top. In that case add to it:

1 teaspoon vanilla
3 tablespoons confectioners' sugar

GELATINE PINEAPPLE CHIFFON PIE
A 9 Inch Pie

Prepare by any rule, page 564:

A baked Pie Shell

Soak:
    1 tablespoon gelatine
in:
    ¼ cup cold water
Beat until light:
    4 egg yolks
Add gradually:
    ¼ cup sugar
Stir in:
    1¼ cups canned crushed pineapple
    1 tablespoon lemon juice
Cook and stir these ingredients over
boiling water until they thicken. Stir
in the soaked gelatine until it is dissolved. Cool these ingredients until
they are about to set. Whip until stiff:
    4 egg whites
    ¼ teaspoon salt
Fold in:
    ¼ cup sugar
Fold these ingredients lightly into the
pineapple mixture. Fill the pie shell.
Chill the pie thoroughly. Serve it
topped with:
    Whipped cream

GELATINE APRICOT CREAM PIE
A 9 Inch Pie
Prepare by any rule, page 564:
    A baked Pie Shell
Soak:
    1 tablespoon gelatine
in:
    ¼ cup cold water
Put through a ricer:
    1 cup drained cooked or canned
        apricots
Add to the pulp and heat:
    ½ cup apricot juice
    2 tablespoons lemon juice
    ⅓ cup sugar
    ¼ teaspoon salt
Stir in the soaked gelatine until it is
dissolved. Chill these ingredients until
they are about to set. Whip until stiff:
    1 cup heavy cream
Fold into the apricot mixture ¾ of the
cream. Fill the pie shell. Chill the pie
thoroughly. Top it with the remaining
cream.

GELATINE RASPBERRY OR LOGANBERRY CREAM PIE
A 9 Inch Pie
Prepare by any rule, page 564:
    A baked Pie Shell
Drain the contents of:
    1 No. 2½ can raspberries or
        loganberries: 3½ cups
Soak:

1 tablespoon gelatine
in:
    ¼ cup of the juice
Dissolve it in:
    ¾ cup of the hot juice or juice
        and water
Chill the gelatine until it is about to
set. Whip it with a wire whisk until it
is fluffy. Whip until stiff:
    1 cup heavy cream
Fold in:
    3 tablespoons confectioners' sugar
Fold the cream into the gelatine. Fold
in the drained berries. Fill the pie shell.
Chill the pie thoroughly. Garnish the
top with:
    (Whipped cream)

GELATINE FRUIT CHIFFON PIE
A 9 Inch Pie
Prepare by any rule, page 564:
    A baked Pie Shell
Peel and cut into very thin slices:
    1 banana
Soak the slices for 1 hour in:
    ¾ cup orange juice
    ¼ cup lemon juice
Add:
    (¼ cup drained canned crushed
        pineapple)
Soak:
    2 tablespoons gelatine
in:
    ½ cup cold water
Dissolve it in:
    ¾ cup boiling water
Add and stir until it is dissolved:
    1 cup sugar
    ¼ teaspoon salt
Cool these ingredients slightly and
combine them with the banana mix-
ture. Chill the jelly until it is about to
set. Beat it with a wire whisk until it
is fluffy. Whip until stiff:
    1 cup heavy cream
Fold it into the jelly. Chill the jelly
until it is fairly stiff. Heap it into the
baked pie shell. Chill it thoroughly
before serving it.

GELATINE COFFEE CHIFFON CREAM PIE
A 9 Inch Pie
Prepare by any rule, page 564:
    A baked Pie Shell
Soak:
    2 tablespoons gelatine
in:
    ½ cup cold water
Dissolve it in:

2 cups hot coffee
Stir in:
 ½ cup sugar
Pour these ingredients slowly onto:
 2 well-beaten egg yolks
Cook and stir these ingredients in a double boiler until they thicken. Cool the filling until it is about to set. Beat it with a wire whisk until it is fluffy. Add:
 1 teaspoon vanilla
 (1 tablespoon brandy)
Whip until stiff:
 1 cup heavy cream
Fold in:
 1 tablespoon sugar
Whip until stiff:
 2 egg whites
 ⅛ teaspoon salt
Fold the whipped cream into the coffee mixture. Fold in the egg whites. Pour the filling into the pie shell. Chill the pie thoroughly before serving it.

GELATINE COFFEE CHIFFON PIE

You may fill a 9 inch baked Pie Shell or Crumb Crust, page 567, with Mocha Sponge, page 739. Good garnished with whipped cream.

CHOCOLATE TOPPED GELATINE CHIFFON CUSTARD PIE
A 9 Inch Pie

Prepare by any rule, page 564:
 A baked Pie Shell
Soak:
 1 tablespoon gelatine
in:
 ¼ cup cold water
Heat in a double boiler:
 1 cup milk
 (¼ teaspoon nutmeg)
Beat until light:
 3 egg yolks
Add gradually:
 ½ cup sugar
Beat these ingredients until they are well blended. Pour the hot milk over this mixture. Place it in the double boiler and cook and stir it until it is the consistency of thick cream. Remove it from the fire. Add the soaked gelatine. Add:
 1 teaspoon vanilla
 (3 tablespoons rum)
Chill these ingredients until they are nearly set. Beat them until they are light with a wire whisk. Whip until stiff:

3 egg whites
 ¼ teaspoon salt
Fold them lightly into the custard. Fill the pie shell. Chill it well. Whip until stiff:
 (1 cup heavy cream)
Fold in:
 3 tablespoons confectioners' sugar
Pile it on the pie. Sprinkle the top with:
 ¼ cup grated unsweetened chocolate or 2 tablespoons cocoa
 ½ cup blanched, shredded, toasted almonds

BLACK BOTTOM PIE

Prepare by the rule, pages 567, 564, a deep 9 inch baked:
 Crumb Crust or Pie Crust
Soak:
 1 tablespoon gelatine
in:
 ¼ cup cold water
Scald:
 2 cups rich milk
Combine:
 ½ cup sugar
 4 teaspoons cornstarch
Beat until light:
 4 egg yolks
Stir the scalded milk in slowly. Stir in the sugar mixture. Cook these ingredients over hot water, stirring occasionally, about 20 minutes, until the custard will coat a spoon heavily. Take out 1 cupful of the custard. Add to it:
 1½ oz. melted chocolate
Beat these ingredients until well blended and cool. Add:
 ½ teaspoon vanilla
Pour this custard into the pie shell. Dissolve the soaked gelatine in the remaining custard. Be sure it is hot. Let it cool, but do not permit it to stiffen. When it is cool stir in:
 1 tablespoon or more rum
Beat until well blended:
 3 egg whites
 ¼ teaspoon salt
Add:
 ¼ teaspoon cream of tartar
Beat the egg whites until they are stiff. Beat in gradually, a teaspoonful at a time:
 ¼ cup sugar
Fold the egg whites into the custard. Cover the chocolate custard with the rum-flavored custard. Chill it until it sets. Whip until stiff:
 1 cup heavy cream
Add gradually:

2 tablespoons confectioners' sugar
Cover the custard with the cream.
Sprinkle over the top:
½ oz. shaved chocolate

GELATINE RUM CREAM PIE

Minus egg whites, and headier than any of its preceding tamer relatives. Prepare by one of the rules on pages 567 or 564:

A 9 inch baked Crumb Crust or Pie Shell

Beat until light:
6 egg yolks
Beat in gradually:
⅞ cup sugar
Soak:
1 tablespoon gelatine
in:
½ cup cold water

Place these ingredients over low heat and stir until the gelatine is dissolved. Pour this over the egg yolks in a slow stream, beating constantly. Cool the mixture. Stir in:
½ cup Jamaica rum
Whip until stiff:
1 pint heavy cream: 2 cups
When stiff, fold it into the egg mixture. Cool the filling but before it begins to set pour it into the pie shell. When set sprinkle the top with:
Grated bittersweet chocolate
Finely shaved pistachio nuts
Serve the pie well chilled.

GELATINE MAPLE CHIFFON PIE

A 9 Inch Pie
Prepare by any rule, page 564:
A baked Pie Shell
Soak:
1 tablespoon gelatine
in:
2 tablespoons cold water
Heat and stir in a double boiler:
½ cup milk
½ cup maple sirup
⅛ teaspoon salt
Pour part of this over:
2 beaten egg yolks
Return it to the double boiler. Stir and cook the custard until it thickens. Add the soaked gelatine. Stir until the gelatine is dissolved. Chill these ingredients until they begin to thicken. Whip until stiff:
1 cup heavy cream
Fold into ¾ of it:
⅓ cup broken nut meats
1 teaspoon vanilla

Whip until stiff:
2 egg whites
Fold them into the custard. Fill the pie shell. Garnish it with the remaining cream. Chill the pie.

GELATINE CHOCOLATE CHIFFON PIE WITH BANANAS

A 9 Inch Pie
Prepare by any rule, page 564:
A baked Pie Shell
Soak:
1 tablespoon gelatine
in:
¼ cup cold water
Combine and stir until smooth:
6 tablespoons cocoa or 2 oz. melted chocolate
½ cup boiling water
Stir in the soaked gelatine until it is dissolved. Stir in:
4 lightly beaten egg yolks
½ cup sugar
Chill these ingredients until they are about to set. Add:
1 teaspoon vanilla
Beat them with a wire whisk until they are light. Whip until stiff:
4 egg whites
¼ teaspoon salt
Fold them into the chocolate mixture with:
½ cup sugar
Fill the pie shell. Chill the pie thoroughly. Shortly before serving it cover the top with thinly sliced:
Bananas
Spread it with:
Whipped cream

GELATINE PUMPKIN CHIFFON PIE

A 9 Inch Pie
Prepare by any rule, page 564:
A baked Pie Shell
Soak:
1 tablespoon gelatine
in:
¼ cup cold water
Beat slightly:
3 egg yolks
Add:
½ cup sugar
1¼ cups canned or cooked pumpkin
½ cup milk
¼ teaspoon salt
½ teaspoon cinnamon
½ teaspoon nutmeg
Cook and stir these ingredients over hot water until they are thick. Stir in

the soaked gelatine until it is dissolved. Chill these ingredients. Whip until stiff:

3 egg whites
¼ teaspoon salt

When the pumpkin mixture begins to set stir in:

½ cup sugar

and fold in the egg whites. Fill the pie shell. Chill the pie for several hours.

Serve it garnished with:
Whipped cream

___

Pumpkin Pie, page 573.

___

See Refrigerator Cakes, page 657.
There are several recipes in that chapter that might be classed as gelatine chiffon pies.

Cakes and Cookies

If you wish to be glamorous, become a cake baker. It is a simple accomplishment, rewarding beyond its desserts! At weddings and birthdays as well as on more casual occasions a cake is frequently a center of interest, and this interest has been known to extend to the cook.

A cake should be a treat to the eye and the palate but good or bad it is unfailingly reliable as a conversation piece. The old definition of "lady" is "cake-giver." Whether you bake a cake as an attention for a friend, send a box of cookies to a homesick child or hand a pan of gingerbread over a back fence, the gesture is one of fellowship that adds to your stature and enriches your life. Besides, it's fun to be a "lady."

To bake a perfect cake you must observe these processes where they are called for:

To stir is to blend ingredients with a horizontal circular motion. For this use a spoon.

To cream is to work fat and sugar with the hand or the back of a spoon and the sides of a bowl until these ingredients are smooth and creamy.

To beat is to blend ingredients rapidly with a vertical circular motion to enclose as much air as possible. For this use a slotted spoon.

STIR CREAM BEAT

To whip, a term usually applied to light mixtures and creams, is like "to beat." Use a flat wire egg whip for the egg whites, a spiral wire whip for the cream.

To fold in is to combine 2 previously beaten mixtures. Heap the lighter on the heavier mixture. Use a spoon or a rubber or plastic cake scraper. Cut through the mixtures to the bottom with a downward stroke. Lift the lower mixture gently

TO FOLD IN

and place it over the top mixture. Repeat this motion until the 2 mixtures are blended. Be careful to enclose, as much as possible, the air that has been beaten into the mixtures.

The best cakes result when the advice below is carefully followed:

The ingredients used in cakes must be measured accurately. The majority of recipes are very carefully balanced, and this balance must not be disturbed by careless measurements. All the measurements given in this book are level, unless otherwise stated. All ingredients should be at room temperature.

Flour and sugar should be sifted, the former before it is measured. After being measured, the flour should be sifted 3 times. The sugar need not be sifted again unless the recipe calls for it. These ingredients should be handled separately. It is a help to use paper plates or squares of stiff paper in sifting the sugar and flour. Bend the paper or plates when you wish to transfer these ingredients.

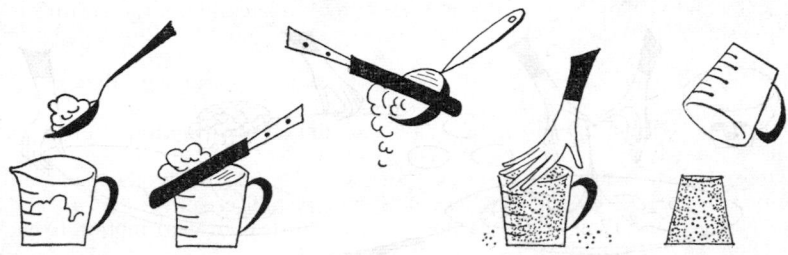

Use a tablespoon or a small scoop to handle the sugar and flour when measuring them. Heap the flour lightly into a cup. Do not shake the cup. Fill it to overflowing, then level off the top with a knife. All dry ingredients are measured this way except brown sugar, which is packed into the cup firmly so that it will hold its shape, sand castle wise, when inverted. Descriptions of hard and soft flour will be found on page 499. Also suggestions for substituting one flour for the other.

If flour has been exposed to moisture it will make a "streaky" cake. Be sure to spread flour in shallow pans and dry it well in a slow oven before using it if there is any doubt about its being dry, or sift it 4 or 5 times before the open door of a hot oven. A discussion of baking equivalents, terms and additional rules will be found on pages 502-505.

When you have an obstinate cake that sticks to the bottom of the pan wring a cloth out of hot water and place it under the tin until the cake loosens.

Cakes are divided into 2 classes, sponge cakes and butter cakes.

Sponge cakes are made without butter.

Butter cakes call for butter or other shortening.

Bulk butter or shortening is most easily measured by the displacement method shown below. When butter comes in 4 sections to the pound each section equals ½ cupful or 4 ounces.

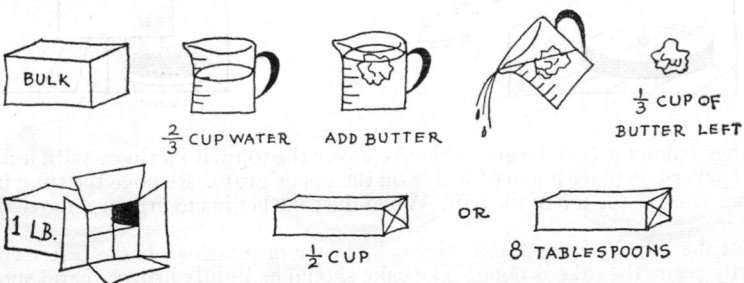

BULK

⅔ CUP WATER   ADD BUTTER

⅓ CUP OF BUTTER LEFT

1 LB.

½ CUP   OR   8 TABLESPOONS

Sponge Cakes

Be sure to have all ingredients, unless directed otherwise, at room temperature.
Beat the egg yolks until they are light and lemon colored. Add the remaining ingredients as directed in the recipes, using sifted sugar and sifted flour.

Do not beat a sponge cake batter unless the recipe calls for it. Fold in the ingredients lightly until they are blended only—enclosing as much air as possible.

Either the flour or the beaten egg whites may be folded in last. Do not beat the egg whites until you are ready to use them. Add a few grains of salt to the egg whites and beat them on a large platter, using a flat wire egg beater. Beat them until they are stiff, stand up well in peaks and keep their shape when the beater is

lifted, but not until they are dry. They should still be glossy. While slower than mechanical beating, hand beating incorporates more air.

Fold (page 592) the stiffly beaten egg whites into the cake batter. Enclose all the air, do not stir or beat it out. A pliable plastic scraper is handy for this and for removing the last bit of batter from the bowl.

Have an ungreased cake pan ready and pour the batter into it. The batter will cling to the sides of the ungreased pan and will rise higher than if it were greased.

Bake a sponge cake in a moderate oven, preheated to 325°, or place it in a somewhat slower oven, 300°, and bake it with a slightly increasing heat. Heat the oven about 15 minutes before using it. The oven should be heated to the degree indicated before the cake is put into it. Do not crowd the oven with pans. Place the pans so that the air may circulate freely as shown on the right below.

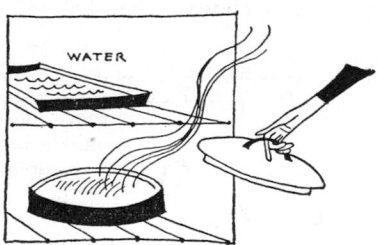

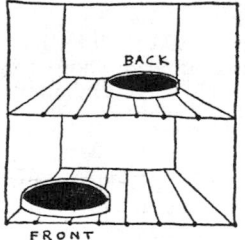

When baking a very large mold cake cover the top with a tin or with a piece of waxed paper and place a pan of water on the upper grate. Remove the tin when the cake has risen to the top of the pan. When the cake begins to brown remove the pan of water.

Test the cake by inserting a wire cake tester or a straw. If the tester emerges perfectly clean, the cake is done. The cake should be lightly browned and should be beginning to shrink from the sides of the pan. If pressed with a finger, it should at once come back into shape.

Remove the cake from the oven and invert the pan until the cake is entirely cold. This may be done by placing it on 3 inverted cups. Right the pan, run a knife around the sides and across the bottom and remove the cake from the pan. Trim off the hard edges if there are any. There really should not be any. Sprinkle the cake with powdered sugar or cover it with icing.

Rule for Mixing Sponge Cake with an Electric Mixer

Beat egg whites and salt in the large bowl at high speed until stiff, about 2 to 3 minutes. Turn to low speed and add sugar gradually. Then in the small bowl, without washing beater, beat egg yolks, lemon, water and vanilla at high speed for 4 minutes. Sift flour twice and fold it by hand into beaten egg whites alternately with beaten yolks.

Butter Cakes

A discussion of baking terms and additional rules will be found on page 504.

Be sure to have all ingredients at room temperature. Remove the butter called for in the recipe from the refrigerator and put it in a warm room. Permit it to become fairly soft but do not permit it to melt, unless the recipe calls for melted butter. When the butter has softened somewhat, beat it with a wooden cake spoon or work it with the hand until it is creamy. Sift the sugar. Brown sugar may be sifted in a food mill. Add it slowly and beat or work it into the butter until it is entirely dissolved. This first step in the making of a butter cake is a very important one. Do not hasten it. Cream the butter and sugar until they are fluffy and foamy, like very thick cream, until the mixture will drop from a spoon when the spoon is shaken.

Next beat in the egg yolks one by one.

Sift the flour, measure it and resift it with the baking powder. Add the sifted ingredients in 3 or 4 parts to the butter mixture alternately with one third or one fourth of the milk, or whatever liquid is called for, until all the ingredients have been used. Beat the batter after each addition of flour or liquid until the ingredients are well blended. This will give the cake a fine grain. If beaten too long, the cake will be close.

Place the egg whites on a large platter, add a few grains of salt and whip them with a flat wire egg beater until they are stiff, stand in peaks and hold their shape, but not until they are dry. They should still be glossy. Do not beat the egg whites until you are ready to use them. Fold in (page 592) the beaten egg whites.

Have a greased cake pan ready or a cake pan lined with waxed paper, which may also be greased. To determine the size of a cake pan, measure it across the top. Pour the batter into it and bake the cake in a moderate oven, preheated to 350°, or place it in a somewhat slower oven, 325°, and bake it with a slightly increasing heat. Light the oven about 15 minutes before using it. The oven should be heated to the degree indicated before the cake is put into it. To place pans in the oven or to bake a large cake see page 594.

Test the cake by inserting a wire cake tester or a straw. If the tester emerges perfectly clean, the cake is done. The cake should be lightly browned and should be beginning to shrink from the sides of the pan. If pressed with a finger, it should at once come back into shape.

Cool the cake on a rack for 5 minutes, then loosen it from the sides and the bottom of the pan, invert it onto a plate and turn it right side up on a cake cooler or on a rack so that the air may circulate from the bottom. This will keep the crust dry and prevent it from becoming soggy. Sprinkle the cake with powdered sugar or cover it with icing.

Rule for Mixing Butter Cakes with an Electric Mixer

1. Combine sugar, shortening, eggs or egg yolks, and flavoring in large mixing bowl and beat at high speed for 3 to 4 minutes. The shortening should be soft but not melted unless the recipe specifies melted shortening.
2. Sift dry ingredients together while above mixture is being beaten.
3. Turn switch to medium speed.
4. Add sifted dry ingredients, about ½ cupful at a time, alternately with liquid, beating not more than 2 minutes. Combine as quickly as possible to avoid overbeating. Overbeating makes a very fine-grained cake so it is better to add the dry ingredients by hand.
5. Remove mixture from sides of bowl either by turning bowl in opposite direction or by scraping sides.
6. If beaten egg whites are to be added separately, beat them in a small bowl before mixing the cake. Fold them into cake mixture last, using low speed, or preferably fold them in with a spoon.

Sponge Cakes

The 3 following sponge cakes call for water and are exceptions to the rule that sponge cake batter must not be beaten:

ECONOMY SPONGE CAKE
Grate, then stir:
    1 teaspoon lemon or orange rind
into:
    1 cup sifted sugar
Beat until very light:
    3 egg yolks
Beat in the sugar gradually. Beat in:
    ¼ cup boiling water
When cool beat in:
    1 tablespoon lemon juice
    1 teaspoon vanilla or grated lemon rind or 3 drops anise oil
Sift before measuring:
    1 cup cake flour
Resift with:
    2 teaspoons tartrate or phosphate baking powder or 1½ teaspoons combination type (see Baking Powder, page 501)
Add the sifted ingredients gradually to the yolk mixture. Beat the batter until they are blended. Whip until stiff but not dry:
    3 egg whites
    ¼ teaspoon salt
Fold them lightly into the batter. Bake the cake in an ungreased 9 inch tube pan in a slow oven 325° for about 50 minutes. Invert it to cool. Remove it from the pan when cold. Some cooks prefer to beat the egg yolks with cold water, then add the sugar gradually and to continue with the other ingredients as suggested above.

SPONGE CAKE DE LUXE
This is made with the ingredients for Economy Sponge Cake, using in all 6 eggs.

ORANGE SPONGE CAKE
Follow the preceding rule for:
    Economy Sponge Cake
Substitute for ¼ cupful water:
    2 tablespoons water
    2 tablespoons orange juice
Substitute for the lemon rind or vanilla:
    1 tablespoon grated orange rind

COFFEE SPONGE CAKE
Follow the rule for:
    Economy Sponge Cake or
    Sponge Cake De Luxe
Substitute for the water:
    Strong coffee
Omit the lemon rind and juice.

YELLOW ANGEL CAKE OR SPONGE CAKE
This makes a large, melting superb cake. Be sure that the cream of tartar is fresh.
Sift before measuring:
    1½ cups cake flour
Resift it 5 times with:
    1 cup sugar
    ½ teaspoon any baking powder
    ¼ teaspoon salt
Beat until light and lemon colored:
    5 egg yolks
Beat in gradually:
    ½ cup sugar

Combine:
>   1 tablespoon lemon juice
>   ½ cup cold water

Stir in the flour mixture in about 3 parts alternately with thirds of the liquid ingredients. Beat until foamy:
>   5 egg whites

Add:
>   ¾ teaspoon cream of tartar

Beat until the egg whites are stiff but not dry. Fold them into the flour mixture. Bake the cake in a 10 inch tube pan in a moderate oven 325° from 50 to 60 minutes.

One teaspoonful grated lemon rind may be added or all lemon flavoring may be omitted. In that case, substitute 1½ teaspoonfuls vanilla or the popular and delicious 4 drops anise oil.

SPONGE CAKE MADE WITH YOLKS

A quick little cake, good for strawberry shortcake, layer or loaf cake. Beat until light:
>   3 egg yolks

Sift twice, then beat in gradually:
>   ½ cup sugar
>   ⅛ teaspoon salt

Add:
>   ¼ cup boiling water

Sift before measuring:
>   ¾ cup cake flour

Resift with:
>   2 teaspoons any baking powder

Add the sifted ingredients to the sugar mixture. Beat the batter until it is smooth. Add:
>   1 teaspon vanilla
>   (½ teaspoon grated lemon or orange rind)

Bake the cake in an 8 inch layer pan or in a small loaf or tube pan in a moderate oven 350° for about 30 minutes. Spread the layers with:
>   Jelly, stewed fruit or a
>   Cake Filling, page 705

QUEEN MARY'S SPONGE CAKE

When King George was sick, his wife, who is reputed to have that inborn thing, "a light hand with pastry," bought a book of Marie Corelli's and baked a sponge cake for him. Her cake contains neither baking powder nor cream of tartar, but depends for its lightness upon the air that is first beaten and then folded into it. This recipe makes a large, delicate, fine-grained cake, which, if somewhat un-interesting, makes up for that by being highly digestible.

Sift:
>   1 cup sugar

Grate onto the sugar, then stir in:
>   Rind of 1 lemon

Beat until very light:
>   6 egg yolks

Add the sugar gradually, beating constantly. Add:
>   3 tablespoons lemon juice or 1
>   teaspoon vanilla and 1 teaspoon
>   water

Beat these ingredients until they are blended. Whip until stiff but not dry:
>   6 egg whites
>   ¼ teaspoon salt

Fold them lightly into the yolk mixture until they are partly blended. Sift:
>   1 cup cake flour

Fold the flour into the cake batter 1 tablespoonful at a time. When it is blended pour the cake batter into an ungreased 9 inch tube pan. Bake the cake in a slow oven 325° for about 1 hour.

RICE FLOUR SPONGE CAKE

Sift:
>   ½ cup rice flour
>   ½ cup sugar

Beat until light:
>   4 egg yolks
>   ½ teaspoon vanilla

Fold in the sifted ingredients. Whip until stiff but not dry:
>   4 egg whites
>   ⅛ teaspoon salt

Fold them into the yolk mixture. Pour the batter into a greased 7 inch tube pan. Bake the cake in a slow oven 300° for about 20 minutes, or until done. Permit it to cool in the pan.

POTATO FLOUR SPONGE CAKE

Beat until light:
>   4 egg yolks
>   ½ teaspoon vanilla

Add and beat:
>   6 tablespoons potato flour
>   ¼ cup sugar

Beat until stiff but not dry:
>   4 egg whites
>   ⅛ teaspoon salt

Beat in gradually:
>   6 tablespoons sugar

Fold the egg whites into the yolk mixture. Pour the batter into a greased 7 inch tube pan sprinkled with sugar. Bake the cake in a slow oven 300° for about 45 minutes. Permit it to cool in the pan.

HOT MILK SPONGE CAKE
Follow the rule on page 605 for:
Hot Milk Cake
Omit the butter. Bake the cake in an ungreased 9 inch tube pan in a moderate oven 325° for about 1 hour.
Ice it with:
Lemon Icing, page 703

Chocolate Sponge Cake, page 608.

FILLED SPONGE CAKES
There are various suggestions for Filled and Iced Angel Cake on page 646. Sponge cake may be substituted.

SUNSHINE CAKE
Sift 4 times:
1 cup sugar
Into a separate bowl sift before measuring, then measure and resift 3 times:
1 cup cake flour
Beat until light and lemon colored:
7 egg yolks
Beat the sugar in gradually.
Whip until foamy:
7 egg whites
Add:
½ teaspoon cream of tartar
¼ teaspoon salt
Whip the egg whites until they are stiff but not dry. Add:
1 teaspoon vanilla
Fold in the yolk mixture lightly. Fold in the flour, 2 tablespoonfuls at a time. Bake the cake in an ungreased 9 inch tube pan in a slow oven 325° for about 1 hour.

IMPERIAL SUNSHINE CAKE
Sift before measuring:
⅞ cup cake flour—1 cup less 2 tablespoons
Resift with:
½ teaspoon cream of tartar
Boil to the soft ball stage 240° (see rule for White Icing, page 693):
⅓ cup water
1¼ cups sugar
Whip until stiff but not dry:
5 egg whites
¼ teaspoon salt
Pour the sirup over them in a fine stream. Beat constantly until the mixture is cool. Add:
1 teaspoon vanilla
Beat well and fold in:
5 egg yolks

Fold in the sifted flour 1 tablespoonful at a time. Bake the cake in an ungreased 9 inch tube pan in a moderate oven 350° for 30 minutes. Reduce the heat to 325° and bake it about 20 minutes longer.

Graham Cracker Sponge Cake, page 642.
The batter may be baked in a loaf pan.
Ice the cake with:
Chocolate Icing, page 699

RULE FOR ANGEL FOOD CAKES
It seems to be the desire of every novice to bake a perfect angel cake. Fortunately, the accomplishment of this desire is entirely within reach, although the goal may be attained by various ways. Use a finely granulated sugar. Use fresh cream of tartar. Egg whites that have been kept for some time do not make as delicate a cake as freshly separated egg whites. Chilled eggs separate easily. Egg whites at room temperature whip easily. Whip the egg whites on a platter. Use a wire egg beater. Keep the egg beater below the surface while beating. This makes the cake light. Whip the egg whites until they are stiff but not dry. Stop when they barely will hold a point that curls over and are still moist and foamy. Combine the cake as directed in the following recipes. If you bake your cake in a pan which has been greased previously for other use, be sure every vestige of grease is removed before filling it with the batter.
Bake it in a moderate to slow oven—see Angel Cakes I and II. Or bake it by a new and very good method. Heat the oven to 425°. Place the cake in it and bake it for 30 minutes. The high temperature will crack the top of the cake. This is of no consequence, as the cake will be inverted when it is done. The texture of an angel cake baked in this way is wonderful.
Invert all angel cakes when taken from the oven. Remove them from the pan 1½ hours later. The following cakes differ both in proportions and in the manner of combining the ingredients. The first is light; the second is so light it seems to melt away.
Serve the cakes dusted with:
Powdered sugar
Or spread with any desired:
Icing
Do not cut a fresh angel or sponge

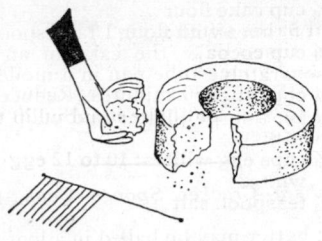

cake with a knife. Use a cake cutter or pull the cake lightly apart with 2 forks, as shown above.

Filled Angel Cake, page 646; Filled Cup Cakes, page 647; Angel Cake Bars or Balls, page 666.

ANGEL CAKE I
Sift twice:
   1½ cups sugar
Sift separately before measuring:
   1 cup cake flour
Resift the flour 3 times with ½ cupful of the sifted sugar and:
   ½ teaspoon salt
Whip on a platter until foamy:
   1¼ cups egg whites: 10 egg whites
      (2 tablespoons water or 1 table-
      spoon water and 1 tablespoon
      lemon juice)
Add:
   1 teaspoon cream of tartar
Whip the egg whites until stiff but not dry. Gradually whip in, about 1 teaspoonful at a time, 1 cupful of the sifted sugar. Fold in:
   ½ teaspoon vanilla
   ½ teaspoon almond extract
Sift about ¼ cupful of the sugar and flour mixture over the batter. Fold it in gently and briefly with a rubber scraper. Continue to do this until all the mixture is used. Pour the batter into an ungreased 9 inch tube pan. Run a knife through the batter in widening circles to break up the air bubbles. Bake the cake in a moderate oven 375° for 15 minutes. Reduce the heat to 250° and bake it until done, for about ½ hour in all.
See preceding rule for Angel Cakes.
A good angel cake may be made by this rule using:
   1¼ cups sugar
   1 cup egg whites

RULE FOR MIXING ANGEL CAKE WITH AN ELECTRIC MIXER
Beat egg whites and salt in the large bowl at high speed until frothy, about 1 minute. Add cream of tartar. Beat 3 minutes; add lemon juice or water. Continue beating at high speed until whites will stand in peaks, about 3 to 4 minutes. Turn mixer to low speed; add sugar gradually and flavoring. Beat about ½ minute longer. Sift flour twice and fold in by hand.

ANGEL CAKE II
Part I
Combine and set aside:
   1½ cups egg whites
   2½ tablespoons cold water
   1½ teaspoons cream of tartar
   1 scant teaspoon vanilla
   1 teaspoon almond extract
   ½ teaspoon salt
Part II
Sift, then measure:
   1 cup cake flour
Add and resift 6 times:
   ½ cup sugar or confectioners'
      sugar
Beat Part I by hand or with an electric mixer until well blended. Then beat with an egg beater until stiff but not dry. Stop beating while the mixture is still glossy. Fold in, about 2 table-spoonfuls at a time:
   1 cup sifted sugar
Fold in Part II lightly with a rubber scraper, a little at a time. You may then fold in:
   1 cup chopped black walnut
      meats or ¾ cup blanched
      thinly sliced toasted almonds
Bake the batter in an ungreased 10 inch tube pan. Run a knife through the batter in widening circles to break up the air bubbles. Bake the cake in a moderate oven 375° for ¼ hour. Reduce the heat to a slow oven 250° and bake it about 15 minutes longer, or until done. Invert the cake until it is cold. Remove it from the pan and ice it as desired.

SPICED ANGEL CAKE
Add to the flour for Angel Cake:
   1 teaspoon cinnamon
   ½ teaspoon nutmeg
   ¼ teaspoon cloves

NUT ANGEL CAKE
Fold into the batter for Angel Cake I:
   ¾ cup finely chopped nut meats

Yellow Angel Cake or Sponge Cake, page 596.

DAFFODIL CAKE

A marble cake effect of Angel Food and Orange Sponge Cake that is delicious. Sift before measuring:

1⅛ cups cake flour—1 cup and 2 tablespoons

Resift it twice. Sift separately:

1¼ cups sugar

Whip on a platter until frothy:

10 egg whites

Add:

½ teaspoon salt
1 teaspoon cream of tartar

Whip until they hold a point. Fold the sifted sugar in gradually. Separate the mixture into halves. Fold into one half a little at a time ¾ cupful of the sifted flour and:

6 beaten egg yolks
Grated rind of 1 orange

Fold into the other half a little at a time ½ cupful of the sifted flour and:

1 teaspoon vanilla

Place the batters, a cupful or more at a time, in an ungreased 9 inch tube pan, alternating the colors. Bake the cake in a slow oven 250° for 30 minutes. Increase the heat to 325° and bake it for about 20 minutes longer.

Filled Daffodil Cake, page 646.

CHOCOLATE ANGEL OR FEATHER CAKE

This is incredibly delicate.
Sift before measuring:

¾ cup cake flour

Resift 5 times with:

¼ cup cocoa

Sift separately:

1¼ cups sugar

Place on a large platter and whip until foamy:

1¼ cups egg whites: 10 to 12 egg whites
¼ teaspoon salt

Add:

1 teaspoon cream of tartar

Whip them until they are stiff but not dry. Fold in the sifted sugar, 1 tablespoonful at a time. Add:

1 teaspoon vanilla
½ teaspoon lemon extract

Sift a small amount of the flour mixture over the batter and fold it in. Repeat this process until the flour is used. Bake the cake in an ungreased 9 inch tube pan in a slow oven 275° for 30 minutes. Increase the heat to a moderate oven 325° and bake it 30 minutes longer. When it is cool cover the cake with:

White Icing, page 694, and Chocolate Coating, page 695, or with Cocoa Coffee Icing, page 703

MARBLE ANGEL CAKE

Prepare:

Angel Cake I or II, page 599

Prepare the preceding:

Chocolate Angel Cake

Alternate the batters in 2 ungreased 9 inch tube pans. Bake the cake by any rule for Angel Cake.

Butter Cakes

WHITE CAKE

Method I.

This cake is usually made in layers and iced with a nut, raisin or other icing. It is the batter for the famous Lady Baltimore Cake, page 641. White Cake II calls for less butter and fewer eggs. It is more economical than White Cake I and a third smaller. Both cakes are superlative.
Sift:

2 cups sugar

Beat until soft:

1 cup butter

Add the sifted sugar gradually. Blend these ingredients until they are very light and creamy. Sift before measuring:

3½ cups cake flour

Resift it twice with:

5 teaspoons tartrate or phosphate baking powder or 4 teaspoons combination type (see Baking Powder, page 501)
½ teaspoon salt

Add these ingredients in 3 parts to the butter mixture alternately with thirds of:

1 cup milk

Beat the batter until it is smooth after each addition. Beat in:

1 teaspoon vanilla
(¼ teaspoon almond extract)

Whip until stiff but not dry:

7 or 8 egg whites
⅛ teaspoon salt

Fold them lightly into the cake batter. Bake the cake in a greased 9 x 13 inch pan in a moderate oven 350° for about 40 minutes, or in 3 greased 8 inch layer pans in a moderate oven 375° for about 25 minutes. Spread the cake with:

Icing, page 693

Method II.
Please read the comment under Method I.
Sift:

1¼ cups sugar

Beat until soft:

½ cup butter

Add the sugar gradually. Blend these ingredients until they are very light and creamy. Sift before measuring:

2¼ cups cake flour

Resift twice with:

> 3 teaspoons tartrate or phosphate baking powder or 2½ teaspoons combination type (see Baking Powder, page 501)
> ¼ teaspoon salt

Add these ingredients in 3 parts to the butter mixture alternately with thirds of:

1 cup milk

Add:

> 1 teaspoon vanilla or ½ teaspoon vanilla and ¼ teaspoon almond extract

Whip until stiff but not dry:

4 egg whites
⅛ teaspoon salt

Fold them lightly into the cake batter. This batter may be baked in a 9 inch tube pan, or in two 9 inch layer pans or in a 9 x 13 inch cake pan. It is fine baked in the latter, iced with any thick icing, decorated with nut meats and cut into cubes. Place the pans in a moderate oven 350°. Allow about 1 hour for a loaf cake and ½ hour or more for a flat cake.

I use this rule frequently to make a Marble Cake, page 603. Sometimes I bake 1 white and 1 dark layer and use a Chocolate Icing. There are not even crumbs left to mark its passing.

Rule for Mixing Butter Cakes with an Electric Mixer, page 596.

CAKE FOR A LAMB MOLD
Children love this cake.

The metal mold, in which this cake is baked in the shape of a lamb, is made in 2 parts. The lamb is covered with white icing and sprinkled generously with grated coconut. A blue ribbon with a little bell or a garland of decorative icing roses is placed around the lamb's neck, a redhot or colored icing forms its lips, and raisins or chocolate chips are used for its eyes.

The 2 halves of a standard mold hold in all 7 cupfuls of water. This rule will fill the front half. The heat will cause the cake to rise and fill the second half.

Cream until fluffy:

1 cup sugar
5 tablespoons butter

Sift before measuring:

2½ cups plus 2 tablespoons cake flour

Resift with:

> 2½ teaspoons tartrate or phosphate baking powder or 2 teaspoons combination type (see Baking Powder, page 501)

Combine:

⅔ cup milk
1 teaspoon vanilla

Add the sifted ingredients to the butter mixture in about 3 parts alternately with thirds of the liquids. Beat the batter after each addition until it is blended.

Whip until stiff but not dry:

2 large egg whites
¼ teaspoon salt

Fold the egg whites into the batter. Have ready a well greased or oiled lamb mold. To do this use a pastry brush and be rather lavish about it. Place the batter in the front half, cover it with the second half. Bake the cake in a moderate oven 350° for about 1 hour.

Do not be at all alarmed if when you take the cake from the mold the lamb promptly loses its head. It probably will. If you lift off the top mold and let the cake cool first this danger may be averted. If the head does break off, stick it on with some icing, using a few toothpicks as armatures.

Prepare:
White Icing, page 694, or Seven Minute Icing, page 700
This makes a light coat. Increase the proportions by ½ for a heavier coating of wool.
Spread the icing. Press into it lightly:
¼ to ½ lb. grated coconut
If the tail is lost to sight, make a new one with additional icing. Bed the lamb on ferns or shredded green paper and place a few small flowers about it. One newlywed had to call upon all the inhabitants of her apartment house to assist in the "accouchement" of her first lamb. The neighbor who produced an old-fashioned hatpin to keep the head from toppling until the icing hardened was voted the heroine of the hour. At that, the ungrateful husband said the joint work of art looked "like an unknown grave in winter," but even he had to admit that a second attempt was a triumph.

Rabbit molds of the same capacity are also available and the use of coconut, which is optional, gives an angora effect.

QUICK WHITE CAKE
A great deal can be said for this little cake. It is easily made, remains moist a long time and calls for only 2 egg whites.
Sift before measuring:
2 cups cake flour
Resift 3 times with:
2 teaspoons any baking powder
1 cup sugar
Blend in:
4 tablespoons soft butter
Whip until stiff, then fold in:
2 egg whites
¼ teaspoon salt
Combine:
¾ cup milk
¼ teaspoon almond extract
½ teaspoon vanilla
Add the liquids to the other ingredients. Stir them until the flour is dampened, then beat them vigorously for 1 minute. Bake the cake in 2 greased 8 inch layer pans in a moderate oven 375° for about 25 minutes, or in a 9 x 4 inch bread pan for a somewhat longer time. Spread the cake with:
Chocolate Icing, page 699
Use only ½ the amount of ingredients given. Or spread between the layers:
Lemon Filling, page 708
This is fine as a complete dessert. Try

icing the cake with White Icing, page 694, or serve it uniced with Foamy Sauce, page 754.

WHIPPED CREAM CAKE
Here is something delicious. This recipe makes good cup cakes served with hot sauce and ice cream. See page 647.
Sift before measuring:
2 cups cake flour
Resift twice with:
1⅓ cups sugar
3½ teaspoons tartrate or phosphate baking powder or 2¾ teaspoons combination type (see Baking Powder, page 501)
¾ teaspoon salt
Whip until stiff:
1 cup heavy cream
Whip until stiff but not dry:
3 egg whites
¼ teaspoon salt
Combine the cream and the egg whites. Fold in:
½ cup water
1½ teaspoons vanilla or almond flavoring
Fold the sifted ingredients into the whipped cream mixture about ⅓ at a time. Bake the cake in two 9 inch layer pans in a moderate oven 350° for about 25 to 30 minutes. Spread it with any good:
Icing, page 693

Sweet or Sour Cream Cake, page 606.

LADY CAKE
The following recipe is a good tube pan cake or loaf cake. It tastes and looks like a traditional wedding cake, that is, traditional since fruit cake fell from grace.
Sift:
1 cup sugar
Beat until soft:
¾ cup butter
Add the sugar gradually. Blend these ingredients until they are very light and creamy. Sift before measuring:
1¾ cups cake flour
Resift twice with:
2 teaspoons any baking powder
Add these ingredients in 3 parts to the butter mixture alternately with thirds of:
½ cup milk
Beat the batter for a few minutes after each addition. Beat in:
1 teaspoon almond extract
Grated rind of 1 lemon

Whip until stiff but not dry:
    3 egg whites
    ¼ teaspoon salt
Fold them lightly into the cake batter. Bake the cake in a greased 9 inch tube pan in a moderate oven 350° for about 45 minutes. Sprinkle it with:
    Powdered sugar
or spread it with:
    White Icing, page 694

MOCK POUND CAKE
The following recipe calls for milk, so it is not the "genuine article," but it is mighty fine cake.
Follow the rule for:
    White Cake I, page 600
Use only:
    6 egg whites or 4 eggs separated
If you use whole eggs beat the yolks into the butter mixture.
Flavor the cake as directed. The old recipes add:
    1 teaspoon lemon juice
    6 drops rose water or 1 or more tablespoons brandy
    1 cup chopped nut meats

Bake the cake in a greased tube pan in a moderate oven for about 1 hour.

MARBLE CAKE
This old-fashioned cake is still a favorite when served, but one seldom encounters it.
Prepare:
    White Cake II, page 601
Before whipping the egg whites separate the batter into 2 parts. Add to ½ the batter:
    1½ oz. melted cooled chocolate
    1 teaspoon cinnamon
    ¼ teaspoon cloves
    ⅛ teaspoon soda
Whip the egg whites as directed and fold ½ into the light and ½ into the dark batter. Grease a 9 inch tube pan. Place large spoonfuls of batter in it, alternating the light and the dark dough. Bake the cake for about 1 hour in a moderate oven 350°. Sprinkle it with:
    Confectioners' sugar
or spread it with:
    Lemon Icing, page 703,
    White Icing, page 694, etc.

Yellow Cakes

ONE EGG LOAF OR LAYER CAKE
Sift:
    1 cup sugar
Beat until soft:
    ¼ cup butter
Add the sugar gradually. Blend these ingredients until they are very light and creamy. Beat in:
    1 egg yolk
Sift before measuring:
    2 cups cake flour or 1¾ cups all-purpose flour
Resift with:
    3 teaspoons tartrate or phosphate baking powder or 2 teaspoons combination type (see Baking Powder, page 501)
    ½ teaspoon salt
Add these ingredients in 3 parts to the butter mixture alternately with thirds of:
    ¾ cup milk
Beat the batter for several seconds after each addition. Beat in:
    1 teaspoon vanilla
    ⅓ teaspoon almond extract
    ¼ cup chopped nut meats
Whip until stiff but not dry:
    1 egg white

Fold it lightly into the cake batter Bake the cake in a greased 4 x 8 inch loaf pan in a moderate oven 350° for about 30 minutes, or in 2 greased 8 inch layer pans at 375° for about 25 minutes.

TWO EGG YELLOW CAKE
Follow the rule on page 607 for:
    Hurry-Up Cake

GOLD LAYER CAKE WITH THREE EGG YOLKS
One of the best layer cakes. Sift:
    1 cup sugar
Beat until soft:
    ½ cup butter
Add the sugar gradually. Blend these ingredients until they are creamy. Beat in:
    3 well-beaten egg yolks
Add:
    1 teaspoon vanilla or 1 teaspoon grated lemon rind
Sift before measuring:
    2 cups cake flour
Resift with:
    3 teaspoons tartrate or phosphate baking powder or 2 teaspoons

combination type (see Baking Powder, page 501)
¼ teaspoon salt

Add the sifted ingredients to the butter mixture in 3 parts with thirds of:

¾ cup milk

Beat the batter until it is smooth after each addition. Bake it in 2 greased 8 inch layer pans in a moderate oven 375° for about ½ hour. Spread the layers with:

Lemon, page 703, or other icing

or spread between the layers:

Lemon Filling, page 708

This cake is delicious filled with a layer of good raspberry jam. Dust the top with:

Powdered sugar

GOLD LOAF SPICE CAKE

Follow the above rule for:

Gold Layer Cake

Add to the dry ingredients before sifting:

½ teaspoon freshly grated nutmeg
1 teaspoon cinnamon
¼ teaspoon cloves

Bake the cake in a lightly greased tube pan in a moderate oven 375° for about 45 minutes, or until done.

THREE EGG YELLOW CAKE

Follow the rule on page 605 for:

Hot Milk Cake

FOUR EGG YELLOW LOAF OR LAYER CAKE

The old time One-Two-Three-Four Cake slightly modernized.
Sift:

2 cups sugar

Beat until soft:

1 cup butter

Add the sugar gradually. Blend these ingredients until they are very light and creamy. Beat in one at a time:

4 egg yolks

Add:

1½ teaspoons vanilla or 1 teaspoon vanilla and ½ teaspoon almond extract

Sift before measuring:

2⅔ cups cake flour

Resift with:

2 teaspoons tartrate or phosphate baking powder or 1½ teaspoons combination type (see Baking Powder, page 501)
½ teaspoon salt

Add the sifted ingredients to the butter mixture in about 3 parts alternately with thirds of:

1 cup milk

Beat the batter until it is smooth after each addition.

Whip until stiff but not dry:

4 egg whites
¼ teaspoon salt

Fold them lightly into the batter. Bake the cake in an 8 x 12 inch pan lined with greased waxed paper in a moderate oven 350° for about 45 minutes, or in 3 greased 9 inch layer pans from 30 to 35 minutes. Spread the layers with:

Pineapple or other cake filling, page 705

Spread the top with:

White or some other icing, page 694

NUT LOAF CAKE

Follow the preceding rule for:

Four Egg Yellow Loaf or Layer Cake

Add to the batter before folding in the egg whites:

1 cup chopped nut meats
¼ teaspoon salt

Bake the cake in a greased 8½ inch tube pan in a moderate oven 350° for about 1 hour. Sprinkle it with:

Confectioners' sugar

or ice it with:

Caramel Icing, page 698

COCONUT LOAF OR LAYER CAKE

Follow the preceding rule for:

Four Egg Yellow Loaf or Layer Cake

Add to the batter before folding in the egg whites:

¾ cup shredded coconut
1½ teaspoons grated lemon rind
¼ teaspon salt

Bake the batter in a greased 8½ inch tube pan in a moderate oven 350° for about 1 hour.

GOLD LOAF OR LAYER CAKE WITH EGG YOLKS

This recipe calls for 8 egg yolks. The cake, I find, is a great favorite.
Sift:

1¼ cups sugar

Beat until soft:

¾ cup butter

Add the sugar gradually. Blend these ingredients until they are very light and creamy. In a separate bowl beat until light and lemon colored:

8 egg yolks

Beat them into the butter mixture. Sift before measuring:

2½ cups cake flour

Resift 3 times with:

3 teaspoons tartrate or phosphate baking powder or 2⅓ teaspoons combination type (see Baking Powder, page 501)
¼ teaspoon salt

Add the sifted ingredients to the butter mixture in 3 parts alternately with thirds of:

¾ cup milk

Beat the batter thoroughly after each addition. Add and beat for 2 minutes:

1 teaspoon vanilla
1 teaspoon lemon juice or grated lemon rind

Bake the cake in a greased 9 inch tube pan in a moderate oven 350° for about 45 minutes, or in 3 greased 9 inch layer pans in a moderate oven 375° for about 20 minutes. Sprinkle it with:

Powdered sugar

or spread it with:

Uncooked Orange Icing, page 702 or with one of the Seven Minute Icings, page 700

RULE FOR MIXING GOLD LOAF CAKE WITH AN ELECTRIC MIXER

Have all ingredients at room temperature. The butter should be soft but not melted unless the recipe calls for melted butter. Beat it at high speed for 1 minute. Scrape the sides of the bowl. Continue to beat at high speed. Add the egg yolks, unbeaten, 1 at a time. Add the sugar gradually. Scrape the sides of the bowl. Continue to beat for 1 minute. Turn to low speed. Add the sifted ingredients in about 3 parts alternately with thirds of the liquid. Do this quickly. These ingredients may be stirred with a spoon until blended only. It is unwise to beat or stir a cake unnecessarily after adding the sifted ingredients. Overbeating results in close, tough cake. Scrape the sides of the bowl. Beat in the scrapings until blended only.

HOT MILK LOAF OR LAYER CAKE

A light, fine-grained cake easily made. This rule makes good cup cakes.

Sift:

1½ cups sugar

Beat until very light:

3 eggs

Add the sugar very slowly, beating constantly. Beat for 5 minutes by hand, 2½ with a mixer. Sift before measuring:

1½ cups cake flour

Resift with:

1½ teaspoons tartrate or phosphate baking powder or 1 teaspoon combination type (see Baking Powder, page 501)
½ teaspoon salt

Fold these ingredients quickly and briefly, all at one time, into the egg mixture. Combine and heat but do not boil:

¾ cup milk
1½ tablespoons butter

Add these ingredients all at one time. Fold them in quickly and briefly. Add:

1 teaspoon vanilla or
½ teaspoon grated lemon rind

Bake the batter in a greased 8 x 8 inch cake pan, in two 8 inch layer pans or in muffin tins. The oven may vary from 350° to 375°. Use the hotter oven for the small cakes. Time about 35 minutes for layer cake, about 25 minutes for cup cakes.

COFFEE-FLAVORED LOAF OR LAYER CAKE

Follow the preceding rule for:

Hot Milk Cake

Substitute for an equal amount of milk:

¼ to ½ cup very strong coffee

BLITZKUCHEN OR LIGHTNING CAKE

A delicious tea cake and a good accompaniment to a heavy dessert. It should be about ⅓ inch high and closely covered with sugar and cinnamon.

Sift:

1 cup powdered or granulated sugar

Beat until light:

½ cup butter

Add the sugar gradually. Blend these ingredients until they are very light and creamy. Stir in:

4 well-beaten egg yolks

Add:

½ teaspoon vanilla or 1 teaspoon grated lemon rind

Sift before measuring:

1⅛ cups cake flour
Resift with:
    1 teaspoon any baking powder
Beat the sifted ingredients gradually
into the butter mixture. Add:
    (3 tablespoons milk)
Whip until stiff but not dry:
    4 egg whites
    ¼ teaspoon salt
Fold them lightly into the batter mixture. Place the batter in 2 greased
8 x 12 inch pans. Spread it with:
    (1 egg white diluted with 1 tablespoon water)
Sprinkle the top with:
    ¾ cup sugar
    2 tablespoons cinnamon
    ½ cup blanched shredded almonds
    or other chopped nut meats
Bake the cake in a moderate oven 375°
for about 20 minutes. Cut it into diamond shaped pieces. It may be served
hot or cold.

Blitztorte, page 656.

SWEET OR SOUR CREAM CAKE

Beat until light and lemon colored:
    2 eggs
Sift, then beat in gradually:
    1 cup sugar
Add:
    1 teaspoon vanilla
Sift before measuring:
    1⅔ cups cake flour
Resift with:
    2½ teaspoons tartrate or phosphate
    baking powder or 2 teaspoons
    combination type (see Baking
    Powder, page 501)
    ¼ teaspoon soda if sour cream is
    used
    ¾ teaspoon salt
Add these ingredients to the egg mixture in about 3 parts alternately with
thirds of:
    1 cup rich sweet or sour cream
Beat after each addition until the batter is smooth. Bake the cake in 2
greased 8 inch layer pans, or in a
greased 8 inch tube pan in a moderate
oven 350°. Allow about 25 minutes
for the layers and about 45 minutes
for the loaf cake.

SWEET OR SOUR CREAM SPICE CAKE

Follow the preceding rule for:
    Sweet or Sour Cream Cake
Add to the flour before resifting:

½ teaspoon nutmeg
1 teaspoon cinnamon
Fold into the batter:
    1 cup raisins
    ½ cup broken nut meats

Mock Pound Cake, page 603.

POUND CAKE

This contribution, gratefully acknowledged, comes from an unknown Seattle
friend whose family has used this rule
for many years. She writes: "I use an
electric mixer so creaming is easy."
Cream thoroughly:
    2 cups butter, no substitutes
When you think you have creamed it
enough cream some more. Slowly
"dribble in":
    2 cups sugar
beating and creaming well. Cream for
quite a while after the sugar is added.
Beat in one at a time:
    9 eggs
Beat the batter well after each addition. Add:
    1 teaspoon vanilla
    ½ teaspoon mace
You may add:
    (2 tablespoons brandy or 8 drops
    rose water)
Sift before measuring:
    4 cups cake flour
Resift with:
    ½ teaspoon cream of tartar
    ½ teaspoon salt
"Dribble in" the sifted ingredients
slowly, at lowest speed, mixing until
thoroughly blended only. Pour the
batter into 2 greased 9 x 5 inch loaf
pans lined with heavy waxed paper.

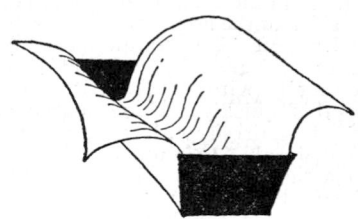

Allow the paper to project as shown
for easy removals. Bake the cake in a
slow oven 325° for about 1 hour.
Sometimes I add to ½ the mixture ½
cupful each of candied cherries, pineapple, citron and white raisins and
have a delicious fruit cake.

ENGLISH CURRANT CAKE

This old-fashioned cake keeps fresh for a long time. Its fragrance is a reminder of the period when rose jars were in vogue.
Follow the preceding rule for:
Pound Cake
Use only ½ the amount of ingredients and 4 eggs in all. Stir in:
1 lb. washed dried currants: 3 cups
Bake the cake in a greased 9 inch tube pan lined with heavy waxed paper in a moderate oven 325° for 1 hour or more.

SAND TORTE

This is a German stand-by that seems to keep indefinitely in tin. It has a fine grainy quality from which it derives its name.
Sift:
1 cup sugar
Grate into it:
Rind of 1 lemon
Beat until soft:
1 cup butter
Add the sugar gradually. Cream these ingredients until they are light and fluffy. Beat well, then beat in:
6 egg yolks
Add:
1½ tablespoons lemon juice or
2 tablespoons brandy or rum
Sift before measuring:
1 cup all-purpose flour
1 cup cornstarch
Resift with:
2 teaspoons tartrate or phosphate baking powder or 1¾ teaspoon combination type (see Baking Powder, page 501)
½ teaspoon salt
Stir the sifted ingredients into the butter mixture. This batter is stirred and stirred. Whip until stiff but not dry:
6 egg whites
Fold them into the batter. Bake the cake in a greased 9 inch tube pan in a moderate oven 350° for about 45 minutes.

HURRY-UP CAKE

The name of this cake speaks for itself. It is surprisingly good. It is best as a flat cake, iced and cut into cubes, or as a layer cake.
Three fine variations of this cake are noted below.
Be sure to have all ingredients at room temperature. Sift before measuring:
1¾ cups cake flour
Resift with:
1 cup sugar
Add:
½ cup soft butter
2 eggs
½ cup milk
½ teaspoon salt
2¼ teaspoons tartrate or phosphate baking powder or 1¾ teaspoons combination type (see Baking Powder, page 501)
1 teaspoon vanilla
Beat these ingredients vigorously with a wire whisk or a rotary beater for 2 or 3 minutes. Bake the cake in a greased 9 x 13 inch pan lined with greased waxed paper, or in two 8 inch layer pans in a moderate oven 350° for about ½ hour. Spread it with:
Chocolate Butter Icing, page 703, or Lemon Icing, page 703

VARIATION I. QUICK SPICE CAKE

Add:
1 teaspoon cinnamon
½ teaspoon cloves
When done, dust the cake with:
Confectioners' sugar

VARIATION II. QUICK CHOCOLATE CAKE

Deduct:
4 tablespoons flour
Add:
4 tablespoons cocoa
Ice the cake with:
Chocolate Icing, page 699

One Bowl Cakes, page 620.

Caramel Cakes

VARIATION III. QUICK CARAMEL CAKE

Follow the above rule for:
Hurry-Up Cake
Substitute for the white sugar:
1 cup firmly packed medium brown sugar

You may add to the batter:
¾ cup nut meats
¾ cup chopped dates
Spread the cake with:
Caramel Icing, page 698
Decorate it with:
(Nut meats)

The addition of the dates and nut meats calls for three 8 inch cake pans or 2 somewhat larger pans. If served at tea, it is easier to handle baked in a 9 x 12 inch pan lined with greased waxed paper. Ice the cake. Cut it into squares. Decorate each square with a nut meat.

CARAMEL CAKE

A fine-grained, delicate cake. Sift:

2 cups brown sugar

Beat until soft:

½ cup butter

Add the sugar gradually. Beat these ingredients until they are very light and creamy. Beat in one at a time:

4 egg yolks

Sift before measuring:

1½ cups cake flour

Resift with:

1 teaspoon any baking powder

Beat these ingredients into the butter mixture in 3 parts alternately with thirds of:

¼ cup milk

Add:

2 teaspoons vanilla
(1 cup chopped nut meats)

Whip until stiff but not dry:

4 egg whites
½ teaspoon salt

Fold them lightly into the cake batter. Bake the cake in 2 greased 8 inch layer pans in a moderate oven 375° for about 20 minutes. Spread it with:

White Icing, page 694, or
Caramel Icing, page 698

Add to the icing:

(¼ cup or more chopped nut meats)

Caramel Banana Cake, page 643.

BURNT SUGAR CAKE

This cake is made with a burnt sugar sirup. A handsome and luscious creation.

Sirup

Stir and melt in a skillet, then permit to burn until black:

½ cup sugar

Stir in slowly:

½ cup boiling water

Boil the sirup until it is the consistency of molasses. Cool it.

Cake Batter

Sift:

1½ cups sugar

Beat until soft:

½ cup butter

Add the sugar gradually. Blend these ingredients until they are very light and creamy. Beat in one at a time:

2 egg yolks

Sift before measuring:

2½ cups cake flour

Resift with:

2½ teaspoons any baking powder
¼ teaspoon salt

Add these ingredients in 3 parts to the butter mixture alternately with thirds of:

1 cup water

Beat the batter after each addition until it is smooth. Stir in:

3 tablespoons burnt sugar sirup
1 teaspoon vanilla

Whip until stiff but not dry:

2 egg whites

Fold them lightly into the cake batter. Bake the cake in 2 greased 9 inch layer pans in a moderate oven 375° for about 25 minutes. Spread the cake with:

White Icing, page 694

When making the icing flavor it in addition to the vanilla with:

4 teaspoons burnt sugar sirup

Place any remaining sirup in a closed jar. It will keep indefinitely.

Chocolate Cakes

After entertaining, I often wonder whether it is worth while to bake anything but chocolate cake. What unusual quality gives this particular food such an overwhelming popularity? Undoubtedly, chocolate cake has "it."

The following recipes have been very carefully chosen. Each cake is distinctive in flavor and texture.

CHOCOLATE SPONGE CAKE

This is a fine, light chocolate cake. As it requires no butter, it is not rich and is therefore a good cake to bake for children. It gives a very generous return for the little it calls for.

Sift:

2 cups sugar

Melt over hot water:

3½ oz. chocolate

Add:

1 cup milk

and 1 cupful of the sifted sugar. Cook and stir the mixture until it is smooth. Beat until light:

 4 egg yolks

Add gradually the second cupful of sifted sugar. Beat until these ingredients are well blended. Stir in the hot chocolate mixture.

Sift before measuring:

 1¼ cups cake flour

Resift with:

 3 teaspoons tartrate or phosphate baking powder or 2½ teaspoons combination type (see Baking Powder, page 501)
 ¼ teaspoon salt

Add these ingredients to the batter with:

 ½ teaspoon vanilla

Stir them until they are well blended. Whip until stiff but not dry:

 4 egg whites

Fold them lightly into the batter. Bake the cake in an ungreased 9 inch tube pan, or in three 8 inch layer pans in a slow oven 325°. Allow about 50 minutes for a loaf and 20 to 25 minutes for layer cake. Permit the cake to become cold in the pan. Do not invert it. Ice it with:

 White Icing and Chocolate Coating, page 695, or Chocolate Icing, page 699

Chocolate Date Cake or Torte, page 647. A sponge cake much like the preceding one. It may be baked in a 9 inch tube pan as well as in layers. A marvelous cake. Thanks to the orange rind it tastes like curaçao.

CHOCOLATE CAKE

Known as "Rombauer Special." A delicious, light chocolate cake always in demand.

Melt over hot water:

 2 scant oz. chocolate

Add:

 5 tablespoons boiling water

Cool this mixture slightly. Sift:

 1½ cups sugar

Beat until soft:

 ½ cup butter

Add the sugar gradually. Blend these ingredients until they are very light and creamy. Beat in one at a time:

 4 egg yolks

Add the chocolate mixture. Sift before measuring:

 1¾ cups cake flour

Resift with:

 4 teaspoons tartrate or phosphate baking powder or 3 teaspoons combination type (see Baking Powder, page 501)
 ¼ teaspoon salt

Add these ingredients in 3 parts to the butter mixture alternately with thirds of:

 ½ cup milk

Beat the batter until it is smooth after each addition. Add:

 1 teaspoon vanilla

Whip until stiff but not dry:

 4 egg whites

Fold them lightly into the cake batter. Bake the cake in a greased 9 x 13 inch pan in a moderate oven 350° for about ½ hour. Spread the top with thick:

 White Icing, page 694, with Chocolate Coating, page 695, or Chocolate Peppermint Icing, page 695

BLACK WALNUT CHOCOLATE CAKE

Follow the preceding rule for:

 Chocolate Cake

Fold into the batter before the egg whites are added:

 1 cup coarsely chopped black walnut or other nut meats or ¾ cup grated coconut

TWO EGG CHOCOLATE NUT CAKE

This cake has a candy quality but more body than the following fudge cake.

Melt, then cool:

 2½ squares chocolate: 2½ oz.

Blend until creamy:

 ⅓ cup butter
 1 cup sugar

Beat in the cooled chocolate and:

 2 egg yolks
 1 teaspoon grated orange rind or vanilla

Sift before measuring:

 1½ cups cake flour

Resift with:

 2¼ teaspoons tartrate or phosphate baking powder or 1½ teaspoons combination type (see Baking Powder, page 501)
 ½ teaspoon salt

Combine:

 1 cup thin milk
 1 teaspoon vanilla

Add the sifted ingredients to the butter mixture in about 3 parts alternately

with the milk. After each addition, beat until blended only. Beat in:
(½ to ¾ cup broken nut meats)
Beat until stiff:
    2 egg whites
Add gradually, beating constantly:
    ½ cup sugar
Fold the batter gently into this meringue. Bake the cake in a 9 x 12 inch pan, or in 2 deep 8 inch layer pans lined with greased waxed paper in a moderate oven 350° for about ½ hour. When it is cool, ice it with:
    White or Chocolate Icing, pages 694, 699

ONE EGG FUDGE LOAF OR LAYER CAKE

Fudge Pie on page 583 is another version of Fudge Cake. Good, less rich than the preceding cake.
Sift, then measure:
    1¾ cups cake flour
Add, then sift 3 times:
    2¼ teaspoons phosphate or tartrate baking powder or 1¾ teaspoons combination type (see Baking Powder, page 501)
    ½ teaspoon salt
Beat until light and creamy:
    ½ cup butter
Add gradually, stirring constantly:
    1 cup sifted sugar
Cream these ingredients until they are fluffy. Beat in:
    1 egg
Melt, cool slightly, then beat in:
    2 oz. chocolate
Add the flour mixture in about 3 parts to the butter mixture alternately with:
    ¾ cup milk
Beat after each addition until the batter is blended. Beat in:
    1 teaspoon vanilla
Bake the cake in a greased 8 x 8 inch pan in a moderate oven 325° for about 45 minutes, or in two 8 inch layer pans in a 350° oven for about 25 minutes. Ice it as desired.

HALF-HOUR CHOCOLATE CAKE OR ECONOMY CHOCOLATE CAKE

It is claimed that the following cake can be prepared, baked and iced in ½ hour and the claim is justified.
Melt, then cool:
    2 oz. chocolate
Sift:
    1 cup sugar

Beat well:
    2 tablespoons soft butter
    1 egg
Add the sifted sugar gradually. Beat these ingredients well with a wire whisk. Sift before measuring:
    1 cup cake flour
Resift with:
    1 teaspoon any baking powder
    ¼ teaspoon salt
Combine:
    ¾ cup milk
    1 teaspoon vanilla
Add the sifted ingredients to the egg mixture in 3 parts alternately with thirds of the combined liquids. Beat the batter until it is smooth with a wire whisk after each addition. Add the cooled chocolate. Bake the cake in a greased 7 inch ring mold in a moderate oven 350° for about 25 minutes. Spread it while it is hot with:
    Chocolate Icing II, page 699
Make only ½ the amount given. This cake may be served uniced, the center filled with:
    Whipped cream, ice cream or Three Minute Icing, page 632
Or serve it with:
    Hot Chocolate Sauce, page 757

FUDGE CAKE

A flat, soft, rich cake. Good served any way. Fine cut into squares, topped with rum or orange-rind flavored whipped cream or ice cream.
Sift:
    1 cup sugar
Beat until soft:
    ½ cup butter
Add the sugar gradually. Blend these ingredients until they are creamy. Melt over hot water and add:
    2 oz. chocolate
Beat in one at a time:
    2 eggs
Add:
    1 teaspoon vanilla
Sift, then measure:
    ¾ cup all-purpose flour
Add the flour, beating until well blended only.
Fold in:
    1 cup coarsely chopped nut meats
Line with greased waxed paper an 8 x 8 inch pan or a 9 inch pan. Pour the batter into it. Bake the cake in a moderate oven 350° for about 30 minutes.

CHOCOLATE FEATHER CAKE

Neither rich nor sweet. A good tea cake, quickly made.
Cream until fluffy:
> 1/4 cup butter
> 1/2 cup sugar

Beat in:
> 1 egg

Melt, then cool and beat in:
> 1 oz. chocolate

Sift before measuring:
> 7/8 cup cake flour—1 cup less 2 tablespoons

Resift with:
> 2 1/2 teaspoons tartrate or phosphate baking powder or 2 teaspoons combination type (see Baking Powder, page 501)
> 1/4 teaspoon salt

Add the sifted ingredients to the batter in about 3 parts alternately with:
> 1/2 cup milk
> 3/4 teaspoon vanilla

Beat the batter until smooth after each addition. Bake the cake in a greased 8 x 8 inch pan in a moderate oven 350° for about 25 minutes. It is too light to ice well. You may dust it with:
> Confectioners' sugar

and stud it with:
> Nut meats

Serve it cut into squares.

CHOCOLATE DEVIL'S FOOD
Method I.
This good cake, made with cocoa and white sugar, keeps moist for a long time.
Part I
Combine and beat until well blended:
> 1 cup sugar
> 1/2 cup cocoa
> 1/2 cup sour milk

Part II
Sift:
> 1 cup sugar

Beat until soft:
> 1/2 cup butter

Add the sugar gradually. Blend these ingredients until they are creamy. Beat in one at a time:
> 2 eggs

Sift before measuring:
> 2 cups cake flour

Resift with:
> 1 teaspoon soda
> 1/2 teaspoon salt

Add the flour in about 3 parts to the butter mixture alternately with thirds of:
> 1/2 cup sour milk

Beat the batter after each addition until it is smooth. Add:
> 1 teaspoon vanilla

Beat in the cocoa mixture (Part I). Bake the cake in a greased 9 inch tube pan in a moderate oven 350° for about 60 minutes. It may be baked in 2 greased 9 inch layer pans in a 375° oven for about 35 minutes. Spread the cake with:
> White or Chocolate Icing, pages 694, 699

Add to the icing if desired:
> Nut meats

Method II.
A light rich cake with a strong flavor of brown sugar.
Sift before measuring:
> 1 lb. medium brown sugar: 2 3/4 cups

Beat until soft:
> 1/2 cup butter

Add the sugar gradually. Blend these ingredients until they are very creamy. Beat in one at a time:
> 2 eggs

Add:
> 1 teaspoon vanilla

Sift, then measure:
> 2 1/2 cups cake flour

Resift with:
> 1 teaspoon soda
> 1/2 teaspoon salt

Add the sifted ingredients to the butter mixture in 3 parts alternately with thirds of:
> 1 cup sour milk

Beat the batter until smooth after each addition. Dissolve:
> 1/4 cup cocoa

in:
> 1/2 cup boiling water

Beat this into the batter. You may add:
> (3/4 cup chopped nut meats)

Bake the cake in 2 greased 9 inch layer pans in a slow oven 300° for 25 minutes, then in a moderate oven 375° for 10 minutes longer. Spread the layers with:
> Chocolate Icing, page 699, or Peppermint Icing, page 701

CHOCOLATE DEVIL'S FOOD OR CUSTARD CAKE
A smooth, fine-grained cake. Two chocolate measurements are given. When the larger amount of chocolate is used it is a very rich, black devil's food.

Prepare the following custard:
Cook and stir in a saucepan over a very low flame:

 2 to 4 oz. chocolate
 ½ cup milk
 1 cup light brown sugar
 1 egg yolk

Keep the custard below the boiling point. Remove it from the fire when it is thick and smooth. Cool it. Sift:

 1 cup white sugar

Beat until soft:

 ½ cup butter

Add the sugar gradually. Blend these ingredients until they are very light and creamy. Beat in one at a time:

 2 egg yolks

Sift before measuring:

 2 cups cake flour

Resift with:

 1 teaspoon soda
 ½ teaspoon salt

Add the flour to the butter mixture in 3 parts alternately with thirds of:

 ¼ cup water
 ½ cup milk
 1 teaspoon vanilla

Beat the batter until it is smooth after each addition. Stir in the custard. Whip until stiff but not dry:

 2 egg whites

Fold them lightly into the cake batter. Bake the cake in 2 greased 9 inch layer pans in a moderate oven 375° for about 25 minutes. Spread it with:

 Caramel Icing, page 698, or
 Chocolate Icing, page 699

RED DEVIL'S FOOD CAKE

Generally popular—but not with me, which is not to be taken as a criterion, "likes" being what they are.
Measure:

 1½ cups sifted cake flour

Resift with:

 1½ teaspoons tartrate or phosphate
 baking powder or 1 teaspoon
 combination type (see Baking
 Powder, page 501)
 ½ teaspoon salt
 1 teaspoon soda

Cream until light and fluffy:

 4 tablespoons butter
 1 cup sugar

Add one at a time and beat well:

 2 eggs

Melt:

 2 oz. chocolate

in:

 ½ cup boiling water

Cool slightly, then stir these ingredients into the egg mixture. Add the dry ingredients in about 3 parts alternately with thirds of:

 ½ cup sour milk

Add:

 1 teaspoon vanilla

Stir the batter after each addition until it is well blended. Bake it in 2 greased 9 inch layer pans in a moderate oven 350° for about 25 minutes. Spread the cake with:

 Mocha Icing with Confectioners' Sugar, page 703

CHOCOLATE POTATO CAKE

This chocolate cake has an excellent quality.
Boil, chill, then grate:

 2 medium-sized potatoes

Sift:

 2 cups sugar

Beat until soft:

 1 cup butter

Add the sugar gradually. Blend these ingredients until they are very light and creamy. Beat in one at a time:

 4 egg yolks

Stir in:

 1 cup grated chocolate
 (1 cup ground unblanched
 almonds or 1 cup finely chopped
 black walnuts)

Add the grated potatoes. There should be 1 cupful. Sift before measuring:

 1½ cups cake flour

Resift with:

 ½ teaspoon cinnamon
 2 teaspoons any baking powder
 ½ teaspoon salt

Add the sifted ingredients to the butter mixture in 3 parts alternately with thirds of:

 ½ cup cream or milk
 1 teaspoon vanilla

Beat the batter until it is smooth after each addition. Whip until stiff but not dry:

 4 egg whites
 ⅛ teaspoon salt

Fold them lightly into the cake batter. Bake the cake in a greased 9 inch tube pan in a moderate oven 350° for about 1 hour. Spread the cake with any:

 White or Chocolate Icing,
 pages 694, 699

CHOCOLATE OLD WORLD SPICE CAKE WITH CITRON

A tempting loaf cake, a bit solid, with an unusual flavor.

Beat until soft:

 ½ cup butter

Add gradually and cream until light and fluffy:

 1½ cups sugar

Beat in 1 at a time:

 4 eggs

Stir in:

 4 oz. grated sweet chocolate
 ½ cup very finely shaved citron, candied orange or lemon peel

Sift before measuring:

 2⅓ cups cake flour

Resift with:

 1½ teaspoons any baking powder
 ½ teaspoon cloves
 1 teaspoon cinnamon
 ¼ teaspoon freshly grated nutmeg

Stir the sifted ingredients into the butter mixture in about 3 parts alternately with thirds of:

 ⅞ cup milk

Beat the batter well after each addition until blended. Most European cakes are stirred a long time. This gives them a close sandy texture. Bake the cake in a 9 inch tube pan, or in a loaf pan in a moderate oven 350° for about 1 hour. Ice the cake with:

 Chocolate Butter Icing, page 703

CHOCOLATE SPICE CAKE

A very slightly spiced, rich, light loaf or layer cake.

Having firmly made up my mind that this collection contained enough chocolate cakes, I have lost my strength of character sufficiently to lower the bars to let this one in. Its epitaph might well be—"If I am so soon done for, what was I begun for?"

Sift:

 2 cups sugar

Beat until soft:

 ½ cup butter

Add the sugar gradually. Blend these ingredients until they are very light and creamy. Beat in one at a time:

 4 egg yolks

Melt, cool and add:

 2 oz. chocolate

Sift before measuring:

 2 cups cake flour

Resift with:

 1 teaspoon cinnamon
 ¼ teaspoon cloves
 2 teaspoons any baking powder
 ¼ teaspoon salt

Add these ingredients in 3 parts to the butter mixture alternately with thirds of:

 1 cup milk

Beat the batter until it is smooth after each addition. Whip until stiff but not dry:

 4 egg whites
 ⅛ teaspoon salt

Fold them lightly into the cake batter. Bake the cake in 2 greased 9 inch layer pans in a moderate oven 375°, or in a greased 9 inch tube pan at 350°. Spread it with any:

 Chocolate Icing, page 699

Try this recipe without spices and with sour milk. Add to the dry ingredients from ¼ to ⅓ teaspoonful soda, according to the acidity of the milk.

CHOCOLATE PRUNE CAKE

A delightful dessert. It may be served with whipped cream or pudding sauce.

Remove the pits and cut into pieces:

 1 cup cooked, lightly sweetened, well-drained Prunes, page 450

Sift:

 ¾ cup sugar

Beat until soft:

 ⅓ cup butter

Add the sugar gradually. Blend these ingredients until they are creamy. Melt, cool slightly and add:

 1 oz. chocolate

Beat well:

 2 eggs

Reserve ¼ of the eggs. Add the remainder to the butter mixture. Sift before measuring:

 1 cup and 6 tablespoons cake flour

Resift with:

 2 teaspoons tartrate or phosphate baking powder or 1⅓ teaspoons combination type (see Baking Powder, page 501)
 ¼ teaspoon soda
 ¼ teaspoon salt

Add the sifted ingredients to the butter mixture in 3 parts alternately with thirds of:

 ½ cup milk

Beat the batter until it is smooth after each addition. Add the prunes and:

 ½ teaspoon vanilla

Bake the cake in 2 greased 8 inch layer pans in a moderate oven 375° for about 25 minutes. Spread the layers with:

 Chocolate Butter Icing, page 703

Only ½ the amount given will be sufficient for the top of this moderate-sized cake. Put the left-over ½ egg in the icing.

CHOCOLATE APRICOT CAKE
Follow the preceding rule for:
Chocolate Prune Cake
Substitute for the prunes:
1 cup cooked, lightly sweetened,
well-drained apricots

Banana Chocolate Cake, page 643.

CHOCOLATE CHIP OR POLKA DOT CAKE
Shaved semisweet chocolate may be added to any cake batter in about the same proportion as nut meats or raisins. The heavier commercial chocolate shot, chips, or variously named chocolate morsels that are used in cookies, are a little heavy for light batters, so sprinkle ½ the chocolate bits over ½ the batter and scatter the other ½ over the top of the cake before baking it. Approximately 2 ounces semisweet chocolate shaved equals ½ cupful of chips. Use a recipe for loaf or layer cake. Bake it as directed. Ice it as desired.

Spice Cakes

VELVET SPICE CAKE
This cake is well named, as it has a very delicate consistency. Its flavor is unequaled in spice cakes.
Sift:
1½ cups sugar
Beat until soft:
¾ cup butter
Add the sifted sugar gradually. Blend these ingredients until they are very light and creamy. Beat in:
3 egg yolks
Sift before measuring:
2 cups cake flour
Resift twice with:
1 teaspoon any baking powder
½ teaspoon soda
1 teaspoon freshly grated nutmeg
1 teaspoon cinnamon
½ teaspoon cloves
½ teaspoon salt
If the sour milk is very acid add an extra ½ teaspoonful soda. Add the sifted ingredients to the butter mixture in 3 parts alternately with thirds of:
⅞ cup sour milk or buttermilk
Beat the batter after each addition until it is smooth. Whip until stiff but not dry:
3 egg whites
Fold the egg whites lightly into the cake batter. Bake the cake in a greased 9 inch tube pan in a moderate oven 350° for 1 hour or more. Spread it with:
Chocolate Icing I, page 699 or White Icing, page 694

Sour Cream Spice Cake, page 606; Gingerbread I, page 538.

MYSTERY CAKE
This curious combination of ingredients makes a good cake. It would not occur to me to bake it for my own purposes as I have many others to choose from that are better, although I have been called to task severely for this statement by a fan whose family prefers this to any cake. It is suited ideally to the needs of numerous allergic friends, as it calls for neither eggs, milk nor butter. The following Economy Spice Cake comes under the same heading.
Sift:
1 cup sugar
Beat until soft:
2 tablespoons shortening
Add the sifted sugar gradually and blend these ingredients well. Sift before measuring:
2 cups all-purpose flour
Resift with:
½ teaspoon salt
1 teaspoon cinnamon
½ teaspoon cloves
½ teaspoon nutmeg
1 teaspoon soda
Stir the sifted ingredients in about 3 parts into the sugar mixture alternately with thirds of the contents of:
1 can condensed tomato soup:
10½ oz.
Beat the batter until it is smooth after each addition. Fold in:
1 cup nut meats
1 cup raisins
Bake the cake in a greased 9 inch tube pan in a moderate oven 350° for about 45 minutes. Spread the cake with:
White Icing II, page 702

ECONOMY SPICE CAKE
Boil for 3 minutes:
1 cup water
2 cups seeded raisins
1 cup brown sugar
⅓ cup shortening

½ teaspoon cinnamon
½ teaspoon allspice
½ teaspoon salt
⅛ teaspoon nutmeg
Cool these ingredients. Sift before measuring:
2 cups cake flour
Resift with:
1 teaspoon any baking powder
1 teaspoon soda
Stir the flour gradually into the other ingredients. Beat the batter until it is smooth. Add:
(1 cup chopped nut meats)
Bake the cake in a greased 7 inch tube pan in a slow oven 325° for 1 hour or more. Spread the cake with:
Caramel Icing, page 698, or
White Icing, page 694
By the addition of 1 cupful chopped dates, figs and citron this becomes an acceptable fruit cake.

QUICK SPICE CAKE
See Hurry-Up Cake, Variation I, page 607.

BROWN SUGAR SPICE CAKE WITH SWEET MILK AND A BAKED FROSTING
This and the following cake bring about much the same results, both good. The first is the sweeter of the 2, the second the richer. Also they differ slightly in method. In the first the meringue or frosting is added after the cake is baked, in the second it is baked at the same time. The choice is yours.
Cream until fluffy:
1½ cups firmly packed brown
sugar
½ cup butter
Beat in:
3 egg yolks
Sift before measuring:
2½ cups cake flour
Resift with:
1 teaspoon salt
¼ teaspoon soda
3 teaspoons tartrate or phosphate baking powder or
2½ teaspoons combination type
(see Baking Powder, page 501)
1 teaspoon cinnamon
½ teaspoon cloves
¼ teaspoon nutmeg
(2 teaspoons grated orange rind)
Stir these ingredients into the butter mixture in about 3 parts alternately with thirds of:
1 cup milk

Stir the batter after each addition until it is blended. Have ready a greased 9 x 4 inch loaf pan. It may be lined with greased waxed paper. Bake the cake in a moderate oven 375° for about 30 minutes, or until done. Remove it from the oven. Permit it to remain in the pan. Reduce the oven heat to 350°. Cover the top of the cake with the following:
Meringue
Beat until stiff:
3 egg whites
⅛ teaspoon salt
Add gradually:
1½ cups brown sugar
Beat constantly. Pile the meringue on the cake. Top it with:
½ cup chopped nut meats
Return the cake to the oven until the meringue is set, about 20 minutes.

CRUMB SPICE CAKE
This really deserves mention of some kind but I have run out of adjectives.
Sift before measuring:
2½ cups all-purpose flour
Sift into the same bowl:
2½ cups dark brown sugar
In another bowl beat until soft:
¾ cup butter or shortening
Add the combined flour and sugar gradually and blend the ingredients lightly until they crumble. Work them with a pastry blender or the fingertips. Do not permit them to become oily. Measure 1 cupful of the crumbs thus formed. Add to them:
¾ teaspoon cinnamon
¼ cup blanched shredded
almonds or other chopped nut
meats
Reserve these crumbs. To the remainder add:
½ teaspoon soda
½ teaspoon salt
¼ teaspoon nutmeg or cloves
½ teaspoon cinnamon
2 teaspoons any baking powder
Beat well, then add:
1 cup sour milk
2 eggs
Beat the batter until it is smooth. Spread it in a greased 9 x 12 inch pan. Bake the cake in a moderate oven 375° for 20 minutes. Sprinkle the reserved crumbs over the top. Bake it about 10 minutes longer.
The spices may be omitted from the cake batter but retained in the crumb topping. We have never been able to

make up our minds about the matter so I am passing it on unsolved for your consideration.

Roman Apple Cake, page 637.

APPLESAUCE CAKE
Sift:

> 1 cup white or firmly packed brown sugar

Beat until soft:

> ½ cup butter

Add the sugar gradually. Blend these ingredients until they are very light and creamy. Beat in:

> 1 egg

Sift before measuring:

> 1¾ cups cake flour

Sift a little of the flour over:

> 1 cup raisins
> 1 cup currants or nut meats

Chopped walnuts are super. Resift the remainder with:

> ½ teaspoon salt
> 1 teaspoon soda
> 1 teaspoon cinnamon
> ½ teaspoon cloves

Or the flavoring may be varied by adding:

> 2 tablespoons cocoa

In that case deduct the same amount of flour.
Stir the sifted ingredients gradually into the butter mixture until the batter is smooth. Add the raisins and nut meats. Heat:

> 1 cup thick lightly sweetened applesauce

Beat it into the batter. Bake the cake in a greased 9 inch tube pan in a moderate oven 350° for about 40 minutes.
Spread it with:

> Caramel Icing, page 698

Chocolate Old World Spice Cake with Citron, page 612; Chocolate Spice Cake, page 613.

PRUNE SPICE CAKE
A moist, rich cake, which keeps fresh for a week or more. It is good as a loaf or layer cake with any kind of icing but is best baked in 1 large layer, iced with unboiled white icing flavored with rum, decorated with nuts and cut into small shapes. Recently I have been serving it uniced with foamy sauce—and great success. This may be done with other rich spice cakes.

Choose a sauce that is less rich if you prefer it. See page 753.
Sift:

> 1 cup sugar

Beat until soft:

> ½ to 1 cup butter

Add the sugar gradually. Blend these ingredients until they are very light and creamy. Beat in one at a time:

> 2 eggs

Beat in:

> 1 cup prune pulp

Use 1 pound prunes, seeded and put through a colander or ricer or substitute about 8 ounces prune pulp, baby food.
Sift before measuring:

> 1½ cups cake flour

Resift with:

> 1½ teaspoons soda
> 1 teaspoon cinnamon
> ¾ teaspoon cloves
> ½ teaspoon salt

Add the sifted ingredients in 3 parts to the butter mixture alternately with thirds of:

> ½ cup sour milk

Beat the batter after each addition until it is smooth. Stir in:

> ½ cup broken nut meats

This makes two 9 inch layers or one 9 inch spring form. Grease the pans. Bake the layers for 25 minutes in a moderate oven 375°. Bake the spring form cake in a slower oven 350° with slightly increasing heat for about 1 hour. Spread the cake with any:

> Icing, page 693

FIG SPICE CAKE
It is difficult to choose between this and the preceding prune cake. They are both unusual and delicious.
Stew (page 450):

> 1 lb. dried figs

Preserved figs, well drained, may be substituted, in which case add 1 teaspoonful lemon juice.
Cool, drain, then cut the figs into ¼ inch cubes. Measure, packing rather closely, 2 cupfuls of figs. Combine:

> ½ cup fig juice
> ½ cup sour milk

Sift before measuring:

> 1 cup sugar

Beat until soft:

> ½ cup butter

Add the sugar gradually. Blend these ingredients until they are very light and creamy. Beat in one at a time:

> 2 eggs

Sift before measuring:
  2 cups cake flour
Resift with:
  1 teaspoon any baking powder
  1 teaspoon salt
  ½ teaspoon cinnamon
  ¼ teaspoon cloves
  ½ teaspoon soda
Add the sifted ingredients to the butter mixture in about 3 parts alternately with thirds of the milk and fig juice. Beat the batter after each addition until it is smooth. Add the figs and:
  1 teaspoon vanilla
  1 cup broken nut meats or
    raisins
Bake the cake in a greased 9 inch tube pan or an 8 by 10 inch pan lined with greased waxed paper in a moderate oven 350° for about 50 minutes. Spread it with:
  Unboiled Chocolate, Coffee or
  Mocha Icing, page 703

DATE SPICE CAKE
Cut into small pieces:
  1 cup dates
Pour over them:
  1 cup boiling water or coffee
Cool these ingredients. Cream:
  3 tablespoons butter
  1 cup sifted sugar
Stir in:
  1 beaten egg
Sift before measuring:
  1½ cups cake flour
Resift with:
  2 teaspoons tartrate or phosphate baking powder or 1½ teaspoons combination type
    (see Baking Powder, page 501)
  ¾ teaspoon freshly grated nutmeg
  ¼ teaspoon salt
  ¼ teaspoon soda
Add the sifted ingredients to the sugar mixture in about 3 parts alternately with thirds of the date mixture. Beat the batter well after each addition. Fold in:
  1 cup raisins
  1 cup broken pecan meats
Bake the cake in a greased 9 inch loaf pan in a slow oven 325° for about 45 minutes.

ROMBAUER JAM CAKE
Cream until fluffy:
  6 tablespoons butter
  1 cup brown sugar

Beat in one at a time:
  2 eggs
Beat in:
  3 tablespoons sour cream
Sift, then measure:
  1½ cups all-purpose flour
Resift with:
  1 teaspoon any baking powder
  ½ teaspoon soda
  ½ teaspoon cloves
  1 teaspoon cinnamon
  1 teaspoon freshly grated nutmeg
Beat these ingredients into the butter mixture until barely blended. Beat in:
  1 cup rather firm raspberry or
    blackberry jam
  (½ cup broken nut meats)
Pour the batter into a greased 7 inch tube pan. Bake it in a moderate oven 350° for about ½ hour, or until done. When cool ice the cake with:
  Quick Brown Sugar Icing,
  page 698

TUTTI FRUTTI CAKE
A well-flavored summer fruit cake.
Sift:
  1½ cups brown sugar
Beat until soft:
  ½ cup butter
Add the sugar gradually. Blend these ingredients until they are fluffy. Beat in 1 at a time:
  2 eggs
Sift before measuring:
  2 cups and 2 tablespoons cake
    flour
Resift with:
  1 teaspoon cloves
  1 teaspoon cinnamon
  1 teaspoon nutmeg
  1 teaspoon soda
  ½ teaspoon salt
Stir the sifted ingredients into the butter mixture in about 3 parts alternately with thirds of:
  1 cup lightly drained crushed
    pineapple
Stir in:
  ½ cup raisins
  ½ cup currants
  1 cup broken nut meats
Bake the cake in a greased 9 inch tube pan in a moderate oven 350° for about 1 hour.

ORANGE RAISIN CAKE
Unusual in flavor, this dough makes fine tiny cup cakes for tea.
Juice:
  1 orange

Reserve the peel. Put through a grinder, using a fine knife:

    1 cup raisins
    ½ cup nut meats
    The orange peel

Beat until soft:

    ½ cup butter

Add gradually and cream until fluffy:

    1 cup sugar

Beat in 1 at a time until light:

    2 eggs

Sift before measuring:

    2 cups cake flour

Resift with:

    1 teaspoon soda
    1 teaspoon salt

Combine:

    1 cup sour milk
    1 teaspoon vanilla

Add the sifted ingredients to the butter mixture in 3 parts alternately with thirds of the liquid ingredients. Beat the batter after each addition until blended. Last fold in the ground ingredients. Bake the cake in a greased 9 x 14 inch pan lined with greased waxed paper or in muffin tins similarly prepared in a slow oven 300° for about 40 minutes. Combine with the orange juice and stir well:

    ⅞ cup sugar—1 cup less 2 tablespoons

Pour this sirup slowly over the cake as soon as you take it from the oven. This cake is at its peak on the second day.

Fruit Cakes

Here are 3 recipes for very good dark fruit cake. Basically they have nearly the same ingredients, but they differ in flavor. While they all call for brandy or wine, fruit juice may be substituted. No. II calls in addition for grape jelly and grape juice. No. III, Lucy's Fruit Cake, calls for molasses and is the darkest and the heaviest of the 3.

Use scissors that have been dipped in water for greater ease in cutting up raisins, dates, figs.

FRUIT CAKE
Method I.   About 12 Pounds

Sift:

    1 lb. brown sugar: 2⅔ cups

Beat until soft:

    1 lb. butter: 2 cups

Add the sugar gradually. Blend these ingredients until they are very light and creamy. Beat in:

    15 beaten egg yolks

Sift before measuring:

    4 cups all-purpose flour

Reserve 1 cupful. Resift the remainder with:

    1 tablespoon cinnamon
    1 tablespoon cloves
    1 tablespoon allspice
    1 tablespoon nutmeg
    ½ tablespoon mace
    1½ teaspoons salt if butter is unsalted

Add the sifted ingredients to the butter mixture alternately with:

    ¼ cup whisky and ¼ cup wine or
    ½ cup thick fruit juice: prune, apricot, grape, etc.

Wash:

    2½ lbs. currants

Cut up:

    2½ lbs. raisins
    1 lb. citron

Break coarsely:

    1 lb. pecan meats

Sprinkle these ingredients well with the reserved flour. Beat until stiff but not dry:

    15 egg whites

Fold them into the butter mixture. Fold in the floured ingredients. Place the dough in loaf pans lined with a layer of heavy waxed paper or with 4 layers of thin waxed paper. Cover the bottom of the oven with shallow pans filled with 1 inch of hot water and bake the loaves in a very slow oven 300° from 2 to 3 hours. The pans of water may be removed for the last 15 minutes. Permit the loaves to cool and remove them from the pans. Remove the waxed paper, wrap the loaves in fresh waxed paper and store the cake in tightly covered tin boxes in a cool place. Should the cake become dry, place it in a closed container over hot water until it is hot. Heat wine or grape juice, but do not let it boil. Pour it from a small pitcher very slowly, drop by drop, onto the hot cake. Use as much as the cake will absorb.

Method II.   About 11 Pounds

Sift:

    2 cups sugar

Beat until soft:

    1 lb. butter: 2 cups

Add the sugar gradually. Blend these

ingredients until they are very soft and creamy. Beat in:

12 beaten egg yolks

Sift before measuring:

4 cups all-purpose flour

Reserve 1 cupful. Resift the remainder with:

1 teaspoon cinnamon
½ teaspoon cloves
½ teaspoon nutmeg
1 teaspoon salt if butter is unsalted

Add the sifted ingredients to the butter mixture ½ cupful at a time alternately with:

½ cup grape jelly
½ cup grape juice
½ cup brandy or wine

Sprinkle the reserved flour over:

2 lbs. seedless raisins
1 lb. chopped citron
¼ lb. orange peel and lemon peel
1 lb. coarsely chopped figs
2 lbs. whole pecan meats
12 candied cherries

Stir these ingredients into the batter. Whip until stiff but not dry and fold in:

12 egg whites
¼ teaspoon salt

To bake the cake follow the preceding rule.

LUCY'S FRUIT CAKE
About 11 Pounds

Work until creamy:

4 cups brown sugar
2 cups butter

Beat in:

8 beaten egg yolks
1 cup dark molasses

Sift before measuring:

5 cups all-purpose flour

Resift with:

2 teaspoons soda
2 teaspoons cinnamon
1 teaspoon cloves
1 teaspoon freshly ground nutmeg

You may sift over and work in a cupful of this with the fruit given below in order to separate it. Beat the sifted ingredients in several parts into the butter mixture alternately with:

½ cup brandy or wine

Stir in:

4 lbs. raisins
½ lb. cut-up citron
1¼ lbs. cut-up dates
1 lb. cut-up figs
¾ lb. broken pecan meats

Beat until stiff, then fold in:

8 egg whites
½ teaspoon salt

Line loaf pans with 3 layers of greased wrapping paper. Bake the cake in a slow oven 300° for 3 to 4 hours. Place a pan of hot water on the bottom of the oven. Remove it for the last hour of baking. Remove and wrap the loaves as directed under Fruit Cake I.

SCOTCH CAKE

Sift:

1 cup white sugar
1⅓ cups brown sugar

Beat until soft:

1 cup butter

Add the sugar gradually. Blend these ingredients until they are very light and creamy. Stir in:

6 beaten egg yolks

Sift before measuring:

4 cups cake flour

Reserve 1 cupful. Resift the remainder with:

5 teaspoons tartrate or phosphate baking powder or 4 teaspoons combination type (see Baking Powder, page 501)
½ teaspoon nutmeg
½ teaspoon salt if butter is unsalted

Add the sifted ingredients to the batter alternately with:

½ cup whisky
½ cup molasses

Sprinkle the reserved flour over:

1 lb. pecan meats
2 lbs. seeded raisins

Stir them into the batter. Whip until stiff but not dry and fold in:

6 egg whites
⅛ teaspoon salt

Bake the cake in 2 greased 9 inch tube pans in a slow oven 300° for 45 minutes, increase the heat to 350° and bake it until it is done.

FRUIT CAKE IN CANDIED ORANGE CUPS

These are attractive in a Christmas box.

Remove all pulp and membrane from:

8 orange halves

Cover the halves with boiling water. Cook them until the skins are tender. Drain and dry them. Stir and bring to the boiling point:

2 cups sugar
1 cup light corn sirup
1 cup water

Add the orange halves. Cook them to a temperature of 230°, about 10 minutes. Lift out the shells onto a cookie sheet. Let the excess sirup drop from them, then roll them in:

Sugar

Permit them to dry on inverted cups. Fill the shells to within ½ inch from the top with:

Fruit cake batter

Place the filled cups on a greased cookie sheet. Bake them in a slow oven 250° for about 45 minutes. Test them with a straw.

WHITE FRUIT CAKE

Prepare by the rule on page 607:

English Currant Cake

Before folding the egg whites into the batter beat in the following fruit mixture:

1 cup chopped nut meats, preferably blanched slivered almonds
½ cup finely sliced citron, candied orange or lemon peel
½ cup finely shredded coconut
1 cup white raisins
¼ cup chopped candied pineapple
¼ cup candied cherries cut in two

Bake the cake as directed.

See Pound Cake, page 606, last paragraph.

One Bowl Cakes

After Betty Crocker's "Double-Quick Cakes."

Before You Start to Mix: For best results it is desirable to have all ingredients at normal room temperature, 72°. Turn on oven to moderate heat 350°.

Select Right Size of Pans: Pan size—2 round layers, 8 inch diameter, 1¼ inch deep, or 9 inch diameter, 1½ inches deep, or oblong 9 x 13 x 2 inches.

Prepare Pans Carefully: Grease them generously. Dust layer pans with flour; shake out excess. Line square and oblong pans with plain paper. Let paper extend over sides for easy removal. Grease over paper. Line bread loaf pans with 3 thicknesses of paper.

To Mix: Sift cake flour, measure and place in sifter set in mixing bowl, or over square of paper. Measure all ingredients accurately, level, with standard measuring cups and spoons.

Measure eggs in measuring cup—eggs vary in size.

Sift dry ingredients—flour, sugar, salt, baking powder, soda, cocoa or spices—into mixing bowl.

Shortening—Important Note: These cakes call for homogenized vegetable shortening. Drop in shortening. Add part or all of liquid as indicated in recipe. Measure flavoring into liquid.

Now You Are Ready to Mix: Beat with a spoon for 2 minutes by clock, 150 strokes per minute. You may rest a moment; just count actual beating time. Or mix with electric mixer on medium speed for 2 minutes. *Scrape bowl constantly.* Add any remaining liquid, and unbeaten eggs or whites or yolks. Beat 2 more minutes, scraping bowl constantly. Batter for some cakes is quite thin.

If recipe calls for chocolate, nuts or fruits, directions for adding are given in recipe. Pour batter into prepared pans and bake according to directions in each recipe.

These cakes are based on the use of Softasilk Cake Flour and Calumet Baking Powder.

ONE BOWL SILVER WHITE LAYER CAKE

Follow general directions above. Sift together:

2¼ cups sifted cake flour
1½ cups sugar
3½ teaspoons double-action baking powder
1 teaspoon salt

Add:

½ cup high grade shortening
1 teaspoon flavoring
⅔ cup milk

Beat 2 minutes. Add:

⅓ cup milk
½ to ⅔ cup unbeaten egg whites:
4 large

Beat 2 minutes. Bake in a moderate oven 350°, 30 to 35 minutes for layers, 40 to 45 minutes for oblong. Frost with white, chocolate or caramel icing. Or use special fillings with white icings.

ONE BOWL DEVIL'S FOOD
CAKE
Follow general directions above. Sift
together:
   1¾ cups sifted cake flour
   1½ cups sugar
     1 teaspoon double-action baking
      powder
   ½ teaspoon soda
    1 teaspoon salt
Add:
   ½ cup high grade shortening
   ⅔ cup milk
Beat 2 minutes. Add:
   ⅓ cup milk
   ⅓ to ½ cup unbeaten eggs: 2
    medium
    2 squares melted unsweetened
    chocolate: 2 oz.
   (¼ teaspoon red food coloring)
Beat 2 minutes. Bake in a moderate
oven 350°, 30 to 35 minutes for layers.
Frost with White or Chocolate Icing,
pages 694, 699.

---

*Other One Bowl Cakes to be found else-
where: Hurry-Up Cake, page 607; Hurry-Up Chocolate Cake, page 607; Quick
Caramel Cake, page 607.*

ONE BOWL GOLDEN
LAYER CAKE
Follow general directions above. Sift
together:
   2¼ cups sifted cake flour
   1½ cups sugar
   2½ teaspoons double-action
    baking powder
    1 teaspoon salt
Add:
   ½ cup high grade shortening
    1 teaspoon flavoring
   ⅔ cup milk
Beat 2 minutes. Add:
   ⅓ cup milk
   ⅓ to ½ cup unbeaten eggs:
    2 medium
Beat 2 minutes. Bake in a moderate
oven 350°, 30 to 35 minutes for layers,
40 to 45 minutes for oblong. Frost or
fill in any way desired, pages 693 and
705.

Chiffon Cakes

    This new type of cake calls for oil instead of the more usual shortenings. Betty
Crocker of General Mills, Inc., originated it, and the following rules are based on
the General Mills findings and are used with their approval. This same organization also previously perfected the time-saving one-bowl or "Double-Quick" method
of cake preparation, see page 620.
    Chiffon cakes, while somewhat less flavorsome than those made with butter or
vegetable fats, have an amazingly light texture. They are all based on the use of
Softasilk Cake Flour and Calumet Baking Powder.

CHIFFON CAKE WITH
VARIATIONS
Method I. 16 to 20 Servings
Preheat oven. This takes from 10 to
20 minutes. See below. See pan size
and corresponding temperature below.
Step 1. Measure (level measurements
throughout) and sift together into
mixing bowl:
   2¼ cups sifted cake flour
   1½ cups sugar
    3 teaspoons any baking powder
    1 teaspoon salt
Spoon the flour lightly into cup; don't
pack it.
Make a well and add in order:
   ½ cup cooking or salad oil
    5 unbeaten egg yolks: medium-
    sized
   ¾ cup cold water
    2 teaspoons vanilla

    Grated rind of 1 lemon, about 2
    teaspoons, if desired
One teaspoonful almond extract and 1
teaspoonful vanilla may be used. In
this case omit lemon rind.
Beat with spoon until smooth.
Step 2. Measure into large mixing
bowl:
    1 cup egg whites: 7 or 8
   ½ teaspoon cream of tartar
Whip until whites form very stiff
peaks. They should be much stiffer
than for angel food or meringue. **Do
not underbeat.**
Step 3. Pour egg yolk mixture gradually in thin layers over the entire surface of the whipped egg whites, gently
folding with rubber scraper just until
blended. **Do not stir!** Pour into ungreased pan immediately. Bake in 10
inch tube pan 4 inches deep in a 325°

oven for 55 minutes. Then in 350° oven for 10 to 15 minutes, or until the top springs back lightly when touched. For a 9 x 13 x 2 inch oblong pan bake in 350° oven 45 to 50 minutes. Measure width of pans across top and depth from inside. Immediately turn pan upside down, placing tube part over neck of funnel or bottle, or resting edges of square, oblong or loaf pans on 2 other pans. Let hang, free of table, until cold. Loosen from sides and tube with spatula. Turn pan over and hit edge sharply on table to loosen.

Method II. Small Cake
8 to 10 Servings
Preheat oven. This takes from 10 to 20 minutes. See below. See pan size and corresponding temperature below.
Step 1. Measure (level measurements throughout) and sift together into mixing bowl:
> 1⅛ cups sifted cake flour—1 cup plus 2 tablespoons
> ¾ cup sugar
> 1½ teaspoons any baking powder
> ½ teaspoon salt
Spoon the flour lightly into cup; don't pack it.
Make a well and add in order:
> ¼ cup cooking or salad oil
> 2 unbeaten egg yolks: medium-sized
> ⅜ cup cold water—¼ cup plus 2 tablespoons
> 1 teaspoon vanilla
> Grated rind of ½ lemon, about 1 teaspoon, if desired
One-half teaspoonful almond extract and ½ teaspoonful vanilla may be used. In this case omit lemon rind.
Beat with spoon until smooth.
Step 2. Measure into large mixing bowl:
> ½ cup egg whites: 4 whites
> ¼ teaspoon cream of tartar
Whip until whites form very stiff peaks. They should be much stiffer than for angel food or meringue. **Do not underbeat.**
Step 3. Pour egg yolk mixture gradually in thin layers over the entire surface of the whipped egg whites, gently folding with rubber scraper just until blended. **Do not stir!** Pour into ungreased pan immediately. Bake in 8 x 8 x 2 inch or 9 x 9 x 2 inch square pan in a 350° oven for 30 to 35 minutes, or until the top springs back lightly when touched. If you use a 5 x 10 x 3 inch loaf pan or a 9 inch tube pan 3½ inches deep, bake it in a 325° oven for 50 to 55

minutes. Immediately turn pan upside down, placing tube part over neck of funnel or bottle, or resting edges of square, oblong or loaf pans on 2 other pans. Let hang, free of table, until cold. Loosen from sides and tube with spatula. Turn pan over and hit edge sharply on table to loosen.

ORANGE CHIFFON CAKE
Omit vanilla. Substitute for the lemon rind:
> About 3 tablespoons grated orange rind
For small cake use 1½ tablespoonfuls grated orange rind.

BANANA CHIFFON CAKE
Omit lemon rind and use only:
> 1 teaspoon vanilla
Add with the cold water:
> ½ to ⅔ cup sieved banana: about 2 medium-sized
For small cake use half the amount of vanilla and banana mentioned above.

NUT CHIFFON CAKE
Immediately before pouring the batter for Chiffon Cake into the pan, fold in gently:
> 1 cup very finely chopped nut meats
For small cake use only ½ cupful nut meats.

SPICE CHIFFON CAKE
Omit vanilla and lemon rind. Sift with the dry ingredients:
> 1 teaspoon cinnamon
> ½ teaspoon freshly grated nutmeg
> ½ teaspoon cloves
> ½ teaspoon allspice
For small cake use only half the proportions mentioned above.

COCOA CHIFFON CAKE
Method I. 16 to 20 Servings
Preheat oven. This takes from 10 to 20 minutes. See below. See pan size and corresponding temperature below.
Sift an ample amount of cake flour onto a square of paper.
Stir until smooth, then cool:
> ¾ cup boiling water
> ½ cup cocoa
Step 1. Measure (level measurements throughout) and sift together into mixing bowl:
> 1¾ cups sifted cake flour
> 1¾ cups sugar
> 3 teaspoons any baking powder
> 1 teaspoon salt

Spoon the flour lightly into cup; don't pack it.

Make a well and add in order:
½ cup cooking or salad oil
7 unbeaten egg yolks: medium-sized
The cooled cocoa mixture
1 teaspoon vanilla
(¼ teaspoon red food coloring if desired)

Beat with spoon until smooth.

Step 2. Measure into large mixing bowl:
1 cup egg whites: 7 or 8
½ teaspoon cream of tartar

Whip until whites form very stiff peaks. They should be much stiffer than for angel food or meringue. **Do not underbeat.**

Step 3. Pour egg yolk mixture gradually in thin layers over the entire surface of the whipped egg whites, gently folding with rubber scraper just until blended. **Do not stir!** Pour into ungreased pan immediately. Bake in 10 inch tube pan 4 inches deep in a 325° oven for 55 minutes, then raise heat to 350° and bake for 10 to 15 minutes, or until the top springs back when lightly touched. Immediately turn pan upside down, placing tube part over neck of funnel or bottle, or resting edges of square, oblong or loaf pans on 2 other pans. Let hang, free of table, until cold. Loosen from sides and tube with spatula. Turn pan over and hit edge sharply on table to loosen. When cold spread the cake with any desired:

Chocolate Icing, page 699

Method II. Small Cake
8 to 10 Servings
Preheat oven. This takes from 10 to 20 minutes. See below. See pan size and corresponding temperature below. Sift an ample amount of cake flour onto a square of paper. Stir until smooth, then cool:
⅜ cup boiling water—¼ cup plus 2 tablespoons
¼ cup cocoa

Step 1. Measure (level measurements throughout) and sift together into mixing bowl:
⅞ cup sifted cake flour—¾ cup plus 2 tablespoons
⅞ cup sugar
1½ teaspoons any baking powder
½ teaspoon salt

Spoon the flour lightly into cup; don't pack it.

Make a well and add in order:
¼ cup cooking or salad oil
4 unbeaten egg yolks: medium-sized
The cooled cocoa mixture
½ teaspoon vanilla
(⅛ teaspoon red food coloring if desired)

Beat with spoon until smooth.

Step 2. Measure into large mixing bowl:
½ cup egg whites: 4 whites
¼ teaspoon cream of tartar

Whip until whites form very stiff peaks. They should be much stiffer than for angel food or meringue. **Do not underbeat.**

Step 3. Pour egg yolk mixture gradually in thin layers over the entire surface of the whipped egg whites, gently folding with rubber scraper just until blended. **Do not stir!** Pour into ungreased pan immediately. Bake in an 8 x 8 x 2 inch or 9 x 9 x 2 inch square pan in a 350° oven for 50 to 55 minutes, or until the top springs back when lightly touched. If you use a 5 x 10 x 3 inch loaf pan or a 9 inch tube pan 3½ inches deep, bake it in a 325° oven for 50 to 55 minutes. Immediately turn pan upside down, placing tube part over neck of funnel or bottle, or resting edges of square, oblong or loaf pans on 2 other pans. Let hang, free of table, until cold. Loosen from sides and tube with spatula. Turn pan over and hit edge sharply on table to loosen. When cold spread the cake with any desired:

Chocolate Icing, page 699

Coffee Cakes

Is there anything better than good coffee cake? I am told that the deposed King of Spain "dunked." Perhaps that afforded him some comfort.

BASIC RULE FOR YEAST COFFEE CAKE DOUGH
For a richer dough see the rule for Coffee Cake Wreath on page 626. This is sufficient for one 9 x 13 inch coffee cake, 1 fruit cake baked in an 8 inch

pie pan and fourteen or sixteen 2½ inch crescents. See the following recipes.

Warm a large mixing bowl. Place in it:
½ cup all-purpose flour

Crumble over it:

  2 cakes yeast

Make a hollow in the flour and pour into it:

  ½ cup lukewarm milk and water

Add:

  1½ teaspoons sugar

Stir these ingredients until they are well blended. Cover them and put them in a warm place to rise for 20 minutes. Beat until soft:

  ½ cup butter

Add gradually:

  ¼ to ½ cup sugar

Blend these ingredients until they are creamy. Add:

  ½ teaspoon salt
  1 teaspoon grated lemon rind
  2 beaten eggs
  ½ cup water and milk
  (½ tablespoons lemon juice)
  (1 teaspoon vanilla extract)

Sift:

  4 cups all-purpose flour

Stir part of it into the butter mixture, then knead in the rest with the hands. Add the yeast mixture and knead the dough well. Cover it and permit it to rise in a warm place for 1½ to 2 hours, until it has doubled in bulk. Shape the dough as desired. Add to it a filling, page 626, or cover it with butter, sugar, etc. Permit it to rise for ½ hour. Bake it in a moderate oven 350° for about 20 minutes.

PLAIN COFFEE CAKE

Prepare:

  Coffee Cake Dough, see above

When it has doubled in bulk spread it in flat greased pans to the depth of ½ inch. Permit it to rise in a warm place for ½ hour. Spread the cakes with:

  Melted butter or milk

Sprinkle them with:

  Cinnamon
  Sugar
  Chopped nuts

Bake them in a moderate oven 350° for about 20 minutes.

HONEY-BEE TOPPING FOR COFFEE CAKES

Stir and bring to the boiling point over a low flame:

  ½ cup sugar
  ¼ cup milk
  ¼ cup butter
  ¼ cup honey
  ½ cup crushed nut meats

Spread these ingredients on coffee cakes that are ready to be baked.

BUTTER TOPPING FOR COFFEE CAKES

Cream:

  ¼ cup butter

with:

  ½ cup sugar

Stir in:

  1 beaten egg
  ½ teaspoon vanilla
  6 tablespoons all-purpose flour

Add:

  About 3 tablespoons milk

that is, enough to make the topping a good consistency to spread. Spread it on coffee cakes that are ready to be baked.

YEAST COFFEE CAKE WITH CRUMBS OR STREUSSEL

Prepare:

  Coffee Cake Dough or Coffee
  Cake Wreath Dough, page 626

After spreading it with butter combine:

  2 tablespoons all-purpose flour
  2 tablespoons butter
  5 tablespoons sugar

Blend these ingredients until they crumble. Add:

  ½ teaspoon cinnamon

Sprinkle the crumbs over the coffee cake and bake it as directed. This amount is sufficient for a round or square 8 inch cake.

APRICOT GLAZE FOR COFFEE CAKE

Spread baked coffee cake with:

  Apricot Glaze, page 634

You may decorate the edges with:

  Chopped nut meats

YEAST COFFEE CAKE WITH APPLES, PEACHES, PLUMS, ETC.

Prepare:

  Yeast Coffee Cake Dough

After permitting the dough to rise in the pans, cover the entire surface of the cakes closely with rows of:

  Fruit: cored sliced apples,
  peaches, seeded cherries or
  plums

Sprinkle the tops with:

  Cinnamon
  Sugar, according to the acidity
  of the fruit

Dot them generously with:

  Butter

Or, in place of the butter pour around the fruit the following:

Custard
Beat:
   1 egg yolk
   4 tablespoons cream
Bake the cake in an 8 inch round pan in a hot oven 400° until it is done and the fruit is soft.

CINNAMON CRESCENTS
Prepare:
   **Coffee Cake Dough or Coffee
   Cake Wreath Dough, page 626**
Use only ¼ cupful sugar and omit the vanilla, the lemon and the lemon rind if you want a more breadlike dough. After the dough has doubled in bulk, roll it on a floured board to the thickness of ¼ inch. Cut the dough into 3

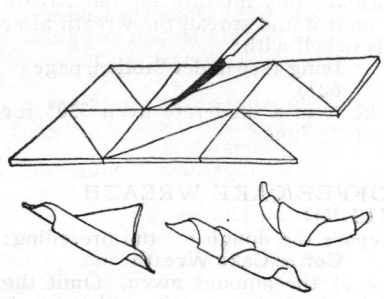

inch squares. Cut across the squares on the bias, making 2 triangles out of every square. Spread the triangles with:
   Melted butter
Sprinkle them with:
   **Brown or white sugar
   Cinnamon**
Start with the long end and roll the triangles into little rolls. Twist the rolls into half circles. Place the crescents on a greased baking sheet. Permit them to rise in a warm place for ½ hour. Spread the tops lightly with:
   Melted butter
Bake the crescents in a moderate oven 350° for about 30 minutes.

CINNAMON BUNS OR SNAILS
Prepare:
   **Coffee Cake Dough or Coffee
   Cake Wreath Dough, page 626**
When it has doubled in bulk, roll it on a floured board to the thickness of ¼ inch. Spread it generously with:
   Melted butter

Sprinkle it with:
   **Cinnamon
   Brown sugar**
Add if desired:
   **Chopped nut meats
   Seedless raisins
   Chopped citron
   Grated lemon rind**
Roll the dough like a jelly roll (page 648). Cut it into 1 inch slices. Rub muffin tins generously with:
   Butter
Sprinkle them well with:
   **Brown sugar
   (Chopped nut meats)**
Place each slice of roll firmly on the bottom of a greased muffin tin. Permit

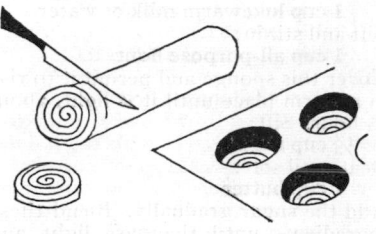

the rolls to rise in a warm place for ½ hour. Bake them in a moderate oven 350° for about ½ hour.

CARAMEL BUNS
Prepare the preceding:
   Cinnamon Buns
Roll and cut the dough as directed. Cut it into 1 inch slices. Brush the sides with:
   Melted butter
Cream:
   **6 tablespoons butter
   6 tablespoons brown sugar**
Spread this mixture on the bottom and sides of an iron skillet or pan about 7 inches in diameter. Sprinkle on the bottom:
   **Whole or broken pecan meats,
   or blanched shredded almonds**
Place the slices close together in the skillet, with the flat side down. Permit them to rise for ½ hour. Bake them in a moderate oven 350° for about 30 minutes.

REFRIGERATOR COFFEE CAKE
There are a number of rules for Refrigerator Rolls—see chapter on Bread,

page 499—that may be used as a basis for very plain coffee cake.

Spread the dough in greased pans. Cover it with:

> Cinnamon and Sugar, page 624,
> Streussel, page 624, or Fruit,
> page 624

Let the dough rise as directed by the rule you are following. Bake the cake in a moderate oven 400° for about 25 minutes.

COFFEE CAKE WREATH OR HEFENKRANZ

For a dough that is less rich, see basic rule for Coffee Cake Dough, page 623.

Dissolve:

> 2 cakes yeast

in:

> 1 cup lukewarm milk or water

Sift and stir in:

> 1 cup all-purpose flour

Cover this sponge and permit it to rise in a warm place until it is light, about ½ hour. Sift:

> ½ cup sugar

Beat until soft:

> 1 cup butter

Add the sugar gradually. Blend these ingredients until they are light and creamy. Beat in one at a time:

> 2 or 3 eggs

Add:

> 1 teaspoon salt
> 2 teaspoons grated lemon rind

Beat in the sponge. Sift and beat in gradually:

> 3½ cups all-purpose flour

Beat the dough for 5 minutes. Add:

> (⅞ cup chopped citron)
> (¼ cup raisins or chopped candied
> pineapple)
> (1 cup broken nut meats)

Cover the bowl with a cloth and permit the dough to rise in a warm place for about 2 hours, or until it has doubled in bulk. This amount will make

2 wreaths 9 inches in diameter. Roll ½ the dough into 3 long strips. Braid them and shape them into a wreath. Or, make a rectangle about 9 x 12 inches of the dough about ¼ inch thick. Put the filling down the center lengthwise, cut the outer thirds into 2 inch strips and lace them as shown, folding the ends inside. This is optional. The dough may be shaped in any way desired or it may be placed in greased pans. Place the wreath on a greased baking sheet or in a greased 9 inch tube pan. Permit the dough to rise for ½ hour. Brush the top with:

> Melted butter

If you have added no fruit or nut meats to the batter combine:

> ½ cup blanched shredded almonds
> ¼ cup sugar

Sprinkle this mixture on the wreath or omit it and spread the wreath after it is baked with:

> Icing (see under Stollen, page
> 627)

Bake it in a moderate oven 350° for about ½ hour.

COFFEE CAKE WREATH FILLED

Prepare the dough for the preceding:

> Coffee Cake Wreath

Use ½ the amount given. Omit the raisins and citron. When the dough has doubled in bulk roll it or pat it on a greased surface into an oblong ⅓ inch thick. Spread it evenly with one of the following fillings.

Roll the dough like a jelly roll. Shape it into a ring. Place it on a greased sheet or in a greased 9 inch tube pan. Permit it to rise for ½ hour. Brush, sprinkle the top and bake the wreath as directed in the preceding rule.

ALMOND FILLING I

Cream:

> 3 tablespoons butter
> ½ cup sugar

Beat in:

> ½ cup blanched ground almonds
> ¼ teaspoon grated lemon rind
> 1 slightly beaten egg

ALMOND FILLING II OR EDELWEISS

Fills one 9 inch wreath.

Cream:

> ½ cup confectioners' sugar
> ½ cup butter

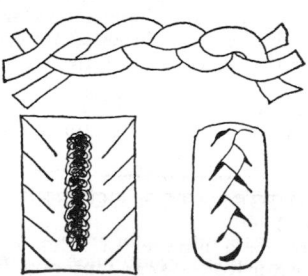

Stir in:
    ½ teaspoon vanilla or grated
        lemon rind
    ½ cup blanched shredded or
        ground almonds

HAZELNUT FILLING
Fills one 9 inch wreath.
Combine:
    ½ cup ground hazelnut meats
    ½ cup sugar
    2 teaspoons cinnamon
    ½ teaspoon vanilla
    2 tablespoons finely chopped
        citron or orange peel
Beat well and add:
    1 egg
Thin these ingredients with:
    Water
until they are the right consistency to
spread over the cake.

POPPY SEED FILLING
Fills one 9 inch wreath.
Soak for 2 hours:
    ½ cup poppy seed
in:
    ¼ cup milk
Add:
    ¼ cup sugar
    ½ teaspoon vanilla or grated
        lemon rind
Beat and add gradually:
    1 small egg
It may not be necessary to add all of
the egg as the filling should be moist
but not liquid. If it becomes too moist,
add more poppy seed.

RAISIN, NUT AND CITRON FILLING
Fills one 9 inch wreath.
Chop:
    ¼ cup blanched almonds
    ¼ cup citron
    ¼ cup raisins
Melt:
    ¼ cup butter
After rolling the dough, spread it with
the melted butter and the chopped in-
gredients. Sprinkle it with:
    (Sugar)
    (Cinnamon)

FILLED COFFEE CAKE CRESCENTS
Prepare the dough for:
    Coffee Cake Wreath, page 626
Omit the raisins and citron. Permit
the dough to rise as directed. Roll or
pat the dough to the thickness of ¼
inch. Cut it into 4 inch squares. Spread
the squares with 2 tablespoonfuls of
one of the preceding fillings or spread
them with melted butter, cinnamon
and sugar. Roll the squares on the
bias. Curve the rolls into crescents
(page 625). Place them on a greased
sheet. Permit them to rise for ½ hour.
Brush, sprinkle and bake them as directed in the rule for Coffee Cake
Wreath, page 626.

*High Coffee Cake with Baking Powder,
page 631.*

STOLLEN OR YEAST RAISIN CAKE
Sift before measuring:
    6 cups all-purpose flour
Dissolve:
    1½ cakes yeast
in:
    1½ cups lukewarm milk
Add 1 cupful of the sifted flour. Permit
this sponge to rise in a warm place for
several hours.
Sprinkle a little of the sifted flour over:
    ½ lb. raisins
    ½ lb. blanched chopped almonds
Sift:
    ¾ cup sugar
Beat until soft:
    1½ cups butter
Add the sifted sugar gradually. Blend
these ingredients until they are light
and creamy. Beat in one at a time:
    3 eggs
Add:
    ¾ teaspoon salt
    ¾ teaspoon grated lemon rind
Add the sponge and the remaining
flour and knead the dough until it is
smooth and elastic. Add the raisins
and nuts. Permit the dough to rise
until it doubles in bulk. Toss it onto a
floured board. Divide it into 3 or more
parts. Shape the parts into loaves.
Place them in greased loaf pans. Brush
the tops with:
    Melted butter
Let the loaves rise until they double
in bulk. Bake them in a moderate oven
350° for about 45 minutes. When they
are cool, brush them with the following:
Icing
Blend until the right consistency to
spread:
    1 cup confectioners' sugar
    2 tablespoons or more boiling
        water
    ½ teaspoon vanilla or
    1 teaspoon lemon juice

HIGH COFFEE CAKE OR YEAST BUNDKUCHEN OR KUGELHOPF

This is usually made in a tube pan with a fluted bottom. It is a good rule for Baba or Savarin, page 657. Sift before measuring:

    4 cups all-purpose flour

Dissolve:

    3 cakes yeast

in:

    1 cup lukewarm milk

Only 2 cakes yeast may be used but the rising process will be slower. Beat in 1 cupful of the sifted flour and set the sponge to rise in a warm place until about doubled in bulk. Sift:

    ¾ cup sugar

Beat until soft:

    1 cup unsalted butter

Add the sifted sugar gradually. Blend these ingredients until they are very light and creamy. Beat in one at a time:

    5 eggs

Beat in:

    1 teaspoon salt

Add the sponge, the remaining flour and:

    ½ teaspoon grated lemon rind
    1 cup seedless raisins

Beat the batter well until it is smooth and elastic. Place in the bottom of a greased 9 inch tube pan:

    ⅓ cup blanched almonds

Place the dough on top of them and permit it to rise until it is very light, about 1½ hours. Bake the cake in a moderate oven 350° from 45 to 60 minutes. When it is cold, sprinkle the top with:

    Confectioners' sugar

High Coffee Cake with Baking Powder, page 631.

CHRISTMAS STOLLEN WITHOUT EGGS— CURRANT BREAD

Sift before measuring:

    6 cups all-purpose flour

Make a hollow in the center into which pour:

    3 cups milk
    ½ lb. melted butter
    1 cup sugar
    ½ teaspoon grated lemon rind
    1½ tablespoons lemon juice
    ½ lb. raisins
    ½ lb. washed dried currants
    ¼ lb. blanched shredded almonds
    ¼ lb. diced citron

    ¾ teaspoon salt
    1 cake yeast dissolved in 2 tablespoons lukewarm water
    ¼ teaspoon mace

Work these ingredients into the flour. Cover the bowl with a damp towel and permit the dough to rise for 12 hours in a warm place. Beat it well with a spoon. Place it in 3 greased 4½ x 9½ inch pans. Cover them and permit the dough to rise until doubled in bulk. Bake them in a moderate oven 350° for about 1 hour. Spread them while hot with:

    Melted butter

Cover them with a heavy coating of:

    Confectioners' sugar

Sprinkle them lightly with:

    (White rose water)

ALMOND STOLLEN WITHOUT EGGS

Follow the preceding rule for:

    Christmas Stollen

Omit the raisins and currants. Use in all:

    1 lb. blanched, coarsely shredded almonds
    1 lb. diced citron

DANISH PASTRY OR COFFEE CAKE

This falls between a rich coffee cake and a rich pastry. It is usually classed as a coffee cake since it is combined with much the same fillings and toppings. Sometimes it is iced with a sugar and water icing. This rule is, I think, a lot of bother with a result that is not superior to Coffee Cake Wreath on page 626. However, taste varies and this is a popular cake. People buy it by the gobs in bakeries, so here goes. Scald:

    1 cup milk

Let it cool to lukewarm, then add:

    2 crumbled cakes yeast

Sift, measure and beat in:

    1 cup all-purpose flour

Cover this sponge and permit it to rise for ½ hour. Cream:

    ¾ cup butter

Add gradually:

    6 tablespoons sugar

Beat in:

    2 or 3 eggs
    1 teaspoon salt
    2 tablespoons grated lemon rind

Beat in the sponge. Beat in gradually, then knead in the last of:

    2½ cups all-purpose flour

Cover the bowl and permit the dough

to rise until it has doubled in bulk. Work with the hands under cold water until it is pliable:

1 cup butter: 8 oz.

Place it where it will remain cool. When the dough has risen, pat or roll it out into a square to the thickness of about ¼ inch. Dot the surface with ⅓ of the butter. Fold the right side of the dough to the center. Fold the left side to the center. Fold the edges to let top and bottom meet. Pat or roll out the dough. This process—rolling, dotting with butter and folding—should be done 3 times in all. At this point the dough may be closely covered and chilled; an advantage in handling it and also a convenience if you wish to prepare the dough one day and bake it the next. If you chill the dough allow about 1 hour longer for the rising period. If you do not wish to chill the dough, permit it to rest for 20 minutes. Shape the dough into rounds, twists or oblongs. Place them on tins covered with brown paper. If you wish to add fillings suitable to coffee cake mixtures, do so when shaping the dough. Place the filling on squares of dough. Fold over the corners. Brush the tops with:

Melted butter or beaten egg

Permit the dough to rise for ½ hour. Bake it in a moderate oven 350° for about 25 minutes. Spread it, if you wish, with the following icing for coffee cake.

Blend until the right consistency to spread:

    1 cup confectioners' sugar
    2 tablespoons or more boiling water
    1 teaspoon lemon juice or 1 teaspoon vanilla

You may sprinkle the top with:

    Chopped nut meats

SCANDINAVIAN COFFEE BREAD OR CAKE

6 Large Servings

So good that if your family is large you might as well double the recipe as the bread may be reheated satisfactorily. It is cakelike and delicate, tender and crisp at the same time. Crumble into a medium-sized bowl:

    1 cake yeast

In hot weather use ⅔ this measurement. Sprinkle over it:

    1 tablespoon sugar

Permit these ingredients to stand for about 10 minutes, or until both sugar and yeast are dissolved. Beat these ingredients. Beat into them:

    1 egg
    ⅔ cup milk at room temperature
    ¼ teaspoon salt

Stir in at first, then work in by hand to make a soft dough about:

    2 cups all-purpose flour

Handle the dough lightly, just long enough to have it hold together. Work with the hands until pliable but not soft:

    ¾ stick butter: 6 tablespoons

Roll out the dough lightly into a square on a lightly floured board. Dot the surface with about ¼ of the butter. Fold the dough over from east to west and again from north to south. Roll it out. Dot it with butter. Follow this process 4 times in all. Place the dough in a bowl covered with a piece of waxed paper in the refrigerator for 5 hours or longer. Roll it out lightly to the thickness of about ¼ inch. You may now do about anything you like with it. Try cutting it into 3 inch squares. Brush them lightly with:

    Melted butter

Place on each square:

    1 tablespoon raisins and nut meats
    1 teaspoon sugar
    A dash of cinnamon

Or use in place of this mixture a tablespoonful of any desirable coffee cake filling.

Pinch the corners together to make a pocket. You may moisten the edges with a little water to make them stick. Permit the dough to rise in a moderately warm place for 1 hour. Have the oven heated to 500°. Bake the buns in it for about 10 minutes or more if necessary. While hot spread the rolls with:

    Melted butter

and sprinkle them with:

    Sugar

This last touch is sublime. Serve the bread piping hot. This dough makes delicious triangles spread with melted butter, sugar and cinnamon and rolled, or it may be made into an oblong spread with melted butter, sugar, cinnamon, raisins and nut meats and then rolled into one large roll.

SWEDISH TEA RING

Prepare (page 623):

    Basic Coffee Cake Dough

After the first rising of the dough, punch it down and let it rise again until doubled in bulk, for about 45 minutes. Pat out the dough on a lightly floured board into a 9 x 18 inch oblong. Brush the top with:

Melted butter

Spread it with:

½ cup raisins
½ cup chopped nut meats
¼ cup sugar mixed with 2 teaspoons cinnamon
(⅛ cup chopped citron)

Or you may use as a filling 1 cupful brown sugar mixed with 1½ teaspoonfuls each of granulated sugar and cinnamon. Roll the dough like a jelly roll, page 648. Use a knife or a spatula to lift it if it sticks. Shape it into a ring.

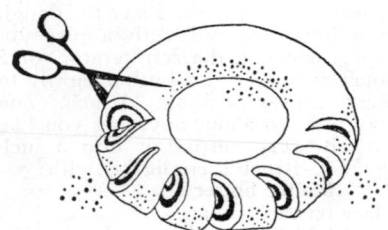

You may use a little water to hold it together. Place the ring on a greased sheet. Hold floured kitchen scissors perpendicularly to cut bias gashes into the outer edges of the ring. Cut to within 1 inch of the inner edge. The slices should be about 1½ inches wide at the rim, tapering to ½ inch at the center. As you cut, turn each partially cut slice flat on the tin. Cover the ring with a damp cloth. Permit the dough to rise until doubled in bulk, about ½ hour. The top may be brushed lightly with:

Melted butter or cream

Bake it in a moderate oven 375° from 25 to 30 minutes. Spread it while hot with the following butter icing:
Combine:

1 tablespoon butter
1 cup confectioners' sugar

Add to make a good consistency to spread:

Cream

Spread the cake with the icing. Sprinkle the top with:

Chopped nut meats

Place the ring in the oven for 1 minute to glaze it.

Baking Powder Coffee Cakes

QUICK COFFEE CAKE WITH BAKING POWDER

Sift:

¼ to ½ cup sugar

Beat until soft and creamy:

¼ cup butter

Add the sugar gradually. Blend these ingredients until they are light and creamy. Beat in:

1 egg
⅔ cup milk

Sift before measuring:

1½ cups all-purpose flour

Resift with:

¼ teaspoon salt
2 teaspoons any baking powder

Add the sifted ingredients to the butter mixture. Add:

(¾ teaspoon grated lemon rind or
½ teaspoon vanilla)

Beat the batter until it is smooth. Spread the dough in a shallow greased 8 x 10 inch pan. Sprinkle the top with:

Cinnamon
Sugar
(½ cup chopped nut meats)

Dot it with:

Butter

Bake the cake in a moderate oven 375° for about 25 minutes. The dough may be spread with 1½ tablespoonfuls melted butter, and ½ teaspoonful cinnamon, ¼ cupful sugar and 1 tablespoonful flour may be combined and sifted over it. This makes a good topping.

BAKING POWDER CRUMB COFFEE CAKE

Sift before measuring:

3 cups all-purpose flour

Sift and add:

¾ cup sugar

Beat until soft and add:

½ cup butter

Blend these ingredients lightly until they crumble. Do not permit them to become oily. Reserve 1 cupful. To the remainder add:

4 teaspoons tartrate or phosphate baking powder or 3 teaspoons combination type (see Baking Powder, page 501)

Combine and add:
>2 beaten eggs
>1 cup milk
>¼ teaspoon salt
>Grated rind of 1 lemon

Beat the batter and spread it to the thickness of ¾ inch in a greased 8 x 13 inch pan. Sprinkle the reserved crumb mixture over the top with:
>½ cup blanched shredded almonds or other nut meats

Bake the cake in a moderate oven 375°.

SOUR CREAM COFFEE CAKE WITH BAKING POWDER

This cake may be made with sour top milk. It is light and very good. Combine and beat well:
>1 cup sour cream
>2 eggs

Sift before measuring:
>1½ cups all-purpose flour

Resift with:
>1 cup sugar
>2 teaspoons any baking powder
>½ teaspoon soda
>¼ teaspoon salt

Add the sifted ingredients to the cream mixture. Beat the batter until it is smooth. Spread the dough in a lightly greased 8 x 10 inch pan. Bake the cake in a moderate oven 350° for about 25 minutes. While it is hot sprinkle it with:
>Confectioners' sugar and chopped nut meats, or with butter, cinnamon and sugar, or Topping for Baking Powder Coffee Cake

---

TOPPING FOR BAKING POWDER COFFEE CAKE

Beat until stiff:
>2 egg whites
>⅛ teaspoon salt

Fold in, a little at a time:
>1 cup brown sugar

Spread this topping on:
>Quick Coffee Cake, page 630, or Sour Cream Coffee Cake Batter, below

Sprinkle it with:
>½ cup chopped nut meats

Bake the cake in a moderate oven 350° for about ½ hour, or until done.

See Streussel, page 624.

HIGH COFFEE CAKE— KUGELHOPF WITH BAKING POWDER

Sift:
>1 cup sugar

Beat until soft:
>1 cup shortening: butter or half butter and half lard

Add the sugar gradually. Blend these ingredients until they are very light and creamy. Beat in one at a time:
>5 eggs

Sift before measuring:
>3½ cups all-purpose flour

Resift with:
>5 teaspoons tartrate or phosphate baking powder or 3 teaspoons combination type (see Baking Powder, page 501)
>½ teaspoon salt

Add the sifted ingredients to the butter mixture in 3 parts alternately with thirds of:
>1 cup milk

Beat the batter until it is smooth after each addition. Add:
>1 cup seedless raisins
>1 teaspoon grated lemon rind
>1 teaspoon vanilla

Bake the cake in a greased 7 inch tube pan in a moderate oven 350°. When it is cold sprinkle it with:
>Confectioners' sugar

Cakes with Fruit, Cream and Fillings that Serve as a Complete Dessert Course

RULE FOR WHIPPING CREAM

Cream when whipped about doubles in bulk.

Chill the cream, the bowl and the beater in a refrigerator for at least 2 hours. Use a heavy wire whisk. Beat:
>1 cup heavy cream

Beat it until it is fairly stiff. Be careful not to beat it until it is warmer than 45° or it will turn to butter. Should it start to turn buttery, whip in 2 or more tablespoonfuls cold milk. Fold in:
>2 tablespoons confectioners' sugar
>1 teaspoon vanilla, coffee or other flavoring

If you wish the cream to keep stiff for a day or two, add to it:

1 teaspoon gelatine soaked in
1 tablespoon cold water
Dissolve the gelatine over hot water.
Cool it.
When whipping cream with an electric
beater use medium speed.

RULE FOR GELATINE
Gelatine must be soaked in a cold
liquid before it is dissolved. Dissolve
it by adding it to a hot liquid—water,
milk, custard, etc.—or by placing the
receptacle holding it in boiling water
or over a low flame. If a mold is to be
used for gelatine puddings wet it before filling it or grease it lightly with
oil. This will prevent the pudding
from sticking to the mold. To set a
gelatine dish rapidly, place the receptacle containing it in a bowl of ice
water.

SUBSTITUTES FOR WHIPPING CREAM
I.
Use **light or cereal cream** after permitting it to stand undisturbed for 48
hours in the refrigerator. Whip it by
the rule on page 631.
II.
Use **cream from the top of milk** after
permitting it to stand undisturbed for
48 hours in the refrigerator. Two
quarts of milk will yield 1 cupful
whipped cream.
III.
Prepare **18% cream** as follows:
Soak:
    1 teaspoon gelatine
in:
    2 tablespoons cold water or fruit
    juice
Heat:
    ½ cup 18% cream
Dissolve the soaked gelatine in it. Stir
these ingredients into:
    1½ cups 18% cream
You may add:
    1 tablespoon powdered sugar
Place the cream in the refrigerator.
Stir it from time to time. Add:
    ½ teaspoon vanilla
The cream will be thoroughly chilled
after 4 to 6 hours. Beat it until it is
stiff.
IV.
Use **evaporated milk.** Milk prepared
with gelatine holds up longer, but
merely chilling it may be more con-
venient at times. When whipping

evaporated milk with an electric beater
use medium speed.
Either soak:
    ½ teaspoon gelatine
in:
    2 teaspoons cold water
Scald in a double boiler:
    1¼ cups evaporated milk
Add the soaked gelatine. Stir until the
gelatine is dissolved. Chill the milk
until it is icy cold, then whip it like
cream. A small amount of vanilla,
caramel, coffee, etc., may be added to
the milk to flavor it.
Or, chill evaporated milk for 12 hours.
Less time is needed if you place it in a
refrigerator tray for about 15 minutes
or a few minutes in a freezer. When it
is cold you may add a little lemon
juice, about ½ teaspoonful to a cupful
of milk. This will help to stiffen it.
When crystals form around the edges,
whip it until stiff.
V.
Sprinkle equal parts of:
    Dry milk solids
on equal parts of:
    Water or milk
Blend with a rotary beater, electric
mixer or blender. For a more stable
foam add to each cupful of this mixture:
    1½ teaspoons lemon juice

Meringue, page 578.

THREE MINUTE ICING
Use this icing as a substitute for
whipped cream or meringue.
Beat until blended, then place in a
double boiler over boiling water:
    2 egg whites
    ½ cup sugar
    ⅛ teaspoon salt
    2 tablespoons cold water
Beat these ingredients for 3 minutes or
until stiff with a wire whisk. Remove
the icing from the fire. Add:
    1 teaspoon vanilla or almond
    extract
Beat the icing well. Spread it over
jellied fruit, pies or tarts, cakes, etc.,
that have been cooled. Top it with:
    Chopped nut meats or coconut

QUICK SPONGE CAKE WITH FRUIT
Sift before measuring:
    1 cup all-purpose flour
Resift it into a bowl with:

1 teaspoon any baking powder
¼ teaspoon salt
⅞ cup sugar
Make a hole in the center of these ingredients. Place in it:
3 lightly beaten eggs
1½ tablespoons water
1 teaspoon vanilla
Beat the batter until it is smooth. Bake
the cake in a 10 inch layer pan in a
moderate oven 350° for about 20 minutes. Spread the cake with:
Sugared or cooked fruit
Serve it with:
Cream or whipped cream
Or prepare:
Economy Sponge Cake, page 596
Use only ½ the amount. Bake the
cake in an 8 x 8 inch pan. Cut it into
pieces or keep it whole.
Serve it as suggested above.

SPONGE CAKE WITH FRESH FRUIT AND CREAM
Almost an effortless "quickie" when
"store" cake is used. Remember to
serve this good combination:
Sponge Cake
Uncooked fresh or frozen
crushed berries, sugared
peaches, sweetened cream,
whipped cream or ice cream
Plain sponge cake is good served with
this sauce:
5½ oz. puréed peaches—baby food
Grated rind and juice of 1 orange
Sugar to taste
Rum, a good dash, about 2
tablespoons

INDIVIDUAL SHORTCAKES
Prepare:
Fluffy Biscuit Dough, page 506
Cut the dough into 3 inch rounds.
Bake the biscuits, split them while
they are hot and spread them with:
Butter
Place between the biscuit halves and
pour over them:
Sugared or cooked fruit

LARGE SHORTCAKE
See the comment under Hazelnut
Torte, page 650.
Prepare:
Fluffy Biscuit Dough, page 506,
Scone Dough, page 509, or any
of the plain sponge cakes, pages
596 and 597
Roll it and place it in 2 layers in a
greased pan. Bake it. Separate the
layers. If desired spread the inner
surface with:
Butter
Place between the layers and over
them:
Sugared or cooked fruit

MOCK SHORTCAKE
Toast on one side:
4 thick slices of bread
Spread the untoasted side with a mix-
ture of:
Soft butter
Sugar and cinnamon
Toast the second side. Place on the
spread side:
Sugared strawberries, cherries,
blueberries, drained stewed fruit
or baby-food fruit
Dot them with:
Butter
Sprinkle them with:
Cinnamon
Broil or bake the toast in a 350° oven
until the berries are hot.

BREAD TARTS
4 Servings
Cut into slices 1 inch thick:
White bread
Cut them with a cutter into large
rounds. Cut into them partially with a
smaller cutter. Hollow the bread to
make shells about ½ inch thick. Spread
them with:
Honey or with butter and
brown sugar
Toast them in a slow oven 325° until
they are delicate brown. Fill the centers with:
Fresh berries or other fruit or
drained canned fruit
Serve them topped with:
Whipped cream

GLAZED STRAWBERRIES
Method I.
Sufficient for Glazing 3 Cupfuls of
Berries
Boil to the jelly stage, page 800, then
strain:
1 cup water
1 cup sugar
1 cup hulled strawberries
2 medium-sized chopped apples
A little red coloring
Cool these ingredients. When the jelly
is about to set pour it or spread it over
3 cupfuls of berries that have been
placed in a baked 9 inch pie shell or in

six 2½ inch tarts. Chill the pie until ready to serve it.

Or use jelly, light in flavor, diluted with a little hot water. Liquefy it over hot water, cool it and use as a glaze.

Method II.
Sufficient for a 9 Inch Pie Shell or Six 2½ Inch Tarts
Hull and crush:

  3 cups strawberries

Strain them first through a ricer, then through a fine sieve. Add to the juice:

  ⅓ cup sugar
  1 tablespoon lemon juice
  1 tablespoon cornstarch
  A little red coloring

Cook and stir these ingredients over low heat until they are thick and transparent. Cool them. Spread them over:

  3 cups hulled strawberries

Chill the dessert until ready to serve it.

APRICOT GLAZE FOR FRUIT
This glaze has the advantage of being available at any season of the year and of keeping for a long time. Soak for 12 hours:

  ¼ lb. dried apricots

in:

  1 cup water

Add:

  ⅓ cup sugar

Cook these ingredients slowly until the apricots are soft. Strain them through a fine sieve. Or add the sugar to 1 cupful cooked, sieved, hot apricot pulp. Place the glaze while hot in a sterilized jar. Seal it. When ready to use the glaze dilute it with water to make it a good consistency to spread and spread it over fruit that has been placed on cake or in baked pie shells.

DUTCH APPLE, PLUM OR PEACH CAKE
Sift before measuring:

  1 cup all-purpose flour

Resift with:

  2 teaspoons tartrate or phosphate baking powder or 1 teaspoon combination type (see Baking Powder, page 501)
  ¼ teaspoon salt
  2 tablespoons sugar

Add:

  1½ tablespoons butter

Work these ingredients like pastry, page 592. Beat in:

  1 egg
  ½ teaspoon vanilla
  About 2 tablespoons milk

to make a stiff dough. Spread it with a lightly floured palm in a round greased 9 or 10 inch oven-proof dish. Cover the top very closely with:

  Fruit

Sprinkle it with:

  Sugar
  Cinnamon

Dot it with:

  Butter

Bake the cake in a hot oven 425° for about 25 minutes. This dough may be used as an upside-down cake (page 764) over berries or other fruit. Try this base:

  1 cup pitted cherries
  1 cup light brown sugar
  ½ teaspoon cinnamon
  4 tablespoons butter

PINEAPPLE, APRICOT OR PEACH SKILLET CAKE OR UPSIDE-DOWN CAKE
Melt in a 9 or 10 inch heavy skillet:

  ¼ or ½ cup butter

Add, cook gently and stir until dissolved:

  1 cup brown sugar

Remove the pan from the fire and add:

  (1 cup pecan meats)

Drain and place on the bottom of the skillet:

  8 slices canned drained pineapple:
  contents of 1 No. 2½ can

Cover the fruit with the following batter. Sift:

  1 cup cake flour

Resift with:

  1 teaspoon any baking powder

Beat in a separate bowl:

  4 egg yolks

Add:

  1 tablespoon melted butter
  1 teaspoon vanilla

Sift in a separate bowl:

  1 cup sugar

Whip until stiff but not dry:

  4 egg whites
  ¼ teaspoon salt

Fold in the sugar 1 tablespoonful at a time. Fold in the yolk mixture, then fold in the sifted flour ¼ cupful at a time. Bake the cake in a moderate oven 325° for about ½ hour. Serve it upside down.

Vary this recipe by using canned peaches or apricots which call for only ½ cupful sugar. Fresh fruit, peaches, cherries, apples, etc., may call for more than 1 cupful, according to the acidity of the fruit.

When done sprinkle the fruit with:
 (Brandy or rum)
The cake may be served with:
 Whipped cream or Rich
 Pudding Sauce, page 756

FRENCH APPLE OR PEACH CAKE

Grease a deep 8 inch pie pan or oven-proof dish. Cover the bottom well with:
 2 cups or more sliced apples,
 peaches or other fruit
Sprinkle the fruit with:
 ⅔ cup sugar
 Cinnamon or nutmeg
 Rind and juice of 1 lemon
Dredge it with:
 1 tablespoon flour or 1 well-beaten
 egg
Dot it with:
 2 to 4 tablespoons butter
Prepare the following batter. Sift before measuring:
 1 cup all-purpose flour
Resift with:
 ½ cup sugar
 1 teaspoon any baking powder
 ¼ teaspoon salt
Beat and add:
 2 egg yolks
 1 tablespoon melted butter
 ¼ cup milk
Beat these ingredients with swift strokes until they are blended. Cover the fruit with the batter. Bake the cake in a hot oven 425° for about 30 minutes. Reverse it on a platter. Cool it slightly. Use the egg whites for:
 Meringue, page 578
Cover the cake with it and bake it in a slow oven 300° for 15 minutes.

Yeast Coffee Cake with Apples, Peaches, Plums, Etc., page 624.

COBBLER
6 Servings
A cobbler is a rich Biscuit Dough, page 505, covered with fruit and baked, or baked with the fruit in the bottom of the pan and the dough on top. It is usually served with Hard Sauce, Butter Sauce, etc., see Pudding Sauces, page 753. It is advisable to thicken the fruit. Combine:
 3 cups prepared fruit: apples,
 peaches, plums, etc.
 ⅔ cup sugar—approximately
 1 tablespoon flour or 1 beaten egg
If you are using flour, permit the mix-

ture to boil. If egg is used, stir the mixture over low heat without boiling until the egg thickens somewhat. Prepare:
 Fluffy Biscuit Dough, page 506
Use ½ the amount given. Place the dough in a greased 8 x 8 inch pan and cover it closely with the fruit, or place the fruit in the bottom of an 8 inch baking dish and cover it with the dough. When using cooked fruit have it boiling hot. Dot the fruit with:
 4 tablespoons butter
Sprinkle it with:
 (¾ teaspoon cinnamon)
Bake the cobbler in a hot oven 425° for about ½ hour.

CHERRY COBBLER
6 Servings
Place in a baking dish:
 3 cups pitted drained cherries:
 1 No. 2 can
The flavor of canned cherries is improved by the addition of a few drops of almond flavoring or ½ teaspoonful cinnamon. Combine and pour over them:
 ¾ cup cherry juice or water
 ½ to ¾ cup sugar
 3 tablespoons flour
Heat this mixture on top of the stove. Prepare ½ the amount of:
 Fluffy Biscuit Dough, page 506
Use in all:
 3 tablespoons butter
 2 tablespoons sugar
Roll the dough on a slightly floured board to the thickness of ⅓ inch. Place it in a greased shallow pan. Cover it with the heated cherries. Bake the cobbler in a hot oven 425° for about 30 minutes.
Or, in preparing the fruit you may omit the flour. Drop the batter by the spoonful onto the hot fruit. Bake it as directed.

German Cherry Cake with Custard, page 637; Blueberry Tart or Kuchen with Custard, page 570; Custard and Fruit Pie, page 581. Don't overlook these good desserts.

FRUIT ROLL OR ROLY POLY
8 Servings
Prepare:
 Fluffy Biscuit Dough, page 506
Use in all:
 4 tablespoons butter
Roll the dough on a floured board to

the thickness of ⅓ inch. Brush it with:
White of an egg
This will keep it from being soggy.
Place a filling, see recipe below, upon
the dough and roll it like a jelly roll.
Cut the roll, if desired, into 1 inch
slices or leave it whole. Bake the roll
in a greased pan in a hot oven 425° for
about 30 minutes. Serve it hot with:
**Hard Sauce, etc., Sauces, page
753, or cream**

FILLINGS FOR FRUIT ROLL
Apple Filling
Boil for 2 minutes:
1 cup water
¾ cup sugar
Pare, core and slice:
3 lbs. apples: 7 large apples
Add the apples to the sirup and cook
them until they are nearly tender.
Drain and cool them. Spread them on
the dough. Sprinkle them with:
¼ cup brown sugar
⅓ teaspoon cinnamon
⅓ cup butter

Apricot Filling
Stew:
¾ lb. Apricots, page 450
Drain them. Reserve ⅓ of the apricots. Spread the remainder on the
dough and dot them with:
⅓ cup butter
Bake the roll. Serve it hot with:
Apricot Sauce
Cream:
4 tablespoons butter
1 cup confectioners' sugar
Beat in:
1 egg yolk
Strain the reserved apricots. Add them
to the above. Chill the sauce.

Mincemeat Filling
Combine:
1½ cups mincemeat
⅔ cup tart finely sliced apples
¼ teaspoon salt
**2 teaspoons lemon juice or
2 tablespoons brandy**
Serve the roll with:
Lemon Sauce, page 757

BLACKBERRY ROLL
Prepare the dough for:
Fruit Roll, page 635
Roll out the dough. Omit the egg
white. Brush the dough with:
2 tablespoons melted butter
Sprinkle it with:

3 cups blackberries
½ cup sugar
(½ teaspoon cinnamon)
Roll the dough like a jelly roll. Place
it in a large well-greased pan. Surround it with:
3 cups blackberries
½ cup sugar
Bake it in a hot oven 425° for about 30
minutes. Cut it into slices and serve
them with the sauce from the pan.

PINEAPPLE MERINGUE CAKES
Attractive served in custard cups. Fol-
low the rule on page 580 for:
Pineapple Meringue Pie
Substitute for the pie shell:
**Lady fingers or pieces of sponge
cake**

APPLE STRUDEL
Strudel is to the Hungarian what pie
and biscuit are to the American. Flour,
egg and water are combined with a
little salt and are kneaded until they
become so elastic that the dough can
be stretched until it is as thin as paper.
This is done on a large table covered
with a cloth. The dough is then sprinkled with fruit or vegetables, butter or
cream and nuts, rolled like a huge jelly
roll, twisted into a pan and baked in a
moderate oven. The result is superlative.
Sift into a bowl:
1½ cups all-purpose flour
¼ teaspoon salt
Add:
1 beaten egg
Heat until lukewarm and add:
⅓ cup water or milk
Combine the ingredients quickly with
a pastry blender. Knead the dough on
a board until it is elastic and no longer
sticks to the board. Place it on a
floured board and cover it with a warm
bowl for 30 minutes. Work into the
dough:
2 tablespoons melted butter
Place it in the center of a large table
covered with a floured cloth. Gently
pull and stretch the dough, placing
both hands under it, until it is as thin
as paper. Be careful not to tear it.
Strudel is stretched to tremendous
dimensions, 2 x 2 yards or more.
Spread the dough with:
4 lbs. finely chopped tart apples
1½ cups raisins and currants
1½ teaspoons cinnamon

¼ lb. blanched shredded almonds
1 cup sugar
5 tablespoons melted butter

Do not feel bound by these ingredients or proportions. Spread the dough with 6 tablespoonfuls dry bread crumbs if a juicy fruit is substituted.

Fold the dough over one side, hold up the tablecloth and let the strudel roll into a huge roll. Twist the roll into a large, greased pan or cut it into pieces and trim the edges. Bake the strudel for ½ hour in a hot oven 400°, reduce the heat to 350° and bake it until it is crisp and brown. Serve it before it is cold.

APPLE CRISP OR FRUIT PARADISE
6 Servings

This is the best dessert imaginable when made with good cooking apples. It is a very indifferent one made with poor ones.

Peel, core and slice into a 7 x 7 inch pan:
    3 lbs. tart apples: 7 or 8 large
    cooking apples

If you wish to serve the cake at table, use an oven-proof pie dish.

Four cupfuls of diced rhubarb flavored with lemon juice and rind or 3 cupfuls of pitted cherries may be substituted. Add sugar to taste.

The apple layer when cooked should be about ¾ inch thick. If the apples are dry and sweet, dot them with:
    Butter
Sprinkle them with:
    Lemon juice and grated rind

The success of this dish depends upon the flavor of the apples, which should be tart. A good apple needs no additional ingredients. Work like pastry with a pastry blender or a knife or the finger-tips may be used, but the mixture must be lightly worked so that it does not become oily:
    1 cup all-purpose flour
    1 cup brown sugar
    ½ cup butter
    ½ teaspoon salt if butter is unsalted
    (1 teaspoon cinnamon)

Some cooks find this topping too heavy and prefer using only ½ of these measurements.

Spread these ingredients over the apples. They may crumble, but that is unimportant. Bake the cake in a moderate oven 375° for about 30 minutes,

or until the apples are done. Serve it hot or cold, with or without:
    Cream

GRANDMOTHER'S SOUR CREAM APPLE CAKE OR SOUFFLÉ
Serves 12 People or More

This dish is always referred to as Apfelkuchen but it is really a Torte. When properly made it might be classed as a soufflé, but no matter what it is called or how it is made, it is a remarkably good dessert.

Pare, core and slice:
    5 cups tart apples
Melt in a skillet:
    ¼ cup butter

Add the apples and cook them covered over a very low fire, stirring them from time to time until they are tender. Combine and pour over the apples:
    ½ cup sour cream
    Rind and juice of 1 lemon
    1 cup sugar, scant unless apples
    are very tart
    2 tablespoons all-purpose flour
    8 egg yolks
    (½ cup blanched shredded almonds)

Stir these ingredients over a low fire until they thicken. Remove the skillet from the fire. Cool the mixture. Whip until stiff but not dry:
    8 egg whites
    ½ teaspoon salt

Fold them lightly into the apple mixture. Spread the soufflé to the thickness of 1 inch in a large pan or oven-proof dish. Sprinkle the top with a mixture of:
    Sugar
    Cinnamon
    Dry bread crumbs
    ¼ cup blanched shredded almonds

Bake it in a moderate oven 325° until it is firm, about 45 minutes. It may be served hot, but it is best very cold, covered with:
    Whipped cream flavored with
    vanilla or with Angelica Ice
    Cream, page 764

ROMAN APPLE CAKE
Method I.

A rich delight, beloved of "mankind." Without the apples, a superb coffee cake.

Sift:
    1½ cups all-purpose flour
Add:
    ½ cup brown sugar

½ cup white sugar
½ cup cold butter cut into bits
½ teaspoon cinnamon
⅛ teaspoon salt

Use the hands to crumble this mixture until blended but not oily. Divide the crumbs into 2 parts. Stir into ½ the crumbs the following ingredients, combined and beaten:

1 teaspoon soda
½ cup buttermilk or sour milk
1 egg

Place ½ this batter in a deep greased oven-proof 9 inch pie plate. Pare, core, slice thinly and scatter over the batter:

1 large or 2 small tart apples

Cover it with the remaining crumbs. You may dot the top with:

Butter and cinnamon

Bake the cake in a moderate oven 325° for about 1 hour.

Method II.
Or, for an excellent cake that is less rich than the above, prepare:

Crumb Spice Cake, page 615

To serve 6 persons use only ½ the amount of the ingredients given. Reserve the crumbs as directed. Place ½ the batter in a greased 9 inch glass oven-proof pie plate. Pare, slice finely and spread over the surface:

1 large tart cooking apple

Cover it with the second half of the batter. Bake the cake in a moderate oven 375° for 20 minutes. Sprinkle the reserved crumbs over the top. Bake it for about 15 minutes longer, or until done. My best gauge for this cake is to remove it when it begins to shrink from the sides. You may serve either cake with:

Cream or whipped cream

SOUR CREAM CHERRY CAKE
8 Servings

Combine and work with the finger-tips until well blended:

1½ cups zwieback crumbs: 4½ oz.
¾ cup sugar
¾ teaspoon cinnamon
½ cup melted butter

Press the crumbs on the bottom and against the sides of a 9 inch oven-proof baking dish to form a shell less than ¼ inch thick. This shell may be filled at once, but it is much better when chilled for several hours. Fill the shell with:

Cherry Custard

Beat:

3 eggs

Add:

½ cup sugar
¾ cup sour cream
2 cups fresh or canned drained cherries

Bake the cake in a moderate oven 325° until the custard is firm. Serve it hot or very cold.

Cheese Cake, page 585.

GERMAN CHERRY CAKE
About 5 Servings—A 9 Inch Cake

The Germans who became political refugees in 1832 and 1848 brought with them to their new American home this treasured rule for Cherry Cake. There are, of course, different versions of the same cake. Mine is a fairly modern one which may call displeasure down on my head. However, even a German Cherry Cake rule must bow to the Zeitgeist.

Drain well the contents of:

2 No. 2½ cans pie cherries or use fresh cherries: 2½ cups solid pitted fruit

Pour over the cherries:

6 tablespoons sugar

Very acid cherries may require more sugar. Permit them to stand for about 1 hour, or until the sugar is dissolved. Stir them gently several times. Drain them. Meanwhile prepare:

1½ cups sifted flour

Resift it with:

1½ teaspoons cinnamon
6 tablespoons sugar
⅛ teaspoon salt

Cut into these ingredients with a pastry blender or 2 knives until blended:

½ cup butter: 1 stick

Add to the above:

1 beaten egg

Now wade in with your hands and work the dough until it will hold together, but no longer. Chill it. Pat it into a 9 inch glass oven-proof pie pan. Let it come to the upper edge of the pan. See that it is spread evenly. Crimp the dough around the edge with the tines of a fork. Now back to our cherries. Measure the sirup drained from them. There should be ¾ cupful. If there is less, add cherry juice to make up that amount. Taste it. Add sugar if it seems to be too sour. Reserve ¼ cupful. Place the rest on a low fire. Stir into the ¼ cupful until smooth:

4 teaspoons cornstarch

When the rest of the juice is boiling stir in the cornstarch mixture. Stir and cook over low heat for 2 or 3 minutes until the mixture is no longer cloudy. You may add:

(¼ teaspoon almond extract)

Place the cherries in the tart shell, pour the hot juice over them, pop the cake into a moderate oven 350° and bake it from 50 to 60 minutes.

PEACH CRISP OR CRUMBLE

4 Servings

Pare and slice:

8 fresh peaches

Place them in a greased baking dish. Sprinkle them with:

¼ cup water
2 teaspoons lemon juice

Combine until the mixture resembles corn meal:

¾ cup all-purpose flour
⅛ teaspoon salt
1 cup brown sugar
2 tablespoons butter
(¼ teaspoon cinnamon)

Sprinkle this over the peaches. Bake them in a moderate oven 350° until the fruit is tender and the top is brown.

WASHINGTON OR BOSTON CREAM PIE

Sift:

¾ cup sugar

Beat until soft:

⅓ cup butter

Add the sugar gradually. Blend these ingredients until they are very light and creamy. Beat in one at a time:

2 eggs

Add:

1 teaspoon vanilla

Sift before measuring:

1½ cups cake flour

Resift with:

2 teaspoons tartrate or phosphate baking powder or 1½ teaspoons combination type (see Baking Powder, page 501)
⅓ teaspoon salt

Add the sifted ingredients in about 3 parts to the butter mixture alternately with thirds of:

½ cup milk

Beat the batter after each addition until it is smooth. Bake the cake in 2 greased 8 inch layer pans in a moderate oven 375° for about 25 minutes. Place between the layers a filling of:

Whipped cream
A cooked Cake Filling, page 705, usually custard filling, or jam, jelly, cooked or sugared fruit

Sprinkle the top with:

Confectioners' sugar

or spread it with:

Whipped cream

In Italy I was served a similar cake baked in 3 layers. One layer was spread with raspberry jam, one with custard filling flavored with rum. The cake was spread with uncooked white icing. A superb combination.

Layer Cakes

A layer cake is a complete course. Unfortunately, it is frequently served in addition to a dessert, which dwarfs it.

After a long period abroad nothing could make me more homesick or emotional than an American magazine ad of a luscious layer cake, except a pictured lemon pie.

When serving layer cake you need not stick to the usual white or chocolate icing. Try a cream, butterscotch or fruit filling. There isn't anything better than plain sponge cake layers filled with sweetened pie cherries topped with whipped cream. Or serve a cake as suggested under the preceding Washington or Boston Cream Pie. Also see the section on Cake Icings and Fillings, page 693.

PLAIN LAYER CAKE

Sift:

1 cup sugar

Beat until soft:

¼ cup butter

Add the sifted sugar gradually. Blend these ingredients until they are very light and creamy. Beat in one at a time:

2 eggs

Add:

1 teaspoon vanilla

Sift before measuring:

1⅔ cups cake flour

Resift with:

2½ teaspoons tartrate or phosphate baking powder or 1½ teaspoons combination type (see Baking Powder, page 501)
¼ teaspoon salt

Add the sifted ingredients to the butter mixture in about 3 parts alternately with thirds of:
½ cup milk
Bake the cake in 2 greased 9 inch layer pans in a moderate oven 375° for about 25 minutes. Spread between the layers:
Jam or jelly
Chocolate, Vanilla, Lemon Filling, etc., page 705, or any Cake Icing, page 693

WHITE LAYER CAKE

Use the recipes for:
White Layer Cake I or II, page 600
No. I will make three 9 inch layers.
No. II will make two 9 inch layers.
Spread them with any desired icing, pages 693-705.

EIGHT LAYER CAKE

This cake was once the pièce de résistance of the American hostess. Follow the rule on page 604 for:
Four Egg Yellow Loaf or Layer Cake using the combination type baking powder
Bake it in 8 layers. Spread them with:
Jelly or Chocolate Filling, page 706
Sprinkle the top with:
Confectioners' sugar

SOUR MILK LAYER CAKE

Sift:
1 cup sugar
Beat until soft:
⅓ cup butter
Add the sugar gradually. When these ingredients are creamy, beat in:
2 beaten egg yolks
1 teaspoon vanilla
Sift before measuring:
1¾ cups cake flour
Resift with:
¼ teaspoon soda
2 teaspoons tartrate or phosphate baking powder or 1¾ teaspoons combination type (see Baking Powder, page 501)
¼ teaspoon salt
Add the sifted ingredients to the butter mixture in 3 parts alternately with thirds of:
⅔ cup sour milk
Beat the batter after each addition until it is smooth. Whip until stiff but not dry:
2 egg whites
¼ teaspoon salt

Fold them lightly into the batter. Bake the cake in 2 greased 8 inch layer pans in a moderate oven 375° for about ½ hour. Spread it with:
Fig Filling, page 708, or any desired filling or icing, page 693

PEPPERMINT CANDY CAKE

The sort of thing most children like: a decorative Christmas cake.
Prepare by the preceding rule:
Sour Milk Layer Cake
Pour the batter into 2 well-greased lightly floured 8 inch layer pans. Crush so that no piece is larger than ¼ inch:
⅓ cup peppermint candy
Use the soft red and white sticks. Sprinkle the candy over the cake at this time or bake the batter for exactly 7 minutes and sprinkle it over the layers without removing the pans from the oven. Bake the cake in a moderate oven 375° for about ½ hour. Remove the cake from the pans at once. The candy should be in creamy lumps throughout the cake. Spread the cake with:
White Icing, page 694, or Chocolate Icing, page 699
Sprinkle over the cake:
(⅓ cup crushed peppermint candy)

MOLASSES LAYER CAKE

This is a fine change from the usual white or yellow cake. It is richly flavored and easily made.
Sift:
½ cup brown sugar
Beat until soft:
¼ cup butter
Add the sugar gradually. Blend these ingredients until they are very light and creamy. Beat in one at a time:
2 egg yolks
Beat in:
½ cup molasses
Sift before measuring:
2 cups cake flour
Resift with:
1 teaspoon soda
Add the sifted ingredients to the butter mixture in about 3 parts alternately with thirds of:
¾ cup water
1 teaspoon vanilla
Whip until stiff but not dry:
2 egg whites
¼ teaspoon salt
Fold them lightly into the batter. Bake the cake in 2 greased 9 inch layer pans in a moderate oven 375° for about 30

minutes. Spread it with:
Pineapple Icing, page 704,
Raisin Smash Icing, page 694, or
Mocha Icing, page 703

CHOCOLATE LAYER CAKE
The chocolate cakes are all massed under one heading in the preceding section, page 608. Among them are many fine layer cakes and the loaf cakes given may be used for that purpose as well.

Many of the loaf cakes given on and after page 603 make fine layer cakes.

DOBOS TORTE
The many-tiered Hungarian chocolate cake that looks rich, is rich and enriches all who eat it.
Beat until light and lemon colored:
5 egg yolks
Beat in gradually:
½ cup sugar
My old recipe says cheerfully beat for ½ hour or longer. Add:
½ teaspoon vanilla
Sift before measuring:
½ cup cake flour
Resift 4 times with:
¼ teaspoon salt
Beat in the sifted ingredients gradually. Whip until stiff but not dry:
5 egg whites
Fold them into the batter. Bake the cake in 9 layers using well-greased 7½ or 8 inch layer cake pans in a moderate oven 375° for about 5 to 8 minutes. Work rapidly. Spread between the layers the following filling.
Place in a double boiler:
½ cup sugar
4 large eggs
1 inch vanilla bean
Or add 1 teaspoonful of vanilla extract after the filling has cooled.
Beat until the eggs begin to thicken. Cool the filling slightly. Cut into pieces and dissolve:
¼ lb. bittersweet chocolate
in:
2 tablespoons boiling water
Keep this warm. Cream until light:
⅞ cup butter: 1¾ sticks
Add the chocolate mixture. Beat this into the egg mixture. This filling may also be spread over the top and sides of the cake, but the true Hungarian will content himself with the filling spread between layers only. The best-looking layer is reserved for the top and a caramel glaze crowns the chef-d'oeuvre. Melt and brown in a skillet:
3 tablespoons sugar
Pour it over the cake. Spread it with a hot knife. "Rest" the cake in a cool place for 12 or more hours.

MAPLE BUTTERNUT CAKE
Follow the rule on page 601 for:
White Cake II
Fold into the batter before adding the egg whites:
½ cup chopped butternuts
Bake the cake in 2 greased 9 inch layer pans. Line the bottoms of the pans with lightly greased waxed paper. Bake in a moderate oven 375° for about 25 minutes, or until done. When cool ice the cake with:
Maple Sugar Icing, page 698

LADY BALTIMORE CAKE
Prepare the batter for:
White Cake I, page 600
Bake it in 3 layers. Place the following filling between the layers: Chop:
6 figs
½ cup seeded raisins
1 cup nut meats
Prepare:
White Icing or Seven Minute White Icing, page 700
Reserve a generous third of this. To the rest add the nuts, figs and raisins. Spread the filling between the layers. Spread the reserved icing over the top.

POPPY SEED CAKE WITH CUSTARD FILLING
Ruth Buchan bakes this cake in a 9 x 12 inch pan, sprinkles it when cool with powdered sugar and serves it for tea with great success.
Combine and soak for 2 hours:
⅔ cup poppy seed
¾ cup milk
Beat until soft:
⅔ cup butter
Add gradually:
1½ cups sugar
Cream these ingredients until they are fluffy. Sift before measuring:
2 cups cake flour
Resift with:
3 teaspoons tartrate or phosphate baking powder or 2½ teaspoons combination type (see Baking Powder, page 501)
½ teaspoon salt

Combine the soaked poppy seeds and:
¼ cup milk
1 teaspoon vanilla
Add the sifted ingredients to the butter mixture in about 3 parts alternately with the liquid ingredients. Beat the batter after each addition until it is blended. Whip until stiff but not dry, then fold in:
4 egg whites
Bake the cake in two 9 inch layer pans in a moderate oven 375° for about 20 minutes. Place between the layers:
Custard Filling, page 705
Serve the cake with:
Chocolate Sauce, page 757

CHARLOTTE POLONAISE
The recipe of an old Southern family, who remember that the colored cook crushed the almonds with a flatiron. The donor added that she liked the cake better on the second day when the filling was well soaked in.
Prepare:
Eight Layer Cake, page 640
Bake it in 5 or more layers. Prepare double the amount of:
Custard Filling, page 705
Add to ½ the filling:
4 cups ground or crushed, blanched or unblanched almonds: 1 lb.
Add to the other ½:
½ lb. citron cut into small pieces
Place these fillings alternately between the cake layers. The almond filling is best on top.

GRAHAM CRACKER SPONGE CAKE WITH OR WITHOUT NUT MEATS
Sift:
1 cup sugar
Beat until light:
6 egg yolks
Add the sugar gradually and beat these ingredients until they are very light and creamy. Add:
1 teaspoon vanilla or ½ teaspoon grated lemon rind
Roll graham crackers until they are very fine. Combine and add to the egg mixture:
1 cup graham cracker crumbs
1 teaspoon any baking powder
Add:
(1 cup chopped English walnut meats)
Whip until stiff but not dry:

6 egg whites
¼ teaspoon salt
Fold them lightly into the cake batter. Bake the cake in an ungreased 9 inch tube pan, or in 3 layer pans, in a moderate oven 350°. Place a cooked cake filling between the layers:
Custard Cake Filling, page 705, etc.

GRAHAM CRACKER BUTTER CAKE
Beat until soft:
3 tablespoons butter
Add gradually and cream until fluffy:
⅞ cup sugar
Beat in:
3 egg yolks
1 teaspoon vanilla
(1 cup finely chopped nut meats)
Crush:
2¼ cups graham cracker crumbs
Sift them with:
2½ teaspoons tartrate or phosphate baking powder or 2 teaspoons combination type (see Baking Powder, page 501)
½ teaspoon salt
Add the crumb mixture in about 3 parts to the butter mixture alternately with:
¾ cup milk
Whip until stiff, then fold in:
3 egg whites
⅛ teaspoon salt
Pour the batter into 2 greased 9 inch layer pans. Bake it in a moderate oven 350° for about ½ hour. Place between the layers:
Raspberry jam and whipped cream or Custard Filling, page 705
This cake is good iced with Caramel Icing, page 698.

BANANA CAKE
I wish I might comment on all the cakes in this book. Please try this one if you like bananas and make the comments yourself.
Sift:
1½ cups sugar
Beat until soft:
½ cup butter
Add the sifted sugar gradually. Blend these ingredients until they are very light and creamy. Beat in 1 at a time:
2 eggs
Sift before measuring:
2¼ cups cake flour

Resift with:
    ½ teaspoon any baking powder
    ¾ teaspoon soda
    ½ teaspoon salt
Prepare:
    1 cup lightly mashed bananas
Add:
    1 teaspoon vanilla
    ¼ cup sour milk
Add the sifted ingredients to the butter mixture in about 3 parts alternately with thirds of the banana mixture. Beat the batter after each addition until it is smooth. Bake the cake in 2 greased 9 inch layer pans in a moderate oven 350° for about ½ hour.
Place between the layers:
    2 sliced bananas
Spread the cake with:
    White Icing, page 694
Use ½ the amount given if only the top of the cake is to be iced. Use the full amount if the icing is to be spread between the layers and on top. This cake is good uniced sprinkled with powdered sugar or served with whipped cream.

BANANA CHOCOLATE CAKE
Sift:
    1 cup sugar
Beat until soft:
    ½ cup butter
Add the sugar gradually. Blend these ingredients until they are very light and creamy. Beat in:
    1 cup sliced bananas
    ½ teaspoon vanilla
Beat in one at a time:
    3 eggs
Sift:
    2½ cups cake flour
Resift with:
    ½ teaspoon salt
    2½ teaspoons tartrate or phosphate baking powder or 2 teaspoons combination type (see Baking Powder, page 501)
    3 tablespoons cocoa
Add the sifted ingredients to the butter mixture in about 3 parts alternately with thirds of:
    1 cup top milk or ½ cup evaporated milk diluted with ½ cup water
Bake the cake in 2 greased 9 inch layer pans in a moderate oven 375° for about 20 minutes. Spread the layers with:
    Chocolate Icing, page 699, or
    Creamy Chocolate Filling, page 706

CARAMEL BANANA CAKE WITH WHITE OR CARAMEL ICING
Bake in layers:
    Quick Caramel Cake, page 607
Cover the bottom layer closely with:
    Sliced bananas
Spread the cake between the layers and over the top with:
    White Icing, page 694, or
    Caramel Icing, page 698
Decorate it with whole:
    (Walnut meats)

PINEAPPLE CAKE
Unusual, as crushed pineapple is added to the cake batter with a very pleasing result.
Sift:
    1 cup sugar
Beat until soft:
    ½ cup butter
Add to this and cream until fluffy ¾ cupful of the sugar. Beat in one at a time:
    3 egg yolks
Sift before measuring:
    2½ cups cake flour
Resift with:
    2 teaspoons tartrate or phosphate baking powder or 1½ teaspoons combination type (see Baking Powder, page 501)
    ½ teaspoon soda
    ½ teaspoon salt
Combine:
    ½ cup orange juice
    ½ teaspoon almond or 1 teaspoon vanilla extract
The contents of:
    1 can crushed pineapple: 9 oz.
Add the sifted ingredients to the butter mixture in 3 parts with thirds of the liquid ingredients. Beat the batter until it is smooth after each addition. Whip until stiff but not dry:
    3 egg whites
Add gradually, beating constantly, the remaining ¼ cupful of sugar. Fold the egg whites into the batter. Bake the cake in 2 greased 9 inch layer pans in a moderate oven 350° for about ½ hour.
Spread the layers with:
    Seven Minute Icing, page 701, or Lemon Icing, page 703

ORANGE CAKE
Most rules for orange cake prove to be disappointing, for upon reading them you find that they are merely sponge

or butter cake with an orange filling. This one calls for orange juice in the batter plus orange icing. A gorgeous gilded lily presented without apologies. Grate:

Rind of 1 orange

into:

1½ cups sugar

Cream this until fluffy with:

¾ cup butter

Beat in one at a time:

3 eggs

Sift, then measure:

3 cups cake flour

Resift with:

¾ teaspoon salt
4½ teaspoons tartrate or phosphate baking powder or 3½ teaspoons combination type (see Baking Powder, page 501)

Measure:

½ cup orange juice
½ cup water
2 tablespoons lemon juice

Add the sifted ingredients in about 3 parts to the butter mixture alternately with the liquid. Beat the batter until it is smooth after each addition.

Bake the cake in 2 deep or 3 shallow layers in 9 inch cake pans in a 375° oven for about ½ hour. Ice it with:

Orange Icing, page 702

Orange Raisin Cake, page 617.

ORANGE CREAM LAYER CAKE

Sift:

1 cup sugar

Beat until light:

4 egg yolks

Add the sugar gradually. Beat these ingredients until they are well creamed. Add:

3 tablespoons cold water
1½ teaspoons grated orange rind
½ teaspoon vanilla

Sift before measuring:

1 cup cake flour

Resift with:

1¼ teaspoons tartrate or phosphate baking powder or 1 teaspoon combination type (see Baking Powder, page 501)

Add the sifted ingredients to the sugar mixture. Beat the batter until it is smooth. Whip until stiff but not dry:

4 egg whites
¼ teaspoon salt

Fold them lightly into the batter. Bake the cake in 2 greased 9 inch layer pans

in a moderate oven 325° for about ½ hour. When the cake is cool spread the following filling between the layers.

Orange Cream Filling

Soak for 5 minutes:

1 teaspoon gelatine

in:

1 teaspoon water

Sift into a double boiler:

2 tablespoons cornstarch
2 tablespoons flour
¾ cup sugar

Add:

¾ cup boiling water

Stir and cook these ingredients over boiling water for 20 minutes. Add:

1 tablespoon butter

Pour part of this mixture over:

2 egg yolks

Beat them and pour them into the double boiler. Cook and stir the custard long enough to permit the yolks to thicken. Add the soaked gelatine. Stir it until it is dissolved. Remove the custard from the fire. Add:

Grated rind of 1 orange
3 tablespoons orange juice
3 tablespoons lemon juice

Cool the custard. Beat until stiff:

½ cup heavy cream

Fold it into the custard. Chill it for 1 hour. Spread it between the layers. Spread the cake with:

Orange Icing, page 702

ORANGE LAYER CAKE

Follow the preceding rule for:

Orange Cream Layer Cake or any white or yellow layer cake

Spread the layers with:

Orange Filling, page 708

Spread the cake with:

Orange Icing, White Icing or Chocolate Icing, page 699

LEMON LAYER CAKE

This is, after chocolate cake, the most popular everyday cake served at my table. It is a light and delightful dessert, quickly made and economical. Prepare:

Gold Cake, page 603, or any yellow or white layer cake

Spread between the layers:

Lemon Filling, page 708

Sprinkle the top of the cake with:

Powdered sugar

or, if preferred, spread it with:
Lemon Icing or White Icing,
page 694

CHOCOLATE LAYER CAKE WITH FRUIT FILLING

Prepare:
Chocolate Devil's Food or
Custard Cake, page 611
Bake the cake in two 9 inch layer pans.
Prepare the following filling. Cook in
a double boiler:
¾ cup evaporated milk
¼ cup water
¾ cup sugar
⅛ teaspoon salt
When the sugar is dissolved add and
cook until thick:
¼ cup chopped dates
¼ cup chopped figs
¼ cup chopped raisins
Cool these ingredients and add:
1 teaspoon vanilla
½ cup chopped nut meats
Spread the filling between the layers.
Spread the cake with:
Chocolate Icing, page 699

RASPBERRY LAYER CAKE

Prepare two 9 inch cake layers by any
rule for:
Layer Cake
When cold spread between the layers:
Raspberry jam
Cover the top with:
Marzipan, page 783, or almond
paste
Whip until stiff:
1 cup heavy cream
Fold in:
1 tablespoon sugar
1 teaspoon vanilla or 1 tablespoon
rum
Decorate the top with the cream. Stud
it with:
Blanched almonds

RASPBERRY RUM CAKE OR ENGLISH TRIFLE

This is usually rather a dry sponge
cake baked in layers and spread with
jam. It may be garnished with whipped
cream. Sometimes the cake, or 1 layer
of it, is sprinkled with rum. Sometimes
rum is added to the custard filling.
This is good with sweetened, thickened pie cherries, apricot jam or other
fruit or preserves.

Prepare by any rule:
Sponge Cake, page 596
Bake the sponge cake in layers. While
the layers are hot sprinkle them gener-
ously with:
Rum
Spread between the layers:
Raspberry or other jam
Serve the cake with:
Custard Sauce, Whipped Cream
or Rich Pudding Sauce, page 756

WHITE LAYER CAKE WITH CREAM NUT FILLING

Prepare:
White Cake I or II, page 600
Bake it in layer pans. Spread between
the layers:
Almond or Hazelnut Custard
Filling, page 707
Sprinkle the top with:
Confectioners' sugar
or spread it with:
White Icing, page 694

NUT LAYER CAKE WITH JAM FILLING

It is always a pleasure to serve this
good little cake.
Sift:
1 cup sugar
Beat:
6 egg yolks
Add the sugar gradually and beat these
ingredients until they are very creamy.
Sift:
¾ cup cake flour
Resift with:
½ teaspoon any baking powder
Beat these ingredients into the egg
mixture. Stir in:
½ cup finely chopped nut meats
1 teaspoon vanilla
Whip until stiff but not dry:
6 egg whites
¼ teaspoon salt
Fold them lightly into the cake batter.
Bake the cake in two 9 inch layers in a
moderate oven 350°. Spread between
the layers:
Tart jam
Ice the top and the sides of the cake
with:
White Icing, page 694
or serve it uniced with:
Whipped cream

Filled Cakes: Cup Cakes, Rings, Rolls and Meringues, Torten, Tarts, Cream Puffs, Etc.

FILLED DAFFODIL CAKE

Prepare:
> Daffodil Cake, page 600

Cut the cake crosswise into 2 layers.
Place between the layers:
> Orange Filling, page 708

Spread the top with:
> Orange Icing, page 702

FILLED ANGEL OR SPONGE CAKE

There are many attractive ways of serving a filled Angel or Sponge Cake. Cut the cake in 2 crosswise layers with a slightly thicker lower layer. Or, hollow a cake leaving a shell of about 1 inch. Use a piece of top crust to close the hole in the bottom; use the rest of the removed cake shredded in the filling. See Cake Fillings, page 705. Or cut a cake into pieces suitable for individual servings. Allow 2 pieces of cake per person, fill the slices and garnish the tops with cream, nut meats, cherries, etc. These cakes may be served with sauce.

FILLED ANGEL CAKE

This makes a marvelous dessert. Bake by the rule on page 599:
> Angel Cake I or II

When the cake is cold cut it crosswise into 2 layers.

I.
Spread between the layers and over the top and sides of the cake:
> Seven Minute White Icing, page 700

Top the cake with:
> ½ cup blanched, shredded, toasted almonds

II.
Or, prepare the following:
Almond Cream Filling
Cook in a double boiler and stir until thick:
> 3 egg yolks
> 1 cup sweet or sour cream
> ¼ cup sugar
> 2 teaspoons cornstarch
> ⅛ teaspoon salt

Remove from the fire, cool and add:
> 1 teaspoon vanilla, 1 tablespoon rum or ¼ teaspoon almond extract

Spread the filling between the layers.
Spread the top of the cake with:
> Seven Minute White Icing, page 700. Use only ½ the amount given

Sprinkle it with:
> 1 cup blanched, shredded, toasted almonds

III.
Spread between the layers:
> Chocolate Whipped Cream Filling, page 706, Whipped Cream and Cocoa Filling, page 707, or Almond Filling, page 707

IV.
A famous hostess serves the following:
Immediately before serving place between 2 layers of angel cake:
> Ice cream: vanilla, strawberry, etc.

Spread the entire cake with a blanket of:
> Whipped cream

covered with:
> Freshly shredded coconut

Garnish the cake with:
> (Berries)

V.
Serve pieces of angel or sponge cake with:
> Sweetened thickened pie cherries, page 570, or crushed pineapple or Pineapple Meringue Pie Filling, page 580, or apricots, etc.

Top with:
> Ice cream or whipped cream

VI.
Prepare an angel or sponge cake shell (see first paragraph). Shred the removed cake. Combine it with:
> 18 oz. crushed pineapple
> 1 cup shredded coconut
> 20 diced marshmallows
> 12 or more maraschino cherries
> 1 cup heavy cream, whipped

Fill the shell. Cover the top with:
> 1 cup heavy cream, whipped

to which you may add:
> (1 teaspoon vanilla or 1 tablespoon rum)

Chill the cake for 6 hours.
VII.
Make an angel or sponge cake shell (see first paragraph). Shred the removed cake. Combine it with:

Chocolate or Maple Charlotte,
Charlotte Russe, Strawberry,
Coffee or some other Bavarian,
one of the fillings for Refrigerator Cakes, Mocha, Chocolate or
some other sponge
Garnish the top with:
Whipped cream, chopped nut
meats, strawberries or other
berries, toasted almonds or
crushed nut brittle

VIII.
Cut an angel cake into 2 layers. Soak:
2 teaspoons gelatine
in:
⅓ cup water
Place it over hot water. Stir until it is
dissolved. Remove from heat. Stir in:
1 cup confectioners' sugar
2 tablespoons strong coffee
Cool slightly. Beat until light and
add:
8 egg yolks
1 teaspoon vanilla
Whip until stiff. Then fold in:
1 pint heavy cream: 2 cups
Chill until nearly set. Spread between
layers and on top of the cake. Sprinkle
top with:
½ cup blanched, slivered, toasted
almonds
Chill in refrigerator for 2 or 3 hours.

IX.
Place on a serving plate:
Angel Cake
Combine and beat with an electric
mixer for 2 minutes:
1 cup red raspberries
1 egg white
1 cup sugar
⅛ teaspoon salt
Fill the hole and spread the cake with
this mixture. Decorate it with a few
choice:
Raspberries
Chill until ready to serve.

RULE FOR FILLED CUP CAKES
These tempting cakes are convenient to
serve at large dinners, teas or picnics.
Bake:
Cup Cakes
Remove a thin slice from the top of
each and make a slight hollow in each
center. Fill the hollow with a cooked:
Cake Filling
Replace the thin slices. Spread the
cakes with:
Icing
Or fill the cakes with jam. Serve them
with Custard Sauce, page 754.

SUGGESTIONS:
Daffodils
White or yellow cup cakes
Orange or lemon filling
Orange or lemon icing
Chocolate Gems
Cocoa or chocolate cup cakes
Chocolate or custard filling
Chocolate or white icing

CHOCOLATE OR OTHER CUP CAKES À LA MODE
Prepare the batter for:
Chocolate Custard Cake or any
Devil's Food, pages 611, 612,
Cocoa Cup Cakes, page 661, or
other chocolate cake
Bake it in large well-greased muffin
tins in a moderate oven 375°. When
the cakes are cold cut them crosswise
into halves. Place between the halves
a round slice of:
Vanilla Ice Cream, page 761
Cut it with a biscuit cutter the same
size as the cakes. Serve the cakes with:
Hot Chocolate Sauce, page 757

FILLED SPONGE CAKE RING
Bake in a ring mold:
Sponge Cake, page 596
Stir and beat until a good consistency
to spread:
Currant jelly
Spread it over the cake. Sprinkle the
top with:
Chopped nut meats
You may fill the center shortly before
serving with:
Whipped cream or Custard
Sauce, page 754
(Drained canned pineapple)
You may flavor the cream with brandy
or rum or use white cherries or some
other stewed or canned fruit, drained
and sprinkled with brandy or rum.

CHOCOLATE DATE TORTE
A richly flavored exceedingly good
cake.
Prepare:
Chocolate Sponge Cake, page
608
Sprinkle:
2 tablespoons sifted flour
over:
¾ cup chopped dates
1 tablespoon grated orange rind
(½ cup chopped nut meats)
Beat these ingredients into the cake
batter before folding in the egg whites.

Bake the cake as directed in a 9 inch tube pan. Sprinkle it with:
Powdered sugar
I serve this to everybody's intense satisfaction with:
Rich Pudding Sauce, page 756, or Foamy Sauce, page 754

Prune Spice Cake, page 616. This makes a good dessert served uniced with some pudding sauce flavored with rum or brandy.

JELLY ROLL

This was the first cake I ever attempted, "so many years ago." It was then an old recipe. It is interesting to note that it has held its own as the standard roll cake without the slightest change through all this time.
Sift:
¾ cup sugar
Beat until light:
4 egg yolks
Add the sugar gradually. Beat these ingredients until they are creamy. Add:
1 teaspoon vanilla
Sift before measuring:
¾ cup cake flour
Resift with:
¾ teaspoon any baking powder
Add the flour gradually to the egg mixture. Beat the batter until it is smooth. Whip until stiff but not dry:
4 egg whites
¼ teaspoon salt
Fold them lightly into the cake batter. Line a 15 x 10 inch pan with heavy greased unglazed brown paper. Spread the dough in it and bake it in a moderate oven 375° for about 13 minutes.

While it is hot invert the cake onto a sheet of unglazed brown paper or a tea towel sprinkled with confectioners' sugar. Cut the hard edges. Spread the cake with:

Jelly
Roll it. Wrap the roll in waxed paper. Before serving it sprinkle it with:
Confectioners' sugar

LEMON ROLL
Prepare by the preceding rule:
Jelly Roll
Substitute for the jelly:
Lemon Filling, page 708
Proceed as directed.

CHOCOLATE FILLED ROLL
Prepare by the preceding rule:
Jelly Roll
Substitute for the jelly:
Chocolate Icing II, page 699
Serve it with:
Whipped cream

SOUR CREAM ALMOND ROLL
Prepare by the preceding rule:
Jelly Roll
To roll and fill it, see below.
Substitute for the jelly the following:
Almond Filling
Combine and beat:
1 cup sour cream
1 cup sugar
1 cup ground or chopped unblanched almonds
2 teaspoons vanilla
Proceed as directed.

NUT CREAM ROLL
Prepare by the preceding rule:
Jelly Roll
Sprinkle a damp towel with:
Confectioners' sugar
Invert the cake on it and roll it while it is hot. Cool it. Whip:

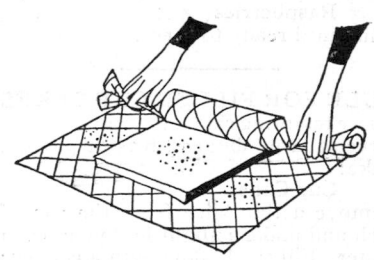

2 cups heavy cream
Flavor it with:
1 teaspoon vanilla, coffee essence, sherry, etc.
Fold into it:

¼ cup confectioners' sugar
1 cup ground or chopped hazel
or other nut meats
When ready to serve the cake unroll it. Spread it with the cream, roll it and serve it with:
  Caramel Sirup, page 754

ALMOND CAKE ROLL
Beat until light:
  8 egg yolks
Beat in gradually:
  ½ cup sugar
Add:
  ½ cup blanched ground almonds
Beat until stiff:
  8 egg whites
  ¼ teaspoon salt
Fold in:
  1 teaspoon vanilla
Fold the egg whites into the yolk mixture. Bake the cake on greased unglazed brown paper in a shallow pan 10 x 15 inches in a moderate oven 325° for about 15 minutes. Roll it as directed in the preceding rule. When cold spread it with:
  1 cup heavy cream, whipped,
  flavored with 1 teaspoon
  vanilla or rum

ANGEL CAKE ROLL
Follow the rule on page 599 for:
  Angel Cake I
Use the smaller amount of egg whites and sugar as suggested at the end of the recipe. Make only ½ the amount if you wish to have 1 roll. Bake the batter in a shallow 10 x 15 inch pan lined with greased unglazed brown paper in a slow oven 300° for about 20 minutes. To roll and fill it follow the rule on page 648 for Sour Cream Almond Roll. Use any of the fillings suggested for the various Cake Rolls in this chapter. Raspberry or apricot jam and whipped cream are fine.

SPICE BUTTERSCOTCH ROLL
Place in a bowl over hot water:
  4 eggs
  ¼ teaspoon salt
Beat until the eggs are thick and lemon colored. Beat in gradually:
  ¾ cup sugar
Remove from heat. Sift before measuring:
  ¾ cup cake flour
Resift with:

¾ teaspoon any baking powder
1 teaspoon cinnamon
½ teaspoon cloves
Fold in the sifted ingredients and:
  1 teaspoon vanilla
Bake the batter in a 10 x 15 inch pan lined with greased unglazed brown paper in a hot oven 400° for about 13 minutes. Roll it as directed under Nut Cream Roll, page 648. Make by the rule on page 706:
  Butterscotch Filling
Cool the filling, spread the cake and roll it as directed.

GRAHAM CRACKER CAKE ROLL
Follow the rule on page 642 for:
  Graham Cracker Sponge Cake
To bake, roll and fill the roll, see Nut Cream Roll, page 648.

CHOCOLATE OR COCOA ROLL WITH WHIPPED CREAM AND CHOCOLATE SAUCE
Sift:
  ½ cup powdered sugar
Beat until light:
  3 egg yolks
Add the sugar gradually and beat these ingredients until they are creamy. Add:
  1 teaspoon vanilla
Sift and add:
  2 tablespoons cocoa
  2 tablespoons all-purpose flour
  ⅛ teaspoon salt
Whip until stiff and rather dry:
  3 egg whites
  ½ teaspoon cream of tartar
Fold them lightly into the cake batter. Line a shallow 8 x 12 inch pan with heavy greased paper and spread the dough in it to the thickness of ¼ inch. Bake the cake in a moderate oven 325° for about 25 minutes. Let it cool in the pan for 5 minutes, then invert the contents onto a moist hot cloth. Trim off the hard edges of the cake. Roll it, see page 648. Whip until stiff:
  1 cup heavy cream
Flavor it with:
  ½ teaspoon vanilla or coffee
  essence or
  ⅓ cup crushed peppermint candy
Unroll the cake. Spread it with the cream. Roll the cake in the cloth like jelly roll and chill it for 1 hour. Remove the cloth, place the cake on a

platter and cut it into slices. Cover them with:

Chocolate Sauce, page 757

Fudge Pie, page 583; Fudge Cake, page 610.

GIRAFFE TORTE

A Viennese rule contributed by the professional cake-baker par excellence of St. Louis, Mrs. Nina Mayer. Not at all troublesome to make once the ingredients are assembled. This fabulous cake is feather-weight. Bake it in an ungreased 9 inch pan with a re-

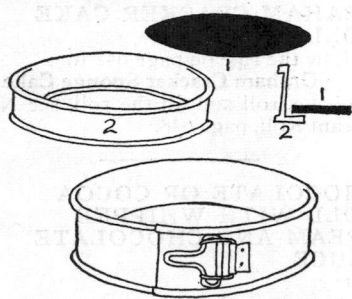

movable rim, shown above, or in a tube pan from which you can loosen it easily from the bottom. Combine and work with the fingers until blended:

½ teaspoon grated lemon rind
¾ cup sugar

Grind in a nut grinder:

¾ cup almonds

Grate:

2 oz. sweet chocolate

Sift:

3 tablespoons dry bread crumbs

Measure:

1½ tablespoons cornstarch

Separate:

5 eggs

Now we're off! Beat the yolks until very light. Beat in the sugar gradually. Beat in the almonds. Add:

¼ teaspoon salt

to the egg whites and beat them in a separate bowl until stiff. Fold them into the yolk mixture. Separate the batter into 2 fairly equal parts. Fold into the first part the cornstarch. Fold into the second part the chocolate and bread crumbs. Use a large spoon to place the batter in alternate blobs in the pan. This should really be called Zoo Torte, for you may make your effects leopard or giraffe as you please. Bake the cake in a moderate oven

350° for about 1 hour. Let it cool in the inverted pan. You may serve it with whipped cream or sauce, but I say just good black coffee.

HAZELNUT TORTE

Sift:

1 cup sugar

Beat:

12 egg yolks

Add the sugar gradually and beat these ingredients until they are very creamy. Grind in a nut grinder:

¼ lb. hazelnut meats
¼ lb. pecan or walnut meats

Whip until stiff but not dry:

8 egg whites
¼ teaspoon salt

Fold them lightly into the other ingredients. Bake the cake in an 8 inch pan with a removable rim in a moderate oven 325° for about 40 minutes. When it is cold spread between the layers:

Whipped cream flavored with vanilla or sherry

Spread the cake with:

(Coffee or caramel icing)

One half the amount of this cake served in the following manner will make a wonderful dessert for 8 people. Bake the cake in 1 layer. Garnish it with 1 cupful whipped cream and 1 pint strawberries.

ALMOND CAKE OR TORTE

The following recipe is the well-known German Mandeltorte. In order to have the right result the almonds should be put through a nut grinder, not a meat grinder. This recipe must be starred as "the" nut cake my friends so frequently ask for. It may be baked in a loaf or in layers. This amount serves 6 to 8 people.

Sift:

1 cup sugar

Beat:

6 egg yolks

Add the sugar gradually and beat until these ingredients are very creamy. Add:

Grated rind and juice of 1 lemon or 1 small orange
1 teaspoon cinnamon
1 cup ground unblanched almonds
½ cup toasted white bread crumbs
(½ teaspoon almond extract)

Whip until stiff but not dry:

6 egg whites
¼ teaspoon salt

Fold them lightly into the batter. This cake is very light and consequently difficult to remove from the pan. Bake it in an 8 inch tube pan in a moderate oven 350° for about 40 minutes. Permit it to cool in the pan. Spread it with:

> Chocolate Butter Icing, page 703

or bake it in two 8 inch layer pans lined with greased waxed paper. Spread between the layers:

> Lemon and Orange Filling, page 708

Spread the top with:

> Confectioners' sugar

When making a large cake, double or triple this recipe and use pans with a removable rim in order to facilitate handling it. Spread the layers with:

> Lemon and Orange Filling, page 708

Spread the cake with:

> White Icing, page 694, or
> Chocolate Butter Icing, page 703

PECAN CAKE

For a richer moister cake use the preceding recipe substituting pecans for almonds.

FILLED NUT TORTE

The 3 preceding cakes are frequently served baked in layers filled with a cream filling. Use:

> Custard Filling flavored with rum, Coffee or Mocha Bavarian Cream, etc.

BREAD TORTE

In the following recipe for the well-known Brodtorte, the ingredients differ only slightly from those in the preceding Mandeltorte, but the results, thanks to the wine bath, are amazingly different.
Sift:

> 1 cup sugar

Beat:

> 6 egg yolks

Add the sugar gradually. Beat these ingredients until they are creamy.
Combine and add:

> 1⅙ cups bread crumbs
> ½ teaspoon baking powder
> ¼ teaspoon cinnamon
> ⅛ lb. citron, cut fine
> 1 cup unblanched almonds ground in a grinder
> Rind and juice of 1 lemon

Whip until stiff but not dry:

> 6 egg whites
> ¼ teaspoon salt

Fold them lightly into the cake batter. Bake the cake for 1 hour or more in a 9 inch pan with a removable rim in a moderate oven 350°. Heat but do not boil:

> ¾ cup sherry
> 2 tablespoons water
> 2 whole cloves
> 1 stick cinnamon
> ¼ cup sugar

Strain these ingredients and place them in a small pitcher. Pour them very slowly onto the hot cake. When all the liquid has been absorbed cool the cake and remove it from the pan. Spread the cake with:

> Creamy Chocolate Filling or Icing, page 706

YAEGERTORTE

A wine-soaked almond cake served with jam and a meringue.
Soak:

> 1 cup dry bread crumbs

in:

> 2 tablespoons sherry
> 3 tablespoons lemon juice

Blanch and shred:

> 1 cup almonds

Sift:

> 1 cup sugar

Beat until light:

> 5 egg yolks

Add the sugar gradually. Beat these ingredients until they are very creamy. Add the bread crumbs, ¾ cupful of the almonds and:

> 1½ teaspoons tartrate or phosphate baking powder or 1 teaspoon combination type (see Baking Powder, page 501)

Whip until stiff but not dry:

> 5 egg whites
> ½ teaspoon salt

Fold them lightly into the batter. Bake the cake in a greased 9 x 12 inch pan in a moderate oven 350° for about 40 minutes. Cool it slightly. Spread it with:

> Jam or jelly

Cover it with a:

> Meringue, page 578: use 4 egg whites

Sprinkle the meringue with the remaining almonds. Bake the meringue in a slow oven 300° for 15 minutes.

CHOCOLATE WALNUT TORTE

Sift:

7/8 cup sugar—1 cup less 2 tablespoons

Beat until light:

6 egg yolks

Add the sugar gradually. Beat these ingredients until they are well blended. Add:

½ cup finely crushed sifted
cracker crumbs
¼ cup grated chocolate
¾ cup chopped walnut meats
2 tablespoons brandy or rum
½ teaspoon any baking powder
½ teaspoon cinnamon
¼ teaspoon cloves
¼ teaspoon nutmeg

Whip until stiff but not dry:

6 egg whites
¼ teaspoon salt

Fold them lightly into the cake batter. Bake the cake in a 9 inch pan with a removable rim in a moderate oven 325° for about 1 hour. Spread the cake with:

Chocolate Butter Icing, page 703

or serve it with:

Wine Custard, page 712

LINZERTORTE

The following recipe is for a delicious German "company" cake. It looks like an open jam pie and, being rich, is usually served in thin wedges. Sift:

1 cup sugar

Beat until soft:

7/8 cup butter—1 cup less 2 tablespoons

Add the sugar gradually. Blend these ingredients until they are very light and creamy. Add:

1 teaspoon grated lemon rind

Beat in one at a time:

2 eggs

Stir in gradually:

1¼ cups sifted all-purpose flour
1 cup unblanched almonds
ground in a nut grinder
½ teaspoon cinnamon
¼ teaspoon cloves
1 tablespoon cocoa
¼ teaspoon salt

The recipe reads, "Stir for one hour," but of course no high-geared American has time for that. If the dough is very soft, chill it. Roll it to the thickness of ⅛ inch between sheets of waxed paper. Put it into an oven-proof dish, giving it a good edge. Cover the bottom of the cake generously with a good quality of:

Jam, preserves or apple butter

Roll the remaining dough into strips. Make a lattice over the preserves. If the room is warm and the dough is temperamental, place the dough in a pastry tube and make the strips by forcing the dough through the bag. Bake the cake in a hot oven 400°. Before serving it fill the hollows with additional preserves.

FIG TORTE

Sift:

7/8 cup sugar—1 cup less 2 tablespoons

Beat until light:

5 egg yolks

Add the sugar gradually. Beat these ingredients until they are well blended. Crush and add:

½ cup cracker or toasted white
bread crumbs

Grind in a meat grinder and add:

⅛ lb. chopped candied orange
peel
½ cup blanched chopped almonds:
⅛ lb.
¼ lb. chopped figs

Stir in:

½ teaspoon cinnamon
¼ teaspoon nutmeg
¼ teaspoon allspice
¼ teaspoon cloves
1 teaspoon tartrate or phosphate
baking powder or ½ teaspoon
combination type (see Baking
Powder, page 501)
1 tablespoon brandy or other
strong wine
Grated rind and juice of ½
lemon

Whip until stiff but not dry:

5 egg whites
¼ teaspoon salt

Fold them lightly into the cake batter. Bake the cake in a 9 inch pan with a removable rim in a moderate oven 325° for about 1 hour. The cake may be spread with:

Seven Minute Icing, page 701

or it may be served with:

Whipped cream

SACHERTORTE

A recipe of the famous restaurant keeper Frau Sacher, who fed the impoverished Austrian nobility long after they had ceased to pay. She is the hotel proprietress in "Reunion in Vienna."

This cake was considered worthy of her name. Beat until soft:

½ cup butter

Add gradually:

½ cup and 2 tablespoons confectioners' sugar

Beat these ingredients until they are well blended. Put in a warm place until it is as soft as butter:

4 oz. sweet chocolate

Beat in 1 at a time:

6 egg yolks

Stir in:

1 tablespoon grated lemon rind
1 teaspoon cinnamon
½ teaspoon cloves
1 cup and 2 tablespoons very fine toasted white bread crumbs

Whip until stiff but not dry:

6 egg whites
¼ teaspoon salt

Fold them lightly into the cake batter. Bake the cake in 2 greased 8 inch pans in a moderate oven 325° for about 25 minutes. Spread between the layers:

Apricot jam or pulp, page 806

Spread the cake with:

Chocolate Butter Icing, page 703

CREAM PUFFS

Please cease to think of these as something to try out in your more adventurous moments. No need to shine up your rabbit's foot—just have all ingredients at room temperature. But once the cream puffs are filled with custard, be sure that they are stored in a cool or refrigerated place, as they are subject to bacterial activity which may be highly toxic although they give no evidence of spoilage.

This is the rule to use for Puff Shells I and II. It will make 6 large puffs or éclairs or thirty-five 1 inch puffs.

Sift before measuring:

½ cup all-purpose flour

Heat:

½ cup milk or water

Add:

¼ cup butter

Bring these ingredients to the boiling point. Add the sifted flour and:

⅛ teaspoon salt

Cook and stir the batter until it leaves the sides of the pan and forms a ball. Remove it from the fire. Beat in 1 at a time:

2 eggs

Be careful to beat 1 egg until well blended before adding the other. Place spoonfuls of batter in 2 inch rounds on a greased tin, heaping them well in the center. Allow 2 inches between the puffs. In France the dough is chilled before being baked. Bake them in a hot oven 400° for ½ hour. Reduce the heat to 350°. Bake them 5 minutes longer. Test the puffs by removing one from the oven. If it does not fall it is thoroughly done. When the puffs are cool cut a gash in the side of each puff and fill them with:

Sweetened flavored whipped cream, Custard, Chocolate or Coffee Filling, see below

Ice the éclairs with:

(Chocolate Icing, see this page)

Children like cream puffs filled with cream or ice cream, to which crushed peppermint candy has been added, served with chocolate sauce.

CUSTARD FILLING

Scald:

1½ cups milk

Combine and add:

1½ tablespoons cornstarch
¼ teaspoon salt
5 tablespoons sugar

When these ingredients are well blended pour them over:

2 slightly beaten egg yolks

Stir and cook the custard in a double boiler or over a very low flame until it is thick. Cool it and add:

½ teaspoon vanilla

COFFEE FILLING

Follow the preceding rule for:

Custard Filling

Substitute for the milk:

½ cup strong coffee
1 cup cream or rich milk

Ice the puffs with:

French Coffee Icing, page 703

CHOCOLATE FILLING

Follow the preceding rule for:

Custard Filling

Add to the hot milk:

1 oz. melted chocolate
3 tablespoons sugar

CHOCOLATE ICING

Use ½ the amount of:

Chocolate Butter Icing, page 703

In Europe an individual is frequently served with 5 or 6 small puffs. They are filled with sweetened and flavored whipped cream and are glazed with burnt sugar. Stir and melt sugar in a heavy skillet over moderate heat. When it is clear and brown, spread it on the puffs with a hot spatula.

CHOCOLATE ÉCLAIRS
Prepare by the rule above:
Cream Puffs
Shape the batter with a spoon or a tube into oblongs. Heap it well in the centers. Bake the puffs as directed. Fill them with:
Whipped cream or Custard or Chocolate Custard Filling, see above
Cover them with:
Chocolate Icing, page 653

MERINGUES
About Twelve 3 Inch Meringues
If you are cursed with a mental hazard in regard to meringues, dismiss it. This is an easily made, delicious dessert. Its success depends upon having the egg whites at room temperature, beating them until they are stiff, adding the sugar very slowly and in baking the meringues as directed. Meringues may be made several days in advance.
Sift:
1½ cups sugar
Place on a platter:
7 egg whites
⅛ teaspoon salt
Beat them until they are very stiff (see page 578). Add the sifted sugar very slowly, ½ teaspoonful at a time. Beat the eggs constantly. Continue to beat for several minutes after the last of the sugar has been added. Add:
1 teaspoon vanilla
Fold in:
¾ cup sugar
Place large spoonfuls of this mixture on a baking sheet or shape the meringues with a pastry bag into ovals. For easy removal you may cover the sheet with heavy brown unglazed paper that has been well moistened. Bake them in a very slow oven 225° from 45 to 60 minutes. Shrinkage is caused by draughts or rapid changes of temperature. You may turn off the heat and permit the meringues to dry in the oven, with a partly open door, for 10 minutes. Remove them from the sheet. If they are to be filled, and this is optional, crush the smooth side with the thumb while the meringues are warm.

Shortly before serving the meringues fill the hollows with:
Sweetened and flavored whipped cream or a frozen mixture
Placed 2 filled meringues together. Serve them with:
Sweetened crushed fruit,
Chocolate Sauce, page 757, or
Butterscotch Sauce, page 756

GRAHAM CRACKER MERINGUE
6 Servings
Chop until fine:
½ cup nut meats
Roll until fine:
11 graham crackers
Add to the crumbs:
1 teaspoon any baking powder
Beat until stiff:
3 egg whites
Beat in a very little at a time:
1 cup sugar
Fold in the cracker mixture lightly, then fold in the nut meats. To shape and bake the batter into 6 meringues follow the above rule for meringues. Cool them. Fill them with:
1 pint vanilla ice cream
If preferred the meringue may be baked in pie shape like the following Meringue Tart. When cool fill it with the ice cream.

MERINGUE TART OR PINCH PIE
6 Servings
While the preceding meringue mixture may be shaped into a tart, this rule is so much better for the purpose that it is advisable to follow it. This is a surefire hit as a dessert. It deserves all the asterisks in the printing press. I never serve it to newcomers without sending them home happy, replete and with the recipe in their pockets.
Sift:
1 cup sugar
Place on a platter:
3 egg whites
½ teaspoon any baking powder
⅛ teaspoon salt
Combine in a small pitcher or cup:
1 teaspoon vanilla
1 teaspoon vinegar
1 teaspoon water
Whip the egg whites until they are very stiff. Add the sifted sugar very slowly, ½ teaspoonful at a time, alternately with a few drops of the com-

bined liquids. Beat constantly. When all the ingredients have been added continue to beat the meringue for several minutes. When making meringue tart with an electrical beater combine all the ingredients except the sugar. Use high speed. When the egg whites are stiff add the sugar, a tablespoonful at a time. Heap it upon the lightly greased platter or dish from which it is to be served or in a pan with a removable rim. Subsequent baking will not affect the platter or dish, or heap the meringue lightly onto an oven-proof plate or a piece of well-greased unglazed brown paper placed on a tin. Shape the meringue like a pie or tart with a heavy edge, using a spatula or knife. Bake it in a very slow oven 275° for 1 hour or longer. Remove the paper when the pie is cool. Slide the pie onto a platter or plate. When ready to serve the meringue fill the center with:

Sweetened fresh or stewed fruit

Top it with lightly sweetened and flavored:

Whipped cream

Combinations of fruit are good in this tart. Fresh strawberries or raspberries and sliced bananas, or canned peaches or apricots, pineapple and bananas. The tart is delicious filled with orange or pineapple ice topped with whipped cream.

A famous cook recommends as a gala dessert filling the cooled meringue with a cold custard (See Posie's Custard, page 713) covered with the contents of a package of frozen raspberries garnished with 1 cupful of heavy cream, whipped.

SCHAUM TORTE

This delicious dessert, capable of infinite variations, is much like the preceding Meringue Tart or Pinch Pie. While troublesome to make it in 2 batches, the result seems better, although it may be made with 8 eggs, etc., all at once. Follow the above rule for Meringue Tart, but use:

    4 egg whites
    1 cup sugar
    1 teaspoon vanilla
    1 teaspoon vinegar

Beat without interruption until your first batch is in the pan and the oven, then if you like beat a second batch. Place each batch in a greased 10 inch tin about 1¾ inches high with a re-

movable rim or in a pan that has that little scraper effect on the bottom for easy removal of the tart. Bake the tarts in a slow oven 275° until firm, for 1 hour or longer. Leave them in the oven, the door open, for about 5 minutes longer to avoid shrinkage. Cool them gradually. Remove them from the pan when cold. Place between the layers:

Ice cream

Garnish the top with rum or vanilla flavored:

Whipped cream

You may add:

Cherries, red and green candies, etc.

The fillings for the preceding Meringue Tart and for Cream Tart, page 656, may be used.

ANGEL PIE

Prepare by the rule on page 654:

Meringue Tart

Place it in a deep buttered 10 inch oven-proof pie plate. Bake it as directed. Permit it to cool in the oven with the door open. Prepare the following filling in a double boiler:

    4 beaten egg yolks
    ½ cup sugar
    Juice and rind of 1 lemon
    1 tablespoon flour
    ½ cup water

Stir and cook the filling until it is thick. Cool it. When the pie and the filling are cool, whip:

    1 cup heavy cream

Fold in:

    ½ teaspoon vanilla

Place a layer of cream in the pie, then the filling, then another layer of cream. Chill the pie for several hours.

CREAM MERINGUE TART

The following recipe deserves a chapter to itself. It serves from 8 to 10 people, is delicate and delicious and is not at all difficult to make. The result is an optical as well as a gastronomic treat. It is a de luxe dessert complete in itself and comparatively inexpensive. The cake batter and the meringue are baked at the same time.

Blanch and shred:

    (⅓ cup almonds)

Sift:

    1½ cups sugar

Beat until soft:

    ¼ cup butter

Add ½ cupful of the sifted sugar gradually. Blend these ingredients until they are light and creamy. Beat in one at a time:

4 egg yolks

Add:

½ teaspoon vanilla

Sift before measuring:

1 cup cake flour

Resift with:

2 teaspoons tartrate or phosphate baking powder or 1 teaspoon combination type (see Baking Powder, page 501)

¼ teaspoon salt

Add the sifted ingredients to the butter mixture alternately with:

5 tablespoons cream

Beat the batter until it is smooth. Spread it in 2 greased 9 inch layer pans. Cover it with the following meringue. Whip until stiff:

4 egg whites

⅛ teaspoon salt

Add the remaining cupful sifted sugar very slowly, ½ teaspoonful at a time. Beat constantly. When all the sugar has been added continue to beat for several minutes. Fold in:

1 teaspoon vanilla

Spread the meringue lightly over the cake batter in both pans. Stud one meringue with the blanched shredded almonds, placing the shreds very close together. Bake the layers in a slow oven 350° for about 40 minutes. Remove the layers from the oven. Permit the cakes to cool in the pans. Shortly before serving the cake place one layer, meringue side down, on a cake plate. Spread one of the following cream fillings over it, reserving 4 tablespoonfuls for the top. Place the almond studded layer, meringue side up, on the cream filling and place the reserved filling in the center on top.

FILLINGS FOR CREAM TART

Apricot Cream Filling

Whip until stiff:

1 cup heavy cream

Fold in:

¾ cup apricot pulp: stewed and sweetened Apricots, page 450, put through a ricer

Pineapple Cream Filling

Whip until stiff:

1 cup heavy cream

Fold in:

1½ tablespoons confectioners' sugar

1 cup drained crushed pineapple

¼ teaspoon vanilla

Plain Cream Filling

Whip until stiff:

1 cup heavy cream

Fold in:

1½ tablespoons confectioners' sugar

½ teaspoon vanilla

Fresh Fruit Filling

Whip until stiff:

1 cup heavy cream

Fold in:

1 teaspoon vanilla

Cover the lower cake layer with:

Sugared fruit: strawberries, raspberries, sliced peaches, bananas, etc.

Heap the cream on top of it. Reserve 4 tablespoonfuls for the top. Decorate the top with the cream and, if berries are used, with a few whole berries.

Orange Pineapple Filling

Place in a double boiler and beat well:

5 egg yolks

2 tablespoons cornstarch

½ cup sugar

3 tablespoons lemon juice

6 tablespoons orange juice

1 teaspoon grated orange rind

2 cups crushed or diced pineapple

Cook and stir these ingredients until they are thick. Add:

¼ cup butter

¼ teaspoon salt

Cool the filling.

BLITZTORTE

This is the German mother of the preceding Cream Tart. A little more frugal, a little less flossy—mighty good. Bake the batter and the meringue as directed in the rule for:

Cream Tart, page 655

Place between the layers:

Custard Filling

Beat:

1 egg

Add:

3 tablespoons sugar

1 tablespoon cornstarch

1 cup sour cream

Cook and stir these ingredients over hot water until they are thick. Cool the custard, flavor it with:

½ teaspoon grated lemon rind

1 teaspoon vanilla

Spread it between the cake layers. Serve the tart with:

(Strawberries or raspberries)

BABA AU RHUM

Beloved by the French, who frequently serve it with tea. This is an American version.

Prepare:

High Coffee Cake, page 631, or Brioche Dough, page 522

Make only ½ the amount given for the latter. Place it in a greased 8 inch tube pan. Permit it to rise and bake it as directed. Remove it from the pan, cool it and return it to the pan. Prepare a sirup by boiling for 10 minutes:

½ cup water
1 cup sugar

Cool the sirup slightly. Flavor it generously with:

Rum or whisky: at least ¼ cup

Place the sirup in a small pitcher. One hour before serving the Baba pour the sirup slowly drop by drop onto the cake. Use as much as it will absorb. Permit the Baba to stand until ready to serve. Remove it from the pan. If it is to be a dessert top it with:

Whipped cream

You may serve individual Baba cakes. Bake them in muffin tins. Soak them as directed, or cut a slice from the top, hollow the cakes slightly and fill the hollows with raspberry or apricot jam. Serve the cakes with:

Lemon Sauce, page 757

Or, slice the muffins in half, cover each half with a slice of fresh pineapple and currant jelly sprinkled with confectioners' sugar and kirsch.

Refrigerator Cakes

REFRIGERATOR CAKES

Line a bowl with waxed paper. Place around the sides and over the bottom about:

30 Lady Fingers, page 683, slices of Sponge Cake, page 596, or Angel Cake, page 599

Prepare:

Custard, see below

Put part of the custard in the bowl, then a layer of the lady fingers or cake, then more custard and last a layer of lady fingers or cake. Cover the bowl and place it in the refrigerator for 12 hours or more. Invert the contents of the bowl onto a plate. Whip until stiff:

1 cup heavy cream

Fold in:

4 tablespoons confectioners' sugar
½ teaspoon vanilla

Spread the cream over the cake.

FILLINGS FOR REFRIGERATOR CAKES

Lemon Custard

Grate:

Rind of 1 lemon

over:

1 cup sugar

Beat until soft:

½ cup butter

Add the sugar gradually. Blend these ingredients until they are light and creamy. Beat in one at a time:

4 egg yolks

Add:

3 tablespoons lemon juice

Whip until stiff but not dry:

4 egg whites
⅛ teaspoon salt

Fold them lightly into the butter mixture. Add if desired:

4 tablespoons apricot pulp:
stewed Apricots, page 450, put through a ricer, or 4 tablespoons well-drained crushed pineapple

This filling is uncooked. One teaspoonful gelatine soaked in 1 tablespoonful cold water, then dissolved over heat, may be added if desired.

Chocolate Custard

Melt:

⅜ lb. sweet chocolate

Add:

3 tablespoons sugar
3 tablespoons water
4 egg yolks

Stir and cook these ingredients over a very low flame or over boiling water until they are thick. Cool the mixture. Place on a platter and whip until stiff but not dry:

4 egg whites
⅛ teaspoon salt

Fold them lightly into the chocolate mixture.

Cocoa Custard

A substitute seldom compares favorably with an original recipe, but this acceptable cocoa custard may be used when sweet chocolate is not available. Cook and stir over hot water until thick and smooth:

2 tablespoons cocoa
⅓ cup water
½ cup sugar
4 egg yolks

Cool these ingredients. Add:

1 teaspoon vanilla

Whip until stiff and add as directed in the preceding rule:

4 egg whites
⅛ teaspoon salt

Charlotte Polonaise, page 642.

This may be classed as a refrigerator cake.

EGGNOG REFRIGERATOR CAKE

Soak:

1 tablespoon gelatine

in:

2 tablespoons cold water

Dissolve it over heat. Cool it slightly. Cream:

¾ cup butter
1 cup confectioners' sugar

Beat in:

4 egg yolks
¼ cup brandy or rum
¾ cup chopped blanched almonds
or 12 or 14 crushed macaroons

Stir in the dissolved gelatine. Whip until stiff, then fold in:

4 egg whites
¼ teaspoon salt

Line a bowl as directed under Refrigerator Cakes with:

Angel Cake, page 599

Fill it with the eggnog mixture. Chill the cake. Serve it decorated with:

Whipped cream

COFFEE FLAVORED PORCUPINE

The tenth birthday celebration of the Manhattan Baking and Cooking School was a joyous occasion upon which the guests were served luscious and varied native dishes of many countries. The food editors present, as well as the other guests, after sampling all sorts of delicacies, came back repeatedly to praise and to resample the German Porcupine, or Igel, the rule for which the school director, Louise Schwarz, kindly wrote out for me.

Cream until thoroughly blended:

1 cup butter
½ cup confectioners' sugar

Beat in:

3 egg yolks
⅛ teaspoon salt
1 tablespoon coffee extract

Arrange on a platter in oval shape:

12 lady fingers

Spread the top with ½ the butter mixture. Cover it with a layer of:

12 lady fingers

and a second layer of the butter mixture. Chill the dish for several hours. Whip until stiff:

1 cup heavy cream

Cover the entire surface of the porcupine with the cream. Now give him his quills by sticking into him:

3 tablespoons lightly toasted, blanched slivered almonds

You may reserve a little of the cream with which to garnish the edge of the pudding. Use a pastry bag for this.

STRAWBERRY REFRIGERATOR CAKE

Line a bowl as directed under Refrigerator Cakes. Fill it with:

Strawberry or Raspberry Bavarian, page 743

Chill it for about 6 hours. Garnish the dish with:

Whipped cream
Whole berries

The cake or lady fingers may be omitted in the filling.

See Filled Angel or Sponge Cake, page 646.

REFRIGERATOR CHEESE CAKES

Distinctions between rules are sometimes trifling but slight changes in ingredients result in marked variations of flavor and texture. Here are 3 rules for Refrigerator Cheese Cake. No. I calls for cottage cheese and whipped cream; No. II calls for cream cheese and plain cream; No. III calls for cream cheese and thick sour cream. No. I is fine for a family dinner; No. II is larger and suitable for company; and No. III is distinctive as it has an unusual sour cream topping. Choose between them, I cannot, "and may digestion wait on appetite." These cakes are usually made in a spring mold but an oven-proof glass dish may be substituted.

REFRIGERATOR CHEESE CAKE

Method I.

Line a deep 9 inch pie pan with:
     Zwieback Crust, page 567
Reserve ½ cupful of the mixture.
Soak:
     2 tablespoons gelatine
in:
     ½ cup cold water
Cook and stir in a double boiler until the custard begins to thicken:
     2 egg yolks
     ½ cup sugar
     ½ cup milk
     1 teaspoon salt
Stir in the soaked gelatine until dissolved. Chill the custard by placing the pan in a bowl of ice water. Beat until very smooth, then stir into the cooled custard:
     2 cups smooth cottage cheese
     1 teaspoon grated lemon rind
     3 tablespoons lemon juice
     1 teaspoon vanilla
Whip until stiff, then fold in:
     1 cup heavy cream
Whip until stiff, then fold in:
     2 egg whites
Fill the pie shell. Place the reserved crumbs on top. Chill the cake for 12 hours or until ready to serve.

Method II.

This sumptuous Torte will serve 18 persons. It is handsome and delectable and has the valuable quality of keeping well so that it may be made a day in advance.
Crush:
     1 package zwieback or graham crackers: about 6 oz.
Work into the crumbs:
     ½ cup butter
     ¼ to ½ cup sugar
Reserve ¼ of the crumbs. Spread or pat the rest in a thin layer over the bottom and sides of a 10 inch spring mold about 3 inches deep. Bake the crust in a moderate oven 375° for 15 minutes. Cool it. Beat in the top of a double boiler:
     4 egg yolks
     ¾ cup sugar
     ¼ teaspoon salt
     ⅓ cup milk
Heat and stir this custard over hot water until it thickens. Soak:
     2 tablespoons gelatine
in:

     ½ cup water
Stir this into the hot custard until dissolved. Cool the custard. Work with a fork until smooth:
     1½ lbs. soft cream cheese:
       about 9 packages
Stir it into the custard until well blended. Whip until stiff:
     4 egg whites
Whip in gradually:
     ½ cup sugar
Fold these into the custard. Beat until stiff, then fold in:
     1 cup heavy cream
Fill the zwieback crust with the custard. Sprinkle the reserved crumbs over the top. Chill the Torte well in the refrigerator until ready to serve.

REFRIGERATOR CREAM CHEESE CAKE WITH SOUR CREAM

12 Servings

Make this a day before serving it. Line a 9 inch spring form 2½ inches deep with:
     Zwieback Crust, page 567
Chill the crust well. Mix well, then pour into the shell:
     2 well-beaten eggs
     4 packages soft cream cheese:
       ¾ lb.
     ½ cup sugar
     1 teaspoon lemon juice or ½ teaspoon vanilla
     ½ teaspoon salt
Bake the cake in a moderate oven 375° for 20 minutes. Remove the cake from the oven. Increase oven heat to 425°. Dust the top of the cake with:
     Cinnamon
Let the cake cool to room temperature. Mix well and pour over the cake:
     1½ cups thick sour cream
     2 tablespoons sugar
     ½ teaspoon vanilla
     ⅛ teaspoon salt
Bake the cake in the hot oven for 5 minutes. Permit it to cool, then chill it thoroughly until ready to serve.

PINEAPPLE REFRIGERATOR CHEESE CAKE

8 Servings

Prepare by the rule on page 567:
     Zwieback Crust
Line a deep 10 inch dish with it.
Drain:

1 No. 2 can pineapple gems
Soak:
2 tablespoons gelatine
in:
½ cup water
Beat until light:
3 egg yolks
Beat in gradually:
½ cup sugar
½ cup pineapple juice
Cook and stir these ingredients in a double boiler until they thicken. Add the soaked gelatine. Stir until it is dissolved. Cool the custard. Stir in:

1 lb. smooth cottage cheese
1 teaspoon grated lemon rind
3 tablespoons lemon juice
¼ teaspoon salt
Fold in ¾ of the pineapple gems and:
1 cup heavy cream, whipped
Fold in:
3 stiffly beaten egg whites
Fill the pie shell. Garnish the top with the remaining pineapple gems. Sprinkle it with:
Cinnamon
Chill the pie for at least 3 hours, or until ready to serve.

Small Cakes and Cookies

Rule for Cup Cakes

Cup cakes are easy to bake and to serve. They may be baked in well-greased muffin tins filled two thirds full, but a more attractive way to make them is to fill paper baking cups about one third full and bake them on a sheet or in muffin pans in the oven. When the cakes are done they will have risen to within a quarter of an inch of the frilled edge. Cup cakes may be iced attractively and garnished with half a nut meat, 3 blanched almonds, a candied cherry, raisins, etc. See the rule for Filled Cup Cakes, page 647. They are delicious.

To ice a cup cake quickly place upon the hot cake a small piece of sweet or semisweet chocolate bar. Spread it as it melts. To ice cakes rapidly dip them in

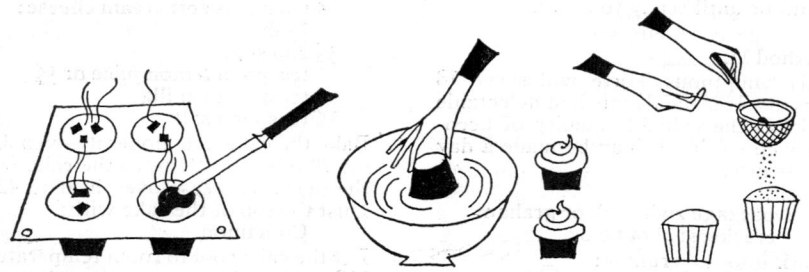

rather thin icing and swirl them. Baked cup cakes may be sprinkled with confectioners' sugar. Sift it from a tea strainer directly onto the cakes. The result is a thin even coating.

Suggestions for Handling Nut Meats

Almonds are easily shelled. They are used blanched, page 505, or unblanched. Walnuts, pecans, hazel and brazil nuts are best used directly after shelling. If the shells of pecans are hard to crack, pour boiling water over the nuts and allow them to cool. Crush from end to end.

It is important to use a special nut grinder, not meat grinder, which will keep the nuts grated and dry rather than mashed and greasy, especially if the nuts are to be used in baking. If only a few crushed nuts are needed they may be prepared in a small rotary hand grinder or placed in a clean towel and rolled with a rolling pin. Nuts slice and shred more easily when warm and moist.

YELLOW CUP CAKES WITH NUTS, RAISINS OR CURRANTS
About Twenty-Eight 2 Inch Cakes
Sift:
> 1 cup sugar

Beat until soft:
> ⅓ to ½ cup butter

Add the sugar gradually. Blend these ingredients until they are very light and creamy. Beat in one at a time:
> 2 eggs

Sift before measuring:
> 1¾ cups cake flour

Sift a little of this over:
> 1 cup broken nut meats
> 1 cup raisins or 1 cup washed dried currants

Resift the remainder with:
> 2 teaspoons tartrate or phosphate baking powder or 1½ teaspoons combination type (see Baking Powder, page 501)
> ⅛ teaspoon salt

Add the sifted ingredients to the butter mixture in 3 parts alternately with thirds of:
> ½ cup milk

Beat the batter after each addition until it is smooth. Add:
> 1 teaspoon vanilla
> (½ teaspoon almond extract or ¼ teaspoon grated lemon rind)

Fold in the nuts and fruit. Bake the cakes in greased pans in a moderate oven 350° for about 25 minutes.

ONE EGG CUP CAKES
Prepare:
> One Egg Loaf or Layer Cake, page 603

Add to the batter:
> (1 cup raisins or washed dried currants)

Test for doneness with a toothpick. When cool, sprinkle the tops with confectioners' sugar (page 705).

SPONGE CUP CAKES
Queen Mary's Sponge Cake, page 597, baked in this way is similar to the French Marguerite—a fine-grained dry tea cake.
See the Rule for Cup Cakes, page 647. Permit them to cool in the pans.

GOLD CUP CAKES
About Twelve 2 Inch Cakes
An excellent rule for using 4 extra egg yolks.
Sift:
> ½ cup sugar

Beat until soft:
> ¼ cup butter

Add the sugar gradually. Blend these ingredients until they are creamy.
Add:
> Grated rind of 1 orange or 1 lemon

Beat in 1 at a time:
> 4 egg yolks

Add:
> ½ teaspoon vanilla

Sift before measuring:
> ⅞ cup all-purpose flour—1 cup less 2 tablespoons

Resift with:
> 1 teaspoon any baking powder

Add the sifted ingredients to the butter mixture in 3 parts alternately with thirds of:
> ¼ cup milk

Stir in:
> (¼ cup currants)

Bake the cakes in greased muffin tins in a moderate oven 375° for about 20 minutes. Dust them with:
> Confectioners' sugar

or spread them with:
> Orange Icing, page 702, or other icing

ANGEL CUP CAKES
6 Big Cakes or 8 Small Ones
Prepare ½ the batter for:
> Angel Cake I, page 599

Place it in ungreased muffin tins. Bake it as directed for Angel Cake. When cold split and fill them. See Filled Cup Cakes, page 647, Angel Cake Bars and Balls, page 666.

COCOA CUP CAKES
About Twenty 2 Inch Cakes
Sift:
> 1 cup white or brown sugar

Beat until soft:
> ½ cup butter

Add the sugar gradually. Blend these ingredients until they are very light and creamy. Beat in:
> 1 egg

Sift before measuring:
> 1½ cups cake flour

Resift with:
> 2 teaspoons tartrate or phosphate baking powder or 1½ teaspoons combination type (see Baking Powder, page 501)
> ¼ teaspoon salt
> ½ cup cocoa

One ounce chocolate melted and cooled may be substituted for the cocoa. Beat it into the creamed sugar and butter. Add the sifted ingredients to the butter mixture in 3 parts alternately with thirds of:

    1 teaspoon vanilla
    ½ cup milk

Or if you use sour milk, omit the baking powder and add ½ teaspoonful soda to the dry ingredients. Beat the batter until it is smooth after each addition. Bake the cakes in greased pans in a moderate oven 375° for about 20 minutes. Spread the tops with:

    White Icing, page 694, or Chocolate Butter Icing, page 703, or Cocoa Coffee Icing, page 703

CHOCOLATE CUP CAKES

Follow one of the rules in the Cake chapter, page 608, for Chocolate Cake. Test the cakes for doneness with a toothpick.

CARAMEL SPONGE CUP CAKES
Ten 2 Inch Cakes
Sift:
    1 cup loosely packed light brown sugar
Beat until light:
    2 egg yolks
Beat in the sugar gradually until well blended. Sift:
    ½ cup cake flour
Resift with:
    ¼ teaspoon any baking powder
    ¼ teaspoon salt
Stir these ingredients into the yolk mixture. Add:
    ½ cup finely chopped nut meats
Beat until stiff but not dry:
    2 egg whites
Stir about ⅓ of these into the batter, fold in the rest lightly. Bake the cakes in greased pans in a moderate oven 325° for about 25 minutes, or until done. Permit the cakes to cool in the pans.

SOUR CREAM CUP CAKES
14 to 16 Cakes
Cream:
    1 egg
    1 cup light brown sugar
Combine, then add:
    ½ teaspoon vanilla
    ¼ teaspoon almond extract
    1 cup sour cream
Sift:
    1½ cups cake flour
Resift with:

    1 scant teaspoon soda
    ¼ teaspoon salt
Combine liquid and dry ingredients like muffins with few strokes. Bake the cakes in a moderate oven 375° for about 40 minutes.

SOUR MILK SPICE CUP CAKES
Twenty-Four 2 Inch Cakes
Very lightly spiced.
Sift:
    1 cup brown sugar
Beat until soft:
    ½ cup butter
Add the sugar gradually. Blend these ingredients until they are very light and creamy. Beat in one at a time:
    2 eggs
Add:
    1 teaspoon vanilla
Measure:
    ½ cup sour milk
Sift before measuring:
    2¼ cups all-purpose flour
Resift with:
    2 teaspoons tartrate or phosphate baking powder or 1½ teaspoons combination type (see Baking Powder, page 501)
    ⅛ teaspoon salt
    ½ teaspoon cinnamon
    ¼ teaspoon cloves
    ½ teaspoon soda
Add the sifted ingredients to the butter mixture in 3 parts alternately with thirds of the sour milk. Beat the batter after each addition until it is smooth. Fold in:
    ¾ cup nut meats or currants
Bake the cakes in greased pans in a moderate oven 375° for about 20 minutes.

PEANUT BUTTER CUP CAKES
About Twenty-Two 2 Inch Cakes
Delicate and well flavored.
Beat until soft:
    ⅓ cup butter
Add gradually:
    1 cup medium brown sugar
When these ingredients are light and fluffy, beat in and blend well:
    ½ cup peanut butter
Combine and beat until light:
    2 eggs
    ½ cup medium brown sugar
Add:
    1 teaspoon vanilla
Sift before measuring:
    2 cups all-purpose flour

Resift with:
    ½ teaspoon salt
    2½ teaspoons tartrate or phosphate
        baking powder or 2 teaspoons
        combination type (see Baking
        Powder, page 501)
Beat the egg mixture into the butter
mixture. Add the sifted ingredients in
about 3 parts alternately with thirds
of:
    ¾ cup milk
Bake the cakes by the Rule for Cup
Cakes on page 660 in a moderate oven

350° for about 25 minutes. Ice them
with:
    Maple Icing, page 704

ORANGE RAISIN CUP CAKES
Prepare the batter for:
    Orange Raisin Cake, page 617
Bake it in small greased muffin tins.

JAM CUP CAKES
Prepare the batter for:
    Jam Cake, page 617
Bake it in greased muffin tins.

Squares and Bars

The most quickly made of all small cakes. The following batters are baked in
shallow pans. Sometimes the cakes are iced; sometimes they are rolled in confectioners' sugar; but as a rule they merely are cut into shapes and served.

Grease pans with unsalted shortening. To flour a tin, place a teaspoonful or
two of flour on a greased tin. Tip the tin until it is coated evenly with a thin film
of flour. Reverse the tin to discard excess flour.

BROWNIES I OR FUDGE SQUARES
Fifty-Four 1 x 2 Inch Bars
"Than which there are no others."
Sift:
    2 cups sugar
Melt, then cool:
    4 oz. chocolate
    ½ cup butter
Beat until light:
    4 eggs
    ¼ teaspoon salt
Add the sifted sugar gradually. Con-
tinue to beat until these ingredients are
light and creamy. Fold in the melted
mixture and:
    1 teaspoon vanilla
Sift and add:
    1 cup all-purpose flour
Beat the batter until it is just smooth.
Fold in:
    1 cup nut meats
Grease and flour a 9 x 13 inch pan.
Pour in the batter. Bake the cake in a
moderate oven 325° for about 30 min-
utes. When it is cold cut it into oblongs
or squares.

BROWNIES II OR BAKED FUDGE
About Forty-Two 1½ Inch Squares
A lighter bar than Brownies I, even
better.
Sift:
    1 cup sugar
Beat until soft:
    3 tablespoons butter

Beat until light:
    2 eggs
Add the sugar gradually to the butter.
As it is difficult to cream this small
amount of butter, add ½ the eggs.
Blend these ingredients until they are
creamy. Beat in the remaining egg.
Melt, then cool and add:
    2 oz. chocolate
Stir in:
    3½ tablespoons all-purpose flour
    1 teaspoon vanilla
    1 cup broken nut meats
Grease an 8 x 12 inch pan. Spread the
batter in it. If there is no pan of that
size, spread the batter in some other
pan to the depth of about ¼ inch. Bake
the fudge in a 325° oven for about 30
minutes. Cut it into squares.

BUTTERSCOTCH BROWNIES
Thirty-Two Thin 1 x 2 Inch Bars
An all-time favorite, easily made.
Melt in a saucepan:
    ¼ cup butter
Stir into it until dissolved:
    1 cup brown sugar
Cool these ingredients slightly. Beat
in well:
    1 egg
    1 teaspoon vanilla
Sift, then measure:
    ½ cup all-purpose flour
Resift it with:
    1 teaspoon any baking powder
    ½ teaspoon salt

Stir these ingredients into the butter mixture. Add:

½ to 1 cup finely chopped nut meats

Chopped dates and figs may be substituted entirely or in part. Use a little of the flour over them. Pour the batter into a greased and floured 8 x 8 inch pan. Bake it in a moderate oven 350° for about 30 minutes. Cut the cake into bars.

COCONUT BARS OR CHEWS

Follow the preceding rule for:

Butterscotch Brownies

Omit the nut meats. Substitute:

¾ cup grated coconut

CHOCOLATE MOLASSES BROWNIES
Thirty-Two 1 x 2 Inch Bars

Melt:

⅓ cup butter
2 oz. chocolate

Add:

½ cup sugar
½ cup molasses

Cool slightly. Add:

2 beaten eggs
½ teaspoon vanilla

Combine and stir in:

⅔ cup sifted all-purpose flour
½ teaspoon any baking powder
⅛ teaspoon salt
½ cup nut meats

Bake these ingredients in a greased 8 x 8 inch pan in a moderate oven 325° for about ½ hour.

DATE BARS
Method I.
Forty-Two 2½ x 1 Inch Bars

This delicious date bar remains soft and fresh for a long time.

Sift:

1 cup sugar

Beat until light:

3 eggs

Add the sugar gradually. Blend these ingredients until they are very light. Add about:

2 cups chopped dates
1 cup broken nut meats

Sift before measuring:

1 scant cup all-purpose flour

Resift with:

1 teaspoon baking powder
⅛ teaspoon salt

If spices are desired add:

¼ teaspoon cloves
(¼ teaspoon cinnamon)

Add the sifted ingredients to the egg mixture with:

1 teaspoon vanilla

Beat the batter until the ingredients are well blended. Pour it into a greased and floured 9 x 13 inch pan. Bake it in a moderate oven 325° for about 25 minutes. When the cake is cool cut it into bars. Roll them in:

Confectioners' sugar

Method II.
Forty-Two 2½ x 1 Inch Bars

The virtue of this bar is that it calls for egg yolks only.

Sift:

1 cup sugar

Beat until soft:

½ cup butter

Add the sugar gradually. Blend these ingredients until they are very light and creamy. Add:

½ teaspoon vanilla
⅛ teaspoon salt

In a separate dish beat well:

5 or 6 egg yolks

Add and beat:

2 tablespoons cold water

Stir these ingredients into the creamed butter mixture. Sift:

1½ cups cake flour

Stir it gradually into the batter. Add:

2 cups chopped dates
½ cup broken nut meats

Spread the dough in a greased and floured 9 x 13 inch pan. Bake the cake in a moderate oven 325° for about 25 minutes. When it is cool cut it into bars and roll them in:

Confectioners' sugar

DATE HONEY BARS
Forty-Two 2½ x 1 Inch Bars

These are valuable for their keeping qualities. They may be made 2 or 3 weeks before they are served.

Beat well:

3 eggs

Beat in gradually:

1 cup strained honey

Combine, sift, then stir in:

1½ cups sifted cake flour
½ teaspoon salt
1 teaspoon any baking powder

Stir in:

2 cups ground dates
1 cup ground nut meats

Place the batter in a greased and floured 9 x 13 inch pan. Bake it in a moderate oven 350° for about ½ hour. When cool cut the cake into bars. Roll them in:

Confectioners' sugar

You may wrap the bars individually in waxed paper or for the decorative effect in aluminum foil.

FIG BARS

Mme. Bu Wei in her charming book, "How To Cook and Eat in Chinese," tells us that the little cakes served between meals in her native country are called "dot hearts." These are endearing morsels.

Follow the rule on page 664 for:

Date Bars I

Substitute for the dates:

Dark moist chopped figs

Of course other figs may be substituted. If dry, steam them in a double boiler until soft or soak them in wine or water. Dry them between towels.

Christmas Cakes with Molasses and Chocolate, page 688; Christmas Chocolate Bars, page 688. Do not overlook these cakes. Whatever I might say in their praise would be an understatement.

FRUIT BARS

Fifty-Four 1 x 2 Inch Bars

These bars keep well. They are a bit moist at first. Beat until light:

3 eggs

Beat in gradually:

1 cup firmly packed brown sugar

Sift, then measure:

½ cup and 1 tablespoon cake flour

Part of the flour may be dusted over the raisins and fruit. Turn them over lightly to distribute it. Resift with:

½ teaspoon any baking powder
½ teaspoon allspice
½ teaspoon cloves
1 teaspoon cinnamon

Stir these ingredients into the egg mixture. Stir in:

½ cup seedless raisins
1½ cups chopped figs, dates and/or prunes

Bake the batter in a greased and floured 9 x 12 inch pan in a moderate oven 350° for about 20 minutes. When cool cut it into bars. Roll them in:

Confectioners' sugar

FILLED BARS

Cover the bottom of a greased pan with a very thin layer of any good Cookie Dough, page 669. Spread it with a filling: jam, fig, raisin, nut,

mincemeat, etc. Cover it with a very thin layer of cookie dough. Bake the cake by the rule for Cookie Dough. While warm, cut the cake into bars.

PLAIN JAM OR JELLY SQUARES

Very popular. Much like the preceding rule but cut before being baked. Prepare:

Sugar Cookie Dough, page 669, or Quick Oatmeal Cookie Dough, page 672

Roll it into a thin sheet. Cut it into 1½ inch squares. Spread a square lightly with rather firm:

Jam, jelly or marmalade

Cover it with a similar square. Bake the cookies on a well greased and floured sheet in a moderate oven 375° for about 10 minutes. You may decorate the tops with:

A bit of candied cherry

JAM AND ALMOND PASTE BARS

Luscious—may be made in advance and cut into slices when ready to serve. Prepare by the rule on page 669:

Sugar Cookie Dough

Chill it. Divide it into ⅔ and ⅓. Roll or pat the larger part to fit the greased and floured bottom of an 8 x 8 inch pan. Spread the dough with:

Jam, marmalade, jelly, etc.

Roll out the remaining dough. Cut it into ½ inch strips. Place them ¾ inch apart over the jam. Beat:

1 egg white

Whip in gradually:

½ cup sugar
¼ cup confectioners' sugar

Work into it:

¾ cup almond paste

Spread this mixture over the jam between the strips. Bake the cake in a moderate oven 375° for about 12 minutes, or until done. Leave it in the pan until cold. Cut it into bars. These cookies may be iced with:

Confectioners' sugar

thinned to a good consistency with:

Lemon juice

But why give earrings to an elephant?

ANGEL JELLY BARS

This rule sounds wild but is really quite tame.

Grate:

½ lb. unblanched almonds

Stir well:

2 unbeaten egg whites
⅔ cup sugar
⅛ teaspoon salt
1 teaspoon vanilla

Stir in the almonds. Form a long oblong of this paste, about 2½ inches wide and ½ inch thick, on a lightly greased and floured tin. Make a depression down the center lengthwise with a wooden spoon handle. Fill it with:

Jelly or firm jam

Bake the meringue in a moderate oven 325° from 20 to 30 minutes. When cold spread the top with:

Lemon Icing, page 703

Slice the meringue on the bias.

NUT BARS
About Forty-Eight 1 x 2 Inch Sticks

These, like the following Pecan Slices, are made on a pastry base. The cakes are equally good and popular. This filling calls for egg whites, no yolks. Cream until well blended:

½ cup butter
(¼ cup sugar)

Beat in well:

1 egg

Combine:

1¼ cups sifted all-purpose flour
⅛ teaspoon salt

Add these dry ingredients in about 3 parts to the butter mixture, blending them well. You may work in:

(½ teaspoon vanilla)

You may use your hands to spread the dough evenly in a 9 x 12 inch pan. Bake it in a moderate oven 350° for 15 minutes. Beat in a heavy saucepan:

2¼ cups finely chopped pecans
1 cup sugar
1½ teaspoons cinnamon
4 egg whites

Cook and stir this mixture over low heat. After the sugar has dissolved you may increase the heat slightly. Stir and cook until the mixture leaves the sides of the pan, but remove it from the fire before it is dry. Spread it over the pastry base. Bake the cake in a moderate oven 350° for 15 minutes longer. When cool cut the cake into sticks.

PECAN SLICES OR BARS
About Forty-Eight 1 x 2 Inch Bars

Many a copy of the "Joy" has been sold on the strength of this recipe. Line a pan with dough as directed for the preceding Nut Bars. Bake it as directed. Spread it with the following mixture:

Combine:

2 beaten eggs
1½ cups brown sugar
½ cup grated coconut
1 cup chopped pecan meats
2 tablespoons flour
½ teaspoon any baking powder
½ teaspoon salt
1 teaspoon vanilla

If preferred, omit the coconut and use in all 1½ cupfuls nut meats. Bake the cake in a moderate oven 350° for 25 minutes. When it is cool spread it with:

1½ cups confectioners' sugar

thinned to a good consistency to spread with:

Lemon juice

Cut the cake into oblongs.

GUMDROP BARS
About Fifty-Four 1 x 2 Inch Bars

Well liked by children. The better the gumdrop, the better the bars. See Gumdrop Cookies, page 683. Combine, then sift:

1 cup sifted all-purpose flour
¼ teaspoon salt
½ teaspoon cinnamon

Prepare:

¼ cup chopped pecans
½ cup shredded gumdrops, licorice flavor omitted

Sprinkle about ¼ of the flour mixture over these ingredients. Beat until light:

2 eggs
½ tablespoon water

Add gradually:

1 cup light brown sugar

When the sugar is well blended stir in the flour mixture and last the nut meats and gumdrops. Spread the batter in a greased 9 x 12 inch pan. Bake it in a moderate oven 350° for about ½ hour. Ice the cake while warm with the icing given under the preceding Pecan Slices. Cut it into bars while warm and remove from the pan.

SPONGE CAKE OR ANGEL CAKE BARS OR BALLS

These are light, dainty and a bit unusual served among the well-known cookies or bars at teas. Please do not overlook them. Bake in bread pans:

Sponge Cake, page 596, or
Angel Cake I, page 599

When the cake is cold, cut it into 1

inch slices, then into bars 1 inch thick
and about 2 inches long. Spread the
bars with any good:

Uncooked Icing or other icing, page 702

Let the icing be rather soft, as that will
make it easier to spread on these light
cakes.
Roll them in:

Chopped nut meats or shredded coconut

To make balls, bake the batter in deep
muffin tins. While warm shape the
cakes into balls with the hands. Ice
them as directed or use Boiled White
Icing, page 694.

CHOCOLATE ALMOND BARS
About Fifty-Four 1 x 2 Inch Bars
Blanch and shred:

1 cup almonds

Melt, then cool:

1½ oz. chocolate

Six tablespoonfuls cocoa may be substituted. Fold it into the egg and sugar
mixture.
Sift:

6 tablespoons sugar

Whip until stiff:

3 egg whites

Add the sifted sugar very slowly.
Whip constantly. Fold in the melted
chocolate, ½ cupful of the almonds
and:

½ teaspoon vanilla

Spread the batter in a greased 9 x 13
inch pan. Sprinkle the top with the
remaining almonds. Bake it in a slow
oven 320° for about 40 minutes. When
cold cut the cake into bars with a hot
knife.

Blitzkuchen, page 605. This excellent
tea cake and Hot Milk Cake, page 605,
are quickly made. They may be cut
into bars.

MOLASSES BARS
Method I.
Thirty-Two 1 x 2 Inch Bars
It is difficult to choose between the 2
following recipes for Molasses Bars,
as they seem to be equally good. No. I
is richer than No. II, but it yields a
smaller crop.
Sift:

⅓ cup powdered sugar

Beat until soft:

6 tablepoons butter

Add the sugar gradually. Blend these

ingredients until they are very light
and creamy. Beat in:

1 egg
⅓ cup molasses
⅛ teaspoon salt
⅛ teaspoon soda

Sift before measuring:

⅞ cup all-purpose flour

Add the flour in 3 parts to the butter
mixture. Stir in:

1 teaspoon vanilla

Beat the batter after each addition
until it is smooth. Fold in:

1 cup broken nut meats

Bake the batter in a greased 8 x 8 inch
pan in a moderate oven 375° for about
15 minutes. Cut the cake into bars
before it is cold. Roll them in:

Powdered sugar

Method II.
About Fifty-Four 1 x 2 Inch Bars
Sift:

½ cup sugar

Beat until soft:

5 tablespoons butter

Add the sugar gradually. Blend these
ingredients until they are very light
and creamy. Beat in:

1 egg
½ cup molasses

Sift before measuring:

2 cups all-purpose flour

Resift with:

¼ teaspoon salt
¼ teaspoon soda
1½ teaspoons any baking powder

Add the sifted ingredients in 3 parts
to the butter mixture alternately with
thirds of:

½ cup milk

Beat the batter after each addition
until it is smooth. Stir in:

1 cup broken nut meats
1 cup chopped figs, dates and raisins

Bake it in a greased 9 x 13 inch pan in
a moderate oven 375°. Cut the cake
into bars.

COCONUT GRAHAM CRISPS
About Forty 2 x 1 Inch Bars
This was a prize-winning cookie in a
household magazine contest.
Sift:

1¼ cups brown sugar

Beat until soft:

⅓ cup butter

Add the sugar gradually. Blend these
ingredients until they are creamy. Beat
in one at a time:

2 eggs

Add:

½ teaspoon vanilla

Sift before measuring:

1 cup all-purpose flour

Resift with:

½ cup rolled oats or crushed
cornflakes

½ cup graham cracker crumbs

½ teaspoon salt

Stir the sifted ingredients gradually into the butter mixture. When they are well blended stir in:

½ cup chopped nut meats

½ cup shredded coconut

Spread the dough on a greased sheet. Bake it in a hot oven 400° for about 30 minutes. Cut the cake into squares while it is warm.

SCOTCH SHORTBREAD
About Forty-Eight 1½ Inch Squares

These are rich crumbly cookies.

Sift:

½ cup confectioners' sugar

Sometimes ½ of this amount is granulated sugar, or 1⅓ cupfuls brown sugar are sometimes substituted. Beat until soft:

1 cup butter

Add the sugar gradually. Cream these ingredients until they are blended. Add:

1 teaspoon vanilla or ¼ teaspoon
freshly ground nutmeg

Combine, then work in with the hands:

2 cups sifted all-purpose flour

¼ teaspoon salt

¼ teaspoon any baking powder

Roll the dough to the thickness of ⅓ inch or pat it between pieces of waxed paper. Cut it into squares. Bake them on a greased tin in a moderate oven 375° for about 20 minutes.

The vanilla and baking powder are American touches.

Cookies

Rule for Rolling Cookies

Avoid the use of flour if possible when rolling cookie dough. An easy way is to roll it between sheets of waxed paper. This obviates the use of flour on the board and on the roller. But of course the use of a pastry canvas and roller cover does this too. It is not necessary to roll cookie dough. It may be patted with the palm of the hand. Chilled dough may be handled more readily than warm dough. If there is time, chill it for an hour or more. It is wise to bake a trial cookie. If the batter is too thin, add a very little flour, if it is too thick, a little liquid. These rules are supposed to be correct, but eggs differ in size, and honey, molasses and some other ingredients vary slightly in quality. A small pancake turner or a spatula is helpful when removing cookies from the pan. Place the hot cookies on cake racks to cool.

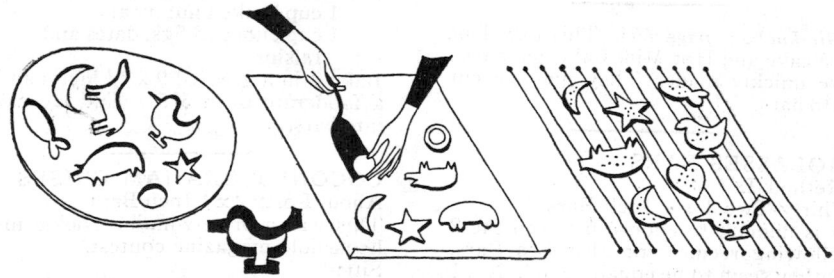

A good way to handle very thin cookie dough is to roll it directly on the bottom of an inverted greased and lightly floured cookie sheet. Cut the dough into shapes and remove the surplus dough between them. This method eliminates the transference of the thin dough from the board to the sheet and keeps the cookies shapely.

To keep cookies from sticking to the pans spread the pans with hydrogenated fat or other unsalted fat or use heavy waxed paper and grease this lightly. If a cookie is of a spreading variety you may drop the dough onto a tin that is greased and very lightly floured. To flour a tin, see page 672. Permit very thin cookies to cool for a minute or two before removing them from the pan. If they become too hard reheat them briefly.

The economical housewife will be tempted to substitute shortening for butter in these recipes. If this is done, for the sake of the flavor it is advisable to use half butter and half shortening.

PLAIN COOKIES
About 30 Crisp 3 Inch Cookies
Sift:
>   1 cup sugar

Beat until soft:
>   4 tablespoons butter

Add the sugar gradually. Blend these ingredients until they are creamy.
Combine and beat:
>   1 egg
>   3 tablespoons milk
>   1 teaspoon vanilla

Sift before measuring:
>   2 cups all-purpose flour

Resift with:
>   1 teaspoon any baking powder
>   ¼ teaspoon salt

Add the flour to the butter mixture in about 3 parts alternately with thirds of the milk mixture. Beat the batter after each addition. Chill the dough until it is firm enough to roll. Roll it into a thin sheet. See the preceding Rule for Rolling Cookies. Cut it into shapes. Sprinkle the cookies with:
>   Sugar

Bake them on a greased tin in a moderate oven 375° for about 9 minutes.

SUGAR COOKIES
About Forty 3 Inch Cookies
These are richer than the preceding plain soft cookies.
Sift:
>   1 cup sugar

Beat until soft:
>   ½ cup butter

Add the sugar gradually. Blend these ingredients until they are creamy. Beat in:
>   1 egg

Combine:
>   1 teaspoon vanilla or 1 teaspoon
>   grated lemon rind
>   ⅓ cup sour cream

Sift before measuring:
>   2 cups all-purpose flour

Resift with:
>   ⅓ teaspoon soda
>   ½ teaspoon salt
>   1 teaspoon any baking powder

Add the flour to the butter mixture in 3 parts alternately with thirds of the cream. Beat the batter until it is smooth after each addition. Chill the dough for 12 hours or more. Roll it out until it is very thin. Use as little flour as possible or roll the dough between sheets of waxed paper. Cut it into shapes. Decorate each cookie with a:
>   Nut meat

Sprinkle the cookies with:
>   Sugar

Bake them on greased tins in a moderate oven 350° for about 5 minutes.

CRISP SUGAR COOKIES, EGGLESS
Prepare the preceding:
>   Sugar Cookies

Omit the egg. Substitute for the soda:
>   1 teaspoon any baking powder

Resift the flour with the baking powder.

CHOPPED NUT COOKIES
About Two Hundred 1¼ Inch Squares
Place in a bowl and mix well:
>   3 cups sifted all-purpose flour
>   2 teaspoons any baking powder
>   1 cup sugar

Cut in until the mixture is like coarse corn meal:
>   1 cup butter or ½ cup butter and
>   ½ cup butter substitute

Stir in:
>   4 unbeaten egg yolks
>   1 whole egg

Use your hands to combine this crumbly mixture. Roll or pat it out until paper thin on a lightly floured board. Cut it into shapes. Combine, beat, then spread the cookies with:
>   1 egg yolk
>   1 tablespoon milk

Sprinkle them with:
>   Granulated sugar
>   Chopped nut meats

Bake them on a greased and floured tin in a moderate oven 350° for about ¼ hour. Decorate each cookie when cool with a dab of:

Chocolate Icing, page 699
½ pecan meat

JAM COOKIES

Prepare by one of the preceding rules:

Dough for cookies

Roll it into 1 inch balls. Make a depression in each ball. Fill it with:

Jam or preserves

Close the opening. Place the balls well apart on a greased cookie sheet. Bake the cookies as directed.

FILLED COOKIES

Use one of the preceding rules for:

Plain Cookies or Sugar Cookies

Roll the dough until it is thin, then cut it into rounds. The upper round may be cut with a doughnut cutter to permit the filling to show through. Place

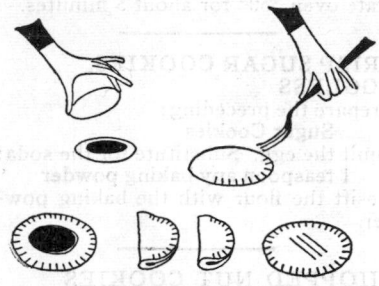

a filling between 2 rounds or place a filling on half of a round and fold over the other half. Press the edges of the cookies with a floured fork to hold in the filling.

Raisin, Fig or Date Filling

Boil and stir until thick:

1 cup chopped raisins, figs or dates
6 tablespoons sugar
5 tablespoons boiling water
½ teaspoon grated lemon rind
2 teaspoons lemon juice
2 teaspoons butter
⅛ teaspoon salt

BURIED TREASURE

Here's something new. For these cookies you must have chocolate candy wafers, the paper-thin kind, either plain, mint or rum flavored. Prepare any dough that will roll out well:

Sugar Cookies, page 669, Butter Cookies, page 675, Yolk Cookies I, page 692, etc.

Chill it for easier handling. Encase each:

Chocolate candy wafer

in about 1 tablespoonful dough. Place on top of each cookie:

½ nut meat

Bake the cookies on a lightly greased and floured sheet as directed for the dough you are using until lightly browned, usually in a 375° oven from 10 to 12 minutes.

VANILLA WAFERS

Cream:

¼ lb. butter: 1 stick

Sift, then measure and beat in:

1 cup confectioners' sugar

Beat until smooth. Add:

1 teaspoon vanilla

Sift, then measure:

1¾ cups all-purpose flour

Resift and add to the creamed mixture alternately with:

½ cup milk

Beat until creamy. Butter a baking sheet lightly. Chill the sheet. Then, with a spatula spread about 2 tablespoonfuls of the mixture over it as thin and evenly as possible. Sprinkle with:

Chopped nut meats

It is well to press them down a bit so that they will stick. Take a sharp knife and mark off the batter into 1½ inch squares. Bake in 325° oven until brown. When done take from oven and, while still hot, quickly cut through the marked squares. Slip a knife under to remove from sheet. The cakes grow crisp as soon as they cool and break easily so you have to work fast. These cookies must be kept in covered tins as they tend to grow soft if too long exposed to the air, and they are best when crisp.

SAND TARTS

About Eighty 1½ Inch Cookies

The only objection to sand tarts is that they go so very fast.

Sift:

1¼ cups sugar

Beat until soft:

¾ cup butter

Add the sugar gradually. Blend these ingredients until they are very soft and creamy. Beat in:

1 egg
1 egg yolk

1 teaspoon vanilla
1 teaspoon grated lemon rind
Sift before measuring:
3 cups all-purpose flour
Resift with:
¼ teaspoon salt if butter is
unsalted

Stir the flour gradually into the butter mixture until the ingredients are well blended. Chill the dough for several hours. Roll it until it is very thin. See page 668 for Rolling Cookies. Cut it into rounds. Brush the tops of the cookies with:
The white of an egg
Sprinkle them generously with:
Sugar
Garnish them with:
(Blanched split almonds)
Bake them on greased tins in a quick oven 400° for about 8 minutes.
A good sand tart with a slightly different flavor may be made by following this rule and substituting for white sugar 1⅓ cupfuls brown sugar.

Soft Molasses Drop Cakes, page 676.

GINGER SNAPS
About Eighty 2½ Inch Cookies
Sift:
1 cup brown sugar
Beat until soft:
1 cup shortening
Add the sugar gradually. Blend these ingredients until they are creamy. Beat in:
1 egg
1 cup dark molasses
1 tablespoon vinegar
Sift before measuring:
4 cups all-purpose flour
Resift with:
A few grains cayenne
1 teaspoon soda
1 teaspoon salt
3 to 4 teaspoons ginger
If you like a more heavily spiced cookie add:
½ teaspoon cinnamon
½ teaspoon cloves
Stir the sifted ingredients into the sugar mixture. Roll the dough until it is very thin. Cut it into rounds. Bake them in a moderate oven 350° for about 8 minutes.

GINGERBREAD MEN
About Eight 5 Inch Long Fat Men or 16 Thinner Ones
Blend until creamy:

¼ cup butter
½ cup white or brown sugar
Beat in:
½ cup dark molasses
Sift:
3½ cups all-purpose flour
Resift with:
1 teaspoon soda
¼ teaspoon cloves
½ teaspoon cinnamon
1 teaspoon ginger
½ teaspoon salt
Add the sifted ingredients to the butter mixture in about 3 parts alternately with:
5 tablespoons or more water
You will have to work in the last of the flour mixture with your hands. If you want crude men, roll a ball for a head, a larger ball for the body and cylinders for the arms and legs. Stick them together on a greased pan to form a fat boy. If you want something looking less like primitive man, roll the dough to any thickness you like. A good way to do this is to grease the bottom of a baking sheet and to roll the dough directly onto it. Now cut out your figures, either with a floured cookie tin or make a pattern of your own in the following way:

Fold a square of stiff paper or light cardboard lengthwise and cut it as indicated in the diagram. Unfold it and you have a symmetrical pattern. Grease one side of the pattern and place it on the rolled dough. Cut around the outlines with a sharp knife. Remove the scraps of dough between the figures. Use the scraps to make more men. Decorate the figures before baking them with small raisins, bits of candied cherry, redhots, decorettes, citron, etc., indicating features, buttons, etc. After baking, the men may receive further decorations as described below. Bake the cookies in a

moderate oven 350° for about 8 minutes or according to their thickness.
Test them with a toothpick. Remove
them at once from the pans. Let them
cool. Stir in a small bowl to make a
paste:

    ¼ cup confectioners' sugar
    A few drops water

You may add:

    A drop or two of coloring

Apply the icing with a toothpick or a
small knife to make additional garnishes—caps, hair, mustaches, belts,
shoes, etc. Children love to make
these.

QUICK OATMEAL COOKIES
About Twenty-Four 2½ Inch Cookies
Sift and place in a bowl:

    ½ cup brown sugar

Sift and add:

    1 cup all-purpose flour

Add:

    6 tablespoons soft butter
    ¾ cup rolled oats
    1 beaten egg
    ½ teaspoon soda
    ½ teaspoon grated lemon rind
    ¼ teaspoon salt
    (1 teaspoon cinnamon)

Use a pie blender to cut the butter into
the dry ingredients. When all the ingredients are well blended combine
and stir in:

    2 tablespoons water or milk
    1 teaspoon vanilla

Chill the dough for an hour or so. Roll
it into 1 inch balls. Flatten them well
between the hands. Place them on a
lightly greased and floured tin, or you
may drop the batter from a teaspoon,
about 1 inch apart. Bake the cookies
in a moderate oven 375° from 10 to 15
minutes.

Drop and Other Cookies

Whoever invented drop cookies deserves a decoration—that is so much more
effective than a vote of thanks.

Here they are—a varied array—delicious to eat, fine to keep on hand and pain-
less to manufacture.

Cookie batter may be dropped from a teaspoon well apart, on a prepared tin or,
if the dough is stiff, it may be pushed off the spoon with a finger or the back of a
second spoon.

Chilled cookie dough may be rolled into small balls and flattened between
palms that are lightly floured or spread with confectioners' sugar. In the case of

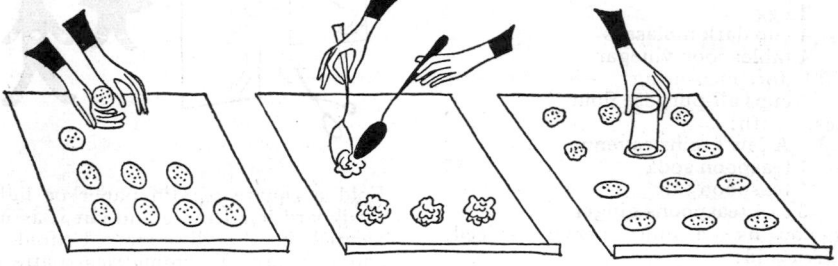

chocolate or cocoa cookies dust the palms with cocoa. Or the balls may be placed
on a prepared tin and flattened with the bottom of a glass lightly dusted with flour
or cocoa as shown above, or may be flattened with a spatula dipped in ice water or
rubbed with an ice cube.

To Prepare Cookie Pans: Spread them lightly with unsalted butter or shortening. Sprinkle a teaspoonful or two of flour on them. When making chocolate
or cocoa cookies sprinkle the tin with cocoa. Tip the tin and shake it to distribute
the flour evenly. Pour off the excess flour.

The 3 following rules are for very light cookies that are good to serve with
rich desserts.

VANILLA WAFERS OR DROP COOKIES

About Thirty 2½ Inch Cookies

This cookie is supposed to live up to its name and be very thin.

Sift:

> ½ cup sugar

Cream it with:

> 1½ tablespoons butter

Beat in:

> 1 egg
> ½ teaspoon vanilla
> ½ teaspoon grated lemon rind

Sift:

> ¾ cup all-purpose flour

Resift with:

> ⅛ teaspoon salt
> 1 teaspoon any baking powder

Add the sifted ingredients to the sugar mixture in 3 parts alternately with:

> 3 tablespoons milk

Beat the batter after each addition until it is smooth. Drop it from a teaspoon onto a greased baking sheet. Place the spoonfuls well apart, as the dough spreads readily. Bake the cookies in a moderate oven 350° for about 7 minutes.

LEMON WAFERS OR DROP COOKIES

Follow the preceding rule for:

> **Vanilla Wafers**

Substitute for the vanilla:

> 1 teaspoon lemon juice

Add:

> ½ teaspoon grated lemon or orange rind

COCOA WAFERS OR DROP COOKIES

Follow the preceding rule for:

> **Vanilla Wafers**

Deduct 3 tablespoonfuls of flour. Substitute:

> 3 tablespoons cocoa

YOLK DROP COOKIES WITH CURRANTS

About Sixty 2 Inch Cookies

Sift:

> 1½ cups sugar

Beat until soft:

> ½ cup butter

Add the sugar gradually. Blend these ingredients until they are very light and creamy. Beat in:

> 3 egg yolks
> 1 teaspoon vanilla
> ½ teaspoon grated lemon rind

Sift before measuring:

> 2¼ cups all-purpose flour

Resift with:

> 1½ teaspoons tartrate or phosphate baking powder or 1 teaspoon combination type (see Baking Powder, page 501)

Add the sifted ingredients to the butter mixture in 3 parts alternately with thirds of:

> ½ cup milk

Beat the batter until smooth after each addition. Stir in:

> ½ to 1 cup currants, washed dried raisins or nut meats

Drop the batter from a teaspoon onto a greased baking sheet. Bake the cookies in a moderate oven 350° for about 10 minutes.

CHOCOLATE, RAISIN AND NUT DROP COOKIES

About Fifty 2½ Inch Cookies

Reminiscent of the Sunday motorist who said, "Nice town we are coming to, wasn't it?"

Stir and boil until dissolved, then cool:

> ½ cup water or milk
> ¼ cup sugar
> 3 oz. cut-up chocolate

Sift:

> 1 cup sugar

Beat until soft:

> ½ cup butter

Add the sugar gradually. Blend these ingredients until they are very light and creamy. Beat in one at a time:

> 2 eggs

Stir in the chocolate mixture and:

> 1 teaspoon vanilla

Sift before measuring:

> 1½ cups cake flour

Resift with:

> 2 teaspoons tartrate or phosphate baking powder or 1½ teaspoons combination type (see Baking Powder, page 501)

Stir the sifted ingredients into the butter mixture. Beat the batter until it is smooth. Fold in:

> 1 cup broken nut meats
> 1 cup chopped raisins, dates, figs or dried apricots

Drop the batter from a teaspoon, well apart, onto a greased sheet. Bake the cookies in a moderate oven 375° for about 8 minutes.

SOUR CREAM DROP COOKIES

About Forty 2 Inch Cookies

Cream:

> 2 tablespoons butter
> 1 cup sugar

Beat in:
  1 egg
  1 teaspoon vanilla or grated
    orange or lemon rind
  ¼ cup sour cream
Sour milk may be substituted. In that
case use 4 tablespoonfuls butter. Sift,
then beat in:
  1¼ cups sifted all-purpose flour
  ¼ teaspoon soda
  ¼ teaspoon baking powder
  ½ teaspoon salt
Drop the batter from a teaspoon, well
apart, onto a greased cookie sheet.
Sprinkle the cookies with sugar. Garnish each cookie with a nut meat or a
raisin (optional). Bake them in a
moderate oven 375° for about 15 minutes.

SUGAR DROP COOKIES
About Forty-Five 2 Inch Cookies
Cream:
  ½ cup butter
Add gradually and beat until creamy:
  6 tablespoons brown sugar
  6 tablespoons white sugar
Beat in:
  1 egg
  ½ teaspoon vanilla
Sift and stir in:
  1 cup and 2 tablespoons sifted
    all-purpose flour
  ½ teaspoon salt
  ½ teaspoon soda
Stir in:
  1 cup chopped nut meats, raisins,
    dates, figs or currants
Drop the batter from a teaspoon, well
apart, on a greased cookie sheet. Bake
the cookies in a moderate oven 375°
for about 8 minutes.

CHOCOLATE CHIP DROP COOKIES OR TOLL HOUSE COOKIES
A specially prepared chocolate may be
bought for use in cookies. Any semisweet chocolate may be substituted,
cut into pea-sized pieces. Use it as you
would raisins, nut meats, etc. Follow
the preceding recipe for:
  Sugar Drop Cookies
Use only:
  ½ cup chopped nut meats
Add:
  ½ cup chipped chocolate

HONEY DROP COOKIES
About 65 Soft, Chewy 2 Inch Cookies
Sift:

  1 cup sugar
Beat until soft:
  ½ cup butter
Add the sugar gradually. Blend these
ingredients until they are very light
and fluffy. Add:
  2 tablespoons honey
  ¼ teaspoon salt
Beat in one at a time:
  2 eggs
Add:
  ½ teaspoon vanilla
Sift before measuring:
  1½ cups all-purpose flour
Resift with:
  2 teaspoons tartrate or phosphate
    baking powder or 1½ teaspoons
    combination type (see Baking
    Powder, page 501)
Stir the sifted ingredients into the
butter mixture. Drop the batter, ½
teaspoonful at a time, 2 inches apart on
a greased sheet. Garnish each cookie
with a:
  Nut meat
Bake the cookies in a hot oven 400°
for about 12 minutes.

ORANGE DROP COOKIES, ICED OR FILLED
About Thirty 2 Inch Cookies
Cream:
  ⅔ cup light brown sugar
  6 tablespoons butter
Beat in:
  1 egg
Add:
  1 teaspoon grated orange rind
  ¼ cup orange juice
Sift before measuring:
  1⅓ cups all-purpose flour
Resift with:
  ⅓ teaspoon soda
  ⅔ teaspoon any baking powder
Stir these ingredients into the sugar
mixture. Drop the batter from a teaspoon onto a greased baking sheet.
Bake the cookies in a moderate oven
350° for about 7 minutes. Ice or fill
the cookies with:
  Orange Icing, page 702

ORANGE MARMALADE DROP COOKIES
About Forty-Eight 2 Inch Cookies
This cookie, like the following one, is
chewy and besides is pleasantly acid
in flavor.
Sift:
  ⅔ cup sugar
Beat until soft:

⅓ cup butter
Add the sugar gradually. Blend these
ingredients until they are light and
creamy. Beat in:

  1 whole egg
  6 tablespoons orange marmalade

Sift:

  1½ cups all-purpose flour

Resift with:

  2 teaspoons tartrate or phosphate
    baking powder or 1¼ teaspoons
    combination type (see Baking
    Powder, page 501)

Stir the sifted ingredients into the butter mixture. Drop the batter from a
teaspoon, well apart, on a greased
sheet. Bake the cookies in a moderate
oven 375° for about 8 minutes.
It is difficult to gauge the right amount
of flour to be used as marmalades
differ a great deal in consistency. Follow this rule, then try out 1 or 2 cookies. If they are too dry, add a little
more marmalade; if they are too moist,
add a little more flour.

RICH BROWN SUGAR OR BUTTERSCOTCH DROP COOKIES

A number of cookbooks have much-
vaunted recipes for these cookies. I
have tried many of them and find that
they are all practically the same as
Butterscotch Brownies on page 663,
only they are more troublesome and
since they call for more flour are not
quite so good as that chewy, flavorful
mouthful. Please try out the Brownies
and see for yourself, then if you still
persist in wanting a drop cookie instead of a bar, just follow the recipe
and add 2 tablespoonfuls of flour.

BUTTER COOKIES

There are so many versions of this
versatile dough that I have tried to
condense them into the recipe given
below. It is used as a basis to make a
variety of cookies, as is the reliable rule
for Yolk Cookies I, page 692.

BUTTER THINS

About Twenty-Eight 2 Inch Cookies
Blend until creamy:

  6 tablespoons to ½ cup butter
  ⅓ cup sugar

Beat in:

  1 egg or 2 egg yolks
  ½ teaspoon vanilla or almond
    extract

¼ teaspoon grated lemon rind
  1 cup sifted all-purpose flour
  ⅓ teaspoon salt

In warm weather chill the dough for
several hours. Roll it into 1 inch balls.
Flatten them between lightly floured
hands. Place them on a lightly greased
and floured cookie sheet. You may
decorate them with:

  Sugar, sugar and cinnamon or
    colored sugar
  ½ nut meat or a candied cherry

Bake them in a moderate oven 375°
from 10 to 12 minutes, until the edges
are light brown. Chilled, this dough
may be put through a cookie press.

POPPY SEED COOKIES

Follow the preceding rule for:

  Butter Thins

Use the larger amount of butter.
Stir in:

  2 tablespoons poppy seed

Garnish and bake the cookies as directed.

BUTTER WAFERS

About Thirty-Six 2½ Inch Cookies
These wafers are as thin as paper and
have light brown edges. Follow the
preceding rule for:

  Butter Thins

Use:

  ½ cup butter
  ¾ cup all-purpose flour

Drop the batter from the tip of a
spoon, well apart, onto a lightly
greased and floured cookie sheet. Bake
the cookies as directed, ungarnished.

DEEP WELL COOKIES

About Forty-Two 1¼ Inch Cookies
You may call these Hussar Balls,
Thimble Cookies, Thumbprint Cookies or Pits of Love, the latter borrowed
from the French, but a rose by any
other name, etc. I find that these may
be made economically or not, according to your preference. Good either
way and highly decorative.
Prepare the dough for:

  Butter Thins

Use the larger amount of butter. Roll
the dough into a ball. You may chill it
briefly for easier handling. Pinch off
pieces to roll into 1 inch balls.
I.
Roll the balls in:

  1 slightly beaten egg white

then in:

  1 cup finely chopped nut meats

II.

Or, omit the egg white and nut meats.
Roll the balls in:

    Sugar

Place them on a lightly greased and
floured tin. Bake them in a moderate
oven 375° for 5 minutes. Depress the
center of each cookie with a thimble or
thumb, as shown on the left below.
Continue baking them until done, for
about 8 minutes. When cool fill the
pits with:

    **A preserved strawberry, a bit of
jelly or jam, a candied cherry or
a dab of icing**

MACAROON JAM TARTS

About Fourteen 3 Inch Cakes
The star of stars.
Blend until creamy:

    2 tablespoons sugar
    ½ cup butter

Beat in:

    1 egg yolk
    ½ teaspoon grated lemon rind
    1½ tablespoons lemon juice

Stir in gradually until well blended:

    1½ cups sifted all-purpose flour

alternately with:

    2 tablespoons cold water

Chill the dough for 12 hours. Roll it
out to the thickness of ⅛ inch. Cut it
into 3 inch rounds. Whip until stiff:

    3 egg whites

Beat in gradually:

    1⅓ cups confectioners' sugar
    1 teaspoon vanilla

Fold in:

    **½ lb. almonds blanched and
ground in a nut grinder**

Place this mixture around the edge of
each cookie, making a border ¾ inch
wide. Use a pastry bag, as shown on
the right above, a spatula or a spoon.
Bake the cakes in a moderate oven
325° for 20 minutes, or until done.
When they are cold fill the centers
with:

    Jam

MERINGUE JAM COOKIES OR RUSSIAN COOKIES

About Thirty-Five 1 x 2 Inch Cookies
The addition of jelly and meringue
makes this a distinctive cookie.
Prepare the dough for:

    Butter Thins, page 675

Chill the dough for several hours. Roll
it until it is very thin. Cut it into
oblongs. Spread the cookies with:

    Tart jam or jelly

Cover them with the following meringue. Whip until stiff:

    1 egg white

Add very slowly, beating constantly:

    5 tablespoons sugar

Fold in:

    1 teaspoon cinnamon
    6 tablespoons chopped nut meats

Bake the cookies on a greased tin in a
moderate oven 350° for about 12 minutes.

INDIVIDUAL ALMOND OR NUT TARTS

Prepare:

    **Galette Dough, page 565, or
Sugar Cookie Dough, page 669**

Chill it for 12 hours. Pat or roll it until
it is very thin. Line muffin pans with
the dough. Beat until light:

    3 egg yolks

Beat in gradually:

    1 cup sugar
    ¼ teaspoon salt

Grind in a nut grinder and add:

    **1 cup blanched almonds or other
nuts**

Stir in:

    1½ tablespoons lemon juice

Fold in:

    3 stiffly beaten egg whites

Fill the lined muffin tins with this mixture. Bake the tarts in a moderate
oven 350° until done, for about 20
minutes.

SOFT MOLASSES DROP COOKIES

About Thirty 2½ Inch Cookies
Sift:

    ½ cup brown or white sugar

Beat until soft:

    ½ cup shortening

Add the sugar gradually. Blend these
ingredients until they are very light
and creamy. Beat in:

    1 egg
    ½ cup molasses

Sift:

    1½ cups all-purpose flour

Resift with:
  1 teaspoon ginger
  1 teaspoon cinnamon
  ¼ teaspoon cloves
  ¼ teaspoon salt
  1½ teaspoons any baking powder
  ¼ teaspoon soda
Combine:
  ½ teaspoon vinegar
  ¼ cup coffee or water
Add the sifted ingredients to the butter mixture in 3 parts alternately with thirds of the coffee mixture. Beat the batter after each addition until it is smooth. Drop it from a teaspoon onto a greased tin. Flatten the dough with a spatula dipped in cold water. Bake the cookies in a moderate oven 350° for about 10 minutes.
These cookies may be iced with Icing for Christmas Cakes, page 705.

Molasses Nut Drop Cookies, page 680.

MOLASSES DROP COOKIES
About Forty-Two 2 Inch Cookies
Follow the above rule for:
  Soft Molasses Drop Cookies
Substitute for the liquid:
  ½ cup sour milk
Use in all:
  2¼ cups all-purpose flour
  1 teaspoon soda
You may add:
  ½ cup chopped raisins

ROCKS
About Fifty-Five 2½ Inch Cookies
Blend until creamy:
  1 cup sifted sugar
  1 cup butter
Beat in one at a time:
  3 egg yolks
Stir in:
  1 teaspoon cinnamon
  ½ teaspoon cloves
  1½ tablespoons water or milk
  1 teaspoon vanilla
Sift, then measure:
  2½ cups all-purpose flour
Sift a little of this over:
  1 cup broken nut meats
  1 cup chopped raisins or dates
  ½ cup chopped citron
Add to the rest of the flour:
  ¾ teaspoon soda
Stir it into the butter mixture. Stir in the raisins, etc. Whip until stiff:
  3 egg whites
  ⅛ teaspoon salt

Fold them into the batter. Drop it from a teaspoon, well apart, onto a greased sheet. Bake the rocks in a moderate oven 375° for about 12 minutes.

COLUMBIA DROP COOKIES
About Thirty 2 Inch Cookies
Sift:
  ¾ cup brown sugar
Beat until soft:
  ½ cup butter
Add the sugar gradually. Blend these ingredients until they are very light and creamy. Beat in one at a time:
  2 eggs
Sift before measuring:
  1½ cups all-purpose flour
Resift with:
  ½ teaspoon soda
  1 teaspoon cinnamon
  ½ teaspoon cloves
  ¼ teaspoon allspice
  ⅛ teaspoon salt
Add the sifted ingredients in 3 parts to the butter mixture alternately with thirds of:
  ¼ cup water
Beat the batter until it is smooth after each addition. Stir in:
  1 cup broken nut meats
  1 cup raisins, chopped dates or figs
Drop the batter from a teaspoon onto a greased tin. Bake the cookies in a moderate oven 375° for about 12 minutes.

HERMITS
About Thirty 2 Inch Cookies
Sift:
  1 cup brown sugar
Beat until soft:
  ½ cup butter
Add the sugar gradually. Blend these ingredients until they are very light and creamy. Beat in:
  1 egg
  ½ cup sour cream, sour milk or strong coffee
Sift before measuring:
  1⅓ cups all-purpose flour
Resift with:
  ¾ teaspoon cinnamon
  ½ teaspoon cloves
  ¼ teaspoon soda
If coffee has been used above, the spices are optional.
Add the sifted ingredients to the butter mixture. Beat the batter until it is smooth. Stir in:
  ½ cup chopped raisins
  ¼ cup hickory or other nut meats

¼ cup coconut may be added if desired

Drop the batter from a teaspoon onto a greased sheet. Bake the cookies in a moderate oven 375° for about 15 minutes.

ROLLED OATS MACAROONS
About Thirty-Six 2 Inch Cookies
Inexpensive and good.
Combine and beat well:
  2½ teaspoons melted butter
  1 cup sugar or firmly packed brown sugar
  2 egg yolks
  2 cups rolled oats
  2 teaspoons tartrate or phosphate baking powder or 1⅓ teaspoons combination type (see Baking Powder, page 501)
  1 teaspoon vanilla
Whip until stiff:
  2 egg whites
  ⅛ teaspoon salt
Fold them into the other ingredients. Drop the batter from a teaspoon 3 inches apart on a lightly greased baking tin. Bake the cookies in a moderate oven 375° for about 10 minutes.

SPICED OATMEAL COOKIES
About Forty 2½ Inch Cookies
Sift:
  1 cup all-purpose flour
Resift with:
  ¼ teaspoon soda
  ½ teaspoon salt
  ½ teaspoon cinnamon
  ¼ teaspoon cloves or freshly grated nutmeg
  ½ cup brown sugar firmly packed
Work in with the hands or with a pie blender until well incorporated:
  ½ cup soft butter or shortening
Beat until light, then add:
  1 egg
Stir in:
  ¾ cup rolled oats
  2 tablespoons molasses or sour milk or buttermilk
Stir in:
  (½ cup chopped nuts)
  (¾ cup chopped raisins or dates or figs)
From a teaspoon drop the batter well apart onto lightly greased and floured cookie sheets. Flatten the cookies with a spatula moistened in cold water. Chill the cookies for ½ hour. Bake in

a moderate oven 375° for 15 to 20 minutes or until well browned.

CHOCOLATE CHIP OATMEAL COOKIES
About 48 Cookies
Good crunchy cookies—nutless, but tasting nutty.
Cream well:
  ½ cup butter
  1 cup firmly packed brown sugar
Beat in:
  1 egg
  Grated rind of 1 orange
  1 teaspoon vanilla
  ½ cup all-purpose flour
  1½ cups rolled oats
  ¼ teaspoon salt
Fold in:
  7 oz. chocolate chips
Drop the batter from a teaspoon onto lightly greased and floured cookie sheets. Bake the cookies in a moderate oven 375° for 15 to 20 minutes.

CEREAL CHOCOLATE DROP COOKIES, UNBAKED
Melt in a double boiler or over very low heat:
  Sweet chocolate bars
Use the common drugstore variety, with or without nut meats. Stir in:
  Cornflakes, Post Toasties or Rice Crispies, etc.
as much as the chocolate will absorb. Drop the mixture from a spoon onto oiled paper. Chill it.

Coconut Graham Crisps, page 667.

COCONUT DROP COOKIES I OR KISSES WITH EGG WHITES
About Fifty 1½ Inch Kisses
Sift:
  1 cup sugar
Beat until stiff:
  3 egg whites
  ⅛ teaspoon salt
Add the sugar very slowly, beating constantly. Fold in:
  1 teaspoon vanilla
  1¼ cups shredded coconut
Drop the batter from a teaspoon onto a greased and well-floured tin. Bake the cookies in a slow oven 300° for about 30 minutes.

COCONUT DROP COOKIES II WITH CONDENSED MILK
About Twenty 1 Inch Cookies

Chop:

    ¼ lb. shredded coconut

Add:

    1 teaspoon vanilla

    ⅛ teaspoon salt

Combine these ingredients with sufficient:

    Sweetened condensed milk

to make a thick paste. Roll the paste into balls or drop it from a teaspoon onto greased tins about 2 inches apart. These cookies are much improved by folding into the batter:

    1 to 3 stiffly beaten egg whites

Drop this batter from a spoon. Bake the cookies in a slow oven 250° until they are lightly browned. Take them from the oven when they can be removed from the tin without breaking. The balls may be rolled in:

    Confectioners' sugar

CHOCOLATE COCONUT DROP COOKIES
Prepare the preceding:

    Coconut Drop Cookies II

Heat the milk and add:

    2 tablespoons cocoa or ¾ oz. chocolate

Cool the mixture before adding it to the coconut.

FLORENTINES
48 Very Thin 4 Inch Cookies

The European public is familiar with this unusually delicious confection but it is only since World War II that it has become generally known here, through refugees who make it commercially.

Stir well:

    ½ cup whipping cream: 40%

    3 tablespoons sugar

Stir in:

    ⅓ cup blanched slivered almonds

    ¼ lb. preserved diced orange peel

    ¼ cup all-purpose flour

Spread a cookie sheet with unsalted shortening, flour it lightly. Drop the batter on it from a teaspoon, well apart. Bake the cookies in a moderate oven 350° from 10 to 12 minutes. They burn easily so watch them. When cold spread the bottoms of the cookies with:

    Melted sweet chocolate

Use a spatula or impale a cookie on a fork and dip it into the chocolate. Dry them on waxed paper, bottoms up.

MACAROONS
About Thirty 2 Inch Macaroons

Work with the hands until well blended:

    1 cup shaved Almond Paste, page 783: ½ lb.

    ⅞ cup sugar

Work in:

    3 egg whites

    ½ teaspoon vanilla

Sift, then add and blend in:

    ⅓ cup powdered sugar

    2 tablespoons cake flour

    ⅛ teaspoon salt

Put these ingredients through a pastry bag, well apart, onto unglazed paper. Permit them to stand for 2 hours or more. Bake the macaroons in a slow oven 300° for about 25 minutes. Place the paper on a moist cloth. Remove the macaroons.

White Macaroons, page 689.

MINCEMEAT DROP COOKIES
30 Cookies

Sift:

    ½ cup white or brown sugar

Beat until soft:

    ¼ cup butter

Add the sugar gradually. Beat these ingredients until they are well blended. Beat in:

    1 egg

    1 cup mincemeat

Sift before measuring:

    1¼ cups all-purpose flour

Resift with:

    2 teaspoons tartrate or phosphate baking powder or 1½ teaspoons combination type (see Baking Powder, page 501)

Stir the sifted ingredients into the mincemeat mixture until they are blended. Drop the batter by the teaspoonful, well apart, on a greased sheet. Bake the cookies in a hot oven 400° for about 10 minutes.

NUT SQUARES, FLOURLESS
Combine in a stewpan:

    1½ cups ground almonds or pecans

    1 cup brown sugar

    1 egg white

    1½ teaspoons butter

Stir these ingredients over a very low fire until they are well blended. Cool the mixture. Shape it into small balls or roll it out and cut it into shapes. If the dough is hard to handle, use a little confectioners' sugar. Place the cookies on a very well-greased sheet. Bake them in a moderate oven 325° for 30 to 40 minutes. Leave them on the sheet until cold. The cookies may be iced with confectioners' sugar and lemon juice or with some chocolate icing.

Nut Wafers, Small Cakes and Rolled Cookies

The following recipes for nut wafers are delicious. They are not at all alike. The first, made with ground nut meats, is crisp and delicate; the second and third call for similar ingredients, but are different in texture; the fourth differs in flavor. These rules deserve all the stars in the firmament.

To grease and flour a tin, see page 672.

PECAN DROP COOKIES WITH BROWN SUGAR AND GROUND PECANS
About Fifty 1½ Inch Wafers
Grind in a nut grinder:
    1 cup pecan meats
Put through a food mill or crush the lumps from:
    1⅓ cups firmly packed brown sugar
Whip until stiff:
    3 egg whites
Add the sugar very slowly, beating constantly. Fold in the ground pecans and:
    1 teaspoon vanilla
Drop the batter from a teaspoon, well apart, onto a greased and floured tin. Bake the cookies in a moderate oven 325° for about 15 minutes.

LUCY'S COOKIES
30 Cookies
Work:
    1 tablespoon flour
into:
    1 cup brown sugar
Beat until stiff, then fold in:
    1 egg white
Fold in:
    ¾ teaspoon vanilla
    1⅛ cups coarsely chopped pecans
Drop the batter from a teaspoon onto a greased and floured cookie sheet. Bake the cookies in a moderate oven 325° for about 15 minutes, or until done.

PECAN WAFERS
About Fifty 2½ Inch Wafers
Do not attempt these cookies in moist hot weather. Put through a food mill or crush the lumps from:
    1⅓ cups firmly packed brown sugar
Whip until light:
    2 eggs
Add the sugar gradually. Beat these ingredients until they are well blended. Add:
    5 tablespoons all-purpose flour
    ⅛ teaspoon salt
    ⅛ teaspoon any baking powder
    1 teaspoon vanilla
Beat the batter until it is smooth, then add:
    1 cup broken nut meats
Grease and flour tins. Drop the batter on them, well apart, from a teaspoon. Bake the cookies in a moderate oven 375° for about 8 minutes. Remove them from the tins while still warm.

MOLASSES NUT DROP COOKIES
About Fifty 2½ Inch Wafers
Sift:
    1 cup dark brown sugar
Whip until light:
    2 eggs
Add the sugar gradually. Beat these ingredients until they are well blended. Add:
    1 tablespoon dark molasses
    ¼ teaspoon any baking powder
    6 tablespoons all-purpose flour
    ⅛ teaspoon salt
Beat the batter until it is smooth. Stir in:
    1 cup black or English walnuts, hazelnuts or mixed nut meats
To bake the cakes follow the above rule for Pecan Wafers.

COCONUT CRISPS
About Twenty-Eight 2 Inch Cookies
Remember these? They are the kind the grocer, in days gone by, drew out of a highly decorated tin canister to put into the hand of an expectant child.
Blend until creamy:
    ½ cup soft butter
    1 cup sifted brown sugar

Beat in:
    1 egg
Combine, then stir in:
    2 tablespoons molasses, preferably
        black-strap
    ½ teaspoon vanilla
Sift:
    2 cups all-purpose flour
Resift with:
    ¾ teaspoon any baking powder
    ¼ teaspoon soda
    ⅛ teaspoon salt
Stir the sifted ingredients into the
butter mixture. Fold in:
    1 to 1¼ cups grated coconut
Chill the dough for 3 hours or more.
Roll it into ¾ inch balls. Flatten them
as thin as you can between very lightly

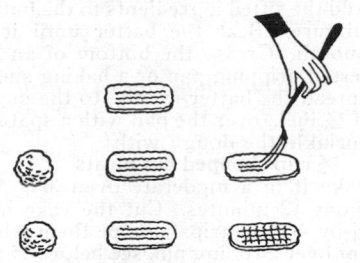

floured hands. Score them in parallel
lines to give a corrugated effect with a
fork dipped in flour. Bake the cookies
on lightly greased and floured tins in a
moderate oven 375° from 10 to 12
minutes.

PECAN PUFFS
About Thirty-Two 1½ Inch Cakes
There is a strong family resemblance
between this and the next rule.
Rich and devastating.
Beat until soft:
    ½ cup butter
Add and blend until creamy:
    2 tablespoons sugar
Add:
    1 teaspoon vanilla
Measure, then grind in a nut grinder:
    1 cup pecan meats
Sift before measuring:
    1 cup cake flour
Stir the pecans and the flour into the
butter mixture. Roll the dough into
small balls. Place them on a greased
baking sheet. Bake them in a slow
oven 300° for about 45 minutes. Roll
the puffs while hot in:
    Confectioners' sugar

When cold roll them again in confectioners' sugar.

JELLY TOTS
Method I.
Artemus Ward, who, by the way, once
edited a cookbook, called his pet kan-
garoo an "amoosing little cuss." This
rule makes 28 amusing little cakes.
Combine:
    ½ cup melted butter
    1½ tablespoons sugar
    1 cup finely chopped pecan meats
    ½ teaspoon grated lemon rind
    1 teaspoon vanilla
    ⅛ teaspoon salt if the butter is
        unsalted
Sift and stir in:
    1½ cups all-purpose flour
Place the bowl containing the dough
over hot water so that the dough will
become soft enough to handle. Roll
it into 1 inch balls. Make a depression
in each ball. Place in the depression
a bit of:
    Drained strawberry preserves
    ½ pecan meat
Bake the tots on a greased sheet in a
moderately hot oven 400° for about 10
minutes. Sprinkle them with:
    Confectioners' sugar

Method II.
The following version is nutless and
more economical.
Combine in the order given above:
    ½ cup butter
    ⅓ cup confectioners' sugar
    ½ teaspoon almond extract
    ½ teaspoon vanilla
    1¼ teaspoons cinnamon
    ⅛ teaspoon salt
    1 cup cake flour
Roll, depress, add the jelly and bake.

Method III.
Or use confectioners' sugar to roll
the dough into sticks. Shape them into
rings. Bake them in a slow oven 300°
for about 15 minutes. You may sprinkle the rings while hot with cinnamon
and confectioners' sugar.

RUM DROPS, UNCOOKED
About Forty-Five 1 Inch Balls
Fine served with tea or with lemon
ice, etc. Place in a mixing bowl:
    2 cups finely sifted, toasted sponge
        cake, zwieback or graham
        cracker crumbs

Add:
> 2 tablespoons cocoa
> 1 cup sifted powdered sugar
> ⅛ teaspoon salt
> 1 cup finely chopped nut meats

Combine:
> 1½ tablespoons honey or sirup
> ¼ cup rum or brandy

Add the liquid ingredients slowly to the crumb mixture. Use your hands in order to tell by the "feel" when the consistency is right. When the ingredients will hold together nicely stop adding the liquid. If the mixture is too dry, add a few drops more of the liquid. Roll the mixture into 1 inch balls. Roll the balls in:
> Powdered or granulated sugar

Set the drops aside in a tin box for 12 hours to ripen.

ROLLED CARAMEL COOKIES
About 24 Cornucopias
Cream well:
> ¼ cup butter
> ½ cup brown sugar

Beat in:
> 1 egg

When well blended beat in:
> ½ teaspoon vanilla
> ⅛ teaspoon salt
> 3 tablespoons all-purpose flour

Stir in:
> ¼ cup ground or minced nut meats

Black walnuts are excellent.
Drop the batter from a teaspoon, well apart, on a greased cookie sheet, about 6 to a sheet. Flatten them with the back of a spoon. Bake the cookies in a hot oven 400° for 8 or 9 minutes. Cool them slightly, remove them from the pan with a small pancake turner.

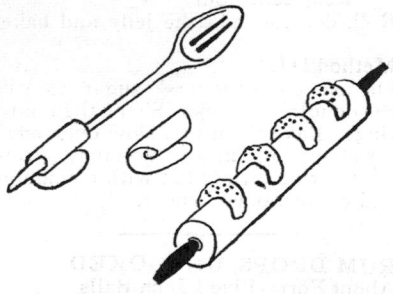

Then roll them over a wooden spoon handle as shown on the left above or with the hands. If the cookies cool too quickly, return them for a minute to the oven.

ROLLED NUT WAFERS
About 20 Wafers
Sift:
> ⅔ cup sugar

Beat until soft:
> 2 tablespoons butter
> 2 tablespoons lard

Add the sugar gradually. Blend these ingredients until they are very light and creamy. Beat in:
> 1 egg
> 2 tablespoons milk
> ½ teaspoon vanilla
> ¼ teaspoon almond extract

Sift before measuring:
> 1⅓ cups all-purpose flour

Resift with:
> 1 teaspoon any baking powder
> ½ teaspoon salt

Add the sifted ingredients to the butter mixture. Beat the batter until it is smooth. Grease the bottom of an inverted dripping pan or a baking sheet. Spread the batter evenly, to the depth of ⅛ inch, over the pan with a spatula. Sprinkle the dough with:
> ⅓ cup chopped nut meats

Bake it in a moderate oven 375° for about 12 minutes. Cut the cake into ¾ by 4 inch strips. Shape them while hot over a rolling pin, see below. If the strips become too brittle before they are shaped, return them to the oven until they become pliable again.

PEANUT BUTTER COOKIES
After many try-outs I find these the only peanut butter cookies that are really good. Perhaps I do not know all the recipes extant, but I have struggled with many. This recipe makes about sixty 1½ inch cookies. They are rich and crumbly. Sift:
> ½ cup brown sugar
> ½ cup granulated sugar

Beat until soft:
> ½ cup butter

Add the sugar gradually and blend these ingredients until they are creamy. Beat in:
> 1 egg
> 1 cup peanut butter
> ½ teaspoon salt
> ½ teaspoon soda

Sift before measuring:
> 1½ cups all-purpose flour

Add the flour to the batter and:
> ½ teaspoon vanilla

Roll the dough into small balls. Place them on a greased tin. Press them flat with a fork. Bake them in a moderate oven 375° for about 15 minutes.

GUMDROP COOKIES
About Forty 2 Inch Cookies
Good for school boxes, as they keep fresh and travel well.
Beat until soft:
   ½ cup shortening
Beat in gradually until light and creamy:
   ½ cup brown sugar
   ½ cup white sugar
   1 teaspoon vanilla
Sift before measuring:
   1 cup all-purpose flour
Resift with:
   ½ teaspoon soda
   ½ teaspoon any baking powder
   ¼ teaspoon salt
Sprinkle ¼ of this over:
   ½ cup small gumdrops or large ones cut
   1 cup quick-cooking oatmeal
   (½ cup grated coconut or chopped nut meats)
Beat the sifted ingredients into the butter mixture in about 2 parts alternately with:
   1 beaten egg
Stir in the coconut, gumdrops and oatmeal mixture. Pinch off small pieces of dough. Roll them into 1 inch balls. Flatten them with a spatula dipped in milk. Bake the cookies in a moderate oven 350° for about 10 minutes.

Gumdrop Bars, page 666.

LADY FINGERS
About 30
Sift:
   ⅓ cup confectioners' sugar
Beat until thick and lemon colored:
   1 whole egg
   2 egg yolks
Sift before measuring:
   ⅓ cup cake flour
Resift it 3 times. Whip until stiff but not dry:
   2 egg whites
   ⅛ teaspoon salt
Fold the sugar gradually into the egg whites. Beat the mixture until it thickens again. Fold in the egg yolk mixture and:
   ¼ teaspoon vanilla
Fold in the flour. Shape the dough into oblongs with a paper tube, see page 696, on ungreased paper placed in a pan, or pour it into greased lady finger or small muffin tins or put through a cookie press. Bake the cakes in a moderate oven 375° for about 12 minutes.

Cookie Press Cookies

A number of cookie doughs may be put through a cookie press. All the Refrigerator Cookies and many others may be made into these attractive little cakes. The press seems to call for rather a firm dough. See Poppy Seed Cookies, page 675. If the dough you wish to use does not do well in the press, try chilling it until it is ready to be used successfully.

Refrigerator Cookies

The following recipes for Refrigerator Cookies are all so good that it is hard to decide upon the best. The addition of nut meats, which is optional, is considered an improvement to the plain cookie, but the cookie *au naturel* is mighty good.

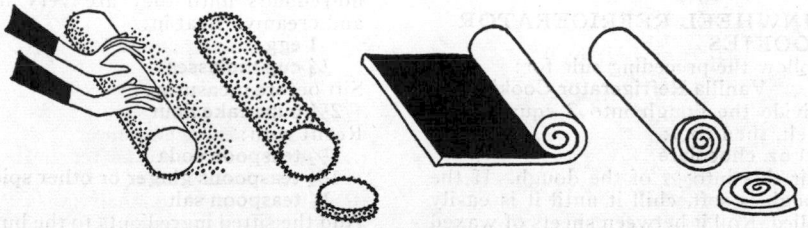

For a description of ways to shape these cookies see the next page.

Rule for Refrigerator Cookies

Combine the ingredients as directed and shape the dough into long rolls about 2 inches in diameter. If the dough is too soft to roll, chill it until it can be handled easily. Do not use additional flour. Cover the rolls with waxed paper and place them in the refrigerator for about 24 hours until they are thoroughly chilled. Cut the rolls into the thinnest possible slices. Bake them on a greased sheet in an oven heated to 400° for about 10 minutes. The whole nut meats may be combined with the dough or they may be used to garnish the slices, or the entire roll of dough may be rolled in chopped nuts, as shown on page 683, so as to make a border when the cookie is cut. Two sheets of different-colored dough may be rolled together, see preceding page. These, when sliced, become pinwheel cookies. See rule below.

VANILLA REFRIGERATOR COOKIES
About Forty 2 Inch Cookies
This cookie resembles a Sand Tart and is less troublesome to prepare. It makes a good Filled Cookie, page 670.
Sift:
> 1 cup sugar

Beat until soft:
> ½ cup butter

Add the sugar gradually. Blend these ingredients until they are very light and creamy. Beat in:
> 1 egg

Add:
> 1 teaspoon vanilla
> (½ teaspoon grated lemon rind)

Sift before measuring:
> 1¾ cups all-purpose flour

Resift with:
> ¼ teaspoon salt
> 2 teaspoons tartrate or phosphate baking powder or 1½ teaspoons combination type (see Baking Powder, page 501)

Stir the sifted ingredients into the butter mixture. Add:
> (½ cup nut meats)

Follow the preceding Rule for Refrigerator Cookies. Sprinkle the cookies with:
> (Sugar)

to make them sandy and with:
> (Chopped or half nut meats)

Bake them as directed.

PINWHEEL REFRIGERATOR COOKIES
Follow the preceding rule for:
> Vanilla Refrigerator Cookies

Divide the dough into 2 equal parts. Melt, then cool:
> 1 oz. chocolate

Stir this into ½ of the dough. If the dough is soft, chill it until it is easily rolled. Roll it between sheets of waxed paper. Roll the white and the brown dough separately into oblongs to the

thickness of ⅛ inch, see Rule for Cookies, page 668. Place the dark dough on the light dough and roll the layers like a jelly roll. Follow the Rule for Refrigerator Cookies.

BUTTERSCOTCH REFRIGERATOR COOKIES
Follow the preceding rule for:
> Vanilla Refrigerator Cookies

Substitute for the white sugar:
> 1¼ cups firmly packed brown sugar

COCONUT REFRIGERATOR COOKIES
Follow one of the rules on these pages for:
> Butterscotch Refrigerator Cookies, Vanilla Refrigerator Cookies, or Spiced Refrigerator Cookies

The Butterscotch seems best for this purpose. Omit the nut meats. Substitute:
> 1 cup grated coconut

SPICED REFRIGERATOR COOKIES
About Sixty 2 Inch Cookies
Sift:
> ½ cup sugar

Beat until soft:
> ½ cup butter

Add the sugar gradually. Blend these ingredients until they are very light and creamy. Beat in:
> 1 egg
> ¼ cup molasses

Sift before measuring:
> 2¼ cups cake flour

Resift with:
> ½ teaspoon soda
> 1½ teaspoons ginger or other spices
> ½ teaspoon salt

Add the sifted ingredients to the butter mixture. Follow the Rule for Refrigerator Cookies above.

CHOCOLATE REFRIGERATOR COOKIES

About Sixty 2 Inch Cookies

Sift:

1½ cups sugar

Beat until soft:

½ cup butter

Add the sugar gradually. Blend these ingredients until they are very light and creamy. Beat in:

1 egg

2 oz. melted cooled chocolate

½ teaspoon vanilla

Sift before measuring:

2½ cups all-purpose flour

Resift with:

½ teaspoon salt

2 teaspoons tartrate or phosphate baking powder or 1 teaspoon combination type (see Baking Powder, page 501)

Add the sifted ingredients to the butter mixture alternately with:

¼ cup milk

Add:

(½ cup unbroken nut meats)

Follow the Rule for Refrigerator Cookies, page 684.

CREAM CHEESE REFRIGERATOR COOKIES

About Sixty 2 Inch Cookies

All of these Refrigerator Cookies are good but this one is especially tempting.

Blend until creamy:

½ cup butter

1 cup sugar

1 well-beaten egg

Soften slightly:

1 package cream cheese: 3 oz.

Beat it into the butter mixture with:

2 tablespoons sour milk

1 teaspoon vanilla

Beat in:

2 cups all-purpose flour

⅛ teaspoon soda

½ teaspoon any baking powder

½ teaspoon salt

Follow the Rule for Refrigerator Cookies, page 684. Be sure to sprinkle the cookies with sugar, to which you may add cinnamon. This dough, after being chilled, may be rolled to paper thinness, cut into shapes and baked. Bake them in a moderate oven 350° from 12 to 15 minutes.

OATMEAL REFRIGERATOR COOKIES

About Fifty-Six 2 Inch Cookies

Stir until well blended:

½ cup white sugar

½ cup brown sugar

¾ cup sifted all-purpose flour

½ teaspoon soda

½ teaspoon salt

½ cup soft butter

1 egg

1½ teaspoons grated orange or lemon rind

½ teaspoon almond or vanilla extract

Work in with the hands:

1½ cups rolled oats

To vary the flavor, you may use 1½ tablespoonfuls of molasses and 2 additional tablespoonfuls of flour. Follow the Rule for Refrigerator Cookies, page 684.

Quick Refreshments for Tea

ORANGE MARMALADE SANDWICHES

Cut the crusts from:

¼ inch slices of bread

Spread them with:

Marmalade

Roll the slices and secure them with toothpicks. Toast them under a broiler or on a toaster. Turn them to brown evenly. Serve them hot.

Cinnamon Toast, page 539.

LADY FINGER SANDWICHES

Spread:

Lady fingers or small cookies

with:

Jam or marmalade

Place one upon another to form a sandwich.

PINEAPPLE FINGERS

Method I.

Cut into strips 3 by 1½ inches wide and 1½ inches thick:

White bread

Toast them on 3 sides. Place them on a baking sheet with the untoasted side up. Drain:

Pineapple sticks

Place them on the untoasted sides. Sprinkle them well with a mixture of:

Brown sugar and cinnamon

Dot them with:
Butter
Brown them under a broiler.

Method II.
Or prepare by any rule:
Pie Dough, page 564
Roll it until it is very thin. Cut it into

oblongs. Sprinkle:
Pineapple sticks
with:
Cinnamon and brown sugar
Wrap the sticks in the oblongs. Moisten the edges with water. Bake the sticks in a hot oven 450° for about 20 minutes.

Meringue Kisses

For large Meringues, see page 654.
For Meringue Tart or "Pinch Pie," see page 654.

Rule for Meringue Kisses

Meringue cakes or kisses are made with egg whites, sugar and other ingredients. A small quantity of salt is added to the egg whites and they are whipped on a platter with a flat wire egg beater until they are stiff and hold a peak, but not until they are dry. The sugar is then added very slowly during continuous beating. When the last of the sugar has been blended thoroughly, the remaining ingredients are folded in. The batter is dropped from a spoon onto a lightly greased tin and shaped into cones. The kisses are baked in a very slow oven 250° until they are partly dry and will retain their shape. They are removed from the pan while hot.

NUT KISSES
About Forty 1 Inch Kisses
Perhaps Falstaff anticipated these when he spoke of "pretty little tiny kickshaws." Decorate the kisses if you wish with a bit of cherry or a filbert, etc.
Sift:
  1 cup sugar
Whip until stiff:
  2 egg whites
  ⅛ teaspoon salt
Add the sugar very slowly. Whip constantly. Add:
  ½ teaspoon vanilla
  ½ teaspoon grated lemon rind
Fold in:
  1 cup broken or chopped nut
  meats or a combination of nut
  meats and ½ cup chopped citron
Follow the preceding Rule for Meringue Kisses.

DATE AND NUT KISSES
About Fifty 1 Inch Kisses
Follow the rule for the preceding:
  Nut Kisses

Add:
  1 cup chopped dates

Coconut Drop Cakes I, page 678; Almond Rings, page 689.

COCOA KISSES
About Forty 1 Inch Meringues
Sift:
  1 cup sugar
Whip until stiff:
  3 egg whites
  ⅛ teaspoon salt
Add gradually ½ of the sugar. Combine:
  2 teaspoons water
  1 teaspoon vanilla
Add the liquid, a few drops at a time, alternately with the remaining sugar. Whip constantly. Fold in:
  3 tablespoons cocoa
Follow the Rule for Meringue Kisses on this page. Decorate each kiss with a:
  Nut meat

Christmas Cakes

The following are various forms of German Christmas Cakes. They are so good that one wonders why they are limited to one short period of the year. If the cakes become hard keep half an apple in the cookie jar. Replace it frequently.

GERMAN HONEY CAKES

Honey, like molasses, is apt to be troublesome. Old German cooks used to insist on its being over a year old. Very good cakes are made with fresh honey but then the amount of flour is a little hard to gauge. These cakes will keep for 6 months and longer if placed in a closed tin. This recipe may be cut to ⅓ if preferred.

Heat slightly in a large saucepan:

6 lbs. honey or molasses

Add and melt:

1 cup butter

Sift and add sufficient:

Bread flour

to make a semi-liquid dough. Add:

1 lb. blanched shredded almonds
½ lb. chopped citron
4 cups sugar
½ cup mixed spices: cinnamon, cloves, nutmeg, mace, allspice
4 teaspoons grated lemon rind

When the dough is nearly cold add:

1 oz. carbonate of powdered ammonia dissolved in ½ cup water, wine or rum

Sift and add sufficient:

All-purpose flour

to make a dough that will stick to the hands. The dough may be baked at once, but the cakes are better when the dough has been aged. It will keep for weeks in a cool place. Roll out the dough or pat it. It may even be necessary to warm it. Spread it to the thickness of ¼ inch in shallow greased pans. In doing this use as little flour as possible or roll the dough between sheets of waxed paper. Bake it in a moderate oven 350°. Cut the cake into squares and ice them with the following:

Lemon Icing

Whip until stiff:

2 egg whites
⅛ teaspoon salt

Sift and add sufficient:

Confectioners' sugar and grated rind and juice of 1 lemon

to make the icing a good consistency to spread.

GERMAN HONEY CAKES WITH EGGS

Method I.

Cut into small pieces and combine:

3 oz. citron
3 oz. candied orange peel
3 oz. candied lemon peel

Add:

1 cup chopped blanched almonds
1 teaspoon grated lemon rind
3 tablespoons cinnamon
1 tablespoon cloves
3⅓ cups confectioners' sugar

Beat until light and add:

6 eggs
¼ cup orange juice

Bring to the boiling point, then cool until lukewarm:

1 pint honey
2 tablespoons hot water

Stir this into the egg mixture with:

5 cups sifted all-purpose flour
1 tablespoon soda

Permit the dough to stand for 12 hours or more. Drop it from a spoon, well apart, on a greased baking sheet. Bake the cakes in a moderate oven 350° until light brown. When cool decorate the cakes with:

Icing for Christmas Cakes, page 705

Or decorate them before baking with:

Blanched almonds

Method II.

These are more lightly spiced than Honey Cakes with Eggs I. They are very delicate.

Blanch and shred:
 1 lb. almonds
Chop:
 ¼ lb. citron
Sift:
 4 cups all-purpose flour
Resift with:
 1 teaspoon cinnamon
 1 teaspoon cloves
 ½ teaspoon nutmeg
 ¼ teaspoon allspice
Dissolve:
 1 teaspoon carbonate of powdered
  ammonia
in:
 ¼ cup brandy
Boil:
 1 quart honey
Cool it slightly. Stir in part of the flour. Beat in one at a time:
 4 eggs
Stir in the brandy, almonds, citron and the rest of the flour. Chill the dough for 12 hours. Drop it from a spoon, well apart, onto a greased baking sheet. Honey is a difficult ingredient. Sometimes it "acts up." It may become necessary to use more flour in the dough. Bake it in a moderate oven 350°. Ice it with:
 Icing for Christmas Cakes, page 705

CHRISTMAS CAKES WITH MOLASSES AND CHOCOLATE

The chocolate does not predominate in these cakes. Their marvelously blended flavor makes them Christmas cakes to remember.
Sift:
 1½ cups sugar
Beat until soft:
 ¼ cup butter
Add the sugar gradually. Blend these ingredients until they are creamy. Beat in one at a time:
 9 eggs
Beat in:
 2 tablespoons whisky
 1 cup molasses
 2½ teaspoons cinnamon
 ½ teaspoon cloves
 ½ teaspoon allspice
Grate and add:
 2 oz. sweet chocolate
 (1 cup chopped citron, orange or
  lemon rind)
Stir in:
 2 cups broken pecan meats
Sift before measuring:
 3 cups all-purpose flour

Resift with:
 3 teaspoons tartrate or phosphate
  baking powder or 2 teaspoons
  combination type (see Baking
  Powder, page 501)
Stir the flour into the other ingredients. Spread the dough in two 9 x 13 inch pans lined with waxed paper. Bake the cakes in a moderate oven 350°. Do not permit them to become very dry. When slightly cooled cut the cakes into shapes. Ice them with:
 **Glaze for Christmas Cakes,
  page 705**

CHRISTMAS CHOCOLATE BARS

These differ very much from the preceding cakes for they are richly flavored with chocolate. As it is difficult to choose between them, better bake them both and ice one with white and the other with chocolate icing. The question of preference is then up to the family.
Sift:
 2¾ cups brown sugar: 1 lb.
Beat until light:
 6 small eggs or 5 large ones
Add the sugar gradually and beat these ingredients until they are well blended. Grate and add:
 4 oz. chocolate
Combine and sift:
 3 cups all-purpose flour
 1 tablespoon cinnamon
 1½ teaspoons cloves
 ½ teaspoon allspice
 1 teaspoon soda
Add the sifted ingredients to the egg mixture alternately with:
 ½ cup honey or molasses
Chop and add:
 1 cup citron
 ¼ to 1 lb. broken nut meats, preferably blanched shredded almonds
Spread the dough with a spatula in two 9 x 13 inch pans lined with waxed paper. Bake it in a moderate oven 350°. When the cake is cold ice it with:
 **Chocolate Butter Icing, page
  703**
Cut it into bars.

CHRISTMAS MOLASSES WAFERS OR CAKES

This treasured rule comes from the Becker family archives. Adele gave it to me for my first cookbook but her children and mine think that this, their

favorite Christmas cake, should be presented to you with "a little more rhapsody," so I am giving it all I can. The yield from this recipe depends on your strength. It has been known to produce a chip basket full of crisp, amazing paper-thin delicacies.
Heat in a saucepan:

> 1/2 gallon New Orleans molasses

Add and melt:

> 1/2 cup butter
> 1/2 cup lard

Remove the pan from the fire. Stir in:

> 3/4 cup sugar
> 1 lb. unblanched almonds ground in a nut grinder
> 3/4 lb. finely chopped citron
> 1/4 lb. finely chopped orange rind
> 1/4 lb. finely chopped lemon rind
> 2 teaspoons any baking powder
> 1 teaspoon mace
> 2 teaspoons cloves
> 12 hulled ground cardamon seeds
> 2 teaspoons grated lemon rind

Sift and add sufficient:

> All-purpose flour

to make a rather stiff dough. You may begin to work in the flour with a spoon, but as soon as the dough begins to cool work it in with your hands. Add flour sparingly as the dough will be stiffer when cold. When it is cool work in:

> 2 teaspoons powdered carbonate of ammonia

dissolved in:

> 1 tablespoon hot water

Permit the dough to stand covered in a cold place for 2 or 3 weeks. Sift, then knead in:

> All-purpose flour

Knead and knead and knead until the dough can be rolled to paper thinness. Cut into diamond shapes with a pie cutter. Place the dough on greased tins. Brush it with:

> A beaten egg

Decorate the center of each diamond with:

> Blanched almonds

Bake the cakes in a fairly hot oven 400° until they begin to color.

TORTELETTES
About Forty 1½ Inch Cookies
A very old recipe. Anything as good as these should survive.
Grate:

> Rind of ½ lemon

onto:

> 1 cup sugar

Cream the sugar with:

> 3/4 cup butter

Beat in one at a time:

> 2 egg yolks

Add gradually to make a stiff dough:

> 1½ cups or more all-purpose flour

Pinch off about a teaspoonful of dough at a time. Roll it into a ball. Flatten the balls until the dough is very thin.
Beat slightly:

> 1 egg white
> 1 tablespoon water

Brush the cakes with this mixture.
Blanch, then shred coarsely:

> 1 cup almonds or other nut meats

Combine them with:

> ½ cup sugar
> 1 tablespoon cinnamon
> 1/4 teaspoon nutmeg
> 1/8 teaspoon salt

Sprinkle the cakes with this mixture. Bake them in a moderate oven 375° until light brown.

Meringue Jam Cookies, page 676; Macaroon Jam Tarts, page 676.

ALMOND RINGS
This recipe is like the saxophone which belongs neither with the wood winds nor with the brasses. It is a kind of meringue but it is always found among the Christmas Cakes. By the way, the various forms of Meringue Kisses, page 686, are very decorative in Christmas boxes.
Blanch:

> 1/4 lb. almonds

Cut them lengthwise into thin shreds. Toast them lightly. Whip until stiff:

> 2 egg whites

Add gradually, beating constantly:

> 1 cup confectioners' sugar

My old recipe says "stir" for ½ hour, but of course you won't do that, so whip until you are tired or use an electric beater. Fold in the almonds and:

> 1 teaspoon vanilla

Shape the batter into rings on a greased tin. Bake them in a slow oven 300° until they are light brown.

WHITE MACAROONS
About Forty 1 x 1½ Inch Rich Macaroons
Very pretty. Seasonable when decorated with a redhot or a bit of candied cherry.
Sift:

> 1 cup sugar

Whip until stiff:

3 egg whites

Add the sugar very slowly. Whip constantly. Combine and fold in:

½ teaspoon cornstarch
½ teaspoon any baking powder
½ lb. almonds blanched and ground in a nut grinder

Drop the batter from a teaspoon, well apart, onto a greased tin. Decorate the centers of the cookies with:

Redhots (cinnamon drops) or bits of candied cherry

Bake them in a slow oven 275° until they are done. Remove them from the oven before they begin to color.

___

The 2 following rules are for German Nut Cakes—both delicious. The nuts are put through a nut, not a meat, grinder.

___

CINNAMON STARS
About Forty-Five 1½ Inch Stars

Deservedly one of the most popular Christmas cakes.

Sift:

2 cups confectioners' sugar

Whip until stiff:

6 egg whites
⅛ teaspoon salt

Add the sugar gradually. Whip these ingredients well. The old recipes say for ¾ of an hour. Add:

1 teaspoon cinnamon
1 teaspoon lemon rind

Whip constantly. Reserve ⅓ of the mixture. Fold into the remainder:

1 lb. ground unblanched almonds

Spread a board or pastry canvas lightly with confectioners' sugar. Pat or roll the dough to the thickness of ⅓ inch. Cut the cakes with a star or other cutter. Glaze the tops with the reserved mixture. Bake the cakes on a greased tin in a slow oven 325°. This recipe requires no flour.

___

HAZELNUT CAKES
About Sixty 1½ Inch Cookies

This flavor is unusual and perfectly delicious.

Grind in a nut grinder:

1 lb. hazelnut meats: 2 lbs. in the shell

Sift:

2¾ cups brown sugar

Whip until stiff:

6 egg whites
⅛ teaspoon salt

Add the sugar gradually. Whip constantly. Add:

1 teaspoon vanilla

Fold in the ground nuts. Shape the batter lightly into 1 inch balls. Roll them in:

Granulated sugar

Bake them on a greased tin in a moderate oven 325°.

___

CHOCOLATE ALMOND SHELLS

This batter is pressed into a little wooden mold in the shape of a shell. Any attractive mold will do.

Grind in a nut grinder:

1 lb. unblanched almonds

Sift:

2 cups sugar

Whip until stiff:

8 egg whites
¼ teaspoon salt

Add the sugar gradually. Whip constantly. Fold in the ground almonds and:

3 teaspoons cinnamon
¼ teaspoon cloves
1 teaspoon grated lemon rind
3 tablespoons lemon juice
5 oz. grated chocolate

Permit this batter to stand in a cold place for 12 hours. Shape it into balls. Prepare molds by dredging them with a mixture of:

Sugar and flour

Press the balls into the molds. Unmold them. Bake them on a greased tin in a moderate oven 350°.

___

NUT AND DATE COOKIES

Not a German classic but very much like Baseler Leckerle in flavor. Grind in a nut grinder:

1 cup nut meats
1 cup seeded dates

Sift:

1 cup sugar

Whip until stiff:

2 egg whites
⅛ teaspoon salt

Add the sugar gradually. Whip constantly. Fold in:

1 tablespoon cream

Sift before measuring:

1 cup all-purpose flour

Resift with:

1 teaspoon any baking powder

Fold in the sifted ingredients, the nuts and dates. It may be necessary to combine these ingredients with the hands. Grease and flour a baking tin. Place the batter on it and pat it down to the thickness of ¼ inch. If the batter is sticky, dip the palm of the hand in confectioners' sugar. Bake the cake in a moderate oven 350°. Spread the cake while it is hot with:

Confectioners' sugar moistened with lemon juice

Cut it while it is hot into bars or squares.

HARD-COOKED EGG COOKIES

I add this recipe to my book in self-defense. I am tired of hearing from friends who felt injured when they failed to find it in an earlier edition. These cookies seem to have a nostalgic hold that does not lessen with the years. Therefore, to keep my hold on my friends I am complying with their request to have this rule included.

Grate:

Rind of 1 lemon

onto:

10 tablespoons sugar

Beat until soft:

1 cup butter

Add the sugar gradually. Cream these ingredients until they are fluffy. Beat in:

1 egg

Put through a ricer, then add:

4 hard-cooked eggs

Stir in:

3 cups all-purpose flour

Roll the dough into 1 inch balls. Flatten them into cakes. Dip them in:

1 slightly beaten egg white

then in a mixture of:

Sugar, cinnamon and chopped nut meats

Bake them in a slow oven 325°.

CHRISTMAS PRETZELS

This and the 3 following rules are for rich, crumbly white cakes with blanched chopped almonds. They are variously shaped and flavored.

Sift:

1 cup sugar

Beat until soft:

1 cup butter

Add the sugar gradually. Blend these ingredients until they are very light and creamy. Beat in:

2 egg yolks
2 eggs
¼ cup sour cream

Sift and stir in:

2½ cups all-purpose flour

You may add:

1 teaspoon any baking powder
1 teaspoon cinnamon
1 teaspoon grated lemon rind

Chill the dough for several hours until it is easy to handle. Shape it into long thin rolls and twist these into pretzel shape. Place the pretzels in a greased tin. Brush them with:

Yolk of an egg

Sprinkle the tops with:

Blanched chopped almonds
Sugar

Bake them at once in a moderate oven 375°.

WHITE ALMOND WAFERS OR MANDELPLAETTCHEN

Sift:

1 cup sugar

Beat until soft:

1 cup butter

Add the sugar gradually. Blend these ingredients until they are very light and creamy. Beat in one at a time:

2 eggs
1 egg yolk

And:

1 teaspoon grated lemon rind
⅛ teaspoon salt
½ lb. blanched finely chopped almonds
½ teaspoon rose water

Sift and add:

All-purpose flour—about 3 cups

to make the dough the right consistency to roll. Chill the dough. Roll it to the thickness of ⅛ inch. Cut it into shapes. Combine and beat:

1 egg yolk
2 tablespoons milk

Brush the top of the cakes with this mixture. Bake them on a greased tin in a moderate oven 375°.

ALMOND CRESCENTS

Sift:

½ cup confectioners' sugar

Beat until soft:

1 cup butter

Add the sugar gradually. Blend these ingredients until they are very light and creamy. Beat in:

1 egg yolk

Sift and stir in:

2½ cups all-purpose flour

Add:

¼ lb. blanched chopped almonds

Chill the dough, roll it to the thickness of ¼ inch. Cut it into crescent shape. Bake the cakes on a greased tin in a moderate oven 375°. Dip them when baked in:

Vanilla Sugar, page 709

ALMOND FINGERS
About 66 Bars
Grind:

¼ lb. citron

Blanch, then chop:

¼ lb. almonds

Measure:

2 cups sugar

Grate into it:

Rind of 1 lemon

Stir into it:

1 tablespoon ground cloves
1 tablespoon ground ginger
1 teaspoon any baking powder

Beat until light:

4 eggs

Stir in the sugar mixture gradually. Add enough all-purpose flour to make a stiff dough. Roll the dough into strips. Cut them into 2 inch lengths. Bake them on a greased or waxed paper covered sheet in a moderate oven 375° for about 12 minutes. Ice the bars with:

Icing for Christmas Cakes, page 705

Place on each bar:

A cinnamon drop (redhot)

SPECULATIUS
About Thirty-Four 2½ Inch Cookies
Miscalled "Speculazzis" and eagerly devoured by us and our fellow small fry. A traditional Christmas cookie of Danish origin—probably the original refrigerator cookie. It is eggless and very rich.

Cream until well blended:

½ cup butter
½ cup brown sugar

Sift:

1¼ cups sifted all-purpose flour
⅛ teaspoon soda
⅛ teaspoon salt
1 teaspoon cinnamon
¼ teaspoon cloves
¼ teaspoon freshly grated nutmeg

Beat these ingredients into the butter mixture alternately with:

2 tablespoons sour cream

Beat in:

½ cup broken nut meats

Shape the dough into a roll with floured hands. As it is very soft you may have to chill it first. Then chill it for 12 hours or more. Cut it into very thin slices. Bake them on a greased

and floured tin in a 375° oven for about 12 minutes, or until done.

YOLK COOKIES I
This and the 3 following recipes are good rules for utilizing the many yolks left over from baking Christmas nut cakes. In Germany the dough of No. 1 is invariably used to form the letter S. I have used it successfully for engagement parties—shaping the initials of the betrothed. The letters are very dainty. This amount makes about 250 letters. Don't worry, they will all be eaten.

Sift:

1 cup sugar

Beat until soft:

1 cup butter
½ teaspoon salt if unsalted butter is used

Add the sugar gradually. Blend these ingredients until they are very light and creamy. Add:

½ teaspoon grated lemon rind
1½ tablespoons lemon juice

Beat in:

8 egg yolks

Stir in:

4 cups all-purpose flour

Chill the dough for 1 hour, then roll it into sticks ¼ inch in diameter. Shape these into letters. Brush them with:

Yolk of an egg

Sprinkle them with:

Colored or white sugar

Bake them on a greased tin in a moderate oven 375°.

Faith Bryan, an expert cookie baker, has found this dough to be very satisfactory as a cookie base. She rolls it to paper thinness, cuts it into small varied shapes, which she tops with a dab of nut meringue and a bit of candied cherry or citron before baking. She uses a slow oven 275° for most decorated cookies. This is her:

Meringue Topping
Beat until stiff:

2 egg whites
⅛ teaspoon salt

Beat in gradually:

1 cup powdered sugar
2 teaspoons cornstarch
2 cups chopped nut meats

YOLK COOKIES II OR GELBE PLAETTCHEN
About Two Hundred 1½ Inch Cookies
They are very light, not at all rich

Sift:
2 cups confectioners' sugar
Beat until light:
1 egg
8 egg yolks
Add the sugar gradually. Beat these
ingredients until light. Add:
1 teaspoon grated lemon rind
3 tablespoons lemon juice
Sift and stir in:
1¼ cups all-purpose flour
Add:
(2 tablespoons crushed anise
seed)
Beat the dough well. Drop it from a
teaspoon, well apart, on a greased tin.
Permit the cookies to dry for 12 hours
at room temperature. Bake them in a
slow oven 325°.

_____

Butter Wafers, page 675.

_____

ANISE CAKES
About Fifty 1½ Inch Cakes
Sift:
1 cup sugar
Beat until light:
3 eggs
Add the sugar gradually. Beat until
light, then add:
½ teaspoon vanilla
Sift before measuring:
1½ to 2 cups all-purpose flour
Resift with:
1 teaspoon any baking powder
Add:
1½ tablespoons crushed anise seed

Beat the batter well. Drop it from a
teaspoon, well apart, on greased tins.
Permit it to dry at room temperature
for 12 hours. Bake the cakes in a moderate oven 350° until they begin to
color.

_____

SPRINGERLE
This recipe is for the well-known German Anise Cakes which are stamped
with a wooden mold into quaint little
designs and figures. This calls for the
same ingredients as the preceding
Anise Cakes recipe, but it is much
heavier in flour. If these cakes become
too hard, keep an apple in the cookie
jar. Replace it frequently.
Sift:
2 cups sugar
Beat until light:
4 eggs
Add the sugar gradually. Beat the ingredients until they are creamy. Sift
before measuring about:
4 cups all-purpose flour
Add the flour until dough is stiff. Roll
it to the thickness of ¼ inch. Flour a
springerle board. Press it hard upon
the dough to get a good imprint. Separate the squares, place them on a
board and permit them to dry for 12
hours. Butter tins and sprinkle them
with:
1 tablespoon crushed anise seed
Place the cakes on them. Bake them
in a slow oven 300° until the lower
part is light yellow.

Icings and Cake Fillings

Boiled Icings

Rule for White Icing

Boil the amount of water and sugar given in the recipes until the sirup forms a
soft ball when dropped into cold water, or when it forms a thread about 3 inches
long when dropped from a spoon. This thread should be thin enough to curl or
wave. In either case the sirup will have reached about 238°.

Have the egg whites at room temperature.

Add the salt to the egg whites. Egg whites may be whipped until they are stiff,
whipped until they are frothy, or they need not be whipped at all before the sirup
is added.

The sirup is poured upon them while it is very hot in a very fine stream, the eggs
being beaten constantly during the addition of the sirup and afterward until the
icing becomes creamy and of the right consistency to spread. If you have any difficulty in keeping the bowl steady, place it on a folded wet dish cloth.

When the last of the sirup has been added, ⅛ teaspoonful of cream of tartar to 2
egg whites or a few drops of lemon juice or a few teaspoonfuls of corn sirup may be
added to keep the icing from becoming gritty.

Beat in the flavoring as the icing cools.

When the sirup has been cooked to the right stage, the icing will spread readily and will stay where it is put. If it has not been boiled long enough and the icing does not thicken, beat it in strong sunlight or near an open oven door, or place the bowl containing the icing over, not in, boiling water and beat the icing until it becomes the right consistency to spread. You may do this in a double boiler.

If the sirup has been cooked too long and the icing threatens to harden too soon, beat in a few drops of lemon juice or a teaspoonful or more of boiling water.

Have a bowl of very hot water in readiness before making a white icing. You are then prepared for any emergency.

Never place a thin or doubtful icing on a cake. Do everything you can to thicken it before taking this step.

When the icing begins to thicken around the sides of the bowl, it is usually ready to be spread, but if you are in doubt about it, spread a small quantity only and see how it behaves. A little patience at this stage of the icing will save endless trouble and will insure a good-looking cake. You may spread the sides of the cake first with a spatula or knife or you may pile the icing on top of the cake and spread it quickly, working it toward the edges and sides of the cake. Reverse cakes that have uneven tops and ice the bottom. Dip the spatula in hot water as the icing thickens. Beat in a very little hot water, if necessary, to soften the last icing in the bowl.

If raisins, nut meats, or other ingredients are to be added to the icing, wait until the last moment to do so. Acid or oil is apt to thin the icing beyond repair if the fruit is added too soon.

When icing large or small cakes decorate them with nut meats, with candied cherries, angelica, etc.

WHITE ICING I
Sufficient to Cover the Top and Sides of Two 9 Inch Layers
The following icing has the consistency of a marshmallow icing. As this and the Seven Minute White Icing answer all purposes, they are the only white icings I use. They may be used interchangeably. Stir until the sugar is dissolved, then boil to the thread stage without stirring (see preceding page):

> 2 cups sugar
> 1 cup water

Whip until frothy:

> 2 egg whites
> ⅛ teaspoon salt

Add the sirup in a thin stream. Whip constantly. When it is all whipped in add:

> (⅛ teaspoon cream of tartar or a
> few drops lemon juice)

Add:

> 1 teaspoon vanilla

Follow the Rule for White Icing on page 693.

White Icing II, page 702.

RAISIN SMASH ICING
Chop:

> 1 cup seeded raisins

Add them to:

White Icing or Seven Minute Icing, page 700
immediately before spreading it, or sprinkle the raisins over the cake and spread the icing over them.

ORIENTAL ICING
Prepare the preceding:

> **Raisin Smash Icing**

Use only ½ cupful chopped seeded raisins and add:

> ½ cup chopped nut meats

COCONUT ICING
If possible, use fresh grated coconut. To prepare it, heat an oven to 350°. Punch holes in 2 of the 3 eyes at the end of the coconut. Drain off the milk to use later in cooking or to cover the coconut if you intend to deep-freeze it (see page 863). Heat the coconut for about 15 minutes, during which time the shell may crack. Continue to remove the shell by knocking it with a mallet or hammer if necessary. Pare the inner brown skin off with a knife. Sliver or grate the white portion for use.

Canned or boxed coconut may be substituted. A little lemon or orange rind may be added to any grated coconut for flavor. Sprinkle the grated coconut over the freshly spread:

White Icing I, page 694, or Seven Minute White Icing, page 700

NUT ICING

Just before spreading:

White Icing I, page 694, or Seven Minute White Icing, page 700

add:

1/4 to 1/2 cup chopped nut meats

or sprinkle the nut meats over the freshly spread icing before it hardens.

CHOCOLATE COATING OVER WHITE ICING

A very good touch to something that is good in itself.

Melt:

2 oz. chocolate

Cool it and spread it with a broad knife or spatula over:

White Icing I, page 694, or Seven Minute White Icing, page 700

This may be done as soon as the white icing is set. Allow several hours for the coating to harden. In summer or moist weather add to the chocolate before spreading it:

1/4 teaspoon melted paraffin

This coating **will** run. Transfer the cake to a fresh plate before serving it. Do not attempt to make this coating in excessively hot weather unless the cake can be put in a refrigerator until the chocolate hardens.

CHOCOLATE PEPPERMINT ICING

Prepare:

White Icing I, page 694, or Seven Minute White Icing, page 700

Before spreading it add:

A few drops peppermint extract

Cover it as directed in the preceding rule with:

Chocolate Coating

WHITE MOUNTAIN ICING

Made with an Electric Mixer

Sufficient to Ice a 9 Inch Cake

Stir until the sugar is dissolved, then cook covered until the sirup boils rapidly:

1 tablespoon white corn sirup
1 cup sugar
1/3 cup water

Beat for about 2 minutes in a small bowl at high speed:

1 egg white

Add 3 tablespoonfuls of the boiling sirup. Continue to beat until the sirup reaches the thread stage 238°. Pour the remaining sirup gradually into the egg mixture while continuing to beat at high speed. Add while beating:

1 teaspoon vanilla

Beat the icing until it is ready to spread, from 4 to 6 minutes.

DECORATIVE ICING OR TWICE COOKED ICING

Sufficient to Cover and Decorate a Round 9 Inch Cake About 4 Inches High

This is a fine recipe for decorative icing. It will keep without hardening for a long time if closely covered with waxed paper.

Stir until the sugar is dissolved, then boil without stirring:

1 cup sugar
1/2 cup water

Meanwhile whip until stiff:

2 egg whites
1/8 teaspoon salt

Sift and add very slowly, whipping constantly:

3 tablespoons sugar

When the sirup begins to fall in heavy drops from a spoon add a small quantity of it to the eggs and sugar and continue beating. Repeat this process, adding the sirup to the eggs in 4 or 5 parts. If these additions are properly timed, the last of the sirup will have reached the thread stage. Beat the icing constantly. Have a pan ready partly filled with water. Place it over heat. The bowl in which the icing is being made should fit closely into this pan so that the bowl will be over, but not in, the water. When the water in the pan begins to boil add to the icing:

1/4 teaspoon icing powder—equal parts of baking powder and tartaric acid

Continue to beat the icing until it sticks to the sides and the bottom of the bowl and holds a point. Remove the icing from the heat. Place as much as is required for the decoration, usually about 1/3, in a small bowl. Cover it closely with waxed paper. To the remainder add:

1 teaspoon or more hot water

to thin it to the right consistency to spread. Beat it well and spread it on the cake. Decorate the cake with the

reserved icing. Color it daintily with:
Color paste or liquid
Have on hand bakers' paper or heavy bond paper cut into sheets of about 9 x 11 inches. The advantage of paper over a pastry bag with metal tube points is that it gives a softer, more pleasing effect to the icing. Roll the sheets into cornucopias. As the icing softens the paper within 20 minutes or so have plenty of empty bags ready and make them in two sizes, cutting the sheets in two for the smaller bags. Use the larger bags for the principal work, for instance: the garlands and roses. Use the smaller bags for leaves, stems and dots, etc.

To roll a bag, take the paper in hand as shown in the illustration. Roll the paper into a cornucopia and play it to and fro with the right hand at what is going to be the point of the bag, and

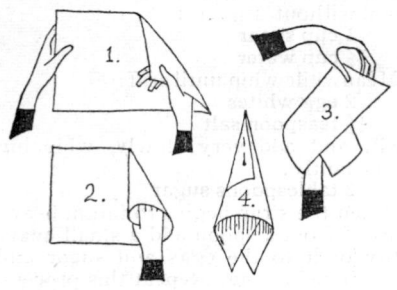

the middle of the bag, so that the rolled part will be tight toward the bottom and able to hold the icing when pressure is put upon it later. A bag rolled too loosely at the point and too large through the middle will make a bad job. Pull the paper tightly over the well-rolled end with the right hand before you secure it. Secure the bag about 1½ inches above the point with a pin or a strip of Scotch tape. You must put the pin in right the first time. Having punctured the bag you cannot withdraw the pin and put it in again. You may cut the point of the bag into shape before filling it. I find this easier to do than when the bag is filled, but in either case flatten the tip slightly before cutting it.

The cut of the point will produce different shapes. The shapes will differ not only due to the cut but also due to the way the bags are manipulated both as to pressure and position in relation to the decorated surface while the icing is being released. This is not all so complex as it sounds, so some leisurely day try your hand on a few cake or bread slices. It is amazing how individual a style you can develop within the limits of the medium.

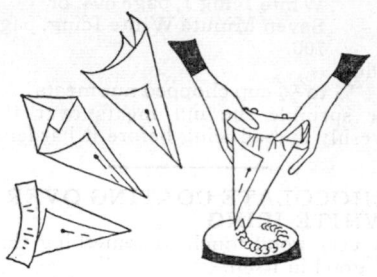

Fill the cornucopias not more than half full of variously colored icings. Then press the open edges of the bag together. Fold the points over far enough to seal the tops well to make a platform against which both your thumbs can apply pressure on the icing mass within the bag, while both forefingers lie along the slope of the bag to steady it, as shown above.

If a bag becomes soft or is unsatisfactory, cut a generous piece off the point and press the icing directly into a new bag. If you have not cut the point of the new bag, be sure to do so before transferring the icing.

Shape 1 has a simple horizontal cut which produces straight or curved lines, letters, numerals or dots. With this cut there is little difference in result whether the icing is applied from an upright bag or one held almost parallel to the decorated surface. Both hands are used in applying pressure on the icing supply as shown above. All the designs in the drawing below are

made with shape 1 except the long leaf which is made with shape 2 and applied with a one-handed longer slower pressure on the bag during a slightly turning motion. When beginning to release the icing hold bag shape 2 so that the cut at base is in the position shown in the detail below.

Bag shape 2 is the most versatile of all. Not only will it produce long leaves, or short ones when handled as described above but it will make ruchings or petals or buds, depending on the angle and the pressure applied. Held flat and inched along it makes the continuous ruching so typical of bakers' cakes. Applied in curves it makes ruching garlands. Held flat and released at each small squeeze it makes typical wild rose petals or the base for a fullblown rose. Held upright it produces the center enveloping petals of the rose. Or held flat and released quickly it makes a fat bud. So by combining shapes 1 and 2 with these motifs, a result like that shown at the base of the drawing below is achieved.

Shape 3 is the most flamboyant. It is useful for chrysanthemum and daisy-type flowers, although the botanist might not recognize the structures below as such.

It is a great temptation when preparing fancy icings to overload cakes with both decoration and color. Try to work for simple, asymmetrical floral compositions. For luxurious effects bind the top and sides of the cake with garlands, heavy in relief but light in values—and remember to leave plenty of undecorated space to set them off.

FLOWER CANDLES

Here is a charming quick-trick cake decoration. Just before serving an iced cake, select some delicately colored, open-petaled flowers, like hollyhocks. Remove the stamen. Cut off all but ¾ inch of the stem. Arrange the flowers on the cake. Place a small candle in the center of each one.

SOUR CREAM ICING
Sufficient for the Tops of Two 9 Inch Layers

Stir until the sugar is dissolved, then boil to 238°, the soft ball stage (see page 693):

> 1 cup sour cream
> 1 cup sugar

Cool the sirup until it is lukewarm. Beat it until it is creamy. Add:

> 1 teaspoon vanilla
> ½ cup chopped nut meats

LUSCIOUS ORANGE ICING
Sufficient for the Tops of Two 8 Inch Layers

This icing becomes firm on the outside and remains soft on the inside. Cook to the soft ball stage:

> 1 cup granulated sugar
> 1 tablespoon white corn sirup
> ⅛ teaspoon cream of tartar
> ½ cup water

Pour the sirup in a slow stream over:

> 2 beaten egg whites

Beat for 10 minutes. Beat in:

> ¼ cup powdered sugar
> 1 teaspoon grated orange rind
> 1 tablespoon orange juice or ¾ teaspoon vanilla

Beat the icing until it is the right consistency to spread.

SEA-FOAM ICING I WITH 1 EGG WHITE
Sufficient for the Tops of Two 9 Inch Layers

Stir until the sugar is dissolved, then boil without stirring to 238°, the soft ball stage (see page 693):

2 cups brown sugar
⅔ cup water
Whip until frothy:
  1 egg white
  ⅛ teaspoon salt
Pour the sirup over the egg white in a thin stream. Whip constantly. Place the bowl containing the icing over, not in, boiling water. Beat the icing until it will hold a point. Add:
  ½ teaspoon vanilla
Spread the icing. Sprinkle it with:
  (¼ cup chopped nut meats)

SEA-FOAM ICING II WITH 2 EGG WHITES
Sufficient for the Tops and Sides of Two 9 Inch Layers
Stir until the sugar is dissolved, then boil without stirring to 238°, the soft ball stage (see page 693):
  2½ cups brown sugar
  ½ cup water
Whip until frothy:
  2 egg whites
  ⅛ teaspoon salt
Pour the sirup over the egg whites in a thin stream. Whip constantly. Add:
  1 teaspoon vanilla
Place the bowl containing the icing over, not in, boiling water. Whip the icing until it will hold a point. Spread it. Sprinkle it with:
  (⅓ cup chopped nut meats)

MOCHA SEA-FOAM ICING
Follow the preceding rule for Sea-Foam Icing II. Substitute for the water:
  ½ cup strong coffee

CARAMEL ICING
Sufficient for the Top and Sides of Two 9 Inch Layers
Stir until the sugar is dissolved, then boil without stirring to 238°, the soft ball stage (see page 693):
  2 cups brown sugar
  1 cup milk or cream
Add:
  3 tablespoons butter
Remove the icing from the fire and cool it. Add:
  1 teaspoon vanilla
Beat the icing until it is thick and creamy. If it becomes too heavy, thin it with a little:
  Cream
until it is the right consistency to spread.

CARAMEL FILLING OR ICING
Sufficient for the Tops and Sides of Two 9 Inch Layers
Stir over low heat until dissolved:
  2 cups brown sugar
  ½ cup butter
  ½ cup cream
Boil these ingredients to 238°, the soft ball stage (see page 693). Beat them until they are cool. Add:
  1 teaspoon vanilla
Spread the icing.

QUICK SUGAR ICINGS
Method I.
Sufficient for the Tops of Two 8 Inch Layers
A quick, acceptable, rather coarse icing.
Combine, stir and cook slowly to the boiling point:
  1½ cups brown sugar
  5 tablespoons cream
  2 teaspoons butter
  ⅛ teaspoon salt
Remove from fire. Cool slightly, add:
  ½ teaspoon vanilla
Beat the icing until it is a good consistency to spread. You may add:
  ½ cup chopped nut meats
Method II.
Melt and stir in a skillet until a golden brown:
  6 tablespoons butter
Blend in gradually:
  1½ cups confectioners' sugar
Add 1 tablespoonful at a time until the icing is a good consistency to spread:
  Hot water
Add:
  1 teaspoon vanilla

CLEAR CARAMEL COATING
Sufficient for the Top of an 8 x 8 Inch Cake
This brittle topping is used on many European cakes.
Place in a large heavy skillet over a moderate flame:
  1 cup sugar
Cook and stir it until it melts. When clear and brown spread it at once with a hot spatula.

MAPLE SUGAR ICING
Combine and cook, stirring frequently:
  2 cups maple sugar
  1 cup cream
When a small quantity dropped into cold water forms a soft ball, 234°, re-

move the icing from the fire. Cool it slightly. Beat it well until it is creamy. Fold in:

½ cup chopped nut meats, preferably butternut meats

Not a traditional Yankee touch, but chopped toasted almonds are wonderful with maple sirup mixtures.

MAPLE SIRUP ICING
Sufficient for the Sides and Tops of Two 8 Inch Layers
Cook almost to the firm ball stage, 242°:

1 cup maple sirup

Beat this in a fine stream into:

2 unbeaten egg whites

Use an electric mixer or beat the mixture until it stiffens somewhat, although this icing remains soft. Spread the icing. Scatter over it:

¼ cup chopped nut meats

BROWN SUGAR MARSH-MALLOW ICING
Sufficient for the Tops of Two 8 Inch Layers
Cut into small cubes:

12 marshmallows

Boil over a slow fire without stirring:

2 cups brown sugar
½ cup milk

Cover the pan with a lid for the first 3 minutes. When the sirup has reached 238°, the soft ball stage, remove it from the fire. Add the marshmallows and:

4 tablespoons butter

When these ingredients are melted and the icing is cool beat it until it is a good consistency to spread. If too heavy, it may be thinned with a little:

Cream

Add it a few drops at a time. You may add:

(½ cup chopped nut meats)

CHOCOLATE ICING BOILED
Method I.
Sufficient for the Tops and Sides of Two 9 Inch Layers
This icing is like soft fudge. Stir until the sugar is dissolved, then cook slowly without stirring to 238°, the soft ball stage (page 693):

2 cups sugar
2 oz. chocolate
2 tablespoons white corn sirup
¾ cup milk

Add:

2 tablespoons butter

Remove the sirup from the fire. Place the saucepan in cold water. When the icing is lukewarm, add:

1 teaspoon vanilla

Beat it until it is the right consistency to spread. If the icing hardens too quickly, add a few drops of hot water or place the saucepan containing the icing in hot water. This icing may be beaten with an electric mixer. Use high speed.

Method II. Sufficient for the Top and Sides of an 8 x 8 Inch Cake
This icing is similar to the preceding one, but it is richer and not so sweet. Stir until the sugar is dissolved, then cook slowly without stirring to 238°, the soft ball stage (page 693):

2 oz. chocolate
1 cup sugar
½ cup cream

Add:

2 tablespoons butter

Cool the icing. Add:

½ teaspoon vanilla

Beat it until it thickens, then spread it.

Method III.
Melt over hot water:

Sweet chocolate bars or chocolate peppermints

Cool, then spread the icing.

RICH CHOCOLATE ICING
Follow the above rule for:

Chocolate Icing I

Substitute brown sugar for white, cream for milk, and increase the chocolate measurement to 8 ounces. Oh, yes! You may double the vanilla. Is all this worth while? If you are a poor calorie counter, try it and see.

GLOSSY CHOCOLATE ICING WITH EVAPORATED MILK
Sufficient for the Tops of Two 8 Inch Layers
This icing has an outstanding quality—it may be made long before it is spread. Melt in the top of a double boiler:

3 oz. chocolate

Combine and stir into the chocolate:

1 well-beaten egg
¾ cup evaporated milk
¼ cup water
1 cup sugar

Cook the icing over hot water for 20 minutes. Remove it from the steam. Beat it with a rotary beater for 1 minute or until well blended. Stir in:

1 teaspoon vanilla

Cool the icing before spreading it. If this icing is tightly covered and placed in the refrigerator, it will keep several days.

CHOCOLATE MARSHMALLOW ICING
Sufficient for the Tops and Sides of Two 9 Inch Layers
Stir until the sugar is dissolved, then boil to 238°, the soft ball stage (page 693):

  1½ cups sugar
  1½ cups water

Add:

  2 oz. grated chocolate
  1 dozen marshmallows cut into eighths and steamed until soft

Permit these ingredients to stand for several minutes. Add:

  ⅛ teaspoon cream of tartar

Whip until stiff:

  2 egg whites
  ⅛ teaspoon salt

Pour the sirup over the egg whites in a thin stream. Whip constantly until the icing is the right consistency to spread.

QUICK CHOCOLATE ICING
Sufficient for the Tops and Sides of Two 8 Inch Layers
Melt:

  1 to 2 oz. chocolate

Add:

  ½ cup sugar

Stir in slowly:

  ½ cup boiling water

Boil these ingredients. Dissolve:

  1½ tablespoons cornstarch
  ⅛ teaspoon salt

in:

  3 tablespoons water

Stir these ingredients into the chocolate mixture. Boil the icing until it thickens to a good consistency to spread. Add:

  1½ tablespoons butter
  1 teaspoon vanilla

Spread the icing at once. Place the cake in the refrigerator if you wish the icing to chill quickly. This is a rather soft icing.

Creamy Chocolate Icing or Filling, page 706; Seven Minute Icing, made with an electric mixer, page 701.

SEVEN MINUTE WHITE ICING
Sufficient for the Tops and Sides of Two 9 Inch Layers
A very fluffy, delightful icing that never fails. Please read the comment under White Icing, page 694.

One half this amount will make a light icing for a 9 inch loaf cake. Use the full amount for a heavy icing.

Place in the top of a double boiler and beat until thoroughly blended:

  2 unbeaten egg whites
  1½ cups sugar
  5 tablespoons cold water
  ¼ teaspoon cream of tartar
  (1½ teaspoons light corn sirup)

Place these ingredients over rapidly boiling water. Beat them constantly with a rotary beater or with a wire whisk for 7 minutes. Remove the icing from the fire. Add:

  1 teaspoon vanilla

Continue beating until the icing is the right consistency to spread.

SEVEN MINUTE NUT OR COCONUT ICING
Spread the preceding:

  Seven Minute White Icing

Sprinkle it with:

  ½ cup chopped nut meats or grated coconut

SEVEN MINUTE LEMON ICING
Prepare:

  Seven Minute White Icing, above

Use only:

  3 tablespoons water

Add:

  2 tablespoons lemon juice
  ¼ teaspoon grated lemon rind

SEVEN MINUTE SEA-FOAM ICING
Method I.
Sufficient for the Tops and Sides of Two 9 Inch Layers
Place in the top of a double boiler and beat until thoroughly blended:

  2 unbeaten egg whites
  1½ cups firmly packed brown sugar
  ⅛ teaspoon salt
  5 tablespoons water

Place these ingredients over rapidly boiling water. Beat them constantly for 5 minutes with a rotary beater or a wire whisk. Remove them from the fire but allow them to remain over hot water. Beat them for 2 minutes longer.

Place the icing in cold water. Beat it for 3 minutes. Add:

1 teaspoon vanilla

Spread the icing and sprinkle it with:

¾ cup chopped nut meats

Method II.

Or, cook Seven Minute White Icing for 8 minutes. Fold in:

4 teaspoons burnt sugar (Caramel Sirup, page 754)

Don't forget the vanilla.

SEVEN MINUTE ORANGE ICING

Sufficient for the Tops and Sides of Two 9 Inch Layers

Place in the top of a double boiler and beat until thoroughly blended:

1½ cups sugar
2 egg whites
1 tablespoon lemon juice
½ teaspoon orange rind
¼ cup orange juice

Follow the rule for Seven Minute White Icing, page 700.

SEVEN MINUTE PEPPERMINT ICING

Prepare:

Seven Minute White Icing, page 700

Just before spreading it add:

1 stick crushed peppermint candy

SEVEN MINUTE ICING

Made with an Electric Mixer

Sufficient for the Tops of Two 9 Inch Layers

Stir, then boil in a covered pan until the sugar is dissolved:

3 tablespoons hot water
1 cup confectioners' sugar

Place in a small mixing bowl:

1 unbeaten egg white
¼ teaspoon cream of tartar
⅛ teaspoon salt

Add the hot sirup. Beat these ingredients at high speed until the icing is the right consistency to spread, from 3 to 4 minutes. Add while beating:

1 teaspoon vanilla

Three Minute Icing, page 632.

DIPPING ICINGS
Method I.

Dip tops and sides of small cakes in icing, see page 660, then right them on a cake rack to drip. Catch the drippings on a pan and use them to ice other cakes.

Stir over heat, then boil for 1 minute:

1 cup sugar
½ cup butter
½ cup milk

Cool slightly. Add:

1¼ cups confectioners' sugar
½ teaspoon salt
½ teaspoon vanilla
A few drops of coloring
(¼ teaspoon almond flavor)

Method II.

Place over hot water and stir until smooth:

3 oz. cut-up chocolate
3 tablespoons butter

Pour:

5 tablespoons scalding hot milk

over:

2 cups confectioners' sugar
¼ teaspoon salt

When dissolved add the chocolate mixture and:

1 teaspoon vanilla

Beat until the right consistency to dip or spread.

CORN SIRUP OR HONEY ICING
Method I.

Sufficient for the Tops of Two 9 Inch Layers

Combine and cook to the thread stage (page 693):

1½ cups light honey or corn sirup

Whip until stiff:

2 egg whites
⅛ teaspoon salt

Pour the sirup onto the egg whites in a thin stream. Whip constantly. Flavor the icing with:

½ teaspoon vanilla
⅛ teaspoon almond extract

Follow the rule on page 694 for:

White Icing

A quick icing, good but with staying qualities of about 12 hours only, may be made in the following way:

Method II.

Combine, then beat with a rotary or an electric beater until it is a good consistency to spread:

½ cup honey or corn sirup
⅛ teaspoon salt
2 egg whites
½ teaspoon vanilla
⅛ teaspoon almond extract

BAKED ICING
Sufficient for a Cake 8 Inches Square
Double this amount for a 9 x 13 inch cake.
This icing is baked at the same time as the cake. Use it on a thin cake only, one that will require 25 minutes' baking or less.
Sift:

> ½ cup brown sugar

Whip until stiff:

> 1 egg white
> ⅛ teaspoon salt

Fold in the sugar or beat it in slowly. Spread the icing on the cake. Sprinkle it with:

> ¼ cup broken nut meats

Bake the cake in a moderate oven 375° until it is done.

To vary the flavor fold in 2 tablespoonfuls of cocoa after adding the sugar.

BROILED ICING
Sufficient for a Cake 8 Inches Square
Combine and spread upon a cake while it is warm:

> 3 tablespoons melted butter
> 10 tablespoons brown sugar
> 2 tablespoons cream
> ⅛ teaspoon salt
> ½ cup shredded coconut or other nut meats

Place the cake very low under a broiler with the flame turned low. Broil the icing until it bubbles all over the surface but do not permit it to burn.

Uncooked Icings

Rule for Uncooked Icings

Uncooked icings are very good and very quickly made. Their one drawback is that they sometimes have a slightly raw taste.

Let uncooked icings made with confectioners' sugar stand over hot water for 10 or 15 minutes to overcome this raw taste. Make the icing soon after putting the cake in the oven. Let it stand over hot water until you are ready to spread it. Beat it until it is cool and the right consistency to spread easily. If a delicate flavoring such as vanilla, rum or sherry is used, it is wise to add it after the icing is removed from the hot water.

The following uncooked icings may be made with an electric mixer. Combine the ingredients, using soft butter and only ½ the sugar. Beat them at high speed from 3 to 5 minutes. Add the remaining sugar gradually until the icing is a good consistency to spread.

FRENCH ICING
Sufficient for the Tops of Two 9 Inch Layers
This is a richer icing than the following one.
Sift:

> 2 cups confectioners' sugar

Beat until soft:

> 4 tablespoons butter

Add the sugar gradually. Blend these ingredients until they are creamy. Beat in:

> 1 egg
> 1 teaspoon vanilla

See the Rule for Uncooked Icings above.

WHITE ICING II
Sufficient for the Top of an 8 or 9 Inch Cake
Sift:

> 1 cup confectioners' sugar

Beat until soft:

> 1½ tablespoons butter

Add the sugar gradually. Blend these ingredients until they are creamy. You may substitute for the butter 1 egg yolk beaten until light or 1½ tablespoonfuls hot cream. Add:

> ⅛ teaspoon salt
> 1 teaspoon vanilla or 1 tablespoon sherry, rum, coffee, etc.

If the icing is too thin add:

> Confectioners' sugar

See the Rule for Uncooked Icings above.

White Icing I, page 694.

ORANGE ICING
Sufficient for the Tops of Two 9 Inch Layers
Place in the top of a double boiler:

> 2 cups sifted confectioners' sugar
> 1 tablespoon melted butter
> 1 tablespoon grated orange rind
> ¼ cup orange juice

One tablespoonful of this may be lemon juice.
Place these ingredients over hot water for 10 minutes. Beat the icing until cool and a good consistency to spread. See Rule for Uncooked Icings, page 702.

LEMON ICING
Sufficient for the Tops of Two 9 Inch Layers
Blend well:
　　2 cups confectioners' sugar
　　¼ cup soft butter
Beat in:
　　Grated rind and juice of 1 lemon
　　1 or more teaspoons cream
Note on orange and lemon rind:
A subtle flavor may be obtained by grating orange or lemon rind coarsely. Place it in a piece of cheesecloth. Wring the juice onto sugar. Stir it in. Permit the sugar to stand for 15 minutes or more.

BUTTERSCOTCH ICING
Sufficient for the Tops of Two 9 Inch Layers
Combine, stir and heat in a double boiler until smooth:
　　4 tablespoons butter
　　½ cup brown sugar
　　⅛ teaspoon salt
　　⅓ cup rich or evaporated milk
Cool this slightly. Beat in to make a good consistency to spread:
　　2 cups more or less of confectioners' sugar
You may add:
　　½ teaspoon vanilla or 1 teaspoon rum
　　½ cup chopped nut meats

CHOCOLATE BUTTER ICING
Sufficient for the Tops of Two 9 Inch Layers
Melt over a very low flame:
　　2 oz. chocolate
Add and melt:
　　2 teaspoons to 3 tablespoons butter
Add:
　　¼ cup hot water, cream or coffee
　　⅛ teaspoon salt
Remove these ingredients from the fire. When they are cool add:
　　1 teaspoon vanilla
Sift and add gradually:
　　2 cups confectioners' sugar

Slightly less sugar may be required. Stir the icing until it is a good consistency to spread. See Rule for Uncooked Icings, page 702.
One-fourth cupful cocoa may be substituted for the chocolate. In that case combine it at once with the hot water and butter.
One egg may be substituted for the water, etc. Remove the icing from the fire before the egg is added.

COCOA COFFEE ICING
Sufficient for the Tops of Two 9 Inch Layers
Beat until well blended:
　　1½ tablespoons butter
　　2½ tablespoons cocoa
Sift and beat in gradually:
　　2 cups confectioners' sugar
Add sufficient:
　　Strong black coffee
to make the icing a good consistency to spread. See Rule for Uncooked Icings, page 702.

FRENCH COFFEE ICING
Sufficient for the Tops of Two 9 Inch Layers
Sift:
　　1⅔ cups confectioners' sugar
Beat until soft:
　　¼ to ½ cup butter
Add the sugar gradually. Blend these ingredients until they are creamy. Add:
　　⅛ teaspoon salt
　　3 tablespoons strong hot coffee
Beat these ingredients for 2 minutes. When the icing is cool add:
　　1 teaspoon vanilla or rum
Permit it to stand for 5 minutes. Beat it well and spread it.

MOCHA ICING WITH CONFECTIONERS' SUGAR
To the preceding:
　　French Coffee Icing
Add:
　　1 tablespoon cocoa
Use only:
　　½ teaspoon vanilla

MOCHA ICING WITH BROWN SUGAR
Prepare the preceding:
　　Mocha Icing
Substitute light brown sugar for the confectioners' sugar.

APRICOT ICING
Sufficient for the Tops of Two 9 Inch Layers
Put sweetened Stewed Apricots, page 450, through a ricer until you have:
  ½ cup apricot pulp
Canned puréed baby food apricots may be substituted. Sift:
  1½ cups confectioners' sugar
Stir the sugar into the pulp until it is smooth. Beat in:
  1 tablespoon soft butter
  ½ tablespoon lemon juice
This is a soft icing. Add more confectioners' sugar if needed.

BANANA ICING
Sufficient for the Tops of Two 9 Inch Layers
Put soft bananas through a ricer until you have:
  ½ cup banana pulp
Sift:
  2 cups confectioners' sugar
Stir the sugar into the pulp until it is smooth. Beat in:
  ⅛ teaspoon salt
  1 teaspoon lemon juice
  ½ teaspoon vanilla
Add more confectioners' sugar if needed.

PINEAPPLE ICING
Sufficient for the Tops of Two 9 Inch Layers
Sift:
  2 cups confectioners' sugar
Beat until soft:
  ¼ cup butter
Add the sugar gradually. Blend these ingredients until they are creamy. Beat in:
  1 teaspoon lemon juice
  ⅛ teaspoon salt
  ½ teaspoon vanilla
  ½ cup chopped drained pineapple
Permit these ingredients to stand for 5 minutes. Beat the icing until it is creamy. Add more sugar if necessary.

MAPLE ICING
Sufficient for the Tops of Two 9 Inch Layers
Sift:
  2 cups confectioners' sugar
Add and blend:
  1 tablespoon butter
  ¼ teaspoon salt
  ½ teaspoon vanilla
Beat in to make a good consistency to spread:
  Maple sirup, or a combination of maple sirup and cream

QUICK HONEY PEANUT BUTTER ICING
This appeals mainly to the small fry. Combine and bring to a boil:
  2 tablespoons shortening
  2 tablespoons butter
  ¼ cup honey
Remove from fire and add:
  ½ cup coarsely ground peanut butter
Stir until well blended. Spread on a warm cake. Toast it very lightly under a broiler at medium heat. Watch it carefully.

CREAM CHEESE ICING
Sift:
  ¾ cup confectioners' sugar
Work until soft and fluffy:
  2 packages cream cheese: 6 oz.
  1½ tablespoons cream or milk
Beat in the sugar gradually. Beat in:
  1½ teaspoons grated lemon or orange rind
or:
  1 teaspoon vanilla and
  ½ teaspoon cinnamon
or:
  A good dash rum or liqueur

CREAM CHEESE ORANGE ICING
This is sweeter and less cheesy than the rule above.
Cream until soft:
  1 tablespoon butter
  1 package cream cheese: 3 oz.
  2 tablespoons grated orange rind
  ⅛ teaspoon salt
Work in until well blended:
  2 cups sifted confectioners' sugar

JELLY ICING
Sufficient for the Top of One 9 Inch Layer
Beat until light:
  1 egg white
  ⅛ teaspoon salt
Add gradually bit by bit, beating constantly:
  ½ to ¾ cup jelly
Beat until the icing is a good consistency to spread.

ICING FOR CHRISTMAS CAKES

Sift:

Confectioners' sugar

Flavor it with:

Grated lemon rind

Moisten it with:

Lemon juice

Drop a small quantity from a teaspoon onto a cake and permit it to spread and harden.

QUICK LACE TOPPING

A very quick decorative effect, good for tea cakes, is gained by using a lace paper doily and confectioners' or colored granulated sugar. Use a sifter-top shaker filled with the sugar or a strainer and a spoon to dust the sugar lavishly over the doily, being careful that it sifts into the interstices of the doily. Lift off the doily gingerly with a straight upward motion and you will find a clearly marked lacy design on your cake top. Shake the surplus sugar on the doily into a bowl. Reserve it for future use.

GLAZE FOR CHRISTMAS CAKES

Sift:

2 cups confectioners' sugar

Moisten it with:

3 tablespoons or more boiling water

Flavor it with:

1 teaspoon vanilla

See Rule for Uncooked Icings, page 702. Beat the icing until it is a good consistency to spread.

Cake Fillings

Fillings for cakes seem to hold better when the cake layers are placed with the bottom crusts together.

CUSTARD FILLING
Sufficient to Spread Between Three 9 Inch Layers

Combine:

½ to ¾ cup sugar
⅓ cup flour
¼ teaspoon salt

Add and stir until smooth and thick:

2 cups scalded milk or cream

Pour these ingredients over:

2 slightly beaten eggs or 4 egg yolks

Stir and cook the custard in a double boiler over, not in, hot water until the eggs thicken. Cool it and add:

1 teaspoon vanilla

Add, if desired:

(1 cup blanched chopped almonds)
(1 tablespoon sherry, rum, etc.)

Coffee Filling, page 653.

BANANA CUSTARD FILLING

Prepare the preceding:

Custard Filling

Before spreading the custard add to it:

2 or more thinly sliced bananas

ORANGE CUSTARD FILLING
Sufficient to Spread Between Two 9 Inch Layers

Stir in the top of a double boiler:

⅓ cup sugar
5 tablespoons all-purpose flour
¼ teaspoon salt

Stir in until smooth:

1 cup milk

Then stir in:

½ cup orange juice

Cook this over boiling water for 10 minutes, stirring frequently. Beat slightly:

1 egg

Beat about ⅓ of the sauce into it. Return it to the pan, continuing to cook and stir for 2 minutes. Cool, then spread the filling.

BANANA FILLING

Prepare:

White Icing I, page 694, or
Seven Minute White Icing, page 700

Spread the cake layers closely with:
   Thinly sliced bananas
Cover them with the icing.

PINEAPPLE FILLING
Sufficient to Spread Between Three 9 Inch Layers
Spread layers with:
   Pineapple Meringue Pie Filling, page 580
or spread the layers with:
   Drained chopped or crushed pineapple
and cover it with:
   White Icing I, page 694, or Seven Minute White Icing, page 700

Almond Filling, page 626.

BUTTERSCOTCH FILLING
Sufficient to Spread Between Three 9 Inch Layers
Cook and stir in a double boiler or over very low heat until clear and brown:
   ¾ cup brown sugar
   ¼ cup butter
Add and cook until scalded:
   1½ cups milk
Stir until blended:
   5 tablespoons all-purpose flour
   ½ cup milk
   ¼ teaspoon salt
Add these ingredients to the butter mixture. Cook and stir them for 15 minutes. Pour part of the sauce over:
   2 beaten eggs
Return it to the double boiler. Cook the custard for 3 minutes longer. Cool it. Flavor it with:
   ½ teaspoon vanilla or
   2 teaspoons rum

Caramel Filling or Icing, page 698.

CREAMY CHOCOLATE FILLING OR ICING
Sufficient to Spread Between Three 9 Inch Layers or to Cover the Tops and Sides of Two 9 Inch Layers
This filling adheres to the cake and remains soft and creamy.
Place in a saucepan:
   2 cups sugar
   ½ teaspoon salt
   ½ cup cocoa
Beat and add to the sugar mixture:

   2 egg yolks or 1 egg
   1 cup milk
Stir and cook these ingredients to 238°, the soft ball stage (page 693). Cool the filling and beat it until it is the right consistency to spread. Add to it:
   1 teaspoon vanilla

CHOCOLATE FILLING
Sufficient to Spread Between Two 9 Inch Layers
Sift:
   ½ cup sugar
Beat until light:
   4 egg yolks or 2 eggs
Add the sugar gradually. Beat these ingredients until they are well blended. Add slowly:
   1 cup milk
Add:
   2 teaspoons butter
   1 oz. grated or chopped chocolate
   ⅛ teaspoon salt
Cook these ingredients in a double boiler until they are thick. Cool the filling. Add:
   1 teaspoon vanilla

Glossy Chocolate Icing or Filling, page 699.

CHOCOLATE CUSTARD FILLING
Prepare:
   Custard Filling, page 705
Add to the milk mixture:
   1½ oz. chocolate

CHOCOLATE WHIPPED CREAM FILLING
Sufficient to Spread Between Two 9 Inch Layers
This is good as a filling for cream puffs, tarts or cakes that are to be served at once.
Heat in a double boiler:
   4 tablespoons sugar
   ⅛ teaspoon salt
   1 oz. chocolate cut in pieces
   2 tablespoons cream
When the sugar is dissolved and the chocolate is melted, beat the filling with a wire whisk until the ingredients are well blended. Cool them. Whip until stiff:
   1 cup heavy cream
Add:
   ½ teaspoon vanilla
Fold in the chocolate mixture.

WHIPPED CREAM AND COCOA FILLING FOR ANGEL OR SPONGE CAKE

Combine and sift:

1/2 cup confectioners' sugar
6 tablespoons Droste's cocoa
1/8 teaspoon salt

Add them to:

2 cups whipping cream

Chill these ingredients for 2 hours or more. Add:

1 teaspoon vanilla

Whip the mixture until it is stiff. If a 9 inch angel or sponge cake is cut into 2 layers it can be filled with the cream and there will be enough to ice the tops and sides of the cake. Sprinkle the top of the cake with:

2/3 cup blanched, shredded, toasted almonds

Droste's cocoa or an equally well-flavored cocoa is needed for the success of this filling.

Three Minute Icing, page 632.

CHOCOLATE COFFEE FILLING FOR SPONGE OR ANGEL CAKE

Cut crosswise:

A sponge or angel cake

Combine, cook and stir in a double boiler until smooth:

2 oz. chocolate
2/3 cup cream
1 1/3 cups strong coffee

Combine and beat:

4 egg yolks
1 egg
1/4 teaspoon salt

Beat in gradually:

1 3/4 cups sugar

Combine until smooth, then add:

2 teaspoons cornstarch
2 tablespoons cold coffee

Add these ingredients to the mixture in the double boiler. Stir and cook the filling until it is a good consistency to spread. Cool it. You may add:

1/2 teaspoon vanilla or
1 teaspoon rum

Spread between the layers and cover the top and sides of the cake.

WHIPPED CREAM AND JAM FILLING

Whip until stiff:

1 cup heavy cream

Fold into the cream:

1 cup jam

Spread the filling between 2 layers and over the top and sides of a 9 inch cake.

Almond Cream Filling, page 646; Almond Filling, page 626; and other fillings for Angel Cake.

ALMOND OR HAZELNUT CUSTARD FILLING

Sufficient to Spread Between Three 9 Inch Layers

Stir and heat in a saucepan over a very low flame:

1 cup sugar
1 cup sour cream
1 tablespoon flour

Do not permit these ingredients to boil. Pour them over:

1 beaten egg

Place them in a double boiler. Stir and cook the custard until it is thick. Add:

1 cup blanched or unblanched, shredded or ground almonds or
1 cup ground hazelnuts

When the custard is cool add:

1/2 teaspoon vanilla

ALMOND RAISIN FILLING

Sufficient for the Tops of Three 9 Inch Layers

Blanch, sliver, then toast:

3/4 cup almonds

Combine:

1/2 cup sugar
1 tablespoon orange rind
1/2 cup orange juice
3 tablespoons flour
3/4 cup water
2 cups chopped or ground seeded raisins
1/8 teaspoon salt

Simmer these ingredients for 5 minutes. Stir constantly. Add the almonds and:

1/2 teaspoon vanilla

TOASTED WALNUT OR PECAN FILLING

Sufficient for the Tops of Two 8 Inch Layers

Chop, then toast:

3/4 cup walnuts or pecans

Combine, stir and heat in a double boiler until sugar is dissolved:

1/2 cup brown sugar
1/4 teaspoon salt
2 tablespoons butter
1 tablespoon water

Stir part of this into:
  1 slightly beaten egg yolk
Return all to the double boiler. Stir
and cook until the egg yolk is slightly
thickened. Cool the filling. Add the
nut meats and:
  ½ teaspoon vanilla

FIG FILLING
**Sufficient to Spread Between Two 9
Inch Layers**
Cook in a double boiler until thick:
  ½ lb. chopped figs
  ⅓ cup sugar
  ⅓ cup boiling water
  1 tablespoon lemon juice
  ¾ teaspoon grated lemon rind
  (1 tablespoon cornstarch)
Cool the filling.

---

*Lady Baltimore Filling, page 641; Fruit
Filling for Cake (dates, figs, raisins and
nut meats), page 645.*

The following fillings deserve some
kind of mention, honorable, to say the
least. It is a pleasant surprise to find
them in a cake of strongly contrasting
flavor—let us say in a chocolate cake
spread with white icing or some other
good combination. Superb in Almond
Torte, page 650, spread with Chocolate
icing.

LEMON FILLING
**Sufficient to Spread Between Two 9
Inch Layers**
Stir and cook in a double boiler until
thick:

  2½ tablespoons lemon juice
  6 tablespoons orange juice
  ⅓ cup water
  ½ cup sugar
  2 tablespoons flour
  ⅛ teaspoon salt
  3 egg yolks
  (½ teaspoon grated lemon rind)
Cool the filling.

APRICOT FILLING
Follow the preceding rule for:
  Lemon Filling
Add:
  ¼ cup sugar
  ½ to ⅔ cup thick apricot pulp:
  Apricots Stewed without sugar
  and strained, page 450

ORANGE FILLING
Method I.
Follow the rule for:
  Lemon Filling
Use:
  Grated orange rind
and only:
  1 tablespoon lemon juice

Method II.
Stir and cook in a double boiler until
thick:
  ⅓ cup sugar
  2 tablespoons butter
  1 tablespoon flour
  1 tablespoon grated orange rind
  1 cup orange juice
  ⅛ teaspoon salt
  2 eggs

Orange Cream Filling, page 644.

Desserts

A family I know had a cook who always urged the children to eat sparingly of the meat course so as to leave a little room for the "hereafter." I have prepared so many, many "hereafters" for children and grownups that I feel like Christopher Morley's heroine, who made an anthology of the loaves of bread she had baked.

The majority of the following recipes are simple, require only staple ingredients and are very quickly made. If you make them in the electric mixer follow the rule below.

Rule for Puddings Made with an Electric Mixer:
Whip egg whites at high speed.
Whip egg yolks at medium speed.
Whip gelatine mixtures that are nearly set at medium speed.
Whip cream at medium speed.
Whip snow pudding and similar desserts after all the ingredients are combined at high speed until the mixture holds its shape.

You will find a number of suggestions for fruit desserts in the section on Cooked Fruits To Be Served with Meats, page 442.

As cream toppings are so often used with puddings, see the Rule for Whipping Cream, page 631, Rule for Whipping Evaporated Milk, and Substitute for Whipping Cream, page 632, Whipped Dried Milk Solids, page 632.

Flavorings are also important and the following lend interest and variety.

THE VANILLA BEAN AND EXTRACT

The ever popular vanilla bean is far more flavorful than the extract drawn from it. To use a vanilla bean cut off a small piece and place it in the liquid that is to be heated for a dessert. Use about a ½ inch piece for 2 cupfuls of liquid.

The bean is taken out or left in. As children we used to quarrel as to who was to suck the bean still floating in the custard sauce. The French sense of frugality urges that it be taken out, washed carefully, dried and used in Vanilla Sugar, see below.

To flavor a cold dessert split the piece of bean, scrape it well and add the seeds and pulp to the other dessert ingredients. When you use vanilla extract be sure to add it to cooled ingredients only. It has an alcohol base and when added to hot substances resolves itself into that wonderful fragrance that is one of the treats of the kitchen—but gives you a much diminished flavor in the food.

VANILLA SUGAR

A good French cook will have in readiness containers filled with variously flavored sugars to be used in desserts. Place in a bowl:

A split piece vanilla bean, either fresh or used—see above

Add about:

The same quantity sugar

Pound these ingredients to extract the vanilla flavor. Add:

2 cups sugar

Place it in a tightly closed container. Use it in desserts omitting other vanilla flavor. The sugar may be strained and the bean used again until it loses all flavor.

ORANGE OR LEMON SUGAR

Combine:

Sugar

Grated orange or lemon rind

Place these ingredients in tightly closed containers. Use the sugar in desserts omitting other orange or lemon rind.

ALMOND MILK

This French touch makes a most delicately flavored dish.

Pound in a mortar:

1 cup blanched almonds

709

ɪu pound:

ɪts until they are
ɪid through a fine
ɪqueeze it. Use
ɪd milk to 1 part
sserts. You may

or kirsch

For aɪɪ ɪ hurry-up version
that will shock the painstaking French,
use a blender to grind the almonds.
Add the water gradually. Strain the
almond milk or not, as you wish.

_____

Milk Pudding II, page 741.

ORANGE, LEMON AND LIME FLAVORINGS

These fruit flavors may be added as
juice or as rind. If used as rind a little
goes a long way. Grate only the colored portion of the rind; the white is
bitter. If you grate your peel diagonally it will not stick so annoyingly to
the grater.
To extract a maximum of juice from
citrus fruit, roll the fruit before slicing
or juicing it. If only part of the fruit is
used, store the remainder in a tightly
covered jar in the refrigerator. If only
a small quantity is wanted puncture
the fruit, squeeze what is needed and
store the fruit as above for further use.

Custards

Custard sauces and puddings are prepared over boiling water or over a very
low flame. They must be stirred constantly while they are cooking and they must
not be permitted to boil at any time. A high degree of heat destroys their delicate
flavor and solidifies the eggs so rapidly that they curdle or separate. Should a custard sauce separate, remove it at once from the fire, dump it quickly into a cold
bowl and whip it with a wire whisk, see page 592. Beat it well and it may become
smooth. Always store cooked custards or custard puddings, pies, eclairs, sauces in
a cool or refrigerated place as they are very susceptible to bacterial activity although they may give no evidence of spoilage.

CUP CUSTARD
5 Servings
For speed and good results see both
Blender Custard, page 898, and Pressure Cooker Custard, page 893.
Scald:
   2 cups milk
   ¼ cup sugar
   ⅛ teaspoon salt
Pour these ingredients slowly over:
   **3 beaten egg yolks or 2 whole
   eggs**
Add:
   **½ teaspoon vanilla
   (⅛ teaspoon nutmeg)**
Beat the custard until it is well
blended. Pour it into a baking dish or
into individual molds. Place the molds
in a pan of hot water in a moderate
oven 325° for about 1 hour or more, or
until the custard is set. To test, insert
a silver knife or spoon. If the custard
does not adhere to the spoon it is ready
to be removed from the oven. Chill
and serve it with:
   **Caramel Sirup, page 754, fruit
   juice or Maple Sauce, page 755**
For a company dessert serve cup custard with cored pear halves, fresh or
stewed, sprinkled with rum, the centers filled with a stewed pitted prune
dusted in cinnamon.

CARAMEL CUSTARD
4 Servings
Place in a small heavy skillet and stir
over a quick fire until melted:
   ½ cup sugar
Add:
   1 tablespoon hot water
Stir until the sugar is dissolved. Scald:
   2 cups milk
Add the melted sugar. Pour these ingredients slowly over:
   3 beaten egg yolks
Add:
   **½ teaspoon vanilla or almond
   extract**
   ⅛ teaspoon salt
Beat the custard until it is well
blended. Place it in a 7 inch ring mold
set in a dish of hot water and bake ɪt
in a moderate oven 325° until it is firm.
To test it see the rule for Cup Custard
on this page.

_____

DANISH OR QUICK CARAMEL-IZED CUSTARD
5 Servings
Beat until light:
   3 eggs
Add:
   ¼ cup sugar
   ⅛ teaspoon salt

Scald and stir in slowly:
>   2 cups milk

Add:
>   ½ teaspoon vanilla or 1 teaspoon
>   rum

Beat the custard until it is well blended. Sift:
>   ½ cup light brown sugar

If more sauce is desired, double this amount. Place it in the bottom of a baking dish or mold and pour the custard on top of it. Place the baking dish in a pan of hot water in a moderate oven and bake the custard until it is firm. To test it see rule for Cup Custard on page 710. Cool it and invert the contents of the dish onto a platter. The brown sugar will form a caramel sauce.

CARAMELIZED CUSTARD
4 to 5 Servings

Melt in a heavy skillet:
>   ½ cup sugar

Stir it slowly and constantly. Place it in a 7 inch ring mold or other mold. Turn the mold to permit the caramel to spread evenly, then push it with a spoon until the entire surface is coated. Prepare by the rule on page 710 and add:
>   Cup Custard or Danish Custard

In case of the latter, omit the brown sugar in the bottom of the dish. Bake the custard as directed. Invert it when cold onto a platter. The center may be filled with:
>   Whipped cream

Sprinkle the top with:
>   Shredded toasted almonds or
>   crushed nut brittle

MAPLE CUSTARD
4 to 6 Servings

Beat:
>   4 egg yolks
>   ¾ cup maple sirup

Add:
>   3 cups milk
>   (½ cup chopped nut meats)

Place on a platter and whip until stiff:
>   4 egg whites
>   ⅛ teaspoon salt

Fold the custard into the egg whites. Fill individual custard cups, place them in a pan of hot water and bake the custard in a moderate oven 325° until it is firm. To test it see rule for Cup Custard, page 710.

COFFEE CUSTARD
4 Servings

Combine and scald:
>   1 cup strong coffee
>   1 cup top milk
>   4 tablespoons sugar
>   ⅛ teaspoon salt

Pour these ingredients slowly over:
>   2 whole beaten eggs or 3 egg
>   yolks

Beat these ingredients until they are well blended. To bake the custard follow the rule on page 710 for Cup Custard. Serve it cold with:
>   Cream or whipped cream

COFFEE AND CHOCOLATE CUSTARD

Follow the preceding rule for:
>   Coffee Custard

Add:
>   ⅓ cup grated chocolate
>   1 tablespoon sugar

"BOILED" CUSTARD OR CUSTARD SAUCE
About 2½ Cupfuls

This custard has acquired a celestial association thanks to the incomparable "Green Pastures." It is badly named as it must not be permitted to boil at any time.

Beat slightly:
>   3 or 4 egg yolks

Add:
>   ¼ cup sugar
>   ⅛ teaspoon salt

Scald and stir in slowly:
>   2 cups milk

Place the custard over a very slow fire. Stir it constantly. Take care that it does not boil. Or stir over simmering water until it begins to thicken. Strain and cool the custard. Add to it:
>   1 teaspoon vanilla, rum or sherry
>   or a little grated lemon rind

Chill it thoroughly. This is not a firm custard. It is really a custard sauce.

FLOATING ISLAND
Method I. 4 Servings

Children call this "eating clouds."
Prepare by the above rule:
>   "Boiled" Custard (flavored
>   with lemon rind)

Place it in a baking dish. Whip until stiff:
>   3 egg whites
>   ⅛ teaspoon salt

Add very slowly, whipping constantly:

3 tablespoons sugar
½ teaspoon vanilla or a few drops
almond extract

Heap the egg whites on the custard. Place the dish in a hot oven 500° for 2 minutes, or under a broiler until the tips of the meringue are brown. Serve the custard hot or cold.

Method II.

Or do them the delicate French way and call them Oeufs à la Neige: Whip until stiff:

3 egg whites

Beat in gradually:

4 tablespoons sugar

Scald:

2 cups milk

Drop the meringue mixture from a tablespoon in rounds onto the milk. Poach them gently without letting the milk boil, for about 4 minutes, turning them once. Lift them out carefully with a skimmer onto a towel. Use the milk to make:

"Boiled" Custard, page 711

Cool the custard. Place the meringues on top of it. Chill the custard before serving it.

CRÈME BRULÉE
4 Servings

A French custard made in an unusual way, which gives it an unusual flavor. Stir, bring to the boiling point and boil for exactly 1 minute:

1 pint 40% cream: 2 cups

Remove the cream from the fire. Pour it in a slow stream into:

4 well-beaten egg yolks

Beat it constantly. Return the cream to the fire. Stir and cook it over a low flame until it is nearly boiling, or stir and cook it for 5 minutes in a double boiler. Place the cream in a greased baking dish. Chill it well. Cover the cream with a ⅓ inch layer of:

Brown sugar or maple sugar

Place it under a broiler, keeping the oven door open, to form a crust and to caramelize the sugar. Chill it again. The cream may be made one day and caramelized the next.

ZABAGLIONE OR SABAYON
6 Servings

This is served as a sauce, as a custard or as a beverage. Any heavy wine may be used: Madeira, sherry, etc. Beat until very light:

8 egg yolks
1 cup confectioners' sugar

Place these ingredients in the top of a double boiler over, not in, boiling water. Do not permit the water to touch the bottom of the double boiler top. This is important. Beat the custard constantly with a wire beater. When it is foamy add gradually:

½ cup Madeira, sherry, etc.

Continue to beat the custard until it doubles in bulk and begins to thicken. Remove it from the heat. Whip until stiff:

8 egg whites
⅛ teaspoon salt

Fold in the custard. Serve the Sabayon at once in sherbet glasses.

WINE CUSTARD OR WEINSCHAUM
6 Servings

Place in the top of a double boiler over, not in, boiling water:

2 cups white wine
½ cup water

Add:

4 unbeaten eggs
½ cup sugar

Beat these ingredients vigorously with a wire whisk. Cook the custard until it thickens. Beat it constantly. Serve it hot or cold.

LADY FINGER CUSTARD
5 Servings

Split:

12 lady fingers

Spread them generously with:

Tart jelly

Put them together again. Place them in the bottom of an 8 inch baking dish. You may use slices of dry sponge cake or macaroons. You may substitute for the jelly well-drained canned cherries, not too sour. Line the sides of the dish with cake, place the cherries in the bottom and proceed as directed. Beat until creamy:

2 egg yolks
¼ cup sugar

Scald:

1¼ cups milk

Pour this over the yolk mixture. Dissolve:

1½ tablespoons cornstarch

in:

¼ cup milk

Stir this into the yolk mixture. Stir and cook these ingredients over a very low fire until they are thick. Cool them slightly. Season them with:

1 teaspoon vanilla

Pour the custard over the lady fingers. Beat until stiff:

2 egg whites

Add very slowly, beating constantly:

2 tablespoons sugar
1 teaspoon lemon juice

When the meringue is stiff heap it onto the pudding. Dot the top with bits of:

Tart jelly

Bake the pudding in a slow oven 325° until the meringue is set, about 15 minutes.

FRUIT CUSTARD
5 Servings

Prepare:

½ cup toasted crushed nut meats

Prepare by the rule on page 710:

Cup Custard

Butter custard cups. Line them with the nut meats. Place in each cup:

An apricot or peach half, round side down, or a pineapple slice

You may sprinkle the fruit with:

A few drops kirsch, rum, brandy or vanilla

Fill the cups with custard. Bake them by the rule for Cup Custard. Cool, then remove the custard from the cups. Serve it with:

Fruit juice drained from fruit

APPLE CUSTARD
3 Servings

Such a good dessert on a lonely evening. Cut the ingredients down to about ⅓ for one serving:

Pare, core and slice thinly:

3 tart apples

Sprinkle them with:

2 tablespoons sugar
2 tablespoons lemon juice

Permit them to stand for 10 minutes. Beat until light:

3 eggs
2 tablespoons white wine
1 teaspoon melted butter

Fold in the apples. Bake them in a lightly greased oven-proof dish in a moderate oven 325° until the custard is firm. Serve at once with:

Cinnamon and sugar

POSIE'S CUSTARD WITH WHIPPED CREAM
6 Servings

Combine and beat:

4 egg yolks
¾ cup sugar
2 tablespoons cornstarch

Scald, then stir in:

2 cups milk and cream mixed

Add:

2 tablespoons butter
⅛ teaspoon salt

Cook and stir these ingredients in a double boiler over, not in, boiling water until thick. Cool, then add:

1½ teaspoons vanilla

Fold in:

1 cup heavy cream, whipped

Chill the custard. Serve it with:

Brandied fruit, Fruit Sauce, page 759, or Dampfnudeln, page 422

ORANGE CUSTARD WITH MERINGUE
6 Servings

Grate the rind of:

2 oranges

onto:

⅓ cup sugar

Peel:

6 oranges

Separate the sections and remove the membrane (page 472). Place the sections in a baking dish. Scald:

3 cups milk

Pour it over:

3 beaten egg yolks

Beat these ingredients until they are well blended. Combine the sugar with:

2 tablespoons cornstarch
¼ teaspoon salt

Stir this mixture into the custard. Cook and stir it in a double boiler until thick, for about 7 minutes, or cook over a very low flame. Cool the custard. Pour it over the oranges. Top it with a Meringue, page 578, made with:

3 egg whites
⅛ teaspoon salt
6 tablespoons sugar
1 teaspoon vanilla

Bake the meringue in a slow oven 325° for about 15 minutes. Serve the custard chilled.

PUDDING CUSTARDS AND PIE FILLINGS

The rules that follow for Orange, Lemon and Pineapple Sponge Custard make delicious puddings and pie fillings. They are known also as angel pudding, orange, lemon or pineapple pudding. The batter separates while cooking, leaving a spongy top and a saucelike substance on the bottom. If you prefer a meringuelike quality, beat about ¼ the sugar slowly into the beaten egg whites before folding them into the egg yolk mixture. These and Applesauce Pudding, page 722, served ice cold with thick cream are among my favorite summer desserts.

ORANGE SPONGE CUSTARD
4 to 6 Servings

Please read the preceding comment.
Cream:
>   ¾ cup sugar
>   1½ tablespoons butter
>   1 tablespoon grated orange rind

Add and beat well:
>   2 or 3 egg yolks

Stir in:
>   3 tablespoons all-purpose flour

alternately with:
>   ⅓ cup orange juice
>   1 cup milk

Beat until stiff:
>   2 or 3 egg whites
>   ⅛ teaspoon salt

Fold them into the yolk mixture. Place the batter in greased custard cups, or in a 7 inch oven-proof dish, set in a pan filled with 1 inch of hot water. Bake the sponge in a moderate oven 350° for about 45 minutes for the cups and about 1 hour for the baking dish, or until set. Serve it hot or ice cold with:
>   (Thick cream)

LEMON SPONGE CUSTARD
4 to 6 Servings

Follow the above rule for:
>   Orange Sponge Custard

Substitute for orange peel:
>   2 teaspoons lemon peel

Substitute for orange juice:
>   ¼ cup lemon juice

CHOCOLATE SPONGE CUSTARD

Follow the rule on page 577 for filling for
>   Chocolate Sponge Cake Pie

PINEAPPLE SPONGE CUSTARD
4 Servings

Combine and stir in the order given:
>   5 tablespoons sugar
>   3 tablespoons all-purpose flour
>   ½ cup pineapple sirup
>   1 teaspoon grated lemon rind
>   2 tablespoons lemon juice

>   2 or 3 beaten egg yolks
>   ½ cup milk
>   1½ tablespoons melted butter

Whip until stiff, then fold in:
>   2 or 3 egg whites
>   ⅛ teaspoon salt

Place in the bottom of a 7 inch baking dish or in four 3½ inch individual ones:
>   1¼ to 1½ cups coarsely cut drained pineapple

Pour the custard mixture over the fruit. Place the dishes in a pan in 1 inch of hot water. Bake the custard in a moderate oven 350° for about 1 hour for the dish and 45 minutes for the cups. Serve the sponge hot or cold.

SPONGE CAKE PUDDING

Place in a baking dish:
>   Slices of sponge cake, lady fingers or macaroons

Cover them with a thick layer of:
>   Drained stewed cherries, oranges, bananas or peaches

Pour over them:
>   Boiled Custard, page 711

Flavor it with:
>   (Rum or sherry)

Make a Meringue, page 578, of:
>   3 egg whites
>   ⅛ teaspoon salt
>   6 tablespoons sugar
>   1 teaspoon vanilla

Heap it on the fruit. Bake the pudding in a slow oven 300° for 15 minutes. Serve it hot or cold with:
>   Cherry juice or cream

BAKED CHOCOLATE CUSTARD WITH MERINGUE
6 Servings

The delight of all children.
Dissolve:
>   2½ tablespoons cornstarch

in:
>   ¼ cup milk

Scald:
>   1¾ cups milk

Add and stir until dissolved:
>   ½ cup sugar
>   1¾ oz. chocolate
>   ⅛ teaspoon salt

Add the cornstarch mixture. Stir and cook these ingredients over a very low fire or in a double boiler until they have thickened. The cornstarch is cooked, when you can no longer taste it. Pour them over:
>   4 beaten egg yolks

Beat these ingredients until they are

well blended. Place the custard in a baking dish. Cool it. Cover it with meringue made with:

    4 egg whites
    ⅛ teaspoon salt
    ½ cup sugar
    1 teaspoon vanilla

Place the baking dish in a pan of hot water and bake the custard in a slow oven 300° until the meringue is set. Serve the pudding hot or cold with:

    Cream

FRENCH CHOCOLATE CUSTARD
Pot de Crème
6 Servings

Combine and cook over very low heat:

    2 cups milk
    ½ lb. grated, best quality sweet chocolate

Cook and stir these ingredients until they are blended and the milk is scalded. Remove them from the heat. Beat into them:

    6 lightly-beaten egg yolks

Strain the custard. Pour it into custard cups. Chill it well.

French Chocolate Cream, page 745.

POT DE CRÈME BAKED
12 Servings

Heat in the top of a double boiler:

    1½ cups milk and 1½ cups cream
    3 tablespoons sugar
    5 oz. sweet chocolate

Stir well. When chocolate is melted pour it over:

    6 well-beaten eggs

Add:

    1 teaspoon vanilla

Strain through a fine sieve into individual ramekins and bake like Custard, page 710. While hot grate some semisweet chocolate over each custard. Cool and then chill.

FROZEN LEMON PIE
6 Servings

You may substitute 1 cupful whipping cream for the milk, but my followers in far away places will probably welcome this rule as it is.

Chill for 12 hours:

    1 cup evaporated milk

Butter well a 1 quart refrigerator tray. Grind or crush about:

    7 graham crackers: ½ cup

Use your fingers to spread ½ of these on the bottom and sides of the tray. Measure:

    ½ cup sugar

Reserve 2 tablespoonfuls of this. To the rest add:

    2 slightly beaten egg yolks
    Grated rind of ½ lemon
    ⅓ cup lemon juice

Cook and stir these ingredients over hot water until they form a custard. Cool it. Whip until stiff:

    2 egg whites
    ⅛ teaspoon salt

Whip in the reserved sugar gradually. Fold the egg whites into the custard. Whip the evaporated milk until stiff in a chilled bowl. Fold in:

    1 tablespoon confectioners' sugar

Fold the milk into the custard and fill the tray. Top it with the reserved crumbs. Freeze the pie until it is firm.

Cereal Puddings

FARINA PUDDING BOILED
6 Servings

Another good dish for children. Boil:

    2 cups milk
    ¼ cup sugar

Add:

    ½ cup farina

Stir and cook the farina over a low fire until it is thick. Add and stir until melted:

    1 tablespoon butter

Remove the pan from the fire. Beat in one at a time:

    2 egg yolks

Cool the mixture. Add:

    1 teaspoon vanilla
    (½ teaspoon grated lemon rind)

Place on a platter and whip until stiff:

    2 egg whites
    ⅛ teaspoon salt

Fold the egg whites into the farina mixture. Serve the pudding cold with:

    Cream, fruit juice, stewed fruit or crushed sweetened berries

----

FARINA PUDDING BAKED

Prepare the preceding:

    Farina Pudding

Use:

1 teaspoon grated lemon rind
3 eggs instead of 2

Place the pudding in a greased pan. Spread it to the thickness of 1 inch. Bake it in a moderate oven 350° until the edges are crisp. Serve it hot with:

> Raspberry or loganberry juice or crushed sweetened berries
> Hot Claret Sauce, page 760

INDIAN PUDDING
8 Servings

Boil in the top of a double boiler:

> 4 cups milk

Stir in:

> ⅓ cup corn meal

Place these ingredients over boiling water. Cook them for 15 minutes. Stir into them and cook for 5 minutes:

> ¾ cup dark molasses

Or use 1 cupful molasses and omit the sugar. Remove them from the heat. Stir in:

> ¼ cup butter
> 1 teaspoon salt
> 1 teaspoon ginger
> 3 tablespoons sugar
> (1 well-beaten egg)
> (½ cup raisins)
> (½ teaspoon cinnamon)

Pour the batter into a well-greased baking dish. To have a soft center you may pour over the top:

> 1 cup milk

Bake the pudding in a slow oven 325° from 1½ to 2 hours. Serve the pudding hot with:

> Hard Sauce, page 753, or cream

It is a New England custom to serve it with:

> Vanilla Ice Cream, page 761

MILK RICE
6 to 8 Servings

A very simple dessert and the basis of many more elaborate ones. Measure:

> 1 cup rice

Brown rice may be used for added nutrition and a richer flavor. Put it in a double boiler with:

> 6 cups hot milk
> 1 teaspoon salt

Cover it and steam it until it is tender, for about 1 hour. Stir it frequently. Add to it:

> (2 tablespoons butter)
> (½ teaspoon vanilla)

Serve the rice hot or cold with:

> Crushed or stewed fruit

or with a combination of:

> 4 tablespoons sugar
> 1 tablespoon cinnamon

RICE RINGS
6 Servings

This dessert is frequently served in Europe, where rice puddings are highly appreciated.
Cook by the preceding rule:

> ¾ cup rice
> 3 cups milk
> ¾ teaspoon salt

When the rice is tender cool it slightly and add to it:

> 1½ tablespoons butter
> 2 teaspoons vanilla or 1 teaspoon vanilla and 1 teaspoon lemon rind
> 2 teaspoons sugar

Pack the rice into buttered individual ring molds. Chill it. Turn it out onto plates. Fill the centers with:

> Stewed or canned fruit, or crushed sweetened berries

Or serve the rice with:

> Caramel Sauce, page 755, or Hot Caramel Sauce, page 755

RICE PUDDING
6 to 8 Servings

Cook (page 103):

> ⅔ cup rice: 2 cups cooked rice

Combine, beat well and add:

> 1⅓ cups milk
> ⅛ teaspoon salt
> 3½ tablespoons sugar
> 1 tablespoon soft butter
> 1 teaspoon vanilla
> 2 eggs

Add:

> ½ teaspoon grated lemon rind
> 1 teaspoon lemon juice
> (⅓ cup raisins)

Combine these ingredients lightly with a fork. Grease a baking dish and cover the bottom and sides with:

> (Bread crumbs)

Put the rice in it and cover the top with bread crumbs. Bake the pudding in a moderate oven 325° until it is set. Serve it hot or cold with:

> Cream, Strawberry or Raspberry Hard Sauce, page 754, fruit juice or Hot Sherry Sauce, page 760

CARAMEL RICE PUDDING

Prepare the preceding:

> Rice Pudding

Omit the white sugar. Substitute:
½ cup brown sugar
Omit the lemon rind and juice.

FRUIT AND NUT RICE PUDDING
5 Servings
Cook by the rule on page 716 ½ the quantity given for:
Milk Rice
Stir in lightly with a fork:
3 tablespoons sugar
¼ teaspoon freshly grated nutmeg
½ cup cooked chopped apricots or prunes
½ cup chopped nut meats
Grated rind and juice of ¼ lemon
2 beaten egg yolks
Place this in a greased baking dish. Top it with a Meringue, page 578, made of:
2 egg whites
¼ teaspoon salt
4 tablespoons sugar
½ teaspoon vanilla
Bake the pudding in a moderate oven 325° from 15 to 20 minutes.

Baked Pineapple and Rice, page 109.

FAITH'S RICE PUDDING
4 Servings
This has a fine caramelized quality.
Stir in an oven-proof dish:
¾ cup rice
1 can evaporated milk: 13 oz., and water to make 4 cups liquid
3 tablespoons sugar
Bake the pudding in a slow oven 275° for 3 hours. Stir it frequently. If it becomes stiff add:
Milk or cream

Stir in when cooked:
1 teaspoon vanilla
1 teaspoon butter

BAKED RICE CREAM
4 Servings
This dish is not like a pudding, for long cooking gives the rice the consistency of cream. It is served chilled. Combine and place in a baking dish in a very slow oven 225°:
4 cups milk
2 tablespoons rice
⅓ cup sugar
½ teaspoon salt
Stir the mixture every ½ hour until the rice is completely dissolved, a matter of about 3 hours. The rice may then be flavored with:
1 teaspoon vanilla or grated lemon rind
Serve it with:
Cream

CARAMEL CORNFLAKE RING
8 Servings
Very quickly made—crisp and good—a fine emergency dish, as it takes the place of cake.
Stir, melt and cook to the soft ball stage 238°:
1 cup brown sugar
1½ tablespoons light corn sirup
⅓ cup milk
2½ tablespoons butter
Place in a large buttered mixing bowl:
4 cups cornflakes
Stir in the hot sirup until blended. Pack the flakes in a buttered 8 inch ring mold or into 8 small molds. Invert and serve, with the center filled with:
Sugared or stewed fruit
Cream

Tapioca

Java produces the cassava plant and the cassava root produces tapioca, but the commercial article as we know it is processed in the United States.

When tapioca puddings are sticky they have been cooked too long.

QUICK TAPIOCA CUSTARD
4 Servings
Combine and stir in a double boiler:
3 tablespoons quick-cooking tapioca
⅓ cup sugar
⅛ teaspoon salt
1 or 2 beaten egg yolks
2 cups milk

Cook these ingredients without stirring over rapidly boiling water for 7 minutes. Stir and cook them 5 minutes longer. Remove them from the steam. The tapioca thickens as it cools. Whip until stiff:
1 or 2 egg whites
⅛ teaspoon salt
Beat in gradually:

2 tablespoons sugar

Fold a small amount of the tapioca into the egg white, then fold the egg white into the rest of the tapioca. Fold in:

½ teaspoon vanilla or 1 teaspoon grated orange or lemon rind

Chill the pudding. Serve it with:

Cream, fresh berries, crushed or canned fruit or Chocolate or other sauce, page 753

Additions may be made to this recipe. In that case the eggs may be omitted. Suggestions:

¼ cup or more coconut or toasted almonds
½ cup or more chopped dates
½ crushed banana and ½ diced banana

These eggless puddings are good served with custard sauce.

BUTTERSCOTCH TAPIOCA CUSTARD

4 Servings

Follow the preceding rule for:

Quick Tapioca Custard

Melt:

2 tablespoons butter

Stir in until it melts and bubbles:

⅓ cup brown sugar

Add this mixture to the cooked tapioca. Omit the citrus peel.

CLARA'S PEARL TAPIOCA PUDDING

8 Servings

This luxurious pudding, rich and delicate enough to make a fine party dish for children, is also relished by adults. If an added cookie is wanted for the festivities, try Vanilla Wafers, page 670, an incredibly thin and distinguished cookie, the recipe for which comes from the same source.

Soak overnight:

1 cup pearl tapioca

in:

1 cup milk

Add these ingredients to:

3 cups milk

and cook them for three hours in the top of a double boiler. Cool this mixture.

Beat and add:

5 egg yolks
Grated rind of 1 lemon
Juice of ½ lemon
¾ cup sugar

Beat until stiff but not dry:

5 egg whites
½ teaspoon salt

Line a baking dish with a layer of the tapioca mixture, a layer of the egg whites, another layer of tapioca, and end with the egg whites on top. Bake in a moderate oven, 325° for 15 minutes. Serve hot or cold, with or without a fruit sauce.

If adults are doing the eating try Hot Fruit Sauce for Fritters or Pudding, page 759. For the children use Fruit Sauce, page 759, without the wine.

PINEAPPLE TAPIOCA

4 Servings

Follow the rule on page 717 for:

Quick Tapioca Custard

Melt:

2 tablespoons butter

Stir in until it melts and bubbles:

2 tablespoons brown sugar

Stir in:

½ cup crushed pineapple

Add this mixture to the cooked tapioca.

CRUSHED FRUIT TAPIOCA PUDDING

8 Servings

This may be made with pineapple, prunes, berries, etc. It is eggless.

Boil in the top of a double boiler over direct heat:

2 cups water

Combine and stir in gradually:

⅓ cup quick-cooking tapioca
½ cup sugar
¼ teaspoon salt

When these ingredients are boiling place them over rapidly boiling water. Cook and stir them for 5 minutes. Remove them from the heat. Cool them slightly. Fold in:

2½ cups canned crushed pineapple
1 tablespoon lemon juice or
2 cups cooked prune or apricot pulp
2 tablespoons lemon juice or 1½ to 2 cups crushed sweetened berries
1 tablespoon lemon juice

Chill the tapioca. It may be served in sherbet glasses with:

Whipped cream, plain cream or custard sauce

Cornstarch Puddings

CORNSTARCH BLANCMANGE
6 Servings
When carefully prepared and thoroughly chilled this simple pudding is delicious. Scald:
    2¼ cups milk
Combine and stir until well blended:
    ¾ cup milk
    2 tablespoons sugar
    ¼ teaspoon salt
    ¼ cup cornstarch
Or if you wish to mold the pudding use ⅓ cupful cornstarch. Add these ingredients to the hot milk. Stir and cook them over a very low flame, or in a double boiler, until they thicken. The cornstarch is cooked when you can no longer taste it. Beat until light:
    1 egg
    2 tablespoons sugar
Pour the hot mixture over the egg, beat it and return it to the fire for a minute or two. Stir it constantly until the egg thickens, then remove it from the fire. When cool add:
    ½ teaspoon vanilla
Chill the pudding. Serve it with:
    Crushed sweetened fruit, fruit juice or cream
Canned strained loganberries make a very piquant sauce.

CARAMEL CORNSTARCH PUDDING
4 Servings
Place in a skillet over a quick fire:
    1 cup sugar
Stir it until it melts. Permit it to burn slightly. Heat to the boiling point:
    1¾ cups milk
Stir the milk slowly into the sugar. Cook it until the sugar is dissolved. Dissolve:
    2 tablespoons cornstarch
in:
    ¼ cup milk
Add these ingredients to the sugar mixture. Reduce the heat to a low flame or cook the pudding in a double boiler. Stir it until it thickens. The cornstarch is cooked when you can no longer taste it. Add:
    ⅛ teaspoon salt
    1 tablespoon butter
Pour part of this mixture over:
    2 slightly beaten egg yolks
Beat it until it is well blended. Return

it to the saucepan. Cook and stir the custard until it thickens. Cool it and add:
    1 teaspoon vanilla
    (½ cup chopped nut meats)
Chill the pudding. Serve it with:
    Cream

Variation I
After adding the vanilla, cover the pudding with a Meringue, page 578, made with:
    2 egg whites
    ⅛ teaspoon salt
    ¼ cup sugar
    ½ teaspoon vanilla
Bake the pudding in a slow oven 300° for about 15 minutes or until the meringue is set. Chill it. Serve it with:
    Cream

Variation II
Whip until stiff:
    2 egg whites
    ⅛ teaspoon salt
After adding the vanilla fold the egg whites lightly into the pudding mixture. Chill it and serve it with:
    Cream
Variation II makes a creamy substance that freezes well in a refrigerator tray.

CHOCOLATE CORNSTARCH PUDDING
4 Servings
Melt in a double boiler:
    1 oz. chocolate
Stir in slowly:
    ½ cup sugar
    1¾ cups milk
    ⅛ teaspoon salt
Heat these ingredients to the boiling point.
Dissolve:
    3 tablespoons cornstarch
in:
    ¼ cup milk
Stir the cornstarch slowly into the hot milk mixture. Cook the pudding over boiling water for 20 minutes, or cook and stir it over a very low flame until it thickens. The cornstarch is cooked, when you can no longer taste it. Cool it. Add:
    ½ teaspoon vanilla
Pour it into a wet mold. Chill it. Unmold it and serve it with:
    Cream

Baked Chocolate Custard with Meringue, page 714. This is really a cornstarch pudding and a mighty good one.

COCOA CORNSTARCH PUDDING
4 Servings

Prepare the preceding:
    Chocolate Cornstarch Pudding
Use only:
    2 tablespoons cornstarch
Substitute for the chocolate:
    2 tablespoons Droste's cocoa or
    4 tablespoons other cocoa

ICY LEMON FLUFF
6 Large Servings

This is as good as it sounds and much better than you think it is going to be when you first make it.
Combine, stir, then cook without stirring for 2 minutes:
    2 cups water
    1½ cups sugar
Stir in a cup until smooth:
    3 tablespoons cornstarch
    ¼ cup water
Add these ingredients to the boiling sirup. Boil them, stirring occasionally, over a low flame for 5 minutes. Cool them. Add:
    ½ cup lemon juice
Chill this mixture well. Whip until stiff:
    3 or 4 egg whites
    A pinch salt
Fold them well into the cornstarch mixture. Place the fluff in an ice tray in the refrigerator for 4 to 5 hours. Serve it with chilled:
    Boiled Custard, page 711

ROTHE GRUETZE OR FRUIT JUICE THICKENED WITH FARINA OR CORNSTARCH
Method I. 4 Servings

This good German pudding is usually made with raspberry juice but the juices of other fruits may be substituted.
Boil:
    2 cups fruit juice
Sweeten it palatably with:
    Sugar
Season it with:
    ⅛ teaspoon salt
Stir into the boiling juice:
    ⅓ cup farina
Or you may substitute 2⅔ tablespoonfuls tapioca. Add it to the hot liquid. Cook it in a double boiler for 20 minutes. Stir the pudding until it thickens. Pour it into a wet mold. Chill it. Serve it very cold with:
    Cream

Method II.
Or dissolve:
    3 tablespoons cornstarch
in:
    ¼ cup fruit juice
Boil:
    1¾ cups fruit juice
Sweeten it with:
    Sugar
Season it with:
    ⅛ teaspoon salt
Stir in the dissolved cornstarch. Continue to stir until the pudding thickens. Place it in a bowl. You may sprinkle the top lightly with sugar which will prevent a crust from forming. Chill it. Serve it very cold with:
    Cream

Bread Puddings

BREAD PUDDING WITH MERINGUE
6 Servings

Well-made bread pudding is an excellent dish, particularly if one is clever about "jazzing up" the hard sauce that accompanies it.
Cut bread into slices and trim away the crusts. Soak for 15 minutes:
    5 cups diced fresh bread or 3⅓ cups stale bread or stale or unsuccessful cake
The bread should be measured lightly, not packed. Soak in:
    3 cups warm milk
Add:

    ¼ teaspoon salt
Combine and beat well:
    3 egg yolks
    ⅓ to ½ cup sugar
    1 teaspoon vanilla
    (½ teaspoon nutmeg)
Add:
    (¼ cup raisins or nut meats)
Pour these ingredients over the soaked bread. Stir them lightly with a fork until they are well blended. If preferred the meringue may be dispensed with and the stiffly beaten egg whites may be folded in at this time. Cook the pudding in a baking dish set in a pan of hot water in a moderate oven

350° for about ¾ hour. Cool the pudding. Cover it with a Meringue, page 578, made with:

- 3 egg whites
- ⅛ teaspoon salt
- 6 tablespoons sugar
- ½ teaspoon vanilla

Bake the pudding in a slow oven 300° until the meringue is set, for about 15 minutes. Serve it hot with:

Hard Sauce, page 753, Strawberry Hard Sauce II, page 754, or cream or fruit juice

You may vary the flavor of bread pudding by adding: ½ cupful dates, figs, bananas or some orange marmalade.

QUEEN OF PUDDINGS

Prepare the above:
Bread Pudding
Place on the baked and cooked bread mixture:
Dabs of tart jelly
Heap the meringue on top. Bake it as directed above. Serve the pudding with:
Cream

CARAMEL BREAD PUDDING

Prepare the preceding:
Bread Pudding
Substitute for the white sugar:
½ cup brown sugar
Add:
2 tablespoons Caramel Sirup, page 754

CHOCOLATE BREAD PUDDING

Prepare by the basic rule above:
Bread Pudding
Use the larger amount of sugar. Add to the milk:
1½ oz. melted chocolate

LEMON BREAD PUDDING

6 Servings
Soak for ½ hour:
1 cup dry bread crumbs or
1½ cups soft bread crumbs
in:
2 cups milk
Cream until fluffy:
4 tablespoons butter
½ cup sugar
Beat in:
2 egg yolks
Grated rind and juice of ½ lemon
Stir in the soaked crumbs. Place the

pudding in a baking dish. Bake it in a moderate oven 325° for about 20 minutes. Cool it. Top it with a Meringue. See Caramel Cornstarch Pudding I, page 719.
Serve the pudding hot or cold with:
Cream

PINEAPPLE BREAD PUDDING

5 Servings
Cook and stir for 2 minutes:
1½ cups soft bread crumbs
1 cup milk
Cool these ingredients slightly.
Beat in:
1 egg yolk
2 tablespoons soft butter
1 tablespoon brandy or 1 teaspoon vanilla
¼ cup blanched shredded almonds or raisins
½ cup sugar
½ teaspoon cinnamon
¼ teaspoon ginger or cloves
A grating of nutmeg
1½ teaspoons grated lemon rind
Add:
1 cup crushed drained pineapple
1½ tablespoons lemon juice
Whip until stiff:
1 egg white
⅛ teaspoon salt
Fold it lightly into the other ingredients. Place the pudding in a greased baking dish. Bake it in a moderate oven 375° for about 35 minutes. Serve it with:
Cream or some kind of hard sauce, foamy sauce, etc.

SPICED DATE BREAD PUDDING

6 Servings
Combine:
2 cups warm milk
½ cup sugar
¼ teaspoon salt
1 teaspoon freshly grated nutmeg
¼ teaspoon cinnamon
1 teaspoon vanilla
½ cup pineapple or other fruit juice
Pour this over:
2 cups cubed day-old bread
Permit this to soak for 10 minutes.
Stir in lightly with a fork:
¾ cup chopped dates
3 beaten eggs
(½ cup nut meats)
Bake the pudding in a greased baking dish set in a pan of hot water in a

moderate oven 350° for about 1 hour.
Serve it hot or cold with:
> Hard Sauce, page 753, or cream

APPLE BREAD PUDDING
5 Servings
Cook and stir for 2 minutes:
> 1½ cups soft bread crumbs
> 1 cup milk

Cool these ingredients slightly. Beat in:
> 2 egg yolks
> 2 tablespoons soft butter
> 2 tablespoons brandy or 1 teaspoon vanilla
> 1 cup blanched shredded almonds, raisins and citron
> ½ cup sugar
> ¼ teaspoon cinnamon
> ¼ teaspoon cloves
> A grating of nutmeg
> 1½ teaspoons grated lemon rind

Add:
> 1½ cups peeled chopped apples

Whip until stiff:
> 2 egg whites
> ⅛ teaspoon salt

Fold them lightly into the other ingredients. Place the pudding in a greased baking dish. Bake it in a moderate oven 375° for about 35 minutes. Serve it with:
> Cream or some kind of hard sauce, foamy sauce, etc.

RHUBARB BREAD PUDDING
6 Servings
Wash, peel and dice:
> Rhubarb

There should be 2 cupfuls. Add:
> 10 tablespoons sugar
> 2 cups soft bread crumbs
> 1 tablespoon grated lemon rind
> 1½ tablespoons lemon juice

Beat well:
> 1 cup milk
> 1 egg

Stir these ingredients into the rhubarb mixture. Place the pudding in a buttered baking dish. Dot the top generously with:
> Butter

Bake the pudding covered in a moderate oven 375° for about 1 hour.

Other Baked Puddings

APPLESAUCE PUDDING
4 Servings
The following recipe calls for fresh or canned applesauce. The latter is recommended when the cook is pressed for time. It makes a simple, unusually good summer or winter dessert. Place in a bowl:
> 3 cups sweetened applesauce

Beat in:
> 3 egg yolks
> 1 teaspoon grated lemon rind
> ½ teaspoon vanilla or ¼ teaspoon almond extract or 2 teaspoons lemon juice

One third of the meringue may be folded into the yolk mixture. This makes a lighter pudding. Place these ingredients in a baking dish. Make a Meringue, page 578, with:
> 3 egg whites
> ⅛ teaspoon salt
> 6 tablespoons sugar
> ½ teaspoon vanilla

Heap it upon the pudding mixture. Set the dish in a pan of hot water. Bake the pudding in a slow oven 300° for 15 minutes. Serve it hot or very cold with:
> Cream

APPLE PUDDING
4 Servings
Very good made with a well-flavored apple—flat with a poor one. Beat:
> 1 egg

When it is light beat in slowly:
> ¾ cup sugar

Stir in:
> 1 tablespoon all-purpose flour
> 1 teaspoon any baking powder
> 1 teaspoon vanilla

Add:
> ½ cup chopped nut meats
> 4 medium-sized peeled, cored, diced tart apples

Bake the pudding in a covered dish in a moderate oven 325° until the apples are nearly tender, about ½ hour. Remove the cover to brown the top. Serve the pudding cold with:
> Cream

QUICK BAKED FRUIT SPONGE OR "AUFLAUF"
6 Servings
A perfect light dessert with a great appeal to children. Spread an ovenproof 8 inch dish with:
> Butter

Sprinkle it with:
1/4 cup brown sugar
Fill the dish about 3/4 full with:
Tart sliced apples or peaches
If hard apples are used, bake them
with the sugar in a 350° oven covered
for about 15 minutes. If uncooked
pour over the fruit at once the following:

Sponge Cake Batter
Beat:
2 egg yolks
2 tablespoons water
Beat in gradually:
1/2 cup sugar
1 teaspoon vanilla
Stir in:
1/2 cup sifted all-purpose flour
1/4 teaspoon salt
1/2 teaspoon any baking powder
Beat until stiff but not dry, then fold
into the batter:
2 egg whites
Bake the sponge in a moderate oven
350° for about 30 minutes. It may be
served with:
Custard, page 710, Vanilla
Sauce, page 758, or whipped
cream
A good fruit sponge may also be made
with:
1 package frozen blueberries:
11 oz.
1/2 cup sugar
1 tablespoon lemon juice
1/8 teaspoon cinnamon

BROWN BETTY
5 Servings
Combine:
1 1/2 cups dry bread or graham
cracker crumbs
1/4 cup melted butter
Line the bottom of a baking dish with
1/3 of the crumb mixture. Prepare:
2 1/2 cups peeled diced or sliced
apples
Sift:
3/4 cup brown sugar
1 teaspoon cinnamon
1/4 teaspoon nutmeg
1/4 teaspoon cloves
1/2 teaspoon salt
Add:
1 teaspoon grated lemon rind
(1 teaspoon vanilla)
Place 1/2 the apples in the dish. Cover
the layer with 1/2 the sugar mixture.
Sprinkle them with:
1 tablespoon lemon juice

Add:
2 tablespoons water
Cover the apples with 1/3 the crumb
mixture and:
(1/4 cup raisins or currants)
Add the remaining apples and sprinkle
them as before with the sugar mixture
and:
(1 tablespoon lemon juice)
(2 tablespoons water)
(1/4 cup raisins or currants)
Place the last 1/3 of the crumb mixture
on top. Cover the dish and bake the
pudding in a moderate oven 350° for
about 40 minutes, until the apples are
nearly tender. Remove the cover, increase the heat to 400° and permit the
pudding to brown for about 15 minutes. Serve it hot with:
Hard Sauce, page 753, or cream,
or Lemon Sauce, page 757

APRICOT BETTY
Follow the preceding rule for:
Brown Betty
Use only:
2 tablespoons sugar
Substitute for the apples:
1 1/2 cups stewed, drained, sweetened
apricots
Substitute for the lemon juice and
water:
3/4 cup apricot juice

PANCAKE AND WAFFLE DESSERTS
Serve:
Pancakes or waffles
spread with:
Thick sour cream
Strawberry or other preserves

WAFFLES WITH CRUSHED FRUIT
Serve:
Waffles, page 556
with:
Crushed sweetened strawberries,
raspberries or other fruit, and
cream

MINCEMEAT WITH COOKIES OR PASTRY ROUNDS
6 Servings
Bake:
Sugar Cookies, page 669, or
pie crust cut into rounds
Heat:
2 cups mincemeat
Add:

2 tablespoons grated orange rind

Heap the mincemeat on an oven-proof plate. Surround it with cookies. Pour over the mincemeat:

  ⅓ cup brandy or rum

Ignite at table.

BAKED FIG PUDDING
14 Servings

Beat until soft:

  ½ cup butter

Add and beat until fluffy:

  2 eggs
  1 cup molasses

Add:

  2 cups finely chopped figs
  ½ teaspoon grated lemon rind
  1 cup sour milk
  (½ cup broken black walnut meats)

Sift before measuring:

  2½ cups all-purpose flour

Resift with:

  ½ teaspoon soda
  2 teaspoons any baking powder
  1 teaspoon salt
  1 teaspoon cinnamon
  ½ teaspoon nutmeg

One teaspoonful ginger may be substituted for the cinnamon and nutmeg. Stir the sifted ingredients into the pudding mixture.

Bake the pudding in a greased 9 inch tube pan in a slow oven 325° for about 1 hour. Serve it hot with:

  Brown Sugar Hard Sauce, page 754, or Rich Pudding Sauce, page 756, or Hot Sherry Sauce, page 760

BAKED DATE RING OR CHRISTMAS WREATH
6 Servings

You may bake this in a ring mold. When cold unmold it onto a platter, cover it well with whipped cream and stud it with maraschino cherries. Surround it with holly leaves. Very effective, but it tastes just as good baked in a shallow pan, cut into squares and served with Rich Pudding Sauce, page 756.

Prepare:

  1 cup stoned minced dates
  1 cup chopped nut meats

Combine these ingredients with:

  ½ cup white or brown sugar
  1 tablespoon flour
  1 teaspoon any baking powder
  2 beaten egg yolks
  1 teaspoon vanilla

Fold in:

  2 stiffly beaten egg whites
  ⅛ teaspoon salt

Bake the pudding in a well-greased 9 inch ring mold in a moderate oven 350° for about ½ hour. You may sprinkle over the pudding while hot ¼ cupful Madeira or sherry or 3 tablespoonfuls brandy or rum. Permit it to cool in the pan.

Whip until stiff:

  1 cup heavy cream

Fold in:

  2 tablespoons powdered sugar
  1 teaspoon vanilla

Garnish the ring as suggested above.

BAKED PLUM PUDDING
10 Servings

Sift:

  1 cup sugar

Beat until soft:

  ½ cup butter

Add the sugar gradually. Blend these ingredients until they are creamy. Beat in one at a time:

  6 eggs

Combine:

  1 cup raisins, currants and pecans

Sprinkle them lightly with:

  Flour

Add these ingredients to the butter mixture. Combine:

  2 cups bread crumbs
  2 teaspoons cinnamon
  ½ teaspoon cloves
  ½ teaspoon allspice

Stir these ingredients into the butter mixture. Bake the pudding in a greased pan or baking dish in a moderate oven 375° for about ½ hour. Serve it with:

  Hard Sauce, page 753, Lemon Sauce, page 757, or Hot Wine Sauce, page 760

COTTAGE PUDDING
6 Servings

Jane Austen would probably have pronounced this pudding only "moderately genteel" but it persists as a favorite that "grandmother used to make."

Sift:

  ½ cup sugar

Beat until soft:

  ¼ cup butter

Add the sugar gradually. Blend these ingredients until they are creamy. Beat in:

  1 egg
  1 teaspoon vanilla

Sift before measuring:

1½ cups all-purpose flour
Resift with:
  **2 teaspoons tartrate or phosphate
  baking powder or 1½ teaspoons
  combination type (see Baking
  Powder, page 501)
  ¼ teaspoon salt**
Add the sifted ingredients to the batter
in 3 parts alternately with thirds of:
  ½ cup milk
Beat the batter until it is smooth after
each addition. Pour it into a greased
8 x 8 inch pan. Bake the pudding in a
hot oven 400° for about 25 minutes.
Serve it cut into squares with:
  **Crushed fruit, stewed fruit,
  Fluffy Orange Sauce, page 757,
  Raisin Sauce, page 758, Coffee
  Sauce, page 755, Wine Custard,
  page 712, or Hot Brown Sugar
  Sauce, page 755**
A friend writes: "Here is something
we like and maybe it is new to you.
When making Cottage Pudding I put
peaches or plums after they have been
halved on top of the unbaked dough,
facing up. I then put a teaspoonful of
sugar in the hollow of the fruit and
push the fruit gently down into the
dough. The dough will rise around it
and the sugar will melt in the hollows,
making a sirup to sweeten it."

CHOCOLATE FEATHER PUDDING
8 Servings
This might be placed among the
steamed puddings, but steamed puddings are troublesome and it might be
overlooked in those surroundings. It is
an inexpensive and delightful dessert.
Sift:
  1 cup sugar
Beat until light:
  1 egg
Stir the sugar in gradually. When
these ingredients are well blended stir
in:
  **1 cup milk
  1 tablespoon melted butter
  1½ oz. melted chocolate**
Sift:
  1½ cups all-purpose flour
Resift with:
  **¼ teaspoon salt
  2 teaspoons tartrate or phosphate
  baking powder or 1½ teaspoons
  combination type (see Baking
  Powder, page 501)**
Stir these ingredients into the egg
mixture. Add:

  ½ teaspoon vanilla
Place the batter in well-greased deep
custard cups. Fill them ⅔ full. Cover
them with heavy waxed paper held in
place with rubber bands or with aluminum foil. Steam the pudding by
setting it in a pan of hot water in a
moderate oven 350° for about ½ hour,
or by placing the pan of hot water
over a low flame. Serve the pudding
at once with:
  **Vanilla Sauce, page 758, flavored
  with rum**

CHOCOLATE CAKE PUDDING
Hard to classify, neither fish, fowl nor
good red herring, but a mighty fine
dessert by any name.
Sift before measuring:
  1¼ cups cake flour
Resift 3 times with:
  **¾ cup sugar
  2 teaspoons tartrate or phosphate
  baking powder or 1½ teaspoons
  combination type (see Baking
  Powder, page 501)
  ¼ teaspoon salt**
Melt over hot water:
  **2 tablespoons butter
  1 square chocolate: 1 oz.**
Remove from heat. Stir in:
  **½ cup milk
  1 beaten egg
  1 teaspoon vanilla**
Stir the liquid ingredients all at once
into the sifted ingredients. Stir in:
  ½ cup coarsely chopped nut meats
Place the batter in a well-greased
round 8 inch oven-proof dish about 1
inch deep.
Prepare a topping by combining:
  **2 tablespoons cocoa
  ½ cup firmly packed brown sugar
  ½ cup granulated sugar**
Sprinkle this over the batter. Pour
over it:
  1 cup boiling water
Bake the cake (pudding?) at once in a
moderate oven 350° from 45 to 50
minutes. Serve warm with:
  Whipped cream or ice cream

SNOWBALLS
About 12 Cakes
Sift:
  ½ cup sugar
Beat until soft:
  ¼ cup butter
Add the sugar gradually. Blend these
ingredients until they are light and
creamy. Add:

1 teaspoon vanilla
Sift before measuring:
    1 cup cake flour
Resift twice with:
    1½ teaspoons tartrate or phosphate
    baking powder or 1 teaspoon
    combination type (see Baking
    Powder, page 501)
Add the sifted ingredients to the butter mixture in 3 parts alternately with thirds of:
    ¼ cup milk
Beat the batter until it is smooth after each addition. Whip until stiff but not dry:
    3 egg whites
    ⅛ teaspoon salt
Fold them lightly into the batter. Grease small molds or cups. Dust them with:
    Flour
Pour the batter into them. Fill them ⅔ full. Cover the tops with heavy waxed paper or aluminum foil. Place the molds in a pan of hot water. Steam the snowballs in a moderate oven 350° for about 35 minutes. Invert them. Sprinkle them with:
    Powdered sugar
Garnish them with:
    Unhulled strawberries
Serve them with:
    Strawberry Hard Sauce, page
    754
If strawberries are not available, substitute raspberries, raspberry juice, loganberry juice, etc. Or serve the snowballs with:
    Rum Sauce, page 760, or Butter
    Sauce I or II, page 756
The snowballs may be rolled in:
    Grated coconut

SWEET POTATO PUDDING
Method I. 6 Servings
This Southern dish has many variations. Raisins, currants, nut meats and shaved citron are frequently added and molasses is substituted for part of the sugar.
Pare, then grate:
    Sweet potatoes
There should be 2 cupfuls. Beat until light:
    2 eggs
Beat in gradually:
    1 cup white or brown sugar
Stir in:
    1 cup rich milk
    ¼ cup melted butter
    ½ teaspoon lemon rind and 1

tablespoon lemon juice or ½
    teaspoon cinnamon
    ¼ teaspoon ginger
    ¼ teaspoon cloves
    ½ teaspoon salt
Place the pudding in a greased baking dish. Bake it in a moderate oven 350° for about ½ hour. Stir it with a spoon. Bake it 15 minutes longer. Serve it with:
    Tart jam and cream

Method II. 8 Servings
Combine and beat well:
    2 cups cooked mashed sweet
    potatoes
    1 cup sugar
    ½ cup melted butter
    6 beaten egg yolks
    1½ teaspoons grated lemon rind
    1 cup orange juice
    ¼ teaspoon nutmeg or
    2 tablespoons rum
Fold in:
    2 stiffly beaten egg whites
Bake the pudding in a greased baking dish in a moderate oven 350° for about 1 hour. The top may be sprinkled before baking with:
    Sliced citron
    Broken nut meats
Or, after the pudding is baked and cooled, it may be topped with a Meringue, page 578, made with the remaining egg whites. Bake it in a moderate oven 325° for 15 minutes.

PERSIMMON PUDDING
8 Servings
Put through a colander:
    1 quart persimmons
There should be about 2 cupfuls pulp.
Beat in:
    3 eggs
    1¼ cups sugar
    1½ cups all-purpose flour
    1 teaspoon any baking powder
    1 teaspoon soda
    ½ teaspoon salt
    ½ cup melted butter
    2½ cups rich milk
    2 teaspoons cinnamon
    1 teaspoon ginger
    ½ teaspoon freshly grated nutmeg
One cupful raisins or nut meats may be added to the batter.
Bake the pudding in a greased 9 x 9 inch baking dish in a moderate oven 325° until it is firm, about 1 hour.
Serve it with:
    Cream or hard sauce

Sweet Soufflés and Omelets

It may be helpful to read the rules given on page 217 for combining and baking soufflés. The cook who has mastered the very simple art of making soufflés has added an exceedingly convenient and palatable dish to her list of economical desserts.

A soufflé is usually baked in a moderate oven until firm, but a good result may be obtained by steaming it in a greased 2 quart double boiler over, not in, boiling water for about 45 minutes. Invert the soufflé onto a plate.

CHOCOLATE SOUFFLÉ
4 Servings
Heat but do not boil:
   1 cup milk
   1 oz. chocolate cut in pieces
Stir these ingredients over a low flame until the chocolate is melted. In a separate saucepan melt:
   2 tablespoons butter
Stir in until blended:
   1 tablespoon all-purpose flour
Stir in the hot milk mixture. When the sauce is smooth, stir in until dissolved:
   ⅓ cup sugar
Beat until light:
   3 egg yolks
Beat part of the sauce into them, then add them to the liquid in the pot and stir the custard over a very low flame to permit the yolks to thicken slightly. Cool the custard well. Add:
   1 teaspoon vanilla
Whip until stiff:
   3 egg whites
   ⅛ teaspoon salt
Fold them lightly into the chocolate mixture. Bake the soufflé in a 7 inch baking dish set in a pan of hot water in a moderate oven 325° for about 30 minutes, or until it is firm. Serve it at once with:
   Cream, Vanilla Sauce, page 758, Foamy Sauce, page 754, or Rich Pudding Sauce, page 756

LEMON SOUFFLÉ
4 Servings
Sift:
   ¾ cup sugar
Beat until very light:
   5 egg yolks
Add the sugar gradually. Beat constantly until the eggs are creamy. Add:
   1 teaspoon grated lemon rind
   4 tablespoons lemon juice
   (½ cup chopped nut meats)
Whip until stiff:
   5 egg whites
   ⅛ teaspoon salt

Fold them lightly into the yolk mixture. Bake the soufflé in a 9 inch baking dish set in a pan of hot water in a moderate oven 325° for about 50 minutes, or until it is firm. Serve it at once with:
   Cream

Lemon Bread Pudding, page 721.
Rum Soufflé II, page 730.

PINEAPPLE SOUFFLÉ
4 Servings
This soufflé may be made in advance. It is equally good hot or very cold. As it calls for bread crumbs instead of flour, it is not apt to shrink or fall. Cream until light:
   ½ cup butter
   ¾ cup sugar
Beat in:
   5 egg yolks
   4 tablespoons dry bread crumbs
   1 cup crushed drained pineapple
   1 tablespoon lemon juice
Whip until stiff, then fold in:
   3 egg whites
   ⅛ teaspoon salt
Place the soufflé in a baking dish. Cover it with a Meringue, page 578, made with:
   2 egg whites
   ⅛ teaspoon salt
   4 tablespoons sugar
   ½ teaspoon vanilla
Bake it set in a pan of hot water in a moderate oven 325° for about 30 minutes. Serve it with:
   Cream or whipped cream

PINEAPPLE MACAROON SOUFFLÉ
4 Servings
Melt over a low fire:
   3 tablespoons butter
Stir in:
   3 tablespoons flour
When blended stir in:
   1 cup crushed pineapple

When thick and smooth stir in:
   ⅔ cup dry crushed macaroons
   3 egg yolks
Permit the yolks to thicken slightly.
Cool the mixture. Beat until stiff:
   3 egg whites
   ⅛ teaspoon salt
Beat in gradually:
   2 tablespoons sugar
   ½ teaspoon vanilla
Fold this into the soufflé mixture.
Bake it in a 7 inch baking dish in a
moderate oven 325° for about 30
minutes.

VANILLA SOUFFLÉ OR SPONGE PUDDING
8 Servings

For a smaller serving use 2 eggs and
½ the other ingredients.
Sift before measuring:
   ½ cup all-purpose flour
Resift with:
   ¼ cup sugar
Stir in:
   ½ cup cold milk
Boil:
   2 cups milk
Stir in the flour mixture with a wire
whisk. Cook and stir these ingredients
over a low flame until they thicken.
Remove them from the fire. Stir in:
   ¼ cup butter
   5 beaten egg yolks
You may add:
   ¾ cup chopped nut meats
Cool the batter. Add:
   1 teaspoon vanilla
Whip until stiff:
   5 egg whites
   ¼ teaspoon salt
Fold them lightly into the batter. Bake
the pudding in a 9 inch baking dish in
a moderate oven 325° for about 1 hour.
Serve it with:
   Fluffy Strawberry Sauce, page
   758, Maple Sauce, page 755,
   Rum Sauce II, page 760, or fruit
   juice
For a change in flavor use in place of
the sugar:
   ¼ cup ginger sirup
Use in place of the vanilla:
   ¼ cup chopped preserved or
   candied ginger
Serve the pudding with:
   Cream

MOCHA SOUFFLÉ
4 Servings
Melt:

3 tablespoons butter
Stir in until blended:
   3 tablespoons flour
Stir in slowly:
   ⅓ cup top milk or cream
   ¾ cup strong coffee
Cook the sauce until it is thick.
Beat until creamy:
   4 egg yolks
   ½ cup sugar
Add the sauce slowly to these ingredients. Beat them until they are blended.
Place them over a low fire. Stir them
for 1 minute to permit the yolks to
thicken slightly. Cool them. Add:
   ¾ teaspoon vanilla
Whip until stiff:
   5 egg whites
   ¼ teaspoon salt
Fold them lightly into the sauce.
Bake the soufflé in a 7 inch baking dish
in a moderate oven 325° for about 35
minutes. Serve it at once with:
   Cream or whipped cream

FRESH PEACH SOUFFLÉ
5 Servings
Prepare by peeling and mashing ripe
peaches:
   1 cup peach pulp
Or use an equal amount of canned
puréed baby food peaches or other
raw or canned fruit pulp. Add:
   1½ tablespoons lemon juice
   ¼ cup sugar
   4 beaten egg yolks
   ⅛ teaspoon salt
   (1 tablespoon grated orange rind)
Fold in:
   4 stiffly beaten egg whites
Place the mixture in a 7 inch oven-
proof dish. Bake it in a moderate oven
325° for about 45 minutes. Serve it
hot with:
   Cream

PRUNE SOUFFLÉ OR WHIP
4 to 6 Servings
Drain and pit:
   Stewed Prunes, page 450:
   approximately 1 lb. dried prunes
Put them through a ricer. There
should be 1 cupful thick prune pulp.
Whip until foamy:
   5 egg whites
   ⅛ teaspoon salt
Add:
   ¼ teaspoon cream of tartar
Or substitute ¼ teaspoonful lemon
juice for the cream of tartar, adding it
to the prune pulp. Whip the eggs until

they are stiff. If the prunes are unsweetened, fold in:

> ½ cup sugar

Fold in the prune pulp and:

> (½ cup broken nut meats)
> (1 teaspoon grated lemon rind)

Place the soufflé in a 9 inch baking
dish. Set it in a pan of hot water. Bake
it in a slow oven 275° for about 1 hour,
or until it is firm. Serve it hot or cold,
preferably the former, with:

> Cream, Custard Sauce, page
> 754, or Rich Pudding Sauce,
> page 756

This and similar whips may be made
with an electric mixer. Add the sugar
to the prunes. Beat the egg whites at
high speed for about 3 minutes. Add
the other ingredients gradually. Beat
the mixture until it is fluffy, for about
5 minutes.

APRICOT SOUFFLÉ OR WHIP

Follow the preceding rule for:

> Prune Soufflé

Substitute for the prune pulp:

> 1 cup apricot pulp, see Stewed
> Apricots, page 450

Applesauce Pudding, page 722.
This is a form of soufflé that is delicious served very cold with cream.

BANANA SOUFFLÉ OR WHIP

6 Servings

A good, very simple California dish.
Put through a colander or ricer:

> 6 medium-sized peeled bananas

Beat into the pulp:

> 6 tablespoons powdered sugar
> 1 tablespoon lemon juice
> A little yellow or red coloring
> (½ teaspoon vanilla)
> (½ cup broken nut meats)

Whip until stiff:

> 4 egg whites
> ⅛ teaspoon salt

Fold them lightly into the banana
mixture. Place these ingredients in a
baking dish. Bake the soufflé in a
moderate oven 325° for about 30 minutes. Serve it hot or cold with:

> Cream or Custard Sauce, page
> 754

CHESTNUT SOUFFLÉ WITH CARAMEL SAUCE

4 Servings

Combine:

> ¾ cup sugar

> ¼ teaspoon cinnamon
> ⅛ teaspoon freshly ground nutmeg
> ½ teaspoon vanilla
> 3 egg yolks

Beat these ingredients until they are
well creamed. Add:

> ½ lb. raw shelled chestnuts,
> ground or crushed

Stir these ingredients vigorously until
they are frothy. Whip until stiff:

> 3 egg whites
> ⅛ teaspoon salt

Fold them into the chestnut mixture.
Bake the soufflé in a buttered dish in a
moderate oven 325° for about 45 minutes. Invert the soufflé onto a platter.
Serve it with:

> Caramel Sauce, page 755, or
> whipped cream

HAZELNUT SOUFFLÉ

Beat until light:

> 3 egg yolks

Beat in gradually:

> 3 tablespoons sugar
> 3 tablespoons flour
> ⅛ teaspoon salt

Put through a nut grinder:

> ¾ cup hazelnuts

Pour over them and heat to just below
the boiling point:

> 1 cup milk

Stir in the egg mixture. Stir and cook
these ingredients over low heat to
permit the yolks to thicken slightly.
Stir in:

> 3 tablespoons butter

Cool the custard. Beat in:

> ½ teaspoon vanilla or 1 tablespoon
> rum

Beat until stiff:

> 3 egg whites

Fold them into the custard. Bake the
soufflé in a buttered mold in a moderate oven 325° for about 30 minutes.
Serve it hot or cold with:

> 1 cup heavy cream, whipped

flavored with:

> Caramel or coffee

MACAROON SOUFFLÉ

4 Servings

Scald:

> 1 cup milk

Pour it slowly over:

> 12 macaroons

Beat and add:

> 4 egg yolks

Cook these ingredients in a double
boiler until they are thick. Cool them.
Add:

½ teaspoon vanilla or
1 tablespoon rum
Whip until stiff:
4 egg whites
⅛ teaspoon salt
Fold them lightly into the macaroon
mixture. Place the pudding in an 8
inch buttered baking dish. Set it in a
pan of hot water. Bake it in a moderate oven 325° for about 35 minutes.
Serve it hot from the baking dish with:
Cream
or invert the contents of the dish onto
a plate and garnish the soufflé with:
Candied Kumquats, page 797
Serve it with:
Caramel Sauce, page 755

ENGLISH ALMOND SOUFFLÉ
8 Servings
Sift:
⅔ cup sugar
Beat until very light:
8 egg yolks
Add the sugar gradually. Beat constantly until the yolks are creamy.
Fold in:
2 teaspoons grated lemon rind or
1 teaspoon vanilla
½ lb. blanched ground almonds
Whip until stiff:
8 egg whites
¼ teaspoon salt
Fold them lightly into the yolk mixture. Place the batter in a greased
baking dish. Set it in a pan of hot
water. Bake it in a moderate oven 325°
until it is firm, about 45 minutes. Serve
it hot or cold with the following sauce:
Stir with a wire whisk in a double
boiler until thick and frothy:
½ cup sugar
2 tablespoons grated lemon rind
2 teaspoons lemon juice
½ cup water or ½ cup wine
3 beaten eggs

POSIE'S WALNUT SOUFFLÉ
8 Servings
Follow the above rule for:
English Almond Soufflé
Substitute for the almonds:
¾ cup ground walnuts
Posie uses the vanilla in place of the
lemon rind and substitutes:
1¼ cups confectioners' sugar
for the granulated sugar. She serves
the soufflé with:
Fruit sauce and/or whipped
cream flavored with rum

OMELET SOUFFLÉ OR
OMELETTE AUX CONFITURES
2 Servings
Beat until light:
2 egg yolks
Beat in gradually:
¼ cup confectioners' sugar
Add:
½ teaspoon vanilla or a grating of
orange or lemon rind
Whip until stiff:
4 egg whites
⅛ teaspoon salt
Fold them lightly into the yolk mixture. Melt in a skillet:
1½ teaspoons butter
Pour in the omelet mixture. Cook it
over a slow fire. Cover it with a lid. As
it cooks slash across it several times
with a knife to permit the heat to
penetrate the slight crust on the bottom. When done fold over the omelet,
which should be soft on the inside.
Sprinkle it with:
Confectioners' sugar
Serve it with:
Preserves or jelly
Before folding the omelet it may be
spread with:
Applesauce, prune or apricot
pulp, drained canned fruit,
sugared berries

RUM SOUFFLÉ OR RUM
OMELET
You may use bourbon in this and in
the following omelet.
Prepare the preceding:
Omelet Soufflé
Add to the yolk mixture:
1 tablespoon rum
Omit the preserves.
The rum may be omitted and the
soufflé may be served with:
Caramel Sirup, page 754,
flavored with rum

RUM SOUFFLÉ OR BAKED
RUM OMELET
4 Servings
Beat until very light:
4 egg yolks
¼ cup sugar
Add:
½ teaspoon vanilla
Whip until stiff:
4 egg whites
⅛ teaspoon salt
Fold them lightly into the yolk mixture. Place these ingredients in a flat
baking dish. The soufflé should be

about 1 inch high. Bake it in a moderate oven 325° until it is firm, about 25 minutes.
Cover it with:
    ¼ cup rum

Ignite the rum at table and let it burn down. This may be served with:
    Crushed sweetened berries

Sweet Omelet, page 85.

Steamed Puddings

Rule for Steaming Puddings

Steam the pudding mixture in a pudding mold, or tin cans with tightly fitting lids like baking powder tins. Grease the molds well, then sprinkle them with sugar. Fill them only ⅔ full. Place the mold on a trivet in a steamer over 1 inch of boiling water or place it on a trivet in a heavy kettle over 1 inch of boiling water. Cover the steamer or kettle closely. Use high heat at first, then as the steam begins to escape use low heat for the rest of the cooking. True steam puddings need complete circulation of steam, so do not expect uniform results if you use a greased double boiler or covered custard cups as suggested as alternatives in some of the recipes.

STEAMED BROWN PUDDING
14 Servings
Combine and blend well:
    1 cup light brown sugar
    ½ cup shortening
Add:
    1 cup milk
    1 cup molasses
    1 cup dry bread crumbs
    2 beaten eggs
    2 cups chopped seeded raisins
Sift before measuring:
    2 cups all-purpose flour
Resift with:
    2 teaspoons any baking powder
    ½ teaspoon soda
    1 teaspoon cinnamon
    ½ teaspoon ginger
    ½ teaspoon cloves
    ¼ teaspoon grated nutmeg
Add the sifted ingredients to the molasses mixture. Pour the batter into a well-greased pudding mold. Steam the pudding for 1 hour, see Rule for Steaming Puddings above. Serve it hot with:
    Hard Sauce, page 753, or
    Foamy Sauce, page 754

STEAMED MOLASSES PUDDING
4 Servings
Cream well:
    ¼ cup sugar
    ¼ cup butter
Beat in:
    1 beaten egg
Measure:
    1 cup sifted all-purpose flour
Resift with·

    ½ teaspoon soda
    ⅛ teaspoon salt
    ½ teaspoon cinnamon or freshly grated nutmeg
Combine and beat:
    ¼ cup molasses
    ¼ cup sour milk
Stir the sifted ingredients into the butter mixture in about 3 parts alternately with the liquid ingredients. Beat the batter until smooth after each addition. Partly fill a greased 1 pound coffee tin, or other mold, not more than ⅔ full of batter. Cover it closely. Steam the pudding for 2 hours, see Rule for Steaming Puddings above. Serve it hot with:
    Hard Sauce, page 753, or
    whipped cream

STEAMED FIG PUDDING
12 Servings
A wonderful winter wind-up to a good meal. All these steamed puddings make me wish that I had never heard of carbohydrates.
Beat until soft:
    1 cup suet: ½ lb.
Add gradually:
    1 cup sugar
When these ingredients are well blended beat in:
    3 egg yolks
Stir in:
    1 cup milk
    3 tablespoons brandy
Put through a grinder and add:
    1 lb. figs
Grate and add:
    2 teaspoons grated orange rind
    1 nutmeg

Ground nutmeg may be substituted, but it is done at your peril.
Combine and add:

1½ cups dry bread crumbs
2 teaspoons any baking powder

Whip until stiff, then fold in:

3 egg whites
⅛ teaspoon salt

Pour the ingredients into a greased mold. Steam the pudding for 4 hours, see Rule for Steaming Puddings, page 731. Serve the pudding with:

Fluffy Orange Sauce, page 757, or Hot Wine Sauce, page 760

Flavor the sauce with:

2 teaspoons or more brandy

STEAMED DATE PUDDING
8 Servings

Not so rich as the preceding fig pudding but equally good.
Sift:

1 cup brown sugar

Beat until soft:

¼ cup butter

Add the sugar gradually. Blend these ingredients until they are creamy. Beat in:

1 egg
½ teaspoon vanilla

Sift before measuring:

1¼ cups all-purpose flour

Resift with:

4 teaspoons tartrate or phosphate baking powder or 2⅔ teaspoons combination type (see Baking Powder, page 501)
½ teaspoon salt

Add the sifted ingredients to the butter mixture in 3 parts alternately with thirds of:

1 cup milk

Beat the batter until it is smooth after each addition. Fold in:

1 cup chopped dates
1 cup broken nut meats

Pour the batter into a greased pudding mold. Cover it. Steam it for 2 hours, see Rule for Steaming Puddings, page 731. Serve the pudding hot with:

Foamy Sauce, page 754, or Rich Pudding Sauce, page 756

STEAMED CHOCOLATE PUDDING
Method I. 4 Servings

Melt, then cool:

2 oz. chocolate

Sift:

½ cup sugar

Beat until light:

1 egg

Add the sugar gradually. Beat these ingredients until they are creamy. Add the melted chocolate. Melt, cool and add:

1 tablespoon butter

Beat in:

1 tablespoon jelly or 1 teaspoon vanilla

Sift:

1 cup all-purpose flour

Resift with:

1 teaspoon any baking powder
⅛ teaspoon salt

Add the sifted ingredients in 3 parts to the egg mixture alternately with thirds of:

½ cup milk

Beat the batter until it is smooth after each addition. Pour it into a greased pudding mold. Cover it closely. Steam it for 1 hour, see Rule for Steaming Puddings, page 731. Serve the pudding hot with:

Cream
Custard Sauce, page 754,
Nut Sauce, page 758, or
Almond Sauce, page 758

Method II. 6 Servings

Beat until light:

6 egg yolks

Beat in gradually:

1 cup sugar

Stir in:

¾ cup grated chocolate
2 tablespoons finely crushed crackers or toasted bread crumbs
1 teaspoon any baking powder
1 teaspoon vanilla
½ teaspoon cinnamon
(½ cup grated nut meats)

Beat until stiff:

6 egg whites
¼ teaspoon salt

Fold them lightly into the batter. Place it in a greased pudding mold. Steam the pudding for 1½ hours, see Rule for Steaming Puddings, page 731. Serve it with:

Hard sauce or cream

Chocolate Feather Pudding, page 725.

STEAMED CARAMEL PUDDING
6 Servings

This is a delicious company pudding.
Melt in a heavy skillet:

⅓ cup sugar

When it is light brown stir in very slowly:

¾ cup hot milk

Cool this sirup. Beat until soft:

2 tablespoons butter

Beat in one at a time:

5 egg yolks

Add the sirup and:

1 teaspoon vanilla
1½ tablespoons all-purpose flour
1 cup ground unblanched almonds

Beat the batter until it is smooth. Place on a platter and whip until stiff:

5 egg whites
⅛ teaspoon salt

Fold them lightly into the batter. Pour it into a greased pudding mold sprinkled with:

Sugar

Cover it closely. Steam it for 1 hour, see Rule for Steaming Puddings, page 731. Serve the pudding hot with:

Whipped cream or
Caramel Sirup, page 754

STEAMED GINGER PUDDING
10 Servings

Beat:

1 egg

Add and beat well:

1 cup molasses
½ cup melted butter
1 cup chopped figs, dates or raisins

Sift before measuring:

2½ cups all-purpose flour

Resift with:

1 tablespoon ginger
1 teaspoon soda

Add the sifted ingredients to the egg mixture. Beat them until they are well blended. Stir in:

1 cup hot water

Place the pudding in a greased mold or in greased shallow cups. Cover them with heavy waxed paper or aluminum foil. Place the pudding in a pan of hot water in a moderate oven 375° for about ½ hour. Serve it hot with:

Lemon Sauce, page 757, or
Vanilla Sauce, page 758

STEAMED SUET PUDDING
8 Servings

Chop until fine:

1 cup suet: ½ lb.

Add:

2 cups dry bread crumbs
1 cup raisins

½ cup chopped citron or nut meats
1 cup sugar or 1½ cups brown sugar
½ cup milk
1 beaten egg
½ teaspoon soda
1 teaspoon cinnamon
½ teaspoon cloves
½ teaspoon allspice
½ teaspoon salt

Pour the batter into a greased pudding mold. Cover it closely. Steam it for 2 hours, see Rule for Steaming Puddings, page 731. Serve it hot with:

Whipped cream or
Wine Sauce, page 760

STEAMED APPLE SUET PUDDING

This is a fine variation of the above Suet Pudding.

Substitute closely packed brown sugar for white sugar. Add 5 medium-sized tart apples, peeled, cored and finely sliced, and substitute black walnuts for the citron. When about to serve soak the pudding with ⅓ cupful rum. Ignite the rum at the table. Serve it with:

Rich Pudding Sauce, page 656, flavored with vanilla

STEAMED APPLE PUDDING
6 Servings

Cream until fluffy:

¼ cup butter
½ cup brown sugar

Beat in:

1 egg
¼ cup molasses
1 tablespoon orange rind

Measure:

1½ cups sifted all-purpose flour

Resift with:

½ teaspoon soda
1 teaspoon any baking powder
1 teaspoon ginger
1 teaspoon cinnamon

Add these ingredients to the butter mixture alternately with:

½ cup sour milk

Stir in:

1 cup chopped apples

Place the pudding in a greased mold. Steam it for 1½ hours, see Rule for Steaming Puddings, page 731. Serve it with:

Lemon Sauce, page 757

STEAMED PLUM PUDDING
24 Servings
Sift:
 1 cup all-purpose flour
Prepare and dredge lightly with part
of the flour:
 1 lb. chopped suet: 2 cups
 1 lb. seeded raisins
 1 lb. washed dried currants
 ½ lb. chopped citron
Resift the remaining flour with:
 1 grated nutmeg
 1 tablespoon cinnamon
 ½ tablespoon mace
 1 teaspoon salt
 6 tablespoons sugar or
 ½ cup brown sugar
Combine the dredged and the sifted
ingredients. Add:
 7 egg yolks
 4 tablespoons cream
 ½ cup brandy or sherry
 3 cups grated bread crumbs
Place on a platter and whip until stiff:
 7 egg whites
 ⅛ teaspoon salt

Fold them lightly into the raisin mixture. Pour the batter into a greased
pudding mold. Cover it closely. Steam
the pudding for 6 hours, see Rule for
Steaming Puddings, page 731. Serve it
with:

Sauce
Cook and stir in a double boiler until
thick:
 1 cup sugar
 ½ cup butter
 2 eggs
 ⅛ teaspoon salt
 5 tablespoons heavy wine: tokay,
  muscatel, Madeira, etc.
Or serve it with:
 Hot Sherry or Rum Sauce
 page 760, or Wine Sauce,
 page 760
You may substitute ½ cupful orange
juice and 2 tablespoonfuls grated orange rind for the brandy.

Baked Plum Pudding, page 724.

Gelatine Puddings

LEMON JELLY
4 Servings
Soak:
 4 teaspoons gelatine
in:
 ¼ cup cold water
Dissolve it in:
 2 cups boiling water
Add and stir until dissolved:
 ¾ cup sugar
 ¼ teaspoon salt
Add:
 ½ cup lemon juice
 (1 teaspoon grated lemon rind)
Pour the jelly into a wet mold. Chill
it until it is firm. Serve it with:
 Cream or Custard Sauce,
 page 754

ORANGE JELLY
4 Servings
Soak:
 1½ tablespoons gelatine
in:
 ¼ cup cold water
Dissolve it in:
 ½ cup boiling water
Add and stir until dissolved:
 ½ cup sugar
 ¼ teaspoon salt

Add:
 6 tablespoons lemon juice
 1½ cups orange juice
 (1½ teaspoons grated orange rind)
Pour the jelly into a wet mold. Chill
until it is firm. Unmold it and serve
it with:
 Cream or Custard Sauce,
 page 754

GRAPEFRUIT JELLY
5 Servings If No Solid Ingredients
Are Added
Soak:
 1 tablespoon gelatine
in:
 ¼ cup cold water
Stir and boil for 3 minutes:
 ½ cup water
 ½ cup sugar
Dissolve the soaked gelatine in the
hot sirup. Cool it. Combine it with:
 ¾ cup grapefruit juice
 ¼ cup orange juice
 ¼ cup lemon juice
 ⅛ teaspoon salt
Chill the jelly until it is about to set.
One or 2 cupfuls solid ingredients:
grapefruit, apples, nut meats, celery,
peppers, olives, etc., may be added at
this time. Place the jelly in a wet mold.

Chill it until it is firm. Unmold it. If it is to be a salad serve it with:

Cream Mayonnaise, page 496

If it is to be a dessert serve it with:

Cream

PINEAPPLE JELLY
8 Servings
Soak:

2 tablespoons gelatine

in:

1 cup cold water

Dissolve it in:

1½ cups boiling pineapple juice

Be sure to note that fresh pineapple must be boiled before being added to any gelatine. Add:

1 cup boiling water

Add and stir until dissolved:

¾ cup sugar

⅛ teaspoon salt

Chill the gelatine until it is about to set. It will fall in sheets from a spoon. Add the contents of:

1 No. 2 can shredded drained pineapple

3 tablespoons lemon juice

Pour the jelly into a wet mold. Chill it until it is firm, unmold it and serve it with:

Cream or
Custard Sauce, page 754, etc.

Pineapple Sponge, page 737; Pineapple Soufflé, page 727.

FRUIT MOLDED INTO LEMON OR ORANGE JELLY
Prepare by one of the preceding rules:

Lemon or Orange Jelly

When it is nearly set it will fall in sheets from a spoon. Combine it with well-drained:

Cooked or raw fruit

Add to it, if desired:

Nut meats
Marshmallows cut into quarters

Do not use more than 3 cupfuls of solids in all.
Fresh pineapple must be boiled before it is added to any gelatine mixture.

FRUIT GELATINE
12 Servings
This is good made in a ring mold. Fill the center with ice cream.
Stir:

The grated rind of 2 oranges
The grated rind of 2 lemons

into:

1 cup sugar

Stir in and boil for 1 minute:

1½ cups water or part fruit juice and water

Soak:

2 tablespoons gelatine

in:

½ cup cold water

Dissolve the gelatine in the hot sirup. Cool the mixture slightly. Add:

1 No. 2½ can riced apricots
2 riced bananas
Juice of 2 oranges
Juice of 2 lemons
⅛ teaspoon salt

Chill these ingredients until they are firm. Serve the gelatine with:

Cream or whipped cream

PRUNE JELLY
8 Servings
Cook by the rule on page 450, omitting the sugar:

1 lb. prunes

Drain them, reserving the juice. Replace the prune pits with:

Blanched toasted almonds or with walnuts

Dissolve:

2 tablespoons gelatine

in:

¼ cup cold water

Bring to a boil:

2 cups prune juice

Add and stir until dissolved:

1 cup sugar

Dissolve the gelatine in the hot juice. Remove from fire and add:

Juice of 3 lemons

Strain the juice and chill it until it is nearly set. It will fall in sheets from a spoon. Combine it with the prunes in a wet mold. Chill it until firm. Unmold and serve with:

Cream or whipped cream or
Boiled Custard, page 711

Berry Marshmallow Cream, page 744.

CHERRY NUT GELATINE
8 Servings
Combine and heat to the boiling point the contents of:

1 No. 2 can pie cherries

Add and stir until dissolved:

⅞ cup sugar

Drain the cherries, reserving the fruit and juice. Dissolve in the hot juice the contents of:

1 package lemon-flavored
gelatine: 3¼ oz.
Chill this mixture over cracked ice.
When it begins to thicken add the
cherries and:
3/4 cup broken nut meats
Chill the gelatine until it is firm. Serve
it with:
Cream or whipped cream

WINE JELLY
8 Servings
Soak:
2 tablespoons gelatine
in:
¼ cup cold water
Dissolve it in:
3/4 cup boiling water
These proportions of water, fruit juice
and wine may be varied. If the wine is
not strong, use less water to dissolve
the gelatine and increase the amount
of wine accordingly. This makes a soft
jelly of a very good consistency to
serve in sherbet glasses or from a
bowl. If a stiff jelly is desired for
molds, increase the gelatine to 3 tablespoonfuls.
Stir in until dissolved:
½ cup or more sugar
It is difficult to give an accurate sugar
measurement. One-half cupful is sufficient if both the oranges and the

wine are sweet. Taste the combined
ingredients and stir in additional sugar
if it is needed.
Cool these ingredients. Add:
1 3/4 cups orange juice
6 tablespoons lemon juice
1 cup well-flavored wine
If this mixture is not a good color add:
A little red coloring
Chill the jelly until it is firm. Serve it
with:
Cream, whipped cream or
Boiled Custard, page 711

COFFEE MARSHMALLOW JELLY
4 Servings
Place in a double boiler over boiling
water:
1 full lb. marshmallows
Pour over them and stir until they are
dissolved:
2 cups boiling coffee
Stir in:
1 cup nut meats
Place these ingredients in a wet mold.
Chill them until they are firm. Invert
the jelly onto a plate. Serve it with:
Cream or whipped cream

---

*Coffee Marshmallow Jelly with
Whipped Cream, page 744.*

Gelatine Fruit Whips and Sponge Puddings

FRUIT WHIPS
6 to 8 Servings
Oranges, raspberries, peaches, strawberries, apricots, prunes, etc., raw or
cooked, may be used alone or in combination. If fresh pineapple is added it
must be cooked before being added to
any gelatine mixture.
Stir:
1 teaspoon grated lemon rind
into:
1 scant cup sugar: 7/8 cup
Soak according to the juiciness of the
fruit:
2½ teaspoons to 1 tablespoon
gelatine
in:
¼ cup cold water
Dissolve it in:
¼ cup boiling water
Stir in the sugar until it is dissolved.
Add:
3 tablespoons lemon juice
1 cup crushed or riced fruit

If a single fruit is used, add:
1 teaspoon vanilla
Place the pan holding these ingredients in ice water. When they are
chilled whip them with an egg beater
until they are frothy. Whip until stiff:
4 egg whites
1/8 teaspoon salt
Whip these ingredients into the gelatine mixture until the jelly holds its
shape. Pour it into a wet mold. Chill
it thoroughly. Serve it with:
Cream or Boiled Custard,
page 711

CHERRY WHIP
6 Servings
Boil to the consistency of sirup:
1 cup sugar
1/3 cup water
Drop into it and cook until soft, for
about 3 minutes:
1 quart stoned cherries

Drain the cherries. Reserve the juice.
Soak:

1 tablespoon gelatine

in:

2 tablespoons cold water

Dissolve it in 1 cupful hot cherry juice.
Chill these ingredients until they are
thick. Whip them with an egg beater
until they are fluffy. Whip until stiff:

3 egg whites
⅛ teaspoon salt

Fold them into the cherry mixture.
Pour part of this into a wet mold.
Alternate the whip with layers of the
drained cherries. Chill the pudding
until it is set.
Serve it with:

Cream or Boiled Custard,
page 711

ORANGE WHIP
10 Servings
A delicious winter dessert. Light and
refreshing—good to serve after a
heavy meat course. It depends for
success upon the quality of the orange
juice used.
Soak:

1½ tablespoons gelatine

in:

¼ cup cold water

Dissolve it in:

¼ cup boiling water

Add:

1½ tablespoons lemon juice
¾ cup orange juice

Chill these ingredients until the jelly
falls in sheets from a spoon.
Whip until stiff:

5 egg whites
⅛ teaspoon salt

Beat in the gelatine mixture. Have
ready:

¾ cup sugar

Beat this in, ½ the amount at a time.
When the whip begins to thicken,
fold in:

5 egg yolks

Place the pudding in a wet mold or
in the bowl from which it is to be
served. Chill it thoroughly. Serve it
with:

Cream

MARSHMALLOW PUDDING
6 to 8 Servings
This pudding is named for its marsh-
mallowlike consistency. It is very
quickly made.
Sift:

1 cup sugar

Soak:

1½ tablespoons gelatine

in:

½ cup cold water

Dissolve it in:

½ cup boiling water

Cool these ingredients. Whip until
stiff:

4 egg whites
⅛ teaspoon salt

Add the gelatine to the egg whites in
a slow stream. Whip the pudding
constantly. Add the sugar ½ cupful at
a time. Whip the pudding well after
each addition. Whip in:

1 teaspoon vanilla

Continue to whip until the pudding
thickens. Chill it thoroughly. Serve it
with:

Boiled Custard, page 711

Flavor the custard when it is cold
with:

Rum or sherry

or serve the pudding with:

Crushed sweetened fruit

SNOW PUDDING
6 Servings
An ideal summer dessert.
Soak:

1 tablespoon gelatine

in:

¼ cup cold water

Dissolve it in:

1 cup boiling water

Add and stir until the sugar is dissolved:

¼ cup lemon juice
¼ cup sugar

Chill these ingredients until they fall
in sheets from a spoon. Whip until
stiff:

3 egg whites
¼ teaspoon salt

Whip the jelly into them. Continue
to beat until the mixture begins to
stiffen. Pour the pudding into the
bowl from which it is to be served.
Chill it thoroughly. Serve it with:

Boiled Custard, page 711

PINEAPPLE SPONGE
5 Servings
Soak:

2 teaspoons gelatine

in:

¼ cup cold water

Dissolve it in:

¼ cup boiling water

Add:

½ cup sugar
¼ teaspoon salt
2 tablespoons lemon juice
1 cup canned crushed pineapple
If fresh pineapple is used be sure it is cooked before being added to the gelatine.

Cool these ingredients until they are nearly set. Beat them with a wire whisk until they are frothy. Whip until stiff:

2 egg whites
⅛ teaspoon salt

Fold them lightly into the gelatine mixture. Chill the sponge until it is firm. Serve it with:

Boiled Custard, page 711

Molded Pineapple Cream, page 743.

BANANA SPONGE
6 Servings
Mash lightly with a fork:
3 bananas
There should be about 1 cupful of pulp. Soak:
1 tablespoon gelatine
in:
2 tablespoons water
Dissolve it in:
½ cup boiling water
Stir in until dissolved:
½ cup sugar
Cool this mixture. Stir in the banana pulp and:
2 teaspoons lemon juice
Chill the jelly until it begins to thicken. Whip it. Beat until stiff:
3 egg whites
¼ teaspoon salt
Fold them into the gelatine. Fill sherbet cups or a serving dish. Top the dessert with:
1 cup whipped cream
to which add:
½ teaspoon vanilla

APRICOT SPONGE
8 Servings
Cover:
½ lb. apricots: 1½ cups
with:
2 cups cold water
Permit them to soak for 12 hours. Bring them slowly to the boiling point. Simmer them until they are tender. Drain the fruit. Put it through a ricer. Reserve the juice. Soak:
1½ tablespoons gelatine
in:
½ cup apricot juice

Cook and stir until the sugar is dissolved:
½ cup apricot juice
1¼ cups sugar
Add the gelatine and stir it until it is dissolved. Add:
3 tablespoons lemon juice
Combine the liquid with the apricot pulp. Chill these ingredients until they are thick. Whip until stiff:
4 egg whites
⅛ teaspoon salt
Fold them lightly into the jelly mixture. Chill the pudding thoroughly. Serve it with:
Vanilla Sauce I, page 758,
Boiled Custard, page 711,
cream or whipped cream

Prune Whip, page 728.

EGGLESS PRUNE WHIP
6 Servings
Not only has the following dish the virtue of being good and cheap, but it provides in addition a dessert for those who are unable to eat milk and eggs. Soak for 12 hours:
½ lb. prunes
in:
2 cups cold water
Add:
(½ sliced lemon)
(1 stick cinnamon)
Stew the prunes gently for ½ hour. Add and cook for 10 minutes, or until the prunes are tender:
½ cup sugar
Drain the prunes. Save the juice. Remove the pits and put the prunes through a ricer. Soak:
1 tablespoon gelatine
in:
½ cup cold prune juice or part prune, part orange
(1½ tablespoons lemon juice)
Dissolve it in:
1 cup hot prune juice
Chill this mixture until it is thick. Whip it with a wire whisk until it is fluffy. Fold in the prune pulp and place the whip on ice until it is well chilled. Serve it with:
Cream or Boiled Custard, page 711

EGGLESS APRICOT WHIP
Follow the preceding rule for:
Eggless Prune Whip
Substitute for the prunes:
Dried apricots

QUICK FRUIT WHIP
2 Servings
Soak:
> 1 teaspoon gelatine

in:
> ½ cup fruit juice

Dissolve it over hot water. Add the contents of:
> 1 can puréed apricots and apple-
> sauce, peaches, etc.: 4½ oz.
> 3 tablespoons sugar
> ½ teaspoon vanilla

Chill these ingredients until set. They may be whipped. Serve with:
> Cream

LEMON FLUFF
5 to 6 Servings

A quickly made light dessert much like a lemon pie filling of which there never seems to be enough.
Soak:
> 2 teaspoons gelatine

in:
> 3 tablespoons cold water

Beat in the top of a double boiler until light:
> 4 egg yolks
> Juice of 2 lemons

Beat in gradually:
> ⅔ cup sugar

Add the soaked gelatine. Continue beating over boiling water until the custard thickens somewhat. Cool it. Beat until stiff:
> 4 egg whites
> ⅛ teaspoon salt

Beat in gradually:
> 3 tablespoons sugar

Fold the egg whites lightly into the custard. Place the fluff in a bowl or in individual glasses. They may be lined with:
> Lady fingers or cookies

The tops may be garnished with a:
> Maraschino cherry or a dab of
> bright jelly

COCOA SPONGE
5 Servings
Soak:
> 1 tablespoon gelatine

in:
> ¼ cup cold water

Dissolve it in:
> ¾ cup boiling milk or water

Add and stir until dissolved:
> ⅓ cup sugar
> 3 tablespoons cocoa

Cool these ingredients until they are thick. Add:

> 1 teaspoon vanilla

Whip the mixture until it is fluffy. Whip until stiff:
> 3 egg whites
> ⅛ teaspoon salt

Combine them with the jelly and whip the sponge until it will hold its shape. Pour it into a wet mold. Chill it thoroughly. Unmold it and serve it with:
> Almond Sauce, page 758,
> cream or whipped cream

CHOCOLATE SPONGE
6 Servings
Soak:
> 2 tablespoons gelatine

in:
> ½ cup cold water

Melt over hot water:
> 3 oz. chocolate

Add and heat to the boiling point:
> ½ cup boiling water
> 1 cup sugar
> ⅛ teaspoon salt

Cool these ingredients slightly.
Scald:
> 3 cups milk

Dissolve the soaked gelatine in it. Stir in the chocolate mixture. Cool these ingredients. Add:
> 1 teaspoon vanilla

Whip until stiff, then fold in:
> 2 egg whites

Place the sponge in an oiled ring mold. Chill it until it is set. When firm unmold it. Serve it with the center filled with:
> Whipped cream

You may top this with:
> Chopped nut meats or
> crushed nut brittle

MOCHA SPONGE
6 Servings

This is good frozen in a refrigerator tray. If it is to be made in this way, use ¾ cupful sugar in all.
Soak:
> 1 tablespoon gelatine

in:
> ¼ cup cold water

Dissolve it in:
> 1½ cups strong boiling coffee

Add:
> ⅓ cup sugar
> ½ cup milk

Cook and stir these ingredients over a low flame until they are hot. Do not permit them to boil. Beat in a separate dish:

3 egg yolks
¼ cup sugar

Pour part of the hot mixture over them. Return it to the pan and cook and stir it for 2 minutes over low heat to permit the yolks to thicken slightly. Do not permit it to boil. Cool these ingredients until they are thick. Add:

½ teaspoon vanilla

Whip them with a wire whisk until they are fluffy. Whip until stiff:

3 egg whites
⅛ teaspoon salt

Fold them into the gelatine mixture. Pour the sponge into a wet mold. Chill it thoroughly. Unmold it and serve it with:

Cream

Coffee Jelly with Marshmallows, page 736.

MAPLE CREAM
6 Servings

Place in the top of a double boiler:

2½ cups milk
1 tablespoon gelatine

Place the container over hot water. Heat and stir the milk to dissolve the gelatine. Pour this mixture slowly, beating constantly, onto:

3 beaten egg yolks

Return it to the double boiler top. Cook and stir it until it begins to thicken. Remove it from the heat. Cool it. Stir in slowly:

⅔ cup maple sirup
1 teaspoon vanilla

Beat until stiff:

3 egg whites
¼ teaspoon salt

Fold them into the gelatine mixture. Place the cream in a large mold rinsed in cold water, or into individual molds. Chill it. Unmold it. Serve it as it is or with:

Whipped cream

PERSIAN CREAM
6 Servings

Soak:

1 tablespoon gelatine

in:

¼ cup cold milk

Scald:

1½ cups milk

Dissolve the gelatine in it. Beat:

2 egg yolks
⅓ cup sugar

Beat a little of the hot milk into the

yolks, then return it to the saucepan. Cook and stir these ingredients over very low heat until they begin to thicken. Cool them. Add:

1 teaspoon vanilla or rum

Whip until stiff:

2 egg whites
⅛ teaspoon salt

Fold them lightly into the gelatine mixture. Chill the cream. Serve it very cold with:

Crushed fruit or fruit sauce

CARAMEL CREAM I
4 Servings

Soak:

1 tablespoon gelatine

in:

¼ cup cold water

Stir and melt in a heavy skillet until light brown:

½ cup sugar

Stir in slowly:

1 cup hot water

When the sugar is dissolved add the soaked gelatine. Stir it until it is dissolved. Scald:

½ cup milk

Beat into it:

2 egg yolks

Add:

½ cup sugar

Cook and stir these ingredients over low heat until the yolks begin to thicken. Add the caramel mixture. Chill these ingredients until they are about to set. Whip until stiff:

2 egg whites
⅛ teaspoon salt

Fold in:

½ teaspoon vanilla

Fold these ingredients lightly into the custard. Chill the pudding thoroughly. Serve it with:

Cream or whipped cream

Caramel Bavarian Cream, page 742.

MILK PUDDING
Method I. 4 Servings

This sounds flat but it is not without character. One of my favorite easy desserts.

Soak:

1 tablespoon gelatine

in:

3 tablespoons water

Heat until scalded:

¾ cup milk
¼ cup sugar
⅛ teaspoon salt

Dissolve the gelatine in this mixture. Cool it slightly. Add it to:

1 cup cream

Two cupfuls rich milk may be substituted for the milk and cream. Flavor the pudding with:

½ teaspoon vanilla
½ teaspoon almond extract

Beat it from time to time as it solidifies. The pudding may be chilled in a bowl of ice. One to 1¼ cupfuls cooked, drained fruit may be molded into the pudding shortly before it is firm. Pour it into an oiled mold. Chill it until it is firm. Serve it with the following sauce:

Rum Sauce
Combine:

¾ cup puréed peaches, baby food
Peach or other slightly sweetened preserves

1 teaspoon grated orange rind
¼ cup orange juice
2 tablespoons rum

Or use a sauce of preserves like orange marmalade or fresh or stewed fruit.

Method II.

Made in the following way Milk Pudding becomes blancmange, one of the outstanding triumphs of French art. Substitute for the milk and cream in the above rule about:

1¼ cups Almond Milk, page 709
¾ cup milk

Substitute for the flavoring:

1 teaspoon rum or kirsch

Serve the pudding very cold with:

Fresh or stewed fruit

Whipped Cream Puddings

RICE PUDDING WITH WHIPPED CREAM

10 Servings

Boil (page 103):

⅓ cup rice: about 1 cup cooked rice

Drain off any excess liquid. Soak for 5 minutes:

2 teaspoons gelatine

in:

¼ cup cold water

Dissolve it over heat. Add it to the rice. Stir into it:

6 tablespoons sugar
(½ cup blanched shredded almonds)

Chill the rice. Whip until stiff:

1 pint heavy cream: 2 cups

Fold into it:

2 teaspoons vanilla

Fold the cream into the rice. Place the pudding in a wet mold. Chill it thoroughly. Unmold it and serve it very cold with:

Cold Currant Jelly Sauce, page 758, or Hot Butterscotch Sauce, page 756

PINEAPPLE SNOW

8 Servings

A pretty Christmas pudding.

Soak:

1 tablespoon gelatine

in:

¼ cup cold water

Heat:

2 cups crushed canned pineapple

If fresh pineapple is used, be sure it is cooked before adding it to the gelatine mixture. Stir in:

1 cup sugar
⅛ teaspoon salt

When these ingredients are boiling add the soaked gelatine. Remove the pan from the fire and stir in the gelatine until it is dissolved. Chill the jelly until it is about to set. Whip until stiff:

2 cups heavy cream

Add:

½ teaspoon vanilla

Fold in the pineapple. Place the pudding in a wet mold. Chill it thoroughly. Unmold it and serve it with:

(Maraschino cherries)

Quick Fruit Fluff, page 743.

RICE AND FRUIT CREAM

5 Servings

Combine:

1 cup cooked rice
1 cup drained apricots, pineapple, etc.

Whip until stiff:

½ cup heavy cream

Fold in the rice mixture and:

12 diced marshmallows

Place the cream in individual dishes. You may top it with:

Crushed nut brittle or shaved semisweet chocolate

BAVARIAN CREAM WITH MILK AND CREAM

8 Servings

This dessert is an elaborate version of Blancmange, page 719. You may improvise many pleasant variations of flavoring and accompaniments with fruits and sauce. Various kinds of cake and fruit may be molded into it. It may be served in a ring mold, in a large mound, in individual rings or mounds, or it may be molded in a block and served sliced, covered with fruit, etc.

Soak:

> 1 tablespoon gelatine

in:

> 2 tablespoons cold water

Scald:

> 1¾ cups milk

If preferred, ½ cupful milk and 2 cup-fuls cream, whipped, may be used. This makes a richer pudding. Add:

> ⅓ to ½ cup sugar
> ¼ teaspoon salt

Stir the gelatine into this mixture until it is dissolved. Chill it. As it thickens flavor it with:

> 1½ teaspoons vanilla
> (¼ teaspoon almond extract)

Whip it with a wire whisk until it is fluffy. Beat until stiff:

> 1 cup heavy cream

Fold it into the gelatine mixture. Place the pudding in a wet mold. If desired, alternate the pudding mixture with:

> 6 broken macaroons or lady
> fingers soaked in rum or sherry,
> and ½ cup ground nut meats,
> preferably almonds

Chill the pudding thoroughly. Un-mold it. Serve it with:

> Whole or crushed berries or
> stewed fruit and whipped cream

BAVARIAN CREAM WITH EGGS AND CREAM
8 Servings

Place in a cup and soak:

> 1 tablespoon gelatine
> ¼ cup cold water

Dissolve it by setting the cup in hot water. Cool the gelatine. Beat until light:

> 5 egg yolks
> ¼ cup sifted sugar

Add the gelatine and:

> 1½ teaspoons vanilla

In a separate bowl whip until stiff:

> 5 egg whites
> ⅛ teaspoon salt

Whip in slowly:

> ¼ cup sifted sugar

In a separate bowl whip until stiff:

> 2 cups heavy cream

Combine the cream, the egg whites and the egg yolks by folding them lightly together. Place the pudding in a wet mold. Chill it thoroughly. Unmold it and serve it with:

> Crushed fruit, brandy peaches,
> etc.

CHOCOLATE BAVARIAN CREAM
Prepare:

> Bavarian Cream with Milk and
> Cream, page 741

Add to the hot milk:

> 2 oz. chocolate or
> 6 tablespoons cocoa

HAZELNUT BAVARIAN CREAM
8 Servings

Soak:

> 1 tablespoon gelatine

in:

> 2 tablespoons cold water

Combine and beat:

> ½ cup scalded milk
> ¼ cup sugar
> 4 egg yolks
> ⅛ teaspoon salt

Cook and stir these ingredients over low heat until they begin to thicken. Stir in the soaked gelatine until it is dissolved. Grind and add:

> ¾ cup hazelnuts

Add:

> 1 teaspoon vanilla

Chill these ingredients until they are about to set. Whip until stiff:

> 2 cups heavy cream

Fold it into the other ingredients. Place the pudding in the dish from which it is to be served or in a wet mold. Chill it thoroughly. Serve it with:

> Raspberry Juice, page 759

CARAMEL BAVARIAN CREAM
8 Servings

Soak:

> 1 tablespoon gelatine

in:

> ¼ cup water

Place in a large heavy skillet over low heat:

> ¾ cup sugar

Stir it until it melts and is a clear brown. Stir in slowly over low heat:

> ½ cup hot water

Stir and boil this sirup for about 1 minute. Add:

1 cup rich hot milk
¼ cup sugar
¼ teaspoon salt
Heat until scalded, then pour part of this mixture over:
3 beaten egg yolks
Return this to the skillet. Stir and cook it over low heat until it coats a spoon heavily. Stir in the soaked gelatine. Stir it until it is dissolved. Cool the custard. Add:
1 teaspoon vanilla or
1 tablespoon rum
Fold in:
1 cup heavy cream, whipped
Place the bavarian in an oiled mold. Chill it thoroughly.

STRAWBERRY BAVARIAN CREAM
8 Servings
Crush:
1 quart hulled strawberries
Add:
1 cup sugar
Permit them to stand for ½ hour. Soak:
2 teaspoons gelatine
in:
3 tablespoons water
Dissolve it in:
3 tablespoons boiling water
Stir this into the berries. You may add:
1 tablespoon lemon juice
Cool the gelatine. When it is about to set fold in lightly:
2 cups heavy cream, whipped
Pour the cream into a wet mold. Chill it until it is firm. Serve it with the following sauce:
Strawberry Sauce
2 cups strawberries
½ cup sugar
1 teaspoon lemon juice
Permit these ingredients to stand for 2 hours. Put them through a ricer or sieve.

RASPBERRY BAVARIAN CREAM
Follow the preceding:
Strawberry Bavarian Cream
Substitute for the strawberries:
Raspberries

MOLDED PINEAPPLE CREAM
4 Servings
Soak:
1 tablespoon gelatine

in:
¼ cup cold water
Combine and stir constantly over very low heat until slightly thickened:
2 egg yolks
½ cup sugar
2 cups unsweetened pineapple juice
⅛ teaspoon salt
Add the soaked gelatine. Stir it until it is dissolved. Pour ½ this mixture into a wet mold. Chill it. Chill the remaining gelatine until it begins to set. Then fold into it:
½ cup heavy cream, whipped
Fill the mold; chill the cream until it is firm.

QUICK FRUIT FLUFF WITH CREAM
5 Servings
This whip takes a good beating, but is worth it. Good in a crumb crust or baked pie shell.
Beat:
½ cup heavy cream
Combine and beat long and hard until light and fluffy:
1 cup fruit or hulled berries
1 egg white
1 cup sugar or less depending on your choice of fruit
½ teaspoon vanilla or 2 teaspoons lemon juice
Fold this mixture into the cream. Heap it into sherbet glasses. Chill it thoroughly.
Try 1 cupful grated raw apple, riced banana, cooked apricot or prune pulp, raw crushed peaches or apricots or canned drained pineapple.

Gelatine Fruit Whips and Sponge Puddings, page 736.

RHUBARB FOOL
4 Servings
Cut up:
6 cups young rhubarb
Cook it in boiling water that barely covers it for about 6 minutes, or until tender. Drain it. Put it through a ricer or food mill. Add to taste:
Sugar
Stir the rhubarb over a slow fire for about 10 minutes, until it is a thick purée. Cool to lukewarm. Combine it with an equal amount of:
Thick cream
Chill well before serving.

CHILLED APPLESAUCE CREAM
4 Servings
Whip until stiff:
    1 cup heavy cream
Fold in:
    1 cup applesauce
    1½ teaspoons grated lemon rind or
    ¼ teaspoon almond extract
Place the mixture in the bowl from which it is to be served. Sprinkle the top with:
    Grated semisweet chocolate
Chill the cream thoroughly.

BANANA CREAM
3 Servings
Beat until stiff:
    1 cup heavy cream
Put through a ricer:
    3 ripe bananas
Stir in:
    2 tablespoons confectioners' sugar
    1 teaspoon vanilla
    ⅛ teaspoon salt
Fold the cream into these ingredients. Serve the fluff in sherbet glasses with:
    Orange juice or other fruit juice
Or omit the vanilla and use:
    4 tablespoons sugar
Add:
    1½ tablespoons lemon juice
Serve this combination without additional fruit juice.

BERRY MARSHMALLOW CREAM
6 Servings
Cut into eighths:
    1 cup marshmallows
Whip until stiff:
    1 cup heavy cream
In a separate bowl whip until stiff:
    1 egg white
    ⅛ teaspoon salt
Fold in the marshmallows. Fold in the cream. Chill these ingredients thoroughly. Shortly before serving fold in:
    1 cup crushed raspberries or
    strawberries

COFFEE MARSHMALLOW JELLY WITH WHIPPED CREAM
6 Servings
Melt in the top of a double boiler over boiling water:
    1 lb. diced marshmallows
in:
    1 cup hot very strong coffee
Stir and cook these ingredients until the marshmallows are dissolved. Chill the mixture until it is about to set. Fold in:
    1 cup heavy cream, whipped
Place the jelly in an oiled ring mold. Chill it well. Invert it and cover the top with:
    Slivered toasted almonds or
    crushed nut brittle

Coffee Marshmallow Jelly, page 736.

CHARLOTTE RUSSE
Method I. 6 Servings
Soak:
    ¾ tablespoon gelatine
in:
    ¼ cup cold water
Dissolve it in:
    ⅓ cup scalded milk
Beat in:
    ⅓ cup powdered sugar
Cool these ingredients. Flavor them with:
    ½ teaspoon maple flavoring
    2 tablespoons strong coffee
Whip until stiff:
    1 cup heavy cream
Fold it lightly into the chilled ingredients. Line a mold with:
    Lady fingers
Pour the pudding into it. Chill it thoroughly. Unmold it and serve it with:
    Boiled Custard, page 711,
    flavored with rum

Method II. 10 to 12 Servings
Soak:
    2 tablespoons gelatine
in:
    ¼ cup cold water
Dissolve it in:
    2 cups scalded milk
Add and stir until dissolved:
    ½ cup sugar
Pour part of this over:
    4 egg yolks or 2 or 3 whole eggs
Return it to the fire and cook and stir the custard over a very low flame until it begins to thicken. Cool it. Add:
    1 teaspoon vanilla or
    1 tablespoon brandy or other
    strong liquor
Whip until stiff:
    4 egg whites
    ⅛ teaspoon salt
Fold them lightly into the custard.

Whip until stiff:
1 pint heavy cream: 2 cups
Fold it lightly into the custard. Line
a mold with:
Lady fingers
Fill it with custard. Chill it thoroughly. Unmold the pudding. Garnish it
with:
(Maraschino cherries)
Serve it with:
(Whipped cream)

CHOCOLATE CHARLOTTE
6 Servings
Soak:
1 tablespoon gelatine
in:
¼ cup cold water
Dissolve it in:
¾ cup scalded milk
Add and stir until dissolved:
1 oz. chocolate broken into pieces
Chill these ingredients until they begin
to thicken. You may add at this time:
¾ cup ground nut meats
Whip until stiff:
1 pint heavy cream: 2 cups
Whip until stiff in a separate bowl:
1 egg white
⅛ teaspoon salt
Fold into the egg white:
⅞ cup sugar—1 cup less 2 table-
spoons
1 teaspoon vanilla
Fold these ingredients into the cream.
Fold in the gelatine mixture. Pour the
pudding into a wet mold. Chill it thoroughly. Unmold it. Serve it with:
Cream or whipped cream

UNCOOKED CHOCOLATE CREAM
4 Servings
Place over low heat and stir until
smooth:
¼ lb. sweet chocolate
3 tablespoons water
Cool the chocolate. Add:
1 teaspoon vanilla
Whip until stiff:
1 cup heavy cream
Fold in the chocolate mixture and if
you wish:
½ cup chopped nut meats
Line a bowl or individual glasses with:
Lady fingers or slices of cake
generously sprinkled with rum. Fill it
with the cream. If you have not used
nut meats in the cream, place it over:
Macaroons

FRENCH CHOCOLATE CREAM
6 Servings
Stir and scald in a saucepan over low
heat:
2 cups milk
¼ cup sugar
3 oz. grated sweet chocolate
Pour part of these ingredients over:
3 beaten egg yolks
Return the sauce to the pan. Stir the
custard constantly over low heat until
it thickens. Strain it. Cool the custard
by placing the pan in cold water. In a
separate bowl whip until stiff:
¾ cup heavy cream
Add:
1 teaspoon vanilla
2 tablespoons brandy
Fold the cold custard into the whipped
cream mixture until it is well blended.
Fill custard cups with the pudding.
Chill it thoroughly before serving it.

French Chocolate Custard, page 715.

MAPLE CHARLOTTE
10 Servings
Soak:
1 tablespoon gelatine
in:
¼ cup cold water
Dissolve it in:
¾ cup hot maple sirup
Chill the jelly until it falls in heavy
sheets from a spoon. Whip until stiff:
1 pint heavy cream: 2 cups
Beat in with a spoon:
(½ cup blanched chopped almonds)
Beat in the gelatine until it is well
blended. Line a bowl with pieces of:
Sponge Cake, page 596, or
Lady Fingers, page 683
Pour the gelatine into it. Chill it until
it is firm. Unmold it and serve it garnished with:
Whipped cream

CHESTNUT CREAM
6 Servings
Place in a moderately hot oven until
the shells and inner skins peel off
easily:
1 lb. Italian chestnuts
Peel the chestnuts. Drop them into
boiling water to cover. Add to the
water:
3 tablespoons sugar
¼ teaspoon salt
Boil the chestnuts until they are very
tender. Remove them from the fire.

Add to them:

½ cup sugar

Chill them thoroughly. Remove the chestnuts from the sirup. Reserve 8 or 10 of them. Put the remainder through a ricer. Let them fall onto a platter. Make a high mound of them. Top the mound with:

Whipped cream

Place a border of whipped cream around the base of the mound. Decorate it with the reserved chestnuts. Serve it, if desired, with the:

Sirup

Add to the sirup:

1 tablespoon rum

Or, if preferred, after draining the chestnuts reserve:

8 or 10 of them

Mash the remainder with:

4 tablespoons cream
4 tablespoons sherry
1 teaspoon vanilla

Heap them into a mound. Garnish with the reserved chestnuts and:

Whipped cream

CHESTNUT MOUND OR MONT BLANC

6 Servings

Boil in water for 8 minutes:

2 lbs. chestnuts

Remove the shells. Cook the hulled nuts in a double boiler over hot water in:

1 quart milk

Add:

¼ teaspoon salt
1 cup sugar
1 teaspoon vanilla or 2 or more tablespoons brandy, curaçao, etc.

When the chestnuts are mealy and are easily pierced with a straw, drain them. Put them through a ricer. Let them fall lightly onto a large plate into a mound. If necessary to touch them, try to do so very lightly so that they will not be mashed. Whip until stiff:

1 cup heavy cream

Fold in:

1 teaspoon vanilla
2 tablespoons confectioners' sugar

Place the cream on the mound and let it overflow to the sides. Chill well before serving. You may cover the top of the cream with a grating of:

Sweet chocolate

And then, as my dear old French friend would have said: "I'd be so pleased I would not thank the King to be my uncle."

DATE LOAF

12 Servings

Crush:

½ lb. graham crackers

Remove the pits and cut into pieces:

1 lb. dates: 2 cups

Cut into pieces:

½ lb. marshmallows

Chop fine:

1 cup pecan meats

Whip until stiff:

1 cup heavy cream

Fold in:

1 teaspoon vanilla

Combine ½ the cracker crumbs with the dates, marshmallows, nuts and whipped cream. Shape them into a roll. Roll it in the remaining cracker crumbs. Chill the roll for 12 hours. Serve it cut into slices with:

Cream or whipped cream

Macaroon Puddings

A rule for macaroons will be found on page 679.

NESSELRODE PUDDING

12 Servings

Soak:

2 tablespoons gelatine

in:

1 cup cold milk

Scald in a double boiler:

2 cups milk

Add:

⅔ cup sugar

Beat and stir in:

5 egg yolks

Cook and stir these ingredients for 1

or 2 minutes to permit the yolks to thicken slightly. Stir in the soaked gelatine until it is dissolved. Add:

⅔ cup chopped raisins
3 tablespoons ground almonds
¼ lb. broken macaroons

Cool these ingredients. Add:

1 tablespoon brandy or rum
2 teaspoons vanilla

Whip until stiff:

5 egg whites
⅛ teaspoon salt

Fold them lightly into the other ingredients. Place the pudding in a wet mold. Chill it well. Unmold it on a plate and garnish it with:

Maraschino cherries

Serve it with:

Whipped cream

MACAROON CHARLOTTE
6 Servings
Roll until fine:

12 macaroons

Place on a platter and whip until stiff:

2 egg whites
1/8 teaspoon salt

Fold in:

1/4 cup confectioners' sugar
1/2 teaspoon vanilla
1/4 teaspoon almond extract

Fold in the macaroons. Whip until stiff:

1 cup heavy cream

Fold it into the other ingredients. Line a mold, or individual molds, with:

Lady Fingers or Sponge Cake, pages 683, 596

Fill it with the charlotte. Chill it for 2 hours or more. Unmold it and serve it with:

Maraschino cherries
Caramel sauce

CHOCOLATE MACAROON CHARLOTTE
6 Servings
Soak:

1 tablespoon gelatine

in:

2 tablespoons water

Beat and stir until blended:

1 1/4 oz. chocolate
1 1/2 cups milk

Dissolve the gelatine in the milk. Add:

1/2 cup sugar
1/4 teaspoon salt

Chill these ingredients until they begin to set. Whip until stiff:

1/2 cup heavy cream

Fold in:

1/2 cup dry macaroon crumbs
1/2 teaspoon vanilla or
2 teaspoons rum

Fold in the chocolate mixture. Place it in 1 large moist mold or in sherbet glasses. Garnish the top with:

1/4 cup macaroon crumbs
A maraschino cherry

CABINET PUDDING
8 Servings
This delicate pudding is not to be confused, please, with the indifferent bread pudding, alias Cabinet Pudding, frequently served in public eating places. Soak:

1 1/2 tablespoons gelatine

in:

6 tablespoons water

Dissolve it over hot water. Beat until very light:

6 egg yolks
6 tablespoons sugar

Beat in the dissolved gelatine and:

1 teaspoon vanilla

Whip until stiff:

6 egg whites
1/8 teaspoon salt

Fold them lightly into the yolk mixture. Soak:

16 macaroons

in:

Rum, sherry or arrack

Line a mold with:

Lady fingers or soaked macaroons

Place in it a layer of custard and a layer of macaroons. Repeat the process. Custard should form the top layer. Chill the pudding until it is firm. Unmold it on a platter. Garnish it with:

(Maraschino cherries)

Serve it with:

Whipped cream

Fruit and Cheese Desserts

Fresh Fruits

When planning a dessert remember that a light course is always in order. In these calorie-conscious days it is usually preferable to a heavy one. Follow the French custom of serving:

A bowl of choice fruit or fruits
Cheese: Camembert, Roquefort, Philadelphia cream, etc.
French bread, toasted wafers or other crackers.
Toasted walnuts or salted almonds

Or serve:
Cream cheese
Choice preserves or jam
Lightly toasted crackers
The calorie counters may decline the cheese and nut meats. This is less embarrassing than to leave a plateful of barely touched baked Alaska or other rich "unhappy ending."

PETIT SUISSE
4 Servings
Beat until soft:
2 packages cream cheese: 6 oz.
Beat in:
2 teaspoons confectioners' sugar
Beat into a smooth, even consistency:
2 or more tablespoons cream
Place the mixture in moist custard cups. Chill it. Unmold it. Serve it surrounded with:
Unhulled strawberries or other fruit
Place on one side of the plate a small mound of:
Confectioners' sugar

FRENCH CHEESE CREAM OR FRÔMAGE À LA CRÈME
6 Servings
This very simple dessert is as good as any elaborate concoction I know.
Whip until stiff:
1 cup heavy cream
Beat until soft:
3 or 4 packages soft white cream cheese: 3 oz. each
2 tablespoons cream
⅛ teaspoon salt
Fold the cheese into the whipped cream. Place these ingredients in a wet mold or in individual molds or in

the traditional heart shaped wicker basket lined with cheesecloth. Chill the cheese thoroughly. Unmold it. Serve it with:
Fresh unhulled strawberries, raspberries or other fresh fruit

COTTAGE CHEESE DISH
Put through a fine sieve:
Cottage cheese
Thin it to the consistency of applesauce with:
Cream
Sweeten it as desired with:
Sugar
Vanilla
Place it in a bowl. Sprinkle the top with:
Cinnamon
Serve the mixture very cold with:
Cranberry Relish, page 443, stewed cranberries, stewed cherries, crushed sweetened strawberries, etc.
The cheese and the fruit may be placed side by side in small dishes and served with turkey, chicken, veal, etc.

CREAM CHEESE PARFAIT
8 Servings
Beat until smooth:
1 cup cottage cheese
Whip until stiff, then fold in:
1 cup heavy cream
½ teaspoon almond extract
Beat until stiff, then fold in:
1 egg white
½ teaspoon salt
Alternate spoonfuls of this mixture in a bowl or parfait glasses with:
Frozen fruit, stewed fruit or sweetened fresh fruit
Chill it.

BAR-LE-DUC DESSERT
A pleasant summer dish. Serve it with toasted crackers.
Stir to a smooth paste:
2 packages cream cheese: 6 oz.
1 or 2 tablespoons cream
Fold in:
2 tablespoons currant preserves
Freeze the mixture or chill it well.

DEVONSHIRE CREAM
Place in an oven-proof dish for 12 hours:
Milk
Move it very gently onto a stove and heat it very slowly until bubbles ap-

pear around the edges. Do not let the milk boil. Remove it from the fire and permit it to stand for 24 hours in a cool place. Skim the cream. It will be thick and clotted. Serve it very cold with:
  Berries

See *Sour Cream, page 192; Yogurt, page 818.*

STRAWBERRIES AND SOUR CREAM

Formerly we had a short, intensive strawberry season. Now, like poor relations, they are always with us. No longer a thrill, just an everyday "happenstance" that leaves us unmoved. Serve:
  Strawberries
Do not remove the hulls. To eat them dip them in:
  Brown or white sugar
Then in:
  Sour cream or smooth cottage cheese

STRAWBERRIES OR RASP-BERRIES IN CREAM CHEESE
4 Servings
Wash if gritty, drain and hull:
  1 quart strawberries
Chill them. Work to a smooth paste:
  2 packages cream cheese: 6 oz.
  4 tablespoons or more cream
The mixture should be thin. Work in:
  ⅓ cup confectioners' sugar
Chill this. Reserve a few of the finest berries to garnish the dish. About ½ hour before serving combine the remaining berries and cheese mixture. Fold one into the other until the strawberries are well coated. Chill them until ready to serve.

STRAWBERRIES IN SAUCE
6 Servings
Wash if gritty, then hull:
  2 quarts strawberries
Reserve about ½ the choice berries. Put the remaining berries through a sieve. Measure them. Add an equal amount of:
  Sugar
Stir them over heat, then permit them to cook until they are reduced about ½. Cool this sauce. You may add to it:
  2 tablespoons kirsch or brandy
Make a mound of the reserved berries. Pour the sauce over them. Chill them well. A delicious dessert is strawber-

ries in meringues with either this or a similar sauce made with raspberries.

STRAWBERRIES AND PINE-APPLE WITH KIRSCH
4 Servings
Prepare:
  1½ cups hulled strawberries
  1½ cups fresh diced pineapple
Chill them. Make a sirup of:
  ½ cup sugar
  ¾ cup water
Chill it. Shortly before serving add to the cold sirup:
  1 or 2 tablespoons kirsch
Place the fruit in a bowl or in individual glasses. Pour the sirup over it.

STRAWBERRY AND KIRSCH CREAM
6 Servings
Wash if gritty:
  1 quart ripe strawberries
Reserve 8 unhulled berries. Hull, then cut into halves the remaining berries. Sprinkle over them:
  ½ cup confectioners' sugar
Permit them to stand for 10 minutes. Whip until stiff:
  1 cup heavy cream
Flavor it with:
  3 tablespoons kirsch
Fold the berries into the cream. Serve it in sherbet glasses garnished with the unhulled berries.

FRESH PINEAPPLE IN WINE
4 to 6 Servings
Remove the top from:
  A large pineapple
Cut out the pulp, leaving a shell. Cut the pulp into dice. Return it to the shell in layers alternately with:
  1 cup sugar
Pour over it:
  1 cup Madeira
Chill the pineapple for at least 2 hours.

AMBROSIA
4 Servings
This is an old favorite, especially popular in the South. The rule has many variations.
Peel carefully, removing all membrane:
  2 large Valencia oranges
Peel and cut into thin slices:
  3 ripe bananas
Pineapple is sometimes added, so are other fruits. Combine and stir:

¼ cup confectioners' sugar
1½ cups shredded coconut
Arrange alternate layers of oranges
and bananas in individual serving
dishes or in a bowl. Sprinkle each
layer with a part of the coconut mixture, reserving some for the top. Chill
the dish well before serving it.

SLICED APPLES OR PEARS AND CREAM

Pare and cut into thin slices:
Apples or pears
To keep them from discoloring sprin-
kle them with:
(Lemon juice)
Just before serving sprinkle them with:
Sugar
Cinnamon
Serve them with:
Thick sweet or sour cream
or with smooth cottage cheese
or serve sliced apples or pears with:
Crumbled Roquefort cheese

Apple Fritters, page 543.
While on the subject of apple dishes
remember how good the various forms
of fritters are as desserts. Apple rings
are especially good, so are French
fritters with lemon sauce.

BROILED APPLE SLICES

Core, then cut crosswise into ½ inch
slices:
Apples
Spread the slices on one side with:
Butter
Place them in a buttered pan. Spread
the other side with:
Honey
Broil them slowly. Serve them with:
Cinnamon
Cream

*A number of fruit dishes suitable for
desserts will be found in the section on
Cooked Fruits to be Served with Meats,
page 442.*

BAKED APPLES AND MINCEMEAT

Prepare by the rule on page 446:
Baked Apples and Mincemeat
Add to the mincemeat:
Grated orange rind
Substitute for the water:
Orange juice
Serve the apples with:

Soft cream cheese balls and hard
crackers, or with Hard Sauce,
page 753

APPLES BAKED IN FRUIT JUICE

Prepare:
Baked Apples, page 445
Substitute for the water:
½ cup fruit juice
Bake the apples covered until they are
nearly tender. Uncover them and bake
them until they are tender. Baste
them frequently.

ALMOND APPLES IN SIRUP

4 Servings
Boil for 5 minutes:
1⅓ cups water
1 cup sugar
Pare, core and add:
4 large tart apples
Cook the apples gently in the sirup,
partly covered with a lid, until they are
tender. Place them in a baking dish.
Add to the sirup and boil until thick:
⅛ teaspoon cloves
¼ teaspoon cinnamon
2 teaspoons butter
Fill the centers with the sirup. Stud
the apples with:
⅓ cup blanched slivered almonds
Place them in a moderate oven 375° to
brown the almonds lightly. Chill them.
Serve with:
Cream

For other Apple Dishes see the Index.

APPLES OR OTHER FRUIT BAKED IN WINE

4 Servings
An attractive garnish for Custard,
Blancmange or Milk Pudding.
Pare:
4 peaches, apples or pears
Place them in a baking dish. Combine, heat but do not boil, stir and
pour over them:
⅔ cup red wine
⅔ cup sugar
½ stick cinnamon
4 whole cloves
⅛ teaspoon salt
½ thinly sliced seeded lemon
Bake the fruit covered in a 350° oven
until it is tender when tested with a
fork. Baste it every 10 minutes. Turn
it so that it will cook evenly.

FLAMING APPLES
4 Servings
Make this with a well-flavored cooking apple only, like a Jonathan.
Core so as to leave a small plug at the base and cut a slice of peel from the top of:
> **4 apples**
The centers may be filled with a combination of:
> **2 tablespoons chopped nut meats**
> **3 tablespoons well-drained crushed pineapple, chopped figs or dates**
> **6 tablespoons light brown sugar**
Have ready an oven-proof dish, the bottom covered with:
> **6 tablespoons water**
Place the apples on it. Bake them in a moderate oven 375° for ½ hour, or until done. Baste them frequently. Add water if necessary. Place them on a small platter or in individual dishes. Pour the apple juice over them. Sprinkle the tops with:
> **Confectioners' sugar**
> **A dash of cinnamon**
Heat in a double boiler, then pour on each apple while warm:
> **2 tablespoons rum**
Light the rum and serve the apples aflame.

FLAMING PEARS
Allow 1 Pear for a Serving
Cut into halves, then core:
> **Ripe unchilled pears**
Place them on an oven-proof plate. Prick them. Sprinkle them with:
> **Confectioners' sugar**
Pour over each ½:
> **1 tablespoon brandy**
Ignite the brandy at the table.

Fresh Pears in Liqueur, page 3.

FLAMING PEACHES OR PÈCHES FLAMBÉES
Cook in sirup:
> **Whole Peaches, page 444**
Allow 1 peach to each person. Drain them. Bring them to the table while warm. Pour over each peach:
> **1 or 2 tablespoons sugar**
> **2 or more tablespoons kirsch**
Light the liquor and let it burn down.

---

*Peaches and Mincemeat, page 446;
Stewed Pears with Rum, page 444.*

PEACHES AND RASPBERRIES OR BLUEBERRIES
6 Servings
Peel and halve:
> **4 chilled peaches**
Place them in a bowl. Combine and stir:
> **2 cups chilled raspberries or blueberries: 1 pint**
> **6 tablespoons sugar**
> **1½ tablespoons lemon juice**
> **½ cup broken nut meats**
If you are in California, try "green almonds."
Pour the berries over the peaches. Serve the fruit with:
> **Whipped cream**

STUFFED PEACHES WITH MERINGUE
4 Servings
Pare, then cut in halves:
> **4 large freestone peaches**
Crack one peach stone. Pound the kernel to a pulp. Crush or roll:
> **6 macaroons**
Hollow the peach halves slightly. Combine the kernel, the macaroons, the peach pulp and:
> **2 beaten egg yolks**
Fill the peach halves with this mixture. Bake them in a moderate oven 350° until they are done. Make a Meringue, page 578, of:
> **2 egg whites**
> **3 tablespoons sugar**
> **½ teaspoon vanilla**
Heap it on the peaches. Brown the meringue in a 325° oven.

CANNED FRUIT IN BRANDY SAUCE
Drain:
> **Canned fruit**
Add to the sirup:
> **Brandy, liqueur or sherry**
Pour the sirup over the fruit. Chill it well. It may be served in sherbet glasses topped with:
> **Whipped cream**

CHILLED FRESH FRUIT IN SIRUP WITH LIQUEUR
Prepare for the table and place in a bowl:
> **An assortment of fresh fruits: hulled, pared and cored peaches, apricots, berries, grapes, etc.**
Boil for 10 minutes:
> **1 cup sugar**

⅛ teaspoon salt
1 cup water
Or substitute for this mixture the sirup from canned or stewed fruits. Cool the sirup. Add to it:
1 tablespoon or more liqueur
Partly cover the fruit with the sirup. Chill it for at least 2 hours.

BAKED CANNED FRUIT
4 Servings
Drain the contents of:
1 No. 2½ can fruit salad
or other canned fruits or pineapple slices covered with fruit cocktail and juice. Place the fruit in rows in a baking dish. Sprinkle it with:
½ cup ground macaroons, ground pine nuts or other nut meats
Juice of 1 lemon
3 or 4 tablespoons maraschino, brandy, etc., or fruit juice
Dot it with:
2 tablespoons butter
Bake the fruit in a moderate oven 350° for about ½ hour. Serve it hot.

AVOCADO DESSERT
Pare, then put through a fine strainer:
Ripe avocados
Flavor them with:
Lime juice
Powdered sugar
(A dash of cloves)
Beat the mixture until fluffy with an egg beater. Chill it well.

For attractive ways to serve fresh pineapple, see page 4.

APRICOTS WITH CURAÇAO
5 Servings
Drain the contents of:
1 No. 2½ can apricots
Place them in a serving dish. Place the apricot juice in a saucepan, add and boil for 10 minutes:
2 tablespoons sugar
Yellow rind of 1 orange
Remove the rind. Stir in:
2 tablespoons curaçao, brandy, etc.
Pour the juice over the apricots. Serve hot or cold. Wonderful with very cold Rice Rings, page 716.

ORANGE COMPOTE
4 Servings
Cut the yellow rind from:

2 Valencia oranges
Cut it into thin slices, add to it and boil for 20 minutes:
1 cup water
¾ cup sugar
⅛ teaspoon salt
Remove membrane from the 2 oranges and the rind and membrane from:
3 additional oranges
Place the sections in a serving bowl. Pour the hot sirup and rind over them. Chill the compote. You may add to it before serving:
1 tablespoon rum or liqueur

BAKED BANANAS WITH RUM
4 Servings
Melt in a baking dish:
3 tablespoons butter
Place in it:
6 peeled bananas
Sprinkle them with:
3 tablespoons brown or white sugar
(1 tablespoon lemon juice)
Bake the bananas uncovered in a moderate oven 350° until tender, about 20 minutes. Turn them while baking. Sprinkle them generously with:
(Rum)
Or, if you wish, you may pour over the bananas ½ cupful rum and light it at the table.

BANANAS AND PINEAPPLE JUICE
Slice:
Bananas
Cover them with:
Chilled pineapple juice
Garnish them with:
Maraschino cherries

See Fresh Pineapple Cocktail, page 2.

BANANAS BAKED IN PIE CRUST
Peel:
Bananas
Cut them in two crosswise. Roll them in:
Sugar
Cinnamon
Wrap them in oblongs of:
Thin Pie Crust, page 561
Bake the bananas in a hot oven 450° for 15 minutes. Serve them with:
Lemon Sauce, page 757

For other Banana Dishes, see the Index.

Caramel Cornflake Ring with Fruit, page 717.

CANTALOUPE FRUIT CUPS
8 Servings
Cut into halves and remove the seeds from:
    4 cantaloupes
Scallop the edges. Chill the fruit. Combine the following ingredients:
    2 cups peeled sliced oranges
    2 cups peeled sliced fresh peaches
    2 cups peeled diced pineapple:
        fresh or canned
    1 cup peeled sliced bananas
    1 cup skinned grapefruit sections
    1 cup sugar dissolved in the
        various fruit juices
Chill the fruit thoroughly. Just before serving fill the cantaloupe cups with the fruit. Pour over each cup:
    (1 tablespoon sherry or rum)
Top each cup with:
        Orange or Lemon Ice, page 773,
        or Sherbet, page 775

CANTALOUPE FILLED WITH PINEAPPLE AND CHOPPED MINT
Peel and cut into cubes:
    A fresh pineapple
Sprinkle the cubes with:
    Confectioners' sugar
Chill the fruit. Cut into halves:
    Chilled cantaloupes
Fill them with the cubed pineapple. Sprinkle the tops with:
    Chopped mint leaves

See Cocktail Chapter for numerous dessert suggestions.

Dessert Sauces

Rum, sherry, brandy, Madeira, kirsch, etc., add flavor and piquancy to desserts and sauces. Be very careful to vary all flavors as the same flavor should not be repeated too frequently.

Plain custard sauce, cream and fruit juice are excellent if served with the right pudding at the right time. With pudding sauces the "object all sublime" is "to let the punishment fit the crime." A sauce should complement a pudding. If a pudding is acid, serve a bland sauce; if a pudding is bland, serve a sauce with character; and if a pudding is rich, shun whipped cream and try a fruit sauce. The success of the pudding with sauce will depend upon your sense of discrimination.

HARD SAUCE
About 1 Cupful
Hard sauce is given different flavors but its basis is always the same although its proportions may differ. Any kind of sugar may be used for hard sauce. The sauce may be spread in a dish to the thickness of ¾ inch. Chill it. When it is firm cut it into small shapes suitable to individual servings. Use a cookie cutter.
Sift:
    1 cup confectioners' sugar
Beat until soft:
    2 to 5 tablespoons butter
Add the sugar gradually. Beat these ingredients until they are well blended. Add:
    ⅛ teaspoon salt
    1 teaspoon or more vanilla, coffee,
        rum, whisky, brandy, lemon or
        orange juice, etc.
If desired, beat in:
    1 egg or ¼ cup cream

When the sauce is very smooth chill it thoroughly.

HARD SAUCE MADE WITH AN ELECTRIC MIXER
Use the ingredients given for the preceding rule. Cream the softened butter in a small bowl at high speed. Add the sugar gradually. Add the flavoring. Beat the sauce until it is creamy, about 5 minutes. Scrape the sides of the bowl once or twice while beating. Chill the sauce.

FLUFFY HARD SAUCE
About 1½ Cupfuls
Sift:
    1 cup sugar
Beat until soft:
    1 tablespoon butter
Add the sugar gradually and:
    1 tablespoon cream

Beat these ingredients until they are well blended. Whip until stiff:

    3 egg whites
    ⅛ teaspoon salt

Fold them into the sugar mixture. Add:

    2 tablespoons cream
    1 teaspoon or more vanilla, rum or sherry

Beat the sauce well. Pile it in a dish. Chill it thoroughly.

SPICY HARD SAUCE
About 1 Cupful
Sift:

    1⅓ cups powdered sugar

Beat until soft:

    ⅓ cup butter

Add the sugar gradually. Beat these ingredients until they are creamy. Beat in:

    ½ teaspoon cinnamon
    ¼ teaspoon cloves
    1 teaspoon vanilla
    ½ teaspoon lemon juice
    ⅛ teaspoon salt if butter is unsalted

Chill the sauce.

BROWN SUGAR HARD SAUCE
About 1⅔ Cupfuls
Sift:

    1½ cups brown sugar

Beat until soft:

    ½ cup butter

Add the sugar gradually. Beat these ingredients until they are well blended. Beat in slowly:

    ⅓ cup cream

Beat in drop by drop:

    2 tablespoons wine or 1 teaspoon vanilla

When the sauce is very smooth chill it thoroughly. One-fourth cupful nut meats may be added at this time.

STRAWBERRY HARD SAUCE
About 1⅔ Cupfuls
Sift:

    1 cup confectioners' sugar

Beat until soft:

    ⅓ cup butter

Add the sugar gradually. Beat these ingredients until they are well blended. Beat in:

    ⅔ cup crushed strawberries

Chill the sauce thoroughly. This makes a good sauce, but it is better with the addition of:

    ¼ cup cream
    1 stiffly beaten egg white

Fluffy Strawberry Sauce, page 758; Strawberry Cream Sauce, page 758.

RASPBERRY OR BANANA HARD SAUCE
Follow the above rule for:

    Strawberry Hard Sauce

Substitute for the strawberries:

    ½ cup crushed raspberries or bananas

If you use bananas, add:

    1 teaspoon vanilla

FOAMY SAUCE
About 2 Cupfuls
Sift:

    1 cup powdered sugar

Beat until soft:

    5 tablespoons to ½ cup butter

Add the sugar slowly. Beat these ingredients until they are well blended. Beat in:

    1 egg yolk
    1 teaspoon vanilla or 2 tablespoons wine

Place the sauce over hot water. Beat and cook it until the yolk has thickened slightly. Whip until stiff:

    1 egg white
    ⅛ teaspoon salt

Fold it lightly into the sauce. Serve it hot or cold.

CUSTARD SAUCE
Follow the rule for:

    Boiled Custard, page 711

Posie's Custard, page 713.

CARAMEL SIRUP
About 3 Cupfuls
Place in a large heavy skillet over low heat:

    3 cups sugar

Stir it constantly as it melts. If a strong caramel flavor is desired, burn the sugar slightly. When making caramel for coloring for soups, etc., burn it until it loses all sweetness. Stir into the sugar slowly over low heat:

    3 cups boiling water

Be careful that the steam caused by this operation doesn't burn you. Cook these ingredients until they are the consistency of maple sirup. This sirup may be kept indefinitely in a closed jar or bottle. It may be flavored with rum.

CARAMEL SAUCE
Combine and stir until blended:
> 1 part Caramel Sirup, page 754
> 2 parts cream or top milk
> Vanilla as desired
> 1/8 teaspoon salt

HOT CARAMEL SAUCE
About 1 1/3 Cupfuls
Melt in a heavy skillet over very low heat:
> 1 1/4 cups sugar

Stir in very slowly:
> 1/3 cup hot cream

Cook and stir the sauce until it is smooth. Remove it from the fire. Add:
> 1/2 teaspoon vanilla

Keep the sauce hot over hot water. Add if desired:
> Chopped nut meats

COFFEE CARAMEL SAUCE
About 1 1/2 Cupfuls
Melt in a heavy skillet:
> 1 cup sugar

Stir into it gradually over low heat:
> 1 1/2 cups strong coffee

Dissolve:
> 2 tablespoons cornstarch

in:
> 3 tablespoons water

Stir it into the sugar mixture. Cook the sauce until it boils and thickens. Add:
> 2 tablespoons butter
> 1/8 teaspoon salt

COFFEE SAUCE
About 1 1/2 Cupfuls
Beat:
> 2 eggs

Beat into them very slowly:
> 1/2 cup strong boiling coffee

Add:
> 1/4 cup sugar
> 1/8 teaspoon salt

Cook and stir the sauce in a double boiler until it coats a spoon. Chill it. Shortly before serving fold in:
> 1/2 cup heavy cream, whipped, or
> 1/2 cup cream

MAPLE SAUCE
1 Cupful
Boil for 5 minutes:
> 1 cup maple sirup

Add:
> 2 or 3 tablespoons chopped nut meats or toasted almonds

Serve the sauce at once over:
> Pudding or ice cream

Maple Nut Sauce, page 779.

HOT BROWN SUGAR SAUCE
About 1 1/2 Cupfuls
Cook for 5 minutes:
> 1 cup brown sugar
> 1/2 cup water

Pour the sirup in a fine stream over:
> 1 beaten egg

Beat the sauce constantly. Cook and stir it over hot water for 2 minutes. Add:
> 3 tablespoons sherry
> 1/8 teaspoon salt

Serve the sauce hot.

BROWN SUGAR CREAM SAUCE
About 1 1/2 Cupfuls
Place in a double boiler:
> 3 beaten egg yolks
> 3/4 cup cream
> 3/4 teaspoon salt
> 1/2 cup brown sugar

Stir and cook until thick and creamy. Add a little at a time:
> 3 tablespoons butter
> 1 1/2 tablespoons lemon juice

BROWN SUGAR BUTTER SAUCE
About 1 Cupful
Fine with hot puddings or waffles. Cream in a small saucepan:
> 1/4 cup butter
> 1 cup closely packed brown sugar

Add gradually:
> 1 cup warm thin cream

Stir this over low heat until it boils. Remove from fire. Add:
> 1/4 cup bourbon or brandy

Beat with egg beater until smooth.

MARSHMALLOW SAUCE
About 2 Cupfuls
Did you ever try to make a marshmallow sauce? It usually becomes grainy and settles down when cold to a cementlike consistency. This sauce, the result of many struggles, welcomed by Jane's three boys and the neighbors' children, remains smooth and reheats readily.
Stir over low heat until the sugar is dissolved:
> 3/4 cup sugar
> 1 tablespoon light corn sirup
> 1/4 cup milk

Bring it to a boil, then simmer it gently for 5 minutes. Dissolve in top of double boiler by stirring over boiling water:

½ lb. marshmallows
2 tablespoons water

Pour the sirup over the dissolved marshmallows, beating well. Add:

1 teaspoon vanilla

Serve the sauce hot or cold. It may be reheated in a double boiler. Beat well before serving.

WHIPPED CREAM NUT SAUCE
About 2 Cupfuls

Adds glamour to "store" or other cake. Whip until stiff:

1 cup heavy cream

Fold in:

1 teaspoon vanilla or rum
2 tablespoons grated coconut or crushed nut brittle

RICH PUDDING SAUCE
About 2¾ Cupfuls

This is so good that it will glorify the plainest pudding or cake. It is less extravagant than it sounds, as only a small amount is needed over gingerbread, cake, cottage pudding, etc.
Beat well:

2 egg yolks

This sauce may be made with 1 egg. In that case do not bother to separate it. Beat in gradually:

1 cup confectioners' sugar

Add:

1½ teaspoons vanilla or 2 tablespoons brandy, sherry, etc.

Whip until stiff:

1 cup heavy cream

Whip until stiff, in a separate bowl:

2 egg whites

Fold first the cream into the yolk mixture, and then the egg whites.

HOT BUTTER SAUCE WITH WATER
About 1 Cupful

Melt:

4 tablespoons butter

Stir in until blended:

2 tablespoons flour

Add slowly:

1 cup boiling water
4 tablespoons brown sugar

Cook and stir the sauce until it boils, then cook it in a double boiler over a very low flame for about 15 minutes. If the butter is unsalted add:

⅛ teaspoon salt

Season the sauce well with:

Brandy, whisky, sherry, or with lemon juice or vanilla

Serve it hot.

HOT BUTTER SAUCE WITH EGG YOLKS AND CREAM
About 1½ Cupfuls

Beat until soft in the top of a double boiler:

⅓ cup butter

Add gradually and beat until creamy:

1 cup confectioners' sugar

Beat in slowly:

3 tablespoons brandy or other strong liquor

Beat in 1 at a time:

2 egg yolks

Add:

½ cup cream

Cook these ingredients over boiling water until they are hot and slightly thickened. Serve the sauce at once.

BUTTERSCOTCH SAUCE
About ¾ Cupful

Boil to the consistency of heavy sirup:

⅓ cup white corn sirup
⅝ cup light or medium brown sugar—½ cup plus 2 tablespoons
2 tablespoons butter
A few grains salt

Cool these ingredients. Add:

⅓ cup evaporated milk or cream

Serve the sauce hot or cold. Reheat it in a double boiler.

GRATED CHOCOLATE OR CHOCOLATE SHOT OR CHIPS

Sprinkle:

Grated sweet or bitter chocolate or chocolate shot or chips

over:

Whipped cream or ice cream

HOT FUDGE SAUCE

The grand kind that, served hot, grows hard on ice cream.
Melt in a double boiler:

2 oz. unsweetened chocolate: 2 squares

Add and melt:

1 tablespoon butter

Stir and blend well, then add:

⅓ cup boiling water

Stir well and add:

1 cup sugar
2 tablespoons corn sirup

Permit the sauce to boil rapidly but not too furiously over direct heat. Do not stir it. If you wish a usual sauce, boil it for 5 minutes. If you wish a hot sauce that will harden when poured over ice cream, boil it for about 8 minutes. Add just before serving:

1 teaspoon vanilla or 2 teaspoons
   rum

When cold, this sauce is very thick. It
may be reheated over boiling water.

CHOCOLATE SAUCE
About 1 Cupful

Stir until dissolved, then cook without
stirring to the sirup stage, about 5
minutes:
   ½ to 1 cup water
   ½ cup sugar

Cool the sauce. Melt:
   1 to 2 oz. chocolate

Stir it into the sirup. Add:
   1 teaspoon vanilla

If the sirup is too thick, thin it to the
right consistency with:
   Cream, sherry or brandy

Serve it hot or cold. Keep it hot in a
double boiler.

CHOCOLATE SAUCE WITH BROWN SUGAR
About 1 Cupful

Melt:
   4 oz. chocolate

Stir in:
   1 cup brown sugar
   ½ cup cream

Cook these ingredients until the sauce
is thick. Stir it constantly.

CHOCOLATE CUSTARD SAUCE
About 2¼ Cupfuls

Heat in a double boiler:
   2 cups milk
   2 oz. cut-up chocolate

Beat well:
   4 egg yolks
   ¾ cup sugar
   ⅛ teaspoon salt

Beat the hot sauce into the yolk mixture. Cook and stir the sauce in the
double boiler for 5 minutes. Cool it.
Add:
   1 teaspoon vanilla

Serve it hot or cold over:
   Filled Cream Puffs, page 653
   puddings or ice cream

SOUR CREAM ORANGE SAUCE
About 1 Cupful

Cream until well blended:
   ¾ cup confectioners' sugar
   3 tablespoons butter

Beat in:
   ⅓ cup thick sour cream
   1 teaspoon grated orange rind
   3 tablespoons orange juice

Good over dry cake or hot pudding.

LEMON SAUCE WITH CORNSTARCH
About 1 Cupful

Combine and stir constantly over a
low flame until thickened:
   ¼ to ½ cup sugar
   1 tablespoon cornstarch
   1 cup water

In about 5 minutes remove the sauce
from the fire. Stir in:
   2 to 3 tablespoons butter
   ½ teaspoon grated lemon rind
   1½ tablespoons lemon juice
   ⅛ teaspoon salt

LEMON SAUCE
About 1½ Cupfuls

Sift:
   ¾ cup confectioners' sugar

Beat until soft:
   3 tablespoons butter

Add the sugar gradually. Blend these
ingredients until they are creamy. Beat
in:
   3 egg yolks or 2 eggs

Stir in slowly:
   ½ cup boiling water

Cook and stir the sauce in a double
boiler or over a very low flame until it
thickens. Remove it from the fire. Stir
in:
   1 teaspoon grated lemon rind
   3 tablespoons lemon juice or
   2 tablespoons brandy

LEMON CUSTARD SAUCE
About 1 Cupful

Beat until light:
   2 eggs

Beat in gradually:
   ½ cup sugar
   ½ teaspoon grated lemon rind
   ⅛ teaspoon salt

Place the bowl over hot water. Beat
the custard until the sugar is dissolved
and the sauce is warm. Add:
   ½ cup lukewarm milk

Beat for 1 minute longer. Add:
   1 tablespoon lemon juice

FLUFFY ORANGE SAUCE
About 1¼ Cupfuls

Combine and stir constantly over a
low flame until thick:
   ½ cup orange juice
   1 teaspoon grated lemon rind
   1½ teaspoons lemon juice
   5 tablespoons sugar
   2 beaten egg yolks

Remove the sauce from the fire. Cool
these ingredients lightly.

Whip until stiff:
    2 egg whites
    ⅛ teaspoon salt
Fold them lightly into the sauce. Fold in:
    1 teaspoon vanilla
Keep the sauce hot in a double boiler, or chill it and serve it cold.

VANILLA SAUCE
Follow the rule on page 757 for:
    Lemon Sauce I
Use the smaller amount of sugar and substitute for the lemon juice:
    1 teaspoon vanilla or
    1 inch of Vanilla Bean, page 709, or 1 tablespoon rum

ALMOND SAUCE
Prepare:
    Boiled Custard, page 711
Add:
    ½ cup blanched ground almonds
Flavor the sauce with:
    Vanilla or 1 teaspoon grated lemon rind and 2 teaspoons lemon juice or brandy

NUT SAUCE
About 1½ Cupfuls
Stir and bring slowly to the boiling point:
    ¼ cup soft butter
    1 cup brown sugar
    ⅓ cup cream
Simmer these ingredients for 2 minutes. Remove them from the fire. Add:
    ⅓ cup chopped nut meats
    1 teaspoon lemon juice
    1 teaspoon vanilla
    ⅛ teaspoon salt
Serve the sauce hot or cold.

STRAWBERRY OR RASPBERRY CREAM SAUCE
About 2¼ Cupfuls
Whip until stiff:
    1 egg white
Add:
    1 beaten egg yolk
Beat in slowly:
    1 cup confectioners' sugar
Combine and beat into this mixture:
    ½ cup thick cream
    ¼ cup milk
Beat in:
    ½ cup hulled crushed strawberries or raspberries
You may add:
    1 teaspoon rum

RAISIN SAUCE
About 1⅔ Cupfuls
Boil for 15 minutes:
    1½ cups water
    ⅓ cup seeded raisins
    ¼ cup sugar
    ⅛ teaspoon salt
Melt:
    2 tablespoons butter
Stir in until blended:
    1 teaspoon flour
Add the hot sauce slowly. Stir and cook it until it boils. Add:
    A grating of nutmeg or lemon rind

JELLY SAUCE
About ¾ Cupful
Dilute over hot water:
    ¾ cup currant or other jelly
Thin it with:
    ¼ cup boiling water
Serve it hot or cold. This sauce may be thickened. Melt:
    1 tablespoon butter
Blend in:
    1 tablespoon flour
Add the diluted jelly. Cook and stir the sauce over a low flame until it thickens.

FLUFFY STRAWBERRY SAUCE
About 1½ Cupfuls
Hull, then mash with a silver fork:
    2 cups strawberries
Add:
    ½ cup powdered sugar
    1 teaspoon lemon juice
Whip until stiff:
    1 egg white
    ⅛ teaspoon salt
Add it to the strawberry mixture. Whip the sauce until it is light and fluffy.

SUMMER SAUCE OF RHUBARB AND STRAWBERRIES
Cut into ½ inch pieces without peeling:
    Rhubarb
There should be about 2 cupfuls. Sprinkle over it:
    1 cup sugar
Permit these ingredients to stand for at least 6 hours. Add:
    2½ cups hulled strawberries
Cook the sauce until the fruit is tender. Serve it over:
    Cottage Pudding, page 724, Rice Rings, page 716, etc.

RASPBERRY SAUCE
Combine in a small saucepan:
    ¼ cup raspberry jam
    2 tablespoons sugar
    ½ cup water
Stir and boil these ingredients for 2 minutes. Add:
    1 teaspoon kirsch or ¼ teaspoon almond extract
Serve the sauce hot or cold.

CHERRY SAUCE
About 2½ Cupfuls
Drain well:
    2 cups canned cherries
Add to the cherry sirup and simmer for 10 minutes:
    ¼ cup sugar
    ¼ cup corn sirup
    1 stick cinnamon: 2 inches
    1 tablespoon lemon juice
Remove the cinnamon. Mix:
    2 teaspoons cornstarch
    1 tablespoon cold water
Stir this into the hot cherry juice. Cook and stir it until it boils. Add the cherries. Serve hot or cold.

NESSELRODE SAUCE FOR DESSERTS
Combine and stir well the contents of:
    1 bottle maraschino cherries: 6 oz.
    1 can citron or orange peel, etc.: 3 oz.
Add:
    1 cup orange marmalade
    ½ cup coarsely chopped candied ginger
    ½ the maraschino juice
    1 cup nut meats, preferably unsalted cashews
    ½ cup or more rum to make the sauce a good consistency
Place in jars and seal. Let ripen for 2 weeks. Candied fruits may be added: pineapple, apricots, etc.

HOT FRUIT SAUCE FOR FRITTERS OR PUDDING
About 1¼ Cupfuls
Heat over hot water:
    1 cup apricot preserves
Add:
    1 jigger rum
    1 jigger brandy
Serve at once.

FRUIT SAUCE
About 1½ Cupfuls
Combine, stir and heat to boiling:

    1 cup unsweetened fruit juice
    ½ to ¾ cup sugar
    1 tablespoon cornstarch or
    2 tablespoons flour
Remove the sauce from the fire. Stir in:
    2 teaspoons lemon juice
    (2 tablespoons butter)
Cool the sauce. You may add:
    1 cup crushed shredded fruit, fresh or stewed
Cook and stir the sauce until it is thick. Flavor it, if desired, with:
    Sherry or other wine
Serve it hot or cold.

FRUIT CUSTARD SAUCE
About 3 Cupfuls
Cream:
    ¼ cup butter
Add gradually and beat until fluffy:
    1 cup sugar
Beat in one at a time:
    2 eggs
Beat in slowly:
    1 cup boiling milk, well, nearly boiling
Beat thoroughly. Fold in:
    1 cup crushed berries or sliced peaches, etc.

FRUIT SIRUP
About 2½ Cupfuls
Chop or crush:
    2 cups fruit: raspberries, loganberries, etc.
Add to it:
    1 cup sugar
Place these ingredients in a warm place for 1 hour. Strain the fruit. Serve the juice. If you wish to thicken the sauce, cook it until it is the consistency you like.

CANNED RASPBERRY OR LOGANBERRY JUICE
Put through a strainer:
    Canned raspberries or loganberries
Use the juice for sauce. Discard the seedy pulp. It is one of the few things I have been unable to utilize but you might feed it to the chickens.

CIDER SAUCE FOR STEAMED PUDDINGS
About 2 Cupfuls
Melt over heat:
    1 tablespoon butter
Stir in until blended:

¾ tablespoon flour
Add:
 1½ cups cider
 Sugar and spices if required
Stir and boil these ingredients for 2
minutes. Serve the sauce hot or cold.

CLARET SAUCE
Boil for 5 minutes:
 1 cup sugar
 ½ cup water
Add:
 ¼ cup claret or other wine
 ½ teaspoon grated lemon rind

WINE SAUCE
Prepare:
 Wine Custard, page 712

HOT WINE SAUCE
About 1½ Cupfuls
Cream:
 1 cup sugar
 ½ cup butter
Beat and add:
 1 egg
Stir in:
 ¾ cup sour wine or 6 tablespoons
  sherry
 1 teaspoon grated lemon rind
 (¼ teaspoon nutmeg)
Shortly before serving beat the sauce
over hot water. Heat it thoroughly.

HOT SHERRY SAUCE
About 1¼ Cupfuls
Cream:
 ½ cup butter
 1 cup sugar
Stir these ingredients over heat. Permit them to boil. Remove them at
once. Add:
 ¼ cup sherry
 A few grains of nutmeg
Serve the sauce hot.

RUM SAUCE
Method I. About 1¼ Cupfuls
Follow the preceding rule for:
 Hot Sherry Sauce
Substitute for the sherry:
 ¼ cup rum

Method II. About 2½ Cupfuls
Beat:
 2 egg yolks
 1 cup confectioners' sugar
Add slowly:
 6 tablespoons rum
Beat these ingredients until they are
well blended. Whip until stiff:
 1 cup heavy cream
Fold in:
 1 teaspoon vanilla
Fold the egg mixture into the cream.

CARAMEL RUM SAUCE
Add to:
 Caramel Sirup, page 754
 1 or 2 tablespoons rum

FRUIT RUM SAUCE
Combine equal parts of:
 Preserves or puréed fruit
 Orange juice
Flavor the sauce with:
 Rum

*Sauces and Garnishes for Frozen Des-
serts, page 779.*

Ice Cream, Ices and Frozen Desserts

The frozen dessert is not as old as the hills whence snow was brought in Renaissance times to freeze it, but it is no newcomer in our culinary world. When and where it was introduced into the colonies is shrouded in mystery but when it came it was speedily made welcome. The soda fountain is our forum and "make mine vanilla" is comprehensible to any American. Were it not for pie, ice cream might be called our favorite dessert. Here, like Charlie McCarthy, we are torn "between vice and versa."

Ice Creams and Ices To Be Made in an
Ice Cream Freezer

Rule for Making Ice Cream and Ices in a Freezer

Preparing the ice cream mixture the day before it is frozen will make the ice cream smoother and will increase its yield.

Cream that is 24 hours old makes a finer grained dish than fresh cream. When it is possible to do so, dissolve the sugar in liquid over heat before adding it to the cream.

Add ⅛ teaspoonful, or more, of salt to the sirup. Cool the sirup before adding it to the cream. Chill the mixture to be frozen before placing it in the ice cream container.

Fill the ice cream container only three fourths full to allow for the expansion of the frozen cream.

To Pack a Freezer: Allow from 3 to 6 measures of ice to 1 measure of coarse rock salt, according to the rapidity with which you wish to freeze the cream. The larger proportion of salt will bring quicker results, but the cream is finer grained when it is frozen slowly. Pack the freezer one third full of ice before adding any salt, then add the salt and the remaining ice and salt in alternate layers around the container until the freezer is filled.

Turn the cream slowly at first until a slight pull is felt, then turn it rapidly.

If the ice cream is to be used at once, turn it until it is very stiff. If the ice cream is to be packed, turn it only until it is the consistency of thick sauce. Ices and sherbets are treated in the same way.

Pour off the salt water in the freezer. Wipe the lid carefully, remove it, remove the dasher, scrape it and pack the cream down with a spoon. Place a heavy piece of waxed paper over the top of the container. Place a cork in the lid, fit it closely on the container and repack the ice cream in additional salt and ice. Cover the freezer with newspapers and a piece of carpet or other heavy material.

There is no flavoring extract comparable in quality to the vanilla bean. Add it to the milk in which the sugar is dissolved for ice cream. You may add it to sugar in the French way. See page 709.

VANILLA ICE CREAM I
About 1½ Quarts

Warm over low heat but do not boil:
    1 cup cream
Stir in until dissolved:
    ¾ to 1 cup sugar
    ⅛ teaspoon salt

Chill these ingredients. Add to them:
    3 cups cream
    1½ teaspoons vanilla
Freeze the cream as directed in the preceding rule. Serve it with:
    Tutti Frutti, page 809, Cherries Jubilee, page 779, Crushed Nut Brittle, page 794

761

Vanilla Ice Cream with Evaporated Milk, page 766.

VANILLA ICE CREAM WITH EGG YOLKS
About 1½ Quarts
Scald over low heat but do not boil:
 1½ cups milk
Stir in until dissolved:
 ¾ cup sugar
 ⅛ teaspoon salt
Pour the milk slowly over:
 2 or 3 beaten egg yolks
Beat these ingredients until they are well blended. Stir and cook them over low heat or in a double boiler until they are thick and smooth. Do not let them boil. Chill them. Add:
 1 tablespoon vanilla
Whip until stiff:
 1 pint heavy cream: 2 cups
Fold it into the custard. Freeze the cream as directed (page 761).
Serve it with:
 Crushed Caramelized Nut Brittle, page 794

CHOCOLATE CHIP ICE CREAM
Prepare the above:
 Vanilla Ice Cream I
or other vanilla ice cream. When partially frozen stir in:
 2 cups chipped semisweet chocolate
Freeze until it is firm.

CARAMEL ICE CREAM I
Prepare:
 Caramel Sirup, page 754
Prepare:
 Vanilla ice cream
Add:
 2 tablespoons or more caramel sirup
Freeze the cream as directed (page 761). This is good served with:
 Chopped pecans or toasted almonds

Caramel Ice Cream with Evaporated Milk, page 767.

CHOCOLATE ICE CREAM
About 1¾ Quarts
Dissolve in a double boiler:
 2 oz. chocolate in
 2 cups milk
Stir in:
 1 cup sugar
 ⅛ teaspoon salt

Remove these ingredients from the heat. Beat them with a wire whisk until they are cool and fluffy. Add:
 1½ teaspoons vanilla
Whip until stiff:
 1 pint heavy cream: 2 cups
Fold the cream into the chocolate mixture. Freeze it as directed (page 761).
You may serve the ice cream in:
 Meringues, page 654
with:
 Chocolate Sauce, page 757

Chocolate Ice Cream with Evaporated Milk, page 767.

COFFEE ICE CREAM
About 1½ Quarts
Scald over low heat but do not boil:
 2½ cups rich milk
Stir in until dissolved:
 1½ cups sugar
Pour the milk slowly over:
 2 beaten eggs
Beat these ingredients until they are well blended. Stir and cook them over low heat or in a double boiler until they are thick and smooth. Do not permit them to boil. Chill them. Add:
 ½ cup strong cold coffee
 ½ teaspoon salt
Whip until stiff:
 1 cup heavy cream
Fold in:
 1 teaspoon vanilla
 (3 tablespoons rum)
Fold it into the other ingredients. Freeze the cream as directed (page 761).

COFFEE FRAPPÉ
2 Quarts or More
Dissolve:
 1¾ cups sugar
in:
 3 cups strong coffee
Chill these ingredients. Add:
 3 cups cream
Partly freeze the mixture (page 761). Beat until stiff and fold in:
 3 egg whites
 ¼ teaspoon salt
Freeze the frappé until it is firm. Serve it garnished with:
 Whipped cream

COFFEE PARFAIT
About 1 Quart
Combine:
 2 tablespoons cornstarch
 ⅔ cup sugar

⅛ teaspoon salt
Stir into this:
   2 tablespoons milk
Beat, then add:
   2 egg yolks
   1 cup strong coffee
Stir and cook this custard over very low heat or in a double boiler until it thickens. Chill it. Whip until stiff, then fold in:
   1½ cups heavy cream
Freeze the parfait as directed (page 761). Serve it in tall glasses topped with:
   Whipped cream

TOASTED NUT ICE CREAM
Add to the mixture for Vanilla Ice Cream I, page 761:
   1 cup toasted, ground or chopped almonds, pecans or Brazil nuts or 1 cup crushed nut brittle
To toast the nut meats place them in a slow oven 300° until lightly browned. The almonds may be ground without being blanched.

PISTACHIO ICE CREAM
About 1¾ Quarts
This is a pretty Christmas dessert served in a meringue tart garnished with whipped cream and cherries.
Shell:
   4 oz. pistachio nuts
Blanch them. Pound them in a mortar with:
   A few drops rose water
Add to them:
   ¼ cup sugar
   ¼ cup cream
   1 teaspoon vanilla
   ½ teaspoon almond extract
   A little green coloring
Stir these ingredients until the sugar is dissolved. Heat but do not boil:
   1 cup cream
Add and stir until dissolved:
   ¾ cup sugar
   ⅛ teaspoon salt
Chill these ingredients. Add the pistachio mixture and:
   3 cups cream
Freeze the cream as directed (page 761).

MOCK PISTACHIO ICE CREAM
Prepare:
   Vanilla Ice Cream I, page 761
Before freezing it add:
   1 teaspoon almond extract
   1½ teaspoons vanilla
   A little green coloring

Freeze the cream as directed (page 761). Serve it in:
   Meringues, page 654
or in a:
   Meringue Tart, page 654
Garnish it with:
   Whipped cream, maraschino cherries or fresh strawberries

PEPPERMINT STICK ICE CREAM
About 1½ Quarts
Grind or crush:
   ½ lb. peppermint stick candy
Soak it for 12 hours in:
   2 cups milk
Add to it:
   1 pint cream: 2 cups
If the cream is heavy, whip it by all means. Freeze the mixture as directed (page 761). Serve the ice cream with:
   Chopped Chocolate, page 756, or Chocolate Sauce, page 757

RASPBERRY ICE CREAM
Put through a sieve:
   2 cups raspberries: 1 pint
Add them to one of the rules for:
   Vanilla ice cream
You may stir in when the ice cream is partially frozen:
   2 tablespoons kirsch or 1 teaspoon almond extract

STRAWBERRY ICE CREAM I
About 1½ Quarts
Hull:
   1 quart strawberries
Crush them. Stir in:
   ⅞ cup sugar—1 cup less 2 tablespoons
Chill the berries thoroughly. Combine them with:
   1 quart cream: 4 cups
Freeze the cream as directed (page 761).

PEACH ICE CREAM
About 1½ Quarts
Pare, slice and mash:
   4 lbs. ripe peaches
Stir in:
   ½ cup sugar
   ⅛ teaspoon salt
Cover the peaches and permit them to stand until the sugar is dissolved. Combine:
   1 teaspoon vanilla
   ½ cup sugar
   1 quart cream: 4 cups

Partly freeze these ingredients as directed (page 761). When they are half frozen add the peach mixture and finish freezing the cream.

APRICOT ICE CREAM
Prepare the preceding:
Peach Ice Cream
Substitute for the peaches:
Fresh apricots

DRIED APRICOT ICE CREAM
About 1½ Quarts
Cook by the rule on page 450:
½ lb. dried apricots: 1½ cups
with 1 to 1¼ cups sugar
Put them through a ricer. Cool the pulp. Add:
2 tablespoons lemon juice
1 quart cream: 4 cups
Freeze the mixture as directed (page 761).

BANANA ICE CREAM
Prepare:
Vanilla Ice Cream I, page 761
Use the larger amount of sugar. Partly freeze the mixture. Stir in until blended:
1 cup riced banana pulp
½ cup lemon juice
Finish freezing the cream.

ORANGE ICE CREAM
About 1½ Quarts
Scald:
1½ cups heavy cream
Stir in until dissolved:
1½ cups sugar
Chill the mixture. Add:
1½ cups heavy cream
Freeze the cream as directed (page 761) until it is the consistency of mush. Add:
3 tablespoons lemon juice
1¼ cups orange juice
Finish freezing the cream.

BAKED ALASKA
6 Servings
Cover a breadboard with heavy paper. Place on it squares of:
Sponge Cake, page 596, or
Angel Cake, page 599
cut into slices about ½ inch thick.
Place on each piece a slice of:
Ice cream
Use ice cream frozen in brick form. The ice cream should be cut 1 inch shorter than the cake so that it will come within ½ inch from the edge when placed upon it.
Cover the ice cream and cake well with a Meringue, page 578, made with:
6 egg whites
⅛ teaspoon salt
6 tablespoons confectioners' sugar
1 teaspoon vanilla
You may dust the top well with confectioners' sugar. Bake the Alaska in a hot oven 450° until the meringue is brown. Slide it from the paper onto a plate. Serve the Alaska at once.
One large slice of cake may be used and the whole brick of ice cream or ice cream frozen in a round mold may be placed upon it. The ice cream may be hollowed slightly and filled with preserves or crushed sweetened fruit. Or cake may be baked in individual "Mary Jane" or upside-down pans, as shown

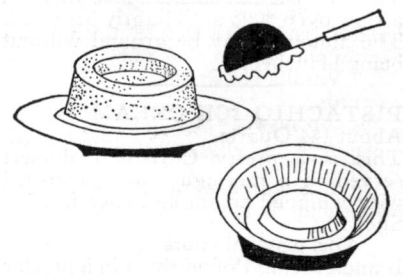

here, the centers filled with ice cream and the whole covered with meringue. For 6 such cakes use 1 pint of ice cream and 4 egg whites.

ANGELICA I OR PARFAIT
About 1½ Quarts
Boil to the thread stage (page 781):
¾ cup water
1 cup sugar
Whip until stiff:
3 egg whites
⅛ teaspoon salt
Continue to whip while pouring the sirup in a slow stream onto the egg whites. Whip constantly until the mixture is cool. Add:
1 teaspoon vanilla
Whip until stiff and fold in:
1 or 2 cups heavy cream
Freeze the mixture as directed (page 761). Serve it with:
Crushed berries, Chocolate Sauce, page 757, or over Sour Cream Apple Soufflé, page 637

FROZEN EGGNOG I
Prepare:
Vanilla Ice Cream with Egg Yolks, page 762
When partially frozen make a funnel-shaped hole in the center. Place in it:
Several tablespoons rum, brandy or whisky
Stir the liquor into the ice cream.

MACAROON ICE CREAM
Follow the rule on page 761 for:
Vanilla Ice Cream I
Use:
¾ cup sugar
Crush and add:
12 macaroons: 1 cup
You may sprinkle them with:
2 tablespoons rum or sherry
Freeze the cream as directed (page 761).

BURNT ALMOND ICE CREAM
Follow the rule on page 761 for:
Vanilla Ice Cream I
Use only:
½ cup sugar
Crush with a rolling pin until fine or grind:
½ lb. Sugared Almonds, page 794
Add them to the cream. Freeze the cream as directed (page 761).

MARSHMALLOW NUT MOUSSE
About 1 Quart
Whip until stiff:
1 pint heavy cream: 2 cups
Fold in:
½ cup and 2 tablespoons confectioners' sugar
2 tablespoons Caramel Sirup, page 754
2 teaspoons vanilla
Partly freeze this mixture (page 761).
Beat in:
½ cup broken pecan meats
¼ lb. marshmallows cut into pieces
Freeze the cream until it will hold its shape.

NUT BRITTLE MOUSSE
A Scant Quart
Crush:
¾ lb. Nut Brittle, page 794
Whip until stiff:
1 pint heavy cream: 2 cups
Fold the brittle into the cream. Freeze the mousse as directed (page 761).
Serve it with:
Chocolate Sauce, page 757

Ice Creams, Ices and Desserts To Be Made in Refrigerator Trays or in Molds

Rules for Making Frozen Desserts with Mechanical Refrigeration

In order to freeze ices and ice creams successfully in a mechanical refrigerator, or in a mold packed in ice and salt, it is advisable to add some thickening substance to the mixture to be frozen. This substance may be dissolved gelatine, flour or cornstarch, egg yolks in custard or hot sirup poured over egg yolks or egg whites.

When cream or evaporated milk is used in creams or mousses it must be stiffly whipped and folded into the other ingredients just before the mixture is put into a refrigerator tray or mold.

Mechanically frozen ice creams and ices have not the light consistency characteristic of churned ice creams and ices, but in the case of mousses and bombes, excellent results are obtained.

In the case of ices and sherbets vigorous beating at intervals during the freezing time will give the ice the quality of a frappé or coarsely frozen water ice.

Corn sirup added to water ice, ice cream or mousse helps to prevent an icy consistency. A good proportion is 1 part corn sirup to 2 parts sugar.

Combinations that are too sweet will not freeze in a mechanical refrigerator. A good proportion is 1 part sugar to 4 parts liquid.

Sherbets are water ices to which a small amount of dissolved gelatine is added. When partly frozen the ice is combined with stiffly beaten egg whites.

Parfaits are stiffly beaten egg whites over which a thick hot sirup is poured. When the mixture is cool it is combined with stiffly whipped cream.

Mousses are heavy cream whipped and combined with flavors of different kinds, eggs, fruit pulp, chocolate, gelatine, macaroons, etc.

Bombes are mousses frozen into various shapes.

The length of time for freezing ices and ice creams depends upon the refrigerator used. Companies manufacturing refrigerators issue time charts for freezing desserts. The period varies but is usually from 2 to 4 hours.

It is advisable to use 2 trays in preference to 1. Be sure to moisten the outer bottoms of the filled trays with water for faster freezing.

All mixtures frozen in refrigerator trays are improved by frequent stirring while being frozen. They may be beaten with a wire whisk or an electric beater shortly before being served. Preparing ice cream mixtures a day in advance makes a smoother cream and increases the yield.

To Beat Cream or Evaporated Milk, see pages 631, 632.

Rule for Sealing and Packing Molds:

Molds fitted with tightly closing lids are made for freezing creams and ices. If there is no mold available, a baking powder can, or other tin receptacle that will close tightly, may be used.

Fill the mold with any desired mixture suited to the purpose of still freezing, cover the top of the can with a piece of heavy waxed paper and adjust the lid. Let the waxed paper protrude for an inch or more. Lift the paper and spread a generous coating of lard around the container under the paper, then plaster the paper down firmly and spread lard around the edge of the lid. This will keep the salt water from penetrating.

Have ice ready that has been pounded into small pieces, and set the mold in a bed of ice. Allow from 2 to 6 portions of ice to 1 of salt, and cover the mold completely. A bucket or pail is best that will allow for about a 3 inch packing. Freeze the cream from 4 to 6 hours.

VANILLA ICE CREAM II
About 1½ Quarts
Soak:
    2 teaspoons gelatine
in:
    2 tablespoons cold milk
Heat but do not boil:
    1 cup cream
Stir into it until dissolved:
    ¾ to 1 cup sugar
    ⅛ teaspoon salt
Stir in the soaked gelatine. When this mixture is cool add:
    2 teaspoons vanilla
Place it in refrigerator trays until it is thoroughly chilled. Whip it with a wire whisk. Whip until stiff:
    1½ pints heavy cream: 3 cups
Fold it into the chilled and beaten gelatine mixture. Freeze the cream in a mold (page 766) or in refrigerator trays (page 765). Serve it with:
    Chocolate Mint Sauce, page 780,
    or Maple Nut Sauce, page 779
or cover it with:
    Shredded coconut
    Chocolate sauce
An attractive way to serve vanilla ice cream in summer is to place balls of cream in the center of a large platter and surround it with mounds of red raspberries, black raspberries and pineapple, pared and cut into finger lengths.

VANILLA ICE CREAM WITH EVAPORATED MILK
4 Servings
Stir over heat but do not boil:
    ⅓ to ½ cup sugar
    ¼ cup cream
Chill this mixture. Add:
    1½ teaspoons vanilla
Prepare for whipping by the rule on page 632:
    1¼ cups evaporated milk
Whip it. Combine it lightly with the sugar mixture. Freeze the cream in refrigerator trays (page 765).

CARAMEL ICE CREAM II
Follow the above rule for:
    Vanilla Ice Cream II
Add to the gelatine mixture:
    2 tablespoons or more Caramel
    Sirup, page 754

CARAMEL ICE CREAM WITH EVAPORATED MILK
4 Servings
Prepare by the preceding rule:
  Vanilla Ice Cream II
Use:
  ⅓ cup sugar
Just before freezing the cream fold in:
  4 tablespoons Caramel Sirup, page 754

DELMONICO ICE CREAM
6 Servings
Beat:
  2 egg yolks
Beat in until well blended:
  ½ cup confectioners' sugar
  ¼ cup cream
Cook and stir these ingredients in a double boiler until they are slightly thickened. Chill them. Add:
  1 teaspoon vanilla or 1 tablespoon or more sherry
Whip until stiff:
  ½ pint heavy cream: 1 cup
In a separate bowl whip until stiff:
  2 egg whites
  ⅛ teaspoon salt
Fold the cream and the egg whites into the custard. Freeze the cream in a mold (page 766) or in refrigerator trays (page 765).
Serve it with:
  Sauce under Milk Pudding, page 741

GINGER ICE CREAM
Add to:
  Vanilla Ice Cream II, page 766
  ½ cup or more chopped preserved ginger
  2 tablespoons ginger sirup

CHOCOLATE ICE CREAM WITH EVAPORATED MILK
About 1½ Pints
Chill until ice-cold:
  1 cup evaporated milk
Combine:
  6 tablespoons cocoa or 1½ oz. melted chocolate
  6 tablespoons sugar
  ¼ teaspoon salt
Stir in gradually:
  ½ cup evaporated milk
  ½ cup water
Stir and cook these ingredients over boiling water until they are smooth. Add and stir until melted:
  16 marshmallows: ¼ lb.
Cool this mixture. Whip the chilled milk until stiff, then fold it in. Freeze

the cream in a mold or refrigerator trays (page 765).

ECONOMICAL CHOCOLATE ICE CREAM
3 Quarts
Boil:
  1 cup evaporated milk
  1 cup water
  2 cups sugar
Soak:
  1½ tablespoons gelatine
in:
  2 tablespoons cold water
Dissolve it in the hot sirup. Stir in until dissolved:
  ½ lb. minced chocolate
When cool stir in:
  1 teaspoon vanilla
  1 cup chilled evaporated milk
  1 cup Whipped Evaporated Milk, page 632
Freeze the cream in refrigerator trays (page 765).

CHOCOLATE ICE CREAM III
A Scant Quart
The custard for this good creamy ice cream may be made a day in advance and the egg whites folded in just before it is finally frozen. See below.
Melt over low heat:
  2 oz. chocolate: 2 squares
Three tablespoonfuls cocoa may be substituted. Beat well:
  2 egg yolks
Add gradually, beating constantly:
  ¾ cup sugar
Add the chocolate. Scald:
  1 cup evaporated milk
  1 cup milk
Pour a little of this mixture over the chocolate mixture. Beat it in. Return it to the pan. Cook and stir the custard over low heat until it is slightly thickened. Chill the custard. Add:
  1 teaspoon vanilla
Freeze it in a refrigerator tray (page 765) until it is nearly firm. Beat until stiff:
  2 egg whites
  ⅛ teaspoon salt
Fold them into the custard. Replace it in the refrigerator until it is firm. It may be beaten a second time before it is served. This gives it a fine fluffy consistency.

STRAWBERRY ICE CREAM II
4 Servings
Wash and hull:
  1 pint strawberries

Drain the berries. Crush them. Stir into them to sweeten them well:

Confectioners' sugar

Whip until stiff:

½ pint heavy cream: 1 cup

Fold it into the berry mixture. Freeze the cream in a mold or in refrigerator trays (page 765).

STRAWBERRY ICE CREAM III
6 Servings

Hull and cut into pieces or crush:

1 pint strawberries

Add:

1 cup sugar

Cook and stir the berries until they reach the boiling point. Chill them and add:

3 tablespoons lemon juice

Whip until stiff:

½ pint heavy cream: 1 cup

In a separate bowl whip until stiff:

2 egg whites
⅛ teaspoon salt

Fold the cream and the egg whites lightly into the berry mixture. Freeze the cream in a mold or in refrigerator trays (page 765).

Fruit Bombe or Mousse, page 770.

ANGELICA II
2 Quarts

Boil to the thread stage (page 781):

1½ cups sugar
½ cup water

Whip until stiff:

2 egg whites
⅛ teaspoon salt

Pour the sirup over them in a slow stream. Whip constantly. When the mixture is cool add:

1 teaspoon vanilla or
1 tablespoon or more sherry

Whip until stiff:

1½ pints heavy cream: 3 cups

Fold it lightly into the egg mixture. Freeze the cream in a mold or in refrigerator trays (page 765). Serve it with:

Raspberry Juice, page 759

RASPBERRY PARFAIT
About 1½ Quarts

Crush:

1 quart raspberries

The raspberries may be strained through 2 thicknesses of cheesecloth. Boil to the thread stage (page 781):

¾ cup water
1 cup sugar

Whip until stiff:

3 egg whites
¼ teaspoon salt

Pour the sirup over them in a slow stream. Whip constantly until they are cool. Fold in the crushed berries. In a separate bowl whip until stiff:

1 pint heavy cream: 2 cups

Fold it lightly into the other ingredients. Freeze the parfait in a mold or in refrigerator trays (page 765).

MAPLE PARFAIT
About 1½ Quarts

Cook and stir over boiling water until thick:

6 egg yolks
¾ cup maple sirup
⅛ teaspoon salt

When the custard will coat a spoon remove it from the heat. Pour it into a bowl and beat it with a wire whisk until it is cold. Whip:

1 pint heavy cream: 2 cups

Fold it lightly into the custard. You may add:

½ cup crushed nut brittle

Freeze the parfait in a mold or in refrigerator trays (page 765).

BUTTERSCOTCH PARFAIT
About 1 Quart

Stir and melt in a saucepan over low heat, then boil for 1 minute:

⅔ cup brown sugar
2 tablespoons butter

Add:

½ cup water

Cook the butterscotch until it is smooth and sirupy. Beat:

4 egg yolks

Add the sirup slowly, beating constantly. Cook and stir these ingredients over low heat until they are light and fluffy. Chill them. Whip until stiff:

1 cup heavy cream

Add:

A few grains salt
2 teaspoons vanilla

Fold in the egg mixture. Freeze the parfait in a mold or in refrigerator trays (page 765).

CARAMEL PARFAIT
About 1½ Quarts

Soak:

1½ teaspoons gelatine

in:

½ cup cold water

Melt and stir in a skillet until it is brown:

  ½ cup sugar

Burn it slightly. Stir in and cook until the sugar is dissolved:

  ½ cup boiling water

Beat:

  2 egg yolks

Beat in slowly:

  ½ cup sugar

Beat these ingredients until they are well blended. Add the caramel mixture. Stir these ingredients over slow heat or in a double boiler until they will coat a spoon. Stir in the soaked gelatine. Cool the custard. Add:

  2 teaspoons vanilla

Chill the custard until it is about to set. Whip until stiff:

  1 pint heavy cream: 2 cups

Fold it lightly into the custard. Freeze the parfait in a mold or in refrigerator trays (page 765).

TUTTI FRUTTI PARFAIT
About 1 Quart
Soak:

  1 cup chopped candied fruit

in:

  Brandy, rum, liqueur or sirup
  from canned or stewed fruit

Drain it well. Soak:

  1 teaspoon gelatine

in:

  2 tablespoons water

Dissolve it over hot water. Boil to the thread stage:

  ½ cup water
  ½ cup sugar

Beat until stiff:

  2 egg whites
  ¼ teaspoon salt

Pour the sirup over the egg whites in a fine stream, beating constantly. Beat in the dissolved gelatine. Continue beating until the mixture thickens somewhat. Beat in the drained fruit. Whip until stiff:

  1 cup heavy cream
  1 teaspoon vanilla

Fold this into the fruit and egg mixture. Freeze the parfait in a mold or in refrigerator trays (page 765). Serve it topped with:

  Whipped cream
  Candied cherries

Icy Lemon Fluff, page 720.

FROZEN CARAMEL PUDDING
This is a rather hefty but acceptable everyday dessert.
Follow the rule for:

  Caramel Cornstarch Pudding,
  page 719

Freeze it in refrigerator trays.

FROZEN COFFEE PUDDING
Follow the rule on page 762 for:

  Coffee Ice Cream

Soak:

  2 teaspoons gelatine

in:

  2 tablespoons cold water

Dissolve it in the hot coffee. Freeze the mixture in refrigerator trays.

Bombes, Mousses

The 3 following bombes, or mousses, are old treasured family recipes. These mixtures were placed in molds, packed in ice and salt and served on "occasions."

Today similar recipes are to be found in any book on Iceless Refrigeration. Modern equipment has made these dishes commonplace, but for me they retain a certain glamour associated with distinguished company, conviviality and the easy flow of intellectual conversation.

CHOCOLATE BOMBE
About 1¾ Quarts
Soak:

  1½ teaspoons gelatine

in:

  1 cup cold water

Stir and bring to the boiling point:

  1 cup milk
  1½ cups sugar
  2 tablespoons cocoa

Dissolve the gelatine in the mixture. Cool it. Add:

  1 teaspoon vanilla

Chill the gelatine until it is about to set. Whip until stiff:

  1 pint heavy cream: 2 cups

Fold it lightly into the gelatine. Freeze the bombe in a mold (page 766) or in refrigerator trays.

VANILLA BOMBE
About 2½ Quarts
Soak:

  1½ teaspoons gelatine

in:
    ¼ cup cold water
Stir and bring to the boiling point:
    2 cups milk
    1½ cups sugar
Dissolve the gelatine in the hot milk.
Pour part of this mixture over:
    2 beaten egg yolks
Beat these ingredients until they are
blended. Stir and cook them over a
very low fire until the eggs thicken
slightly. Cool the custard. Add:
    1 teaspoon vanilla
Chill it until it is about to set. Whip
until stiff:
    1 quart heavy cream: 4 cups
In a separate bowl whip until stiff:
    2 egg whites
    ⅛ teaspoon salt
Fold the cream and the egg whites
lightly into the custard. Have ready:
    18 macaroons
soaked in:
    Wine
Spread them with:
    Tart jelly
Place alternate layers of the cream and
the macaroons in a mold (page 766) or
in refrigerator trays. Freeze the
cream by packing it or by placing
it in the refrigerator.

APRICOT BOMBE
Method I. About 2 Quarts
Soak:
    1½ teaspoons gelatine
in:
    ¼ cup cold water
Bring to the boiling point:
    2 cups apricot pulp and juice
For this, Stewed Apricots, page 450,
cooked without sugar, can be put
through a ricer.
Dissolve the gelatine in the hot juice.
Add:
    1 cup sugar
    3 tablespoons lemon juice
Chill the mixture until it is about to
set. Whip until stiff:
    1 pint heavy cream: 2 cups
Fold it lightly into the apricot mixture.
Freeze in a mold (page 766) or in
refrigerator trays.

Method II. About 1¼ Quarts
Canned apricots make this recipe a
little bit less troublesome than No. I.
Drain the contents of:
    1 No. 3 can apricots
Put the pulp through a ricer. There
should be about 2¼ cupfuls. Chill it in

a refrigerator tray for 1 hour. Place it
in a bowl with:
    2 unbeaten egg whites
    ⅛ teaspoon salt
Beat it until light and fluffy. Whip:
    1½ cups heavy cream
Beat in gradually:
    ½ cup sugar
    ½ teaspoon vanilla
Fold this into the apricot mixture.
Freeze it in a mold (page 766) or in
refrigerator trays.

FRUIT BOMBE OR MOUSSE
About 1½ Quarts
Prepare:
    2 cups crushed fruit: peaches,
        apricots, bananas
Stir in:
    ⅛ teaspoon salt
    ¾ to 1 cup confectioners' sugar
Soak:
    1½ teaspoons gelatine
in:
    2 tablespoons cold water
Dissolve it in:
    ¼ cup boiling water
You may add:
    2 tablespoons lemon juice
Stir this into the fruit mixture. Whip
until stiff:
    2 cups heavy cream
Fold it into the fruit mixture. Freeze
the bombe in a mold (page 766) in
refrigerator trays.

MACAROON PEACH OR
APRICOT BOMBE
About 1¼ Quarts
Beat:
    1 egg
Beat in gradually:
    ½ cup sugar
Stir in:
    2 cups scalded milk
Stir and cook this custard over low
heat until the egg thickens slightly.
Chill it. Add:
    1 cup dry macaroon crumbs
    1 cup fresh peach or apricot pulp
Fold in:
    ½ cup heavy cream, whipped
    ½ teaspoon vanilla
Freeze it in a mold (page 766) or in
refrigerator trays.

BISCUIT TORTONI OR
MACAROON BOMBE
About ¾ Quart
Combine:
    ¾ cup crushed macaroons
    ¾ cup rich milk

¼ cup confectioners' sugar
A few grains salt
Permit these ingredients to stand for
1 hour. Whip until stiff:
1 cup heavy cream
Fold in the macaroon mixture and:
1 teaspoon vanilla
Place the mixture in paper muffin cups
set in a refrigerator tray. Either before
freezing or when it is partly frozen
decorate the tops with:
> Maraschino cherries
> Unsalted toasted almonds
> Angelica, etc.

MACAROON RASPBERRY BOMBE

A marvelous combination. Prepare:
Raspberry Ice II, page 775
Place it in refrigerator trays. Prepare:
Biscuit Tortoni, page 770
Heap it on the raspberry mixture in
the trays or place the raspberry mixture in a mold, heap the biscuit tortoni
upon it and freeze it as directed (page
766).

MACAROON STRAWBERRY BOMBE
About 1 Quart
Wash and hull:
1 pint strawberries
Sprinkle them with:
⅓ cup sugar
Permit these ingredients to stand for 1
hour. Put them through a ricer. Add:
A few grains salt
3 tablespoons corn sirup
Soak:
1 teaspoon gelatine
in:
3 tablespoons cold water
Dissolve it over hot water. Cool it.
Add it to the strained berries. Whip
until stiff:
1 cup heavy cream
Fold in the gelatine mixture and:
½ cup finely crushed macaroons
Freeze the cream in a mold (page 766)
or in refrigerator trays.

STRAWBERRY OR RASPBERRY BOMBE
About 1¼ Quarts
Hull and wash:
1 quart berries
Combine them with:
1½ cups sugar
2 tablespoons lemon juice
Chill them for 1 hour. Rub them
through a sieve or 2 thicknesses of
cheesecloth. Soak:

1¼ teaspoons gelatine
in:
2 tablespoons cold water
Dissolve it in:
3 tablespoons boiling water
Add it to the fruit juice. Chill the juice
until it is about to set. Whip until
stiff:
1 pint heavy cream: 2 cups
Add:
1 teaspoon vanilla
Fold it lightly into the gelatine mixture. Freeze the cream in a mold (page
766) or in refrigerator trays.

PEPPERMINT BOMBE
Follow the rule on page 763 for:
Peppermint Stick Ice Cream
Whip the cream. Serve the bombe
sprinkled with:
Chocolate decorettes or
Chocolate Sauce, page 757

BUTTER PECAN ICE CREAM
About 1 Quart
Boil for 2 minutes:
1 cup light brown sugar
½ cup water
⅛ teaspoon salt
Beat:
2 eggs
Beat in the sirup slowly. Cook these
ingredients over hot water, stirring
constantly, until they are slightly
thickened. Add:
2 tablespoons butter
Cool, then add:
1 cup milk
1 teaspoon vanilla extract
1 tablespoon sherry
Beat until thickened but not stiff:
1 cup heavy cream
Fold it into the egg mixture. Fold in:
½ cup broken toasted pecan meats
Place the cream in refrigerator trays
until it is partly frozen. Beat it well.
Freeze it until it is firm.

PERSIMMON ICE CREAM
4 Servings
A California recipe.
Put through a ricer:
2 ripe Japanese persimmons
Add:
1 tablespoon sugar
3 or more tablespoons lemon
juice
Fold in:
1 cup heavy cream, whipped
Freeze the cream in a mold (page 766)
or in refrigerator trays.

FRESH PINEAPPLE MOUSSE WITH LIQUEUR
About 1¼ Quarts
Prepare by putting through a grinder:
>Fresh pineapple to make
>1 cup pulp and juice

Combine it with:
>1 cup sugar
>¾ cup water
>¼ teaspoon salt

Bring these ingredients to the boiling point. Boil them for 10 minutes. Soak:
>1 teaspoon gelatine

in:
>2 tablespoons water

Dissolve it in the hot sirup. Chill, then add:
>2 tablespoons or more kirsch, Madeira, rum or liqueur

Whip until stiff:
>1 cup heavy cream

Fold in the fruit sirup. Freeze the mousse in a mold (page 766) or in refrigerator trays.

CHOCOLATE MOLASSES CHIP MOUSSE
About 1½ Quarts
Crush or grind:
>½ lb. Chocolate-Covered Molasses Chips, page 791

Soak:
>2 teaspoons gelatine

in:
>2 tablespoons cold water

Heat but do not boil:
>2 cups top milk

Stir in:
>¼ teaspoon salt
>⅓ cup sugar

Stir in the soaked gelatine. When these ingredients are dissolved cool the mixture. Add:
>½ teaspoon vanilla

Whip until stiff:
>2 cups heavy cream

Fold it into the milk mixture. Fold in the crushed candy. Freeze the mousse in a mold (page 766) or in refrigerator trays. Serve it sprinkled with:
>(Grated bitter chocolate)

APRICOT MOUSSE WITH EVAPORATED MILK
6 Servings
Soak for 12 hours:
>¼ lb. dried apricots: ¾ cup

in:
>1 cup water

Bring them slowly to the boiling point. Add:
>½ cup sugar

Cook the apricots for 2 minutes. Drain them. Cool them. Put the apricots through a ricer. There should be ¾ cupful pulp and ¼ cupful juice. Soak:
>1 teaspoon gelatine

in:
>2 tablespoons cold juice

Dissolve it in:
>2 tablespoons hot juice

Add the gelatine to the pulp and the remaining juice. Chill it until it is about to set. Prepare for whipping by the rule on page 632:
>1¼ cups evaporated milk

Whip it. Add to it:
>½ teaspoon vanilla
>⅛ teaspoon salt

Fold it lightly into the gelatine mixture. Freeze the mousse in refrigerator trays.

BLACK RASPBERRY MOUSSE
About 1¼ Quarts
Cook for 10 minutes:
>½ cup water
>1½ cups sugar

Cool the sirup. Add:
>1 tablespoon lemon juice

Press through a sieve:
>1 quart black raspberries

Add the juice to the sirup. Freeze it to a mush. Whip until stiff:
>1 cup heavy cream

Beat it into the raspberry mixture. Freeze it in refrigerator trays until it is nearly firm. Beat it again. Freeze it until it is stiff.

MACAROON MOUSSE WITH EVAPORATED MILK
4 Servings
Prepare by the rule on page 766:
>Vanilla Ice Cream with Evaporated Milk

Use:
>¼ cup sugar

Just before freezing the cream fold in:
>2 tablespoons Caramel Sirup, page 754
>10 crushed macaroons: about ¾ cup

PINEAPPLE MARSHMALLOW MOUSSE
About 1 Quart
Cut into small pieces:
>20 marshmallows

Pour over them and stir until dissolved:
>1 cup hot milk

Chill this mixture. Whip until stiff:
>1 cup heavy cream

Fold in the marshmallow mixture. Fold in the contents of:

    1 can crushed pineapple: 9 oz.

Freeze the mousse in refrigerator trays.

NUT BRITTLE MOUSSE

Follow the rule on page 765. Freeze the mousse in a mold (page 766) or in refrigerator trays.

FROZEN EGGNOG II

Follow the rule on page 765. Freeze the eggnog in a mold (page 766) or refrigerator trays.

MARSHMALLOW NUT MOUSSE

Follow the rule on page 765. Freeze the mousse in a mold (page 766) or in refrigerator trays.

Ices To Be Made in an Ice Cream Freezer

Ices may be frozen in an ice-cream freezer or in a refrigerator tray. When still frozen it is advisable to add gelatine to the mixture to avoid the formation of ice crystals.

Ices served in a meringue tart topped with whipped cream make a showy dessert. They may be served in individual meringues or the ice may be shaped in a ring on a platter and the ring may be filled with fresh or canned fruits.

Any one of the following ices may be frozen in a freezer, then used to line a mold or tray which is filled with whipped cream, sweetened lightly with powdered sugar and flavored with vanilla. The mold is packed in ice and salt until the cream is frozen (page 766), or the tray is placed in the refrigerator until the cream is frozen.

Decorate the dessert, when unmolded, with berries, kumquats or fruit that harmonizes in color and flavor with the ice.

A delicate flavor may be added to the following citrus fruit ices by using moderately strong tea in place of water.

LEMON ICE

About 1½ Quarts

Grate:

    2 teaspoons lemon rind

onto:

    2 cups sugar

Add, stir over heat until the sugar is dissolved, then boil for 5 minutes:

    4 cups water
    ¼ teaspoon salt

Chill this sirup. Add:

    ¾ cup lemon juice

Freeze the ice as directed (page 765). Serve it in a mound or ring with:

    Fresh or canned fruit used in some attractive combination flavored with curaçao, Cointreau or rum

-----

ORANGE AND LEMON ICE

About 1½ Quarts

This and the following Pineapple Ice are delicious served with rum. Place the ice in sherbet glasses and pour a teaspoonful of rum over each glass, or pass a small decanter of rum at table. Combine and stir:

    2 teaspoons grated orange rind
    2 cups sugar

Stir in and boil for 5 minutes:

    4 cups water
    ¼ teaspoon salt

Chill the sirup. Add to it:

    2 cups orange juice
    ¼ cup lemon juice

Freeze the ice as directed (page 765).

PINEAPPLE ICE

About 1½ Quarts

Boil for 5 minutes:

    1 cup sugar
    4 cups water

Chill the sirup and add:

    1 cup crushed pineapple
    ⅛ teaspoon salt
    6 tablespoons lemon juice

Freeze the ice as directed (page 765). Good served with:

    Chopped Chocolate, page 756

RASPBERRY ICE I

Follow the rule for Raspberry Ice II, page 775. Omit the gelatine. Freeze the ice as directed on page 765.

LOGANBERRY ICE I

About 1½ Quarts

An excellent substitute when fresh berries are not available.

Stir until the sugar is dissolved, then boil for 5 minutes:

2 cups water
2 cups sugar
¼ teaspoon salt

Chill the sirup. Strain the contents of:

1 No. 2½ can loganberries

There should be about 3 cupfuls juice. The juice may be strained through 2 thicknesses of cheesecloth. Add it to the sirup. Freeze the ice as directed (page 765).

STRAWBERRY ICE I

Strain or rice:

2 quarts strawberries

The juice may be strained through 2 thicknesses of cheesecloth. There should be about 2 cupfuls pulp and juice. Combine, stir until the sugar is dissolved, then boil for 3 minutes:

4 cups water
2 cups sugar

Chill the sirup. Add the strawberry pulp and:

1 tablespoon lemon juice

Freeze the ice as directed (page 765).

FRUIT ICE WITH BANANA I
About 1½ Quarts

Banana imparts a pleasant flavor to ices.

Combine and stir:

1 teaspoon grated lemon rind
1 teaspoon grated orange rind
1 cup sugar

Add:

1½ cups water

Stir over low heat until the sugar is dissolved, then boil the sirup for 5 minutes. Chill it. Add to it:

1 cup riced canned apricots with juice
5 tablespoons lemon juice
½ cup orange juice
1½ peeled riced bananas

Freeze the ice as directed (page 765).

APRICOT ICE
About 1½ Quarts

Put through a ricer or sieve the contents of:

1 No. 2½ can apricots

Add:

2¼ cups orange juice
6 tablespoons lemon juice

Stir in:

1 cup sugar

Freeze the ice as directed (page 765).

PEACH ICE
About 2 Quarts

Combine:

2 cups peach pulp: fresh peaches peeled and riced
6 tablespoons lemon juice
¾ cup orange juice

Boil for 5 minutes:

3 cups water
1 cup sugar

Chill the sirup. Combine it with the fruit pulp and juices. Freeze the ice as directed (page 765).

Ices To Be Made in a Mold or a Refrigerator Tray

FRUIT ICE WITH BANANA II

Soak:

2 teaspoons gelatine

in:

2 tablespoons cold water

Follow the rule on this page for:

Fruit Ice I

After the sirup has boiled for 5 minutes dissolve the gelatine in it. Chill the sirup. Add the fruit and proceed to pack the ice in a mold (page 766) or to freeze it in refrigerator trays.

ORANGE ICE AND FROZEN WHIPPED CREAM
6 Servings

Strain:

2 cups orange juice

If it is very acid stir into it a little:

Confectioners' sugar

Soak:

1 teaspoon gelatine

in:

1 tablespoon cold water

Heat ¼ cupful of the orange juice, dissolve the gelatine in it and return it to the remaining orange juice.

Whip until stiff:

1 pint heavy cream: 2 cups

Fold into it:

1 teaspoon vanilla
1 tablespoon or more powdered sugar
(½ cup broken nut meats)

Place the orange juice in the bottom of a mold or tray. Pile the cream on top of it. Freeze it packed in a mold (page 766) or in refrigerator trays.

RASPBERRY ICE II

To be used as a lining for a bombe or in the bottom of a refrigerator tray. See Macaroon Raspberry Bombe, page 771.

Soak:

    1 teaspoon gelatine

in:

    1 tablespoon cold water

Crush:

    1 quart red raspberries

Loganberries may be substituted. They have character and a delicious flavor. Put them through a fine strainer or 2 thicknesses of cheesecloth.

Strain through the pulp:

    ½ cup water

Combine and boil for 3 minutes:

    ½ cup sugar
    ½ cup water

Dissolve the soaked gelatine in the hot sirup. Cool it. Combine it with the raspberry juice. Add:

    1½ teaspoons lemon juice

Place the mixture in a chilled mold or in a refrigerator tray. Cover it with:

    Biscuit Tortoni, page 770

or with:

    2 cups heavy cream, whipped

to which add:

    1 teaspoon vanilla
    2 tablespoons confectioners' sugar
    (½ cup chopped nut meats)

Pile it on the fruit juice. Freeze the cream in a mold (page 766) or in refrigerator trays.

LOGANBERRY ICE II

Follow the rule on page 773 for:

    Loganberry Ice I

Soak:

    2 teaspoons gelatine

in:

    ¼ cup cold water

Dissolve it in the hot sirup. Use ½ of these ingredients and ½ the amount given in the recipe if you wish to line a mold or tray. Freeze the ice in a mold (page 766) or in refrigerator trays.

STRAWBERRY ICE II

6 Servings Crushed, 4 Servings Strained

This is the right amount to fill a 3 egg Meringue Tart, page 654. Top the tart with ½ pint (1 cupful) heavy cream, whipped, and a few unhulled strawberries. Crush or strain:

    1 quart berries

Soak:

    1 teaspoon gelatine

in:

    1 tablespoon cold water

Boil for 3 minutes:

    1 cup water or ½ cup water and ½ cup pineapple juice
    ¾ to 1 cup sugar
    ⅛ teaspoon salt

Add:

    1 to 2 tablespoons lemon juice

Dissolve the gelatine in the hot sirup. Chill it. Combine the crushed berries or juice with the sirup. Freeze the ice in a mold (page 766) or in refrigerator trays.

Sherbets To Be Made in an Ice Cream Freezer

These sherbets may be frozen in refrigerator trays. See Milk Sherbets, page 776.

LEMON, ORANGE OR PINEAPPLE SHERBET I

About 1½ Quarts

Follow the rules on page 773 for:

    Lemon, Orange or Pineapple Ice

Use only:

    2 cups water

Freeze the sherbet as directed (page 761) until it is the consistency of mush. Whip until stiff:

    2 egg whites
    ⅛ teaspoon salt

Fold them lightly into the sherbet. Continue to freeze it until it is firm. Pack the sherbet in ice and salt for at least 1 hour before serving it.

Please read the paragraph on Ices, page 773. Sherbets may be served in the same way.

MINT SHERBET

About 1½ Quarts

Combine and stir:

    1 teaspoon grated lemon rind
    1 teaspoon grated orange rind
    1½ cups sugar
    2 cups water

Stir over low heat until the sugar is dissolved, then boil the sirup for 5 minutes. Pour it over:

    12 sprigs chopped fresh mint

Use the tender leaves only and steep the mint for 1 hour. Strain the sirup. Add to it:

> ¾ cup orange juice
> 6 tablespoons lemon juice
> A little green coloring

Freeze these ingredients as directed (page 761) until they are the consistency of mush. Whip until stiff:

> 1 egg white
> ⅛ teaspoon salt

Fold them lightly into the sherbet. Continue to freeze it until it is firm. Pack it in salt and ice for at least 1 hour before serving it. Serve it garnished with:

> Mint leaves

The following milk sherbets are so good that they offer an "embarrassment of choice." Please try them out.

LEMON MILK SHERBET
About 1½ Quarts
Dissolve:

> 1⅓ cups sugar
> 7 tablespoons lemon juice

Stir these ingredients slowly into:

> 3½ cups milk or milk and cream

If the milk curdles it will not matter after it is frozen. Freeze the sherbet as directed (page 761). Pack it in ice and salt for at least 3 hours before serving it.

ORANGE MILK SHERBET
About 1¾ Quarts
Chill until very cold:

> 4 cups milk

While it is chilling, combine and stir:

> 1½ teaspoons grated orange rind
> 1½ cups sugar

Dissolve the sugar in:

> ¼ cup lemon juice
> 1½ cups orange juice

Stir these ingredients gradually into the chilled milk. If the milk curdles slightly it will not matter after it is frozen. Freeze the sherbet as directed (page 761). Pack it and permit it to stand for 3 hours before serving it.

PINEAPPLE MILK SHERBET
About 1¾ Quarts
Combine and stir:

> 1 cup unsweetened pineapple juice
> 1 teaspoon grated lemon rind
> ¼ cup lemon juice
> 1 cup sugar
> ⅛ teaspoon salt

Stir these ingredients slowly into:

> 4 cups chilled milk

Freeze the sherbet as directed (page 761). Pack it and permit it to stand 3 hours before serving it.

FRUIT MILK SHERBET
About 2 Quarts
Combine:

> 1½ riced bananas
> 10 tablespoons lemon juice
> 1¼ cups orange juice
> 3 cups milk
> 1½ cups sugar

Freeze the sherbet (page 761). Pack it and permit it to stand 3 hours before serving it.

Sherbets To Be Made in a Mold or a Refrigerator Tray

To freeze sherbet place the sherbet in trays in the refrigerator. At ½ hour intervals stir it from the back to the front. Freeze the sherbet for 4 hours or more. Beat it with a wire whisk or an electric beater before serving it.

FOUNDATION RULE FOR FRUIT SHERBET FROZEN IN A REFRIGERATOR
5 Servings
Soak:

> 2 teaspoons gelatine

in:

> ¼ cup cold water

Boil for 10 minutes:

> ¾ cup sugar
> 1¾ cups water

Dissolve the gelatine in the hot sirup. Chill it. Combine it with:

> 1 cup fruit juice

Place the mixture in a refrigerator tray for about 45 minutes until it begins to solidify. Turn it into a chilled bowl. Whip it with a wire whisk until it is fluffy. In a separate bowl whip until stiff:

> 2 egg whites
> ⅛ teaspoon salt

Fold them lightly into the fruit mixture.
Additional fruit juice or fruit pulp may be used in all sherbets except lemon

and orange. Subtract the amount of fruit juice added from the amount of water given in the recipe.
A delightful way to serve sherbet is to place on individual plates, or on a large platter, sugared fruits. Top them with sherbet.

LEMON SHERBET II
5 Servings
Soak:
    2 teaspoons gelatine
In:
    ¼ cup cold water
Boil for 10 minutes:
    2¼ cups water
    ¾ cup sugar
Dissolve the gelatine in the hot sirup. Chill it. Grate:
    1 teaspoon lemon rind
Add to it:
    ¾ cup lemon juice
Add these ingredients to the sirup. Fold into this chilled mixture:
    2 stiffly beaten egg whites
    ⅛ teaspoon salt
To freeze the sherbet, see page 776.
Serve it topped with finely chopped candied orange or lemon rind.

MINT SHERBET II
Follow the preceding rule for:
    Lemon Sherbet II
Strip the tender leaves from:
    12 sprigs mint
Chop them. Pour the hot sirup over them. Steep them for 1 hour. Strain and chill the sirup. Add to it:
    A little green coloring

GRAPEFRUIT SHERBET
4 Servings
The sherbets given in this chapter are all good but this one is outstanding.
Soak:
    2 teaspoons gelatine
in:
    ½ cup cold water
Boil for 10 minutes:
    1 cup sugar
    1 cup water
Dissolve the gelatine in the hot sirup. Chill it. Add to it:
    ¼ cup lemon juice
    2 cups fresh grapefruit juice
    ⅓ cup orange juice
    ¼ teaspoon salt
Fold into this chilled mixture:
    2 stiffly beaten egg whites
    ⅛ teaspoon salt
To freeze the sherbet, see page 776.

ORANGE SHERBET II
5 Servings
Soak:
    2 teaspoons gelatine
in:
    ¼ cup cold water
Boil for 10 minutes:
    1 cup water
    ⅔ to ¾ cup sugar as needed
Dissolve the gelatine in the hot sirup. Cool it. Add to it:
    1 teaspoon grated lemon rind
    1 teaspoon grated orange rind
    1½ cups orange juice
    ⅓ cup lemon juice
Fold into this chilled mixture:
    2 stiffly beaten egg whites
    ⅛ teaspoon salt
To freeze the sherbet, see page 776.

LIME SHERBET
4 Servings
Boil for 10 minutes:
    ⅔ cup sugar
    1¾ cups water
Stir in:
    1¼ teaspoons gelatine dissolved in
    ¼ cup cold water
Cool the sirup slightly. Add to it:
    ½ cup lime juice
    2 drops green coloring
Fold into this chilled mixture:
    2 stiffly beaten egg whites
    ⅛ teaspoon salt
To freeze the sherbet, see page 776.

THREE FRUIT SHERBET
6 Servings
Boil for 5 minutes:
    ¾ cup sugar
    1 cup water
Soak:
    1 teaspoon gelatine
in:
    2 tablespoons cold water
Dissolve it in the hot sirup. When the gelatine is dissolved chill the mixture. Stir in:
    ½ cup lemon juice
    1 cup orange juice
    1¼ cups riced banana pulp
Fold into this chilled mixture:
    1 stiffly beaten egg white
    ⅛ teaspoon salt
To freeze the sherbet, see page 776.

RASPBERRY SHERBET
5 Servings
Soak:
    2 teaspoons gelatine
in:

¼ cup cold water
Press through a sieve or ricer:
    1 quart fresh or frozen raspberries
Add to them:
    4 tablespoons lemon juice
Boil for 10 minutes:
    1¾ cups water
    ¾ cup sugar
Dissolve the gelatine in the hot sirup.
Cool it. Add the raspberries. Chill this
mixture. Fold into it:
    2 stiffly beaten egg whites
    ⅛ teaspoon salt
To freeze the sherbet, see page 776.

STRAWBERRY SHERBET
Follow the preceding rule for:
    Raspberry Sherbet
Substitute for the raspberries:
    1 quart strawberries

CRANBERRY SHERBET
8 Servings
Boil until soft:
    1 quart cranberries
    1¾ cups water
Strain the juice and put the berries
through a sieve. Add to them and boil
for 5 minutes:
    1¾ cups sugar
    1 cup water
Soak:
    2 teaspoons gelatine
in:
    ¼ cup cold water
Dissolve the gelatine in the hot juice.
Chill this mixture. Fold into it:
    2 stiffly beaten egg whites
    ⅛ teaspoon salt
To freeze the sherbet, see page 776.

BANANA PINEAPPLE SHERBET
About 1¼ Quarts
Combine and stir until dissolved:
    1½ cups crushed pineapple
    ¾ cup confectioners' sugar
Add:
    1½ cups banana pulp: about 3
        large bananas
    ½ cup orange juice
    6 tablespoons lemon juice
Place these ingredients in refrigerator
trays. Freeze them until they are near-
ly firm. Beat until stiff but not dry:
    2 egg whites
    ¼ teaspoon salt
Add the fruit mixture gradually. Beat
the sherbet until it is light and fluffy.
Return it to the trays. Freeze it until
it is firm.

REFRIGERATOR MILK SHERBETS
Simple and refreshing desserts. Superlative!
Follow one of the rules on page 776
for:
    Lemon, Orange, etc., Milk
    Sherbet
These sherbets may be frozen without
the addition of gelatine but they are
somewhat lighter when it is added.
Soak:
    2 teaspoons gelatine
in:
    2 tablespoons cold water
Dissolve it over heat. Add it to the
other ingredients. Place the sherbet
in trays in the refrigerator. When it is
fairly firm beat it well with a wire
whisk or an electric beater. Freeze it
until it is firm. Beat it well shortly
before serving it.

BUTTERMILK SHERBET
Method I. 6 Servings
This remarkable combination has
come into favor.
Combine:
    2 cups buttermilk
    ½ cup sugar
    ·1 cup crushed pineapple
Freeze these ingredients until they are
the consistency of mush. Place them
in a chilled bowl. Add:
    1 egg white
    1½ teaspoons vanilla
Beat the sherbet until it is light and
fluffy. Replace it in the refrigerator
trays. Freeze it until it is firm. Stir it
frequently.

Method II. About 1½ Quarts
Combine in a large bowl and beat well:
    1 quart buttermilk
    2 tablespoons grated lemon rind
    ¼ cup lemon juice
    ½ cup sugar
    1½ cups white corn sirup
    ⅛ teaspoon salt
Place these ingredients in 2 refrigerator trays until partly frozen. Pour
them into a cold bowl and beat them
with a wire whisk until smooth. For
best results freeze and beat the sherbet
3 times in all.

FROZEN RHUBARB
Sugarless but good.
Wash, then cut into ½ inch lengths:
    1½ lbs. young rhubarb
Cook it until soft in:

1½ cups light corn sirup
Add:
A few drops red coloring
Freeze the rhubarb in refrigerator trays. You may add:
1 package frozen strawberries

CANNED FRUIT FROZEN
Freeze:
A can of fruit

Follow the Rule for Packing a Mold, page 766. When it is frozen, place it horizontally and open it with a can opener by running the opener around the side of the can near the top. Invert the contents of the can and slice the iced fruit and juice. Serve each slice topped with:
Whipped cream
Fruit may be placed in a refrigerator tray but it must not be frozen too long. Two hours is usually sufficient.

Sauces and Garnishes for Frozen Desserts

Commercial ice cream may be glorified by the addition of a good sauce or a few tablespoonfuls of curaçao, brandy, rum or one of the following toppings:

Whipped cream and maraschino cherries
Honey and chopped citron
Crumbled macaroons
Crushed toasted or burnt almonds or hazelnuts
Decorettes
Chopped nut meats: black walnuts, hazelnuts, etc., plain or in maple sirup
Preserved chopped ginger with sirup

Finely chopped sweet or bitter chocolate
Hot maple sirup
Crushed sweetened fruit or cooked fruit
Crushed peppermint candy
Crushed or ground nut brittle
Shredded fresh coconut over vanilla ice cream served with chocolate sauce
Chopped candied orange or lemon rind

Crushed chocolate molasses chips

SPIKED BING CHERRY SAUCE
Drain well:
A can of pitted Bing cherries
Soak them for 2 hours in:
Brandy, whisky or rum
Stir them several times. Serve them over:
Orange ice

CHERRIES JUBILEE
6 Servings
Heat well the contents of:
A bottle of the best preserved cherries: about 1 cup
Add:
¼ cup brandy
Set the brandy on fire. When the flame is dead add:
2 tablespoons kirsch
Serve the sauce hot on:
Vanilla ice cream
If you do not wish to light the brandy, you may soak the cherries in it well in advance. If you wish to light the sauce be sure the fruit is at room temperature. Other preserves may be substituted for the cherries.

ORANGE MARMALADE SAUCE WITH CREAM
6 Servings
Combine and stir:
¾ cup orange marmalade
¼ to ½ cup cream

PEACH PRESERVE SAUCE
8 Servings
Combine and stir:
¾ cup peach preserves
2 teaspoons grated orange rind or
2 tablespoons orange marmalade
¾ cup orange juice
2 tablespoons brandy or rum
Other preserves may be substituted. A good combination:
Apricot preserves
prepared as directed above, flavored with:
Apricot brandy

MAPLE NUT SAUCE
10 Servings
Stir over low heat until dissolved, then boil without stirring to a thin sirup:

1 lb. maple sugar
½ cup evaporated milk
Add:
  ¼ cup corn sirup
  ½ teaspoon vanilla
  ½ cup shredded nut meats
Don't overlook Maple Sauce, page 755.

CHOCOLATE MINT SAUCE
6 Servings
Melt over hot water:
  10 large chocolate peppermints
Add:
  3 tablespoons cream
Stir the sauce well. Serve it over:
  Ice cream

CHOCOLATE NUT BRITTLE SAUCE
8 Servings
Melt over hot water:
  3 oz. sweet chocolate
Add:
  1¼ cups crushed nut brittle
Stir in slowly:
  ½ cup boiling water
Heat the sauce until the candy is melted. Cool it slightly. Before serving it add:
  1 tablespoon brandy
Serve it over:
  Ice cream

CRÈME DE MÊNTHE AS SAUCE
A handsome dessert.
Place in a bowl:
  A mound of vanilla ice cream
Pour over it:
  Crème de mênthe
Garnish the top with:
  A few maraschino cherries

FRESH FRUIT
Serve sliced peaches, crushed berries, etc., over frozen desserts. Sweeten the fruit. It may be topped with whipped cream.

HONEY SAUCE
4 Servings
Combine and stir well:
  ¼ cup hot water
  ½ cup honey
  ¼ cup chopped nut meats
  ¼ cup minced candied orange or
    lemon peel
Chill the sauce.
Candied ginger or grated orange or lemon rind may be substituted for the candied peel.

Candied Mint Leaves, page 490.
An attractive decoration for ices and sherbets.

FROZEN FRUIT SAUCE
Barely thaw frozen fruit, strawberries, peaches, etc. Slice the fruit. Add to it vanilla, brandy or rum. Peaches are improved by a few drops of almond flavoring.

CANNED FRUIT
Serve combinations of canned fruit, preferably with ices. Flavor the fruit with rum, brandy, etc.

SEMISWEET CHOCOLATE CASES
Line the insides of crinkle baking cups with:
  Melted chocolate chips
Allow the chocolate to harden. Carefully remove the paper. Fill the chocolate cases with ice cream or custard just before serving.

CARAMEL CREAM SAUCE
8 Servings
Combine and stir in a double boiler over hot water until melted:
  ½ lb. caramels
  1 cup rich cream or evaporated
    milk

Candies and Confections

The rainy day fudge pot is responsible for many an early stirring of culinary curiosity and the subsequent development of a good cook. When we were children inexperience frequently caused an aromatic, sublimely smooth substance to change mysteriously into a grainy mass of blighted hope, but only the chicken-hearted were discouraged by one failure. After devouring the hot debris voraciously, we were soon off to another attempt at candy making. I can still feel the burns on my finger-tips.

Our mothers bore the brunt of a general household and a specific stomach upset with patience. Had they not traveled the same sticky road to success? And success it was in the end although our rules were vague, candy thermometers and stabilizers such as corn sirup, cornstarch and cream of tartar being beyond our ken. It is easier today with all these aids and explicit directions to attain near professional results, but the fudge pot remains the young cook's initial baptism by fire, so please, in spite of its drawbacks, give your children free rein.

If you are using a thermometer, the following chart gives a good approximation of the various stages referred to in the recipes:

Thread	230° to 234°	Very Hard Ball	254° to 260°
Soft Ball	234° to 238°	Light Crack	270° to 285°
Firm Ball	244° to 248°	Hard Crack	290° to 300°
Hard Ball	248° to 254°	Caramelized Sugar	310° to 338°

To test the accuracy of your thermometer heat it gradually in water to avoid breakage, and keep it in boiling water for 10 minutes. It should register 212°. If there is any variation add or subtract the number of degrees necessary to make it conform. Clean the thermometer after using it for cooking by placing it in warm water.

If you are not using a thermometer, the following descriptions approximate the degrees given above. The thread stage has arrived when sirup dropped from a spoon spins a thread of about 3 inches. For the ball and crack stages have a cupful of cold water, not ice water, ready. Drop a little of the boiling sirup into it. When the sirup can be gathered up in the fingers into a soft ball that will hold its shape, until pressure is removed, it has reached the soft ball stage, 238°. When the sirup can be gathered up so as to hold its shape, it has reached the firm ball stage, 244°. When the sirup can be made into a ball and is still plastic but not rigid, it has reached the hard ball stage, 248°. When the cooled sirup is knocked against the side of a cup and a cracking sound is heard, it has reached the crack stage, 270° to 300°. Another test for the crack stages is to drop the hot sirup into the cold water. When the sirup separates into threads that are hard but not brittle, the light crack stage, 270°, has been reached. If the threads are brittle, the hard crack stage, 290°, has been reached.

Weather Conditions:

The weather is a big factor in candy making. It is impossible to make good hard candies in a moist, hot atmosphere. They become sticky, then sugary. It is advisable to take this into consideration when making all candies and to cook them to 2 degrees higher than in dry, cold weather.

Utensils:

Use a heavy aluminum pot and a long wooden spoon. Choose a pot that is large enough to let the sirup boil up without running over—one that holds about 4 times as much as the ingredients used. Grease the edge of the pot to the depth of 2 inches with butter to prevent the sirup from boiling over. A candy thermometer is a big help. Marble slabs are ideal cooling surfaces. A spatula or pot scraper is an aid in making smooth finishes.

Cooking:

Cook candies by stirring them over slow heat until the sugar is dissolved. Cover the pan for the first 3 minutes of boiling. The steam will prevent crystals from forming on the sides of the pan. Or wipe away the crystals that may form on the sides of the pan with a dampened pastry brush or with a wet cloth wrapped around the tines of a fork. Candies made with corn sirup must be cooked to slightly higher temperatures than those made without it.

Fondant, candies calling for water and hard candies are then cooked, without stirring, over rapid heat. This makes the latter crisp and brilliant. Remove the sirup gently from the fire and permit it to "settle" for a minute or 2 before pouring it.

Candies that call for butter, cream, milk, chocolate or molasses are apt to burn if not stirred while cooking. Dissolve the ingredients for these candies over quick heat. Cook them slowly after they reach the boiling point. Do not beat candies until they are cool—almost cold.

Drop butter on the surface when you remove the pot from the heat. Beat it in later.

If candy curdles while cooking, do not be alarmed; it will probably become smooth when it is beaten. You may add water to sugared candy and boil it again.

Greasing:

Grease pans or slabs that are to be used for all candy except fondant with salad oil or butter. Use a brush to spread it. Do not at any time oil marble that is to be used for fondant. Moisten it with water.

Pulling:

When pulling candy dip the hands frequently in cold water. If gloves are used, grease them lightly and dip them in flour. A candy hook is a great help when pulling large quantities of candy. It should be placed on a level with the eyes.

Dipping:

This is best done in a room that is about 65°. Melt chocolate for dipping at a very low heat.

Wrapping:

Wrap candies in small squares of waxed paper or aluminum foil. Store them in tin boxes.

Beating Candy Mixtures with an Electric Mixer:

Pour the cooked candy mixtures, while hot, into a large bowl. Add the butter and the flavoring. You may allow the candy to cool. Cooling it makes a creamier texture. Beat the candy at high speed for about 5 to 6 minutes. Add the nut meats and pour the candy onto oiled platters.

COOKED FONDANT

Stir in a saucepan over slow heat until dissolved:

> **3 cups sugar**
> **1 cup cold water**

Wipe the sides of the pan with a damp pastry brush or a damp cloth wrapped around the tines of a fork, so that no sugar will adhere to it. Cook these ingredients quickly, without stirring, to the soft ball stage 238°, page 781. An inexperienced candy maker may make sure of her results by adding to the boiling sirup:

> **¼ teaspoon cream of tartar**

Add, if desired, a little:

> **Coloring**

Pour the sirup onto a marble slab, a buttered enameled table top or large platter. Use only what will pour; do not scrape the pan. When thoroughly cool stir the sirup with a spatula or fork. Always work from the edges to the center. When the sirup begins to cream knead it well with the hands. Cover it with a damp cloth and permit it to stand for 10 minutes before using it.

The fondant may be set aside in an airtight container, like a sealed jar, tin box, etc., in a cold place where it will keep fresh for a long time.

Flavor the fondant as you use it with a few drops of:

> Oil of peppermint, wintergreen or almond extract

CREAMY FONDANT

A soft melting fondant.

Place in a saucepan:

> 2 cups sugar
> 1 cup water
> ¼ teaspoon glycerine
> 1 tablespoon white corn sirup

Stir these ingredients until the sugar is thoroughly dissolved. Place the pan over slow heat. When the mixture begins to boil cover it so that the steam will wash down any crystals that may form on the side of the pan. Cook the sirup for 3 minutes. Remove the cover. Continue cooking the sirup until it reaches the soft ball stage 238°, page 781. Remove it gently from the fire. Pour it onto a wet slab or platter. Cool the sirup until it is lukewarm.

Spread over it with a spatula:

> 1 well-beaten egg white

Follow the preceding rule for Cooked Fondant to work and shape it. Dip the fondant in:

> Chocolate Coating, page 784

This must be done at once as the egg white causes this fondant to soften quickly.

ALMOND PASTE

About 2 Pounds

In some parts of Europe this confection is traditional at Christmastime. It is molded into fancy shapes and frequently into flat cakes that are pie shaped and elaborately decorated. A thin wedge is served a visitor together with a glass of dessert wine.

Blanch:

> 1 lb. almonds

Grind them. All my other rules for grinding almonds read: "Put through a nut grinder." This is the only rule that says: "Put them through a meat grinder." This time you want the nuts to be oily. Use the finest knife and grind the almonds at least 4 times. Cook just past the soft ball stage to 240°:

> 2 cups sugar
> 1 cup water

Add the grated almonds and:

> 6 to 8 tablespoons orange juice
> A few drops rose water

Rose water is highly desirable as a traditional flavor, but other flavors may be substituted. Stir these ingredients until they are thoroughly blended and creamy. Knead them toward the end. There are 2 things that make kneading easier: put confectioners' sugar on your hands or cover the paste and permit it to rest for about 12 hours. Flatten it on a hard surface dusted with confectioners' sugar. Permit the paste to cool. Pack it in a closely covered tin or in a fruit jar. Permit it to ripen from 6 to 8 days.

MARZIPAN

Whip until fluffy:

> 1 egg white

Work in gradually:

> 1 cup almond paste, see above

Add:

> Confectioners' sugar

until it makes a paste that is easy to handle. Should it become too thick, work in drop by drop:

> Lemon juice

Knead the paste. Mold it into any desired shape. Use a pastry brush to color it, if you wish, with a little diluted coloring, or you may roll it in:

> Equal parts of cocoa and
> powdered sugar

Wrap each piece separately in waxed paper. Store the marzipan closely covered in a cool place. It dries out easily.

CHOCOLATE-COATED FONDANT BALLS OR UNCOOKED FONDANT

Tempting, opulent-looking—not for reducers. This candy is the specialty of a very clever hostess, whose parties seem incomplete without them. Her son calls them "knockout drops" because he once indulged in 13 and suffered the consequences.

Beat until soft:

> ½ cup butter

Add very slowly and cream until very light:

> 1 lb. confectioners' sugar

Add:

> 4 tablespoons rich, thick cream
> 1 scant teaspoon vanilla

Work the fondant well with the hands and shape it into 1½ inch balls. To roll the balls use about:

¼ lb. confectioners' sugar

A maraschino cherry, drained and wiped dry, a piece of date or fig, a few raisins or nut meats or a bit of candied fruit may be rolled into the center of the balls. Place the balls on waxed paper in the refrigerator until they are hard. Follow the rule below for:

Chocolate Coating

Cool it slightly. Dip the balls into the chocolate coating with a fork. Place them on waxed paper. Permit them to harden. Place the balls in a closed fruit jar in the refrigerator until ready to serve them.

BUTTER CREAM FONDANT

Follow the preceding rule for the fondant part of Chocolate-Coated Fondant Balls.

UNCOOKED FONDANT

Beat until well blended:

    1 egg white
    1 tablespoon cold water and
    2 tablespoons evaporated milk or
    3 tablespoons cream
    1 teaspoon vanilla or a few drops peppermint or wintergreen

Add very slowly until the fondant is thick enough to knead:

    Sifted confectioners' sugar

Knead and work it until it is smooth. A very little coloring matter may be added. Cover it with a damp cloth and permit it to stand for 1 hour before using it. It may be set aside in a sealed jar in a cool place and used when desired.

CHOCOLATE COATING

Choose crisp dry weather for dipping and work in a temperature between 60° and 70°. Special dipping chocolate is available but other types suggested below may be used. In any case grate the chocolate and melt it in the top of a double boiler, over, not in, hot water. Stir the chocolate until it reaches 130°. Remove it from the heat and cool it to about 83°. Heat water in the bottom of the double boiler to 85°. Place the chocolate in the double-boiler top over it. Immerse the centers one at a time in the chocolate. Lift them out with a fork, shake off the excess coating and use the drippings falling from the fork, as you remove it, to make designs by which you may identify the various fillings. Dip quickly. Place the candies on waxed paper to dry, or on a piece of white oilcloth stretched on a board. The latter process is the better of the two.

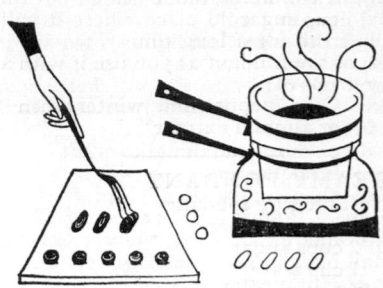

I am giving a recipe for chocolate coating that is in general use. However, both bitter chocolate and milk chocolate may be melted by a very slow process, over warm, not hot, water and used for dipping, after the chocolate has been melted and is almost cold, with excellent results.

If you find milk chocolate too sweet, use milk and bitter chocolate in equal parts.

Place in a shallow pan over warm water:

    4 oz. chocolate
    2 tablespoons butter
    1 inch square paraffin

Stir these ingredients until they are melted and blended. Add:

    5 drops vanilla

Remove them from the heat and follow the dipping process above.

UNCOOKED MAPLE WALNUT CREAMS OR MAPLE FONDANT

Combine and stir:

    1 egg white
    2 tablespoons evaporated milk
    1 teaspoon maple extract

Work in sufficient:

    Confectioners' sugar

to make a firm creamy fondant. Work in:

    1 cup chopped walnut meats

Press the candy into a buttered tin. Mark it into squares. Let it ripen for 24 hours. Break it into pieces.

PATIENCE CANDY OR CARAMEL FONDANT

Stir over quick heat until the sugar is dissolved:

1½ cups sugar
½ cup milk
¼ cup butter
Permit these ingredients to boil very slowly without stirring. Meanwhile melt in a skillet without stirring:

½ cup sugar

When the sugar is a light brown stir it very slowly into the boiling sirup. Cook the candy to the soft ball stage 238°, page 781. At this time beat in, if desired:

12 or more marshmallows cut into quarters

Cool the candy. Beat it until it is creamy. Pour it into a pan and mark it into squares or form the candy into small balls. Place them between:

Nut meats

or use the fondant as a filling for:

Dates or figs

This fondant may be dipped in:

Chocolate Coating, page 784

NEWPORT CREAMS
Stir over low heat until the sugar is dissolved:

⅔ cup corn sirup
2 cups brown sugar
6 tablespoons hot water

Cook these ingredients quickly, without stirring, to the thread stage 234°, page 781.
Whip until stiff:

1 egg white
A few grains of salt

Pour the sirup slowly onto the egg white. Whip constantly. Add:

1 teaspoon vanilla
1¼ cups nut meats

When you can no longer stir the candy flatten it out on a greased tin. When it is cold cut it into squares.

ALMOND CREAMS
Blanch and toast lightly:

Almonds

Cover them with:

Cooked Fondant, page 782, or
Uncooked Fondant, page 784

Dip them at once in:

Chocolate Coating, page 784

Place them on waxed paper to dry.

OPERA CREAMS
About 1¼ Pounds
Stir over quick heat until the sugar is dissolved:

2 cups sugar
¾ cup rich cream
1 cup milk

2 tablespoons light corn sirup
⅛ teaspoon salt

Cook and stir these ingredients over slow heat to the soft ball stage 238°. Remove them from the heat. Cool them. Add:

1 teaspoon vanilla

Beat the mixture until it is creamy. Add:

1 cup pecan meats
1 cup English walnut meats

Pour the candy into a buttered pan. When it is cold cut it into squares. Place it in an airtight container. This candy improves with age.

PEPPERMINT CREAMS
Stir over slow heat until the sugar is dissolved:

2 cups sugar
¼ cup light corn sirup
¼ cup milk
¼ teaspoon cream of tartar

Cook and stir these ingredients slowly to the soft ball stage 238°, page 781. Remove them from the heat. Cool them slightly. Beat the candy until it is creamy. Flavor it with:

½ teaspoon peppermint

Color it lightly as desired. Drop it from a teaspoon onto waxed paper.

PEPPERMINT DROPS
Stir over slow heat until the sugar is dissolved:

2 cups sugar
½ cup cold water
¼ teaspoon cream of tartar

Cook these ingredients quickly, without stirring, to the soft ball stage 238°, page 781. Remove them from the heat. Permit them to stand for 2 minutes. Add:

8 to 12 drops oil of peppermint

Beat the candy until it becomes creamy and begins to cool. Drop it from the side of a teaspoon onto waxed paper.

COCOA FUDGE
This makes the best fudge imaginable—rich, soft and creamy. As the ingredients used do not differ materially from dozens of other fudge recipes, the manner of making it is undoubtedly responsible for the success. When you eat this observe the feed limit.
Stir over quick heat until the sugar is dissolved:

2 cups sugar
6 tablespoons cocoa
¾ cup milk

Cook these ingredients very, very slowly to the soft ball stage 238°, page 781. Do not stir them, unless they threaten to burn, after they reach the boiling point. Remove the saucepan from the fire and add, without stirring:

2 tablespoons butter

Cool the sirup. Do not be disturbed if the butter fails to combine with the sirup. Time enough to beat it in later. If in haste, place the pan in cold water. When the sirup is nearly cold, add:

1 teaspoon vanilla

Beat the sirup until it is creamy. Grease a platter lightly with:

Butter

When the sirup thickens, just before it is ready to pour onto the platter, add:

1 cup broken nut meats

Black walnut meats or grated coconut are sometimes a welcome change. Pour the candy onto the platter. Cut it into squares before it hardens.

CHOCOLATE FUDGE
About 1¼ Pounds

If a fudge mixture becomes too hard or if it sugars, add enough milk to it to melt it and cook it again to the right temperature.

Stir over quick heat until the sugar is dissolved:

2 oz. chocolate
2 cups sugar or ½ cup sugar and
1½ cups brown sugar
⅛ teaspoon salt
¾ cup rich milk
5 tablespoons white corn sirup

Cook the sirup slowly to the soft ball stage 238°, page 781. Stir it frequently. Remove it from the fire. Add:

4 tablespoons butter

Cool the candy slightly. You may place the pan in cold water. Beat it until it begins to harden. Add:

1 teaspoon vanilla
(⅓ cup broken nut meats)

Pour it onto an oiled platter. Cut it into squares before it hardens.

For a good fudge that is less rich and a bit grainier, reduce the corn sirup to 2 tablespoonfuls and use only 2 tablespoonfuls butter.

To substitute cocoa for chocolate, see page 946.

BROWN SUGAR FUDGE
Follow the preceding rule for:

Chocolate Fudge

Omit the chocolate. Substitute for white sugar:

Brown sugar

COFFEE FUDGE
About 1½ Pounds

Stir over slow heat until the sugar is dissolved:

2 cups sugar
1 cup strong coffee
1 tablespoon cream
1 tablespoon butter
⅛ teaspoon salt
¼ teaspoon cream of tartar

Boil these ingredients quickly, stirring them constantly, to the soft ball stage 238°, page 781. Remove the candy from the fire. Cool it slightly. Add:

½ teaspoon almond extract or ½
teaspoon cinnamon

Beat it until it begins to harden. Add:

1 cup broken pecan or hickory
nut meats

Pour the candy onto an oiled platter. Permit it to cool and harden before cutting into oblongs or squares.

MAPLE SUGAR FUDGE
Break into small pieces and place in a saucepan:

2 cups maple sugar

Add:

⅛ teaspoon salt
½ cup boiling water

Cook and stir the mixture until the sugar is dissolved. Add:

1 cup cream or rich milk

Boil the sirup slowly, stirring it frequently, to the soft ball stage 238°, page 781. Cool it. When it is lukewarm beat it until it is creamy. Beat in:

(1 cup or more broken nut meats)

Pour the candy into a greased pan. Permit it to cool and harden before cutting it into oblongs or squares.

CANDY PUDDING
Stir over quick heat until the sugar is dissolved:

5 cups light brown sugar
¾ cup light corn sirup
1 tablespoon butter
¼ teaspoon salt
1 cup cream
¼ cup water

Boil these ingredients slowly, stirring them constantly, to the soft ball stage 238°, page 781. Add:

1 lb. blanched shredded almonds
¼ lb. chopped figs
1 lb. seeded chopped raisins

Stir the candy well, remove it from the fire and beat it hard until it begins to cream. Shape it into a roll. Cover it with a damp cloth. When it is cold and firm, cut it into pieces.

CHOCOLATE PECAN SQUARES WITH SOUR CREAM

Stir over quick heat until the sugar is dissolved, then boil slowly, without stirring, to the soft ball stage 238°, page 781:

> 2½ cups brown sugar
> 3 oz. chocolate
> 1 cup thick sour cream

Cool the candy. Beat it until it begins to harden. Add:

> ⅔ cup chopped pecan meats

Pour these ingredients onto a buttered pan. When cool cut the candy into squares.

CHOCOLATE BALLS OR TRUFFLES I WITH CONDENSED MILK

Melt over hot water:

> 6 oz. milk chocolate

Add:

> ½ teaspoon cinnamon
> 1½ teaspoons butter

When the butter is melted add:

> A scant ½ cup sweetened condensed milk—½ cup less 1½ teaspoons
> ½ teaspoon vanilla

Stir these ingredients until they are thoroughly blended. Pour the mixture onto a shallow platter and chill it for 2 hours or more. Form it into balls. Roll the balls in:

> Chocolate decorettes or chopped nut meats

Chill the candy until it is hard.

CHOCOLATE BALLS OR TRUFFLES II WITH EVAPORATED MILK

Melt in a double boiler:

> ½ lb. bittersweet dipping chocolate cut in pieces

Add:

> ¾ cup evaporated milk
> ¼ teaspoon cinnamon

Cook and stir these ingredients over boiling water for 15 minutes. Cool them. Shape the candy into balls. Roll them in:

> Chocolate decorettes or chopped nut meats

FRENCH TRUFFLES

Grate:

> 3 oz. chocolate

Work into it:

> ¼ cup butter
> 7 tablespoons confectioners' sugar

Add to this:

> 2 tablespoons thick cream

Shape the candy into balls. Roll them in:

> Granulated sugar or cocoa

CHOCOLATE BALLS WITH NUTS

Cook over a slow fire, stirring constantly, until thick:

> 1 egg yolk
> ¼ cup sugar
> 2 tablespoons flour
> 1 cup milk
> ⅛ teaspoon salt

Remove these ingredients from the fire. Cool them. Melt in a separate saucepan:

> ½ lb. sweet chocolate

Cool it. Combine it with the egg mixture. Shape the candy into small balls. Roll them in:

> Confectioners' sugar

Place each ball between:

> 2 half walnut or pecan meats

GINGER CANDY

Stir over quick heat until the sugar is dissolved:

> 2 cups white sugar
> 1 cup brown sugar
> ¾ cup milk
> 2 tablespoons white corn sirup

Cook these ingredients slowly to the soft ball stage 238°, page 781. Stir them frequently. Add:

> 2 tablespoons butter

Remove the sirup from the fire. Cool it. Beat it until it begins to thicken. Add:

> 1 teaspoon vanilla
> ¼ lb. finely chopped ginger

If preserved ginger is used, drain it well. If candied ginger is used, wash the sugar from it in the milk, dry the ginger and chop it.

Pour the candy onto a greased platter. Cut it into squares before it hardens. These candy squares may be dipped in:

> Chocolate Coating, page 784

HAWAIIAN CANDY

This has the acid flavor of pineapple and the spicy flavor of ginger—a fine combination.

Stir over quick heat until the sugar is dissolved:

½ cup brown sugar
1 cup sugar
½ cup crushed drained pineapple
1 cup cream

Boil these ingredients slowly to the soft ball stage 238°, page 781. Stir them constantly. Remove them from the fire. Add:

1 tablespoon butter
1 teaspoon confectioners' ginger
½ cup broken pecan meats
1 teaspoon vanilla

Cool the candy. Beat it until it is creamy. Pour it into a shallow greased pan. Cut it into squares before it is cold.

MEXICAN ORANGE CANDY

Heat in a double boiler:

1 cup evaporated milk

Melt in a deep saucepan:

1 cup sugar

When the sugar is a rich brown, stir in slowly:

¼ cup boiling water or orange juice

Add the hot milk. Stir in until dissolved:

2 cups sugar
¼ teaspoon salt

Cook the sirup slowly to the soft ball stage 238°, page 781. Stir it frequently. Add:

Grated rind of 2 oranges

Cool these ingredients. Beat them until they are creamy. Stir in:

1 cup nut meats

Pour the candy onto a greased platter and cut into squares when it is cold, or drop it from a spoon onto waxed paper.

HONEY NOUGAT
About ¾ Pound

Blanch:

¾ cup almonds
¼ cup pistachio nuts

Dry them well in a slow oven 250°. Have ready a large bowl in which to whip the eggs that fits closely over a saucepan. Line a 4 x 8 inch pan, bottom and sides, with rice paper. Goldfish wafers will do. Place in an enameled saucepan:

1 cup sugar
⅓ cup corn sirup
⅓ cup strained honey
¼ teaspoon melted paraffin

Cook these ingredients over low heat, stirring constantly, until the sugar is dissolved, then cook them, stirring occasionally, to the firm ball stage 248°, page 781. Shortly before the sirup is ready beat until stiff:

2 egg whites
¼ teaspoon salt

Pour about ½ of the sirup in a slow steady stream over the egg whites, whipping constantly. Return the remaining sirup to the fire. Cook it to the crack stage 290°, page 781. Pour this gradually onto the egg whites, whipping constantly. Place the bowl over the saucepan partly filled with hot water. Bring the water to the boiling point. Beat the candy constantly until it begins to harden, until it is crisp by the cold water test. Beat in the nut meats and:

1 teaspoon vanilla

Pour the candy into the pan. Smooth over the top. Cover the candy closely with rice paper. Place waxed paper over this. Set the candy aside to cool. When cold, invert the pan, cut the nougat into oblong blocks with a knife or candy scissors. Wrap each piece in a square of waxed paper. The nougat may be chocolate dipped, page 784, in which case it requires no wrapping.

DIVINITY

Place in a saucepan and stir over low heat until dissolved:

3 cups sugar
¾ cup water
¾ cup white corn sirup

Cook these ingredients without stirring over medium heat to the crack stage 290°, page 781. Meanwhile beat until stiff:

3 egg whites
⅛ teaspoon salt

Pour a little of the hot sirup gradually over the egg whites, beating constantly with an egg beater or an electric mixer. Keep the remaining sirup boiling over a slow flame. Add it, little by little, to the egg whites. When all of it is beaten in, add:

1 teaspoon vanilla

Use a large spoon to beat in:

1 cup broken nut meats

Continue to beat until the mixture stands up well and loses its gloss. Drop it from a spoon in rounds on waxed paper.

CARAMEL CREAM DIVINITY

A smooth, rich, melting candy. Stir over quick heat until the sugar is dissolved:

3 cups sugar
1 pint cream: 2 cups
1 cup white corn sirup

Cook and stir these ingredients slowly

to the soft ball stage 238°, page 781. Remove the sirup from the fire. Cool it slightly. Beat it until it is very stiff. Beat in:

1 cup pecan meats

Pour the candy into a buttered pan. Cut it when it is cold.

DIVINITY ROLL

Put through a grinder:

1 cup raisins
2 cups stoned dates
1 cup figs
1 cup nut meats

Moisten these ingredients to make a thick paste with:

Orange juice

Boil to the soft ball stage 238°, page 781:

2 cups sugar
2 tablespoons white corn sirup
¼ cup hot water

Whip until stiff:

2 egg whites
⅛ teaspoon salt

Pour the sirup on the egg whites in a steady stream, whipping constantly. When thick pour the divinity onto a sheet of waxed paper. Cover it with fruit paste. Roll it while hot. Chill it. Cut into slices.

SEA FOAM

Stir over slow heat until the sugar is dissolved:

3 cups light brown sugar
1 cup water or ½ cup water and ½ cup light corn sirup
1 tablespoon vinegar

Cook these ingredients quickly to the soft ball stage 238°, page 781. Whip until stiff:

2 egg whites
⅛ teaspoon salt

Pour the sirup over the eggs in a thin stream. Beat them constantly. Place the bowl containing the candy over, not in, boiling water and beat the candy until it is thick and creamy. Add:

1 teaspoon vanilla
1 cup broken nut meats

Pour the candy onto an oiled platter. Cut it into squares while it is hot.

CHOCOLATE CARAMELS I WITH CREAM

40 Caramels

Stir over quick heat until the sugar is dissolved:

1 cup sugar
¾ cup light corn sirup
3 oz. chocolate
¼ teaspoon salt
½ cup cream

Boil these ingredients slowly to the soft ball stage 238°, page 781. Stir them constantly. Add:

½ cup cream

Cook the candy until it again reaches the soft ball stage 238°. Add:

½ cup cream

Cook the candy until it reaches the firm ball stage 248°, page 781. Remove the candy from the fire and pour it into an 8 x 4 inch tin that has been lightly oiled. Do not scrape the pan. When the candy is cold, mark it with a knife into squares, invert it onto a slab, turn it right side up and cut the squares with a long sharp knife. Permit it to dry for 3 or 4 hours. Wrap each piece of candy in waxed paper or aluminum foil.

CHOCOLATE CARAMELS II WITH MILK

Stir over quick heat until the sugar is dissolved:

3 cups sugar
1 cup light corn sirup
1 cup milk
1½ tablespoons butter

Cut into small pieces and stir in:

3 oz. chocolate

Stir and boil these ingredients slowly to the firm ball stage 248°, page 781. Add:

1 teaspoon vanilla

Pour the candy into lightly oiled tins. Follow the preceding rule for Chocolate Caramels I.

CHOCOLATE CARAMELS III WITH MOLASSES AND BROWN SUGAR

Stir over a quick fire until the sugar is dissolved:

1 cup molasses
1 cup brown sugar
1 cup white sugar
1 cup grated chocolate
1 cup milk or cream

Boil and stir these ingredients slowly until they reach the firm ball stage 248°, page 781. Add:

1 tablespoon butter
1 teaspoon vanilla

Pour the candy into lightly oiled tins. Follow the rule on this page for Chocolate Caramels I.

CREAM CARAMELS

Stir over quick heat until the sugar is dissolved:

    2 cups sugar
    1 cup cream
    1 tablespoon butter

Stir and cook these ingredients slowly to the soft ball stage 238°, page 781. Remove the candy from the fire. Cool it. Beat it until it is creamy. Pour it onto an oiled platter. Cut it into squares.

MAPLE CARAMELS

Stir over quick heat until the sugar is dissolved:

    2 cups brown sugar
    1½ cups maple sirup
    ½ cup cream

Stir and cook these ingredients slowly to the soft ball stage 238°, page 781. Add:

    1 tablespoon butter

Pour the candy into an oiled tin. Cut it into squares as it hardens. Nuts may be added to the candy just before removing it from the fire, or they may be sprinkled on the greased tin.

CARAMELS

Combine:

    2 cups white corn sirup
    2 cups white sugar
    ⅛ teaspoon salt

Cook these ingredients slowly, stirring constantly until they are clear. Add bit by bit:

    ½ cup butter

Add drop by drop:

    1 can evaporated milk: 14½ oz.

Continue to cook the candy very slowly to the soft ball stage 238°, page 781. You may add at this time:

    1 cup broken nut meats or
      chocolate chips

Pour it into a buttered pan. When cool, cut it.

VANILLA CARAMELS
About 1¼ Pounds

Place in a deep saucepan and stir over quick heat until the sugar is dissolved:

    1 cup sugar
    ½ cup brown sugar
    ¼ cup light corn sirup
    ¼ cup cream
    ½ cup milk
    6 tablespoons butter

Cook these ingredients over slow heat, stirring them rarely, to the firm ball stage 248°, page 781. Remove the candy from the fire. Add:

    1 teaspoon vanilla
    ⅛ teaspoon salt

Permit this to stand for about 15 minutes. Stir in:

    1 cup nut meats

Stir the candy only enough to incorporate the nut meats. Pour it into a shallow lightly buttered pan. When firm, invert the candy onto a wooden board. Cut it with a long thin-bladed knife, using a sawing motion. Place in a cool place for 2 hours, then wrap the candy in waxed paper or aluminum foil.

OLD-FASHIONED BUTTER-SCOTCH

Place in a deep kettle to allow for foaming:

    2 cups brown sugar
    ¼ cup molasses
    ½ cup butter
    2 tablespoons water
    2 tablespoons vinegar

Stir these ingredients over a quick heat until the sugar is dissolved. Boil them quickly, stirring them frequently, to the hard crack stage 300°, page 781. Pour the candy onto buttered tins and mark it into squares as it hardens or drop it from a teaspoon onto waxed paper.

BUTTERSCOTCH
About 1¾ Pounds

Stir in a saucepan:

    2 cups sugar
    ⅔ cup dark corn sirup
    ¼ cup water
    ¼ cup cream

Cook these ingredients to just below the hard ball stage 260°, then stir constantly until they almost reach the hard crack stage 288°. Pour the candy into an oiled pan. When cool and almost set mark it off into squares or bars. When cold, cut or break it apart.

ENGLISH TOFFEE

Combine in a deep saucepan and stir over quick heat until the sugar is dissolved:

    1¾ cups sugar
    ⅛ teaspoon cream of tartar
    1 cup cream

Stir and boil these ingredients for 3 minutes. Add:

    ½ cup butter

Cook and stir the sirup until it is light colored and thick to the hard crack stage 290°, page 781. Remove the sirup from the fire. Add:

1 teaspoon vanilla or 1 teaspoon
  rum
Pour the candy into a buttered pan.
When it is cold cut it into squares.

PLAIN WHITE PULL CANDY
Combine and stir over slow heat until
the sugar is dissolved:
  1¼ cups sugar
  ¼ cup water
  2 tablespoons mild vinegar
  1½ teaspoons butter
Cook these ingredients quickly, without stirring, to just between the very
hard ball and light crack stages, 268°-
270°, page 781. Add:
  ½ teaspoon vanilla or other
    flavoring
Pour the candy onto an oiled platter or
onto a marble slab and let it cool until
a dent can be made in it when pressed
with a finger. Gather it into a lump and
pull it with the finger-tips until it is
light and porous, page 782. Pull any
desired flavoring or coloring into the
candy. Roll it into long thin strips and
cut them into 1 inch pieces. Place the
candy in a tightly covered tin if you
wish it to become creamy.

CHOCOLATE PULL CANDY
Spread an oiled dish with:
  Grated chocolate
Follow the preceding rule for:
  Plain White Pull Candy
Pour it onto the chocolate. Pull the
chocolate into the candy.

SALT WATER TAFFY
Combine and stir over slow heat until
the sugar is dissolved:
  2 cups sugar
  1 cup light corn sirup
  1½ cups water
  1½ teaspoons salt
  2 teaspoons glycerine
Cook the sirup without stirring to the
early stages of the hard ball stage
256°, page 781. Remove it from the
heat. Add:
  2 tablespoons butter
Pour these ingredients onto a greased
platter, then follow the preceding rule
for Plain White Pull Candy. Pull in
flavoring and coloring.

CREAM PULL CANDY
Stir over slow heat until the sugar is
dissolved, then boil quickly without
stirring for 6 minutes:

  2½ cups sugar
  ¾ cup water
  ⅛ teaspoon salt
Skim these ingredients. Pour in very
slowly so that the boiling is not disturbed:
  ½ cup cream
Cook the sirup to between the firm
ball and the light crack stage 262°,
page 781. Remove it from the fire.
Add:
  ½ teaspoon vanilla
Follow the rule on this page for:
  Plain White Pull Candy

MOLASSES PULL CANDY
Stir over quick heat until the sugar is
dissolved:
  1 cup molasses
  2 teaspoons vinegar
  1 cup sugar
  ⅛ teaspoon salt
Boil the sirup rather quickly to just
below the firm ball stage 240°. Add:
  2 tablespoons butter
Boil the sirup slowly just past the very
hard ball stage, 265°. Stir it from time
to time as it tends to stick. Follow the
rule on this page for Plain White Pull
Candy.

MOLASSES PEPPERMINT CANDY
Follow the preceding rule for:
  Molasses Candy
Flavor it with:
  4 drops peppermint oil

CHOCOLATE-COVERED MOLASSES CHIPS
Stir over a quick flame until the sugar
is dissolved:
  1 cup molasses
  1 cup sugar
  2 tablespoons vinegar
  2 tablespoons butter
Boil these ingredients slowly to the
hard crack stage 290°, page 781. Stir
the sirup as it thickens. Add:
  1 teaspoon vanilla
Pour the candy onto a buttered platter.
To pull it follow the rule on this page
for Plain White Pull Candy. Pull it into
long thin strips. Cut them into 1 inch
pieces. When they are cold dip them in:
  Chocolate Coating, page 784

PEANUT TAFFY
Stir over quick heat until the sugar is
dissolved:

1 cup sugar
⅓ cup molasses
⅓ cup water
Boil these ingredients slowly to the hard crack stage 290°, page 781. Add:
½ teaspoon vinegar
2 tablespoons butter
Spread in a buttered pan:
1 cup chopped peanuts
Pour the taffy over them evenly. Cut the candy into squares when it is cold.

GUMDROPS OR TURKISH PASTE
About 1¾ Pounds
Soak:
2 tablespoons gelatine
in:
½ cup cold water
Pour:
¾ cup boiling water
over:
2 cups sugar
⅛ teaspoon salt
Stir the mixture over slow heat until the sugar is dissolved. Add the soaked gelatine. Bring these ingredients to the boiling point and boil them slowly for 15 minutes. Remove the sirup from the fire. Add:
1 teaspoon grated lemon rind
1 tablespoon lemon juice
1 teaspoon vanilla or other flavoring
A little coloring
It is well to taste the candy to see that it is flavored sufficiently. Pour it into a pan that has been dipped in cold water and permit the sirup to harden for 12 hours. Cut it into squares or oblongs with a hot knife and roll the pieces in powdered sugar or in granulated sugar. Fruit juice may be substituted for the water or diluted with water to make up ¾ cupful of liquid. Additional orange and lemon juice and rind add a great deal to this rather bland but popular paste.

ORANGE PASTE WITH NUTS
This is a winter confection as it will soften readily in hot weather. It is a great favorite with young people. Mine have nicknamed it "amoebas."
Soak for 5 minutes:
2 tablespoons gelatine
in:
¼ cup cold water
Stir and boil over slow heat until the sugar is dissolved:
2 cups sugar
½ cup water

Add the soaked gelatine. Boil the sirup for 10 minutes over a quick flame. Use an asbestos plate under the saucepan to keep the sirup from burning, or cook it in a double boiler for 20 minutes. Place on a lightly greased platter:
½ lb. finely chopped nut meats
Grate over them:
The rind of 1 lemon
The rind of 1 orange
Sprinkle over them:
The juice of 1 lemon
The juice of 1 orange
½ teaspoon vanilla
(6 drops rose water)
Pour the sirup over these ingredients. The paste should be about ¼ inch thick. Chill it for 6 hours or more. Cut it into squares. Roll them in:
Confectioners' sugar

APPLE CANDY SQUARES
About 2 Pounds
In order to utilize a surplus apple crop, an energetic Northwestern woman concocted a confection now sold all over that section of the country and known as Applets. It is delicious. This rule approximates an applet, at least it is as close to that confection as one can get to a professional secret.
Cook until tender, with the skin and cores, enough apples to make, when strained:
2 cups apple pulp
Use a well-flavored apple only. Add:
2 cups sugar
⅛ teaspoon salt
Cook the pulp slowly, stirring it frequently, until it is very thick and forms sheets from a spoon. Soak:
2 tablespoons gelatine
in:
⅔ cup cold water
Stir it into the hot pulp. Add, when the pulp begins to cool:
1½ cups broken walnut meats
¼ teaspoon orange extract
¼ teaspoon vanilla extract
Pour the candy into a buttered 8 x 8 inch pan. When firm cut it into oblongs or squares. They may be rolled in:
Confectioners' sugar

QUICK CHOCOLATE PECAN OR PEANUT CLUSTERS
Melt over hot water:
½ lb. package chocolate bits or other semisweet chocolate
Stir in slowly:
¾ cup sweetened condensed milk

When well blended add:

1 cup whole pecan meats or
shelled peanuts

Drop the clusters from a teaspoon onto
waxed paper.

HEAVENLY HASH
Dice:

12 marshmallows

Chop:

1 cup nut meats

Boil water in the bottom of a double
boiler. Turn off the heat. Place in the
top:

1 lb. milk chocolate

Stir it occasionally. Line a tray with
waxed paper. When melted pour in ½
the chocolate. Cover it with marshmallows and nut meats. Pour on the
other half. Cool and break the candy
into pieces.

TOFFEE COATED WITH CHOCOLATE AND NUTS
Chop until fine:

1½ cups nut meats

Combine, stir and heat to boiling:

1 cup sugar
¼ teaspoon salt
¼ cup water
½ cup butter

Cook without stirring to the light
crack stage 285°, page 781. Add ½
cupful of the nut meats. Pour the
candy onto a greased cookie sheet.
Permit it to cool. Melt over hot water:

12 oz. semisweet chocolate or
chocolate chips

Spread ½ of this over the candy.
Sprinkle it with ½ cupful of the nut
meats. Permit this to cool. Turn the
candy and spread it with the remaining
chocolate and nut meats. When cold
break the candy into pieces.

COCONUT STACKS
Combine in a deep saucepan:

1½ cups sugar
½ cup corn sirup
½ cup top milk
¼ cup molasses
⅛ teaspoon salt

Stir these ingredients over heat until
the sugar is dissolved, then cook them
slowly to the soft ball stage 238°, page
781. Stir in:

1¼ cups shredded coconut
3 tablespoons butter

Pour the candy onto a greased platter.
When cold enough to handle, shape it
into small cones. Place them on
greased waxed paper to dry.

COCONUT SQUARES
Stir over quick heat until the sugar is
dissolved:

2 cups sugar
2 tablespoons butter
½ cup milk

Cook these ingredients slowly and stir
them constantly until they reach the
soft ball stage 238°, page 781. Remove
them from the fire. Stir in:

1 cup shredded coconut
1 teaspoon vanilla

Beat the candy until it is creamy.
Place it in a buttered dish. Cut it at
once into squares.
Or, make patties by cooking the sugar
and the milk (omitting the butter) as
directed to the soft ball stage. Stir in:

1½ cups coconut
1 teaspoon vanilla

Drop the candy from a teaspoon onto
waxed paper. The centers may be
decorated with:

Cinnamon drops (redhots)

COCONUT MOLASSES CHEWS
Combine:

½ cup white corn sirup
½ cup New Orleans molasses
1 tablespoon vinegar
2 tablespoons butter

Stir and cook these ingredients over
quick heat until they boil. Cover them
with a lid for 3 minutes. Continue
cooking, stirring occasionally, until
the sirup reaches the firm ball stage
248°, page 781. Remove from heat.
Work in with 2 forks:

2 cups moist shredded coconut
⅛ teaspoon salt

Drop the chews on waxed paper.

RAISIN DROPS
Melt in a heavy skillet:

2 tablespoons butter

Stir in:

1 cup brown sugar

When the sugar is dissolved, stir in
until blended:

½ cup ground raisins
½ cup ground nut meats

Remove the candy from the fire. Add:

½ teaspoon vanilla

Drop the candy from a teaspoon onto
waxed paper.

PENUCHE
Stir over slow heat until the sugar is
dissolved:

2 cups brown sugar
¼ teaspoon salt
1 cup water

One cupful milk, cream or evaporated milk may be substituted for the water. In that case boil the sirup slowly and stir it frequently. Boil these ingredients slowly, without stirring, to the soft ball stage 238°, page 781. Add:

    1 tablespoon butter

Place the saucepan containing the candy in cold water. When the bottom of the saucepan is cool begin to beat the candy. Beat it until it is smooth and creamy. Add:

    1 teaspoon vanilla
    1 cup nut meats

Drop the candy from a spoon onto an oiled surface or waxed paper.

PRALINES

The preceding rule for Penuche may be used for Pralines. Separate the nut meats as the candy dries.
Stir over quick heat until the sugar is dissolved:

    4 cups light brown sugar
    2/3 cup rich milk or cream
    2 tablespoons butter
    1/8 teaspoon salt

Bring these ingredients to the boiling point. Stir them. Cook them slowly, stirring constantly, as brown sugar and milk have a tendency to curdle. After they have boiled for 4 minutes stir in:

    2 cups broken nut meats

Pour the candy onto a greased surface. Cool it. Separate the nut meats. Or drop the candy from a spoon into patties on waxed paper. Keep the pan over hot water while doing this.
Penuche and praline crumbs, if any, are fine added to or sprinkled over ice cream.

WHITE PRALINES

Stir over quick heat until the sugar is dissolved:

    3 cups sugar
    1 cup cream

Boil and stir these ingredients over low heat for 15 minutes. Remove them from the heat. Stir in carefully:

    1 teaspoon vanilla
    1 lb. pecan meats

Pour the candy onto a greased surface. Cool it. Separate the nut meats.

NUT BRITTLE.
Peanut, Almond, Etc.

This candy, ground or crushed, is delicious over ice cream and other desserts.

Melt in a skillet over low heat:

    1 cup sugar

Stir it constantly. When the sirup is light brown stir in until they are well coated:

    1 cup nut meats

Pour the candy onto an oiled platter. When it is cold break it into pieces.

PEANUT BRITTLE

Place in a heavy skillet and cook slowly to the thread stage 230°, page 781:

    1 cup white corn sirup
    2 cups sugar
    1/2 cup water

Add:

    2 cups raw Spanish peanuts with red skins

Stir and cook these ingredients just beyond the hard crack stage 301°-302°. Remove from the heat. Stir in until blended:

    1 1/2 tablespoons butter
    1 1/2 teaspoons vanilla
    2 teaspoons soda

Pour the brittle onto a greased surface, preferably marble. Turn it at once and stretch it quickly until it is very thin. When cold break into pieces.

SUGARED ALMONDS

Cook over slow heat, stirring constantly:

    2 cups sugar
    1/2 cup water
    1 teaspoon or more cinnamon

Boil the sirup rapidly. When it is clear and falls in heavy drops from a spoon, add:

    1 lb. unblanched almonds

Stir the almonds until they are well coated. Remove the candy from the heat and stir it until the nuts are dry. Sift them to remove the superfluous sugar. Add a very little water to the sifted sugar, a few drops of red coloring and as much additional cinnamon as is desired. Boil the sirup until it is clear, then add the almonds and stir them until they are well coated.

SPICED NUTS

Sift into a shallow pan:

    1/2 cup sugar
    1/4 cup cornstarch
    1/8 teaspoon salt
    1 1/2 teaspoons cinnamon
    1/2 teaspoon allspice
    1/3 teaspoon nutmeg
    1/3 teaspoon ginger

Combine and beat slightly:

1 egg white
2 tablespoons cold water
Dip in this mixture:
¼ lb. nut meats
Drop them one at a time in the sifted
ingredients. Roll them about lightly.
Keep the nut meats separated. Place
them on a cookie sheet. Bake them
in a very slow oven 250° for about 1½
hours. Remove them from the oven
and sift the sugar from them. When
cold they will be crisp and spicy.

---

*Salted Nuts (Almonds, Brazil Nuts,
Etc.), page 28; Toasted Pumpkin or
Squash Seeds, page 29.*

CHOCOLATE-COATED NUTS
Dip whole nut meats in:
Chocolate Coating, page 784

STUFFED APRICOTS
The following recipe makes a delicious
confection.
Wash and scrub in hot water:
1 lb. apricots
Steam them over hot water in a covered colander for 20 minutes. Make a
sirup of:
1 cup sugar
½ cup water
Boil it until it spins a thread 240°, page
781. Place the apricots in this and stir
them about gently with a fork. Permit
them to drain on a board for a few
minutes. Place in the center of each
apricot:
A piece of marshmallow
Roll the fruit in:
Granulated sugar

STUFFED PRUNES
Wash:
1 lb. large prunes
Steam them over hot water until they
are tender. Cool them. Remove the
stones. Stuff the prunes with one or
two of the following:
Fondant, page 782
Hard Sauce, page 753
Nut meats
Candied pineapple
Marshmallows, etc.
The prunes may be rolled in:
Granulated or powdered sugar

STUFFED DATES OR FIGS
Soak:
Dates or figs
in a little:

Wine, rum, whisky, lemon or
orange juice
or steam them for 10 minutes over hot
water. Remove the date seeds. Fill
the cavities with pieces of:
Marshmallow and nut meats
Shape the fruit in its original form and
roll it in:
Powdered sugar
The fruit may be stuffed with:
Candied ginger, candied fruit,
nuts or Fondant, page 782
Or steam dates as directed or buy
moist dates in bulk. Wrap a date
around a nut meat. Surround the date
with 3 nut meats. Surround the nut
meats with 2 dates. Roll these ingredients in the palm of your hands into a
firm ball. Roll the balls in granulated
sugar. Cut the balls into halves crosswise of the nut meats. Decorative and
good!

APRICOT ORANGE BALLS
About 45 Balls ¾ Inch in Diameter
Wash:
1 lb. best dried apricots
Smaller apricots may be used if they
are steamed for 5 minutes in a double
boiler before they are ground. Dry
them. Cut into pieces:
1 seedless orange
Put these ingredients through a meat
grinder. Place them in a double boiler
with:
1 or 2 cups sugar
Steam and stir them until the sugar is
dissolved. Cool them. Shape the candy
into balls. Roll the balls in:
Granulated sugar

APRICOT COCONUT BALLS
34 Balls ¾ Inch in Diameter
Wash:
¾ cup dried apricots
Steam them in the top of a double
boiler for 5 minutes. Put them through
a meat grinder with:
¾ cup shredded coconut
½ cup nut meats
Add:
1 teaspoon grated lemon rind
1 teaspoon lemon juice
Shape the mixture into balls about ¾
inch in diameter. Roll them in:
Granulated sugar
If the mixture seems dry, a little
orange juice may be added. If it is too
moist, a little powdered sugar may be
worked into it.

DATE ROLL

Boil to the soft ball stage 238°, page 781:

  3 cups sugar
  1 cup evaporated milk
Stir in:
  1 cup chopped dates
  1 cup chopped nut meats
When cool enough to handle, form these ingredients into a roll with buttered hands. Wrap the roll in a damp cloth or in waxed paper. Chill it. Slice it.

DATE BALLS

Remove the seeds from:
  1 lb. dates, or use ½ lb. seeded dates
Put them through a food chopper with:
  1 cup chopped pecan meats
Add:
  ¼ teaspoon salt
  1 teaspoon grated orange rind
Shape the candy into tiny balls. Roll them in:
  Confectioners' sugar

MERINGUE DATE BALLS

Follow the rule above for:
  Date Balls
Beat until stiff:
  2 egg whites
  ⅛ teaspoon salt
Add gradually, beating steadily:
  ½ cup sugar
  ½ teaspoon vanilla
Place the balls on a fork. Dip them in the egg mixture until well coated. Place them on a greased baking sheet. Sprinkle the tops with:
  Grated coconut
Bake them in a slow oven 250° for about ½ hour.

PERSIAN BALLS

Remove the seeds from:
  1 lb. dates, or use ½ lb. seeded dates
Cut the stems from:
  1 lb. dried figs
Put these ingredients through the coarsest cutter of a meat grinder with:
  1 lb. seeded raisins
  1 lb. pecan meats
  ½ lb. crystallized ginger or orange peel
Shape these ingredients into balls. If very stiff, add 1 or 2 tablespoonfuls lemon juice. Roll them in:
  Confectioners' sugar

FRUIT ROLL

Follow the above rule. Roll the mixture into long rolls. Roll them in:
  Confectioners' sugar
Wrap them in waxed paper. Serve them cut into slices.

PEACH AND APRICOT LEATHER

Use high grade of fruit for best results. Put through a food chopper twice, using the finest knife:
  2 lbs. dried apricots
  1 lb. dried peaches
Place on a board:
  Powdered sugar, not confectioners'
Roll out a small part of the fruit mixture at a time using powdered sugar on the rolling pin. Roll it to the thickness of ⅛ inch or less. Cut it into 1¼ x 2 inch strips. Roll the strips into tight rolls.

GLAZED FRUITS AND NUTS

Stir over slow heat until the sugar is dissolved:
  2 cups sugar
  1 cup water
  ¼ teaspoon cream of tartar
  or ⅔ cup light corn sirup
Cook these ingredients quickly without stirring until they become pale yellow, about 310°, almost to the caramelized stage, page 781. Or the sirup may be boiled to 290° and the lemon juice may be omitted. Remove the sirup from the fire and add:
  4 drops lemon juice
Plunge the pot containing the sirup for a moment into very cold water to check the boiling, then place it in hot water to keep the sirup from hardening. Begin dipping in the sirup at once:
  Nut meats, pieces of canned pineapple, cherries, figs, dates, prunes, grapes, sections of orange, etc.
Drop the candies on tin and they will not stick.
All the fresh fruits dipped must be perfect. Discard those that have been pricked or broken. Leave a bit of stem on grapes.

Frosted Grapes, page 450.

GLAZED PINEAPPLE

Drain the contents of:
  1 No. 2½ can pineapple
Dry the slices with a cloth. Add to the sirup from the can:

2 cups sugar
⅓ cup white corn sirup
Stir and bring these ingredients to a boil in a large kettle. Add the fruit but do not crowd it. Simmer the sirup until the fruit is clear. Lift it from the sirup; dry it on racks. Place it between waxed paper.

CANDIED KUMQUATS
Wash:
1 quart kumquats
Prick a hole in the stem ends. Cover the fruit with:
4 cups cold water
Bring it slowly to the boiling point. Simmer the kumquats until they are tender, about 10 minutes. Drain them well. Boil:
1 cup water
Stir in until dissolved:
2 cups sugar
Add:
⅛ teaspoon cream of tartar
Boil these ingredients to the soft ball stage 238°. Add the kumquats. Cook them slowly for 10 minutes. Remove them from the sirup. Drain them. When they are cool enough to handle roll them in:
Granulated sugar

Ornamental Cranberries, page 443.

CANDIED APPLES
Cook the sirup for:
Glazed Fruits, page 796

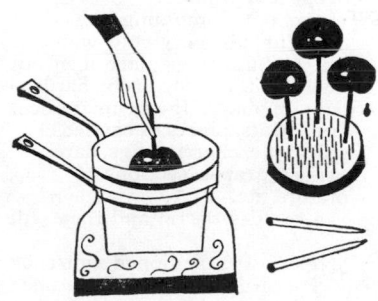

Add:
A few drops of coloring
Dip in:
Apples on skewers
Place them on a well-greased surface or on a metal flower holder to harden.

Candied Mint Leaves, page 490.

LOLLYPOPS
Stir over low heat until dissolved:
2 cups sugar
⅔ cup light corn sirup
½ cup water
Cook these ingredients, without stirring, over quick heat to just past the crack stage 310°, page 781. Remove the sirup from the heat. Stir in:
A few drops of coloring
1 teaspoon vanilla or fruit flavoring or a few drops peppermint oil, etc.
Pour the sirup by the tablespoonful onto a greased sheet. Press into each disk a wooden skewer or cardboard loop. Remove the lollypops when cold.

POPCORN BALLS OR LOLLYPOPS
½ Cup Corn Equals About 6 Cups Corn When Popped
Pop:
½ cup corn
Discard the imperfect kernels. Sprinkle the corn with:
½ teaspoon salt
Prepare one of the sirups given below. Stir it slowly into the popped corn until every kernel is coated. You may add to the corn:
2 cups shelled peanuts
Shape the corn lightly into balls with slightly floured or buttered hands as soon as it is cool enough to handle. Or you may shape the corn into inch thick lozenge shaped lollypops by inserting a wooden skewer or cardboard loop.

Molasses Sirup:
Melt:
1½ teaspoons butter
Add:
½ cup molasses
¼ cup sugar
Stir these ingredients until the sugar is

dissolved. Boil them without stirring to the hard crack stage 290°, page 781.

Caramel Sirup:
Melt:
　1½ tablespoons butter
Add:
　1½ cups brown sugar
　6 tablespoons water
Stir these ingredients until the sugar is dissolved. Boil them without stirring to the soft ball stage 238°, page 781.

White Sugar Sirup:
Stir until the sugar is dissolved:
　⅔ cup sugar
　½ cup water
　2½ tablespoons white corn sirup
Boil these ingredients without stirring to the firm ball stage 248°, page 781. Add and cook nearly to the hard crack stage 290°:
　⅛ teaspoon salt
　1 teaspoon vanilla
　⅓ teaspoon vinegar

Candied Fruit Peel

Here are 2 recipes for grapefruit or orange peel—both very good. The first can be made in an hour or 2; the second requires 24 hours' soaking. The first is a moist peel; the second has a more sugared quality.

CANDIED GRAPEFRUIT OR ORANGE PEEL
Method I.
Cut into strips:
　Grapefruit or orange peel
Cover it with cold water. Bring it slowly to the boiling point. Remove it from the fire. Drain it well. Repeat this process, boiling the peel in 5 waters in all. Drain it well each time. Make a sirup allowing:
　¼ cup water and ½ cup sugar
to the peel of 1 grapefruit or 2 large oranges. Add the peel and boil it until all the sirup is absorbed. Cool the peel. Roll it in:
　Sugar
Spread it to dry. The sugared peel, when thoroughly dry, may be dipped in:
　Chocolate Coating, page 784

Method II.
Cut into strips:
　Grapefruit or orange peel
Soak it for 24 hours in:
　Salt water to cover
Use 1 tablespoonful salt to 4 cupfuls water. Drain the peel, rinse it and soak it for 20 minutes in fresh water. Drain it, cover it with fresh water and boil it for 20 minutes and drain it again. Measure in equal parts with the peel:
　Sugar
Cook the peel, adding a very little water only if necessary, until it has absorbed the sugar. Shake the pot as the sirup diminishes so that the peel will not burn. This method does not call for rolling the peel in additional sugar.

Jellies, Jams, Preserves and Marmalades

The abundance that is summer may be translated into engaging rows of well-filled jelly glasses to carry you through the dearth that is winter. But if you feel akin to the grasshopper that "just sang" happily through the harvest months, and I have always envied her her good times, follow the recipes for the various preserves that you may now put up at any old time thanks to improved methods of transportation and storage. Of course the moral of the fable goes kiting partly because jellies and jams, for all their deliciousness, are almost without nutritive value and partly because there is much to be said in favor of this unseasonable convenience.

Jellies, jams and marmalades are made by boiling fruit juice and sugar, or fruit and sugar, until these ingredients reach a stage when they will form a jelly.

Rule for Making Jelly, Jam, Etc.

Fruit:

The best results are obtained by using fruit that is slightly underripe, when its pectin content is highest. Fruit that is ripe or overripe does not form a jelly readily. Slightly underripe fruit combined with fully ripened fruit produces a full flavor and a good consistency.

Some fruits like raspberries, pineapple, cherries and strawberries contain so little pectin that the addition of another fruit rich in pectin is needed to make their juices thicken. Apples, crab apples, currants, grapes, gooseberries, plums and cranberries may be added measure for measure or in smaller quantities to the fruits lacking the necessary amount of pectin.

Commercially prepared pectin is on sale at all groceries, and is in favor with many people. No recipes for jellies and jams made with commercially prepared pectin are given, because a much greater proportion of sugar to fruit is required and because special instructions invariably accompany the purchase of this product.

Sugar:

Tests show that beet and cane sugar produce the same results in jellies.

Water:

Water is added to fruit in varying quantities. Strawberries and some other berries may be preserved without the addition of water. Apples, plums and pears require it.

Water may be added to these fruits until it can be seen through the top layer, but the fruit must never float in water.

Juice for Jelly:

When the fruit has been cooked until it is soft, extract the juice by putting it through a jelly bag. Wet the bag, then wring the water from it. A dry bag takes up a lot of juice. If the jelly is to be clear and sparkling, do not squeeze the bag.

Special racks and bags are sold for jelly making. If there is no available jelly rack and bag, make a jelly bag of material that is to hold back the particles that will cause the jelly to be cloudy, a material like flannel, heavy muslin, or 3 or 4 layers of cheesecloth. Sew the bag well so that it will be strong. The top may be bound with tape and loops of tape may be sewed to it from which to hang it. Or, instead of hanging the bag, place it on a strainer and permit the juice to drip through both bag and strainer. When the juice stops dripping from the bag, you may return the pulp in the bag to the kettle. Add about half as much water and boil it from 10 to 15 minutes. This second extraction will give you a second-grade jelly, acceptable but inferior to the jelly made with the first extraction.

After using the bag rinse it in boiling water.

The strained juice may be reheated, poured boiling hot into sterilized jars covered with screw tops and simmered in a hot water bath 185° for 20 minutes. See page 850. Seal the jars completely. Keep them in a cool dark place. The juice will keep for about 6 months and can be made into jelly at your convenience.

Sugar:

Use ¾ cupful of sugar to every cupful of juice or fruit, except in cases where the fruit is extremely acid. Then use 1 cupful of sugar to 1 cupful of fruit or juice. The sugar may be preheated by being placed in a slow oven. Many cooks recommend this.

A jelly that contains too little sugar will not thicken, but a jelly that contains too much sugar will become sirupy and will not thicken either. The following helpful test has been contributed by the wife of an instructor in physics.

Test for Pectin:

To determine if fruit juice contains sufficient pectin to jell, put 1 tablespoonful of the cooled fruit juice in a glass. Add the same quantity of grain alcohol and shake gently. The effect of the alcohol is to bring together the pectin in a jelly. If a large quantity of pectin is present it will appear in 1 mass or clot when poured from the glass. This indicates that equal quantities of sugar and juice should be used. If the pectin does not slip from the glass in 1 mass, less sugar will be required. If the pectin collects in 2 or 3 masses, use two thirds or three fourths as much sugar as juice. If it collects in several small particles, use one half as much sugar as juice.

To Boil Jelly:

The best jelly is made by cooking a small quantity of juice at a time, about 4 to 6 cupfuls. Measure the juice and place it in a deep kettle that will allow for the boiling up of the liquid.

Boil the juice rapidly for 5 minutes and skim it, if necessary. Add the sugar, which may have been warmed, stir it until it is dissolved, and continue to boil the juice rapidly, without stirring it, until it is ready to be removed from the fire.

To Test Jelly:

Begin to test the juice 5 minutes after the sugar has been added. Place a small amount of jelly in a spoon, cool it slightly and let it drop back into the pan from the

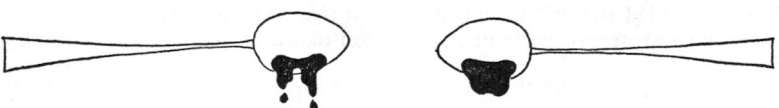

side of the spoon. As the sirup thickens, 2 large drops will form along the edge of the spoon, 1 on either side. When these 2 drops come together and fall as 1 drop, as shown to the right above, the "sheeting stage," 220° to 222°, has been reached.

This makes a firm jelly. If you like a somewhat softer jelly, cook the sirup only until it falls in 2 heavy drops from the spoon as shown to the left above.

The jelly is then ready to be taken from the fire. The time for cooking required will probably be between 8 and 30 minutes, dependent upon the kind of fruit and the amount of sugar used.

Place the jelly at once in sterilized glasses. Fill them to within ¼ inch of top. Do not boil jelly unnecessarily. Quick, short cooking preserves both its color and its flavor.

Preserves:

Preserves are fruits cooked with sugar until the sirup thickens, the fruit being permitted to remain whole.

Apply the test given for jelly. If you like a "loose" quality in preserves, cook them until 2 heavy drops form on the edge of the spoon and not until the 2 drops combine and fall together.

Jams:

Jam is fruit cooked with sugar until the ingredients thicken and the fruit loses most of its shape.

To Sterilize Glasses or Jars:

Fill glasses or jars three-fourths full of water and place them well apart in a shallow pan partly filled with water. Simmer the glasses 15 or 20 minutes. Keep hot until ready to fill. If the lids are placed lightly upon the glasses they will be sterilized at the same time.

Paraffin:

Melt paraffin over very low heat or over hot water. If the paraffin is permitted to become very hot it is apt to pull away from the sides of the jelly glass. Pour it from a small teapot or pitcher to cover the jelly as soon as it is cold with a very thin coating of paraffin. On the second day place a string across the paraffin allowing it to protrude somewhat. The string will help in removing the paraffin. Cover the jelly again with a thin film of paraffin, tilting the glass to permit the paraffin to cover every bit of the surface. The 2 coatings should not be more than ⅛ inch thick. A heavy coating of paraffin is apt to pull away from the sides of the glass. Besides it is wasteful and unsightly.

A simpler way of handling paraffin is to put 1½ to 2 teaspoonfuls of shaved paraffin in the bottom of a jelly glass. Pour the hot jelly on it. The paraffin will melt and rise. In the case of preserves place the paraffin in the hot sirup on top.

Cover the jelly glasses with tin lids and store the jelly in a cool, dark place. If placed in a warm, light place, it may "weep" and ooze from the glass.

Jellies

CURRANT JELLY

Wash:

Currants

It is not necessary to stem them. Place them in a kettle. Currants may be cooked with or without water. This is a matter of taste. Cooking them without water makes a very concentrated jelly. If water is used, allow about ¼ as much water as there is fruit. If no water is used, crush the bottom layer of currants and pile the rest on top of them. Cook the currants over low heat until they are soft and colorless. Drain them through a jelly bag (page 799). Allow to each cupful of juice:

¾ to 1 cup sugar

Cook only 4 cupfuls of juice at a time. Follow the Rule for Making Jelly on page 799.

CURRANT AND RED RASPBERRY JELLY

Prepare currants by the preceding rule for:

Currant Jelly

Crush:

Raspberries

Add them to the currants. Cook the fruit until the currants are soft and colorless. Strain the fruit through a jelly bag (page 799). Equal parts of raspberries and currants may be used, or 2 parts raspberries to 3 parts currants, and even 1 part raspberries to 3 parts currants will impart a delicious flavor to the jelly. Allow to each cupful of juice:

¾ to 1 cup sugar

Cook only 4 cupfuls of juice at a time. Follow the Rule for Making Jelly, page 799.

CURRANT AND BLACK RASPBERRY JELLY

Follow the preceding rule for:
    Currant and Red Raspberry
    Jelly
Substitute black raspberries for red. If they are rather dry, add a little water to them.

BLACK RASPBERRY AND GOOSEBERRY JELLY

Place in a saucepan and stew until soft:
    4 quarts black raspberries
    ¼ cup water
Place in a separate saucepan and stew until soft:
    2 quarts gooseberries or about 2
    cups sliced green apples with
    peel and core
    ½ cup water
Combine the fruits and strain them through a jelly bag (page 799). Allow to each cupful of juice:
    ¾ to 1 cup sugar
Cook only 4 cupfuls of juice at a time. Follow the Rule for Making Jelly, page 799.

CRAB APPLE JELLY

Follow the rule below for:
    Apple Jelly
Do not quarter the crab apples. Cut them into halves.

QUINCE JELLY

Scrub and cut into quarters:
    Quinces
Remove the seeds. Follow the rule below for:
    Apple Jelly
See rule for Quince Jam, page 806.

APPLE JELLY

Wipe, quarter and remove the stems and blossom ends from:
    Tart apples
Place them in a saucepan. Add water until it can be seen through the top layer of apples. Cover the pan. Cook the apples until they are soft. Drain them through a coarse sieve. Put the juice through a jelly bag (page 799). Boil the juice for 20 minutes. Allow to each cupful of juice:
    ¾ to 1 cup sugar
Cook only 4 cupfuls at a time. Follow the Rule for Making Jelly, page 799.
For a delicious flavor add to every 6 pounds of apples 1 pound of frozen raspberries. Place them in the apple juice for the last 5 minutes of boiling. Strain them before adding the sugar.

MINT JELLY

Follow the preceding rule for:
    Apple Jelly
Before removing the jelly from the fire bruise the leaves of a bunch of:
    Fresh mint
Hold the stems in the hand and pass the leaves through the jelly until the desired strength of mint flavor is obtained. Add a small amount of:
    Green coloring

ROSE GERANIUM JELLY

See Flavored Jellies, page 803.

PARADISE JELLY

Wash and cut into quarters:
    20 medium-sized apples
Peel and cut into quarters:
    10 medium-sized quinces
Remove the seeds. Place the apples in a pan with:
    1 quart cranberries
Barely cover them with water. Boil them until they are soft. Cover the quinces with water. Boil them until they are soft. Strain the juices of all the fruits through a jelly bag. Boil them for 12 minutes. Allow to each cupful of juice:
    1 cup sugar
Cook only 4 cupfuls at a time. Follow the Rule for Making Jelly, page 799.

GRAPE JELLY

Wash underripe:
    Grapes
They are preferable to ripe or overripe grapes on account of their tart flavor and pectin content.
Remove them from their stems. Place them in a kettle with a small quantity of water—about ½ cupful of water to 4 cupfuls of grapes. A quartered:
    Apple
may be added to this amount of grapes, but the addition is optional. It is supposed to keep grape jelly from sugaring. Boil the grapes until soft. Strain them through a jelly bag. Allow to each cupful of juice:
    ¾ to 1 cup sugar
Cook only 4 cupfuls at a time. Follow the Rule for Making Jelly, page 799.

WATERLESS GRAPE JELLY

This recipe is included for when it succeeds it is superlative. Some grapes

do not co-operate. In this case nothing is lost as you then proceed by the Rule for Grape Jelly, page 802.
Wash:

Concord grapes

Mash them in a large pot. Cook them until soft. Strain the juice from them. Measure it. Bring juice to a rolling boil. Remove it from the fire. Add the same amount of sugar as you have juice. Stir it over heat until it is dissolved. Pour the jelly into sterilized glasses and seal them.

PLUM JELLY

Goose plums make delicious jelly or jam.
Wash:

Small red plums

Place them in a saucepan. Add water to them until it can be seen through the top layer. Boil the plums until they are soft, then strain them through a coarse strainer and put the juice through a jelly bag. Allow to each cupful of juice:

¾ to 1 cup sugar

Boil only 4 cupfuls at a time. See Rule for Making Jelly, page 799, and rule for making Plum Jam, page 806.

FLAVORED JELLIES

Place in the bottom of a jelly glass and cover with boiling jelly:

A rose geranium leaf or
A sprig lemon verbena or mint

You may add herbs to a tart jelly that is to be served with meat. Follow the above method. Add a small sprig of:

Tarragon
Basil, etc.

SPICED GRAPES

Wash, then remove from their stems:

15 lbs. Concord grapes

Drain them. Place ½ the grapes in a kettle. Add to them:

4 cups vinegar
4 two inch sticks cinnamon
2 tablespoons whole cloves
without heads

Cover them with the remaining grapes. Cook them until they are soft. Strain the juice through a jelly bag. Allow to each cupful of juice:

1 cup sugar

Cook only 4 cupfuls of juice at a time. Follow the Rule for Making Jelly, page 799.

Preserves

It is advisable to weigh both sugar and fruit when making preserves. Best results are obtained by cooking preserves in small quantities, about 4 cupfuls of fruit at a time.

STRAWBERRY PRESERVES

Wash and remove hulls from:

Firm, tart, uniform strawberries

Use:

¾ cup sugar to
1 cup berries

If very acid, use cupful for cupful. Cook only 4 cupfuls of berries in 1 batch. Place alternate layers of berries and sugar in a preserving kettle. The sugared fruit may be permitted to stand from 3 to 10 hours before cooking. Heat them very slowly with as little stirring as possible until the sugar is dissolved. Boil the preserves rapidly for 15 to 20 minutes, taking care to prevent burning. Two minutes before taking the preserves from the stove you may add to every 4 cupfuls of berries:

⅓ cupful lemon juice

Pour the preserves at once into hot sterilized jars and seal them.

SUNSHINE STRAWBERRIES

Arrange in a large kettle:

2 layers of washed, hulled, perfect
strawberries

Sprinkle the layers with an equal amount of:

Sugar

Permit them to stand for ½ hour. Heat them over low heat until they reach the boiling point, then boil them rapidly for 15 minutes. Pour the berries onto platters. Place glass about ¼ inch above the platters, covering them completely. Permit the berries to stand in the sun for 2 or 3 days until the juice forms a jelly. Turn the berries very gently twice daily. These preserves need not be reheated. Place them in hot sterilized glasses. Seal them.

STRAWBERRY PRESERVES

Pick over, hull and wash:

2 quarts strawberries

Cover them with boiling water for 2 minutes. Drain them well. Add:

    4 cups sugar
    1 teaspoon lemon juice

Boil the berries for 15 minutes. Add:

    4 cups sugar

Boil the berries for 5 minutes. Place the preserves in a bowl uncovered for 24 hours. They are then ready to be placed in hot sterilized glasses and sealed.

STRAWBERRY AND PINE-APPLE PRESERVES

Combine:

    1 quart hulled berries
    4 cups sugar
    1 cup canned pineapple
    Rind and juice of ½ lemon

Boil these ingredients for 20 minutes. Stir them frequently. To cook fresh pineapple and strawberries combine and cook for 10 minutes:

    1 cup shredded pineapple
    3 cups sugar

Add:

    2 cups hulled strawberries

Cook the preserves until thickened, about 20 minutes longer. Stir them frequently.

STRAWBERRY AND RHUBARB PRESERVES

Cut into small pieces:

    1 quart rhubarb

Sprinkle over it:

    8 cups sugar

Permit these ingredients to stand for 12 hours. Bring them quickly to the boiling point. Wipe and hull:

    2 quarts strawberries

Add them to the rhubarb. Boil the preserves until they are thick, about 15 minutes.

GOOSEBERRY PRESERVES

These, being tart, are good with a meat course, with soft cream cheese or a sweet cake. Wash:

    1 quart gooseberries

Remove the stems and blossom ends. Place the berries in a saucepan. Add to them:

    ½ cup water

Place them over a quick fire. Stir them. When they are boiling add:

    3 to 4 cups sugar

Boil the preserves quickly until the berries are clear and the juice is thick, about 15 minutes.

DAMSON PRESERVES

Wash, cut into halves and remove the seeds from:

    Damson plums

Stir into the plums an equal amount of:

    Sugar

The sugar may be moistened with a very little water or the fruit and sugar may be permitted to stand for 12 hours before it is cooked. Boil the preserves until the sirup is heavy.

PEACH PRESERVES

Use firm, slightly underripe, well-flavored peaches.
Peel and cut into lengthwise slices:

    Peaches

The fruit may be dipped briefly in boiling water to facilitate the removal of the skins. Reserve the stones. Crack some of them and remove the kernels. Measure the peaches. Allow to each cupful:

    ¾ cup sugar
    2 tablespoons water

Stir this sirup and cook it for 5 minutes. Add the fruit. Cook it rapidly until it is transparent. Place it in glasses or jars. If the fruit is juicy and there is too much sirup, place the peaches in jars and boil down the sirup until it is thick. Add to each glass 1 or more peach kernels. This is optional but they give the preserves a distinctive flavor.
You may add to the sirup if desired:

    Lemon juice—about 2 teaspoons
    to every cup of peaches

If preferred, omit the water. Pour the sugar over the peaches and permit them to stand for 2 hours before preserving them.
See Peach Marmalade, page 808.

APRICOT PRESERVES

Follow the preceding rule for:

    Peach Preserves

QUINCE PRESERVES

Scrub:

    Quinces

Pare them. Cut them into eighths. Reserve the peelings. Remove the cores and discard them. Weigh the quince slices. Cover the peelings well with water. Measure the water as you pour it over them. To each quart of water allow:

    1 sliced seeded lemon
    1 sliced seeded orange

Simmer the fruit until the rinds are tender. Strain the juice. Add the quince slices to the juice. Cook them until they are almost tender. Add:

Sugar

Allow as much sugar as the weight of the quince slices. Continue cooking the fruit. When it is tender lift out the fruit and place it in jars. Boil the sirup until it is heavy. Pour it over the quince slices.

CHERRY PRESERVES

Stem and seed:

Cherries

Bring them to the boiling point. Stir them frequently. Add:

Sugar

Unless the cherries are very sweet these ingredients should be used pound for pound. Fruit and sugar may be placed in alternate layers and permitted to stand 8 or 10 hours. Stir the preserves carefully while heating slowly to the boiling point. Cook rapidly for 20 minutes. Put them in a crock or bowl for 12 hours before placing them in glasses. If the cherries are very juicy, they may be removed from the sirup after 20 minutes' boiling and the sirup may be boiled down until it thickens. Pour it over the cherries and permit them to stand as directed.

BAR LE DUC

Wash and stem:

3 quarts currants

Crush a few in the bottom of the pot. Bring the currants to the boiling point. Boil them for 2 minutes. Add:

6 cups heated sugar

Boil the currants for 2½ minutes. Add in a slow stream so as not to disturb the boiling point:

½ cup strained honey

Boil the currants for 2½ minutes longer. Place them in sterilized glasses (page 801). Cover them with paraffin.

CITRON PRESERVES

About 2 Pints

Peel and remove the seeds from a:

6 lb. citron melon

Dice it or cut it into thin slices. To 8 cupfuls sliced melon allow:

5 cups sugar
4 cups water

Cook these ingredients for 6 minutes. Add the citron. Cook it until it is tender and transparent. Test it with a straw. Add:

Rind of 1 lemon
Juice of 1 lemon
(6 cloves without heads)

Cook the preserves 20 minutes longer. Add:

3 tablespoons chopped candied ginger

Place the preserves in sterilized jars.

TOMATO PRESERVES

Scald and skin:

1 lb. tomatoes

Small yellow tomatoes or green tomatoes may be used with fine results and need not be scalded or pared. If red or green tomatoes are used, slice them. Cover the tomatoes with:

An equal amount of sugar

Permit them to stand for 12 hours. Drain the juice. Boil it until the sirup falls from a spoon in heavy drops. Add the tomatoes and:

Grated rind and juice of 1 lemon or 2 thinly sliced seeded lemons
2 oz. gingerroot or preserved ginger or 4 inches stick cinnamon

Cook the preserves until they are thick.

Jams

Jams are usually made with ¾ cupful sugar to 1 cupful fruit unless the fruit is acid, in which case a scant cupful of sugar may be used. Stir and cook jam slowly until the sugar is dissolved, then cook it rapidly to retain both flavor and color. If necessary, use a tablespoonful or two of water to keep it from sticking or grease the pot with olive oil. Cook the jam until it will stay in place when dropped from a teaspoon onto a plate to cool.

Pack it while boiling hot in hot sterilized jars and seal them at once. This will prevent spoilage or weeping. Jam may be packed in tin cans and sealed. Leave ¼ inch head room.

Jam may be "stretched" by adding peeled diced rhubarb. Weigh the rhubarb and the fruit. Use as much rhubarb as fruit. For best results remember to cook jam in small quantities, about 4 cupfuls of fruit at a time.

RASPBERRY, BLACKBERRY OR STRAWBERRY JAM

Crushing a few berries, combine:

4 cups raspberries, blackberries or strawberries

with:

3 cups sugar

If the berries are tart, use a scant cupful of sugar to 1 cupful of fruit. Stir and cook them over low heat until the sugar is dissolved. Boil them rapidly. Stir them frequently from the bottom to keep them from sticking. Boil them until a small amount dropped on a plate will stay in place.

Place them while hot in hot sterilized jars. Seal them at once.

QUINCE JAM

When making:

Quince Jelly, page 802

put the pulp left in the strainer and in the jelly bag through a ricer or fine sieve. To 3 cupfuls of pulp add 1 cupful quince juice and:

3 to 4 cups sugar

Cook about 4 cupfuls of jam at a time until it is thick and smooth, about 20 minutes. Stir it frequently from the bottom as it is apt to stick. Place it while boiling hot in hot sterilized jars. Seal them at once.

PLUM JAM

Method I.

Follow the preceding rule for:

Quince Jam

Substitute plum pulp and juice for quince pulp and juice.

Method II.

If you are not making jelly, select plums of a tart variety. Wash the fruit and drain. To each pound of fruit allow ¾ pound of sugar and 1 cupful of water. Boil the plums in the water for 10 to 15 minutes, or until the skins are tender. Add the sugar and stir while boiling until the jelly stage is reached. See page 799. Pour into hot sterilized jars and seal.

APRICOT JAM

Wash:

Fully ripe apricots

Cut them, unpeeled or peeled, into small pieces. Measure the fruit. Add to every cupful of fruit:

¾ cup sugar
(1½ teaspoons lemon juice)

Permit this to stand for 12 hours. Stir this mixture over a quick fire. Permit it to boil until it is thick. Stir it if necessary to keep it from sticking to the bottom of the pot. Place the jam while hot in hot sterilized glasses. Seal them.

SPICED PEAR JAM WITH PINEAPPLE

About 2 Quarts

Peel and core:

7 or 8 firm cooking pears: about 3 lbs.

Wash well:

1 orange
1 lemon

Put the fruit through a grinder using a coarse blade. Save the juices. Add them to the pulp with:

1 cup crushed pineapple
4 to 5 cups sugar
3 or 4 whole cloves
About 6 inches stick cinnamon
1 one inch piece ginger

Stir the mixture while heating it. Boil it for 30 minutes. Pour it into hot sterilized glasses. Seal them with paraffin and cover them with lids. As it is hard to gauge the acidity of the pear used, taste the jam as it cooks. Add sugar or lemon juice as needed.

FIVE FRUITS JAM

The following is a marvelous blend and sometimes blends are desirable. On the whole I like food to retain its natural flavor. My sympathy goes out to the cowboy movie actor who is reported to have said after his first formal dinner: "I et for two hours and I didn't recognize anything I et except an olive."

Hull:

Strawberries

Place as much sugar as you have strawberries in a glass or china bowl and soak them for 12 hours. Bring them quickly to the boiling point and boil them with as little stirring as possible until the juice thickens, about 15 minutes. As strawberries are apt to come a little in advance of the other fruits these preserves may be placed in sterilized and sealed fruit jars and set aside until the later fruits are available.

Stem and seed:

Cherries

Stem:

Currants

Pick over:

Raspberries

Stem and head:
Gooseberries
The first 4 fruits are best used in equal proportions but gooseberries have so much character that it is well to use a somewhat smaller amount or their flavor will predominate. Bring the fruits separately or together to the boiling point. Add to each cupful of fruit and juice:
¾ cup sugar
Boil the jam until it is thick, about 20 minutes. Combine it with the strawberry preserves.

Fruit Butters

APPLE BUTTER
About 5 Pints
Use Jonathan, Winesap or other well-flavored apples for good results.
Wash:
4 lbs. apples
Remove the stems, quarter the apples. Cook them slowly until soft in:
2 cups water, cider or cider vinegar
Put the fruit through a fine strainer. Add to each cupful of pulp:
½ cup sugar
Add:
2 teaspoons cinnamon
1 teaspoon cloves
½ teaspoon allspice
(Grated lemon rind and juice)
Cook the butter over low heat, stirring constantly, until the sugar is dissolved. Then cook it rapidly stirring frequently until it sheets from a spoon, or place a small quantity on a plate. When no rim of liquid separates around the edge of the butter it is done. You may reduce the heat as the butter thickens. Pour it into boiling hot sterilized jars and seal.

PAULA'S BAKED APPLE BUTTER
About 5 Pints
A revolutionary rule given by a superb cook.
Wash and remove cores from:
12 lbs. apples: Jonathan or Winesap
Cut them into quarters. Nearly cover them with water. Cook them gently for about 1½ hours. Put the pulp through a fine strainer. Measure it. Allow to each cupful of pulp:
½ cup sugar
Add:
Grated rind and juice of 2 lemons
3 teaspoons cinnamon
1½ teaspoons cloves
½ teaspoon allspice
Bring these ingredients to the boiling point. Chill them. Stir into them:
1 cup port, claret or dry white wine
Place about ¾ of the purée in fruit jars or in a large crock. Keep the rest in reserve. Put the jars in a cold oven. Light the oven and set the regulator at 300°. Permit the apple butter to bake until it thickens. As the purée shrinks, fill the jars with the reserved apple butter. When the apple butter is thick, but still moist, seal the jars.

PEACH OR APRICOT BUTTER
About 1½ Quarts
Wash, peel, remove pits and crush:
4 lbs. peaches or apricots
Cook them very slowly until soft in their own juice. Stir them. Put the fruit through a fine strainer. Add to each cupful of pulp:
½ to ⅔ cup sugar
Add:
2 teaspoons cinnamon
1 teaspoon cloves
½ teaspoon allspice
(Grated lemon rind and juice)
To cook and place in containers follow the directions under Apple Butter.

Marmalades

ORANGE MARMALADE
About 8 Glasses
Cut into quarters and remove the seeds from:
2 large oranges
2 large or 3 small lemons
Soak the fruit for 24 hours in:
11 cups water
Drain it. Cut it into very small shreds. Return it to the water in which it was soaked. Boil it for 1 hour. Add to it:
8 cups sugar
Boil the marmalade until the juice forms a jelly when tested. Follow the Rule for Making Jelly, page 799.

ORANGE, LEMON AND GRAPEFRUIT MARMALADE
About 20 Glasses
Cut in halves, remove the seeds and slice into very small pieces:
  1 grapefruit
  3 oranges
  3 lemons
Measure the fruit and juice and add 3 times the amount of water. Soak the fruit for 12 hours. Boil it for 20 minutes. Permit it to stand again for 12 hours. For every cupful of fruit and juice add:
  ¾ cup sugar
Cook these ingredients in small quantities, about 4 to 6 cupfuls at a time, until they form a jelly when tested. Follow the Rule for Making Jelly, page 799.
Here is a popular variation:
  2 oranges
  2 grapefruit
  2 lemons
Follow the above recipe. For every cupful of juice add 1 cupful of sugar.

LIME MARMALADE
Cut the thin outer rind from:
  6 small limes or 2 Persian limes
  3 lemons
Follow the above rule for:
  Orange, Lemon and Grapefruit Marmalade

APRICOT AND PINEAPPLE MARMALADE
About 11 Glasses
Wash:
  1 lb. dried apricots
Soak them for 12 hours in water that covers the fruit by 1 inch. Bring them slowly to the boiling point. Drain them. Reserve the juice. Put them through a ricer. Add the juice and the contents of:
  1 No. 2 can crushed pineapple:
  2½ cups
Allow for every cupful of pulp and juice:
  ¾ cup sugar
Add:
  3 tablespoons lemon juice
Boil the marmalade for 15 minutes, or until it thickens. Stir it frequently.

APRICOT, PINEAPPLE AND ORANGE MARMALADE
Follow the preceding rule for:
  Apricot and Pineapple Marmalade

Grind and add to the apricots:
  1 lemon
  1 orange
Omit the additional lemon juice in the recipe.

PEACH MARMALADE
Peel and slice:
  Firm peaches
Allow to each cupful of sliced peaches:
  1 cup sugar
Allow to every 5 cupfuls of peaches:
  1 seeded minced orange
Permit these ingredients to stand for 2 hours. Boil them, stirring them frequently, until the sirup is heavy.

SEEDLESS WHITE GRAPES AND ORANGE MARMALADE
Cut into very thin slices:
  1 small seeded orange
Soak it for 3 hours in:
  ¾ cup water
Add:
  2 cups seedless grapes
Soak them for 30 minutes. Bring the fruit slowly to the boiling point. Boil it quickly for 5 minutes. Add:
  1½ cups sugar
  1 tablespoon lemon juice
Boil the marmalade for 5 minutes.

TOMATO, APPLE AND GINGER MARMALADE
Skin, cut up and drain:
  2 cups ripe tomatoes
Peel, core and chop:
  2 cups apples
Put through a grinder or mince:
  1 lemon
Combine the tomatoes, apples and lemon. Cook them for 15 minutes. Add:
  3 cups sugar
Cook these ingredients until they are the consistency of marmalade. Add for the last 10 minutes of the cooking:
  4 tablespoons chopped preserved or candied ginger

SPRING MARMALADE
Dice:
  2 lbs. rhubarb
Grind:
  1 seedless orange
Add:
  4 cups sugar
and the contents of:
  1 No. 2½ can crushed pineapple
Cook these ingredients for 30 minutes. Stir them frequently.

Conserves

BLACK CHERRY CONSERVE
Slice into very thin slices:

2 seeded oranges

Barely cover the slices with water. Cook them until they are very tender. Stem, seed and add:

1 quart black cherries
6 tablespoons lemon juice
3½ cups sugar
¾ teaspoon cinnamon
(6 cloves)

Cook the conserve until it is thick and clear.

SPICED RHUBARB CONSERVE
Cut into very thin slices:

1 seeded orange
1 seeded lemon

Tie in a small bag:

1 oz. gingerroot
¼ lb. cinnamon candy: redhots
1 blade mace
2 whole cloves

Add the spices to the fruit with:

½ cup water
¼ cup vinegar

Boil these ingredients until the fruit is tender. Add and cook until the conserve is thick:

1½ cups strawberry rhubarb
3 cups sugar
(¼ cup white raisins)

BLUE PLUM CONSERVE
Peel and chop:

The thin yellow rind of 2 oranges and 1 lemon

Add:

The juice and chopped pulp of 3 oranges and 1 lemon
1¼ lbs. ground seeded raisins
9 cups sugar

Seed and add:

5 lbs. blue plums
4 pared cubed peaches

Cook the conserve slowly until it is fairly thick. Stir it frequently. Add:

½ lb. broken walnut meats

Cook the conserve 10 minutes longer.

APRICOT AND ALMOND CONSERVE
Wash:

Apricots

Scrub them. Cut them in halves and remove the stones. Weigh the apricots. Allow to every pound and add:

½ cup blanched shredded almonds
6 tablespoons white raisins

Weigh these ingredients. Add an equal weight of:

Sugar

Stir the conserve over heat until the sugar is dissolved. Cook it until it is thick. Stir it occasionally. Add when the conserve is cool, in any quantity desired:

(Brandy)

GOOSEBERRY CONSERVE
Wash, stem and hull:

4 quarts gooseberries

Add:

The thin chopped yellow rind of 4 oranges
Juice and chopped pulp of 4 oranges

Boil these ingredients until they are nearly tender. Add:

10 cups heated sugar
1½ lbs. seeded raisins

Boil the conserve 30 minutes longer.

RASPBERRY, RHUBARB AND ORANGE CONSERVE
Prepare:

8 cups diced rhubarb

Sprinkle over it:

5 cups sugar

Permit it to stand for 12 hours. Add to it:

Grated rind of 2 oranges

Skin and seed the oranges. Cut them into very thin slices. Add them to the rhubarb with:

1 quart raspberries

Boil these ingredients until they thicken.

TUTTI-FRUTTI
The following conserve, a tradition in our family, is unusually good served with a meat course or as a sauce over puddings and ices.

Place in a stone crock with a closely fitting lid:

1 quart brandy

Add, as they come into season, about:

1 quart strawberries
1 quart cherries
1 quart raspberries
1 quart currants
1 quart gooseberries

1 quart peeled sliced apricots
1 quart peeled sliced peaches
1 quart peeled sliced pineapple,
  etc.

With each addition of fruit add the same amount of:

Sugar

Stir the tutti-frutti every day until the last of the fruit has been added. Cover the crock well. Place it in a cool place. The mixture will keep indefinitely. These are the clearest instructions I can give for making it. Had I known, when I was permitted to go to the cellar as a small child on tutti-frutti stirring expeditions, that I should one day write a cookbook, I might have paid some attention to proportions. I am told they are immaterial, which is fortunate, as I remember only the excitement of the undertaking and the delicious aroma of the brew.

This conserve may be made successfully with less sugar. Add to the brandy 2 cupfuls of sugar to sweeten the pot. From then on add ½ as much sugar as you add fruit, instead of equal parts. Avoid using apples, too hard; bananas, too soft; grapes, unless skinned as their skins become tough.

Beverages

Hot Beverages

Coffee, to be good, should be freshly ground and served just as soon as it is made. Buy only a small quantity of ground coffee at a time. Put it in an airtight container—a glass container, for instance, a fruit jar, is ideal. Keep the filled container, if possible, in a refrigerator.

Keep all coffee-making utensils scrupulously clean. To keep a coffeepot fresh when not in use, fill it with water to which you may add 3 teaspoonfuls of baking soda. When possible avoid using metal equipment in brewing coffee or tea. Use freshly boiling water for both tea and coffee as this makes a finer brew than when water is used that has been boiling for some time. To keep coffee hot, place the pot in hot water. Soft but not softened water usually makes better tea and coffee than hard water.

Store tea in a tightly covered container in a cool place. Teas vary greatly in flavor depending on how they are processed. Green teas are unfermented and astringent. Oolong and Ceylon types are partially fermented, and black teas, which are completely fermented, have the least tannin.

Cocoa and chocolate are both made from different parts of the same plant. But the fat content of chocolate gives drinks made from it a richer, smoother quality.

The aroma of the steaming coffee pot ranks in allure above Chanel No. 5, "My Sin" and all the rest of the perfume counter. Add to this fragrance a whiff of homemade bread or coffee cake and immediately visions arise of sociability, good cheer, gossip and true *Gemutlichkeit*.

Tea is equally attractive in fragrance and effect, but it is so much more delicate that it does not proclaim its presence so readily as the more out-going coffee. A cupful of either at the right moment—but why stop at one cupful?—is a true boon to mankind.

STEEPED COFFEE
1 Cupful
Steeped or drip coffee are both preferable to the old boiled coffee because the lower heat used in brewing does not allow the bitter undesirable tannic acid flavor to develop.

Preheat the pot by scalding with hot water. Place in the pot:

2 tablespoons coffee

Pour on:

¾ to 1 cup freshly boiling water

Stir the coffee for at least ½ minute. Let it stand covered from 5 to 10 minutes depending on the grind and the strength of the brew desired. Pour the coffee off the grounds through a strainer. Or you may settle the grounds by stirring into the pot:

1 slightly beaten egg

DRIP COFFEE
1 Cupful
Preheat the coffeemaker by scalding it with boiling water. If you are using cloth filters, never wash them with soap and always keep them in cold water in the refrigerator when not in use. Place in a drip filter or in filter paper in a chemical glass:

2 tablespoons finely ground coffee

Pour over it slowly:

¾ to 1 cup freshly boiling water

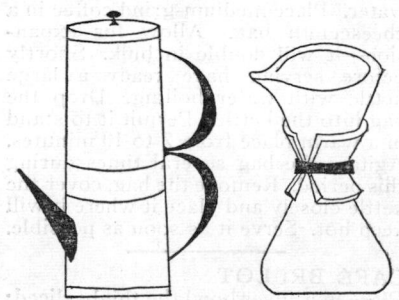

When the dripping process is over, remove the grounds and serve the coffee at once.

811

PERCOLATED COFFEE

For best results make the amount of coffee your equipment calls for. Place in the percolator:

> 3/4 to 1 cup cold water for every 2 tablespoons coffee you have measured into the percolator basket

When the water boils, remove the percolator. Put in the basket. Cover the percolator, return it to the heat and allow it to percolate slowly 6 to 8 minutes. Remove the coffee basket and serve.

VACUUM METHOD COFFEE

Allow:

> 2 tablespoons coffee for every 3/4 to 1 cup water

Measure the water into the lower bowl. Place it on the heat. Place the wet filter in the upper bowl and add the ground coffee. Insert the upper bowl into the lower one with a slight twist to insure a tight seal. Insert it at this time or not depending on your equipment. If your equipment has a vented stem, you may place it on the heat already assembled. If it does not have this small hole on the side of the tube above the hot-water line, wait until the water is actively boiling before putting the upper bowl in place. When nearly all the water has risen into the upper bowl (some will always remain below), stir the water and coffee thoroughly. In 1 to 3 minutes, the shorter time for the finer grinds, turn off the heat. Or if electricity is used, remove the coffee from the unit.

COFFEE IN QUANTITY

One pound of coffee will serve 40 to 50 people. Cook it with 6 to 8 quarts of water. Place medium-grind coffee in a cheesecloth bag. Allow for expansion—it will double in bulk. Shortly before serving have ready a large kettle with water boiling. Drop the bag into the kettle. Permit it to stand in a warm place from 7 to 10 minutes. Agitate the bag several times during this period. Remove the bag, cover the kettle closely and place it where it will keep hot. Serve it as soon as possible.

CAFÉ BRÛLOT

Place in a silver bowl the thinly sliced:

> Peel of 1 orange
> 4 sticks cinnamon
> 12 whole cloves
> 6 lumps sugar

Pour over these ingredients:

> 1/2 cup brandy or cognac

Ignite it and ladle it until the sugar is dissolved. Add:

> 4 cups freshly made coffee

Serve Café Brûlot in demitasses.

CAFÉ AU LAIT

The famous milk coffee of France. Combine equal parts of:

> Strong coffee
> Scalded milk

TEA

The care with which tea is brewed is as important as the variety of tea you choose. Make the tea in a china or earthenware pot. A metal pot is apt to spoil its flavor. Scald the pot. Allow:

> 1 teaspoon tea for every cup boiling water

Place the tea in the scalded pot. Bring cold, fresh water to a bubbling boil. Pour a small quantity of boiling water over the tea just when the bubbling boil is reached. Cover the pot. Permit the tea to steep for 1 minute, add the rest of the boiling water, stir the tea and permit it to steep in a warm place for 2 minutes before serving it. It may then be strained if desired.

Iced Tea, page 813.

COCOA

About 4 Cupfuls

Combine, stir and boil for 2 minutes in the top of a double boiler over direct heat:

> 4 tablespoons cocoa
> 1/8 teaspoon salt
> 1 cup boiling water
> 2 to 4 tablespoons sugar
> (1/2 teaspoon cinnamon or 1 teaspoon vanilla)

Place the top of the boiler over boiling water. Add:

> 3 cups scalded milk

Stir and heat the cocoa. Cover it, if there is time, and keep it over hot water for 10 minutes. Beat it before serving.

CHOCOLATE

About 4 Cupfuls

Melt over hot water:

> 1 1/2 oz. chocolate

Stir in:

> 1/4 cup sugar
> 1/4 teaspoon salt

Stir in slowly:

> 1 cup boiling water

When these ingredients are well blended add:

3 cups scalded milk

Boil the chocolate for 1 minute. Beat it with a wire whisk until it is frothy. Add:

½ teaspoon vanilla

RUSSIAN CHOCOLATE
About 5 Cupfuls

Melt:

1 oz. chocolate

Add:

¼ cup sugar
⅛ teaspoon salt
1¾ cups boiling water

Stir and cook these ingredients for 5 minutes. Add:

½ cup milk
½ cup cream

Reheat but do not permit this to boil. Add:

1 teaspoon vanilla
2 cups hot freshly made coffee

Beat the mixture well. Serve it at once.

HOT OR MULLED CIDER

Good on a cold night with canapés or sandwiches.

Heat well but do not boil:

Apple cider

You may add to it:

A few cloves
A stick of cinnamon

Cold Beverages

Cold drinks are frequently served when fresh herbs and fruits are available. Drinks may be garnished appropriately with a sprig of common mint or velvety, frosted-looking apple mint, a few borage leaves and bright starry blossoms, or a spray of sweet woodruff, or waldmeister, shown in order on the left below.

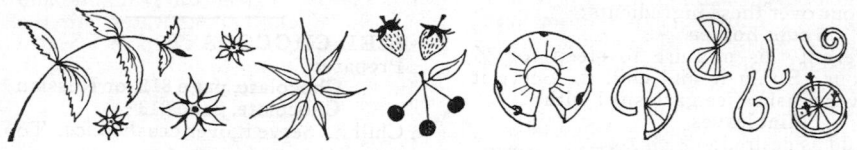

You may garnish some drinks with strawberries, cherries, pineapple slices or citrus fruits cut into attractive shapes. For winter drinks put a few cloves in the citrus slices. Garnish the glasses with these slices or put a few thin twisted citrus rind shavings in the drink itself.

ICED COFFEE

Prepare:

Boiled, Drip or Percolated Coffee, pages 811, 812

Sweeten it with:

(Sugar)

Chill it. Just before serving it add for every cupful of coffee:

(2 tablespoons cream)

Serve the coffee over crushed ice or pour chilled and sweetened coffee into glasses and top the coffee with:

Whipped cream or Vanilla Ice Cream, page 761

Coffee may be frozen in cubes and added to chilled coffee in the place of ice.

CUBE COFFEE

Prepare:

Strong coffee

Place it in trays with separators. Freeze it. Place several cubes in a glass. Pour over them:

Cream or ice cream
Freshly made hot weak coffee

COLD CHOCOLATE COFFEE

Place in a glass:

3 or 4 tablespoons chocolate ice cream

Fill the glass with:

Fresh made coffee that has been cooled

ICED TEA

Prepare:

Double-strength hot Tea, page 812

Strain it and pour it over crushed ice. Serve it with:

Lemon slices and sugar
Sprigs of mint

ICED TEA WITH COLD WATER
Method I.
Fill a quart fruit jar with:
> Cold water

Add:
> 2 tablespoons tea

Place the jar in the sun for 2 hours, strain the tea at once, replace it in the fruit jar and keep it in the refrigerator ready for use.

Method II.
This effortless brew has a fine flavor, will keep for several days and never clouds. Make it in a quart jar or a milk bottle.
Combine:
> 4 teaspoons tea
> 1 quart cold water

Store this covered overnight. Strain the leaves from it before using it.

ICED TEA WITH MINT LEAVES
Bruise the leaves of:
> 4 sprigs mint

Add:
> 6 tablespoons lemon juice

Pour over these ingredients:
> 6 cups hot tea

Permit this mixture to steep for ½ hour. Strain it and chill it. Serve it over crushed ice garnished with:
> Mint leaves

Add as desired:
> Sugar

DECORATIVE ICE CUBES TO BE USED IN ICED DRINKS
Fill a refrigerator tray with water. Place in each section one of the following:
> A maraschino cherry
> A preserved strawberry
> A piece of lemon or pineapple
> A sprig of mint, etc.

You may flavor the cubes with:
> 1 teaspoon rum, sherry or whisky

Freeze the water. Serve the cubes in tea, lemonade, punch or other cold drinks.

ICED TEA WITH RUM
Add to each serving of iced tea:
> 1 teaspoon rum

or fill refrigerator trays with water and add to each section:
> 1 teaspoon rum

Serve 1 or more of the frozen blocks in iced tea. Garnish the glasses with:
> Slices of lemon
> Sprigs of mint

ICED TEA WITH LEMON, MINT AND GINGER ALE
Combine:
> 2 quarts strong hot tea
> Juice of 6 lemons
> 1 cup sugar
> Several sprigs twisted mint

Chill the tea. When ready to serve, strain and add:
> 1 quart ginger ale

Place in each glass:
> A sprig of mint

MINTED ICED TEA WITH LEMON ICE
Allow:
> 1½ teaspoons tea

to:
> 1 cup boiling water

While hot add:
> A dozen crushed mint leaves

Strain the tea and chill it. Fill iced tea glasses ¼ full with:
> Lemon Ice or Sherbet, page 773

Add the tea. Garnish the glasses with:
> Mint
> Confectioners' sugar to taste

ICED CHOCOLATE
Prepare:
> Chocolate, page 812, or Russian Chocolate, page 813

Chill it. Serve it over crushed ice. Top it with:
> Whipped cream or ice cream

LEMONADE
Allow to:
> 1 cup water
> 1½ tablespoons lemon juice
> 3 to 4 tablespoons sugar
> A few grains salt

The sugar and water need not be boiled but the quality of the lemonade is improved if they are. Boil the sugar and water for 2 minutes. Chill the sirup and add the lemon juice. Orange, pineapple, raspberry, loganberry, white grape juice and other fruit juices may be combined with lemonade. Chilled tea may be added to these combinations in any quantity desired.

LEMONADE FOR 100 PEOPLE
Boil for 10 minutes:
> 4 cups water
> 4 lbs. sugar: 8 cups

Cool the sirup. Add:
> 7½ cups lemon juice

Stir in the contents of:

2 No. 2½ cans pineapple
Add:
    8 sliced oranges
    4 gallons water
Chill. Serve over ice.

LEMONADE SIRUP
Boil for 5 minutes:
    2 cups sugar
    1 cup water
    Rind of 2 lemons cut into thin
      strips
    ⅛ teaspoon salt
Cool and add:
    Juice of 6 lemons
Strain the sirup. Store it in a covered
jar. Add:
    2 tablespoons sirup
to:
    1 glass ice water or charged water
Or add:
    1 tablespoon sirup
    2 tablespoons orange, apricot or
      pineapple juice
to:
    1 glass ice water or charged water

ORANGEADE
Serve undiluted:
    Orange juice
over:
    Crushed ice
or, if preferred, add to the orange
juice:
    Water, lemon juice and sugar
in any quantity desired.

MINT CUP
About 2 Quarts
Remove the tips and the leaves from:
    4 sprigs mint
Add to them:
    2 cups sugar
    2 cups water
Boil these ingredients for 5 minutes.
Strain the sirup. Add:
    2 cups lemon juice
    ¼ teaspoon salt
    A little green coloring
Chill these ingredients well. Immedi-
ately before serving add:
    1 quart chilled ginger ale

GINGER ALE CUP
About 2 Quarts
Combine and boil for 5 minutes:
    1 cup sugar
    1 cup water
Cool the sirup. Add to it the:
    Juice of 6 oranges
    Juice of 6 lemons

Chill these ingredients. Immediately
before serving add:
    1 quart chilled ginger ale

PINEAPPLE PUNCH
18 Servings
Place in a large bowl:
    2 cups strong tea
Add and stir well:
    ¾ cup lemon juice
    1⅓ cups orange juice
    2 tablespoons lime juice
    1 cup sugar
    Leaves from 12 sprigs mint
Place these ingredients on ice for 2
hours. Shortly before serving, strain
the punch and add:
    8 slices pineapple and juice from
      can
    4 pint bottles ginger ale
    4 pint bottles plain soda
    Crushed ice

GINGER ALE AND PINEAPPLE JUICE
Combine equal parts of:
    Chilled pineapple juice
    Chilled ginger ale
Serve at once over ice.

GINGER ALE AND GRAPEFRUIT JUICE
Combine equal parts of:
    Chilled unsweetened grapefruit
      juice
    Chilled ginger ale
Serve at once over ice.

GINGER ALE AND GRAPE JUICE OR MOCK CHAMPAGNE
Boil for 3 minutes, then cool:
    ½ cup sugar
    ½ cup water
Add:
    ½ cup fresh or bottled grape juice
    ¼ cup orange juice
Chill these ingredients. Just before
serving add:
    1 pint chilled ginger ale

STRAWBERRY FRUIT PUNCH
12 Quarts or More
Boil for 5 minutes:
    2 quarts water: 8 cups
    8 cups sugar
Cool the sirup. Combine:
    3 quarts hulled strawberries
    8 sliced bananas
    2 cups sliced canned or fresh
      pineapple

2 cups mixed fruit juice: pineapple, apricot, raspberry, etc.
Juice of 12 large oranges
Juice of 12 large lemons

Add the chilled sirup or as much of it as is palatable. Chill these ingredients. Immediately before serving add:

4 quarts Apollinaris or club soda
6 cups or more crushed ice

This is a strong punch. It is given purposely this way as the ice will thin it, and water may be added if desired.

FRUIT PUNCH WITH TEA
About 1½ Quarts

Pour:

⅓ cup strong hot tea

over:

1 cup sugar

Stir until the sugar is dissolved. Add:

¾ cup orange juice
½ cup lemon juice

Chill this sirup. Place in a bowl or pitcher large pieces of ice. Pour the sirup over it. Add:

1 pint chilled ginger ale
1 pint Apollinaris or club soda

Serve the punch at once in glasses garnished with:

Orange slices

PUNCH FOR 50 PEOPLE

Make a sirup by boiling for 10 minutes:

1¼ cups water
2½ cups sugar

Reserve ½ cupful of this. Add to the remainder, stir, cover and permit to stand for 30 minutes or more:

1 cup lemon juice
2 cups orange juice
1 cup strong tea
2 cups white grape juice, grape-fruit juice, pineapple juice or crushed pineapple
1 cup maraschino cherries with juice
2 cups fruit sirup

The fruit sirup, I find, is the hitch. Your punch is apt to be just as good as this touch. Strawberry jam may be diluted and strained, canned raspberry or loganberry juice may be sweetened and boiled until heavy. Strain these ingredients. Add ice water to make about 2 gallons of liquid or add ice water to make 1½ gallons of liquid and add at the last minute:

1 quart charged water

If you find the punch lacking in sugar, add part or all of the reserved sugar sirup.

FRUIT PUNCH
About 4 Quarts

Boil for 10 minutes:

1 cup sugar
1 cup water

Add:

2 cups strong hot tea

Cool the mixture. Add:

¾ cup crushed pineapple
2 cups strawberry juice or other fruit juice
Juice of 5 lemons
Juice of 5 oranges

Chill these ingredients for 1 hour. Add sufficient water to make 1 gallon (4 quarts) of liquid. Immediately before serving add:

1 cup maraschino cherries
1 quart carbonated water

CHOCOLATE MILK SHAKE
20 Servings
Sirup

First, melt in the top of a double boiler over hot water:

7 oz. unsweetened chocolate: 7 squares

Stir slowly into the melted chocolate:

1 can sweetened condensed milk: 1⅓ cups
1 cup boiling water

Stir in until dissolved:

½ cup sugar

Cool the sirup and put it in a clean jar. Cover it tightly and place it in the refrigerator. It will keep for a week or 10 days. To make chocolate milk shakes for 4 people: Measure into a bowl:

½ cup chocolate sirup

Stir in slowly:

4 cups chilled milk

Beat the mixture well with an egg beater or blend it. For increased food value you may add:

(½ cup milk solids)
(2 teaspoons debittered brewers' yeast)

Pour the liquid into tall glasses over:

Cracked ice

Serve it at once.

To make a frosted chocolate omit the ice and add for each glass a dip of chocolate or vanilla ice cream. Beat or blend it in.

To make a chocolate float omit the ice and add to each glass a dip of chocolate, mint or vanilla ice cream.

COCOA MILK SHAKE

First make a cocoa sirup. Place in a saucepan:

1 cup sugar
½ cup cocoa
½ teaspoon vanilla
(½ cup malt)

Stir in slowly with a spoon:

¼ cup cold water

Place the pan over low heat. Stir the mixture constantly until it boils. Stir and boil it for 2 minutes. Cool it. This is a good place to slip in a few fortifying tablespoonfuls dried milk solids or a few teaspoonfuls powdered brewers' yeast. Pour the sirup into a clean jar, seal it tightly and keep it in the refrigerator. Use:

2 tablespoons sirup

to:

1 cup chilled milk

To make cocoa milk shake for 4 people use:

4 cups chilled milk
½ cup cocoa sirup
(4 tablespoons malt)

Beat the mixture well with a rotary beater or blend it. Pour it into 4 tall glasses.

Hot chocolate drinks may be cooled and served with cracked ice and whipped cream, page 631.

CHOCOLATE MINT DRINK

About 1½ Quarts

Combine and stir until dissolved:

1 cup hot milk
½ cup cocoa malt

Add:

3 cups cold milk
¼ teaspoon salt
1 teaspoon vanilla
¼ teaspoon peppermint extract

Chill this mixture. Just before serving pour it into a shaker. Add:

½ pint vanilla ice cream

Shake the mixture well.

ORANGE MILK PUNCH

Individual Serving

Combine and beat well with a wire whisk:

¼ cup orange juice
¾ cup milk
1 teaspoon sugar

Chill the punch well. Beat it before serving it.

Grape Juice, page 851.

MOCHA PUNCH

12 Servings

Prepare, then chill well:

4 cups freshly made coffee

Whip until stiff:

1 cup whipping cream

You may prepare an additional ½ cupful whipped cream and then reserve about a cupful to garnish the tops. Have in readiness:

1 quart chocolate ice cream

Pour the chilled coffee into a large chilled bowl. Add ½ the ice cream. Beat until the cream is partly melted. Add:

2 tablespoons rum or ½ teaspoon almond extract
⅛ teaspoon salt

Fold in the remainder of the ice cream and all but a cupful of the whipped cream. Place the punch in tall glasses. Garnish the tops with the reserved cream. Sprinkle them with:

Freshly grated nutmeg or grated sweet chocolate

SOYA BEAN MILK

This substance is very valuable nutritionally. It is commonly used as food for babies in the Orient. It may be substituted cup for cup in any recipe calling for milk, and the taste of the finished product is hardly distinguishable from a drink made with real milk. Soak, well covered in water for 12 hours:

1½ lbs. dried soya beans

Drain the beans. Put them through a food grinder, pouring on them while grinding a slow steady stream of:

Water

Continue pouring the water until the entire mixture reaches 1 gallon. Heat this mixture until it is disagreeable to hold a finger in it, 131°. Put the mixture in a cloth bag and allow it to drip. Heat the drippings in a double boiler for 45 minutes, stirring frequently. Sweeten with dextrose or honey to taste. Add enough water to make in all 5 quarts. Keep the soya milk under refrigeration.

Or:

Mix gradually so as to avoid lumping:

1 quart soya bean flour
4 cups water

Strain this mixture in a cloth bag. Heat the drippings for 15 minutes in a double boiler, stirring frequently. Cool and keep the milk under refrigeration.

Fermented Milks

The long life of the Arabs, Bulgars and other Eastern peoples is often attributed to their diet of fermented milks. This subject is now engrossing the Florida bench-sitters and their counterpart the country over. It is also captivating their progeny, but oldies are especially agog as they drink their daily dose of acid cheer with the fervent toast "and may the friendly bacteria win." Withstanding body heat, these so-called friendly bacteria of fermented milks settle in the intestines where they break down sugar into lactic acid, thereby lording it over hostile bacteria who cannot procreate in the presence of the acid. Koumiss and yogurt are among the most palatable of these unique foods. Koumiss, made with yeast, is a thick foamy creamy drink. Yogurt, almost solid in consistency, must be made by adding to milk a special culture or a small quantity of the prepared yogurt, both of which are available in health stores.

TO MAKE AMERICAN-STYLE KOUMISS

Heat to 75°:
    1 quart milk
Stir in to the milk:
    ¼ cake yeast
    1½ tablespoons sugar dissolved in
        ¼ cup lukewarm water

Fill sterilized bottles with this mixture to within 2 inches of the top. Cork the bottles firmly, tying or sealing the corks, as the gas produced by subsequent fermentation tends to force the corks loose. Invert the bottles. Let them stand for 10 hours at 70°. Refrigerate them, still inverted, for 24 hours. Shake them occasionally during this period. The koumiss is then ready to serve. When opening the bottles beware of a "spit in the eye." Koumiss is as effervescent as hope.

TO MAKE YOGURT

Let stand covered from 2 to 3 hours at room temperature:
    2 to 4 tablespoons prepared yogurt

This is available at most health stores or from your dairy. Place it in the top of a double boiler with:
    1 quart skimmed or whole milk

Float a dairy thermometer in the milk and heat the milk until it reaches 120°. Cool the mixture slightly and set it, still in the top of the double boiler, and with the thermometer in it, over not in, hot water. Keep the water hot enough so that the thermometer registers between 90° and 105°. Continue at this heat between 2 and 3 hours, until the mixture becomes as thick as custard. Chill the yogurt at once and refrigerate it. Yogurt will keep from 2 to 5 days. It may be served alone or as a base or garnish for soup; or it may be used in salad dressings. Try serving it with brown sugar or black strap molasses and cinnamon, or with fruits. Keep 2 to 4 tablespoonfuls of this batch covered and refrigerated as a starter for the next batch. Allow it to stand covered at room temperature for 2 to 3 hours before adding it to the new quart of milk.

Cocktails and Other Alcoholic Beverages

A country woman summed up my philosophy for drinking in a single sentence. After promising to marry a gay young blade she said to him, "You can drink but you can't pour."

A commentator says: "Alcohol does not give you courage. It simply makes you see things as they should be." How is your eyesight?

If you can pry your family loose from the generally accepted American custom of serving a cocktail before dinner, serve dry sherry at room temperature or vermouth cold—temperature about 45°.

If you mix drinks in your kitchen, your equipment probably includes the essential strainer, squeezer, bottle opener, ice pick and sharp knife.

Basic bar equipment also includes a heavy glass cocktail shaker, a Martini pitcher, an ice bucket, a muddler, a bar spoon, a jigger, a corkscrew and a bitters bottle with a dropper-type top.

The following recipes call for a variety of glasses and the distinctive shapes used are shown under each section. For Garnishes see page 813.

Measurements

1 dash	= 6 drops	1 standard	
3 teaspoons	= ½ ounce	whisky glass	= 2 ounces
1 pony	= 1 ounce	1 pint	= 16 fluid ounces
1 jigger	= 1½ ounces	1 fifth	= 25.6 fluid ounces
1 large jigger	= 2 ounces	1 quart	= 32 fluid ounces

Sirup for Beverages

A simple sirup is a useful ingredient when making drinks. Keep it in a bottle in the refrigerator and use it as needed. Boil for 2 minutes 2 parts water to 1 part sugar or half as much sugar as water.

In addition to various liquors, it is advisable for the home bartender to have on hand a stock of: bitters, olives, cherries, club soda, lemons, oranges and limes.

See the chapters on Canapés and Hors d'Oeuvres for suitable accompaniments, besides a steady head, for cocktails.

Cocktails

The cocktail is probably an American invention, and most certainly a typically American kind of drink. Whatever mixtures you put together—and part of the fascination of cocktail making is the degree of inventiveness it seems to encourage—hold fast to a few general principles.

The most important of these is to keep the quantity of the basic ingredients—gin, whisky, rum, etc.—up to about 60% of the total drink, never below half. Remember, as a corollary, that cocktails are before-meal drinks, appetizers; for this reason they should not be either oversweet or overloaded with cream and egg, and so spoil the appetite instead of stimulating it.

Serve cocktails very cold from a chilled shaker into chilled glasses.

Note the two types of cocktail glasses shown on the left below. Both are so designed that the heat of the hand is not transferred to the contents of the glass. These hold about 3 ounces each. The old-fashioned glass next holds about 6 ounces, and retains its chill through means of a heavy base. The next two drawings show typical sour and daiquiri glasses. Each holds about 4 ounces. Champagne cocktails, also about 4 ounces each, are often served in the saucer-bowl footed glass used for daiquiris. The small glass shown last is for straight whisky.

Mix only one round at a time. Your stock as a bartender will never go up on the strength of your "dividend" drinks.

The cocktails below are some fundamental ones, listed according to their basic ingredients. Each recipe, unless otherwise noted, makes about 4 drinks. When cracked, not crushed, ice is indicated use about ½ cupful.

Gin Cocktails

Gin is perhaps the most frequently used base because of its excellent blending characteristics.

Cream cocktails are generally omitted as being too rich for apéritif purposes. I pass on one great favorite as an example: the Alexander.

ALEXANDER
Shake with ½ cupful cracked ice:
    1 jigger sweet cream
    1½ jiggers crème de cacao
    5 jiggers gin

BRITTANY
Shake well with ½ cupful cracked ice:
    ½ jigger sugar sirup
    1½ jiggers lime juice
    1 jigger apricot brandy
    2 egg whites
    3 dashes orange bitters
    4 jiggers gin

BRONX
Shake, using ½ cupful cracked ice:
    1 jigger French vermouth
    1 jigger Italian vermouth
    1 jigger orange juice
Add:
    4½ jiggers gin
Shake again. Strain into glasses. Add a twist of orange peel to each glass.

PARADISE
Shake well with ½ cupful cracked ice:
    1½ jiggers orange juice
    1 jigger apricot brandy
    4½ jiggers gin
Top with a twist of orange peel.

MARTINI
Stir well:
    1½ jiggers French vermouth
    1½ jiggers Italian vermouth
    5 jiggers gin
Add to each drink:
    1 dash orange bitters
    (1 dash angostura bitters)
Serve with olive in bottom of glass.

DRY MARTINI
Stir, using ½ cupful cracked ice:
    2 jiggers French vermouth
    7 jiggers gin
Add to each drink:
    1 dash orange bitters
With a small onion, this cocktail becomes a Gibson.

ORANGE BLOSSOM
Shake, using ½ cupful cracked ice:
    1 tablespoon sugar sirup
    1 tablespoon lime juice
    2½ jiggers orange juice
    4½ jiggers gin
See Bronx directions, page 820, but omit peel.

PINK LADY
Shake, using ½ cupful cracked ice:
    ½ jigger grenadine
    1 jigger lemon or lime juice
    1 jigger apple brandy
    2 egg whites
    4½ jiggers gin
See Bronx directions, page 820, but omit peel.

CLOVER CLUB
Shake, using ½ cupful cracked ice:
    1 jigger grenadine or raspberry
        sirup
    1½ jiggers lemon juice
    4½ jiggers gin
    2 egg whites
See Bronx directions, page 820, but omit peel.

GIN BITTER
Individual Serving
Half fill an old-fashioned glass with cracked ice. Shake, using 1 cupful cracked ice:
    2 jiggers gin
    2 dashes angostura or orange
        bitters
Strain into glasses and top with twist of orange peel.

GIN SOUR
Shake, using ½ cupful cracked ice:
    1 jigger sugar sirup
    2 jiggers lemon or lime juice
    5 jiggers gin
This recipe becomes a whisky, rum or brandy sour if the base is changed.

GORDON
Shake, using ½ cupful cracked ice:
    2 jiggers dry sherry
    6 jiggers gin
Place a twist of lemon peel over top of each drink.

WHITE LADY
Shake, using ½ cupful cracked ice:
    1½ jiggers lemon juice
    1 jigger cointreau
    2 egg whites
    4½ jiggers gin
See Bronx directions, page 820, but omit peel.

Whisky Cocktails

These are, of course, to be made with bourbon or rye whisky.

FRISCO
Shake with ½ cupful cracked ice:
    1½ jiggers benedictine
    1 jigger lemon juice
    5 jiggers whisky

DRY MANHATTAN
Stir well with ice cubes:
    3 jiggers French vermouth
    5 jiggers whisky
Add to each drink:
    1 dash angostura bitters

SAZERAC
Stir with ice cubes until thoroughly chilled:
    4 teaspoons sugar sirup
    4 dashes Peychaud bitters
    4 dashes anisette or absinthe
    7 jiggers whisky
Pour into chilled glasses. Add a twist of lemon peel to each glass.

MEDIUM MANHATTAN
Stir well with ice cubes:
    1½ jiggers French vermouth
    1½ jiggers Italian vermouth
    5 jiggers whisky
Add to each drink:
    1 dash angostura bitters

OLD-FASHIONED
1 Serving
Put into an old-fashioned glass and stir:
    ½ teaspoon sugar sirup
    2 dashes angostura bitters
    1 teaspoon water
Add:
    2 cubes ice
Fill glass to within ½ inch of top with:
    Whisky
Stir. Decorate with a twist of lemon peel, thin slice of orange and a maraschino cherry.

MILLIONAIRE
Shake with ½ cupful cracked ice:
 1 jigger grenadine or raspberry
 sirup
 2 jiggers curaçao
 2 egg whites

Add and shake again:
 4½ jiggers whisky

Whisky Bitter, see Gin Bitter. Substitute whisky for the gin.
Whisky Sour, see Gin Sour.

Rum Cocktails

All rum cocktails should be mixed with light-bodied Cuban rum only. Jamaica rum is good too, but save it for longer drinks.

Some people like the taste and look of a frosted glass and consider it the final fine touch to cocktails of the rum type.

To Frost a Cocktail Glass: Cool the glass and swab the rim with a section of lemon from which the juice is flowing freely, or dip it in grenadine. Swirl the glass to remove excess moisture, then dip the rim to the depth of ¼ inch in powdered or very finely granulated sugar. Lift the glass and tap it gently to remove any excess sugar.

BENEDICTINE
Shake with ½ cupful cracked ice:
 1½ jiggers lime juice
 1½ jiggers benedictine
 4½ jiggers rum

CUBANA
Shake with ½ cupful cracked ice:
 ½ jigger sugar sirup
 1½ jiggers lime juice
 2 jiggers apricot brandy
 3½ jiggers rum

DAIQUIRI OR PINK DAIQUIRI
With grenadine substituted for sugar sirup this cocktail becomes a Pink Daiquiri or Daiquiri Grenadine.
Shake well with ½ cupful cracked ice:
 ½ jigger sugar sirup
 1½ jiggers lime juice
 5½ jiggers rum
Add to each drink:
 2 dashes grenadine
Serve in tall chilled glasses (page 823).

FROZEN DAIQUIRI
Spectacular and delicious frozen cocktails may be made using an electric blender, page 895. By increasing the amount of crushed ice in the Daiquiri recipe, for instance, to between 2 and 3 cupfuls, using powdered sugar instead of granulated, and "blending" the ingredients until they reach a snowy consistency, you will achieve a hot weather triumph. Serve it in champagne glasses.

EL PRESIDENTE
Shake with ½ cupful cracked ice:
 1½ jiggers French vermouth
 1½ jiggers lemon juice
 2 dashes grenadine
 2 dashes curaçao
Add and shake again:
 4½ jiggers rum
Decorate each glass with a twist of orange peel and a cherry.

KNICKERBOCKER
Shake well with ½ cupful of cracked ice:
 ½ jigger raspberry sirup and
 ½ jigger pineapple sirup
 1½ jiggers lemon juice
 5 jiggers rum
Serve with a twist of orange peel.

LARCHMONT
Shake with ½ cupful cracked ice:
 ½ jigger sugar sirup
 1½ jiggers lime juice
 1½ jiggers Grand Marnier liqueur
 4 jiggers rum
Serve with a twist of orange peel in each glass.

MIAMI
Shake with ½ cupful crushed ice:
 1 jigger white crème de menthe
 1½ jiggers lemon juice
 5 jiggers rum

Rum Sour, see Gin Sour.

Brandy Cocktails

The brandy you use may be either the grape type, like cognac, or applejack, which makes an entirely different, but equally good drink. Brandy cocktails may be served in frosted glasses, page 822. Grenadine may be substituted for the lemon juice in preparing the glass for frosting.

Brandy Bitter, see Gin Bitter.
Brandy Sour, see Gin Sour.

CHAMPAGNE
1 Serving
Pour into large champagne glass:
   ½ teaspoon sugar sirup
   ½ jigger chilled brandy
Fill glass almost to top with:
   Chilled dry champagne
Add:
   2 dashes yellow chartreuse
   2 dashes orange bitters

SIDECAR
Sometimes this drink is served in a frosted glass, page 822. Using apple brandy changes a Sidecar into a Jack Rose.
Shake with ½ cupful cracked ice:
   1 jigger cointreau
   2 jiggers lemon juice
   4½ jiggers brandy
Serve with a twist of lemon peel.

COFFEE
Shake well with ½ cupful cracked ice:
   1 jigger sugar sirup
   3 jiggers port
   2 small eggs
Add and shake again:
   3 jiggers brandy

CURAÇAO
Shake well with ½ cupful cracked ice:
   2 jiggers curaçao
   1 jigger lemon juice
   4½ jiggers brandy
Add to each drink:
   1 dash angostura bitters
Add a twist of lemon peel to each drink.

STINGER
Shake with ½ cupful finely crushed ice:
   1 jigger lime juice
   2 jiggers white crème de menthe
   5 jiggers brandy

Tall Drinks, Punches and Toddies

Glasses and cups for tall drinks vary greatly in size and shape. Collins glasses, lemonade and highball glasses, shown to the left below, are similar in shape and vary in content from 16 to 8 ounces.

Silver cups with a handle, so that the frost remains undisturbed, are highly favorable. Some persons dislike drinks served in metal, but if straws are used no metallic taste is noticeable. If not using straws, serve juleps in very thin glassware. To frost the glasses see page 822.

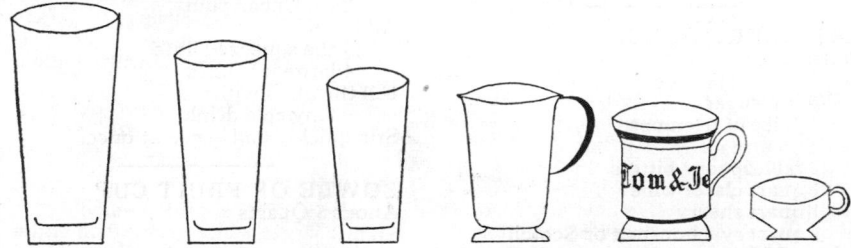

Tom and Jerry mugs, shown next, are usually porcelain and hold about 8 ounces. Punch glasses or cups hold about 4 ounces. The latter are frequently porcelain, an advantage when serving mulled drinks or flaming drinks.

HIGHBALL OR RICKY

Use rye, bourbon or gin. Put ice cubes in a 6 ounce glass. Add:

    1 jigger of the liquor chosen

And for a ricky add:

    Juice of ½ lime

Fill up glass with club soda or water, stir and serve.

TOM COLLINS

Individual Serving

Combine:

    1 tablespoon powdered sugar
    Juice of 1 lemon or 2 limes
    1½ jiggers gin
    (3 or 4 mint leaves)

Shake well with cracked ice and strain into a 10 or 12 ounce glass. Add cubes of ice and fill glass with:

    Club soda

Stir just enough to mix.

RUM COLLINS

Individual Serving

Combine:

    1 large jigger rum
    1 teaspoon sugar
    Juice of 1 lime or ½ lemon

Shake well with ice. Strain into a tall glass. Fill up with club soda. Stir.

RUM PUNCH

Individual Serving

Combine:

    1 part lemon juice or lime juice
    ½ part pure maple sirup
    1¾ parts rum
    2 dashes grenadine

Shake well with ice. Pour into a 10 ounce glass filled with crushed ice. Decorate with:

    Pineapple stick
    A slice of orange
    A cherry

ARTILLERY PUNCH

20 Servings

Combine and stir well:

    1 cup sugar
    Juice of 6 lemons

Add and mix well:

    2 tablespoons bitters
    1 quart claret wine
    1 quart sherry
    1 quart rye, bourbon or Scotch
        whisky
    1 quart brandy

Pour over a block of ice in a punch bowl. Add:

    1 quart club soda

PLANTER'S PUNCH

Individual Serving

Fill a 10 ounce glass with crushed ice. Add and stir:

    2 jiggers rum
    Juice of ½ lemon
    Dash of grenadine

Fill the rest of the glass with:

    Club soda

Decorate with:

    Fruit
    A cherry

WHISKY TODDY

Individual Serving

Dissolve:

    1 lump sugar

in:

    A jigger cold water

Add:

    1 twist lemon peel
    1 jigger bourbon whisky

Add a lump of ice and stir.

If a hot toddy is desired, use hot water to dissolve sugar and after adding whisky fill the glass with hot water.

WHISKY CUP

16 Servings

Combine and stir:

    1½ cups sugar
    Juice of 3 lemons

Stir in until well blended:

    2 quarts whisky
    2 quarts club soda

Pour over large block of ice in punch bowl. Add:

    ½ cup grenadine
    2 sliced oranges
    1 cup sliced pineapple

CUBA LIBRE

Individual Serving

Combine in a 14 ounce glass:

    Juice of 1 small lime
    2 oz. Cuban rum

Add:

    ½ the squeezed lime
    4 large ice cubes

Fill the glass with:

    Any cola drink

Stir quickly and serve at once.

BOWLE OR FRUIT CUP

About 5 Quarts

Stem:

    1 quart strawberries

or peel:

    1 quart peaches

Sprinkle over them:

    ½ cup sugar

Add:

1 quart bottle white wine

Permit these ingredients to stand for 12 hours. Add:

4 cups water
2 quart bottles white wine

Boil for 10 minutes:

1 cup sugar
¾ cup water

Chill the sirup. Add as much of the sirup to the fruit cup as desired. Cover the cup and set it in a refrigerator until it is thoroughly chilled. If available, add tender sprigs of sweet woodruff (Waldmeister) to give the Bowle distinction and a fillip that is all its own.

CLARET CUP
About 7 Cupfuls Without Ice
Place in a pitcher:

2 slices pineapple, cut in pieces
2 small unpeeled peaches, cut in halves
2 peach stones
1 sliced orange
½ sliced lemon
A few small strips cucumber rind
1 tablespoon sugar

Permit these ingredients to stand for 4 hours. Add:

2 tablespoons brandy
2 tablespoons maraschino
1 quart claret or Burgundy

Place the cup in a refrigerator for 1 hour. When ready to serve, remove the cucumber, peaches and stones and add:

1 pint Apollinaris
A large piece of ice

Garnish the cup with:

Mint

Remove the mint before it gives too strong a flavor. Serve the cup in punch glasses.

MULLED WINE
About 2 Quarts
This is fine for an after-the-theater party, served with hors d'oeuvres or assorted cookies.
Make a sirup by boiling for 5 minutes:

1 cup sugar
½ cup water
2 sticks cinnamon
½ lemon cut into slices
2 dozen cloves

Strain the sirup. Add to it:

4 cups hot fruit juice: lemon, orange, pineapple, etc.

If very sweet fruit juice is used, reduce the amount of sugar.

Heat but do not boil:

1 quart or more red wine

Combine the fruit juices and the wine. Keep the wine hot in a double boiler. Serve it very hot with slices of:

Lemon and pineapple

Do not hesitate to vary these proportions.

Hot Mulled Cider, page 813.

HOT BUTTERED RUM
Individual Serving
Place in a hot tumbler:

1 teaspoon powdered sugar

Add:

¼ cup boiling water
¼ cup rum
1 tablespoon butter

Fill glass with boiling water. Stir well. Sprinkle on top:

Freshly grated nutmeg

This is an old-time New England conception of an individual portion. It may be modified. Curious, isn't it, that the Pilgrims made rum—especially a drink like this one, which has been said to make a man see double and feel single.

HOT RUM LEMONADE
Individual Serving
Combine:

1 lump sugar
Juice of ½ lemon
2 tablespoons or more Jamaica rum

Fill the glass with hot water. Add:

A slice of lemon

HOT TOM AND JERRY
6 Servings
Beat to a very stiff froth:

6 egg whites

Beat in gradually:

6 teaspoons powdered sugar

Beat until blended, then beat into the egg whites:

6 egg yolks

Pour 2 tablespoonfuls of this mixture into a china mug. Add to each serving:

½ jigger brandy
1 jigger rum

Fill the mug with very hot water, stir well and sprinkle the top with:

Grated nutmeg

EGGNOG
Method I. About 5 Quarts
A rich and extravagant version that is

correspondingly good. I shall not attempt to give the number of servings as I am a poor judge of thirst and capacity. An authority (Mark Twain) says, "Too much of anything is bad, but too much whiskey is just enough."
Beat until light:
12 egg yolks
Beat in gradually:
1 lb. confectioners' sugar
Add very slowly, beating constantly:
1 quart rum, brandy or whisky
2 quarts cream
1 quart milk
Whip until stiff:
6 egg whites
½ teaspoon salt
Fold them lightly into the other ingredients. Serve the eggnog sprinkled with:
Freshly grated nutmeg

Method II.
Beat until light:
6 egg yolks
Beat in gradually:
½ cup sugar
Add very slowly, beating constantly:
1 cup brandy
2 cups cream
2 cups milk
Whip until stiff:
⅛ teaspoon salt
6 egg whites
You may cut this to 2 egg whites and whip ½ the cream. Fold them lightly into the other ingredients. Serve the eggnog sprinkled with:
Freshly grated nutmeg

Method III. 8 Servings
This must be prepared a day ahead of time. It is smooth, good and made with ingredients one is apt to have on hand. Less "calorious" than the usual eggnog.
Beat until light:
3 eggs
Beat in gradually:
6 tablespoons sugar
A few grains salt
2 tablespoons vanilla
Stir in:
2¼ cups evaporated milk
Diluted with:
¾ cup water
If an alcoholic flavor is desired, omit the vanilla and add:
½ cup brandy, whisky, etc.
Place the eggnog in a jar with a screw top. Permit it to ripen in the refrigerator for 24 hours. Serve it sprinkled with:
Freshly ground nutmeg

EGGNOG
Individual Serving
Beat until light:
1 egg yolk
Beat in slowly:
1 tablespoon sugar
¼ cup cream
⅛ to ¼ cup rum, brandy or whisky
Whip until stiff:
1 egg white
A few grains salt
Fold it lightly into the other ingredients.

MILK PUNCH
Individual Serving
Shake with cracked ice:
1 glass sweet milk
1 teaspoon powdered sugar
1 large jigger bourbon, rye or brandy
Strain into 10 ounce glass. Sprinkle with:
Nutmeg
Or, heat milk and add to each glass:
2 teaspoons rum

MINT JULEP
The "New Yorker" had a most amusing story of a bartender who thought he knew how to make mint julep. As he was following his favorite formula one day he was interrupted by a southern gentleman, who was horrified to find that the bartender was chopping the mint. The southerner, apparently a man of authority, told him that the mint must be bruised, not chopped. So he followed his instructions until one day he was vehemently interrupted by another southerner, who told him that mint must never be bruised, it must be left whole—and so on through endless experiences and endless corrections, until the poor bartender had a nervous breakdown and still did not know the really correct way to prepare a mint julep. Neither do I. It is without any feeling of superiority that I venture to give the following recipe, which I offer as a suggestion only:

TO FROST A MINT JULEP
The quickest way is to place the julep cup on several folds of dry newspaper. This acts as an insulator. Fill the cup with ice and julep mixture and stir it vigorously with a bar spoon or an iced-tea spoon. A slower way is to mix the julep and place it for ½ hour in a refrigerator.

TO PREPARE A MINT JULEP

Chill silver julep cups or 12 ounce glasses. Pick from stem and place in cup:

4 or 5 mint leaves

Muddle with:

1 teaspoon powdered sugar
1 teaspoon water

Fill cup with finely crushed ice. Pour in:

1 jigger bourbon whisky

Stir energetically until the ice has dropped 1 or 2 inches and frost begins to appear. Then fill remainder of julep cup with crushed ice and pour in:

1 jigger bourbon whisky

Decorate the julep with:

Sprigs of mint dusted with powdered sugar

Insert short straws. Long straws are apt to short-circuit the flavor of the drink and make it too strong. Place the julep in the refrigerator for ½ hour, if you are not too impatient. A connoisseur I know likes to add to each julep a finger length of fresh pineapple and a slice of orange.

MINT JULEPS FOR PARTIES

Mint julep in mass production becomes a problem. You may solve it by mixing simple sirup, page 819, and mint leaves ahead of time. Refills may be poured from a pitcher. Place whisky mixed with mint sirup in the pitcher around a single piece of ice and have it passed with separate bowls of mint and crushed ice. For refills metal cups may be prechilled in the refrigerator.

Wines and Cordials

GRAPE, BLACKBERRY OR OTHER BERRY WINE

Mash in a stone jar:

20 lbs. grapes or other fruit

Add:

5 quarts boiling water

Cover the jar. Permit these ingredients to stand for 3 days. Strain the fruit through a cheesecloth bag. Return the juice to the jar. Add:

10 cups sugar

Cover the jar. Permit these ingredients to stand until fermentation has ceased. Remove the scum. Strain the juice. Bottle it tightly. Seal the bottles with sealing wax.

BLACKBERRY CORDIAL

Boil:

Blackberries

Add a little water to keep them from scorching. When they are soft put the juice through a jelly bag. Add to each quart of juice:

2 cups sugar
½ stick cinnamon
2 tablespoons cloves
¼ oz. mace or allspice

Boil these ingredients for 20 minutes. Strain them. Add to each quart of juice:

1 pint French brandy

CHERRY BOUNCE

Stem and place in a crock:

6 lbs. cherries

Add:

1 pint alcohol
5 lbs. sugar: 10 cups

This measurement is for acid cherries. Use less if the cherries are not acid. Cover the crock. Stir the cherries twice a day until the sugar is dissolved, about 3 days. Cover the crock tightly. After 5 months add:

1 pint distilled water

Strain the liquid. Bottle it.

QUINCE LIQUEUR

The formula for this delicious and unusual liqueur was given by a French priest to his friends. When you drink it remember the advice of an old German who said when serving a fine vintage, "Don't gullop it, zipp it!"

Wash and core:

Quinces

Put them through a food grinder. Add to 4 quarts ground quince:

3 gallons rye whisky
1 oz. cardamon seed
½ oz. mace
1 oz. anise seed
½ vanilla bean
1 oz. broken nutmeg

Place these ingredients for 3 weeks in a stone jar with a tight cover. Stir them frequently. Strain them through a flannel jelly bag.

Make a rich sirup of:

10 lbs. granulated sugar
7 pints water

Cool, then add it to the liqueur. Bottle and seal it.

Wine Chart

Course	Wine	How To Serve
Shellfish or Hors d'oeuvre	Chablis Graves Rhine or Moselle	Cold—40° to 45°
Soup	Sauterne Dry Sherry Madeira	Cold—40° to 45° Room Temperature Cool—50°
Fish	White Bordeaux White Burgundy Rhine or Moselle	Cool—50° " " " "
Entrées	White wine Claret	Cold—40° to 45° Room Temperature
Roasts Red Meats	Fine Claret Red Burgundy Sparkling Burgundy	Room Temperature " " Cold—40° to 45°
Roasts White Meats	White Bordeaux White Burgundy Champagne	" " Cool—50° Cold—40° to 45°
Fowl or Game	Fine Claret Red Burgundy Rhone	Room Temperature " " " "
Cheese	Fine Claret Red Burgundy Port Old Sherry Full-bodied Madeira	Room Temperature " " " " " " " "
Dessert	Madeira Rich Old Sherry	Room Temperature " "
Coffee	Cognac Old Port, Sherry Madeira Liqueur	Room Temperature " " " " " "

Wine Cookery

Wine cookery calls for discretion. Its flavor is a pleasant addition to food, but it must never predominate over the natural flavor of the food.

Recipes using wine are found throughout this book. The following can only be the broadest generalization. You must experiment on your own and familiarize yourself with wine flavors to see what you enjoy.

Here are some traditional suggestions recommending which wines to use with which foods:

For soups, use sherry and Madeira; for fish, use dry white wine; for meats, use dry red wine; for desserts, use port, sweet sherry or Madeira, liqueurs, brandy or rum.

Poor wine will not improve any dish. If wine is not good enough to drink, don't combine it with food. Watch the strength of wine, as it varies. Two table-spoonfuls sherry will about equal ½ cupful dry red table wine in strength. A small quantity of Madeira will flavor a dish as well as a cupful or 2 of red wine in cooking a meat dish.

Any hot soup is improved by the addition of 1 or 2 tablespoonfuls dry sherry or Madeira to each soup bowl.

Add little sherry to fish, but do not hesitate to poach it in dry white table wine.

On the Serving of Wines

Here are a few suggestions to guide the inexperienced hostess.

With few exceptions wines are served at 45° to 60°.

Champagne is always served cold—35° to 40°. It should be cooled gradually in a refrigerator and placed in ice shortly before being used. The younger vintages of champagne call for 35°, the older for 40°.

The wine glasses below are a hollow-stemmed champagne glass, a Roemer for Rhine wine, a glass for red or white table wine, a pipestem sherry glass, a glass for port, a brandy inhaler or snifter and liqueur glasses.

Either champagne or a medium dry sherry is suitable to serve at all times and with all foods and throughout a meal.

Some of the generally accepted customs on the serving of wine are:

Serve dry wines before sweet wines; white wines before red ones; light wines before heavier ones; white wines with hors d'oeuvres, fish and white meats; red wines with dark meats, game and cheeses.

On the Serving of Beer and Ale

The beer connoisseur, like the wine fancier never forgets the living quality of his brew. Even today's pasteurized beer is still full of living organisms subject to deterioration and shock. So if he wants to savor beer at its height, he looks at the date to make sure it won't be over 2 months old when it is served. He keeps it stored in a dark place. He chills it slowly before serving and once it is cold it is not allowed to warm up again and be rechilled, nor is it ever allowed to freeze.

Like the wine connoisseur, he is very fussy about the temperatures at which he serves beer. Forty degrees is favored as producing the fullest flavor, a not too great contrast between the temperature of the drink and the taste buds.

A slightly higher serving temperature is suggested for ale. This drink is made from the same ingredients as beer, except for the strain of the yeast. It is fermented rapidly and at room temperature rather than at the almost freezing temperatures modern beer demands in its long, slow and intricately controlled processing.

Beers vary greatly in alcoholic and sugar content depending on how they are brewed. Bock, which appears at Eastertime is frequently advertised by a picture of a monk, for Shrove Tuesday was the traditional tasting and testing day in the old monasteries. This brew is dark and is usually higher in alcoholic content than beer set in the spring. Beer is light and tart or dark and sweet depending whether the barley is processed with low, slow heat or with high, swift heat. Which to serve is a matter of personal taste.

Here are the traditional beer and ale glass or mug shapes.

Steins, heirloom and everyday, the Pilsener glass for light beer and an ale glass and mug are shown above. The true connoisseur is probably happiest drinking beer from an opaque container which does not allow him to see the small imperfections in the appearance of beer which are visible when it is served in improperly washed glasses. Grease is the natural enemy of beer for it kills the foam. So wash glasses with soda, not with soap. The glasses should never be dried with a cloth but be allowed to drain on a soft cloth which has been washed with a detergent.

Glasses may be chilled before using, but in any case they should be rinsed just before using in cold water and the beer should be poured into a tilted wet glass.

You may like a high or a low collar but the usual size is one fourth the height of the glass or mug. A bottle of beer, despite popular superstition, is not so caloric as the average cocktail, but since it lacks the disembodied quality of table wines it is usually served with snacks and suppers.

Herbs

Numerous books and articles have been written recently on herbs, how to grow them and how to use them. It is impossible to condense all this lore into a few paragraphs, as the approach to the subject is handled reverently by some writers and exhaustively by all.

Marion and I have firm friends in Mrs. Otto Rosenfelder and Mrs. Harold Downing of Lebanon, Ohio, mother and daughter. They pursue their hobby, gardening, with vigor and intelligence. Their charmingly planned herb garden is a joy to see and smell, their horticultural and practical knowledge extensive. Their gardening experience has greatly enriched this chapter.

Our country, after decades of neglect, is being made nationally herb-conscious. Many cooks smile at this vibrant revival of a custom they have never permitted to lapse into oblivion. They have always found room for a sprout of tarragon in a garden corner, a bit of chervil, basil, etc., or if minus a garden, they have persuaded a neighbor or truck gardener to grow them. Now suddenly the cultivation of herbs has become a cult and it threatens to engulf us.

My rules are elastic, culled from various authorities with assailable but unbending convictions. I fully expect some protest about whatever I may say, for social ostracism seems to follow in the wake of a vagrant savory or a misplaced camomile. Epicures are insistent upon wedding the right herb to the right dish and in some circles only the brave venture forth on a doubtful alliance. However, a break in the conventions cannot be much worse than a split infinitive or a double negative and they certainly have been known to creep into the best of families.

Herbs are a delightful addition to our everyday cooking, but even the most enthusiastic grower should use them with discretion. A pinch of herb adds a wonderful touch to a creamed dish, salad, soup or meat. Use herbs fresh or dried. Keep an assortment of the latter on your pantry shelf.

Cooks seem to agree that flavors resulting from blended herbs are in most cases preferable to the use of a single flavor except in the case of basil, rosemary and tarragon, which stand unusually well alone.

For cooking purposes the fine herbs—basil, chervil, sweet marjoram, thyme, rosemary and tarragon—may be paired as they are listed here with the addition of chives, or may be used in other combinations. Watch rosemary and tarragon in blending for they tend to dominate. Parsley frequently replaces the more delicate chervil.

Borage, fennel, dill, caraway, sorrel, orégano and summer savory are standbys in many households, along with the more common mint, sage and horseradish.

Many herb blends are said to come from a hoary and sophisticated past, but you may prefer to mix your own. If not, try the following which my friend, Herman Smith, has kindly allowed me to use from his incomparable *Stina: The Story of a Cook.*

"The herb powder without which Stina declared she could not cook was prepared at the end of summer before the flowers bloomed. Gathered and dried, the herbs would be weighed on Stina's small balancing scale; two ounces each of sweet marjoram, summer savory, parsley and thyme; an ounce of basil, a half-ounce each of sage, bay leaves, dried celery tops and dried lemon peel. This she would pound with a wooden pestle, and it was this delicious concoction which was the secret of so many of Stina's masterpieces."

For soups and stews use a faggot or "bouquet garni." These vary in makeup

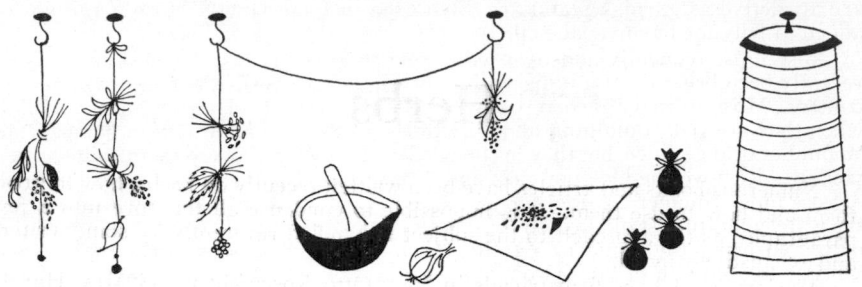

but usually include a bay leaf, thyme and parsley. Basil, sweet marjoram, summer savory, celery or lovage and chervil are often added. Tie the fresh herbs in a bouquet and use immediately. Wrap the dried ones, about ½ teaspoonful each of the herbs to 1 small bay leaf, in 4 inch squares of heavy cheesecloth. Gather the 4 corners together and bind them securely. The bouquets of dried ingredients may be made in advance and stored in a closely covered container, preferably light-proof. In any case never use a bouquet more than once. Add it only the last ½ hour of cooking at the longest and remove it before serving.

There are also many famous combinations of ingredients and herbs, so basically successful that they have names of their own, like ravigote, remoulade, Mirepoix and Duxelles (see Index).

Many spices combine well with herbs and their uses should be experimented with. Ginger, peppers, cinnamon, caraway, mustard and cumin seed are common favorites, used singly and in combination. Combined they make the basis for curry powder. Paprika, especially the imported Hungarian variety, nutmeg, freshly grated, mace, coriander, cardamon and cloves all contribute wonderfully characteristic flavors. Vinegar is also a classic agent for herb infusions (see page 494).

Most herbs are extremely simple and undemanding to grow, needing little space, normal garden soil and plenty of sun. They are picked for drying just before they come into flower. After careful washing, they are hung in small bunches in a shady, airy room or dried in a 250° oven. When thoroughly dry, the leaves are stripped from the stems and stored in closed containers. They retain their flavor better if pulverized just before using. One-third to ½ teaspoonful dried herbs, or ¼ teaspoonful powdered herbs is substituted for 1 tablespoonful fresh chopped herbs. In recipes where the seeds themselves are called for, use them sparingly for the flavor is very strong.

You may also preserve some herbs by salting them down green in a covered crock, alternating ½ inch layers of salt with ½ inch layers of herbs. Begin and end with slightly heavier salt layers. After a few weeks the salt will take on the flavor of the herbs you have chosen to combine and will be ready for use. The herbs which remain green may also be used.

Fine herbs are added the last minute to soups and sauces so that their essential oils are not evaporated. More heavily flavored herbs which are cooked longer with the food are often strained off before the food is served. In light colored or finely textured dishes, dried herbs are best tied in a cloth which can be easily removed before the end of the cooking process.

A stronger infusion results when dry or fresh herbs are soaked in milk, stock or vinegar, or mixed with the cooking butter about an hour before being added to ground meats, stuffing, chicken or veal.

For long drinks, bruised herbs, such as borage, mint, burnet, sweet woodruff, lemon balm and costmary are steeped in the cold or hot liquid and removed before serving. Borage blossoms or sweet woodruff leaves are sometimes floated on top of punch as a garnish. See Bowle, page 824. Lemon verbena and rose geranium are attractive as garnishes and are often used in fingerbowls. Rose geranium is added to jelly for flavor (page 803).

Rose hips frequently added to jellies and marmalades for tartness have more recently been brewed for mixing with fruit juices because of their high vitamin C content. Most ordinary garden rose seed pods may be used. They are most valuable when they are red, containing about 25 times as much vitamin C as a comparable amount of orange juice, but they may be picked at any time. Keep them chilled after picking. Remove the blossom ends and stems. Use 2 parts of boiling water to 1 of rose hips. Simmer covered for 15 minutes. If soft mash, if hard grind, and let the watery mixture stand in a covered pottery jar for 24 hours. Strain, discard the pulp, and bring the liquid to a rolling boil. Add 2 teaspoonfuls lemon juice or vinegar to each pint of fluid. Pour into sterile jars and seal.

This recent discovery of the vitamin C potency of rose hips may lead to more scientific revelations of the vitaminic values of herbs. Some are undoubtedly a digestive aid, like horseradish, in cutting the fat on naturally greasy foods; some are considered aphrodisiac; some wear an aura of benevolent superstitions, but whatever the reason the subtle use of herbs will continue in all interesting cuisine.

Some herbs and foods are so mutually flattering in flavor that their use has become classic. Try some of these time-tested favorites:

Basil with:

Tomato, fish and egg dishes, in ground meats, with calves' livers and fricassees of poultry, in salad dressings, spaghetti, and with eggplant, peas, beans, turnips and onions.

Borage with:

Lentils or cauliflower, in green salads, in marinade of beef. You may also use the leaves and blossoms in tea, lemonade or wine. Cooked as a vegetable, borage comes very close to spinach in flavor.

Caraway with:

Cottage cheese or potatoes, broccoli, cabbage, sauerkraut or turnips, in vegetable stock or on breads and appetizers with or without cheese.

Chervil with:

Egg dishes and sauces, especially Béarnaise, in cold soups like Vichyssoise, with veal and chicken, potato, celery root, artichoke hearts and in French dressing.

Chives with:

All onion-seasoned recipes, as a substitute. Be careful to add them the last moment of cooking and in cold dishes do not let them stand long before serving, as they tend to become strong.

Cumin with:

Bean or rice dishes, pork chops, codfish, sauerkraut or corn.

Dill with:

Shrimp and fish sauces, potato salad, beans or cucumbers with sour cream and of course in pickles. Use either green or as seed.

Fennel with:

Lentils and rice, and as a substitute in recipes calling for celery as seasoning. Use the seed in apple pie.

Horseradish with:

Sauces for fatty meats, in potato salad, with cold meats and fish.

Mint with:

Peas, lamb sauce, jellies, juleps, teas and chocolate.

Orégano with:

Lamb, all fowl, stuffings, lentils and broccoli, spaghetti and hot Mexican dishes.

Parsley with: ,

Practically everything, as you know—but with restraint. A Japanese cook once served it with ice cream. Minced finely, its high vitamin content is made more easily available to the human system.

Rosemary with:

Soup, spinach soufflé, roast beef or pork, in veal and chicken stews and with peas.

Sage with:

Salt fish and pork dishes, in stuffings for goose or duck, in cream or cottage cheese, but sparingly in all instances.

Summer Savory with:

Lentil, pea or vegetable soup, in liver sausage, veal stuffing, minced or roast beef or pork, with snap beans, Lima beans and potatoes, and in stuffed tomatoes and French dressing.

Sweet Marjoram with:

Omelets, eggs and cream cheese, chopped meats and sausages, roast chicken, lamb or pork, spinach, squash, tomatoes, mushrooms, potatoes, cabbage, slaw, broccoli, Brussels sprouts, cauliflower and green salads.

Tarragon with:

Fish, chicken, egg and tomato dishes, cream or butter sauces, salad dressings, ham and boiled meats, mushrooms, peas, pot greens, cabbages, celery root, in green salads and aspics.

Thyme with:

Cheeses, aspics, onions and clam chowders, sparingly in chopped meats, stews, fricassees, especially rabbit, in stuffings and with peas, carrots and onions.

There are also a few mystic ingredients without which some gourmets seem to find cooking dull.

Saffron, the fabulously renowned and expensive stigmas of Crocus sativus, used in rice dishes, breads, buns and bouillabaisse both for its flavor and color.

Filé powder, a concoction of sassafras used in gumbos, casseroles and Creole cooking.

Monosodium glutamate, the mysterious "white powder" of the Orient, which, by stimulating the taste buds, intensifies the basic flavors of many foods except sweets and egg dishes. Use about ½ teaspoonful for each pound of meat or fish, or each quart of stock. Use about ½ teaspoonful to each cupful gravy. "M. S. G.," as it is nicknamed by its devotees, may be added at any time to stews, sauces and vegetables, but it is usually rubbed into meats before boiling, roasting or sautéing them. This is now available under trade names or at the druggist under its own.

Pickles

Peter Piper must have been pretty well pickled himself when he picked that peck of previously pickled peppers, for less privileged persons have to pick and then pickle the produce themselves.

Pick, pickle and process peppers and pickles promptly. Plump, fresh produce pickles superbly. Limp produce pickles poorly.

Brine:

Brine is a solution of salt and water. Use 1 part coarse salt to 9 parts water. Combine the salt with a little water, dissolve it and add the remaining water. For best results use soft water.

Avoid the use of iodized salts in pickles. Barrel or coarse salt is preferable to table salt. One cupful of salt equals about 10 ounces or ⅔ pound.

When following recipes use a 5 per cent vinegar, a white one if the pickles are light in color or a cider vinegar if they are not.

Use glass, pottery or enamel vessels for soaking pickles. Cook them in enamel pots.

Store pickles in well-sealed crocks or in jars with glass tops, rather than metal tops, to avoid corrosion.

MUSTARD PICKLE
About 6 Quarts

Since making the following mild and palatable pickle for the first time I have abandoned all other mixed pickles and have clung to this one as it meets with general and enthusiastic approval.
Slice, unpeeled if tender:
1 quart or more green cucumbers
Cover them for 12 hours with:
Brine, see preceding rule
Drain them well. Keep them separate. Slice to make 4 quarts with the cucumbers:
Green vegetables: green tomatoes, beans, etc.
Keep them separate. Pour boiling salted water, 1 teaspoonful salt to 1 quart water to cover, over the vegetables and bring them to the boiling point. Drain them well. If the beans are not very young, boil them until they are nearly tender. Peel and slice:
2 dozen small onions
Break into flowerets:
1 large cauliflower
If the cauliflower is not very tender, boil it until it is partly done. Slice:
2 dozen or more small gherkins
Keep them separate. Pour boiling salted water over them. Bring them to the boiling point. Drain them well. Combine all the vegetables. Prepare the following mustard sauce.

Combine and stir until smooth:
1½ cups flour
6 tablespoons dry mustard
1½ tablespoons turmeric
2 cups mild cider vinegar
Bring to the boiling point:
2 quarts mild cider vinegar: 8 cups
2½ cups sugar
3 tablespoons celery seed
Slowly stir in the flour mixture. Stir constantly. When the sauce is smooth and boiling combine it with the drained vegetables. Add if needed:
Salt
Place the pickle in jars and seal them.

GREEN TOMATO PICKLE
Wash and cut into thin slices:
1 peck green tomatoes
Peel and cut into thin slices:
12 large onions
Sprinkle them with:
1 cup coarse salt
Permit them to stand for 12 hours. Wash them in clear water. Drain them. Heat to the boiling point:
3 quarts cider vinegar
12 green peppers sliced thin
6 sweet diced red peppers
12 minced cloves garlic
4 lbs. brown sugar
Add the tomatoes and onions. Add

and cook slowly until the tomatoes are transparent, about 1 hour:

    2 tablespoons dry mustard
    2 tablespoons whole cloves
    2 tablespoons broken stick
      cinnamon
    2 tablespoons powdered ginger
    1 tablespoon salt
    1 tablespoon celery seed

Stir these ingredients frequently. Place the pickle in jars and seal them.

YELLOW CUCUMBER PICKLES OR SENFGURKEN
About 14 Quarts

These large, luscious, firm slices are served very cold with meat.
Pare, cut into strips of about 1½ x 2½ inches and seed:

    1 bushel large yellow cucumbers

Soak the strips for 12 hours in:

    Brine, page 835

Drain them well. Sterilize 14 quart fruit jars (page 844). Place in each one:

    A slice of peeled horseradish
    1½ inches long, ⅓ inch wide
    and ⅓ inch thick
    A ½ inch piece long hot red
    pepper
    4 sprigs dill blossom with seeds
    1 tablespoon white mustard seed

If pint jars are used, halve these amounts. Combine:

    3 cups water
    1 cup sugar
    1½ gallons white pickling vinegar

If the vinegar is very acid, use 1¼ cupfuls sugar.
Other vinegar may be substituted but it will darken the pickle. Taste these ingredients. They should be palatable, not raw. Boil about 3 cupfuls at a time, enough to cover the bottom of a large saucepan to the depth of about ½ inch. Keep several pans going to hasten the process. Immerse in the boiling vinegar sufficient cucumber strips to cover the bottom of the pan. Let them come to the boiling point. Remove them at once to the jars. Do not cook the strips longer, as it will soften them. When a jar is filled with cucumber strips cover them with boiling vinegar. Seal the jars. Permit the pickles to ripen for at least 6 weeks before serving them.

SOUR-SWEET SPICED CUCUMBER PICKLES

These are wonderfully good. Scrub:

    20 lbs. very small cucumbers

Soak them for 24 hours in brine made of:

    1 cup coarse salt
    3 quarts water: 12 cups

Remove them from the brine and pour boiling water to cover over them. Drain them quickly in a colander and pack them closely while hot in sterilized jars (page 844). Cover them at once with the following vinegar mixture. Bring to the boiling point:

    1 gallon cider vinegar
    11 cups sugar
    2 oz. whole mixed spices
    1 oz. stick cinnamon
    1 teaspoon cloves
    1 teaspoon alum

Seal the jars at once.

SOUR-SWEET YELLOW CUCUMBER PICKLES OR SENFGURKEN
About 9 Quarts

Peel, cut into strips and seed:

    12 large yellow cucumbers

Place them in Brine, page 835, for 12 hours. Drain them. Have ready 8 or 10 sterilized quart fruit jars (page 844). Prepare the following mixture:

    1 gallon pickling vinegar
    8 cups sugar
    ¼ cup mustard seed

Place in a bag and add:

    ¾ cup whole mixed spices

Boil about 5 cupfuls of the mixture at a time, enough to cover the bottom of a large pan to the depth of about ½ inch. Place the bag of spices in the pan. Immerse in the boiling vinegar sufficient strips to cover the bottom of the pan. Bring the vinegar to the boiling point. Remove the strips at once. Place them in the jars. Fill the jars with the boiling vinegar mixture. Seal them at once.

BREAD AND BUTTER PICKLES
About 6 Quarts

Wash well:

    1 gallon medium-sized cucumbers:
    4 quarts
    6 to 12 large onions or 3 cups or
    more small white ones
    2 green or red peppers

Proportions for this rule may vary, as onion fanciers use the larger amount and even more of their beloved vegetable. Cut the unpared cucumbers and the peeled onions into the thinnest slices possible. Remove the seeds and fibrous membranes from the peppers. Shred or chop the peppers. Place the vegetables in a bowl. Pour over them:

    ½ cup coarse salt

Place them in a refrigerator for 3 hours. A weighted lid may be placed over them. Drain the vegetables. Rinse them in cold water. Drain them well this time. A cloth bag is frequently used to let all the moisture drip from them. Prepare the following sirup:

    5 cups well-flavored mild cider
      vinegar
    5 cups white or brown sugar
    1½ teaspoons turmeric or allspice
    2 tablespoons mustard seed
    1½ teaspoons celery seed
    ½ teaspoon ground cloves or 1
      inch stick cinnamon

Bring these ingredients to the boiling point. Add the vegetables gradually with very little stirring. Heat them to the scalding point but do not permit them to boil. Place the pickles in hot sterilized jars. Seal the jars at once.

OZARK PICKLES

This recipe makes fine, hard, crisp pickles.

Thoroughly scrub with a brush:

    About 350 small cucumbers
    about 2 inches in length

Place them in Brine, page 835, heavy enough to float a small potato, for 24 hours. Pour boiling water to cover over:

    Small pickling onions

Permit them to stand for 2 minutes. Drain them. Cover them with cold water. Remove the outer skin. Peel them. Place them in Brine, page 835, for 12 hours. Drain them. Pour boiling water over them. Drain them. Have ready sterilized pint jars. Place in the bottom of each jar:

    A head of dill

Cover this with a row of pickles. Peel:

    Horseradish

Add to each jar a block of horseradish about ¼ x ¼ inch high and wide and ½ inch long. Add 5 to 6 of the onions and:

    ½ inch or more gingerroot
    ¼ inch long red pepper

Barely fill the jar with pickles. Place 5 or 6 onions on top. Bring to the boiling point and pour over these ingredients:

    ¼ cup cider vinegar
    ¼ cup water
    1 cup sugar

Permit the pickles to stand for about 15 minutes. Pour off the liquid. Boil it again. Add to each jar:

    ¼ teaspoon mustard seed
    ¼ teaspoon celery seed
    A pinch alum

Pour on the boiling liquid and seal the jars.

CURRY SAUCE PICKLE

Peel and chop fine:

    12 large green cucumbers
    6 large onions
    2 sweet red peppers

Sprinkle these ingredients with:

    ¼ cup coarse salt

Permit them to stand for 1 hour. Drain them. Peel and stew until soft:

    12 large tomatoes

Combine the salted vegetables with the stewed tomatoes. Add and boil for 30 minutes:

    4 teaspoons curry powder
    2 teaspoons celery seed
    2 tablespoons brown sugar
    2 cups cider vinegar

Pack the pickle into jars and seal the jars.

OLIVE OIL PICKLE
About 3 Quarts

This pickle is not for reducers, but even they will be tempted by it.

Wash:

    24 cucumbers 3 to 4 inches long

Cut them, unpeeled, into very thin slices. Sprinkle them with:

    ½ cup coarse salt

Permit them to stand for 3 hours. Drain them well. Peel, slice very finely and add:

    2 small onions

Combine and add:

    1 cup white mustard seed
    1 tablespoon celery seed
    ½ cup olive oil
    4 cups cider vinegar

Mix all the ingredients thoroughly. Place the pickle in jars. Permit it to ripen for 3 weeks before serving it.

COLD PICKLES

Combine and stir:

    1 gallon cider vinegar
    ½ cup coarse salt
    3 cups sugar
    1 cup finely diced horseradish

Wash and trim the stems from:

    1 peck 4 inch cucumbers

Place them in a 3 gallon crock. Pour the vinegar mixture over them. Cover them with a plate. Place a weight on the plate. Permit the pickles to ripen for several days before serving them.

DILL PICKLES
About 4 Quarts
Sterilize four 1 quart jars. Place in each jar:
    1 clove garlic
    6 peppercorns
    1 clove
    Sprigs of dill with seeds
Scrub well, then dry:
    ½ peck straight 3 inch cucumbers
Pack them closely into the jars. Bring to the boiling point:
    2 quarts cider vinegar
    1 quart water
    1 cup coarse salt
Fill the jars with this mixture. Seal the jars. Permit the pickles to ripen for 5 days before serving them.

PICKLED ONIONS
Cover with water:
    Small white onions
Add:
    1 tablespoon coarse salt to every quart water
Permit the onions to soak for 2 hours. Remove the outer skins. Soak the onions for 48 hours in:
    Brine to cover, page 835
Drain them well. Bring to the boiling point:
    White vinegar
To each gallon vinegar add:
    1 cup sugar
Add the onions and boil them for 3 minutes. Place them at once in sterilized jars (page 844). Cover them with the boiling vinegar. Add to each quart jar:
    ½ inch long red hot pepper pod
    ⅛ bay leaf
    (3 cloves without heads)

Midwinter Pickles

MIDWINTER PICKLES IN MUSTARD SAUCE
About 7 Quarts
Slice into ⅓ inch slices:
    24 large sour cucumber, not dill, pickles
Peel and cut into thin slices:
    (3 large onions)
Dissolve:
    4 tablespoons cornstarch
    1 tablespoon dry mustard
    1 teaspoon turmeric
in:
    1 cup cider vinegar
Combine and heat to the boiling point:
    1 cup white or brown sugar
    1 teaspoon salt
    ½ teaspoon paprika
    A few grains cayenne
    3 cups cider vinegar
    2 teaspoons celery seed
Stir in the cornstarch mixture. Stir and boil these ingredients until they thicken. Combine the pickles, the onions and the boiled dressing. Place the pickles in jars.

SOUR-SWEET MIDWINTER PICKLES WITH OR WITHOUT SPICES
About 4 Pints
Cut into 1 inch slices:
    12 large sour cucumber pickles
Cover them with:

    3 cups brown or white sugar
    3 tablespoons mustard seed
    3 tablespoons celery seed, or in place of these seeds, 6 tablespoons mixed whole spices
Permit them to stand in an earthen receptacle until the sugar is dissolved, about 3 days. Stir them daily. The crock may be rubbed with:
    Garlic, or 3 or 4 finely sliced cloves garlic may be added to the pickle
Remove the garlic. Place the pickle in jars.

MIDWINTER GARLIC PICKLES
About 6 Pints
Place in a stone jar:
    6 sliced cloves garlic
    25 sour cucumber pickles cut into 1 inch slices
Pour over them:
    ⅓ cup olive oil
Bring to the boiling point and boil for 10 minutes:
    3 cups cider vinegar
    ¼ cup whole spices
    1 tablespoon black peppercorns
    ½ cup tarragon vinegar
    4 lbs. brown sugar
    6 tablespoons mustard seed
Pour these ingredients over the ingredients in the jar. Permit the pickle to ripen for 3 weeks before serving it.

MIDWINTER SWEET CUCUMBER PICKLES WITH RAISINS, GINGER AND SPICES

About 5 Quarts

Cut into ⅓ inch slices:

32 cucumber pickles in brine: about 8 lbs., or dill pickles

Boil:

2 cups water
1 quart cider vinegar
5 lbs. granulated sugar

Place in a small bag and add:

4 tablespoons mustard seed
4 tablespoons celery seed
1 tablespoon freshly grated nutmeg
1 tablespoon ground clove
1 tablespoon ground mace
2 or 3 small red peppers

Boil these ingredients until the sirup drops heavily from a spoon. Remove the bag. Add the pickles. Cut into small pieces and add:

½ lb. candied ginger
½ lb. candied orange peel

Add:

½ lb. raisins

Boil these ingredients until the sirup is thick. Place the pickles in sterilized covered jars.

MIDWINTER PICKLED ONIONS

Save the liquid from any kind of pickle.

Add:

Small or medium-sized dry onions cut in halves

Permit them to stand for 1 week before serving them.

UNCOOKED SPICED CABBAGE PICKLE

Shred:

1 gallon cabbage: 4 quarts

Place it in layers in a stone jar. Sprinkle each layer generously with:

Coarse salt

Permit it to stand for 12 hours. Wash off the salt. Drain the cabbage well. Place it in layers in sterilized jars. Combine and sprinkle each layer with some of the following mixture:

2 cups sugar
1 tablespoon cinnamon
1 tablespoon cloves
1 tablespoon allspice
3 tablespoons dry mustard
1 tablespoon white mustard seed
1 tablespoon grated horseradish

Cover the pickle with cold:

Cider vinegar

Seal the jars.

Relishes

PICCALILLI

Approximately 5 Quarts

Cut into very thin slices:

½ peck small green cucumbers

Seed and slice:

4 medium-sized green peppers

Skin and slice:

4 medium-sized onions

Place these ingredients in Brine, page 835, for 12 hours. Drain them well. Bring to the boiling point:

1 quart cider vinegar
4½ cups sugar

Place in a bag and add:

2½ tablespoons whole mixed spices
½ tablespoon celery seed
½ tablespoon mustard seed

Add the drained vegetables. Bring them to the boiling point. Remove the spices. Place the pickle in jars.

CHILI SAUCE

Method I. About 4½ Quarts

Scald, peel and slice:

½ bushel tomatoes: 16 quarts

Bring them to the boiling point. Add:

14 seeded, finely chopped large green peppers
12 peeled, finely chopped large white onions
1 cup sugar
¼ cup coarse salt
1 teaspoon ground cloves
2 cups cider vinegar
(¼ cup celery seed)

Boil the sauce until it is thick, about 3 hours. Stir it frequently. Taste it. Add if needed:

Salt

Bottle the sauce.

Method II. About 5 Quarts

Wash, peel and quarter:

3 dozen large tomatoes

Put through a food grinder:

12 seeded green peppers
3 small seeded hot red peppers
12 large skinned white onions

Add the tomatoes and:

2 lbs. brown sugar
1 quart cider vinegar

½ cup coarse salt
1 tablespoon black pepper
1 tablespoon allspice
1 teaspoon ground cloves

Cook these ingredients slowly until thick, about 3 hours. Stir them frequently to prevent burning. Add salt if needed. Place in jars.

TOMATO CATSUP

Wash and cut into pieces:

1 peck tomatoes: 8 quarts

Add:

8 medium-sized sliced onions
½ clove garlic
1½ bay leaves
2 long red peppers without seeds

Boil these ingredients until they are soft. Strain them. Add:

¾ cup closely packed brown sugar

Tie in a bag and add:

1 tablespoon whole allspice
1 tablespoon whole cloves
1 tablespoon whole mace
1 tablespoon celery seed
1 tablespoon black peppercorns
2 inches stick cinnamon

The spices may be varied. Boil these ingredients quickly, stirring frequently, until they are reduced to ½ the quantity. Remove the spice bag. Add:

2 cups cider vinegar
Cayenne and coarse salt if desired

Boil the catsup for 10 minutes longer. Bottle it at once. Seal the bottles with sealing wax.

CORN RELISH

Method I.

Cut the kernels from:

18 ears corn

Prepare:

4 cups shredded cabbage
1 stalk chopped celery
2 chopped green peppers, seeds and membranes removed
2 skinned chopped onions

Place these ingredients in a kettle with the corn. Pour over them and stir in:

1 quart cider vinegar

Combine:

1 quart cider vinegar
2 cups sugar
1 cup flour
½ cup coarse salt
½ tablespoon dry mustard
¼ tablespoon cayenne
½ tablespoon turmeric

Stir these ingredients until they are well blended. Pour them into the kettle. Bring the relish to the boiling point. Stir it gently. Simmer it for 40 minutes. Place it in covered jars.

Method II. About 10 Pints

Cut the kernels from:

18 ears corn

Put through a food grinder:

1 head green cabbage
8 white onions
6 green peppers, seeds and membranes removed
6 small hot red peppers or 2 tablespoons dried crushed pepper pods

The pepper pods may be bought in powdered form. Combine these ingredients with the corn and:

2 teaspoons celery seed
2 teaspoons mustard seed
2 quarts vinegar
¼ cup salt
2 cups sugar
(⅓ cup minced pimiento)

Boil the relish for 20 minutes. Place in jars.

VEGETABLE RELISH

3 Quarts

Peel and chop until very fine:

2 large carrots
4 white onions

Seed and chop until very fine:

4 large red sweet peppers
4 large green sweet peppers

Chop until very fine:

1 small head cabbage

Add to the vegetables and permit them to stand for 3 hours:

¼ cup coarse salt

Drain them well. Combine, stir well and add:

3 cups cider vinegar
2 cups sugar
1 tablespoon celery seed
1 tablespoon mustard seed
⅛ teaspoon red pepper

Pack the relish into sterilized jars. It should be well covered with vinegar. Seal the jars.

INDIAN RELISH

About 4 Quarts

Put through a food chopper or chop until they are very fine:

12 green tomatoes
12 tart peeled cored apples
3 peeled onions

Boil:

5 cups vinegar
5 cups sugar

1 teaspoon red pepper
3 teaspoons ginger
1 teaspoon turmeric
1 teaspoon salt

Add the chopped ingredients. Cook them for ½ hour. Pack the relish in sterilized jars. Seal them.

APPLE CHUTNEY
Method I. About 1½ Quarts
Chutney is a highly spiced condiment. The ingredients used vary greatly. The following is a good peppy chutney. Cook until the fruit is tender:

1 seeded chopped lemon
1 skinned chopped clove garlic
5 cups peeled chopped apples
2¼ cups brown sugar
½ lb. seeded raisins: 1½ cups
3 oz. chopped crystallized ginger: ¾ cup
1½ teaspoons salt
¼ teaspoon cayenne
2 cups cider vinegar

Place the chutney in jars and seal them.
Pears may be substituted for apples. In either case the fruit should be firm and slightly underripe.

Method II. About 1½ Quarts
Similar to the preceding rule but with onions and tomatoes added.
Combine, cook slowly for 3 hours, then seal in sterilized jars:

2 cups chopped seeded raisins
2 cups chopped green apples
1 cup minced onions
¼ cup coarse salt
6 medium-sized ripe, skinned, quartered tomatoes
1½ lbs. brown sugar
1 pint cider vinegar
4 oz. white mustard seed
2 oz. preserved ginger
⅛ teaspoon cayenne pepper

PEACH CHUTNEY
About 8 Quarts
Wash well:

12 lbs. firm peaches
½ lb. sweet green or red peppers

Remove the seeds and membranes from the peppers. Get out your grinder. Grind the peppers and:

⅛ lb. green ginger
2 skinned cloves garlic

Pare and slice the peaches and cut up:

3 lbs. seeded raisins

Make a sirup by boiling:

2 quarts cider vinegar
4 lbs. brown sugar
6 oz. mustard seed
1 tablespoon salt

Add the other ingredients. Cook them for 2 or 3 hours, or until they are thick and transparent. Add salt if needed. Place the chutney in sterilized jars. Seal the jars.

Pickled Rind and Fruit

WATERMELON PICKLE
Cut the green rind and the red meat from:

Watermelon rind

The rind may be cut into rounds with a biscuit cutter or into balls with a melon scoop or any desired shape. Weigh the rind. Cover it well with:

Salted water—¼ cup coarse salt to 1 quart water

Soak it for 12 hours. Drain it well. Boil it rapidly in boiling water to cover until it is tender but not soft, about 10 minutes. Drain it. Allow for every pound of rind:

1 cup water
1 cup cider vinegar
2 cups sugar
3 inches stick cinnamon
8 cloves without heads

Tie the spices in a bag. Place it in the kettle with the other ingredients. Boil them for 5 minutes. Add the drained rind. Boil it for 30 minutes, or until it is clear. Remove the spice bag. Place the rind in jars. Cover it with the boiling vinegar mixture. Seal the jars.
If you like the flavor of anise, place in each jar on top of the pickles a star anise, a wonderful addition.
If you are not using anise, gingerroot and finely sliced lemon and orange may be added at this time. Allow to every 6 pounds of rind:

1 orange and 1 seeded lemon
1 oz. gingerroot or 4 tablespoons chopped preserved ginger

GINGER WATERMELON PICKLE
About 5 Pints
Remove the green peel and all red meat from:

Watermelon rind

There should be 5 pounds of peeled

rind. Cut it into strips or balls. Soak it for 12 hours in cold water. Keep the water cold if possible. Drain the rind. Boil the rind rapidly in boiling water to cover until it is tender but not soft, about 10 minutes. Drain it. Reserve the water. Combine and boil to the consistency of heavy sirup, about ½ hour:

    10 cups of the watermelon water
    10 cups sugar

Add for the last 10 minutes:

    ¼ lb. gingerroot or 6 tablespoons crystallized or chopped preserved ginger
    5 thinly sliced seeded lemons
    1 teaspoon salt

Add the rind. Bring the sirup again to the boiling point. Place the rind in sterilized jars (page 844). Cover the jars. Permit the sirup to boil until it is heavy. Cover the rind with boiling sirup. Seal the jars at once.

PICKLED PEACHES
About 4 Quarts
Pour boiling water over:

    1 peck clingstone peaches: 16 lbs.

Drain them. Peel them. Place in each peach:

    5 cloves minus heads

Stir until the sugar is dissolved, then bring to the boiling point and boil for 10 minutes:

    1 quart mild cider vinegar: 4 cups
    7 cups sugar

Tie in a bag and add:

    6 two inch sticks cinnamon

Add enough peaches to fill a jar. Boil them until they are thoroughly hot. Remove them from the liquid. Place them in a sterilized jar (page 844). Cover them to keep them hot. When all the peaches are cooked boil the sirup for about 10 minutes. This is optional. Pour it boiling hot over the peaches. Discard the spice bag. Seal the jars at once.

BRANDIED PEACHES
Select ripe, firm:

    Peaches

Weigh them. Rub the fuzz from the peaches with a coarse towel.
Make a thick sirup of equal parts of:

    Sugar and water—allow 1 cup sugar and 1 cup water for every lb. of fruit

Boil the peaches in the sirup for 5 minutes. Place them in sterilized jars (page 844). If the sirup is thin, add more sugar and boil it until it is heavy. Pour the sirup over the fruit, filling the jars ¾ full. Add to fill the jars:

    Brandy

SPICED PEARS I OR WINTER PEARS
Boil:

    6 cups cider vinegar
    8 cups brown sugar
    2 teaspoons cloves minus heads
    A 3 inch stick cinnamon

Cut into slices, core and add:

    8 lbs. winter pears: Kiefer

Boil them until they are tender. Drain them. Place them in jars. Cover them with the sirup. Seal the jars at once. The excess sirup may be saved and used a second time or used for basting a ham.

SPICED PEARS II OR SECKEL PEARS
Leave the stems on:

    Seckel pears

Pare the pears. Follow the above rule for Spiced Pears I.

PICKLED CRAB APPLES
Leave the stems on:

    Crab apples

Cut out the blossom ends. Follow the above rule for Spiced Pears I.

Canning

It is a thrill to possess shelves well stocked with home-canned food. In fact, you will find their inspection, often surreptitious, and the pleasure of serving the fruits of your labors comparable only to a clear conscience or a very becoming hat.

Chapters on this subject usually begin with a dry-as-dust definition of the word "canning." Let us assume that you know the meaning of the word although you may be unfamiliar with the process.

The information in this chapter is based on practical experience and recent government and state bulletins. These bulletins are published periodically and are available gratis or for a small charge.

In the scientific and praiseworthy bulletins issued by these authorities and in the blurbs of manufacturers of canning equipment, several points are stressed. One is that definite techniques must be followed to make canned products nutritious and safe.

For the maximum nutritional value only the freshest and best food should be used for canning. The ideal rule is: "Two hours from garden to can."

But freshness and safety are not synonymous.

Safe canning means first that foods be made free of bacteria which might cause ferments. If such bacteria are not destroyed, the result of their work is obvious, for the molds, color changes, acids and gases they cause are easily seen, tasted or smelled, and such products should, of course, be discarded at once.

But there is another insidious bacterium known as Cl. Botulinum which may sometimes be present, usually in non-acid canned foods. More details for handling these low-acid foods like meats and some vegetables are given below. The Botulinum bacterium may or may not give an indication of its presence. If the spores have been active, the food may be soft in consistency and some gas may be present. But the toxin that this bacterium produces may be present without showing any evidence. Botulinus spores may remain resistant to 212° temperatures after several hours of processing and subsequently they can produce a deadly toxin in the canned product. This toxin is destroyed by cooking the canned food in boiling liquid uncovered for 10 minutes in a pan over direct heat before serving it.

Good organization and the right equipment simplify canning and give you, with a minimum of effort, gay-looking shelves of glistening, jewellike jars filled with canned fruits and vegetables, all labeled, dated and ready for use.

A careful reading of the canning steps described below and a bit of forethought as to the best management of your task will both speed and ease it.

Heat, seasonal heat and heat from the range, inevitably accompanies canning. Hot fluids in hot jars and heavy pots have to be handled carefully. Have a funnel, plenty of pot holders and a strong tongs or jar lifter at hand.

Steps in the Canning of Food by Pressure
or in a Boiling Water Bath

Follow these general steps in the canning of foods, whether processed in a pressure canner, cooker, or in a boiling water bath. Work quickly on those steps which involve the exposure of the food to air. Prepare for a smooth-running canning operation by first getting together and checking over all necessary utensils and materials.

1. To Test Rubbers, Jars and Lids

If you are using lids that call for separate rubbers, test the rubbers even though they may be newly purchased. Unused left-over rubbers may deteriorate from one canning season to another. To test the rubbers bend them into small pleats. If the rubbers crack, discard them. Or stretch the rubbers to see if they will return to their original shape. If not, they are worthless. Wash the rubbers and lids.

If you are using a pressure canner, see illustration page 845, make sure that the jars are the type which can stand 240° or more of heat. In any case, check all jars to make sure they are not chipped, cracked or blemished. Wash them well in soap and hot water.

Next before filling or processing, check the closures between the jars and lids. If using screw types, first place them on sound jars without a rubber. Screw them tight. They are usable if it is impossible to insert a thin penknife blade or a thumbnail between the jar and the lid. Unscrew them. Put the rubbers in place and fill the jars with water. Screw down the lids. Invert the jars. If there is no seepage, the jars and lids may be used. This test may also be used for the clamp or wire-bail type closure.

Jars and lids used for processing need not be sterilized but merely well washed. If they are to be used for open kettle canning, they must be sterilized. To do this submerge them in water to cover and boil them for 15 minutes. Leave them in the water and remove them one at a time when ready to use them. Do not boil vacuum-type lids as they contain a sealing composition. Scald these and let them stand in hot water until ready to use them.

2. The Preparation of the Food

Clean and pare or cut up food just as you would if planning to cook it for immediate use. Remember that vitamins escape quickly, so prepare only small batches of food at a time—about 1 quart. The size of pieces may depend upon convenience of packing in jars. Make any sirups that may be needed for fruit, allowing about 1 cupful of sirup for each quart of fruit, see page 848.

3. Precooking or Blanching and Steaming of the Food

Blanching or precooking foods shrinks them and drives out the air. This preliminary step allows the packing of more produce in each jar than would otherwise be possible. Large fruits and all vegetables should be put in a wire basket and immersed, about 1 quart at a time, in boiling liquid and boiled 5 minutes—counting from the time the water begins to boil again—then dipped up and down quickly in cold water 2 or 3 times to keep shape better and make handling easier.

To steam food use a perforated utensil like a strainer without a handle, or place the food in a cheesecloth bag. Steam only a small quantity at a time. Do not crowd the food as the steam must penetrate all of it. Use a kettle with a tightly fitting lid. Have the kettle filled with several inches of boiling water. Suspend the filled strainer or bag over it. Close the lid tightly. Steam the food the length of time given in the individual recipes for fruit or vegetables. See pages 848 and 852.

Berries, soft fruits and tomatoes may be canned without precooking. The liquid in which the foods were precooked or steamed should be used to fill the jars, thus saving valuable minerals.

Meat may be partially cooked about two thirds done by simmering or roasting. For more details about meat, see page 856.

4. The Packing of the Food

Pack prepared food in the clean hot jars. They need not be sterilized by boiling. Pack the jars firmly but not so tightly that the material is crushed. Pack fruits and vegetables to within ½ inch of top of jars, excepting Lima beans, dried beans, peas and corn, which swell considerably more than other vegetables. These and meats should be packed to within 1 inch of top of jars. Then fill the jars with boiling water to within ½ inch of the top. Add 1 teaspoonful salt to each quart and ½ teaspoonful of salt to each pint. Fill jars of fruit with sugar sirup to within ½ inch of top. For Sugar Sirup Formulas, see page 848.

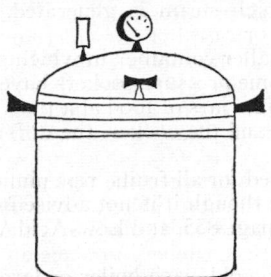

Before preparing to put on the lids make sure that air which may be trapped beneath the liquid is expelled. Run a long thin spatula down between the inside of the jar and the produce, changing the position of the jar contents enough to release the trapped air. Then wipe the top of the jar carefully.

5. Adjustment of Lids

When jars are packed, if the lid you are using requires a separate rubber, adjust the rubbers and the lids. Have the rubbers wet. It is always wisest to follow the manufacturer's directions. Lids are of two main types, those which need separate rubbers and adjustment both before and after processing, and those which have an attached rubber and are adjusted once before processing and close automatically when cooling. The latter type is shown first on the left below.

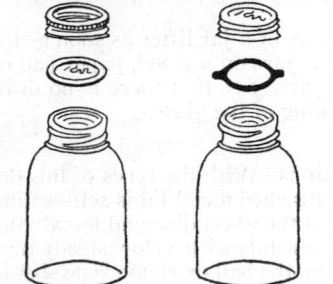

The type above, the zinc porcelain-lined screw top and the two-piece glass disc and metal ring top all fit on the regular grooved-top canning jar. You may use them on a jar of pint, quart or half-gallon size. The zinc and glass disc tops, shown second and third above, are placed on the rubber ring and then screwed as tight as possible clockwise and then turned counterclockwise ¼ inch.

The jar with the all-glass lid shown next has a wire bail or clamp closure. It is processed with the longer wire resting in the groove of the lid. The shorter wire is not snapped down in its final position until after processing. The slight openings provided by all these adjustments allow excess air to be forced out of the jars and keep the jars from possible explosion during processing.

6. Processing in a Pressure Canner or Cooker or in a Boiling Water Bath

Pressure cooker canning is the only method recommended for meats and non-acid vegetables. It is an easier, quicker and safer method than the boiling water bath and takes less fuel. A pressure canner is a good investment for those who plan a lot of canning. It is also a convenience in other forms of cookery. Detailed directions for the use of a pressure canner are furnished by the manufacturers and should be followed carefully.

As the words pressure canner and pressure cooker are used frequently in this chapter they should be defined in order to avoid confusion.

A pressure canner is a large container in which steam is generated, used principally for processing, i.e., canning food in jars or cans.

A pressure cooker was until recently a much smaller container in which steam is generated to cook meat, vegetables, soups, etc. Some pressure cookers have now been enlarged so that they may be used to process a few jars of food at a time. The principle is generally the same for both the canner and the cooker, the difference between the two being largely a matter of size.

Processing in a boiling water bath is recommended for all fruits, ripe pimientos and rhubarb. This method is reasonably dependable though it is not advised without reservations. See Canning of Low-Acid Meats, page 855, and Low-Acid Vegetables, page 852.

A regular hot-water canner may be bought, or the old wash boiler or lard can, clean, of course, may be used if it has a tight-fitting cover. Other utensils needed are a rack to fit in the bottom of the boiler so the jars will not crack from direct contact with heat; a wire one may be bought for this purpose, or a slatted wooden one may be made at home. Have ready a holder for lifting jars out of boiling water. Fill the boiler with water to about the height of the jars. When the water is boiling lower the jars into the boiler. The jars must not touch one another or the sides of the container. Leave a 2 inch space between them. The jars should rest on the wire rack. Add more boiling water to cover the jars at least 1 inch above the tops. Continue to add boiling water as the water in the boiler evaporates. Make a note of the time when the processing will be completed. Process the required length of time for the particular food chosen (pages 847 and 856), counting from the time the water begins to boil after the jars have been added.

7. To Remove the Jars from the Hot Water

Remove the jars from the boiling water with tongs or a jar lifter as soon as the time is up. Do not lift the jars by the lids. Place the jars on a wood, paper pad or cloth surface, allowing several inches between the jars. See that there is no draft on the hot jars, as a sudden cooling may cause cracking of the glass.

8. To Seal the Jars

Seal all jars according to manufacturers' directions. With the types of lids described in Step 5, proceed as follows: The rubber-attached metal lid is self-sealing and should not be touched. The zinc screw type and the glass disc and metal ring lid should be turned clockwise as far as possible. Screw lids with a slow steady turn so as not to displace the rubbers. The shorter wire on the bail or clamp type should be snapped down into place. Whatever type you have used, be sure to leave the jars upright and undisturbed for 12 hours. If you have used the lid types shown first and third from the left under Step 5, remove the metal ring.

9. To Test the Seal

Test-seal the metal tops by tapping the lids lightly with a metal spoon or knife. A ringing note indicates a safe seal. If the contents touch the inner side of the lid the sound may be dull but not hollow. If the note is both dull and hollow reprocessing with a new lid is in order. Or, if you prefer, use the food right away.

10. To Label and Store Jars

Label the jars and store them in a cool dark place. Storage temperatures between 45° and 60° make foods retain good color and also inhibit Cl. Botulinus which is still capable of development after many months, especially in higher temperatures.

The Handling of Cans

Use only unbent perfect cans of the rim steel or sanitary type. Bright gold R-enamel type is recommended for squash, pumpkin, red fruit and vegetables; the dull gold C-enamel type for corn and succotash. Lids are of two types with a paper or composition gasket. They must be crimped on with a special sealer. Keep the lids in the paper packing until ready to use. Just before use, wash the cans in clean water. Reverse them to drain. Merely wipe the lids with a damp cloth. Do not wash the paper ones as this may injure the gasket. Adjust the sealer for the can size you are using. Before filling the cans be sure that the food is heated to at least 170°. Fill the cans to within ¼ inch of the top, except for Lima beans, peas or corn which are filled to within ½ inch. Seal the can at once. Then to test the can for a perfect seal submerge the sealed, processed and cooled can in a pot of boiling water. If air bubbles rise the seam is not tight. This test is not absolutely infallible because sometimes a particle of food may have plugged the seam temporarily.

Time Chart for Canning by Pressure or in a Boiling Water Bath

	Pressure Cooker	Boiling Water Bath
Fruit		15 to 30 minutes
Fruit Juices		30 minutes
Vegetables	40 to 70 minutes at 10 lbs.	1½ to 3½ hours
Meats and Poultry	65 to 75 minutes at 10 lbs.	3 hours

The above Time Chart is based upon a 1 quart pack at altitudes up to 1,000 feet for processing in a boiling water bath. Increase the time 10% for each additional 500 feet. For processing in a pressure canner or cooker, add 1 pound of pressure for each additional 2,000 feet of elevation after the first 2,000 feet.

For the Open Kettle Method see page 850. This method is confined generally to the making of jellies, preserves, pickles and relishes or highly acid fruits.

The Canning of Fruit

Approximate Yield of Fruits

Fruit	Weight	Units	Yield	Yield Per Bushel
Apples	2½ lbs.	7 to 8	1 quart	28 quarts
Berries	1¼ to 1½ lbs.	5 cups	1 quart	24 quarts
Cherries	1¼ to 1½ lbs.	6 cups	1 quart	20 quarts
Peaches	2 to 2½ lbs.	8 to 10	1 quart	20-22 quarts
Pears	2 to 2½ lbs.	5 to 6	1 quart	30 quarts
Plums	1½ to 2½ lbs.	24 to 32	1 quart	28 quarts
Tomatoes	2½ to 3½ lbs.	8 to 10	1 quart	18 quarts

Choose fresh, firm, perfect fruit that is not overripe. Imperfect fruit may be used but it must be carefully gone over and all blemishes removed.

Wash the fruit. Prepare as for table use. If it is to be pared it may be dipped in boiling water until the skins loosen and then dipped for a moment in cold water. It is best to do this with a small quantity—about a quart of fruit at a time.

Discoloration Solution

To prevent the darkening of certain fruits like peaches, apples, apricots, etc., during preparation, drop them as soon as the skins are removed into a solution of 2 tablespoonfuls vinegar and 2 tablespoonfuls salt for 1 gallon water, or use the solution suggested on page 863. Drain the solution off before canning the fruit.

Sirup for Canning

Sirup for canned fruit varies in consistency, depending upon the fruit or the use to which it will be put. Although claims are made for a fresher taste in pie cherries and some other sour fruits canned without sugar, there is an actual saving when sugar is added to cooked fruit. See page 442. The following recipes will help you decide which proportions of sugar to water to use.

Thin Sirup

One cupful sugar to 3 cupfuls water. Stir well before heating and bring slowly to a boil. Use for naturally sweet fruits and to approximate the quality of fresh fruits.

Medium Sirup

One cupful sugar to 2 cupfuls water. Prepare as for thin sirup. Good for canning fruits that are not highly acid.

Heavy Sirup

One cupful sugar to 1 cupful water. Stir and boil very carefully to prevent crystallization and scorching. For very sour fruits like rhubarb; also suitable for dessert use. If too heavy a sirup is used the fruit may rise to the top of the jar during processing.

Directions for Canning Fruit

The following directions are for 1 quart jars processed in a boiling water bath. Reduce the processing time 10% if pint jars or No. 2 or No. 3 tin cans are used. See page 846. Increase the processing time by 5 minutes if half-gallon jars are used.

Apples

Select firm, sound tart varieties. Wash, pare and core; cut into quarters or halves. Drop into discoloration solution (see 847). Drain. Boil 1 minute in thin or medium sirup. Pack in jars, cover with boiling sirup and process 20 minutes in boiling water bath. Apples may be baked, packed, covered with boiling sirup and processed 15 minutes in a boiling water bath.

Applesauce

Prepare applesauce, pack boiling hot. Process at once for 10 minutes in a boiling water bath.

Apricots

Select ripe, firm fruit. Blanch to remove skins. Pack whole or halves into jars and cover with boiling medium sirup, process 25 minutes in a boiling water bath.

Berries

Pick over, wash if gritty, stem, pack closely in jars, fill with boiling medium sirup and process 20 minutes in a boiling water bath.

For strawberries this more complicated procedure will yield plump, bright-colored canned berries. Wash if gritty, then hull. Add 1 cupful sugar to each quart prepared berries, placing in alternate layers in shallow pans and let stand 2 hours. Simmer them for 5 minutes in their own juice. Fill jars full, add boiling thin sirup if additional liquid is needed. Process at once 15 minutes in a boiling water bath.

Cherries

Wash, stem. Can whole or pitted. To seed use the rounded end of a hairpin or use a cherry pitter. If not seeded, prick with a pin. Use heavy sirup for sour cherries; medium sirup for sweet cherries. Pack, cover with boiling sirup and process at once 20 minutes in a boiling water bath.

Cranberries

Wash and stem. Boil 3 minutes in heavy sirup. Pack hot, cover with boiling sirup. Process 3 minutes in a boiling water bath.

Currants

Same as for berries.

Grapes

Use only sound, firm grapes. Wash and stem. Bring to a boil in medium sirup. Cover with boiling sirup. Process 20 minutes in a boiling water bath.

Peaches

Use firm, ripe fruit. Scald to remove skins. Halve peaches. Drop into discoloration solution (page 847). Pack in jars, cover with boiling medium sirup and process at once for 20 minutes in a boiling water bath.

Pears

Pare, core, halve, quarter or slice. Drop into discoloration solution (page 847). Drain. Boil gently about 5 minutes in medium sirup. Pack into jars, cover with boiling sirup, process for 20 minutes in a boiling water bath. Hard pears are best if cooked in water only until nearly tender. Then the sugar is added in sirup proportions and the whole is brought to a boil. Pack into jars and proceed as above. See page 845.

Pineapple

Slice, pare, core, remove eyes. Shred or cut in cubes. Pack, cover with boiling thin or medium sirup, depending upon sweetness of fruit. Process at once for 35 minutes in a boiling water bath.

Plums

Use moderately ripe fruit. Wash and prick skins. Pack firmly but don't crush into jars. Cover with boiling sirup, thin for sweet plums, and medium for tart varieties. Process at once for 20 minutes in a boiling water bath.

Quinces

Use well-ripened fruit. Pare, cut into convenient-sized pieces and boil gently in a medium or heavy sirup about 1½ minutes. Or for easier handling wipe the fuzz from the quince, cut out the stem and blossom ends and cook the quinces gently in several inches of water, covered, for 20 minutes. Drain the water for use in the canning sirup. Pare or simply cut the fruit from the core unpared. Pack into jars, cover with boiling sirup and process at once for 60 minutes in a boiling water bath.

Rhubarb

Wash stalks and cut into ½ inch pieces. Pack, cover with boiling heavy sirup, process at once for 20 minutes in hot water bath.

Tomatoes

Use firm fresh tomatoes, scald 1 minute and then dip 1 minute in cold water to remove skins. Cut out cores. Leave whole, halve or quarter. Pack closely in jars, fill with boiling water or tomato juice, add 1 teaspoonful salt per quart jar. Process at once for 30 minutes in a boiling water bath. If tomatoes are not of high quality, process 45 minutes.

Directions for Canning Fruit Purées and Juices by Pressure or in a Boiling Water Bath

Purées

Use ripe, soft fruit. Simmer it until it can be forced through a strainer or fine sieve or, if there are no objectionable seeds, put it in a blender (page 895). Add sugar to taste. Reheat the purée, fill the jars, seal and process them for 20 minutes in a boiling water bath.

Fruit Juices

Select sound, ripe fruit, crush and heat slowly to simmering point. Strain through several layers of cheesecloth. Heat again to simmering. Pour into clean hot jars, process below boiling, 180°-185°, for 5 minutes or in a regular boiling water bath for 30 minutes.

Juices from uncooked fruit may be pressed out in a cider press and heated to lukewarm before being poured into jars, and processed as above. Peach, cherry and apple juice, canned this way, are less likely to taste flat. Use this method for apple cider.

The addition of sugar to tart fruit juices before canning is more satisfactory than sweetening after canning. One cupful sugar to 1 gallon juice is a moderate proportion.

Grape Juice

Wash sound, ripe grapes. Cover with boiling water and heat slowly to simmering. Do not boil. Cook slowly until fruit is very soft, then strain through a bag and add ½ cupful sugar to each quart juice. Process for 5 minutes in a boiling water bath. For Open Kettle Grape Juice see page 851.

Pineapple Juice

Discarded eyes, cores and skins of fresh fruit can be used in making pineapple juice. Cover with cold water. Cook slowly in covered kettle from 30 to 40 minutes. Strain through a jelly bag. Measure juice, heat and add one sixth as much sugar as juice. Boil rapidly 10 minutes and process for 5 minutes in boiling water bath. Juice may also be extracted from pineapple by putting the pared fruit through fine blade of food chopper with large bowl beneath to catch it. See Fruit Juices above.

Rhubarb Juice

Cut rhubarb in small pieces, add just enough water to cover and simmer until very soft. Strain through a jelly bag. Add 2 cupfuls sugar to each quart juice. Heat until sugar is dissolved, bring to boiling point and process for 5 minutes in a boiling water bath.

Tomato Juice

Use soft but perfect tomatoes. Wash tomatoes, remove stem ends and cores. Chop or cut into small pieces. Small quantities of onion, parsley and celery are often added at this time so that the juice is full-flavored for cocktails and clear tomato soup without any additions later. Heat these ingredients in a covered kettle until the juice flows freely. Put through a fine sieve. Pack hot into jars to within ½ inch from top and add 1 teaspoonful salt to each quart. Process in a boiling water bath for 30 minutes.

Fruits Canned by the Open Kettle Method

This old-fashioned way of canning fruit is not generally recommended because there is more danger of spoilage if utensils, jars and spoons are not thoroughly sterile. It is, however, a convenient method and the housewife frequently resorts to it.

If you use this method be sure to sterilize all jars and lids by boiling them for 20 minutes in clean water. If you are reusing old porcelain-lined zinc caps boil them for 30 minutes. Leave the jars and lids in the water until you are ready to use them.

Prepare fruit as for immediate use. Be careful to use enamel, stainless steel or shiny aluminum pans for the cooking, never iron or tin. Prepare Sirup for Canning Fruit, page 848.

Fruits

Add a small quantity of fruit to the boiling sirup, about enough for one jar. Boil the fruit until it is tender.

Cook hard fruits like pineapple, some apples, quince, etc., in boiling water until nearly tender. Drain them well. Finish cooking them in sirup. Use the water in which the fruit was cooked for the sirup.

Boil small fruits slowly. Test the fruit with a straw or cake tester. If not seeded, prick cherries several times with a large pin. Boil them for 5 minutes. Have ready a hot sterilized jar with a sterilized rubber in place. Work quickly. Fill the jar with fruit. Fill it to overflowing with boiling sirup. You will retrieve sirup if you place the jar in a small pan. Run the handle of a sterilized spoon around the fruit to make the air bubbles rise (page 845). Wipe the top of the jar free from seeds, pulp and sirup. Seal the jar at once tightly with a hot sterilized lid.

Set the jars well apart on several thicknesses of cloth. Cool them as rapidly as possible. Avoid drafts that might crack the jars. Seal screw lids completely. Do not touch self-sealing lids again. Try to tighten other screw lids further as the jars cool. To test for perfect seal, see page 846.

In cooking berries, *except strawberries,* wash them by putting them in a colander and dipping it up and down in water. Wash 1 quart at a time. Pick them over. Add 1½ cupfuls sugar to 1 quart berries. Permit them to stand for about 2 hours. Cook them with as little stirring as possible for 20 minutes. Pack boiling hot into sterilized jars. Use sterilized rubbers and lids. Complete seal at once.

Tomatoes are officially a fruit. They are one of the safest of fruits to can by the open kettle method, provided that all equipment used is sterile (page 850). Also because of their acid content they retain their vitamins well during processing. Wash firm tomatoes. Dip them in boiling water, 4 to 6 at a time. As soon as the skins are loose, after 1 or 2 minutes, remove the tomatoes. Put them briefly in cold water. Core, stem and slip the peel from the tomatoes. They may be cut into pieces. Place them in an open kettle. Season them with salt—about 1 teaspoonful salt to 4 cupfuls tomatoes.

Bring them very slowly to the boiling point. Stir them frequently to keep them from sticking to the bottom. Cook them for ½ hour. Fill hot sterilized jars on which sterile rubbers have already been placed. Wipe rubbers free of seeds and juice. Seal the jars at once with sterilized lids.

Tomato Purée

Follow the above rule. Boil the tomatoes until they form a thick paste. Put them through a strainer. Reheat the purée, season it and place it in jars as directed above.

Fruit Juice Canned by the Open Kettle Method

Tomato Juice

Wash and cut into small pieces ripe tomatoes. Simmer them, about 4 cupfuls at a time, long enough to have the juice flow freely. Put them through a fine sieve. Allow 1 teaspoonful salt to 1 quart of tomato juice. You may also add bay leaf, herbs, etc. As spices discolor the juice it is better to add them before serving rather than at this time. Bring the strained juice to the boiling point. Fill sterilized jars, on which sterilized rubbers have already been placed, to overflowing. Seal them at once.

Grape Juice

Wash Concord grapes. Pick them from the stems. Cover the grapes with cold water. Boil them until they are broken and the seeds are separated. Strain them through a colander. Strain the juice twice through a jelly bag (page 799). Measure the juice. Allow 1 cupful sugar to 4 cupfuls juice. Boil the juice and the sugar for 20 minutes. Bottle the juice. Cool it. Cork it and seal it with paraffin.

Uncooked Grape Juice

A highly unorthodox but successful method.

Wash grapes. Remove them from the stems. There should be 2 cupfuls. Place them in a 1 quart sterile fruit jar. Add to them 1 cupful sugar. Cover them with boiling water. Seal the jar with a sterilized lid. Shake the jar well to dissolve the sugar. Permit the juice to stand until the liquid looks like commercial grape juice, for about 6 weeks. When ready to use it, strain the contents of the jar.

Vegetable Canning and Brining

Approximate Yield of Vegetables

Vegetable	Weight	Yield
Asparagus	3 lbs.	1 quart
Beans, Lima	2 lbs.	1 quart
Beans, snap	1¾ lbs.	1 quart
Beets, baby	2½ to 3 lbs.	1 quart
Carrots	2½ to 3 lbs.	1 quart
Corn on the cob	6 to 8 small ears	1 quart
Greens, spinach, etc.	2¾ to 3 lbs.	1 quart
Peas, green, shelled	4 lbs.	1 quart
Tomatoes	3 lbs.	1 quart

Preparation of Vegetables for Canning

Vegetables must be very carefully and quickly washed, through several waters if necessary, or under running water, to remove all soil.

Prepare only one canner load at a time. Work quickly to preserve the vitamins.

Jars of prepared, boiling hot, precooked vegetables are filled with boiling water, preferably that in which they were precooked, and seasoned with 1 teaspoonful of salt to each quart jar, ½ teaspoonful to each pint. Fill the jars to within ½ inch of the top with boiling water, or with the boiling water in which they were precooked.

Corn, peas and shell beans are apt to swell, so allow about 1 inch head space between the liquid and the top of the jar.

The U. S. Department of Agriculture (Bulletin AW 1-93) does not recommend the home canning of the following vegetables:

Cabbage (except sauerkraut)   Baked beans   Parsnips
Cauliflower   Eggplant   Turnips
Celery   Lettuce   Vegetable mixtures
Cucumbers   Onions

Great care must be exercised in the canning of non-acid foods to prevent the development of Cl. Botulinus, a deadly germ which may be present even though no odor or color changes indicate the danger of its presence (page 843).

The government warns that all non-acid home-canned vegetables should be boiled in an open pan for 10 minutes before tasting or serving.

Directions for Canning Vegetables

These directions are for 1 quart glass jars, unless otherwise specified, processed in a steam pressure canner at 10 pounds pressure or in a boiling water bath.

Asparagus

Wash, remove loose scales and tough ends. Grade for uniformity. Place in wire basket or square of thin cloth. Hold in boiling water which reaches just below tips for 3 minutes. Or cut in 1 inch lengths and boil 2 to 3 minutes. Pack, fill with boiling water, add 1 teaspoonful salt and process 40 minutes at 10 pounds in pressure canner or 2¼ hours in boiling water bath.

Beans, Green, Snap or Wax

Wash, remove strings and tips. Break into small pieces. Precook 5 minutes.

Reserve water. Pack, fill jars with boiling reserved water, add 1 teaspoonful salt. Process 40 minutes at 10 pounds in pressure canner or 2¼ hours in boiling water bath.

Beans, Green Lima

Sort and grade for size and age. Boil young beans 5 minutes, older beans 10 minutes. Pack loosely allowing 1 inch head space. Cover with boiling water. Add 1 teaspoonful salt. Process 55 minutes at 10 pounds in pressure canner.

Beans, Dried Navy, Soy, Kidney or Pinto

Look over carefully, wash, soak overnight in a cool place. Simmer 5 to 10 minutes. Pack hot, filling containers 7/9 full. Cover with boiling water, add 1 teaspoonful salt and 1 tablespoonful sugar or molasses to each quart. Process at once. Small pieces of salt pork may be added and tomato juice used instead of water. Process 90 minutes at 10 pounds in pressure canner or 4 hours in boiling water bath.

Beets

Boil small whole beets with 1 inch top stem and all the root 15 minutes. Trim off roots. Slip off skins, pack in jars, add boiling water and salt. Process 45 minutes at 10 pounds in pressure canner or 2½ hours in boiling water bath.

Carrots

Sort and grade for uniformity. Wash and scrape. Boil 5 minutes. Reserve water. Slice or pack whole, fill jars with boiling reserved water, add salt. Process 45 minutes at 10 pounds in pressure canner or 2½ hours in boiling water bath.

Corn, Whole-Kernel

Use tender, freshly gathered corn. Cut corn from cob. Do not scrape cobs. To each quart of corn add 1 pint boiling water and 1 teaspoonful salt. Heat to boiling. Pack at once. Add no more salt or water. Process for 75 minutes at 10 pounds in pressure.canner or 3¼ hours in boiling water bath.

Corn, Cream-Style

Pack in pints only. Cut off the tops of kernels, scrape cobs with back of knife or corn scraper (page 184) to remove all pulp. Add half as much boiling water as corn, by weight, and 1 teaspoonful salt per quart. Heat to boiling. Pack at once. Process pints for 75 minutes in pressure canner at 15 pounds.

Greens

Use fresh, tender greens. Wash thoroughly, discard any decayed leaves and tough stems. Steam about 8 minutes, or until wilted. Pack quickly and loosely. Fill jars with boiling water, add ½ teaspoonful salt per quart. Process in pressure canner for 1¾ hours at 10 pounds or 3½ hours in boiling water bath.

Hominy

Pack loosely, boiling hot. Leave 1½ inches head space. Cover with boiling liquid. Process at once, 60 minutes in pressure canner at 10 pounds or 3 hours in boiling water bath.

Mushrooms

Wash well. Peel if wilted or old. Drop into hot water with 1 tablespoonful vinegar and 1 teaspoonful salt per quart. Cover and precook 3 to 4 minutes. Drain, pack hot, covering with freshly boiled water. Add 1 teaspoonful salt to each quart. Process 40 minutes at 10 pounds in pressure canner or 2¼ hours in boiling water bath.

Nut Meats

Heat nut meats in a shallow pan in a slow oven until well heated. Pack in hot *dry* jars. They may be processed in a steamer or a water bath which contains only 2 to 3 inches of boiling water for 20 minutes. If processed in pressure canner, run the pressure up to 5 pounds and release at once.

Okra

Use tender pods only. Wash and remove caps without cutting into pod. Cover with boiling water, bring to a boil. Pack hot, cover with boiling liquid. Process 40 minutes in steam pressure canner at 10 pounds or 2¼ hours in boiling water bath.

Peas

Pack in pint jars only or No. 2 cans because they overcook and become mushy if packed in quart jars. Shell, sort for size. Cover with boiling water, boil 5 minutes. Pack loosely into jars. Cover with boiling cooking liquid to within 1 inch of top of jars. Add ½ teaspoonful salt per pint jar. Process 45 minutes in pressure canner at 10 pounds or 2½ hours in boiling water bath.

Pumpkin and Squash

Peel and cut into 1 inch cubes. Add enough water to prevent sticking. Cook or steam until tender. Mash and pack hot in jars. Add salt but no water. Process 90 minutes at 10 pounds in pressure canner or 4 hours in boiling water bath.

Sweet Potatoes

Wash well. Boil about 15 minutes, or until skins will slip off easily. Skin, cut into pieces. Pack hot, cover with fresh boiling water. Add 1 teaspoonful salt for each quart jar. Process 110 minutes in pressure canner at 10 pounds or 4 hours in boiling water bath.

Tomatoes

See directions under Fruits, page 851.

Preparation and Cooking of Brined Vegetables

Salted and brined vegetables have less food value than fresh, frozen or canned vegetables. They do provide a variety of taste for winter meals.

Use only sound, tender, freshly gathered vegetables. Soft water and dairy salt make the best brine. But the most important factor about the salt is to use the right amount for each vegetable as indicated in each recipe. Too little salt may prevent the product from keeping, too much will shrivel and toughen the vegetables. When used in great excess salt will inhibit fermentation. The salt must extract enough juice to cover the vegetables with brine during the first 24 hours and the brine must continue to cover the vegetables all during the fermentation period.

Pack and cover the vegetables as indicated in each recipe. A 10 pound weight will usually be needed for a 5 gallon crock. A jug filled with water makes a conveniently adjustable weight. Fermentation time will vary but is complete if no bubbles rise to the surface when the side of the crock is pounded with the hand.

The same precaution is necessary before serving brined vegetables as for canned products. Boil all non-acid vegetables 10 minutes before tasting them. See page 852.

Salted Sauerkraut I

A 2 gallon crock holds about 15 pounds of kraut.

Choose sound, mature heads of cabbage. Use 1 pound salt for 40 pounds cabbage, 2 teaspoonfuls salt for 1 pound. Remove outside leaves, quarter heads, cut out cores. Cut cabbage fine into 1/16 inch shreds and mix with salt. Pack firmly in stone crocks to within 2 inches of top. Cover with clean cloth and a board, not pine, or a plate. Place a weight on the plate heavy enough to make the brine come up to the cover and wet the cloth. When fermentation begins remove the scum daily. Place with a clean cloth over the cabbage and wash the board.

The best quality kraut is made at a temperature below 60°, requiring at least a month of fermentation. It may be cured in less time at higher temperatures, but the kraut will not be so good. When fermentation has ceased, store the kraut in a cool place after sealing by either of the following methods:

Pour a layer of hot paraffin over the surface of the crock. Or heat kraut to simmering temperature, about 180°. Pack firmly in hot jars, add sufficient kraut juice or a weak brine, 2 tablespoonfuls salt for 1 quart water, to cover kraut. Leave ½ inch head space. Process in boiling water bath 25 minutes for pints, 30 minutes for quarts. Cook the sauerkraut 10 minutes before serving (page 843).

Salted Sauerkraut II

For small quantities.

Pack shredded cabbage tightly into quart jars to within 1 inch of the top. Add 1 scant tablespoonful of salt to each quart. If packed closely the kraut will draw enough juice to nearly fill the jar. The sauerkraut should be kept at a temperature of 85°. It is cured in 6 weeks. After fermentation ceases, the lids should be tightly sealed. Cook the kraut 10 minutes before serving (page 843).

Salted Turnips

Use same method as Salted Sauerkraut, page 854.

Salted Snap Beans

Wash fresh, tender, stringless beans. Leave whole, cut lengthwise or shred with kraut cutter. Use 1 pound salt to 8 pounds beans. Pack in clean crock, alternating layers of beans and salt. If brine that forms is not enough to cover beans, add brine made of 1 part salt to 8 parts water by weight. When fermentation has ceased, seal with paraffin and store in a cool place.

Before serving, rinse the beans. Cook them until tender in fresh unsalted boiling water, at least 10 minutes (page 843).

Brined Snap Beans

Wash and string beans. Leave whole. Blanch 10 minutes in rapidly boiling water. Drain well, pack firmly into jars. Cover with a brine of 1 cupful vinegar, ¾ cupful salt to each gallon of water. Use about half as much brine as beans by volume. After a few days, when fermentation has ceased, seal with paraffin and store in a cool place.

Before serving, rinse the beans well. Cook them in fresh unsalted boiling water until tender, at least 10 minutes (page 843).

Brined Corn

Cut corn from the cob. Do not scrape cobs. Add 1 cupful sugar and 1 cupful salt for every 12 cupfuls corn. Mix and permit to stand overnight. Add just enough water for cooking, cook 20 minutes, or until tender. Place in hot sterilized jars, fill brim full, seal at once. Store in cool dark place.

To serve drain the corn. Cover it with fresh unsalted boiling water to cover and cook for at least 10 minutes (page 843).

Canning of Meat, Poultry and Game

Methods for canning fish are not given in this book because the various recommended processes are both controversial and complicated. Government bulletins call for long processing and again, before the food is served, long cooking of home-canned fish and sea food, causing great loss of flavor and food value. The freezing of fish is recommended for better retention of both these values. See page 868. But the canning of meats, poultry and game in homes can be both a safe and economical procedure and a much more convenient one than the old-fashioned method of preserving by salting and smoking, although not so satisfactory as freezing (page 868).

For safe serving of home-canned meat products, process all these non-acid foods in a pressure canner. Make sure that the temperature reaches at least 240°. Foods canned in this manner may then be served hot or cold. If a boiling water bath is used, a further precaution must be taken.

The government warns that all home-canned meats should be boiled in an open pan for 10 minutes before tasting or eating.

Preparation of Meat, Poultry and Game for Canning

After killing, meats and poultry should be well bled and cooled to below 40°, preferably for 24 hours, before canning. Beef is better if allowed to age for a week or 10 days at 34° to 38°. Large game animals are prepared and processed like beef; small game like poultry.

Frozen meat may be canned, but it does not yield a high quality product. Do not thaw it first. Saw or cut it into 1 to 2 inch strips and drop it into boiling water and precook it as other meats are prepared.

Copper or iron utensils may discolor meat. Meat should not be left in galvanized utensils for more than ½ hour or it may take up harmful quantities of zinc.

Spices, onions, garlic, etc., should be used sparingly. White pepper retains a better flavor than black pepper in meat products. If you like, use 1 teaspoonful salt for each quart container. Place it in the empty containers. It does not help to preserve the meat.

Precooking of Meats

1. In moderate oven (350°): Cut the meat into pieces about 1 pound each. Place in uncovered pans in the oven. Roast until the red or pink color of the meat has almost disappeared at center of pieces, about 20 to 40 minutes. Cut the meat into smaller pieces. Place salt, ½ teaspoonful per pint, in empty jar. Pack hot in hot jars. Pack closely, at least 2 pieces to a pint jar. Skim fat from drippings. Add enough boiling water or broth to them to cover the meat, leaving ½ inch head space. Remove air bubbles with blade of knife (page 845).

2. In water: Cut meat in uniform pieces about 1 pound each, drop in boiling water and simmer 12 to 20 minutes, or until the raw color has disappeared at center of pieces. Cut meat into smaller serving pieces, salt, pack closely, cover with the boiling broth. Remove air bubbles with blade of knife (page 845).

Frying is the least desirable method of precooking. It makes the surface of meat hard and dry and often gives an undesirable flavor to the finished product.

Packing of Meats

Meat that is not covered with liquid will discolor and lose some flavor in storage. One to 1½ pounds meat will fill a pint jar or No. 2 can.

Directions for Canning Meat, Poultry and Game by Pressure or in a Boiling Water Bath

Pint jars are preferable to larger containers, especially if processed by water bath, as the heat penetrates more readily to the center of the container. Plain tin cans are better for meats and poultry than enameled ones.

Processing Time

Most meat is processed at 10 pounds steam pressure (240°). If you live high above sea level, you add 1 pound pressure for each 2,000 feet. Process for the length of time given below.

Roasts and Steaks

Remove all large bones, gristle and excess fat, leaving just enough fat for flavor. Precook in oven or hot water except for pork which has a better flavor when precooked in an oven. Pack hot and cover with boiling liquid in which the meats were cooked. Process pints for 1¼ hours, quarts for 1½ hours in pressure cooker at 10 pounds. Or process pints for 3½ hours in boiling water bath.

Ground Beef

Be sure the meat is fresh and is kept clean and cold. Grind lean meat, using plate with ⅛ inch holes. Add 1 teaspoonful salt per pound ground meat or 1 cupful for 25 pounds. Mix thoroughly. Form into flat cakes that can be packed without breaking. Precook in moderate oven 350° until medium done. Pack hot. Skim fat from drippings. Cover cakes with drippings and boiling water. Leave 1 inch head space. Process for same length of time as roasts or steaks above.

Meat for Stews or Hash

Use less tender cuts and small pieces. Cut meat into 1 inch cubes. Add boiling water to cover. Simmer until raw color is gone. Pack hot, cover with boiling broth. Process pints for 75 minutes, quarts for 90 minutes in pressure canner at 10 pounds. Or process pints for 3½ hours in boiling water bath.

Liver

Wash, remove veins and membranes, slice or cut as desired. Drop in boiling salted water, simmer about 5 minutes. Pack, cover with boiling water. Process as for stew above.

Hearts

Wash, remove thick connective tissue. Precook by Method 2. Pack, add salt and boiling broth to cover. Process as for stew above.

Tongue

Wash, place in boiling water, simmer about 45 minutes, or until skin can be removed. Skin, slice, or cut into pieces. Reheat to simmering in broth. Pack, add salt and broth to cover. Process as for stew above.

Soup Stock and Broth

Crack or saw bones. Simmer them in salted water until the meat is tender. Strain the stock to remove bones. Skim off excess fat. Meat may be returned to stock. Reheat to boiling, pour into jars. Process pints for 20 minutes, quarts for 25 minutes at 10 pounds pressure, or process pints for 1½ hours in boiling water bath.

Sausage

Make sausage according to favorite recipe, but omit sage. One-fourth beef may be used. Form into flat cakes. Brown in moderate oven 350° or on top of stove in heavy skillet over moderate heat, pouring off fat as it accumulates. Pack hot, cover with boiling pan gravy and water. Leave 1 inch head space. Process like Ground Beef, page 856.

Poultry

Chickens should be dressed, cut as for frying, and cooled at 40° or lower for at least 8 hours, preferably 24, before canning.

Mature chickens yield a more flavorful canned product than do younger ones, though either may be used.

Separate the meat into 3 piles—the meaty pieces, the bony pieces and the giblets. The giblets will flavor and discolor the meat and are best canned alone. Trim off all lumps of fat, as too much would make the chicken difficult to process.

To precook the chicken prepare a broth by simmering the bony pieces until tender. Add broth to meaty pieces and simmer until medium done. Skim fat from broth. Pack meaty pieces with or without bone, add boiling broth to cover, leaving 1 inch head space. Work out air bubbles with a knife. Remove meat from bony pieces, cut in uniform pieces and can, covered with boiling broth, using the boned chicken for salad, creamed chicken, etc. Process pints for 65 minutes, quarts for 75 minutes at 10 pounds pressure, or pints for 3½ hours in boiling water bath.

It is desirable to can livers separately, gizzards and hearts together. Cover giblets with boiling chicken broth or water. Cover and cook until medium done. Pack hot, cover with boiling broth. Leave 1 inch head space. Work out air bubbles. Process pints for 75 minutes at 10 pounds pressure.

Rabbit

Prepare the meaty pieces, precook and process as for chicken.

Frozen Foods

The Freezer and Its Contents

We are indebted to an Arctic explorer for the following Eskimo rule for a frozen dinner:

"Kill and eviscerate a medium-sized walrus. Net several flocks of small migrating birds and remove only one small wing feather from each wing. Store birds whole in interior of walrus. Sew up walrus and freeze. Then two years or so later, find the cache if you can, notify clan of a feast, partially thaw walrus. Slice and serve." Simplicity itself.

Simple, too, are the mechanics of home freezing, this rather new to us and comparatively easy method of food preservation which has been advertised as all things to all men. The result is that some frozen food enthusiasts toss any type of food into the poor freezer and expect fabulous results. Yes, some foods can be preserved by freezing more successfully than in any other way, but quality produce comes out only if quality produce goes in, and then only if suitable foods are chosen, and all the necessary steps are followed meticulously, i. e.: quick and careful preparation, moisture-vapor-proof sealed wrapping, constant zero degree or lower temperatures during storage, and the observance of the proper thawing and cooking methods. In spite of this rather formidable list, these conditions are easily met for meats, fish, poultry, fruits and precooked foods. They all require care, but vegetables, because of the necessity of blanching, require both more time and more care.

As compared with canning, freezing takes one third to one half the amount of time and labor. The yields per bushel of produce are about the same. See page 847.

The economy of having a well-filled freezer presents what I have heard called a "mooty" point. Unless you are a determined planner and dispenser it may lead to extravagance. If you are faced with an emergency, it is a great temptation to use that choice cut of meat reserved for company, and children love to draw on the seemingly unlimited freezer resources of ice cream and desserts. It is only by unsparing effort and good husbanding of supplies that the satisfactions as well as the cash savings from the use of a freezer are apparent and well worth while.

You profit especially if you raise your own meat and produce and are a sharp trader when markets are glutted seasonally with raw or already frozen goods. But remember that some frozen foods stored too long suffer excessive vitamin loss so that buying foods that have been held too long is a doubtful procedure.

In any case the freezer is not meant for miserly hoarding but should be managed on an over-all continuously shifting plan—a seasonal plan—geared to your family's food needs and preferences. But keep the freezer stocked with favorites so the family will continue to ask: "What's thawing?"

Space

Space estimates differ depending on family appetites, but the allowance of 6 to 8 cubic feet per person is average. Allow 6 cubic feet per person if you plan to use half the fruits and vegetables served during the year from your frozen store, supplementing the other half by the use of fresh vegetables or canned goods. Plan for about 3 pounds of frozen meat per person per week. This amount of space does not permit more than half your year's meat supply to be in the freezer at any given time. Allow 8 cubic feet of space per person if you also plan to freeze half your supply of baked goods, desserts and precooked foods.

858

Quality

Whatever quantity you freeze the quality of the food you use is of first importance. Remember that quality cannot be made in the freezing process itself. It is lost sometimes even though well-fed animals, and fruits and vegetables from rich soils are used. For example, the keeping qualities of varieties of the same fruit or vegetable differ. Elberta peaches grown in New York are considered tops for freezing, but Elberta peaches grown in Virginia are often reported poor for that purpose.

Time and conditions of harvest or slaughter are also factors to reckon with. Most crops are best when they have sun just before maturing. Undue rain before harvest may cause the entire pack to be mediocre. Crops such as early apples, the first asparagus, etc., keep their flavor the best. Because new discoveries are being made constantly it is wise, if you are barging into freezing in a big way, to consult your county agricultural agent about the best varieties of fruits and vegetables to grow and to buy from your neighborhood. Also watch government bulletins and state experiment station publications, for these agencies continue to make discoveries in the science of home freezing.

The retention of nutritional values and flavors depends on the speed with which food can be processed after harvesting. From the time of harvesting on it must be kept at such favorable temperatures that microbial and enzymatic activities are held to a minimum. See page 865. The freezing process arrests both these activities, but they can get very lively during thawing, especially the bacterial, if contamination happens to have taken place before freezing.

Wrapping, Packaging and Sealing

After selecting quality food decide how to package it. Excess air within the frozen food package is a real enemy. Choose only those wrappings which will insure an absolutely moisture-proof and vapor-proof seal, both to protect the food from drying out and to keep odors from penetrating into the freezer and causing off-flavors in other foods. Air left in the containers dries out the food during the inevitable temperature variations of storage, drawing moisture from the food itself to form a frost in the package—a frost made from the juices and seasoned with the flavors of the food itself. So pack always to exclude as much air as possible from the package. Liquid foods must be stored in leak-proof containers, and enough space must be allowed for the expansion of the liquid during the freezing process. Allow ½ inch in pint and ¾ inch in quart cartons. If you use glass, allow 1 inch for a pint and 1½ inches for a quart container. For cans see page 847.

Choose containers that are vapor and moisture-proof and of convenient size and shape. Cubic containers almost double the storage space as compared to cylindrical shapes. Meats and irregularly formed foods are wrapped in aluminum foil or special laminated papers. The foil, which should have a weight of .0015 or thicker, needs no sealing, but profits from an overwrap of stockingnet. In some cases old nylon stockings are used in place of stockingnet. Plastics and papers vary in quality, and it is often hard to judge their efficiency. They need careful sealing with tapes adapted to low temperatures. Some may be sealed with heat. A special iron is available for heat sealing, although a not-too-hot curling or pressing iron will do.

All sheet wrappings are applied with the lock-seal or drugstore wrap or, where size demands, with the costlier butcher wrap. Both are shown in detail on page 860. To make the drugstore or lock-seal wrap, place the food in the center of a piece of paper large enough so that when the ends are brought together they can be folded into an interlocking seam as shown on the left. Make the seam and draw the paper down against the food to enclose it tightly as shown in the center. Reverse the package so that the seam lies on the table. Now turn the package so

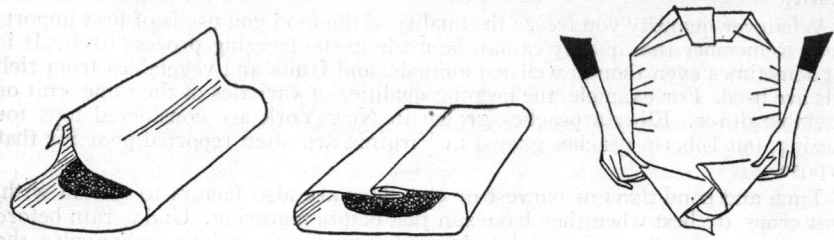

that the closed ends are at right angles to your body. Fold the end farthest from you in a pleated fold and make an extra fold in the end before pressing the folded end against the package. Spin the package around so that the doubly folded end can be braced against your body, as shown on the right above. Now very carefully force any excess air from the package. Then fold the remaining open end as described and shown on the right above. Seal the package with a tape that is adapted to low temperature.

To make the butcher wrap, the food is placed on a large square of paper on the diagonal. One corner is brought over it generously as shown on the left below. The adjoining corners are then folded over as shown in the center drawing and then the

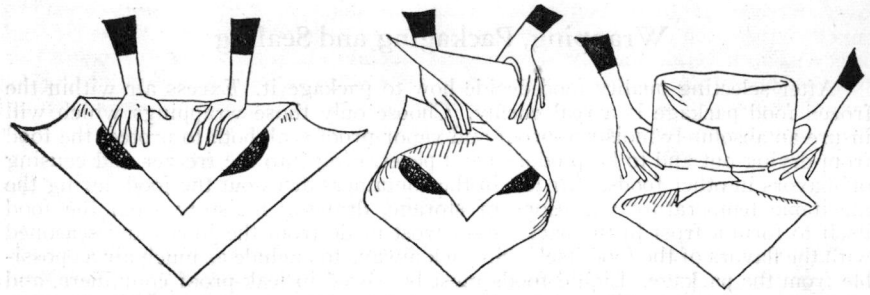

entire package is folded over as shown on the right above. This wrap requires great care if excess air is to be excluded from the package and the food kept flat.

Easiest to handle are polyethylene bags made of a plastic which can be heat-sealed, but it is equally good and simpler to twist them tightly into a goose neck and secure them closely with a rubber band. These bags remain pliable even at zero temperature, need no overwrap, and can be re-used. Pliofilm bags may also be re-used if handled carefully, but an overwrap of stockingnet, etc., is advisable. Cellophane bags may be the cheapest, but they are not re-usable and must be heat-sealed.

Some frugal housewives keep their old butter and ice cream cartons and line them with pliofilm bags, but any such cartons must be considered as merely protective overwraps for a moisture and vapor-proof liner. Plastic boxes and heavily waxed cartons are good for liquids, but watch for a tight seal. Both may be re-used. Before re-using, wash the wax cartons with a detergent and cold water to keep the wax firm.

If storing food to be frozen in cans, seal the cans (see page 847) but allow head space (page 847) for expansion when filling the cans. Aluminum foil cartons are particularly satisfactory for foods that can be served with a mere reheating, but be extremely careful to seal them tightly. They are also satisfactory for rapid chilling before storage and can come out of the freezer to the oven without further handling or loss of food.

If packing vegetables in cartons, size them carefully. A device such as the one shown on the right below can be made out of a wooden box. Adjusted to your carton size, it is a great aid for quick, close packing.

If several servings of meat, cookies or other small items are combined in 1 package, they separate more easily when 2 thicknesses of moisture-proof paper are placed between each 2 units, as shown on the left below, or when they are slid into folded foil as shown in the center below before the outside wrapping is put on. In packaging your foods wrap in convenient serving or meal-size quantities: holding

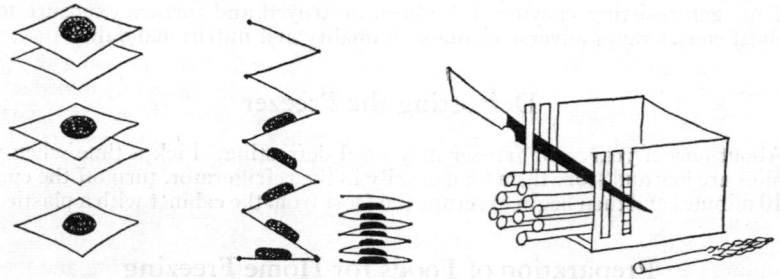

over or recooking thawed left-overs is not advisable. Since good results depend so much on the speed with which the fresh foods are prepared and put into the freezer, it is wise to have all filling, wrapping and labeling equipment ready at hand. Use proper funnels for filling cartons to keep liner edges dry for a perfect seal. Rectangular ones can be bought or they can be made by removing both ends from tin cans and compressing the lower end to fit the cartons.

Labeling and Dating

Soft wax or china-marking pencils or marking pens do well for cartons. Labels may be slipped between stockingnet and other wrappings or under transparent wrappings. Small tough different-colored tags with strings attached are helpful in quick identification of stored opaque packages. Keep a master record of dates of freezing as well as poundage on meats and portions of other foods you store. Labeling and dating of the packages themselves, needless to say, are essential. While many foods keep satisfactorily from one season to the next, there are some exceptions noted in detail later, such as fat meats, poultry, prepared doughs and precooked foods. But whatever you are processing, remember to start with quality food, get it properly prepared, well cooled, wrapped and labeled before storing it.

Filling the Freezer

Do not overload your freezer. Doing so causes too great a rise in temperature and impairs the condition of the other foods stored in it. Several hours before adding new foods set the freezer to the coldest point. Freeze no more than 35 to 40 pounds of food per 12 cubic feet of freezer space in any 24-hour period unless your manufacturer says you may freeze more. Place the new packages, with the exception of sandwiches and baked goods, against the freezer plates or the walls of the freezer, unless the manufacturer directs otherwise, until the new produce is well frozen. Then when you finally go to use these treasures allow enough time for proper thawing and cooking, see pages 869-875, if you want prime results.

Power Break

The bugaboo of power failure is lessened by the advice of experts who say that even a small freezer, if loaded, can last 2 days, a half-loaded one, 1 day. Should the power break last longer, 5 pounds of dry ice added to a 20-cubic-foot cabinet will increase the time to 3 or 4 days for a loaded and 2 or 3 days for a half-loaded freezer. In any case do not open the freezer during a power failure except to put in the dry ice. Food that still retains ice crystals can be frozen, but meats, poultry and fish registering more than 50° must be cooked and used at once. All frozen foods once thawed should be used at once. Especially if they have been blanched, their oxygen-resisting enzymes have been destroyed and further exposure to air and heat causes rapid adverse changes in quality and nutritional value.

Defrosting the Freezer

About once a year your freezer may need defrosting. Pick a time when your supplies are low and store them temporarily in the refrigerator, turn off the current for 10 minutes and then begin to scrape the frost from the cabinet with a plastic tool.

Preparation of Foods for Home Freezing

It may seem repetitious to begin this section with the caution: "The retention of nutritional values and flavors depends on the speed with which food can be processed after harvesting and the favorable temperatures at which it is held until frozen," but this principle bears repetition. Work quickly with small quantities of fruits and vegetables and keep the rest chilled in the refrigerator.

Freezing Fruits

Choose almost any firm, sound, uniformly sun-ripened fruit. Exceptions are pears, which seldom freeze well but do somewhat better if ripened off the tree, and bananas which had better be kept out of the freezer. It is not essential to use sugar in freezing fruit but it is sometimes preferable. See page 864.

Small Fruits

Those who grow their own berries may freeze them successfully without washing them. It is safer to wash berries that are not home grown. Fragile fruits like berries or cherries may be washed twice in cold or ice water to clean and firm them. Drain the fruit well, then spread it out on several thicknesses of paper toweling and cover it lightly with paper toweling to absorb as much surface moisture as possible. In order to avoid crushing or bruising the fruit use very gentle movements. After the fruit is picked over and hulled or stemmed, it is ready for packaging with or without the addition of sugar. For different methods of preparation see page 863. Blueberry skins remain tender if the fruit is blanched (page 864) before sugar is added. If whole strawberries are to be packaged without sugar, prick them with a fork to release the air. Raspberries may be frozen without sugar by being placed unwrapped in a single layer on trays in the freezer until solidly frozen and then packaged closely, properly sealed and stored.

Some fruits keep better if packed in dry sugar or in Sirup, page 863. The dry method of sweetening is preferable, as the addition of water tends to weaken the flavor of the fruit.

To Sugar Fruit

Place the fruit on a shallow tray. Sift the sugar over it until it is evenly coated. For amounts of sugar see page 864. When the fruit is coated pack it gently into suitable cartons. Seal, label and freeze the fruit.

Large Fruits

Sort the fruit carefully, removing pits, cores and stems, and paring it when necessary. Treat fruits that tend to discolor before freezing and during thawing, such as pared apples, peaches, apricots, pears, by 1 of the 2 following methods:

1. Drop the prepared fruit into a mixture of lemon juice and water—3 tablespoonfuls of lemon juice to 1 quart of water—or ½ teaspoonful ascorbic acid crystals dissolved in 1 quart water. To dissolve the crystals, see below. One quart of either of these mixtures is enough for about 4 quarts of fruit. Drain the fruit well before adding it to the sirup. It is advisable to blanch (page 865) sliced apples. Or:

2. Drop the prepared fruit directly into the sirup, see below, in which it is to be frozen, adding to it 1½ teaspoonfuls lemon juice or ¼ teaspoonful ascorbic acid to 2 cupfuls of sirup. To distribute the acid evenly dissolve ¼ teaspoonful of the ascorbic acid powder or crystals in 1 teaspoonful of water. Do this in a small bottle and shake the contents until dissolved before adding it to 1 cupful of sirup. Add the lemon juice or acid to the sirup shortly before putting the fruits into the sirup.

If fruits that tend to discolor are packed in mixtures with citrus fruits, the lemon juice or acid may be omitted.

Sirups

Sirups may be made several days in advance and stored in the refrigerator so as to be well chilled when combined with the fruit.

For light or 40% sirup use 1¾ cups sugar to 1 pint water
For medium or 50% sirup use 2½ cups sugar to 1 pint water
A heavier sirup is not recommended
For suggested amounts of fruit and sirup, see below

Some people prefer to combine sugar with corn sirup. If this combination is desired, never use more than ⅓ cupful corn sirup to ⅔ cupful sugar. Any of these sirups may be made by merely dissolving the sugar and corn sirup in water, but it is preferable to boil the mixture until the sugar is dissolved. Chill well before using.

Amounts of Fruit and Sirup

Use enough sirup to cover the fruit well. When using sirup with small or sliced fruits or berries allow about 1½ cupfuls of fruit and ⅓ to ½ cupful of sirup for a pint container. Halved fruits require about 1½ cupfuls of fruit and ¾ to 1 cupful of sirup to a pint container.

If the fruit tends to rise above the sirup, crush a piece of moisture-proof paper lightly and put it on top to keep the fruit submerged until the expansion of freezing makes the sirup fill the carton. Leave the paper in the carton.

Purées

Some fruits such as plums, prunes, avocados, persimmons and melons keep better in uncooked purée form. Bananas should not be frozen. Applesauce is one of the most delicious of cooked frozen purées, especially if made with early apples. When packaging with sugar allow as much per pound of fruit as is indicated on the Chart below.

Fruit Juices

Fruit juices such as apple and cider, raspberry, plum and cherry keep very well. The cherry and apple juice should have ½ teaspoonful ascorbic acid or 2 teaspoonfuls of lemon juice added for each gallon of juice. Raspberry is best if the whole berries are mixed with 1 pound of sugar to each 10 pounds of fruit and frozen. Extract the juice when ready to use. In freezing citrus juices it is difficult to retain their vitamin content without an elaborate vacuum process. If you do freeze these juices, store them in specially lined cans. Fruit for jelly and jam may be frozen unsugared, and the juice extracted later, without any cooking. To make the jelly, proceed as usual (see page 799). Fruit sauces or cobbler fillings made from seedy berries, especially blackberries, are smoother if the frozen berries are broken apart and put unthawed through a meat grinder. Use a fine blade.

Suggested Amounts of Sugar for Frozen Fruits

Use 1 pound sugar to the pounds of fruit indicated below.

*5 lbs. apples	4 to 5 lbs. dewberries	4 lbs. raspberries, whole
4 to 5 lbs. blackberries	3 to 4 lbs. gooseberries	or crushed
**4 lbs. blueberries	*3 lbs. peaches, sliced	4 to 5 lbs. rhubarb, diced
*3 to 5 lbs. sour cherries	3 lbs. pineapple	†4 lbs. strawberries, whole
3 lbs. currants	*3 to 4 lbs. plums	or crushed

*Mix ½ teaspoon dry ascorbic acid crystals with every 5 lbs. of dry sugar.
**Steam-blanch (page 866) ½ to 1 minute to keep skins tender.
†After washing, prick whole strawberries with fork to release excess air before combining with sugar.

Light or medium sirup. For relative amounts of fruit and sirup see page 863.

*‡L Apples	L Grapefruit	L-M Papaya, ½ inch
*L-M Apricots, peeled or	L Guavas, pulp and rind	cubes
unpeeled	L Grapes	L-M Pomegranate
L Blackberries	L-M Loganberries	*L-M Plums
L Blueberries	*L Nectarines	L-M Prunes
L-M Boysenberries	L Oranges, sections	L-M Raspberries, whole
*M Cherries, sweet	*L Peaches	or crushed
M Dewberries	*L Pears	L-M Strawberries
*L-M Figs	L-M Pineapple	L-M Youngberries

*Use lemon juice or ascorbic acid (page 863).
‡Blanch 1½ minutes in sirup.

No sugar is required for these fruits.

*Apples	Loganberries	Prunes
*Apples, sliced	Melons	Rhubarb
**Blueberries	Pineapple	Raspberries
Cranberries	*Plums	Youngberries

* Use lemon juice or ascorbic acid (page 863).
**Steam-blanch (page 866) ½ to 1 minute to keep skins tender.

Preparation of Vegetables for Freezing

Vegetables such as peas, asparagus, green beans, Lima beans, broccoli and corn take well to freezing. If the produce was garden fresh and properly processed the taste is hardly distinguishable from fresh vegetables when served. Others, such as kale, New Zealand spinach, white potatoes and salad materials (tomato, cucumber and onions) are distinct failures. Still others, such as sweet potatoes, the squashes, celery and cabbage, are possible only when precooked before they are frozen.

A long processing list is given on page 866 in case there is some reason for wanting to freeze the less successful types of vegetables rather than to can them or to keep them in root storage.

Blanching of Vegetables

Since enzymes continue to be active in vegetables even after harvesting and unless arrested will bring about changes which lead to nutritional loss and off-flavors, blanching, which lessens activity, is imperative before freezing. There are 2 methods of blanching, by boiling or by steaming. Steaming usually takes about ½ to 1 minute longer, but these methods are used more or less interchangeably. Exceptions are leafy vegetables which must be boiled if the heat is to penetrate quickly, and watery vegetables like squashes and cut sweet corn which loose flavor badly through leaching and must be steamed. Since blanching is not meant to be a cooking process but merely a preparatory one, it should be carefully timed to avoid textural and nutritional breakdowns. Removal of excess moisture after blanching (page 866) and proper chilling before packaging are extremely important.

Choose young tender vegetables. The starchy ones such as peas and corn and Lima beans should be slightly immature. If not prepared and frozen at once, vegetables should be kept fresh by being chilled from harvesting to processing. Prepare them quickly as for regular cooking. In order to blanch them evenly and to pack them as efficiently as possible in the containers sort the vegetables for size before blanching them. Several handy devices for sizing and cutting are available and a corn scraper for preparing corn cream-style or for scraping is a great asset. Better food values and flavor are retained if vegetables are not shredded or frenched.

Blanching Equipment

Whether you boil or steam-blanch, blanching equipment consists preferably of a special blanching kettle with a tight-fitting lid and a wire basket. In either case handle no more than 1 pound of vegetables at a time.

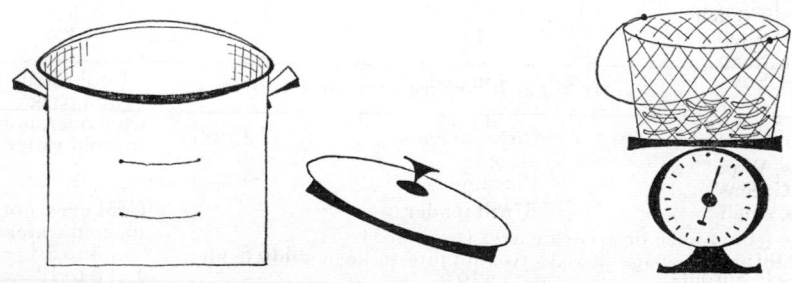

Boil-Blanching

To blanch by boiling allow 6 to 10 quarts of boiling water to 1 pound of vegetables. The larger amount of water is preferable as the boiling process resumes more rapidly with the larger quantity after the vegetables are added and tends to leach them less. Put 1 pound of vegetables in the wire basket. Submerge them completely in the boiling water and wait until the water again reaches a boil. Then begin to time the blanching. See Chart on this page. Shake the wire basket several times during this period to allow even penetration of the heat.

Steam-Blanching

To blanch by steaming put 6 quarts of water in the kettle and bring to an active boil. Put the vegetables, again not more than a pound at a time, in the wire basket and suspend them above the water. Cover the kettle and when the steam starts to escape under the lid begin to time for blanching. Shake the basket several times during this period to make sure that all the vegetables are uniformly exposed to the steam.

Whether you have used the boiling or the steam method, when the time is up remove the vegetables from the heat at once. Since the blanching process is not meant to cook the vegetables, but merely to halt the enzymatic action, the vegetables must be chilled at once to stop further softening of the tissues by heat. If your tap water is 60° or less, hold the vegetables under the running cold water. If not, immerse them in ice water or chill them over ice water as directed in the Chart on this page. Then drain the vegetables well and spread them on several thicknesses of paper toweling and also cover them with paper toweling to absorb as much of the surface moisture as possible before packaging them. Except for greens like spinach, which should have a ½ inch head space, the containers should be closely and completely filled but not stuffed. Some vegetables keep best as purées. If frozen vegetables toughen consistently, the water used may be too hard for good results.

Blanching Chart for Vegetables

(Showing preferred method)

Vegetable	Minutes to boil	Minutes to steam	Minutes to chill in ice water
†Artichoke	7		10 to 12
Asparagus, medium size	3 to 12		3 to 5
Beans, Lima	1½		3
Beans, French		2	5
Beans, Shell	1¾		3
Beans, Snap	2		5
Beans, Soy	4 in pod		Cool, shell and pack
*Bean Sprouts	4 to 6		Cool over, not in, cold water
Beans, Wax	2		5
Beet Greens	2		5
Beets, small	Until tender		Cool over, not in, cold water
Broccoli		3 to 5	4 to 5
Brussels Sprouts	4 to 6		8 to 12

Vegetable	Minutes to boil	Minutes to steam	Minutes to chill in ice water
*Cabbage, leaf or shredded	Until tender	3 to 4	Cool over, not in, cold water
Carrots, scrubbed	3		5
Cauliflower, flowerets		3	4
*Celery, diced		Until tender	Cool over, not in, cold water
Chard	2		5
*Chinese Cabbage, shredded	1½		Cool over, not in, cold water
Collards	2		5
Corn, cream-style, white or yellow		3 to 5 off the cob 8	Cool over, not in, cold water 15
Corn, medium size, cut, yellow		8 on the cob	15 on cob, then cut off for packing
Corn on Cob			
Corn, scraped for pudding (see page 873)			
†Eggplant, 1½ inch slices	4		‡4 in ascorbic acid solution
*Kale	4 to 6		4 to 5
Kohlrabi, diced		1¾	5
*Mushrooms, medium, whole	3½		5
*Mustard Greens	Until tender		Cool over, not in, cold water
Okra, medium, whole	2		5
Parsnips		3	5
Peas, Black-eyed	2		5
Peas, Green		3¾ to 1⅓	2 to 5
Peppers	2		2 to 5
*Potatoes, Sweet, purée	Until tender		Cool over, not in, cold water. Add 1 teaspoon ascorbic acid to every quart potatoes
*Pumpkin, purée	Until tender		Cool over, not in, cold water
Spinach	2½		3
*Squash, Winter, purée	Until tender		Cool over, not in, cold water
Turnip Greens	2½		4
Turnips, sliced, peeled		1½	5
Vegetables, mixed	Blanch separately as directed above; combine after chilling		

* Cook before freezing

† Add 1 teaspoon ascorbic acid to each quart of water used in blanching

‡ Ascorbic acid solution—2 teaspoons acid to 2 pints of ice water

Freezing Meats

Meats should be slaughtered, chilled and aged as for canning, with the exception of Poultry, below, and divided into meal-size quantities, not more, for packaging. Serve left-overs cold rather than hot: the reheating of once-thawed cooked meats does not make for very tasty or nutritious eating. For packaging, see page 859.

The same advice as with all frozen produce applies to the choice of meats: watch quality. Storage at low temperatures does not produce enough change to make tough meats tender. If you are used to buying quality cuts over the counter, make sure you can trust your new source when you buy elsewhere in quantity. Beef, lamb and mutton must be properly aged in a chill-room before being frozen, but not too long (see below); pork and poultry should be frozen as soon as they cool after slaughtering to forestall the tendency of the fat to turn rancid.

Although some meats may be held over a year it is a questionable economic or gastronomic procedure. Hold corn-fed beef, lamb and mutton a year if necessary; pork, veal and young chicken no more than 8 to 9 months; old chickens, turkeys and variety meats 3 to 4 months. Game storage depends in part on the type of game and in part on the laws of your state, which may limit the holding time. For large game, see directions for meat above. For birds, see directions for poultry below. Ground and sliced meats keep less well than solid cuts. Salted or fat meats such as fresh sausage ought never to be held longer than a month as the salt tends to make the fats rancid. Smoked meats like bacon and ham will keep 2 to 4 months but extra precautions should be taken in wrapping any smoked meats to keep the odor from penetrating other foods. Bones, which add flavor to meats during cooking, take up considerable locker space and may also cause tearing in wrappings. Removing of bones takes both skill and time. If they are removed, be sure to cook them with the meat trimmings for concentrated stock, which is valuable for soups and gravies or for packaging precooked meats (page 872). Frozen in ice-cube-size trays and removed and wrapped for storage, these concentrates make quick gravy or soup.

Broilers, fryers and roasting chickens are most desirable for freezing. For stewers, see Precooked Foods, page 871. Starve the chickens but give them plenty of water for 24 hours before slaughter. Then bleed them well. Clean and dress them (page 389) immediately. Be careful not to tear or bruise the flesh. Chill not longer than 2 hours. Do not age them. Remove the excess cavity fat. Wrap giblets separately in moisture-vapor-proof wrappings and store in the cavity. Wrap and seal (page 859), label and freeze. Storage space is saved if chickens are halved or disjointed before packaging. The halves are wrapped with double moisture-proof paper between them. The pieces may be stored in cartons. Necks, backs and less meaty pieces may be cooked at once for concentrated Stock, page 47. Strain and freeze the stock. Store young chickens no longer than 9 months, older ones 3 to 4 months, and stuffed chicken 2 to 3 months at the most. Keep ducks and turkeys 6 to 9 months. If you stuff poultry before freezing, avoid watery vegetables in the dressing, such as celery, onion, etc. A slight discoloration of the bones may occur during storage. It is harmless.

Freezing Fish

Fish, shellfish and frog legs freeze successfully if they can be cleaned and frozen immediately. If this is impractical, keep fish under refrigeration from catching to freezing, but in no case over 24 hours. Fish weighing 2 pounds or less, minus viscera, head, tails and fins, are frozen whole. For fish weighing 2 to 4 pounds filleting is advised (page 227). Larger fish are usually cut into steaks (page 228). Separate fillets or steaks with a double thickness of waterproof paper (page 861).

Lobster and crab are best if cooked as for the table but without salt. Shrimp, minus the head, are best frozen uncooked as they toughen if frozen after cooking. In fact, most shellfish are apt to toughen cooked or uncooked if held over 4 months. These may all be closely dry-packed. Oysters, clams and scallops are shelled and drained. The liquor is saved. Scallops may be washed after shelling, but not the other shellfish. Package in liquor to cover and freeze. Hold no longer than 6 months.

Freezing Butter, Cream and Milk

Unsalted butter stores well, but if salt is added, 5 months should be the limit of storage. Cream, whether in butter or stored separately, should be pasteurized first (page 503). The uses for thick cream are limited on thawing mainly to whipped or ice cream as its oil rises on contact with coffee and the texture is not good for cereals. If making ice cream for freezing, use a recipe calling for heating the cream. If the milk is frozen, pasteurize first (page 503) and allow 2 inches for expansion in freezing.

Freezing Eggs

Eggs must be removed from the shell before freezing. For short periods the shelled egg may be frozen whole individually in an ice-cube container, then packaged and stored. Usually the yolks and the whites are stored separately. The whites are simply packaged in moisture-vapor-proof, small recipe-sized containers (perhaps in the exact amount for your favorite angel cake rule). The yolks need a stablilizer and must be labeled for subsequent use, depending on what is added. If for salad dressing, add 2 teaspoonfuls of salt for each pint of yolks. If for desserts, use 2 tablespoonfuls of sugar, honey or corn sirup for each pint of yolk. If you prefer to package whole eggs, stir in with them 2 tablespoonfuls of sugar or corn sirup or 1 teaspoonful of salt to each pint of egg. In packaging allow a small head space for expansion during freezing. Thaw all eggs before using in recipes. To reconstitute a whole egg from your separately packaged whites and yolks, allow 1 table-spoonful of the yolks and 2 tablespoonfuls of the whites.

Freezing Dried Fruits, Etc.

Dried fruits, nut meats, coconut and whole cereals keep well frozen. Wrap them in usable quantities, taking the usual precautions to exclude air from the packages. If storage space permits, jellies and jams, especially raspberry and strawberry, retain for many months that fresh taste and clear color they have just after preserving.

Thawing and Cooking of Frozen Foods

Certain changes take place in frozen foods during storage that call for distinctive handling before and during cooking. A tendency to mushiness in vegetables, dryness of meat and a lack of juiciness in fish can be lessened by proper thawing and heating.

Always thaw frozen foods in their original containers. When time allows it is preferable to place them on a refrigerator shelf (with the exception of unbaked doughs, page 874). Thawing them, still packaged, at room temperatures takes about half as long, and if the package is put before a fan about one third as long as the refrigerator method. For emergencies, if the package is absolutely waterproof, it may be immersed in cool, not warm, water. This method should be used only when pressed for time as the result is poor. Use all frozen foods immediately after thawing.

Thawing and Cooking of Frozen Vegetables

Most frozen vegetables, because of previous blanching and a tenderizing process induced by temperature changes during storage, cook in from one third to one half the time that fresh vegetables require. See page 262. Uncooked frozen vegetables may be substituted in recipes calling for fresh vegetables if it is possible to shorten the cooking time. Example: add them to stews for the last minutes of cooking. As with fresh vegetables it is imperative, if flavor and food values are to be retained, not to overcook them, especially if you use a pressure pan. See Chart, page 882.

The question of thawing or not thawing before cooking vegetables is disputed. If you thaw, cooking must follow immediately. To thaw vegetables allow about 6 hours in the refrigerator, 3 at room temperature or 1 hour before a fan, for a 12 to 16 ounce package. In any case broccoli and spinach profit by partial thawing and corn on the cob should always be completely thawed. Corn on the cob is delicious if buttered and rewrapped in the aluminum foil in which it was frozen, then baked at 400° for 20 minutes. Thawed vegetables must be cooked immediately; otherwise adverse changes take place very rapidly.

Unthawed vegetables should be broken apart sufficiently to allow the heat to penetrate rapidly and evenly. To cook them use the smallest possible amount of boiling water—¼ cupful is enough for most vegetables, although Lima beans take almost a cupful and soybeans and cauliflower about ½ cupful. They should be covered at once with a lid. Once the boiling has begun again, simmer the vegetables until tender. They will take from one third to one half the time required for fresh vegetables. As the addition of water is ruinous to the flavor of some frozen vegetables, steaming, double boiler cooking or baking is recommended, especially for corn cut from the cob, or squash. These methods are slower but superior to boiling.

Thawing and Cooking of Frozen Meats

Meats may be cooked thawed or unthawed, but partial or complete thawing helps retain juiciness in thick cuts. Variety meats or meats prepared by breading or dredging must be completely thawed. Always defrost in the original wrappings and when possible on a refrigerator shelf. Allow 5 hours for each pound in thick cuts and less for thinner cuts. Defrosting wrapped cuts at room temperature takes about half as long, and about a third as long as the refrigerator method when put before a fan. Thin cuts and patties may toughen if they are not thawed. Unthawed meats need 12 to 25 minutes more per pound added to the usual cooking time. In any roasting process use only the slow method of roasting meats (see page 335). A meat thermometer (see page 335) is a reassuring aid.

Thawing and Cooking of Frozen Poultry

Poultry is always best when thawed before cooking unless used for fricassee (see page 401). The usual method is to thaw in the original wrappings and allow 2 hours per pound on the refrigerator shelf, 1 hour per pound wrapped at room temperature, 20 minutes per pound if the package is placed before a fan. Poultry, however, sometimes profits by thawing in the presence of moisture. To thaw a large rooster or a turkey by this method, wrap the frozen bird completely in Turkish toweling which has been immersed in water and wrung out well. Place the bird so wrapped on a sink drain, allowing a portion of the toweling to be steeped in water. The towel is then kept moist evenly. Allow the bird to thaw this way for 12 hours if large or for 6 or 7 hours if small. Cook when thawed.

Thawing and Cooking of Frozen Fish

Slowly thawed fish loses less juice and is more delicate when cooked than quickly thawed fish. Thaw fish in the original wrappings and allow about 8 hours per pound if thawing on a refrigerator shelf, 4 hours per pound wrapped and at room temperature, 2½ hours per pound if the package is put before a fan. Lobster takes slightly longer; scallops, oysters, shellfish and uncooked shrimp slightly less time than given above. Cooked shrimp need not be thawed before further cooking. Unthawed fish must be cooked both longer and at much lower temperatures than usual for fresh fish.

Handling of Partially or Completely
Prepared Frozen Foods

Shades of Aladdin's feasts—without the lamp! The precooked meal is a reality. There are many discoveries still to be made in this field, so be adventurous. The following suggestions embody experiments which have been found acceptable. There is a definite earned increment in precooking and preparing foods like school lunches and canapés. Gains are made in time and dishwashing if several pies rather than one are prepared—one for immediate use and others for storage—or if bread, roll or cake recipes are doubled and half or more of the dough or baked goods is stored.

As with all frozen foods careful selection not only of quality but of type is important, for some things like potatoes, green salads and some uncooked doughs do not freeze successfully. Many frozen creamed dishes can be ready for the stove at once; others need planning and long slow thawing periods. Some precooked foods can be held in storage 3 months or more; others only a few weeks. The importance of bringing precooked foods to room temperature and, when this temperature has been reached, of packaging and sealing them properly at once for storage cannot be overemphasized. Use the same methods as for wrapping other frozen foods, and take the same precautions to exclude air (see page 859). In storing pies, cakes and all fragile commodities use additional cartons or tins to protect them from the weight of other objects in the freezer. Open sandwiches, rolls, unbaked biscuits and pies can be frozen on trays before packaging if desired.

Perhaps the most important thing to consider in precooking frozen foods is not to overcook before storing the foods that are to be served hot; also to watch seasonings carefully. Baffling changes take place. Onion and salt tend to vanish, as do herb flavorings, even the indomitable sage. Garlic and clove grow stronger and curry gets a musty flavor. Use only true vanilla extract or bean and avoid all synthetic flavorings.

Sauces have their own peculiar reactions. Avoid all egg sauces. Sauces heavy in fat have a tendency to separate but often recombine with stirring. Sauces with much milk or cheese tend to curdle. Thickened sauces may need thinning.

Frozen Stews and Creamed Dishes

Goulashes and stews, which often improve in flavor on reheating, and creamed dishes and croquettes, which are coated against drying, are among the most successful precooked frozen foods. Fried foods almost without exception tend to rancidity, toughness and dryness. Starchy foods like macaroni, noodles, rice and potatoes should be omitted from precooked frozen foods.

Frozen Canapés and Sandwiches

Canapés and sandwiches should not be stored longer than 2 weeks. Make them up quickly to keep the bread from drying out. For mass production methods, see page 9. Be sure to spread all bread well and to make the fillings rather heavy in fats so that the bread will not become saturated. You may prefer to prepare and freeze sandwich spreads for use later with fresh bread. In choosing recipes for fillings avoid mayonnaise and boiled salad dressings, hard-cooked egg whites, jellies and all crisp salad materials. Garnishes like cress, parsley, tomato and cucumber cannot be frozen, so add these the last moment before serving. Ground meats, fish, butter, cream and Cheddar type cheeses, peanut butter, nut meats, dried fruits and olives are all suitable for freezing.

You may freeze the canapés on trays first or wrap them carefully and then freeze them. In either case keep the different kinds separated from one another and keep them away from the freezing plates as this contact makes the bread soggy.

Canapés and sandwiches should always be thawed in the wrappings. They take from 1 to 2 hours to thaw on a refrigerator shelf and from 15 to 45 minutes at room temperature, depending on size.

Frozen Soups

To freeze soups make them as for regular use. Chill them rapidly over ice water. Store them in any containers suitable for liquids (see page 859), allowing head space of ½ inch in pint and 1 inch in quart containers (see page 859). Concentrated meat or fish stock, the stock that has been simmered until it is reduced to one half or one third its original quantity (see Soup Stock, page 43), or cream soup and chowder bases to which liquids are added after thawing are the most space-saving soups to store. If the chowder calls for potato it is preferable to add freshly cooked potato just before serving. If you do freeze the potato, undercook it. Fish and meat stock thawed and combined in a blender with fresh vegetables make delicate soups in short order (see page 895).

To serve frozen soups bring them to a boil in a saucepan unless they are thick or on a cream base, when a double boiler is recommended. For cold soups thaw until liquid and serve while still chilled. For quick Vichyssoise, see page 896.

Frozen Main Dishes

Precooked main dishes of the creamed type, stews, casserole dishes, meat pies, croquettes and spaghetti sauces are among the most convenient and successful precooked foods.

Prepare them as usual following your favorite recipes, but in all instances where vegetables are called for undercook the vegetables. Omit potatoes if possible. Chill these precooked foods rapidly over ice water and package closely and carefully (see page 859) before freezing. Reheat stews and creamed dishes in a double boiler. Stir as little as possible. Allow 1½ times as long as normal to heat a frozen casserole at the usual temperature. Put frozen meat pies into a 350°-375° oven until brown. Thaw croquettes 6 hours on a refrigerator shelf and reheat in a 400°-450° oven.

Oven-prepared meats, fish and fowl hold much better than fried ones, which tend to get rancid, tough and dry even when covered with gravy before packaging. Stewed meats keep best in heavy sauces; if they are to be used for salads, in clear concentrated stock. Cook as for regular use. Chill rapidly to room temperature. Cut in meal-sized portions, as refreezing and holding is not advised. Package closely (see page 859) and freeze; hold no longer than 3 months. Thaw in original wrappings on a refrigerator shelf, allowing about as much time to thaw as for uncooked meats. Reheat in a double boiler.

Frozen Vegetable Dishes

A number of vegetables such as squash, boiled and candied sweet potatoes and creamed celery are best cooked before freezing and are convenient to have on hand. See Chart, page 866, for these and other suggestions. They may be heated in a double boiler or in a 400° oven without thawing.

Corn Pudding, page 184, was once a seasonal treat but it is now available at any time. Prepare the pudding as for immediate use. Put it into aluminum cartons, heat it in a moderate oven 325° for 10 minutes. Cool it over, not in, cold water. Cover, seal and freeze it. To serve, heat it in a 250° oven for about 1 hour until brown. If you plan keeping the corn longer than 4 months merely scrape it, heat, chill and seal it as above. Then when ready to serve it thaw in a 250° oven until soft, add the butter, cream and salt and continue to heat the pudding until brown. For an attractive way to serve Corn on the Cob, see page 870.

Frozen Salad Ingredients

The materials that the word salad brings to mind—fresh crisp greens, tomatoes, cucumbers and aspics—are impossible to freeze, but some of the ingredients traditionally served with them are good to have on hand. Frozen precooked meats and fish, whole or diced, sliced and covered with concentrated stocks may be used for salad. Cooked ground meats, ham, etc., may be packed with cream cheese. Do not hold these ground meat bases longer than 3 weeks, especially if salted. Precooked snap beans evenly sized and unsliced may be packaged and frozen and later coated in French dressing. Fruit mixtures, excluding bananas and pears, may be frozen for use in fruit salads.

Frozen Cheeses

Cheeses of the hard or Cheddar type may be stored for 6 months. Cream cheese, but not cottage cheese, may be stored for 2 weeks.

Frozen Doughs

You may feel that the freshly baked quality of rolls or pie is so good that it is worth a chance. Leavens are highly variable under frozen storage conditions, so frozen batters are really a gamble. Store uncooked doughs in the containers in which they are to be baked to avoid further jostling. Doughs previously baked are quicker and easier to freeze and give more satisfactory results.

Precooked baked goods heavy in fats like pies and rich cookies are more surely successful. They have a 3 months' storage limit. Bread and bread rolls may be kept for 6 months or more. Whether you bake before or after freezing, careful packaging is essential. See page 859. Plan to serve just the amount of baked goods needed, for they dry out very rapidly after thawing.

Baked yeast bread has the most lasting storage possibilities of all baked goods. Bake as usual, cool and package as for frozen foods (see page 859). Bread stored over 1 year, if necessary, is still in good condition. If it is used for toast it is not necessary that it be thawed. If not toasted, thaw wrapped 1 hour at room temperature before serving.

Unbaked yeast bread dough is best when stored only a week or 10 days. It is prepared as usual, kneaded and allowed to rise once until double in bulk. Knead again and shape into loaves not thicker than 2 inches before packaging. These thin loaves will thaw with much greater rapidity than thicker loaves. Frozen bread dough is the great exception to the rule that frozen foods are best when thawed slowly, for it is best when rapidly thawed. Place it in a 250° oven for 45 minutes. Then bake it as usual (see page 524), cool and serve. It is best to use it as soon as possible, for unless it is refrozen after cooling it dries out very rapidly.

Baked yeast rolls can be held for 3 months or more if they are well packaged. Bake as usual, cool, wrap and store. To serve, thaw them wrapped at room temperature for 1 hour and then reheat them in a 400° oven for 5 minutes. Unbaked dough for yeast rolls should not be held longer than 1 week. Follow the procedure for unbaked yeast dough for bread above. Grease all roll surfaces and freeze them 2 to 4 hours on trays set against freezing units. Package them within 24 hours after freezing. Or wrap them before freezing, separating the rolls with double sheets of moisture-vapor-proof material (see page 861). To bake, remove the rolls from the package, cover with a cloth and put in a warm place to rise until they have doubled in bulk, about 2 to 4 hours. Bake as usual and serve.

Biscuits baked before freezing are packaged closely after cooling. Thaw them wrapped at room temperature for 1 hour. Reheat them in a 400° oven for 5 minutes. Unbaked biscuits are frozen on trays or packaged before freezing (see unbaked frozen yeast rolls). Biscuits rise well if they are rolled thin for quick thawing. Thaw them wrapped at room temperature for 1 hour and bake as usual. Muffins, like biscuits, are prepared as usual. Baking cups are filled ⅔ full of batter. Bake as usual and package and freeze as for baked frozen yeast rolls (see above).

Frozen Cookies

Freezer cookies are among the greatest favorites, so it is hard to keep them on hand. Cookies when baked before freezing will keep about 3 months. Bake as usual, cool and package closely, separating each cookie with moisture-vapor-proof material. To avoid breakage store in extra carton after wrapping. Let the cookies thaw ½ to ¾ hour wrapped at room temperature before serving.

If cookie dough is unbaked before freezing and you want to save time, freeze cut dough on pans ready to bake and wrap each pan. If you are trying to save freezer space rather than time, freeze the dough in a roll and cut and bake it later. Wrap the roll in moisture-vapor-proof material and seal. Uncooked cookie dough keeps 2 months. Package preferably in batch-sizes or open package at one end, fold back wrapping, thaw only until amount needed is cut off, roll, then rewrap and freeze the remainder at once. Cut individual cookies and bake in a 350° to 375° oven for 10 to 12 minutes.

Frozen Cakes

Sponge cake, angel food and similar cakes must be baked before freezing. When baked, these and butter cakes, cup cakes and loaf cakes will keep 3 to 4 months unfrosted, but only 2 months if frosted. Filled cakes tend to sogginess and any filling with an egg base is to be avoided. It is preferable to wait and add fillings just before serving. If frosted cakes are frozen, use icings with a confectioners' sugar and butter base. All icings containing egg whites or sirups tend to crystallize and to freeze poorly, including, of course, fudge and brown sugar icings. Do not wrap iced cakes until the icing has been well firmed by chilling. Place waxed paper over iced portions before putting on the outer wrap. Seal. Protect cakes with an extra carton to avoid crushing.

Thaw cakes wrapped at room temperature for 2 hours or wrapped before a fan for 40 minutes before serving.

Frozen Pies

There are a number of differences in the handling of pie, depending on whether you bake it before freezing or freeze it before baking. Pie crust may be frozen ready for rolling or rolled and cut ready to put in the pan. Unrolled crust must be handled while it is still very cold if it is to remain tender. The best fillings for either method are fresh fruits, pumpkin, squash or mince meat, and their storage limit is 4 to 6 months. If the pie is to be frozen unbaked, the filling should have about 1½ times more cornstarch or tapioca than usual. If the fruits are like peaches or apricots, which darken on exposure to air, they should be treated with ascorbic acid (see page 863). In covered pies that are frozen unbaked no vents should be cut before packaging. Cut the vents after the first 10 minutes of baking. Chiffon pies can be frozen only if baked before freezing. They can be defrosted wrapped at room temperature for 1 to 2 hours and garnished with whipped cream before serving. If a meringue topping is preferred, add it while the pie is still frozen and bake in a 325° oven for 15 minutes. Serve within the hour. Custard pies should never be frozen. Whether you bake first and store, or store and then bake, use metal rimmed or oven-proof pans so the pie can be stored and cooked in the container. After lining the pan with the crust brush the crust with lard or egg white to keep it from becoming soggy. Allow about 1 pint of filling for an 8 inch pie. Freeze wobbly fillings before packaging or be very careful to keep them level during packaging and freezing. Package pies closely, seal carefully and protect with carton or tin against the weight of other objects in the freezer.

Thaw a baked pie at room temperature for 8 hours if it is to be served cold. If it is to be served hot, place it unthawed in a 400° preheated oven for 30 to 50 minutes, depending on size. Bake uncooked unthawed pies in a 450° preheated oven 15 to 20 minutes and reduce heat to 375° until done, about 1 hour in all.

Frozen Desserts

The same principles that apply to still frozen and refrigerator desserts apply to those made in zero storage cabinets. Whipped cream, whipped egg white or a gelatine base are necessary to prevent the formation of undesirable graininess or crystals. If these stabilizing ingredients are not used, the dessert mixture must be beaten several times during the freezing to break up these crystals. Such desserts should be used shortly after being frozen and not be stored for any length of time. Turned ice cream is best if the recipes call for heating of the cream; and a final beating and refreezing may be necessary if these ice creams have been stored longer than 3 weeks. Remove frozen ice creams and desserts from storage 10 or 15 minutes before serving.

Pressure Cookery

A man once summed up his wife's life with an epitaph: "She died of things." And well she might have! Gone is the cluttered home with its jumble of superimposed hangings, its vase-laden double mantel shelves and the so-called "objets d'art" that covered every other available horizontal surface. Gone is the feather duster in use on the china figurines, animal families, fancy busts and Nubian slaves and with it the patient maids who slaved from dawn to dusk to keep order in those complicated households. In the place of all this superfluity we have sanity and sanitation. Necessity and the housewife's determination to enjoy freedom from "things" have resulted in the simplification of her belongings and the streamlining of her home.

Among our numerous functional improvements and timesavers the pressure cooker is supreme for cooking certain types of food.

The sound approach to a pressure cooker is an appreciation of its good qualities and a knowledge of its limitations.

It cooks soups and vegetables superbly. Some meats like tongue, oxtails, flank steak, pot roast and many others are well and expeditiously prepared by this method, but I have only scorn for those who suggest that a juicy chop or steak, a tender chicken or a rib roast be sacrificed to a steam bath. Experiment. Use your judgment, your good cooking standards and, above all, your sense of taste to determine what you find desirable and undesirable when cooking by pressure. Do not permit yourself to regard this timesaving method as the answer to all good cooking. Accept it gratefully as a wonderful boon—but use it with discretion, for it is not a kitchen schmoo.

Frequently when I sing the praises of my pressure cooker I am asked: "How dare you use it? Why, it frightens me to death!" Then I explain that there is nothing complicated about pressure cooker technique, that mastering a few simple rules insures safety. Aldous Huxley found the Mexicans "anti-mechanical." So am I, but I use my pressure cooker daily with ease.

The economical and practical features of all pressure cookers are unquestioned, but as the various makes of cookers now available differ somewhat it is not possible to treat them as one.

First of all, after acquiring a pressure cooker, have someone familiar with that particular make demonstrate its use. Then read the booklet issued by the manufacturer until you are thoroughly familiar with the mechanism of your cooker.

How To Cook with a Pressure Cooker

Place the food to be cooked in the pressure cooker, *never* filling it more than ½ to ⅔ full. Adjust the cover, unless directed otherwise. Place the cooker over *high* heat, unless directed otherwise. When the steam arises freely from the vent, but not until it does, close or cover the vent with a gauge or weight. It is very important in order to retain vitamins in pressure cooking to exhaust the air from the cooker at the start of cooking. When the indicator shows that the desired degree of pressure has been reached, or the gauge or weight jiggles, place the cooker over *low* heat. Cooking time is counted from this moment on. The pressure pan should show a mild form of activity by hissing occasionally during the cooking period. If you have a stop clock, use it; if not, watch the time carefully as overcooking results very quickly. As soon as the cooking time is up reduce the pressure in your cooker as directed, gradually or instantly, the latter by placing it in cool water or by letting cool water run over the side.

The cover must not be removed until all the steam is out of the cooker. Here again handle your particular type of cooker exactly as you are instructed. When a cover is difficult to remove, do not force it; there is still steam in the container which will be exhausted if you wait a few minutes.

Some cookers are geared to 15 pounds pressure. Others permit you to vary the pressure from 3¾ pounds to 20 pounds. Fifteen pounds of steam is standard pressure. Soups and vegetables are cooked at this degree of heat. A lower heat is recommended by some manufacturers for cereals, meats, desserts, etc. Consult your booklet for these variations.

Points To Remember

Cook as small a quantity of food as you wish but use the full amount of liquid given in the recipe for pressure cooking. Do not reduce or increase the amounts of liquid given in your recipes. These amounts have been gauged in relation to the cooker to insure best results. Allow the same amount of time for a reduced amount of food as for the full quantity.

When cooking foods that require different periods of cooking begin with the ingredient that requires the longest period of time. Always reduce the pressure as directed in the manufacturer's booklet before opening the lid to add the ingredient that requires the shorter period of cooking. Readjust the cover, place the cooker again over high heat and proceed as before, see page 876. When the desired degree of pressure has been reached reduce the heat and begin to count the rest of the cooking time.

When adding vegetables that require an unequal period of cooking, equalize them by cutting into small dice those that require the longer period of time, like potatoes, turnips, etc.

A trivet is useful for keeping food above the water. It is usually used for vegetables, some meats, puddings, etc. *Caution:* When cooking foods like Lima beans and cereals which tend to sputter be careful to see that the vent pipe is not clogged. It is well to acquire the habit of always checking the vent before sealing the lid. The cooking of applesauce and dried peas is not recommended by all manufacturers.

Mrs. Joseph Conrad wrote a delightful cookbook in which she says that no woman need spend more than 2½ hours preparing dinner, but that she must never leave the kitchen during this time. Shades of the past! It is wise to stay put, however, during the short periods of pressure cooking—at least not to wander out of earshot.

High Altitude Pressure Cooking, see page 901.

Rules for Cooking by Other Methods
Applied to Pressure Cookery

Compare general cookbook recipes with similar recipes in this chapter and your pressure cooker booklet. Use only the amount of water called for in similar pressure cooker recipes, even though the general recipe may call for a larger amount. Never have the cooker more than half full of liquid or two thirds full of liquid and food unless a full pressure pan is recommended by the manufacturer.

Use less seasoning in pressure cooked food as there is less liquid to dilute it. Correct the seasoning later. Use about one fourth less fat. In order to time food that is cooked in the pressure cooker consult the time for pressure cooked food in the recipes in this chapter or in your pressure cooker booklet.

The Pressure Cooker as an Adjunct

There are a large number of general rules that may be followed with the entire or partial use of the pressure cooker. On the whole I find husbands object to a too general use of the pressure cooker, condemning the results as "messes." This is unfair to the cooker and to the cook. Where this is the case the cook will find it expedient instead, let us say, of making Hot Potato Salad, page 464, or Bean Salad, page 465, from scratch in the cooker to put on the vegetable and prepare the dressing while the vegetable cooks. This takes about the same amount of time as doing it all in the pressure cooker and insures crispness. Here again it is wise to stress discretion.

General Directions for Pressure Cooker Soups

Cook soup at 15 pounds pressure. Time: soups with raw meat, ½ hour; with cooked meat, 20 minutes.

When cooking soup by the usual method a large quantity of liquid is used as some of it will be lost during the cooking period. As there is practically no loss of liquid through evaporation in pressure cooked soups, a much smaller amount of liquid is used, usually about 4 cupfuls in a 4 quart cooker. If the result is a too highly concentrated soup it may be diluted later with stock, vegetable juices, water or milk. Have your pressure cooker no more than half full of liquid or two thirds full of liquid and food combined at any time unless a full pressure cooker is recommended by the manufacturer.

Cook soup with as little fat as possible. An excess of fat is apt to clog the vent pipe. Remember to underseason soup and to correct the seasoning when ready to serve it.

If you wish a clear vegetable soup, cook the meat, water and mild seasonings until the soup is almost done, then reduce the pressure and remove the cover. Add the vegetables and pressure cook them until tender, from ½ to 5 minutes. See Chart, page 882. Reduce the pressure. Strain the soup.

A long-cooking cereal may be added to soup at once. Or, if a cereal calls for a shorter cooking period than the soup, reduce the pressure as directed, add the cereal to the soup and then pressure cook it until the cereal is done. See Rule for Cooking Cereal, page 100, Thickenings for Soup, page 41.

General Recipes for Soups Applied to Pressure Cooking

Please read the above General Directions for Pressure Cooker Soups and be guided by them. Also read the beginning of the Soup Chapter, page 40. Cut the meat into 1 inch cubes. Beef may be browned in 3 tablespoonfuls fat. Crack or crush bones to extract full food value. Remember to reduce the liquid in soups and to season them lightly. For instance, in Soup Stock II, page 44, use about half as much water and do the same for chicken broth and left-over chicken soup. A specific rule for soup stock is given below. Do not have the pressure cooker more than half full of liquid or two thirds full of liquid and solids.

PRESSURE COOKER ECONOMY SOUP
See:

Scrap Stock or Soup, page 44

Use 2 to 4 cupfuls of water dependent on the amount of left-overs to be utilized. Season lightly. Do not overload your cooker, see preceding rule. Cook at 15 pounds pressure for 10 to 15 minutes, the longer time when raw meat and uncooked bone are used. See To Thicken Soups, page 41.

PRESSURE SOUP STOCK
4 to 6 Servings
Wash and cut into 1 inch cubes:
2 lbs. lean beef: soup meat
Brown it (page 887) slowly in the pressure cooker in:
2 tablespoons melted fat
Add:
1 quart boiling water
Soup bone that has been cracked
1 medium sliced onion
1 diced carrot

4 stalks diced celery with leaves
½ bay leaf
4 peppercorns
1½ teaspoons salt

Adjust cover. Cook (page 876) at 15 pounds pressure for 30 minutes. Reduce pressure instantly. Strain, remove grease. Correct seasoning. See General Rules for Cooking Soup, page 878.

OXTAIL SOUP OR STEW

4 Servings

Sear:

1 oxtail, joints separated
1 small diced onion

in:

3 tablespoons fat

Add:

4 cups hot water or ½ water, ½ tomato juice
1 teaspoon salt
2 peppercorns

Adjust cover. Cook (see page 876) at 15 pounds pressure for 45 minutes. Reduce pressure quickly. Remove cover. Remove ox joints. Add to liquid in cooker:

1 diced carrot
4 diced ribs celery

Readjust cover. Pressure cook the soup for 5 minutes longer. If you do not like grease, chill the soup and remove the fat. Reheat the soup, correct the seasoning. You may add:

2 tablespoons sherry or tomato catsup

Separate the meat from the ox joints. Add it to the soup. Serve it with:

Chopped parsley

Oxtail Stew

Reserve 1 cupful of oxtail soup. Chill it. Remove the fat. Melt:

2 tablespoons soup fat

Stir in:

1½ tablespoons flour

Stir in the reserved stock. Stir this sauce over heat until it is smooth and boiling. Add the oxtail joints or the meat cut from the bones. This is a matter of preference, mine being for the inclusion of the joints. Suck them if you dare. Add, if you wish, 1 cupful of diced pressure cooked carrots, celery, onion, etc. Correct the seasoning. Serve the stew. See Braised Oxtails, page 386. You may follow this rule using the pressure cooking method. Pressure cook the oxtails at 15 pounds pressure for 45 minutes. Add the vegetables for the last 5 minutes only.

ONION SOUP

4 Servings

Follow the rule on page 52 for:

Onion Soup

Use 4 cupfuls stock. Cook (see page 876) at 15 pounds pressure for 4 minutes. Season and serve as directed in the rule for Onion Soup, page 52.

POTATO SOUP

Follow the rule on page 57, using 1 cupful of water, for:

Potato Soup

Cook it (see page 876) for 3 minutes at 15 pounds pressure.

QUICK VEGETABLE SOUP

4 Servings

Place in pressure cooker:

3 tablespoons bacon fat or butter

Sauté briefly in the fat:

¼ cup diced carrots
½ cup diced onions

Add:

½ cup sliced celery
3 cups hot water
1 cup canned tomatoes
1 tablespoon chopped parsley
½ teaspoon salt
⅛ teaspoon pepper
(½ cup chopped cabbage)

Adjust cover. Cook (see page 876) at 15 pounds pressure for 3 minutes. Remove from heat and let stand for 5 minutes, then reduce pressure instantly. Correct seasoning.

Dried Legume Soups

Peas form a frothy purée that tends to clog the vent pipe and are not recommended for pressure cooking by all manufacturers. Follow directions on the label. Many dried legumes are soaked (see page 268). Some packaged legumes do not require soaking. Follow directions on the label. Soak legumes if required. Drain them. Combine them as directed with water, etc., vegetables and seasonings. Do not have the cooker more than about half full of combined ingredients. Adjust cover, place cooker over low heat. To cook, see page 876. Reduce heat gradually. For about 6 to 8 servings use:

Legume	Liquid	Salt	Time at 15 Pounds Pressure
Lima beans, 1 cup	4 cups water	1 teaspoon	45 minutes
Navy beans, 1 cup	4 cups water	1 teaspoon	45 minutes
Lentils, 1 cup	4 cups water	1 teaspoon	30 minutes
Split peas, 1 cup	4 cups water	1 teaspoon	15 minutes

The liquid may be water, ham stock or other stock. To this you may add ½ cupful tomato juice or purée. Good additions to the pot are a ham bone, a broken-up turkey or chicken carcass or a 2 inch cube diced salt pork.

For vegetables and seasoning use: ½ to 1 cupful diced celery with leaves, 1 diced green pepper, seeds and fibrous portions removed, 1 minced onion, 1 skinned and sliced carrot, ½ bay leaf, 1 teaspoonful salt, ½ teaspoonful celery salt, ¼ teaspoonful pepper or 3 peppercorns. Correct seasoning when the soup is to be served. These soups may be strained. Chill them. Remove the fat. They may be thinned with stock, tomato juice or milk. Navy bean soup calls for milk. Lentil and pea soup may be "bound" as follows: Combine 1 tablespoonful flour, 1 tablespoonful fat, add a little cold stock. Stir this into hot stock and cook it until it boils. For Combinations and Garnishes, see page 72.

You may follow any of the general rules for making Legume Soups, page 48, provided you fill the pressure cooker only half full. These soups may be thinned later. Cut the usual time down to one third.

CREAM SOUPS

Please read about Cream Soups, page 56. Pressure cook the vegetables in ¼ to ½ cupful of water. For time, consult the Vegetable Chart, page 882. Put them through a strainer or blender. Proceed as directed.

SPANISH RICE

4 Servings

Wash well in 4 waters:

½ cup rice

Cook slowly in pressure cooker until lightly browned:

4 slices minced bacon

Pour off surplus drippings, leaving about 2 tablespoonfuls. Sauté lightly in these:

¼ to ½ cup chopped onion
¼ cup chopped green pepper

Stir in the rice and brown lightly. Stir in:

1 cup diced celery
2½ cups canned or fresh tomatoes
1 teaspoon brown or white sugar
½ cup water
1 teaspoon salt
¼ teaspoon white pepper
(1 clove minced garlic)

Bring these ingredients to the boiling point. Reduce heat. Adjust cover. Bring slowly to 15 pounds pressure (see page 876). Cook 10 minutes. Reduce heat gradually.

Macaroni, Spaghetti, Noodles and Rice

Boil the amount of water and salt given below in the pressure cooker. Place the macaroni, etc., in it. Stir briefly to keep the macaroni, etc., from sticking to the bottom of the cooker. Adjust cover. To cook, see page 876. When cooking time is up, reduce heat gradually. Not all manufacturers recommend cooking cereals by pressure.

Spaghetti and macaroni will about double in bulk. Noodles will increase about one third of original measure. They may be rinsed after cooking (see page 91).

	Water	Salt	Minutes at 15 Pounds Pressure
Macaroni			
Yield about 3 cups			
Long, 6 ounces			
Stir into:	6 cups boiling water	1 tablespoon	7 minutes
Elbow, 6 ounces			
Stir into:	6 cups boiling water	1 tablespoon	5 minutes
Noodles			
Yield about 3½ cups			
Narrow noodles, 4 ounces			
Stir into:	4 cups boiling water	1 tablespoon	2 minutes
Broad noodles, 4 ounces			
Stir into:	4 cups boiling water	1 tablespoon	4 minutes
Rice			
Yield about 3 cups			
White, 1 cup			
Stir into:	4 cups boiling water	2 teaspoons	8 minutes
Wild or brown			
Yield about 4 cups			
Stir 1 cup into:	4 cups boiling water	2 teaspoons	15 minutes
Spaghetti			
Yield about 3 cups			
Thin, 6 ounces			
Stir into:	6 cups boiling water	1 tablespoon	8 minutes
Regular, 6 ounces			
Stir into:	6 cups boiling water	1 tablespoon	9 minutes

SPAGHETTI SAUCE
8 Servings
Sufficient for 8 to 12 ounces spaghetti.
Brown in pressure pan:
    1½ cups chopped onion
    1½ lbs. ground beef
in:
    ⅓ cup salad oil or bacon drippings
Add:
    1 small minced clove garlic
    ½ to 1 tablespoon chili powder
    1 tablespoon Worcestershire
        sauce
    ½ cup diced green pepper
    ½ cup diced celery
    ½ teaspoon pepper
    ½ teaspoon salt
    ½ cup mushrooms or 4 oz. canned
        mushrooms
    Contents of 2 cans tomato paste:
        12 oz.
    1 No.2 can tomatoes
Adjust cover. Cook (see page 876) at
15 pounds pressure for 20 minutes.
Reduce pressure instantly. If not the
desired consistency, simmer sauce uncovered until it thickens. Correct seasoning. You may add ½ teaspoonful
dried basil. Serve over spaghetti sprinkled with grated Parmesan cheese.

QUICK NOODLE DISH
6 Servings
Melt:
    3 tablespoons butter or oil
Sauté in it lightly:
    3 tablespoons grated onion
Brown in it lightly:
    ½ lb. ground beef or pork
Add:
    1 cup uncooked noodles
    1 teaspoon salt
    ⅛ teaspoon pepper
    1 cup tomato soup and 1 cup water
The liquids may be 1½ cupfuls stewed
tomatoes and ½ cupful water or stock.
You may use diluted tomato purée or
paste. Go easy on salt when making
these changes and correct seasonings
later.
Adjust cover. Place over high heat.
When steam escapes close vent. When
15 pounds pressure has been reached
reduce heat and cook for 4 minutes.

Reduce pressure instantly. Remove cover. Add:

1 cup cut-up celery or whole-kernel corn
⅓ cup chopped ripe olives or ½ cup mushrooms
¼ teaspoon basil or thyme
½ clove garlic

Adjust cover. Place over high heat. When steam escapes close vent. When 15 pounds pressure has been reached reduce heat and cook for 1½ minutes. Reduce heat instantly. Garnish with lots of:

Chopped parsley, chives or grated cheese

Pressure Cooked Vegetables

Prepared by this method vegetables are superlative. As they differ in age and freshness the cooking period varies slightly. The younger and fresher the vegetable the faster it cooks. Be careful not to overcook vegetables. They are best when barely tender.

The amount of water given in the chart is for a 4 quart pressure cooker and is sufficient for the maximum amount of vegetables. For a 7 quart cooker use no less than 1 cupful of water. Stock may be substituted for water for zest and flavor. Do not reduce the amount of liquid when cooking a smaller amount of vegetables.

Never crowd your cooker. Unless recommended otherwise by the manufacturer, have it only about two thirds full. The exception to this rule is spinach. That wilts down at once when cooking, but even so, do not pack it down hard when filling the cooker.

Vegetables are salted preferably after cooking. When cooked, drain vegetables. Reserve the liquor for the sauce or the stock pot. Dress them as directed in the Vegetable Chapter, page 262.

Time Chart for Fresh Vegetables in Pressure Cooker

Cooking time begins when pressure reaches 15 pounds. Reduce pressure instantly at end of cooking period.

Artichokes, French
Prepare for cooking (page 264). Drain. Place in cooker heads up. Add ½ cup water. Cook large ones 15 minutes; small ones, 8 minutes.

Artichokes, Jerusalem
Peel, cut into halves. Add ⅓ cup water. Cook 10 minutes.

Asparagus
Wash, remove tough portions. Add ⅓ cup water. Cook 3 minutes.

Beans, Snap, Green or Wax
Wash, stem, cut into 1 inch pieces. Add ⅓ cup water. Cook 2½ minutes; whole, 3 minutes; Frenched, 1 minute.

Beans, Lima
Shell, wash. Add ½ cup water. Cook small, 1 minute; large, 2 minutes.

Beet Greens
Wash thoroughly in several waters. Add ¼ cup water. Cook 3 minutes.

Beets
Wash, scrub. Add ⅓ cup water. Cook whole, small, young ones 10 minutes; whole, large, young ones 15 minutes. For whole, large, old ones add ½ cup water and cook 20 minutes.

Broccoli
Wash, remove outer leaves and tough part of stalk. Slash ends up 2 inches. Add ¼ cup water. Cook 1½ minutes.

Brussels Sprouts
Wash. Remove wilted leaves. Add ¼ cup water. Cook 2 minutes.

Cabbage, new
White or red—wash and shred, or cut into 2 inch wedges. Add ⅓ cup water. Cook 1 minute.

Cabbage, old
White or red. Add ⅓ cup water. Cook 4 minutes.

Carrots, sliced or diced
Scrape, cut into ⅛ inch slices or dice. Add ⅓ cup water. Cook 2 minutes.

Carrots, strips
Wash, scrape, cut into 2 inch strips. Add ⅓ cup water. Cook 1½ minutes.

Carrots, whole
Medium-sized. Add ⅓ cup water. Cook 5 minutes.

Cauliflower
Wash, separate into flowerets. Add ⅓ cup water. Cook 1 minute.

Celeriac
Peel, slice or dice into ¼ inch pieces. Add ½ cup water. Cook 3 minutes.

Celery
Cut into uniform 2 inch pieces. Add ¼ cup water. Cook 1½ minutes.

Celery, diced
Scrub, cut into ½ inch pieces. Add ¼ cup water. Cook 1 minute.

Corn cut from Cob
Add ¼ cup water. Cook 1 minute.

Corn on Cob
Remove husk and silk. Wash. Add ½ cup water. Cook 4 minutes.

Cucumber
Wash, peel, leave whole. Add ¼ cup water. Cook 2½ minutes.

Eggplant
Wash, cut into ½ inch slices. Pour water into cooker before placing eggplant into it. Add ½ cup water. Bring pressure to 15 pounds only.

Eggplant, whole for stuffing
Wash. Add ½ cup water. Cook 5 minutes. When cooked cut in half for stuffing.

Kale
Wash, remove tough stems. Add ¼ cup water. Cook 4 minutes.

Kohlrabi
Scrub, peel, cut into cubes. Add ¼ cup water. Cook 2 minutes.

Leeks
Cut off root ends and part of top, leaving only crisp green section. Add ¼ cup water. Cook 2 minutes.

Mushroom Caps
Large. Wipe clean, cut off stems. Add ⅓ cup water. Cook 1 minute.

Mushrooms, sliced
Caps and stems. Wipe clean, slice. Add ¼ cup water. Cook 1 minute.

Mustard Greens
Wash, remove tough portions. Add ½ cup water. Cook 5 minutes.

Okra, cut
Wash, stem, cut into ½ inch pieces. Add ½ cup water. Cook 1½ minutes.

Okra, whole
Wash, stem. Add ½ cup water. Cook 3 minutes.

Onions, large
Quartered or halves. Add ⅓ cup water. Cook 9 minutes.

Onions, sliced
Peel and slice. Add ¼ cup water. Cook 3 minutes.

Onions, whole
To precook before placing around a roast in the oven, add ½ cup water. Cook 7 minutes.

Onions, whole
Small. Leave whole only if small. Add ⅓ cup water. Cook 7 minutes.

Oyster Plant or Salsify
Wash, scrape and slice. Add ½ cup water. Cook 10 minutes.

Oyster Plant, whole
Wash and scrape. Add ½ cup water. Cook 15 minutes.

Parsnips, halved
Peel, cut into halves. Add ⅓ cup water. Cook 8 minutes.

Parsnips, sliced
Peel and cut into ½ inch slices. Add ⅓ cup water. Cook 3 minutes.

Peas, normal size
Shell, wash. Add ¼ cup water. Cook 1½ minutes.

Peas, small and very fresh
Shell, wash. Add ¼ cup water. Cook 15 seconds.

Potatoes
To precook for browning around a roast in the oven, add ½ cup water. Cook 5 minutes.

Potatoes, large
Halved. Peeled or unpeeled. Add ½ cup water. Cook 15 minutes.

Potatoes, medium
Whole. Peeled or unpeeled. Add ½ cup water. Cook 13 minutes.

Potatoes, sliced
Add ½ cup water. Cook 2½ minutes.

Potatoes, Sweet
Halved. Peel or not as desired. Add ½ cup water. Cook 12 minutes.

Potatoes, Sweet
Sliced. Add ½ cup water. Cook 4 minutes.

Potatoes, White
Small, whole. Peeled or unpeeled. Add ½ cup water. Cook 11 minutes.

Pumpkin
Wash, cut into 3 inch wedges. Add ⅓ cup water. Cook 10 minutes.

Rutabagas
Wash and pare. Cut into ½ inch slices or cubes. Add ¼ cup water. Cook 6 minutes.

Salsify
See Oyster Plant

Spinach
Wash thoroughly and rinse 3 or 4 times. Remove tough stems. Add ¼ cup water. Cook 1 minute.

Squash, Acorn
Cut into halves. Remove seeds. Add ½ cup water. Cook 8 minutes.

Squash, Hubbard
Scrub, cut into pieces. Add ½ cup water. Cook 10 minutes.

Squash, Summer
Wash, cut into 1 inch slices, do not peel. Add ¼ cup water. Cook 1 to 3 minutes.

Squash, Yellowneck
Cut into ½ inch slices, pared or unpared. Add ¼ cup water. Cook 1 to 2 minutes.

Squash, Zucchini, old or very large
Add ¼ cup water. Cook 3 minutes.

Squash, Zucchini, young
Cut into 1 inch slices. Add ¼ cup water. Cook 1 minute.

Swiss Chard
Wash thoroughly in several waters. Add ¼ cup water. Cook 1½ minutes.

Tomato Juice
Wash and core ripe tomatoes. Do not peel. Cut into quarters. Add no water. Cook ½ minute.

Tomatoes, whole
Peel, remove core. Use firm tomatoes. Add ¼ cup water. Cook 1 minute.

Turnip Greens
Wash, remove tough stems. Add ¼ cup water. Cook 2 minutes.

Turnips, diced
Peel, cut into 1 inch cubes. Add ⅓ cup water. Cook 3 minutes.

Turnips, sliced
Peel, cut into ¼ inch slices. Add ⅓ cup water. Cook 3 minutes.

CREAMED POTATOES
6 Servings

Wash, pare, cut into ¾ inch cubes and put into a pressure cooker:

    4 cups cubed raw potatoes

Add:

    2 tablespoons grated onion
    1¼ cups milk

Combine by stirring:

    2 tablespoons soft butter
    2 tablespoons flour
    2 teaspoons salt

    ¼ teaspoon pepper
    (½ teaspoon paprika)

Place this mixture in the center of the potatoes. Do not stir. Adjust cover. Place over medium heat. When 15 pounds pressure is reached (see page 876) remove from heat. Permit the potatoes to stand until pressure is reduced. Stir until thickening and liquid are blended. You may stir in:

    1 cup grated cheese
    3 tablespoons chopped parsley or chives

Pressure Cooked Dried Legumes

	Amount	Salt	Hot water	Soaked	Unsoaked
Beans, Garbanzo					
(Chick-pea)	2 cups	2 teaspoons	4 cups	30 minutes	80 minutes
Beans, Great Northern	2 cups	2 teaspoons	4 cups	25 minutes	50 minutes
Beans, Kidney	1 cup	1 teaspoon	2½ cups	25 minutes	60 minutes
Beans, Lima, large	1 cup	1 teaspoon	3 cups	35 minutes	55 minutes
Beans, Lima, small	1 cup	1 teaspoon	2½ cups	30 minutes	45 minutes
Beans, Navy	2 cups	2 teaspoons	4 cups	30 minutes	80 minutes
Beans, Pinto	2 cups	2 teaspoons	4 cups	30 minutes	45 minutes
Lentils	1 cup	1 teaspoon	3 cups	20 minutes	45 minutes
Peas, split	1 cup	1 teaspoon	2½ cups		15 minutes
Peas, whole	1 cup	1 teaspoon	2½ cups		20 minutes
Soybeans	1 cup	1 teaspoon	3 cups	30 minutes	45 minutes

See Index for dishes made with dried beans, peas and lentils.

For Peas, see page 271.

Some packaged legumes do not require soaking. See instructions on label. Soak dried legumes if necessary. See page 268. Drain them. Place them in the cooker. Add hot water to cover. Add for each cupful of legumes 1 teaspoonful salt. Do not fill the cooker more than ½ full of legumes and water. Adjust the cover. Place cooker over low heat. Cook (see page 876) at 15 pounds pressure. Reduce heat gradually.

BOSTON BAKED BEANS
6 Servings

Soak (page 268):

  2 cups dried navy beans

Drain them.

Brown in the pressure cooker:

  ¼ lb. diced salt pork

Place beans in cooker and add:

  ¼ cup chopped onion
  1½ teaspoons dry mustard
  4 tablespoons catsup
  ⅓ cup brown sugar
  2 tablespoons molasses
  1 teaspoon salt
  2 cups water
  (1½ teaspoons Worcestershire sauce)

Adjust cover. Cook (see page 876) at 15 pounds pressure for 1 hour. Reduce pressure gradually. Shake or roll the beans gently. Place them in greased baking dish. You may decorate the top with:

  ⅛ lb. sliced salt pork or 4 strips bacon

Brown in a 400° oven for ½ hour.

Frozen Vegetables Pressure Cooked

Te prepare, see Cooking of Frozen Vegetables, page 870.

Frozen vegetables cook in a shorter time than fresh vegetables so give them your full attention. Time them carefully. Have them slightly underdone rather than overdone.

Use a trivet if possible. If you cover the steam outlet as soon as the steam emerges steadily, you will find that ¼ cupful boiling water is sufficient for cooking frozen vegetables except in the case of Lima beans where you must use ⅓ cupful. Always reduce pressure instantly when cooking time is up (see page 876) in order to check further cooking promptly, for every second counts in preserving the flavor and nutritional values of the vegetables.

Time Chart for Frozen Vegetables in Pressure Cooker

When cooking time is up reduce heat instantly.

Frozen Vegetable	Amount of boiling water	Minutes to cook at 15 pounds pressure
Asparagus Cuts or spears Break into sections	¼ cup	1½ minutes
Asparagus Tips Break or separate before cooking	¼ cup	1 minute
Beans, Green, Frenched Break or separate before cooking	¼ cup	30 seconds
Beans, Green or Wax Break or separate before cooking	¼ cup	1 minute
Beans, Lima Break or separate before cooking		
Baby	½ cup	1 minute
Large	½ cup	2 minutes
Broccoli Separate stalks	¼ cup	1 minute
Brussels Sprouts Separate before cooking	¼ cup	1 minute
Carrots and Peas Break or separate before cooking	¼ cup	45 seconds
Cauliflower Separate flowerets	¼ cup	30 seconds
Corn		
Cut	¼ cup	30 seconds
On cob	¼ cup	1 minute
Always defrost completely covered at room temperature		
Mixed Vegetables Separate into pieces	½ cup	1 to 1½ minutes
Peas Separate into pieces	¼ cup	0 minutes
Spinach Cut into 1 inch cubes with a strong knife	¼ cup	30 seconds
Succotash Separate into pieces	½ cup	1 minute

Meats

Meat and stewing chicken are pressure cooked in approximately one third of the usual cooking time required by other methods. This is frequently an important consideration.

If you have a fine piece of choice meat, give it its just due and cook it with care and appreciation by some method other than by pressure, unless you have found through experience that you prefer this method. If you wish to prepare meat of commercial or utility grade by stewing or pot roasting, cook it by all means in the pressure cooker. It will be tender and juicy. You may add vegetables for the last few minutes of cooking.

Meats are usually browned in the pressure cooker, or in a skillet, fat being added for lean meat. Browning adds to flavor but may be omitted. To avoid unnecessary shrinkage brown the meat slowly. The meat may be lightly floured. The meats that are never browned are corned beef, salt pork, tongue and tripe. Do as you like about oxtails. Heat about 2 tablespoonfuls or more of fat or oil in the cooker or in a skillet. Sear the meat in it slowly on all sides. The meat may be seasoned lightly at this time and fully seasoned later. If you, as a novice, find it difficult to use this small amount of fat without scorching the meat, you may increase it to 4 or 5 table-spoonfuls. In this case pour off any fat that will pour after the meat is browned and before the liquid and other ingredients are added.

Cool the cooker to avoid undue evaporation when the liquid is added. Place the meat on a trivet in the cooker, add a hot liquid and cook as directed. Add only the amount of liquid specified in each recipe. There should always be some water or liquid in the bottom of the cooker to produce the necessary steam for cooking. The juice which remains in the pan after cooking will make delicious gravy.

If you wish the meat to be browned and are willing to sacrifice some juiciness for appearance, place it briefly under a broiler after it is cooked.

The time given for cooking meats is approximate, not exact. It is difficult to gauge the exact cooking time for cuts of meat and poultry, as age, shape, quality, amount of fat or bone, etc., must be taken into consideration. The thickness of the cut is more important than the size and shape in judging cooking time. A chunky piece of meat will take longer than a flat thinner cut. Follow instructions given in this chapter or in your pressure cooker booklet carefully.

Some manufacturers urge you to cook all meats at 10 pounds pressure or under. Others claim that much the same results are obtained by cooking meat at 15 pounds pressure. Some cookers are adjusted to 15 pounds only.

A few specific rules follow to acquaint the cook with the detailed manner of pressure cooking meats. The time chart, page 889, is a condensed version of the process, minus, for reasons of space, some of the vegetables and spices that may be added to the rule and that are to be found under similar rules in the Chapters on Meat and Poultry.

Go easy at first on seasoning. This may be added later to the finished dish.

POT ROAST
4 to 5 Servings
Heat in the cooker (see above):
    2 tablespoons fat
Brown in it slowly on all sides:
    A 2 or 3 lb. piece shoulder of
    beef, chuck, rump or top round
Remove the meat from the cooker.
Add and stir about:
    1 sliced onion
Place the meat in the cooker on a trivet. Add to the pot:
    4 tablespoons hot water
    1 teaspoon pepper
Place on the beef:
    ½ bay leaf
Adjust cover. Cook the meat (see page 876) at 15 pounds pressure for 11 minutes to the pound. Reduce heat instantly.

BEEF STEW
4 to 6 Servings
Cut into 1 inch cubes:
    1½ lbs. lean beef
Brown it (see above) slowly in the cooker in:

    2 tablespoons hot fat
Add, if desired:
    ½ diced or sliced onion
Add:
    2 cups boiling water
    ½ teaspoon salt
    2 peppercorns
    ½ bay leaf
Adjust cover. Cook (see page 876) at 15 pounds pressure for 25 minutes. Reduce pressure instantly.

SHORT RIBS OF BEEF
4 Servings
Cut into 8 pieces:
    2 lbs. short ribs
Dredge them with:
    ⅓ cup flour
Season with:
    Salt and pepper
Brown them (see above) slowly in the pressure cooker or in a skillet in:
    2 tablespoons hot fat
Add:
    ½ cup water
Adjust cover. Cook (see page 876) at 15 pounds pressure for 20 minutes. Re-

duce pressure instantly. If desired, add pared carrots and potatoes for the last 10 minutes of the cooking time (see page 876). See Anna's Short Ribs of Beef, page 344.

BARBECUED SHORT RIBS OF BEEF
6 Servings
Brown slowly but well in pressure cooker (page 887):

    3 lbs. short ribs of beef
in:
    2 tablespoons hot bacon fat
Add:
    ½ cup diced onion
Combine, heat and pour over the meat:
    ⅓ cup catsup
    ¼ cup vinegar
    2 tablespoons water
    2 teaspoons chili powder
    ½ teaspoon salt
Adjust cover. Cook the meat (see page 876) at 15 pounds pressure for 20 minutes. Reduce pressure instantly. Thicken liquid in the pan (page 887) with flour. Correct seasoning.

SWISS STEAK
6 to 8 Servings
Combine:
    ¾ cup flour
    2 teaspoons salt
    ¼ teaspoon pepper
Pound as much of this mixture as possible with the edge of a plate into:
    2 lbs. round steak ¾ inch thick
You may leave the steak whole or cut it into individual pieces. Brown the steak (see page 887) slowly in the cooker in:
    3 tablespoons hot fat
Add:
    ½ teaspoon brown sugar
    ¾ cup strained hot tomatoes or tomato juice
A nice variation is to substitute for the tomato juice the contents of:
    1 bottle pickled onions: 10 oz., the onion liquid mixed with water to make ¾ cup liquid in all
Adjust cover. Cook (see page 876) at 15 pounds pressure for 25 minutes. Reduce pressure instantly. Correct the seasoning.

STUFFED FLANK STEAK
4 Servings
Trim the edges of a:
    1¼ to 1½ lb. flank steak
Season it lightly with:

Salt and pepper
Spread it with dressing (see page 348) and roll it loosely. Tie it with string. Brown it slowly (see page 887) in the pressure cooker in:
    2 tablespoons hot fat
Add:
    1 cup hot tomato juice
    ¾ teaspoon brown sugar
    ½ teaspoon salt
Adjust cover. Cook the steak (see page 876) at 15 pounds pressure for 35 minutes. Reduce pressure instantly.

Dressing
Prepare the dressing under Flank Steak, page 348, or try this one. Combine:
    ¼ cup sausage meat
    1 pared sliced tart apple
    1½ cups fresh bread crumbs
    ½ teaspoon grated onion
    2 tablespoons chopped celery or parsley
    ⅓ cup hot water
    ¼ teaspoon salt
    (¼ teaspoon dried savory)

CORNED BEEF
6 to 8 Servings
Soak for 1 hour in cold water:
    3 to 4 lbs. corned beef: brisket
Drain it. Place it on a trivet in a cooker with:
    2 cups cold water
Add:
    1 bay leaf
    5 peppercorns
    1 small sliced onion
    3 whole cloves
    1 cut-up carrot
    ¼ cup cut-up celery with leaves
    (1 clove garlic)
Adjust cover. Cook the meat (see page 876) at 15 pounds pressure from 20 to 25 minutes to the pound. Reduce the heat instantly. Correct the seasoning.

MEAT LOAF
4 Servings
Combine and shape into a loaf:
    1 lb. ground beef
    2 lightly beaten eggs
    1 cup soft bread crumbs
    1 small chopped onion
    2 stalks chopped celery
    ¼ cup chopped green pepper
    2 tablespoons milk
    1 tablespoon horseradish
    ½ teaspoon dry mustard

2 tablespoons catsup
1¼ teaspoons salt
⅛ teaspoon pepper
If time permits, wrap the loaf in waxed paper and chill it in the refrigerator. Remove paper. Brown the loaf (or cook it slowly without browning in a greased loaf pan, or cook it wrapped in moistened parchment paper) slowly in:
3 tablespoons hot fat
Place it on a trivet. Add:
¼ cup hot water
Adjust cover. Cook the loaf (see page 876) at 15 pounds pressure for 15 minutes. Reduce heat instantly.

LIVER LOAF
The ingredients for the good Liver Loaf on page 384 may be steamed in containers, see Steamed Puddings, page 894, for 15 minutes, valve closed, at 15 pounds pressure.

CHILI CON CARNE
4 to 6 Servings
Never increase the amount of this recipe when using a 4 quart cooker as thick masses like this in a large quantity may clog the vent pipe.
Brown (page 887):
1 lb. ground beef
in:
2 tablespoons hot fat
Add and sauté lightly:
⅓ cup chopped onion
(1 minced clove garlic)
Add:

2 cups tomato purée or canned tomatoes: No. 2 can
2 cups cooked or canned kidney beans: No. 2 can
1½ teaspoons salt
⅛ teaspoon pepper
1 teaspoon chili powder
Adjust cover. Cook (see page 876) at 15 pounds pressure for 15 minutes. Reduce heat instantly. Correct the seasoning and add more chili powder if desired. Simmer for several minutes in cooker without cover until desired consistency is reached.

CHICKEN WITH CREAM GRAVY
3 to 4 Servings
Disjoint (page 390):
A 2 to 3 lb. chicken
Make Chicken Stock, page 394, of the wing tips, neck, back and gizzard. Dredge the other pieces in:
Seasoned Flour, page 540
Brown them slowly in a pressure cooker in:
4 tablespoons butter
Add:
¼ cup hot chicken stock
Adjust cover. Cook the chicken (see page 876) for 12 minutes at 15 pounds pressure. Reduce the pressure instantly. The chicken may be crisped in a 400° oven for a few minutes. Serve the chicken with:
Dumplings, page 420, and
Chicken Gravy, page 394

Time Chart for Meats and Fowl in Pressure Cooker

If you wish to cook meats at a lower pressure than 15 pounds, consult the booklet furnished with your pressure cooker.

Use seasoning lightly in food to be pressure cooked as there is very little liquid to dilute it. Correct the seasoning later as needed. Some of the following rules call for little or no seasoning. Do not hesitate to vary the flavor of these dishes by the substitution of tomato juice or stock for the water and the addition of a bay leaf, peppercorns, whole cloves, celery with leaves, carrots, onions, parsley, horseradish, mustard, catsup, etc. *in moderation.*

For amounts of meat per serving see page 334.

Cooking time begins when pressure reaches 15 pounds. Reduce pressure instantly at end of cooking period. Where asterisk appears reduce pressure gradually.

Beef, Flank Steak
Cut into serving pieces 1½ pounds flank steak. Dredge with flour. Brown slowly on all sides in 2 tablespoons hot fat (page 887). Cool. Season lightly. Add ½ cup boiling water. Cook 30 minutes in all.

Beef Heart
Remove fat, veins and arteries from a 2 pound beef heart. Brown heart slowly in 2 tablespoons hot fat in cooker (page 887). Cool. Season lightly. Add 1 cup boiling water. Cook 2 hours. See Stuffed Heart, page 381.

Beef Kidneys, sliced

Remove white center and tubes (page 380). Slice. Season lightly. Add 1 cup boiling water. Cook 7 to 8 minutes. See Creole Kidney Stew, page 380.

Beef Kidneys, whole

Remove white center and tubes (page 380). Season lightly. Add 1 cup boiling water. Cook 9 to 10 minutes. Use liquid in cooker for gravy.

Sauerbraten*

Prepare for cooking as directed on page 344 3 pounds beef. Brown slowly on all sides in 2 tablespoons hot fat (page 887). Cool. Add 2 cups liquid in which meat was soaked. Cook 45 minutes.
Make gravy from liquid left in pan. See page 426.

Short Ribs, see page 344.

Beef Tongue, corned

Add 2 cups water. Cook 20 minutes per pound. See page 385.

Beef Tongue, smoked

Soak in cold water for 2 hours. Bring to boil in fresh water. Drain. Season. Add 2 cups water. Cook 28 minutes per pound.
See Smoked Tongue Boiled, page 385.

Chicken, baked type*

Prepare and stuff a 3½ pound chicken as directed on page 390. Place in cooker. Add ¼ cup hot water. Cook 20 to 30 minutes in all. Brown under broiler or in a 400° oven after cooking.

Chicken, fried*

Use a 3½ pound frying chicken cut into pieces. Dredge in ½ cup of flour mixed with 1 teaspoon salt and ½ teaspoon pepper. Brown slowly on all sides in cooker in 3 tablespoons hot fat (page 887). Cool. Add 2 tablespoons hot water. Cook 14 minutes.

Chicken, stewed*

Singe, wash, clean and cut into pieces a 3½ pound chicken. Place in cooker with ½ cup diced celery, 2 teaspoons salt, ½ cup sliced onion. Add 2 cups water. Cook 20 minutes.

Lamb Breast

Stuff, brown slowly in 2 tablespoons hot fat (page 887). Season. Add 2 tablespoons hot water. Cook 35 minutes.

Lamb Kidney

Remove skin, tubes and fat. See page 380. Season. Add 2 tablespoons hot water. Cook 4 minutes.

Lamb Shanks

Split in half and brown slowly in 2 tablespoons hot fat (page 887). Add 1 small onion chopped. Cool. Season. Add ¼ cup hot water. Cook 90 minutes.

Lamb Shoulder

Brown slowly in 2 tablespoons hot fat 3 pounds lamb shoulder. Season. Add ¼ cup hot water. Cook 60 minutes. Add vegetables for the last few minutes of cooking. See Braised Roast of Lamb, page 361.

Lamb Stew

Cut meat in 1 inch pieces. Dredge with flour. Season. Brown slowly in 2 tablespoons hot fat. Cool. Add ½ cup hot water. Cook 20 minutes in all.

Lamb Tongues

To prepare, see page 385. Add ¾ cup water. Cook 20 to 25 minutes.

Oxtails, see page 386.

Pork Chops

Rub flour into 4 chops, each ¼ inch thick. Brown slowly on both sides in 1 tablespoon hot fat. Pour off excess fat. Season. Cool. Add 2 tablespoons hot water. Cook 12 minutes.

Pork Loin

3 or 4 pounds. Brown slowly on all sides in 2 tablespoons hot fat. Pour off excess fat. Season. Cool. Add ½ cup hot water. Cook 20 minutes per pound.

Pork Shoulder

Brown slowly on all sides in 2 tablespoons hot fat. Pour off excess fat. Season. Cool. Add ½ cup hot water. Cook 18 to 20 minutes per pound.

Ham Slice, tenderized

¾ inch thick. Brown slowly in 1 teaspoon hot fat. Cool. Add 2 tablespoons hot water. Cook 6 minutes in all.

Ham Slice, not tenderized

Add 2 tablespoons hot water. Cook 15 minutes.

Ham Butts

2 smoked bones ham butts, ¼ cup granulated sugar, ¼ teaspoon dry mustard, ¼ teaspoon powdered cloves, ¼

teaspoon cinnamon, 2 tablespoons grated orange rind. Add 1⅓ cups hot water or fruit juice—orange, pineapple, etc. Cook 6 minutes per pound.

Spareribs

2 pounds. Brown slowly in 2 tablespoons hot fat. Cool. Season with salt and pepper. Add 2 tablespoons hot water. Cook 15 minutes in all. If further browning is desired when cooked, place under broiler, brush with barbecue sauce. Watch carefully to prevent burning. Cook sauerkraut separately.

Spareribs Barbecued

Follow recipe on page 369. Add ½ cup hot liquid. Cook 15 minutes in all.

Rabbit

Clean, cut into pieces. Dredge with seasoned flour. Brown slowly in 2 tablespoons hot fat (page 887). Cool. Add 3 tablespoons hot water. Cook 20 to 25 minutes in all.

Tripe

Honeycomb, see page 387 for preparation. Add 2 cups boiling water. Cook 1 hour.

Regular. See Tripe, page 387. Add 2 cups boiling water. Cook 1½ to 2 hours.

Veal Birds*

Prepare veal birds for cooking as directed on page 359. Brown slowly in 2 tablespoons hot fat (page 887). Add ¼ cup hot water. Cook 15 minutes.

Veal Roast

Brown veal shoulder slowly on both sides in 2 tablespoons hot fat (page 887). Cool the pot. Place the roast on a trivet. Season with salt and pepper. Add 2 tablespoons hot water. Cook 20 minutes per pound.

Veal Stew

Brown cubes of veal slowly in 2 tablespoons hot fat (page 887). Season. Add 1 cup hot water. Cook 15 to 20 minutes in all.
See Veal Stew, page 358.

Veal Tongue, large

For preparation see Calf Tongue, page 386. Add 1 cup hot water. Cook 45 minutes in all.

DUMPLINGS

Follow the rule on page 420 for:
Dumplings
You may add:
3 tablespoons chopped parsley or chives or 1 tablespoon grated onion
Drop the batter from a spoon into hot stew, or into at least 3 cupfuls stock or water in the pressure cooker. Adjust cover. Steam over low heat, vent open, for 5 minutes.

SPOON BREAD

This will taste as good as oven-baked spoon bread but will look less tempting. Prepare by the rule on page 423:
Spoon Bread
Fill a greased tin or mold ⅔ full of batter. Cover it with aluminum foil or 3 thicknesses of waxed paper secured with string. Place mold on trivet. Add to the cooker 2 cupfuls water. Cook the bread (see page 876) without pressure with the valve open for 4 minutes. Close valve, bring pressure to 15 pounds and cook it for 12 minutes. Reduce heat gradually.

SHRIMP
3 or 4 Servings
Wash and drain:
1 lb. shrimp
Cover the bottom of a pressure cooker with:
¼ inch water
to which you may add:
A slice of onion
¼ bay leaf
1 slice lemon
2 diced ribs celery
⅛ teaspoon salt
A few grains cayenne
Adjust cover. Cook the shrimp (see page 876) at 15 pounds pressure from 2½ to 5 minutes, according to size. Reduce pressure instantly. See Index for dishes calling for boiled shrimp.

STEAMED CLAMS
4 Servings
Prepare for cooking (see page 251):
36 live clams
Place in cooker:
¼ cup hot water
Add clams. Adjust cover, cook (see page 876) at 15 pounds pressure for 3

minutes. Reduce pressure instantly. Serve clams in shells with:

Melted butter and lemon juice

LOBSTER TAILS

Bring to a rolling boil in cooker:

2 cups water

Plunge into it:

Lobster tails

Adjust cover. Cook (see page 876) at 15 pounds pressure for 8 minutes. Reduce pressure instantly.

FROZEN MEATS, FOWL AND SHELLFISH

Please read the paragraph in the introduction to Pressure Cooked Meats, page 887, about the difficulty of gauging the exact time for cooking meats. Have all roasts partially or entirely thawed, page 870. Frozen chops should be partially defrosted, a whole fowl entirely thawed. A cut-up fowl need only be defrosted to the point where it may be broken apart.

Meat that is not defrosted may be pressure cooked but it has a tendency to cook unevenly. It calls for a longer cooking period than fresh meat. Allow about ½ to ¾ again as much time as given in the Meat Chart on page 889 and increase the water measurement to about double the amount.

When browning frozen meats be sure to use a moderate temperature to avoid unnecessary shrinkage. See Browning Meats, page 887. Read about Pressure Cooked Meats on page 886.

Shellfish—clams, lobster, shrimp, etc.—need not be defrosted before cooking.

BAKED APPLES

4 Servings

Wash, remove core to ½ inch of stem end, then cut a strip of peel from one of the hollowed ends of:

4 large tart apples

Combine:

4 tablespoons brown sugar
1 tablespoon cinnamon

Fill the centers with this. Dot the tops with:

Butter

Place trivet in cooker, add ½ cupful hot water. Place apples on trivet. Adjust cover. Cook (see page 876) the apples 3 to 4 minutes at 15 pounds pressure. Reduce the pressure instantly.

PURÉED FRUITS

Place prepared fruit, sugar and water in a cooker. Have the cooker only ½ full. Allow ½ cupful of sugar and ½ cupful of water to 1 pound of fruit, unless the fruit is very dry like apricots, when 1 cupful of water is required. Proceed to pressure cook the fruit, page 876. Rhubarb and fresh apricots are brought up to 15 pounds pressure and the pressure is reduced instantly. Peaches and pears, if hard, may require 5 minutes' cooking at 15 pounds pressure. Reduce heat instantly. Apples, rhubarb and cranberries tend to sputter. Do not remove cover until all steam is exhausted. The cooking of these fruits is not recommended by all manufacturers.

DRIED FRUITS

These are not soaked. Sugar is added after the fruit is cooked. Fill the pressure cooker only ⅔ full. When cooking pressure is reached (see page 876) start counting cooking time. After cooking time is up, allow the fruit to stand until pressure is reduced.

Fruit	Amount of water	Time to cook at 15 pounds pressure
Apricots		
1 cup	1½ cups	0 minutes
Figs		
1 cup	1 cup	4 or 5 minutes
Peaches		
1 cup	1½ cups	0 minutes
Pears		
1 cup	1 cup	0 minutes
Prunes		
1 cup	1 cup	0 minutes
Raisins		
1 cup	1 cup	0 minutes

EXTRACTING FRUIT JUICE FOR JELLY

When fruit for jelly making is cooked in a pressure cooker instead of in an open kettle, anywhere from ⅕ to ¼ more juice is extracted. As jelly should always be made in small quantities for best results, a cooker is ideally suited to this purpose. Wash and prepare the fruit according to your usual recipe. Add the desired amount of water, remembering that the less water used the more concentrated a fruit flavor will be obtained. Adjust the cover and quickly bring the pressure up to its highest point. Remove at once from the heat and let pressure recede of its own accord. Strain the juice through a jelly bag without squeezing and proceed as usual.

BOSTON BROWN BREAD
2 Loaves
Follow the rule on page 537, using ½ the ingredients, for:
Boston Brown Bread
Partially fill two 1 pint greased molds or tins. Cover them with aluminum foil or 3 thicknesses of waxed paper secured with string. Place the molds on a trivet or rack in the pressure cooker. Add 2 cupfuls hot water. Adjust cover. Steam over low heat for 15 minutes without pressure, that is, with the valve open, then cook (see page 876) for 30 minutes at 15 pounds pressure. Reduce heat instantly.

MOCK BOSTON BROWN BREAD
2 Loaves
Sift:
　¾ cup all-purpose flour
　4 teaspoons tartrate or phosphate baking powder or 3 teaspoons double-acting baking powder (see Baking Powder, page 501)
　1 teaspoon soda
　½ teaspoon salt
Add:
　1 cup fine graham cracker crumbs
Cut in with a pastry blender or 2 knives:
　3 tablespoons shortening
Stir in:
　(½ cup raisins)
Mix together and add to the dry ingredients:
　1 well-beaten egg
　¾ cup buttermilk or sour milk
　½ cup molasses
Divide the batter equally between 2 well-greased No. 2 tin cans. Cover the cans with aluminum foil or 3 thicknesses of waxed paper secured with string. Bring to the boiling point in the pressure cooker:
　1 cup water
Place the cans in the cooker and adjust cover. When 15 pounds pressure is reached (see page 876) reduce heat and cook for 30 minutes. Reduce pressure instantly.

BROWN BETTY
Follow the rule on page 723 for:
Brown Betty
Place it in a greased baking tin or mold, filling it only ⅔ full. Cover it closely with aluminum foil or 3 thicknesses of waxed paper secured with string. Add to the cooker:
　¾ cup water
Place trivet in cooker and mold upon it. Secure cover. Steam for 5 minutes, vent open. Close vent. Cook at 15 pounds pressure (page 876) for 10 minutes.

RICE PUDDING
6 Servings
Soak for 15 minutes:
　½ cup rice
In:
　¼ cup water
Place it in a pressure cooker and bring it to the boiling point with:
　2¾ cups milk
Stir it gently. Adjust cover. Cook it (see page 876) at 15 pounds pressure for 1½ minutes. Remove pan from heat. When pressure is down, mix together and add while rice is still hot:
　2 well-beaten eggs
　¼ cup sugar
　½ teaspoon salt
　½ cup washed raisins
　1 teaspoon vanilla or grated lemon rind
Stir well. Cover and let stand for 5 minutes or more. Serve hot or cold with:
　Cream

CUSTARD
Follow the rule on page 710 for:
Danish Custard
Use the brown sugar sauce or omit it. This without the brown sugar is much like the delicate French flan; with the brown sugar it has a caramel sauce. Pour the ingredients into an oiled casserole. Cover it closely. Place in the pressure cooker ½ cupful hot water. Place the casserole on a trivet in the cooker and adjust cover. Bring to 15 pounds pressure (see page 876) and cook for 2 minutes. Reduce heat gradually.

CHOCOLATE CUSTARD
Prepare:
　Danish Custard, page 710
Cut into small pieces and add to the milk:
　1½ oz. unsweetened chocolate:
　1½ squares
Stir until the chocolate is dissolved. Proceed as for custard above, omitting brown sugar.

"STEAM" PUDDINGS

Thanks to the pressure cooker we may now have the popular old-time steamed puddings in short order.

Puddings may be cooked in custard cups or a deep mold or bowl, the tops covered with aluminum foil or 3 thicknesses of waxed paper secured well with string, in a casserole similarly covered, or covered with a tightly fitted lid. For easy handling allow at least ½ inch of space all around between the mold and the cooker. Do not fill mold more than ⅔ full. Place it on a trivet. Pour around the mold 2 to 2½ cupfuls of boiling water. This is sufficient for a 4-quart cooker.

Most pressure cooked puddings that contain baking powder or soda are cooked at first without pressure; that is, with the lid of the pressure cooker adjusted but with the vent open and without the pressure weight. Exact time is given in the following rules for this preliminary step. Then the vent is closed and the puddings are cooked at 15 pounds pressure until done.

PLUM PUDDING

6 Servings

Sift:

½ cup flour
½ teaspoon baking soda
½ teaspoon salt
½ teaspoon cinnamon
¼ teaspoon nutmeg

Add:

½ cup dry bread crumbs

Mix together and add to the dry ingredients:

½ cup raisins
¾ cup currants
¼ cup chopped citron or candied lemon peel

Combine and beat:

½ cup ground suet
½ cup firmly packed brown sugar
¼ cup milk
1 well-beaten egg

Mix these ingredients with the fruit mixture and the dry ingredients. Place the batter in a well-greased pudding mold; a 1 pound coffee can will do. Cover it closely with a lid or 3 thicknesses of waxed paper secured with string. Place in the pressure pan on a trivet with 2 cupfuls of boiling water. Adjust cover. Place it over low heat and steam for 30 minutes with the valve open, then cook (see page 876) at 15 pounds pressure for 50 minutes. Reduce pressure instantly. Serve plum pudding hot with:

Hard Sauce, page 754

To serve flaming, see page 751.

CHOCOLATE PUDDING

Melt:

2½ oz. chocolate

If preferred, ¼ cupful cocoa may be substituted. Sift it with the dry ingredients. Blend until creamy:

3 tablespoons butter
⅔ cup sugar

Beat in:

1 egg

Sift before measuring:

2¼ cups flour

Resift with:

4½ teaspoons phosphate or tartrate baking powder or 3¼ teaspoons combination type (see Baking Powder, page 501)
¼ teaspoon salt

Add the flour mixture to the butter mixture in about 3 parts alternately with:

1 cup milk

Add the melted chocolate. Pour the batter into a greased mold, filling it only ⅔ full. Cover the top closely with a lid, or with aluminum foil or 3 thicknesses of waxed paper tied with string. Place pudding on a trivet or rack in cooker, add 2 cupfuls hot water. Adjust cover. Steam over low heat for 15 minutes without pressure, vent open, then cover vent and bring to 15 pounds pressure and cook (see page 876) for 25 minutes. Reduce heat at once.

MOLASSES PUDDING

4 Servings

Follow the rule on page 731 for:

Steamed Molasses Pudding

Cover the top with aluminum foil or 3 thicknesses of waxed paper secured with string. Place the mold on a trivet in a pressure cooker. Put 2 cupfuls hot water in the pressure pan. Adjust cover. Steam the pudding over low heat without pressure, vent open, for 20 minutes. Close the vent, bring pressure to 15 pounds (see page 876) and cook it for 20 minutes. Reduce the heat gradually. Serve the pudding with sauce as directed.

The Electric Blender

Throw away your tamis cloth and hair sieve, if you still have these relics of a by-gone age, and replace them with the piece of equipment that makes them obsolete, the electric blender. Only the ghost of an old-time medicine man could do justice to its usefulness and fascination, so please give it a chance to speak for itself. Besides, it is so much better than its reputation, that of making an A-1 alcoholic drink.

What else will a blender do? It will crush, blend and purée food in a few seconds with a better result than you could possibly achieve by any other means in a very much longer time. An electric mixer needs special attachments to do a similar job. A blender will liquefy fruits and vegetables and some blenders will grind nut meats, raisins, citron, meat, lentils, etc. It will purée spinach, make a Vichyssoise, a cream soup, a fresh or cooked vegetable bisque of a velvety smoothness, a sherbetlike fresh fruit drink, etc., in a few minutes of effortless application. It will also blend ingredients for batters like popovers, muffins, pancakes and waffles in short order, but the results are not quite so good as when conventional methods are used.

One of the few things the blender will not do satisfactorily is to whip egg whites. These become too fluffy, too airy. Otherwise, says a correspondent, it will do everything but "put out the cat."

There are several makes of blender on the market, one of them invented by a bandmaster. If your budget permits, buy a blender by all means; if it does not, pinch, scrape and sacrifice to be the possessor of this kitchen marvel. In the long run it is an economy, for it is ready to utilize refrigerator scraps and to make them into palatable dishes.

Suggestions for Hot Blender Soups

Marion says that she no longer has "hang-over" food remnants in her refrigerator, for her noon menu is often left-over blender soup. Dump a bit of meat, cubed, or fish, an odd carrot, cut up, some cress or lettuce and the last of last night's Lima beans into the blender with a liquid like milk, stock or tomato juice and in a split minute a soup of fine smooth consistency is ready to be heated. Some of these and other soups are improved by the addition of 1 or 2 tablespoonfuls of sherry.

It is advisable to cut up raw food coarsely before putting it into the blender. Raw meat may form disagreeable curds in cooking which can be made to vanish by reblending after heating.

Mushrooms cooked or uncooked are a fine addition.

Rub the container with garlic or add onion very sparingly for good additional flavor.

Combine ingredients in any proportion to suit your taste or convenience. Chiffonade effects are gained with parsley, cress, celery leaves, outer lettuce leaves, spinach, etc., added to clear stock. A "cream" quality is gained with cream sauce, cream, egg yolks, milk and the use of canned cream soups or such vegetables as Lima beans and potatoes or small chunks of cooked veal stew or steak.

Good Combinations:

1 can cream of chicken soup, 1 cupful cress, ½ cupful parsley, a fresh pared cucumber, seeded if old, plus a cupful or two stock-pot liquor or milk. This is good, especially when chilled.

1 can green pea soup, left-over blender spinach or raw spinach, parsley, ham bone stock or milk, or both.

1 can tomato soup, milk or stock, parsley, celery leaves, etc.

General Comments:

Raw rhubarb, pineapple, outer celery stalks and foods with a fairly tough cellulose structure become stringy or grainy and are only recommended for concoctions which are further softened by cooking or straining.

One teaspoonful grated onion may be added to a mixture that is to be served uncooked, but if raw onions in quantity are used their flavor will be disagreeably strong and they must be cooked until the flavor is mild.

Avoid adding boiling hot liquids to blender. Cool them to prevent cracking the container. Fill the container only about ⅔ full to avoid overflowing. If you have a larger amount of ingredients to blend, put them through in several batches.

Always place the lid on the container before turning on the blender to avoid spurting.

BLENDER VICHYSSOISE
3 Servings
Superlative! Made in about 20 minutes by using a blender and pressure cooker. Serve it hot or chill it quickly by placing it in a refrigerator tray or deep freeze. Follow the rule on page 64 for:

Vichyssoise
Use ½ the amount of ingredients given. After adding the potatoes and stock, pressure cook the soup for 3 minutes at 15 pounds pressure. Cool it. Blend it covered until smooth, about 1 minute. Place the soup in a jar. Chill it thoroughly. You may add the cream, but you will probably like the velvety result just as well without cream. Hot or cold, sprinkle the top with:

Chopped chives

BLENDER BORSCH
3 Servings
Canned beets are fine for this. Blend covered for 2 minutes:

1 cup bouillon or stock
1 cup beet liquor
2 tablespoons sour cream
2 teaspoons lemon juice
½ teaspoon salt
A grating of pepper
Thin lemon peel, about 1 tablespoon
1 cup canned or cooked sliced beets

Serve hot or thoroughly chilled topped with:

½ cup whipped sour cream
Chopped chives

In summer keep a can of beets and one of consommé on ice. Combine these with ½ cupful water and 1 or 2 tablespoonfuls catsup. Blend, season and serve as directed, or combine the beets,

1 can of consommé and 1 can of cream of chicken soup. Blend. Season and serve.

BLENDER COLD CUCUMBER SOUP
See Rule on page 64. Place ingredients in blender. Cover. Blend the mixture until it is smooth. Chill it. Serve it with chopped chives.

BLENDER ONION SOUP
3 Servings
Sauté covered over low heat for ¼ hour, stirring frequently:

2 cups sliced onions

in:

3 tablespoons fat

Remove cover for the last 5 minutes. Place in the container the cooled onions and:

2 cups beef or chicken stock
2 or 3 tender ribs celery with leaves
2 or 3 sprigs parsley

Cover container and run blender for 30 seconds. Serve hot like Onion Soup, page 52.

BLENDER CREAM SOUPS
4 Servings
Place in container, cover and blend until smooth:

2 cups milk or part cream, part stock or vegetable stock
2 tablespoons flour
2 tablespoons soft butter
½ teaspoon salt
⅙ teaspoon pepper
1 thin slice onion
2 to 3 sprigs parsley or
¼ cup celery leaves
Raw, canned or cooked vegetables cut up coarsely

Stir and cook over low heat until soup boils, about 5 minutes. Season as needed with salt. For vegetables use: Asparagus, ⅔ cupful; corn, 1 cupful; raw unpeeled cucumber, 2 cupfuls; 6 to 8 mushroom caps, stems sautéed. Spinach, if raw, 2 cupfuls tightly packed; if cooked, ⅓ cupful. If you use 1 cupful peas, cut the flour to 1 tablespoonful. If using cooked leftover food, do not season soup until ready to serve it. Heat and serve.

BLENDER BISQUES

Use the basic ingredients given above for blender cream soups. Omit seasoning, depending on how rich a soup you like, add or reduce flour to 1 tablespoonful, substitute for the raw, canned or cooked vegetables:

> ½ cup cooked chicken, ⅔ cup cooked or canned crab meat or fish flakes, ½ cup lobster meat, ½ cup salmon, ⅔ cup shrimp, 3 raw oysters or ½ cup diced cooked meat: beef, lamb, veal or ham

Stir and cook over heat as directed for blender cream soups. Season and serve.

BLENDER CHICKEN EGGNOG

3 Servings
Heat:

> 2 cups chicken broth

Blend covered for about 15 seconds:

> 2 eggs
> 1 tablespoon lemon juice
> ⅛ teaspoon salt
> A grating of pepper
> 2 tablespoons sherry

Remove cover. Add the hot broth very slowly to container with blender running. Place in jar and chill thoroughly. Serve with:

> Chopped parsley

SUGGESTIONS FOR COLD BLENDER FRUIT SOUPS OR SHERBETS

A frothy thick texture is achieved by adding to fruit juice a raw apple, cooked rhubarb or cracked ice cubes. A smoother, heavier result comes from use of egg yolks and cream. A fairly creamy result comes from a fresh peach, a banana or canned pineapple juice. A velvety concoction is:

> 1 small banana
> 1 cup milk

Add vanilla or rum, no sugar needed. You may add to this 1 tablespoonful chocolate sirup or 4 tablespoonfuls vanilla ice cream.

Also try stewed or canned apricots with milk, apricot, pineapple and lemon juice with cracked ice cubes, frozen strawberries with sour or sweet cream. Interesting flavors may be added through the use of small quantities of jelly or jam. Vary flavor with honey sweetening. Almost any fruit is usable unless it is very seedy or has long tough fibers like pineapple.

BLENDER GRAPE DRINK

Individual Serving
Combine:

> ½ cup grape juice
> 1 tablespoon lime or lemon juice
> 1 teaspoon sugar or honey
> 1 egg yolk

Put cover on blender and run it about 30 seconds.

BLENDER HEALTH DRINK

Individual Serving
Place in blender container and run until thoroughly blended:

> 1 peeled and sectioned navel orange
> 2 tablespoons lemon juice
> 1 egg yolk
> 1 tablespoon sugar or honey
> (1 cup finely chopped ice)

BLENDER PURÉED VEGETABLES

The blender is a find for mothers of young children. Raw vegetables may be blended and then cooked until they boil. Or, vegetables may be barely cooked, the pressure cooker is wonderful for this, cooled and then blended. Butter and cream may be added.

BLENDER SPINACH

4 Servings
Wash, remove coarse stems from about 12 ounces of spinach. Place ½ cupful milk, sour cream, stock or water in the container. Run blender. Feed the spinach into it gradually. When blended, heat, add butter and seasoning, or cream it (page 313).
Or cook spinach (page 313), put it very briefly through a blender. Cream it as directed.
Or, as a timesaver when making creamed spinach follow the next rule.

BLENDER SPINACH DISH

4 Servings

Place in blender:

    1 cup milk
    1 thin slice onion
    3 tablespoons soft butter
    2 tablespoons flour
    ½ teaspoon salt
    ⅛ teaspoon paprika
    A fresh grating of nutmeg or
    lemon rind
    (½ skinned clove garlic)

Turn on blender. Feed into it gradually:

    12 oz. spinach, coarse stems
    removed

When smooth, stir this mixture over low heat for about 2 minutes, until it bubbles and the flour is cooked. Serve with:

    Buttered crumbs
    4 slices cooked crumbled bacon
    2 sliced hard-cooked eggs

CUSTARD

Follow any rule for custard. Blend ingredients briefly without heating, pour into cups and bake as directed on page 710. This makes a good quick custard:

    2 cups milk
    3 whole eggs
    ¼ to ⅓ cup sugar
    1 teaspoon vanilla
    A pinch of salt

QUICK BLENDER TRICKS

For meat loaf. When in haste place all ingredients, except the meat, in a blender. Combine the blended ingredients with the ground meat.

For Spaghetti Sauce, page 92. Blend all the ingredients for spaghetti sauce after sautéing and cooling the onion. Cook the sauce.

For Fish Mousse, page 479, and similar dishes. You may avoid grinding the raw fish by using the blender.

For quick mixing and improving texture of pie fillings, commercial puddings and cocoa before heating.

For cheese spreads. Blend hard cheeses with a little cream and your favorite seasonings.

For French Dressing, page 491. Blended French dressing does not separate or need shaking for 4 or 5 days.

For ice creams. Many ice cream mixtures may be rapidly and satisfactorily combined in a blender. Example: Put in the container some of the liquid called for in the ice cream recipe you choose. Add fruit, sugar and flavoring, etc. If you use frozen fruit, break up the block into pieces. Blend and combine with remaining ingredients.

For cleaning. Even the messiest mixtures are freed from blades by adding soap chips or detergents to water and running the blender for a few seconds.

High Altitude Cookery

Miss Emma Thiessen, of whom more later on, reminds us that "Boiling water's not so hot, way up on the mountain top" and that it becomes increasingly cooler the higher the elevation. In fact, it may boil when lukewarm on some of the higher mountain peaks. This means that rules used successfully at sea level and up to about 2,000 feet may fail dismally when applied in the higher regions.

Betty Ely, an experienced General Foods Home Economist, now of Denver, writes: "Bewilderment is the general state of the new cook in high altitudes." It is also the state of the cookbook writer who must in this case rely on the experience of others.

A great deal of serious research has been done by scientists in food laboratories and the information given here is derived from their findings and published with their consent.

Water boils at sea level at 212° and after that the boiling point drops 1 degree every 500 feet above it. This condition affects the timing of boiled foods—stews, vegetables, fruits, sirups, etc., and deep fat frying. It also affects the following foods:

Yeast bread dough rises more rapidly at high altitudes, and it may become overproofed if it is not watched carefully and allowed to rise only until it is doubled in bulk. Less yeast may be used, but most bakers prefer to let the dough rise for a shorter time. Because flour dries out faster at high altitudes, it may be necessary to use more liquid to compensate for this loss and to make the dough the proper consistency.

With *biscuits, muffins* and *quick breads,* the baking powder may be decreased slightly, but the structure of the product is such that it will withstand the increased internal pressure quite well.

Pie crust is not affected by altitude except for the higher rate of evaporation; slightly more liquid may be required.

Cookies usually do not need adjustment for altitude, although a slight reduction in baking powder and sugar may improve them.

Cake doughs are subject to a pixylike variation of mood that seems to defy all general rules. Not only must cake ingredients be adjusted to suit the altitude but also to suit the locality. The newcomer must therefore adapt herself to these changes before she can serve her meals on time and produce once more the opulent, featherweight cakes she has been accustomed to baking.

The expectant cake baker is sometimes presented with a graph. Can you read a graph? Among the fairies that stood at my cradle the mathematical one was conspicuously absent—or on a binge—for I struggle helplessly with graphs and assume that others are similarly afflicted. If you have a vagrant mind and wish to sally forth to bake on your own, armed with your old general rules plus a graph, there is no restriction placed on your venture. Paper, pencil and persistence may lead you past guesswork to genuine achievement. But if you have a stay-at-home mentality, do not despair. There are many authoritative booklets available with usable recipes that are fully understandable. So, instead of struggling with slide rule and perplexities comprehensible only to the trained mind, such as: "Each and all of these adjustments may be required to a greater or lesser degree, for every recipe is different in richness and balance of ingredients and only repeated experiments with each recipe can give you the most successful proportions to use," you may turn with appreciation and relief to the definite information of such blessed publications as the following which may be had "for free" or for a small charge:

"Cake Making at High Altitudes," Frances Barton,
  General Foods Corporation, 250 Park Avenue, New York.
"Cakes—Cookies, Recipes for Different Altitudes."
  Colorado Agricultural Experiment Station, Colorado A. and M. College,
  Fort Collins, Colorado.
"Mile High Cakes" by Elizabeth Dyer and Elizabeth Cassel,
  Colorado Agricultural Experiment Station, Colorado A. and M. College,
  Fort Collins, Colorado.
"Food Preparation at High Altitudes" by Mariana W. Kulas,
  Colorado Agricultural Experiment Station, Colorado A. and M. College,
  Fort Collins, Colorado.
"Baking Quick Breads and Cakes at High Altitudes" by Marjorie W. Peterson,
  Colorado State College, Colorado.
"High Altitude Vegetable Cookery" by Emma J. Thiessen,
  University of Wyoming Agricultural Experiment Station,
  Laramie, Wyoming.
"Deep Fat Frying at High Altitudes,"
  University of Wyoming Agricultural Experiment Station,
  Laramie, Wyoming.

Now while we are waiting for one or all of these helpful booklets to arrive, let us consider a few rules taken from the above and other authoritative sources to use in an emergency:

Baked vegetables and meats require no adjustment up to 7,000 feet. After that a somewhat longer period of time may be required. Mrs. House of Nederland, Colorado, who has experimented for the Pet Milk Company, writes that she frequently adds a small amount of water to the pan near the end of the roasting period for meats.

Sugar cookery is affected by high altitudes. You may decide to discard your candy thermometer and disregard all degrees given for cooking sirups at sea level and to revert to the old-fashioned tests—thread stage, soft, hard ball and crack stage—given on page 781.

Doughs for deep fat frying, fritters, doughnuts, etc., have to be adjusted. The temperature of the fat is reduced somewhat for these foods, and sometimes for potato chips. See the rule for Doughnuts on page 544 and the Deep Fat Frying booklet mentioned above.

Vegetable Cookery at High Altitudes

In Miss Thiessen's explicit booklet from which the following facts are gleaned you will find much additional valuable information, as well as charts to guide you.

The rules given in the vegetable chapter of The Joy, page 262, for the preparation and cooking of vegetables may be applied for the cooking of similar vegetables at high altitudes with the following exceptions. Since boiling water at 7,200 feet is 13.1° cooler than at sea level the cooking periods for vegetables must be lengthened; also it may be necessary to use more water. Experiments made at the University of Wyoming at this elevation show that beets, cauliflower and onions required the greatest increase in time, around 55% to 60% more time or an increase of about 9% to 11% for each 1,000 feet rise of elevation. Mature snap beans needed 44% to 50% more time or an increase of about 7% to 8% for each 1,000 feet rise. Squash, green cabbage, turnips and parsnips required approximately 20% to 25% more time or an increase of about 4% for each 1,000 feet in rise. If vegetables such as carrots and beets are old, the cooking time is further increased.

In these tests cabbage, turnips, cauliflower, broccoli and other strong-flavored vegetables were cut up or divided into pieces of small size to facilitate quicker cooking, thereby preventing the development of strong odors and flavor through long boiling. As cooking leafy vegetables often results in a tough rib and an overcooked leaf, the tough ribs of kale, mustard greens and mature spinach were removed and discarded. Since vegetables vary in size, age and freshness in any altitude only approximate cooking periods can be given for them.

Rules for the handling of vegetables at sea level, page 262, apply to vegetables in high altitudes as well, and here as elsewhere the best general method is cooking by pressure. For particulars see the paragraphs below on vegetable cookery at high altitudes and read the general directions for vegetables in the Chapter on Pressure Cookery, page 882.

Frozen Vegetable Cookery at High Altitudes

For the preparation of frozen vegetables see page 870. Cook them closely covered in a pan or in a pressure cooker. Tests showed that such frozen vegetables as snap beans and vegetable mixes required about 5 to 12 minutes more cooking at the high compared with a low elevation. The majority of frozen vegetables need but 1 to 2 minutes additional cooking.

Baked Vegetables

Vegetables may be baked at high altitudes in approximately the same time required at low altitudes when similar temperatures are used.

Pressure Cookery in High Altitudes

It is a decided advantage to use a pressure cooker in high altitudes as elsewhere, since it is possible to raise temperatures within it high enough to insure the complete sterilization of canned products and the quick cooking of other foods. Canning temperatures, however, as well as those used for everyday cooking do not escape the effects of altitude and adjustments are therefore necessary. See paragraph under Time Chart for Canning, page 847, and Processing Time for Meat, page 856.

A cooker geared to 5, 10 and 15 pounds of steam is recommended for the highest quality in cooked foods. It is essential that your cooker be provided with an accurate gauge. The extension division of most land grant colleges will test your gauge free of charge.

Charts are also provided by the same authority that enable the cook to achieve the best results possible in high altitude vegetable cooking.

Repeated experiments at the Wyoming State College show that the cooking of vegetables at 15 pounds pressure at both sea level and at 7,200 feet brought about varied results. Vegetables that required the greatest increase in time were Irish potatoes, whole beets, whole yams and mature snap beans. Asparagus, sliced carrots and celery need only 1 or 2 minutes additional time. Spinach, corn, peas and cabbage cooked in similar periods of time at both high and low altitudes.

Cabbage, if shredded, was overcooked when the gauge reached 15 pounds pressure and was considerably better when cooked at 10 pounds. Texture and color of asparagus, celery, turnips and cauliflower were all better cooked at 10 pounds pressure than at 15. If a chart is not available to you, make your own by jotting down the results of your trials and errors. Test vegetables both at 10 and at 15 pounds of steam in order to determine your preference. Your notes will soon enable you to arrive at accurate cooking periods provided the age and the condition of the vegetable will co-operate.

The water measurement for 2 cupfuls of vegetables when cooked is usually ¼ cupful for a short cooking period and ½ cupful for longer ones. The 2 tablespoonfuls suggested in some publications for leafy vegetables at sea level did not prove sufficient to hold a pressure of 15 pounds in high altitudes.

It is always advisable to undercook rather than to overcook vegetables. Should you find your vegetable objectionably underdone a very brief period of additional cooking will remedy the evil.

Pressure Cooked Meats

Tests showed that these have less shrinkage and more flavor if cooked at 10 rather than at 15 pounds pressure. The subject of high altitude cooking is like a greased pig, but even a greased pig has been known to be brought to slaughter. In my fan mail there is a letter from a seasoned mountain cook who is now living at sea level. She is in despair, burns or overcooks all her food and doesn't know how to bake. Her situation is deplorable, but newcomers to high altitudes may find it amusing in reverse.

Cakes

The following suggestions are to be found in the booklet, "Cakes—Cookies, Recipes for Different Altitudes":

"Sheet and layer cakes are easier to bake than loaf cakes. . . .

"Dried-out flour has caused many baking failures. . . .

"You cannot incorporate more air in a sponge cake batter after the flour has been added. However, you can remove air from a sponge cake batter that is too light by continuing the folding after the flour has been added. . . .

"Most natural shortenings, such as butter and lard, should be used in cakes that are relatively low in sugar and liquid. Use hydrogenated shortenings for richer cakes."

And, of course, I cannot resist the touch of humor in: "Old sayings are based on experience, more often they are grounded on fiction."

The following rules for cakes are from Frances Barton's booklet, "Cake Making at High Altitudes." They are published with the consent of The General Foods Corporation of New York. These cakes are based on the use of Swans Down Cake Flour and Calumet Baking Powder.

They may be variously filled and iced. For suggestions see pages 693 and 705.

SILVER MOON WHITE CAKE
I. For 5,000 Feet Altitude

Preparations:

Have the shortening at room temperature. Line bottoms of pans with paper; grease. Use 2 round or square 9 inch layer pans, 1½ inches deep. Start oven for moderate heat 375°. Sift flour once before measuring.

Measure into sifter:

2½ cups sifted cake flour
2¼ teaspoons double-action baking powder
1 teaspoon salt
1¼ cups sugar

Measure into mixing bowl:

⅔ cup vegetable shortening

Measure into a small bowl:

1¼ cups milk
1½ teaspoons vanilla

Have ready meringue of:

5 egg whites
½ cup sugar

Mix-Easy Mixing Method:

Stir shortening just to soften. If butter, margarine, or lard is used, decrease sugar and milk. Use 1 cupful plus 2 tablespoonfuls of each. Sift in dry ingredients. Add ¾ of the milk and mix until all the flour is dampened. Then beat 2 minutes.

Add remaining milk, blend; then add meringue mixture and beat 1 minute longer.

Mix cake by hand or at low speed of electric mixer. Count only actual beating time. Or count beating strokes. Allow about 150 full strokes per minute. Scrape bowl and spoon often.

Turn batter into pans. Bake in a moderate oven 375° 25 minutes, or until done.

This cake may also be baked in a 13 x 9 x 2 inch pan 35 minutes, or until done. Spread with icing, page 693.

II. For 3,000 Feet Altitude

Measure into sifter:

2½ cups cake flour
2½ teaspoons double-action baking powder
1 teaspoon salt
1¼ cups sugar

Measure into a mixing bowl:

⅔ cup vegetable shortening

If the shortening used is butter, margarine or lard, decrease milk to 1 cupful.

Measure into a small bowl:
> 1 cup plus 2 tablespoons milk
> 1½ teaspoons vanilla

Have ready meringue of:
> 5 egg whites
> ½ cup sugar

Follow the Mix-Easy Mixing Method above.

III. For 7,000 Feet Altitude

Measure into sifter:
> 2½ cups cake flour
> 2 teaspoons double-action baking powder
> 1 teaspoon salt
> 1 cup plus 2 tablespoons sugar

Measure into a mixing bowl:
> ⅔ cup vegetable shortening

If the shortening used is butter, margarine or lard, decrease sugar and milk. Use 1 cupful sugar and 1 cupful plus 2 tablespoonfuls milk.

Measure into a small bowl:
> 1¼ cups milk
> 1½ teaspoons vanilla

Have ready meringue of:
> 5 egg whites
> ½ cup sugar

Follow the Mix-Easy Mixing Method above.

SWANS DOWN QUICK CAKE
I. For 5,000 Feet Altitude

Preparations:
Have the shortening at room temperature. Line bottoms of pans with paper; grease. Use 2 round 8 inch layer pans, 1¼ inches deep. Start oven for moderate heat 375°. Sift flour once before measuring.

Measure into sifter:
> 2 cups sifted cake flour
> 1¾ teaspoons double-action baking powder
> ¾ teaspoon salt
> 1¼ cups sugar

Measure into mixing bowl:
> ½ cup vegetable shortening

Measure into cup:
> 1 cup minus 2 tablespoons milk
> 1 teaspoon vanilla

Have ready:
> 2 unbeaten eggs

Mix-Easy Mixing Method:
Stir shortening just to soften. If the shortening used is butter, margarine or lard, decrease sugar and milk. Use 1 cupful plus 2 tablespoonfuls sugar and ¾ cupful milk. Sift in dry ingredients. Add ¾ of the milk and mix until all flour is dampened. Then beat 2 minutes.

Add remaining milk and the eggs and beat 1 minute longer.

Mix cake by hand or at low speed of electric mixer. Count only actual beating time. Or count beating strokes. Allow about 150 full strokes per minute. Scrape bowl and spoon often.

Turn batter into pans. Bake in moderate oven 375° for 25 minutes, or until done.

Or bake in a 9 x 9 x 2 inch pan or 10 x 10 x 2 inch pan in moderate oven 375° 25 to 35 minutes, or until done.

II. For 3,000 Feet Altitude

Measure into sifter:
> 2 cups sifted cake flour
> 1¾ teaspoons double-action baking powder
> ¾ teaspoon salt
> 1¼ cups sugar

Measure into mixing bowl:
> ½ cup vegetable shortening

If the shortening used is butter, margarine or lard, decrease milk to ¾ cupful.

Measure into cup:
> ¾ cup plus 1 tablespoon milk
> 1 teaspoon vanilla

Have ready:
> 2 unbeaten eggs

Follow the Mix-Easy Mixing Method above.

III. For 7,000 Feet Altitude

Measure into sifter:
> 2 cups sifted cake flour
> 1½ teaspoons double-action baking powder
> ¾ teaspoon salt
> 1 cup plus 2 tablespoons sugar

Measure into mixing bowl:
> ½ cup vegetable shortening

If the shortening used is butter, margarine or lard, decrease milk and sugar. Use 1 cupful sugar and ¾ cupful plus 1 tablespoonful milk.

Measure into cup:
> 1 cup minus 1 tablespoon milk
> 1 teaspoon vanilla

Have ready:
> 2 unbeaten eggs

Follow the Mix-Easy Mixing Method above.

SWANS DOWN GOLD CAKE
I. For 5,000 Feet Altitude

Preparations:
Have the shortening at room temperature. Line bottom of 10 x 5 x 3 inch

loaf pan with paper; grease. Start oven for moderate heat 350°. Sift flour once before measuring.
Measure into sifter:
  2 cups sifted cake flour
  1½ teaspoons double-action baking powder
  ¾ teaspoon salt
  1 cup sugar
Measure into mixing bowl:
  ½ cup vegetable shortening
Measure into cup:
  1 cup minus 2 tablespoons milk
  1 teaspoon vanilla
Have ready:
  5 unbeaten egg yolks
Mix-Easy Mixing Method:
Stir shortening just to soften. If the shortening used is butter, margarine or lard, decrease the milk to ¾ cupful. Sift in dry ingredients. Add egg yolks and ½ cupful of the milk and mix until all flour is dampened. Then beat 2 minutes.
Add remaining milk and beat 1 minute longer.
Mix cake by hand or at low speed of electric mixer. Count only actual beating time. Or count beating strokes. Allow about 150 full strokes per minute. Scrape bowl and spoon often.
Turn batter into pan. Bake in moderate oven 350° for 1 hour, or until done. Spread with icing, page 693.

II. For 3,000 Feet Altitude
Measure into sifter:
  2 cups sifted cake flour
  1¾ teaspoons double-action baking powder
  ¾ teaspoon salt
  1 cup sugar
Measure into mixing bowl:
  ½ cup vegetable shortening
If the shortening used is butter, margarine or lard, decrease milk to ⅔ cupful.
Measure into cup:
  ¾ cup milk
  1 teaspoon vanilla
Have ready:
  5 unbeaten egg yolks
Follow the Mix-Easy Mixing Method above.

III. For 7,000 Feet Altitude
Measure into sifter:
  2 cups sifted cake flour
  1½ teaspoons double-action baking powder
  ¾ teaspoon salt
  1 cup minus 1 tablespoon sugar
Measure into mixing bowl:

  ½ cup vegetable shortening
If the shortening used is butter, margarine or lard, decrease sugar and milk.
Use 1 cupful minus 2 tablespoonfuls sugar and ¾ cupful milk.
Measure into cup:
  1 cup minus 2 tablespoons milk
  1 teaspoon vanilla
Have ready:
  5 unbeaten egg yolks
Follow the Mix-Easy Mixing Method above.

MIX-EASY DEVIL'S FOOD
I. For 5,000 Feet Altitude
Preparations:
Have the shortening at room temperature. Line bottoms of pans with paper; grease. Use 2 round 9 inch layers 1½ inches deep. Start oven for moderate heat 350°. Sift flour once.
Measure into sifter:
  2 cups sifted cake flour
  ½ teaspoon double-action baking powder
  ¾ teaspoon soda
  ¾ teaspoon salt
  1⅓ cups sugar
  ½ cup cocoa
Measure into mixing bowl:
  ⅔ cup vegetable shortening
Measure into small bowl:
  1¼ cups milk
  1 teaspoon vanilla
Have ready:
  2 unbeaten eggs
Mix-Easy Mixing Method:
Sift dry ingredients together twice. Stir shortening just to soften. If butter, margarine or lard is used, decrease sugar and milk to 1¼ cupfuls sugar and 1 cupful plus 2 tablespoonfuls milk. Sift in dry ingredients. Add ¾ of the milk and mix until all flour is dampened. Then beat 2 minutes.
Add remaining milk and the eggs, and beat 1 minute longer.
Mix cake by hand or at low speed of electric mixer. Count only actual beating time. Or count beating strokes. Allow about 150 full strokes per minute. Scrape bowl and spoon often.
Turn batter into pans. Bake in moderate oven 350° for 25 minutes, or until done. Spread with Seven Minute Icing, page 700.
This cake may also be baked in a 13 x 9 x 2 inch pan in moderate oven 350° for 30 to 35 minutes.

II. For 3,000 Feet Altitude
Measure into sifter:

2 cups sifted cake flour
½ teaspoon double-action baking
   powder
1 teaspoon soda
¾ teaspoon salt
1⅓ cups sugar
½ cup cocoa
Measure into mixing bowl:
   ⅔ cup vegetable shortening
If the shortening used is butter, margarine or lard, decrease milk to 1 cupful.
Measure into small bowl:
   1 cup plus 2 tablespoons milk
   1 teaspoon vanilla
Have ready:
   2 unbeaten eggs
Follow the Mix-Easy Mixing Method above.

III. For 7,000 Feet Altitude
Measure into sifter:
   2 cups sifted cake flour
   ½ teaspoon double-action baking
      powder
   ¾ teaspoon soda
   ¾ teaspoon salt
   1¼ cups sugar
   ⅓ cup cocoa
Measure into mixing bowl:
   ½ cup vegetable shortening
If butter, margarine or lard is used, decrease sugar and milk. Use 1 cupful plus 2 tablespoonfuls of each.
Measure into small bowl:
   1¼ cups milk
   1 teaspoon vanilla
Have ready:
   2 unbeaten eggs
Follow the Mix-Easy Mixing Method above.

FAMILY-SIZE ANGEL FOOD
I. For 5,000 Feet Altitude
Preparations:
Have eggs at room temperature. Start oven for moderate heat 375°. Sift flour once before measuring. Use 9 inch tube pan.
Ingredients:
   1 cup sifted cake flour
   1 cup plus 2 tablespoons sifted
      granulated sugar
   1 cup egg whites plus 1 white
   ¼ teaspoon salt
   1 teaspoon cream of tartar
   1 teaspoon vanilla
   ¼ teaspoon almond extract
The Mixing Method:
Measure sifted flour, add ¼ cupful sugar and sift together 4 times.
Beat egg whites and salt with flat wire whisk or rotary egg beater until foamy. Sprinkle in cream of tartar and continue beating until egg whites are stiff enough to hold up in soft peaks, but are still moist and glossy. Sprinkle remaining sugar over egg whites, about 4 tablespoonfuls at a time, and beat after each addition to blend (25 strokes). Beat in flavoring (10 strokes). Sift about ¼ of the flour over mixture and fold in lightly with whisk or spoon (15 fold-over strokes), turning bowl gradually. Continue folding in flour by fourths in this way, folding well after last addition (25 strokes).
Turn into ungreased round 9 inch tube pan. Bake in moderate oven 375° for 30 minutes, or until done. Remove from oven, invert pan and let stand 1 hour, or until cake is cool. Spread with icing, page 693.

II. For 3,000 Feet Altitude
Ingredients:
   1 cup sifted cake flour
   1¼ cups sifted granulated sugar
   1 cup egg whites
   ¼ teaspoon salt
   1 teaspoon cream of tartar
   1 teaspoon vanilla
   ¼ teaspoon almond extract
Follow the Mixing Method given above.

III. For 7,000 Feet Altitude
Ingredients:
   1 cup sifted cake flour
   1 cup sifted granulated sugar
   1 cup egg whites plus 1 white
   ¼ teaspoon salt
   1¼ teaspoons cream of tartar
   1 teaspoon vanilla
   ¼ teaspoon almond extract
Follow the Mixing Method given above.

SWANS DOWN SPONGE CAKE
I. For 5,000 Feet Altitude
Preparations:
Have eggs at room temperature. Start oven for moderate heat 375°. Sift flour once before measuring. Use 9 inch tube pan.
Ingredients:
   1 cup sifted cake flour
   1 cup minus 1 tablespoon sifted
      granulated sugar
   5 egg yolks
   1½ teaspoons grated lemon rind
   1½ teaspoons lemon juice
   2 tablespoons water
   5 egg whites

¼ teaspoon salt
¼ teaspoon cream of tartar
The Mixing Method:
Measure sifted flour, add ¼ cupful sugar and sift together 4 times.
Place egg yolks in small bowl. Add lemon rind and beat with rotary egg beater until thick and lemon-colored. Add lemon juice and water gradually, beating until thick and light.
Beat egg whites and salt with flat wire whisk or rotary egg beater until foamy. Sprinkle in cream of tartar and continue beating until egg whites are stiff enough to hold up in soft peaks but are still moist and glossy. Add remaining sugar in three additions, beating 50 strokes after each. Then fold in egg yolk mixture with flat wire whisk or spoon until well blended.
Sift about ¼ of flour over mixture and fold in lightly with whisk or spoon (15 fold-over strokes), turning bowl gradually. Continue folding in flour by fourths in this way, folding well after last addition (25 strokes).
Turn into ungreased round 9 inch tube pan. Bake in moderate oven 375° for 30 minutes, or until done. Remove

from oven, invert pan and let stand 1 hour, or until cake is cool.

II. For 3,000 Feet Altitude
Ingredients:
    1 cup sifted cake flour
    1 cup sifted granulated sugar
    5 egg yolks
    1½ teaspoons grated lemon rind
    1½ tablespoons lemon juice
    2 tablespoons water
    5 egg whites
    ¼ teaspoon salt
    ¼ teaspoon cream of tartar
Follow the Mixing Method given above.

III. For 7,000 Feet Altitude
Ingredients:
    1 cup sifted cake flour
    1 cup minus 2 tablespoons sifted
      granulated sugar
    5 egg yolks
    1½ teaspoons grated lemon rind
    1½ tablespoons lemon juice
    2 tablespoons water
    5 egg whites
    ¼ teaspoon salt
    ½ teaspoon cream of tartar
Follow the Mixing Method given above.

The following recipes are published through the courtesy of Dr. W. E. Pyke, Ph.D., professor of chemistry at the A. and M. College, of Fort Collins, Colorado. They are to be found in the booklet "Cakes—Cookies, Recipes for Different Altitudes" previously referred to.

DOUGHNUTS
About 3½ Dozen
Ingredients:
    2 tablespoons shortening
    1 cup sugar
    2 eggs
    1 cup sour milk or buttermilk
    1 teaspoon soda
    4 to 4½ cups sifted all-purpose
      flour
    1½ teaspoons baking powder
    1 teaspoon salt
    1 teaspoon nutmeg
Cream shortening and sugar. Add eggs and beat well. Add sour milk. Sift dry ingredients and add to first mixture. Mix well, chill. Roll out and fry in deep fat 350°.

FORT COLLINS BROWNIES
24 Brownies
Ingredients:
    ⅔ cup sifted all-purpose flour
    ½ teaspoon baking powder
    ¼ teaspoon salt
    ⅓ cup shortening

    2 squares unsweetened chocolate
    1 cup sugar
    2 well-beaten eggs
    ½ cup nut meats
    1 teaspoon vanilla
At 7,500 and 10,000 feet use:
    ¼ teaspoon baking powder
Melt shortening and chocolate over boiling water. Add sugar to egg gradually, beating thoroughly. Add chocolate mixture and blend. Add sifted dry ingredients and mix well. Add nuts and vanilla. Bake in a greased pan, 8 x 8 x 2 in a moderate oven 350° for 35 minutes. While still warm, cut into squares. Remove from pan and cool on cake rack.

THIN SUGAR COOKIES
About 8 Dozen 2 Inch Cookies
Ingredients:
    1 cup shortening
    1 cup sugar
    3 cups sifted all-purpose flour
    2 eggs
    1 teaspoon water

½ teaspoon salt
1 teaspoon vanilla
1 teaspoon baking powder

Cream shortening, sugar and water. Add well-beaten eggs. Sift dry ingredients and add to other mixture. Roll very thin and cut in desired shapes. Sprinkle with sugar or cinnamon if desired. Bake in a hot oven 425° about 8 minutes.

CHOCOLATE CHIP COOKIES

50 Cookies
Ingredients:
½ cup shortening
6 tablespoons sugar
6 tablespoons brown sugar
1 beaten egg
½ teaspoon soda
1⅛ cups sifted all-purpose flour
½ teaspoon salt
Few drops hot water
½ cup chopped nuts
1 package chocolate chips: 7 oz.

Cream shortening and sugar. Add egg and mix well. Sift dry ingredients and add. Add few drops of hot water and mix until well blended. Add nuts and chocolate chips. Flavor with ½ teaspoonful vanilla. Drop ½ teaspoonfuls on a greased cookie sheet. Bake in 375° oven about 10 minutes.

REFRIGERATOR COOKIES

About 50 Cookies
I. Vanilla
Ingredients:
½ cup shortening
1 cup granulated sugar
1 well-beaten egg
1 teaspoon vanilla
1½ cups sifted all-purpose flour
½ teaspoon baking soda
½ teaspoon salt

Cream shortening, add sugar gradually and cream well. Add egg and vanilla. Mix well. Sift dry ingredients and gradually add, beating after each addition. Shape into roll 1¾ inches in diameter. Wrap in waxed paper and chill for several hours or overnight. Cut slices ⅛ inch thick and bake on greased cookie sheet in a 375° oven about 10 minutes.

II. Butterscotch
Make Vanilla Refrigerator Cookies, substituting 1 cupful brown sugar, firmly packed, for the granulated sugar. If desired, ½ cupful chopped nuts may be added.

III. Chocolate
Make Vanilla Refrigerator Cookies, adding 1 square melted, unsweetened chocolate to the egg mixture. If desired, ½ cupful chopped nuts may be added.

IV. Pinwheel
Make half of recipe each of butterscotch or vanilla cookies and chocolate cookies. Roll or pat chocolate dough on waxed paper without flour, into a rectangle 8 x 7 inches. Place vanilla or butterscotch dough on top of chocolate and roll or pat until the same size as the chocolate. Roll jelly-roll fashion (page 648). Wrap in waxed paper. Chill. Slice crosswise and bake.

V. Spice
Make vanilla or butterscotch cookies, sifting ½ teaspoonful cinnamon and ¼ teaspoonful nutmeg with dry ingredients.

Menus

The menus of the past bear about the same relationship to those of the present as does the mastodon to the canary.

We envision stupendous banquets still being served in the homes of the wealthy, in restaurants and on steamships, but a changed attitude toward food values, budget restrictions, lack of domestic service and limited time discourage such great expense and effort in the average home.

So, generally speaking, great repasts remain steeped in a bygone aura of luxuriousness, bounded by overwrought iron, lambrequins and the rubber plant except when reproduced in a mild form for some gala occasion. The dinners recorded by chefs and gourmets of the Victorian era seem fabulous and, say I, with a green-eyed glance, gluttonous in retrospect. Among them is an entertaining book by a Monsieur Francatelli, a cook celebrated for towering monstrosities that might have inspired the Albert Memorial but reveal themselves on closer inspection merely as fish or pudding.

A visitor to the Kensington Museum will remember the exhibit of Queen Victoria's wardrobe on replicas of her person. Her gowns are fascinating, her gradual acquisition of girth impressive. It is difficult to believe that the slender maiden who mounted the throne at 18 bore any relation to the sumptuously upholstered matron who relinquished it, reluctantly, 64 years later.

Was her famous chef responsible for this study in gastronomy? His obituary reads: "A great cook is dead. Mr. Charles Edme Francatelli left this world on the 10th of August. He was 71 years old. He was once chief cook to Queen Victoria. He was an exceedingly expensive genius and it was said that if he had a fault it was that he was a little too much addicted to the use of truffles." Let us bury the estimable man with appreciation and a whiff of lavender and resurrect him now and then for the pleasure of licking our chops reflectively before turning to our daily menu problems, which are not apt to have a speaking acquaintance with truffles.

"Or clog the appetite with bare recollections of a feast?" No, William, we are going to eat well, just differently. It is hoped, not too confidently, that helpful suggestions may be gleaned from this menu chapter, but individual taste, standards, budget and diet restrictions make it as difficult as it is unrewarding to tell others what to eat.

Far be it for me to try to pry the American public loose from its well-known national and regional dishes, for they are tops and, besides, it can't be done. Our culinary horizon may be broadened, however, and that is what this chapter attempts to do. But never forget that one meal alone doesn't balance your diet. It is your entire intake day after day which must meet your bodily requirements. See Nutrition, page 931. Dress those requirements with inspiration.

Breakfast Menus

The feminine tendency to make breakfast as light as possible is discouraged by physicians who recommend that it be a rather hearty meal. If you wish to cut on calories, it seems that it is wiser to do so later in the day. So enjoy your breakfast eggs, bacon, cream, milk, grits, cakes or waffles, etc., on prescription.

If, omitting breakfast, your preference is for brunch, you may find among the following menus a few that are sufficiently filling for that practical repast.

1.
Hot Pitted Prunes, p. 450, or
Hot Applesauce, p 447, between
slices of French Toast with
Cinnamon, p. 539, or chilled prunes
sprinkled with cinnamon and brown
sugar, served with cream and
French toast
Link sausages
Coffee

2.
Orange juice
Creamed Chipped Beef, p. 161, on
Fried Mush, p. 100, or on squares
of Hot Corn Bread, p. 515
Hot Pineapple Slices, p. 448
Coffee or milk

3.
Sliced peaches
Beef Kidney Stew, p. 380
Buckwheat Cakes or Popovers,
pp. 549, 514
Lime marmalade
Coffee or milk

4.
Apples Filled with Sausage Meat,
p. 208, or Small Sausages, p. 375
with Cinnamon Apples, p. 446, or

Sausage Ring, p. 150, filled with
Scrambled Eggs, p. 81, surrounded
by Fried Apples, p. 447
Graham Muffins, p. 512
Plum jelly
Coffee or milk

5.
Fresh Pineapple, p. 4
Poached Eggs Blackstone or
Benedict, p. 81
Toasted English Muffins, p. 524
Orange marmalade
Coffee or milk

6.
Broiled grapefruit
Smoked Salmon on toast with
Poached Egg, p. 83, or Broiled
Ham, p. 373, and Sautéed Eggs
Coffee Cake, p. 623
Apple butter
Coffee or milk

7.
Sliced rounds of Honeydew melon
filled with red raspberries
Ham Cakes and Eggs, p. 147
Fried Grits, p. 100, with maple sirup
Coffee

Suggestions for Luncheons

A luncheon menu is usually determined by the breakfast that precedes it and the dinner that follows it. Some of the simple luncheon dishes given below are suitable for late breakfasts. Some of the breakfast dishes above are suitable for luncheons. The Luncheon Chapter, page 77, offers a wealth of further suggestions.

Suggestions for Luncheons

Chop Plate: Liver, bacon, sausages, chops and mushrooms, baked potatoes, green salad, popovers, jam, melons.

Vegetable Plate: Baked tomatoes, baked onions, peas, poached eggs, Hollandaise sauce, whole-grain bread, honey.

Fried smelts, buttered peas and carrots in a creamed potato ring, stewed apricots.

Cold ham, rice croquettes, creamed asparagus or peas, flaming peaches or fresh fruit.

Creamed chicken giblets with mushrooms on corn-meal mush, lettuce salad, chocolate cookies.

Creamed mushrooms with cheese on tomatoes and toast, crumb spice cake.

Welsh rarebit over asparagus on graham toast, tomato aspic, cup cakes.

Gnocchi with gravy and mushrooms, apple salad with cheese balls.

Chilled tomato filled with celery and pineapple, mayonnaise, crackers, cheese, brownies or a fruit tart.

Creamed veal or chicken with celery on French toast, grilled tomatoes, fruit.

Chicken or vegetable timbale and mushroom sauce (or left-over timbale and tomato sauce), cucumber salad, hot rolls, cream cheese balls, fruit gelatine.

For additional luncheon suggestions see how to serve cold soups on page 63, the Hot Weather Menus on page 915 and Supper Menus, page 913.

Luncheon Menus

1.
Meal-in-One Sandwich, p. 132
Petit Suisse with Strawberries, p. 748
A beverage

2.
Honeydew Melon or Cantaloupe Filled with Cottage Cheese, garnished with Seedless Green Grapes and Mayonnaise, p. 471
Nut Bread, p. 535
A beverage

3.
Chicken Livers or Oysters in Batter, p. 139, or cold tongue
Vegetable Soufflé, p. 218
Pulled Bread, p. 76
Cucumber Salad, p. 458
Fresh Pears in Liqueur, p. 3
A beverage

4.
Grits Ring, p. 157, filled with Southern Shrimp, p. 128
Grapefruit Aspic or Salad, pp. 480, 473
Sour Milk Biscuits, p. 507
English Trifle, p. 645
A beverage

5.
Molded Pineapple Ring, p. 486, filled with Chicken Salad, p. 470, on lettuce
Clover Leaf Rolls, p. 519
Chocolate Spice Cake, p. 613
A beverage

6.
Chicken Bouillon, p. 47
Cauliflower Timbales, p. 212, with Mushroom Sauce, p. 436
Japanese Persimmon Salad with French Dressing, p. 470
Hot Rolls, p. 517
Rombauer Jam Cake, p. 617
A beverage

7.
Rice, Tuna Fish and Cheese Sauce, p. 117
Water Cress and Cucumber Salad with Chiffonade Dressing, p. 492
Toasted bran bread
Apples with Orange Juice, p. 750
Chocolate Drop Cookies, p. 679
A beverage

8.
Mushrooms under Glass, p. 175, or Oysters Baked in Mushroom Sauce, p. 114
Buttered Broccoli, p. 273
Luncheon Bread, p. 534
Seedless Grape Ring, p. 484
A beverage

9.
Waffles, p. 556, and Creamed Chicken, p. 143, or Tuna, p. 122
Tomatoes Filled with Pineapple, p. 458
Molasses Nut Drop Cookies, p. 680
Lemon Ice with Rum, p. 773
A beverage

10.
Crab Meat with Piquant Sauce and Rice, p. 124
French Endive with Pearl Onions and French Dressing, p. 491
Graham Muffins, p. 512
Pineapple Sponge, p. 737
Pecan Wafers, p. 680
A beverage

11.
Strawberry Cocktail, p. 4, or Melon Ball Cocktail, p. 5
Braised Sweetbreads, p. 377
New Potatoes Browned, p. 306
Salad Caesar, p. 453
English Muffins, p. 524
Grandmother's Apple Cake, p. 637
A beverage

Plate Luncheon Menus

How men hate to balance plates on their knees! Make it as easy as you can for them by serving plate luncheons with such food only that may be cut readily with a fork while the plate is held in mid-air. Plate service is awkward at best for anyone in a crowded room, but it's the most convenient way to serve food easily to a large number of people.

1.
Caviar canapés
Bouillon
Noodle Baskets, p. 98, or Patty Shells, p. 567, with Creamed Chicken, p. 143, or Oysters, p. 111
Buttered Asparagus, p. 265
Tomato Aspic on Water Cress, p. 476
Clover Leaf Rolls, p. 519
Lime sherbet
Hazelnut cakes, Coffee

2.

Ragout Fin, p. 174, or Creamed
Eggs and Asparagus, p. 88
Black Cherry and Almond Aspic on
Lettuce with Mayonnaise, p. 488
Hot buttered Biscuits, p. 505
Peppermint Ice Cream, p. 763, with
Chocolate Sauce, p. 757
Pecan Slices, p. 666
A beverage

3.

Chicken Timbales or Croquettes, p.
214, with Mushroom Sauce, p. 436
Grapefruit Aspic on Lettuce with
Mayonnaise, p. 480
Olives
Hot buttered Muffins, p. 510
Meringues, p. 654, filled with Rasp-
berry Ice Cream, p. 763
A beverage

Dinner Menus

1.

Ham Loaf, p. 374
Zucchini or Onions with Sherry,
p. 295
New Potatoes, Butter and Chives,
p. 300, or Baked Rice, p. 104
Orange, Grapefruit Salad, p. 473
Chocolate Feather Cake, p. 611
Coffee

2.

Rombauer Rice Dish, p. 109
Snap Bean Salad on Water Cress,
p. 461
Orange Whip, p. 737
Butterscotch Brownies, p. 663
Coffee

3.

Pot Roast, p. 343, or other roast
Potato and Onion Pie Roll, p. 158
Chilled Tomato Cases, p. 458, with
Celery and French Dressing on Let-
tuce
Rum Drops, p. 681
Coffee

4.

Melon cocktail
Broiled Steak with Sauce, p. 345
French Fried Potatoes, p. 307
Tomatoes with Mushrooms, p. 201
Rye toast melba
Orange Cake, p. 643, or Chocolate
Roll, p. 649
Coffee

5.

Tomato Aspic with Cheese Centers,
p. 36
Chicken Pot Pie, p. 141, or Stewed
Chicken and Dumplings, p. 420
Asparagus with Buttered Crumbs,
p. 265, or Sautéed Okra, p. 293
Spinach salad
Lemon Milk Sherbet, p. 776
Chocolate Chip Cookies, p. 674
Coffee

6.

Pineapple Grapefruit Cocktail, p. 2
Frog Legs, p. 244, with Tartar

Sauce, p. 439, or Fried Chicken, p.
398
Braised Celery, p. 282
New Potatoes Browned, p. 306
Snowballs with Strawberry Sauce,
p. 758, or Hazelnut Soufflé, p. 729
Coffee

7.

Tomatoes, p. 458, Filled with Crab
Meat and Vinaigrette Sauce, p. 493
Fillet of Beef with Mushrooms, p.
292, or Marchand de Vin Sauce, p.
436
Red Cabbage in Green Peppers, p.
202
French Potato Balls, p. 302
Refrigerator Cheese Cake, p. 659
Coffee

8.

Shrimp in Grapefruit, p. 6
Clear Soup with Marrow Balls, p.
74
Celery
Crackers
Duck with Orange Sauce, p. 437, or
Goose, p. 405, dressed with Sweet
Potatoes and Apples, p. 419
Turnip Cups Filled with Peas, p.
207, or White Asparagus with
Almonds, p. 265
Parker House Rolls, p. 518
German Cherry Cake, p. 638, or
Mint Sherbet with Fig Bars, p. 665
Coffee

9.

Herring and Onions in Sour Cream
on Shredded Lettuce, p. 131
Crown Roast of Lamb with Dress-
ing, p. 361, gravy and Mint Sauce,
p. 439
Kale or Spinach, pp. 290, 313
Apricot Bombe, p. 770
Pecan Drop Cakes, p. 680
Coffee

10.

Small tomatoes filled with slaw and
anchovies

Clear Soup with Cracker Balls, p. 74
Celery, radishes or olives
Squab Stuffed with Wild Rice, p. 411
Cauliflower and Mushrooms, p. 178, or creamed broccoli
Rye Bread Rolls, p. 522
Cabinet Pudding, p. 747, or English Almond Soufflé, p. 730
Coffee

11.
Cantaloupe Baskets, p. 5, or Shrimp Bisque, p. 60
Broiled Spring Chicken, p. 395
Green Peas and Mushrooms, p. 299
Corn Fritters, p. 184, or Green Corn Pudding, p. 184
Beaten Biscuits, p. 509
Jelly
Cream Tart with Apricot or other Filling, p. 655
Coffee

12.
Chicken broth
Broiled Lobster, p. 248, with Broiled Tartar Sauce for Fish, p. 260
New Potatoes and Parsley, p. 300
Summer Squash with Onions, p. 316
Corn Dodgers, p. 516, or Garlic Bread, p. 76
Endive Salad with Lorenzo Dressing, p. 491
Pineapple Ice Garnished with Fresh or Canned Fruit, p. 780
Velvet Spice Cake, p. 614
Coffee

13.
Onion Soup, p. 52
Baked Fish, p. 230, or Fillet of Sole or Trout with Almonds, p. 242, garnished with Tomatoes Filled with Mashed Potatoes, p. 199
Clothespin Rolls, p. 519
Cucumber Salad with Sour Cream Dressing II, p. 496
Bombe lined with raspberry ice filled with Biscuit Tortoni, p. 770
Coffee

14.
Creamed Oyster Canapés, p. 15
Tomato Juice Cocktail, p. 1
Baked Ham, p. 371
Asparagus, p. 265
Creamette Loaf, p. 96
Meringue Tart, p. 654, filled with

Lemon or Orange Ice Flavored with Rum and Garnished with Whipped Cream, p. 773
Coffee

15.
Caviar Canapés, p. 18
German Meat Balls, p. 163
Noodles with Buttered Crumbs, p. 97
Spinach, p. 313, or Buttered Green Beans, p. 266
Hawaiian Salad, p. 471
Vanilla ice cream with Cherries Jubilee, p. 779
Coffee

16.
Mushroom Broth with Sherry, p. 50
Roast Suckling Pig, p. 365, with Onion Dressing, p. 419
Sweet Potatoes in Baked Apples, p. 311
Red Cabbage or Sauerkraut, p. 277
Toasted rye bread
Pineapple Macaroon Soufflé, p. 727, or Almond Torte, p. 650, with Lemon and Orange Filling, p. 708
Coffee

17.
Clam Juice Cocktail, p. 1
Celery and olives
Turkey with Oyster or Sausage Dressing, p. 416
Cranberry Jelly, p. 443
Corn-Bread Sticks, p. 515
Acorn Squash Filled with Creamed Spinach, p. 206
Grapefruit Salad on Water Cress with French Dressing, p. 473
Steamed Fig or Date Pudding with Sauce, p. 731, or Chocolate Date Torte, p. 647, with sauce
Coffee

18. Game Dinner
Consommé into Cream Soup, p. 69
Soufflé Crackers, p. 76
Wild Duck, p. 406
Orange Salad for Game, p. 471
Parsley Potatoes, p. 300
Brussels Sprouts with Lemon Butter, p. 431
Crème de Menthe over vanilla ice cream or Pineapple Ice, p. 773
Russian Cookies, p. 676
Coffee

Suggestions for Simplified Service

If you wish to simplify service, serve from one or two platters only. Garnish the food with parsley, celery tops, chives, lemon slices, olives, etc. Consider:

Spinach ring filled with buttered parsley carrots.

Acorn squash filled with tomatoes creole or buttered peas.

Baked potatoes filled with sautéed onions, or creamed onions au gratin in a casserole surrounded by potato balls and glazed carrots.

Broccoli ring filled with creamed mushrooms surrounded by parsley potatoes.

A ring of snap beans filled with Harvard beets.

Cauliflower surrounded by beets or by small mounds of snap beans alternated with beets.

Grits ring, rice or wild rice ring filled with Brussels sprouts Hollandaise surrounded by mushroom caps.

Onions filled with sauerkraut around a mound of mashed potatoes.

Scalloped potatoes, macaroni, noodles, etc., may be baked in a ring. Fill it as you please.

Your entire course may be arranged attractively on one platter:

Creamed oysters in a bowl surrounded by pickled beets stuffed with eggs and herbs and baked potato balls.

Pork tenderloin, olives and cream in a noodle ring surrounded by broccoli and carrots.

Chicken pot pie surrounded by small mounds of snap beans and celeriac salad.

Tartar sauce (in a small bowl) surrounded by fish rolls, potato apples and green peas in paper cups or halves of acorn squash.

Veal stew in a mushroom rice ring, glazed onions, carrots in bunches with parsley tops.

Stuffed eggplant surrounded by chops and new potatoes.

Sautéed fish, tomatoes filled with spinach, browned potatoes, carrots.

Roast pork, apples filled with sweet potatoes, a green vegetable—and so on indefinitely.

Supper Menus

1.
Sweetbreads on Skewers, p. 194
New Potatoes in Sour Cream with Chives, p. 300
Fruit Salad with Lemon and Sherry Dressing, p. 494
Cheese Straws, p. 517
Chocolate Devil's Food or Custard Cake, p. 611
A beverage

2.
Sautéed Mushroom Caps and Broiled Sausages, p. 32, or Stuffed Mushrooms, p. 34
Noodles with Poppy Seed, p. 97
Prunes in Wine, p. 450
Molasses Nut Wafers, p. 680
A beverage

3.
Cheese, Bread and Egg Dish, p. 190
Green Salad with Chopped Bacon, Chives and Catsup Dressing, p. 491
Fresh peaches
Oatmeal Chocolate Chip Cookies, p. 678
A beverage

4.
Cocktail
Water Cress Canapés, p. 19
Chicken Soufflé, p. 221, with Mushroom Sauce, p. 436
Green Peas, p. 298
Biscuits, p. 505
Fresh Pineapple in Wine, p. 749
Brown Sugar Drop Cookies, p. 675
A beverage

Suggestions for a Formal Buffet Supper

Begin by serving cocktails, if you wish, and some simple canapés or crackers. Let the guests go to the buffet and help themselves. Have the table attractively set with china, flat silver and napkins. Choose good color combinations for decorations and food and have the dishes sufficiently varied in texture and taste to be interesting.

One of Jane Austen's characters is left in 1813 "to the comfort of cold ham and chicken." Translated into our terms—cold ham and turkey. How long has this been our usual buffet supper food? Good as it is, too long, perhaps, so it is better to strike a new note and to vary the dishes with something less hackneyed such as:

Fillet of beef	Cold boiled tongue and jambolaya
Baked Canadian ham	Spiced beef
Curried shrimp or shrimp creole	Food on skewers
Chicken livers with baked rice	Glazed salmon
Creamed chicken in a mushroom ring	Welsh rarebit in a chafing dish served
Chicken chop suey	with toast fingers
Tongue in aspic	Gaston beef stew

To be served from a tureen in cold weather: onion soup, oyster stew, chowders, fish bisques and bouillabaisse.

Jellied soups, chilled borsch, cucumber soup and Vichyssoise are fine in hot weather.

Place on the table an attractive salad—tossed, molded cucumber, grapefruit, potato, fruit and cottage cheese, aspic or individual aspic, celeriac, ginger ale, etc.; also potato chips and cooked shrimp, chunks of cooked lobster tails, etc., for dunking in one of the good cocktail sauces given in the Chapter on Hors d'Oeuvres; and, of course, you may serve the usual olives, stuffed celery and radishes.

Sweets served at a buffet supper are less stressed than meats and salad dishes, but orange raisin cup cakes, sponge cake bars, jelly tots, etc., and all the Christmas cakes are acceptable. So is grandmother's apple cake, refrigerator cheese cake or one of the other more elaborate cakes. If you wish, skip the sweet course and substitute mints, salted nuts or something similar.

Serve coffee, of course, and possibly tea, the latter iced in hot weather. Mulled wine or cider is good in cold weather if you are omitting cocktails.

Suggestions for a Cocktail Party

La Brinvilliers, a notorious poisoner, was beheaded for her crimes. According to a French wit, the only difference between La Brinvilliers and the average cook is the intention.

This is particularly true of menu building, wherein many a hostess sins grievously, but at a "help yourself" party she may give her fancy free reign and let her guests assume full responsibility.

Alcoholic or non-alcoholic cocktails—either or both. A choice of the following suggestions:

Olives, radishes, stuffed celery	Tiny broiled sausages with mustard
Marinated mushrooms	cream
Potato chips and cheese	Chicken livers in blankets (tidbits)
Antipasto	Broiled sardine canapés
Lobster spread sandwiches	Deviled sardines
Caviar and cucumber canapés	Rolled tongue or chipped beef hors
Very small hot toasted sandwiches or	d'oeuvres
puff shells (mushroom, cream	Lettuce sandwiches
cheese, liver sausage, oyster, etc.)	Crab or lobster canapés
Pastry snails	Pickles, onions and bacon
Shrimp surrounding a small hollowed	Bacon and saltine canapés
cabbage filled with mayonnaise or	Oyster canapés
pink sauce for shrimp	Salted nuts
Meat in pie dough (Rissoles)	

See page 27 for Attractive Ways of Serving Canapés and Hors d'Oeuvres.

Suggestions for an Informal Tea

Serve tea, coffee or cocoa accompanied by cinnamon toast or a light sandwich: marmalade, pecan, water cress, etc., or nut, prune, fig or orange bread spread with cream cheese. You may follow this with a cup cake or other small cake or cookie, i.e., filled cup cakes, lightning cake, rum balls, etc. Serve a sandwich without nut meats if you plan to have a nutty cake and vice versa.

Menus for a Formal Tea

1.
Open Tomato Sandwiches and/or
Open Cucumber Sandwiches, p. 26
Tiny Bran Biscuit with Cheese
Spread (served hot), p. 12
Sponge or Angel Cake Bars, p. 666
Jelly Tots, p. 681
Butter Wafers, p. 675
Candies
Coffee or tea

2.
Toasted Mushroom or Braun-
schweiger Sandwiches, p. 11
Puff Shells I, p. 13, filled with
creamed oysters
Pineapple and Cream Cheese Sand-
wiches, p. 26
Lettuce and mayonnaise sandwiches
Pecan Drop Cakes, p. 680
Chocolate Cake with White Icing
and Chocolate Coating, p. 695
Kisses
Tea or coffee

3.
Water Cress Sandwiches, p. 19
Olive Sandwiches, p. 24, or

Chicken Salad Sandwiches, p. 20
Cheese Puff Canapés, p. 12
Thin Ham on Beaten Biscuits, p. 509
Peach or Strawberry Ice Cream, p. 763
Honey Drop Cakes, p. 674
White Cake with White Icing and
Coconut—cut into squares, p. 694
Candied orange peel
Salted nuts
Tea or coffee

4.
Ripe Olive Sandwiches, p. 24
Pickle Canapés, p. 19
Stuffed Brussels Sprouts, p. 38
Tomato and Shrimp Canapés, p. 18
Puff Shells II, p. 21, filled with
chicken salad, lobster salad, caviar
or cheese
Orange and Lemon Ice, p. 773
Glazed fruits or nuts
Hazelnut Cakes, p. 690
Sand Tarts, p. 670
Peppermint creams
Tea or coffee

Please see the above suggestions for a cocktail party as many of the things listed may be served at formal teas.

Hot Weather Menus

Charles Dudley Warner to the contrary, "Everybody talks about the weather, but nobody does anything about it," there are a few things within our power to make heat more bearable—a simplified household, the right clothes, or lack of them, and appropriate food.

This means light food, both cold and hot, for it is not palatable, though equally nutritious, to serve only chilled food day after day. Serve clear soup, jellied soups, creamed soups, hot and cold green vegetables, salads, egg dishes, lean fish, lean meat, light desserts, sherbets, ices and lots of fruit, fresh and stewed. Please read the paragraph under Chilled Soups, page 63. Here are a few menus, to some of which you may add, or from which you may prefer to subtract a dish or two.

1.
Chilled vegetable juice
Chops or Steak, p. 345
Corn Pudding, p. 184
Tossed salad
Biscuits, p. 505
Melons or berries and cream
Iced coffee

2.
Quick Aspic Salad, p. 480, or Fish
in Aspic, p. 477

Cucumbers in Sour Cream Herb
Dressing, p. 497
Popovers, p. 514
Chilled Rice Rings, p. 716, with
Fruit Rum Sauce, p. 760
Coffee

3.
Clear hot soup
Cold roast, tongue or ham
Chilled Pickled Beets Filled with
Eggs and Herbs, p. 37

Hot French Bread, p. 534
Chilled fruit
Cocoa Kisses, p. 686
Coffee

4.

Madrilène with Shad Roe, p. 481, on endive
Green Peas, p. 298
Corn-Meal Zephyrs, p. 516
Cottage Cheese and Chilled Stewed

Cherries, p. 748
Coffee

5.

Chilled Spinach Soup, p. 65, or Cold Cucumber Soup, p. 64
Cheese Soufflé, p. 218
Buttered Snap Beans, p. 266
Rye bread toast
Chocolate Angel Cake, p. 600
A beverage

Cold Weather Menus

To fortify themselves against the cold, northern people eat heavy food. If you are not condemned to be a calorie counter, or if you are, but happen to be a poor mathematician, winter is the open season for thick soups, fat fish and meats, heavy sauces, fried foods, rich desserts, ice creams and cakes. Don't feel obliged to serve them all at one time, for ours is not the Arctic zone; but indulge your liking for them when "the northwind doth blow" rather than in the devastating, drooping, dripping summertime when they may spell discomfort to the gastric juices. Among the Dinner Menus, page 911, you will find a number suitable for serving in cold weather.

1.

Tomato bouillon
Salt Pork and Cream Gravy, p. 375
Onion Shortcake, p. 169
Hot Slaw, p. 456, or green salad
Orange Compote, p. 449, or cheese and crackers
Coffee

2.

Clam Broth, p. 50
Anna's Short Ribs of Beef, p. 344
Noodle Ring, p. 98, or Mushroom Rice Ring, p. 105, filled with buttered peas
Hot rolls
Apricot soufflé
Coffee

3.

Hard-cooked egg slices on toast rounds garnished with anchovies
Sauerbraten or Beef à la Mode, p. 344
Potato Dumplings, p. 422
Kale, p. 290, or some other green vegetable
Apple Pudding, p. 722
Coffee

4.

Tomato and Shrimp Canapés, p. 18
Spareribs, p. 369, or Pork Roast, p. 365
Sauerkraut with Mushrooms, p. 177
Puréed Lentils, p. 271, or Mashed Potato Mounds, p. 303
Flaming Pears, p. 751

Butter Thins, p. 675
Coffee

5.

Red caviar on toast
Hasenpfeffer, p. 413
Farina Balls, p. 72, with Croutons, p. 73
Broccoli, p. 273, or Spinach, p. 313, or Buttered Leeks in Wine Sauce, p. 437
Apricots with Curaçao, p. 752
Pecan Slices, p. 666
Coffee

6.

Cocktail of avocado and grapefruit slices in French dressing
Boiled Beef and Horseradish Sauce, p. 351
Baked Potatoes, p. 301
Buttered Cabbage, p. 275
French Fritters with Lemon Sauce, p. 543
Coffee

7.

Black Bean Soup or Consommé, p. 43
Broiled Pigs' Feet or Stuffed Pork Chops, pp. 141, 368
Celeriac Salad, p. 464, on lettuce with French Dressing
French bread
Wine Jelly, p. 736
Molasses Cookies, p. 676
Coffee

Economical Meat Menus

Please read the introductions to Sweetbreads, Brains, Kidneys, Liver, Heart, Tongue, Oxtails, etc., on page 376.

These menus will probably satisfy moderate eaters. For hearty appetites add a soup or another vegetable.

1.

Broiled Beef Kidneys, p. 380
Baked Potatoes or Baked Potato Wafers, p. 302
Creamed Onions au Gratin, p. 295
Baked Apples, p. 445
Coffee

Jane says, "Please remember the good Kidneys Creole, p. 380, and serve them with rice." A roasted Veal Kidney, p. 379, makes a fine little roast for one person. Also see Veal Kidney, Mushroom and Onion Casserole, p. 140, and other Kidney Dishes, pp. 379-380, a bit out of the economy class but not much.

2.

Baked Calf Tongues, p. 386, or Baked Heart, p. 381
Potato Cakes, p. 309, or Green Rice, p. 104
Slaw, p. 455
Fruit Custard, p. 713, or Orange Cream Pie, p. 582
Coffee

3.

Liver Loaf or Patties, p. 384

Creamed Potatoes with Chives, p. 308
Pickled Beets, p. 461
Orange Marmalade Cookies, p. 674
Coffee

4.

Broiled Calf Brains on Tomatoes, p. 140, or Calf Brain Fritters, p. 140, with Stewed Tomatoes, p. 318
Health Bread, p. 531
Water cress salad
Milk Rice, p. 716, with fruit sauce
Coffee

5.

Braised Oxtails, p. 386
Corn-Meal Noodles, p. 97
Snap Beans, p. 266
Fruit, fresh, stewed or in gelatine

6.

Tripe by any rule on pp. 387-388
Boiled potatoes in their jackets with sour cream
A green vegetable: cabbage, spinach, kale, etc., p. 290
Apricot Fritters, p. 543
Coffee

Picnic Menus

1.

Wieners or hamburgers rolled in pancakes
Chilled tomatoes
Rye crisp
Cheddar cheese
Gingerbread in cup cake pans, p. 538
Pears and grapes
Coffee

2.

Sautéed Canadian bacon on hard rolls
Snap Bean Salad with Lettuce, p. 461, Onions and French Dressing, p. 461, or Potato Salad, p. 463, with lots of lettuce
Deviled Eggs with Liver Sausage, p. 89
Watermelon
Poppy Seed Cake, p. 641
Coffee

3.

Baked ham

Italian Salad, p. 463
Bran Muffins II, p. 513
Roquefort Cheese Balls Rolled in Chives, p. 489
Sour Cream Apple Pie, p. 568, or Berry Pie, p. 569
Coffee

4.

Broiled Steak, p. 345
Canned French fried potatoes
Picnic Salad*
Soft buns spread with butter†
Pickles
White Cake I or II with Chocolate Icing, p. 699
Salted nuts
Coffee

* Cubed cucumbers, tomatoes and onions with French dressing.

† If some other salad is served, cover the buns with slices of Bermuda onions.

5.

Sautéed eggs with bacon or sausages
Baked Beans, p. 268, or Jambolaya,
p. 107
Olives
Toasted Buttered French Bread
Loaf, p. 76
Apples
Gold Layer Cake with Caramel
Icing, p. 698
Coffee

6.

Fried fish or chicken*

Baked potatoes†
Potato chips or green corn‡
Cole Slaw, p. 455
Dill pickles
Beaten Biscuits, p. 509
Banana Chocolate Cake, p. 643
Peaches
Coffee

* Sautéed in the open.

† Baked in a campfire.

‡ Broiled over a campfire.

Envoi

The verse below is from the title page of *My Mother's Cook Book,* St. Louis, Missouri, 1875, as quoted in the Missouri Historical Society Bulletin for October 1950:

> Cookery is an Art,
> Still changing and of momentary triumph.
> Know, on thyself thy genius must depend;
> All books of Cookery, all helps of Art
> Are vain, if void of genius, thou wouldst cook.

Dear sentimentalist of a bygone age, your exalted statement is most discouraging!

What if a cook were like Mr. F. A. Pottle's poetaster "with only shivers of genius," or worse still, with none at all!

Would her family have to go hungry while she wooed the muse (if there is a tenth muse)? Would they wait patiently until inspiration rippled down her spine before she began pot-wrestling the food that was to ripple down their esophagus? Not the average family! Definite means would be found to convince the cook that an inspiration need not be personal in order to produce satisfying results—or art and appetite would come to grips.

But even if she cannot follow your high-flown dictum on inspiration first, any cook will appreciate your "momentary triumph," for cooking is hard work and eating is fleeting.

Spirit must be maintained to carry on the daily grind of kitchen effort, and some response must be apparent besides a family's increasing waistline. Expressed appreciation will help soften the disposition of a cook as well as uphold her interest, patience and courage. Give it to her wholeheartedly—she has been at pains to please you—lest she lapse into a blue mood and exclaim with truth and pessimism: "All day to cook, now look it!"

Entertaining and Table Service

This chapter is addressed mainly to the untried hostess who may soon be much tried if she allows herself to become flustered, but who may enjoy the greatest pleasure in sharing her home with others if she takes things serenely. Remember that hospitality has been defined as "making your guests feel at home even when you really wish they were."

Poise is an admirable quality. "Saki" advises us to observe the dignity and grace of a cat, which he thinks equaled in only a few fortunate human beings. As a cat is not called upon to be a cook or a hostess she may well have poise.

Poise is more difficult to attain and sustain when a woman must emulate the mental quickness of Groucho Marx and the physical agility of a flea. Sometimes it takes a superhuman effort to fling aside her kitchen apron as the door bell rings announcing the arrival of the first guests, and to assume a manner devoid of exhaustion or concern when greeting them. But the average woman, who is frequently endowed with tact, grace and other good qualities derived from her precious American heritage of hospitality, is capable of this effort and makes it successfully.

No matter whom you are entertaining, try not to be unduly impressed with the fact that something unusual is expected of you as a hostess. It isn't. Distinguished persons are usually simple. They dislike ostentation, and nothing is more disconcerting to a guest than the impression that his coming is causing a household commotion. Confine all noticeable efforts for his comfort and entertainment to the period that precedes his arrival. Work like a demon, if you must, satisfy yourself that you have anticipated every known emergency—the howling child, the last-minute search for studs, your husband's exuberance, your cook's ill humor—and then relax and enjoy your guests.

If something happens to upset your well-laid plans, rise to the occasion. The mishap may be the making of your party. Capitalize on it, but not too heavily.

If you plan to serve cocktails before a meal, place glasses filled with alcoholic and non-alcoholic beverages on a tray. With these you may pass some form of cracker, canapé or hors d'oeuvre. Keep this preliminary pickup rather light, as too much food at this time is apt to result in a jaded appetite for the dinner to follow.

Correct table setting is much more complicated than an easy formula: "forks to the left except the small fish fork, knives and spoons to the right," or "place silver that is to be used first farthest from the plate."

The table reflects the habits of the household and, no matter how unassuming its setting, its appearance should enhance the food. A change in its daily decor is as stimulating as a change in the seasoning of the food. Keep your basic forms in silver and dishes simple and not too pronounced in color. Vary your accessories. Choose a table top that will resist heat, so that you may set it, if you prefer, without a cloth, mats or trivets.

Change occasionally from covered soup bowls to a tureen and soup dishes. Replace your vegetable dishes with an outsize platter holding several vegetables attractively garnished. Parsley and cress may be varied by the use of small raw vegetables and fruits to give the platter a festive air. Exchange your matching dessert dishes for contrasting bowls.

For a rustic effect serve a hearty menu on your everyday dishes and use bright linens and wooden salad bowls, with a centerpiece of wooden scoops filled with pears and hazelnuts, as shown on the left at the top of page 920.

For a more elegant effect serve a dainty meal on the same dishes against a polished board with fragile glasses and flowers as shown on the right on page 920.

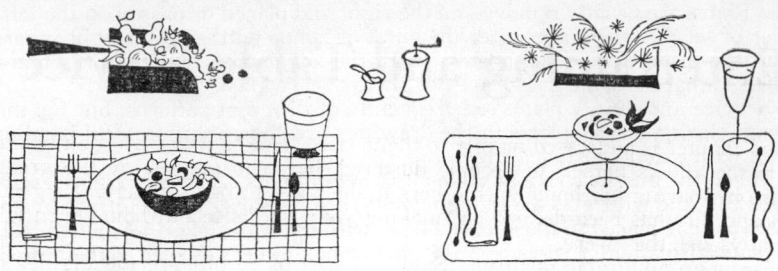

Choose as a centerpiece an ivy ring surrounding a figurine, shown on the left below, a basic evergreen arrangement, accented differently from day to day with blossoms or shrub florets, shown in the center, or a grouping of fruits or dried materials that add a seasonal touch to the everyday table.

To hold down expense use simple means to gain decorative effects. Several mullein-rosettes or other leaf clusters against a large red candle, as shown on the right above, create a holiday table; a silvery head of cabbage, scooped out to hold sauce, while its partially unfurled leaves hold shrimp or other tidbits for dipping, enhances a cocktail setting.

Whatever your decorative scheme, flower arrangements should be low or lacy. Tall arrangements that obstruct the view discourage across-the-table conversation. There is nothing more distracting than dodging a floral centerpiece while trying to establish an intimate relationship with your guests. For the same reason candles should be placed strategically. On a formal buffet or tea table, which is viewed from above, the decorations may be as tall as you wish.

Whether for friends or family always check the freshness of the air, the temperature of the dining area and the proper heat or chill for plates, food and drinks. Be sure that each guest at the table has plenty of elbow room, about two feet from the center of one plate service to the center of the next.

Formal meals given in beautifully appointed homes served by competent, well-trained servants who can be artists in their own right, are a treat. Even though we cannot expect to have these ideal conditions at all times in the average home, it is well to know how a semi-formal meal should be served. No matter what the degree of informality always keep the table attractive-looking through its immaculate cleanliness, and maintain an even rhythm to the service.

Individual ash trays and cigarettes may be placed on the table. Although smoking between courses is frowned on by all epicures because it deadens the sensitivity of the palate, guests must be permitted to do what pleases them. You may prefer to place the ash trays and cigarettes on the table just before the dessert is brought on.

Correct service is always a controversial subject, as there are several schools of thought about it. The procedures below present dignified and simple current practice. Plates are usually removed on the right and placed or passed on the left. The order of serving the guests after the guest of honor on the host's right is served is up to the discretion of the hostess, with the suggestion that the presentation be varied so that the same guests are not always served last.

Service and dinner plates are frequently of different patterns, but for the purpose of clarity service plates in the drawings are shown with a solid banding, hot plates with a double-banded edge.

When the guests arrive at table all is in readiness. The water glasses are two thirds full, the wine glasses, though empty, are in place. For a formal luncheon a butter plate is placed to the left on a level with the water glass. A butter ball is on the plate, also a butter spreader. But for formal dinners the use of the butter plate is optional.

A table setting forecasts the menu to be served, up to the dessert. The dessert service is brought on later. Let us consider two alternative menus from the beginning through the dessert.

The setting in the first drawing shown on the left below indicates a sea-food cocktail, a soup, a meat course, a salad course, water and two wines. Water and wine are poured from the right without lifting the glasses. The glasses may stay in place throughout the meal or the wine glass may be removed after a particular wine is no longer being served.

Once the guests are seated the server's steady but unobtrusive labor begins. There is a plate, filled or unfilled, before each guest throughout a formal meal. The server usually removes a plate from the right and replaces it immediately with another from the left.

The courses follow one another in unbroken rhythm. The passing of crackers, breads, relishes, the refilling of water glasses and the pouring of wines take place during, not between, the appropriate courses. The host may prefer to pour the wines himself, either from the bottle which may be wrapped in a napkin, or from a decanter. When the party is less formal the hostess may pass relishes to the guest at her right and the guests may continue to pass them on to one another. But in any case the work of the server is one that calls for nicely calculated timing and it is easy to see why one server should not be called upon to take care of more than 6 or 8 guests if smooth going is expected.

For this dinner the sea food, which is served in a specially iced glass, is in place when the guests are seated, as shown on the left above. The sea-food cocktail is removed, leaving the service plate in place, as shown on the right above. The soup plate is then placed on the service plate from the left. Relishes are passed during this course.

Let us assume that the meat course is to be carved and served in the dining room. The server removes the soup and service plate from the right, and from the left places an empty hot plate before the guest, as shown on the left at top of next page.

When the meat platter has been put before the host the server, holding an extra hot plate on a napkin, stands to the left of the host. When the host has filled the hot plate before him, the server removes that plate and replaces it with the empty hot plate he has been holding. Then, after removing the empty hot plate before the guest of honor from the right, the server gives the guest the filled hot plate from the left. He then returns to the host and waits to replace the hot plate being filled by the host for another guest.

The server then passes in turn the gravy, the vegetables—with a serving spoon and fork face down on the platter—and the hot breads. During the course he replenishes water and wine.

The menu we have been serving has consisted of a sea-food cocktail, a soup and a meat course. A salad and a dessert course will follow, but first let us consider a different menu—one that omits the cocktail and introduces a fish course. This alternate menu calls for a different setting of silver. You may read by the setting on the right above that the dinner menu is a soup, a fish, a meat and a salad course, water and two wines. The napkin is on the service plate, the place card on the napkin. Cigarettes, matches and an ash tray may be placed just above the service plate. No food is on the table when the guests are seated.

For this second menu soup in a soup plate is served from the left and placed directly on the service plate. If the soup is served on its own place plate, the service plate is removed first. The fish course which follows has been arranged on individual plates in the pantry. The soup and service plate are removed from the right when the pantry-arranged plate is placed, as shown in the first drawing below.

After the server has removed the fish plate from the right, a hot plate is put before the guest from the left, as shown next above. The meat course follows as previously described when served by the host, or the meat may be passed on a pantry-arranged platter.

An alternate to a salad course is a handsomely arranged fruit compote passed during the meat course. In this case a separate plate is used as shown right at the top of page 923. If a compote is substituted for a salad, a spoon for it is put on the right of the setting instead of a salad fork on the left. The salad course follows as shown on the left, page 923. After the salad course is removed the table is denuded for a short time. Any unused silver, salts and peppers—usually one set to two guests—and relishes are removed. The table is crumbed. The server uses a folded napkin and brushes the crumbs lightly onto a plate.

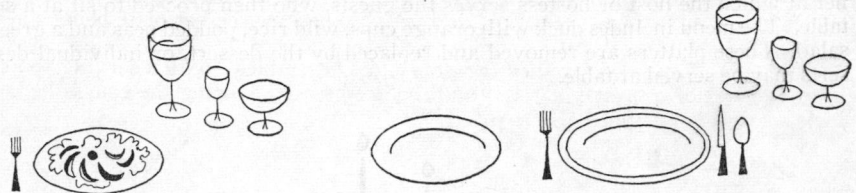

Next, the dessert setting is brought on, as shown on the left below, and is placed directly on the tablecloth. This consists of a partially filled finger bowl on a sheer doily on the dessert plate. Also on the dessert plate are the dessert fork and spoon, the fork to the left, the spoon to the right. The guest places the fork and spoon on the table, the fork to the left and the spoon to the right, and removes the doily with

the finger bowl on it to the upper left opposite the water glass, as shown on the right above. The dessert is passed by the server. If fruit is served after the dessert, the finger bowl is omitted at this time and the dessert plate has only the silver on it. In this case, the dessert plate is replaced with a fruit plate with a doily, finger bowl and knife and fork on it.

Coffee may be poured at table by the hostess or served individually from the pantry by the server. Coffee spoons are on the filled cups. Cream and sugar are passed by the server. Cream is optional. If the dinner is small the hostess may ask the guests' preference and add the sugar and cream herself.

Usually men like to loiter at the table. Being left to their own conversation and a bottle of port is dear to them. The hostess may serve the coffee to her guests and somewhat later retire to the drawing room with the women guests, or she may pour coffee for her reassembled guests in the drawing room. By this time good food, wine and conviviality have usually broken down the minor social inhibitions and the serving of coffee may be informal. Liqueur may be served in the wake of coffee.

If you cannot meet the exacting requirements of so formal a meal, make your dinner less formal by all means. Your chances for success will be greater if you do not attempt the impossible and your standards need not be lowered in the least. Plan to have the kind of food that will simplify last-minute preparation and subsequent serving. Plan to have fewer courses and to put more than one kind of food on one platter. But please do not let your guests sit, trying to make conversation, with a gradually congealing slice of meat before them waiting longingly for the vegetables and the reluctant gravy boat to follow.

If you must rely on indifferent service or if your harassed cook is to pinch hit as a waitress, plan to serve the main course yourself from an attractively arranged platter. For informal meals where the hostess may be both waitress and cook it pays to spend lots of time planning menus that can be prepared in advance and served with little fuss. Here again, in order that food will reach the table at the right temperatures, it is wise to choose co-operative equipment: covered dishes, double dishes with provision for ice and for buffets especially, steam tables or chafing dishes, and a samovar arrangement for hot drinks.

The following layouts show typical buffet settings. The first represents a dinner at which the host or hostess serves the guests, who then proceed to sit at a set table. The menu includes duck with orange cups, wild rice, podded peas and a green salad. These platters are removed and replaced by the dessert, or individual desserts may be served at table.

The second drawing shows a buffet at which the guests serve themselves and proceed to sit at small tables. If there are no tables, individual trays are helpful. If using trays have the consideration to plan food that does not call for the use of a knife.

Shown above are a meat casserole dish, artichokes vinaigrette filled with deviled eggs, relishes and rolls. A dessert may be on the table at the beginning of the service. If the table becomes too crowded move the water and hot drinks to another serving surface.

When service is completely lacking it is sensible to decide what concessions to make to achieve the most peaceful and satisfying conditions for everyone. Trays or a cart prepared in the kitchen and ready to carry or wheel into the dining area and placed to the right of the hostess are often a solution. If the meals are for 4 or less it is practical to fill the plates in the kitchen, but for more than 4 it is hard to keep the food good and hot. For a larger number of persons attractive platters and casseroles placed at table so that serving responsibilities are divided ease matters for the hostess.

Tray meals for invalids should be given the greatest care. The recipient is often helpless, finicky and wanting attention. Here again variety of setting is a stimulant, and a surprise element in the form of a beautiful pitcher or an unusual bowl, a small flower arrangement or some small attention other than food is much appreciated. Make sure that all needed utensils are present and that the food is fresh-looking, hot or cold as required, sufficient in portion but dainty in appearance.

The same injunctions as to having everything present on the tray and having the food look fresh and attractive applies to the afternoon tea tray. Both this and the table for the large tea have their conventionalities, but both may be enhanced by a wide choice of equipment and decor.

The drawing below shows the coffee service at the end of a large formal tea table. It is wise to instruct a maid to keep in frequent touch with the pourers to anticipate their need for additional hot water, coffee or cups. It is also canny to have additional platters ready to replace those at table that become rather ragged-looking. Medium-size rather than large platters are easier to keep in trim and handier for passing among the guests who are standing far from the table.

Not all types of service can be detailed here. But whatever the occasion for entertaining, assemble your tried skills in cooking and presentation and make your party conform to the dictates of your home and flavor it well with your own personality.

Left-Over Food Suggestions

A judicious use of left-over food is commendable provided the housewife knows how far her economical impulses may carry her without a family protest.

Some of the most tempting luncheon dishes are made from refrigerator scraps. Do not disdain them, but please learn to resist the temptation of the too comprehensive dish. Recently *Time* reported that:

"In Memphis, a queasy husband seeking a divorce complained to the court that his wife cooked him up a one-dish breakfast composed of a layer of beans, one of sardines, one of salmon, topped with a cake."

His wish was granted.

Many left-overs are transformed by the blender. For suggestions, see page 895.

Both soufflés and timbales lend themselves readily as a basis for using up odds and ends.

Tomatoes, peppers, onions, eggplant, acorn squash, summer squash, turnips, avocados, cucumbers, pimientos, baked potatoes and carrots may be filled with left-over meat, fish, potatoes, rice or vegetables, alone or in some good combination. Moisten these ingredients with gravy, cream sauce, butter, eggs, bacon fat, milk or cream and combine them with dry bread, bread crumbs, onions, nut meats, etc. Prepare and fill the cases and cook them as directed (pages 198-210).

Waffle, pancake and fritter batter combine well with meat, fish or vegetables. Add ¾ to 1 cupful of finely minced or ground left-over food to waffle batter, cook the waffles and serve them with cream or other sauce, or gravy, etc. See Filled Pancakes, page 162, Fritters, page 543.

Deep custard cups are useful for serving small amounts of left-overs. Fill them with moistened seasoned food, cover the tops with pieces of buttered paper secured with string or rubber bands, and place the cups in a pan partly filled with boiling water. Steam the food on top of the stove or in the oven until it is thoroughly heated. Remove the papers. If desired, the tops may be sprinkled with bread crumbs dotted with butter or sprinkled with cheese and browned under a broiler.

To utilize the following articles of food try the recipes suggested. I hope they will relieve the dreariness Eugene Field complained of as "The review of reviews."

APPLESAUCE:
Applesauce pudding
Applesauce cake
BACON DRIPPINGS:
Bacon drippings will keep indefinitely. Use them for sautéing meats, potatoes, mushrooms, eggs, etc.
BONES:
Chicken bone soup
Ham bone—split pea or bean soup
Ham bone stock—split pea or bean soup
Left-over soup
Turkey soup
Chicken feet soup
BREAD:
Bread, egg and cheese dish
Bread dressing
Croutons
Crumb muffins
Crumb griddle cakes

In tomato cases—see introduction of this chapter
Crumb pie crust
Crumb pie
Bread pudding
Caramel bread pudding
Brown betty
Queen of puddings
Panade
BREAD CRUMBS:
Place stale bread in a slow oven. When it is dry, put it through a food mill or blender or crush it with a rolling pin and place the crumbs in a covered fruit jar. Use them for breaded dishes, oysters, cutlets, etc.
COOKED CEREALS:
Cut into slices. Sauté slowly in drippings. See Cereal Cakes, page 100. Add to soups or use in bread doughs and stuffings.

CHEESE:
Macaroni
Rarebit
Croquettes
Popovers
Noodle ring
Rice
Tomato rice
Ramekins
Welsh rarebit over grilled tomatoes
Cheese soufflé
Cheese and ham soufflé
Cereals
Scrambled eggs with cheese
Baked eggs with cheese
Cheese omelet
Scalloped oysters with cheese
Cabbage stuffed with rice and cheese
Cheese sauce
Baked onions and cheese on toast
Cheese custard pie
Gnocchi
Cheese timbales
Au gratin dishes
Cheese spread
Grated in canapé spreads or sandwiches
Blender cheese spreads

CHICKEN: See Index under Chicken

CHICKEN FAT:
Use chicken fat in place of bacon drippings or clarified and chilled, as a substitute for butter in baking, using ⅔ cupful for every cupful of butter.

COFFEE:
Coffee jelly with marshmallows
Coffee marshmallow jelly with whipped cream
Coffee-flavored layer cake
Soft ginger cookies
Soft molasses drop cakes
Coffee fudge
Mocha sea-foam icing
Mocha torte
Mocha sponge
Mocha sauce
Coffee icebox cake

CREAM SAUCE:
Creamed potatoes
Soufflés
Creamed eggs
Waffles—see introduction to this chapter
Creamed meats, vegetables, hash, etc.

EGG YOLKS:
Scrambled in tomato soup
Scrambled
Egg drops for soup
Mayonnaise
Hollandaise sauce

Sponge cake made with yolks
Yellow loaf or layer cake
Gold cup cakes
Gold layer cakes
Yolk cookies
Yolk drop cakes
Date bars
Butter wafers
Cup custards
Custard filling
Caramel custard
Boiled custard sauce
Lemon sauce
Almond sauce
Drop yolks into simmering water, cook them under the boiling point until they are firm. Rice them and use them as a garnish for salads, etc.
Add egg yolks to cream sauce, gravy or soup. Do not boil the liquid after adding them. Yolks may be kept for days in a refrigerator covered with milk or water.

EGG WHITES:
Angel cup cakes
Angel cake
Angel cake—chocolate
Cinnamon stars
Meringue tart
Meringues
Pecan drop cakes
Prune, apricot and date whip
Apricot sponge
Brown sugar drop cookies
Pound cake
White cake
Marshmallow pudding
Fluffy hard sauce
Sea-foam candy
Chocolate almond bars
Hazelnut cakes
Kisses
Lady cake
Divinity
White and other icings
Marble cake
Whipped cream cake
Poppy seed cake
Chocolate almond shells
Date and nut cookies
Almond rings
Macaroons
Caramel nut cakes
Snow balls
Use egg whites to brush insides of pie shells or before breading fish or meat.

FISH:
Fish timbales
Fish and nut timbales
Fish salad
Fish soufflé

In tomato cases
Aspic salad
Creamed on toast
Steamed fish pudding
Fish and rice ramekins
Fish hash
Fish salad in aspic
Eggs stuffed with fish
Baked rice and fish balls
Three-fourths to 1 cupful of flaked fish may be added to waffles—see first paragraph of this chapter.

FRUIT JUICES:
Cocktails and other drinks
Fruit gelatine
Wine jelly
Substitute for water in seven minute cake icing
To baste ham, pot roast, etc.
Substitute for water in applesauce, dried prunes or apricots
Baked apples, pears, etc.
Fruit sauce (plain or thickened with cornstarch) for baked custards or puddings. You may add grated orange or lemon rind
Fruit salad dressing
Lemonade
Molded fruit salad
In brown betty, tapioca and rice pudding or mincemeat

GRAVY:
Combine gravy with cooked rice, spaghetti, etc., adding chopped onions, celery, carrots or peppers. Serve gravy with waffles or pancakes, with corn oysters, sautéed cereals, or cold sandwiches.

GRAPEFRUIT, ORANGE AND LEMON PEEL:
Candied grapefruit peel
Candied orange peel
Orange bread
Grated lemon peel for flavoring cakes, breads or puddings.

HASH:
In biscuit or pie dough
In pie shells
In tomato cases
Shepherd's pie
On toast
Hash with potatoes
Hash with celery
Hash with waffles
Meat roll
Corn-meal mush pie
On rounds of fried grits
In a grits ring, carrot ring, rice ring, noodle ring, etc.

ICE CREAM:
Stir into 1 pint soft ice cream 1 tablespoonful gelatine soaked in 2 table-

spoonfuls water dissolved over heat. Chill the cream. Serve it with pudding sauce.

JELLIES:
Dissolve bits of jelly and jam with a small quantity of boiling water and use them for pudding sauce.
Use jelly in place of applesauce in turnovers.
Lady finger sandwiches

OATMEAL:
Oatmeal griddle cakes
Oatmeal muffins

PICKLE VINEGAR:
Pickled onions or beets
With salad oil in salads

PICKLED FRUIT JUICE:
Mincemeat
For basting baked ham or other meats

POTATOES:
Potatoes au gratin
Baked mashed potatoes
Creamed potatoes
Eggs in a nest
Hashed brown
O'Brien
Mashed potato puffs
Pear potatoes
Potato balls rolled in cornflakes
Potato cakes
Potato cheese puffs
Potato soufflé
Sautéed potatoes
Shepherd's pie
Mashed potato pie
Mashed potato tuna fish balls
Mashed potato salad

PRUNES OR APRICOTS:
Eggless apricot whip
Eggless prune whip
Soufflé
Apricot bread
Apricot ice cream
Prune or apricot juice
Prune or apricot eggnog
In fruit gelatine
To baste baked ham
Prune muffins
Chocolate prune cake
Prune cake
Apricot whip
Stuffed with cheese for salad
Stuffed with nuts as a confection

RICE:
Cheese rice boiled
Cheese rice baked
Eggs with rice and tomato sauce
Rice ramekins
In tomato cases
Rice croquettes
Rice timbales

Rice pudding
Rice corn-meal griddle cakes
Caramel rice pudding
Rice waffles
Rice served with cinnamon, sugar and cream or fruit juice
Creamed with left-over food
Rice muffins
Batter bread or muffins
Corn-meal rice muffins
In clear soup or blend as base for thick soups

SANDWICHES:
Toast left-over sandwiches

SAUSAGES:
Liver sausage and tomato spread
Liver sausage sandwiches
Frankfurter or Vienna sausages sliced, in thick soups
Cervelat slices filled with cream cheese and rolled in baked beans
Noodle and rice dishes

SOUP:
Jellied soup
Aspic salads
Dumplings
Gravy, brown sauce or other sauces

SOUR MILK:
Biscuit
Muffins
Bran muffins
Graham muffins
Cottage cheese
Doughnuts
Gravy
Gingerbread waffles
Griddle cakes
Graham griddle cakes
Corn bread
Mock venison
Fig spice cake
Spice cup cakes
Sour milk layer cake·
Pancakes
Spoon bread
Velvet spice cake
Prune cake
Chocolate spice cake
Devil's food
Banana cake

SOUR CREAM:
Almond cake filling
Almond roll
Cream sauce for mulled cucumbers and other vegetables
Gravy
Sour cream cake
Sour cream cookies
Sour cream icing
Salad dressing
Sour cream and horseradish sauce
Baked fish with sour cream

Veal paprika
Chicken paprika
Coffee cake
Sour cream cherry cake
Grandmother's apple cake
Hermits
Jam cup cakes
Old-fashioned molasses drop cakes
In ice cream with soda added to cut the acid
Waffles
Crumb muffins
Sour cream muffins
Borsch
Doughnuts with sour cream
Ice cream pie
Sour cream pie
Breaded veal slices
Dressing for fruit

MEAT:
(See beginning of this chapter)
Aspic salad
Bacon left-overs as garnish
Chicken à la king
Chicken and ham creamed
Chicken and ham spread
Chicken and ham soufflé
Chicken and ham timbales
Chicken bisque
Chicken croquettes
Chicken giblets creamed
Chicken livers—see Index
Chicken in tomato cases
Chicken mousse
Chicken salad
Chicken salad in aspic
Chicken or veal forcemeat
Creamed chicken or veal in rice or noodle ring
Club sandwich
Diced meat in French dressing
Eggs in a nest
Ham à la king
Ham cakes with eggs
Ham cakes with pineapple
Ham in tomato cases
Ham, jellied mousse
Ham sandwich spread
Ham soufflé
Ham loaf
Ham noodles
Ground ham on pineapple slices
Ham rolls with rice
Baked potatoes filled with minced ham
Left-over meat loaf
Left-over meat in rice balls
Left-over meat in batter
Left-over meat in soup
Left-over meat deviled
Blend for thick soups
Meat pie roll or pinwheels

Meat scraps in soup
Meat loaf in pastry or meat soufflé
Meat in tomato aspic or fritters
Meat on skewers
Meat in puff shells or meat pie
Meat shortcakes or in corn-meal mush
Hot biscuits baked with fillings—chicken, ham roast, etc.
Rombauer rice dish
Baked potatoes with hash and vegetables
Cold roast beef and tomato sauce
Chow mein
Ham and veal loaf
Curried veal and rice
Terrapin, chicken, lamb
In spaghetti, noodles, rice, etc.
Scrapple

MEAT AND VEGETABLE SCRAPS:

Bacon left-overs
Creamed on toast
Eggplant filled with left-over food
Economy soufflé
Filled pancakes
In a meat roll
In corn-meal mush pie
In fritters or croquettes
In pastry

In soup
In tomato cases
Shepherd's pie
Vegetable casserole
Left-over timables

VEGETABLES:

Vegetable bisque
Vegetable parings—see soups
Vegetables in tomato cases
Vegetable soufflé
Vegetable stock
Creamed vegetables with omelet
Carrot timbales or other timbales
Cream of cauliflower soup
Upside-down vegetable pie
Economy soufflé or other soufflés
Left-over vegetable dish with cheese
Left-over vegetable dish with hamburger
Brussels sprouts, etc., in cheese sauce

CORN:

Corn oysters or corn pudding
In pepper or tomato cases
Corn timbales

LETTUCE:

Cabbage or lettuce and rice dish
Braised or wilted lettuce
In soup

Staples for the Average Family

Beverages, coffee, tea
Bacon
Cereals, breakfast foods, rice, macaroni, spaghetti, noodles, farina, corn meal, tapioca
Cheese
Chocolate, cocoa
Coconut
Butter, lard or other shortening
Flour, whole-grain, all-purpose and cake flour
Sugar, granulated, confectioners', brown, loaf, maple sugar
Bread, crackers
Fruits, fresh, dried and canned
Tomato juice
Potatoes, white and sweet
Onions and garlic
Sirups, corn and molasses
Salad oil and vinegar
Milk, cream and eggs
Canned meats, soup and fish
Beef and vegetable cubes
Nuts
Vegetables, fresh and canned
Molasses
Mayonnaise and French dressing
Honey, preserves, marmalade, jelly
Commercial coloring for soups and sauces

Raisins and currants
Peanut butter
Debittered brewers' yeast
Milk solids, evaporated and condensed milk
Worcestershire and Tabasco sauce
Gelatine, flavored and unflavored
Catsup, chili sauce and horseradish
Flavorings, vanilla, almond, etc.
Baking powder and baking soda
Cornstarch
Ground and stick cinnamon
Ground and whole cloves
Ground ginger
Allspice
Whole nutmeg
Bay leaves
Salt
Celery seed
Celery salt
Dry and prepared mustard
Black and white peppercorns
Paprika and cayenne
Curry powder
Garlic and onion salt
Chili powder
Dried herbs, tarragon, basil, savory, sage, etc.
Monosodium glutamate

Nutrition and Calorie Chart

To live we must eat. To live in health we must eat intelligently. By whose intelligence, how guided?

Will our own intuitive desires lead us to a balanced diet, the same cravings that made our forebears gather greens each spring? Shall we follow scientists ceaselessly at work to uncover the secrets of human nutrition? Or shall we listen to the dicta of health faddists or the croaking of quacks?

Sufficient facts have come from scientific sources to enable us to make some definite statements about nutrition. Since much research is still going on and since not all scientists are in agreement, even rather conservative ideas may, however, be disputed.

A calorie chart that gives the caloric values of ordinary quantities of common foods will be found on page 934. But our total caloric intake is not the whole story, for it is the distribution of the foods that provide our caloric intake that is important to our health.

Scientists recommend that we divide our daily caloric intake of energy foods in approximately this proportion:

Protein .... 10 to 20%
Fats .... 20 to 30%
Carbohydrates .... 50 to 60%

In addition to other functions, the main task of protein foods is the building and repairing of body cells. People living in cold climates, growing children, pregnant women and nursing mothers consequently require a larger proportion of protein than average adults.

Proteins are known to contain amino acids. These complex acids are still being studied by chemists, but it is known that some of them are essential to growth and life. All of these acids are not found in complete form in all protein foods. They are most fully represented in meat, fish, eggs, milk and cheese. They are present but less well represented in nuts, legumes and cereals. Since the vegetable groups are incomplete in themselves, it is wise to draw half to two thirds of the daily protein intake from the animal sources given above. Meats should be fresh, not pickled, salted or highly processed.

Many proteins are likely to lose some of their appetite appeal and to become less digestible if cooked with too great heat, because high heat toughens them. For instance, it may make eggs curdle, cheese string and meat or fish dry out.

Fats act as fuel, as insulation for the body against cold, as cushioning for the internal organs, and as lubricants. In addition to transporting the fat-soluble vitamins, some fats contain unsaturated fatty acids which harbor necessary growth factors, and help with the digestion of other fats. Therefore, the use of a variety of fats from animal and vegetable sources is recommended.

We are apt to eat more fat than we realize as it lurks in unexpected places. Egg yolk is one third fat; pork may be more than one half; and the leg of a young fryer may yield over a teaspoonful. Again, avocado, chocolate and pecans may be from one fourth to three fourths fat, not to mention the large amounts present in some of the lightest textured cakes and pastries, and in the smoothest gravies and sauces. All fats are sensitive to high temperatures, light and air. For fat storage and cooking temperatures see pages 541, 542 and 940.

While all fats are slow to leave the stomach and therefore leave us with a satisfied feeling, properly fried foods should have no adverse effect on normal digestion.

Carbohydrates constitute about 60% of our daily intake. Vegetables and fruits are included in this group as well as flour, cereals and sugars. The caloric value of fruits and vegetables is frequently low, while that of cereals and sweets is high. It is possible for children and athletes to consume a larger amount of sugars and starches with less harm than other people, but most of us are likely to eat an undue amount and are less well equipped to take care of it. Our consumption of sweet and starchy foods, in addition to highly sweetened beverages, is frequently excessive. An imbalance results that is acknowledged to be one of the major causes of malnutrition, for the demands excess carbohydrates make on the system cause a deficiency of vitamin B complex.

We must now consider the importance of vitamin and other accessory substances to the functioning of the system. The body requires some of these substances in only minute quantities. It can store few of them in quantity. So they must be replenished daily from food sources. There are over forty known minerals, vitamins, hormones and enzymes which the body demands. They are often the fragile elements in foods that are readily lost through indifferent handling, poor cooking and excessive processing. For the proper handling and cooking of vegetables, meats, fish and cereals so that they will retain these elements as much as possible, read the forewords to the chapters on these subjects.

During the last fifty years a great change has taken place in the processing and preserving of foods. We have drifted into assuming that sanitary and keeping qualities are synonymous with nutritive values, but preservatives and purifying processes frequently tend to be destructive of vital elements in food. Freezing seems to preserve more values than most canning. Canning by pressure retains more than old-fashioned canning exposed to air. Both freezing and canning are usually better methods than drying, pickling, salting or brining.

We have reviewed our calorie needs and the distribution of calories among the energy foods. We have still to assure ourselves a practical method of including optimal amounts of accessory factors. If we list the prime sources of minerals and vitamins we find many duplications; for often foods rich in one vitamin or mineral are also rich in others. It happens, too, that some of the foods heavily weighted with biologic values are the best quality proteins. Many of the foods rich in accessory values also have bulk, a factor to be considered in planning our daily intake so as to include more high than low-residue foods.

Here is our shopping guide for accessory factors. We should fill our baskets so they hold a minimum of 2 fruits and 3 vegetables daily.

First on the list are vegetables, preferably highly colored ones. Concentrate on raw dark green salad materials, and for cooking, on leafy greens and the green and yellow vegetables. Close runners-up are the cabbage family, especially the loose leaved, greener types to be used either raw or cooked. Add root vegetables prepared with their tops, tomatoes, potatoes, especially sweet potatoes, and peppers, both green and red.

Make a place next for quantities as large as the pocketbook will allow of fresh fruits and juices, especially citrus fruits and yellow fruits like apricots, peaches and melons. Add, in season, small berried fruits; and use prunes, pineapple, bananas and, if available, guavas. Don't neglect the canned acid fruit juices, like grapefruit or tomato.

Prime choices in our protein allowance are milk, cheese and eggs, fish and fish roe, organ meats such as liver, kidneys, heart and brains, lean-muscle cuts of beef, pork and lamb, dried peas and beans, especially soybeans and peanuts. Use yeast as a leaven or as an addition in autolyzed form to baked goods, soups, puddings, gravies and meat dishes. Bake with whole grains and flavor with brown sugar, molasses, wheat germ and butter. Don't forget the cheapest of all accessory factors, outdoor exercise, to whet your appetite, tone your muscles and get you out where you absorb the sunlight vitamin D.

Other incidentals to bear in mind are to drink seven or eight glasses of fluid a day and to use iodized salt if you live in a region that calls for it.

The plan outlined above is not necessarily a costly one. It is nearly always possible to substitute cheaper but equally nutritious items from the same food groups. Vegetables of similar accessory value, for example, may be differently priced. Seasonal foods, which automatically give us menu variations, are usually higher in food value and lower in cost. Whole-grain cereals are no more costly than highly processed ones. Fresh fruits are frequently less expensive than canned fruits loaded with sugar.

If you are willing to cut down the refined starch and sugar items, especially fancy baked goods, bottled drinks and candies, a higher proportion of the budget will be released for dairy products, vegetables and fruits. Do not buy more perishable foods than you can store properly. Use left-overs cold, if possible.

Our fundamental effort always must be to provide this highly versatile body of ours with those elements it needs for efficient functioning, and to provide them in such proportions as to put the least strain on our systems.

Natural foods are usually our best sources for complete nourishment. A proper choice of them should in most cases supply our needs without the use of synthetic vitamin preparations.

The subject of nutrition is of the greatest importance and the housewife who has the responsibility of supplying her family with food will do well to make a real study of the advances in this field.

Food Energy: Recommended Daily Allowances [1]

Man (154 lbs.)
Moderately active	3000 calories
Very active	4500 "
Sedentary	2500 "

Woman (123 lbs.)
Moderately active	2500 "
Very active	3000 "
Sedentary	2100 "
Pregnancy (latter half)	2500 "
Lactation	3000 "

Children up to 12 years
Under 1 yr. [2]	100 calories per kilogram (2.2 lbs.)
1-3 years [3]	1200 calories
4-6 years	1600 "
7-9 years	2000 "
10-12 years	2500 "

Children over 12 years
Girls, 13-15 years	2800 "
16-20 years	2400 "
Boys, 13-15 years	3200 "
16-20 years	3800 "

[1] Recommended Dietary Allowances, Committee on Food and Nutrition, National Research Council, p. 3. May 1941. Reprinted by permission.

[2] Needs of infants increase from month to month. The amounts given are for children of approximately 6-8 months of age.

[3] Allowances are based on needs for the middle year in each group (as 2, 5, 8, etc.) and for moderate activity.

Calorie Chart

"Personal size and mental sorrow have certainly no necessary proportions. A large, bulky figure has as good a right to be in deep affliction as the most graceful set of limbs in the world. But, fair or not fair there are unbecoming conjunctions, which reason will patronize in vain—which taste cannot tolerate—which ridicule will seize." Jane Austen.

This chart is given hopefully to offset those "unbecoming conjunctions." When you read it remember that a gram of carbohydrate or protein is 4 calories—a gram of fat is 9 calories. In addition, "Let your contours be your guide."

Food	Calories
Almonds, 12 salted	100
Almonds, 12 to 14 shelled	100
Apple, 1 medium baked with 2 tablespoons sugar	200
Apple, 1 large raw	100
Apple butter, 1 tablespoon	75
Apple dumpling, 1 medium	300
Apple pie, 3" cut	200
Applesauce, ½ cup	150
Apricots, 5 halves canned with juice	150
Apricots, ½ cup dried, stewed, sweetened	200
Apricots, 3 whole fresh	60
Artichoke, 1	100
Artichoke, 1 large tuber Jerusalem	80
Asparagus, 8 stalks	25
Asparagus soup, cream of, 1 cup	200
Avocado, ½ medium	200
Bacon, 5 crisp slices	100
Banana cream pie, average serving	250
Banana, 1 medium	100
Batter cakes, 2	200
Beans, baked, 2 cups canned	150
Beans, green or snap, ½ cup	26
Beans, Lima, ½ cup fresh or canned	100
Bean soup, 1 cup	130
Bean sprouts, 1 cup	35
Beef, corned, boiled, average slice	100
Beef, corned, hash, ½ cup	190
Beef, dried, 4 thin slices	100
Beef, 1 fillet of	275
Beef, hamburger, broiled, 1 cake 2½" diameter	100
Beef, rib roast, lean, slice 5" x 2½" x ¼"	100
Beef broth, 1 cup	30
Beef heart, 4 oz.	118
Beef liver, 1 medium slice	100
Beef loaf, average slice	100
Beefsteak, sirloin, slice 2" x 1½" x ¾"	100
Beef stew with vegetables, 1 cup	225
Beef tongue, 2 small slices	65
Beer, 1 can or bottle (12 oz.)	140
Beer, 1 glass (10 oz.)	115
Beet greens, ½ cup cooked	30
Beets, ½ cup	40
Berry pies, average slice	350
Biscuits, 2 small	100
Blackberries, ¾ cup fresh	52
Blueberries, ¾ cup fresh	50

Food	Calories
Bologna sausage, 6 slices	180
Bouillon, clear, 1 cup	25
Brazil nut, 1 shelled	50
Bread, bran, 1 slice (1 oz.)	75
Bread, gluten, 1 slice (1 oz.)	50
Bread, commercial whole wheat, 1 slice (1 oz.)	75
Bread, rye, 1 slice (1 oz.)	70
Bread, white, 1 slice (1 oz.)	75
Bread, whole grain, 1 slice (1 oz.)	80
Bread pudding, ½ cup	200
Broccoli, 1 cup cooked	50
Brown betty, ¼ cup	125
Brussels sprouts, ¾ cup	55
Butter, 1 square ¼" thick	50
Buttermilk, 1 glass	80
Cabbage, ½ cup chopped, raw	10
Cabbage, ½ cup cooked	25
Cake, angel, plain, 3" slice	150
Cake, chocolate layer, 2" slice	400
Cake, coffee, 1 piece 1½" square	100
Cake, cup, 1 plain	100
Cake, fruit, 1 small slice ½" thick	100
Cake, sponge, 2" slice	100
Cantaloupe, ½ average melon	50
Caramels, 1 plain	100
Carrots, ½ cup cooked	30
Carrot, 1 whole raw	20
Cashew nuts, 5	100
Catsup, 1 tablespoon	10
Cauliflower, 1 cup	30
Caviar, 1 tablespoon	100
Celeriac, 1 medium	40
Celery, 10 to 12 ribs	30
Celery cabbage, 1 cup raw	20
Celery soup, cream of, ½ cup	100
Charlotte Russe, 1 serving	250
Cheese, American, 3" x 2" x ¼" slice	118
Cheese, Camembert, 2" wedge	122
Cheese, cottage, ½ cup	100
Cheese, cream, ½ of 3 oz. cake	125
Cheese, Edam, 1" cube	61
Cheese, Liederkranz, 2" x 1¼" x 1" piece	119
Cheese, Parmesan, ¼ cup	75
Cheese, Roquefort, 1 oz. piece	100
Cheese, Swiss, 4½" x 3½" x ⅛" piece	100
Cheese soufflé, ½ cup	100
Cheese straws, 3	100
Chef salad without dressing, average serving	90
Cherries, canned, ½ cup	100
Cherries, fresh, 20 large	100

Food	Calories
Chicory, 5 or 6 leaves	21
Chicken, ½ medium broiler	125
Chicken, roast, average serving	125 to 150
Chicken salad, ½ cup	200
Chocolate, beverage, 1 cup made with milk	230
Chocolate bar, milk, 1 small	285
Chocolate creams, 1 medium	100
Chocolate eclair, 1 small	250
Chocolate fudge, 1″ square	100
Chocolate ice cream, ½ cup	250
Chocolate malted milk, 13 oz.	514
Chocolate milk shake, 13 oz.	472
Chocolate soda, 1 glass	400
Cinnamon bun, 1 average	200
Clam chowder, 1 cup	130
Cocoa made with milk and water, 1 cup	135
Coconut, shredded, dried, 2 tablespoons	70
Coconut custard pie, 1 average piece	350
Codfish, creamed, ½ cup	200
Codfish balls, 2 large	200
Cod liver oil, 1 tablespoon	100
Coffee, clear, 1 cup	None
Coffee with 1 tablespoon cream, 1 cup	30
Coffee with 1 lump sugar, 1 cup	25
Cola beverages, 1 bottle (7 oz.)	75
Consommé, 1 cup	25
Cookies, plain, two 3″	100
Corn, canned, ½ cup	120
Corn on cob, 1 medium	60
Corn bread, 1 slice 2″ x 2″ x 1″	100
Cornflakes, ¾ cup	100
Corn meal, cooked, ⅔ cup	100
Corn sirup, 1 tablespoon	75
Corn soup, cream of, ½ cup	100
Cornstarch blancmange, ½ cup	200
Cottage pudding, average serving	100
Crab meat, canned, ½ cup	75
Crab, soft shell, 1	75
Cracked wheat, ¼ cup	115
Cracker, graham, 1	35
Crackers, oyster, twelve 1″	50
Cracker, saltine, 1 double	30
Cracker, soda, 1	20
Cranberry jelly, 2 tablespoons	100
Cream, thick (40% fat), 2 tablespoons	120
Cream, thin (18.5% fat), 2 tablespoons	59
Cream of wheat, cooked, ¾ cup	100
Cream sauce, white, ¼ cup	100
Cucumbers, 12 slices	10
Custard, ½ cup	125
Custard pie, average piece	200
Daiquiri cocktail, 1 cocktail glass (3 oz.)	130

Food	Calories
Dates, 3 or 4	100
Divinity, 1 square	100
Doughnut, 1	200
Duck, roast, 1 medium piece	300
Dumpling, 1	100
Eggnog, 1 scant cup	200
Eggplant, 3 slices 4″ x ½″	50
Egg, 1 whole boiled	75
Egg, 1 fried with 1 teaspoon butter	105
Egg, 1 poached	75
Egg, 1 scrambled, with 2 tablespoons milk, 1 teaspoon butter	140
Farina, ¾ cup cooked	100
Fig, 1 large dried	65
Figs, 3 large fresh	60
Flounder, average serving	100
Frankfurters, 1 average	125
French dressing, 1½ tablespoons	100
French toast, 1 piece	135
Frog legs, 2	50
Fruit cocktail or salad, ½ cup with 1 tablespoon dressing	200
Gin, 2 tablespoons (1 oz.)	70
Ginger ale, 1 cup	75
Gingerbread, one 2″ square	200
Ginger snap, 1	20
Goose, roast, 1 average serving	300
Gooseberries, cooked, ½ cup	100
Grapefruit, ½ large	50
Grapefruit juice, unsweetened, 1 cup	100
Grape juice, 1 glass (8 oz.)	160
Grapes, Malaga, 20 to 25	100
Gravy, thick, 3 tablespoons	100
Green pepper, 1 whole	20
Griddle cakes, 1 cake 4½″ in diameter	100
Grits, hominy, cooked, ¾ cup	100
Gum drop, 1 large	25
Haddock, average serving	100
Halibut steak, cooked, 3″ x 1½″ x 1″ piece	125
Ham, baked, medium, fat, 4½″ x 4″ x ¼″ slice	400
Ham, boiled, no fat, 4¼″ x 4″ x ⅛″ slice	100
Hamburger, 1 cake 2″ in diameter	100
Hard sauce, 1 tablespoon	100
Hermits, one 2″ in diameter	50
Herring, fresh, 3 oz.	128
Herring, smoked, 3 oz.	268
Hickory nuts, about 12	100
Hollandaise sauce, 1 tablespoon	100
Honey, 1 tablespoon	100
Honeydew melon, ¼ medium melon	100
Horseradish, 1 tablespoon	25
Ice cream, commercial, plain, ½ cup	190

Food	Calories
Jam or jelly, 1 tablespoon	60
Kale, 1 cup cooked	50
Kidneys, 1 medium broiled, beef or veal	250
Kisses, 1 small	50
Kohlrabi, ½ cup	35
Kumquats, 3	35
Lady fingers, 1	50
Lamb, leg, roast, 3½″ x 4½″ x ⅛″ slice	100
Lamb chops, broiled, 1 average	100
Leek, 1	10
Lemon, 1 medium	30
Lemonade, 1 cup	75
Lemon ice, scant ½ cup	100
Lemon jelly, ½ cup	100
Lemon juice, 3 tablespoons	15
Lemon meringue pie, ⅙ of pie	250 to 300
Lentil soup, 1 cup	250
Lettuce, 1 large head	50
Lettuce, loose leaf, 6 large leaves	18
Lime juice, 1 tablespoon	10
Liver, 1 medium slice	100
Lobster, canned, scant ¾ cup	84
Lobster, fresh, ½ cup	125
Loganberries, canned, ½ cup	100
Macaroni, cooked, ½ cup	89
Macaroni and cheese, ⅔ cup	200
Mackerel, broiled, average serving	125
Malted milk, 1 glass	200
Manhattan cocktail, 1 cocktail glass	160
Maple sirup, 1 tablespoon	72
Margarine, 1 tablespoon	100
Marmalade, 2 tablespoons	200
Marshmallows, 5	100
Martini cocktail, 1 cocktail glass	135
Mayonnaise, 1 tablespoon	100
Meat loaf, 1 medium slice	100
Melba toast, 1 slice	25
Milk, cream removed, 1 glass (8 oz.)	80
Milk, evaporated, ½ cup	150
Milk, powdered, skim, 1 tablespoon	25
Milk, powdered, whole, 1 tablespoon	40
Milk, whole, fresh, 1 glass (8 oz.)	160
Mincemeat pie, average serving	500
Mints, chocolate cream, 3 small	100
Molasses, 1 tablespoon	55
Muffin, 1 small	125 to 150
Mushrooms, canned, ½ cup	85
Mushrooms, fresh, 25 medium	100
Mustard greens, 1 cup	35
Mutton, leg, roast, lean, average serving	100
Noodles, cooked, ½ cup	60
Oatmeal, cooked, ½ cup	66

Food	Calories
Okra, 10 pods	38
Old-Fashioned cocktail, 1 old-fashioned glass	150
Olive oil, 1 tablespoon	100
Olives, green, 2 small or 1 large	20
Olives, ripe, 2 small or 1 large	25
Onions, 4 medium	100
Onions, creamed, ⅓ cup	100
Onions, green, raw, 5 medium	10
Orange, 1 average	75
Orange ice, ½ cup	110
Orange juice, 1 cup (8 oz.)	110
Oxtail soup, 1 cup	150
Oysters, 7 medium	50
Oyster stew with milk, 1 cup	225
Pancake, 1	100
Parsley, ½ cup	24
Parsnips, cooked, ½ cup	65
Peaches, canned, 2 large halves with juice	100
Peach, fresh, 1 large	50
Peanut butter, 2 scant tablespoons	200
Peanuts, 20 to 24 nuts	100
Pears, canned, 2 halves with juice	100
Pear, 1 medium fresh	60
Peas, canned, ½ cup	50
Peas, dried, cooked, ½ cup	175
Peas, fresh, cooked, ½ cup	65
Pea soup, cream of, 1 cup	150
Pecans, 5 halves	75
Pepper, green, 1 medium	25
Perch, 3 medium	280
Pickles, cucumber, 4 small	25
Pigs' feet, pickled, 1 small	100
Pineapple, canned, 1 slice with juice	100
Pineapple, fresh, ½ cup sliced	60
Pineapple ice, ½ cup	200
Pineapple juice, 1 cup	150
Plums, 3 or 4	100
Popcorn, 1½ cups, no butter	100
Popover, 1	100
Pork chop, broiled, 1 lean	200
Pork roast, ¼ pound	300 to 620
Pork tenderloin, 1 piece	200
Potato, baked, 1 medium	100
Potato, sweet, baked, 1 medium	200
Potato chips, 8 to 10 large	100
Potatoes, boiled, 2 small	100
Potatoes, mashed, 1 scant cup	200
Potato salad, ½ cup	200
Praline, 1	300
Preserves, 1 tablespoon	75
Pretzel, 1	20
Prune juice, 1 cup	180
Prune, dried, 1 large	35
Prunes, stewed, 4 medium with juice	200
Prune soufflé, ⅔ cup	100
Pumpkin, 1 cup	70
Pumpkin pie, ⅙ of pie	150

Food	Calories
Radishes, 5 medium	10
Raisins, ¼ cup seeded or 2 tablespoons seedless	100
Raspberries, fresh, ½ cup	45
Raspberry ice, ½ cup	120
Red snapper, average serving	100
Rhubarb, stewed, sweetened, ½ cup	100
Rice, brown, cooked, ¾ cup	115
Rice, white, cooked, ¾ cup	115
Rolls, French, 1 average	80
Roll, Parker House, 1	100
Rum, 1 jigger (1½ oz.)	110
Salmon, canned, ½ cup	100
Salmon, fresh, average serving	200
Sardines, 4 large	100
Sauerkraut, ⅔ cup	27
Sauerkraut juice, ½ cup	20
Sausage, pork link, 2 medium	100
Scallops, 6 large	100
Shad roe, average serving	100
Sherbets, ½ cup	200
Sherry, 1 wine glass (3 oz.)	120
Shortcake with fruit, average serving	300
Shredded wheat biscuit, 1	100
Shrimp, 5 large	50
Shrimp cocktail with sauce, ½ cup	100
Sirup, corn, 1 tablespoon	85
Smelts, 2	100
Snow pudding, ⅔ cup	100
Sole, fillet of, average serving	100
Soybeans, dried, cooked, ½ cup	108
Spaghetti, cooked, ¾ cup	125
Spareribs, 4	150
Spinach, cooked and chopped, ½ cup	20
Spinach soup, cream of, ⅔ cup	150
Split pea soup, 1 cup	165
Squab, 1 small	300
Squash, Hubbard, ½ cup cooked	50
Squash, summer, ½ cup	15
Strawberries, ½ cup	30
Strawberry shortcake, average serving	300
Succotash, canned, ⅓ cup	100
Sugar, brown, 1 tablespoon	50
Sugar, granulated, 1 tablespoon	50
Sweetbreads, 2 broiled	125

Food	Calories
Sweetbreads, ½ cup creamed	125
Swordfish, average serving	180
Tangerine, 1	35
Tapioca pudding, scant ½ cup	100
Tartar sauce, 1 tablespoon	150
Tea, 1 cup, unsweetened	None
Tea, with lemon, 1 cup	15
Tomatoes, canned, 1 cup	50
Tomato, fresh, 1 medium	25
Tomato juice, 1 cup	50
Tomato salad, whole, raw or canned, ½ cup	30
Tomato soup, clear, 1 cup	50
Tomato soup, cream of, 1 cup	200
Tongue, 2 small pieces	75
Tripe, boiled, average serving	150
Trout, brook, 2	75
Trout, lake, average serving	125
Tuna fish, canned in oil, ½ cup	130
Turkey, 4" x 2" x ¼" slice	100
Turnip greens, 1 cup	23
Turnips, 1 cup	50
Veal chop, 1 lean	100
Veal cutlet, breaded, 1 medium	250
Veal roast, leg, 2" x 2¾" x ⅛" slice	100
Veal stew, 1 cup	200
Vegetable juice, 1 cup	48
Vegetable soup, 1 cup	100
Waffle, 1	250
Waldorf salad, average serving	100
Walnuts, English, 4 to 8 nut meats	50
Water cress, 1 bunch	20
Watermelon, 1 slice ¾" thick 6" in diameter	100
Welsh rarebit, 1½ tablespoons rarebit, ½ slice toast	100
Whisky, bourbon, 1 jigger (1½ oz.)	125
Whisky, Scotch, 1 jigger (1½ oz.)	110
Whitefish, average serving	100
White sauce, medium, ¼ cup	112
Yeast, 1 cake	20
Yeast, brewers', 2 teaspoons	40
Yogurt, ½ cup	150
Zucchini, 1 cup	25
Zwieback, 1 slice	35

Cooking and Kitchen Hints

Household Needs

If you are establishing a new household it pays to give time and thought to your equipment. Storage space at convenient heights, even in a large kitchen, is limited. Choose your pots and pans, mixing bowls, baking dishes and sheets so that they can be nested or stacked. Wire lid racks and sliding pot hangers are great space savers. Tightly covered canisters for cereals, crackers, flours and sugars, and clearly labeled spice, herb and condiment jars give you immediate identification without confusion. Nonrusting, well-designed hand tools save your towels and your temper. The best quality sharp knives are a long-range economy. With the following equipment you are ready to produce the recipes in this book, but don't feel that equipment is the whole answer. Some of the best cooking is done with virtually no tools.

For Cooking

2 saucepans with covers
2 frying pans (large and small)
1 deep fat fryer
1 Dutch oven
1 double boiler
1 mold for steaming
1 large stewing or soup kettle
   (5 quarts or over)

1 dessert mold
3 strainers
1 steamer
1 colander
1 bean pot
Coffee maker
Tea kettle
Earthenware or china teapot

For Baking

1 open roasting pan with rack
3 round cake pans
1 square cake pan
1 loaf pan or bread pan
2 cake racks for cooling
1 muffin tin

1 pie tin
2 cookie sheets
1 casserole
6 custard cups
1 nine inch tube pan
1 shallow 9 x 12 inch pan

For Preparation

1 set of mixing bowls
2 measuring cups
1 set of measuring spoons
2 teaspoons
2 tablespoons
1 wooden spoon
1 wooden slotted spoon for cake
   mixing
1 large fork
1 small fork
2 paring knives
1 bread knife
1 meat knife
Grapefruit knife
Spatula
1 egg beater
Ladle
2 graters
1 nut or cheese grater
1 sugar or flour scoop
Funnel
Tongs
Deep fat fryer

Flour sifter
Potato ricer or food mill
Potato masher
Wooden chopping bowl and chopper
Meat grinder
Wooden salad bowl
Salad basket
Doughnut cutter
Cutting board
Biscuit cutter
Pastry blender
Pastry board
Pastry brush
Vegetable brush
Rolling pin
Pastry cloth and cover for rolling pin
Pancake turner
Apple corer
Vegetable slicer or parer
Rubber scraper
Weighing spoon or scales
Ice-cream freezer
Griddle

938

Accessories

4 canisters	Salt and pepper shakers
1 bread box	Knife sharpener
1 cake box	Set of refrigerator containers
1 dish drainer	Waxed paper
1 sink strainer	Plastic storage bag
1 garbage can	Aluminum foil
1 waste basket	Paper towels
1 vegetable bin	Dishpan
1 or more trays	Whisk broom
Bottle opener	1 broom
Corkscrew	1 dust mop
Can opener	1 scrubbing brush
Pot holders	Pan and brush
1 bucket	Toaster
Kitchen shears	Waffle iron
Toothpicks for testing cake	12 dish towels
Malted milk shaker	2 dish cloths
Nutcracker	2 dust cloths

For Timesaving

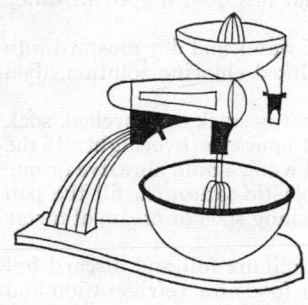 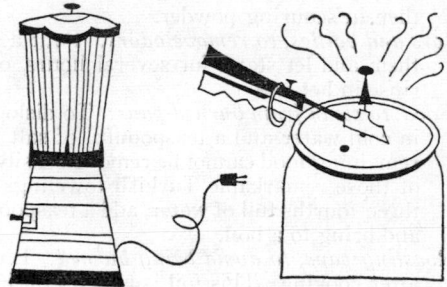

Electric Mixer   *Blender*   *Pressure cooker*

Helpful hints appear where they are germane to the text. If you are interested in how to sour milk for baking, look in the Index for: Milk, how to sour. If you want to find out whether your baking powder is still active, look under: Baking powder, test for activity; or how to core an artichoke quickly, look under: Artichoke, how to core.

In fact, a perusal of the Index may give you some wonderful ideas. There are a number of handy hints, however, that are not part of cooking processes nor described in the recipes. Safeguarding yourself from burns is a most important one.

Burns and Burning

If you are burned badly, get a doctor. If you should be burned slightly, apply a paste of baking soda and water. If grease catches fire, throw a handful of salt or flour on it. Water will only cause the fire to spread. Do the same for spilled juices from pies in the oven.

To prevent being burned from the popping of hot fat, sprinkle a little flour in the frying pan and the spattering will stop at once. Or cover the skillet with a colander.

In pouring hot liquids into a glass, put a metal spoon in first to absorb some of the heat.

To save scorched food, plunge it into cold water before transferring it from the burned pan to a fresh one. The burned taste is greatly lessened.

And speaking of disguises, it is sometimes possible in emergencies to hide the taste of excess salt by adding a small quantity of sugar or vinegar.

Cleaning of Equipment

Glasses, to wash: When washing glasses do not put them in hot water bottom first, as they may crack from sudden expansion. Glasses may be safely washed in very hot water if slipped in edgewise.

Glasses or pitchers which have been used for milk: To wash, rinse first with cold water before putting them into warm water.

How to separate two stuck glasses: Set bottom one in warm water and pour cold water into the top one.

Egg cups or spoons: To wash, rinse first in cold water before washing in warm water. Hot water used first cooks the egg and makes it difficult to remove it.

Silver spoons tarnished by egg: They can be cleaned with damp salt.

Vinegar cruets, to clean: Fill with warm water to which a few drops of household ammonia has been added. Let stand for an hour then rinse well with lukewarm water.

Knives, to clean: Rub kitchen knives with a cork that has been dipped in water then in scouring powder.

Jars and bottles, to remove odors: Pour a solution of water and dry mustard into them and let stand for several hours, or use a diluted chlorine solution, then rinse in hot water.

Food, to clean from burned pans: To dislodge food that is stuck or scorched, soak in cold water and a teaspoonful of salt for several hours, or overnight. If the remaining food cannot be removed easily with steel wool, a mild abrasive or one of those remarkable Turkish towelings that are plastic-saturated, fill the pan three-fourths full of water, add a teaspoonful of washing soda or cream of tartar and bring to a boil.

Roasting pans, to avoid being burned: Line with aluminum foil and discard foil after cooking. This foil is also useful in wrapping foods for refrigeration and storage.

Grease, to store: Save excess fats in paper cups that are suitable for hot foods; discard when through using.

Skillets, to clean: A skillet should be wiped with a clean paper towel after all grease is poured off. It can then be easily washed.

Skillets, iron, new, to treat: Grease them well, place them in a hot oven 450° for about 30 minutes. Scour them well with steel wool.

Aluminum utensils, to clean: Spots and discolorations on aluminum pans may be removed by using a solution of 2 tablespoons cream of tartar dissolved in 1 quart of water. This solution may be stored in a jar and used as needed.

Silverware, to clean: Use prepared silver polish; or remove tarnish by the electrolytic method, as follows: Put an old piece of aluminum in a large pot or dish pan. Do not use an aluminum utensil still in use for cooking as this process will quickly corrode it. Add 2 tablespoonfuls of salt and 2 tablespoonfuls of soda. Add 2 quarts of boiling water and put silver in water so that each piece is touching aluminum or another piece of silver. Let stand about 5 minutes until tarnish is deposited on aluminum. Wash silver with soapy water, rinse and dry. Rub with clean, dry flannel cloth. Hollow ware or knives with hollow handles should not be cleaned in this way.

Waffle iron, electric, to clean: Wipe grids with a clean, dry cloth. If particles stick, remove with brush; never wash. Wipe batter spilled on the outside with a damp cloth, polish with a dry one.

Refrigerator, to clean: Wash inside with a mixture of 1 tablespoonful powdered borax to 1 quart water.

Bread box, to deter mold: Wash out bread box with mixture of 2 tablespoonfuls vinegar to 1 quart water.

Toaster, care of: Do not insert a knife into toaster to lift out toast. Do not put buttered bread in the toaster. Do not shake toaster upside down to remove the crumbs. Once a week remove the plate on the bottom and brush it with a soft brush. Do not wrap the cord around the toaster until the toaster had cooled.

Household Stains

Gum, adhesive tape, etc.: Lemon juice will remove adhesive tape, gum, etc., from hands and clothes. Lemon juice will also remove ink, fruit, other stains, and onion odors from the hands.

Vegetable stains, to remove from hands: Rub them with a slice of lemon or raw potato.

Wax or paraffin, to remove from cloth: Scrape off the hardened wax. Place blotting paper under the cloth and press with warm iron.

Chocolate and cocoa: To remove stain from washable material use soap and hot water. On unwashable materials scrape off what you can and apply cleaning fluid.

To remove cod liver oil stains: Prepare and store the following paste. Apply it to the spot as soon as possible and then wash it and the oil out in warm suds. Dissolve one tablespoonful of soap flakes in 3 tablespoonfuls of boiling water. Cool and blend this mixture with 2 tablespoons of banana oil.

Coffee: Boiling water poured from a height of 2 feet is good for fresh stains. For old stains try laundering. If fabric is unwashable, place stained portions between damp cloths and press.

To remove egg stains: Launder or use dry cleaning fluid.

Fruit stains: To remove pour boiling water from height of 2 or 3 feet onto stretched fabric. If stain remains, try bleaching in sun after moistening stain with lemon juice.

Linoleum and furniture: To clean grease from linoleum dust with baking soda and follow with boiling water.

Odds and Ends

Butter, to cut hard butter cleanly: Cover the blade of the knife with waxed paper or use knife heated in hot water.

Food chopper, to fasten securely: Place a potholder on the table and put the food chopper on it before tightening the screws.

Bowl, to keep steady when mixing or whipping ingredients: Place bowl on a wet folded cloth or a Mason jar rubber.

Jars, to open: To open Mason-type or glass-top jars, pull out the jar rubber with a pair of pliers, then there is no danger of injuring either the lid or the jar.

Broken glass: To remove small slivers from any rug press scotch tape against it. To remove from a smooth surface use moist woolen cloth, absorbent cotton or wet toilet tissues.

To make a cork smaller: Remove small wedge from the center so edges still fit closely.

If doing much paring: Use rubber office finger to protect finger.

To store baked goods: Keep cake and bread in different tin containers as cake draws the moisture from bread.

Store crackers and cereals in tins on shelves above stove or electric refrigerator.

Salt shakers: In damp weather add cornstarch or a few grains of rice to salt in shakers to keep it dry for easy pouring.

Definitions and Tables

À la king:
Food served in rich cream sauce sometimes flavored with sherry.

À la mode:
A term used for braised food or for pies and cakes to which ice cream is added as a garnish.

Au gratin:
Food creamed or moistened with other ingredients like eggs, milk or stock, covered with bread crumbs and butter or cheese and baked or broiled until the top is brown.

Au jus:
Meat served in its natural juice or gravy.

Au lait:
Food prepared or served with milk. See Café au lait, page 812.

Au naturel:
Food either plainly cooked or in the natural state.

Bain Marie:
A hot water bath used for keeping foods warm or sometimes for cooking them. See double boiler, page 265.

Bake:
To cook by dry heat usually in an oven.

Baste:
To moisten roasting meat or other food while baking with juices from the pan or with additional liquid.

Bavarian:
Pudding with a gelatine and cream base.

Beat:
To blend by mixing thoroughly using an over-and-over or rapid rotary motion. See page 592.

Bisque:
A thick cream soup usually made from fish; also a rich frozen dessert, or ice cream with crushed macaroons.

Blanch:
To parboil or to pour boiling water over a food, then drain and rinse it with cold water. Used to whiten or remove skins from almonds, to shrink vegetables for canning and freezing, etc.

Blanquette:
A stew with a white sauce.

Blend:
To mix two or more ingredients until well combined.

Boil:
To cook in liquid, usually water, in which bubbles constantly rise to the surface and break. After boiling point is reached heat may be reduced, provided water is kept in constant motion.

Bombe:
A still-frozen rich cream or custard pudding.

Bonne Femme:
Cooked in plain home style.

Botulinus:
A deadly bacterium which forms in some improperly canned foods. To avoid, see page 843.

Brochettes:
See Skewers.

Brush:
To spread with butter, egg, etc., thinly with a brush or a small paper or cloth.

Calorie:
Amount of heat required to raise 1 kilogram of water 1 degree centigrade.

Caramelize:
To heat sugar in a skillet until melted and brown, about 338°, or to heat foods containing sugar until light brown and of caramel flavor.

Casserole:
Special earthenware or other fire-proof dish in which food is first cooked and then served. See Casserole of Veal

and Spinach, page 165, Spanish Casserole, page 167.

Caviar:

The roe of sturgeon or other large fish, pressed and salted as a relish.

Cepes:

A kind of edible mushroom.

Chantilly:

A dish containing whipped or plain cream.

Charlotte:

Usually a gelatine dessert with flavored whipped cream molded in a form lined with cake or lady fingers.

Chiffonade:

Finely minced herbs especially sorrel or lettuce served in soups and salads.

Chowder:

A soup or stew made of clams, fish or vegetables.

Clabber:

Milk soured to a point where there is marked precipitation of curd but no separation from whey. Buttermilk, sour milk, clabber and yogurt may be used interchangeably in cooking.

Condiments:

Food seasonings such as salt, pepper, vinegar, herbs and spices. Relishes are frequently called condiments.

Compote:

Sweetened stewed fruit left whole or in pieces, frequently served with a meat course.

Confectioners' sugar:

Sugar ground to the consistency of cornstarch.

Court bouillon:

A highly seasoned fish broth.

Cracklings:

The crisp residue left when fat, especially hog fat is rendered, or the crisp dark rind of pork roast.

Crêpes:

Thin dessert pancakes. See Crêpes Suzette, page 551.

Croissants:

Rich French crescent rolls.

Croquettes:

A mixture of chopped or ground cooked food, cereals, cheese, meat, etc., bound together by eggs or a thick sauce, shaped, then dipped into egg and crumbs and fried.

Croutons:

Cubes of bread toasted or fried, served over various dishes and in soup.

Cuisine:

Literally "kitchen." Cookery or a style of cooking.

Demi tasse:

A small cup of after-dinner coffee.

Deviled:

Highly seasoned food.

Dissolve:

To liquefy a solid food, to melt.

Dredge:

To coat with flour or sugar.

Drippings:

The residue left in the pan in which meat or poultry has been cooked.

Dust:

To sprinkle lightly with flour or sugar.

Entrée:

The main dish of an informal meal or a subordinate dish served between main courses.

Entremets:

Usually a side dish. It may be a dish served between the principal courses at a meal.

Espagnole:

A basic brown sauce.

Fecula:

Very pure starch used for thickening, but cornstarch, arrowroot, etc., may be used. See page 947 for equivalents.

Fines Herbes:

A combination of finely chopped herbs for flavoring soups, sauces, omelets. See page 832.

Flake:

To break up into small pieces with a utensil.

Flambée:
To cover or combine food with spirits and serve it lighted. See Pears Flambée, Plum Pudding, Cafe Brûlot.

Fondue:
A baked dish not unlike a soufflé usually including bread or cracker crumbs.

Forcemeat:
Pastes of meat, fish, or shellfish bound with egg white, butter or cream for use as soup garnishes or stuffings.

Frappé:
Sweetened fruit juice frozen until of a mushy consistency.

Fry:
To cook in deep fat.

Fumet:
An essence extracted from fish or game and used as a fish or game stock.

Galantine:
A cold preparation of boned, stuffed and seasoned chicken, veal, etc., served in its own jelly; also fowl, fish or game, boned, stuffed and roasted, boiled or braised, left whole or pressed and cut in slices put in molds and covered with aspic.

Glacé:
Frozen, iced or glazed food effects. See Glazed Grapes, page 796, Glazed Strawberries, page 633, Glazed Salmon, page 239.

Glaze:
To cover with aspic or to coat with a glossy covering using a thin sugar sirup that has been cooked to the crack stage or its equivalent with diluted fruit jelly.

Goulash:
A Hungarian thick meat stew.

Gumbo:
A term used for okra or mixtures with okra.

Hollandaise:
A sauce made of eggs and butter, served hot or cold with vegetables or fish.

Julienne:
Food cut into narrow lengthwise strips.

Kirsch:
A cherry cordial.

Lyonnaise:
Usually cold boiled potatoes chopped and sautéed with butter and onions.

Macédoine:
A mixture of vegetables or fruits.

Maître d'hôtel:
A dish which is flavored with chopped parsley, butter and lemon juice.

Marinade:
An oil and acid mixture, such as French dressing, in which food is allowed to stand to gain flavor or tenderness.

Marinate:
To soak in French dressing, vinegar, lemon juice, sour cream, etc.

Marmite:
See Stockpot.

Marzipan:
A confection of almonds reduced to a paste with sugar.

Mask:
To cover completely with a sauce, jelly, aspic, mayonnaise or cream.

Milt:
The soft male roe of fish.

Minestrone:
A thick Italian vegetable soup.

Mousse:
A mixture of sweetened whipped cream and other ingredients frozen without stirring, or combinations of cream, fruit, meat, vegetables, etc., thickened with gelatine.

Mustard:
Seeds used in pickling; used powdered, it is called English mustard; when blended with wine or vinegar it is called French mustard.

Nesselrode:
Frozen dessert which includes chopped fruits and chestnuts.

Panada:
A paste of flour and water or soaked breads frequently used in soups.

Parfait:

A frozen dessert consisting of beaten egg whites or yolks cooked with hot sirup and combined with whipped cream or a mixture of ice cream, fruit and whipped cream.

Pâté de foie gras:

Goose liver paste.

Paysanne:

Country style.

Petit Fours:

Small iced cakes.

Pilaf:

Oriental dishes combining meat and vegetables with rice.

Pimento:

All spice.

Pimiento:

A garden pepper used as a relish or vegetable and as a flavoring for cheese.

Polenta:

Italian dish of corn meal.

Powdered sugar:

A finer grind than granulated, but in which the individual granules are still discernible.

Purée:

To press fruit or vegetables through a sieve, food mill or blender; also a soup made with food put through a sieve, etc., and thinned with cream or stock.

Poach:

To cook under the boiling point in hot liquid to cover.

Ragout:

Being French, a de luxe concoction, but literally a thick, well-seasoned stew.

Ramekins:

Individual baking dishes.

Render:

To free fat from connective tissue by heating slowly until fat melts and can be drained off.

Rennet:

Prepared inner linings of calf or pig stomach used for curdling or coagulating milk.

Rissole:

To sear or brown food with a protective covering, or a baked or fried pastry filled with meat, fish or fruit.

Roe:

Eggs of fish.

Roux:

A melted fat and starch base used mainly for thickening sauces or soups.

Reduce:

To lessen a quantity of fluid by boiling it away.

Sauté:

To cook in a small amount of fat.

Scald:

To heat liquid to a temperature just below the boiling point. To immerse food in boiling liquid for a short time.

Scallop:

To bake food in layers covered with sauce and crumbs in an oven-proof dish.

Score:

To make light cuts in a surface, usually in lines.

Sear:

To brown the surface of meat by the quick application of intense heat, usually in a hot pan or in a hot oven.

Sherbet:

A frozen mixture of fruit juice, sugar, egg whites and milk or water.

Shred:

To cut into very thin slices or strips.

Shortening:

Any kind of fat suitable to baking.

Simmer:

To cook in liquid that is kept just below the boiling point.

Sliver:

To cut or shred into lengths.

Stock:

The liquid resulting from the cooking of meat, fish or vegetables—an invaluable aid in making gravies (page 426), sauces (page 428), soup (page 40), and adding interest to vegetables (page 262).

Trichina:

A harmful nematode which may be present in pork and may not be killed unless the pork is sufficiently cooked. See page 364.

Try out:

Usually applied to bacon. To heat slowly until the fat is liquid.

Until set:

Until a liquid has become firm, usually applied to a gelatine mixture.

Velouté:

A basic white sauce.

Wheat—Farina, Semolina:

Are the wheat particles left in the bolting machine after the flour is extracted. Semolina comes from durum wheats, farina from nondurums.

Yeast:

A commercial substance made of yeast cells. If the cells are dormant or living, the yeast may be used in the raising of doughs (page 000). If autolization has taken place and the yeast cells are no longer active, as in brewers' yeast. It is used as a food supplement rich in some of the B vitamins.

Substitutions

Arrowroot	2 teaspoons	=	1¾ tablespoons flour when used for thickening purposes
Baking powder	1 teaspoon	=	¼ teaspoon baking soda plus ½ teaspoon cream of tartar
Butter	1 cup	=	⅘ cup bacon fat, clarified*
Butter	1 cup	=	⅔ cup chicken fat, clarified*
Butter	1 cup	=	⅞ cup cottonseed, corn, nut oil (solid or liquid)
Butter	1 cup	=	⅞ cup lard
Butter	1 cup	=	½ cup suet*
Chocolate	1 square	=	3 tablespoons cocoa plus 1½ teaspoons fat
Cocoa	3 tablespoons plus 1½ teaspoons fat	=	1 square (1 oz.) chocolate
Cornstarch	1 tablespoon	=	2 tablespoons flour when used for thickening purposes
Cracker crumbs	¾ cup	=	1 cup bread crumbs
Cream, sour, heavy	1 cup	=	⅓ cup butter and ⅔ cup milk in any sour-milk recipe
Cream, sour, thin	1 cup	=	3 tablespoons butter and ¾ cup milk in any sour-milk recipe
Eggs	1 average	=	2 oz.
Flour, all-purpose, sifted	1 cup	=	1 cup plus 2 tablespoons sifted cake flour
Flour, cake, sifted	1 cup	=	⅞ cup sifted all-purpose flour (1 cup less 2 tablespoons)
Flour, rice	2 teaspoons	=	1¾ tablespoons flour (for thickening purposes)
Milk	1 cup	=	½ cup evaporated milk and ½ cup water
Milk	1 cup	=	4 tablespoons powdered milk and 1 cup water
Milk	1 cup	=	1 cup soy milk
Molasses	1 cup	=	1 cup honey
Sugar	1 cup	=	1 cup molasses plus ¼ to ½ teaspoon soda**
Sugar	1 cup	=	1 cup honey plus ¼ to ½ teaspoon soda**
Sugar	1 cup	=	1 cup maple sirup and ¼ cup corn sirup**
Sugar, granulated	1 cup	=	1⅛ cup raw sugar, see page 503

* Increase the liquid ¼ cup.   ** Reduce the liquid ¼ cup.

Table of Equivalents

Almonds	1 cup chopped	⅘ lb. shelled
Apricots	3 cups dried	1 lb.
Apricots	6 cups cooked	1 lb.
Beans, dried	1 cup	½ lb.
Butter	2 cups	1 lb.
Butter	1 stick	½ cup
Butter	1 stick	8 tablespoons
Chocolate	1 square	1 oz.
Chocolate	1 square	5 tablespoons grated
Cocoa	4 cups	1 lb.
Coconut	5 cups	1 lb.
Cheese	4 cups dry	1 lb.
Cheese	5 cups freshly grated	1 lb.
Corn meal	3 cups	1 lb.
Cottage cheese	2 cups	1 lb.
Dates	2 cups pitted	1 lb.
Eggs	5 whole eggs	1 cup
Egg whites	8	About 1 cup
Egg yolks	16	About 1 cup
Figs	3 cups chopped	1 lb.
Flour		
Bread flour..........	4 cups	1 lb.
Cake flour, sifted.....	4½ cups	1 lb.
Graham flour........	3⅓ cups	1 lb.
Lemon	1 juiced	About 2 to 3 tablespoons
Macaroni	3 cups	1 lb.
Macaroni	1 cup	2 cups cooked
Marshmallows	16	¼ lb.
Meat	2 cups diced	1 lb.
Noodles	1 cup raw	1¼ cups cooked
Nut meats	4 cups coarsely chopped..	1 lb.
Orange	1 juiced	6 to 8 tablespoons
Peanuts	3 cups chopped	1½ lbs.
Pecans	3 cups chopped	2½ lbs. unshelled
Prunes	2½ cups dried	1 lb.
Prunes	4 cups cooked	1 lb.
Raisins	2½ cups seeded	1 lb.
Raisins	3 cups seedless	1 lb.
Rice	2⅓ cups uncooked	1 lb.
Rice	1 cup raw	3 to 4 cups cooked
Saccharin	¼ grain	1 teaspoon sugar
Sucaryl	1 tablet	1 teaspoon sugar
Sugar, brown	2¼ cups firmly packed	1 lb.
Sugar, confectioners' ..	3⅓ cups	1 lb.
Sugar, granulated	2 cups	1 lb.
Walnuts, black	3 cups chopped	5½ lbs. unshelled
Walnuts, English	4 cups chopped	2½ lbs. unshelled
Water	2 cups	1 lb.

For Use in Translating Foreign Measurements

1 ounce .... equals	....	Approximately 30 grams
1 pound or 16 ounces....................... "	....	454 grams
½ cup less 1 tablespoon butter (7 tablespoons) "	....	100 grams
¾ cup less 1 tablespoon of all-purpose		
flour (11 tablespoons)................... "	....	100 grams
½ cup less 1 tablespoon sugar (7 tablespoons) "	....	100 grams

Table of Weights and Measures

The recipes in this book call for standard measuring cups and spoons. A standard measuring cup equals ½ pint. All measurements given are level.

A few grains	= Less than ⅛ teaspoon	⅝ cup	= ½ cup plus 2 tablespoons
60 drops	= 1 teaspoon	⅞ cup	= ¾ cup plus 2 tablespoons
1 teaspoon	= ⅓ tablespoon (5 grams)	1 cup	= ½ pint
1 tablespoon	= 3 teaspoons (15 grams)	2 cups	= 1 pint (1 pound)
2 tablespoons	= 1 ounce (30 grams)	2 pints	= 1 quart (2 pounds)
4 tablespoons	= ¼ cup	4 quarts	= 1 gallon (8 pounds)
5⅓ tablespoons	= ⅓ cup	8 quarts	= 1 peck
1 gill	= ½ cup	4 pecks	= 1 bushel
8 tablespoons	= ½ cup	16 ounces	= 1 pound
16 tablespoons	= 1 cup	1 fluid ounce	= 2 tablespoons
⅜ cup	= ¼ cup plus 1 tablespoon	16 fluid ounces	= 1 pint (2 cups)

For measurements for drinks see page 819

Average Can Sizes

The net weight will always be found on the label of every can of food.

Can Size	Weight	Cupfuls
8-oz.	8 oz.	1
No. 1	11 oz.	1⅓
No. 1½	16 oz.	2
No. 2	20 oz.	2½
No. 2½	28 oz.	3½
No. 3	33 oz.	4
No. 10	106 oz.	13

Canned goods will keep without spoilage as long as the can is airtight. Once opened it must be kept under refrigeration. Some acid foods left in open cans act on the metal of the can and the dissolved iron gives an astringent taste which is unpleasant but harmless.

Average Frozen Food Packages

Vegetables ....14 to 16 ounces
Fruits ....12 ounces

INDEX

Index